Dictionary of British Literary Characters:

18th- and 19th-Century Novels

Dictionary of British Literary Characters:
18th- and 19th-Century Novels

Edited By
John R. Greenfield

Associate Editor
David Brailow
With the Assistance of
Arlyn Bruccoli

A Bruccoli Clark Layman Book

New York

Dictionary of British Literary Characters: 18th- and 19th-Century Novels

Facts On File, Inc.
460 Park Avenue South
New York NY 10016

Library of Congress Cataloging-in-Publication Data

Dictionary of British literary characters : eighteenth and nineteenth
  century novel / edited by John R. Greenfield ; associate editor,
David Brailow.
      p. cm.
    "A Bruccoli Clark Layman book."
    ISBN 0-8160-2179-1
    1. English fiction——19th century——Dictionaries. 2. English
fiction——18th century——Dictionaries. 3. Characters and
characteristics in literature——Dictionaries. I. Greenfield, John
R. II. Brailow, David.
PR830.C47D5 1991   90-3998
823'.80927'03——dc20

A British CIP catalogue record for this book is available from the British Library.

Facts On File books are available at special discounts when purchased in bulk quantities for businesses, associations, institutions or sales promotions. Please call our Special Sales Department in New York at 212/683-2244 or 800/322-8755 .

Manufactured by the Maple-Vail Book Manufacturing Group
Printed in the United States of America

10 9 8 7 6 5 4 3 2 1

This book is printed on acid-free paper.

To my teachers, students, and colleagues

Preface

The Dictionary of British Literary Characters: The Novel is a two-volume compendium comprising over a thousand novels and more than ten thousand characters. As the most comprehensive reference work on characters in the English novel, these volumes may have implications for the current controversy over what constitutes the canon of the English novel. The editors' approach concerning the selection of novels has been as democratic and as inclusive as space permits. In addition to comprehensive coverage of established British novelists, the editors have sought to include a representative sampling of novels by lesser-known authors, including many women writers. In general, three broad criteria were followed in selecting the novels included herein: (1) has the novelist or the novel become established so as to have achieved a degree of permanence?; (2) has the novelist or the novel received scholarly or critical attention?; (3) has the novel achieved a degree of popularity in its own time or in later times? A novel or novelist that meets two or in some cases only one of these general criteria may qualify for inclusion.

Volume I begins with *The Pilgrim's Progress*, and includes a strong representation of eighteenth-century and nineteenth-century novels, 486 novels in all and 11,663 characters. Volume II will continue with novelists who published the bulk of their work after 1890 and will cover the span of a century, including some novels from the 1980s. Though certain Victorian novelists, such as Thomas Hardy, published important novels after 1890, these novelists appear in Volume I on the basis of their having produced the bulk of their work before 1890. Other nineteenth-century novelists, who published the bulk of their novels after 1890, are represented in Volume II.

Generally speaking, an effort has been made to include all major characters and all other characters who contribute to the plot or themes of the novel in any significant way. Characters who appear in more than one novel by an author are listed in the *Dictionary* only once with their roles for all the novels in which they appear described in that single entry. Each character is listed alphabetically by surname (when the surname is available). Characters with only first names or with no names are listed alphabetically by first names or, in the case of those with no name, by some salient identifying characteristic, as for example, the Brown Man of the Moors, in Sir Walter Scott's *The Black Dwarf.* Except for a few historical characters whose names identify periods or causes but who do not appear in the novels in person, every individual mentioned by name in another character's entry has an entry of his own, and the name by which he is indicated is sufficient for his location in the *Dictionary*. In addition to providing the author and title for each character entry, the *Dictionary* provides an index, alphabetical by author (with birth/death dates), of all titles (with date of first publications); each title is followed by an alpahbetical list of those characters included in the *Dictionary*; the contributor responsible for the character entries is identified by initials following each title.

Those consulting the *Dictionary* may find useful information about the characters' occupations, family relations, relations with other characters, class, and gender roles as well as the characters' contributions to the novels' plots and themes. In addition to providing students and other readers with factual information about the characters, the *Dictionary* may provide scholars and critics with data for various historical, sociological, or thematic studies of the English novel.

A project of this magnitude could never have been accomplished without the help and cooperation of mant people. I would especially like to thank my colleague David Brailow, the Associate Editor of Volume I, for his help in getting this project started in the summer of 1989, and of course for all the work he has done on the project. John Rogers, who is the Associate Editor of Volume II, also helped in securing contributors for Volume I. The *Dictionary* could never heve been completed without the participation of the many contributors, some few of whom are friends or acquaintances of mine and most of whom I have never met. These contributors deserve and have my gratitude for their promptness in meeting deadlines, for their conscientiousness in compiling character entries, for their willingness to make revisions, and most of all, for their cooperation and patience over the long duration of this project. I would also like to thank Danyelle Warden, a former student of mine, for her valuable editorial assistance performed under the auspices of the McKendree College internship program. Three secretaries at McKendree College, Naomia Severs, Ella Doty, and Nancy Ferguson, deserve thanks for the help they gave me in handling the correpsondence associated with this project. Finally, as the dedication suggests, I would like to thank all my best students, teachers, and colleagues for helping to keep me continually and vitally interested in the English novel.

—John R. Greenfield

Dictionary of British Literary Characters:

18th- and 19th-Century Novels

A

Lord A—— Aristocratic husband of Lady A—; he once proposed to Mrs. Darnford and occasionally comments on her letters in Clara Reeve's *Plans of Education*.

M. A—— A French Academician, who dines with Mr. Home de Bassompierre in Charlotte Brontë's *Villette*.

Marquis of A—— Wily and successful statesman, who is a member of the Scottish Privy Council and a kinsman to Edgar Ravenswood; he aids Edgar in his struggle against Sir William Ashton in Sir Walter Scott's *The Bride of Lammermoor*.

Louisa, Lady A—— Aristocratic recipient of Mrs. Darnford's letters on education; she seeks to hire Mrs. Darnford as a governess for her daughters, who are to be educated at home in Clara Reeve's *Plans of Education*.

Aaron Jewish moneychanger hired by the Prior of Saint Mary's to testify against Hugh Woodreeve in Ann Radcliffe's *Gaston de Blondeville*.

Abarak Failed seeker after the sword of Aklis; he assists Shibli Bagarag in finding the sword and afterward in George Meredith's *The Shaving of Shagpat*.

Abate Abbot who refuses to help Vincentio di Vivaldi in releasing Ellena Rosalba from the clutches of the Abbess of the San Stefano convent in Ann Radcliffe's *The Italian*.

Abate Maniacal, politically ambitious abbot of the Saint Augustin monastery, who betrays Julia de Mazzini to her father the Marquis in Ann Radcliffe's *A Sicilian Romance*.

Abbess Elqidia's sister, who has a bad temper and is jealous of the relationship between her sister and Natura in Eliza Haywood's *Life's Progress Through the Passions: or, the Adventures of Natura*.

Abbess Sadistic abbess of the San Stefano convent, who gives Ellena Rosalba the ultimatum to become a nun, to marry the man of Marchesa di Vivaldi's choice, or to be locked in the dungeon in Ann Radcliffe's *The Italian*.

Benedictine Abbess Norman aunt of Eveline Berenger; when Eveline refuses to take her advice to break the engagement to Hugo de Lacy, she withdraws her protection from Eveline in Sir Walter Scott's *The Betrothed*.

Lady Abbess Head of the convent to which the Lady Lucy is taken after being attacked and abandoned by her husband; the Abbess later spreads the story of Lucy and Lewis Augustus Albertus so that all may be inspired by the example of virtue and religion in Penelope Aubin's *The Life and Adventures of the Lady Lucy*.

Lady Abbess Isabella's aunt, who hopes to gain Isabella's estate for the nunnery if Isabella takes holy orders in Aphra Behn's *The History of the Nun*.

Abbess of Ursuline Convent Prim and earnest recluse, who shelters Isabelle de Croye and is anxious to have her become a nun in Sir Walter Scott's *Quentin Durward*.

Mrs. Abbot A widow after the suicide of her journalist husband; she takes in two children deserted by their father and ultimately remarries in George Gissing's *The Whirlpool*.

Martha Abbot Officious lady's maid at Mrs. Reed's residence, who has no kind words for Jane Eyre in Charlotte Brontë's *Jane Eyre*.

Abderames Emperor of the Moors; Julian the Apostate, as a Spanish king, forces him into war by refusing to pay the yearly tribute of one hundred virgins in Henry Fielding's *A Journey From This World to the Next*.

Moses Abednego Jewish clerk in the Independent West Diddlesex Fire and Life Insurance Co.; his father precipitates its collapse in William Makepeace Thackeray's *The History of Samuel Titmarsh and the Great Hoggarty Diamond*.

Abellino See Count Rosalvo.

Princess Abenaide of Morocco Exquisite daughter of Sultan Abenamin of Morocco and Eloisa Clinton; her father smuggles her out of Morocco disguised as a male page; she marries young Harry Clinton in Henry Brooke's *The Fool of Quality*.

Emperor Abenamin of Morocco Rescuer of Eloisa Clinton, whom he marries after his conversion to Christianity; the father of Abenaide, he flees to England to protect his daughter and to be among Christians in Henry Brooke's *The Fool of Quality*.

Abencerrage Rebellious son of Sultan Abenamin of Morocco and a concubine; his threat to the throne and his lust for his half sister Abenaide contribute to the sultan's reasons for fleeing to England in Henry Brooke's *The Fool of Quality*.

Raphael Aben-Ezra Rich, educated Jew, actually Miriam's son; initially a troublemaker and enamored of Hypatia, he loses all faith in human nature, gives up his wealth, and becomes the student of his dog, Bran; he recovers some faith, is finally converted to Christianity by Augustine, marries Victoria, and tries to save Hypatia in Charles Kingsley's *Hypatia*.

Abigail Servant in the household of Count Melvil; she is the victim of the scheme by Ferdinand and Teresa to cheat Mademoiselle de Melvil in Tobias Smollett's *The Adventures of Ferdinand Count Fathom*.

Mrs. Abigail Any of several maidservants in Henry Fielding's *The History of Tom Jones*. Also see Honour Blackmore.

The Misses Ablewhite Godfrey Ablewhite's two giggling sisters, dubbed the Bouncers by Gabriel Betteredge; they are guests at Rachel Verinder's birthday celebration, where the yellow diamond is shown off and stolen in Wilkie Collins's *The Moonstone. A Romance*.

Mr. Ablewhite Apoplectic father of Godfrey; angered by Rachel Verinder's refusal to marry his son, he refuses to become her guardian as desired by the will of her late mother, Lady Julia Verinder, in Wilkie Collins's *The Moonstone. A Romance*.

Mrs. Ablewhite Downtrodden mother of Godfrey and two daughters; she escorts Rachel Verinder to London, where she and her irascible husband intend to provide Rachel with shelter after her mother's death in Wilkie Collins's *The Moonstone. A Romance*.

Godfrey Ablewhite Suave lay preacher and cousin of Rachel Verinder, to whom he becomes engaged for a while in order to gain her fortune; he sees Franklin Blake remove a diamond from Rachel's room, and then he makes off with it himself; he is murdered by Hindu priests to recover the jewel sacred to their temple, where it originally lodged in Wilkie Collins's *The Moonstone. A Romance*.

Abner Incompetent, disloyal shepherd employed by George Fielding on his ranch in Australia; he leaves and is followed and "killed" by Jacky but recovers to return and complain to George in Charles Reade's *It Is Never Too Late to Mend*.

Abner Arthur Abner's son, a Jew whom Matey Weyburn protects as a schoolboy in George Meredith's *Lord Ormont and his Aminta*.

Arthur Abner Man who arranges for Lady Charlotte to hire Matey Weyburn as a tutor in George Meredith's *Lord Ormont and his Aminta*.

Aboan A friend of Oroonoko; he seduces the king's old wife, Onahal, so that Oroonoko may see Imoinda, who is under her guardianship, in Aphra Behn's *Oroonoko*.

Abraham The Biblical patriarch, who almost loses his wife to Totis, king of Egypt; he refuses gifts of Charoba, but when he discovers she slipped jewels into his supplies, he spends them on pious works in the appended romance "The History of Charoba, Queen of Egypt" in Clara Reeve's *The Progress of Romance*.

Abraham Faithful servant of Richard Annesly in Henry Mackenzie's *The Man of the World*.

Achilles Hero whose spirit the author encounters in Elysium in Henry Fielding's *A Journey From This World to the Next*.

Anophel Achthar Villainous fop, who unsuccessfully attempts to have his way with Anthelia Melincourt in Thomas Love Peacock's *Melincourt*.

Luke Ackroyd Intelligent working man in love with Thyrza Trent; he is rejected and temporarily falls into evil ways in George Gissing's *Thyrza*.

Lawrence Acorn Horse thief and accomplice of John Burrows in the murder of Farmer Trumbull in Anthony Trollope's *The Vicar of Bullhampton*.

Actor Traveler on the wagon who intercepts the Ale-Wife's bottle and who mimics everyone in Charles Johnstone's *Chrysal: or, The Adventures of a Guinea*.

Actress Traveler on the wagon who speaks in "heroicks" and turns up her nose at everything and everyone in Charles Johnstone's *Chrysal: or, The Adventures of a Guinea*.

Mr. Adair Pamphlet writer on the Irish question; he is conceded to be helpful to Mr. Gladstone, but is considered a bore by the debutantes in George Moore's *A Drama in Muslin*.

Adam the First Old man from the town of Deceit; he tries to stop Faithful at the Hill of Difficulty in John Bunyan's *The Pilgrim's Progress From this World to That Which Is to Come*.

Adams Head boy at Dr. Strong's school in Charles Dickens's *The Personal History of David Copperfield*.

Mrs. Adams Long-suffering, self-interested wife of Parson Adams; she objects to his support of Fanny Goodwill and Joseph Andrews against Lady Booby, which threatens the welfare of Adams's own family in Henry Fielding's *The History of the Adventures of Mr. Joseph Andrews and of his Friend Mr. Abraham Adams*.

Abraham Adams Learned country parson, whose virtue prompts him to support the innocent or afflicted and condemn the hypocritical despite the consequences; he accompanies Joseph Andrews and Fanny Goodwill to their home parish in Henry Fielding's *The History of the Adventures of Mr. Joseph Andrews and of his Friend Mr. Abraham Adams*. He is the editor's friend, who perused and evaluated the manuscript that is published as *A Journey From This World to the Next*.

Dick (Jack) Adams Parson Adams's favorite child, who is reported drowned and prompts the parson's disproportionate grief; this behavior contradicts his admonition to Joseph Andrews to love in moderation in Henry Fielding's *The History of the Adventures of Mr. Joseph Andrews and of his Friend Mr. Abraham Adams*.

John Adams English sailor who escapes from Africa with Peter Wilkins in Robert Paltock's *The Life and Adventures of Peter Wilkins*.

Jack Adamson Unscrupulous partner of John Caldigate in a gold-mining venture in New South Wales; he conspires with Timothy Crinkett to blackmail Caldigate over his alleged bigamous marriage; he confesses to perjury in the case in Anthony Trollope's *John Caldigate*.

Jack Adderly Northerton's fellow ensign, who joins him in teashing and insulting the new volunteer, Tom Jones, in Henry Fielding's *The History of Tom Jones*.

Joseph Addison Essayist whose soul the author encounters in Elysium in Henry Fielding's *A Journey From This World to the Next*. He appears as a critic and poet in William Makepeace Thackeray's *The History of Henry Esmond*.

Adelaide Mistress of Charles the Simple; she procures the downfall of Julian the Apostate, in his incarnation as court jester, after he makes fun of her appearance in Henry Fielding's *A Journey From This World to the Next*.

Adelhu The heir and only son of King Oeros of Hypotosa and the lover and husband of Eovaai; after he is exiled through the evil machinations of Ochihatou, he disguises himself as Ihoya and acts as protector of Ijaveo in Eovaai's absence; he rescues her from Ochihatou and they are happily reunited in Eliza Haywood's *Adventures of Eovaai, Princess of Ijaveo*.

Adeline Innocent young woman abandoned to thieves by her "father," Louis de St. Pierre (Jean d'Aunoy); she is rescued by the La Mott family and remains with them in an abandoned abbey until La Mott plans to relinquish her to the evil Phillippe, Marquis de Montalt; captured by Montalt, she escapes with her lover, Theodore Peyron, only to be recaptured by Montalt and returned to the abbey; she is released by La Mott to escape to Savoy, where she is sheltered by the clergyman Arnand La Luc; ultimately she testifies against Montalt, is discovered to be his niece and heir to the Montalt fortune, and marries Theodore in Ann Radcliffe's *The Romance of the Forest*.

Adept Alchemist who, while searching for the philosopher's stone, manages to free the spirit Chrysal from a small portion of pure gold and records the narration of the spirit in Charles Johnstone's *Chrysal: or, The Adventures of a Guinea*.

Euthanasia dei Adimari Beautiful, virtuous childhood friend and later the lover of Castruccio Castracani dei Antelminelli; she becomes Countess of Valperga and a benevolent ruler; she tries unsuccessfully to maintain neutrality in the Guelph-Ghibelline conflict of Florence and Lucca; an innocent idealist, she becomes disillusioned by the corrupt power tactics of her lover and finds her love for him changed to grief in Mary Shelley's *Valperga*.

Lauretta dei Adimari Cousin of Euthanasia dei Adimari and wife of Leodino de Guinigi; she is consoled by Euthanasia at Valperga after her husband's execution by Castruccio dei Antelminelli in Mary Shelley's *Valperga*.

Messer Antonio dei Adimari Chief of the Guelph party in Florence, father of Euthanasia, and a blind scholastic, who engrains love of peace and liberty in his daughter in Mary Shelley's *Valperga*.

Admiral Achiever of rank through phlegmatic indolence and servility of soul; he sells contracts to pursers at a great profit and accepts bribes in Charles Johnstone's *Chrysal: or, The Adventures of a Guinea*.

Admiral's Clerk Employee who keeps track of the Admiral's accounts and enriches himself at the same time in Charles Johnstone's *Chrysal: or, The Adventures of a Guinea*.

Admiral's Executive Officer Active man who appeals to his sailors' sense of patriotism and greed before he leads them into battle; he gives Chrysal to the sailor who first spots land in Charles Johnstone's *Chrysal: or, The Adventures of a Guinea*.

Adon-Ai Male spirit who is the friend and familiar of Zanoni in Edward Bulwer-Lytton's *Zanoni*.

Adonijah The old Jewish doctor who provides a haven for Alonzo de Monçada after Fernan di Nunez is interred; he makes a study of Melmoth the Wanderer and tells Alonzo de Monçada of Donna Isadora di Aliaga (Immalee), who was shipwrecked as an infant and grew up on an uninhabited island until she was visited by the Wanderer in Charles Maturin's *Melmoth the Wanderer*.

Adrian   Poetic, sensitive second Earl of Windsor, son of the late King of England, and true friend of Lionel Verney; he vainly loves Evadne Zaimi, assumes the duty of Lord Protector, believes in republican government, and leads the last of mankind toward the safety of the Alps in Mary Shelley's *The Last Man*.

Aearchus   A parasite who ingratiates himself with the duchess, Gigantilla, and has an affair with her but forsakes her in the end in Eliza Haywood's *The Perplex'd Dutchess; or, Treachery Rewarded*.

Agatha   Beloved of Redhead and wily waiting maid to the queen of Utterbol; she assists Ursula to escape the evil king of the Kingdom of the Tower in William Morris's *The Well at the World's End*.

Aged Gallant   Aurora's titled and rich admirer, who lives a life of gallantry and cannot divert himself from the passion of love in Francis Coventry's *The History of Pompey the Little*.

Michael Agelastes (Elephas, The Elephant)   Philosopher and highly influential court wit; publicly an austere sage, in private he is a voluptuary; though seemingly attached to Emperor Alexius Comnenus, he secretly plots to ascend the throne himself but is killed before succeeding in Sir Walter Scott's *Count Robert of Paris*.

Agellius   Callista's suitor, a farmer, who first tells her of the Christian faith; his uncle Jucundus and his brother try to dissuade him from it in John Henry Newman's *Callista*.

Agent   Go-between who arranges Her Grace's patronage interviews for a gift of cash in Charles Johnstone's *Chrysal: or, The Adventures of a Guinea*.

Agnes   Ill-disposed servant of Mme. Walravens; she lives off the generosity of M. Paul Emanuel in Charlotte Brontë's *Villette*.

Agnes   Aged attendant on Maud, Lady Rookwood in William Harrison Ainsworth's *Rookwood*.

Sister Agnes   See Laurentini di Udolpho.

Agni of the Daylings   Warder of the Thingstead or holy place of the Markmen, where Thiodolf and Otter are chosen as war-dukes to lead the Gothic clans in their resistance against the Romans in William Morris's *A Tale of the House of the Wolfings*.

Agon   Tall, aquiline-featured, white-bearded and vindictive high priest of the Zu-Vendi people; he fiercely hates Allan Quatermain and his English party; he joins General Nasta in rebellion against Queen Nyleptha and is killed by Umslopogaas in H. Rider Haggard's *Allan Quatermain*.

Ah Wing (Ah Sing)   Chinese cook of the *Flying Scud*, wounded and buried alive at sea by the crew of the *Currency Lass*; his place is taken by Joseph Amalu in Robert Louis Stevenson's *The Wrecker*.

Mme. Aigredoux   Pauline Home's former schoolmistress, who did not like Mr. Home constantly in her school in Charlotte Brontë's *Villette*.

Aimor   Rebellious Jamaican slave, who protects Matilda from his hostile compatriots in Sophia Lee's *The Recess*.

Mary Ann Ainley   An ugly, unselfish old maid, whose good works Caroline Helstone takes as a model but finds too difficult to follow in Charlotte Brontë's *Shirley*.

Earl of Ainslie   High-principled father of Lady Muriel Orme; he has an interest in science, particularly botany, in Lewis Carroll's *Sylvie and Bruno*. He appears in *Sylvie and Bruno Concluded*.

John de Aire   Calais citizen who urges Eustace St. Pierre to sacrifice his kinsmen to English conquerors in a parable told by Charles Meekly in Henry Brooke's *The Fool of Quality*.

Miss Airish   A loose lady of the town in Eliza Haywood's *The History of Miss Betsy Thoughtless*.

Mr. Akerman   Keeper of Newgate Prison in Charles Dickens's *Barnaby Rudge*.

Alan   Honest hand on the *Hispaniola* who won't join the mutiny; he is killed by Long John Silver in Robert Louis Stevenson's *Treasure Island*.

Chevalier de Alancon   Father of the young nobleman Katherine de Maintenon loves; he gives her and Belinda (Madam de Beaumont) shelter when they run away from their convent in Penelope Aubin's *The Life of Madam de Beaumont*.

Colonel de Alancon   Young nobleman loved by Katherine de Maintenon; she runs away from her convent to marry him in Penelope Aubin's *The Life of Madam de Beaumont*.

Alanthus (Formator)   The hero, who rescues Amoranda and falls in love with her immediately; he disguises himself as the elderly guardian Formator in Mary Davys's *The Reform'd Coquet*.

Demetrius Alasco (Dr. Doboobie)   Evil alchemist and

astrologer, who poisons Thomas Ratcliffe, Earl of Sussex, tries to poison Amy Robsart Dudley, plays on the fears and ambitions of Robert Dudley, Earl of Leicester, with his astrological forecasts, and dies from inhaling his own concoction in Sir Walter Scott's *Kenilworth*.

Alaster Rob Roy MacGregor's minstrel in Sir Walter Scott's *Rob Roy*.

Albany Misanthrope born in Jamaica who haunts Cecilia Beverley to burden her conscience as a rich woman; he takes her to people who need her assistance and tells her his life story of disappointed love in Frances Burney's *Cecilia*.

Duke of Albany (Robert Stewart) Younger brother of King Robert III and uncle of the Duke of Rothsay; he conspires with John Ramorny in the murder of Rothsay in Sir Walter Scott's *The Fair Maid of Perth*.

Earl of Albemarle Host of the masquerade at which young Harry Clinton displays his dancing skills and parries the flirtations of several women in Henry Brooke's *The Fool of Quality*.

Alberic de Montemar Duke Richard of Normandy's young vassal, who becomes his trusted friend and advisor in Charlotte Yonge's *The Little Duke*.

Albert Older son of Lionel Verney and Idris in Mary Shelley's *The Last Man*.

Henrietta Albertus Beautiful and virtuous daughter of Lady Lucy and Lewis Augustus Albertus; she marries a nobleman of great fortune from Heidelberg in Penelope Aubin's *The Life and Adventures of the Lady Lucy*.

Lewis Augustus Albertus Handsome and gentlemanly but jealous German officer, who marries Lady Lucy; falsely believing she and Frederick are having an affair, he kills Frederick and stabs Lucy, leaving her to die in the woods; he leads a life of debauchery until wounded in battle, whereupon he begins to feel remorse and vows to live virtuously; he lives in a hut as a hermit, vindicates Arminda and reunites her with her husband, falls sick, and is nursed by Father Joseph, who discovers his identity and reunites him with Lady Lucy and his family in Penelope Aubin's *The Life and Adventures of the Lady Lucy*.

Lewis Augustus Albertus (the younger) Son of Albertus and Lady Lucy; he lives in the convent with his mother until he is five; then he stays with Father Joseph in the abbey, where he meets his father, who is living as a hermit in Penelope Aubin's *The Life and Adventures of the Lady Lucy*.

Lucy Albertus Beautiful and virtuous daughter of Lady Lucy and Lewis Augustus Albertus; she marries the noble son of Henrietta and Lord Lycidas in Penelope Aubin's *The Life and Adventures of the Lady Lucy*.

Angelo D'Albini Libertine count, who refuses to marry the mother of his children, takes many mistresses, ruins his son by example, and locks his daughter in a convent after killing her lover in Charlotte Dacre's *The Libertine*.

Felix D'Albini Aristocratic son of Angelo D'Albini and Gabrielle Di Montmorency; his self-love and rejection of his mother are encouraged by his nurse; he ends up a thief in Charlotte Dacre's *The Libertine*.

Agnes D'Albini (Ida) Lost daughter of Angelo D'Albini and Gabrielle Di Montmorency; she lived in Germany after her escape from Pierre Bouffuet and fell in love but gave up her lover to please her adoptive parents; she finally ends up locked in a convent by her father in Charlotte Dacre's *The Libertine*.

Rosaline, Lady Albury The Marchesa Baldoni's sister and Sir Harry Albury's wife; she is fond of her cousin Colonel Stubbs; she befriends Ayala Dormer, inviting her to visit and doing all she can to further a match between Ayala and her cousin in Anthony Trollope's *Ayala's Angel*.

Sir Harry Albury Jovial Master of Foxhounds who provides Ayala Dormer with a pony so that she can ride during her visit to his country place in Anthony Trollope's *Ayala's Angel*.

Mrs. Albuzzi Loquacious lady of rank; she finds democratic principles loathsome in William Beckford's *Azemia*.

Alcidiana Miranda's younger sister, upon whose fortune Miranda and Tarquin rely; when Alcidiana threatens to marry against her wishes, Miranda plots her murder; Alcidiana survives two attempts made on her life and eventually obtains a pardon for Tarquin and her sister in Aphra Behn's *The Fair Jilt*.

Mr. Alcock Bath innkeeper who, with the help of his Methodist scullery maid Deborah, guides Geoffry Wildgoose to the Methodist meeting place in Richard Graves's *The Spiritual Quixote*.

Madeline Alcot A young society matron, Lady Kitty Ashe's social rival in Mrs. Humphry Ward's *The Marriage of William Ashe*.

Cytherea Bradleigh Aldclyffe Wealthy unmarried woman who, as the girl Cytherea Bradleigh, fell in love with Ambrose Graye but mysteriously refused his offer of marriage; having inherited a fortune and taken the family name Aldclyffe, she hires Cytherea Graye as lady's maid and Aeneas Manston as steward and resorts to deceit to promote their marriage; after Manston's death she reveals to Cytherea Graye that he was her son by a cousin who deserted her and the reason for her refusal of Ambrose Graye's hand; she dies, leaving her property to Cytherea Graye in Thomas Hardy's *Desperate Remedies*.

Alderigo   Cousin to Castruccio dei Antelminelli; a rich London merchant, he persuades Edward II of England to exile his friend Piers Gavaston and advises Castruccio in affairs of the English court in Mary Shelley's *Valperga*.

Leonora Aldi   Italian aristocrat; she marries an Englishman who is later killed in the Napoleonic wars; she marries Captain Brooks and then dies after the births of Owen and Beatrice Brooks in Caroline Norton's *Lost and Saved*.

Don Gomez d'Aldova   Physician who attends the feverish Amelia de Gonzales and instantly falls in love with her in William Beckford's *Modern Novel Writing; or, the Elegant Enthusiast*.

Father Aldrovand   Norman priest, who serves as Eveline Berenger's father confessor, and who competes with Wilkin Flammock as her chief advisor in Sir Walter Scott's *The Betrothed*.

Mr. Aldworth   Wealthy landowner and magistrate who, over the objections of his clerk Mr. Newland, assumes that Geoffry Wildgoose and Jeremiah Tugwell are innocent until proven guilty with regard to a stolen horse in Richard Graves's *The Spiritual Quixote*.

Alehouse-Keeper's Daughter   Purchaser of Pompey from the Maiden Aunt's footman; she takes him to live in a garret in Smithfield in Francis Coventry's *The History of Pompey the Little*.

Duke of Alencon   Officer in the army of Francis I; he leads a small body of soldiers in an orderly retreat following the battle of Pavia in William Godwin's *St. Leon*.

Ale-Wife   Traveler on the wagon who drinks a great deal and offers a bottle of gin to the Disguised Gentleman in Charles Johnstone's *Chrysal: or, The Adventures of a Guinea*.

Alexis   Servant at Bellfont who acts as one of Philander's go-betweens to Sylvia in Aphra Behn's *Love Letters Between a Nobleman and His Sister*.

Catharina Alexowna   Livonian woman cited as a model of beauty and virtue by Fum Hoam in a letter to Lien Chi Altangi; captured and enslaved by the Russians,

she attracts the notice of Peter the Great, who makes her his wife in Oliver Goldsmith's *The Citizen of the World*.

Ferdinand Alf   Style-conscious literary acquaintance of Lady Carbury and editor of the *Evening Pulpit*; he stands against Augustus Melmotte as Parliamentary candidate for Westminster and loses in Anthony Trollope's *The Way We Live Now*.

Alfonso the Good   Rightful lord of Otranto, poisoned by Prince Manfred's grandfather for his realm; his ghost, represented by an armor-clad giant in a monstrous plumed helmet, throws down the castle walls and ascends to heaven in a catastrophic revenge finale in Horace Walpole's *The Castle of Otranto*.

Alhahuza   Head of the rebel faction in Hypotosa that ousts Ochihatou; he aids Eovaai, giving her shelter and magic herbs to prevent Ochihatou's evil intentions toward her in Eliza Haywood's *Adventures of Eovaai, Princess of Ijaveo*.

Mahbub Ali   Afghan Muslim horse trader and spy for the British; he treats young Kim as a son in Rudyard Kipling's *Kim*.

Clara di Aliaga   Wife of Don Francisco di Aliaga and the overbearing, insensitive mother of Isidora (Immalee) and Fernan di Aliaga in Charles Maturin's *Melmoth the Wanderer*.

Fernan di Aliaga   Hot-tempered brother of Isidora (Immalee); he unsuccessfully defends his sister against and is slain by Melmoth the Wanderer in Charles Maturin's *Melmoth the Wnaderer*.

Francisco di Aliaga   Father of Isidora and Fernan and husband of Clara; his business ventures keep from the di Aliaga estate during Isidora's reorientation; returning to his family, he is accompanied by Mantilla, to whom he has betrothed Isidora, unaware that Isidora has married Melmoth the Wanderer in Charles Maturin's *Melmoth the Wanderer*.

Isidora (Immalee) di Aliaga   Daughter of Don Francisco di Aliaga; as an infant she is shipwrecked and grows up on an uninhabited island where she is visited by Melmoth the Wanderer and falls in love with him; after she is found and returned to Spain, the Wanderer visits her again and they are married in a non-Christian ceremony; her marriage is discovered and she is turned over to the Inquisition; she dies shortly after giving birth to the Wanderer's child in Charles Maturin's *Melmoth the Wanderer*.

Alice   Maid to Ellinor and Matilda and witness of the

marriage of Lord Leicester and Matilda in Sophia Lee's *The Recess*.

Alice Inquisitive but sensible seven-year-old heroine, who follows a rabbit down a hole and into a fantasy land where her size and shape are subject to surprising changes; she keeps her head, literally and figuratively, throughout encounters with creatures that embody various kinds of tyrannical nonsense, finally triumphantly denouncing the "pack of cards" at the trial which concludes Lewis Carroll's *Alice's Adventures in Wonderland*. Aged "seven and a half, exactly," she climbs through a drawing-room mirror into a world laid out like a gigantic chess board; participating in the game, she reaches the eighth square and is crowned queen in *Through the Looking-Glass*.

Alice's Sister Elder sister and afternoon companion who listens to Alice's narration of her dream; she envisions it herself and acknowledges her disadvantage of being an adult and part of the "real" world; she reflects that Alice will grow up to share her dream with her own children in Lewis Carroll's *Alice's Adventures in Wonderland*.

Alick A shepherd on the Poyser farm in George Eliot's *Adam Bede*.

Alithea Ellinor's favorite attendant, who helps her mistress escape from Lord Arlington (2) in Sophia Lee's *The Recess*.

Mr. Allaby Rector of Crampsford; he gives Theobald Pontifex his first job; he is Christina Allaby Pontifex's father in Samuel Butler's *The Way of All Flesh*.

Mrs. Allaby Mother of Christina Allaby Pontifex; she tries to marry off her other daughters but doesn't know how in Samuel Butler's *The Way of All Flesh*.

Allan One of Rob Roy MacGregor's clan in Sir Walter Scott's *Rob Roy*.

Mrs. Allan Guy Mannering's housekeeper, responsible for the womanly aspects of Julia Mannering's upbringing in Sir Walter Scott's *Guy Mannering*.

Allan-a-Dale Robin Hood's gaily dressed minstrel, who captures Prior Aymer in Sir Walter Scott's *Ivanhoe*.

Allchin Grocer's clerk who cannot keep a job but becomes a faithful assistant in Will Warburton's grocer's shop in George Gissing's *Will Warburton*.

Mr. Allen Well-to-do, sensible neighbor of the Morland family; his kindness in including Catherine Morland on a visit to Bath raises speculation that she will be his heir in John Thorpe and, consequently, in General Tilney in Jane Austen's *Northanger Abbey*.

Mrs. Allen Good-humored, indolent, childless matron, fond of fashionable attire, in whose charge Catherine Morland visits Bath in Jane Austen's *Northanger Abbey*.

Mrs. Allen Isaac Allen's wife, disappointed when her son, George, marries Priscilla Broad in Mark Rutherford's *The Revolution In Tanner's Lane*.

Arabella Allen Dark-haired young lady with fur-topped boots, who is an attendant at Isabella Wardle's wedding and the sister of Ben Allen; she elopes with Nathaniel Winkle in Charles Dickens's *The Posthumous Papers of the Pickwick Club*.

Benjamin Allen Coarse, dissolute medical student, who becomes a medical partner with Bob Sawyer in Bristol; he is Arabella Allen's brother in Charles Dickens's *The Posthumous Papers of the Pickwick Club*.

Fanny Allen Isaac Allen's daughter, who is courted by Thomas Broad in Mark Rutherford's *The Revolution In Tanner's Lane*.

George Allen With his father Isaac, a shopkeeper in Cowfold; he marries Priscilla Broad, is politically active in free-trade debate, is falsely accused of infidelity with Marie Pauline Coleman, and emigrates to America with his parents in Mark Rutherford's *The Revolution In Tanner's Lane*.

Isaac Allen An ardent Whig, shopkeeper, and deacon in the Reverend Broad's chapel in Cowfold; a friend of Zachariah Coleman, he emigrates to America with his family after confrontation with Broad in Mark Rutherford's *The Revolution In Tanner's Lane*.

Sir John Allestree London acquaintance of Archibald Reeves; he warns Harriet Byron of the mischievous and revengeful character of Sir Hargrave Pollexfen in Samuel Richardson's *Sir Charles Grandison*.

Mr. Allewinde Erudite Dublin barrister, who leads the Crown case against Thady Macdermot for the murder of Captain Ussher in Anthony Trollope's *The Macdermots of Ballycloran*.

Mrs. Allison Lord Fontenoy's kind, widowed friend, who will not marry him until her son, Lord Ancoats, marries and comes to live at Castle Luton in Mrs. Humphry Ward's *Sir George Tressady*.

Thomas Allworthy Benevolent and generous-spirited squire, who raises as his own the foundling Tom Jones; he is brother to Bridget Allworthy and uncle to Master Blifil, whom he makes his heir until Lawyer Dowling finally reveals the extent of Blifil's hypocrisy; Allworthy is benefactor to many poor and needy individuals throughout Henry Fielding's *The History of Tom Jones*.

Alonzo Nephew of the governor of Flanders; he shares a bed with Sylvia at an inn while she is dressed as the Chevalier Bellumere; he boasts that no woman can capture his heart; Sylvia schemes to win him and, with Brilliard's help, succeeds in spending most of his fortune in Aphra Behn's *Love Letters Between a Nobleman and His Sister*.

Don Alonzo Young lord who loves Arminda and marries her in secret before going to the army; he believes the Duchess and Grizalinda when they claim Arminda betrayed him with Constantine until Augustus the Hermit (Lewis Augustus Albertus) proves Arminda's innocence and they are reunited in Penelope Aubin's *The Life and Adventures of the Lady Lucy*.

Alphones Dapper but cowardly little French cook with enormous black moustachios; he fled to Africa after killing his girlfriend's lover in Marseille; he accompanies Allan Quatermain to the Zu-Vendis and returns to civilization with Quatermain's manuscript narrating their adventures in H. Rider Haggard's *Allan Quatermain*.

Alphonso the Chaste Spanish king and uncle of Julian the Apostate in his incarnation as a king; he educates and trains Julian to be his heir in Henry Fielding's *A Journey From This World to the Next*.

David Alroy The Jewish "Prince of the Captivity" in thirteenth-century Palestine under the rule of the Turkish caliph; he leads a revolt that is initially successful but ultimately fails because Alroy abandons the altruism that created his initial triumph in Benjamin Disraeli's *The Wondrous Tale of Alroy*.

Miriam Alroy David Alroy's sister, who is devoted to her brother and stands with him when he falls from power and is thrown into prison in Benjamin Disraeli's *The Wondrous Tale of Alroy*.

Colonel Altamont (Johnny Armstrong, J. Amory) Mysterious Indian stranger, who turns out to be Lady Clavering's first husband, J. Amory, transported as a convicted felon and long believed dead; his reappearance invalidates her marriage to Sir Francis Clavering until it is discovered that Altamont had previously, as Johnny Armstrong, been married to Madame Fribsby in William Makepeace Thackeray's *The History of Pendennis*.

Lord Altamont A duke, who is brother of the recently widowed Lady Matilda Sufton and the eventual spouse of Adelaide Julia Douglas in Susan Ferrier's *Marriage*.

Altemira Woman disguised as a man because she has been seduced by Lord Lofty and wishes to get even with him; she does so by masking herself as Amoranda and marrying Lofty in Mary Davys's *The Reform'd Coquet*.

Francesca Altifiorla Meddling feminist, who preaches that men on the whole are bad; she persuades Cecilia Holt to break off her relationship with Sir Francis Geraldine; she tries to wreck Cecilia's marriage to George Western by encouraging Sir Francis to tell the husband of his broken engagement with Cecilia in Anthony Trollope's *Kept in the Dark*.

Arthur Danvers, Lord Alton Brave, noble elder brother of Richard Danvers (Lord Alton) and the real father of Julian Danvers; he challenges Fabroni, who had insulted his wife's family and nation, and dies in the duel that follows in William Godwin's *Cloudesley*.

Richard Danvers, Lord Alton Younger brother of Arthur Danvers, Lord Alton; he cheats his nephew, Julian Danvers, of his name and his inheritance; he later feels compunction at his misdeed and hires William Meadows to locate Julian in William Godwin's *Cloudesley*.

Earl of Altringham Good-humoured man of the world; he regularly welcomes George Hotspur to grouse-shooting at his Scottish estate but will never lend him a penny in Anthony Trollope's *Sir Harry Hotspur of Humblethwaite*.

Lady Altringham Hearty consort of the Earl; she loves horseracing and regards Goodwood and Ascot as vital days in the calendar; having a soft spot for George Hotspur, she helps him in his pursuit of Emily Hotspur in Anthony Trollope's *Sir Harry Hotspur of Humblethwaite*.

Duke of Alva Man who raises military support for the Duke of Norfolk in Sophia Lee's *The Recess*.

Sigismund Alvan Hungarian-Jewish Socialist leader, lawyer, and free spirit; he falls in love with Clotilde Von Rüediger but fails to overcome the resistance of her family to her marrying such a disreputable figure and is led to fight a duel with a fellow suitor of Clotilde and is killed in George Meredith's *The Tragic Comedians*.

Alphonso d'Alvarada See Raymond, Marquis de la Cisternas.

Don Alvarez Governor of Puerto Rico and father to Emanuella in Eliza Haywood's *The Rash Resolve; or, the Untimely Discovery*.

Isora D'Alvarez Morton Devereaux's young wife, who is murdered by his brother Aubrey Devereaux in Edward Bulwer-Lytton's *Devereaux*.

Mr. Alworth   Harriot Trentham's cousin and betrothed, who, during their engagement, falls in love with and marries Miss Melman instead; eventually resigned to a bad marriage, he allows Harriot to raise his daughter in Sarah Scott's *A Description of Millenium Hall*.

Mrs. Alworth   Kindly old gentlewoman of large fortune; she raises her grandchildren and hopes for a match between two of them, Harriot Trentham and Mr. Alworth, in Sarah Scott's *A Description of Millenium Hall*.

Alywyn   Master of the many-towered Warding Knowe; he foretells his own death in battle in William Morris's *The Sundering Flood*.

Princess Venetia Corona d'Amagüe   Sister of Lord Rockingham and widow of the Spanish nobleman Beltran Corona d'Amagüe; Bertie Cecil strikes his commanding officer to defend her honor; she becomes Bertie's wife when he has been cleared of forgery charges and has the right to the family estates and title in Ouida's *Under Two Flags*.

Amalia (Princess of Schyll-Weilingen), Duchess of Graaetli, Countess of Pohrendorf   An Austrian aristocrat with affection for Italian patriots; she involves herself in a number of plots involving Vittoria Campa and others in George Meredith's *Vittoria*.

Amalric the Amal   Prince, lover of Pelagia, and leader of the band of warrior Goths searching for the holy city of Asgard whom Philammon meets on the Nile; he falls off a parapet to his death during a fight with Philammon over Pelagia in Charles Kingsley's *Hypatia*.

Joseph Amalu   Hawaiian cook on the *Currency Lass*, whom Loudon Dodd first meets in a bar in San Francisco; he volunteers to go aloft as lookout after murders on the *Flying Scud* in Robert Louis Stevenson's *The Wrecker*.

Monsieur Amand   Melancholy widower who is attracted to Adeline in Ann Radcliffe's *The Romance of the Forest*.

Amanda   Mysterious Flemish young woman, who meets Perry Pickle in a coach from Paris to Ghent; she resists his wooing and finally dismisses him altogether after he embarrasses her in a convent in Tobias Smollett's *The Adventures of Peregrine Pickle*.

Amarantha   A good-natured, innocent, and virtuous woman in love with Theanor in Eliza Haywood's *The Perplex'd Dutchess; or, Treachery Rewarded*.

Giles de Amaury   Grand Master of the Templars and a leader of Christian forces on Crusade; he is jealous of King Richard and sends an assassin against the king; he murders his co-conspirator Conrade, Marquis of Montserrat and is beheaded by Saladin in Sir Walter Scott's *The Talisman*.

Ambroise   French servant of Juliet Granville; he is forced to carry the ransom message to her in England; he marries Margery Fairfield in Frances Burney's *The Wanderer*.

Ambrose   Margaret Borradale's manservant, who, following her death from a stroke brought on by the shock of witnessing the murder of William, enters the service of Travers in order to assist him in pursuing Margaret's jealous husband, Deloraine, in William Godwin's *Deloraine*.

Father Ambrose   See Father Checkley.

Ambrosio   Foundling grown into the austere, revered, proud Abbot of Madrid's Capuchin Monastery; seduced by a demon (Friar Rosario/Matilda de Villanegas), he degenerates into an incestuous rapist and parricide; selling his soul to escape the Inquisition's punishment, he is destroyed by Lucifer in Matthew Lewis's *The Monk*.

Ambrosius   See Edward Glendinning.

Bernard Amedroz   Apathetic, hypochondriac father of Clara and Charles and proprietor of the Belton estate, to which Will Belton becomes heir; resenting him at first, he comes to value his interest in improving the estate and supports Will's courtship of Clara; his sudden death puts Will in possession of the estate in Anthony Trollope's *The Belton Estate*.

Charles Amedroz   Bernard's son, the heir to the Belton estate until debt drove him to suicide; Will Belton succeeds him as heir in Anthony Trollope's *The Belton Estate*.

Clara Amedroz   Resourceful, proud daughter of Bernard Amedroz; she courageously breaks off her engagement with Captain Aylmer when she realizes he was chiefly interested in what she might inherit from Mrs. Winterfield; her distant cousin Will Belton wants to save her from poverty by handing over Belton Castle to her; his generosity and love win her heart in Anthony Trollope's *The Belton Estate*.

Amelia   Amiable cousin and intimate confidante of Felicia; she marries Felicia's rejected suitor Mellifont in Mary Collyer's *Felicia to Charlotte*.

Amelia   Traveling companion of the unnamed narrator in S. J. Pratt's *Travels for the Heart*.

Amelia   Wife of a criminal being defended by Mr. Jaggers, who threatens to drop the case if she keeps pestering him about "My Bill" in Charles Dickens's *Great Expectations*.

Amelia   Beautiful young woman of whom Traffick was enamored and whom Traffick cheated of her fortune; later she marries the Spanish commander of Jamaica in Charles Johnstone's *Chrysal: or, The Adventures of a Guinea*.

Amelia ('Melia)   Servant at Dr. Blimber's school; she is kind to little Paul Dombey in Charles Dickens's *Dombey and Son*.

Amelot   Damian Lacy's page, who leads soldiers during Damian's convalescence, and who marries Rose Flammock at the end in Sir Walter Scott's *The Betrothed*.

Amenartas   Princess of the royal house of Egyptian pharaohs; her exhortation to her son to avenge the death of her husband Kallikrates at the hands of She was passed from generation to generation for two thousand years until it initiated Leo Vincey's and Horace Holly's quest into the African interior in H. Rider Haggard's *She*.

Aminadab   Brother of the Portugese Banker; a Jewish stock-jobber and Her Grace's agent, he feels that he must take revenge upon all Christians for the evils done to his race in Charles Johnstone's *Chrysal: or, The Adventures of a Guinea*.

Young Aminadab   Aminadab's son who debases Chrysal of a quarter of his weight and all of the coin's beauty; he gives his Jewish uncle, the Portugese Banker, to the Holy Office and is himself caught by the Holy Office for clipping coins in Charles Johnstone's *Chrysal: or, The Adventures of a Guinea*.

Count Carlo Ammiani   An ardent revolutionist in the cause of Italian liberation; his traditional ideas concerning female roles hinder his relationship with his sweetheart, later his wife, Vittoria Campa; he is killed after leading a failed revolt in George Meredith's *Vittoria*.

Carlo Merthyr Ammiani   The son of Vittoria Campa and Carlo Ammiani in George Meredith's *Vittoria*.

Countess Marcellina Ammiani   Carlo Ammiani's Venetian mother; she initially disapproves of her son's betrothed, Vittoria Campa, for incomplete submission to her son's authority in George Meredith's *Vittoria*.

(Thaumasus) Ammonius   Catholic monk who hurls a stone at the prefect Orestes, is crucified, and is subsequently canonized in Charles Kingsley's *Hypatia*.

Amoranda   Heroine, who is headstrong and very used to having her own way in Mary Davys's *The Reform'd Coquet*.

Blanche Amory   Beautiful, self-centered stepdaughter of Sir Francis Clavering; she jilts Arthur Pendennis to become engaged to Harry Foker, who breaks with her when he learns she has been corresponding with her disreputable father, Colonel Altamont, in William Makepeace Thackeray's *The History of Pendennis*.

Amos   Old shepherd of the Essene monastery, who wel-comes Jesus back, turning over the flock to him in George Moore's *The Brook Kerith*.

Amy (Cherry, Mrs. Amy, Madam Collins)   Roxana's maid who stays with her after her first husband leaves; she volunteers to sleep with Roxana's landlord to save Roxana from being "undone"; later, she is fired by Roxana for wanting to kill Roxana's daughter Susan, and she has Susan put into debtor's prison falsely; finally, she dies of the "French disease" in Daniel Defoe's *The Fortunate Mistress*.

Amy's Gentleman   Messenger for the Prince of ——; he becomes Amy's lover in Daniel Defoe's *The Fortunate Mistress*.

Anana   Black mistress of Don Pedro de Sylva and benefactress to Mary, Queen of Scots; she arranges Matilda's release from a Jamaican prison in Sophia Lee's *The Recess*.

Anatole   Henry Foker's valet in William Makepeace Thackeray's *The History of Pendennis*.

Edgar, Lord Ancoats   Son of Mrs. Allison and heir to Castle Luton; his involvement with an unsuitable actress causes distress to his relations and friends in Mrs. Humphry Ward's *Sir George Tressady*.

Richard Ancrum   Melancholic minister, who befriends David Grieve in Mrs. Humphry Ward's *The History of David Grieve*.

Anderson   Young husband of an ailing, pregnant wife and father of several children; he has brought his family to destitution by going bail for a ne'er-do-well brother; in desperation he turns highwayman and tries to rob Tom Jones; he becomes an object of Tom's benevolence in Henry Fielding's *The History of Tom Jones*.

Anderson   See Marquis of Montrose.

Captain Anderson   Charlotte Grandison's clandestine suitor and the recipient of her rash and regretted written promise not to marry another man without his consent; though the fortune of £10,000 bestowed on her by Sir Charles Grandison is a contrary inducement, Sir Charles's eloquence convinces him of the unmanliness of not releasing her in Samuel Richardson's *Sir Charles Grandison*.

David Anderson Kind farmer of AultRigh; he hires Robert Colwan and leads the burial party after his suicide in James Hogg's *The Private Memoirs and Confessions of a Justified Sinner.*

Hugh Anderson Lovelorn second secretary at the British Legation in Brussels whose courtship of Florence Mountjoy is rebuffed in Anthony Trollope's *Mr. Scarborough's Family.*

James Anderson Young son of David Anderson; he is the last to speak with Robert Colwan before his suicide in James Hogg's *The Private Memoirs and Confessions of a Justified Sinner.*

Job Anderson The *Hispaniola*'s boatswain, who serves as mate after Arrow goes overboard; he leads the first attack on the stockade, wounds Captain Smollett, tries to stab Jim Hawkins, and is killed by Abraham Gray in Robert Louis Stevenson's *Treasure Island.*

Molly Anderson Peggy Anderson's thirteen-year-old daughter, who faithfully nurses her young brother and mother in Henry Fielding's *The History of Tom Jones.*

Peggy Anderson The pregnant wife of Anderson and the mother of several children; the Andersons are cousins of Mrs. Miller, who uses their example as a warning of the hazards of marrying imprudently for love in Henry Fielding's *The History of Tom Jones.*

Tommy Anderson Peggy Anderson's sick seven-year-old son, who shares a bed with his mother; he is restored to health after his father is aided by Tom Jones in Henry Fielding's *The History of Tom Jones.*

Doge Andreas Elderly prince who grants Count Rosalvo his niece for ridding Venice of assassins and political conspirators in Matthew Lewis's *The Bravo of Venice.*

Andrew Ludovic Lesly's grim and burly yeoman in Sir Walter Scott's *Quentin Durward.*

Mr. Andrew Amiable domestic in the household of Henry Clinton in Henry Brooke's *The Fool of Quality.*

Miss Andrews Isabella Thorpe's off-stage dear friend, frequently mentioned by Isabella for the purpose of showing herself to advantage in Jane Austen's *Northanger Abbey.*

Mr. Andrews (Spanking Jack) Friend and schoolmate to Hector Mowbray; he contends with Hugh Trevor for Olivia Mowbray's affection in Thomas Holcroft's *The Adventures of Hugh Trevor.*

Elizabeth Andrews Farmer's wife and mother of Pamela Andrews; her religious and moral values inspire her daughter to resist and overcome repeated attempts of seduction and sexual assault; she attends her daughter during childbirth in Samuel Richardson's *Pamela, or Virtue Rewarded.* As "Gammar Andrews" she is mother of Pamela Andrews and Fanny Goodwill; she corroborates the peddler's story that Gypsies switched Joseph Andrews and Fanny while they were infants in Henry Fielding's *The History of the Adventures of Mr. Joseph Andrews and of his Friend Mr. Abraham Adams.*

Henrietta Maria Honora Andrews Mother of Shamela Andrews; her astute teachings in manipulating men's passions allow her daughter to improve her situation by marrying Squire Booby in Henry Fielding's *An Apology for the Life of Mrs. Shamela Andrews.*

John (Goodman, Goody) Andrews Farmer and father of Pamela Andrews; his religious and moral values inspire his daughter to resist and overcome repeated attempts of seduction and sexual assault in Samuel Richardson's *Pamela, or Virtue Rewarded.* As "Gaffar Andrews" he is father of Pamela Andrews and Fanny Goodwill; in his youth, he was a sergeant at Gibraltar; he is unaware that while he was overseas, Gypsies switched Fanny, his infant daughter, and Joseph Andrews in Henry Fielding's *The History of the Adventures of Mr. Joseph Andrews and of his Friend Mr. Abraham Adams.*

Joseph Andrews Virtuous brother of the paragon, Pamela Andrews; as footman to Lady Booby, he refuses her impolite advances out of virtue and loyalty to Fanny Goodwill; as the long-lost son of Mr. Wilson, he can marry Fanny in Henry Fielding's *The History of the Adventures of Mr. Joseph Andrews and of his Friend Mr. Abraham Adams.*

Pamela Andrews (later Pamela B———) Serving maid who, at sixteen, attracts the attentions of her young master and suffers kidnapping and attempted sexual assault before her virtue persuades him to marry her; thereafter she is the virtuous wife who struggles to raise and educate a family of seven, maintain her errant husband's affections, and learn aristocratic behavior without qualifying her own standards; her letters to her parents tell the story in Samuel Richardson's *Pamela, or Virtue Rewarded.* She is Joseph Andrews's supposed sister, whose outstanding virtue sets an example to Joseph and brings about her marriage to rather than ruin by Squire Booby; her influence saves Joseph from Bridewell; she reluctantly accepts Fanny Goodwill as a sibling in Henry Fielding's *The History of the Adventures of Mr. Joseph Andrews and of his Friend Mr. Abraham Adams.*

Shamela Andrews Hypocritical heroine, who manipulates Squire Booby into marrying her by feigning maidenhood in Henry Fielding's *An Apology for the Life of Mrs. Shamela Andrews.*

Thomas Andrews Eldest nephew of Pamela (Andrews) B——; he wishes to live with his grandparents after Pamela's husband provides them with a farm to manage in Samuel Richardson's *Pamela, or Virtue Rewarded*.

Angelique A titled pupil at Mme. Beck's boarding school in Charlotte Brontë's *Villette*.

Angelo Cornelia de Vereza's lover who, denied her hand, joins the army and is believed to be killed; later he becomes a priest in order to be near Cornelia; he witnesses her death in the Saint Augustin monastery in Ann Radcliffe's *A Sicilian Romance*.

Angharad Daughter of Seithenyn; she marries Prince Elphin and is the object of Rhûn's lustful pursuit, easily foiled by Taliesin in Thomas Love Peacock's *The Misfortunes of Elphin*.

Duke of Anjou French suitor of Queen Elizabeth, who is flattered by his attention in Sophia Lee's *The Recess*.

Ann Eldest daughter of a poor widow; her chronic melancholy attracts her rich, slightly younger neighbor, Mary, to her aid as caretaker and benefactor; after a period of lingering illness Ann's sudden death at their Lisbon retreat casts Mary into despair in Mary Wollstonecraft's *Mary, A Fiction*.

Anna (The Carline) Older woman who cares for Elfhild and whose magical powers save them from danger while they seek for Osberne Wulfsson in William Morris's *The Sundering Flood*.

Lady Annaly Distant relative of Sir Ulick O'Shane's first wife; O'Shane wishes to regain her goodwill; dignified, intelligent, and highly regarded by the public, she sees promise of good character in O'Shane's ward, Harry Ormond, and is proved correct in Maria Edgeworth's *Ormond*.

Florence Annaly Lady Annaly's charming daughter, who wins Harry Ormond's heart; after various misunderstandings and adventures Ormond wins her hand in Maria Edgeworth's *Ormond*.

Sir Herbert Annaly Honorable but sickly son of Lady Annaly; he befriends Harry Ormond and is an example to him of how a just man can improve the lives of others in Maria Edgeworth's *Ormond*.

Annaple Hobbie (Halbert) Elliot's faithful old nurse in Sir Walter Scott's *The Black Dwarf*.

Anne Woman who is seduced and then abandoned; she educates herself and becomes a famous actress; she is depicted as honorable in Caroline Norton's *The Wife and Woman's Reward*.

Princess Anne, Lady of Beaujeau Louis XI's lovely and cherished eldest daughter in Sir Walter Scott's *Quentin Durward*.

Queen [Anne] Wife of King James; she scorns her husband and neglects Prince Henry in Sophia Lee's *The Recess*.

Mr. Annesley Cheerful incumbent of a Hertfordshire parish and father of Harry; his brother-in-law, Peter Prosper, chides him with Harry's failings in Anthony Trollope's *Mr. Scarborough's Family*.

Mrs. Annesley Peter Prosper's sister and Harry Annesley's mother, a sensible, good-humored woman in Anthony Trollope's *Mr. Scarborough's Family*.

Mrs. Annesley Georgiana Darcy's companion in Jane Austen's *Pride and Prejudice*.

Charles Annesley Frivolous but amiable noble dandy; he is a friend of the young Duke of St. James in Benjamin Disraeli's *The Young Duke*.

Harry Annesley Guileless heir of his uncle Peter Prosper of Burton Hall; innocently caught up in the Scarborough plots concerning property and entail, he begins to lose Prosper's confidence as future squire of Burton; Augustus Scarborough tries to steal his love, Florence Mountjoy, and her mother is set against him; he is restored to favor and marries Florence in Anthony Trollope's *Mr. Scarborough's Family*.

Mary Annesley Youngest daughter of the Rector of Burton and sister of Harry; she is wooed and won by Joe Thoroughbung, the brewer, in Anthony Trollope's *Mr. Scarborough's Family*.

Harriet Annesly Gentle daughter of Richard and Harriet Wilkins Annesly; raped by Sir Thomas Sindall, she dies shortly after giving birth to their illegitimate daughter in Henry Mackenzie's *The Man of the World*.

Harriet Wilkins Annesly Plain but saintly wife of Richard Annesly; she dies giving birth to their third child in Henry Mackenzie's *The Man of the World*.

Richard Annesly Parson who eschews his father's wealth, retires to the country, and dies of a broken heart when his daughter is debauched in Henry Mackenzie's *The Man of the World*.

William (Billy) Annesly Impetuous, passionate son of Richard; led astray by Sir Thomas Sindall, he falls into fornication, theft, gambling, and eventually criminal transportation in Henry Mackenzie's *The Man of the World*.

Annette   Beautiful lover of Alphones; her betrayal and Alphones's killing of her lover in a jealous rage are the subjects of much hilarity in H. Rider Haggard's *Allan Quatermain*.

Annette   Madame Montoni's talkative, superstitious maid, who becomes Emily St. Aubert's companion and informant during her captivity in the Castle di Udolpho; she falls in love with Ludovico, the servant who effects Emily's escape; she ultimately marries Ludovico and becomes housekeeper of the St. Aubert estate in Ann Radcliffe's *The Mysteries of Udolpho*.

Anny   Old workhouse woman who helps nurse Old Sally in Charles Dickens's *Oliver Twist*.

Anodos   Twenty-one-year-old protagonist who, on his birthday, is sent on an eastward journey in Fairyland by his "faerie" grandmother; he is seduced by the Maid of the Alder; Pygmalion-like, he sings the marble lady to life and falls in love with her; he acquires a Shadow, fights the giants with his "brothers," suffers from pride, and loses the Shadow when he learns the true nature of love in George MacDonald's *Phantastes*.

(Sacchi) Father Ansaldo   Former suitor to Olivia di Bruno who, upon her rape by and marriage to Ferando di Bruno, becomes a priest; he is the confessor to whom Ferando admits his murder of his brother; later his testimony at Ferando's trial before the Inquisition results in a verdict of death in Ann Radcliffe's *The Italian*.

Castruccio Castracani dei Antelminelli   Impressively handsome, ambitious, abstemious Italian nobleman, who becomes leader of the Ghibelline party in Lucca, proconsul of Lucca, Lord of Lucca, and Imperial Vicar of Tuscany; high principled at first and naturally ingenuous, he subordinates love to ambition and becomes corrupted by power: a cruel, solitary tyrant in Mary Shelley's *Valperga*.

Ruggieri dei Antelminelli   Ghibeline of Lucca and father of Castruccio; with his family, he is exiled from Lucca by the Guelph party in Mary Shelley's *Valperga*.

Anthony   Coarse English archer in Sir Walter Scott's *Castle Dangerous*.

Anthony   Dupe of Cleopatra's cunning wiles; he is forgiven by his saintly wife, Octavia; he commits suicide after hearing the false report of Cleopatra's death that she has sent out to test her power over him in Sarah Fielding's *The Lives of Cleopatra and Octavia*.

Father Anthony   Priest and friend of Father Benedict; he aids in the escape of Madam de Beaumont; later he meets Count de Beaumont in Muscovy but is killed by robbers before he can inform him his wife lives in Penelope Aubin's *The Life of Madam de Beaumont*.

Dr. Pessimist Anticant   (caricature of Thomas Carlyle) Disputatious pamphleteer; his journal, *Modern Charity*, attacks Mr. Harding in Anthony Trollope's *The Warden*.

Antiquarian   A vain man who has such a desire to collect ancient artifacts that he is easily tricked in Charles Johnstone's *Chrysal: or, The Adventures of a Guinea*.

Antonet   Sylvia's maid, who assists and advises her in her amours; she allows Brilliard, whom she loves, to read letters between Octavio and Sylvia; when Brilliard disguises himself as Octavio in order to go to bed with Sylvia, Antonet dupes him by dressing as Sylvia in Aphra Behn's *Love Letters Between a Nobleman and His Sister*.

Antonio   Olivia's father, a rich merchant who has business with the English, is arrested by the Inquisition as a spy, and is freed by English sailors in Charles Johnstone's *Chrysal: or, The Adventures of a Guinea*.

Padre Antonio (Father Antony)   The Portuguese ship's Catholic priest, who clears young Bob Singleton of the charge that he is a Turk and a heretic in Daniel Defoe's *The Life, Adventures, and Pyracies of the Famous Captain Singleton*.

Earl of Antrim   Kinsman of Alister M'Donnell and commander of the Irish army serving in Montrose's Royalist army in Sir Walter Scott's *A Legend of Montrose*.

Madame D'Anville   Parisian hostess and one of Henry Pelham's amours during his stay in Paris in Edward Bulwer-Lytton's *Pelham*.

Apaecides   Unstable brother of Ione; he is raised by Arbaces to be a priest of Isis and is murdered by him after he becomes a Christian in Edward Bulwer-Lytton's *The Last Days of Pompeii*.

Aph-Lin   Richest man in a commuity of the Vril-ya; he serves as host to the Tish in Edward Bulwer-Lytton's *The Coming Race*.

Nicholas Apjohn   Trusted lawyer of Indefer Jones and maker of several of his wills; he tracks down the missing will, which names Isabel Brodrick true heir of Llanfere estate, at the same time unmasking Henry Jones's pathetic hiding of his knowledge of the will's existence so that he might inherit in Anthony Trollope's *Cousin Henry*.

Apollyon Monster of the Valley of Humiliation; Christian fights him and is wounded but puts him to flight in John Bunyan's *The Pilgrim's Progress From this World to That Which Is to Come.*

Apothecary Servant of the charity who sells useless medicines to the charity and gets into a disagreement with the Cook in Charles Johnstone's *Chrysal: or, The Adventures of a Guinea.*

Apothecary Unnamed medical man who treats the nearly drowned Mr. Watson; he announces the arrival of the Duke of Monmouth to overthrow King James in Henry Fielding's *The History of Tom Jones.*

Mr. Appledom A fifty-year-old suitor to Violet Effingham; she finds his suit highly comic, but he is unexceptionable in Lady Baldock's eyes in Anthony Trollope's *Phineas Finn.*

Nicholas (Nick) Appleyard Tunstall farmer who had fought at Agincourt and is the first victim of a black arrow in Robert Louis Stevenson's *The Black Arrow: A Tale of Two Roses.*

Apsimar Tyrant who threatens to punish Julian the Apostate, in his incarnation as a monk, when he fails to betray his deposed predecessor, Justinian II, as promised in Henry Fielding's *A Journey From This World to the Next.*

Aqilmund Goth warrior and a particular friend of Amalric the Amal in Charles Kingsley's *Hypatia.*

Arabella The title character, who, mistaking French romances for true histories, overestimates both her power and her vulnerability to rape; she loves her cousin Charles Glanville but treats him with queenly disdain; she almost becomes to others what she believes herself to be, but is eventually "cured" (humbled) by a rational clergyman in Charlotte Lennox's *The Female Quixote.*

Mrs. Arabin See Eleanor Harding.

Francis Arabin Scholarly clergyman recruited by Archdeacon Grantly in his struggle against Bishop Proudie and Mr. Slope; he marries Eleanor Harding Bold and becomes Dean of Barchester in Anthony Trollope's *Barchester Towers.* He appears in *Framley Parsonage* and in *Doctor Thorne.* His absence in the Holy Land complicates problems for Mr. Crawley in the stolen-cheque scandal in *The Last Chronicle of Barset.*

Susan (Posy) Arabin Younger daughter of Dean Arabin; adored by her grandfather, Mr. Harding, she comforts him in his old age in Anthony Trollope's *The Last Chronicle of Barset.*

Eugene Aram Gentle scholar and scientist, who is arrested on his wedding day and charged with the murder of Geoffrey Lester (Daniel Clarke), uncle of his bride-to-be, Madeline Lester; his post-execution confession (by letter) maintains that the killing was an accident in Edward Bulwer-Lytton's *Eugene Aram.*

Solomon Aram Wily attorney acting for Lady Mason in her trial; he believes that the forensic skills of Mr. Chaffanbrass will win her case in Anthony Trollope's *Orley Farm.*

Araspes A beautiful captive's protector, who learns that even the most virtuous can be overcome by the bad side of his nature in a parable told by Henry Clinton in Henry Brooke's *The Fool of Quality.*

Arbaces Wicked Egyptian magician, who schemes to win Ione and to destroy Glaucus and Apaecides in Edward Bulwer-Lytton's *The Last Days of Pompeii.*

Miss Arbe Provincial lady of talents; she resigns her part in a play to the Stranger, Juliet Granville, and condescends to patronize Juliet's teaching of the harp in Frances Burney's *The Wanderer.*

Giles Arbe Cousin of Miss Arbe; he befriends the Stranger, Juliet Granville, and helps her to discharge her debts in Frances Burney's *The Wanderer.*

Skipper Arblaster Thirsty captain of the *Good Hope* who never ceases lamenting Tom; he is cozzened out of his ship by Will Lawless and Dick Shelton and is tricked into releasing them; Dick saves his life from Yorkists at the cost of the favor of Richard of Gloucester in Robert Louis Stevenson's *The Black Arrow: A Tale of Two Roses.*

Miss Arbour Old lady who lives in the town where Mark Rutherford receives his first preaching appointment; she tells Mark the secret of her miserable marriage to help him decide about his engagement to Ellen (Butts) in Mark Rutherford's *The Autobiography of Mark Rutherford.*

Lord Arbroath Impulsive leader of Queen Mary of Scotland's van at Langside in Sir Walter Scott's *The Abbot.*

Isabella Staveley Arbuthnot Judge Staveley's elder daughter, who brings her family to the Christmas celebrations at Noningsby, the Staveley home, in Anthony Trollope's *Orley Farm.*

Edith Archbold Matron at Silverton Grove House (asylum), who falls in love with Alfred Hardie and follows him to Drayton House, offering two options: to be made happy by his love or to reduce him to an insane slave in Charles Reade's *Hard Cash.*

Mr. Archdale Annabella Richmond's beloved, whom her father finally allows her to marry in Charlotte Smith's *The Young Philosopher*.

Archer Colonel Mannering's lieutenant, who lies to him about the relationship between Captain Vanbest Brown (Henry Bertram) and Sophie Wellwood and then confesses the truth on his deathbed in Sir Walter Scott's *Guy Mannering*.

Charles Archer See Paul Dangerfield.

Sir John Archer Social catch of the season but more interested in racing than in marriage; Miss Vyner successfully pursues him in George Moore's *A Modern Lover*.

Mr. Archibald Gentleman whose testimony establishes the credibility of Mr. Longfield, a defense witness in the murder-robbery trial of Arabella Clement in Henry Brooke's *The Fool of Quality*.

John Archibald Reserved and efficient groom of John, Duke of Argyle, and confidential agent in Sir Walter Scott's *The Heart of Midlothian*.

Arco Mythical son of Perigen and Philella; he murders his father and, with his wife Telamine, founds a cruel race in Robert Paltock's *The Life and Adventures of Peter Wilkins*.

Julia Arden Priggish young woman from Torquay, Devonshire, who is Catharine Furze's roommate at school in Abchurch in Mark Rutherford's *Catharine Furze*.

Knight of Ardenvohr See Sir Duncan Campbell.

Count Ardolph German nobleman who seduces Marchesa (Laurina) di Loredani, forces her daughter into seclusion, and kills her husband in Charlotte Dacre's *Zofloya; or, The Moor*.

John Ardworth Lawyer and Susan Mivers's kinsman, who is mistakenly believed by Lucretia Clavering to be her lost son, Vincent Braddell, in Edward Bulwer-Lytton's *Lucretia*.

Arentia Female friend to Berentha (Biranthus); she helps with the disguise in Mary Davys's *The Reform'd Coquet*.

Mr. Aresby A young captain in the militia who flirts with Cecilia Beverley from the time he meets her at Mr. Monckton's in Frances Burney's *Cecilia*.

Duchess of Argyle Kind and courteous wife of John, Duke of Argyle; she receives Jeanie Deans warmly while she is in London in Sir Walter Scott's *The Heart of Midlothian*.

Duke of Argyle Chief of the Scottish clan Campbell and present head of the College of Justice during the 1752 Appin murder trial; he is an associate of Prestongrange, Lord Advocate of Scotland, in Robert Louis Stevenson's *Catriona*.

Archibald, Duke of Argyle Brother and successor to John, Duke of Argyle and Greenwich, in Sir Walter Scott's *The Heart of Midlothian*.

John, Duke of Argyle Powerful Scottish nobleman, who champions his country; his influence at the court of King George II makes him unpopular but allows him to assist Jeanie Deans in Sir Walter Scott's *The Heart of Midlothian*.

MacCallum More, Duke of Argyle Rob Roy McGregor's protector, who writes letters of reference for Robert Campbell (Rob Roy) in Sir Walter Scott's *Rob Roy*.

M'Callum More, Marquis of Argyle Lord Justice General of Scotland, and feudal enemy of Montrose; although a coward, he is the potent leader of the Presbyterians; he assumes the name Murdoch Campbell when he visits Dalgetty's cell; the Highlanders dub him Gillespie Grumach (ill-favoured one) in Sir Walter Scott's *A Legend of Montrose*.

Mungo Argyle A proud, newly wealthy upstart and a widely detested exciseman who shoots Lord Eaglesham in a dispute over hunting rights in John Galt's *Annals of the Parish*.

Ariadne Beautiful Neapolitan lady to whom Julian the Apostate, in his incarnation as a wise man, loses his heart; she marries elsewhere when he decides her dowry is insufficient in Henry Fielding's *A Journey From This World to the Next*.

Ariel Ungainly, feeble-minded cousin of and attendant on Miserrimus Dexter; doglike in her devotion, she dies on his grave not long after his death in Wilkie Collins's *The Law and the Lady*.

Arinbiorn of the Bearings Chief of the Bearings; his fury at the invading Romans leads him to launch a premature attack before the forces of Otter are prepared; he goes mad because of his responsibility for Otter's death in William Morris's *A Tale of the House of the Wolfings*.

Aristo Greek artist and brother of Callista; he tries first to dissuade her from Christianity, then to save her from martyrdom in John Henry Newman's *Callista*.

Arithea A woman of the Bashaw's seraglio who is the beloved of Bellamont in Eliza Haywood's *Philidore and Placentia; or, L'Amour trop delicat*.

Lord Arlington (1) Credulous and jealous dupe of Queen Elizabeth; Ellinor is forced to marry him in Sophia Lee's *The Recess*.

Lord Arlington (2) Ignorant naval officer who assumes the family title after the death of his brother in Sophia Lee's *The Recess*.

Allan Armadale Inheritor of an estate worth £8,000 a year and target of the relentless fortune hunter Lydia Gwilt; he is befriended by Ozias Midwinter, his darker self, and saved by him from a murder attempt by Gwilt; he marries Eleanor Milroy in Wilkie Collins's *Armadale*.

Arminda A lady of quality disguised as a shepherdess; her reputation has been ruined by the Duchess and Grizalinda, and her husband, Don Alonzo, has deserted her; vindicated by Lewis Augustus Albertus, she is reunited with Alonzo in Penelope Aubin's *The Life and Adventures of the Lady Lucy*.

Constance Grandison, Lady Armine Wife of Sir Ratcliffe Armine and mother of Ferdinand Armine in Benjamin Disraeli's *Henrietta Temple: A Love Story*.

Ferdinand Armine Member of an old Roman Catholic family but living in genteel poverty; he gets into debt, and, when his grandfather's entire fortune goes to his cousin, Katherine Grandison, he thinks he must, for the sake of his family, marry her even though he does not love her—even after he falls hopelessly in love with Henrietta Temple—in Benjamin Disraeli's *Henrietta Temple: A Love Story*.

Sir Ratcliffe Armine Father of Ferdinand Armine; that he and his wife live quietly on a heavily mortgaged estate largely motivates Ferdinand's decision to marry his rich cousin even though he is in love with Henrietta Temple in Benjamin Disraeli's *Henrietta Temple: A Love Story*.

Mr. Armitage Writer on radical subjects, George Delmont's mentor, and friend of the Glenmorris family in Charlotte Smith's *The Young Philosopher*.

Mr. Armitage A mill owner, who is shot at when there is not enough work in spite of his attempts to conciliate his workers in Charlotte Brontë's *Shirley*.

Captain Armour Officer of an English army corps quartered in Gudetown; he is discovered to be the brother of a girl hanged for child murder; he rises from stable boy to gentleman in John Galt's *The Provost*.

Mr. Armstrong Dean of Winchester and father of Rachel, Viscountess Castlewood, in William Makepeace Thackeray's *The History of Henry Esmond*.

Mr. Armstrong Bigoted Protestant clergyman who takes meat to the Galway poor on Fridays in Anthony Trollope's *The Landleaguers*.

Mr. Armstrong Sixty-year-old vicar near Cowfold; he teaches astronomy to Didymus Farrow and Miriam Tacchi in Mark Rutherford's *Miriam's Schooling*.

Grace Armstrong Hobbie (Halbert) Elliot's distant cousin, as well as his betrothed, and a cherished member of the Elliot household; abducted by Willie Graeme, she is soon released, and she and Hobbie are married in Sir Walter Scott's *The Black Dwarf*.

Joseph Armstrong Protestant clergyman who helps uncover Barry Lynch's plan to have Doctor Colligan murder Barry's sister, Anty, in Anthony Trollope's *The Kellys and the O'Kellys*.

Army Chaplain Cleric considered not well bred in England; in America he becomes a leader of polite society and marries the lost European Lady in Charles Johnstone's *Chrysal: or, The Adventures of a Guinea*.

Army Commander Sinner who rapes, murders, and robs his brother's wife and then buys forgiveness and salvation with the stolen gold and jewels, and who, to avoid secular punishment, joins the Jesuits in Charles Johnstone's *Chrysal: or, The Adventures of a Guinea*.

Arnobius Jucundus's acquaintance, a young man and student who is interested in his advancement and has no religious beliefs in John Henry Newman's *Callista*.

Dr. Arnold Imposing and dominating yet kindly headmaster of Rugby School who brings about the moral and spiritual regeneration of Tom Brown in Thomas Hughes's *Tom Brown's Schooldays*.

Mr. Arnold Genteel and handsome husband of Sidney Bidulph Arnold and owner of Arnold Abbey; estranged from his wife through Mrs. Gerrarde's intrigues, he is happily reunited with Sidney after a long absence; he dies of a wounded skull after a riding accident in Frances Sheridan's *Memoirs of Miss Sidney Bidulph*.

Widow Arnold Former wife of Mr. Arnold's deceased elder brother; she marries the attorney she enlists in her effort to gain the Arnold estate by passing off her illegitimate child as the eldest Mr. Arnold's heiress in Frances Sheridan's *Memoirs of Miss Sidney Bidulph*.

Catherine Sidney Bidulph Arnold Daughter of Lady Bidulph, sister of Sir George Bidulph, wife of Mr. Arnold, mother of two daughters, and best friend of Cecilia, to whom this ill-fated heroine writes copiously of her unconsummated love for Orlando Faulkland and her reasons for renouncing him in an ongoing struggle to live virtuously in Frances Sheridan's *Memoirs of Miss Sidney Bidulph.*

Cecilia Arnold   Younger and less beautiful but well-liked daughter of Sidney Bidulph Arnold and Mr. Arnold in Frances Sheridan's *Memoirs of Miss Sidney Bidulph.*

Charles Arnold   The eldest son of a modest country gentleman and a gallant midshipman aboard the *Amputator*; he falls in love with the captured Azemia; he loses her when she is removed from Mrs. Periwinkle's custody; eventually he rescues her from three poachers and marries her in William Beckford's *Azemia.*

Charlotte Arnold   Romantic, loyal servant to Mrs. James Frost and later to her grandson, James; she marries Thomas Madison in Charlotte Yonge's *Dynevor Terrace.*

Dolly Arnold   Elder and beautiful daughter of Sidney Bidulph Arnold and Mr. Arnold in Frances Sheridan's *Memoirs of Miss Sidney Bidulph.*

John Arnold   Footman on Mr. B——'s Bedfordshire estate; he wins Pamela Andrews's trust by delivering her letters to her parents but betrays that trust by secretly showing the letters to the man who is attempting to seduce her, Mr. B——, before delivering them in Samuel Richardson's *Pamela, or Virtue Rewarded.*

Quilt Arnold   Bodyguard to Jonathan Wild in William Harrison Ainsworth's *Jack Sheppard.*

Andrew Arnot   Archer for Louis XI's Scottish Guard who relates the king's reaction to the Duke of Burgundy's message of war in Sir Walter Scott's *Quentin Durward.*

Mr. Arnott   Brother of Mrs. Harrel; he constantly pays debts for Mr. Harrel and unsuccessfully loves Cecilia Beverley in Frances Burney's *Cecilia.*

Arnulf of Flanders   Treacherous murderer of Duke William of Normandy; he is ultimately forgiven by Duke Richard in Charlotte Yonge's *The Little Duke.*

Lady Arsinoe Arrogant   Woman of rank and the pretentious wife of Colonel Brusque; she finds conversation about poor people distasteful at dinner in William Beckford's *Azemia.*

Arrow   Ship's mate on the *Hispaniola* with Long John Silver's sponsorship; drunk most of time and overfamiliar with the crew, he disappears overboard one night before the discovery of the conspiracy in Robert Louis Stevenson's *Treasure Island.*

Mr. Arrowpoint   Hospitable owner of Quetcham Hall and father of Catherine Arrowpoint in George Eliot's *Daniel Deronda.*

Mrs. Arrowpoint   Catherine Arrowpoint's mother, who is disappointed at her daughter's marriage to Julius Klesmer in George Eliot's *Daniel Deronda.*

Catherine Arrowpoint   Sensible heiress, who disturbs her family by marrying her poor Jewish music teacher, Herr Klesmer, in George Eliot's *Daniel Deronda.*

Artemia   Woman in love with Philamont; Gigantilla discredits her with him; she becomes a Vesta priestess in Eliza Haywood's *The Perplex'd Dutchess; or, Treachery Rewarded.*

Artful Dodger   See Jack Dawkins.

Arthur   King of the kings in Britain in Thomas Love Peacock's *The Misfortunes of Elphin.*

Arthur   Trustworthy son of Rose Cecil's nurse; he conducts Leicester and Matilda to France in Sophia Lee's *The Recess.*

Arthur   The Black Squire, who helps to rescue three imprisoned damsels; he shifts his affections from Atra to Birdalone, whom he ultimately marries in William Morris's *The Water of the Wondrous Isles.*

Mrs. Arthur   Bedfordshire neighbor whose sneers and innuendos become pleasantries once Pamela Andrews is raised from the servant class; she and her husband are given to bickering in Samuel Richardson's *Pamela, or Virtue Rewarded.*

George (Gerdie) Arthur   A delicate boy, orphaned son of a clergyman who ministered in an industrial parish in the Midlands, who is entrusted to the protection of Tom Brown and thus becomes the means of his moral and spiritual regeneration in Thomas Hughes's *Tom Brown's Schooldays.* Arthur is reported as winning a scholarship to Trinity College, Cambridge, in *Tom Brown at Oxford.*

Earl of Arundel   Guardian of the young Lord Leicester, for whom he intends Sir Patrick Lineric's daughter as a wife; he introduces Elizabeth Tudor, later Queen Elizabeth, to Leicester in Sophia Lee's *The Recess.*

Lady Arundel   Sister to Lady Pembroke and Sir Philip Sidney and constant ally of Matilda and Ellinor in Sophia Lee's *The Recess.*

Clare Arundel   Beautiful niece of the Catholic patroness Lady St. Jerome; she shares Lothair's desire to alleviate poverty and nurses Lothair after he is hurt fighting for the liberationists in Italy in Benjamin Disraeli's *Lothair*.

Asbella   Mother of Valerius; she becomes very ill and loses all her beauty and, therefore, the little female power she had in Jane Barker's *Exilius; or, The Banish'd Roman*.

Mrs. Asgill   Charlotte Melmoth's friend, who dies and leaves Charlotte her jointure in Thomas Amory's *The Life of John Buncle, Esq.*

Ash   Tree ogre, who is always trying to fill the hole in his heart; he follows and threatens Anodos throughout his journey in George MacDonald's *Phantastes*.

Lord Ashburnham   Wealthy young nobleman who becomes engaged to Lady Beatrix Esmond but grows tired of her demands; he marries Lady Mary Butler in William Makepeace Thackeray's *The History of Henry Esmond*.

Lady Ashby   Mother of Sir Thomas; she is a patrician devoted to a dissolute son and antagonistic toward her new daughter-in-law, Rosalie (Murray), in Anne Brontë's *Agnes Grey*.

Sir Thomas Ashby   Dissolute owner of Ashby Park, who, when he marries Rosalie Murray, adds her to his list of possessions, leaving her in the country while he continues his bachelor ways in town in Anne Brontë's *Agnes Grey*.

Henry Ashe   Frail, crippled son of Lady Kitty and William Ashe in Mrs. Humphry Ward's *The Marriage of William Ashe*.

Lady Kitty (Bristol) Ashe   Madcap, unstable wife of William Ashe, cabinet minister; her bizarre behavior is caused by her unhappiness with stifling English society; when she publishes a scurrilous attack on this society and nearly ruins her husband's career, she runs away and dies, reunited at the end with her husband in Mrs. Humphry Ward's *The Marriage of William Ashe*.

William Ashe   Aristocrat, Member of Parliament, and under secretary for foreign affairs; he makes a disastrous marriage with Lady Kitty Bristol after a short acquaintance; his career is nearly ruined by the publication of his wife's book on country-house politics in Mrs. Humphry Ward's *The Marriage of William Ashe*.

Owen Asher   Wealthy, fashionable dilettante, an attractive man of forty; he entices Evelyn Innes to Paris, where he has her trained as an opera star; their six-year liaison shapes her life; an atheist, he tries to destroy her Catholicism in George Moore's *Evelyn Innes*. After she rejects him to take the veil, he finds consolation in aestheticism and travel, though he continues to intrude upon her peace, offering marriage in *Sister Teresa*.

Mrs. Gilbert Ashleigh   Kinswoman of Mr. Vigors; she occupies Dr. Lloyd's old house in Edward Bulwer-Lytton's *A Strange Story*.

Lilian Ashleigh   Young heiress and a natural clairvoyant, whose powers are abused by Louis Grayle; she marries Allen Fenwick in Edward Bulwer-Lytton's *A Strange Story*.

Sir Edward Ashton   Proposed husband for Miss Milner; he is rejected as too old and boring in Elizabeth Inchbald's *A Simple Story*.

Henry Ashton   Youngest child of Sir William and Lady Ashton; he succeeds to his father's estates and is the last of the Ashtons in Sir Walter Scott's *The Bride of Lammermoor*.

Lucy Ashton   The lovely and innocent daughter of Sir William and Lady Ashton; she falls in love with Edgar Ravenswood despite a long-standing feud between their families; her mother's pawn, she eventually breaks with her lover to marry Frank Hayston, Laird of Bucklaw, only to go insane and attack her groom before dying herself in Sir Walter Scott's *The Bride of Lammermoor*.

Margaret Douglas, Lady Ashton   Wife of Sir William Ashton and a wily politician; in her attempts to ruin Edgar Ravenswood and dismiss him as a suitor for her daughter, Lucy, she unwittingly incurs the enmity of the Marquis of A—, causing her husband's downfall in Sir Walter Scott's *The Bride of Lammermoor*.

Colonel Sholto Douglas Ashton   Ambitious heir of Sir William and Lady Ashton; he challenges Edgar Ravenswood and is killed in a duel in Flanders in Sir Walter Scott's *The Bride of Lammermoor*.

Sir William Ashton   Wealthy and politically cunning member of the Scottish Privy Council; he feigns approval of his daughter's romance with Edgar Ravenswood in order to avoid a harmful investigation, but his duplicity loses him his position as well as his daughter in Sir Walter Scott's *The Bride of Lammermoor*.

Mrs. Ashwood   Mrs. Stafford's sister-in-law, who takes Emmeline Mobray into her house near London at Mrs. Stafford's request; there Emmeline meets Humphrey Rochely in Charlotte Smith's *Emmeline: The Orphan of the Castle*.

Asisticus (Scipio)   Scipiana's elder brother, who was originally named Scipio but because of his great exploits as a soldier is given a more important name; in love with

Clarenthia, he is the hero of Jane Barker's *Exilius; or, The Banish'd Roman*.

Colonel Askerton   Bluff ex-military man whose wife, Mary, he had rescued from a bullying drunkard; he leases the shooting at Belton Castle, avoids social contacts, and refuses to attend church in Anthony Trollope's *The Belton Estate*.

Mary Askerton   Intimate friend of Clara Amedroz, who is bullied by Lady Aylmer over the friendship; Mrs. Askerton is the subject of gossip in the town of Belton concerning her rescue from an abusive husband by Colonel Askerton; her living with him prior to her husband's death casts a shadow over her social position in Anthony Trollope's *The Belton Estate*.

Mr. Askew   Solicitor who represents Mr. Furze during his bankruptcy in Mark Rutherford's *Catharine Furze*.

Asmund   Ancient Dayling warrior; he foresees the ill effect on Thiodolf of the dwarf-wrought hauberk and penetrates Wood-Sun's disguise as Thorkettle in William Morris's *A Tale of the House of the Wolfings*.

Mr. Asper   Impecunious second lieutenant of H.M.S. *Harpy*; he is not above sponging on Jack Easy in Captain Frederick Marryat's *Mr. Midshipman Easy*.

Constance Asper   Wealthy heiress with an impeccable reputation; she pines away for Percy Dacier until his infatuation with Diana Warwick wanes and the two marry in George Meredith's *Diana of the Crossways*.

Knight of Aspramonte   Countess Brenhilda's loving but prejudiced Norman father in Sir Walter Scott's *Count Robert of Paris*.

Lady of Aspramonte   The loving but prejudiced Norman mother of Countess Brenhilda in Sir Walter Scott's *Count Robert of Paris*.

Robert Asquith   Diplomat and distant cousin of Isabel Clarendon; he proposes to her when they are young but is refused; he later becomes her friend and adviser and is ultimately accepted in George Gissing's *Isabel Clarendon*.

Astarte   Distinguished calligrapher, who serves as Anna Comnena's slave and Violante's companion in Sir Walter Scott's *Count Robert of Paris*.

Mr. Asterias   Ichthyologist who spends his life searching for a mermaid in Thomas Love Peacock's *Nightmare Abbey*.

Astronomer   Learned man whose long solitude has driven him to madness and the delusion that he is in control of the weather; he exemplifies the dangerous prevalence of imagination which preys incessantly on life in Samuel Johnson's *The History of Rasselas, Prince of Abissinia*.

Atamadoul   Monkey on a chain who tells her history to Eovaai as a warning against Ochihatou: a woman of the bedchamber to Princess Syllalippe, she wanted Ochihatou for herself and disguised herself as Syllalippe to get him, but then was transformed by Ochihatou into a monkey when he learned that he had been tricked in Eliza Haywood's *Adventures of Eovaai, Princess of Ijaveo*.

Sir Ethelbert Atawel   Honorable English nobleman, to whom Francesco de Guinigi entrusts the eighteen-year-old Castruccio dei Antelminelli; he dislikes Piers Gavaston; he teaches Castruccio honor, horsemanship, arms, dance, and courtly behavior in Mary Shelley's *Valperga*.

Athalfrida   Sister of the Gothic king Totila; she is in charge of Veranilda in George Gissing's *Veranilda*.

Atheist   One of the flatterers warned of by the four Shepherds; he tries to convince Christian and Hopeful that the Celestial City does not exist in John Bunyan's *The Pilgrim's Progress From this World to That Which Is to Come*.

Philip Athel   Egyptologist father of Wilfrid Athel; he disapproves of his son's engagement to the governess in George Gissing's *A Life's Morning*.

Wilfrid Athel   Oxford University student whose ill health forces him to return home; he becomes engaged to a governess, Emily Hood, who cancels the engagement because of family troubles and disappears; he enters Parliament and becomes engaged to another lady but meets Emily again after six years and finally marries her in George Gissing's *A Life's Morning*.

Athelstane the Unready   A debauched, slow-witted, drunken direct descendant of Edward the Confessor, revered by the Saxons; Lady Rowena's betrothed, he barely escapes being buried alive in Sir Walter Scott's *Ivanhoe*.

Countess Athenry   Richard Devereux's aunt, who takes him under her wing when her husband is cruel to him; when she wants to make all his decisions for him they quarrel and he returns to Chapelizod and the Royal Irish Artillery in J. Sheridan Le Fanu's *The House by the Churchyard*.

Lewis Athenry   Sickly son of Lord Roland Athenry and Captain Richard Devereux's cousin; he travels on the Continent with Dan Loftus as his tutor and dies there, bringing Devereux much closer to the family inheritance in J. Sheridan Le Fanu's *The House by the Churchyard*.

Lord Roland Athenry Selfish, lunatic uncle of Captain Richard Devereux; he shows no fondness for his nephew; he is frequently reported near death in J. Sheridan Le Fanu's *The House by the Churchyard*.

Earl of Athlin Scottish nobleman who is slain by a neighboring baron, Malcolm of Dunbayne, in Ann Radcliffe's *The Castles of Athlin and Dunbayne*.

Captain Atkins Emily Atkins's beleagured father, who failed to instill religious principles in her in Henry Mackenzie's *The Man of Feeling*.

Mr. Atkins Surgeon aboard the *Thunder* when Roderick Random is kidnapped in Tobias Smollett's *The Adventures of Roderick Random*.

Mr. Atkins Clergyman sent for when Mr. Arnold is dying in Frances Sheridan's *Memoirs of Miss Sidney Bidulph*.

Emily Atkins Young prostitute whom Harley rescues from degradation and reunites with her father in Henry Mackenzie's *The Man of Feeling*.

Will Atkins One of three mutineers; he turns against the English Captain but is eventually captured by the captain, Friday, and Robinson Crusoe in Daniel Defoe's *The Life and Strange Surprizing Adventures of Robinson Crusoe of York, Mariner*.

Nurse Atkinson Mother to Joe Atkinson and wet nurse to Amelia Harris; she shelters Amelia and William Booth after they escape Mrs. Harris before their marriage in Henry Fielding's *Amelia*.

Joe Atkinson Foster brother to Amelia Booth; his secret adoration of her prompts his endless friendship and service to both the Booths; he marries Molly Bennet in Henry Fielding's *Amelia*.

Atra First love of Arthur and one of the three damsels imprisoned by the Witch-Wife's Sister and released by the three knights in William Morris's *The Water of the Wondrous Isles*.

William John Attwater Steel-hearted but religious fatalist and aristocrat, who commands a small native settlement and pearl export trade on a secluded South Sea island; he successfully repels attack from three outcast sailors, Captain John Davies, Huish, and Robert Herrick in Robert Louis Stevenson's *The Ebb-Tide: A Trio and a Quartette*.

Mrs. Attwood Widow housekeeper from whom Mag-

dalen Vanstone learns details of the household of Admiral Bartram so that she can insinuate herself there as an employee in Wilkie Collins's *No Name*.

Mr. Auberry Faithful young lover, who, though discharged by Eleanor Grimshaw's father before her marriage, saves her from her wicked husband; they marry, and he joins her father's business in a ghost story interpolated into William Beckford's *Azemia*.

Eloisa, Marchioness D'Aubigny Mother of Louisa D'Aubigny (later Clinton); she assists her daughter's escape from the arbitrary power of the French king; she hires Henry Clinton, believing him a tutor, for her daughter in Henry Brooke's *The Fool of Quality*.

Lewis, Marquis D'Aubigny Brother of Louisa D'Aubigny (later Clinton); he is rescued by Henry Clinton from thugs; he serves as French ambassador to Morocco in Henry Brooke's *The Fool of Quality*.

Edward Aubrey Village priest and mentor to Lady Vargrave (Alice Darvil) and Evelyn Templeton; he knows the secret of Evelyn's birth and was the rejected suitor of her grandmother in Edward Bulwer-Lytton's *Alice*.

Knight of Auchenbreck See Sir Duncan Campbell.

John Auchtermuchty Immoderate and lazy messenger between Kinross and Edinburgh in Sir Walter Scott's *The Abbot*.

Auctioneer A salesman who plays on mankind's desire to buy bargains in Charles Johnstone's *Chrysal: or, the Adventures of a Guinea*.

Lady Audley Socialite English aunt and guardian of Alicia Malcolm (Douglas); she opposes Alicia's marriage to her son, Sir Edmund Audley, in Susan Ferrier's *Marriage*.

Monsieur Audley Swiss brother-in-law of Arnand La Luc; he oversees Theodore Peyron's education in Ann Radcliffe's *The Romance of the Forest*.

Alicia Audley Sir Michael Audley's daughter from his first marriage; she loves her cousin Robert Audley and dislikes her stepmother, is interested in horses, marries Sir Harry Towers, and lives happily in Mary Elizabeth Braddon's *Lady Audley's Secret*.

Charles Audley Aristocratic young clergyman, who works with Edward Underwood in Bexley and, after his death, becomes guardian of the Underwood children; he eventually goes as a missionary to Australia in Charlotte Yonge's *The Pillars of the House*.

Sir Edmund Audley   The only child of Lady Audley and the tempestuous suitor of his cousin, Alicia Malcolm, before her marriage to Archibald Douglas in Susan Ferrier's *Marriage*.

Lucy, Lady Audley (Helen Maldon Talboys)   Protagonist, who marries wealthy Sir Michael Audley, much her senior, and lives happily with him until her supposedly dead first husband, George Talboys, returns; she tries to cover up her secret by murder but is caught and punished by Robert Audley, Sir Michael's nephew, in Mary Elizabeth Braddon's *Lady Audley's Secret*.

Sir Michael Audley   Husband of Lady Audley; he loves her but does not know about her first marriage and her child; he rejects her when he learns the truth from his nephew, Robert Audley, in Mary Elizabeth Braddon's *Lady Audley's Secret*.

Robert Audley   Character through whose thoughts the story is told, though not in the first person; suspicious of Lucy, Lady Audley, his uncle's wife, he hunts for his missing friend, George Talboys, and discovers Lucy's secret; he marries Clara, the sister of George Talboys, in Mary Elizabeth Braddon's *Lady Audley's Secret*.

Audrey   Birdalone's mother, from whom she is stolen in babyhood by the Witch-Wife; mother and daughter meet twenty years later in the City of the Five Crafts in William Morris's *The Water of the Wondrous Isles*.

(Arsenius) Aufugus   Elderly patrician monk, who buys Philammon as a slave before retiring with him from the world to the monastery at the Laura; he returns to Alexandria as a Christian ambassador and watches over the estranged Philammon, with whom he is finally reconciled in Charles Kingsley's *Hypatia*.

August Person (King)   Benevolent and humane monarch, who rewards men who speak and act with honesty and boldness in Charles Johnstone's *Chrysal: or, The Adventures of a Guinea*.

Augusta (Guster)   Mrs. Snagsby's simple-minded maid from the workhouse, who has fits; she is kind to Jo in Charles Dickens's *Bleak House*.

Augustine of Hippo   Celebrated philosopher-monk and Bishop of Hippo, who stays with Synesius at Berenice and influences Raphael Aben-Ezra, eventually converting him to Catholicism in Charles Kingsley's *Hypatia*.

Auld Baldie the Shepherd   Rustic shepherd who introduces the legend of the Black Dwarf in order to impress some tavern mates in Sir Walter Scott's *The Black Dwarf*.

Marchioness of Auld Reekie   Mother of Lord Nidderdale, an aspirant to the hand of Marie Melmotte; her social patronage of the Melmottes assists their climb in Anthony Trollope's *The Way We Live Now*. She appears in *Can You Forgive Her?*.

Marquis of Auld Reekie   Uncle and guardian of Lady Glencora MacCluskie (Palliser); he arranges her marriage in Anthony Trollope's *Can You Forgive Her?*. He orders his son, Lord Nidderdale, to marry Marie Melmotte in *The Way We Live Now*. He appears in *The Small House at Allington*.

Jean d' Aunoy (Louis de St. Pierre)   Thief hired by Phillippe de Montalt to capture Henry de Montalt, to pose as Adeline's father, and then to kill her; unable to kill her, he hires du Bosse to do so; his testimony against Phillippe de Montalt results in the marquis's arrest in Ann Radcliffe's *The Romance of the Forest*.

Aurea   Beloved of Sir Baudoin, who helps to release her with two other damsels from the prison of the Witch-Wife's Sister; she marries a son of Gerard of the Clee in William Morris's *The Water of the Wondrous Isles*.

Aurelia   Estranged daughter of Flavius Anicius Maximus and cousin of Basil; she has married a Goth and become a heretic but agrees to embrace Catholicism secretly in order to inherit her father's property; she is mysteriously spirited away by priests in George Gissing's *Veranilda*.

Aurelian   Only son of a gentleman of Florence, Don Fabio; after a six-year absence he accompanies his Spanish friend Hippolito di Saviolina to Florence; they attend a masked ball where he meets and falls in love with the mysterious Incognita; he presents himself to her as Hippolito in an effort to delay his father's knowledge of his return; Incognita is later revealed to be the Juliana to whom his betrothal was arranged in William Congreve's *Incognita*.

Aurora   Theodosia's younger sister, who is an agreeable woman of fashion, takes an interest in Pompey, and buys him from Mrs. Wilkins in Francis Coventry's *The History of Pompey the Little*.

Seymour Austin   Tory politician; he disappoints Cecilia Halkett when he recommends Blackburn Tuckham to her rather than proposing himself in George Meredith's *Beauchamp's Career*.

Author   Middle-class man of sublime sentiments who gives a guinea to a strange woman because she is in distress in Charles Johnstone's *Chrysal: or, The Adventures of a Guinea*.

Author's Friend   Competitor for admission into the Mock Monastery who proposes to bring down the minister by attacking his public blunders and his private vices and follies, and who is thrown into jail for his efforts in Charles Johnstone's *Chrysal: or, The Adventures of a Guinea*.

Mr. Autumn   Mrs. Autumn's long-suffering husband; he feeds his wife's delusion that he is jealous by showing impatience at her imaginary flirtations in Charlotte Lennox's *Henrietta*.

Mrs. Autumn   Henrietta Courteney's elderly but vain and self-deluded employer, who plagues her husband by inventing love intrigues; she falsely accuses Henrietta of having a lover and dismisses her in Charlotte Lennox's *Henrietta*.

Lady Alice Avenel   Mary Avenel's mother; soft-spoken and polite when prosperous, she is treated courteously when misfortune befalls her; she turns to the Protestant Bible for solace and dies holding what the monks term heretical opinions in Sir Walter Scott's *The Monastery*.

Julian Avenel   Mary Avenel's ruthless uncle, a border baron outlawed by England and Scotland; lawless and formidable, he seizes his niece's inheritance but dies defending the monastery in Sir Walter Scott's *The Monastery*.

Leonora Avenel   Gifted young poet, who secretly marries Audley Egerton, is driven to despair by Baron Levy, and dies giving birth to the boy known as Leonard Fairfield in Edward Bulwer-Lytton's *"My Novel," by Pisistratus Caxton*.

Mary Avenel   Lady Alice's scholarly daughter; deprived of her inheritance, she resides with the Glendinnings; she falls in love with Halbert Glendinning, whom she later marries; born on All-Hallows Eve, she is blessed with intuitive insight and is superstitiously called the Spirit of Avenel in Sir Walter Scott's *The Monastery*. She is Lady of Avenal and wife of Sir Halbert; her childless state causes her to lavish Ronald Graeme with maternal devotion in *The Abbot*.

Richard Avenel   Leonora Avenel's brother, who assists and later quarrels with his nephew Leonard Fairfield in Edward Bulwer-Lytton's *"My Novel," by Pisistratus Caxton*.

Captain Avery   Fellow English pirate, who joins Wilmot and Singleton's group in Madagascar; he persuades Wilmot to split off from Singleton and go with him in Daniel Defoe's *The Life, Adventures, and Pyracies of the Famous Captain Singleton*.

Mr. d'Avora   The Italian master for Louisa Mancel and Miss Melvyn; he later joins the women at Millenium Hall to assist in its management in Sarah Scott's *A Description of Millenium Hall*.

Mrs. Awberry   Widow with two daughters; Harriet Byron's forced marriage to Sir Hargrave Pollexfen was to have taken place in her house in Samuel Richardson's *Sir Charles Grandison*.

Deb Awberry   The younger and more tender-hearted daughter of Mrs. Awberry; she loves William Wilson and marries him, thanks to the magnanimity of Sir Charles Grandison in Samuel Richardson's *Sir Charles Grandison*.

Sally Awberry   The elder and less tender-hearted daughter of the widow Mrs. Awberry in Samuel Richardson's *Sir Charles Grandison*.

Samuel Axworthy   Vicious cousin of Leonard Ward; he terrorizes the young Thomas May in Charlotte Yonge's *The Daisy Chain*. He is finally established by Thomas May as the murderer of his uncle in *The Trial*.

Ayacanora   Indian priestess, actually daughter of John Oxenham; she falls in love with Amyas Leigh during his search for El Dorado; Amyas brings her back to England; her identity is discovered by Salvation Yeo, and she and Amyas finally marry in Charles Kingsley's *Westward Ho!*.

Ayesha   Mistress of Louis Grayle in Edward Bulwer-Lytton's *A Strange Story*.

Lady Aylmer   Domineering mother of Frederick; she successfully encourages him to disentangle himself from Clara Amedroz and marry Lady Emily Tagmaggert in Anthony Trollope's *The Belton Estate*.

Sir Anthony Aylmer   Henpecked husband of Lady Aylmer; he advises his son, Frederick, to remain a bachelor; he is the sole member of the family to show kindness to Clara Amedroz when she visits Aylmer Hall in Anthony Trollope's *The Belton Estate*.

Belinda Aylmer   Meek and adoring sister of Frederick; she is nagged and bullied by her mother in Anthony Trollope's *The Belton Estate*.

Captain Frederick Folliott Aylmer   Cold, egotistical Member of Parliament, who becomes engaged to Clara Amedroz; his snobbish mother snubs her when she visits Aylmer Hall and helps separate the couple; he at last marries Lady Emily Taggmaggert in Anthony Trollope's *The Belton Estate*.

Sir William Aylmer   A trustee of Maud Ruthyn's estate in J. Sheridan Le Fanu's *Uncle Silas*.

Aymer Corrupt prior of Jorvaulx Abbey; he brings great grief to the Saxons and so is captured and held for ransom in Sir Walter Scott's *Ivanhoe*.

Sir Aymeris Castellan of the Castle of the Quest in William Morris's *The Water of the Wondrous Isles*.

Phoebe Ayres Experienced prostitute who, as Fanny Hill's coworker and roommate at Mrs. Brown's bordello, introduces her to lesbian love, voyeurism, and other aspects of life in the professional sisterhood in John Cleland's *Memoirs of a Woman of Pleasure*.

Mr. Ayresleigh Middle-aged, haggard prisoner for debt in the Fleet prison in Charles Dickens's *The Posthumous Papers of the Pickwick Club*.

Azariah Early tutor of Joseph of Arimathea, schooling him in Greek in George Moore's *The Brook Kerith*.

Azemia A beautiful Turkish naif captured by a British warship captain; she is intended as a gift for a lecherous duke, but his jealous paramour removes her from the duke's household; she is in the custody of several aristocrats, the last being the good Mrs. Blandford; she eventually marries Charles Arnold in William Beckford's *Azemia*.

Monsieur D'Azimart A famous good shot with a pistol and an old lover of the Duchesse de Perpignan; after she sets up Henry Pelham for his challenge, he is wounded in their duel, having misfired and shot Pelham's hat in Edward Bulwer-Lytton's *Pelham*.

B

Count de B**** Admirer of Shakespeare and English books; mistakenly believing Yorick is like his namesake, the King's Jester, he promptly acquires the passport Yorick needs to avoid being jailed in the Bastille in Laurence Sterne's *A Sentimental Journey through France and Italy*.

Countess of B— Lord B—'s mother; impressed with Henrietta Courteney's rejection of her son, she introduces her to her sister in order to find her a good situation in Charlotte Lennox's *Henrietta*.

Earl of B— Lord B—'s father; he is anxious for his son to marry Jenny Cordwain's money, but sympathetic toward Henrietta Courteney, whom his son prefers, because she is a distressed gentlewoman in Charlotte Lennox's *Henrietta*.

Lord B— Jenny Cordwain's betrothed; he conspires with Mrs. Eccles to seduce Henrietta Courtney, hoping to marry her (though she is a servant) if she will convert to Catholicism and thereby inherit her aunt's estate in Charlotte Lennox's *Henrietta*.

Lord B— Father of Lady Forester; he raised her to be an atheist and is said to have been highly unpredictable in his treatment of tenants in Richard Graves's *The Spiritual Quixote*.

William B— Rake who attempts to seduce but finally marries his mother's young serving maid; his temper, arrogance, and errant behavior as Pamela's husband provide much of the dramatic tension in Samuel Richardson's *Pamela, or Virtue Rewarded*. As Mr. Booby, he is nephew to Lady Booby and husband to Pamela Andrews; his regard for Pamela leads him to rescue successively Joseph Andrews and Fanny Goodwill from his aunt's ire in Henry Fielding's *The History of the Adventures of Mr. Joseph Andrews and Of his Friend Mr. Abraham Adams*.

William (Billy) B— Son of Pamela (Andrews) and Mr. B— in Samuel Richardson's *Pamela, or Virtue Rewarded*.

W—m B—e Old shepherd who guides the Editor and his companions in an expedition to dig up the suicide's grave in James Hogg's *The Private Memoirs and Confessions of a Justified Sinner*.

Bababalouk Chief of Vathek's eunuchs; he likes to bully the women in the harem in William Beckford's *Vathek*.

Mr. Babchild Primitive Methodist pastor whose preference for Hester Limbrick's cooking angers her mother; the pleasant notion of entertaining him in her own home motivates Hester's disastrous marriage to the drunkard Joel Dethridge in Wilkie Collins's *Man and Wife*.

Madame Babette Concierge with whom Virginie de Crequy takes shelter in Elizabeth Gaskell's *My Lady Ludlow*.

Babie Blind Alice Grey's servant, a slovenly and graceless girl, in Sir Walter Scott's *The Bride of Lammermoor*.

Anthony Babington Childhood friend of Cecily Talbot; his admiration for Mary, Queen of Scots draws him into a plot against Queen Elizabeth and leads him to a horrible death in Charlotte Yonge's *Unknown to History*.

Julia Babington Cousin of John Caldigate much in love with him from youth; when he marries Hester Bolton, she becomes his enemy; she marries the Reverend Augustus Smirkie in Anthony Trollope's *John Caldigate*.

Mary Anne (Aunt Polly) Babington John Caldigate's aunt, who had cared for him when he was little; she turns against him when he declines to marry her daughter, Julia, in Anthony Trollope's *John Caldigate*.

Richard (Mr. Dick) Babley Simple-minded man, who was rescued from incarceration in an asylum by Betsey Trotwood, with whom he lives; he is engaged in writing a memorial of the Lord Chancellor, but the subject of King Charles the First's head always gets in the way; Mr. Micawber calls him Mr. Dixon in Charles Dickens's *The Personal History of David Copperfield*.

Baby Sneezing, howling, squirming infant of the Duchess; encumbered with its care, Alice releases it into the wood after it has undergone improvement by turning into a pig in Lewis Carroll's *Alice's Adventures in Wonderland*.

Mr. Baccani Italian scientist who was Nathan Benjulia's friend in his youth; Mr. Mool gets from him information correcting Benjulia's mistaken evidence impugning the character of Carmina Graywell's mother in Wilkie Collins's *Heart and Science*.

The Bachelor Sexton of the old church in the village where Nell Trent dies; he converses with her and shows her the old well in the church in Charles Dickens's *The Old Curiosity Shop*.

Mr. Bacon Personal enemy and rival publisher of his former friend and partner, Mr. Bungay, in William Makepeace Thackeray's *The History of Pendennis*.

Mrs. Bacon Mr. Bungay's sister and Mr. Bacon's wife

in William Makepeace Thackeray's *The History of Pendennis*.

Badcock Ugly and deformed fellow student of Ernest Pontifex at Cambridge; a leader of the despised Simonites, he invites Ernest to hear Gideon Hawke speak; after the session, Badcock tells Ernest that Hawke enquired after him in Samuel Butler's *The Way of All Flesh*.

Sir Philip Baddely Shallow, oath-using false friend of Clarence Hervey; he asks Belinda to marry him; when she refuses, he circulates malicious rumors about her in Maria Edgeworth's *Belinda*.

Bayham Badger Medical man in Chelsea, with whom Richard Carstone lodges while training to be a surgeon; he is proud to be the third husband of Laura Badger in Charles Dickens's *Bleak House*.

Hugh Badger Gamekeeper at Rookwood Place in William Harrison Ainsworth's *Rookwood*.

Laura Badger Youthfully dressed woman of fifty, who was married twice before marrying Mr. Badger; she speaks fondly of her former husbands, Captain Swosser and Professor Dingo, and has their portraits displayed in Charles Dickens's *Bleak House*.

Shibli Bagarag Wandering barber; he is the brave but vain hero of numerous adventures leading up to his successful attempt to shave the head of Shagpat, particularly a single hair, the Identical, which has rendered the people of the city of Oolb subject to Shagpat; his adventures lead him to shed his vanity in George Meredith's *The Shaving of Shagpat*.

James Bagenhall Extravagant and treacherous employer of William Wilson; his indebtedness makes him a conspirator with Solomon Merceda in Sir Hargrave Pollexfen's kidnapping of Harriet Byron; he acts as Sir Hargrave's agent in attempting to force a duel upon Sir Charles Grandison in Samuel Richardson's *Sir Charles Grandison*.

Mrs. Baggett Domineering housekeeper of William Whittlestaff; once her master has become engaged to his young ward, Mary Lawrie, she is determined that the marriage take place in Anthony Trollope's *An Old Man's Love*.

Sergeant Baggett Drunken, one-legged husband of William Whittlestaff's housekeeper; he reappears to plague her with care in Anthony Trollope's *An Old Man's Love*.

Alderman Baggs Prominent Tory canvasser, who decides to support Aubrey Bohun when the Tory candidate,

Mr. Vavasour, resigns in Benjamin Disraeli's *A Year at Hartlebury; or, The Election*.

M. Bagillard Lecherous Frenchman who cultivates William Booth to seduce Booth's wife, Amelia; Colonel Bath kills Bagillard in a duel in Henry Fielding's *Amelia*.

Mrs. Bagnet Soldierly-looking wife of Matthew Bagnet and the decision maker of the family; she advises Trooper George and reunites him with his mother, Mrs. Rouncewell, in Charles Dickens's *Bleak House*.

Matthew Bagnet Ex-artilleryman who is the good friend of Trooper George (Rouncewell) in Charles Dickens's *Bleak House*.

Mrs. Bagot A possessive mother unable to see her son Billy Bagot marry beneath his social position; she manipulates him and divides him and Trilby O'Ferrall; finally, she recognizes the tragedy she creates by meddling in George Du Maurier's *Trilby*.

Billy (Little Billie) Bagot The young, brilliant painter who goes to Paris to study painting and discovers the model and singer Trilby O'Ferrall; naive and sensitive, he falls in love with Trilby to the point of obsession; he is the tragic hero in George Du Maurier's *Trilby*.

Blanche Bagot The younger, caring sister of Little Billie (Billy Bagot); she nurses him and quietly watches his life slip by; after his death, she marries his friend Taffy Wynne in George Du Maurier's *Trilby*.

Bags (Bad Giants) Lovers (Little Ones) who have grown in body but whose depravity keeps them spiritually and emotionally brutal and underdeveloped in George MacDonald's *Lilith*.

Bob Bagshot Ingenuous acquaintance whom Jonathan Wild easily persuades to rob Count La Ruse and who, in turn, becomes Wild's victim in Henry Fielding's *The Life of Mr. Jonathan Wild the Great*.

Major Joseph Bagstock (Joey B.) Retired, conceited military man, who lives opposite Miss Tox; he believes that she loves him; insulted when her interest fades, he strikes up a friendship with Paul Dombey, introducing him to Mrs. Skewton and Edith Granger in Charles Dickens's *Dombey and Son*.

Samuel Bagwax Dedicated Post Office official, whose detective work proves a forged postmark on a letter involved in a court case which has led to the false imprisonment for bigamy of John Caldigate; he marries Jemima Curlydown in Anthony Trollope's *John Caldigate*.

Captain Bailey One of Miss Larkins's dance partners

at the ball where she dances with David Copperfield in Charles Dickens's *The Personal History of David Copperfield.*

Edward (Neddy) Bailey   Young clerk in a London office who is a friend of Richard in Thomas Hughes's *The Scouring of the White Horse.*

Benjamin Bailey (Bailey Junior, Uncle Ben, Young Brownrigg, Collars)   Assertive servant at Todgers's Commercial Boarding House and later groom to Tigg Montague (formerly Montague Tigg); he is physically "an undersized boy" and behaviorally "an ancient man" in Charles Dickens's *The Life and Adventures of Martin Chuzzlewit.*

Bailie   A portly, bustling, and impatient official in Sir Walter Scott's *The Monastery.*

General Baillie   Skillful Presbyterian officer and Covenanter, who briefly joins his army with Argyle's in Sir Walter Scott's *A Legend of Montrose.*

Annaple Bailzou   Fortune-telling beggar, who buys the Whistler, the illegitimate son of Effie Deans and George Staunton, and later sells him to an outlaw in Sir Walter Scott's *The Heart of Midlothian.*

Monsieur Baise-la-main   Art collector and banker; he becomes patron of Jeremy Watersouchy, who earns immediate success with the precise rendering of the coins in the financier's countinghouse in William Beckford's *Biographical Memoirs of Extraordinary Painters.*

Mr. Baker   Pawnbroker who runs Silverton Grove House asylum entirely for profit in Charles Reade's *Hard Cash.*

Mrs. Baker   Insensitive widow, who laments the burden of supporting the six-year-old orphan, Elizabeth Raby, in Mary Shelley's *Falkner.*

Lizzie Baker   A music-hall barmaid, who becomes Frank Escott's mistress; he nurses her back to health in George Moore's *Spring Days.* He persuades her to marry him, and their happy home is envied by Mike Fletcher in *Mike Fletcher.*

Mary Baker   Niece of George Bertram; she is pursued for her money by Sir Lionel Bertram in Anthony Trollope's *The Bertrams.* She comforts Margaret Mackenzie upset by gossip in *Miss Mackenzie.*

Tom Bakewell   Loyal but somewhat dull-witted laborer Richard Feverel pays to burn Farmer Blaize's hayricks; he becomes Richard's servant and assists Richard and Lucy Desborough before and after their marriage in George Meredith's *The Ordeal of Richard Feverel.*

Janet Balchristie   The Laird of Dumbiedikes's lazy housekeeper, who terrorizes Jeanie Deans in Sir Walter Scott's *The Heart of Midlothian.*

Balderick   Retired rear-admiral who lost a leg in the service; he amuses Matthew Bramble with his recovered friendship at Bath in Tobias Smollett's *The Expedition of Humphry Clinker.*

Agostino Balderini   An old Italian poet who has suffered much in the cause of liberation; the librettist of the opera *Camilla,* he proposes—despite the male chauvinism of other revolutionaries—that when Vittoria Campa sings the disguised revolutionary songs in it, she signal the beginning of the Milanese revolt in George Meredith's *Vittoria.*

Caleb Balderson   Edgar Ravenswood's devoted servant, who fiercely protects his master and loves to talk of the ancient glory of the Ravenswood family in Sir Walter Scott's *The Bride of Lammermoor.*

Lady Baldock   Violet Effingham's outspoken aunt, who promotes the claims of suitors Lord Fawn and Mr. Appledom and is strongly opposed to Lord Chiltern and Phineas Finn; she is an inveterate supporter of good causes, such as emigration for unmarried women in Anthony Trollope's *Phineas Finn.* She visits Violet and Lord Chiltern in *Phineas Redux.*

George (or Gustavus), Lord Baldock   Lady Baldock's son, who corrects her assessments of Violet Effingham's suitors in Anthony Trollope's *Phineas Finn.*

Beatrice, Marchesa D' Baldoni   Outgoing wife of an Italian marquis; she introduces Ayala Dormer to her cousin, Colonel Stubbs, in Anthony Trollope's *Ayala's Angel.*

Nina Baldoni   Close friend and confidante of Ayala Dormer; she marries Lord George Bideford in Anthony Trollope's *Ayala's Angel.*

Archbishop Baldwin   Archbishop of Canterbury, successor of Thomas á Becket; he insists that Hugo de Lacy honor his pledge to go on Crusade in Sir Walter Scott's *The Betrothed.*

Count Baldwin   Crusader and brother to Godfrey of Bouillon in Sir Walter Scott's *Count Robert of Paris.*

Ted Baldwin   Also known as Hargrave, a suitor of Ettie Shafter; he served time for crimes as a member of the Scowrers gang in America; he is shot dead in England in Arthur Conan Doyle's *The Valley of Fear.*

Mr. Bale   Merchant and friend of Henrietta

Courteney's late father; as guardian of the orphaned Henrietta, he is kindly and generous but is ill and abroad during most of her adventures; he ultimately returns to arrange settlements to enable her to marry the Marquis of — with his father's consent in Charlotte Lennox's *Henrietta*.

Mr. Bale (the younger)   Son of Henrietta Courteney's guardian; he falls for Henrietta and plots to abduct her while pretending to help her on his father's behalf in Charlotte Lennox's *Henrietta*.

Mrs. Bale   Shrewish wife of the younger Mr. Bale; she finds out her husband has been helping Henrietta Courteney and confronts her, thus exposing Mr. Bale's designs on her in Charlotte Lennox's *Henrietta*.

Balfour of Pilrig   Edinburgh Laird and kinsman to David Balfour; he writes David a letter of introduction to Prestongrange, Lord Advocate of Scotland, in Robert Louis Stevenson's *Catriona*.

Alan Balfour   Son of David and Catriona (Drummond) Balfour in Robert Louis Stevenson's *Catriona*.

Alexander Balfour   Deceased father of young David Balfour and elder brother of Ebenezer Balfour; he exchanged his claim to his estate for the right to court and wed the brothers' hotly contested lover, Grace Pitarrow, in Robert Louis Stevenson's *Kidnapped*.

Barbara Balfour   Daughter of David and Catriona (Drummond) Balfour in Robert Louis Stevenson's *Catriona*.

David Balfour   Young, courageous, and principled Scottish heir to the "Shaws" estate; he is kidnapped, befriends the Jacobite Alan Breck Stewart, and is subsequently involved in the political imbroglio of the 1752 "Appin" murder of Colin Ray Campbell in Robert Louis Stevenson's *Kidnapped*. He attempts to exonerate alleged murderer James Stewart and falls in love with Catriona Drummond in *Catriona*.

Ebenezer Balfour   David Balfour's miserly and hateful uncle, who tries to cheat his young nephew from any rightful claim to the "Shaws" estate by having him kidnapped and taken aboard the Scottish brig *Covenant*, which is destined for colony slave plantations (and slavery for David) in Robert Louis Stevenson's *Kidnapped*.

Grace Pitarrow Balfour   David Balfour's deceased mother, who married Alexander Balfour after being courted by both Alexander and his brother, Ebenezer, in Robert Louis Stevenson's *Kidnapped*.

John (Burley) Balfour   Renegade rebel soldier, who

was a comrade of Henry Morton's father and is a leader of the Cameronian rebels against King James II; later he refuses to accept William as his king; he becomes increasingly fanatic, merciless, and treacherous and at last drowns while attempting to escape after the ambush and murder of Lord Evandale (William Maxwell) in Sir Walter Scott's *Old Mortality*.

Lady Ball   Disagreeable wife of Sir John Ball and mother of John Ball; she begrudges Margaret Mackenzie's coming into a fortune; her approval of her son's courtship of Margaret is contingent on Margaret's possession of the fortune in Anthony Trollope's *Miss Mackenzie*.

Sir John Ball   Grouchy baronet, a kinsman of Margaret Mackenzie and the owner of an estate in Twickenham; he and his wife resolve a long-standing rift between the families by inviting Margaret to stay at their home in Anthony Trollope's *Miss Mackenzie*.

John Ball   Margaret Mackenzie's cousin, a widower short of cash and with nine children to look after; urged by his mother to set his cap at his spinster cousin, he gradually finds he is in love with her; when it is discovered that he in fact is true heir to the Mackenzie fortune, she agrees to marry him in Anthony Trollope's *Miss Mackenzie*.

John Ball   Hedge priest prominent in Wat Tyler's Rebellion of 1381; he discusses with the Scholar the future of England when feudal slavery will be replaced by wage slavery in William Morris's *A Dream of John Ball*.

Jonathan Ball   Brother of Sir John Ball; he causes an uproar by leaving his money to his Mackenzie cousins in Anthony Trollope's *Miss Mackenzie*.

Francis Balliere   Thief hired by Phillippe de Montalt to ambush his half brother Henry de Montalt in Ann Radcliffe's *The Romance of the Forest*.

Francis (Frank) O'Kelly, Lord Ballindine   Impecunious aristocrat addicted to gambling; he finally wins Fanny Wyndham over her guardian's opposition in Anthony Trollope's *The Kellys and the O'Kellys*.

Mr. Balmy   Elderly gentleman of kindly aspect, who looks like an early Christian and explains the history of Sunchildism; he had been a professor of hypothetical languages when forced out because he urged adoption of Sunchildism in Samuel Butler's *Erewhon Revisited Twenty Years Later*.

Mr. Balsam   Mild, respectable barrister, very learned on points of law, brought in to represent Henry Jones in his libel case against Gregory Evans in Anthony Trollope's *Cousin Henry*.

Balthazar   Julian the Apostate's incarnation as a Jewish miser in Henry Fielding's *A Journey From This World to the Next*.

Balthazar   Patriarch of the Gypsies and friend of Dick Turpin in William Harrison Ainsworth's *Rookwood*.

Frere Balthazar   Capuchin friar, who horrifies Roderick Random with his lust and theft on the road to Paris in Tobias Smollett's *The Adventures of Roderick Random*.

Cardinal John Balue   Lord Bishop of Auxerre and Grand Almoner of France; as Louis XI's favorite, he rose quickly from the lower ranks; a vain and presumptuous meddler, he betrays Louis to the Duke of Burgundy when the king insults him; he is subsequently imprisoned in Sir Walter Scott's *Quentin Durward*.

Baluzzo   Assassin brought to justice by Abellino/Flodoardo (Count Rosalvo) in Matthew Lewis's *The Bravo of Venice*.

Micah Balwhidder   Presbyterian minister from 1760 to 1810 of the parish of Dalmailing (Ayrshire); at first rebuffed, he overcomes the congregation's resentment at his appointment; he writes the parish annals which include mentions of individuals and significant events and developments such as the American War of Independence, the French Revolution, and the agricultural and industrial revolutions in John Galt's *Annals of the Parish*.

Jack Bamber   Elderly, shriveled regular at the Magpie and Stump, who tells a story about a queer client in Charles Dickens's *The Posthumous Papers of the Pickwick Club*.

Mr. Bambridge   A horse dealer who is owed money by Fred Vincy; he overhears John Raffles discussing his information against Bulstrode and later realizes that Raffles was murdered in George Eliot's *Middlemarch*.

Guilio Bandinelli   One of the Italian revolutionists who meet atop Monte Motterone to plan the initial uprising of the Milanese revolt in George Meredith's *Vittoria*.

Mrs. Bangham   Charwoman who attended Mrs. Dorrit at the birth of Amy Dorrit in the Marshalsea Prison in Charles Dickens's *Little Dorrit*.

Peter Bangles   Wine merchant whom Madalina Demolines marries after Johnny Eames's escape in Anthony Trollope's *The Last Chronicle of Barset*.

Mr. Bangrove   Worthy curate in the parish of Arabella Bloomville in William Beckford's *Modern Novel Writing; or, the Elegant Enthusiast*.

Father John Banham   Zealous Catholic priest at Beccles; he dines with Roger Carbury and cannot resist trying to convert his host in Anthony Trollope's *The Way We Live Now*.

Banister   A man who becomes Oroonoko's executioner after his failed uprising; he has Oroonoko burned at the stake and subjected to mutilation in Aphra Behn's *Oroonoko*.

Bank Clerk   Moll Flanders's fifth husband, who divorces his previous wife to marry Moll; after five years of marriage, he dies and leaves Moll and their two children penniless in Daniel Defoe's *The Fortunes and Misfortunes of the Famous Moll Flanders*.

Bank Porter   Edinburgh guide who rudely chastises his employer, David Balfour, for talking with Catriona Drummond in the streets in Robert Louis Stevenson's *Catriona*.

Nanse Banks   Exemplary schoolmistress of Dalmailing who is admired by Micah Balwhidder for her "Christian submission of spirit" in John Galt's *Annals of the Parish*.

Michael Bankwell   Virtuous contrast to the wicked Mr. Sedley in S. J. Pratt's *Pupil of Pleasure*.

Baroness Banmann   Bavarian campaigner for women's rights, a very formidable speechmaker invited to address members of the Rights of Women Institute in the Marylebone Road in Anthony Trollope's *Is He Popenjoy?*.

Angelo Cyrus Bantam   Aging dandy and master of the ceremonies at the Pump Room in Bath, where Samuel Pickwick and friends go to socialize in Charles Dickens's *The Posthumous Papers of the Pickwick Club*.

Mr. Banter   One of the London tavern boys; he leads the "roast" of Dr. Wagtail, becomes a companion of Roderick Random after his return from France, helps Roderick get revenge against Melinda Goosetrap, and leads him to success in gambling; he advises Roderick on a scheme to marry Miss Snapper for her money and Banter's own benefit and refuses Don Rodriguez's offer to buy him a commission in the army in Tobias Smollett's *The Adventures of Roderick Random*.

Banu   Prophet who lives in a cave and is an associate of John the Baptist in George Moore's *The Brook Kerith*.

Mr. Baps   Professor of dancing at Dr. Blimber's boarding school in Charles Dickens's *Dombey and Son*.

Mrs. Baps   Wife of Mr. Baps; she accompanies him to

the dance at Dr. Blimber's boarding school in Charles Dickens's *Dombey and Son*.

Baptista   Servant who informs the evil Marquis de Mazzini that his wife, Maria de Vellorno, is having an affair in Ann Radcliffe's *A Sicilian Romance*.

Baptiste   Rapacious bandit killed by his wife Marguerite as he is about to murder Alphonso d'Alvarada (Raymond, Marquis de la Cisternas) and Rodolpha, Baroness Lindenberg in Matthew Lewis's *The Monk*.

Barak El Hadgi   Fakir and secret agent of Prince Hyder Ali Khan Bahauder; he gives Dr. Adam Hartley friendship in return for his medical attention and arranges an interview with the monarch on Menie Gray's behalf in Sir Walter Scott's *The Surgeon's Daughter*.

Barbacela (Queen of Emmets)   Sorceress who appears to Prince Bonbennin bonbobbin-bonbobbinet as an old woman and promises him the white mouse he covets provided he will marry her; later in the shape of the white mouse she is destroyed by Queen Nanhoa, in an oriental fable told by Lien Chi Altangi in Oliver Goldsmith's *The Citizen of the World*.

Barbara   Derba's granddaughter, whose child nature helps the king overcome his nightmares; she becomes his ward in George MacDonald's *The Princess and Curdie*.

Barbara   Pretty and shy servant girl of the Garlands; she eventually marries Kit Nubbles in Charles Dickens's *The Old Curiosity Shop*.

Barbara   A servant at Lowood School, the boarding school attended by Jane Eyre; she serves the headmistress, Miss Temple, in Charlotte Brontë's *Jane Eyre*.

Lady Barbara   Daughter of the Earl of Huntingdon and one of Queen Eleanor's favorites; she marries Gaston de Blondeville only to see him killed by the ghost of Reginald de Folville within days of their marriage in Ann Radcliffe's *Gaston de Blondeville*.

Barbara's Mother   Kindhearted woman, who becomes a good friend to Mrs. Nubbles and assists her when Kit Nubbles is in prison in Charles Dickens's *The Old Curiosity Shop*.

Barbarsa   Duplicitous minister of the king Georigetti; he seduces Yaccombourse and, with her, is executed for sedition in Robert Paltock's *The Life and Adventures of Peter Wilkins*.

Miss Barbary   Godmother (actually aunt) to Esther Summerson and sister to Lady Dedlock; she is grave, strict, and forbidding; she raised Esther in a repressive

way from birth, telling her that it would have been far better if she had never lived, in Charles Dickens's *Bleak House*.

Martha Bardell   Samuel Pickwick's middle-aged landlady, who sues him for breach of promise in Charles Dickens's *The Posthumous Papers of the Pickwick Club*.

Tommy Bardell   Martha Bardell's son, who likes to kick people in Charles Dickens's *The Posthumous Papers of the Pickwick Club*.

Bardo de' Bardi   Blind father of Romola, descendant of a great family but poor because he has devoted his life to scholarship and used his money collecting rare books for his library; he allows Tito Melema to marry Romola only because he wants help with his studies in George Eliot's *Romola*.

Dino de' Bardi (Fra Luca)   The brother of Romola; he leaves his father's scholarly work to become a Dominican monk; he warns Romola against marriage before he dies in the monastery, but he does not tell her that Tito has left his adopted father in slavery in George Eliot's *Romola*.

Romola de' Bardi   An intellectual, beautiful woman raised in Florence to help her blind, scholarly father; she marries Tito Melema before she realizes his evil nature; the novel ends with Tito's mistress and illegitimate children living with and being taught by Romola in George Eliot's *Romola*.

Mrs. Bardolph   Card-playing gossip at Bath who speaks favorably of Geoffry Wildgoose to Lady Sherwood in Richard Graves's *The Spiritual Quixote*.

Countess of Bareacres   Impecunious aristocrat, who is condescending towards Becky Sharp except when she needs her horses at Waterloo in William Makepeace Thackeray's *Vanity Fair*.

Earl of Bareacres   Impoverished nobleman, whose daughter is the despised daughter-in-law of Lord Steyne in William Makepeace Thackeray's *Vanity Fair*.

Mr. Barfield (the Gaffer)   Bluff retired soldier, devoted to horses and gambling; one of the new landed gentry, he is owner of an estate, Woodfield; though he wins big at gambling, he finally loses the estate in George Moore's *Esther Waters*.

Mrs. Barfield (the Saint)   Mistress of the Barfield estate; well-loved and unassuming, she is a member of the Plymouth Brethren and abhors the family gambling; she respects and likes a fellow worshipper, the cook's helper Esther Waters; in old age and widowhood she invites

Esther to return to the estate as servant; the two share common interests in religion and in their sons in George Moore's *Esther Waters*.

Arthur (Ginger) Barfield Gentleman rider and trainer, son and inheritor of Woodfield estate; he rarely visits his mother and dislikes her middle-class, Dissenter associates in George Moore's *Esther Waters*.

Margaret (Peggy) Barfield Daughter of a rich brewer and cousin of the Barfields; she is attracted physically to William Latch, who marries her to spite Esther Waters; the marriage ends in divorce in George Moore's *Esther Waters*.

Mary Barfield Pleasant, attractive daughter of the Barfields; she shows a preference for Esther Waters among the servants; because of ill health, she is taken to Egypt, where she dies in George Moore's *Esther Waters*.

Everard Barfoot Footloose and irresponsible fellow, who believes in freedom and equality between husband and wife; he offers the feminist Rhoda Nunn an unconventional union but refuses to marry her when she decides she wants marriage in George Gissing's *The Odd Women*.

Mary Barfoot Feminist of moderate aims who runs a school that trains girls to earn their living at various occupations in George Gissing's *The Odd Women*.

Bargeman Anonymous fellow who makes an unsuccessful sexual assault on Catharine Furze while she is staying at Chapel Farm in Mark Rutherford's *Catharine Furze*.

Mr. Bargrove Kindly country gentleman, who agrees to help Eleanor Grimshaw in a ghost story interpolated into the narrative of William Beckford's *Azemia*.

Mrs. Bargrove Benevolent wife of Mr. Bargrove in a ghost story interpolated into the narrative of William Beckford's *Azemia*.

Betty Barker One of the Cranford ladies; her cow has a flannel coat in Elizabeth Gaskell's *Cranford*.

Cecil James Barker Former partner of John Douglas in a gold mine in California and an important witness in the Birlstone Manor case; he is attentive to Douglas's wife in Arthur Conan Doyle's *The Valley of Fear*.

Phil Barker Drunken customer at the Three Cripples public house in Charles Dickens's *Oliver Twist*.

Mr. Barkis Carrier who proposes to Clara Peggotty by sending through young David Copperfield the message

that "Barkis is willin' "; he eventually marries her in Charles Dickens's *The Personal History of David Copperfield*.

Clara Barley Daughter and nurse of Old Bill Barley and Herbert Pocket's bride-to-be in Charles Dickens's *Great Expectations*.

Old Bill Barley (Gruffandgrim) Drunken, bedridden father of Clara Barley and a resident with Abel Magwitch (who has assumed the name Provis) at Mrs. Whimple's house in Charles Dickens's *Great Expectations*.

Mr. Barlow Alderman who is reminded by everything of his obligations to General Barton in William Beckford's *Modern Novel Writing; or, the Elegant Enthusiast*.

Polly (Mary) Barlow Waiting maid to Pamela (Andrews) B——; unheedful of her mistress's example, she agrees to enter into a common-law alliance with the silly, thoughtless gentleman Jackey H——; the affair is thwarted before it is consummated—and Polly's honor ruined—by Pamela's inadvertent discovery of them in flagrante delicto; she ultimately marries a clergyman in Samuel Richardson's *Pamela, or Virtue Rewarded*.

Samuel Barmby Vulgar advocate of materialistic culture; he is in love with Nancy Lord and is made a trustee of the will that deprives her of her inheritance because she is married in George Gissing's *In the Year of Jubilee*.

Mr. Barnabas Clergyman called to Joseph Andrews's apparent deathbed; he prefers visiting with the Towwouses to ministering to a penniless nobody in Henry Fielding's *The History of the Adventures of Mr. Joseph Andrews and of his Friend Mr. Abraham Adams*.

Clarence Barnacle Tite Barnacle's weak-minded son, who sports a monocle, works in the Circumlocution Office, and does his best not to help Arthur Clennam in his inquiries regarding William Dorrit and Daniel Doyce's patent in Charles Dickens's *Little Dorrit*.

Lord Decimus Tite Barnacle Revered head of the Barnacle family and uncle of Tite Barnacle in Charles Dickens's *Little Dorrit*.

Ferdinand Barnacle Sprightly young Barnacle who works in the Circumlocution Office and advises Arthur Clennam to give up his inquiries, stating that the Office's goal is "to be left alone" in Charles Dickens's *Little Dorrit*.

Tite Barnacle Pompous member of the highborn Barnacle family; he has high standing in the inefficient and cumbersome Circumlocution Office; he perpetuates its creed of "how not to do it" and its goal of being left alone and hinders Arthur Clennam in his inquiries in Charles Dickens's *Little Dorrit*.

Mrs. Tite Barnacle (née Stilt-stalking) Expensive and well-connected wife of Tite Barnacle in Charles Dickens's *Little Dorrit*.

William Barnacle Lord Decimus Tite Barnacle's connection who is a Member of Parliament and well versed in the art of "how not to do it" in Charles Dickens's *Little Dorrit*.

Mrs. Barnard Kindly wife of the rector and supporter of Denis Duval in his childhood romance with Agnes de Saverne in William Makepeace Thackeray's *Denis Duval*.

Dr. Thomas Barnard Rector of St. Philip's Church, Winchelsea; he assists the French Protestants and is the staunch protector of Denis Duval's interests in William Makepeace Thackeray's *Denis Duval*.

Barnardini Porter at Castle di Udolpho, who betrays Montoni by participating in Count Morano's attempt to kidnap Emily St. Aubert in Ann Radcliffe's *The Mysteries of Udolpho*.

Barnes Barnabas Tyrrel's steward, who assists in the harassing of the Hawkinses and in the imprisonment of Emily Melville; he objects strongly to Emily's being removed from her sickbed to jail but does as he is ordered by the angry Tyrrel in William Godwin's *Caleb Williams*.

Barnes Maid to Olive and Alice Barton; she connives to help Olive by carrying messages in George Moore's *A Drama in Muslin*.

Mr. Barnes London second-hand bookseller, sixty-five years old, who employs Clara Hopgood as a clerk in Mark Rutherford's *Clara Hopgood*.

Betty Barnes Chambermaid first to Arabella Harlowe and then to her younger sister Clarissa; she is rude and insolent to Clarissa and a spy for other members of the family in Samuel Richardson's *Clarissa: or, The History of a Young Lady*.

George Barnes Lord Kew's younger brother in William Makepeace Thackeray's *The Newcomes*.

Lady Julia Barnes Lady Kew's unmarried daughter, dominated by her sharp-tongued mother in William Makepeace Thackeray's *The Newcomes*.

Will Barnes Local swain who took up with (among others) Betty and Molly Seagrim and probably fathered Molly's child in Henry Fielding's *The History of Tom Jones*.

Mr. Barnet Mrs. Barnet's brother-in-law, secretly married to Miss Groves, proving how far she has fallen socially in Charlotte Lennox's *The Female Quixote*.

Mrs. Barnet Sister of Miss Groves's former maid; she provides Miss Groves a place to give birth to an illegitimate child in Charlotte Lennox's *The Female Quixote*.

John Barnet Scots-speaking servant of the Reverend Wringhim; he reproves Robert Colwan for conceit and hypocrisy and is provoked into leaving his post through Robert's scheming in James Hogg's *The Private Memoirs and Confessions of a Justified Sinner*.

Miss Barnevelt Harriet Byron's London acquaintance, a lady of masculine mind and features, who holds her own sex in contempt; her chief pleasure in being a woman derives from the impossibility of her marrying a woman, but she is much taken with Harriet in Samuel Richardson's *Sir Charles Grandison*.

Barney Waiter at the Three Cripples who speaks through his nose; he is Fagin's confederate in Charles Dickens's *Oliver Twist*.

Mrs. Barnington Social leader in Robert Surtees's *Handley Cross*.

Baronet ("handsome Sir ——") Heavy drinker who is robbed by Moll Flanders but who later has an affair with her for a year in Daniel Defoe's *The Fortunes and Misfortunes of the Famous Moll Flanders*.

Baroni An extremely intelligent and able Jew, who was persecuted in his European home but was given a place in Sidonia's circle of talented associates; he is sent by Sidonia to be the companion of Tancred, Lord Montacute during his travels in Palestine in Benjamin Disraeli's *Tancred; or, The New Crusade*.

Moses Barraclough A Methodist and a hypocritical preacher, who leads the machine breakers; he is eventually transported under Robert Moore's orders in Charlotte Brontë's *Shirley*.

Monsieur Barreaux Reclusive botanist, who is a friend of the St. Aubert family in Ann Radcliffe's *The Mysteries of Udolpho*.

Mrs. Barrett A housekeeper and Lucy Snowe's former nurse, who suggests Lucy might teach English abroad in Charlotte Brontë's *Villette*.

Sir Justinian Barrett Purcell Barrett's father, who dies, leaving his son a title but denying him his inheritance because his mother ran away with another man in George Meredith's *Emilia in England*.

Sir Purcell Barrett A male sentimentalist; his aristocratic poverty endears him to the Poles, and he and Cornelia Pole fall in love, but her abstract ideals lead him to suicide, deserted by her and disinherited by his father in George Meredith's *Emilia in England*.

Madame Barronneau Henri Barronneau's widow, who married Rigaud and was murdered by him in Charles Dickens's *Little Dorrit*.

Henri Barronneau Innkeeper with whom Rigaud lodged while in Marseilles in Charles Dickens's *Little Dorrit*.

Mr. Barrow Bedfordshire apothecary in Samuel Richardson's *Pamela, or Virtue Rewarded*.

Mr. Barry John Grey's not over-scrupulous younger partner, who proposes marriage for reasons of self-interest to Grey's daughter, Dorothy, and is rejected; he eventually takes over the firm in Anthony Trollope's *Mr. Scarborough's Family*.

Bell Brady Barry Energetic, handsome widowed mother of Redmond Barry; she helps him guard his wife, and at last, when he is destitute, she cares for him in prison in William Makepeace Thackeray's *The Luck of Barry Lyndon*.

Cornelius Barry (the Chevalier de Balibari) Sixty-year-old, tall, gaudily dressed, one-eyed Irish adventurer and Redmond Barry's uncle; sent to spy on him, the nephew discovers the uncle's identity; the two become partners in card-sharping in high society on the Continent; eventually the uncle, a lifelong Catholic, retires to a convent in William Makepeace Thackeray's *The Luck of Barry Lyndon*.

Felicia Barry Arthur Ronald's beautiful aunt, who is to Christopher Kirkland the ideal woman in Mrs. Lynn Linton's *The Autobiography of Christopher Kirkland*.

"Roaring" Harry Barry Redmond Barry's late father, a scoundrel, in William Makepeace Thackeray's *The Luck of Barry Lyndon*.

Redmond Barry (later Barry Lyndon) The narrator and protagonist, a braggart and an unscrupulous Irish adventurer; having fought a duel at sixteen, he is shipped off to Dublin, where he escapes the consequences of his debt by joining the army as a private soldier; he deserts, is impressed into the Prussian army, and deserts again; his career as a card-sharp is capped by his marriage to Honoria, Countess of Lyndon, whose name he takes; his dissipation and profligacy worsen; eventually his wife escapes his control, and he becomes an inmate of Fleet Prison in William Makepeace Thackeray's *The Luck of Barry Lyndon*.

Eliza Barrymoore Housekeeper at Baskerville Hall and wife of John in Arthur Conan Doyle's *The Hound of the Baskervilles*.

John Barrymoore Butler at Baskerville Hall, husband of Eliza, and beneficiary of a sum of money from the death of Sir Charles Baskerville in Arthur Conan Doyle's *The Hound of the Baskervilles*.

John Barsad See Solomon Pross.

Dr. Ambrose Bartlett Virtuous tutor who accompanies the vicious young Mr. Lorimer on a European tour; to remove the curb on his licentiousness, Lorimer has Dr. Bartlett imprisoned by the Turkish authorities in Athens, where Sir Charles Grandison rescues him from execution; he becomes Sir Charles's revered companion and is the source of much of Harriet Byron's information about Sir Charles's Italian adventures in Samuel Richardson's *Sir Charles Grandison*.

Jack Bartley Unhappily married and impoverished man whose alcoholic wife deserts him and who becomes involved in a forgery ring and is arrested in George Gissing's *The Nether World*.

General Barton Rakish owner of a mansion near the cottage of Arabella Bloomville; he is among the casualties of a fatal banquet in William Beckford's *Modern Novel Writing; or, the Elegant Enthusiast*.

Lady Barton General Barton's grandmother, who writes poetry and has occasional bouts with insanity; her death nearly unhinges her grandson in William Beckford's *Modern Novel Writing; or, the Elegant Enthusiast*.

Mr. Barton Young, simple-minded rustic convinced by Mrs. Howard that he loves and should marry Sophia Darnley despite her poverty in Charlotte Lennox's *Sophia*.

Mrs. Barton Mr. Barton's mother; resenting Mrs. Howard's attempt to marry the penniless Sophia Darnley to her son, she informs her that young Mr. Howard also loves Sophia; she conspires to brand Sophia as a man-trap in Charlotte Lennox's *Sophia*.

Mrs. Barton Mrs. Allen's friend, who nurses Priscilla (Broad) Allen in childbirth in Mark Rutherford's *The Revolution In Tanner's Lane*.

Mrs. Barton Aggressive, foolish mother of Alice and Olive; her entire interest is in society; she neglects her husband and keeps company with Lord Dungory; she fails to understand either her intelligent daughter, Alice, or her beautiful daughter, Olive, who submits to her match-making schemes in George Moore's *A Drama in Muslin*.

Alice Barton   Neglected and unhappy daughter of Mrs. Barton; she dislikes the marriage market and admires two intellectuals, both socially undesirable; without parental blessing she marries Edward Reed and escapes to London; she becomes a novelist and has a happy home, providing sanctuary for her sister, Olive, and her schoolgirl friends in George Moore's *A Drama in Muslin*.

Arthur Barton   Father of Alice and Olive and an aesthete usually dismissed as boring; he is ineffectual in practical matters and selfishly inadequate in responding to his daughters' needs in George Moore's *A Drama in Muslin*.

John Barton   Factory worker and Trade Unionist father of Mary Barton; he is embittered by the deaths of his wife and son and by the conditions of his life as a Manchester worker; his shooting of Harry Carson is catastrophic in Elizabeth Gaskell's *Mary Barton*.

Johnny Barton   A twenty-year-old carpenter, whose love for a young girl is thwarted by poverty until Robert Lovelace provides a modest marriage settlement in Samuel Richardson's *Clarissa: or, The History of a Young Lady*.

Mary Barton   John Barton's daughter, who is in danger of being tempted like her "fallen" Aunt Esther Fergusson; when Jem Wilson is accused of murdering her would-be seducer, Harry Carson, she proves his alibi and realizes she loves him in Elizabeth Gaskell's *Mary Barton*.

Mary, Mrs. Barton   Mother of Mary Barton; her early death deprives her daughter of guidance and her husband of a softening influence in Elizabeth Gaskell's *Mary Barton*.

Olive Barton   A cameo beauty with "nothing wanting but a mind"; through her mother's scheming she becomes the belle of the Dublin social season; though she loves Captain Hibbert, her mother is ambitious for her to catch a title; she is both outschemed by a rival classmate and thwarted in her plans to elope in George Moore's *A Drama in Muslin*.

Ralph Barton   London politician and an acquaintance of Jery Melford; he unsuccessfully courts Liddy Melford; Tabith Bramble, misunderstanding him, thinks she is the object of his amours in Tobias Smollett's *The Expedition of Humphry Clinker*.

Admiral Arthur Bartram   Lusty ex-seafaring owner of St. Crux who has a soft spot for ladies; he employs as parlour maid the disguised Magdalen Vanstone in Wilkie Collins's *No Name*.

George Bartram   Rich cousin of Norah Vanstone; he inherits the Vanstone family fortune from his uncle, Admiral Bartram, and marries Norah in Wilkie Collins's *No Name*.

Mr. Barvile   A young gentleman deviant, who introduces Fanny Hill to flagellation, active and passive, in John Cleland's *Memoirs of a Woman of Pleasure*.

Felix Bashwood   Broken-down, nervous steward engaged by Allan Armadale to assist Ozias Midwinter through the good offices of the elder Mr. Pedgift; Bashwood is captivated by Lydia Gwilt and seeks unsuccessfully to stop her marrying Midwinter in Wilkie Collins's *Armadale*.

James (Jemmy) Bashwood   Churlish, uncouth son of Felix; his skills as professional private detective are called upon by his father, besotted with Lydia Gwilt, to spy on her and Allan Armadale in Wilkie Collins's *Armadale*.

Basil   Young Roman patrician in love with the Gothic princess Veranilda; he searches for her after she is abducted and suspects her of infidelity when he finds her with his false friend Marcian, whom he kills; he regrets his actions after instruction from St. Benedict at the Abbey of Cassino, is reunited with Veranilda, and receives the Gothic king's promise that they will be married in George Gissing's *Veranilda*.

Basil   Second son of an unnamed widower of fortune and ancient family; having agreed to Mr. Sherwin's demand that Basil's marriage to Margaret Sherwin take place a year before its consummation, the love-sick husband is deranged to discover her unchastity with Robert Mannion; hounded by Mannion after Basil has disfigured him in a beating, Basil narrowly escapes death in Cornwall in Wilkie Collins's *Basil: A Story of Modern Life*.

Basil's Father   Unnamed widower whose austere pride motivates the secrecy of Basil's attachment and marriage to a linen draper's daughter in Wilkie Collins's *Basil: A Story of Modern Life*.

Miriam Baske   Wealthy young widow, whose long residence in Italy enables her to escape her repressed Puritanical tendencies and makes her attractive to Ross Mallard, whom she marries in George Gissing's *The Emancipated*.

Captain Cecil Baskelett   Successful challenger of his cousin Nevil Beauchamp for Parliament; he incites Dr. Shrapnel and Everard Romfrey to great enmity in George Meredith's *Beauchamp's Career*.

Sir Charles Baskerville   Baronet and landowner whose recent death from terror is brought to Sherlock Holmes's attention by James Mortimer in Arthur Conan Doyle's *The Hound of the Baskervilles*.

Sir Henry Baskerville   Nephew and heir of the late Sir Charles Baskerville; he returns to England after some years of farming in Canada in Arthur Conan Doyle's *The Hound of the Baskervilles*.

Miss Batchford   Lucilla Finch's maternal aunt, whose dislike of Madame Pratolungo's revolutionary politics creates a barrier of communication which endangers Lucilla in Wilkie Collins's *Poor Miss Finch*.

Bateman   Student of Nun's College, Oxford, an Anglo-Catholic ritualist, and an early influence on Charles Reding in John Henry Newman's *Loss and Gain*.

Mr. Bates   The doctor who treats the patients at Lowood School in Charlotte Brontë's *Jane Eyre*.

Mrs. Bates   Elderly, deaf mother of the good Miss Bates and grandmother of Jane Fairfax in Jane Austen's *Emma*.

Charley Bates   Sprightly boy who works for Fagin; he is shocked by Nancy's murder and reforms at the end of Charles Dickens's *Oliver Twist*.

Henrietta (Hetty) Bates   Good-natured spinster aunt of Jane Fairfax; her inability to stop talking of trivialities causes Emma Woodhouse to be cruelly rude to her in Jane Austen's *Emma*.

Colonel Bath   Pugnacious brother of Jenny Bath; his exaggerated sense of honor propels him into duels on the slightest pretext in Henry Fielding's *Amelia*.

Lady Bath   Pedantic lady, whose learning only Frank Leigh can match in Charles Kingsley's *Westward Ho!*.

Captain Benjamin Batsby   Fox-hunting half brother of Sir Harry Albury; he fancies himself a lady-killer and pursues Ayala Dormer and Gertrude Tringle, whom he persuades to elope with him to Ostend; his gamble pays off when Sir Thomas Tringle makes a generous wedding settlement in Anthony Trollope's *Ayala's Angel*.

Mr. Battersby   Baker from Dollington who aids Mrs. Page in the food preparations for the Hunt Ball in J. Sheridan Le Fanu's *Wylder's Hand*.

Mr. Battle   Burly solicitor from London engaged by Dean Lovelace to probe the circumstances of the marriage of the Marquis of Brotherton and the legitimacy of his heir in Anthony Trollope's *Is He Popenjoy?*.

Captain Battleax   Commander of the British gunboat which comes to end the presidency of John Neverbend over the independent island of Britannula near New Zealand by training its 250-ton cannon on the capital in Anthony Trollope's *The Fixed Period*.

Mr. Batts   Member of Truth Society [Unitarian], who gives Charles Reding a pamphlet to deter him from becoming Roman Catholic in John Henry Newman's *Loss and Gain*.

Sir Baudoin   The Golden Knight, who helps to free the three imprisoned damsels; he is killed by the Red Knight when rescuing Birdalone in William Morris's *The Water of the Wondrous Isles*.

Count Bauvillers   French nobleman who criticizes Valancourt to Emily St. Aubert in Ann Radcliffe's *The Mysteries of Udolpho*.

Fritz Bawwah   German cutter for Mr. Neefit, the breeches-maker; his employer sends him to Ralph Newton (the heir) to collect money owed to him in Anthony Trollope's *Ralph the Heir*.

Mr. Baxendale   Wealthy mayor of Dunfield, a man of great practical intelligence and a Member of Parliament in George Gissing's *A Life's Morning*.

Mrs. Baxendale   Gracious wife of the town's mayor; she once employed Emily Hood as a governess and advises her and her lover, not always wisely, in George Gissing's *A Life's Morning*.

Mrs. Baxter   Methodist whose interview with Ernest Pontifex causes him again to question his faith in Samuel Butler's *The Way of All Flesh*.

Timothy Baxter   Squire Thornhill's agent in the abduction of Sophia Primrose in Oliver Goldsmith's *The Vicar of Wakefield*.

Fred ("F. B.") Bayham   A gifted mimic and a good-humored Bohemian; assisted in need by Colonel Newcome, he campaigns for the colonel's election to Parliament and is ever ready with helpful advice in a crisis in William Makepeace Thackeray's *The Newcomes*.

Baynard   Old friend of Matthew Bramble; driven toward bankruptcy by the excesses of his wife, he is rescued by the interference of Bramble when his wife dies in Tobias Smollett's *The Expedition of Humphry Clinker*.

General Charles Baynes   Retired Indian officer, timid everywhere but in military action; as trustee of Philip Firmin's fortune, he allows Dr. Firmin to embezzle it; his subjugation to his wife makes him a weak and vacillating friend to Philip's engagement to his daughter Charlotte in William Makepeace Thackeray's *The Adventures of Philip on His Way through the World*.

Charlotte Baynes   General Baynes's daughter, who marries Philip Firmin in spite of her mother's implacable opposition; she is an affectionate and devoted wife but unreasonably jealous of Caroline Brandon in William Makepeace Thackeray's *The Adventures of Philip on His Way through the World.*

Eliza Baynes   Shrewish, domineering wife of General Baynes; their seven children include Charlotte, whose engagement to Philip Firmin is bitterly opposed by the mother when his money has been lost; the marriage estranges mother and daughter in William Makepeace Thackeray's *The Adventures of Philip on His Way through the World.*

Mr. Bayton   Workhouse inhabitant who ordered medicine for his sick wife; he dies in Charles Dickens's *Oliver Twist.*

Mrs. Bayton   Woman who dies shortly after coming to the workhouse in Charles Dickens's *Oliver Twist.*

Mr. Bazin   Large, ill-favored French keeper of the inn at which James MacGregor and his daughter Catriona Drummond stay in exile in Robert Louis Stevenson's *Catriona.*

Mr. Bazzard   Hiram Grewgious's sharp-tongued clerk, who has written a tragedy titled *The Thorn of Anxiety* that reflects Rosa Bud's anxious sexual feelings about John Jasper in Charles Dickens's *The Mystery of Edwin Drood.*

Lord Beaconsfield   Influential member of the Marquess of Carabas's political party; he helps cause Vivian Grey's political downfall by withdrawing his support of Frederick Cleveland, the candidate for Parliament whom Grey had advised the Marquess to nominate in Benjamin Disraeli's *Vivian Grey.*

Harriet (Tattycoram) Beadle   Ill-tempered and jealous maid of Minnie (Pet) Meagles; she runs away to Miss Wade and later returns to Mr. Meagles with the iron box which holds the information about Arthur Clennam's birth in Charles Dickens's *Little Dorrit.*

Beamish   Richard Butler's friend and Catherine Butler's betrothed in Anne Thackeray Ritchie's *The Village on the Cliff.*

Alice Bean Lean   Daughter of Donald Bean Lean; Edward Waverly mistakes her for a serving girl while held in the robber's cave; she helps Waverly recover important letters in Sir Walter Scott's *Waverly.*

Donald Bean Lean   Chieftain of a group of Highland robbers; he rescues Edward Waverly from jail and smuggles him to the Highlands; it is his interception of Waverly's letters which brings charges against Waverly in Sir Walter Scott's *Waverly.*

Madame Bearn   Companion to the Countess de Villefort in Ann Radcliffe's *The Mysteries of Udolpho.*

Beatrice   Elderly housekeeper at Villa Altieri, who witnesses Ellena Rosalba's abduction and later identifies Sister Olivia as the Countess di Bruno and Ellena's mother in Ann Radcliffe's *The Italian.*

Beatrice (Prophetess of Ferrara, Ancilla Dei)   Daughter of the executed heretic Magfreda and the adopted daughter of Bishop Marsilio of Ferrara; a rivetingly beautiful innocent, she has an exalted imagination and is victimized by the Church, the Paterins, and Castruccio dei Antelminelli; she goes mad from henbane poisoning in Mary Shelley's *Valperga.*

Lady Beauchamp   Woman who, disappointed in her romantic attraction to Edward Beauchamp, takes revenge by marrying his widowed father and having the son's income in exile greatly reduced; she is talked out of her meanness by Sir Charles Grandison; her stepson treats her generously when she is widowed in Samuel Richardson's *Sir Charles Grandison.*

Sir Benjamin Beauchamp   Founder of a utopian community who watches it disintegrate under the pressure of human frailties in S. J. Pratt's *Shenstone-Green.*

Caroline Beauchamp   Handsome and wealthy young woman, considered somewhat coarse by some; Stanley Lake tells his sister, Rachel, he might marry Caroline in order to allay Rachel's suspicions about his designs on Dorcas Brandon in J. Sheridan Le Fanu's *Wylder's Hand.*

(Sir) Edward Beauchamp   Sir Charles Grandison's friend and European traveling companion; Sir Charles persuades Edward's father and stepmother to drop their unkind treatment of him; Edward is discouraged by Sir Charles from courting Emily Jervois because of her youth, but their eventual union is anticipated at the end of Samuel Richardson's *Sir Charles Grandison.*

Elizabeth Mary Beauchamp   Aunt of both Nevil Beauchamp and Blackburn Tuckham; she divides her estate between them in George Meredith's *Beauchamp's Career.*

Sir Harry Beauchamp   Baronet who is influenced by his young second wife to withdraw support from his son and heir, Edward; Sir Charles Grandison's good-humored intercession restores family harmony, and when Sir Harry dies, Sir Edward treats his stepmother magnanimously in Samuel Richardson's *Sir Charles Grandison.*

Matilda Beauchamp   Daughter of Sir Benjamin and cofounder of Shenstone-Green; she marries the reformed spendthrift Danvers Davies in S. J. Pratt's *Shenstone-Green.*

Nevil Beauchamp   Patriotic and idealist hero of the Crimean War; he campaigns for Parliament as a Liberal, aided by Dr. Shrapnel, estranging his Tory uncle; his involvement with a Frenchwoman and the radical Dr. Shrapnel loses him the campaign, his beloved, and his health; though he reconciles with his family and marries Shrapnel's ward, Jenny Denham, he dies in an act of heroism in George Meredith's *Beauchamp's Career*.

Beauclair   Honest and gullible lover of Montamour; he disguises himself as a friar in order to get her in Eliza Haywood's *The Injur'd Husband; or, the Mistaken Resentment*.

Count de Beauclair   Nephew of Count de Vinevil; left in charge of the family holdings in France when the count takes his family to Constantinople, he faithfully restores the estate to Ardelisa de Vinevil when she returns in Penelope Aubin's *The Strange Adventures of the Count De Vinevil and His Family*.

Beauclerc   Gambler murdered by Charles Archer (Paul Dangerfield); Lord Dunoran is convicted of the crime on Archer's testimony in J. Sheridan Le Fanu's *The House by the Churchyard*.

De Beaujeu   Keeper of a gambling house in Sir Walter Scott's *The Fortunes of Nigel*.

Helena Beauly   Eustace Macallan's cousin, with whom he was in love and whose marriage helped propel him into marriage with his first wife; a widow and houseguest at the time of Sara Macallan's death, she is important as both suspect and motive for Eustace as suspect in Wilkie Collins's *The Law and the Lady*.

Duchess of Beaumanoir   Dignified and accomplished wife of the duke and mother of Henry Sidney in Benjamin Disraeli's *Coningsby; or, The New Generation*.

Duke of Beaumanoir   Well-meaning but politically uninformed father of Harry Coningsby's friend Henry Sidney in Benjamin Disraeli's *Coningsby; or, The New Generation*.

Lucas Beaumanoir   Grand Master of the Templars; he accuses Rebecca of sorcery and is later banished by King Richard in Sir Walter Scott's *Ivanhoe*.

Percy, Marquis of Beaumanoir   Elder brother of Henry Sidney and Harry Coningsby's frivolous rival for Edith Millbank during her brief estrangement from Coningsby in Benjamin Disraeli's *Coningsby; or, The New Generation*.

Count de Beaumont   Son of the governor of Normandy; he elopes with the Protestant Belinda; separated from her by his father because of her religion, he joins the Swedish Army, is taken prisoner, has several adventures, and refuses women who want to love him; he finally remarries but cannot forget Belinda; he is reunited with her and his daughter after fourteen years in Penelope Aubin's *The Life of Madam de Beaumont*.

Belinda, Madam de Beaumont   Protestant orphan, the virtuous daughter of a French nobleman and an English lady; she marries Catholic Count de Beaumont, with whom she has a daughter before they are separated by her father-in-law's objections to her religion; she lives in a cave in Wales for fourteen years, whereupon she meets Mr. Lluelling, who loves her daughter and finds the count, reuniting the family in Penelope Aubin's *The Life of Madam de Beaumont*.

Miss Beaumont   Principal in Dick Lennox's acting company until she is replaced by Kate Ede in leading roles; she is mollified by the attention she gets from admirers in high society in George Moore's *A Mummer's Wife*.

Mrs. Beaumont   Kinswoman of Lord Orville; she is the Bristol hostess for Orville and Louisa Larpent in Frances Burney's *Evelina*.

Lady de Beaumont   Count de Beaumont's second wife, a young widow with a daughter; she dies from grief after two years because he cannot forget his first wife in Penelope Aubin's *The Life of Madam de Beaumont*.

Hortensia Beaumont   Friend whom Lady Clementina della Porretta visits in Rome and who reveals to the family Clementina's love for Sir Charles Grandison; she believes that only marriage to Sir Charles will cure Clementina's affliction in Samuel Richardson's *Sir Charles Grandison*.

Count de Beaunoir   Whimsical, extravagant Frenchman, who engages in a duel with Coke Clifton, later becoming Coke's friend and a suitor of Anna St. Ives in Thomas Holcroft's *Anna St. Ives*.

Beauvaris   Savillon's epistolary intimate, who eventually dies in Henry Mackenzie's *Julia de Roubigné*.

Beck   Crossing sweeper who baffles Lucretia Clavering's plot against Helen Mainwaring and Percival St. John and is murdered by Lucretia before she discovers he is her lost son, Vincent Braddell, in Edward Bulwer-Lytton's *Lucretia*.

Desiree Beck   Mme. Beck's eldest child, who is brought up according to a system of spying to be sly and destructive in Charlotte Brontë's *Villette*.

Fifine Beck   Mme. Beck's second child, who has her

father's honest nature, and who, when she breaks her arm, brings Dr. John Bretton to the school for the first time in Charlotte Brontë's *Villette*.

Georgette Beck   Mme. Beck's youngest child, who is attached to Lucy Snowe in Charlotte Brontë's *Villette*.

Modeste Maria Beck   Determined, cunning headmistress of a boarding school in Villette, Labassecour, who hires Lucy Snowe without references as a nursery governess, promotes her to English teacher, and actively interposes when her cousin, M. Paul Emanuel, becomes interested in Lucy in Charlotte Brontë's *Villette*.

Mr. Beckendorff   Eccentric, Machiavellian prime minister of Austria, whose political intrigues include arranging the marriage of Baroness Sybilla to the Prince of Reisenburg, thereby preventing her marriage to Vivian Grey in Benjamin Disraeli's *Vivian Grey*.

Adam Bede   An authoritative and rigidly moral man, whose fixed ideas of right and wrong are challenged and softened when his betrothed, Hetty Sorrel, deserts her newborn child of another father; ultimately he finds peace through his marriage to Dinah Morris, the Methodist preacher, in George Eliot's *Adam Bede*.

Adam Bede (the younger)   Son of Adam and Dinah (Morris) Bede in George Eliot's *Adam Bede*.

Lisbeth Bede   Adam Bede's anxious, nagging mother, who depends upon this favorite son completely; when her husband drowns, the importance of mourning rites and traditions in calming a grieving loved one are clear in George Eliot's *Adam Bede*.

Lisbeth Bede (the younger)   Daughter of Adam and Dinah (Morris) Bede in George Eliot's *Adam Bede*.

Matthias Bede   Adam Bede's hard-drinking father, who drowns; this begins his son's regeneration because Adam feels guilty for his ill-feelings towards the old alcoholic in George Eliot's *Adam Bede*.

Seth Bede   The gentle, pious younger brother of Adam Bede; he loves Dinah Morris, but his suit is unsuccessful; when Adam falls in love with Dinah, Seth kindly steps aside to allow his brother full joy in marriage in George Eliot's *Adam Bede*.

Earl of Bedford   English envoy to Mary, Queen of Scots and supporter of the Duke of Norfolk's plan to free the pregnant Mary in Sophia Lee's *The Recess*.

Mrs. Bedonebyasyoudid   See Queen of the Fairies.

Bedos   Henry Pelham's inestimable French valet; he

high-mindedly resists all Pelham's offers to effect a reunion with his wife by providing her with employment in Edward Bulwer-Lytton's *Pelham*.

Mrs. Bedwin   Mr. Brownlow's housekeeper, who nurses Oliver Twist when he is ill in Charles Dickens's *Oliver Twist*.

Beech   Maternal tree-woman, who wants to progress to womanhood; she helps protect Anodos in George MacDonald's *Phantastes*.

Sir Timothy Beeswax   Astute, devious Conservative politician and political enemy of the (younger) Duke of Omnium in Anthony Trollope's *The Prime Minister*. He is a protégé of Mr. Daubeny and rises to become Leader of the House of Commons; a falling out with his chief, Lord Drummond, causes his downfall in *The Duke's Children*. He appears in *The American Senator*.

Callum Beg   Young Highlander of the MacIvor clan; he guides Edward Waverly through much of Scotland in Sir Walter Scott's *Waverly*.

Beggar   Charlatan beggar Harley meets on the way to London; he tells pleasing fortunes to people to earn his living in Henry Mackenzie's *The Man of Feeling*.

Begsurbeck   Pious king of Normnbdsgrsutt and revered ancestor of Georigetti; he receives prophetic notice of Peter Wilkins's mission in Robert Paltock's *The Life and Adventures of Peter Wilkins*.

Mr. Beilby   Senior partner in the engineering firm of Beilby and Burton, in which Harry Clavering becomes apprenticed in Anthony Trollope's *The Claverings*.

Duke of Belfield   An admirer of Caroline Strike in George Meredith's *Evan Harrington*.

Mr. Belfield   Proud though poor brother of Henrietta; he changes his enthusiasms from literature to field labor, is seriously wounded in a duel with Sir Robert Floyer for Cecilia Beverley's attention, and is viewed by Mortimer Delvile as a rival in Frances Burney's *Cecilia*.

Henrietta Belfield   Sister of Mr. Belfield; she nurses him during his illness after his duel; she is befriended by Cecilia Beverley; she secretly loves Mortimer Delvile but marries Mr. Arnott in the end in Frances Burney's *Cecilia*.

John ("Jack") Belford   Rakish principal confidant and chief correspondent of Lovelace but never an accessory to Lovelace's machinations; attending Clarissa Harlowe in her decline helps to effect his reformation; he becomes executor for both Clarissa and Lovelace in Samuel Richardson's *Clarissa: or, The History of a Young Lady*.

Lord Belgrave   Nobleman who dismisses Mr. Gifford as tutor to his bear when Mr. Gifford unwittingly lets the animal eat the latest delivery of butter in William Beckford's *Modern Novel Writing; or, the Elegant Enthusiast*.

Belinda   Subject of a letter from Cynthia to Camilla (Simple); she loves the married Philander; after inheriting money she supports him and his wife and then marries him after his wife dies in Sarah Fielding's *Familiar Letters between the Principal Characters of David Simple and Some Others*.

Lady Belinda   Jealous woman of fashion; she removes the beautiful Azemia from the duke's clutches because her matrimonial plans for the noble are threatened; she takes her to the house of Mr. and Mrs. Wildcodger in William Beckford's *Azemia*.

Mr. Bell   Old friend of Mr. Hale and godfather to Margaret Hale; her inheritance of his wealth enables her to save John Thornton and marry him in Elizabeth Gaskell's *North and South*.

Francis Bell   Clergyman prevented by a rash youthful engagement from marrying his cousin, Helen Thistlewood (later Pendennis), to whose care he bequeaths his daughter, Laura (later Pendennis), in William Makepeace Thackeray's *The History of Pendennis*.

Lady Bellair   A great society hostess in Benjamin Disraeli's *Henrietta Temple: A Love Story*.

Mrs. Bellairs   Wife of Harry D. Bellairs and daughter of the man who ruined Bellairs's family; she is still supported by Bellairs though she ran off with a drummer after two years of marriage in Robert Louis Stevenson's *The Wrecker*.

Harry D. Bellairs   Disreputable San Francisco attorney, who bids against Jim Pinkerton as agent for Norris Carthew; he becomes friends with Loudon Dodd on a ship to Europe as he tracks Carthew in Robert Louis Stevenson's *The Wrecker*.

Bellamont   Placentia's brother, who was thought to be dead but instead was castrated by the Bashaw, thus becoming the Christian Eunuch; he is rescued by Philidore in Eliza Haywood's *Philidore and Placentia; or, L'Amour trop delicat*.

George, Duke of Bellamont   Doting but unworldly and socially reclusive father of Tancred, Lord Montacute; he and his wife have spent most of their lives on their country estate and do not understand their son's need to find spiritual fulfillment during a tour through the Holy Land in Benjamin Disraeli's *Tancred; or, The New Crusade*.

Katherine, Duchess of Bellamont   Wife of the duke and mother of Tancred, Lord Montacute in Benjamin Disraeli's *Tancred; or, The New Crusade*.

Mr. Bellamy   A farmer, friend, and customer of Mr. Furze; he is owner of Chapel Farm, where Catharine Furze likes to visit, in Mark Rutherford's *Catharine Furze*.

Mrs. Bellamy   Childless wife of Mr. Bellamy and friend of Catharine Furze; she nurses Catharine in her mortal illness in Mark Rutherford's *Catharine Furze*.

Bellarmine   French lord whose European dress and manners capture Leonora's heart away from Horatio; Bellarmine abandons her when her father refuses to offer an advantageous dowry in Henry Fielding's *The History of the Adventures of Mr. Joseph Andrews and of his Friend Mr. Abraham Adams*.

Lady Bellaston   Sophia Western's distant relative, with whom Sophia takes shelter in London; having started an affair with Tom Jones, and wanting to dispose of Sophia, she encourages Lord Fellamar to rape her so she will more readily accept his marriage proposal; Tom's proposal of marriage to Lady Bellaston has the desired effect of causing her to break with him in outrage; she actively plots his ruin in Henry Fielding's *The History of Tom Jones*.

Belle   Dowerless sweetheart of Ebenezer Scrooge; she releases him from their engagement because of his "master passion, Gain," and is later seen as a comely matron with a loving family in Charles Dickens's *A Christmas Carol*.

Edith Bellenden   Granddaughter of Lady Margaret Bellenden; she loves Henry Morton, becomes engaged to Lord Evandale (William Maxwell) after she believes Morton is dead, and marries Morton after the death of Lord Evandale in Sir Walter Scott's *Old Mortality*.

Lady Margaret Bellenden   Mistress of Tillietudlem and a strong Jacobite, whose castle is the site of battles between Cameronian rebels and Royalist soldiers; driven out during the wars, she loses her estate to her villainous turncoat cousin Basil Olifant and lives on charity until his death in Sir Walter Scott's *Old Mortality*.

Major Miles Bellenden   Uncle of Edith Bellenden and brother-in-law of Lady Margaret Bellenden; he pleads to Francis Stewart, Sergeant Bothwell, for the life of Henry Morton and leads in the defense of Tillietudlem against the Cameronian rebels in Sir Walter Scott's *Old Mortality*.

Harry Beller   Former toastmaster converted to temperance, mentioned in the "Report of the Committee of the United Grand Junction Ebeneezer Temperance Association," in Charles Dickens's *The Posthumous Papers of the Pickwick Club*.

Captain Gustavus Bellfield   Flashy suitor of Mrs. Greenow, who chooses his raffish charm over the stolidity of Samuel Cheesacre and marries him in Anthony Trollope's *Can You Forgive Her?*.

Count de Bellfleur   Fickle Venetian lover of Melanthe; he transfers his affections to Louisa just as he wins Melanthe in Eliza Haywood's *The Fortunate Foundlings*.

Mrs. Bellingham   The mother of Henry Bellingham; she takes advantage of his illness to drive the pregnant Ruth Hilton away in Elizabeth Gaskell's *Ruth*.

Henry Bellingham   The upper-class seducer of Ruth Hilton; he is maneuvered by his mother into abandoning her while he is ill and she is pregnant; having taken the name Donne as a condition of inheriting wealth, he becomes Member of Parliament for Ecclestone; he reencounters Ruth, who repulses him but nurses him during a cholera epidemic; he recovers, but Ruth is infected and dies in Elizabeth Gaskell's *Ruth*.

Bellipine   Jemmy Jessamy's best friend, who is very poor; he has no honor and manipulates everyone in Eliza Haywood's *The History of Jemmy and Jenny Jessamy*.

Sir George Bellmour   Charles Glanville's rakish friend; loved by Charlotte Glanville, he competes with Glanville in wooing Arabella by inventing romances; he reforms when Glanville stabs him nearly to death in a jealous rage; he buys the Glanvilles' forgiveness by agreeing to marry Charlotte in Charlotte Lennox's *The Female Quixote*.

Mr. Belloni   Emilia Belloni's father, an Italian revolutionary and a violinist, who tries to arrange a mercenary marriage for Emilia, causing her to run away; he later tries to help Pericles send her to Italy to study music in George Meredith's *Emilia in England*.

Mrs. Belloni   Emilia Belloni's good-hearted mother in George Meredith's *Emilia in England* and in *Vittoria*.

Emilia Alessandra (Sandra) Belloni   A pure, half-Italian singer; her friends the Poles, her patron Pericles, and even her father try to exploit her financially and socially; only Merthyr Powys remains true, rescuing her from suicide and arranging for her to go to Italy to study music; she vows to grow to love him in George Meredith's *Emilia in England*. Involved with the struggle for Italian liberation from Austria, she changes her name to Vittoria Campa; her revolutionary efforts are hindered by her loyalties to the Poles and by Pericles; she marries a patriot, Carlo Ammiani, who dies in a failed revolt; she names their son

after him and Merthyr, whom she perhaps marries at last in *Vittoria*.

Chevalier de Bellozane   George Godolphin's Swiss cousin, who is attracted to Emmeline Mobray during her stay with Lord and Lady (Augusta Delamere) Westerhaven at his father's chateau; no rebuff can check his importunities; he follows Emmeline to England, where a liaison with Lady Frances Crofts ends when he kills Frederic Delamere in a duel in Charlotte Smith's *Emmeline: The Orphan of the Castle*.

Lady Belmont   Lady Julia Belmont's devoted and well-meaning mother in Frances Brooke's *The History of Lady Julia Mandeville*.

Lord Belmont   Descendant of ancient English nobility, a benevolent patriarch concerned with the Belmont lineage and securing fitting jointure arrangements for its continuance; he realizes the disastrous effects of his oversolicitude with the deaths of his daughter Julia and her beloved Henry Mandeville in Frances Brooke's *The History of Lady Julia Mandeville*.

Evelina Anville Belmont   Seventeen-year-old daughter of Sir John Belmont; she is not acknowledged by her father until he is forced to recognize her mother in her features; she falls in love with Lord Orville, saves Mr. Macartney from suicide, and marries Orville after her reconciliation with Sir John in Frances Burney's *Evelina*.

Sir John Belmont   English baronet and the father of Evelina Anville Belmont, whom he refuses to acknowledge until he is forced to meet her; he joyously bestows an inheritance upon her when she marries in Frances Burney's *Evelina*.

Lady Julia Belmont   Beautiful heroine of wealth, virtue, and sensibility; her mutual love for Henry Mandeville is supported by her parents and all seems well, but grief at the sudden death of Henry causes her immediate death from fever in Frances Brooke's *The History of Lady Julia Mandeville*.

Lady Mary Belmont   Elderly relative of both Belmonts and Mandevilles, once a member of Queen Mary's court; she bequeaths a fortune to Henry Mandeville, which facilitates jointure arrangements made secretly by their parents for Henry's marriage to Lady Julia Belmont in Frances Brooke's *The History of Lady Julia Mandeville*.

Miss Belmour   Lady D—'s relation and Henrietta Courteney's employer; she confides to Henrietta her passion for a married man; she takes her advice to run away to Paris, where she promotes Henrietta to companion; there she resumes her illicit intrigue, forcing Henrietta to leave her service in Charlotte Lennox's *Henrietta*.

Mr. Beloe　Author of Arabian stories, who, though he likes to criticize the work of others, gets angry when his works are attacked in William Beckford's *Modern Novel Writing; or, the Elegant Enthusiast.*

Charles ("Jack") Belsize (later Lord Highgate)　Aristocratic but impoverished suitor of Lady Clara Pulleyn, with whom he subsequently elopes after her unhappy marriage to Barnes Newcome and after he has succeeded to the title of Lord Highgate in William Makepeace Thackeray's *The Newcomes.*

Squire Beltham　Rich, traditional grandfather of Harry Richmond and the direct opposite of his enemy Richmond Roy, the father of his grandson; he attempts to mold Harry in the Beltham image, but, losing patience with his grandson, disinherits him in George Meredith's *The Adventures of Harry Richmond.*

Dorothy Beltham　Beautiful, sought-after, wealthy aunt of Harry Richmond; she consistently intercedes with her brother, Squire Beltham, in Harry's favor; it is revealed that she loves and supports Harry's profligate father, Richmond Roy, in George Meredith's *The Adventures of Harry Richmond.*

Mary Belton　Beloved crippled sister of Will, whose household she manages; she tries to befriend Clara Amedroz, with whom her brother is much in love, in Anthony Trollope's *The Belton Estate.*

Thomas Belton　Robert Lovelace's libertine friend, who is cruelly treated by his common-law wife and dies of consumption; his death helps to effect John Belford's reformation in Samuel Richardson's *Clarissa: or, The History of a Young Lady.*

Will Belton　Prosperous, industrious, unsophisticated landowner and farmer, who inherits Belton estate; meeting Clara Amedroz he instantly falls in love, but she keeps him at arm's length; when her fortunes decline he offers to give her Belton Castle; his loyalty and generosity finally win her heart in Anthony Trollope's *The Belton Estate.*

Miss Belvawney　Member of the Vincent Crummles Theatrical Company who seldom speaks in Charles Dickens's *The Life and Adventures of Nicholas Nickleby.*

Count of Belvedere　Unexceptionable suitor to Lady Clementina della Porretta; not suspecting her infatuation for himself, even Sir Charles Grandison pleads Belvedere's case; recovered from depression and madness, partly induced by cruel treatment, Clementina is looking at Belvedere with some favor and resignation at the end of Samuel Richardson's *Sir Charles Grandison.*

Colonel Belville　The recipient of Lady Anne Wilmot's correspondence and eventually of her hand in Frances Brooke's *The History of Lady Julia Mandeville.*

Ben　Underling vociferously ordered by Long John Silver in pursuit of Black Dog, whom Jim Hawkins has spotted at the Spy Glass tavern in Robert Louis Stevenson's *Treasure Island.*

Benboaro Benbacaio　Disciple of Og of Basan; he follows his master into the deepest wilds but is abandoned by the tormented Og, who is reported dead by peasants shortly afterward in William Beckford's *Biographical Memoirs of Extraordinary Painters.*

Marcia Bencomb　Young woman who meets Jocelyn Pierston when she is running away from her father; he immediately falls in love with her and jilts his betrothed, Avice Caro; perceiving that he is growing tired of her also, Marcia leaves him to return to her father; she eventually marries and, widowed, raises her husband's son, Henri Leverre; she nurses Jocelyn through a serious illness and they marry comfortably but without love in old age in Thomas Hardy's *The Well-Beloved.*

Lady Bendham　Childless wife of Lord Bendham; after her husband's death she ruins herself by gambling in Elizabeth Inchbald's *Nature and Art.*

John, Viscount Bendham　Neighbor of the elder William Norwynne; he dies from overindulgence in food and drink in Elizabeth Inchbald's *Nature and Art.*

Mr. Bendish　Art dealer who collects indiscriminately, paying little but aiding young artists in George Moore's *A Modern Lover.*

Bend-the-Bow　Courteous English archer in Sir Walter Scott's *Castle Dangerous.*

Father Benecke　Priest excommunicated for his book and a friend of Edward Manisty; he befriends Eleanor Burgoyne and Lucy Foster in their self-imposed exile at Torre Amiata in the Italian hill country in Mrs. Humphry Ward's *Eleanor.*

Benedict　The saint and abbot of Cassino who takes the sick Basil into his monastery and gives him religious instruction in George Gissing's *Veranilda.*

Father Benedict　Priest in France who, when he hears how Maintenon has imprisoned Madam de Beaumont because of her religion, helps her escape and pays for her passage back to England in Penelope Aubin's *The Life of Madam de Beaumont.*

Laird Benenck   Scottish neighbor and friend of Laird Douglas in Susan Ferrier's *Marriage*.

Benevolent Army Officer   Elder brother of the Benevolent Naval Captain; he uses his own money to support his men and demonstrates that moral virtue is the best foundation for true heroism in Charles Johnstone's *Chrysal: or, The Adventures of a Guinea*.

Benevolent Naval Captain   Virtuous and compassionate captain of a Man of War, who, concerned with his sailors and ship, runs his ship with interesting rules: no gaming, no cursing or swearing, no drunkenness in Charles Johnstone's *Chrysal: or, The Adventures of a Guinea*.

Benignus   Virtuous hero thwarted in his benevolence; he retires to a forest hermitage, where he dies, in S. J. Pratt's *Liberal Opinions upon Animals, Man, and Providence*.

Nathan Ben Israel   Jewish physician who lives near Templestowe; he helps Isaac of York gain entrance to Templestowe to try to ransom Rebecca in Sir Walter Scott's *Ivanhoe*.

Little Benjamin   See Mr. Partridge.

Mr. Benjamin   Clerk to Valeria Brinton's late father; he gives her away at her marriage to Eustace Woodville (really Macallan), assists her in her investigations, and performs the important task of piecing together the scraps of the torn-up and long-discarded last letter of the poisoned Sara Macallan in Wilkie Collins's *The Law and the Lady*.

Mr. Benjamin   Junior partner in the firm of shady jewelers Harter and Benjamin, with whom Lady Eustace had dealings before her marriage; he engineers the theft of the Eustace necklace and is convicted of the crime in Anthony Trollope's *The Eustace Diamonds* .

Lemuel Benjulia   A publisher's clerk with a reputation as a lazy sensualist; an antivivisectionist, he hates his brother, Nathan, who in turn holds him in contempt in Wilkie Collins's *Heart and Science*.

Dr. Nathan Benjulia   Specialist in diseases of the brain and nervous system; a gaunt, gloomy scientist, he performs secret chemical experiments on animals, expecting to achieve immortality through the publication of the fruits of his experiments; his only human affection is for the child Zoe Gallilee, whom he likes to tickle and in whose favor he makes his will; he commits suicide when his discoveries are pre-empted by Ovid Vere's book in Wilkie Collins's *Heart and Science*.

Mrs. Benlow   Mathematician of Maria Spence's caliber

and even superior to Azora Burcot and Antonia Fletcher in Thomas Amory's *The Life of John Buncle, Esq*.

Miss Bennet   Servant of Mr. Monckton; her objection stops Cecilia Beverley's first attempt at marriage in Frances Burney's *Cecilia*.

Mr. Bennet   Scholarly, ironic, and detached father of Elizabeth and her four sisters in Jane Austen's *Pride and Prejudice*.

Mrs. Bennet   Silly mother, whose goal in life is to marry off her five daughters in Jane Austen's *Pride and Prejudice*.

Carola Bennet   Exploited woman of London who is forced into prostitution by her aunt, Mrs. Hunfleet, and sold to the rapist Cantalupe; she lives with the wealthy Irishman Frederic Dancer and is converted to Christianity by, and married to, Mr. Tench, a clergyman, in Thomas Amory's *The Life of John Buncle, Esq*.

Catherine (Kitty) Bennet   Silly, fretful Bennet sister, fourth of the five; she thinks of nothing but handsome officers in Jane Austen's *Pride and Prejudice*.

Charley Bennet   Molly Bennet's infant son; the Noble Lord feigns to dote on him in order to win Molly's trust in Henry Fielding's *Amelia*.

Elizabeth Bennet   The witty, intelligent, and clear-sighted heroine, second of the five Bennet sisters; she attracts the proud Mr. Darcy, refuses his first proposal of marriage, but eventually loses her initial prejudice against him and grows to love him in Jane Austen's *Pride and Prejudice*.

Jane Bennet   Sweet, good, and beautiful elder sister of Elizabeth; she loves and eventually marries the pleasant Mr. Bingley in Jane Austen's *Pride and Prejudice*.

Lydia Bennet   The vain, foolish, headstrong youngest of the Bennet sisters; at sixteen she elopes with George Wickham to London, where Mr. Darcy finds her and bribes Wickham to marry her in Jane Austen's *Pride and Prejudice*.

Mary Bennet   Bookish and pedantic, the plain Bennet sister, third of the five, in Jane Austen's *Pride and Prejudice*.

Molly Bennet   Sorrowful young woman, friend to Mrs. Ellison; she reveals her history to Amelia Booth to warn her to shun the Noble Lord's masquerade; she marries Joe Atkinson and restores her fortunes in Henry Fielding's *Amelia*.

Tom Bennet   Impoverished clergyman and husband of

Molly Bennet; he dies in financial ruin and misery after discovering Molly's seduction in Henry Fielding's *Amelia*.

Benson   Butler for the Huntingdons at Grassdale Manor, who is loyal to the family despite Arthur Huntingdon's abuses in Anne Brontë's *The Tenant of Wildfell Hall*.

Faith Benson   Thurstan Benson's sister, who helps him rescue Ruth Hilton; she is the practical support of the household during Ruth's progress and later trouble in Elizabeth Gaskell's *Ruth*.

Sir Harry Benson   Miss Walton's purported betrothed, according to a rumor that proves to be false in Henry Mackenzie's *The Man of Feeling*.

Thurstan Benson   The crippled dissenting minister of Ecclestone, who provides a home for Ruth Hilton and her son by Henry Bellingham; he stands by her when her past is discovered and the wealthy Mr. Bradshaw withdraws the financial support for his ministry; his help when Bradshaw's son gets into trouble assists the reconciliation in Elizabeth Gaskell's *Ruth*.

Mr. Bentham   Lucy Bentham's caddish husband, who lives in Paris and will not give her a divorce; hearing Paris gossip, he blackmails her in George Moore's *A Modern Lover*.

Julia Bentham   Divorced distant relative and companion of Emily Watson; beautiful and intelligent, she attracts Hubert Price but refuses his proposals out of loyalty to Emily; in desperation at Emily's tyranny, she and Hubert flee to London, where their marriage is shadowed by news of Emily's suicide in George Moore's *Vain Fortune*.

Lucy Bentham   Wealthy landowner who decides to sponsor Lewis Seymour's career; she is discreetly but deeply in love with him and jealous of Lady Helen Seely, who marries him; she becomes friends with the couple and later shares Lady Helen's recognition of Seymour's weak character in George Moore's *A Modern Lover*.

Madame la Duchesse Benvolio   French countess, who makes her living preying on male travelers; John Jorrocks becomes a victim of her charms in Robert Surtees's *Jorrocks's Jaunts and Jollities*.

Captain James Benwick   A shy poetry lover, mourning the death of his betrothed; Anne Elliot's suspicion that he is not immune to consolation is borne out by his engagement to Louisa Musgrove in Jane Austen's *Persuasion*.

Beppo   Merthyr Powys's servant, who ministers to the wounded Powys in George Meredith's *Emilia in England*. He acts also on behalf of Vittoria Campa in *Vittoria*.

Robert Berdoe   London ironmonger and relative of Mrs. Cardew; he employs Tom Catchpole upon the Reverend Theophilus Cardew's recommendation in Mark Rutherford's *Catharine Furze*.

Queen Berengaria   Queen of England, wife of King Richard; on pilgrimage to the Holy Land while he fights in the Crusade, she joins in the pranks to tease Lady Edith Plantagenet about Sir Kenneth in Sir Walter Scott's *The Talisman*.

Eveline Berenger   Only child of Sir Raymond Berenger; she is rescued from Gwenwyn's siege of Garde Doloureuse Castle by Hugo de Lacy; betrothed to him, she is faithful to him while he is on the Crusades; she comes to love his nephew Damian de Lacy, who was left behind to protect her, and she marries Damian with Hugo's blessing after his return from the Holy Land in Sir Walter Scott's *The Betrothed*.

Sir Raymond Berenger   Norman knight who, lured onto the open plain by insinuations against his honor, dies in battle to defend his castle, Garde Doloureuse, against the attack of Gwenwyn in Sir Walter Scott's *The Betrothed*.

Il Conte Berenza   Venetian nobleman who marries Victoria di Loredani and is later poisoned by her in Charlotte Dacre's *Zofloya; or, The Moor*.

Mrs. Beresford   Passenger returning to England aboard the *Agra* with her son; both are saved by the heroism of David Dodd in Charles Reade's *Hard Cash*.

Donna Berilla   Hypocrite who pretends to like Emanuella but is malicious and plots against her in Eliza Haywood's *The Rash Resolve; or, the Untimely Discovery*.

Berinthia (Berry)   Good-natured niece of Mrs. Pipchin; she works in the boarding establishment from dawn to dusk and plays with the child boarders in Charles Dickens's *Dombey and Son*.

Lady Augusta de Berkely (Augustine)   Fair English heiress, who promises to marry Sir John de Walton if he holds Castle Douglas for a designated period; she adopts the masculine disguise of Augustine and is captured by Sir James Douglas; after de Walton loses in combat and concedes the castle, she marries him in Sir Walter Scott's *Castle Dangerous*.

Mr. Berkins   Boorish and ridiculed city magnate, who was born a gentleman but came up through poverty; he marries Grace Brookes in George Moore's *Spring Days*.

Chevalier de Berlingier Second to Don Pedro de Gonzales in a farcical duel with Lord Mahogany in William Beckford's *Modern Novel Writing; or, the Elegant Enthusiast.*

John Bernard Physician who attends the disfigured Robert Mannion and the dying Margaret Sherwin; he is recognized as an old friend by Basil's brother, Ralph, and provides important information in Wilkie Collins's *Basil: A Story of Modern Life.*

Bernardin Faithful former servant of Reginald de St. Leon and his family; he provides them with money which eases the hunger and penury they suffer near Lake Constance in William Godwin's *St. Leon.*

Bernardo Cornelia's kind and generous lover, whose faithfulness is tested by several scheming women and a domineering stepmother in Sarah Scott's *The History of Cornelia.*

Louisa Bernini Sweet-tempered wife of the Marquis de Mazzini; she is imprisoned in a cave beneath the castle so that the Marquis can remarry; she is discovered twenty years later by her daughter Julia and is freed in Ann Radcliffe's *A Sicilian Romance.*

Baron Bernstein Beatrix Esmond's second husband, now deceased, a disreputable German nobleman in William Makepeace Thackeray's *The Virginians.*

Baroness Bernstein See Lady Beatrix Esmond.

Bob Berrisfort Learned, well-bred owner of Yeoverin-Green; John Buncle first meets him on a passenger boat; he goes hunting with Buncle and discusses theology and literature with him in Thomas Amory's *The Life of John Buncle, Esq.*

Juliet Berrisfort Bob Berrisfort's sister, whose daring at hunting leads to a harmless accident in Thomas Amory's *The Life of John Buncle, Esq.*

Arthur Berryl Admirable friend of Lord Colambre; he takes care of his penniless family and later marries the heiress Miss Broadhurst in Maria Edgeworth's *The Absentee.*

Sir John Berryl Arthur's father, who borrows from Mr. Mordicai and leaves his family penniless at his death in Maria Edgeworth's *The Absentee.*

Bertha (Agatha) Hereward's betrothed, a Saxon captured by the Norman Knight of Aspramonte, rebaptized and renamed Agatha; she is the Countess Brenhilda's efficient squire and trusted friend; she accompanies Brenhilda on the crusade and marries Hereward at its conclusion in Sir Walter Scott's *Count Robert of Paris.*

Sir Bertie Husband of Lady Diana and a good and helpful friend of the Brooks family in Caroline Norton's *Lost and Saved.*

Signor Bertolini Young Venetian gambler, who is a partner in Montoni's plan to use Udolpho as a fortress for mercenaries in Ann Radcliffe's *The Mysteries of Udolpho.*

Bertram Lady Augusta de Berkely's loyal attendant; an enthusiastic minstrel, he obtains permission to study the old lays in Douglas Castle's library; though imprisoned and threatened with torture, he refuses to betray his mistress in Sir Walter Scott's *Castle Dangerous.*

Edmund Bertram Responsible, kindhearted, clever, somewhat pedantic younger son of Sir Thomas Bertram; his bent for instruction makes him an ideal mentor to his young cousin Fanny Price, who loves him wholeheartedly; his intended profession of clergyman is distasteful and unacceptable to the worldly Mary Crawford, whom he loves in spite of himself; eventually he recognizes Fanny's superiority and marries her in Jane Austen's *Mansfield Park.*

George Bertram (the elder) Rich and disagreeable uncle of George Bertram and grandfather of Caroline Waddington; he leaves his fortune to a college for the children of fishmongers in Anthony Trollope's *The Bertrams.*

George Bertram Intelligent but aimless son of feckless Sir Lionel Bertram; he falls in love with Caroline Waddington, who refuses to marry him until he acquires wealth; their engagement broken off, she marries, but some time after her husband's death they become reconciled in Anthony Trollope's *The Bertrams.*

Godfrey Bertram, Laird of Ellangowan Henry and Lucy Bertram's father; seventeen years after the kidnapping of Henry, he dies from the shock of losing the family fortune, leaving Lucy an impoverished orphan in Sir Walter Scott's *Guy Mannering.*

Mrs. Godfrey Bertram Mother of Henry and Lucy Bertram; she is a depressed and superstitious invalid, who dies giving birth to Henry in Sir Walter Scott's *Guy Mannering.*

Henry (Harry) Bertram (Captain Vanbest Brown) Godfrey Bertram's heir, who is kidnapped at the age of five and renamed Vanbest Brown; while serving under Colonel Mannering in India, he falls in love with Julia Mannering; his true identity is discovered through the efforts of Meg Merriles in Sir Walter Scott's *Guy Mannering*.

Julia Bertram Youngest of the Bertram children; she vies with her sister, Maria, for the attentions of Henry Crawford; humiliated and disappointed by his preference for Maria, she admits the attentions of Tom Bertram's friend Mr. Yates, eventually eloping with and marrying him in Jane Austen's *Mansfield Park*.

Lewis Bertram Godfrey Bertram's prudent father in Sir Walter Scott's *Guy Mannering*.

Sir Lionel Bertram Minor diplomatic official in the Middle East whose charm hides his feckless nature; in Jerusalem he meets his son, George, with whom he has had no contact for many years; he retires to the English countryside and pursues two single ladies for their money in Anthony Trollope's *The Bertrams*.

Lucy Bertram Dutiful daughter of Godfrey Bertram; she remains loyal to her father and her eccentric tutor, Dominie Abel Sampson, and marries Charles Hazelwood in Sir Walter Scott's *Guy Mannering*.

Margaret Bertram Godfrey's selfish, cantankerous relative, who refuses to assist him but leaves her property to his son, Henry Bertram, in Sir Walter Scott's *Guy Mannering*.

Maria Bertram The proud and self-consequential handsome elder daughter of Sir Thomas Bertram; she becomes engaged to an immensely wealthy and stupid young neighbor, Mr. Rushworth, but readily responds to Henry Crawford's attentions by falling in love with him; upon his departure she marries Rushworth out of wounded pride and determination to escape paternal restraint; she runs away with Crawford and is eventually doomed to a life of social isolation in Jane Austen's *Mansfield Park*.

Maria Ward, Lady Bertram Handsome and kind-hearted but self-centered and indolent wife of Sir Thomas Bertram and mother of Thomas, Edmund, Maria, and Julia; she is a sister of Mrs. Norris and Mrs. Price; she is loved by her niece Fanny Price in Jane Austen's *Mansfield Park*.

Sir Thomas Bertram The stern and repressive, though just, parent of Tom, Edmund, Maria, and Julia; he takes on the guardianship of his wife's niece Fanny Price, for whom he is a source of terror but who eventually grows to love him in Jane Austen's *Mansfield Park*.

Tom Bertram The eldest of Sir Thomas Bertram's four children; extravagant and careless of responsibility, he is oblivious to the emotional hazards which threaten his sisters; his triviality is diminished by serious illness at the conclusion of Jane Austen's *Mansfield Park*.

Bertrand One of two thugs hired by Montoni to transport Emily St. Aubert from Udolpho to Tuscany in Ann Radcliffe's *The Mysteries of Udolpho*.

Cecile Bertrand Aristocratic woman living in isolation; she aids Gabrielle di Montmorency by raising her child Agnes D'Albini, only to lose Agnes when she marries the tyrant Pierre Bouffuet in Charlotte Dacre's *The Libertine*.

Edgeworth Bess One of Jack Sheppard's loyal mistresses in William Harrison Ainsworth's *Jack Sheppard*.

Bessas Byzantine commander of Rome whom Heliodora, at Marcian's suggestion, tries to corrupt in George Gissing's *Veranilda*.

Bessie A streetwalker who is asked to model for Dick Heldar; she falls in love with his best friend, Torpenhow, and, to revenge herself for Dick's sending Torpenhow away from her, destroys Dick's masterpiece painting, completed just before he goes blind in Rudyard Kipling's *The Light That Failed*.

Bessie Daughter of the farmer and his wife; she introduces Sylvie and Bruno to her doll, Matilda Jane, and sings a song for the doll that Sylvie taught her in Lewis Carroll's *Sylvie and Bruno Concluded*.

Adam Besso Father of Eva, the "Rose of Sharon"; he is the banker to whom Tancred, Lord Montacute presents the letters of credit secured from Sidonia in Benjamin Disraeli's *Tancred; or, The New Crusade*.

Eva Besso Called the "Rose of Sharon," the daughter of the banker Adam Besso; she enchants Tancred, Lord Montacute with her beauty as well as her passionate and highly intelligent explanations of the mysteries of ancient Judaism in Benjamin Disraeli's *Tancred; or, The New Crusade*.

Mrs. Best The housekeeper at Donnithorne Chase in George Eliot's *Adam Bede*.

Erasmus Bethel Lionel Desmond's former guardian and correspondent, who advises him to extricate himself from involvement with the Verney family, although he assists Geraldine Verney in Desmond's absence; letters exchanged by him and Desmond are vehicles for notions about the French Revolution that inform a large part of Charlotte Smith's *Desmond*.

John Bethune Highland cotter and poet, frequently

cited by Alton Locke as a source of inspiration in Charles Kingsley's *Alton Locke*.

Betsy   The Jorrockses' cook in Robert Surtees's *Jorrocks's Jaunts and Jollities*.

Betsy   Serving girl who works for Mrs. Raddle in Charles Dickens's *The Posthumous Papers of the Pickwick Club*.

Betsy   Prostitute friend of Nancy; she works for Fagin in Charles Dickens's *Oliver Twist*.

Betsy ("Rosebud")   A seventeen-year-old maid whom, as an act of conceit, Robert Lovelace vows not to seduce; instead he provides a marriage settlement for her so that she can marry her beloved in Samuel Richardson's *Clarissa: or, The History of a Young Lady*.

Gabriel Betteredge   Garrulous family retainer in the Verinder household; he prides himself on his common sense but uses random texts from Robinson Crusoe as guides to conduct; he helps Sergeant Cuff investigate the theft of a yellow diamond willed to Rachel Verinder by her wicked uncle, John Herncastle, in Wilkie Collins's *The Moonstone. A Romance*.

Penelope Betteredge   Pert, outspoken daughter of Gabriel Betteredge and servant in the Verinder household; she is protective of Rosanna Spearman and furious at the blundering investigation by Superintendent Seegrave into the loss of a diamond willed to Rachel Verinder in Wilkie Collins's *The Moonstone. A Romance*.

Miss Betterton   A Nottingham tradesman's daughter tricked into flight with Robert Lovelace, who rapes her eighteen months before he tricks Clarissa Harlowe; she dies delivering his son in Samuel Richardson's *Clarissa: or, The History of a Young Lady*.

Betty   Privileged old servant of the Holmans, who counsels Paul Manning and later Phillis Holman in Elizabeth Gaskell's *Cousin Phillis*.

Betty   Unfortunate chambermaid, whom Mrs. Slipslop unjustly accuses of being pregnant by Joseph Andrews; jealousy provokes Lady Booby to dismiss her in Henry Fielding's *The History of the Adventures of Mr. Joseph Andrews and of his Friend Mr. Abraham Adams*.

Betty   Booth family maid, who stole Amelia's last possessions to make her own fortune in Henry Fielding's *Amelia*.

Betty   Compassionate chambermaid at the Dragon Inn who provides clothing for the sick, naked Joseph Andrews; she is fired after Mrs. Tow-wouse discovers her in bed with Mr. Tow-wouse in Henry Fielding's *The History of the Adventures of Mr. Joseph Andrews and of his Friend Mr. Abraham Adams*.

Lady Betty   Friend of Lady Davers; her expectations of Mr. B—- are dashed when he marries Pamela Andrews; she becomes an admirer of Pamela through reading her letters in Samuel Richardson's *Pamela, or Virtue Rewarded*.

Mrs. Betty   Lady Maria Esmond's maid, who gets drunk with Gumbo and Case in William Makepeace Thackeray's *The Virginians*.

Betty Chambermaid   Servant at Robin's inn who, fearing Tom Jones's ghost, refuses to answer his bell until the drawer accompanies her in Henry Fielding's *The History of Tom Jones*.

Betty Jean   Niece of Mrs. Wickam in Charles Dickens's *Dombey and Son*.

Mr. Bevan   The only American young Martin Chuzzlewit and Mark Tapley meet who objectively views the failings of his country; he befriends them by advancing money for their return from Eden to New York and offers further assistance in Charles Dickens's *The Life and Adventures of Martin Chuzzlewit*.

Mr. Bever   Dishonest steward of Sir Thomas Grandison's English estate; he conspires with Mr. Filmer to try to establish Miss Obrien as Sir Thomas's mistress in Samuel Richardson's *Sir Charles Grandison*.

Ben ("Old") Beveridge   Longtime Jago dweller, who accurately observes to Dicky Perrott that the only ways out of the Jago are to join the High Mob, to go to prison, or to die in Arthur Morrison's *A Child of the Jago*.

Cecilia Beverley   Young woman whose estate is in the trust of three London gentlemen; an heiress about to come of age, she is pursued by many admirers in London and in her home county of Suffolk; she deliberately gives away most of her wealth to help the poor and sick; she loves Mortimer Delvile and secretly marries him, but loses her mind for a while when she thinks he has deserted her in London; she is reconciled to his father in the end in Frances Burney's *Cecilia*.

Frank Beverley   An earl's nephew, made into a servant of all work at Drayton House, who sets the fires that free the inmates in Charles Reade's *Hard Cash*.

Captain Beville   Dashing officer murdered by the jealous Don Pedro de Gonzales in William Beckford's *Modern Novel Writing; or, the Elegant Enthusiast*.

Bevis   Attractive young man, who makes love to the

married Monica (Madden) Widdowson, causing a crisis in her marriage in George Gissing's *The Odd Women.*

Mrs. Bevis   A widow at the boarding house in Hampstead where Clarissa Harlowe first hides from Robert Lovelace, who charms her into betraying Clarissa in Samuel Richardson's *Clarissa: or, The History of a Young Lady.*

Sir Bevys   Ghostly victim of murder in a story read by Ludovico as he stands watch in the bedroom of the dead Marchioness de Villeroi in Ann Radcliffe's *The Mysteries of Udolpho.*

Valentine Bewick   Working-class labor-union leader who opposes Sir George Tressady during the strike at Tressady's coal mines in Mrs. Humphry Ward's *Sir George Tressady.*

Muzaffer Bey   Bashaw of Buda and favorite of the Turkish sultan; Reginald de St. Leon, in the guise of the Sieur de Chattilon, petitions him to provide aid to the Christian inhabitants of the province in William Godwin's *St. Leon.*

Signor Bezoni   Learned Italian, whose materialistic philosophy temporarily plunges Morton Devereux into deep despair in Edward Bulwer-Lytton's *Devereux.*

Bianca   Servant-confidante of Princess Matilda in Horace Walpole's *The Castle of Otranto.*

Signora Bianchi   Ellena Rosalba's aunt and guardian, who approves of Ellena's engagement to Vincentio di Vivaldi, only to die and leave Ellena vulnerable to the schemes of the Marchesa di Vivaldi in Ann Radcliffe's *The Italian.*

Julius Washington Merryweather Bib   An American "gentleman in the lumber line" and a member of the delegation that greets Elijah Pogram in Charles Dickens's *The Life and Adventures of Martin Chuzzlewit.*

Miss Bickerton   A parlor boarder at Mrs. Goddard's school; taking a country walk with Harriet Smith, she runs away in fright, abandoning Harriet to the importunities of a group of Gypsies in Jane Austen's *Emma.*

Mrs. Bickerton   Prejudiced Scotswoman afflicted with gout; Jeanie Deans's landlady in York, she also befriends her in Sir Walter Scott's *The Heart of Midlothian.*

John Biddle   Captain of the ship by which Lemuel Gulliver travels back to England after leaving Blefuscu in Jonathan Swift's *Travels into Several Remote Nations of the World. In Four Parts. By Lemuel Gulliver.*

Sprigge Biddlepen   Meek, dapper little clergyman, a

guest at a house party given by Lady Monica Knollys; he eventually marries Milly Ruthyn in J. Sheridan Le Fanu's *Uncle Silas.*

Biddy   Orphan who lives with her harsh grandmother, Mr. Wopsle's great aunt; later she takes care of Mrs. Joe Gargery during her illness and, after Mrs. Joe's death, marries Joe Gargery; Biddy critically observes the development of Pip Pirrip's snobbish attitude toward Joe and his pretentions of gentility; she tells Pip that Estella is not worth having if she does not like him as he is in Charles Dickens's *Great Expectations.*

Mr. Bideawhile   Junior partner in the firm of Slow and Bideawhile; he breaks with Louis Trevelyan over Trevelyan's planned abduction of his son in Anthony Trollope's *He Knew He Was Right.* Bideawhile appears in *Framley Parsonage,* in *Orley Farm,* and in *Miss Mackenzie.* He tells Frank Gresham of Louis Satcherd's death in *Doctor Thorne.* His firm is consulted by the Longestaffes in *The Way We Live Now.*

Lord George Bideford   Hearty, good-natured squire, who marries Nina Baldoni in Anthony Trollope's *Ayala's Angel.*

Peter Bide-the-Bent   Strict Presbyterian minister, whose religious prejudices lead him to assist Lady Ashton in dissolving the engagement between Edgar Ravenswood and Lucy Ashton in Sir Walter Scott's *The Bride of Lammermoor.*

Lady Bidulph   Sensible, strict, and sometimes interfering mother of Sidney Bidulph and Sir George Bidulph; she educates her daughter according to the highest standards of virtue, and her death numbers among her daughter's misfortunes in Frances Sheridan's *Memoirs of Miss Sidney Bidulph.*

Sir George Bidulph   Elder brother of Sidney Bidulph Arnold; he wants his sister to marry his friend Orlando Faulkland; he separates from his wife, Lady Sarah; finally he reconciles with his wife and his sister and gives the report of Faulkland's death in Frances Sheridan's *Memoirs of Miss Sidney Bidulph.*

Lady Sarah Bidulph   Monied and materialistic daughter of a newly created peer; she marriers Sir George Bidulph and behaves coldly and condescendingly toward Sidney Bidulph Arnold while affecting kindness and consolation in Frances Sheridan's *Memoirs of Miss Sidney Bidulph.*

Sidney Bidulph   See Catherine Sidney Bidulph Arnold.

Arnold Biederman   Swiss magistrate who has been disinherited in favor of his brother, the Count of Geierstein; he has cared for his niece, Anne of Geierstein, for seven years; he leads an embassy to negotiate with Charles, Duke of Burgundy, and declares war with the duke on behalf of the Swiss cantons in Sir Walter Scott's *Anne of Geierstein.*

Rudiger Biederman   One of Arnold Biederman's sons; he becomes a companion of Arthur Philipson (Arthur de Vere) and is killed during the battle in which Charles, Duke of Burgundy, is killed in Sir Walter Scott's *Anne of Geierstein.*

Sigismund Biederman   One of Arnold Biederman's sons; he offers safe haven to Arthur de Vere and his father after the death of Charles, Duke of Burgundy, in Sir Walter Scott's *Anne of Geierstein.*

Harold Biffen   Impoverished writer, who devotes himself to a realistic novel about slum life, saves his manuscript from a fire, falls hopelessly in love with Edwin Reardon's widow, and takes his own life when his novel is a failure in George Gissing's *New Grub Street.*

Major Biffin   Boring fellow traveller with George Bertram and Arthur Wilkinson on their return journey from the Middle East in Anthony Trollope's *The Bertrams.*

Mr. Biggs   Boatswain of H.M.S. *Harpy*; he is the butt of Jack Easy's practical jokes in Captain Frederick Marryat's *Mr. Midshipman Easy.*

Martha Biggs   Ingratiating, fawning friend of Mrs. Furnival; she revels in the supposed infidelities of Mr. Furnival, who loathes her spying in Anthony Trollope's *Orley Farm.*

Mr. Bilbo   Agitated divine, who cries out in original Greek in William Beckford's *Modern Novel Writing; or, the Elegant Enthusiast.*

Hezekiah Biles   Rustic, gossiping chorister in Thomas Hardy's *Two on a Tower.*

Bill   Clerk in Mr. Dabb's London shop, who gives Andrew Tacchi a critical unwelcome in Mark Rutherford's *Miriam's Schooling* .

Bill   Grave digger in Charles Dickens's *Oliver Twist.*

Bill   A gamekeeper at Knowl who helps protect Maud Ruthyn from a coach of rough intruders (one of whom is her cruel cousin, Dudley Ruthyn) in J. Sheridan Le Fanu's *Uncle Silas.*

Bill   A lizard whose pathetic willingness and helplessness are exploited by the other creatures; after Alice has grown so large as to fill the White Rabbit's house, blocking doors and windows, Bill is sent down the chimney to investigate but is kicked up and out by Alice; Bill later acts as a juror in the trial of the Knave of Hearts in Lewis Carroll's *Alice's Adventures in Wonderland.*

My Bill   Amelia's husband, a criminal whom Mr. Jaggers is defending in Charles Dickens's *Great Expectations.*

Billali   White-bearded, patriarchal, venerable "Father" or head of an Amahagger tribe; kindly disposed toward the Englishmen Leo Vincey and Horace Holly, he saves their lives from his cannibalistic fellow tribesmen and escorts them into the presence of She in H. Rider Haggard's *She.*

Bill Collector   Irate and surly man, who presents Colonel Jack with a payment; he threatens to become violent in Daniel Defoe's *The History and Remarkable Life of the Truly Honourable Colonel Jacques, Commonly Call'd Colonel Jack.*

Mrs. Billickin   Sharp-tongued British woman, who provides lodgings for Rosa Bud after she flees John Jasper and leaves Miss Twinkleton's academy in Charles Dickens's *The Mystery of Edwin Drood.*

Billson   Biggest operator at Muskegon Commercial Academy; he becomes Loudon Dodd's clerk when a bad stock deal bankrupts him in Robert Louis Stevenson's *The Wrecker.*

Billy   Gentleman loafer and errand boy for Douglas Longhurst in Robert Louis Stevenson's *The Wrecker.*

Billy   Captain Nares's friend, who was wrecked in the *Navigators* and decided to stay in Robert Louis Stevenson's *The Wrecker.*

Mr. Bilson   Profligate reclaimed by his wife's virtue; released from prison after Lady Dently pays his debts, he retires to the country to exercise his philanthropic impulses in Sarah Fielding's *The History of the Countess of Dellwyn.*

Mrs. Bilson   Exemplar of domestic virtues who reclaims her husband from a life of frivolous excess and then extends her beneficence to public acts of generosity in Sarah Fielding's *The History of the Countess of Dellwyn.*

Margery Bimbister   Neil Rolandson's praiseworthy wife in Sir Walter Scott's *The Pirate.*

Mr. Bindloose   Sheriff-clerk and banker, who introduces Meg Dods to Peregrine Touchwood in Sir Walter Scott's *St. Ronan's Well.*

Bindo (Albinois) Albino fool of Euthanasia dei Adimari's court; he predicts the downfall of Valperga and brings Beatrice to the witch of the Luccan forest (Fior de Mandragola) in Mary Shelley's *Valperga*.

Emily Bingham Wealthy ward in Chancery; after attempting unsuccessfully to attract Harry Lorrequer, she becomes engaged to Tom O'Flaherty in Charles Lever's *The Confessions of Harry Lorrequer*.

Caroline Bingley Proud, conceited sister of Mr. Bingley; hoping to marry Mr. Darcy, she views his growing attraction to Elizabeth Bennet with alarm and schemes to separate her brother from Jane Bennet in Jane Austen's *Pride and Prejudice*.

Charles Bingley The handsome, agreeable, rich, and young newcomer to the Bennets' neighborhood; he falls in love with Jane Bennet; too easily persuaded that Jane does not return his affections, he is separated from her by the joint efforts of his sisters and Mr. Darcy but eventually marries her in Jane Austen's *Pride and Prejudice*.

Sir Bingo Binks Quarrelsome English baronet, who challenges Francis Tyrrell to a duel and publicizes Tyrrell's shame for not appearing in Sir Walter Scott's *St. Ronan's Well*.

James Binnie Mrs. Mackenzie's brother and Colonel Newcome's old friend, who, by leaving his money to Rosey Mackenzie, precipitates her marriage to Clive Newcome in William Makepeace Thackeray's *The Newcomes*.

Mr. Binny Curate who proposes to the widowed Amelia (Sedley) Osborne in William Makepeace Thackeray's *Vanity Fair*.

Biranthus (Berentha) Character who disguises himself as a woman, Berentha, to get close to Amoranda; he tries to rape her but instead shoots her coachman in Mary Davys's *The Reform'd Coquet*.

Colonel Frank Birch Friend of Lord Charles Oakley in William Beckford's *Modern Novel Writing; or, the Elegant Enthusiast*.

Jem Bird The one-hundred-year-old pride of the village; he tells the history of Deerbrook and the origins of its name in Harriet Martineau's *Deerbrook*.

Birdalone Young woman who was stolen from her mother, Audrey, as a baby by the evil Witch-Wife; after her escape and her adventures involving the Castle of the Quest, she marries Arthur in William Morris's *The Water of the Wondrous Isles*.

John Ernest Biren See John Ernest Biren, Duke of Courland.

Birkebeba Azemia's judicious and sensible paternal grandmother in William Beckford's *Azemia*.

Birkin London bookseller who loses a pair of boots to the author Tim Cropdale, whom he beats in a footrace, in Tobias Smollett's *The Expedition of Humphry Clinker*.

Lord Biron Commander of military forces besieged by the Parliamentary Army at Chester during the reign of Charles I in J. Henry Shorthouse's *John Inglesant, A Romance*.

Bishop A man who enjoys eating and has great faith in dreams in Charles Johnstone's *Chrysal: or, The Adventures of a Guinea*.

Bishop Fat, immoral London bishop, who preaches a sermon written by Hugh Trevor and who publishes Hugh's *Defense of the Thirty-nine Articles* under his own name in Thomas Holcroft's *The Adventures of Hugh Trevor*.

Bishop of Glasgow Kindly, peaceful prelate, who performs the services on Palm Sunday in the kirk of Douglas in Sir Walter Scott's *Castle Dangerous*.

Mr. Bishopriggs Inn employee who testifies as a witness to the "Scotch marriage" of Anne Silvester and Arnold Brinkworth; he sells Anne the letter he stole from her in Wilkie Collins's *Man and Wife*.

Bishop's Lady A card player who believes in dreams in Charles Johnstone's *Chrysal: or, The Adventures of a Guinea*.

Master Bitherstone Little Paul Dombey's fellow boarder at Mrs. Pipchin's establishment; he wants to run away to his parents in India in Charles Dickens's *Dombey and Son*.

Lady Bittlebrains Lady who is uneasy with her newly acquired title and is eager to attain the friendship of her neighbors, the Ashtons, in Sir Walter Scott's *The Bride of Lammermoor*.

Lord Bittlebrains Quick-witted man who has a flair for earning money; he has used his wealth and power to grant political services and gain his title in Sir Walter Scott's *The Bride of Lammermoor*.

Bitzer Colorless student in Thomas Gradgrind's school; he mechanically adheres to his utilitarian training to be without imagination or sentiment in Charles Dickens's *Hard Times*.

Miss Black Lady O'Shane's companion and "evil genius," who, disliking Sir Ulick O'Shane's son, Marcus, and his ward, Harry Ormond, constantly works mischief by persuading Lady O'Shane to thwart the two whenever possible; she continues to spread malicious gossip and to scheme in opposition to Ormond as Mrs. M'Crule after her marriage in Maria Edgeworth's *Ormond*.

Peggy Black Richard Hardie's servant and mistress, who lures Alfred Hardie away from his wedding day with a letter of assignation for important information in Charles Reade's *Hard Cash*.

Black Bess The celebrated horse on which the highwayman Dick Turpin rides nonstop from London to York in William Harrison Ainsworth's *Rookwood*.

Black Dog One of Flint's crew; he is pale and missing two fingers; he threatens Billy Bones and is stabbed in the shoulder by him; he deserts Pew in the rout at the Admiral Benbow Inn; spotted by Jim Hawkins at Long John Silver's pub, he eludes the pursuit Silver has ostentatiously directed in Robert Louis Stevenson's *Treasure Island*.

Black Kitten Offspring of the cat, Dinah; Alice's playful scolding of the kitten leads to her investigation of the world beyond the drawing-room looking-glass; the Red Queen turns into the kitten at the conclusion of Lewis Carroll's *Through the Looking-Glass*.

Lawyer Blackingson Farmer who loves oppressing the poor and beating his maids; he circulates cruel rumors that Dr. Sanderson has adopted democratic principles in William Beckford's *Modern Novel Writing; or, the Elegant Enthusiast*.

Mr. Blackman Middle-aged client of the London procuress Mrs. Skelton; he sexually harasses Julia Townsend but goes away unsatisfied in Richard Graves's *The Spiritual Quixote*.

Honour Blackmore Sophia Western's maid, who escapes with Sophia to London, calling herself Mrs. Abigail at the Upton Inn; she switches allegiance to Lady Bellaston after Squire Western discharges her in Henry Fielding's *The History of Tom Jones*.

Stephen Blackpool Mistreated but uncomplaining worker in Josiah Bounderby's factory; he is wrongly accused of being a thief; he falls down an abandoned mine shaft and dies in Charles Dickens's *Hard Times*.

Mrs. Stephen Blackpool Slovenly, alcoholic wife of the good Stephen; she will not free him to marry the loving Rachel in Charles Dickens's *Hard Times*.

Lord Blackwater Dissolute late father of Lady Kitty Bristol (Ashe); he married two heiresses in succession, spending the fortunes of both and wasting the dowry of his elder daughter before dying, survived by his second wife and both daughters in Mrs. Humphry Ward's *The Marriage of William Ashe*.

Prince Bladud Young prince featured in "True Legend of Prince Bladud" as legendary founder of Bath, recounted by Samuel Pickwick in Charles Dickens's *The Posthumous Papers of the Pickwick Club*.

Blaise Son of King Peter and successful merchant in Whitwall in William Morris's *The Well at the World's End*.

Giles Blaize Uncle of Lucy Desborough and owner of a farm adjacent to Raynham Abbey; he horsewhips Richard Feverel and Ripton Thompson when they trespass on his land, which impells them to pay Tom Bakewell to set fire to the farmer's hayricks; Blaize thinks poorly of Richard and opposes his marriage to Lucy, to no avail in George Meredith's *The Ordeal of Richard Feverel*.

Mr. Blake Supposed friend of Benignus; he tricks him into suing his wife and then forces him to pay £2,500 damages in S. J. Pratt's *Liberal Opinions upon Animals, Man, and Providence*.

Franklin Blake Energetic amateur sleuth, who helps solve the mystery of the yellow diamond stolen from Rachel Verinder, with whom he is wildly in love; when it is established that he removed the diamond from her room, she will have no more to do with him; Ezra Jennings proves that Blake took the diamond while under the influence of a drug administered by Dr. Candy as a joke; the true thief, Godfrey Ablewhite, is unmasked, and the lovers are united in Wilkie Collins's *The Moonstone. A Romance*.

James Blake Suitor favored by Emma Flather until she becomes convinced she is sought by James, Earl of Bray in Robert Surtees's *Hillingdon Hall*.

Mary (Baby) Blake High-spirited cousin of Charles O'Malley; she endeavors to attract him after his uncle's death but eventually marries Sparks in Charles Lever's *Charles O'Malley*.

Montagu Blake Garrulous young curate, who had been at Oxford with John Gordon; completely absorbed by Kattie Forrester, he constantly sings her praises and has a grand wedding in Winchester Cathedral in Anthony Trollope's *An Old Man's Love*.

Philip Blake Relative and neighbor of the O'Malleys and father of Mary (Baby) Blake in Charles Lever's *Charles O'Malley*.

Thomas Blake   Protestant gentleman in County Galway who sympathizes with Philip Jones in the troubles among the tenantry in Anthony Trollope's *The Landleaguers*.

Walter (Dot) Blake   Gambler and horsetrainer, who encourages the courtship by Frank O'Kelly (Lord Ballindine) of Fanny Wyndham in Anthony Trollope's *The Kellys and the O'Kellys*.

Mr. Blanchard   Minister who preaches morality, warns Robert Colwan against Gil-martin, and becomes Robert's first murder victim in James Hogg's *The Private Memoirs and Confessions of a Justified Sinner*.

Mrs. Blanchard   Former mistress of Thorpe-Ambrose, the Norfolk estate which comes into the possession of Allan Armadale in Wilkie Collins's *Armadale*.

Jane Blanchard   Allan Wrentmore's bride-elect, stolen from him by a subterfuge involving forged letters and other trickery by Fergus Ingleby as prelude to events in Wilkie Collins's *Armadale*.

Sir Carte Blanche   Comic, ostentatious architect, who undertakes excessive and ruinously expensive renovations of the Duke of St. James's London residence (Hauteville House) and country seat (Hauteville Castle) in Benjamin Disraeli's *The Young Duke*.

Algernon Blancove   Cousin of Edward Blancove, Dahlia Fleming's seducer; Algernon arranges to pay Nic Sedgett to marry Dahlia and delays Dahlia's letters to Edward, which restore his love for her, until it is too late for Edward to prevent her marriage to Sedgett in George Meredith's *Rhoda Fleming*.

Edward Blancove   Sir William Blancove's son, who seduces Dahlia Fleming, tires of her, asks his cousin to pay someone to marry her, realizes he loves her and rushes back to England but is unable to stop the marriage; although it proves invalid, he is unable to convince Dahlia to marry him because she has lost all taste for life in George Meredith's *Rhoda Fleming*.

Sir William Blancove   Edward Blancove's father, a banker who marries Mrs. Lovell, once courted by his son in George Meredith's *Rhoda Fleming*.

Lady Emily Blandeville   Youngest daughter of a noble peer; she is wooed by Sir Everard Waverly before marrying Colonel Talbot; her loss of their child causes Edward Waverly to gain Talbot's freedom, placing them in Edward's debt in Sir Walter Scott's *Waverly*.

Mrs. Blandford   Benevolent, rich widow, unsympathetic to the aristocratic defense of an economic and political system that forces the majority of the English to live at a subsistence level; she assumes the care and instruction of Azemia, who loves her benefactress dearly; she gives Azemia a dowry in William Beckford's *Azemia*.

Lady Blandish   Widow and neighbor of Sir Austin Feverel; she attempts to reconcile Sir Austin and Richard Feverel; she falls in love for a time with Sir Austin but, after seeing the tragic end of his system, rejects both the man and the system in George Meredith's *The Ordeal of Richard Feverel*.

Blandly   Squire Trelawney's old friend, who finds the schooner *Hispaniola* and Captain Smollett for him; he is to send a consort if the *Hispaniola* fails to return by end of August in Robert Louis Stevenson's *Treasure Island*.

Niel Blane   Town piper and taverner, who helps Henry Morton find Burley (John Balfour) after Morton returns home from exile in Sir Walter Scott's *Old Mortality*.

Lady Blarney   Strumpet posing as a town lady; she is an acquaintance of Squire Thornhill in Oliver Goldsmith's *The Vicar of Wakefield*.

Mr. Blathers   Bow Street runner who comes to Mrs. Maylie's house to investigate the burglary in Charles Dickens's *Oliver Twist*.

Mrs. Blatherwick   Slum landlady who takes in the wandering Arthur Golding in George Gissing's *Workers in the Dawn*.

Bill Blatherwick   Professional beggar who employs the young Arthur Golding in George Gissing's *Workers in the Dawn*.

Mr. Blattergowl   Minister and friend of Oldbuck (Jonathan Oldenbuck); he visits the ruins of St. Ruth's Priory with Oldbuck and others in Sir Walter Scott's *The Antiquary*.

Colonel Sir Thomas Blazo   Bowler in a cricket match in the West Indies, in an anecdote by Alfred Jingle in Charles Dickens's *The Posthumous Papers of the Pickwick Club*.

Lady Constance Bledlow   Rich, orphaned daughter of Lord and Lady Risborough; she enriches the lives of the family of her uncle, Ewen Hooper, an Oxford don; she marries the financially ruined, aristocratic Douglas, Lord Falloden in Mrs. Humphry Ward's *Lady Connie*.

Bleeding Nun   See Beatrice de las Cisternas.

Emperor of Blefuscu   Ruler of the Lilliputians' neighbors and enemies; he welcomes Lemuel Gulliver when he escapes from Lilliput to Blefuscu by wading in Jonathan Swift's *Travels into Several Remote Nations of the World. In Four Parts. By Lemuel Gulliver.*

Lady Blekensop   Shallow and money-conscious friend of Lady Ashton, with whom she schemes to bring about the marriage of Lucy Ashton and Frank Hayston, Laird of Bucklaw, in Sir Walter Scott's *The Bride of Lammermoor.*

Caroline de Blemont   A beautiful but heartless pupil at Mlle. Reuter's school, who sits in the front row in Charlotte Brontë's *The Professor.*

Joshua Bletson   Intellectual politician who is privately an atheist; he is one of the Parliamentary commissioners sent to take possession of Woodstock in Sir Walter Scott's *Woodstock.*

Mr. Blewitt   Benevolent but financially indiscreet acquaintance of the hero Benignus in S. J. Pratt's *Liberal Opinions upon Animals, Man, and Providence.*

Dr. Blick   Hypocitical clergyman who receives his post because of special favors he did for Lord Grondale in Robert Bage's *Hermsprong.*

Captain Blifil   Avaricious brother of Dr. Blifil; having married Bridget Allworthy, he fathers Master Blifil; his untimely death forestalls his plan to inherit Squire Allworthy's estate in Henry Fielding's *The History of Tom Jones.*

Dr. Blifil   Ill-trained, impoverished medical man, who encourages his brother to court Bridget Allworthy; the match secure, he is cast out by his brother and dies of a broken heart in Henry Fielding's *The History of Tom Jones.*

Master Blifil   Hypocrite and villain, who schemes to ruin his half brother, Tom Jones; he is son to Bridget Allworthy Blifil and nephew to Squire Allworthy; he is undone when circumstance reveals his villainy to Allworthy in Henry Fielding's *The History of Tom Jones.*

Bridget Allworthy Blifil   Sister to Thomas Allworthy, mother to Master Blifil and clandestinely to Tom Jones; her obvious preference for Tom arouses Allworthy's pity for Blifil; Blifil intercepts and conceals her deathbed revelation that Tom is her child in Henry Fielding's *The History of Tom Jones.*

Mr. Bligh   Mr. Weston's predecessor as Mr. Hatfield's curate at Horton in Anne Brontë's *Agnes Grey.*

Sergeant Bligh   Member of the Royal Irish Artillery, in charge of transporting Dr. Sturk back to his house when

he is found badly beaten in the woods in J. Sheridan Le Fanu's *The House by the Churchyard.*

Young Blight   Solicitor Mortimer Lightwood's clerk, who invents imaginary clients in Charles Dickens's *Our Mutual Friend.*

Dr. Blimber   Pompous head of the boys' boarding school in Brighton that little Paul Dombey attends; his unfortunate method of education is to force learning into the boys' heads and overfeed them academically, but he grows very fond of Paul in Charles Dickens's *Dombey and Son.*

Mrs. Blimber   Dr. Blimber's wife; not as learned as her husband or daughter, she pretends to appreciate the classical and the classics in Charles Dickens's *Dombey and Son.*

Cornelia Blimber   Dr. Blimber's daughter and teacher of dead languages at the school; a serious scholar who wears spectacles and cuts her hair short, she marries Mr. Feeder in Charles Dickens's *Dombey and Son.*

Blind Beggar   An artist of begging, who lives well on alms and who takes Pompey to Bath in Francis Coventry's *The History of Pompey the Little.*

Blind White Devil (King of San Francisco)   Blind party boss, who confers with Black Tom and is sketched by Loudon Dodd in Robert Louis Stevenson's *The Wrecker.*

Mrs. Blinder   Landlady of the Necketts, who works in a chandler's shop; she generously forgives the children the rent of their lodging after their father dies in Charles Dickens's *Bleak House.*

Mrs. Blockitt   Florence Dombey's nurse in Charles Dickens's *Dombey and Son.*

Chevalier de Blois   Young Tom Newcome's French tutor, an emigré of ancient family; his daughter marries Comte de Florac but retains a lifelong innocent affection for Newcome in William Makepeace Thackeray's *The Newcomes.*

Nikkel Blok   Crude and brutal butcher of Liège; he kills the Bishop of Liège with his cleaver at William De la Marck's command in Sir Walter Scott's *Quentin Durward.*

Blondel of Nesle   Minstrel who sings to entertain King Richard in Sir Walter Scott's *The Talisman.*

Gaston de Blondeville   French knight favored by Henry III and accused by Hugh Woodreeve of robbing and murdering Reginald de Folville; he marries Lady

Barbara only to be haunted by the ghost of Folville; upon winning in a tournament, he is struck dead by Folville's ghost in Ann Radcliffe's *Gaston de Blondeville*.

Colonel Blood　　Soldier who is employed as a henchman by the Duke of Buckingham to prevent Edward Christian's return to London in Sir Walter Scott's *Peveril of the Peak*.

"Lady" Bloom　　Collaborator with the gamester Pliant in a scheme to cheat George Edwards of his fortune; she feigns love for George in John Hill's *The Adventures of Mr. George Edwards, a Creole*.

Bloomacre　　One of the greatest libertines in Eliza Haywood's *The History of Miss Betsy Thoughtless*.

Mr. Bloomfield　　Irascible owner of Wellwood House and Agnes Grey's first employer; he harangues both his wife and the governess in Anne Brontë's *Agnes Grey*.

Mrs. Bloomfield　　Severe, taciturn woman, blind to her children's faults; she is wife and mother in the family where Agnes Grey is first employed; she renders futile Agnes's efforts at disciplining the children in Anne Brontë's *Agnes Grey*.

Fanny Bloomfield　　A pretty but willful four-year-old child, who has already learned to be deceitful in Anne Brontë's *Agnes Grey*.

Harriet Bloomfield　　The only Bloomfield child still untainted; since she is only two, she is still looked after by a nurse in Anne Brontë's *Agnes Grey*.

Mary Ann Bloomfield　　A naughty, intractable child, almost six years old, who has discovered that throwing tantrums is the easiest method of getting her way in Anne Brontë's *Agnes Grey*.

Tom Bloomfield　　Seven-year-old eldest child of the Bloomfields; he delights in torturing small animals and birds, especially in front of his governess in Anne Brontë's *Agnes Grey*.

Arabella Bloomville　　Lady Fairville's daughter, who was thought to have died as a child; she lives in a pastoral cottage but comes into contact with much of London society; she dresses as a shepherdess, including crooked staff and pocketful of turnips, to search for her missing Henry Lambert; eventually reunited with the mother she thought dead, she marries Henry and becomes Lady Laughable in William Beckford's *Modern Novel Writing; or, the Elegant Enthusiast*.

Sammy Blore　　Rustic, gossiping chorister in Thomas Hardy's *Two on a Tower*.

Mr. Blotton　　Member of the Pickwick Club and quarrelsome rival of Samuel Pickwick in Charles Dickens's *The Posthumous Papers of the Pickwick Club*.

Sir Nicolaus Blount　　Older follower of Thomas Ratcliffe, Earl of Sussex; he is Walter Raleigh's friend and sparring partner in Sir Walter Scott's *Kenilworth*.

William Blow　　Merchant at Bristol on whom Mr. Warner depends for help with benevolent actions on behalf of Mr. Price and his daughter in Frances Sheridan's *Memoirs of Miss Sidney Bidulph*.

Mrs. Blower　　Widow of a smuggler; she unsuccessfully woos the Earl of Etherington (Valentine Bulmer) when he moves through the social circle of St. Ronan's Well in Sir Walter Scott's *St. Ronan's Well*.

Eliza Ridd Bloxham　　John Ridd's youngest sister, who is a smart, sassy, and sarcastic bookworm; she can be agreeable but has no desire to exercise charm; Eliza and John don't get along well in R. D. Blackmore's *Lorna Doone*.

Bully Bluck　　Stentorian leader of the Darlford conservatives who supports Nicholas Rigby's election to Parliament in Benjamin Disraeli's *Coningsby; or, The New Generation*.

Nancy Shaw Bluemits　　Bluestocking daughter of a Scottish friend of the Laird Douglas family; she now resides in Bath and entertains Miss Grizzy Douglas and Mary Douglas in Susan Ferrier's *Marriage*.

Blueskin　　Captain of Jonathan Wild's gang who refuses to give Wild a stolen gold watch; he foments rebellion until Wild has him arrested in Henry Fielding's *The Life of Mr. Jonathan Wild the Great*. He is a swarthy-faced, immensely strong criminal crony of Jonathan Wild; he shifts his allegiance to Jack Sheppard and dies trying to save him from the gallows in William Harrison Ainsworth's *Jack Sheppard*.

Mrs. Bluestone　　Good-hearted wife of the eminent lawyer Serjeant Bluestone; she takes care of Lady Anna Lovel when her mother, the Countess Lovel, turns her out of her home for refusing to marry the young earl, Frederick Lovel, in Anthony Trollope's *Lady Anna*.

Serjeant Bluestone　　Eminent barrister, loud in the courtroom and docile at home, who acts for the Countess Lovel in Anthony Trollope's *Lady Anna*.

Alice Bluestone　　Youngest daughter of Serjeant Bluestone and close friend of Lady Anna Lovel; she advises Lady Anna not to marry Daniel Thwaite, the tailor, because of the social gulf between them in Anthony Trollope's *Lady Anna*.

Blunderbussiana Sixteenth-century painter admired for correctness of anatomical rendering and wild scenes; the son of a bandit, he learns anatomy by dissecting his father's victims; his early life with outlaws provides subjects for paintings; he dies of fever and his body is given to surgeons for dissection in William Beckford's *Biographical Memoirs of Extraordinary Painters*.

Rouzinski Blunderbussiana Father of sixteenth-century painter Blunderbussiana and leader of a murderous gang of bandits; his mountain hideouts and exploits provide images for his son's later paintings; his murder victims provide the youngster with opportunities to study anatomy in William Beckford's *Biographical Memoirs of Extraordinary Painters*.

Lady Blunket Sir Paul Blunket's wife, a confirmed invalid with a surprising appetite; she is one of the houseguests at Marlowe in J. Sheridan Le Fanu's *Guy Deverell*.

Miss Blunket Daughter of Sir Paul and Lady Blunket and a houseguest with them at Marlowe; although she is in her thirties, she giggles and acts very girlish in J. Sheridan Le Fanu's *Guy Deverell*.

Sir Paul Blunket Great agriculturalist and eminent authority on liquid manures; he is a stolid guest at Marlowe in J. Sheridan Le Fanu's *Guy Deverell*.

Mr. Blyth Mr. Goodworth's friend and Valentine's father, a businessman whose support of his son's artistic ambitions produces a good man, though not a great artist in Wilkie Collins's *Hide and Seek*.

Lavinia-Ada (Lavvie) Blyth Valentine's invalid wife, cheerful despite her suffering, whose childlessness is relieved by the adoption of the ten-year-old deaf-mute "Madonna" (Grice); when Madonna's parentage is revealed, Mrs. Blyth wisely encourages Zack Thorpe to travel with Mat Grice, knowing that Madonna is attracted to Zack, her half brother, in Wilkie Collins's *Hide and Seek*.

Valentine Blyth Whole-hearted man, whose dedication to painting results in some professional success in spite of limited talent; he is devoted to his invalid wife and to his adopted deaf-mute daughter, "Madonna" (Grice), in Wilkie Collins's *Hide and Seek*.

Lord Boanerges Old friend of the (old) Duke of Omnium; he teaches Martha Dunstable to blow soap bubbles on scientific principles in Anthony Trollope's *Framley Parsonage*. He appears briefly in *The Bertrams* and in *Orley Farm*.

Mr. Boarham Fashionable suitor of Helen Lawrence (later Huntingdon); he is undaunted in his pursuit of her, notwithstanding her outright refusal in Anne Brontë's *The Tenant of Wildfell Hall*.

Bob Turnkey of the Marshalsea debtors' prison when William Dorrit was first imprisoned; he was a good friend to Amy Dorrit and assisted her in her effort to support her family in Charles Dickens's *Little Dorrit*.

Andrea Boccadolce President of Venice art society; his pronouncement that nut oil is a canvas varnish superior to egg whites leads to the decline of Sucrewasser and the ascent of Og of Basan and Andrew Guelph in William Beckford's *Biographical Memoirs of Extraordinary Painters*.

Bodach Glas Foreboding apparition which has warned the MacIvors of imminent death or captivity for three hundred years in Sir Walter Scott's *Waverly*.

Mr. Boddy Feeble but cheerful old man with a wooden leg; he entertains by playing his fiddle and dies pathetically as a derelict in George Gissing's *Thyrza*.

Sir Boreas Bodkin Windbag secretary of the Post Office; he rebukes the clerk, Samuel Crocker, for bad behavior in Anthony Trollope's *Marion Fay*.

Sir Nicholas Bodkin Conservative landowner in County Galway and opponent of Home Rule; he believes tenants must be kept in their place and that nothing must get in the way of hunting in Anthony Trollope's *The Landleaguers*.

Peter Bodkin Eldest son of Sir Nicholas and supporter of Tom Daly in opposing the guerillas and revolutionaries struggling against the Irish landowners in Anthony Trollope's *The Landleaguers*.

Bodle, Laird of Kilmarkeckle Betty Bodle's father, who is obsessed with snuff in John Galt's *The Entail*.

Betty Bodle Daughter of the Laird of Kilmarkeckle; Claud Walkinshaw arranges her marriage to his son Walter, and she dies in childbirth without producing the male heirs Claud had wanted in John Galt's *The Entail*.

Chevalier De Boeffleurs Corrupt French nobleman, who forces Baron Julius von Konigstein to be his accomplice in cheating Albert St. George at the gambling house in Benjamin Disraeli's *Vivian Grey*.

Mr. Boffin Arch conservative left out of the (younger) Duke of Omnium's coalition government; he allies himself with Sir Orlando Drought to bring the duke's administration down in Anthony Trollope's *The Prime Minister*.

Henrietty Boffin   Noddy Boffin's plump, cheerful wife, who aims to be a "high-flyer" of fashion; she wishes to adopt an orphan to replace John Harmon, and, after the child dies, adopts Sloppy in Charles Dickens's *Our Mutual Friend*.

Nicodemus (Noddy) Boffin   Large, child-like, benevolent foreman of the mounds, who inherited Harmon's estate after John Harmon was presumed dead; he invites Bella Wilfer to live with him and his wife, and gradually changes into a miser, but only to teach Bella the danger of becoming too mercenary in Charles Dickens's *Our Mutual Friend*.

J. G. Bogsby   Landlord of the Sol's Arms in Cook's Court in Charles Dickens's *Bleak House*.

Bohemian Petitioner   Brother of the Jesuit from Peru; he petitions the King of Bulgaria for the return of his wife in Charles Johnstone's *Chrysal: or, The Adventures of a Guinea*.

Bohemond   Prince and Count of Tarentum; he is a crafty Norman-Italian crusader, who becomes Emperor Alexius Comnenus's ally only after receiving several large bribes in Sir Walter Scott's *Count Robert of Paris*.

Aubrey Bohun   Charming, wealthy, influential, but unprincipled owner of Bohun Castle; he is drawn back to his home in Hartlebury after ten years' absence by the political turmoil of the Reform Bill and decides to contest the borough seat of Fanchester as a liberal-independent; he wins by one vote (that of the Whig, Mr. Gainsborough) and makes a great impact in London; at the same time, he courts Helen Molesworth, who accepts his advances but later discovers his unprincipled nature in Benjamin Disraeli's *A Year at Hartlebury; or, The Election*.

Aveline de Bohun   Lady-prize of the tournament held by Henry III in Ann Radcliffe's *Gaston de Blondeville*.

Monsieur Du Bois   French gentleman who accompanies Madame Duval to England; he speaks only French and returns to France without her in Frances Burney's *Evelina*.

Josephine de Boisbelle   Sister of the Marquis de Montfleuri; forced into an early marriage, she is estranged from her husband when she meets Lionel Desmond, whose child she bears and commits to his care and Geraldine Verney's while secluded in England; her reputation thus untarnished when her husband dies, she hopes to marry her first love in Charlotte Smith's *Desmond*.

Brian de Bois-Guilbert   Proud Norman Templar and famed crusader; he is an adherent of Prince John; he falls in love with and kidnaps Rebecca the Jewess, taking her to Templestowe; when she is sentenced to death for witchcraft, he is commanded to fight as the Temple's champion; she spurns his offer to sacrifice his ambitions and escape with her; he is defeated by her champion, Ivanhoe, in Sir Walter Scott's *Ivanhoe*.

Boissec   Scoffing, pompous professor from M. Paul Emanuel's college; he suggests that Lucy Snowe's compositions are plagiarized and forces her to take an examination in Charlotte Brontë's *Villette*.

Mrs. Bokum   Widow who is Mrs. MacStinger's bridesmaid at her marriage to John Bunsby in Charles Dickens's *Dombey and Son*.

Eleanor Bold   See Eleanor Harding.

John Bold   Zealous surgeon and town councilor, who leads the attack on Septimus Harding for alleged abuse of a charitable trust; he marries Eleanor, Mr. Harding's daughter, in Anthony Trollope's *The Warden*.

Johnny Bold   Baby son of the widowed Eleanor Harding Bold; Mr. Slope coos over the child in order to flatter his mother, whom he hopes to marry in Anthony Trollope's *Barchester Towers*.

Mary Bold   Sister of John Bold and friend and later sister-in-law of Eleanor Harding Bold in Anthony Trollope's *The Warden*. She is Johnny Bold's adoring aunt in *Barchester Towers*.

Captain Boldwig   Fierce little man, who catches Samuel Pickwick sleeping on his property in a wheelbarrow and puts him in the stocks in Charles Dickens's *The Posthumous Papers of the Pickwick Club*.

John Boldwood   Gentleman farmer obsessively in love with but rejected by Bathsheba Everdene; expecting at last to win her after the extended absence of her deceitful husband, Frank Troy, Boldwood is deranged by Troy's reappearance and kills him; his death sentence is commuted in Thomas Hardy's *Far from the Madding Crowd*.

Anna Boleyn   Spirit of the ill-fated second wife of Henry VIII; she recounts her experiences to Judge Minos to gain entry to Elysium; her sufferings from her own ambition, as well as at the hands of her scheming father and the king, form the last chapter of Henry Fielding's *A Journey From This World to the Next*.

Skyresh Bolgolam   High Admiral of Lilliput; his malice toward Lemuel Gulliver is increased when Gulliver seizes the Blefuscu fleet; he acts for the wishes of the Empress of Lilliput in trying to gain the capital penalty when Gulliver is impeached in Jonathan Swift's *Travels* *into Several Remote Nations of the World. In Four Parts. By Lemuel Gulliver.*

Farmer Bollens Prosperous, middle-aged country man with whom Adelaide Hinton elopes, freeing Edward Springrove from his engagement in Thomas Hardy's *Desperate Remedies.*

Richard Bollum Nefarious partner of Timothy Crinkett; he persuades John Caldigate to pay Crinkett back part of the purchase price for a gold mine in New South Wales; the payment looks like a bribe and further increases Caldigate's troubles in Anthony Trollope's *John Caldigate.*

Miss Bolo Lady Snuphanuph's card-playing companion, with whom Samuel Pickwick plays whist in a cutthroat match in Charles Dickens's *The Posthumous Papers of the Pickwick Club.*

Bridget Bolster Key witness, along with John Kenneby, at Lady Mason's trial for forgery; she withstands a withering examination from Mr. Chaffanbrass in Anthony Trollope's *Orley Farm.*

Mrs. Bolt Extortionate landlady of the lodging house where Bernard Kingcote and his sister stay in George Gissing's *Isabel Clarendon.*

Sir Simon Bolt Longtime Master of the Brotherton Hunt known far and wide for his expertise with horse and hound in Anthony Trollope's *Is He Popenjoy?* .

John Boltby Family lawyer of Sir Harry Hotspur; he learns of George Hotspur's debts and actress mistress, Lucy Morton, and advises his client to forbid his daughter, Emily, to marry the rogue in Anthony Trollope's *Sir Harry Hotspur of Humblethwaite.*

Bolton Defrauding steward of the Mansfield family in Samuel Richardson's *Sir Charles Grandison.*

Mr. Bolton Fanny Bolton's father, porter of Shepherd's Inn in William Makepeace Thackeray's *The History of Pendennis.*

Mrs. Bolton Fanny Bolton's mother, portress of Shepherd's Inn in William Makepeace Thackeray's *The History of Pendennis.*

Fanny Bolton Daughter of the porter at Shepherd's Inn; Arthur Pendennis is enamored of her until his mother rescues him, fearing a dishonorable liaison; Fanny then marries Samuel Huxter in William Makepeace Thackeray's *The History of Pendennis.*

Harry Bolton Sir Thomas Sindall's virtuous cousin,

heir apparent to the Sindall estate and lover of Lucy Sindall in Henry Mackenzie's *The Man of the World.*

Margaret Bolton Sympathetic wife of Robert Bolton; she joins with her husband in urging Hester Bolton to escape from her repressive mother by marrying John Caldigate in Anthony Trollope's *John Caldigate.*

Mary Bolton Religious fanatic obsessed by the idea of dominating her daughter, Hester, and saving her from John Caldigate; when the young people marry, she becomes nearly deranged, and after a scandal erupts around the husband, she locks Hester up in Puritan Grange; even when Caldigate is cleared of a bigamy charge, she remains implacable towards him in Anthony Trollope's *John Caldigate.*

Nicholas Bolton Cambridge banker devoted to his only daughter, Hester, and deeply pained by her mother's cruel treatment of her; he turns against Hester's husband, John Caldigate, when the young man is said to have committed bigamy in Anthony Trollope's *John Caldigate.*

Nicholas Bolton (the younger) Narrow-minded son of a successful Cambridge banker; he shares his parents' religious bigotry in Anthony Trollope's *John Caldigate.*

Robert Bolton Easy-going, gregarious Cambridge attorney and son of Nicholas by his first marriage; observing his stepmother's tyranny towards her daughter, Hester, he advises Hester to marry John Caldigate in Anthony Trollope's *John Caldigate.*

Stawarth Bolton Brusque but chivalrous captain in the English army; he provides protection for the Glendinning house and family in Sir Walter Scott's *The Monastery.*

William Bolton Successful London barrister son of Nicholas Bolton; he succeeds in reconciling his parents to the marriage of their daughter, Hester, and John Caldigate in Anthony Trollope's *John Caldigate.*

Bonamo Vincentio di Vivaldi's cowardly friend and confidant in Ann Radcliffe's *The Italian.*

Bonbennin bonbobbin-bonbobbinet Exemplary prince, whose name means "Enlightener of the Sun"; he chooses Nanhoa out of seven hundred candidates to be his bride, but then barters her for a white mouse with green eyes in an oriental fable by Lien Chi Altangi in Oliver Goldsmith's *The Citizen of the World.*

Mrs. Boncassen Reticent and awkward American mother of Isabel; she is somewhat overawed at the prospect of her daughter's entering the highest ranks of British society by marrying Lord Silverbridge in Anthony Trollope's *The Duke's Children.*

Ezekiel Boncassen　Forthright American scholar engaged in research at the British Museum; proud of his humble origins, he nonetheless has reservations about his daughter, Isabel, entering British aristocracy through marriage to Lord Silverbridge; seeing the young man's devotion, he gives permission for his daughter's marriage in Anthony Trollope's *The Duke's Children.*

Isabel Boncassen　Comely, charming, and outspoken American, the novelty and belle of the season, and daughter of Ezekiel Boncassen; she enchants Lord Silverbridge but is deemed an inappropriate wife by his father, the (younger) Duke of Omnium, because of her antecedents; she charms the duke, who at last gives consent to the wedding in Anthony Trollope's *The Duke's Children.*

Miss Bond　Mr. Bond's daughter, who loves Major Smyth in Frances Sheridan's *Memoirs of Miss Sidney Bidulph.*

Mr. Bond　Gentleman with a wife, several daughters, and a son home from college; the Faulklands stay with them while their country house is being built in Frances Sheridan's *Memoirs of Miss Sidney Bidulph.*

Francesco Bondelmonti　Italian nobleman who heads the Florentine army; a cousin of Euthanasia dei Adimari, he urges her to join the conspiracy to overthrow Castruccio dei Antelminelli in Mary Shelley's *Valperga.*

Mr. Bondum　Corrupt bailiff, who tricks William Booth to arrest him and tries to multiply the suits against him in Henry Fielding's *Amelia.*

Billy Bones　Seaman with a sabre cut who spends his last violent and frightened days as a drunken guest at the Admiral Benbow Inn; Flint's first mate on the *Walrus*, he has possession of Flint's treasure map and is hiding from his *Walrus* shipmates in Robert Louis Stevenson's *Treasure Island.*

Bonhome　Steward and secretary to Count de Vinevil; he accompanies the family to Turkey and is killed with the count in Penelope Aubin's *The Strange Adventures of the Count de Vinevil and His Family.*

Boniface (Father Blinkhoolie)　Ineffectual abbot of the Monastery of St. Mary's of Kennaquhair; he is kindly and hospitable, though pompous and insecure; incapable of dealing with the Reformation, he is sent a capable sub-prior whom he resents but to whom he is ultimately forced to relinquish his miter in Sir Walter Scott's *The Monastery.* After his abdication he acts as mail-gardener at Kinross; he unwillingly aids the rescuers of Queen Mary of Scotland, after which he disguises himself as Blinkhoolie and enters the Abbey of Dundrennan in *The Abbot.*

Barnaby Boniface　Tenant whose offer to permit a neighbor to decide on the merit of the proprietary claims of Walter Warmhouse is rejected; the ensuing lawsuit has gone thirteen years without progress in an anecdote told by Mr. Fielding in Henry Brooke's *The Fool of Quality.*

Monsieur Bonnac　French nobleman rescued from debtor's prison by Valancourt; later he is given the Castle di Udolpho by Emily St. Aubert in Ann Radcliffe's *The Mysteries of Udolpho.*

Mrs. Bonner　The source of the Countess of Saldar's financial ambitions; she dies, leaving Beckley Court to her granddaughter Julianna in George Meredith's *Evan Harrington.*

Julianna Bonner　Ill-tempered, sickly heiress who dies, leaving Beckley Court to Evan Harrington, with whom she had fallen in love, in George Meredith's *Evan Harrington.*

Mary Bonner　Sir Thomas Underwood's lovely niece, who arrives from the West Indies needing a home, much to her uncle's initial irritation; the philandering Ralph Newton, heir of Newton Priory, makes up to her, but she falls in love with the other Ralph Newton, who plucks up courage finally to propose to her in Anthony Trollope's *Ralph the Heir.*

Miss Bonnicastle　Robust artist who tries to arrange Olga Hannaford's love affairs in George Gissing's *The Crown of Life.*

Mr. Bonnycastle　Cool, elegant private-school headmaster in Holy Orders, who uses the cane to give Jack Easy his first reason for abandoning the absurd egalitarianism of his father, Nicodemus, in Captain Frederick Marryat's *Mr. Midshipman Easy.*

Rachel Bonnyrigg　New wife of Sir Bingo Binks; she helps to spread gossip among the visitors to St. Ronan's Well in Sir Walter Scott's *St. Ronan's Well.*

Mr. Bonteen　Loquacious party underling, who mocks Phineas Finn for going against party discipline in Anthony Trollope's *Phineas Finn.* He staunchly supports Plantagenet Palliser in reforming the coinage in *The Eustace Diamonds.* He befriends Lizzie Eustace and tries to help her escape from her marriage to Mr. Emilius; he is murdered in *Phineas Redux.*

Mrs. Bonteen　Busybody wife of a political hack; she tries to bolster his career by denigrating his rivals in Anthony Trollope's *Phineas Finn.* When her husband is murdered, she is vociferous in accusing Phineas Finn of the crime in *Phineas Redux.*

Bonthron Drunken thug, who is a henchman of John Ramorny and Henbane Dwining; he is defeated in a fight with Henry Smith to adjudicate Bonthron's murder of Oliver Proudfute; he undergoes a mock hanging; he helps to murder the Duke of Rothsay and is summarily executed by Archibald, Earl of Douglas, in Sir Walter Scott's *The Fair Maid of Perth*.

Lady Booby Thomas Booby's widow, who assuages her grief through fickle but prolonged pursuit of Joseph Andrews; her passion turns to hatred, and she abuses her aristocratic power to block Joseph's marriage to Fanny Goodwill in Henry Fielding's *The History of the Adventures of Mr. Joseph Andrews and of his Friend Mr. Abraham Adams*.

Mr. Booby See William B——.

Mrs. Booby Wealthy woman who seeks spiritual guidance from Geoffry Wildgoose at Bath, ostensibly because of her estrangement from her husband but actually because she has been snubbed by her former lover's wife in Richard Graves's *The Spiritual Quixote*.

John Booby Naive young squire, whose lust for Shamela Andrews allows him to believe she is a virgin and to be manipulated into a marriage settlement with her in Henry Fielding's *An Apology for the Life of Mrs. Shamela Andrews*.

Thomas Booby Status-conscious lord of the estate and husband to Lady Booby; he employs both Joseph Andrews and Fanny Goodwill before his death early in Henry Fielding's *The History of the Adventures of Mr. Joseph Andrews and of his Friend Mr. Abraham Adams*.

Captain (Doodles) Boodle Dimwitted friend of Archibald Clavering, similarly engrossed in the turf; he counsels Archie in wooing Lady Ongar via her friend Sophie Gordeloup; he becomes fascinated by Sophie and follows her to the Continent in Anthony Trollope's *The Claverings*. He appears in *Phineas Redux*.

Alfred Booker Shrewd editor of the *Literary Chronicle*, who knows all the tricks of his trade and writes book reviews without troubling himself to read the books through in Anthony Trollope's *The Way We Live Now*. He appears in *The Prime Minister*.

Bookseller A man of business who usually buys poetry by quantity rather than quality in Charles Johnstone's *Chrysal: or, The Adventures of a Guinea*.

Mynheer Bootersac Maternal grandfather of Jeremy Watersouchy; his gifts of engravings inspire the child's first efforts at drawing in William Beckford's *Biographical Memoirs of Extraordinary Painters*.

Amelia (Emily) Harris Booth William Booth's virtuous and loving wife, who supports her husband despite his vices, spurns temptations to sacrifice her virtue to sustain her family, does what virtuous things she can to preserve her family, and patiently waits for her husband to grow up in Henry Fielding's *Amelia*.

Billy Booth Oldest son of William and Amelia Booth; he charms Dr. Harrison with his Christian notions of revenge in Henry Fielding's *Amelia*.

Emily Booth Second child of William and Amelia Booth; she becomes the favorite and heir of Dr. Harrison in Henry Fielding's *Amelia*.

James Booth Gardener at Fieldhead, the Keeldar home in Charlotte Brontë's *Shirley*.

Nancy Booth William Booth's cherished sister, whose death removes Booth from Amelia Harris long enough for Mrs. Harris to approve his rival for Amelia's hand in Henry Fielding's *Amelia*.

William (Billy) Booth Good-hearted but weak husband of Amelia Booth; his belief that dominant passions rule man's behavior allows him to justify infidelity and gambling debts; he discovers true faith after reading sermons while imprisoned, eschews his bad habits and company, and, with Amelia's fortune restored, builds his family a contented life in Henry Fielding's *Amelia*.

Mrs. Boothby Widowed housekeeper/companion who joins the Sindall household after the death of Mrs. Selwyn and who acts as a pander for Sir Thomas Sindall with his ward Lucy Sindall in Henry Mackenzie's *The Man of the World*.

Mr. Boots Young man who functions as a buffer at the Veneering dinner parties in Charles Dickens's *Our Mutual Friend*.

Mr. Borden Impudent auctioneer of wrecked ships who auctions off the *Flying Scud* in Robert Louis Stevenson's *The Wrecker*.

Augusta Boreham Lady Baldock's unmarried daughter, who manages her mother by indirection in Anthony Trollope's *Phineas Finn*. She has converted to Roman Catholicism and become Sister Veronica John to the dismay of her mother in *Phineas Redux*.

Leonie Bornier Housekeeper and foster sister of Julie Le Breton in Mrs. Humphry Ward's *Lady Rose's Daughter*.

Lord Borradale Rich, cultured, and worldly elder brother of Maurice Borradale and sole heir to their deceased father's estate; he seeks to marry Maurice's daughter, Margaret, to his undesirable son; to this end, he provides Margaret and her parents with a cottage on his estate in northern England in William Godwin's *Deloraine*.

Margaret Borradale   Ethereal beauty who loves William, who, she fears, has been lost at sea, but marries Deloraine; at her unexpected reunion with William her obsessively jealous husband murders him, and she suffers a stroke and dies in William Godwin's *Deloraine*.

Maurice Borradale   Father of Margaret; as a result of the prevailing system of primogeniture, he is impoverished and dependent on his elder brother, Lord Borradale, but he resists the latter's plans for marriage between Margaret and her first cousin in William Godwin's *Deloraine*.

King of Borrioboola-Gha   African ruler whose enthusiastic participation in the slave trade jeopardizes Mrs. Jellyby's charitable project of establishing a settlement in his country in Charles Dickens's *Bleak House*.

Helen Borrisoff   Unconventional woman who has married for interest rather than love and recommends this policy to the heroine of George Gissing's *The Crown of Life*.

Borromeo   Veteran of many years' imprisonment in Algeria; he is blunt, indifferent to danger, and considers himself an outcast among men; these qualities awaken sympathy in Cloudesley, who befriends him and trusts him with the secret of Julian Danvers's true parentage in William Godwin's *Cloudesley*.

Cousin Borroughs   Cousin to John Andrews; he wants Andrews to employ his son as farm help after Mr. B—— provides his parents-in-law with a farm to manage in Samuel Richardson's *Pamela, or Virtue Rewarded*.

King of Borsagrass   Rival who invades Gwyntystorm at the urging of the traitorous lord chancellor and is defeated there by Curdie Peterson and the king in George MacDonald's *The Princess and Curdie*.

Robin Boss   Drunken town drummer whose public conduct often causes trouble; he is dismissed after striking up the "firebeat" in the middle of the night in John Galt's *The Provost*.

de Bosse   Criminal hired by Jean d'Aunoy to murder Adeline; instead he releases her to La Mott; his testimony in La Mott's trial incriminates Phillippe de Montalt, resulting in his arrest in Ann Radcliffe's *The Romance of the Forest*.

Lady Clarinda Bossnowl   Young woman who decides

to marry for money and is betrothed to young Crotchet; she is converted to romance by the true love of Captain Fitzchrome when Crotchet goes bankrupt in Thomas Love Peacock's *Crotchet Castle*.

Captain Billy Bostock   Rugged proprietor of a public house and tea garden named Currency Lass; he had sailed on the brig *Jolly Roger* in Robert Louis Stevenson's *The Wrecker*.

Bothwell   Husband of Mary, Queen of Scots; he is presumed dead but is found to be alive after the marriage of Mary and the Duke of Norfolk in Sophia Lee's *The Recess*.

Mr. Bott   Toadying supporter in Parliament of the rising Plantagenet Palliser; he is heartily disliked by Glencora Palliser, who rightly suspects him of spying on her and telling tales about her and Burgo Fitzgerald; he finally marries another busybody, Mrs. Masham, in Anthony Trollope's *Can You Forgive Her?*.

(Jemmy) Lord Bottom   Insolent son of Lord Mansfield; he fights with and makes fun of young Harry Clinton in Henry Brooke's *The Fool of Quality*.

Lady Boucher   Misinformed, "purblind dowager" and gossip, who frequently visits Lady Delacour in Maria Edgeworth's *Belinda*.

Mrs. Boucher   John Boucher's wife, who is left with starving children after his suicide in Elizabeth Gaskell's *North and South*.

John Boucher   A mill worker, discontented with a cautious union policy; a leader in the irresponsible strike riot when Margaret Hale is injured, he later commits suicide in despair at not being able to cope with his family's poverty in Elizabeth Gaskell's *North and South*.

Pierre Bouffuet   Tyrant who marries Cecile Bertrand for her money and property and drives away her adopted daughter, Agnes D'Albini, by his cruelty in Charlotte Dacre's *The Libertine*.

Grace Boultby   Thomas's wife, who spends much of her time pampering her husband in Charlotte Brontë's *Shirley*.

Dr. Thomas Boultby   Rector of Whinbury, a hotheaded Welshman who is doted on by his wife in Charlotte Brontë's *Shirley*.

Mr. Bouncer   Novelist and member of a London club, the Universe, haunt of politicians; he is present during the quarrel between Phineas Finn and Mr. Bonteen on the night Bonteen is murdered; he testifies at Finn's trial in Anthony Trollope's *The Eustace Diamonds*.

Bob Bound   Naive lieutenant, who advises William Booth to pay touch money instead of repaying George Trent's debt in Henry Fielding's *Amelia*.

Josiah Bounderby   Blustery, selfish factory owner, who hypocritically brags about being "self-made," and who marries Louisa Gradgrind in Charles Dickens's *Hard Times*.

Colonel Bouverie   Devoted friend of William; he receives an appointment under General Murray, Governor of Canada, and proposes that William join him there in William Godwin's *Deloraine*.

Herbert Bowater   Julius Charnock's muscular young curate, who neglects his duties until brought to a more serious frame of mind by illness in Charlotte Yonge's *The Three Brides*.

Joanna Bowater   Sister of Herbert Bowater; she has rejected Raymond Charnock Poynsett's offer of marriage before the novel opens and is ultimately reunited with her long-lost lover in Natal in Charlotte Yonge's *The Three Brides*.

Mr. Bower   Prosperous shop foreman, who helps organize lectures to workmen but becomes alienated in George Gissing's *Thyrza*.

Mary Bower   Pious working-class girl, who is intolerant of nonbelievers in George Gissing's *Thyrza*.

William Bowker   Impeccably dressed but penniless friend of John Jorrocks; he is owner of a snuff and cigar shop, a critic of the theater, and a Whig party candidate for a seat in Parliament; his candidacy is bought off by the Duke of Donkeyton to ensure election for James, Marquis of Bray, who then loses to Jorrocks in Robert Surtees's *Hillingdon Hall*.

Lady Bowley   Sir Joseph Bowley's young wife, who shares his patronizing view of the working classes in Charles Dickens's *The Chimes*.

Master Bowley   Twelve-year-old son of Sir Joseph Bowley in Charles Dickens's *The Chimes*.

Sir Joseph Bowley   Baronet and Member of Parliament, who styles himself "the Poor Man's Friend and Father," but whose contributions to the welfare of the working class are limited to pontifical speech making in Charles Dickens's *The Chimes*.

Bat Bowling   Charles Arnold's faithful servant, who discusses his difficulty understanding the logic of customs, excises, and taxes in William Beckford's *Azemia*.

Tom Bowling   Roderick Random's sailor uncle, who helps punish the schoolmaster, sends Roderick to university, and jumps his ship after a fight with his captain; found in France and helped to return to England by Roderick, he commands a ship to South America, where he and Roderick discover Roderick's long-lost father in Tobias Smollett's *The Adventures of Roderick Random*.

Mr. Bowls   Stately butler to Miss Matilda Crawley; he marries Mrs. Firkin in William Makepeace Thackeray's *Vanity Fair*.

Bow-may   Huntress and "damsel at arms," whose accurate archery is effective in peace and in battle; she marries Hart of Highcliff in William Morris's *The Roots of the Mountains*.

Mr. Bows   A crippled fiddler, friend and mentor of Miss Fotheringay (Emily Costigan) and Fanny Bolton; he resents Arthur Pendennis's love for both women in William Makepeace Thackeray's *The History of Pendennis*.

Mr. Bowyer   Kindly, weak, dissenting minister, who frequently drinks tea with Alton Locke's mother and Mr. Wiglinton; he responds sympathetically to the young Alton's questions in Charles Kingsley's *Alton Locke*.

Dick Bowyer   Sly but slow servant of Sir Daniel Brackley; he outfits Brackley's troops at Moat House and volunteers to take Brackley's letter to Wensleydale in Robert Louis Stevenson's *The Black Arrow: A Tale of Two Roses*.

Evelyn Boyce   Upper-class mother of Marcella; her husband's financial misdeeds shame and humiliate her in Mrs. Humphry Ward's *Marcella*.

Marcella Boyce   Beautiful, upper-class defender of the rights of the urban and rural poor; she escapes county social life to take a yearlong course in nursing, after which she works with the urban poor and eventually marries Aldous Raeburn, Lord Maxwell in Mrs. Humphry Ward's *Marcella*. As Lady Maxwell she helps the passage of her husband's Factory Bill through her emotional and moral influence on Sir George Tressady in *Sir George Tressady*.

Richard Boyce   Upper-class Member of Parliament and father of Marcella; his misuse of funds leads to the ostracism of his family in Mrs. Humphry Ward's *Marcella*.

Lorimer Boyd   Friend of Sir Douglas Ross; he acts as narrator when he describes events through his thoughts; he brings Sir Douglas and Gertrude Ross together at the end in Caroline Norton's *Old Sir Douglas*.

Lawrence Boythorn   John Jarndyce's ferocious, loud,

and warmhearted friend, who feuds with Sir Leicester Dedlock over their boundary lines; he once loved Miss Barbary but was rejected by her; he makes his home available to Esther Summerson for her recuperation from smallpox in Charles Dickens's *Bleak House*.

Bozzari Erstwhile friend of the Greek warlord Colocotroni, whom he betrays to the Turks; when Colocotroni escapes from prison, Bozzari murders him in order to have free access to his daughter, Irene Colocotroni, in William Godwin's *Cloudesley*.

Mrs. Bozzle Samuel Bozzle's wife and confidante, who takes Emily Trevelyan's part when her child is kidnapped in Anthony Trollope's *He Knew He Was Right*.

Samuel Bozzle Disreputable private detective engaged by Louis Trevelyan to spy on his wife, Emily, and to arrange the kidnapping of his young son in Anthony Trollope's *He Knew He Was Right*.

Bra Aph-Lin's wife, who likes to read the ancient literature of the Vril-ya, which resembles stories of life in our own world in Edward Bulwer-Lytton's *The Coming Race*.

Lady Brackenshaw Leader of the Pennicote society in George Eliot's *Daniel Deronda*.

Lord Brackenshaw Husband of Lady Brackenshaw in George Eliot's *Daniel Deronda*.

Lady Brackley Tall, remote wife of Sir Daniel Brackley; Goody Hatch waits upon her in Robert Louis Stevenson's *The Black Arrow: A Tale of Two Roses*.

Sir Daniel Brackley Villainous guardian of Dick Shelton; he killed Sir Henry Shelton, stole Ellis Duckworth's lands, and tries to marry Joan Sedley to Lord Shoreby; his allegiance to Lancaster or York follows his convenience, not his conscience in Robert Louis Stevenson's *The Black Arrow: A Tale of Two Roses*.

Sir Harry Bracton Noisy, good-looking landowner; he attends the Hunt Ball, where he courts Dorcas Brandon and then badly wounds Stanley Lake in a duel; later he enters Gylingden to canvass for votes against Lake in the upcoming election in J. Sheridan Le Fanu's *Wylder's Hand*.

Earl Bracy Old friend of Dr. Wortle, at whose preparatory school his son Lord Carstairs had been taught prior to attending Eton; when Carstairs falls in love with Mary, the headmaster's daughter, Lord Bracy gives his blessing to the match in Anthony Trollope's *Dr. Wortle's School*.

Maurice de Bracy Vain leader of a band of mercenar-

ies; he captures Lady Rowena and attempts to force her into marrying him in Sir Walter Scott's *Ivanhoe*.

Lilias Bradbourne Favorite attendant of the Lady of Avenel (Mary Avenel); jealous of her mistress's attention, she is responsible for the dismissal of Roland Graeme in Sir Walter Scott's *The Abbot*.

Vincent Braddell See Beck.

General Braddock Leader of the forces against the French in America; young George Warrington serves in his expedition and, captured by Indians, is believed killed in William Makepeace Thackeray's *The Virginians*.

Mr. Braddock Diana Warwick's solicitor; he defends her successfully when Augustus Warwick sues her for divorce in George Meredith's *Diana of the Crossways*.

Hilkiah Bradford Pious, straight-laced, and kindly protector (and, later, tutor) of the child Charles Mandeville on his perilous journey from Dublin to London during the Irish Uprising in 1641 in William Godwin's *Mandeville*.

Bradley Creditor whose bill for $200 wrecks Jim Pinkerton's firm in Robert Louis Stevenson's *The Wrecker*.

Luke Bradley See Luke Rookwood.

Peter Bradley See Alan Rookwood.

Susan Bradley See Susan Rookwood.

Bradshaw Footman to Dr. Henry Jekyll and fellow servant of Poole, Jekyll's butler, in Robert Louis Stevenson's *The Strange Case of Dr. Jekyll and Mr. Hyde*.

Mr. Bradshaw A wealthy, self-important businessman, and a Dissenter who is the main financial support of Thurstan Benson's chapel; after learning about Ruth Hilton's past and Benson's role in concealing it he harshly rejects them; the misconduct of his son plays a major part in changing his own attitudes in Elizabeth Gaskell's *Ruth*.

Mrs. Bradshaw The wife of Mr. Bradshaw; her more generous nature is dominated by his rigid attitudes in Elizabeth Gaskell's *Ruth*.

Mrs. Bradshaw Conventional-minded wife of Jacob Bradshaw in George Gissing's *The Emancipated*.

Elizabeth Bradshaw Daughter of Mr. Bradshaw and pupil of Ruth Hilton in Elizabeth Gaskell's *Ruth*.

Sir George Bradshaw Dissolute companion of Casimir Fleetwood's revels who introduces him to the bewitching Mrs. Comorin in William Godwin's *Fleetwood*.

Jacob Bradshaw   Strong-minded provincial silk manufacturer who travels in Italy in George Gissing's *The Emancipated*.

Jemima Bradshaw   The spirited daughter of Mr. Bradshaw; she befriends Ruth Hilton but unwittingly learns about and reveals the secret of Ruth's past; she marries Walter Farquhar in Elizabeth Gaskell's *Ruth*.

Mary Bradshaw   Daughter of Mr. Bradshaw and pupil of Ruth Hilton in Elizabeth Gaskell's *Ruth*.

Richard Bradshaw   Mr. Bradshaw's son, who reacts against his rigid upbringing; he forges Benson's signature to get money, and the discovery of this shatters Mr. Bradshaw's complacency in Elizabeth Gaskell's *Ruth*.

Thomas Bradshaw   Minister of the London meeting-house attended by the Colemans; his sermons inspire Zachariah Coleman in Radical political views; he warns Coleman to escape London in Mark Rutherford's *The Revolution In Tanner's Lane*.

Cosmo Comyne Bradwardine   Verbose Baron of Bradwardine, whose speech is full of Latin misnomers; a great friend of Sir Everard Waverly, he entertains Edward Waverly on his Scottish estate before joining Prince Charles Stuart's army and sharing many military adventures; as Rose's father, he eventually becomes Edward's father-in-law in Sir Walter Scott's *Waverly*.

Malcolm Bradwardine of Inch-Grabbit   The Baron of Bradwardine's distant heir, who receives Bradwardine's forfeited estate and then sells it unknowingly to Duncan Macwheeble in Sir Walter Scott's *Waverly*.

Rose Bradwardine   Beautiful but shy daughter of the baron; she loves Edward Waverly and writes to Prince Charles Stuart to arrange his escape; after she nurses him to health and obtains the papers which will clear him, her friendship with Flora MacIvor guarantees his safety in the Highlands in Sir Walter Scott's *Waverly*.

Mrs. Brady   Quarrelsome wife of Michael Brady; she and her sister-in-law, Bell Barry, are on bad terms in William Makepeace Thackeray's *The Luck of Barry Lyndon*.

Benjamin Brady   John Jorrocks's young and clever but slothful groom in Robert Surtees's *Jorrocks's Jaunts and Jollities* and in *Handley Cross*.

Charlotte Brady   Captain Maurice's "ward," who discovers that she is in fact his daughter; she is raised and

educated by Mrs. Darnford in Clara Reeve's *Plans of Education*.

Honoria (Nora) Brady   First cousin and first love of Redmond Barry when he is sixteen and she twenty-three; she is the subject of his duel with Captain Quin, whom she later marries in William Makepeace Thackeray's *The Luck of Barry Lyndon*.

Michael Brady   Redmond Barry's maternal uncle and Nora and Ulick's father; he is a good-humored Irish squire in William Makepeace Thackeray's *The Luck of Barry Lyndon*.

Mick Brady   Michael Brady's eldest son, who resents and persecutes Redmond Barry in William Makepeace Thackeray's *The Luck of Barry Lyndon*.

Mysie Brady   Younger sister of Nora Brady in William Makepeace Thackeray's *The Luck of Barry Lyndon*.

Pat Brady   Broken-nosed manager for Thady Macdermot; he is suborned by Hyacinth Keegan into helping ruin his master in Anthony Trollope's *The Macdermots of Ballycloran*.

Ulick Brady   Redmond Barry's first cousin and friend; Barry helps him kidnap the heiress Amelia Kiljoy, whom he marries by force in William Makepeace Thackeray's *The Luck of Barry Lyndon*.

Mr. Bragwell   One of the London tavern boys who participate in the "roast" of Dr. Wagtail in Tobias Smollett's *The Adventures of Roderick Random*.

Lord Brailstone   Lord Fleetwood's friend, whose failed attempt to seduce Henrietta (Fakenham) Kirby causes her to faint and burn her face in George Meredith's *The Amazing Marriage*.

Earl of Bramber   Proprietor of Ongar Castle, where John Jorrocks sleeps in the bathhouse in Robert Surtees's *Handley Cross*.

Mr. Justice Bramber   Judge in the bigamy case brought against John Caldigate; he directs the jury to convict and gives Caldigate a two-year prison sentence in Anthony Trollope's *John Caldigate*.

Matthew Loyd Bramble   Welsh bachelor landowner, who leads a family expedition through Bristol, Bath, London, Edinburgh, and Glasgow; he sends his correspondent Dr. Lewis reports on scenes, manners, and customs of places visited; he discovers his footman Humphry Clinker is really his natural son; he arranges the affairs of his friend Baynard after the death of Baynard's wife, and he agrees to marriages by his sister, his niece, and his natural son in Tobias Smollett's *The Expedition of Humphry Clinker*.

Tabitha Bramble   Forty-five-year-old sister of Matthew Bramble; she flirts with every available gentleman she encounters during the family expedition; she is forced by Matthew to choose between her dog, Chowder, and continuing on the expedition; she finally marries in Tobias Smollett's *The Expedition of Humphry Clinker*.

Dowager Countess of Brambledown   Eccentric patron of Valentine Blyth in Wilkie Collins's *Hide and Seek*.

Bran   Huge British mastiff, beloved pet of Raphael Aben-Ezra; she travels with her despairing master and leads him back to a belief in human nature in Charles Kingsley's *Hypatia*.

Elias Brand   A credulous, pedantic parson, whose disparaging, false report of Clarissa Harlowe's behavior at the Smiths' boardinghouse keeps the family from relenting in Samuel Richardson's *Clarissa: or, The History of a Young Lady*.

Lord Alan Brandir   Lorna Doone's relative, murdered by Carver Doone in R. D. Blackmore's *Lorna Doone*.

Mrs. Brandley   Woman in whose house in Richmond Estella lives after returning from the Continent; many of Estella's suitors call there, exasperating Pip Pirrip, in Charles Dickens's *Great Expectations*.

Colonel Brandon   Worthy man of thirty-five and the survivor of an unhappy romance; he punishes John Willoughby for the seduction of his ward, Miss Williams, and offers the disinherited Edward Ferrars a living so that Edward may marry; he falls in love with and eventually marries Marianne Dashwood in Jane Austen's *Sense and Sensibility*.

Caroline Brandon   Gentle, loving professional nurse known as the Little Sister; lured into a false marriage by "Dr. Brandon" (Doctor Firmin) in her youth, she expiates this sin and compensates for the death of her infant son by consistently protecting the interests of Dr. Firmin's legitimate son, Philip Firmin, in William Makepeace Thackeray's *The Adventures of Philip on His Way through the World*.

Dorcas Brandon   Grave beauty, proud and solemn, who believes that the family tradition of wicked men and brave and suffering women continues in her generation; engaged to marry Mark Wylder, she loves Stanley Lake, whom she marries when Wylder disappears, in spite of Rachel Lake's warning of Stanley's corruption; Stanley confesses his crime to her in order to coerce her into giving him money to pay blackmail to the lawyer Josiah

Larkin; after Stanley dies, she and Rachel travel abroad together in J. Sheridan Le Fanu's *Wylder's Hand*.

Emma Brandon   Heiress who nearly yields to the twin temptations represented by the Roman Catholic church and the reprobate Mark Gardner in Charlotte Yonge's *Heartsease*.

Julius (Uncle Lorne) Brandon   An elderly relative who must, according to the will, be kept at Brandon Hall; he is mistaken by the narrator of the story, Charles de Cresseron, for the ghost of Uncle Lorne; he believes himself a prophet; he predicts the death and the return of Mark Wylder in J. Sheridan Le Fanu's *Wylder's Hand*.

Lucy Brandon   William Brandon's niece, who believes in the virtue of Paul Clifford and helps him escape from an Australian penal colony to America in Edward Bulwer-Lytton's *Paul Clifford*.

Lady Mary Brandon   Dorcas's mother, beautiful and kind but sad because of an unhappy marriage; she died young before the action of the story begins in J. Sheridan Le Fanu's *Wylder's Hand*.

William Brandon   Hanging judge and uncle of Lucy Brandon; he condemns Paul Clifford to death despite his knowledge that Clifford is his son in Edward Bulwer-Lytton's *Paul Clifford*.

Margaret Brandt   Daughter of Peter the Magician; she is betrothed but not wed to Elias's son Gerard; she bears his son and works in Rotterdam as a doctor's assistant, then washerwoman; hearing Gerard preach, she lures him out of his hermit cave and establishes him as pastor of Gouda; she rescues their son from the plague at Deventer School and dies of the plague in Gerard's arms in Charles Reade's *The Cloister and the Hearth*.

Peter "the Magician" Brandt   Pedantic old scholar of Sevenbergen, who plots Gerard's escape from a prison tower, suffers a paralytic stroke, and dies after a vision of Gerard sore-disfigured, in a boat on a great river in Charles Reade's *The Cloister and the Hearth*.

Mr. Branghton   Forty-year-old nephew of Madame Duval; he is contemptuous of all foreigners in Frances Burney's *Evelina*.

Biddy Branghton   Eldest daughter of Mr. Branghton; she is a nineteen-year-old silly woman of fashion who pursues Mr. Smith for a husband in Frances Burney's *Evelina*.

Polly Branghton   Younger daughter of Mr. Branghton; aged seventeen, she is ignorant but good-natured; she pursues Mr. Brown for a husband in Frances Burney's *Evelina*.

Tom Branghton   Eldest son of Mr. Branghton; twenty years old, he is foolish and spends his time tormenting his sisters in Frances Burney's *Evelina*.

Biddy Brannigan   The maid of John Melmoth's uncle; she recounts the Melmoth family's complicity in Cromwell's carnage against the Irish in Charles Maturin's *Melmoth the Wanderer*.

Branston   Butler at Knowl in J. Sheridan Le Fanu's *Uncle Silas*.

Sally Brass   Tall, gaunt sister of Sampson Brass; she is hard and merciless, lacking Sampson's cowardice; she conspires in the plot to frame Kit Nubbles and is cruel to her servant girl, the Marchioness, in Charles Dickens's *The Old Curiosity Shop*.

Sampson Brass   Tall, angular, and cowardly lawyer, who is at Daniel Quilp's beck and call, assists Quilp in his villainy and constantly sings his praises, hires Dick Swiveller as a clerk, and frames Kit Nubbles for theft in Charles Dickens's *The Old Curiosity Shop*.

Carry Brattle   Beloved daughter of Jacob Brattle; victim of a seducer, she is turned out of her home and becomes a prostitute; aided by Frank Fenwick, she is at last restored to her father, and they are reconciled in Anthony Trollope's *The Vicar of Bullhampton*.

Fanny Brattle   Younger daughter of Jacob Brattle; she supports her parents loyally when her brother Sam is accused of murder in Anthony Trollope's *The Vicar of Bullhampton*.

George Brattle   Prosperous, tight-fisted son of Jacob Brattle; he reluctantly puts up bail for his brother, Sam; he refuses to give shelter to his sister Carry in Anthony Trollope's *The Vicar of Bullhampton*.

Jacob Brattle   Cross-grained, moody, but hard-working miller at Bullhampton sorely beset by troubles when his son Sam is accused of murdering Farmer Trumbull; the Marquis of Trowbridge demands that the Brattles be evicted from the mill; Brattle also endures shame and sorrow for his seduced daughter, Carry, abandoned to a life of prostitution; father and daughter are finally reunited in Anthony Trollope's *The Vicar of Bullhampton*.

Maggie Brattle   Heroic, self-sacrificing mother of Carry, the daughter seduced and turned out of the house; she also bravely endures the anguish of having her son Sam wrongly accused of murder in Anthony Trollope's *The Vicar of Bullhampton*.

Sam Brattle   Youngest son of the miller, Jacob Brattle; he is the prime suspect in the murder of Farmer Trumbull, hounded, imprisoned and brought to trial; he is found not guilty thanks to the efforts and testimony of the vicar, Frank Fenwick, in Anthony Trollope's *The Vicar of Bullhampton*.

Anna Braun   German teacher to Lucy Snowe and Paulina Home in Charlotte Brontë's *Villette*.

Miss Bravassa   Member of the Vincent Crummles Theatrical Company in Charles Dickens's *The Life and Adventures of Nicholas Nickleby*.

Baron Brawl   Loud and arrogant but eminent judge who deigns to dine at Sir Henry Harcout's splendid house in Anthony Trollope's *The Bertrams*. He appears briefly as the (old) Duke of Omnium's guest in *Framley Parsonage*.

Sir Bernard Bray   Member of Parliament and cousin to Mr. Evelyn; he takes Hugh Trevor under his wing and later deserts him to join his previous political opponents in Thomas Holcroft's *The Adventures of Hugh Trevor*.

James, Marquis of Bray   The flirtatious, flamboyantly dressed son of the Duke and Duchess of Donkeyton; he runs for a seat in Parliament against John Jorrocks and loses in Robert Surtees's *Hillingdon Hall*.

Madeline Bray   Loving daughter of Walter Bray; she is willing to sacrifice herself in marriage to Arthur Gride in order to save her father; the plot is foiled by Nicholas Nickleby, who learns of it in his work for the Cheeryble brothers; she marries Nicholas in Charles Dickens's *The Life and Adventures of Nicholas Nickleby*.

Walter Bray   Old man who owes money to Arthur Gride and is willing to sell his daughter to the miser in a marriage arranged by Ralph Nickleby in order to retire his debts and be released from prison in Charles Dickens's *The Life and Adventures of Nicholas Nickleby*.

Breakspeare   Editor of a provincial newspaper who supports Dyce Lashmar's political campaign in George Gissing's *Our Friend the Charlatan*.

Angus Breck   Member of Rob Roy MacGregor's clan in Sir Walter Scott's *Rob Roy*.

Ezekiel Brehgert   Influential city banker, a Jewish widower with grown children; despite her parents' horror and his much-dyed hair, Georgiana Longestaffe accepts his proposal of marriage; caught up in the financial whirlwind of Augustus Melmotte's downfall, he finds he can no longer promise her a London house, and she breaks the engagement in Anthony Trollope's *The Way We Live Now*.

Countess Brenhilda Beloved daughter of the Knight and Lady of Aspramonte and the large, handsome, loving, Amazonian wife of Count Robert of Paris; trained early in arms, she accompanies her husband on the crusade; she is endangered by Caesar Nicephorus Briennius's pursuit at Constantinople in Sir Walter Scott's *Count Robert of Paris*.

Gladys, Zoe, and Emily Brennan Unmarried ladies in their thirties; they are laughed at for their yearly trips to the Sherbourne to be in society in George Moore's *A Drama in Muslin*.

Mrs. Brent Mistress of Sir George Tufto in William Makepeace Thackeray's *Vanity Fair*.

Earl of Brentford One-time Privy Seal and now backroom political power, at whose townhouse Phineas Finn meets eminent people; when the marriage of his daughter, Lady Laura (Standish), to Robert Kennedy breaks down, he is desolate and takes her abroad; his long quarrel with his headstrong son, Lord Chiltern, is healed by Chiltern's marriage to Violet Effingham in Anthony Trollope's *Phineas Finn*. He protects Lady Laura further from her husband in *Phineas Redux*.

Duchess of Brentham Wife of the duke and mother of Lady Corisande Brentham and Lord Bertram Brenthan in Benjamin Disraeli's *Lothair*.

Duke of Brentham Father of Lady Corisande Brentham and Lord Bertram Brentham in Benjamin Disraeli's *Lothair*.

Lord Bertram Brentham Oxford friend of Lothair and heir to the dukedom of Brentham in Benjamin Disraeli's *Lothair*.

Lady Corisande Brentham Daughter of the Duke and Duchess of Brentham; Lothair falls in love with her soon after their meeting; she represents the true England that Lothair finally chooses in Benjamin Disraeli's *Lothair*.

Frank Bret Good-looking tenor in Dick Lennox's acting company; he becomes Lucy Leslie's love after Dick becomes interested in Kate Ede in George Moore's *A Mummer's Wife*.

Dr. Bretton Mrs. Bretton's husband and father to John Graham; he dies young in Charlotte Brontë's *Villette*.

Dr. John Graham Bretton Physician attending Mme. Beck's pupils; Lucy Snowe has known him in her youth as Graham Bretton; he falls in love with Ginevra Fanshawe but later is happily married to Paulina Home in Charlotte Brontë's *Villette*.

Louisa Bretton Devoted mother of John Graham Bretton and godmother to Lucy Snowe; she is a sensible and kind woman, who takes care of Lucy when she becomes ill during a summer vacation from teaching in Villette in Charlotte Brontë's *Villette*.

Brewer Husband of Roxana for eight years; he is a jolly but weak and empty-headed man, who lets his business go to ruin; he abandons Roxana but later emerges in the French military, only to die in the Battle of Mons in Daniel Defoe's *The Fortunate Mistress*.

Brewer's Brother-In-Law Husband of the brewer's sister; he is a charitable man who is moved to pity over the condition of Roxana's children and gets family members to help provide support for them in Daniel Defoe's *The Fortunate Mistress*.

Brewer's Sister Sister-in-law to Roxana; she refuses to take in Roxana and the brewer's children after the brewer abandons his family in Daniel Defoe's *The Fortunate Mistress*.

Dr. Brewer Cambridge-educated physician, whose unprofitable practice has led him to innkeeping in Richard Graves's *The Spiritual Quixote*.

Mr. Brewer Young man who functions as a buffer at the Veneering dinner parties in Charles Dickens's *Our Mutual Friend*.

Mrs. Brewer Amiable wife of the innkeeper Dr. Brewer in Richard Graves's *The Spiritual Quixote*.

Peter Brian Gardener at Belmont who reports to the other servants he has seen Lieutenant Puddock and Becky Chattesworth kiss in the garden in J. Sheridan Le Fanu's *The House by the Churchyard*.

Tom Brice Groom at Bartram-Haugh who Maud Ruthyn erroneously thinks has betrayed her by giving her uncle, Silas Ruthyn, her letter meant for Lady Monica Knollys; Bryce helps Maud escape from Bartram-Haugh the night of Mme. de la Rougierre's murder; later he marries Meg Hawkes in J. Sheridan Le Fanu's *Uncle Silas*.

Jefferson Brick War correspondent for the *New York Rowdy Journal*, who is exceedingly youthful in appearance in Charles Dickens's *The Life and Adventures of Martin Chuzzlewit*.

Mrs. Jefferson Brick A child in appearance but a matron with two children in Charles Dickens's *The Life and Adventures of Martin Chuzzlewit*.

Bride Daughter of Hall-ward; when the affections of her betrothed, Face-of-god, shift to Sun-beam, and after she is wounded during the war in Silver-dale, she marries Folk-might in William Morris's *The Roots of the Mountains*.

Constance Bride   Secretary to Lady Ogram; she likes Dyce Lashmar and pretends to be engaged to him at Lady Ogram's command but manifests her independence by rejecting him when she comes into an inheritance in George Gissing's *Our Friend the Charlatan*.

Sue Bridehead   The intelligent but emotionally immature cousin and lover of Jude Fawley; she marries the aging schoolmaster Richard Phillotson out of a misguided sense of duty, then later leaves him to live with Jude, by whom she bears two children; after the tragic deaths of the children, she returns to Phillotson although still in love with Jude in Thomas Hardy's *Jude the Obscure*.

Alice Bridgenorth   Major Bridgenorth's daughter, who is cared for in the household of Lady Peveril until removed by her father during the Restoration years; taken to London by her uncle, Edward Christian, she is intended as part of a political plot to be made the mistress of King Charles II; rescued by Julian Peveril, she marries Julian in Sir Walter Scott's *Peveril of the Peak*.

Major Ralph Bridgenorth   Presbyterian friend and neighbor of Sir Geoffrey Peveril; he was a justice of the peace during the Protectorate and pursues Charlotte de la Tramouille, the Countess of Derby, for revenge in Sir Walter Scott's *Peveril of the Peak*.

Bridget   Mistress of Sir Stephen Penrhyn both before and after his marriage to Eleanor Raymond; she hates Eleanor and her children; she marries Sir Stephen after Eleanor's death in Caroline Norton's *Stuart of Dunleath*.

Bridget   Widow Wadman's maid, courted by Corporal Trim (James Butler) simultaneously with Captain Toby Shandy's courtship of her mistress in Laurence Sterne's *The Life and Opinions of Tristram Shandy, Gentleman*.

Bridget   Ex-abbess of St. Catherine Nunnery; she becomes a conspirator for Queen Mary of Scotland and the Catholic church in Sir Walter Scott's *The Abbot*.

Mr. Bridgnorth   Lawyer who undertakes Jem Wilson's defense and counsels his family and Mary Barton in Elizabeth Gaskell's *Mary Barton*.

Francis Bridle   Protagonist in Partridge's story proving the existence of ghosts in Henry Fielding's *The History of Tom Jones*.

Nicephorus Briennius   Anna Comnena's handsome husband; though he became Caesar through his marriage, he is indifferent to his wife and pursues Brenhilda at Constantinople; haughty and ambitious, he conspires

to become emperor in Sir Walter Scott's *Count Robert of Paris*.

Monna Brigada   Cousin of Bardo de' Bardi; she reveals to Romola de' Bardi that her brother is not dead but a Dominican friar in George Eliot's *Romola*.

Briggs   Stony young roommate of little Paul Dombey at Dr. Blimber's boarding school in Charles Dickens's *Dombey and Son*.

Mr. Briggs   One of Cecilia Beverley's trustees; a miser who has made money from a life of business, he insults Cecilia with a shabby room when she seeks refuge with him in Frances Burney's *Cecilia*.

Mr. Briggs   The London solicitor who accompanies Richard Mason to interrupt the wedding of Mr. Rochester and Jane Eyre in Charlotte Brontë's *Jane Eyre*.

Arabella Briggs   Faithful companion to Miss Matilda Crawley, who ridicules her but leaves her a legacy; Becky (Sharp) Crawley retains her as a companion to aid in maintaining a façade of respectability and defrauds her of her money in William Makepeace Thackeray's *Vanity Fair*.

Mrs. Brightwalton   Society matron at whose dinner party Jocelyn Pierston improves his acquaintance with Nichola Pine-Avon in Thomas Hardy's *The Well-Beloved*.

Brightwell   Educated and artistic young man, who befriends Caleb Williams while the two are in jail; his death while awaiting trial demonstrates the unfairness of the British system of holding people in jail for extended periods of time without trial in William Godwin's *Caleb Williams*.

Brilliard   Friend of Philander and a penniless cadet, who marries Sylvia in order to bar her father's interference in her affair with Philander; he falls in love with her himself, accuses Octavio of treason to prevent him from marrying her, and eventually assists her in duping Octavio and Alonzo out of their money in Aphra Behn's *Love Letters Between a Nobleman and His Sister*.

John (Jack) Brimblecombe   Schoolmaster's fat son, who is intimidated in his schooldays by young Amyas Leigh; he loves Rose Salterne and is invited by Frank Leigh to join the Brotherhood of the Rose, of which he finally proves to be a worthy member, sailing to rescue Rose from Don Guzman de Soto in Charles Kingsley's *Westward Ho!*.

Vindex Brimblecombe   Stern yet kindhearted master of Bideford grammar school who flogs Amyas Leigh as a way of caring for the fatherless boy, and whose head Amyas breaks in Charles Kingsley's *Westward Ho!*.

Arnold Brinkworth   Naive youth who, because Geoffrey Delamayn saved him from drowning, trusts him; he represents himself as Anne Silvester's husband when he meets her at an inn, bringing Geoffrey's excuses; charged with being Anne's husband by "Scotch marriage," Arnold finds his later marriage to Blanche Lundie in jeopardy in Wilkie Collins's *Man and Wife*.

Miss Brinville   Young pupil of Juliet Granville on the harp; she is dropped by Sir Lyell Sycamore in favor of Juliet in Frances Burney's *The Wanderer*.

Brisk   Would-be seducer of Mercy; he pretends to love her in John Bunyan's *The Pilgrim's Progress From this World to That Which Is to Come*.

Benjamin Britain (Little Britain)   Doctor Jeddler's cheerful manservant, who marries Clemency Newcome for friendship; they become owners of the public house The Nutmeg Grater in Charles Dickens's *The Battle of Life*.

Mr. Brittle   Tea and china merchant to Lady Juliana Douglas after her return from Scotland to London; he is eager to relieve her of her new wealth in Susan Ferrier's *Marriage*.

Mr. Brittlereed   Skillful cricketer who joins Jack Neverbend at the crease and helps the Britannula side beat the British in an epic struggle in Anthony Trollope's *The Fixed Period*.

Sergeant Brittson   English borderer entrusted by Captain Stawarth Bolton with the care of Elspeth Glendinning and her home in Sir Walter Scott's *The Monastery*.

Mrs. Brixham   Major Pendennis's landlady, who is cheated by his valet Morgan in William Makepeace Thackeray's *The History of Pendennis*.

Mrs. Broad   Wife of the Reverend Broad; she is socially ambitious for her children in Mark Rutherford's *The Revolution In Tanner's Lane*.

John Broad   Minister of Tanner's Lane Chapel in the village of Cowfold in 1840, who rules his community with his hypocritical opinions; he is paralyzed when he tries to eject George and Isaac Allen from the chapel in Mark Rutherford's *The Revolution In Tanner's Lane*.

Priscilla Broad   The Reverend and Mrs. Broad's daughter, aged seventeen in 1840, who marries George Allen despite her parents' opposition in Mark Rutherford's *The Revolution In Tanner's Lane*.

Thomas Broad   The Reverend and Mrs. Broad's eldest child, aged eighteen in 1840, who is sent to London to remove him from Fanny Allen, and who attempts to seduce Marie Pauline Coleman in Mark Rutherford's *The Revolution In Tanner's Lane*.

Tryphosa Broad   Youngest child of the Reverend and Mrs. Broad in Mark Rutherford's *The Revolution In Tanner's Lane*.

Dr. Broadbent   A kind man and an eloquent speaker at a Bible Society meeting in Charlotte Brontë's *Shirley*.

Bailie Broadfoot   Alderman of Leith, Scotland, and town guide to Archibald Douglas and his niece and foster daughter, Mary Douglas, on her trip to be reunited with her mother in Susan Ferrier's *Marriage*.

Miss Broadhurst   Intelligent, sensible English heiress and friend to Grace Nugent; she is intended as a wife for Lord Colambre but marries Mr. Berryl instead in Maria Edgeworth's *The Absentee*.

King of Brobdingnag   Enlightened monarch, who questions his guest and plaything, Lemuel Gulliver, about English institutions in Jonathan Swift's *Travels into Several Remote Nations of the World. In Four Parts. By Lemuel Gulliver*.

Marie Broc   An imbecile pupil at Mme. Beck's school, a cretin who is looked after during the long summer vacation by Lucy Snowe and partially personifies her own mental state in Charlotte Brontë's *Villette*.

Signor Brochio   Italian mercenary hired by Montoni; he tries to seduce Emily St. Aubert in Ann Radcliffe's *The Mysteries of Udolpho*.

Lord Brock   Prime Minister succeeded by Lord de Terrier in Anthony Trollope's *Framley Parsonage*. He is the illustrious leader of the Liberal party in *Can You Forgive Her?*. Mrs. Finn recalls him as a model statesman in *The Prime Minister*.

Decimus Brock   Somerset rector who takes as pupil Allan Armadale and witnesses the strange friendship between Allan and Ozias Midwinter in Wilkie Collins's *Armadale*.

Miss Brocklehurst   Mr. Brocklehurst's eldest daughter, whose elegant dress contrasts sharply with the homespun smocks of the pupils at Lowood School in Charlotte Brontë's *Jane Eyre*.

Mrs. Brocklehurst   Mr. Brocklehurst's nosy wife, who comes to inspect Lowood School in her best lace and linen in Charlotte Brontë's *Jane Eyre*.

Augusta Brocklehurst Mr. Brocklehurst's second daughter, who amazes the pupils of Lowood School with the finery of her clothes in Charlotte Brontë's *Jane Eyre*.

Broughton Brocklehurst Mr. Brocklehurst's youngest child, whose piety is amply rewarded with treats in Charlotte Brontë's *Jane Eyre*.

Naomi Brocklehurst Mr. Brocklehurst's mother, whose memory is commemorated in a stone inscription over the door of Lowood School in Charlotte Brontë's *Jane Eyre*.

Robert Brocklehurst Humorless clergyman and treasurer of Lowood School, a semi-charity institution which, in the name of humility and fortitude, he controls in a severely parsimonious fashion in Charlotte Brontë's *Jane Eyre*.

Theodore Brocklehurst Mr. Brocklehurst's third child in Charlotte Brontë's *Jane Eyre*.

Mrs. Brodrick Stepmother of Isabel Brodrick; caught up in caring for her own large family, she is anxious to see Isabel married and well out of sight in Anthony Trollope's *Cousin Henry*.

Isabel Brodrick Favorite niece of Indefer Jones, who leaves his estate to her in the last of several wills; the will being lost, his nephew Henry Jones inherits; she refuses to marry Henry, but at last the missing will establishes her as rightful heir, and she marries her true love, William Owen, in Anthony Trollope's *Cousin Henry*.

Mr. Brogley Bill-broker and owner of a second-hand furniture shop; creditor to Solomon Gills, he is about to execute on the overdue debt but is forestalled by Paul Dombey's payment of the bill in Charles Dickens's *Dombey and Son*.

Laird of Broken-girth-flow Jacobite who complains that the Union has ruined Scottish agriculture, though his is a barren district, in Sir Walter Scott's *The Black Dwarf*.

Mr. Bromley Burly, kindly medical student, who tends to Alton Locke, paying for a bed for him when Alton collapses after having been thrown out of his mother's house in Charles Kingsley's *Alton Locke*.

Bronzebeard Faithful colonel of the guards; he helps the king defeat the King of Borsagrass in George MacDonald's *The Princess and Curdie*.

Lord Brooke Friend of Sir Philip Sidney; he delivers letters from Lord Leicester to Matilda in Sophia Lee's *The Recess*.

Miss Brooke Daughter of the dissenting former Birmingham baker; she marries Captain James, to the distress of Lady Ludlow in Elizabeth Gaskell's *My Lady Ludlow*.

Mr. Brooke A dissenter and a Birmingham baker, who buys a neighboring estate where he builds "Yeast House"; his religion is more distressing than his former trade to Lady Ludlow in Elizabeth Gaskell's *My Lady Ludlow*.

Arthur Brooke The old uncle of Celia and Dorothea Brooke; he is a typical English squire and the owner of Tipton Grange; he invites Will Ladislaw to visit Lowick without consulting Dorothea and asks Will to remain in the area to help with his unsuccessful campaign for Parliament in George Eliot's *Middlemarch*.

Celia (Kitty) Brooke The pretty younger sister of Dorothea; she does not understand her sister's intellect or effort to help the poor; after she marries Sir James Chettam and they have a son, Celia is totally enraptured by her child in George Eliot's *Middlemarch*.

Dorothea (Dodo) Brooke Intelligent, idealistic heroine bent on improving the lives of those in need, originally through the construction of cottages for the poor; she marries Edward Casaubon, a much older man who she mistakingly assumes will teach her about his studies in classical learning; after Casaubon's death, she marries his cousin, Will Ladislaw, a man closer to her own age and temperment in George Eliot's *Middlemarch*.

Sir James Brooke English officer stationed in Ireland; he befriends Lord Colambre and warns him to stay away from the conniving Lady Dashfort and her daughter Lady Isabella in Maria Edgeworth's *The Absentee*.

Brooker Formerly a clerk to Ralph Nickleby; he acts as Smike's father in order to have the boy confined at Squeers's Dotheboys Hall and out of Ralph's life; Brooker's evidence helps prove that Smike is Nickleby's illegitimate son when Nickleby will not help him financially in Charles Dickens's *The Life and Adventures of Nicholas Nickleby*.

Grace Brookes Eldest daughter of James Brookes, whose disapproval of her young officer drives her to marry their wealthy neighbor Mr. Berkins; she entertains for her sister in George Moore's *Spring Days*.

Aunt Hester Brookes Spinster sister of James Brookes; she counsels his daughters with religious advice in George Moore's *Spring Days*.

James Brookes Wealthy, self-pitying widower, who worries about his three marriageable daughters but has not cultivated society; he objects to "villa" commoners' associating with his daughters; he is unable to keep money from dominating their marriage arrangements; he finally sells his house to keep his daughters from becoming subjects of scandal in George Moore's *Spring Days*.

Maggie Brookes   James Brookes's youngest daughter, who falls in love with Frank Escott, among others; her jealousy of Frank's model and her father's awkward insistence on marriage settlements with Lord Mount Rorke derail the marriage plans in George Moore's *Spring Days*.

Mary Brookes   Wife and former mistress of Willy Brookes; she has a crippled child, not Willy's, who charms Frank Escott in George Moore's *Spring Days*.

Sally Brookes   James Brookes's second daughter, a headstrong flirt who likes Jimmy Measons, one of the "villa" persons her father dislikes in George Moore's *Spring Days*.

Willy Brookes   James Brookes's only son, who is too methodical to work with his father; he fails in several businesses; he considers himself unlucky but has a happy secret marriage with his former mistress; he is a school friend and confidant of Frank Escott in George Moore's *Spring Days*.

Reggie Brooklyn   Young friend of Eleanor Burgoyne and Edward Manisty; he is fondly protective of Eleanor's well-being in Mrs. Humphry Ward's *Eleanor*.

Captain Brooks   Father of Beatrice and Owen Brooks and guardian of Mariana, the daughter of his wife, Leonora Aldi; a good, kind man, he keeps up a happy home for the children after his wife dies; he rejects Beatrice when he thinks she has married without his permission in Caroline Norton's *Lost and Saved*.

Mr. Brooks   A rag-and-bottle merchant in the last stages of dropsy, who is fearful of death and a tenant of Mrs. Jupp; Ernest Pontifex, as clergyman, attempts to help him in Samuel Butler's *The Way of All Flesh*.

Mr. Brooks   Pieman who used cats in sausages in an anecdote by Sam Weller in Charles Dickens's *The Posthumous Papers of the Pickwick Club*.

Mrs. Brooks   Bedfordshire neighbor whose sneers and innuendos become pleasantries once Pamela Andrews is raised by marriage from the servant class in Samuel Richardson's *Pamela, or Virtue Rewarded*.

Mrs. Brooks (Tacchi)   Forty-year-old widow with no children, who becomes Giacomo Tacchi's second wife in Mark Rutherford's *Miriam's Schooling*.

Beatrice Brooks   Heroine, who loves Montague Treherne when she is still a child and later marries him in a secret ceremony because his inheritance hinges on secrecy; she is unaware that the ceremony is also a mock one; Treherne leaves her pregnant and alone; she works to support herself and her child, who dies at the age of two; she returns to success and marries a rich marquis in Caroline Norton's *Lost and Saved*.

Owen Brooks   Brother of Beatrice and son of Captain Brooks; he joins the navy; he loves and helps his sister in Caroline Norton's *Lost and Saved*.

Broscomin   Ruler of a small principality who wants to be king of Ginsky; he is unorthodox and sleazy in Eliza Haywood's *Adventures of Eovaai, Princess of Ijaveo*.

Father Brosnan   Firebrand sympathizer with the tenantry in Galway involved in struggles with the landlords; he makes Florian Jones swear not to tell his father what he knows of the conspirators in Anthony Trollope's *The Landleaguers*.

Two Brothers   Knights who, with Adonos, overthrow the giants tyrannizing their father's kingdom; they teach Anodos brotherhood and courage in George Macdonald's *Phantasies*.

Bishop of Brotherton   Mild and urbane bishop greatly perplexed by the wild stories circulating about the dean, Henry Lovelace; he is especially bewildered when the dean throws the Marquis of Brotherton into a fireplace in Anthony Trollope's *Is He Popenjoy?*.

Dowager Marchioness of Brotherton   Ill-tempered defender of her long-absent, malicious eldest son against the claims of her five dutiful children in Anthony Trollope's *Is He Popenjoy?*.

Marchioness of Brotherton   An aging Italian widow who speaks no English; the date of her marriage to the marquis is the object of speculation and investigation in Anthony Trollope's *Is He Popenjoy?*.

Frederick Augustus, Marquis of Brotherton   Idle and self-indulgent landowner, who returns from Europe with an Italian widow he claims is his wife and a son and heir, Lord Popenjoy; he summarily evicts his brother, Lord George Germain, from the family estate, Manor Cross; the eventual deaths of the child and of the marquis enable Lord George and his own child to succeed to the titles and estate in Anthony Trollope's *Is He Popenjoy?*.

Belinda Brough   Affected daughter of John Brough in William Makepeace Thackeray's *The History of Samuel Titmarsh and the Great Hoggarty Diamond*.

Isabella Brough   Blindly devoted wife of John Brough in William Makepeace Thackeray's *The History of Samuel Titmarsh and the Great Hoggarty Diamond.*

John Brough   Head of the Independent West Diddlesex Fire and Life Insurance Co.; reputedly of vast wealth, he is a swindler who decamps, leaving his dupe Samuel Titmarsh to answer for the collapse of the association in William Makepeace Thackeray's *The History of Samuel Titmarsh and the Great Hoggarty Diamond.*

Dobbs Broughton   Unsavory partner of Augustus Musselboro and Mrs. Van Siever in a moneylending business; he kills himself after bankruptcy in Anthony Trollope's *The Last Chronicle of Barset.*

Maria Broughton   Wife of the shady stockbroker Dobbs Broughton, after whose death she marries his partner, Augustus Musselboro, in Anthony Trollope's *The Last Chronicle of Barset.*

Jessie Broun   Mother of the bastard child of the Master (James Durie); she stones Henry Durie for betraying the Master; she is supported by a pension delivered on Henry's authority in Robert Louis Stevenson's *The Master of Ballantrae: A Winter's Tale.*

Nicholas Broune   Influential newspaper editor, who assists the literary career of Lady Carbury; although he recognizes her faults of character and fears her profligate son, he becomes fascinated and proposes marriage; her generous refusal cements the friendship and leads later to a marriage of mutual affection in Anthony Trollope's *The Way We Live Now.* The Brounes appear briefly as guests at Gatherum Castle in *The Prime Minister.*

Mr. Browborough   Tory Member for Tankerville for three Parliaments, unseated by Phineas Finn and later tried for bribery in Anthony Trollope's *Phineas Redux.*

John Browdie   Miller from Yorkshire who marries Matilda Price and who helps Nicholas Nickleby break up Dotheboys Hall school run by Wackford Squeers in Charles Dickens's *The Life and Adventures of Nicholas Nickleby.*

Brown   One of the female servants of the Murrays of Horton Lodge in Anne Brontë's *Agnes Grey.*

Captain Brown   Retired officer, whose honest and generous spirit despite his lack of means overcomes the Cranford prejudice toward men; he dies saving a young girl from a train and is mourned by all in Elizabeth Gaskell's *Cranford.*

Dr. Brown   Exemplary ex-carpenter, who rises above his proletarian beginnings to become a rich and respected Cambridge man, mentioned by Dean Winnstay in Charles Kingsley's *Alton Locke.*

Mr. Brown   A grave, elderly gentleman in Brussels, who finds William Crimsworth, with his letter of introduction from Hunsden, a teaching post at M. Pelet's school in Charlotte Brontë's *The Professor.*

Mr. Brown   London haberdasher who is the object of Polly Branghton's marital designs in Frances Burney's *Evelina.*

Mrs. Brown   London madam who hires the newly arrived innocent country girl Fanny Hill and lures her into prostitution in John Cleland's *Memoirs of a Woman of Pleasure.*

Mrs. Brown   Maid at Beech Park, the residence of Frederick, Lord Lindore and his sister, Lady Juliana Douglas, in Susan Ferrier's *Marriage.*

Parson Brown   Minister to whom Gregory Grooby entrusts the care of his illegitimate son, Gregory Glen, in Robert Bage's *Hermsprong.*

Sir Ferdinando Brown   New governor of Britannula, an ex-British colony off New Zealand, who takes the reins of office from John Neverbend when the British navy combined with the local populace puts an end to Neverbend's compulsory euthanasia program for sixty-eight-year-olds in Anthony Trollope's *The Fixed Period.*

George Brown, Sheriff of Calstoun   One of the four Scottish counsels to James Stewart; he is doubtful of the advantages of David Balfour's testifying in the Appin murder trial in Robert Louis Stevenson's *Catriona.*

Goody Brown   Envious villager, who was thrashing Molly Seagrim in the churchyard brawl when Tom Jones interceded in Henry Fielding's *The History of Tom Jones.*

Jessie Brown   Younger daughter of Captain Brown; she marries her early love, Major Gordon, after the deaths of her father and elder sister in Elizabeth Gaskell's *Cranford.*

John Brown   Harmless, drunk Scottish *Flying Scud* sailor killed by Captain Joe Wicks; Mac assumes his identity in Robert Louis Stevenson's *The Wrecker.*

John Brown   A villager whose son, Charley, is injured by Lord Froth's coach and restored to health by Bryan Perdue, Patrick Mac Neale, Alexander Gordon, and Henry Fairman in Thomas Holcroft's *The Memoirs of Bryan Perdue.*

John Brown   Sturdy Berkshire squire and justice of the peace, who sends his son Tom to Rugby School to learn to become a Christian gentleman in Thomas Hughes's *Tom Brown's Schooldays*. He watches over his son's progress anxiously in *Tom Brown at Oxford*.

Mary Brown   The sickly elder daughter of Captain Brown; her care is the cheerfully borne burden of her father and sister in Elizabeth Gaskell's *Cranford*.

Nancy Brown   An old widow, afflicted with religious melancholy and nearly blind, living on the grounds of Horton Lodge; she is befriended by Agnes Grey in Anne Brontë's *Agnes Grey*.

Tom Brown   Eldest child of Squire Brown; he goes to Rugby School in the 1830s and becomes a scapegrace but reforms morally and spiritually under the influence of George Arthur and Doctor Arnold in Thomas Hughes's *Tom Brown's Schooldays*. He learns much about the problems of society while at St. Ambrose's College, Oxford, before marrying Mary Porter in *Tom Brown at Oxford*.

Lieutenant Vanbest Brown   Smuggler who is involved in Francis Kennedy's murder and Henry Bertram's kidnapping and is killed in a smuggling raid; Henry is given his name by the kidnappers in Sir Walter Scott's *Guy Mannering*.

Brown Man of the Moors   Legendary character, the sighting of whom is an omen of bad tidings; Hobbie (Halbert) Elliot and Patrick Earnscliff mistake Elshender (Sir Edward Mauley) for this character and return from hunting to find Hobbie's farm destroyed in Sir Walter Scott's *The Black Dwarf*.

Mrs. Browne   Self-pitying widow, who spoils her worthless son and disregards her selfless daughter in Elizabeth Gaskell's *The Moorland Cottage*.

Edward Browne   Maggie Browne's selfish brother, who forges Mr. Buxton's name; he dies in a shipwreck when fleeing to America in Elizabeth Gaskell's *The Moorland Cottage*.

Maggie Browne   The heroine, who marries Frank Buxton; her courage, loyalty, and selflessness set the example in Elizabeth Gaskell's *The Moorland Cottage*.

Nosey Browne   Bankrupt Cockney owner of a hunting establishment; John Jorrocks hires him as huntsman; his disregard for land boundaries leads Jorrocks onto Squire Cheatum's property in Robert Surtees's *Jorrocks's Jaunts and Jollities*.

Phoebe Browning   The younger and less stern of two spinster sisters; she defends Molly Gibson when appearances are against her in Elizabeth Gaskell's *Wives and Daughters*.

Sally Browning   The senior of the two Browning sisters; she represents local custom and moral tradition in judging Molly Gibson's conduct in Elizabeth Gaskell's *Wives and Daughters*.

Mr. Brownjohn   Corrupt lawyer, who, because as a married man he cannot himself get Medora Glenmorris's inheritance through forced marriage, kidnaps her as a bride for his half brother, Dicky Darnell, in Charlotte Smith's *The Young Philosopher*.

Mr. Brownlow   Old gentleman who takes Oliver Twist home with him after theft charges are dropped against the boy; an old friend of Oliver's father, he had long been searching for Oliver's mother and the boy in Charles Dickens's *Oliver Twist*.

Mrs. Brownlow   Tactful mother of Edith; she helps ease Sir Gregory Marrable's pain when his long-cherished plan to see Edith marry his son is thwarted when the son dies in Anthony Trollope's *The Vicar of Bullhampton*.

Edith Brownlow   Elegant, carefree companion since childhood of sickly Gregory Marrable, whose father has always planned on their marrying in Anthony Trollope's *The Vicar of Bullhampton*.

Dr. Brownside   Dean of Nottingham, whose shallow preaching disillusions Charles Reding with liberal Anglicanism in John Henry Newman's *Loss and Gain*.

John Bruce   Tutor at Trinity College, Dublin; he teaches John Buncle his Unitarian beliefs in Thomas Amory's *The Life of John Buncle, Esq*.

Matthew Bruff   Kindhearted family lawyer of the Verinders; he follows up the whereabouts of the stolen diamond lodged with Septimus Luker; he shows Rachel Verinder that Godfrey Ablewhite's interest in her is entirely mercenary in Wilkie Collins's *The Moonstone. A Romance*.

General Bruges   Military leader of the "Mary Anne" secret societies pledged to promote liberation movements in Europe; he is Lothair's commander when the young heir is convinced to take part in some of the fighting in Italy in Benjamin Disraeli's *Lothair*.

Lady Brumpton   Lady Mary Jones's sister-in-law, who has a weakness for public admiration and cultivates learned company; fatal illness makes her realize her mistaken priorities in Sarah Scott's *A Description of Millenium Hall*.

Baron de Brunne   Character to whom a ghost appears in the story Ludovico reads while watching in the bedroom of the dead Marchioness de Villeroi in Ann Radcliffe's *The Mysteries of Udolpho.*

Bruno   The Warden of Outland's precocious five-year-old son, the younger brother of Sylvie; good and kind, he is the rightful heir of the ruler of Outland; he is sometimes seen as an Outlander, sometimes as a fairy, sometimes as a human child; he is the counterpart of Arthur Forester in Lewis Carroll's *Sylvie and Bruno.* He returns to Outland for Uggug's banquet and is reunited with his father but remains a fairy in *Sylvie and Bruno Concluded.*

Count di Bruno   Olivia di Bruno's husband, murdered by his brother Ferando di Bruno in Ann Radcliffe's *The Italian.*

Ferando di Bruno (Father Schedoni)   Lascivious younger son who kills his brother, Count di Bruno, out of jealousy and greed; he rapes and then marries his sister-in-law, Olivia; mistakenly thinking he murdered Olivia, he takes refuge in the Church as Father Schedoni, the politically ambitious confessor to the Marchesa di Vivaldi; he plots with her to abduct, imprison, and finally kill Ellena Rosalba, who he mistakenly comes to believe is his daughter; imprisoned by the Inquisition, he is poisoned and dies in Ann Radcliffe's *The Italian.*

Olivia di Bruno (Sister Olivia)   Widow of the Count di Bruno; she is raped by, forced to marry, and believed to be killed by her brother-in-law Ferando di Bruno; she escapes his murder attempt to become a nun in the San Stefano convent, where she befriends Ellena Rosalba and helps her to escape with Vincentio di Vivaldi; she retires to a Neapolitan convent, where she is reunited with Ellena and discovered to be her mother in Ann Radcliffe's *The Italian.*

Signor Brunoni   Stage name of the conjuror Sam Brown; he provides the link with Miss Matty Jenkyns's long-lost brother in Elizabeth Gaskell's *Cranford.*

Signora Brunoni   Purveyor of the information that sets in motion the return of Matilda Jenkyns's brother in Elizabeth Gaskell's *Cranford.*

Colonel Brusque   Military man whose elegant entertainment attracts guests of every kind in William Beckford's *Azemia.*

Brussels Courtier Number One   Son of a low-born father who purchased a title; he is welcome in all the fashionable places in Charles Johnstone's *Chrysal: or, The Adventures of a Guinea.*

Brussels Courtier Number Two   Well-born man whose life of pleasure distresses his fortune and debases

his principles in Charles Johnstone's *Chrysal: or, The Adventures of a Guinea.*

Brutus   Brutal enemy of the reformed Tom Robinson; he becomes a tool of Peter Crawley in attempts to kill Tom and George Fielding in Charles Reade's *It Is Never Too Late to Mend.*

Lady Brydehaven   Sara Macallan's aunt; her testimony tended to incriminate Eustace Macallan in his murder trial that precedes the opening of Wilkie Collins's *The Law and the Lady.*

Dr. Hans Emmanuel Bryerly   Swedenborgian friend of Austin Ruthyn and trustee of Maud Ruthyn's estate; he attempts but fails to remove her from Silas Ruthyn's guardianship; he is somewhat mysterious and intimidating, but a true friend to Maud; later he becomes manager of her estate in J. Sheridan Le Fanu's *Uncle Silas.*

Mrs. Bubb   Landlady of a lodging house in George Gissing's *The Town Traveller.*

Madam Bubble   Witch who tries to tempt Stand-fast and the other pilgrims in Christiana's party to commit various sins in John Bunyan's *The Pilgrim's Progress From this World to That Which Is to Come.*

Mr. Bucket   Steady detective officer, who first investigates the death of Nemo (Captain Hawdon), then pursues Mr. Gridley, and then cleverly finds Lady Dedlock and solves the murder of Mr. Tulkinghorn in Charles Dickens's *Bleak House.*

Lord Buckhurst   Generous but impulsive aristocratic friend of Harry Coningsby at Eton; he becomes a member of the "New Generation" of young English politicians in Benjamin Disraeli's *Coningsby; or, The New Generation.*

George (Steenie) Villiers, Duke of Buckingham   Companion of Prince Charles and a public enemy of Nigel Olifaunt; he witnesses the king's interrogation of Lord Dalgarno on the matter of his marital obligations in Sir Walter Scott's *The Fortunes of Nigel.*

Charles Villiers, second Duke of Buckingham   Nobleman in the court of King Charles II; he conspires with Edward Christian to seize control of the Isle of Man and kidnap Alice Bridgenorth for the king; he is tricked by the allure of Zarah in Sir Walter Scott's *Peveril of the Peak.*

Buckram   Horse trader who provides vicious mounts in Robert Surtees's *Mr. Sponge's Sporting Tour.*

Lady Buckray   Lady of fashion and former friend of Mrs. Blandford; she gives a masquerade ball in William Beckford's *Azemia.*

Rosa Bud Pretty heroine, who lives in Miss Twinkleton's boarding school and is engaged to Edwin Drood, also orphaned like herself; Rosa has taken music lessons from John Jasper but is afraid of him, as she admits to Edwin in Charles Dickens's *The Mystery of Edwin Drood*.

Doctor Buddle Village doctor called in to treat Stanley Lake after his duel with Sir Harry Bracton; later he treats Fairy Wylder in J. Sheridan Le Fanu's *Wylder's Hand*.

Mrs. Budger Wealthy widow courted by Dr. Slammer; she attends the ball at the Bull Inn in Rochester and is pursued by Alfred Jingle in Charles Dickens's *The Posthumous Papers of the Pickwick Club*.

Sir Raffle Buffle Snobbish and authoritarian head of the Income Tax Office and Johnny Eames's chief in Anthony Trollope's *The Small House at Allington*. He suffers from Eames's quick wit in *The Last Chronicle of Barset*.

Mrs. Buggins Margaret Mackenzie's old servant, at whose house Margaret faces up to the formidable Lady Ball in Anthony Trollope's *Miss Mackenzie*.

Colonel Bulder Head of the garrison stationed in Rochester who attends the ball at the Bull Inn in Rochester in Charles Dickens's *The Posthumous Papers of the Pickwick Club*.

Miss Bulder Daughter of Colonel and Mrs. Bulder in Charles Dickens's *The Posthumous Papers of the Pickwick Club*.

Mrs. Bulder Wife of Colonel Bulder in Charles Dickens's *The Posthumous Papers of the Pickwick Club*.

Bulgarian Soldier Clergyman who was happily married but who loses everything and everyone in a French attack, and who is wounded in the course of the battle in Charles Johnstone's *Chrysal: or, The Adventures of a Guinea*.

Bull Nosy Brother of Bull Shockhead; he abducts Ursula but is slain by the lustful Gandolf, King of Utterbol in William Morris's *The Well at the World's End*.

Bull Shockhead Wild mountain man, who becomes the thrall of Ralph; he later revenges his brother's murder by slaying Gandolf, King of Utterbol and becomes Lord of Utterbol and marries the queen in William Morris's *The Well at the World's End*.

Bullamy Solemn and imposing porter, whose presence lends credibility to his employer, the Anglo-Bengalee Disinterested Loan and Life Assurance Company, in Charles Dickens's *The Life and Adventures of Martin Chuzzlewit*.

Mr. Bullbean George Hotspur's card-playing associate, who is willing to testify before a magistrate that George cheats in Anthony Trollope's *Sir Harry Hotspur of Humblethwaite*.

Mrs. Bullen Farmer's wife of Mr. Armstrong's parish who criticizes her vicar for his interest in astronomy in Mark Rutherford's *Miriam's Schooling*.

Sir Thomas Bullford Neighbor of Baynard; he plays a practical joke on Obadiah Lishmahago and is himself a victim of Lishmahago's revenge in Tobias Smollett's *The Expedition of Humphry Clinker*.

Viscount Bullingdon Proud, mistreated stepson of Barry Lyndon; he runs away to volunteer in the British army and is reported killed in America; he returns to his mother and horsewhips his stepfather in William Makepeace Thackeray's *The Luck of Barry Lyndon*.

Mr. Bullivant Shop assistant who courts Monica Madden ineffectively in George Gissing's *The Odd Women*.

Mr. Bullivant Sculptor and poet, a friend of Valentine Blyth in Wilkie Collins's *Hide and Seek*.

Frederick Augustus Bullock Member of a banking family who marries Maria Osborne for her money in William Makepeace Thackeray's *Vanity Fair*.

Bulls-Eye Bill Sikes's much kicked and battered dog; Sikes's attempts to drown the dog to keep it from leading pursuers to him after he murders Nancy are unsuccessful in Charles Dickens's *Oliver Twist*.

Valentine Bulmer The illegitimate half brother of Francis Tyrrel; he claims the title of Earl of Etherington, pursues Clara Mowbray to make their mock marriage legitimate, uses John Mowbray's gambling and need of money to gain his consent for marriage to his sister, and is killed by Mowbray in a duel in Sir Walter Scott's *St. Ronan's Well*.

Harriet Bulstrode Sister of Walter Vincy and wife of a powerful banker; she attempts unsuccessfully to arrange a marriage between Rosamond Vincy and Ned Plymdale and is so angry when this match fails that she arranges a meeting with Dr. Lydgate to question his intentions toward Rosamond in George Eliot's *Middlemarch*.

Nicholas Bulstrode Power-mad banker of Middlemarch; he was once married to a wealthy widow whose daughter was Will Ladislaw's mother; wanting all the family money, he kept the daughter hidden; this secret is carefully guarded, as is the one that he was dealing in stolen goods, until John Raffles arrives in George Eliot's *Middlemarch*.

Mr. Bumble   Fat, choleric beadle of the parish workhouse where Oliver lives; he marries Mrs. Corney in Charles Dickens's *Oliver Twist*.

Sergeant Bumptious   Overzealous counsel on behalf of Squire Cheatum; he wins the court case against John Jorrocks, who is found guilty of trespassing his big toe on Squire Cheatum's property in Robert Surtees's *Jorrocks's Jaunts and Jollities*.

Bunce   Aged bedesman at Hiram's Hospital sorely perplexed by squabbles over alleged misuse of the charity in Anthony Trollope's *The Warden*. He appears in *Barchester Towers*.

Jacob Bunce   Journeyman copyist in a legal stationer's office; he provides Phineas Finn with lodgings and educates him in rights of labor with realistic estimates of political chicanery among the legislators in Anthony Trollope's *Phineas Finn*. He proclaims his belief in Finn's innocence in the murder case in *Phineas Redux*.

Jane Bunce   Stout-hearted wife of Jacob, at whose house Phineas Finn lodges; she loathes politics, her husband's consuming interest, in Anthony Trollope's *Phineas Finn*. She is distressed by Finn's ordeal in being tried for murder in *Phineas Redux*.

Jo Bunce   Workingman of vulgarly radical tastes and fiercely antireligious sentiments who nevertheless cares faithfully for his orphaned children in George Gissing's *Thyrza*.

John Bunce (Frederick Altamont)   Captain Clement Cleveland's lieutenant and devoted friend; a gaudy rake, he despises his plebeian name and wishes to be addressed as Frederick Altamont; arrested for piracy, he is spared hanging because of a past humane deed and gains employment in government service in Sir Walter Scott's *The Pirate*.

Mrs. Bunch   Colonel Bunch's wife in William Makepeace Thackeray's *The Adventures of Philip on His Way through the World*.

Colonel Tom Bunch   General Baynes's friend, who is challenged by the General to a duel because he takes the side of Philip and Charlotte (Baynes) Firmin in William Makepeace Thackeray's *The Adventures of Philip on His Way through the World*.

John Buncle (the elder)   The wealthy and educated father of John Buncle; he is generous to his son until he throws him out after a disagreement over a daily prayer, an estrangement aggravated by the selfishness of his recently wedded young wife and her nephew; he is ulti-mately converted to Unitarianism by his son's writing in Thomas Amory's *The Life of John Buncle, Esq.*

John Buncle   Self-conscious autobiographer, who is estranged from his father because of his Unitarian beliefs; he wanders through the mountains of Ireland and Northern England; he marries seven wives whose premature deaths spur on his alpine and philosophical wanderings; he is at length reconciled with his father, a newly converted Unitarian, in Thomas Amory's *The Life of John Buncle, Esq.*

Mr. Buncombe   Man whose wife has left him for a career but who lives in a large house, hoping she will return in George Gissing's *The Whirlpool*.

Mr. Bunfit   Plodding detective in the case of the stolen diamonds whose theory turns out to be less reliable than that of his police colleague Gager in Anthony Trollope's *The Eustace Diamonds*.

Mrs. Bungall   The late part owner of a Devon brewery; her one-third interest in the company passes to her great-nephew, Luke Rowan, but is insufficient to assure him the partnership he wants in Anthony Trollope's *Rachel Ray*.

Mr. Bungay   Publisher of the *Pall Mall Gazette*; he is the enemy of his former friend and partner, Mr. Bacon, in William Makepeace Thackeray's *The History of Pendennis*.

Mrs. Bungay   Sister of Mr. Bacon and wife of Mr. Bungay in William Makepeace Thackeray's *The History of Pendennis*.

Mrs. Bunkin   Neighbor of Mrs. Susannah Sanders in Charles Dickens's *The Posthumous Papers of the Pickwick Club*.

Captain John (Jack) Bunsby   Captain Cuttle's nautical, mahogany-faced friend, who is regarded by Cuttle as an oracular sage and marries Mrs. MacStinger in Charles Dickens's *Dombey and Son*.

Jacob Bunting   Retired soldier who accompanies Walter Lester on his travels and helps him collect the evidence that leads to the indictment for murder against Eugene Aram in Edward Bulwer-Lytton's *Eugene Aram*.

Buonarotti   Venetian saved from an assassin by Abellino (Count Rosalvo); his ingratitude encourages Abellino to join the bravos in Matthew Lewis's *The Bravo of Venice*.

Mr. Burchell   See Sir William Thornhill.

Miss Burchell (Miss B., Mrs. Jefferis, Mrs. Faulkland) Mrs. Gerrarde's niece, whom Sidney Bidulph Arnold wants Orlando Faulkland to marry in order to legitimize his unborn child; under the name Jefferis, she reveals her true name (Burchell) and delivers a son; when married to Orlando Faulkland, she is shot by him for adultery; finally she dies an unloved wretch in Frances Sheridan's *Memoirs of Miss Sidney Bidulph*.

Mr. Burcot Wealthy gentleman, who squanders his fortune in search of the philosopher's stone; reformed by his daughter, Azora, he sets up a colony in Stanemore in Thomas Amory's *The Life of John Buncle, Esq*.

Azora Burcot Head of the female republic at Burcot Lodge, a self-sufficient colony of one hundred deeply religious women remarkably advanced in mathematics; she takes up lengthy religious discussions with John Buncle in Thomas Amory's *The Life of John Buncle, Esq*.

Simon Burden Ancient coastal-village rustic and beacon watchman during the period of concern over an invasion in the Napoleonic War in Thomas Hardy's *The Trumpet-Major*.

Squire Burdock Matthew Bramble's friend at whose house Bramble meets the Count de Melville (Renaldo de Melvil) and Seraphina Melvilia Grieve in Tobias Smollett's *The Expedition of Humphry Clinker*.

Jonathan Burge Owner of a carpentry firm in Hayslope; he employs Adam Bede and eventually makes Adam his partner in George Eliot's *Adam Bede*.

Mary Burge The daughter of Adam Bede's employer, Jonathan Burge; she wants to marry Adam and thus insure that she will inherit her father's carpentry business in George Eliot's *Adam Bede*.

Bartholomew Burgess Sour, discontented uncle of Brooke Burgess; a long-time resident of Exeter, his strongest passion is his hatred of Miss Jemima Stanbury in Anthony Trollope's *He Knew He Was Right*.

Brooke Burgess Clerk in the Ecclesiastical Record Office and Jemima Stanbury's chosen heir; he courts and marries Dorothy Stanbury in Anthony Trollope's *He Knew He Was Right*.

Eleanor Burgoyne Widowed cousin of Edward Manisty; she acts as his secretary for the writing of his book; she loves Manisty but loses him to Lucy Foster, a young American whom she has befriended in Mrs. Humphry Ward's *Eleanor*.

Bastard of Burgundy Military leader; his troop encounters Denys, who is on leave and has nearly reached home for the first time in three years, and impresses him into service in Charles Reade's *The Cloister and the Hearth*.

Charles the Bold, Duke of Burgundy Louis XI's kinsman, who hates his overlord and frets against his feudal bonds; Louis in turn hates and fears the powerful duke, who presides over an extravagant but well-fortified court in Sir Walter Scott's *Quentin Durward*. He negotiates with John de Vere for an alliance with Margaret of Anjou, refuses peace terms with Swiss cantons, and dies in battle in *Anne of Geierstein*.

Lord Burke The Marquis of Kilcarney, social catch of the season; he favors Olive Barton for much of the season but selects Violet Scully in George Moore's *A Drama in Muslin*.

Mr. Burke Reformist agent of the town Colambre (a part of Lord Clonbrony's estate); he is promoted to be the agent of Colambre and Clonbrony (another part of Lord Clonbrony's Irish estate) when Nicholas Garraghty is fired in Maria Edgeworth's *The Absentee*.

Mr. Burke Catholic husband who cruelly abuses his newly wedded, Protestant wife to convert her to Catholicism in Thomas Amory's *The Life of John Buncle, Esq*.

Elizabeth (Betty) Burke Servingwoman at the Nutters' who tries to protect her mistress from Mary Matchwell in J. Sheridan Le Fanu's *The House by the Churchyard*.

Colonel Francis (Crowding Pat) Burke Irish occasional confederate of the Master (James Durie) in Scotland, America, and France; he announces the Master's survival of both Scottish campaign and India; Mackellar uses parts of his laudatory autobiography to forward the narrative in Robert Louis Stevenson's *The Master of Ballantrae: A Winter's Tale*.

Lord Burleigh Cunning minister to Queen Elizabeth and implacable enemy to the Earl of Essex (2); he forces Ellinor to marry Lord Arlington (1) and to renounce her ties to the Stuart line in Sophia Lee's *The Recess*.

Lord Burleigh Commander of the Covenanters; he is defeated under the walls of Aberdeen in Sir Walter Scott's *A Legend of Montrose*.

Burley See John Balfour.

Burlington One of the partners in Burlington and Smith, a London law firm which conspires with Lawyer Larkin in his plot to take the property of William Wylder in J. Sheridan Le Fanu's *Wylder's Hand*.

Mrs. Burman Elderly legal wife of Victor Radnor; she

married the young Radnor when she was already advanced in years, a disparity that led Victor to abandon her; she refuses to grant a divorce and frustrates Victor's designs of entering society in George Meredith's *One of Our Conquerors.*

Mr. Burnet   Hubert Price's wealthy uncle, who disinherits him in favor of Emily Watson, then reinstates Hubert when Emily refuses his marriage proposal in George Moore's *Vain Fortune.*

Helen Burns   Pensive and intelligent pupil at Lowood School, who befriends Jane Eyre and becomes Jane's spiritual guide through the example of her stoicism and selflessness in spite of her consumptive condition in Charlotte Brontë's *Jane Eyre.*

Mrs. Burrows   Ribald crone, mother of John Burrows; she shelters Sam Brattle for a while in her cottage at Pycroft Common where Mr. Fenwick finds Sam's sister Carry in Anthony Trollope's *The Vicar of Bullhampton.*

Anne Burrows   Sullen and sickly wife of John Burrows; she refuses to cooperate with Constable Toffy over her husband's activities or whereabouts in respect to the murder of Farmer Trumbull in Anthony Trollope's *The Vicar of Bullhampton.*

John Burrows (the Grinder)   Jailbird and prime mover in the murder of Farmer Trumbull in Anthony Trollope's *The Vicar of Bullhampton.*

Mr. Burton   Junior partner in a firm of civil engineers and father of Florence; he trains Harry Clavering, who falls in love with Florence; he shares the family's dismay when Clavering neglects her for a while in Anthony Trollope's *The Claverings.*

Mrs. Burton   Practical and unselfish wife of a civil engineer and mother of Theodore, three married daughters, and Florence; she suffers with her husband when Florence seems to be in danger of losing her betrothed, Harry Clavering, in Anthony Trollope's *The Claverings.*

Cecilia Burton   Stouthearted wife of Theodore and staunch ally of Harry Clavering and supporter of his match with Florence Burton; she calls on Lady Ongar in a brave effort to dissuade her from continuing to draw Harry away from Florence in Anthony Trollope's *The Claverings.*

Florence Burton   Devoted bride-to-be of Harry Clavering; she suffers great sorrow when she learns of his renewed attention to Lady Ongar; she sends a parcel of his love letters to Mrs. Clavering, and Harry, thoroughly shamed, begs forgiveness; they finally marry in Anthony Trollope's *The Claverings.*

Hannah Burton   Clarissa Harlowe's favored chambermaid, who is discharged by the Harlowe family as a means of punishing Clarissa; bad health and Robert Lovelace's machinations stop her from joining Clarissa after the latter escapes from Lovelace in Samuel Richardson's *Clarissa: or, The History of a Young Lady.*

Theodore Burton   Unpretentious, good-natured eldest son of a civil engineer; he is destined to take over the firm; he injures his standing with his future brother-in-law, Harry Clavering, by dusting his boots with his handkerchief in Anthony Trollope's *The Claverings.*

Thomas Burton   One-legged purveyor of cats' meat, converted to temperance, mentioned in the "Report of the Committee of the United Grand Junction Ebeneezer Temperance Association" in Charles Dickens's *The Posthumous Papers of the Pickwick Club.*

Sir Wilfrid Bury   Trustee of Lady Henry's estate and her valued friend; he attempts to mediate the quarrel between Lady Henry and Julie Le Breton in Mrs. Humphry Ward's *Lady Rose's Daughter.*

Brother Bushel   Tory farmer, deacon in the Reverend Broad's chapel, who opposes George Allen on the issue of free trade, and who dies vexed by the railroad survey on his lands in Mark Rutherford's *The Revolution In Tanner's Lane.*

Martha Buskbody   Young dressmaker, who persuades the schoolteacher Mr. Pattieson to complete his narration in Sir Walter Scott's *Old Mortality.*

Dr. Butcher   Eastthorp doctor who is considered second-rate but socially superior in Mark Rutherford's *Catharine Furze.*

Mrs. Butcher   Wife of a doctor in Eastthorp; Mrs. Furze wishes to move into her social circle in Mark Rutherford's *Catharine Furze.*

Catherine Butler   Eldest daughter of the Butler family; her brilliant marriage to Beamish of the Foreign Office contrasts to the dreary career of Catherine George in Anne Thackeray Ritchie's *The Village on the Cliff.*

David Butler   Son of Reuben and Jeanie (Deans) Butler in Sir Walter Scott's *The Heart of Midlothian.*

Deb Butler (Dorcas Wykes, Dorcas Martindale)   Deceitful servant and Robert Lovelace's spy in the London brothel where Lovelace lodges the unsuspecting Clarissa Harlowe; she uses the names Dorcas Wykes and Dorcas Martindale in Samuel Richardson's *Clarissa: or, The History of a Young Lady.*

Donald Butler   Son of Reuben and Jeanie (Deans) Butler in Sir Walter Scott's *The Heart of Midlothian.*

Euphemia Butler   Daughter of Reuben and Jeanie (Deans) Butler in Sir Walter Scott's *The Heart of Midlothian.*

James Butler (Corporal Trim)   Uncle Toby Shandy's lanky, devoted servant, voluble but respectful, and like his master a retired soldier with a war wound (in the knee); he helps design and execute re-creations of famous military sieges on Toby's bowling green in Laurence Sterne's *The Life and Opinions of Tristram Shandy, Gentleman.*

Judith Butler   Reuben Butler's grandmother, who fights against age and poverty to procure Reuben an education in the ministry in Sir Walter Scott's *The Heart of Midlothian.*

Lady Mary Butler   The Duke of Ormonde's daughter, who marries Lord Ashburnham in William Makepeace Thackeray's *The History of Henry Esmond.*

Reuben Butler   A kind and scholarly man, who is somewhat vain about his learning; once educated, he becomes an assistant schoolmaster and is forced to officiate as clergyman at the hanging of John Porteous; he marries Jeanie Deans and receives a comfortable living from the kirk of Knocktarlities in Sir Walter Scott's *The Heart of Midlothian.*

Richard Butler   Kind but lazy painter, who is loved by Catherine George and later aided by her to overcome his social pride and recognize his deep love for Reine Chretien in Anne Thackeray Ritchie's *The Village on the Cliff.*

Sarah Butler   Young pupil of Catherine George in Anne Thackeray Ritchie's *The Village on the Cliff.*

Stephen Butler (Bible Butler, Stephen Scripture)   Reuben Butler's Bible-thumping grandfather; as a soldier, he saved Argyle's grandfather, a debt John, Duke of Argyle repays to Reuben and Jeanie Deans in Sir Walter Scott's *The Heart of Midlothian.*

Butt   Fellow convict, who wants Robert Penfold to give poison to the dog so that he can rob General Rolleston in Charles Reade's *Foul Play.*

Mr. Butterfield   Small butcher who is unwittingly used by Orkid Jim to make Tom Catchpole look like a thief in Mark Rutherford's *Catharine Furze.*

Butterfly Catcher   Nameless man of fifty, whom Mark Rutherford encounters during his lonely walks while preaching at the Unitarian chapel, and who renews Mark's acquaintance in London after Mary Mardon's death in Mark Rutherford's *The Autobiography of Mark Rutherford.*

Mabella Buttermead   Young society woman who banters with Jocelyn Pierston and whom he does not mistake for the "well-beloved" in Thomas Hardy's *The Well-Beloved.*

Mr. Butterwell   Secretary of the General Committee Office; on his promotion Adolphus Crosbie is given his job in Anthony Trollope's *The Small House at Allington.* He lends Crosbie £500 in *The Last Chronicle of Barset.*

Clement (Clem) Butts   Son of the marriage of Miss Leroy and George Butts; Mark Rutherford's boyhood friend who drifts apart from him, he becomes a successful schoolmaster and marries Ellen after her engagement to Mark is broken; he emigrates to Australia with her after he is discovered making love to another woman in Mark Rutherford's *Mark Rutherford's Deliverance.*

Ellen (Mrs. Clem) Butts   Mark Rutherford's betrothed, whom he met while they taught Sunday school before he went to college and to whom he tells his religious doubts to break their engagement in Mark Rutherford's *The Autobiography of Mark Rutherford.* He finally marries her after she is widowed and he lives as a journalist in London in *Mark Rutherford's Deliverance.*

George Butts   A placid miller who marries Miss Leroy and provides her with respectability for her eccentric ways in Mark Rutherford's *Mark Rutherford's Deliverance.*

Marie Butts   Ten-year-old crippled daughter of Clem and Ellen Butts; her selfless nursing of Ellen wins Mark Rutherford's profound love after his marriage to Ellen in her widowhood in Mark Rutherford's *Mark Rutherford's Deliverance.*

Edward Buxley   A suitor of two of the icy Pole sisters in George Meredith's *Emilia in England.*

Mr. Buxton   Wealthy landowner, who disapproves of his son's engagement to Maggie Browne; her conduct wins him over in Elizabeth Gaskell's *The Moorland Cottage.*

Mrs. Buxton   Ailing wife of Mr. Buxton; her death removes a softening influence in Elizabeth Gaskell's *The Moorland Cottage.*

Frank Buxton   Son of the wealthy Mr. Buxton; he saves the life of Maggie Browne, to whom he is engaged, during the shipwreck in Elizabeth Gaskell's *The Moorland Cottage.*

Serjeant Buzfuz   Fat, red-faced lawyer, who represents

Martha Bardell in her breach of promise suit against Samuel Pickwick in Charles Dickens's *The Posthumous Papers of the Pickwick Club*.

Justice Buzzard   London judge who hears the trial of Humphrey Clinker, accused of highway robbery; he knows Clinker did not do it and that Edward Martin did in Tobias Smollett's *The Expedition of Humphry Clinker*.

Byam   Deputy-governor of the colony; he is wounded by an arrow from Imoinda's bow; he urges Oroonoko to surrender after the failed insurrection, then has him brutally whipped in Aphra Behn's *Oroonoko*.

Bessie Byass   Samuel Byass's wife, who is lively and amusing like her husband and his partner in benevolence; they quarrel and become estranged in George Gissing's *The Nether World*.

Samuel Byass   Lively and amusing benefactor to various people; he and his wife and partner in benevolence, Bessie, eventually quarrel and become alienated in George Gissing's *The Nether World*.

Maurice Christian Bycliffe   The real father of Esther Lyon and heir to the Transome estate; just before his death the scheming servant Henry Scaddon usurps his identity in George Eliot's *Felix Holt, the Radical*.

Miss Bydel   Local gossip who mishears the initials on a letter to give the Stranger, Juliet Granville, the name of Ellis in Frances Burney's *The Wanderer*.

By-ends   Traveler from Fair-speech who professes whatever will profit him the most; he hides selfish motives beneath apparent religiosity in his conversations with Christian and Hopeful in John Bunyan's *The Pilgrim's Progress From this World to That Which Is to Come*.

Theresa Bygrave   Maud Enderby's aunt with whom Maud is sent to live after her parents separate in George Gissing's *The Unclassed*.

Emily Byril   A "weak intelligent woman" in love with Mike Fletcher but too possessive in George Moore's *Mike Fletcher*.

Harriet Byron   Beautiful heroine, a universally admired and courted orphan, raised by her grandmother; she is kidnapped by a rejected suitor, Sir Hargrave Pollexfen, and foils a secret marriage ceremony with him; Sir Charles Grandison rescues her, falls in love, and, after some trials, marries her in Samuel Richardson's *Sir Charles Grandison*.

C

Mr. C—— Recipient of Mrs. E——'s letter, which takes him to a rendezvous with Syrena Tricksy, who, though expecting Mr. E——, succumbs to his ardor in Eliza Haywood's *Anti-Pamela: or, Feign'd Innocence Detected*.

Mrs. C—— Jealous wife who surprises her husband and Syrena Tricksy together and has Syrena arrested, in accordance with Mrs. E——'s plot in Eliza Haywood's *Anti-Pamela: or, Feign'd Innocence Detected*.

Countess of C—— Aristocratic confidante of Lady Davers; she reads Pamela Andrews's letters with much excitement and sympathy in Samuel Richardson's *Pamela, or Virtue Rewarded*.

Cadiga Prudent mistress of Nourjahad and sister of Cozro (Schemzeddin); named for the favorite wife of Mahomet, she is identified by a natural rosebud birthmark later painted on by an impersonator who feigns Cadiga's death when Nourjahad stabs her; she transfers Nourjahad's secret to Cozro in Frances Sheridan's *The History of Nourjahad*.

Emily Cadman Godwin Peak's aunt, who helps Godwin obtain financial support for his studies when he is a boy in George Gissing's *Born in Exile*.

Captain George Cadurcis Plantagenet Cadurcis's loyal and noble cousin, who encourages Venetia Herbert's marriage to Plantagenet though he loves her himself, but who finally does become her husband after Plantagenet's death in Benjamin Disraeli's *Venetia*.

Katherine, Lady Cadurcis Bitter, unrefined widowed mother of Plantagenet Cadurcis, with whom she has an increasingly volatile relationship until her death in Benjamin Disraeli's *Venetia*.

Plantagenet, Lord Cadurcis (characterization of George Gordon, Lord Byron) Renowned, aristocratic poet, whose childhood affection for Venetia Herbert grows into an adult love, tragically ended by his untimely death by drowning in Benjamin Disraeli's *Venetia*.

Cadwallader Long-dead giant whose skull Mr. Escott acquires from a sexton and with which he bribes Mr. Cranium's consent to his marriage to Cephalis Cranium in Thomas Love Peacock's *Headlong Hall*.

Elinor Cadwallader Busybody matchmaking wife of the Rector of Tipton Grange and Freshitt Hall in George Eliot's *Middlemarch*.

Humphrey Cadwallader Rector of Tipton Grange and Freshitt Hall; he refuses to interfere with Dorothea Brooke's plans to marry Edward Casaubon, although Sir James Chettam begs him to do so in George Eliot's *Middlemarch*.

Cadwallon (Renault Vidal) Welsh bard; he swears vengeance for the death of Gwenwyn, serves Hugo de Lacy under the assumed name of Renault Vidal, murders Randal de Lacy, whom he mistakes for Hugo, and is hanged by King Henry II in Sir Walter Scott's *The Betrothed*.

Caecilius [St. Cypriian] Bishop of Carthage, who reconverts Agellius to Christianity and saves him from persecution, converts Callista and visits her in prison, and relieves Juba's madness in John Henry Newman's *Callista*.

Castruccio Caesarini Idealistic poet, who is betrayed by Lumley Ferrers, his rival for the hand of Florence Lascilles, and lapses into madness in Edward Bulwer-Lytton's *Ernest Maltravers*. He hunts down and kills Ferrers before drowning himself in *Alice*.

Mrs. Caffyn Widow of fifty who befriends Madge Hopgood during her pregnancy in Mark Rutherford's *Clara Hopgood*.

Cafour Princess Carathis's Negress attendant, who forms love relationships with ghouls and enjoys romping in graveyards and other strange activities in William Beckford's *Vathek*.

Pauline Caillaud Illegitimate child of Victorine and Dupin and the foster daughter of Jean Caillaud; an intellectual, free-thinking dancer, she marries Zachariah Coleman after his release from prison in 1821, bears his daughter, and dies in 1822 in Mark Rutherford's *The Revolution In Tanner's Lane*.

Jean Caillaud (John Kaylow) French shoemaker, a leading member of the London radical political club Zachariah Coleman joins; he is executed for killing a soldier to defend Major Maitland during the march of Manchester Blanketeers in 1817 in Mark Rutherford's *The Revolution In Tanner's Lane*.

Daniel Caldigate Just, hard, outwardly unsympathetic father of John, and squire of Folking, near Cambridge; angered by his son's debts, he disinherits him, but when John returns from Australia having made his fortune in gold mines, the pair are reconciled in Anthony Trollope's *John Caldigate*.

George Caldigate Reliable nephew of Daniel Caldigate; at one point he seems likely to become his uncle's heir in Anthony Trollope's *John Caldigate*.

Hester Bolton Caldigate   Only daughter of Nicholas Bolton; she suffers persecution by her mother, who does all she can to separate her from John Caldigate; when scandal breaks out concerning his allegedly bigamous marriage to her, she stands by him; eventually his name is cleared and they are reunited in Anthony Trollope's *John Caldigate.*

John Caldigate   Restless, improvident son of Daniel Caldigate; he falls in love with Hester Bolton and seeks his fortune gold-mining in Australia; a foolish relationship with an adventuress, Euphemia Smith, almost wrecks his marriage when she turns up later in England; he is jailed on a trumped-up bigamy charge but is finally cleared and released from prison in Anthony Trollope's *John Caldigate.*

Calenus   Venal priest of Isis; he attempts to blackmail Arbaces in Edward Bulwer-Lytton's *The Last Days of Pompeii.*

Lady Calista of Mountfaçon   Lady in waiting to Queen Berengaria and a leader in the prank that lures Sir Kenneth from his sentry post in Sir Walter Scott's *The Talisman.*

Robert Callan   Servant of Lord Stivers; he assists in the robbery of the nobleman's corpse and accuses Arabella Clement of the crime in Henry Brooke's *The Fool of Quality.*

Mrs. Callander   Inquisitive passenger aboard the ship taking John Caldigate to Australia; she reprimands him for his flirtatious behavior towards Euphemia Smith in Anthony Trollope's *John Caldigate.*

Callid   One of Amoranda's suitors, who wants only her money in Mary Davys's *The Reform'd Coquet.*

Callipus   Charmides's friend who tries to warn him about consorting with Christians in the Reverend Theophilus Cardew's story in Mark Rutherford's *Catharine Furze.*

Callista   Greek sculptress and singer, converted by her suitor Agellius and Bishop Caecilius; she denies being a Christian when shown instruments of torture but refuses to sacrifice to Roman gods and undergoes martyrdom following instruction and baptism by Caecilius in John Henry Newman's *Callista.*

Earl of Callonby   Irish landowner and father of Lady Jane Callonby in Charles Lever's *The Confessions of Harry Lorrequer.*

Lady Jane Callonby   Daughter of the Irish landowner the Earl of Callonby; her love is sought by Guy Lorrequer but won by Harry Lorrequer in Charles Lever's *The Confessions of Harry Lorrequer.*

Mr. Calomel   Social-climbing apothecary, who is duped by Lady Riot into wearing his pajamas to a high-toned party in an anecdote told by Mr. Rouvell in Richard Graves's *The Spiritual Quixote.*

Calphurnius   Tribune whose intervention Jucundus seeks; it comes too late to save Callista from martyrdom in John Henry Newman's *Callista.*

Arabella (Bell) Calvert   A prostitute who is eyewitness to young George Colwan's murder and who assists Arabella Logan in seeking evidence against Robert Colwan in James Hogg's *The Private Memoirs and Confessions of a Justified Sinner.*

Baldassare Calvo   Tito Melema's benefactor, who raised the boy as a father but is abandoned by Tito and left to remain a slave of the Turks; he frees himself and kills Tito for revenge in George Eliot's *Romola.*

Frederigo, Count of Camaldoli   Esteemed friend of Franceso Perfetti; he is admired by Julian Danvers; he is considered the very embodiment of the Renaissance ideal in William Godwin's *Cloudesley.*

Dr. Cambray   New parson at Sir Ulick O'Shane's home; his benevolence, intelligence, and understanding make him an excellent adviser to Harry Ormond after Cornelius O'Shane's death in Maria Edgeworth's *Ormond.*

Evelyn Cameron   See Evelyn Templeton.

Camilla   Governess to Lady Clementina della Porretta in Samuel Richardson's *Sir Charles Grandison.*

Camilla   Sister of Matthew Pocket, wife of Cousin Raymond, and one of Miss Havisham's disappointed relatives in Charles Dickens's *Great Expectations.*

Camilla   Governess of Rosabella of Corfu in Matthew Lewis's *The Bravo of Venice.*

Camilla   Sweet-tempered nurse of Julian Danvers in William Godwin's *Cloudesley.*

Mother Camilla   Nun of St. Clare and harsh jailer of Agnes de Medina in Matthew Lewis's *The Monk.*

Vittoria Campa   See Emilia Alessandra (Sandra) Belloni.

Colonel Campbell   Kind friend to the orphaned Jane Fairfax; she is brought up and educated in his home; the Campbells' departure for Ireland to visit their daughter, lately married to Mr. Dixon, causes Jane to return to her grandmother's home near Hartfield in Jane Austen's *Emma*.

Lady Campbell　Sir Duncan's wife and Annot Lyle's grieving mother in Sir Walter Scott's *A Legend of Montrose*.

Mr. Campbell　Kindly Scottish minister who is the longtime family friend and mentor of young David Balfour in Robert Louis Stevenson's *Kidnapped*.

Mr. Campbell　A young Anglo-Catholic rector, who tries to convince Charles Reding to remain Anglican in John Henry Newman's *Loss and Gain*.

Mrs. Campbell　Colonel Campbell's wife and Mrs. Dixon's mother in Jane Austen's *Emma*.

Alan Campbell　Disenchanted intimate friend of Dorian Gray; Dorian blackmails him with the threat of ruining his reputation to force Alan to dispose of Basil Hallward's corpse in Oscar Wilde's *The Picture of Dorian Gray*.

General Colin Campbell　Commander of loyal forces; he captures the Pretender Charles Stewart with Jacobite conspirators and gives all their freedom at the command of King George in Sir Walter Scott's *Redgauntlet*.

Colin Ray Campbell (the Red Fox, Glenure)　Government factor to King George and member of the clan Campbell; he is shot by an unidentified man, supposedly a member of the Jacobite Appin Stewarts; David Balfour meets his road party by chance and witnesses the shooting; afterwards, David is wanted as an accessory to his murder in Robert Louis Stevenson's *Kidnapped*.

Dougal Campbell　Scottish landlord who is host for Matthew Bramble's entourage at Inverary; he dislikes bagpipe music in Tobias Smollett's *The Expedition of Humphry Clinker*.

Sir Duncan Campbell　Knight of Ardenvohr, Knight of Auchenbreck; he is the stately old kinsman of the Marquis of Argyle and principal commander of his army; fatally wounded in battle while trying to rally his men, he is taken prisoner and dies shortly after being reunited with his long-lost daughter, Annot Lyle, in Sir Walter Scott's *A Legend of Montrose*.

Mungo Campbell　Colin Ray Campbell's kinsman and lawyer, who is with him when he is shot, and who draws up and prints the placards advertising David Balfour and Alan Breck Stewart as the wanted criminals in Robert Louis Stevenson's *Kidnapped*.

Murdoch Campbell　See Marquis of Argyle.

Mrs. Campbell-Ward　A professional beauty, the sensation of one of Lucy Bentham's balls; she arrives discreetly with her card-playing husband but is obviously admired by the Marquis of Worthing in George Moore's *A Modern Lover*.

Lady Camper　Wealthy, attractive, intelligent widow who becomes acquainted with General Ople when she detects the romance developing between her nephew and his daughter; General Ople misconstrues her friendliness, forcing her to subject him to trial by ridicule before she eventually marries him in George Meredith's *The Case of General Ople and Lady Camper*.

John Camperdown　Samuel Camperdown's son, the junior member of the firm of Camperdown and son in Anthony Trollope's *The Eustace Diamonds*. An energetic attorney, he establishes the existence of Mr. Emilius's first wife in Anthony Trollope's *Phineas Redux*.

Samuel Camperdown　Thoroughly trusted lawyer of the Eustace family; incensed by Lizzie Eustace's claim that diamonds from her late husband were an outright gift, he insists that as an heirloom they belong to the estate; he is consistently frustrated by her lies and maneuvers in Anthony Trollope's *The Eustace Diamonds*.

Theodora Campian　Mysterious inspiration of the "Mary Anne" movements; her father and brothers died with Garibaldi, and she tries to win Lothair over to the cause of the revolutionary liberals in Benjamin Disraeli's *Lothair*.

Caroline Campinet　Charles Hermsprong's love interest and cousin, Lord Grondale's daughter, and Maria Garnet's grandniece, who, with her friend Maria Fluart, plots to escape from an arranged betrothal to Sir Philip Chestrum in Robert Bage's *Hermsprong*.

Lord Campion　Bryan Perdue's rival for Henrietta Saville's affections; he finally marries Henrietta and becomes Bryan's friend in Thomas Holcroft's *The Memoirs of Bryan Perdue*.

Mr. Campley　Married seducer of Miss Belmour; he follows her to Paris and carries on with her there, endangering the reputation of her companion, Henrietta Courteney, in Charlotte Lennox's *Henrietta*.

Old Camplin　Hard-hearted attorney, who is part of Sir Thomas Sindall's circle in Henry Mackenzie's *The Man of the World*.

Young Camplin　Witty friend of Sir Thomas Sindall; the son of the attorney Old Camplin, he is a reluctant soldier who furthers Sindall's evil schemes in Henry Mackenzie's *The Man of the World*.

Count de Campo-Basso Italian nobleman and the Duke of Burgundy's nefarious favorite; the duke vainly commands Isabelle de Croye to accept him as her husband in Sir Walter Scott's *Quentin Durward*. He proves to be a traitor to the duke in the battle with the Swiss in *Anne of Geierstein*.

Maria Candy Slum mother addicted to drink; she lives with her son and daughter in desperate poverty in George Gissing's *The Nether World*.

Pennyloaf Candy Vigorous girl of the slums; she has an alcoholic mother, marries a cruel and irresponsible husband, and is left a poor widow in George Gissing's *The Nether World*.

Stephen Candy Maria's son, who lives in poverty with his mother in George Gissing's *The Nether World*.

Thomas Candy Fussy local physician, who takes offence at Franklin Blake's disparaging the medical profession; by secretly dosing him with laudanum, he unwittingly sets off a chain of events involving the loss of a yellow diamond and the eventual solving of its theft in Wilkie Collins's *The Moonstone. A Romance.*

Major Caneback Sporting chum of Lord Rufford; he has a nasty accident while fox hunting, and the ensuing drama enables Arabella Trefoil to come closer to her own quarry, Lord Rufford, in Anthony Trollope's *The American Senator*.

Miss Cann Teacher and former governess, who lodges with the Ridleys and is kind to young J. J. Ridley in William Makepeace Thackeray's *The Newcomes*.

Billy Cann Diminutive professional thief, who gives evidence against his associates Mr. Smiler and Mr. Benjamin in Anthony Trollope's *The Eustace Diamonds*.

Martin Cannister A sexton who becomes an innkeeper and marries the maidservant Unity in Thomas Hardy's *A Pair of Blue Eyes*.

Michael Cantacuzene Emperor Alexius Comnenus's grand sewer, or household officer, in Sir Walter Scott's *Count Robert of Paris*.

Cantalupe Villainous male who drugs Carola Bennet at a brothel and rapes her in Thomas Amory's *The Life of John Buncle, Esq.*

Grandfather Cantle Aged, comic rustic figure who seems to know or intuit the proceedings and behavior of those outside his social sphere in Thomas Hardy's *The Return of the Native*.

Christian Cantle Elderly grandson of Granfer Cantle and like him a commentator on Egdon Heath folk customs in Thomas Hardy's *The Return of the Native*.

Lady Cantrip Wife of an eminent Liberal statesman in Anthony Trollope's *Phineas Finn*, in *Phineas Redux*, and in *The Prime Minister*. She acts as adviser to Lady Mary Palliser and reluctantly assists Lord Popplecourt's suit with Mary in *The Duke's Children*.

Lord Cantrip Wise senior statesman friend of Plantagenet Palliser and Phineas Finn's chief at the Colonial Office; he begs Finn not to resign over Irish tenant rights in Anthony Trollope's *Phineas Finn*. He is one of the Whig inner circle in *Phineas Redux*. He adds to the problems of the Duke of Omnium (Palliser) by declining to take office in *The Prime Minister*. He makes a brief appearance in *The Duke's Children*.

Nicolò Caparra Weapons maker of Florence who sells Tito Melema a chain mail vest for protection against knife thrusts in George Eliot's *Romola*.

Count Capece Nobleman of Florence and father of Cavaliere di Guardino and Lauretta Capece in J. Henry Shorthouse's *John Inglesant, A Romance*.

Lauretta Capece Beautiful daughter of Count Capece of Florence; she is betrayed by her brother, Cavaliere di Guardino; she marries John Inglesant and dies of the plague with their son in J. Henry Shorthouse's *John Inglesant, A Romance*.

John Capper One of Ellis Duckworth's men; he goes to summon help to the cottage; he fails to recognize the begging friars Will Lawless and Dick Shelton in their disguises in Robert Louis Stevenson's *The Black Arrow: A Tale of Two Roses*.

Captain Man who is attracted to Charlotte Woodville but who behaves honorably and rescues her from other potential molesters when he learns that she is engaged to Mr. Rivers in Richard Graves's *The Spiritual Quixote*.

Captain Friendly and easily bribed man who makes Jemy E. and Moll Flanders's voyage to America more comfortable by providing them with special amenities in Daniel Defoe's *The Fortunes and Misfortunes of the Famous Moll Flanders*.

Captain Unnamed officer who, following the orders of his master, the unnamed squire, abducts Fanny Goodwill from the inn in Henry Fielding's *The History of the Adventures of Mr. Joseph Andrews and of his Friend Mr. Abraham Adams*.

Captain Sinner from Peru; he joins the Jesuits to save

his life and is the man in charge of the assassination of the king of Portugal in Charles Johnstone's *Chrysal: or, The Adventures of a Guinea.*

Captain of Attacking Vessel Cruel man who proves the maxim "cowardice is the inseparable companion of cruelty" and who is granted a trial in Charles Johnstone's *Chrysal: or the Adventures of a Guinea.*

Captain of English Man of War Miser who is bribed by the Spanish to avoid the Spanish treasure ships and who also avoids attacking any ship sighted so that he can get his gold back to England; later, he disobeys orders by leaving his station in order to get to England with his newfound wealth in Charles Johnstone's *Chrysal: or The Adventures of a Guinea.*

Captain of the *Sainte-Marie-des-Anges* Irish captain of the ship on which the Master (James Durie) and Colonel Francis Burke leave Scotland; he is made to walk the plank by Teach in Robert Louis Stevenson's *The Master of Ballantrae: A Winter's Tale.*

Chief Captain of the Romans Ambitious and inexperienced officer, who is cornered with his remaining troops in the Wolfing homestead; he kills Thiodolf and is slain by Wolfkettle in William Morris's *A Tale of the House of the Wolfings.*

Captain's Widow Moll Flanders's friend, who takes Moll in and tries to help her find a husband; she succeeds in marrying a captain herself in Daniel Defoe's *The Fortunes and Misfortunes of the Famous Moll Flanders.*

Sidney Lorraine, Marquess of Carabas Stupid and pompous political leader, whom young Vivian Grey successfully manipulates for his own political ends until the Marquess and his party repudiate him in Benjamin Disraeli's *Vivian Grey.*

Caradoc of Menwygent Young Welsh bard, who competes with Cadwallon for fame in Sir Walter Scott's *The Betrothed.*

Princess Carathis Vathek's cunning, wicked mother, whose ambition causes her to go to extraordinary lengths to encourage and aid her son's attempt to obtain the treasures offered by the Giaour; she also suffers Vathek's fate in William Beckford's *Vathek.*

Mr. Carbottle Liberal candidate in the election at Polpenno, Cornwall, in which Frank Tregear triumphs in Anthony Trollope's *The Duke's Children.*

Jane Carbuncle Domineering aunt of Linda Roanoke; living alone and with a dubious past, she is noted for her technicolor complexion; she forces her niece to accept the proposal of Sir Griffin Tewett, bringing the young girl to mental breakdown in Anthony Trollope's *The Eustace Diamonds.*

Sir Felix Carbury Wastrel son of Lady Carbury, on whom he sponges unmercifully; to extricate himself from debts he follows his mother's advice by persuading Marie Melmotte to elope; he gambles away the money she has stolen from her father and fails to keep their tryst; his mother is reluctantly persuaded to make him a remittance-man in Prussia with a clergyman in attendance in Anthony Trollope's *The Way We Live Now.*

Henrietta (Hetta) Carbury Lady Carbury's lovely, high-minded daughter, who defies her mother's insistence that she marry her devoted cousin, Roger Carbury, because she loves Paul Montague; she becomes Montague's wife and Carbury's heir in Anthony Trollope's *The Way We Live Now.*

Matilda, Lady Carbury Romantic, foolish, hard-pressed widow of a baronet without property; she works arduously for financial and critical success as a writer, for the marriage of her son to an heiress, and for the marriage of her daughter to the owner of the family property; she succeeds at none of these endeavors but makes an unlooked-for successful marriage of her own to the newspaper editor Nicholas Broune in Anthony Trollope's *The Way We Live Now.*

Roger Carbury Morally upright, unbending head of the Carbury family; he warns his friend Paul Montague against dealings with Augustus Melmotte; he is deeply in love with his cousin, Hetta Carbury, but loses her to Paul Montague; he resigns himself to a lonely bachelor life, gives the bride away at her wedding to Paul, and makes her heir to his property in Anthony Trollope's *The Way We Live Now.*

Jane Cardew Wife of the Reverend Theophilus Cardew; she loves her husband but feels rejected by him in Mark Rutherford's *Catharine Furze.*

Theophilus Cardew Thirty-five-year-old rector in Abchurch, son of a London merchant; he is married already when he falls in love with Catharine Furze in Mark Rutherford's *Catharine Furze.*

Lady Cardiff Wealthy, reclusive, and eccentric noblewoman, who marries John Inglesant's twin brother, Eustace, in J. Henry Shorthouse's *John Inglesant, A Romance.*

Cardinal A commercial traveler in the cloth trade, who lives in London and who is rescued from his despair by Mark Rutherford and M'Kay in their mission in Mark Rutherford's *Mark Rutherford's Deliverance.*

Mrs. Cardinal   Cardinal's wife; she cares nothing for him, but her jealousy makes him miserable until she wins self-esteem with help from Mark Rutherford and M'Kay in Mark Rutherford's *Mark Rutherford's Deliverance*.

Don Fernando de Cardiole   Spanish aristocrat who kills his rival for the affections of Donna Corina, then leaves for Turkey, where he leads a life of plunder and debauchery until his conscience awakens and he lives out his years as a hermit; he is found on his deathbed by Father Francis in Penelope Aubin's *The Strange Adventures of the Count de Vinevil and His Family*.

Mary Cardonnel   Daughter of Guilielmina De Verdon Cardonnel; she is her grandmother Lady Mary De Verdon's heir; she refuses all suitors until she comes of age because of her honorable determination to divide her fortune with her first cousin, Medora Glenmorris Delmont; she feels morally bound to acknowledge a just claim stalled by legal machinations in Charlotte Smith's *The Young Philosopher*.

Mr. Cardonnel   Wealthy young man who becomes Lord Daventry when his family purchases an Earldom for him on the occasion of his marriage to Guilielmina De Verdon; he survives his wife and remarries, leaving his daughter, Mary, in the care of her grandmother, Lady Mary De Verdon, in Charlotte Smith's *The Young Philosopher*.

Kitty Carew   Wealthy and witty popular "courtesan," who is a friend of Mike Fletcher, the young lords, and the aesthetes in George Moore's *Mike Fletcher*.

Sir Danvers Carew   Well-mannered, kindly, and aristocratic white-haired gentleman, who is clubbed to death in Robert Louis Stevenson's *The Strange Case of Dr. Jekyll and Mr. Hyde*.

Mother Carey   See Queen of the Fairies.

Widow Carey   Fanny Matthews's rival for Cornet Hebbers's affection; her superior fortune gains her the prize in Henry Fielding's *Amelia*.

Will Carey   Squire of Clovelly Court and member of the Brotherhood of the Rose who sails with Amyas Leigh to Ireland and sails again to rescue Rose Salterne from Don Guzman de Soto in Charles Kingsley's *Westward Ho!*.

Josiah Cargill   Absentminded minister, who, having presided over the mock marriage of Valentine Bulmer and Clara Mowbray, is in possession of the secret in Sir Walter Scott's *St. Ronan's Well*.

Harriet Carker   Sister of James and John Carker; she chose to live with John after his disgrace, separating from James, and is loved by Mr. Morfin in Charles Dickens's *Dombey and Son*.

James Carker   Manager at Paul Dombey's firm; he pretends subservience to Dombey but plots against him and is successful in wooing Edith (Granger) Dombey away from Dombey; his passion destroys him, and he dies when he falls under a train in Charles Dickens's *Dombey and Son*.

John Carker   Older brother of James Carker; he works for Dombey and Son; he had once stolen money from the firm and was forgiven but never allowed to be promoted; now gray and worn, he takes an interest in Walter Gay but wishes to be left alone in Charles Dickens's *Dombey and Son*.

Carle   Guard who sleeps through Hugh Woodreeve's escape and later testifies in Woodreeve's trial in Ann Radcliffe's *Gaston de Blondeville*.

Carle   Old man who lives alone on the shore where a storm drives the ship of Walter Golden; he warns Walter against entering the lands beyond the high rock wall in William Morris's *The Wood beyond the World*.

Captain Clement Carlisle   Conventional, virtuous hero, who overcomes many obstacles to marry his beloved Lucia de Grey in S. J. Pratt's *Tutor of Truth*.

Carlo   Steward of the Castle di Udolpho who, though kind to Emily St. Aubert, remains faithful to the evil Montoni in Ann Radcliffe's *The Mysteries of Udolpho*.

Carlo   Servant ordered to prevent Julia de Mazzini from escaping her forced marriage to Duke de Luovo in Ann Radcliffe's *A Sicilian Romance*.

Carlo   William Fielding's dog that goes with George Fielding to Australia and saves him and his friends several times from their enemies before being killed by one of the thugs in Charles Reade's *It Is Never Too Late to Mend*.

King Carlo Alberto (Charles Albert)   Italian king leading the forces on the side of Italian liberation, despite his association with Austria, which causes his co-revolutionists some unease; Vittoria Campa's faith in him angers Carlo Ammiani in George Meredith's *Vittoria*.

Carloman   Sickly son of King Louis of France; he is pitied and protected by the young Duke Richard of Normandy in Charlotte Yonge's *The Little Duke*.

Mr. Carlton   Fellow of Leicester College, Oxford, who defends Anglican diversity and makes a last-ditch effort to dissuade Charles Reding from becoming Roman Catholic in John Henry Newman's *Loss and Gain*.

Mr. Carlton Gentleman who shares business with Mr. B—— and whose death persuades Mr. B—— to write his own will in Samuel Richardson's *Pamela, or Virtue Rewarded*.

Mrs. Carlton Henrietta Courteney's maternal grandmother, the widow of a bankrupt army officer; her petition for her husband's pension is turned down by the Earl of —— in Charlotte Lennox's *Henrietta*.

Mr. Carlyle Lawyer who is made joint trustee of Scottish estates with Ephraim Mackellar when Henry Durie's family moves to New York in Robert Louis Stevenson's *The Master of Ballantrae: A Winter's Tale*.

Mr. Carn Attorney who represents Mr. Eggleston's claim against Cecilia Beverley's estate in Frances Burney's *Cecilia*.

Hugh Carnaby Well-traveled outdoorsman who kills a man he thinks is seducing his wife and goes to prison in George Gissing's *The Whirlpool*.

Sybil Carnaby Superior lady of much self-control and luxurious tastes who exposes a rival lady's infidelity in George Gissing's *The Whirlpool*.

Ann Avice Caro Avice Caro's daughter; immediately following her mother's burial she meets Jocelyn Pierston, the man who once jilted her mother; he promptly falls in love with her, but she, like Pierston himself when younger, is inconstant in her affections; she accompanies him to London as a housemaid; when he surprises her by proposing marriage, she reveals that she secretly married a young man before her mother's death; Jocelyn helps her establish a household with her husband and does not see her again until, widowed, she writes to him, intending to promote a match between him and her daughter, Avice Pierston, in Thomas Hardy's *The Well-Beloved*.

Avice Caro Young, ingenuous, pretty woman whom Jocelyn Pierston meets when he returns to the peninsular village of his family origins; she falls in love with him and accepts his proposal, but meeting Marcia Bencomb, he abandons her; she marries a cousin of the same name and has a daughter, Ann Avice Caro; she dies when the daughter has grown up in Thomas Hardy's *The Well-Beloved*.

Caroline Wife of one of Ebenezer Scrooge's debtors; she is relieved at news of Scrooge's death in Charles Dickens's *A Christmas Carol*.

Caroline First bride-elect of Lord Lowborough; she

breaks with him when he loses his fortune through gambling in Anne Brontë's *The Tenant of Wildfell Hall*.

Queen Caroline King George II's wife and a power unto herself; she assists Jeanie Deans through the intercession of John, Duke of Argyle, in Sir Walter Scott's *The Heart of Midlothian*.

Monsieur Caron Old printer and comrade of Max du Parc; he tries to apply socialist principles in his paper mill but is killed in the battle of the Commune in Anne Thackeray Ritchie's *Mrs. Dymond*.

Carpenter A character in Tweedledee's poem; his participation in the deception played on the oysters is not so hypocritical as the Walrus's but he eats as many as he can in Lewis Carroll's *Through the Looking-Glass*.

Arthur Carr See Zachary Thorpe.

Louisa Carrington George Uploft's betrothed; she is prevented from revealing the Harringtons' class origin by her own secret, a skin disease, in George Meredith's *Evan Harrington*.

Judy Carrol Servingwoman at Lieutenant O'Flaherty's quarters; she angers O'Flaherty by showing Major O'Neill and Magnolia Macnamara up to his room when he is half-dressed and hung over in J. Sheridan Le Fanu's *The House by the Churchyard*.

Mrs. Carroll John Grey's sister, married to an impecunious inebriate; Mr. Grey maintains in respectability the Carroll family, including their six daughters; only Mrs. Carroll has feelings of gratitude in Anthony Trollope's *Mr. Scarborough's Family*.

Amelia Carroll Eldest of John Grey's six vulgar nieces, who are all looked after and detested by their cousin, Dolly Grey; her engagement to Mr. Jumper broken, Amelia is enabled by Mr. Grey's dowry of £500 to marry the widower Mr. Matterson in Anthony Trollope's *Mr. Scarborough's Family*.

Brenda Carroll One of John Grey's six vulgar nieces in Anthony Trollope's *Mr. Scarborough's Family*.

Georgina Carroll Third of John Grey's six vulgar nieces and a noisy, romping sixteen-year-old in Anthony Trollope's *Mr. Scarborough's Family*.

Minna Carroll One of John Grey's six vulgar nieces in Anthony Trollope's *Mr. Scarborough's Family*.

Moriarty Carroll Lower-class man shot by Harry Ormond during a quarrel in which Ormond tries to defend Marcus O'Shane; Carroll generously refuses to blame Ormond and becomes his friend in Maria Edgeworth's *Ormond*.

Pat Carroll   Ringleader of the tenantry engaged in mayhem throughout Galway; he refuses to pay rents to Philip Jones and leads a gang to flood some fields in Anthony Trollope's *The Landleaguers*.

Captain Patrick Carroll   Raffish, improvident Irish brother-in-law of John Grey, upon whom he sponges for the maintainence of his wife and six silly daughters in Anthony Trollope's *Mr. Scarborough's Family*.

Potsey Carroll   One of John Grey's six vulgar nieces; her openly acknowledged plainness is the despair of the Carroll family in Anthony Trollope's *Mr. Scarborough's Family*.

Sophy Carroll   Second of John Grey's six vulgar nieces; her status as the beauty of the family does not make her less odious to her cousin Dolly Grey in Anthony Trollope's *Mr. Scarborough's Family*.

Terry Carroll   Ruffian brother of Pat; he is shot in the Galway courtroom as he is about to testify against his brother and the terrorists in Anthony Trollope's *The Landleaguers*.

Lord George de Bruce Carruthers   Horse-faced confidence trickster, who becomes a suspect in the Eustace necklace theft; he approaches Lizzie Eustace's romantic ideal of a corsair lover, but he eludes her grasp, finding her too unscrupulous even for his relaxed standards in Anthony Trollope's *The Eustace Diamonds*. His pecuniary embarrassments may have lowered his standards sufficiently at the end of *Phineas Redux*. His escape is apparent from Lizzie's unchanged marital condition in *The Prime Minister*.

Mr. Carruthers   Lawyer who saves Mr. Furze with full payment of his debts in Mark Rutherford's *Catharine Furze*.

Harry Carson   Son of the mill owner John Carson; his shooting death at the hands of John Barton is blamed on Jem Wilson, the honorable rival of Harry's dishonorable pursuit of Mary Barton in Elizabeth Gaskell's *Mary Barton*.

John Carson   Mill owner whose son is murdered by John Barton; his desire for vengeance finally gives way to recognition that conditions make men desperate in Elizabeth Gaskell's *Mary Barton*.

Carstairs   Servant to Lord Glenalmond in Robert Louis Stevenson's *Weir of Hermiston: An Unfinished Romance*.

Lord Carstairs   Eldest son of Earl Bracy; returning to Bowick School as an old boy, he falls in love with Mary Wortle, the headmaster's daughter, in Anthony Trollope's *Dr. Wortle's School*.

Richard Carstone   Handsome young man, who is John Jarndyce's ward; he falls in love with his cousin, Ada Clare, and tries to pursue a profession but always loses interest after a few months; he becomes obsessed with the Jarndyce and Jarndyce Chancery case, which eventually kills him, in Charles Dickens's *Bleak House*.

Carter   Third witness of the forged will that disinherited Amelia Booth in favor of her sister, Betty Harris, in Henry Fielding's *Amelia*.

Carter   Mentally incompetent prisoner, who tries to solve his problem with "hard labor" by destroying the gauge on the weighted crank he is set to turn; he is then punished by the torturing "jacket," bites Hawes's fingers, and becomes brutish in Charles Reade's *It is Never Too Late to Mend*.

Carter   Edwin Reardon's friend who holds a position as an administrator in a hospital and gives Reardon a job there in George Gissing's *New Grub Street*.

Mr. Carter   Tutor hired by Sir Boyvill Neville to prepare his son, Gerald Neville, to testify against his mother, Alithea Neville, in divorce proceedings in Mary Shelley's *Falkner*.

Mr. Carter   The surgeon who quietly treats Mr. Rochester's mad wife, Bertha, and any victims of her attacks in Charlotte Brontë's *Jane Eyre*.

Mrs. Carter   Fellow lodger with the Colemans in Manchester; she nurses Jane Coleman during her illness in Mark Rutherford's *The Revolution In Tanner's Lane*.

John Carter   Sir Daniel Brackley's servant; wounded, he lies moaning for a priest; Bennet Hatch tells Dick Shelton to ask him about Harry Shelton's murder, but he won't talk in Robert Louis Stevenson's *The Black Arrow: A Tale of Two Roses*.

Joseph Carter   Tenant farmer of Indefer Jones; he and his son witness Jones's last will and by their testimony lead Mr. Apjohn to where Jones had hidden it in Anthony Trollope's *Cousin Henry*.

Miss Carteret   Daughter of the Dowager Viscountess Dalrymple in Jane Austen's *Persuasion*.

Mrs. Carthew   Admiral Fakenham's housekeeper, so blinded by the romance of Carinthia Kirby's marriage to wealthy Lord Fleetwood that she doesn't notice his rudeness and lack of affection in George Meredith's *The Amazing Marriage*.

Lady Ann Carthew   Dignified, exacting mother of Norris Carthew, who tells her the story of the *Flying Scud* before leaving for France in Robert Louis Stevenson's *The Wrecker*.

Henry Carthew   Norris Carthew's brother and Lady Ann Carthew's favorite, killed in a hunting accident in Robert Louis Stevenson's *The Wrecker*.

Norris (Norrie) Carthew (Goddedaal, Dickson, Madden)   Bored, disenchanted English gentleman, whose misfortunes in life and aboard the *Currency Lass* lie behind the mystery of the wreck of the *Flying Scud*; he uses various aliases in his bidding for wrecked ships in Robert Louis Stevenson's *The Wrecker*.

Lord Singleton Carthew   Vain, stupid father of Norris Carthew; after frequent fights he finally banishes Norris to Australia; he dies one year before Loudon Dodd's visit to the Carthew estate in Robert Louis Stevenson's *The Wrecker*.

Cartlett   Second husband of Arabella Donn in Thomas Hardy's *Jude the Obscure*.

Sydney Carton   Dissolute London barrister, whose identical appearance to Charles Darnay (Charles St. Evrémonde) is decisive for both of their lives; he falls in love with Lucie Manette and dies on the scaffold in place of Darnay out of love for Lucie in Charles Dickens's *A Tale of Two Cities*.

Cartwright   Fourteen-year-old boy who helps Sherlock Holmes track down information and brings the detective food on the moor in Arthur Conan Doyle's *The Hound of the Baskervilles*.

Mr. Cartwright   Father of five girls who has been forced to adopt a reduced style of living in George Gissing's *A Life's Morning*.

Mrs. Cartwright   Dominating mother of five girls in George Gissing's *A Life's Morning*.

Althea Cartwright   Upper-class bluestocking, who allows Christopher Kirkland to be her escort in society in his first year in London in Mrs. Lynn Linton's *The Autobiography of Christopher Kirkland*.

General Carver   Insipid friend and visitor of Lady Matilda Sufton and a guest at the home of Lord Altamont and Adelaide Douglas after their marriage in Susan Ferrier's *Marriage*.

Mr. Carver   Art dealer who introduces Lewis Seymour to Lucy Bentham; he accepts a secret annual commission from her to buy Seymour's pictures in George Moore's *A Modern Lover*.

Mrs. Caryle   A wife eloped from her husband; she takes a room above the Milliner's shop in Francis Coventry's *The History of Pompey the Little*.

Mr. Carysbroke.   See Lord Ilbury.

Lady Mary Carysbroke   Well-bred, kindly, engaging sister of Lord Ilbury; she befriends Maud Ruthyn at Elverston in J. Sheridan Le Fanu's *Uncle Silas*.

Edward Casaubon   A clergyman and scholar, who has been writing and researching his text "A Key to All Mythologies" for many years; although he is fifty and she is nineteen, he marries Dorothea Brooke in order to have company when he is not studying; the two can never understand each other, for he is cold-hearted while she is loving; he dies in his garden before he can force a promise from Dorothea that she will compile and publish his notes in George Eliot's *Middlemarch*.

Christopher Casby   Patriarchal landlord of the Bleeding Heart Yard with long, flowing white hair; he is Flora Finching's father; he appears benevolent but is greedy and hard-hearted to his tenants; he is eventually humiliated by his collection agent, Mr. Pancks, in the Bleeding Heart Yard in Charles Dickens's *Little Dorrit*.

Mr. Case   Confidential servant of the Baroness Bernstein (Beatrix Esmond) in William Makepeace Thackeray's *The Virginians*.

Captain Jack Casey   Emma Newcome's first husband, who was abusive and died of drink in William Makepeace Thackeray's *The Newcomes*.

Lady Cashel   Weak-minded aunt of Fanny Wyndham; she supports her niece's loyalty to Frank O'Kelly (Lord Ballindine) in Anthony Trollope's *The Kellys and the O'Kellys*.

Lord Cashel   Uncle and guardian of Fanny Wyndham; he tries to enforce her marriage to his son, Lord Kilcullen, in Anthony Trollope's *The Kellys and the O'Kellys*.

Squire Cass   The wealthiest man in Ravenloe; he is renowned more for his ill-temper and irresponsible nature than for any kindness toward the townspeople; he is the father of Godfrey and Dunston Cass in George Eliot's *Silas Marner*.

Dunston Cass   The drinking, gambling, second son of Squire Cass; he imagines himself to be a lucky fellow who is able to rely on chance; he steals Silas Marner's gold and drowns still clutching the heavy money bags in George Eliot's *Silas Marner*.

Godfrey Cass The oldest son of Squire Cass; he allows his wife Molly to die and makes no attempt to claim Eppie as his daughter until many years after his childless marriage to Nancy Lammeter in George Eliot's *Silas Marner*.

Molly Cass The first wife of Godfrey Cass, but unrecognized as such by anyone except Dunston Cass; she is an opium addict, who dies outside in the snow with her child, Eppie, in her arms in George Eliot's *Silas Marner*.

Miss Casseway Elderly companion to Lady Mabel Grex and a distant cousin of the family; she constantly fears that the country is steadily declining in Anthony Trollope's *The Duke's Children*.

Mr. Casson The fat, satisfied owner of the Donnithorne Arms, a tavern in Hayslope, which he opens after being the rich Donnithorne family's butler for fifteen years in George Eliot's *Adam Bede*.

Gian-Battasta Castaldo (Count of Piadena) Persevering, indefatigable general in the army of the Emperor Charles IV and generous patron of the Chevalier de Damville (Charles de St. Leon) in William Godwin's *St. Leon*.

Julian Casti Bookish, culture-loving chemist's assistant and aspiring writer; he becomes the friend of Osmond Waymark by answering an advertisement and contracts a miserable marriage with his cousin, Harriet Smales, in George Gissing's *The Unclassed*.

Castiglione Italian knight who assists Castruccio dei Antelminelli in the siege of Valperga in Mary Shelley's *Valperga*.

Victor (Cabasse) de Castillonnes Young poet who has improved on his name and is a hanger-on of the Duchesse d'Ivry, who instigates his duel with Lord Kew in William Makepeace Thackeray's *The Newcomes*.

Lord Castledanes Childless earl, who, after the death of his long-insane wife, marries in old age a young half sister of his nephew's wife and has two sons, apparently ruining Adolphus Delmont's hope of inheritance in Charlotte Smith's *The Young Philosopher*.

Lord Castlemallard Nobleman who resides near Chapelizod; he is Mervyn's guardian and a very dull conversationalist in J. Sheridan Le Fanu's *The House by the Churchyard*.

Marquess of Castleton Aging nobleman, who marries Fanny Trevanion to ensure heirs to his estate in Edward Bulwer-Lytton's *The Caxtons*.

Betty Castleton Jenny James's aristocratic friend, at whose card party Amelia Booth encounters the Noble Lord while William Booth becomes reacquainted with George Trent in Henry Fielding's *Amelia*.

Lord Castlewell Eloquent suitor of Rachel O'Mahony, the opera singer; he secures a singing engagement for her at Covent Garden and becomes briefly engaged to her in Anthony Trollope's *The Landleaguers*.

Edward Esmond, Earl and Marquis of Castlewood Father of Lady Dorothea Esmond, who is heir to his property and ancestress of the Viscounts Castlewood in William Makepeace Thackeray's *The History of Henry Esmond*.

Francis, first Viscount Castlewood Son of Lady Dorothea and Henry (Poyns) Esmond; he is made baronet by King James I, and later viscount; his eldest son is the second viscount; his two younger sons are fathers of the third and fourth viscounts in William Makepeace Thackeray's *The History of Henry Esmond*.

George, second Viscount Castlewood Nobleman ruined by his loyalty to the Stuarts; his daughter, Lady Isabel, marries his nephew and heir, Thomas, in William Makepeace Thackeray's *The History of Henry Esmond*.

Thomas, third Viscount Castlewood Colonel Thomas Esmond's son; he is a dissipated soldier whose marriage to Gertrude Maes goes unrecognized; he marries his cousin, Lady Isabel; he brings his son, Henry Esmond, to Castlewood but does not acknowledge him as his legitimate heir before he dies in Ireland in William Makepeace Thackeray's *The History of Henry Esmond*.

Francis, fourth Viscount Castlewood Vain, good-natured first cousin of Henry Esmond's father, Thomas, the third viscount; he inherits the title after Thomas's death; he marries Rachel Armstrong and fathers Beatrix and Frank (later the fifth viscount); angry at Lord Mohun's attentions to his wife, he fights a duel with him and is killed; dying, he confesses to his protegé Henry Esmond that he knows Henry is legitimate and the rightful fourth Viscount Castlewood in William Makepeace Thackeray's *The History of Henry Esmond*.

Francis James (Frank), fifth Viscount Castlewood Henry Esmond's cheerful and charming young second cousin, who serves with him in Marlborough's wars before he marries the Catholic Clotilda Wertheim; he is Beatrix Esmond's brother in William Makepeace Thackeray's *The History of Henry Esmond*. His children are Lady Maria Esmond and Eugene, Earl of Castlewood (by

Clotilda) and the Hon. William and Lady Fanny Esmond (by his second wife, Anna) in *The Virginians*.

Eugene, second Earl of Castlewood   No friend of the Virginian Warringtons, his cousins; he gambles with Harry, fleecing him, and tries to deprive both brothers of their inheritance after his marriage to the wealthy Lydia Van den Bosch in William Makepeace Thackeray's *The Virginians*.

Anna, Dowager Countess Castlewood   Second wife, now widow, of Frank, fifth Viscount and first Earl of Castlewood; she is mother of the Hon. William and Lady Fanny Esmond in William Makepeace Thackeray's *The Virginians*.

Clotilda de Wertheim, Viscountess Castlewood   Lady from Brussels who marries the very young Frank, fifth Viscount Castlewood, converts him to Roman Catholicism, and rules over him in William Makepeace Thackeray's *The History of Henry Esmond*. Her children are Lady Maria Esmond and Eugene, Earl of Castlewood in *The Virginians*.

Lady Isabel, Viscountess Castlewood   Daughter of George, the second Viscount Castlewood; she marries her first cousin, Thomas, the third viscount; vain and ridiculous as she ages, she is nevertheless kind to her supposedly illegitimate stepson, Henry Esmond, bequeathing him her modest fortune in William Makepeace Thackeray's *The History of Henry Esmond*.

Rachel Armstrong, Viscountess Castlewood   Wife of the fourth viscount, who is intellectually and morally her inferior; beautiful and high-minded, she is a warm friend to the boy Henry Esmond; after her husband's death following a duel, she is for a time estranged from Esmond; she becomes a supporter of his courtship of her daughter, Lady Beatrix Esmond, and after Beatrix's flight consoles him by marrying him herself; they emigrate to America in William Makepeace Thackeray's *The History of Henry Esmond*.

Stephanos Castor   Celebrated wrestler, who possesses a magnificent shape but clownish features and a surly disposition; he is a conspirator against Emperor Alexius Comnenus in Sir Walter Scott's *Count Robert of Paris*.

Agnes de Castra   Cousin to Antonia Cranmer in Thomas Amory's *The Life of John Buncle, Esq.*

Catau   Signora di Modena's servant girl, who aids the escape of her prisoner in Charlotte Dacre's *Zofloya; or, The Moor*.

Michael (Mike) Catchpole   Former employee of Mr. Furze; blinded in his work, he is forced to sell shoelaces until his son, Tom, is employed by Furze in Mark Rutherford's *Catharine Furze*.

Tom Catchpole   Son of Mike Catchpole; Mr. Furze's assistant, he falls in love with Catharine Furze after she rescues him from a fire; he helps prevent the Reverend Theophilus Cardew from committing adultery with Catharine; the victim of a plot to drive him away from Eastthorp, he goes to London with a reference from Cardew in Mark Rutherford's *Catharine Furze*.

Caterina   Servant in the Castle di Udolpho in Ann Radcliffe's *The Mysteries of Udolpho*.

Caterina   Servant who helps Julia de Mazzini to escape her father's castle the night before her forced marriage to Duke de Luovo in Ann Radcliffe's *A Sicilian Romance*.

Caterpillar   Arrogant and patronizing creature, who sits on a mushroom, smoking a hookah; after his interrogation of Alice he requires her to recite "You Are Old, Father William" as a test of her memory and then advises her to use the mushroom to control her size in Lewis Carroll's *Alice's Adventures in Wonderland*.

Catesby   One of the attendants on Richard of Gloucester, who explains to him why he is so hungry for glory; Catesby tells Dick Shelton he would be an earl tomorrow if his name were Richard in Robert Louis Stevenson's *The Black Arrow: A Tale of Two Roses*.

Monsignore Catesby   Jesuit of noble family; he is more forceful and cunning than Father Coleman in trying to convince Lothair to become a Catholic in Benjamin Disraeli's *Lothair*.

Mr. Catfield   Deacon at Mark Rutherford's first chapel; he distributes the hymns and is ignorant of most things outside a few verses of the Bible in Mark Rutherford's *The Autobiography of Mark Rutherford*.

Marmaduke Catharines   Elderly clergyman who writes a character reference clearing the woman accused of kidnapping Ned Fielding; he performs the marriage of young Harry Clinton and Abenaide in Henry Brooke's *The Fool of Quality*.

Mrs. Catherick   Mother of Anne, the girl with an uncanny likeness to Laura Fairlie; she reveals that Laura's father had been the father of the illegitimate Anne in Wilkie Collins's *The Woman in White*.

Anne Catherick   Poor, demented woman, whose resemblance to Laura (Fairlie), Lady Glyde makes her the victim of Sir Percival Glyde's plan to defraud his wife of her fortune; she dies and is buried under Laura's name while Laura is incarcerated; Walter Hartright discovers that she was the illegitimate daughter of Laura's father in Wilkie Collins's *The Woman in White*.

Donna Catherina Mother of Violetta and wife of Don Manuel in Penelope Aubin's *The Strange Adventures of the Count de Vinevil and His Family*.

Catherine Employee of the Countess of Somerset (2) and attendant to the imprisoned (younger) Mary, whom she poisons in Sophia Lee's *The Recess*.

Catherine Julian Avenel's beautiful mistress and the mother of his illegitimate son; often ill-treated by him, she is nonetheless devoted, and she dies of grief upon discovering his body in Sir Walter Scott's *The Monastery*.

Catherine Wife of Elias; the mother of nine, she is foolish, obstinate, and ignorant, but completely devoted to her family in Charles Reade's *The Cloister and the Hearth*.

Little Catherine Crippled, saintly daughter of Elias; she aids Gerard in his escape from the burgomaster's prison tower and befriends Margaret Brandt in Charles Reade's *The Cloister and the Hearth*.

Lady Catherine—— Clever, enthusiastic young Irish baroness, who attends Frances (Henri) Crimsworth's school in Brussels in Charlotte Brontë's *The Professor*.

Alfred Emery Cathie A solicitor given power of attorney when Jack Higgs leaves for Erewhon in Samuel Butler's *Erewhon Revisited Twenty Years Later*.

Mademoiselle Cattarina A French ballet dancer who charms Harry Warrington for a time in William Makepeace Thackeray's *The Virginians*.

Elder Miss Cattle Daughter of Mr. and Mrs. Cattle; she leads the gossip about Mr. Cutts in Mark Rutherford's *Miriam's Schooling*.

Mr. and Mrs. Cattle Giacomo Tacchi's visitors, who gossip about Mr. Cutts burning his house in Mark Rutherford's *Miriam's Schooling*.

Carry Cattle Younger sister of Elder Miss Cattle; she adds to gossip about Mr. Cutts in Mark Rutherford's *Miriam's Schooling*.

William, Lord Caulfield Convivial and trustful English Lord Governor of the province of Ulster and resident at Charlemont; he is tricked and taken captive along with his officers and men by the treacherous Sir Phelim O'Neile, leader of the Irish conspiracy, in William Godwin's *Mandeville*.

Cavalier Second son of a Shropshire gentleman; his father tries to settle him with a marriage and an annual income, but he wishes to travel; at the instigation of John Hepburn, he joins the forces of King Gustavus Adolphus of Sweden; upon returning home to England, he joins the Loyalists in fighting for Charles I and details the adventures of his life in Daniel Defoe's *Memoirs of a Cavalier*.

Cavalier's Father Shropshire gentleman, who wishes to settle his son with a wife but consents to allow him to travel and join the military; he too is among the Loyalists in Daniel Defoe's *Memoirs of a Cavalier*.

Jean Baptist Cavalleto Small Italian imprisoned with Rigaud in Marseilles; he later works for Daniel Doyce in the Bleeding Heart Yard and is instrumental in hunting down Rigaud in Charles Dickens's *Little Dorrit*.

Mary Cavanagh Commonplace, uneducated woman, whose marriage to Morton Cavanagh causes him to be socially ostracized and ultimately ruined in Mrs. Lynn Linton's *The Autobiography of Christopher Kirkland*.

Morton Cavanagh Upper-class bohemian artist and best friend of Christopher Kirkland; he sinks into alcoholic depravity because of his unfortunate marriage to a woman beneath him in Mrs. Lynn Linton's *The Autobiography of Christopher Kirkland*.

Mary Cave Wife of the Reverend Mr. Helstone; also loved by Hiram Yorke, she dies after five years of marriage amid rumors of neglect in Charlotte Brontë's *Shirley*.

Martha Cavely Unpleasant widowed sister of Martin Tinman; she assists her brother in his pursuit of Annette Smith in George Meredith's *The House on the Beach*.

Elizabeth (Bess of Hardwicke) Cavendish Formidable wife of Lord Shrewsbury and grandmother of Arabella Stewart in Charlotte Yonge's *Unknown to History*.

Cavigni Robber chieftain who captures Megalena de Metastasio and is killed by Wolfstein in Percy Bysshe Shelley's *St. Irvyne*.

Signor Cavigni Italian gallant who helps the evil Montoni in his suit to marry Madame Cheron in Ann Radcliffe's *The Mysteries of Udolpho*.

Bridget Cawthorne Author of an innocuous letter given to Henry Lambert by mistake in William Beckford's *Modern Novel Writing; or, the Elegant Enthusiast*.

Jacob Caxon Old barber, who dresses the only three wigs in the parish of Fairmont and sometimes serves as a messenger for Oldbuck (Jonathan Oldenbuck) in Sir Walter Scott's *The Antiquary*.

Austin Caxton Father of Pisistratus Caxton; an unworldly, futile scholar, he is absorbed in writing a history of human error in Edward Bulwer-Lytton's *The Caxtons* and in *"My Novel,"* by Pisistratus Caxton.

Blanche Caxton Roland Caxton's daughter, who is groomed by her father and her uncle, Austin Caxton, to be the ideal wife for Pisistratus Caxton in Edward Bulwer-Lytton's *The Caxtons*. She provides commentary in *"My Novel,"* by Pisistratus Caxton.

Herbert Caxton Roland Caxton's lost son, who is the rival of Pisistratus Caxton for Fanny Trevanion; he farms sheep with Pisistratus in Australia and dies as a soldier in India in Edward Bulwer-Lytton's *The Caxtons*.

Katharine (Kitty) Caxton Young ward and later wife of Austin Caxton; she is a model of domestic insipidity in Edward Bulwer-Lytton's *The Caxtons*. She provides commentary in *"My Novel,"* by Pisistratus Caxton.

Pisistratus Caxton Austin Caxton's son, who tells the story of his birth and youth, marries his cousin Blanche, and becomes a novelist in Edward Bulwer-Lytton's *The Caxtons*. He is a novelist in *"My Novel,"* by Pisistratus Caxton and in *What Will He Do With It?* by Pisistratus Caxton.

Roland Caxton Brother of Austin Caxton and a Waterloo veteran; he is obsessed with the family honor in Edward Bulwer-Lytton's *The Caxtons* and in *"My Novel,"* by Pisistratus Caxton.

Mr. Cayenne An American Tory who establishes the first cotton-weaving mill in the area and builds the town of Cayenneville to house the workers; he rivals in power the older aristocracy of the parish in John Galt's *Annals of the Parish*.

Ser Ceccone The underhanded informer who gives information to the party willing to pay the most; he is jealous of Tito Melema's ability to receive and pass information more quickly in George Eliot's *Romola*.

Lord Cecil English aristocrat and husband of Lady Cecil in Mary Shelley's *Falkner*.

Berkeley Cecil Younger brother of Bertie Cecil; he forges the Duke of Rockingham's name to pay a gambling debt but escapes punishment when his brother is blamed instead; he inherits the family estates and title when Bertie is presumed dead in Ouida's *Under Two Flags*.

Bertie Cecil Second-eldest son of the Viscount Royallieu and a member of the elite English guard; accused of forgery and disgraced, he joins the French Foreign Legion under the name of Louis Victor and is sta-tioned in Algiers for twelve years in Ouida's *Under Two Flags*.

Rose Cecil Lord Burleigh's daughter, who selflessly suppresses her love for Lord Leicester and arranges his and Matilda's escape from England; abducted by Mr. Mortimer, she takes her own life rather than submit to a forced and degrading marriage in Sophia Lee's *The Recess*.

Sophia, Lady Cecil Wife of Lord Cecil and the charming stepsister of Gerald Neville; she introduces Elizabeth Raby to English society and narrates her brother's story in Mary Shelley's *Falkner*.

Cecilia Best friend of Sidney Bidulph Arnold since childhood; while living abroad with her husband, who has a station in the court of Vienna, she receives the correspondence containing Sidney's vicissitudes, and upon arriving in London she supplements the correspondence with a narrative describing Sidney's later years in Frances Sheridan's *Memoirs of Miss Sidney Bidulph*.

Cecilia A young Christian in Rome; it is in her house that Marius becomes enamoured of the Christian religion in Walter Pater's *Marius the Epicurean*.

Cedric the Saxon of Rotherwood Wealthy, blustering Saxon, Ivanhoe's father and Lady Rowena's guardian; he longs for the ascendancy of his race, plotting the marriage of Rowena and Athelstane and disinheriting his son because of his love for the lady; eventually, King Richard wins him over in Sir Walter Scott's *Ivanhoe*.

Celadine A self-imagined lady-killer; he chases Jenny Jessamy in Eliza Haywood's *The History of Jemmy and Jenny Jessamy*.

Celia Woman who recounts how she has devoted her life to the pursuit of pleasure to her correspondent Sophronia, whose obsession is philosophy in Sarah Fielding's *Familiar Letters between the Principal Characters of David Simple and Some Others*.

Celia-of-the-Woods Country girl; Jemmy Jessamy is enamored of her, but she becomes the haughty Lady Handy, who loves intrigues in Eliza Haywood's *The History of Jemmy and Jenny Jessamy*.

Celinda Fifteen-year-old English girl, who is seduced by Ferdinand in the guise of music master and is abandoned by him to dissipation in addiction to drugs in Tobias Smollett's *The Adventures of Ferdinand Count Fathom*.

Menico Cennini Florentine goldsmith and money-lender in George Eliot's *Romola*.

Astride (Fru Astrida) de Centeville Nurse to Duke

Richard of Normandy; she maintains his knowledge of the old Norse language and of the sagas in Charlotte Yonge's *The Little Duke*.

Eric de Centeville   Norman baron and guardian of young Duke Richard in Charlotte Yonge's *The Little Duke*.

Osmond de Centeville   Loyal, quick-witted squire of Duke Richard of Normandy; he contrives to escpae from the court of King Louis in Charlotte Yonge's *The Little Duke*.

Princess Claelia Cesarini   Gerard's patroness, who, because he does not return her love, hires the assassin Lodovico to slay him; she relents and orders the assassin killed; upon a pilgrimage of penitence to Loretto, she washes the feet of Friar Clement (Gerard) and confesses her wicked plot to the proposed victim in Charles Reade's *The Cloister and the Hearth*.

Cesario   Gallant young prince and a plotter against the king of France; he is emasculated by his love for Hermione and defeated by his dealings with the sorcerer Fergusano; the king, who can forgive Cesario's treason but not his slander of the king's reputation, executes him in Aphra Behn's *Love Letters Between a Nobleman and His Sister*.

Cesario   Servant to Count Morano; he assists in an attempt to kidnap Emily St. Aubert in Ann Radcliffe's *The Mysteries of Udolpho*.

Colonel Raoul de Châteauroy   Colonel in the French Foreign Legion who is called "the Black Hawk"; his jealousy, hatred and maltreatment of Louis Victor (Bertie Cecil) lead to a scuffle and a charge of insubordination against Victor in Ouida's *Under Two Flags*.

Marian Chabot   Low-born, remarkably gifted friend of Marguerite de St. Leon (Marguerite de Damville), who is similar to her in appearance and gesture in William Godwin's *St. Leon*.

Jack Chace   A young man about town who has the ambition to be thought a man of consummate debauch and who marries Daughter Frippery in Francis Coventry's *The History of Pompey the Little*.

Mr. Chadband   Large, oily, dissenting minister with great oratorical skill, who marries Mrs. Rachael, is patronized by Mrs. Snagsby, and tries to "convert" Jo by discoursing on the "human boy" in Charles Dickens's *Bleak House*.

John Chadwick   Steward of the Bishop of Barchester in charge of Hiram's Hospital accounting in Anthony Trollope's *The Warden*. He appears briefly in *Barchester Towers* and in *Framley Parsonage*. He is called on for legal advice in the Crawley case in *The Last Chronicle of Barset*.

Chaeras   The genteel but ugly middle daughter of Maladie Alamode; her name is explained as a translation of "king's evil" in Henry Fielding's *A Journey From This World to the Next*.

Mr. Chaffanbrass   Scruffy Old Bailey barrister, who specializes in defending criminals and scourging witnesses; he takes on Alaric Tudor's case in Anthony Trollope's *The Three Clerks*. He defends Lady Mason with his customary ferocity in *Orley Farm*. He similarly defends Phineas Finn in a murder trial in *Phineas Redux*.

Mr. Chainmail   Young man who believes in the complete superiority of the twelfth century over the nineteenth; he marries Susanna Touchandgo in Thomas Love Peacock's *Crotchet Castle*.

Mark Challenger   Tailor and friend of Arthur Golding; he is a member of a workingmen's club and arouses Arthur's interest in social problems in George Gissing's *Workers in the Dawn*.

Professor Challenger   Irascible scientist who defies public and scholarly opinion and leads an expedition to the region of dinosaurs in Arthur Conan Doyle's *The Lost World*.

Chalmers   Schoolmaster with a Glasgow M.A., who is jealous of Clement Butt's greater success with lesser education in Mark Rutherford's *Mark Rutherford's Deliverance*.

Chamber Maid at Inn   Player of a trick on the Disguised Gentleman by sending him to the wrong room, starting all the other travelers in a merry game of accusation and counter accusation in Charles Johnstone's *Chrysal: or, The Adventures of a Guinea*.

Henry Fitzackerly Chamberlaine   Handsome, affable, utterly self-centred prebendary of Salisbury Cathedral and uncle of Harry Gilmore; his goal in life is not to become involved, but he is reluctantly drawn into the controversy over the chapel built on glebe land in Anthony Trollope's *The Vicar of Bullhampton*.

Champfort   Lord Delacour's deceitful, conceited servant, who turns him against Lady Delacour and circulates lies about Lord Delacour's relationship with Belinda Portman in Maria Edgeworth's *Belinda*.

Marchioness Champfort   Parisian widow of dubious character, whose parties Valancourt frequents during his separation from Emily St. Aubert in Ann Radcliffe's *The Mysteries of Udolpho*.

Chancellor   A conspirator in the scheme to usurp the Warden of Outland and create a Vice-Warden in Lewis Carroll's *Sylvie and Bruno*. He attends Uggug's birthday banquet and escorts in the beggar in *Sylvie and Bruno Concluded*.

Mr. Chandler   Farmer who is a friend and customer of Mr. Furze in Mark Rutherford's *Catharine Furze*.

Chandler's-Shopkeeper   Woman who explains how she came by the manuscript in Charles Johnstone's *Chrysal: or, The Adventures of a Guinea*.

Countess of Channelcliffe   Hostess at whose assembly Jocelyn Pierston hopes for a glimpse of the "well-beloved" in Thomas Hardy's *The Well-Beloved*.

Mercy Chant   A young lady devoted to church work and seen by Angel Clare's parents as a suitable bride for him; she marries his brother Cuthbert in Thomas Hardy's *Tess of the D'Urbervilles*.

Lady Rose Chantrey   Deceased mother of Julie Le Breton; she chose to flout tradition and bear a daughter out of wedlock rather than live with a husband she no longer loved in Mrs. Humphry Ward's *Lady Rose's Daughter*.

Chaplain of the Charity   Person of some learning; he places his abilities in a conspicuous light in Charles Johnstone's *Chrysal: or, The Adventures of a Guinea*.

Chaplain of the Man of War   Libertine who is reformed by the Benevolent Naval Captain in Charles Johnstone's *Chrysal: or, The Adventures of a Guinea*.

Chapman   Traveling merchant from the Westland Cities of the Plain; he had once been held to ransom by Folk-might for dastardly deeds in William Morris's *The Roots of the Mountains*.

Chapman   Ill-disposed traveling merchant, who lusts after Elfhild but sells her to Sir Mark (the Blue Knight) in William Morris's *The Sundering Flood*.

Mr. Chapman   Bedfordshire neighbor whose love and tenderness toward his wife are a foil to the behavior of aristocratic couples in Samuel Richardson's *Pamela, or Virtue Rewarded*.

Mr. Chapman   Henry Lambert's friend in William Beckford's *Modern Novel Writing; or, the Elegant Enthusiast*.

Mrs. Chapman   Bedfordshire neighbor whose kindness to and love of her husband are a foil to the behavior of aristocratic couples in Samuel Richardson's *Pamela, or Virtue Rewarded*.

Nat Chapman   Rustic, gossiping chorister in Thomas Hardy's *Two on a Tower*.

Charity   One of three virgins of the Palace Beautiful who catechize Christian and later his sons; she shows them the house and its contents in John Bunyan's *The Pilgrim's Progress From this World to That Which Is to Come*.

Charity Supporter Number One (Scrivener)   A huge man who is the principal support of every public charity founded on the principle of the feast; he acquires the money he gives to charity from vice in Charles Johnstone's *Chrysal: or, The Adventures of a Guinea*.

Charity Supporter Number Two (Almoner)   A hypocrite who dispenses other people's charity because of his pious demeanor in Charles Johnstone's *Chrysal: or, The Adventures of a Guinea*.

Charity Supporter Number Three (Clergyman)   A venerable and happy man, who is a true supporter of charity and a blessing to mankind in Charles Johnstone's *Chrysal: or, The Adventures of a Guinea*.

Charity Supporter Number Four   A low-bred avaricious wretch, who marries his pupil's mother and turns her against her son, whom she disinherits in Charles Johnstone's *Chrysal: or, The Adventures of a Guinea*.

Charity Supporter Number Five (Attorney)   A man who is beyond reproach, knowledgeable in his profession, honest, and generous in Charles Johnstone's *Chrysal: or, The Adventures of a Guinea*.

Charity Supporter Number Six   A man of such indolence of mind that he completely submits to his wife's capricious tyranny in Charles Johnstone's *Chrysal: or, The Adventures of a Guinea*.

Charity Supporter Number Seven   Superannuated fop, who in his own home is a perfect cypher for his wife in Charles Johnstone's *Chrysal: or, The Adventures of a Guinea*.

Charity Supporter Number Eight   Large athletic and deprived man, who cheats his ward out of her estate and gives everything to his daughter in Charles Johnstone's *Chrysal: or, The Adventures of a Guinea*.

Charity Supporter Number Nine (Man-Midwife)   A man who becomes a midwife through a desire to alleviate the suffering of the poor but neglects to appreciate the force of public opinion in Charles Johnstone's *Chrysal: or, The Adventures of a Guinea*.

Tom Charke   Gambler associated with the young Silas Ruthyn; his death in a locked room during a visit to

Bartram-Haugh is believed to be a suicide until Maud Ruthyn's experiences reveal how he was murdered in J. Sheridan Le Fanu's *Uncle Silas.*

Honora Charlecote   Wealthy, devout spinster, who adopts the orphaned children of Owen Sandbrook, the man who jilted her, and is bitterly disappointed in them in Charlotte Yonge's *Hopes and Fears.*

Humfrey Charlecote   Worthy, high-minded country squire, who finally wins Honora Charlecote but dies before they can marry in Charlotte Yonge's *Hopes and Fears.*

Humfrey Charlecote (the younger)   A Canadian and the heir to Honora Charlecote's estate; he marries Phoebe Fulmort in Charlotte Yonge's *Hopes and Fears.*

Charles   Lucy Snowe's uncle whom she apparently resembles in Charlotte Brontë's *Villette.*

Charles   Friend and narrator of Harley's story in Henry Mackenzie's *The Man of Feeling.*

Charles   Schoolfriend to whom William Crimsworth writes the letter that forms the first chapter of Charlotte Brontë's *The Professor.*

Charles   Son of an aristocratic family; he marries the heiress Mary by parental arrangement and then leaves for an extended absence on the Continent, fueling the young wife's already active aversion to the empty union in Mary Wollstonecraft's *Mary, A Fiction.*

Uncle Charles   Curate of Chapelizod and the narrator's uncle and godfather; his attendance at the funeral of Lady Darby and the finding of the skull of Barney Sturk precipitate the telling of the story of events in Chapelizod in 1767 in J. Sheridan Le Fanu's *The House by the Churchyard.*

Prince Charles (Stuart)   See Charles Edward Stewart.

King Charles I   Prince Charles and son of King James I in Sir Walter Scott's *The Fortunes of Nigel.* He is the reigning monarch during the English civil war for whom John Inglesant is messenger and courtier in J. Henry Shorthouse's *John Inglesant, A Romance.* As monarch of England he enlists the Cavalier to fight for him in the civil war; he is dejected and constantly plagued with poor advice from his counselors in Daniel Defoe's *Memoirs of a Cavalier.*

King Charles II   British monarch who orders the release of the Peverils from the Tower and tricks Zarah into revealing her identity to Charlotte de la Tremouille, the Countess of Derby, in Sir Walter Scott's *Peveril of the Peak.* He is king of Scotland and deposed king of England;

using the names Charles Stewart and Louis Kerneguy he is in hiding at Woodstock Lodge while escaping to the Continent; he attempts to seduce Alice Lee and narrowly escapes a duel with her lover, Markham Everard, in *Woodstock.*

Charles the Simple   King of France, son of Louis III; he was the butt of many of Julian the Apostate's jokes in his incarnation as court jester in Henry Fielding's *A Journey From This World to the Next.*

Charley   Potboy at the Magpie and Stump in Charles Dickens's *The Posthumous Papers of the Pickwick Club.*

Charley   Adolescent who is in love with Eustacia Vye and mourns her death in Thomas Hardy's *The Return of the Native.*

Charley   Owner of a second-hand marine store in Chatham to whom David Copperfield sells his jacket on the way to Dover in Charles Dickens's *The Personal History of David Copperfield.*

Charlot   Idiot groom assigned to Quentin Durward by Louis XI in Sir Walter Scott's *Quentin Durward.*

Charlotta   Charming young woman, who is insensible of her attractions; she is no coquette in Eliza Haywood's *Life's Progress Through the Passions: or, the Adventures of Natura.*

Charlotte   The Sowerberrys' kitchenmaid, who feeds Noah Claypole oysters and later robs the till and runs off with Noah to London in Charles Dickens's *Oliver Twist.*

Charlotte   London friend and recipient of Felicia's letters; she possesses fashionable society's conventional views about male-female relationships and the virtues of country living, but a visit to Felicia changes her mind in Mary Collyer's *Felicia to Charlotte.*

Mrs. Charlton   Suffolk neighbor of Cecilia Beverley; until her death she provides hospitality to Cecilia as desired in Frances Burney's *Cecilia.*

Charmides   Greek sculptor in Rome who becomes a Christian martyr with a woman he loves in a story written by the Reverend Theophilus Cardew and given to Catharine Furze in Mark Rutherford's *Catharine Furze.*

Felice Charmond   Beautiful former actress, now a lonely widow, who has a love affair with Edred Fitzpiers which costs him his wife and his medical practice; she is killed by a former lover in Thomas Hardy's *The Woodlanders.*

Anne Charnock   South African colonist who comes to

England as the bride of Commander Miles Charnock; her rigid, repressive brand of Evangelicalism comes into conflict with the practices of her worldly new relations in Charlotte Yonge's *The Three Brides*.

Frank Charnock   Fourth son of Julia Charnock Poynsett; he gains the hand of Eleonora Vivian after many vicissitudes and succeeds as a literary man in Charlotte Yonge's *The Three Brides*.

Julius Charnock   An albino and Rector of Compton Poynsett; he introduces High Church practices to his parishioners and reconciles Anne Charnock to her in-laws in Charlotte Yonge's *The Three Brides*.

Commander Miles Charnock   Second son of Julia Charnock Poynsett; he sends home from South Africa his rigidly Evangelical bride, Anne, in Charlotte Yonge's *The Three Brides*.

Lady Rosamond (Lady Rose) Charnock   Daughter of an impoverished Irish earl and the warmhearted wife of Julius Charnock; she is held in contempt by her sister-in-law Cecil but overcomes her natural indolence to become a pattern wife and mother in Charlotte Yonge's *The Three Brides*.

Cecil Charnock Poynsett   Priggish young bride of Raymond Charnock Poynsett; she chafes at living in her mother-in-law's house, dabbles in feminism, and recognizes her passion for her husband only as he is dying in Charlotte Yonge's *The Three Brides*.

Julia Charnock Poynsett   Widowed mistress of a large estate and mother of Raymond Charnock Poynsett and of Miles, Julius, and Frank Charnock (the younger sons bear the patronymic alone); she has been crippled in a riding accident; her abnormally strong hold on her eldest son is partly responsible for the failure of his marriage in Charlotte Yonge's *The Three Brides*.

Raymond Charnock Poynsett   Eldest son of Julia Charnock Poynsett and Member of Parliament, who marries his young cousin Cecil Charnock largely for his mother's sake and suffers for this mistake until he dies of typhoid in Charlotte Yonge's *The Three Brides*.

Charoba   Compassionate and independent daughter of Totis, king of Egypt; she becomes Queen of Egypt when her father is poisoned and rids herself of her unwanted suitor and would-be conqueror, the giant Gebirus, by poisoning him in the appended romance "The History of Charoba, Queen of Egypt" in Clara Reeve's *The Progress of Romance*.

Countess Charolois   Belated patroness of Gerard; at the reminder of his brother, the dwarf Giles, she fulfils

an old promise by bestowing Gouda parsonage upon him in Charles Reade's *The Cloister and the Hearth*.

Arthur Charpentier   Royal Navy sublieutenant initially arrested for the murder of Enoch Drebber in Arthur Conan Doyle's *A Study in Scarlet*.

Sir Patrick Charteris   Provost of Perth, who offers himself as champion of Henry Smith, Simon Glover, and other burgesses in their quarrel with the Duke of Rothsay and John Ramorny in Sir Walter Scott's *The Fair Maid of Perth*.

Billy Chatter   One of the London tavern boys, who becomes a companion of Roderick Random after his return from France and suggests that Roderick court Miss Biddy Gripewell in Tobias Smollett's *The Adventures of Roderick Random*.

Simon Chatterly   Dandified prelate who visits St. Ronan's Well for its waters and gossiping society in Sir Walter Scott's *St. Ronan's Well*.

General Chattesworth   Gertrude's father and Rebecca's brother, the jovial leader of the Royal Irish Artillery and owner of the Belmont estate in J. Sheridan Le Fanu's *The House by the Churchyard*.

Gertrude Chattesworth   Graceful daughter of General Chattesworth; she falls in love with Mervyn, but they keep their engagement a secret until his family's name is cleared; Paul Dangerfield tries to marry her but she resists in J. Sheridan Le Fanu's *The House by the Churchyard*.

Rebecca (Aunt Becky) Chattesworth   Kind-hearted but dictatorial sister of General Chattesworth and thus the matriarch of the Royal Irish Artillery; she administers her benevolences somewhat tyrannically; she opposes Mervyn and promotes Paul Dangerfield as a husband for Gertrude until the truth comes out; she finally confesses a long-standing affection for Lieutenant Puddock and marries him in J. Sheridan Le Fanu's *The House by the Churchyard*.

Squire Cheatum   Landowning neighbor of John Jorrocks; he is jealously vigilant against trespassing on his property in Robert Surtees's *Jorrocks's Jaunts and Jollities*.

Father Checkley   Sinister Catholic priest, who officiates at the secret wedding of Sir Piers Rookwood and Susan Bradley and subsequently murders Susan Bradley; later (as Father Ambrose) he attends the Mowbray family; he is finally strangled to death in William Harrison Ainsworth's *Rookwood*.

John Cheekey   Abrasive London lawyer known for his powers of cross-examination; he acts for Gregory Evans in the libel action Henry Jones brings against Evans in Anthony Trollope's *Cousin Henry*.

Charles Cheeryble   Twin brother of Edwin Cheeryble and a kindhearted philanthropist, who gives Nicholas Nickleby a job as a clerk and later makes him a partner in Charles Dickens's *The Life and Adventures of Nicholas Nickleby*.

Edwin Cheeryble   Twin brother of Charles and also a philanthropist; the two help Madeline Bray resolve her father's debt problems with Arthur Gride and work to bring Ralph Nickleby's schemes to a halt in Charles Dickens's *The Life and Adventures of Nicholas Nickleby*.

Frank Cheeryble   Nephew of the Cheerybles, who marries Kate Nickleby after he and Nicholas Nickleby foil Ralph Nickleby's plans to marry Madeline Bray to Arthur Gride in Charles Dickens's *The Life and Adventures of Nicholas Nickleby*.

Samuel Cheesacre   Stolid Norfolk farmer, who pays court to the rich widow, Arabella Greenow, but loses to his rival, Captain Bellfield; he marries Charlotte Fairstairs in Anthony Trollope's *Can You Forgive Her?*.

Cheeseman   Disreputable old acquaintance of James Hood; he extracts money from him in George Gissing's *A Life's Morning*.

Miss Cheggs   Alick Cheggs's sister, who is present at the party where Dick Swiveller breaks with Sophy Wackles and Alick wins Sophy in Charles Dickens's *The Old Curiosity Shop*.

Alick Cheggs   Market gardener who is Dick Swiveller's rival for Sophy Wackles; he wins Sophy after Dick breaks with her in Charles Dickens's *The Old Curiosity Shop*.

Lady Chelford   Mother of Lord Chelford and a rich, strict, old-fashioned dowager, who often lectures the young people around her; she arranges the engagement between Mark Wylder and Dorcas Brandon in J. Sheridan Le Fanu's *Wylder's Hand*.

Lord Chelford   Respected, intelligent, courteous son of Lady Chelford; he loves Rachel Lake, who loves him in return but refuses him because of her secret knowledge of her brother Stanley's crimes; he helps save William Wylder from the machinations of Lawyer Larkin; he hears Stanley Lake's deathbed confession in J. Sheridan Le Fanu's *Wylder's Hand*.

Madame Cheron, later Madame Montoni
Superficial French gentlewoman and guardian to her niece Emily St. Aubert; her marriage to the evil Montoni leads to her and Emily's confinement in the Castle di

Udolpho and ultimately to her own death in Ann Radcliffe's *The Mysteries of Udolpho*.

Mrs. Ferdinand Cherson   Woman whose gossip about financial matters encourages Diana Warwick to invest and lose a great deal of money in George Meredith's *Diana of the Crossways*.

Cheshire-Cat   Unperturbed creature first encountered in the Duchess's chaotic kitchen; it carries on a conversation with Alice full of logical fallacies about madness; its power to appear and disappear at will annoys the King of Hearts at the croquet party in Lewis Carroll's *Alice's Adventures in Wonderland*.

Edward Chester   Sir John Chester's son, disinherited when he refuses to marry a rich heiress; he falls in love with Emma Haredale, niece of his father's hated enemy, marries her, and leaves England to live abroad in Charles Dickens's *Barnaby Rudge*.

Sir John Chester   Refined but vicious gentleman, who has wronged Geoffrey Haredale and plots to wreck the relationship between his son, Edward, and Emma Haredale because of his hatred of the Haredales in Charles Dickens's *Barnaby Rudge*.

Mr. Chestle   Hop grower in Ashford who marries Miss Larkins in Charles Dickens's *The Personal History of David Copperfield*.

Sir Philip Chestrum   Foppish character who loves Caroline Campinet and convinces his mother to arrange their betrothal in Robert Bage's *Hermsprong*.

Dowager Lady Chettam   Mother of Sir James Chettam in George Eliot's *Middlemarch*.

Arthur Chettam   Celia (Brooke) and Sir James's baby boy, who is the joy of his mother's existence in George Eliot's *Middlemarch*.

Sir James Chettam   Baronet and owner of Freshitt Hall, who, when he is rejected as a suitor of Dorothea Brooke, marries her younger sister, Celia; for many years he does not forgive Dorothea for marrying Will Ladislaw in George Eliot's *Middlemarch*.

Charles Cheviot   Headmaster of the Stoneborough school; he marries Mary May in Charlotte Yonge's *The Trial*.

Jacob Chew   American Indian trader who guides the Master (James Durie) and Colonel Francis Burke through the wilderness; he dies, poisoned, in a canoe in Robert Louis Stevenson's *The Master of Ballantrae: A Winter's Tale*.

Harvey Cheyne　　Spoiled fifteen-year-old son of a millionaire; he falls out of an ocean liner and is rescued by the members of the cod-fishing boat *We're Here*; they gradually help him to mature and discard his mannerisms in Rudyard Kipling's *"Captains Courageous": A Story of the Grand Banks*.

Mr. Chichester　　Member of the Brotherhood of the Rose in Charles Kingsley's *Westward Ho!*.

Sir Arthur Chicester　　The Lord Governor legendary for his success in pacifying Ireland and a contemporary of Charles Mandeville's great-uncle in William Godwin's *Mandeville*.

Frederick Chick　　Son of John and Louisa Chick in Charles Dickens's *Dombey and Son*.

George Chick　　One of John and Louisa Chick's sons in Charles Dickens's *Dombey and Son*.

John Chick　　Stout and bald husband of Louisa Chick; slightly vulgar, he likes to whistle and hum tunes at inappropriate times and is animated by bickering with his wife in Charles Dickens's *Dombey and Son*.

Louisa Chick　　Paul Dombey's sister; she supports him in his pride of Dombey and Son, schemes to have him marry Miss Tox, is active in his household, and drops Miss Tox after Dombey marries Edith Granger in Charles Dickens's *Dombey and Son*.

Anne Chickenstalker　　Proprietress of a grocery shop where Trotty Veck owes money in Charles Dickens's *The Chimes*.

Mrs. Chickerel　　Invalid mother of numerous and variously capable children, including Ethelberta Petherwin; she is the nominal keeper of a lodging house established by Ethelberta after Lady Petherwin's death in Thomas Hardy's *The Hand of Ethelberta*.

Joey Chickerel　　Ethelberta Petherwin's younger brother, infatuated with the lady's maid Menlove; by revealing to Menlove his relationship he jeopardizes Ethelberta's social position and influences her choice of husband and her clandestine marriage; Joey's studying for the clergy is an effect of Lord Mountclere's general benevolence to his young wife's family in Thomas Hardy's *The Hand of Ethelberta*.

Picotee Chickerel　　Ethelberta Petherwin's younger sister; she marries Ethelberta's rejected suitor Christopher Julian in Thomas Hardy's *The Hand of Ethelberta*.

R. Chickerel　　Father of heroine Ethelberta Petherwin; he hides his relationship to his daughter because of his position as servant in Thomas Hardy's *The Hand of Ethelberta*.

Sol Chickerel　　A carpenter and Ethelberta Petherwin's brother; his concern over Lord Mountclere's character causes him to accompany Mr. Mountclere in an unsuccessful effort to prevent the viscount's marriage to Ethelberta in Thomas Hardy's *The Hand of Ethelberta*.

Conkey Chickweed　　Clever robber who kept a public house as related by Mr. Blathers of the Bow Street runners in Charles Dickens's *Oliver Twist*.

The Chief　　The leader of Italian revolutionaries who meet atop Monte Motterone; he supports Vittoria Campa's involvement despite objections about her sex in George Meredith's *Vittoria*.

Chiffinch (Will Smith)　　Servant of King Charles II; he conspires with the Duke of Buckingham and Edward Christian to kidnap Alice Bridgenorth; he also steals letters from Julian Peveril to implicate him in the Popish Plot in Sir Walter Scott's *Peveril of the Peak*.

Cardinal di Chigi　　Cardinal elected Pope upon the death of Pope Innocent X; he is uncle of Don Agostino di Chigi and patron of John Inglesant in J. Henry Shorthouse's *John Inglesant, A Romance*.

Don Agostino di Chigi　　Friend and traveling companion of John Inglesant in *John Inglesant, A Romance*.

E. W. B. Childers　　Horseback rider and trainer in Sleary's circus; he marries Sleary's daughter, Josephine, in Charles Dickens's *Hard Times*.

Lady Childish　　Stereotypical lady of quality who acts thirty years younger than her age in Henry Brooke's *The Fool of Quality*.

Lady Charlotte Chillingsworth　　Emilia Belloni's rival for Wilfrid Pole; she believes, rightly, that Pole's feelings for Emilia are superficial in George Meredith's *Emilia in England*.

Mr. Chillip　　Doctor who delivers David Copperfield in Charles Dickens's *The Personal History of David Copperfield*.

Oswald Standish, Lord Chiltern　　The Earl of Brentford's savage son, much given to gambling at cards and on horses; his sister, Lady Laura Standish, has used her fortune to pay his debts; he quarrels with his father; repeatedly rejected by Violet Effingham, he fights a duel with Phineas Finn, who refuses to promise not to court her; he wins Violet at last because of the unchanged intensity of his love in Anthony Trollope's *Phineas Finn*. He becomes a passionately committed Master of Foxhounds, angry with both Dukes of Omnium for failing to be considerate of his foxes in *The Eustace Diamonds*, in *Phineas Redux*, in *The Prime Minister*, and in *The Duke's Children*. He is Lord Mistletoe's guest in *The American Senator*.

Bruno Chilvers   Pretentious and hypocritical clergyman, who advocates a union of science and religion and has a successful career in George Gissing's *Born in Exile*.

Jack Chinaman   Keeper of an opium den in Charles Dickens's *The Mystery of Edwin Drood*.

Joseph Chinney   Railway porter whose belated evidence that Eunice Manston survived the fire convinces Cytherea Graye that her marriage to Aeneas Manston is illegal in Thomas Hardy's *Desperate Remedies*.

Miss Chit   The ensnarer of Jemmy Jessamy in Bellipine's plan that fails in Eliza Haywood's *The History of Jemmy and Jenny Jessamy*.

Tom Chitling   Young man who comes to Fagin's after being released from prison in Charles Dickens's *Oliver Twist*.

Mrs. Chiverly   Woman of rank, proud of her family connections in William Beckford's *Azemia*.

Mr. Chivery   Turnkey of the Marshalsea debtors' prison and tobacco-shop proprietor; he is the concerned father of John Chivery in Charles Dickens's *Little Dorrit*.

Mrs. Chivery   Prudent and watchful mother of John Chivery in Charles Dickens's *Little Dorrit*.

John Chivery   Weak-eyed and slight son of the Marshalsea turnkey and tobacco shop proprietor; he loves Amy Dorrit although she rejects his marriage proposal; he serves Arthur Clennam when the latter is a prisoner in the Marshalsea, and he reveals Amy's love to Clennam in Charles Dickens's *Little Dorrit*.

Lady Chlegen   The former Lady Fanny Fashion; she competes with Lady Dellwyn for social preeminence in Sarah Fielding's *The History of the Countess of Dellwyn*.

Choang   Korean husband who dies, then revives to find his wife Hansi about to remarry; he survives her himself to marry again in a cynical parable on marital faithlessness told by Lien Chi Altangi in Oliver Goldsmith's *The Citizen of the World*.

General Cyrus Choke   Arrogant and nationalistic American military officer, who insists the Queen of England lives in the Tower of London, and who is a member of the Eden Land Corporation, by which young Mar-

tin Chuzzlewit and Mark Tapley are cheated in Charles Dickens's *The Life and Adventures of Martin Chuzzlewit*.

Major Hannibal Chollop   Migratory, tobacco-spitting proponent of liberty, whom Mark Tapley meets in Eden; he carries a host of weapons which he delights to use on anyone who disagrees with him; he advocates slavery and lynch law in Charles Dickens's *The Life and Adventures of Martin Chuzzlewit*.

Mrs. Cholmondely   A fashionable lady in Villette, who chaperons Ginevra Fanshawe in society in Charlotte Brontë's *Villette*.

Chorsoman   Hunnish governor of Cumae who is persuaded by Marcian to allow Veranilda to leave the city and then comes to occupy and pillage Aurelia's villa in George Gissing's *Veranilda*.

Reine Chretien   Beautiful, capable woman, who manages her father's farm in Normandy; she loves Richard Butler but hesitates to marry him because of his family's contempt for her social position in Anne Thackeray Ritchie's *The Village on the Cliff*.

Christian   Pilgrim who journeys from the City of Destruction to the Celestial City, aided by his faith and the spiritual guides sent to help him; he errs and helps others avoid error along the way; he fights and defeats the demon Apollyon; he is accompanied by Faithful, then by Hopeful; he is welcomed by the King of the Celestial City in Part 1 of John Bunyan's *The Pilgrim's Progress From this World to That Which Is to Come*.

Edward Christian (Ganlesse, Simon Canter)   Hypocritical enemy of Charlotte de la Tremouille, the Countess of Derby; he conspires with the Duke of Buckingham to kidnap Alice Bridgenorth for King Charles II and confesses that he is the father of the mysterious Zarah in Sir Walter Scott's *Peveril of the Peak*.

William Christian   A leader of the Roundheads whose execution had been ordered by Charlotte de la Tremouille, Countess of Derby in Sir Walter Scott's *Peveril of the Peak*.

Christiana   Wife of Christian; she remains behind in the City of Destruction with her children, but after Christian's death decides to follow in his path; joined by her four sons and Mercy, she is guided by Great-heart through the same perils and trials as her husband, ultimately reaching the Celestial City in Part 2 of John Bunyan's *The Pilgrim's Progress From this World to That Which Is to Come*.

Miss Christianson   Friend of Lady Macfarren; she plots to make Eleanor (Raymond) Penrhyn look guilty of adultery when David Stuart, thought to be dead, returns; she marries and rules over Lord Peebles in Caroline Norton's *Stuart of Dunleath*.

Christie Lady's maid to Alison (Graeme); she accompanies Henry Durie's family to New York in Robert Louis Stevenson's *The Master of Ballantrae: A Winter's Tale*.

John Christie London ship chandler who rents rooms to Nigel Olifaunt and Richie Moniplies, believes Nigel has seduced his wife, and pursues Lord Dalgarno to recover his wife in Sir Walter Scott's *The Fortunes of Nigel*.

Nelly Christie John Christie's wife, who flees with Lord Dalgarno and is reclaimed by John when Dalgarno is killed in Sir Walter Scott's *The Fortunes of Nigel*.

Christie of the Clint Hill Julian Avenel's odious chief retainer; crafty and aggressive, he cowers in the presence of his master, whom he faithfully serves and dies beside in Sir Walter Scott's *The Monastery*.

Tom Christmas Porter at the local train station; his report leads Larkin to believe erroneously that Rachel Lake went to London with Mark Wylder in J. Sheridan Le Fanu's *Wylder's Hand*.

Christopher Fisherman who directs John Buncle to the home of Dorick Watson and is employed by Watson at regular intervals in Thomas Amory's *The Life of John Buncle, Esq.*

Christy Laborer who runs errands for Father Oliver Gogarty; he represents the simple and parochial mind of the villagers in George Moore's *The Lake*.

Mr. Chromatic Squire Headlong's guest for whom all other arts are inferior to music in Thomas Love Peacock's *Headlong Hall*.

Graziosa Chromatic Mr. Chromatic's daughter; she weds Sir Patrick O'Prism in Thomas Love Peacock's *Headlong Hall*.

Tenorina Chromatic Mr. Chromatic's daughter; she weds Squire Harry Headlong in Thomas Love Peacock's *Headlong Hall*.

Chrysal The spirit of gold trapped in a guinea who narrates the history of his life while in the hands of men, and who promises to communicate the grand secret of nature and spirits to the Adept in Charles Johnstone's *Chrysal: or, The Adventures of a Guinea*.

Saint Chrysostom Humane fourth owner of Julian the Apostate during his incarnation as a slave; he eventually frees him in Henry Fielding's *A Journey From This World to the Next*.

Mr. Chubb Operator of the Sugar Loaf public house; he has an interest in the electioneering in George Eliot's *Felix Holt, the Radical*.

Lord Chudleigh Duke who kills himself on the death of his sickly son because he has no heart to wield the necessary power to run his estates; his property passes to his nephew, Jacob Delafield, in Mrs. Humphry Ward's *Lady Rose's Daughter*.

Mr. Chuffey Anthony Chuzzlewit's devoted clerk, who is debilitated mentally and physically but remains faithful to Chuzzlewit and his memory, helping to expose Jonas Chuzzlewit's attempt to murder his father in Charles Dickens's *The Life and Adventures of Martin Chuzzlewit*.

Mr. Chumfield Mayor of Hartlebury and local Tory chairman; he decides to support Aubrey Bohun in the Fanchester election when his own candidate resigns in Benjamin Disraeli's *A Year at Hartlebury; or, The Election*.

Martha Chump Wealthy, vulgar Irish widow, scorned by the daughters of her business associate and potential husband, Samuel Bolton Pole, in George Meredith's *Emilia in England*.

Hurree Chunder (the Babu) Although fat and seemingly foolish, an eminent player of the "Great Game" of intrigue for the British army in India; a master of disguise, he joins Kim in tricking the Russian spies in Rudyard Kipling's *Kim*.

Mr. Churchill Maternal uncle of Frank Churchill; a childless man of wealth, he and his wife have brought Frank up as their adopted son; he is under the direction of his wife and, after her death, is easily manipulated by his nephew in Jane Austen's *Emma*.

Mrs. Churchill Arrogant, capricious wife of Frank Churchill's uncle; she caused the rupture between the Churchills and Mr. Weston; her sudden death relieves Frank of the necessity for keeping secret his engagement to Jane Fairfax in Jane Austen's *Emma*.

Frank Weston Churchill Handsome, lively, careless son of Mr. Weston; after his mother's death he was adopted and raised by his wealthy uncle and aunt; secretly engaged to Jane Fairfax, he deflects suspicion by pretending to court Emma Woodhouse; his aunt's opportune death removes the need to keep his engagement secret in Jane Austen's *Emma*.

Anthony Chuzzlewit Wealthy and triumphantly

stingy brother of old Martin Chuzzlewit; he is proud of the avarice and suspiciousness of his son, Jonas, in Charles Dickens's *The Life and Adventures of Martin Chuzzlewit*.

Diggory Chuzzlewit Chuzzlewit family forebear who relied heavily for support on an oft-mentioned uncle whose splendid entertainments he called the "Golden Balls" in Charles Dickens's *The Life and Adventures of Martin Chuzzlewit*.

George Chuzzlewit Bachelor who attends the family gathering at Seth Pecksniff's house; he is so disposed to pimples that the ornaments of his attire seem to have broken out upon him in Charles Dickens's *The Life and Adventures of Martin Chuzzlewit*.

Jonas Chuzzlewit The altogether vile, crafty, abusive, and murderous son and business partner of Anthony Chuzzlewit; he woos Mercy Pecksniff by pretending to court her sister in Charles Dickens's *The Life and Adventures of Martin Chuzzlewit*.

Martin Chuzzlewit Extremely wealthy patriarch of the Chuzzlewit family, who suspects everyone he comes in contact with of coveting his money; the selflessness of Mary Graham and Tom Pinch assist his developing benevolence; he is reconciled to his grandson, Martin, and exposes his cousin Seth Pecksniff's hypocrisy in Charles Dickens's *The Life and Adventures of Martin Chuzzlewit*.

Martin Chuzzlewit (the younger) Grandson to Martin and suitor to his grandfather's paid companion, Mary Graham; having quarreled with old Martin, he ventures abroad to America to make his fortune, taking Mark Tapley as his servant/companion; hardship, illness, and Mark's example of cheerful heroism change him from a selfish man into a more affectionate, appreciative friend and lover in Charles Dickens's *The Life and Adventures of Martin Chuzzlewit*.

Mrs. Ned Chuzzlewit Strong-minded, disagreeable widow with three red-nosed, unmarried daughters; she is a witness to Charity Pecksniff's triumph-turned-humiliation in Charles Dickens's *The Life and Adventures of Martin Chuzzlewit*.

Toby Chuzzlewit Chuzzlewit family member, now dead, through whom the Chuzzlewits claim a bend-sinister connection to Lord No Zoo in Charles Dickens's *The Life and Adventures of Martin Chuzzlewit*.

Cicero Former slave employed to carry young Martin Chuzzlewit's luggage in New York; his life story, recounted by Mark Tapley, exemplifies American brutality towards Negroes in Charles Dickens's *The Life and Adventures of Martin Chuzzlewit*.

Cigarette Young, attractive, boyish-looking, cigar-smoking Frenchwoman, a camp follower who leads the troops of the French Foreign Legion to victory at the Battle of Zaraila; she loves Bertie Cecil and sacrifices her life to save him from execution by a firing squad in Ouida's *Under Two Flags*.

Cincia Countess of Cornwall, sister of Queen Eleanor, and member of the royal entourage in Ann Radcliffe's *Gaston de Blondeville*.

Charles Ringwood, Lord Cinqbars Puny only child of the Earl of Ringwood; his early death signifies the end of Lord Ringwood's title in William Makepeace Thackeray's *The Adventures of Philip on His Way through the World*.

Captain Tom (variously George) Cinqbars Member of Rawdon Crawley's regiment and an admirer of Becky (Sharp) Crawley in William Makepeace Thackeray's *Vanity Fair*.

Cinthia Low companion of the bravos and a foil to Rosabella of Corfu in Matthew Lewis's *The Bravo of Venice*.

Drusilla Clack Officious, busybody maiden aunt of Rachel Verinder; she tries to save souls by distributing religious tracts and adores the plausible lay preacher Godfrey Ablewhite in Wilkie Collins's *The Moonstone. A Romance*.

Madame Clairval Wealthy, elderly widow, who is Valancourt's aunt in Ann Radcliffe's *The Mysteries of Udolpho*.

Lady Camilla Clancarryl Wife of an Irish peer and sister of George Godolphin and Lady Adelina Trelawny, whom she introduces to George Fitz-Edward, her husband's brother, in Charlotte Smith's *Emmeline: The Orphan of the Castle*.

Tom Clancy Owner of a small inn, the Cat and Bagpipe, near Knaresborough; he tells John Buncle of his cruel landlord, Old Cock, in Thomas Amory's *The Life of John Buncle, Esq.*

Lady Clandidlem House guest of the de Courcy family who spreads gossip about Lady Dumbello and Plantagenet Palliser in Anthony Trollope's *The Small House at Allington*.

Lady Clara Clangor Woman of fashion in William Beckford's *Azemia*.

Mr. Clapp Clerk and later landlord to John Sedley in William Makepeace Thackeray's *Vanity Fair*.

Mrs. Clapp The Sedleys' landlady after their loss of fortune requires them to move in William Makepeace Thackeray's *Vanity Fair*.

Mary (Polly) Clapp Former servant of the Sedleys who becomes Amelia Sedley's devoted friend in William Makepeace Thackeray's *Vanity Fair*.

Clara Mr. Rochester's third mistress, an honest but uninspiring German girl, whom he sets up in business in Charlotte Brontë's *Jane Eyre*.

Clara Gentle, high-minded sister of Basil; she disobeys their father by visiting Basil when he is ill; her companionship brings Basil solace and strength in Wilkie Collins's *Basil: A Story of Modern Life*.

Clara Amiable, mature orphaned daughter of Lord Raymond and Perdita; she serves as second mother to the children of Lionel Verney and is one of the three survivors of the plague in Mary Shelley's *The Last Man*.

Mr. Clare Renowned and adored poet, who retires to Ferdinando Falkland's part of England; he takes a liking to Falkland, upsetting Barnabas Tyrrel; he warns Falkland against his too great love of honor and urges him to reconcile with Tyrrel; he makes Falkland the executor of his will, upsetting Tyrrel even more in William Godwin's *Caleb Williams*.

Mr. Clare Clergyman uncle of Alick Keith; he brings about Rachel Curtis's reconciliation with the Church in Charlotte Yonge's *The Clever Woman of the Family*.

Mrs. Clare Angel Clare's mother, a good woman, complacent in her ignorance of danger to her son's wife, Tess (Durbeyfield), in Thomas Hardy's *Tess of the D'Urbervilles*.

Ada Clare Beautiful girl, who is John Jarndyce's ward; she falls in love with her cousin, Richard Carstone, whom she eventually marries in Charles Dickens's *Bleak House*.

Angel Clare Clergyman's son and would-be dairyman, who loves and is loved by Tess Durbeyfield; they marry despite her misgivings over her concealed past; when she confesses to him, his intolerance and self-righteousness prevent him from understanding and result in his separation from her; when he realizes his cruelty to Tess, he returns from Brazil to discover that she has been driven by necessity back to her seducer, Alec Stoke-D'Urberville; Clare escapes with Tess for a few days of happiness after she murders Stoke-D'Urberville in Thomas Hardy's *Tess of the D'Urbervilles*.

Cuthbert Clare Angel Clare's conventional clergyman brother who eventually marries Mercy Chant; like Felix Clare, he snobbishly disapproves of Angel's marriage to Tess Durbeyfield in Thomas Hardy's *Tess of the D'Urbervilles*.

Felix Clare Angel Clare's conventional elder brother, a clergyman like his father; he disapproves of Angel's marriage to Tess Durbeyfield in Thomas Hardy's *Tess of the D'Urbervilles*.

Francis Clare Eccentric widower neighbor and friend of Andrew Vanstone; he is constantly descanting on the worthlessness of his son, Frank, whom he despatches to China to earn a living in Wilkie Collins's *No Name*.

Frank Clare Lazy, selfish lover of Magdalen Vanstone, whom he jilts when he learns that she has lost her inheritance in Wilkie Collins's *No Name*.

James Clare Angel Clare's father, a clergyman, who hoped his son would follow the same occupation; he represents those in society who are well-meaning but narrow-minded; when Tess (Durbeyfield) walks over fifteen miles to visit him for financial help, thoughts of his stern goodness intimidate her and she returns home in Thomas Hardy's *Tess of the D'Urbervilles*.

Mr. Clarendon Husband of Isabel and father of the illegitimate Ada Warren; he mistreats Isabel and injures her after his death by a will which requires her to bring up Ada and which limits her interest in his property to Ada's minority in George Gissing's *Isabel Clarendon*.

Isabel Clarendon Wealthy young widow, whose husband has cruelly provided in his will that she must bring up his illegitimate daughter and then turn over the estate to her when she comes of age; she and Bernard Kingcote become lovers but later disagree; ultimately she retains her estate and marries her old lover, Robert Asquith, in George Gissing's *Isabel Clarendon*.

Clarenthia Daughter of Turpius and an heiress; she is the best friend of Scipiana and suffers like her, being abducted and seduced by her father; she is loved by Hannibal but loves Lysander in Jane Barker's *Exilius; or, The Banish'd Roman*.

Lady Clarice Silly and condescending woman, who marries a man she dislikes and is unhappy in Caroline Norton's *The Wife and Woman's Reward*.

Count of Clarinau Calista's jealous, elderly husband, who has killed his first wife; after Calista and Philander elope, he is killed by Octavio, whom he mistakes for Philander in his attempt at revenge in Aphra Behn's *Love Letters Between a Nobleman and His Sister*.

Calista, Countess of Clarinau Octavio's sister and the

unwilling wife of an old Spanish count; she falls in love with Philander, becomes pregnant, and attempts to elope, wounding Clarinau; she flees to a convent, where she takes holy orders when she learns of Philander's infidelity in Aphra Behn's *Love Letters Between a Nobleman and His Sister*.

Lady Clarinda   One of Major Fitz-David's many woman friends; the later employer of Sara Macallan's maid, Phoebe, she relays important information to Valeria Macallan in Wilkie Collins's *The Law and the Lady*.

Mr. Clark   Stout man who works at the wharves; he sends Joe to find Walter Gay for the lost Florence Dombey in Charles Dickens's *Dombey and Son*.

Richard Clark   Lame young London clerk, who is rescued from his work by M'Kay and Mark Rutherford to become a shorthand newspaper reporter in Mark Rutherford's *Mark Rutherford's Deliverance*.

Mr. Clarke   An honest carpenter, who is mistakenly accused of theft by Hugh Trevor, later restores Hugh to health, and finally is a recipient of Hugh's patronage in Thomas Holcroft's *The Adventures of Hugh Trevor*.

Mrs. Clarke   Beloved housekeeper for Anna St. Ives's mother during her life and aunt to Peggy and Mr. Webb in Thomas Holcroft's *Anna St. Ives*.

Betty Clarke   A poor friend of John Brown's wife; she is assisted as a result of Bryan Perdue's concern in Thomas Holcroft's *The Memoirs of Bryan Perdue*.

Daniel Clarke   See Geoffrey Lester.

Thomas Clarke   Attorney, the nephew of Captain Crowe and the godson of Sir Launcelot Greaves; he fears his uncle is losing his mind imitating Sir Launcelot; he flirts with Dolly Cowslip and eventually marries her in Tobias Smollett's *The Adventures of Sir Launcelot Greaves*.

Mr. Clarkson   Importunate, offensively familiar moneylender, who hounds Phineas Finn to pay up punctually on a bill he had signed as a favor to Lawrence Fitzgibbon in Anthony Trollope's *Phineas Finn*.

Mr. Clarriker   Manager of a financial house where Herbert Pocket is given a job in Charles Dickens's *Great Expectations*.

Claudio   Governor (tutor) to Hippolito on his travels; after Hippolito returns from the masked ball, Claudio ventures out in Don Lorenzo's costume and is rescued from attack by Aurelian; his injuries allow Hippolito to postpone traveling in William Congreve's *Incognita*.

Claudio   Hired assassin who kills his master by mistake in Charlotte Dacre's *The Libertine*.

Clavering   Cultivated, well-known statesman; he loves Mary, influences her education, and marries her when his wife dies; he ignores public gossip and continues his political career in Caroline Norton's *The Wife and Woman's Reward*.

Lady Clavering   Good-natured and long-suffering wife to Sir Francis; the reappearance as Colonel Altamont of her presumed-dead first husband threatens her happiness, as does Sir Francis's gambling in William Makepeace Thackeray's *The History of Pendennis*.

Captain Archibald Clavering   Lazy brother of Sir Hugh and cousin of Harry; he devotes his energies to horse racing and the pursuit of Lady Ongar, whom he wants to marry for her money; he drowns off Heligoland in a stormy sea in Anthony Trollope's *The Claverings*.

Fanny Clavering   Younger daughter of the Reverend Henry Clavering; she falls in love with the curate, Samuel Saul, and despite initial disapproval from her father she marries him in Anthony Trollope's *The Claverings*.

Sir Francis Clavering   Impecunious baronet and Member of Parliament, whose marriage to the rich Lady Clavering is threatened by the reappearance of her first husband in William Makepeace Thackeray's *The History of Pendennis*.

Francis Clavering   Young son of Sir Francis and Lady Clavering, who is devoted to him in William Makepeace Thackeray's *The History of Pendennis*.

Harry Clavering   Impulsive, pliable son of the rector of Clavering parish; having been jilted by Julia Brabazon (now Lady Ongar), he falls in love with Florence Burton, but when Lady Ongar returns a wealthy widow he succumbs to her attractions; repentant at last, he admits his folly, and Florence forgives him; he becomes heir to the Clavering property after the accidental deaths of Sir Hugh and Archibald Clavering in Anthony Trollope's *The Claverings*.

Henry Clavering   Uncle of Sir Hugh and Archibald Clavering; the benign rector of Clavering parish, he is amiable in all things except when his curate, Mr. Saul, dares to fall in love with Henry's beloved daughter Fanny; after opposing the match, he at last relents; he becomes the twelfth baronet and resigns the living to Mr. Saul after the deaths of his nephews in Anthony Trollope's *The Claverings*.

Mrs. Henry Clavering   Sweet-natured mother of Mary, Fanny, and Harry and wife of the rector; when

Fanny confides Mr. Saul's declaration of love, her mother mediates between her and her father's wrath; she is also instrumental in bringing Harry Clavering and Florence Burton back together in Anthony Trollope's *The Claverings*.

Hermione Brabazon, Lady Clavering   Elder sister of Julia Brabazon (Lady Ongar); she is abused and neglected by her husband, Sir Hugh Clavering, but is desperate when he is drowned in Anthony Trollope's *The Claverings*.

Sir Hugh Clavering   Eleventh baronet, totally selfish and tyrannical in his household; he bullies his frightened wife until he drowns off Heligoland during a fishing trip in Anthony Trollope's *The Claverings*.

Hughy Clavering   Sickly young son and heir and only living child of Sir Hugh Clavering; his death destroys any vestige of satisfaction left in his parents' marriage in Anthony Trollope's *The Claverings*.

Lucretia Clavering   Heiress of Miles St. John; her tutoring in evil by Olivier Dalibard leads to the loss of her inheritance and then to a career of crime in the company of his son, Gabriel Varney, in Edward Bulwer-Lytton's *Lucretia*.

Mary Clavering   Elder daughter of the Reverend Henry Clavering; she falls in love with the Reverend Edward Fielding and marries him in Anthony Trollope's *The Claverings*.

Dr. Clay   Somewhat unctuous rector of the parish at Knowl in J. Sheridan Le Fanu's *Uncle Silas*.

Penelope Clay   Ingratiating widowed daughter of Sir Walter Elliot's agent; she establishes herself as a necessary member of the Elliot household, accompanying them to Bath; Elizabeth Elliot ridicules the warning that she might become Lady Elliot, pointing out her freckles and projecting tooth; William Elliot neutralizes the threat by setting her up as his mistress, but her cajoling him into making her his wife is not improbable at the end of Jane Austen's *Persuasion*.

Noah Claypole (Morris Bolter)   Big, large-headed charity boy, who works for Mr. Sowerberry; he is knocked down by Oliver Twist when he insults Oliver's mother and later runs off with Charlotte to London, where he spies on Nancy for Fagin in Charles Dickens's *Oliver Twist*.

Tom Claypool   Gossipy, stupid son of a baronet; he marries Flora Warrington in William Makepeace Thackeray's *The Virginians*.

Mr. Clayton   Former lover of Mrs. Booby, prior to her marriage; his suit having been thwarted by her mother, he is now married to someone else in Richard Graves's *The Spiritual Quixote*.

Mrs. Clayton   Ambitious mother of Sir George Clayton; upon his receiving an additional large inheritance which expands his prospects, she precipitates Emily Montague's decision to break the arrangement for the proposed marriage to him in Frances Brooke's *The History of Emily Montague*.

Sir George Clayton   Moneyed, "civil, attentive and dull" English baronet in Quebec to honor the arrangements made for his marriage to Emily Montague by his mother and Emily's now-deceased guardian uncle in Frances Brooke's *The History of Emily Montague*.

Sir Robert Clayton   Roxana's financial adviser, who assists her in investing her money in Daniel Defoe's *The Fortunate Mistress*.

Captain Yorke Clayton   Zealous joint resident magistrate for several Irish counties who hunts down the law breakers; he marries Edith Jones after she nurses him when he has been shot in Anthony Trollope's *The Landleaguers*.

Cleanthe   A lady of about fifty who behaves like a fifteen-year-old and who has a discussion with Cleora in which she abuses (in polite terms) Hillario in Francis Coventry's *The History of Pompey the Little*.

Fanny Cleaver (Jenny Wren)   Crippled, shrewish girl, who is a dolls' dressmaker and looks after her drunken father; she rents a room to Lizzie Hexam, is a friend of Riah's, and is instrumental in divining that the dying Eugene Wrayburn wishes to marry Lizzie Hexam in Charles Dickens's *Our Mutual Friend*.

Clelia   The extremely beautiful niece of Publius Scipio and one of the heroines of Jane Barker's *Exilius; or, The Banish'd Roman*.

Clement   Chapman of Wulstead whom Ralph accompanies from Whitwall to Goldburg and who participates in the battle at Upmeads in William Morris's *The Well at the World's End*.

Father Clement (Clement Blair)   Heretic priest, who teaches Catherine Glover a religion of love and peace, and who flees for safety to the Scottish Highlands in Sir Walter Scott's *The Fair Maid of Perth*.

Madame Clement   Frenchwoman who offers her church pew to an exhausted Monimia (Serafina de Zelos) in London; she sends the crucial letter written by Monimia for Renaldo de Melvil; she agrees to marry Don

Diego de Zelos in Tobias Smollett's *The Adventures of Ferdinand Count Fathom.*

Mrs. Clement Hammel Clement's unsympathetic stepmother, who is responsible for his father's disowning him in Henry Brooke's *The Fool of Quality.*

Arabella Graves Clement Exquisite wife of Hammel Clement; she kills Lord Stivers while defending herself against rape; she is placed on trial, but the justice system proves effective in protecting the innocent and punishing the guilty in Henry Brooke's *The Fool of Quality.*

Bartholomew Clement Wealthy tradesman who disowns his son Hammel at the urgings of Hammel's stepmother; father and son eventually reconcile in Henry Brooke's *The Fool of Quality.*

(Sergeant) Hammel (Hammy) Clement (Stapleton) Reduced gentleman whose education as a scholar of the classics has rendered him unable to do useful work; he commits crimes to feed his wife and child, who have nearly reached starvation; they are befriended by Henry Clinton, who hires Hammel as a tutor to give Master Harry Clinton moral instruction; Hammel and his father, Bartholomew Clement, are reconciled, and he eventually assumes his father's estate in Henry Brooke's *The Fool of Quality.*

Sir James Clement A baronet who is a Liberal candidate for Parliament in George Eliot's *Felix Holt, the Radical.*

Richard (Dicky) Clement Son of Hammel and Arabella Clement and the occasional companion of Master Harry Clinton in Henry Brooke's *The Fool of Quality.*

Mrs. Clements Kindhearted friend of Anne Catherick as a child; she takes Anne to her London lodging and to Cumberland in quest of Laura (Fairlie), Lady Glyde; she trusts Count Fosco, who dupes her and spirits Anne away from her in Wilkie Collins's *The Woman in White.*

Mrs. Clennam Arthur Clennam's old, crippled, hardhearted stepmother; she is bound to a wheel chair, runs the family business, employs Amy Dorrit for needlework, withholds information from Arthur about his birth, negotiates with Rigaud for the iron box containing that information, and suffers a stroke in Charles Dickens's *Little Dorrit.*

Arthur Clennam Middle-aged, lonely gentleman, who returns to London after working in China for twenty years; he breaks with his stern stepmother, unhappily loves Pet Meagles, becomes Daniel Doyce's business partner, is imprisoned in the Marshalsea after losing the partnership's money, and befriends and later marries Amy Dorrit in Charles Dickens's *Little Dorrit.*

Cleomenes Correspondent of Pharamond on the subject of vanity; he ironically prides himself on his lack of vanity in Sarah Fielding's *Familiar Letters between the Principal Characters of David Simple and Some Others.*

Cleopatra Narrative exemplar of the female vices of ambition, avarice, and pride; she regards Anthony's suicide with satisfaction since it reveals her power, and ends her own life because of her horror at the prospect of the imprisonment that will follow her failure to seduce Caesar in Sarah Fielding's *The Lives of Cleopatra and Octavia.*

Cleora Subject of a letter from Aurelia to Silvia; she entraps a wealthy man into marrying her and then dies of sorrow as her passion for him is matched by the waning of his for her in Sarah Fielding's *Familiar Letters between the Principal Characters of David Simple and Some Others.*

Cleora A celebrated toast (belle) in the meridian of her charms who has a discussion with Cleanthe in which she supports Hillario in Francis Coventry's *The History of Pompey the Little.*

Prince of —— (Count de Clerac) Roxana's lover, who gives her a sizeable pension after the death of the landlord; Roxana has three sons by him and calls him by the pseudonym of Count de Clerac; after his wife dies, he repents of his affair with Roxana in Daniel Defoe's *The Fortunate Mistress.*

Clergyman A man with no money who borrows from everyone to keep up an appearance and to support his style of life in Charles Johnstone's *Chrysal: or, The Adventures of a Guinea.*

Clergyman Scholar who lodged with the Chandler's-Shopkeeper's mother and who first edited the manuscript in Charles Johnstone's *Chrysal: or, The Adventures of a Guinea.*

Clerk of the Custom-house Colonel Jack's confidant, who holds his money for safe keeping, allowing it to draw interest in Daniel Defoe's *The History and the Remarkable Life of the Truly Honourable Colonel Jacques, Commonly Call'd Col. Jack.*

Lord Clermont Man who seduces Lady Dellwyn by manipulating her vanity in Sarah Fielding's *The History of the Countess of Dellwyn.*

Henry Clerval The son of a small-minded merchant, who at first thwarts his university education at Ingolstadt; poetic and loyal, he is the dearly loved friend of Victor Frankenstein; he is strangled by Frankenstein's demon in Mary Shelley's *Frankenstein; or, The Modern Prometheus.*

Jock O'Dawson Cleuch Dandie Dinmont's neighbor,

with whom Dinmont quarrels over boundaries in Sir Walter Scott's *Guy Mannering*.

Mr. Cleveland Tutor and loyal friend to Ernest Maltravers in Edward Bulwer-Lytton's *Ernest Maltravers* and in *Alice*.

Captain Clement Cleveland (Clement Vaughan) The pirate; the handsome son of Basil Vaughan and Norna Troil, he adopts the name of Cleveland; when shipwrecked, he is taken into Magnus Troil's household and falls in love with Magnus's daughter Minna; arrested for piracy, he is pardoned because of his past noble deeds in Sir Walter Scott's *The Pirate*.

Frederick Cleveland Embittered member of Lord Carabas's party, whose failure to win the party's support of his candidacy for Parliament leads to a duel in which he is unintentionally killed by Vivian Grey in Benjamin Disraeli's *Vivian Grey*.

Sir Harry Cleveland An ingenuous youth corrupted by exposure to society and then reclaimed to virtue by Miss Bilson, whom he marries, in Sarah Fielding's *The History of the Countess of Dellwyn*.

Captain Clewline Prisoner for indebtedness who seconds Tapley in a prison fight; an alcoholic and a brute since the death of his child, he is a great quarreller with his wife in Tobias Smollett's *The Adventures of Sir Launcelot Greaves*.

Mrs. Clewline Once a beautiful woman and now an ugly drunkard; in debtors' prison with her husband, she seconds Crabclaw in a prison fight in Tobias Smollett's *The Adventures of Sir Launcelot Greaves*.

Clickett (The Orfling) The Micawbers' maid from the workhouse in Charles Dickens's *The Personal History of David Copperfield*.

Geoffrey Cliffe Upper-class poet and journalist; he is a ladies' man who finally induces Lady Kitty Ashe to run away with him; he is murdered by a notorious actress in Mrs. Humphry Ward's *The Marriage of William Ashe*.

Lord Clifford Sir Philip Harclay's aristocratic friend, who arranges the joust between Sir Philip and Sir Walter Lovel in Clara Reeve's *The Old English Baron*.

Lady Anne Clifford Widowed mother of two boys in Dr. Wortle's school; as gossip circulates about the marital status of two of his staff, she is induced by relatives to remove her children in Anthony Trollope's *Dr. Wortle's School*.

Sir Coniers Clifford Military commander defeated by the Irish in Sophia Lee's *The Recess*.

Lionel Clifford Charles Mandeville's fair-haired, good-natured friend and rival at Winchester, whose father is killed fighting for the Royalist cause at Edgehill; he is in every way the archetypal opposite of Mallison; during the Civil War he vies with Charles to become secretary to Sir Joseph Wagstaff and succeeds; later, he marries Charles's sister, Henrietta, in William Godwin's *Mandeville*.

Paul Clifford (Captain Lovett) Foundling who leads a double life as a man about town and a highwayman; he loves Lucy Brandon and is condemned to death by William Brandon in Edward Bulwer-Lytton's *Paul Clifford*.

Mrs. Clifton Virtuous mother of Coke and Louisa; she initially encourages the engagement of Anna St. Ives and Coke and later encourages Coke to forsake his uncontrolled passions in Thomas Holcroft's *Anna St. Ives*.

Coke Clifton Reckless but extraordinary youth, who vies with Frank Henley for the affection of Anna St. Ives; he later attempts to ruin Anna and Frank in a vengeful kidnapping scheme; he finally learns, under Anna's and Frank's instruction, to subdue his passion and pursue virtue in Thomas Holcroft's *Anna St. Ives*.

Louisa Clifton Anna St. Ives's intimate friend and correspondent, who encourages Anna in her admiration of the noble Frank Henley in Thomas Holcroft's *Anna St. Ives*.

Mr. Climbup Promising young man in the Treasury; he argues it is impossible to separate the poor from their poverty in William Beckford's *Azemia*.

Humphry Clinker (Matthew Loyd) Twenty-year-old man, who is employed as Matthew Bramble's footman when John Thomas quits; he embarrasses Tabitha Bramble with his bare posterior, becomes a Methodist preacher, is mistakenly jailed as a highwayman, flirts with Winifrid Jenkins, saves Matthew from drowning, is discovered to be Matthew's natural son, and is allowed to marry Winifrid in Tobias Smollett's *The Expedition of Humphry Clinker*.

General Clinton Governor of New York; he stands by Henry Durie upon the arrival of the Master (James Durie) in Robert Louis Stevenson's *The Master of Ballantrae: A Winter's Tale*.

Mr. Clinton Dishonest speculator, whom John Meadows uses to get Mr. Merton deep in debt in Charles Reade's *It Is Never Too Late to Mend*.

Mrs. Clinton Housekeeper for Arthur Villars; she identifies Evelina as the real daughter of Sir John Belmont in Frances Burney's *Evelina.*

Eloisa Clinton Daughter of Louisa and Henry Clinton; presumed dead in a boating accident, she is discovered to be the wife of the Sultan of Morocco; the mother of Abenaide, she becomes young Harry Clinton's mother-in-law in Henry Brooke's *The Fool of Quality.*

Harriet Clinton Child of Matilda (Golding) and Henry Clinton; she dies young from smallpox in Henry Brooke's *The Fool of Quality.*

Harry (Henry) Clinton Son of Lord Richard Clinton, second Earl of Moreland; because he is reared by peasant foster parents and subsequently by a fugitive uncle who trains him to be the ideal Christian aristocrat, his natural goodness and compassion are not distorted by fashionable society; his lack of affectation and manners cause the fashionable to consider him a fool; he returns home on the deaths of his mother and brother; he marries Abenaide in Henry Brooke's *The Fool of Quality.*

Henry (Harry, Dada) Clinton An idealized Christian aristocrat, the second son of Richard Clinton, first Earl of Moreland; apprenticed to a London merchant, he becomes wealthy at trade; disgusted at his brother's arrogance, he abducts his nephew Harry Clinton to teach him to be a generous and compassionate steward of God's earthly wealth; he uses the alias Mr. Fenton; he is a generous financial supporter of King William; he is eventually reconciled with his profoundly apologetic brother in Henry Brooke's *The Fool of Quality.*

Jacky Clinton Child of Matilda (Golding) and Henry Clinton; he dies young from smallpox in Henry Brooke's *The Fool of Quality.*

Louisa D'Aubigny Clinton Beautiful sister of the Marquis D'Aubigny; unprotected by law, she flees a forced marriage to a favorite of the French king; Henry Clinton rescues her; though her father objects to Clinton's background in trade, she elopes with him and becomes the mother of Eloisa Clinton in Henry Brooke's *The Fool of Quality.*

Mr. Clippurse Waverly family lawyer who draws up documents necessary to clear Edward Waverly in Sir Walter Scott's *Waverly.*

Clipsby Man in a russet smock who followed the Walsinghams and insults Sir Daniel Brackley to his face in Robert Louis Stevenson's *The Black Arrow: A Tale of Two Roses.*

Mrs. Clod Shrewish wife of Thomas; she urges him to make extra money by selling trees cut on Lucius Manly's estate in Mary Collyer's *Felicia to Charlotte.*

Thomas Clod Dull, henpecked tenant on Lucius Manly's estate; he confesses the theft of trees to a stranger who he does not realize is his landlord; Lucius handles the theft in a generous way in Mary Collyer's *Felicia to Charlotte.*

Clodius Lewd wretch who attacks Fabius in Jane Barker's *Exilius; or, The Banish'd Roman.*

Marcus Clodius Young Roman fop and parasite, who proves a fickle friend to Glaucus in Edward Bulwer-Lytton's *The Last Days of Pompeii.*

Lady Clonbrony English-born but Irish-reared aristocrat, who denounces her Irish heritage to be allowed to mingle with snobbish English society in Maria Edgeworth's *The Absentee.*

Lord Clonbrony Irish absentee uprooted from his Irish home by his wife, Lady Clonbrony, and forced to live in England in Maria Edgeworth's *The Absentee.*

Clotilde French actress who entertains Lord Monmouth after his separation from his wife, Lucretia (Colonna), in Benjamin Disraeli's *Coningsby; or, The New Generation.*

Cloudesdale Sir Harry Hotspur's loyal old butler, who is well aware that George Hotspur does no credit to the house of Humblethwaite in Anthony Trollope's *Sir Harry Hotspur of Humblethwaite.*

Cloudesley Son of a peasant on the Danvers estate at Milwood Park; he enters the service of Arthur Danvers, Lord Alton after the latter saves him from prison; his chameleon-like change of character—from a grateful and utterly faithful servant to a greedy, vengeful egotist—occurs after he agrees to become the infant Julian Danvers's foster father; he dies while searching for Julian when he stumbles into an ambush of mountain bandits led by Francesco Perfetti in William Godwin's *Cloudesley.*

Lady Cloudy Loquacious, empty-headed wife of Sir Christopher Cloudy in Henry Brooke's *The Fool of Quality.*

Sir Christopher Cloudy A stereotypical member of the gentry who says nothing in Henry Brooke's *The Fool of Quality.*

Jennet Clouston Dark and sour-looking Scottish peasant woman, who calls down a curse upon the house of Shaws, the residence of miser Ebenezer Balfour and the future estate of Ebenezer's nephew, David Balfour, in Robert Louis Stevenson's *Kidnapped.*

Charles Clover Young man who secures help from Perry Pickle to marry Julia Pickle in Tobias Smollett's *The Adventures of Peregrine Pickle*.

Louisa Clover Proprietor of a china shop whose missing husband is the object of a search in George Gissing's *The Town Traveller*.

Minnie Clover Young girl in whom Mr. Gammon shows an interest but whose mother firmly rejects him in George Gissing's *The Town Traveller*.

The Misses Clubber Daughters of Sir Thomas and Lady Clubber in Charles Dickens's *The Posthumous Papers of the Pickwick Club*.

Lady Clubber Wife of Sir Thomas Clubber in Charles Dickens's *The Posthumous Papers of the Pickwick Club*.

Sir Thomas Clubber Commissioner of the dockyard and a distinguished personage at a ball at the Bull Inn in Rochester in Charles Dickens's *The Posthumous Papers of the Pickwick Club*.

Captain Cluffe Stout, dandyish member of the Royal Irish Artillery and frequent companion of Lieutenant Puddock; he has designs on Rebecca Chattesworth, but when she becomes engaged to Lieutenant Puddock he claims he brought them together; after Paul Dangerfield's identity is revealed, he realizes he saw him hide the murder weapon the night of the attack on Dr. Barney Sturk in J. Sheridan Le Fanu's *The House by the Churchyard*.

John Clump Country lad who delivers a letter from Ralph Mattocks; he is disappointed to learn that Dolly Cowslip loves Thomas Clarke in Tobias Smollett's *The Adventures of Sir Launcelot Greaves*.

Elizabeth Cluppins Brisk, busy-looking friend of Martha Bardell in Charles Dickens's *The Posthumous Papers of the Pickwick Club*.

Captain Cuthbert Clutterbuck of Kennaquhair An antiquarian and the editor of Benedictine manuscripts containing the stories told in Sir Walter Scott's *The Monastery* and in *The Abbot*.

Roger Cly Partner of Solomon Pross and former servant of Charles Darnay, against whom he testifies falsely; he is a spy for the Old Bailey, London criminal court; supposedly dead and buried, he is actually smuggled out of England into revolutionary France; the hoax is uncovered by Jerry Cruncher in Charles Dickens's *A Tale of Two Cities*.

Codicil Coates Attorney to the Rookwood family in William Harrison Ainsworth's *Rookwood*.

Billy Cobb Sportsman and a houseguest at Marlowe in J. Sheridan Le Fanu's *Guy Deverell*.

Thomas Cobb Serious young man of quasi-plebeian demeanor whose quarrel with his betrothed, Louise Derrick, starts a fire in the house where she is lodging in George Gissing's *The Paying Guest*.

Tom Cobb Keeper of the post office at Chigwell and frequenter of the Maypole Inn in Charles Dickens's *Barnaby Rudge*.

John Cock Barber who brings his whole family back to London at the first sign of the plague's abating; everyone in his household except his maid dies in Daniel Defoe's *A Journal of the Plague Year*.

Old Cock Old lawyer who cruelly controls the inheritances and futures of Martha Tilston and Alithea Llansoy; John Buncle with the help of his servant, Soto O'Fin, effects their escape from the villainous guardian and hides the women at Orton Lodge until Old Cock's death in Thomas Amory's *The Life of John Buncle, Esq*.

Cockburn Keeper of the George Inn near Bristo-port in Sir Walter Scott's *Guy Mannering*.

Miss Codger An American literary lady, who wears on her brow a cameo the size and shape of a raspberry tart in Charles Dickens's *The Life and Adventures of Martin Chuzzlewit*.

Tom Codlin Partner with Harris Short in a traveling Punch and Judy show; he meets with Nell Trent and her grandfather, takes care of the money, is cautious and surly, and states that he is the "open-hearted one" but would turn Nell and her grandfather in for a reward in Charles Dickens's *The Old Curiosity Shop*.

Coffee-house Orator A domestic tyrant but a true-born Englishman, who uses his rights to abuse the government for the exertion of its power in Francis Coventry's *The History of Pompey the Little*.

Tom Coffin Protestant justice of the peace and member of the Brotherhood of the Rose in Charles Kingsley's *Westward Ho!*.

Jan Coggan Gabriel Oak's good friend, a worker on Bathsheba Everdene's farm in Thomas Hardy's *Far from the Madding Crowd*.

Andrew Cogglesby A brewer who marries Harriet Harrington, the snobbish daughter of a tailor; she conceals her origins in George Meredith's *Evan Harrington*.

Harriet Harrington Cogglesby Evan Harrington's

snobbish sister, who conceals her father's occupation as a tailor to rise socially by marrying Andrew Cogglesby, a brewer, in George Meredith's *Evan Harrington*.

Tom Cogglesby   Owner of a brewery with his brother Andrew; he engineers numerous odd schemes, including one designed to humble Andrew's snobbish wife in George Meredith's *Evan Harrington*.

Mrs. Cohen   Mother of Ezra Cohen and assistant in his shop in George Eliot's *Daniel Deronda*.

Addy Cohen   Wife of Ezra Cohen in George Eliot's *Daniel Deronda*.

Adelaide Rebekah Cohen   Daughter of Ezra Cohen in George Eliot's *Daniel Deronda*.

Baruch Cohen   Mathematical-instrument maker and forty-year-old widower and Jewish brother-in-law of Mr. Marshall; he falls in love with Clara Hopgood and marries Madge Hopgood after Clara decides not to encourage him in Mark Rutherford's *Clara Hopgood*.

Benjamin Cohen   Apprentice for optical-instrument makers in York; he convinces his father, Baruch Cohen, that he is an independent man in Mark Rutherford's *Clara Hopgood*.

Ezra Cohen   Poor Jewish man who owns a pawn shop and is at first mistaken by Daniel Deronda for Mirah Lapidoth's lost brother in George Eliot's *Daniel Deronda*.

Jacob Alexander Cohen   Precocious son of Ezra Cohen; Ezra Mordecai Lapidoth tutors him in George Eliot's *Daniel Deronda*.

Samuel Cohenlupe   Tricky politician and business associate of Augustus Melmotte; just as Melmotte's trading empire is about to collapse, he decamps with a large sum of money to Europe in Anthony Trollope's *The Way We Live Now*.

M. de Coigney   Vile unsuccessful pursuer of Charlotta de Palfoy in Eliza Haywood's *The Fortunate Foundlings*.

Mademoiselle de Coigney   Vicious, jealous, and devious pursuer of Horatio; she wants to destroy the Charlotta de Palfoy and Horatio connection in Eliza Haywood's *The Fortunate Foundlings*.

Coil   Rustic servant and bagpipe player for the evening dances of the Laird Douglas family at Glenfern Castle in Susan Ferrier's *Marriage*.

Mrs. Coiler   Toady neighbor of the Pockets in Charles Dickens's *Great Expectations*.

Lord Colambre   Irish-born but English-reared son of Lord and Lady Clonbrony; he is in love with Grace Nugent; he embarks on a journey to discover his Irish heritage and investigate the condition of his father's estate in Maria Edgeworth's *The Absentee*.

Monsieur Colbrand   Swiss attendant of Mr. B——; his appearance and demeanor are frightening in Samuel Richardson's *Pamela, or Virtue Rewarded*.

Lady Colchnaben   Mother of Lorimer Boyd; hypocritical and jealous of Gertrude Ross, she plots with Alice Ross and Kenneth Carmichael Ross's mother, Margaret Carmichael Ross, against Gertrude; she wants her son to be Sir Douglas Ross's heir in Caroline Norton's *Old Sir Douglas*.

Mr. Cole   Well-to-do Highbury tradesman, whose social aspirations Emma Woodhouse deplores; she allows herself to be persuaded to attend his and Mrs. Cole's dinner party in Jane Austen's *Emma*.

Mrs. Cole   Unpretentious, ungenteel wife of a prosperous Highbury tradesman; her dinner party is a success in Jane Austen's *Emma*.

Mrs. Cole   Kindly madam of a high-class bordello; almost a surrogate mother to Fanny Hill, she oversees most of Fanny's career and helps her mature and gain financial success in John Cleland's *Memoirs of a Woman of Pleasure*.

Mr. Coleby   Prisoner for indebtedness who receives a gift of money from Sir Launcelot Greaves in Tobias Smollett's *The Adventures of Sir Launcelot Greaves*.

Father Coleman   Good-hearted Jesuit priest, who discusses the church with Lothair but does not bring enough pressure on him to convert and thus incurs the dissatisfaction of Cardinal Grandison in Benjamin Disraeli's *Lothair*.

Miss Coleman   A woman in poor health because of weak lungs, culpable idleness, and a gentleman who disappointed her; she is reunited with her gentleman, Mr. Evans, after her father loses his wealth in George MacDonald's *At the Back of the North Wind*.

Mr. Coleman   Diamond's father's first employer; he dissipates his wealth in shady speculations urged by his daughter's "gentleman," Mr. Evans; he is finally ruined when North Wind sinks the ship with Mr. Evans aboard in George MacDonald's *At the Back of the North Wind*.

Jane Coleman   Zachariah's wife, who dislikes his political activity and French friends, and who dies in 1819 while he is in Manchester prison in Mark Rutherford's *The Revolution In Tanner's Lane*.

Marie Pauline Coleman Daughter of Zachariah and Pauline (Caillaud) Coleman; she lives alone with her widowed father in London; she loathes Thomas Broad and successfully resists his forceful attentions in Mark Rutherford's *The Revolution In Tanner's Lane*.

Zachariah Coleman Radical Calvinist printer, thirty years old in 1814, who is imprisoned for his connections with the Manchester Blanketeers in 1817; he marries Pauline Caillaud after his release and fathers Marie Pauline Coleman in 1822 in Mark Rutherford's *The Revolution In Tanner's Lane*.

Captain Colepepper (Peppercull) Cowardly soldier, who courts Martha Trapbois for her father's wealth, conspires with Andrew Skurliewhitter to kill and rob old Trapbois, and is killed by Richie Moniplies after Colepepper murders Lord Dalgarno in Sir Walter Scott's *The Fortunes of Nigel*.

Gaspar de Coligny Virtuous, honorable French nobleman, who was acquainted with Reginald de St. Leon in his youth, and who, when they meet many years later at the court of Dresden, demands that St. Leon, as a man of honour, account for the astounding change in his fortunes in William Godwin's *St. Leon*.

Colkitto See Alister M'Donnell.

Selina Collett Schoolgirl friend of Aminta Farrell (Lady Ormont); she passes letters to Aminta from Matey Weyburn when they are in school, and when they are adults she—unknowingly—helps bring them together again in George Meredith's *Lord Ormont and his Aminta*.

Dr. Colligan Physician who treats Anty Lynch for fever; he knocks down her brother, Barry, who has invited the doctor to murder her in Anthony Trollope's *The Kellys and the O'Kellys*.

Mr. Collins Ferdinando Falkland's steward, considered by Caleb Williams to be one of his closest friends; Caleb learns Falkland's history from Collins; when Caleb asks for Collins's help, Collins replies he will do what he can, but not at the risk of his position in William Godwin's *Caleb Williams*.

Mrs. Collins Older woman who divides her time between religion and gossip; she goes to Mrs. Thorpe to suggest that Lucy Bentham is the subject of scandal in George Moore's *A Modern Lover*.

William Collins Prosy, self-important clergyman whose practice of studied flattery is not offensive to his patroness, Lady Catherine de Bourgh; heir to Mr. Bennet's entailed estate, he intends to find a wife among the Bennet sisters; after Elizabeth's rejection he proposes

successfully to Charlotte Lucas in Jane Austen's *Pride and Prejudice*.

Christopher Collop Fun-loving Anglican clergyman revealed in a spurious editor's note to be the author in Richard Graves's *The Spiritual Quixote*.

Collwar Deity worshipped by residents of Normnbdsgrsutt in Robert Paltock's *The Life and Adventures of Peter Wilkins*.

Sir George Colmar An early admirer of Clarissa Harlowe's friend Anna Howe in Samuel Richardson's *Clarissa: or, The History of a Young Lady*.

Colocotroni Greek warlord betrayed and later murdered by Bozzari in William Godwin's *Cloudesley*.

Irene Colocotroni Young Greek woman whom Arthur Danvers, Lord Alton rescues from Bozzari, the murderer of her father; she marries Arthur, but dies in childbirth; her son, Julian, survives but is bilked out of his rightful inheritance by Arthur's younger brother, Richard (Lord Alton), and his accomplice, Cloudesley, in William Godwin's *Cloudesley*.

Comfit Colocynth Physician who certifies for Mrs. Grizzle that Mrs. Pickle is wrong to douse her infant in cold water in Tobias Smollett's *The Adventures of Peregrine Pickle*.

Colonel Veteran who calls the Doctor to task for his opinions and impudence in Charles Johnstone's *Chrysal: or, The Adventures of a Guinea*.

Colonel Well-born man whose confidence in his own understanding allows him to be defrauded by the Servant's Servant in Charles Johnstone's *Chrysal: or, The Adventures of a Guinea*.

Fra Colonna Wealthy, aristocratic Dominican friar; a sceptic in religion but a zealot in the arts, he makes Gerard's fortune as a copyist of Greek and Latin in Charles Reade's *The Cloister and the Hearth*.

Princess Colonna Malicious and greedy second wife, later the widow, of Prince Colonna and friend of Lord Monmouth; she unsuccessfully plots her stepdaughter's marriage to Harry Coningsby and her own marriage to Lord Monmouth in Benjamin Disraeli's *Coningsby; or, The New Generation*.

Princess Lucretia Colonna Sullen and manipulative daughter of Prince Colonna; she initially intends to marry Harry Coningsby but falls in love with Sidonia, whose rejection of her causes her to marry Lord Monmouth in Benjamin Disraeli's *Coningsby; or, The New Generation.*

Paul, Prince Colonna   Dissolute Roman friend of Lord Monmouth; he is killed in a riding accident in Benjamin Disraeli's *Coningsby; or, The New Generation.*

Mrs. Colston   Snobbish wife of the brewer in Eastthorp; she condescends to visit Mrs. Furze to collect for a church memorial in Mark Rutherford's *Catharine Furze.*

Charlie Colston   Mrs. Colston's silly son, who is twenty-eight and eligible for marriage, but whom Catharine Furze rejects when her mother introduces them in Mark Rutherford's *Catharine Furze.*

Little Benjie Coltherd   Boy who teaches Darsie Latimer (Arthur Redgauntlet) the art of fishing and is used as a messenger by Cristal Nixon in Sir Walter Scott's *Redgauntlet.*

Mr. Colville   John Falkner's solicitor in his murder trial who obtains his acquittal in Mary Shelley's *Falkner.*

Mr. Colville   Gentleman with an estate in Jamaica; he knowingly marries the pregnant lover of Lord Scroope (1) and with her raises Anthony Colville in Sophia Lee's *The Recess.*

Anthony Colville   Illegitimate son of Lord Scroope (1); he unknowingly marries his sister Gertrude Marlowe; subsequently, as Father Anthony, he devotes himself to study and is an exacting mentor for Matilda and Ellinor before being murdered by Williams in Sophia Lee's *The Recess.*

Colvin   English officer in the pay of Charles, Duke of Burgundy; he is loyal to his employer to the end in Sir Walter Scott's *Anne of Geierstein.*

Robert Wringhim Colwan   Son of Lady Dalcastle (Rabina Colwan) and ward of the Reverend Wringhim; under the influence of Gil-martin and belief in the infallibility of the elect, he murders his brother, George, and several others, commits crimes as Laird of Dalcastle, and finally commits suicide after writing his memoirs in James Hogg's *The Private Memoirs and Confessions of a Justified Sinner.*

Rabina Colwan ("Lady Dalcastle")   Daughter of Baillie Orde; she is the pleasure-renouncing, pious, disapproving wife of the jovial elder George Colwan; hating the name of her husband, she is called Lady Dalcastle as a courtesy; she is mother of the younger George Colwan and of Robert Colwan in James Hogg's *The Private Memoirs and Confessions of a Justified Sinner.*

George Colwan (the father)   Free-living Laird of Dalcastle, who dotes on his son George but rejects his wife's second son, Robert, and dies of grief at George's murder in James Hogg's *The Private Memoirs and Confessions of a Justified Sinner.*

George Colwan (the son)   Elder son of George Colwan the Laird of Dalcastle; he is shadowed, persecuted, and finally murdered by his brother, Robert, in James Hogg's *The Private Memoirs and Confessions of a Justified Sinner.*

Miss Colza   Determinedly youthful maiden lady much given to curls and pink bows, who spies on Margaret Mackenzie and passes information to Mr. Maguire for gossip articles in a Christian journal attacking John Ball; she ends up marrying Maguire in Anthony Trollope's *Miss Mackenzie.*

Charles Comfort   Low Church rector of Cawston, neighboring parish to Baslehurst, in Devon; a long-time friend of Mrs. Ray, he pours cold water on her daughter's attachment to Luke Rowan in Anthony Trollope's *Rachel Ray.*

James Comfort   Village blacksmith and volunteer soldier in Thomas Hardy's *The Trumpet-Major.*

Philip des Comines   Shrewd politician and historian of the Duke of Burgundy's court, who is persuaded to join Louis XI in France in Sir Walter Scott's *Quentin Durward.*

Commander of British Forces in America   Young, active, and brave Commander with good judgment, who leaves his mother and his beloved to do his duty and fight for his country in Charles Johnstone's *Chrysal: or, The Adventures of a Guinea.*

Commissioner   Government Treasury official who bribes Mr. Secretary to spy on London political radicals in Mark Rutherford's *The Revolution In Tanner's Lane.*

Anna Comnena   The emperor's beautiful and intelligent daughter, who wrote his history, the *Alexiad*; she jealously guards her dignity as a princess and author; though admired by the court for her wisdom and generous nature, she is often neglected by her beloved husband, Nicephorus Briennius, in Sir Walter Scott's *Count Robert of Paris.*

Alexius Comnenus   Emperor of Greece; essentially powerless and ineffectual, he maintains his throne through the wealth and importance of his predecessors; though deeply religious and a defender of the Church, he is nevertheless extremely superstitious in Sir Walter Scott's *Count Robert of Paris.*

Mrs. Comorin Mistress of Casimir Fleetwood; she is distinguished by her pride of heart, ease of manners, and inexhaustible vitality in William Godwin's *Fleetwood*.

Compeyson The swindler who jilted Miss Havisham on her wedding day; later he is Abel Magwitch's fellow convict and mortal enemy; he betrays Magwitch to the police and finally drowns fighting in the river with Magwitch in Charles Dickens's *Great Expectations*.

Sally Compeyson Wife of the swindler Compeyson in Charles Dickens's *Great Expectations*.

Mr. Compton Suitor of Alicia Malcolm in contest with her cousin, Sir Edmund Audley, before her marriage to Archibald Douglas in Susan Ferrier's *Marriage*.

Conachar (Ian Eachin, Hector MacIan) Simon Glover's young apprentice, who rejoins his clan in the Highlands to become its chief; he courts Catherine Glover; he shames himself as a coward when he runs from a fight with Henry Smith; he leaps to his death in a raging torrent in Sir Walter Scott's *The Fair Maid of Perth*.

Conari Procurator of Venice whose murder is feigned in Count Rosalvo's plan to ensnare the political conspirators in Matthew Lewis's *The Bravo of Venice*.

Mr. Concordance Schoolmaster who is a friend of Hugh Strap and who recommends Roderick Random to Mr. Lavement in London in Tobias Smollett's *The Adventures of Roderick Random*.

Condall of Shoreby Old, feverish man, from whom Sir Daniel Brackley extorts a promissory note in Robert Louis Stevenson's *The Black Arrow: A Tale of Two Roses*.

Mrs. Coningsby Harry Coningsby's deceased mother, whose portrait Harry discovers in the house of his grandfather's archenemy, Mr. Millbank, in Benjamin Disraeli's *Coningsby; or, The New Generation*.

Henry (Harry) Coningsby Orphan grandson of Lord Monmouth; he rejects his grandfather's epicurean materialism for the honest enterprise of the Millbank family; he matures into the principled political leader of the "New Generation" of idealistic young aristocrats in Benjamin Disraeli's *Coningsby; or, The New Generation*.

Black (Captain Connal, Monsieur de Connal) Connal French-educated brother of White Connal; he marries Dora O'Shane when his brother, betrothed to her since her birth, dies in an accident; a coxcomb, gambler, and fortune hunter, Black alienates Harry Ormond at their first meeting but later treats Ormond with genuine regard for both Ormond's character and the money he wants to win from him in Maria Edgeworth's *Ormond*.

White Connal Shallow "gentleman" betrothed to Dora O'Shane since her birth; he is hard and niggardly with others but extravagant with personal purchases; luckily for Dora, he dies in an accident before he has a chance to wed her in Maria Edgeworth's *Ormond*.

Connoisseur A collector of paintings who is told that he must shoot himself in order to get a good price for his paintings in Charles Johnstone's *Chrysal: or, The Adventures of a Guinea*.

Mrs. Conquest Woman to whom George Edwards transfers his affections from Miss Oddly; he is arranging the terms of his marriage when July Wentworth, believed to be dead, appears; Mrs. Conquest nobly yields her claim in John Hill's *The Adventures of Mr. George Edwards, a Creole*.

Conrad Homely, favored son and heir of Manfred; he dies horribly on the eve of his wedding when a monstrous helmet of supernatural origin falls on him in Horace Walpole's *The Castle of Otranto*.

Count William Considine Old family friend and adviser to the O'Malleys in Charles Lever's *Charles O'Malley*.

Constable Spokesman for the townspeople of Walthamstow who refuse to allow the poor men from Wapping and the band of thirteen others to pass through their town; he agrees to give the group food if they pass around the town in Daniel Defoe's *A Journal of the Plague Year*.

Constable Officer who arrests Colonel Jack, mistakenly thinking that he is Captain Jack in Daniel Defoe's *The History and the Remarkable Life of the Truly Honourable Colonel Jacques, Commonly Call'd Col. Jack*.

Lady Constance Woman falsely rumored to be engaged to Lord Chelford in J. Sheridan Le Fanu's *Wylder's Hand*.

Sister Constance (formerly Lady Herbert Somerville) Aristocratic widow and member of an Anglican sisterhood; she helps the Underwood family in Charlotte Yonge's *The Pillars of the House* and in *The Long Vacation.*.

Constantine Young lord who falls in love with Arminda and pursues her in spite of her protests; he dies from a wound she inflicts when he breaks into her room in Penelope Aubin's *The Life and Adventures of the Lady Lucy*.

Sir Blount Constantine Viviette's jealous husband, off exploring in Africa; instead of dying of fever as reported, he takes to drink and a native wife and eventually his own life, but on a date subsequent to Lady Constantine's clandestine remarriage; Sir Blount has left her an income too small to compensate for the loss of Swithin St. Cleeve's inheritance, should they now repeat their vows in Thomas Hardy's *Two on a Tower*.

Viviette, Lady Constantine   Melancholy young wife, who lives isolated from society because of a promise to her jealous husband, Sir Blount, now off exploring in Africa; she gradually falls clandestinely in love with Swithin St. Cleeve, a handsome young astronomer, and marries him secretly on learning of her husband's death; discovering the marriage invalid because of news of a later date of Sir Blount's death, she gives up St. Cleeve rather than lose him an inheritance; finding that she is pregnant, she desperately marries Bishop Helmsdale; after the bishop's death St. Cleeve returns to claim her, and she dies of heart failure in his arms in Thomas Hardy's *Two on a Tower*.

Matilda Constanza   Guest at a ball held at the castle of the Marquis de Mazzini in Ann Radcliffe's *A Sicilian Romance*.

Signora Alcesté Contarini   The last of Contarini Fleming's mother's family; she marries Contarini and, after a year of traveling with him, dies in childbirth in Benjamin Disraeli's *Contarini Fleming*.

Contarino   Boastful, profligate youth and conspirator, who kills himself after realizing he has been trapped by Abellino/Flodoardo (Count Rosalvo) in Matthew Lewis's *The Bravo of Venice*.

Contrite   One of the good people of Vanity Fair introduced to Christiana and her party by Mnason in John Bunyan's *The Pilgrim's Progress From this World to That Which Is to Come*.

Isabel Conway   Dreamy, aristocratic wife of James Frost; she adapts to a life of relative poverty and publishes a historical romance in Charlotte Yonge's *Dynevor Terrace*.

John Conyers   Poor tenant farmer, for whom Vivian Grey intercedes by flattering Mr. Stapylton Toad to the point that he agrees to stop foreclosure on Conyers's farm in Benjamin Disraeli's *Vivian Grey*.

Cook   South Sea native cook who fixes delicacies out of affection for Robert Herrick aboard the pirated schooner *Farallone* in Robert Louis Stevenson's *The Ebb-Tide: A Trio and a Quartette*.

Cook   Dr. Benjulia's employee, whose food preparation suffers from her passion for reading novels, especially Samuel Richardson's *Pamela*; until the end of the interview in which Benjulia fires her, she confidently expects

his proposal of marriage in Wilkie Collins's *Heart and Science*.

Cook   Servant of the charity who saves the best food for his fellow servants and starts a brawl with the Apothecary in Charles Johnstone's *Chrysal: or, The Adventures of a Guinea*.

Cook   Violent-tempered servant of the Duchess; the chemical assault of her use of pepper is preliminary to her throwing various objects, including fire irons and dishes, at the Duchess and the baby; later, when she is questioned at the trial of the Knave of Hearts, her temper has not improved in Lewis Carroll's *Alice's Adventures in Wonderland*.

John Douglas Cook   Under the assumed name Mr. Dundas, the editor of the newspaper that Christopher Kirkland worked on in his first job in London; in his own name, the editor of the *Morning Chronicle* in Mrs. Lynn Linton's *The Autobiography of Christopher Kirkland*.

Kiddo Cook   One of the few Jago "rats" who escape a life of crime; he becomes a respectable vendor and marries Pigeony Poll in Arthur Morrison's *A Child of the Jago*.

Margery Cook   London cook who is smitten by Captain Samuel Crowe; she advises him to visit the astrologist in Tobias Smollett's *The Adventures of Sir Launcelot Greaves*.

Moll Cook   Kitchen wench, who discovers Shamela Andrews in the coal-hole after Mrs. Jewkes has dragged the pond, believing her drowned, in Henry Fielding's *An Apology for the Life of Mrs. Shamela Andrews*.

Mr. Cooper   Imprisoned Methodist who praises sin because it may provide grace while he removes William Booth's valuables from his pockets in Henry Fielding's *Amelia*.

Sir Anthony Ashley Cooper   The kinsman of an Oxford friend of Charles Mandeville; to show his appreciation to Charles he provides him with an introduction to Colonel Penruddock in William Godwin's *Mandeville*.

Belinda Coote   Newly wedded wife of Orlando Eustace, who stabs her to death after an argument over the merits of her sister Maria's painted fan in Thomas Amory's *The Life of John Buncle, Esq.*

Maria Coote   Sister of Belinda Coote; she overpraises a painted fan she owns but which Belinda disparages; the disagreement leads to violent domestic tragedy in Thomas Amory's *The Life of John Buncle, Esq.*

Clara Copperfield   See Clara Copperfield Murdstone.

David (Daisy, Trotwood, Doady) Copperfield Hero and narrator, who relates the story of his life from birth, including his mother's death, his pain and poverty before he lived with his aunt Betsey Trotwood, his school-days, his courtship of and marriage to Dora Spenlow, his career as a writer, and his marriage to Agnes Wickfield in Charles Dickens's *The Personal History of David Copperfield*.

Dora Copperfield See Dora Spenlow.

Coralie A pupil at Mme. Beck's school in Charlotte Brontë's *Villette*.

King of Coramantien Oroonoko's grandfather, who desires Imoinda for his own when he discovers Oroonoko's love for her; he finds the lovers together, but believes Imoinda's false claim of rape and sells her into slavery instead of killing her in Aphra Behn's *Oroonoko*.

Charles Corbett Father of the heroine, Emma; he urges her betrothed, Henry Hammond, to renounce either Emma or his commission in the British army; he survives to mourn the deaths of Emma and his son Edward in S. J. Pratt's *Emma Corbett*.

Edward Corbett Ill-fated brother of the ill-fated heroine, Emma Corbett, in S. J. Pratt's *Emma Corbett*.

Emma Corbett Heroine who travels to America to join her lover, Henry Hammond, whose regiment is fighting there; she dies in England months after sucking poison from her betrothed's arrow wound in S. J. Pratt's *Emma Corbett*.

Cordelia Daughter of Nicanor, sister of Oliver, and twin of Ferdinand; she fails to meet a man whom she could marry and remains happily single in Sarah Fielding's *The Cry*.

Cordiala An orphan disguised as a male, Almon; having no one to protect her, she masks herself and runs away to avoid marriage to Clodius; she becomes servant to Clarenthia in Jane Barker's *Exilius; or, The Banish'd Roman*.

Mr. Cordwain Rich packer, who wishes to marry his daughter into the nobility in Charlotte Lennox's *Henrietta*.

Jenny Cordwain A rich packer's daughter, who thinks herself more genteel than the impoverished nobility and hires Henrietta Courteney for the fun of having a gentlewoman as her maid; she is betrothed to Lord B—, who loves Henrietta in Charlotte Lennox's *Henrietta*.

Aspasia Corfield Aristocrat at whose country house Letty Sewell and Sir George Tressady become engaged in Mrs. Humphry Ward's *Sir George Tressady*.

Donna Corina Maid of honor to the Queen of Spain; she is loved by Don Fernando de Cardiole but spurns him for Don Pedro de Mendoza in Penelope Aubin's *The Strange Adventures of the Count de Vinevil and His Family*.

Mrs. Cork London landlady who forces Mrs. Hopgood to move out when she discovers Madge Hopgood is pregnant and unmarried in Mark Rutherford's *Clara Hopgood*.

Cornaro Spanish gentleman who sends men out to retrieve his daughter after she marries without his consent; his men mistakenly seize Cornelia and carry her off to Madrid in Sarah Scott's *The History of Cornelia*.

Butler Cornbury Eldest son of a Devonshire squire; his campaign to represent Baslehurst in Parliament is endorsed by Mrs. Tappitt's social gathering; he kowtows to local gentry, but the Tappitts switch allegiance to his opponent, Mr. Hart, from London; it is a close race, but Cornbury wins the election in Anthony Trollope's *Rachel Ray*.

Patty Comfort Cornbury Onetime beauty of Devon, now wife of Butler Cornbury and mother of five; she works hard among the country gentry to ensure that her husband is elected Member of Parliament for Baslehurst; she remains loyal to Rachel Ray in the face of local jealousy over the girl's attachment to Luke Rowan in Anthony Trollope's *Rachel Ray*.

Walter Cornbury Cousin of Patty Cornbury, who encourages him to dance with Rachel Ray at Mrs. Tappitt's ball in Anthony Trollope's *Rachel Ray*.

Cornelia Miranda's friend who tells the story of Prince Henrik's past and of his taking holy orders in Aphra Behn's *The Fair Jilt*.

Cornelia Virtuous orphan from a well-bred family; she hopes to help the poor, but her great beauty and charm expose her to the jealousy of other women and the lechery of various men in Sarah Scott's *The History of Cornelia*.

Cornelis Brother of Gerard and Sybrandt; expecting to inherit the family business, he dies disappointed at age sixty-five with his mother and father still alive in Charles Reade's *The Cloister and the Hearth*.

Cornelius Aristo's friend, a civil servant who negotiates release for Callista on condition she will sign to having sacrificed to the gods in John Henry Newman's *Callista*.

Cornelius A Roman solider in the Twelfth Legion and companion to Marius; he is known for his purity and his paradoxical severity and hopefulness in Walter Pater's *Marius the Epicurean.*

Mrs. Corney Matron of the workhouse where Oliver Twist was born; she is sweet and sympathetic to Mr. Bumble until she marries him; afterwards, she is shrewish and nags him in Charles Dickens's *Oliver Twist.*

Molly Corney Childhood friend of Sylvia Robson; her coarser nature contrasts with Sylvia's sensitivity and depth of feeling in love and marriage in Elizabeth Gaskell's *Sylvia's Lovers.*

Jim Cornick Sailor from the ship *Victory* who brings Anne Garland news of Bob Loveday's survival after the Battle of Trafalgar and gossip of Bob's fickle affections in Thomas Hardy's *The Trumpet-Major.*

Corrado Italian brigand who leads Cloudesley to the hideout of St. Elmo and his band and who, on reaching their destination, is killed along with Cloudesley in William Godwin's *Cloudesley.*

Colonel Ugo Corte An Italian revolutionist from Bergamo, operating in groups with Carlo Ammiani; he objects to Milan's initiating a revolt and to Vittoria Campa, a woman, signaling it in George Meredith's *Vittoria.*

Corydon Cobbler of Constantinople in Sir Walter Scott's *Count Robert of Paris.*

Mrs. Cosgrove Hostess who brings young marriageable people together, opposing the aims of the feminists in George Gissing's *The Odd Women.*

Samuel Cosgrave Merchant whose letter reveals to Harriet Fitzpatrick her husband's mercenary motives in marrying her in Henry Fielding's *The History of Tom Jones.*

Piero di Cosimo The artist who sees Tito Melema's true nature and shows it in his prophetic paintings in George Eliot's *Romola.*

Costello Kind-hearted policeman, who tends to Alton Locke when he collapses with exhaustion after having been thrown out of his mother's house in Charles Kingsley's *Alton Locke.*

Jim Costello Student at Muskegon Commercial Academy who gets stock tips by telegraph from his father in New York; he is imitated by Loudon Dodd in Robert Louis Stevenson's *The Wrecker.*

Emily Costigan (Miss Fotheringay) Beautiful actress encouraged by her father to accept the proposal of the smitten young Arthur Pendennis; persuaded that he is not rich, she breaks the engagement and subsequently, as Miss Fotheringay, goes on the London stage; she marries Sir Charles Mirabel in William Makepeace Thackeray's *The History of Pendennis.*

Captain Jack Costigan Pathetically drunken Irishman, the father of Miss Fotheringay (Emily Costigan), in William Makepeace Thackeray's *The History of Pendennis* He reappears, behaving indecorously in *The Newcomes.*

William Coulson The fellow shopman and subsequent partner of Philip Hepburn; his lack of Philip's intensity of feeling provides a contrast in love and daily life in Elizabeth Gaskell's *Sylvia's Lovers.*

Mr. Coulter An agricultural "improver" who inspires others with his new, productive farming methods in John Galt's *Annals of the Parish.*

Countess, Dowager of—— Aristocratic widow whose costume as a nun at a masquerade attracts Mr. B——'s interest; she almost commits bigamy with him in Samuel Richardson's *Pamela, or Virtue Rewarded.*

Countess of —— Model noblewoman, romance-reader, unfashionably intelligent; she begins Arabella's cure by explaining that real, good women have no adventures; she leaves Bath before accomplishing her purpose in Charlotte Lennox's *The Female Quixote.*

Country Girl Traveler on the wagon who is very beautiful and attracts the attention of the Disguised Gentleman in Charles Johnstone's *Chrysal: or, The Adventures of a Guinea.*

Country Girl's Mother Traveler on the wagon who is an unpolished, good-looking woman whose false modesty allows her to drink too freely in Charles Johnstone's *Chrysal: or, The Adventures of a Guinea.*

John Ernest Biren, Duke of Courland Consort of the Czarina Anne of Russia and de facto head of state, who jealously guards his power; displeased with William Meadows's growing intimacy with his niece, Isabella Scherbatoff, he orders him arrested in William Godwin's *Cloudesley.*

Court Clerk Official who accepts the Matron's bribe in order to facilitate her case in Charles Johnstone's *Chrysal: or, The Adventures of a Guinea.*

Mr. Courtenay Oxford tutor responsible for the shaping of the strong moral sense of Jacob Delafield in Mrs. Humphry Ward's *Lady Rose's Daughter.*

Mr. Courteney Henrietta Courteney's father; the youngest son of the Earl of —-, he is disinherited for marrying the daughter of a poor army widow; he dies leaving his family desolate in Charlotte Lennox's *Henrietta*.

Mrs. (Miss Carlton) Courteney Henrietta Courteney's mother, the daughter of a former army officer; she inspires Mr. Courteney's pity and love when his father rejects her mother's request to reinstate her father's pension in Charlotte Lennox's *Henrietta*.

Charles (Mr. Freeman) Courteney Marquis of —'s tutor-companion; he tries to procure Henrietta Courteney as mistress to his charge, then recognizes her as his long-lost sister; he opposes her marriage to the marquis because of parental opposition; he gives up a large portion of his inheritance to arrange an acceptable dowry for her in Charlotte Lennox's *Henrietta*.

Henrietta ("Clelia," Miss or Mrs. Benson) Courteney Heroine, an orphan cast off by her relatives because of her father's elopement with her mother; she resists forced marriage and conversion to Catholicism and stands up for old aristocratic values in a mercenary world; she shames her family into accepting her by becoming a lady's maid in Charlotte Lennox's *Henrietta*.

Courtesan of Bologna Owner of Phyllis and Pompey; she gives Pompey to the English fop Hillario in exchange for a gold watch in Francis Coventry's *The History of Pompey the Little*.

Earl of Courtland The wealthy English father of Frederick, Lord Lindore and Lady Juliana (Douglas); he opposes her marriage to Henry Douglas on the grounds that it is for love, not for money, in Susan Ferrier's *Marriage*.

Mr. Courtney Selfish libertine, father of Emma; he spends his money on pleasure, leaving Emma poor, but does teach her to appreciate Roman history and to long for heroic virtue in Mary Hays's *Memoirs of Emma Courtney*.

Emma Courtney Independent-minded but impractical young woman, who repeatedly proposes to Augustus Harley, the last time offering to live common-law; she supports herself by tutoring, loses her money in a bank crash, reluctantly marries Mr. Montague, and becomes his medical assistant in Mary Hays's *Memoirs of Emma Courtney*.

Lord Courtown Influential member of the Carabas party, who withdraws his support of Frederick Cleveland's nomination to Parliament, thereby destroying Vivian Grey's political career in Benjamin Disraeli's *Vivian Grey*.

Couthon Chairman of the French Revolutionary Committee of Public Safety during the Terror in 1793; he

yields to Victorine's pleas to release Dupin from prison in Mark Rutherford's *The Revolution In Tanner's Lane*.

Jack Coverley Bristol fop and horseman who flirts with Evelina Anville Belmont without success in Frances Burney's *Evelina*.

Mrs. Cowey Friend of Mrs. Allaby and wife of the celebrated Professor Cowey; a marriage arranger, she suggests Theobald Pontifex for Christina Allaby in Samuel Butler's *The Way of All Flesh*.

Mrs. Cowslip Landlady of Black Lion Inn who believes her foster child Dolly Cowslip is Tom Clarke's sister in Tobias Smollett's *The Adventures of Sir Launcelot Greaves*.

Dorothy (Dolly) Cowslip Supposed daughter of the landlady at Black Lion Inn; she becomes Aurelia Darnel's servant and traveling companion to London, is courted by Tom Clarke, and marries him after she is discovered to be Sir Launcelot Greaves's niece in Tobias Smollett's *The Adventures of Sir Launcelot Greaves*.

Lieutenant Cox Idle horse-riding crony of Ralph Newton, heir of Newton Priory; he joins in the general dissipation of the Moonbeam pub in Anthony Trollope's *Ralph the Heir*.

Mr. Cox London proprietor of Dick Lennox's acting company; he promises to listen to Montgomery's opera but doesn't in George Moore's *A Mummer's Wife*.

Alcmena Cox Guest at a Harrogate dance, where she meets Mr. Dunkley, whom she later marries in Thomas Amory's *The Life of John Buncle, Esq.*

Countess de Crèvecoeur Philip de Crèvecoeur's beautiful and spirited wife; she befriends Isabelle de Croye in Sir Walter Scott's *Quentin Durward*.

Count Philip de Crèvecoeur Haughty and observant Burgundian knight, marshal of the Duke of Burgundy's household, and Isabelle de Croye's friend; a calming influence on the duke, he serves as his courier in delivering a message of war to Louis XI, who admires him in Sir Walter Scott's *Quentin Durward*.

Launcelot Crab Short, fat surgeon, who is an enemy of Roger Potion; he accepts Roderick Random as an apprentice but sends Roderick off to London when his servant becomes pregnant in Tobias Smollett's *The Adventures of Roderick Random*.

Timothy Crabbe Warwick schoolmaster who deciphers part of the manuscript relating Gaston de Blondeville's story in Ann Radcliffe's *Gaston de Blondeville*.

Dr. Crabclaw   Physician in London debtors' prison; he fights Mr. Tapley in Tobias Smollett's *The Adventures of Sir Launcelot Greaves*.

Timothy Crabshaw   Cowardly squire to Sir Launcelot Greaves; he loves his horse, Gilbert, and consults an astrologer about the horse's fate in Tobias Smollett's *The Adventures of Sir Launcelot Greaves*.

Patience Crabstick   Lady Eustace's personal maid, implicated in the theft of the Eustace necklace; she later marries Mr. Gager, the detective who proved her guilt in Anthony Trollope's *The Eustace Diamonds*.

Cadwallader Crabtree   Misanthropic old man, who becomes Perry Pickle's companion in London and influences him toward misanthropy; he pretends to be a magician and soothsayer in a scheme with Perry in London and begrudgingly agrees to give away the bride in Perry's marriage to Emilia Gauntlet in Tobias Smollett's *The Adventures of Peregrine Pickle*.

Mr. Crabwitz   Unscrupulous clerk to Thomas Furnival; under an assumed name he tries to buy off Samuel Dockwrath with £1000 in the case of the forged will in Anthony Trollope's *Orley Farm*.

Father Joe Crackenthorp   Innkeeper who meets Antony Ewart's ship with horses for Darsie Latimer (Arthur Redgauntlet) and serves the Jacobite conspirators as host for their last meeting in Sir Walter Scott's *Redgauntlet*.

Toby Crackit   Accomplice of Bill Sikes in the attempted housebreaking at Mrs. Maylie's mansion in Charles Dickens's *Oliver Twist*.

Mrs. Craddock   Landlady of Samuel Pickwick's lodgings in Bath in Charles Dickens's *The Posthumous Papers of the Pickwick Club*.

Joseph Cradell   Fellow boarder at Mrs. Roper's with Johnny Eames; he marries Amelia Roper, his landlady's daughter, after she fails to secure Eames in Anthony Trollope's *The Small House at Allington*. He appears briefly in *The Last Chronicle of Barset*.

Mrs. Crafton   Lady renowned for the shell collection in her grotto at Fingal, less impressive only than the variety of shells in Harriet Noel's grotto in Thomas Amory's *The Life of John Buncle, Esq.*

Mrs. Craggs   Thomas Craggs's wife, who is suspicious of Jonathan Snitchey on principle in Charles Dickens's *The Battle of Life*.

Thomas Craggs   Conservative lawyer and family friend of the Jeddlers and best friend of his partner, Jonathan Snitchey; his death leaves Snitchey bereft in Charles Dickens's *The Battle of Life*.

Mr. Craig   A gardener at Donnithorne Chase; he tries to woo the beautiful Hetty Sorrel even though he is near forty, knock-kneed, and has an odd voice in George Eliot's *Adam Bede*.

Captain Craigengelt   Shrewd and sinister-looking swindler pretending to support the Jacobite interest; he attaches himself to Bucklaw (Frank Hayston), becoming his constant companion in Sir Walter Scott's *The Bride of Lammermoor*.

Captain Crail   Captain of smugglers on whose ship the Master (James Durie) arrives at Durrisdeer from France and departs after being stabbed by Henry Durie in Robert Louis Stevenson's *The Master of Ballantrae: A Winter's Tale*.

Cousin Cramchild   Dogmatic Bostonian writer of Conversations, in which it is claimed that fairies do not exist; he is berated for his beliefs by the narrator in Charles Kingsley's *The Water-Babies*.

Corporal Cramp   Captain Thornton's subordinate whose duty it is to play Provost-Marshal and hang Dougal in Sir Walter Scott's *Rob Roy*.

Crampley   Midshipman on the *Thunder* who hates Roderick Random and loses a fight with him; he is assigned as a lieutenant on board the *Lizzard*; he abuses his surgeon, Tomlins, after assuming command of the ship returning to England; he attempts to leave Roderick to drown with the ship in Tobias Smollett's *The Adventures of Roderick Random*.

Ben Cranage (Wiry Ben)   A worker in Burge's carpentry shop; he teases Seth Bede about his belief in the Methodist religion and, thus, nearly has to fight Adam Bede in George Eliot's *Adam Bede*.

Bessy Cranage (Chad's Bess)   The blacksmith's daughter, who wears large, fake garnet earrings to hear Dinah Morris preach and is persuaded to remove her jewelry as a part of her Methodist conversion in George Eliot's *Adam Bede*.

Chad Cranage   Ben Cranage's cousin, an anti-Methodist blacksmith, in George Eliot's *Adam Bede*.

Martha Cranch   A poor sister of Peter Featherstone; her hopes of inheritance are disappointed in George Eliot's *Middlemarch*.

Tom Cranch   Useless son of Martha Cranch in George Eliot's *Middlemarch*.

Arabella Crane Jasper Losely's rejected mistress, who baffles his schemes and provides proof of Sophy's parentage in Edward Bulwer-Lytton's *What Will He Do With It? by Pisistratus Caxton.*

Mr. Cranium Phrenologist, who uses skull structure as an index to human personality; he so covets the skull of Cadwallader that he accepts Mr. Escott as his daughter's suitor in exchange for it in Thomas Love Peacock's *Headlong Hall.*

Cephalis Cranium Daughter of Mr. Cranium; she is sought in marriage by both Mr. Escott and Mr. Panscope in Thomas Love Peacock's *Headlong Hall.*

Antonia Cranmer Wealthy, beautiful, nineteen-year-old woman of Bishoprick; John Buncle's third wife, she dies of smallpox at Orton Lodge after the third year of marriage and is buried at Orton Lodge with Buncle's two earlier wives, Charlotte Melmoth and Statia Henley, in Thomas Amory's *The Life of John Buncle, Esq.*

Eva Crasweller Linguist, musician, and model young citizen of Britannula; she is far from enthusiastic about the euthanasia law condemning her father to be disposed of at sixty-eight years of age; she falls in love with Jack Neverbend in Anthony Trollope's *The Fixed Period.*

Gabriel Crasweller Best friend of President John Neverbend of Britannula, an ex-British colony off New Zealand; he supports the law demanding that citizens prepare for euthanasia at sixty-eight years of age, but when his own time comes his enthusiasm for the law wanes in Anthony Trollope's *The Fixed Period.*

Cratander Correspondent with Lysimachus on the subject of personal criticism in Sarah Fielding's *Familiar Letters between the Principal Characters of David Simple and Some Others.*

Mrs. Cratchit Wife of clerk Bob Cratchit and mother of six children; she keeps a happy home despite poverty in Charles Dickens's *A Christmas Carol.*

Belinda Cratchit Bob Cratchit's second daughter in Charles Dickens's *A Christmas Carol.*

Bob Cratchit Meek, underpaid clerk to Ebenezer Scrooge and loving father of crippled Tiny Tim and five other children in Charles Dickens's *A Christmas Carol.*

Martha Cratchit Bob Cratchit's eldest daughter, a milliner's apprentice, in Charles Dickens's *A Christmas Carol.*

Peter Cratchit Bob Cratchit's son about whose future his father is hopeful in Charles Dickens's *A Christmas Carol.*

Tim (Tiny Tim) Cratchit Crippled young son of clerk Bob Cratchit; he exemplifies the piety, charity, and optimism of which Ebenezer Scrooge must learn the importance in Charles Dickens's *A Christmas Carol.*

Anthony Craven Socialist and Venturist friend of Marcella Boyce in Mrs. Humphry Ward's *Marcella.*

Louis Craven Friend of Marcella Boyce and editor of Harry Wharton's paper, the *Labour Clarion,* in Mrs. Humphry Ward's *Marcella.*

Sergeant Craw Legal advisor whose advice to Walter Warmhouse occasions a lawsuit that remains in British courts for thirteen years in an anecdote told by Mr. Fielding in Henry Brooke's *The Fool of Quality.*

Admiral Crawford Uncle and, formerly, guardian of the orphaned Henry and Mary Crawford; his contempt for women has helped form Henry's character; his bringing his mistress to his house after his wife's death has driven Mary to seek a home with Mrs. Grant; the admiral effects William Price's promotion to lieutenant at Henry's instigation in Jane Austen's *Mansfield Park.*

Lord Crawford Loyal captain of the archers of the Scottish Guard, well trusted by Louis XI; tall and spare, he is a blunt Scottish nobleman who distinguished himself under Jeanne D'Arc's banner in Sir Walter Scott's *Quentin Durward.*

Henry Crawford Charming, clever, selfish, and unprincipled half brother of Mrs. Grant; he simultaneously gains the affections of Maria and Julia Bertram; after Maria's marriage to Rushworth, he, with his sister Mary's complicity, begins a campaign on Fanny Price; her dislike of him stimulates his admiration of her beauty and sweetness, and he falls in love; though her rejection is unequivocal, he persists, but his chances of success are doomed by the lapse of constancy which results in his adulterous elopement with Maria in Jane Austen's *Mansfield Park.*

Mary Crawford Pretty, witty, accomplished, financially secure, cynical, and unprincipled half sister of Mrs. Grant; she falls in love with Edmund Bertram before she knows he is to be a clergyman; she is her brother Henry's willing confidante and assistant in his games of lovemaking; her cool acceptance of his adulterous liaison with Maria (Bertram) Rushworth opens Edmund's eyes to her character in Jane Austen's *Mansfield Park.*

Mr. Crawley Impoverished suitor of Jane Wugsby in Bath in Charles Dickens's *The Posthumous Papers of the Pickwick Club.*

Bob Crawley   Only son of Josiah Crawley; his godfather is Dean Arabin in Anthony Trollope's *Framley Parsonage*. He is a schoolboy in *The Last Chronicle of Barset*.

Bute Crawley   Jovial and impecunious fox-hunting clergyman brother to Sir Pitt Crawley in William Makepeace Thackeray's *Vanity Fair*.

Mrs. Bute Crawley   The rector's managing wife, who tries unsuccessfully to secure Matilda Crawley's fortune for her numerous family in William Makepeace Thackeray's *Vanity Fair*.

Emma Crawley   Accomplished and well-educated but poor and plain and therefore unmarriageable daughter of the Reverend and Mrs. Bute Crawley in William Makepeace Thackeray's *Vanity Fair*.

Fanny Crawley   Emma Crawley's sister and like her in being accomplished, well educated, poor, and plain in William Makepeace Thackeray's *Vanity Fair*.

Frank Crawley   Younger son of the Reverend and Mrs. Bute Crawley in William Makepeace Thackeray's *Vanity Fair*.

Grace Crawley   Josiah Crawley's eldest daughter, a child in Anthony Trollope's *Framley Parsonage*. Lovely, gentle, and remarkably well educated by her father, she is a schoolteacher; her love for Major Henry Grantly is rewarded in their union in Anthony Trollope's *The Last Chronicle of Barset*.

Grizzel, Lady Crawley   Deceased well-born first wife of Sir Pitt Crawley and mother of Pitt and Rawdon Crawley in William Makepeace Thackeray's *Vanity Fair*.

James Crawley   Oafish son of Bute Crawley; his attempts to impress his aunt, Matilda Crawley, are thwarted in William Makepeace Thackeray's *Vanity Fair*.

Jane Crawley   Beloved younger daughter of Josiah Crawley; she comforts her father when he is accused of stealing a cheque in Anthony Trollope's *The Last Chronicle of Barset*.

Lady Jane (Sheepshanks) Crawley   Gentle and virtuous wife of the younger Pitt Crawley in William Makepeace Thackeray's *Vanity Fair*.

Josiah Crawley   High-minded clergyman, once a scholar of promise but unlucky in preferment; he has long been the irascible, melancholy perpetual curate of Hogglestock, whose flock are predominately brickmakers; he is charged with the theft of a cheque; driven almost to madness by his own doubts and believed undoubtedly guilty by almost all, he nevertheless holds his own against Mrs. Proudie before he is exonerated and becomes Vicar of St. Ewold's in Anthony Trollope's *The Last Chronicle of Barset*. His friendship with Francis Arabin is mentioned in *Barchester Towers*. He also appears in *Framley Parsonage*.

Kate Crawley   A daughter of the Reverend and Mrs. Bute Crawley in William Makepeace Thackeray's *Vanity Fair*.

Louisa Crawley   A daughter of the Reverend and Mrs. Bute Crawley in William Makepeace Thackeray's *Vanity Fair*.

Sir Marmaduke Crawley   English baronet who hires Juliet Granville to teach the harp to his two sisters in Frances Burney's *The Wanderer*.

Martha Crawley   A daughter of the Reverend and Mrs. Bute Crawley in William Makepeace Thackeray's *Vanity Fair*.

Mary Crawley   Josiah Crawley's stouthearted wife, much tried by poverty; stricken with typhus, she is nursed by Lucy Robarts in Anthony Trollope's *Framley Parsonage*. Her greatest trials occur when her husband is accused of theft in *The Last Chronicle of Barset*.

Matilda Crawley   Rich sister of Sir Pitt Crawley; dashing in her youth, she is in old age pathetically flattered by members of her family; she prefers her rakish nephew, Captain Rawdon Crawley, and takes to the governess Becky Sharp, but casts them off after their secret marriage; her favor and money are eventually won by the younger Pitt Crawleys in William Makepeace Thackeray's *Vanity Fair*.

Matilda Crawley (2)   A daughter of the Reverend and Mrs. Bute Crawley in William Makepeace Thackeray's *Vanity Fair*.

Matilda Crawley (3)   Daughter of the younger Sir Pitt Crawley; she grows up to marry her cousin, young Rawdon Crawley, though she is also courted by Georgy Osborne in William Makepeace Thackeray's *Vanity Fair*.

Peter Crawley   Cowardly, alcoholic attorney-at-law, who is John Meadows's secret agent of "dirty work," going to Australia to attempt to keep George Fielding from returning to claim Susan Merton as his wife in Charles Reade's *It Is Never Too Late to Mend*.

Sir Pitt Crawley   Rough and coarse baronet, who employs Becky Sharp as a governess and proposes marriage to her before taking up with Miss Horrocks and succumbing to a stroke in William Makepeace Thackeray's *Vanity Fair*.

(Sir) Pitt Crawley   Shy and virtuous elder son and heir of Sir Pitt Crawley; he marries Lady Jane Sheepshanks but has vague hankerings after Becky Sharp in William Makepeace Thackeray's *Vanity Fair*.

Captain Rawdon Crawley   Handsome, dashing, somewhat stupid second son of Sir Pitt Crawley; he marries Becky Sharp and lives with her in style, largely by her wits, until he suspects her of having an affair with Lord Steyne; he places his son in the custody of his brother and becomes governor of Coventry Island, where he dies in William Makepeace Thackeray's *Vanity Fair*.

Rawdon Crawley   Son of Becky (Sharp) and Captain Rawdon Crawley; he is loved by his father but neglected by his mother; eventually inheriting the Crawley property, he supports but will not see his mother in William Makepeace Thackeray's *Vanity Fair*.

Rose, Lady Crawley   An ironmonger's daughter and the sickly second wife of Sir Pitt Crawley; only her stepson Pitt treats her with respect; she is the mother of Rose and Violet Crawley; her death enables Sir Pitt to make his unsuccessful proposal of marriage to Becky Sharp in William Makepeace Thackeray's *Vanity Fair*.

Rose Crawley   The elder of Sir Pitt Crawley's young daughters, whom Becky Sharp is hired to teach in William Makepeace Thackeray's *Vanity Fair*.

Violet Crawley   The younger of Sir Pitt Crawley's daughters, whom Becky Sharp is hired to teach in William Makepeace Thackeray's *Vanity Fair*.

Miss Creakle   Daughter of Mr. Creakle; she is rumored to be in love with James Steerforth in Charles Dickens's *The Personal History of David Copperfield*.

Mr. Creakle   Bald, fiery, sadistic head of Salem House school; he always speaks in a whisper but is cruel to the students, except for James Steerforth, whom he treats with favor; he eventually becomes a Middlesex magistrate in Charles Dickens's *The Personal History of David Copperfield*.

Mrs. Creakle   Wife of Mr. Creakle; she breaks the news to David Copperfield of his mother's death and treats him kindly in Charles Dickens's *The Personal History of David Copperfield*.

Mr. Creamer   Miss Matilda Crawley's physician at Brighton in William Makepeace Thackeray's *Vanity Fair*.

Mrs. Creed   The Costigans' landlady in William Makepeace Thackeray's *The History of Pendennis*.

Robert Creedle   Giles Winterborne's loyal old servant in Thomas Hardy's *The Woodlanders*.

Countess von Crefeldt   Longtime lover of Sigismund Alvan; she has become his staunchest friend by the time he meets Clotilde von Rüdiger, but the Countess feels that marriage to the younger woman would ruin Alvan, and she does not help his suit; she nurses Alvan after he is mortally wounded in George Meredith's *The Tragic Comedians*.

Colonel Creighton   Director of the British Secret Service; impressed with Kim's craftiness and cunning, he recruits him into the "Great Game" of intrigue to collect intelligence for the British army in India in Rudyard Kipling's *Kim*.

Clement de Crequy   Young aristocrat and friend of Lady Ludlow's son; Lady Ludlow tells his story of betrayal and death during the Revolution as an example of the dangers of educating the lower classes in Elizabeth Gaskell's *My Lady Ludlow*.

Virginie de Crequy   Clement de Crequy's cousin, for whom he returns to France; she goes to the guillotine with him in Elizabeth Gaskell's *My Lady Ludlow*.

Charles de Cresseron   Narrator of the story, a lawyer helping to sort out the tangled wills of the Brandon and Wylder families; he is infatuated with Dorcas Brandon in J. Sheridan Le Fanu's *Wylder's Hand*.

Earl of Cresset   Nobleman who dies shortly after his wife, Fanny, runs away in George Meredith's *The Amazing Marriage*.

Fanny, Countess of Cresset   The Earl of Cresset's wife, who runs away from her husband; after his death she marries hardy old Captain Kirby; they have two children, Chillon and Carinthia, in George Meredith's *The Amazing Marriage*.

Penrose Cresswell   A trustee of Maud Ruthyn's estate in J. Sheridan Le Fanu's *Uncle Silas*.

Hugh Paulin (Serenus de Cressy) Cressy   Chaplain and fellow at Merton College, Oxford, who joins a Benedictine monastery in Paris and becomes spiritual advisor to John Inglesant in J. Henry Shorthouse's *John Inglesant, A Romance*.

Monsieur Creutzer   (Sir) Charles Grandison's governor on his European tour; because of Creutzer's licentiousness, Charles petitions for a replacement to Sir Thomas Grandison, who thereupon decides no governor is necessary in Samuel Richardson's *Sir Charles Grandison*.

Dr. Crewe   Gruff but kind Gylingden rector when the narrator was a child in J. Sheridan Le Fanu's *Wylder's Hand.*

Luckworth Crewe   Ambitious advertising agent and entrepreneur with crassly materialistic values; he courts Nancy Lord and participates in Beatrice French's ladies' dress business in George Gissing's *In the Year of Jubilee.*

Mrs. Crewkherne   Fundamentalist Christian and George Delmont's aunt, whose prejudice against radical political and social notions has disastrous consequences for the Glenmorris family when it informs rumors she spreads about their licentious behavior in Charlotte Smith's *The Young Philosopher.*

Caroline Crewler   Eldest sister of Sophy Crewler and the beauty of the family; she lives with Tommy Traddles and Sophy after they are married in Charles Dickens's *The Personal History of David Copperfield.*

Horace Crewler   Vicar in Devonshire and father of Sophy; he opposes her engagement to Tommy Traddles in Charles Dickens's *The Personal History of David Copperfield.*

Mrs. Horace Crewler   Wife of the Reverend Horace Crewler; like her husband, she opposes her daughter Sophy's engagement to Tommy Traddles in Charles Dickens's *The Personal History of David Copperfield.*

Louisa Crewler   Sister of Sophy Crewler; she lives with Tommy Traddles and Sophy after they are married in Charles Dickens's *The Personal History of David Copperfield.*

Lucy Crewler   Sister of Sophy Crewler; she lives with Tommy Traddles and Sophy after they are married in Charles Dickens's *The Personal History of David Copperfield.*

Margaret Crewler   Sister of Sophy Crewler; she lives with Tommy Traddles and Sophy after they are married in Charles Dickens's *The Personal History of David Copperfield.*

Sarah Crewler   Second eldest sister of Sophy Crewler; she has an ailment of the spine and lives with Tommy Traddles and Sophy after they are married in Charles Dickens's *The Personal History of David Copperfield.*

Sophy Crewler   Fourth daughter of a vicar in Devonshire and "the dearest girl in the world," according to her betrothed, Tommy Traddles; the marriage is opposed by her family because she is so useful in the household in Charles Dickens's *The Personal History of David Copperfield.*

Richard Crick   Owner and operator of the dairy farm where Tess Durbeyfield and Angel Clare work and meet in Thomas Hardy's *Tess of the D'Urbervilles.*

Mrs. Cricket   Snooping countrywoman whose discovery of a woman's hair on Aeneas Manston's pillow prepares for the disclosure that he has a wife in Thomas Hardy's *Desperate Remedies.*

David Crimp   Pawnbroker to whom young Martin Chuzzlewit pawns his gold watch; later, as David Crimple, Secretary of the Anglo-Bengalee Disinterested Loan and Life Assurance Company, he lapses into fits of hilarity in Charles Dickens's *The Life and Adventures of Martin Chuzzlewit.*

Mr. Crimsworth   Edward and William Crimsworth's uncle, who is responsible for William until he is nine and then passes on the job of William's education to the Seacombes, the maternal relations, in Charlotte Brontë's *The Professor.*

Mrs. Crimsworth   Edward's attractive wife from a wealthy family, who is later mistreated by her husband in Charlotte Brontë's *The Professor.*

Edward Crimsworth   Tyrannical older brother of William; he runs a successful mill and warehouse, where he employs William for a time; he later goes bankrupt in Charlotte Brontë's *The Professor.*

Victor Crimsworth   Son of William and Frances (Henri) Crimsworth; he is attached to his mother and fears his father in Charlotte Brontë's *The Professor.*

William Crimsworth   A reserved "professor" who, orphaned as a boy, receives his education at Eton, tries and dislikes trade with his brother, becomes a teacher in Belgium in several different schools, meets and finally marries Frances Henri, who has his son, and then returns to England, where he retires in Charlotte Brontë's *The Professor.*

Mr. Cringer   Member of Parliament to whom Launcelot Crab sends Roderick Random in London for help to become a surgeon's mate and who refers Roderick to Staytape in Tobias Smollett's *The Adventures of Roderick Random.*

Timothy Crinkett   Mine owner in New South Wales and a partner of John Caldigate in the Polyeuka mine; he follows him to England and tries to blackmail him concerning his association with Euphemia Smith prior to his marriage to Hester Bolton in Anthony Trollope's *John Caldigate.*

Cripple   Loyalist soldier who disguises himself as a cripple in order to flee after the defeat at Marston Moor;

he goes with the Cavalier and another soldier, who are also in disguise, in Daniel Defoe's *Memoirs of a Cavalier*.

Anthony Cripplestraw   Farm worker for Benjamin Derriman and a volunteer soldier in Thomas Hardy's *The Trumpet-Major*.

Mr. Cripps   Gossip and deadbeat who hangs around Captain Nat Kemp's tavern and tries to use information he gathers to his own advantage in Arthur Morrison's *The Hole in the Wall*.

Mr. Crisp   Chiswick curate who falls in love with Becky Sharp in William Makepeace Thackeray's *Vanity Fair*.

Mrs. Crisparkle   The Reverend Septimus Crisparkle's mother, dainty as a china shepherdess; she is fond of Edwin Drood and Rosa Bud but critical of Neville Landless's character in Charles Dickens's *The Mystery of Edwin Drood*.

Septimus Crisparkle   A minor canon in the Cloisterham Cathedral; he befriends Neville and Helena Landless and prevents John Jasper from assaulting Neville after the disappearance of Edwin Drood in Charles Dickens's *The Mystery of Edwin Drood*.

Samuel Crocker   Post Office clerk who gets into hot water with his superiors for tearing up official papers; he pursues Clara Demijohn but loses her to his rival, Daniel Tribbledale, in Anthony Trollope's *Marion Fay*.

Admiral Croft   Warm-hearted retired rear admiral, who rents the Elliot estate; his devotion to and touchingly comic dependence on his wife make them a model of marital happiness in Jane Austen's *Persuasion*.

Sophia Croft   Wife of the admiral and sister to Captain Wentworth; her good-heartedness, candor, and affection for her husband are admired by Anne Elliot in Jane Austen's *Persuasion*.

Chrystal Croftangery   First-time author, who asks editing advice of his friend Mr. Fairscribe and winds up narrating Menie Gray's history in Sir Walter Scott's *The Surgeon's Daughter*.

Mr. Crofts   Elder son of Sir Richard Crofts; he ingratiates himself with Lord Montreville's daughter, Lady Frances, and secretly marries her; he agrees to maintain separate residences when she begins an affair with the urbane Chevalier de Bellozane in Charlotte Smith's *Emmeline: The Orphan of the Castle*.

Mr. Crofts   Perverse old man, ugly but rich, who pays fifty guineas for first rights to Fanny Hill's virginity, tries to rape her, and fails grotesquely in John Cleland's *Memoirs of a Woman of Pleasure*.

Lady Frances Delamere Crofts   Shameless and unprincipled elder daughter of Lord and Lady Montreville; her affair with Bellozane causes her to separate from her husband; Bellozane kills her brother, Frederic Delamere, in a duel in Charlotte Smith's *Emmeline: The Orphan of the Castle*.

Dr. James Crofts   Physician in Guestwick who marries Bell Dale in Anthony Trollope's *The Small House at Allington*. He appears briefly in *The Last Chronicle of Barset*.

Sir Richard Crofts   Attorney and Member of Parliament; he manages Lord Montreville's affairs and promotes ruthless schemes to prevent a marriage between Frederic Delamere and Emmeline Mobray, whose legitimate claim to the Mowbray estate he suppressed soon after the death of her father in Charlotte Smith's *Emmeline: The Orphan of the Castle*.

Roland de Croisnel   Nevil Beauchamp's close friend, after Beauchamp saves his life; he disapproves of Beachamp's plan to elope with his sister Renée (Rouaillout) in George Meredith's *Beauchamp's Career*.

Captain Unton Croke   Officer of the insurgent forces; relentless in pursuit of Sir Joseph Wagstaff and other Royalist fugitives defeated at the battle of Salisbury, he is hoodwinked by Charles Mandeville, who finds an unlikely hiding place for Sir Joseph in William Godwin's *Mandeville*.

Herr Croll   Augustus Melmotte's confidential secretary, whose refusal to sign as witness papers forged by his employer immediately precedes Melmotte's suicide; he and Madame Melmotte marry in Anthony Trollope's *The Way We Live Now*.

Cromwell (Earl of Essex)   Nobleman engaged in the suppression of monasteries in England during the reign of Henry VIII in J. Henry Shorthouse's *John Inglesant, A Romance*.

Oliver Cromwell   A "firebrand of war"; he and his Roundhead forces rout the overeager Prince Rupert and his army at Marston Moor in Daniel Defoe's *Memoirs of a Cavalier*. He is a soldier and Protector of the Commonwealth, who pursues King Charles II after the triumph of Parliamentary armies over Stuart forces; he narrowly misses capturing the king at Woodstock Lodge in Sir Walter Scott's *Woodstock*. He explains his presence in Elysium as a reward for sufferings in a second incarnation that made reparation for his disloyalty to Charles I in his first incarnation in Henry Fielding's *A Journey From This World to the Next*.

Mr. Crook   Legal representative of Staffordshire iron merchants; he insists upon payment for his creditors from Mr. Furze in Mark Rutherford's *Catharine Furze*.

Sir William Crook   Friend of Harry Annesley; he offers Harry a post as private secretary when it appears that Peter Prosper has withdrawn his support and favor in Anthony Trollope's *Mr. Scarborough's Family*.

Tim Cropdale   London author who tricks Birkin out of a pair of boots in Tobias Smollett's *The Expedition of Humphry Clinker*.

Adolphus Crosbie   Unprincipled and selfish minor civil servant, whose social ambition causes him to jilt Lily Dale and marry Lady Alexandrina de Courcy in Anthony Trollope's *The Small House at Allington*. After Lady Alexandrina's death his renewed suit is firmly rejected by Lily in *The Last Chronicle of Barset*.

William Crosbie   Provost of Dumfries, who is a friend of Alexander Fairford, and whose letter reporting the disappearance of Darsie Latimer (Arthur Redgauntlet) causes Alan Fairford's abrupt departure from the court in Sir Walter Scott's *Redgauntlet*.

Mrs. Cross   Kindly shopkeeper who allows Ernest Pontifex and other schoolboys to run up small debts; Theobald Pontifex's anger results in her shop's being ruled off bounds by the Roughborough school in Samuel Butler's *The Way of All Flesh*.

Mrs. Cross   Bertha Cross's ill-tempered mother, who abuses her servants in George Gissing's *Will Warburton*.

Bertha Cross   Girl of a poor but genteel background with a troublesome mother; a friend of Rosamund Elvan, she earns money as an artist and eventually marries Will Warburton in George Gissing's *Will Warburton*.

Mrs. Crossley   Neighbor of Jim Hawkins and his mother in Robert Louis Stevenson's *Treasure Island*.

John Crossthwaite   Idealistic, intelligent Chartist tailor, to whom Alton Locke is apprenticed; an advocate of self-sacrifice for the common good, he encourages Alton to become involved in the Chartist movement, finally becoming, like Alton, a Christian socialist and sailing with him for Texas in Charles Kingsley's *Alton Locke*.

Katie Crossthwaite   Supportive wife of the Chartist tailor John Crossthwaite; she helps Lady Ellerton nurse Alton Locke through his fever in Charles Kingsley's *Alton Locke*.

Lieutenant Crosstrees   First officer of a British gunboat sent to end the jurisdiction of John Neverbend as president of the South Seas island of Britannula; he has charge of a 250-ton cannon trained on the capital city to enforce British law in Anthony Trollope's *The Fixed Period*.

Young Crotchet   Son of Ebenezer Crotchet; his greed and speculations blight the lives of all around him in Thomas Love Peacock's *Crotchet Castle*.

Lemma Crotchet   Daughter of Ebenezer Crotchet in Thomas Love Peacock's *Crotchet Castle*.

(Shaft-speeder) Crow   Warrior who leads scouting parties and bears messages in war and peace in William Morris's *The Roots of the Mountains*.

Jogglebury Crowdey   Chairman of the Stir-it-stiff union; he believes Soapey Sponge is wealthy and invites him to be his houseguest but tries to get rid of him when he finds out otherwise in Robert Surtees's *Mr. Sponge's Sporting Tour*.

Squire Crowdy   Hearty landowner and husband of Blanche Robarts in Anthony Trollope's *Framley Parsonage*.

Blanche Robarts Crowdy   Buxom sister of Mark Robarts; she marries Squire Crowdy and becomes mistress of Creamclotted Hall in Anthony Trollope's *Framley Parsonage*.

Captain Samuel Crowe   Retired merchant marine captain, who travels with his nephew, Thomas Clarke; he admires and imitates Sir Launcelot Greaves, but gives up his mad ambition when he learns from Ferret he has an inheritance; he marries Dorothy Oakley in Tobias Smollett's *The Adventures of Sir Launcelot Greaves*.

Thaddeus Crowe   Honest, successful lawyer, who handles the arrangements on behalf of Fred Neville by which Captain O'Hara is to be paid an annuity of 200 so long as he stays out of Ireland in Anthony Trollope's *An Eye for an Eye*.

Mrs. Crowhurst   Poor woman who is mother of Phoebe and who nurses her during her mortal illness in Mark Rutherford's *Catharine Furze*.

Phoebe Crowhurst   Mrs. Furze's servant, who quits in disgust when she realizes the plot being prepared against Tom Catchpole; she confesses to Catharine Furze her love for Tom before she dies in Mark Rutherford's *Catharine Furze*.

Mr. Crowl   Newman Noggs's fellow lodger, who rails at him when he will not put enough coals on the fire or get him invited to dinner with the Kenwigs in Charles Dickens's *The Life and Adventures of Nicholas Nickleby*.

Old Crowle   Mean-hearted, rough gatekeeper at Bartram-Haugh; at Silas Ruthyn's order he helps keep Silas's ward, Maud Ruthyn, confined to the estate in J. Sheridan Le Fanu's *Uncle Silas*.

Mrs. Crowling   Procuress for Sir Harry Richmond in Charlotte Smith's *The Young Philosopher*.

Lady Hameline de Croye   Isabelle de Croye's aunt and guardian; fond of gaiety and absurdly romantic, she imagines Quentin Durward to be infatuated with her and is humiliated to discover his interest lies with Isabelle; eventually she marries William de La Marck in Sir Walter Scott's *Quentin Durward*.

Lady Isabelle (Jacqueline) de Croye   Beautiful Burgundian heiress whom the Duke of Burgundy endeavors to bestow on an odious favorite; fleeing to France, where she uses the name Jacqueline, she is betrayed by Louis XI to William de La Marck; she is rescued by Quentin Durward in Sir Walter Scott's *Quentin Durward*.

Jacopo Cruchi   An innkeeper who incites Angelo Guidascarpi's distrust during his escape from Milan; he regains his trust only to betray him in George Meredith's *Vittoria*.

John Crumb   Honest, simple, flour-dusted miller, who is devoted to Ruby Ruggles and jealous of her would-be seducer, Sir Felix Carbury; he thrashes his rival and wins Ruby as his bride in Anthony Trollope's *The Way We Live Now*.

Ned Crummins   Laborer who is delivering to Martin Tinman a large mirror broken by Van Dieman Smith (Ribstone); Crummins runs, starting the quarrel between Smith (Ribstone) and Tinman in George Meredith's *The House on the Beach*.

Mrs. Crummles   Vincent Crummles's wife, who plays tragic roles and dances the hornpipe in her husband's theatrical company in Charles Dickens's *The Life and Adventures of Nicholas Nickleby*.

Charles Crummles   Son of Vincent Crummles and an actor in the company since childhood; he later emigrates to Australia in Charles Dickens's *The Life and Adventures of Nicholas Nickleby*.

Ninetta Crummles (The Infant Phenomenon)   Precocious "child" actress, who is kept small in stature by her father, Vincent Crummles, with applications of gin and few hours of sleep; her top billing is resented by other performers in Charles Dickens's *The Life and Adventures of Nicholas Nickleby*.

Percy Crummles   Second son of Vincent Crummles and an actor in his father's theatrical company since childhood; he leaves with his brother for Australia in Charles Dickens's *The Life and Adventures of Nicholas Nickleby*.

Vincent Crummles   Manager of a traveling theatrical company; he hires Nicholas Nickelby and Smike as actors immediately upon seeing them when they need work and asks Nicholas to translate a French play in Charles Dickens's *The Life and Adventures of Nicholas Nickleby*.

Mr. Crump   Baker in the town of Gylingden who, with John Thomas, brings news of Sir Harry Bracton's entry into the town to try to win the election from Stanley Lake, precipitating Lake's fateful ride past the uncovered hand of Mark Wylder's corpse in J. Sheridan Le Fanu's *Wylder's Hand*.

Mrs. Cruncher   Wife of Jerry Cruncher; she fights with him over his stealing bodies from graves and fears for the safety of her son in Charles Dickens's *A Tale of Two Cities*.

Jerry Cruncher   Tellson's Bank employee, who moonlights as a resurrection-man, retrieving bodies from graves to sell to interested parties; he is devoted to Dr. Manette and Lucie Manette and aids Charles Darnay in his escape from France in Charles Dickens's *A Tale of Two Cities*.

(Young) Jerry Cruncher   Son of the resurrectionist; he accompanies his father on burial excavations much to his mother's displeasure in Charles Dickens's *A Tale of Two Cities*.

Mrs. Crupp   David Copperfield's landlady while he is lodging in the Adelphi when he first lives in London; she is afflicted with 'spazzums,' which require the administration of brandy in Charles Dickens's *The Personal History of David Copperfield*.

Mr. Cruse   Clergyman and tutor of a student making the Grand Tour; he vies with Mr. M'Gabbery in trying to attract ladies of the party in Anthony Trollope's *The Bertrams*.

Mr. Crushton   The Honourable Crushton, a bosom friend of Lord Mutanhed in Bath in Charles Dickens's *The Posthumous Papers of the Pickwick Club*.

Robinson (Bob, Robin) Crusoe (Kreutznaer)   Son of a middle-class merchant; having gone to sea against his father's wishes, he is captured by pirates off the coast of Africa and made a slave for two years before escaping and being brought to Brazil by a Portuguese vessel; later, shipwrecked on the "Island of Despair," he becomes a devout Christian and eventually establishes a home and farm while on the island; after fifteen years of solitude, he discovers another inhabitant, a native whom he names

Friday; with Friday, Crusoe saves a Spaniard, the English Captain, and Friday's father, and eventually both Crusoe and Friday are able to leave the island and come to England in Daniel Defoe's *The Life and Strange Surprizing Adventures of Robinson Crusoe of York, Mariner*.

Mr. Crutchleigh   One of the guests at Brandon Hall's Hunt Ball in J. Sheridan Le Fanu's *Wylder's Hand*.

Mrs. Crutchleigh   A guest at the Hunt Ball at Brandon Hall who disapproves of having a singer performing in J. Sheridan Le Fanu's *Wylder's Hand*.

Corfe Crutchleigh   Guest at Brandon Hall's Hunt Ball in J. Sheridan Le Fanu's *Wylder's Hand*.

Tom Cuckow   Man scolded by Ellis Duckworth for not doing a better job of robbing a pardoner; he is one of the few aboard the *Good Hope* who keep their heads during a storm in Robert Louis Stevenson's *The Black Arrow: A Tale of Two Roses*.

Sergeant Richard Cuff   Grizzled, fatherly detective with a penetrating gaze and a passion for growing roses; he is called in by Lady Verinder to investigate the theft of a valuable diamond, but when his suspicions light on her daughter, Rachel, Lady Verinder discharges him; he helps solve the mystery at last in Wilkie Collins's *The Moonstone. A Romance*.

Cul de Jatte   Fraudulent cripple, who befriends Gerard in Burgundy but is last seen as an inmate of the jail in Hansburgh in Charles Reade's *The Cloister and the Hearth*.

Father Cullen   Outspoken curate of Drumsna and an ally of Father John McGrath in Anthony Trollope's *The Macdermots of Ballycloran*.

Lady Cecilia Cullen   Delicate, shy, titled girl, a hunchback, who is fiercely devoted to Alice Barton and becomes a nun in George Moore's *A Drama in Muslin*.

Rosamund Culling   Everard Romfrey's housekeeper and eventually his wife, a motherlike figure to Nevil Beauchamp; despite her affection for Beauchamp, she inadvertently estranges him from his uncle and from an inheritance in George Meredith's *Beauchamp's Career*.

Lord Culloden   Presbyterian Scottish peer and brother-in-law of Lothair's father; he is one of Lothair's two guardians in Benjamin Disraeli's *Lothair*.

Alderman Cullpepper   Wealthy High Churchman, who allows his young wife to attend Methodist services for diversion, and who good-naturedly opposes Geoffry Wildgoose's assertion that the theater is evil in Richard Graves's *The Spiritual Quixote*.

Mrs. Cullpepper   Young wife of a wealthy alderman; she attends Methodist assemblies and flirts discreetly with Geoffry Wildgoose in Richard Graves's *The Spiritual Quixote*.

Sheriff of Cumberland   Kind and courteous sheriff, who escorts Queen Mary of Scotland to England in Sir Walter Scott's *The Abbot*.

Tom Cummins   Card player in an anecdote related by Mr. Wicks to Dodson and Fogg in Charles Dickens's *The Posthumous Papers of the Pickwick Club*.

Miss Cummyns   Virtuous friend of Lady Dellwyn; she is spurned when she will not toady, and then is falsely embraced by society when Lady Dellwyn is cast out after her divorce in Sarah Fielding's *The History of the Countess of Dellwyn*.

Lady Cumnor   Local benevolent autocrat and matriarch of the Whig aristocratic influence on the Hollingford community in Elizabeth Gaskell's *Wives and Daughters*.

Lord Cumnor   Friendly and unpretentious landowner; relations between his "great house" (the Towers) and the Gibsons mirror some of the social changes of the period in Elizabeth Gaskell's *Wives and Daughters*.

Cunegonda   Governess to Agnes de Medina; she is manipulated by Rodolpha, Baroness Lindenberg to oblige Agnes to enter the convent in Matthew Lewis's *The Monk*.

Archie Cunningham   One of Louis XI's Scottish Guard archers who save Quentin Durward from hanging in Sir Walter Scott's *Quentin Durward*.

Curate   Jacobite frequenter of the Black Bear in Sir Walter Scott's *Rob Roy*.

Curate   Heartless clergyman, who uses the manuscript of Harley's biography for shotgun wadding in Henry Mackenzie's *The Man of Feeling*.

Edmund Curll   Bookseller in London made notorious by Pope's *Dunciad* for his frauds and thefts; he shows John Buncle London life, including brothels, and is instrumental in uniting Buncle with his sixth wife, Agnes Dunk, by helping free her from her cruel father, Old Dunk, in Thomas Amory's *The Life of John Buncle, Esq*.

Mr. Curlydown   Post Office clerk who gives evidence at the bigamy trial of John Caldigate in Anthony Trollope's *John Caldigate*.

Jemima Curlydown   Irrepressible daughter of a Post Office clerk called to give evidence in the bigamy trial of

John Caldigate; she marries another postal official, Samuel Bagwax, in Anthony Trollope's *John Caldigate*.

Lord Curryfin   Handsome young nobleman, whose beauty and money attract women to his lectures on fish; he loses himself in constantly changing interests and experiments but finally marries Miss Niphet in Thomas Love Peacock's *Gryll Grange*.

George Curtis   Lost younger brother of Sir Henry Curtis; excluded from his father's inheritance, he assumes the name Neville and journeys into Africa to find King Solomon's mines; he remains stranded in a desert oasis with his servant, Jim, until Sir Henry rescues him in H. Rider Haggard's *King Solomon's Mines*.

Grace Curtis   Quietly satiric elder sister of Rachel Curtis; she attempts unsuccessfully to curb Rachel's excesses in Charlotte Yonge's *The Clever Woman of the Family*.

Sir Henry (Incubu) Curtis   Powerful, handsome, yellow-bearded Englishman, who accompanies Allan Quatermain on two expeditions into Africa; the first is in search of King Solomon's Mines and Sir Henry's lost brother in H. Rider Haggard's *King Solomon's Mines*. The second expedition is to find a rumored white race, the Zu-Vendi, in *Allan Quatermain*.

Rachel Curtis   Socially conscious young woman, whose attempts to transcend the restricted life of the seaside resort in which she lives fail until she submits to the guidance of a superior male; she marries Alick Keith in Charlotte Yonge's *The Clever Woman of the Family*.

Sir Walter Curtis   Man sent by the Earl of Essex (2) to Rouen in search of Lord Leicester and Matilda in Sophia Lee's *The Recess*.

Alderman Cute   Local justice, red-faced and complacent, determined to "put down" the poor and the distressed in his district in Charles Dickens's *The Chimes*.

Sophy Cutler   Girl who made a play for Jos Sedley in India and whom he likes to speak of in William Makepeace Thackeray's *Vanity Fair*.

Captain Edward (Ned) Cuttle   Loyal friend of Solomon Gills and Walter Gay; he has a hook for a right hand; he supports Gills in his big dreams for Walter, watches the shop while Gills is searching for Walter, and gives Florence Dombey shelter there when she flees her home in Charles Dickens's *Dombey and Son*.

Captain Cutts   Criminal associate of Jasper Losely in

Edward Bulwer-Lytton's *What Will He Do With It? by Pisistratus Caxton*.

Mr. Cutts   Fifty-year-old saddler of Cowfold accused and acquitted of arson; Miriam Tacchi is willing to lie to protect him in Mark Rutherford's *Miriam's Schooling*.

Captain Bartholomew (Uncle Bat) Cuttwater   Gin-drinking uncle of Bessie Woodward; he lodges with her and her three daughters in Anthony Trollope's *The Three Clerks*.

Cylinda   Wealthy young woman who exemplifies the dangers of educating females; her "wild imagination" leads her to reject marriage and become the mistress of Nicanor and Eustace; following her repentance she lives a blameless existence with Ferdinand, Portia, and Cordelia in Sarah Fielding's *The Cry*.

"Cynecia"   Phony heroine sent by Sir George Bellmour to convince Arabella that Charles Glanville is her perjured lover, Ariamenes, in Charlotte Lennox's *The Female Quixote*.

Cynthia   Virtuous wife of Valentine in the happy ending of Sarah Fielding's *The Adventures of David Simple in Search of a Faithful Friend*. She corresponds with Camilla (Simple) in *Familiar Letters between the Principal Characters of David Simple and Some Others*. She suffers greatly after Valentine's death in Jamaica; she returns to England to care for her niece after the death of the latter's parents, David and Camilla Simple, in *David Simple. Volume the Last*.

Humphrey Cypher   Sergeant-at-arms who advises Hammel Clement after his first arrest in Henry Brooke's *The Fool of Quality*.

Mr. Cyprus   Visitor at Nightmare Abbey who takes his ideas from Lord Byron's Childe Harold and delivers the Byronic parody "There is a Fever of the Spirit" in Thomas Love Peacock's *Nightmare Abbey*.

Cyril   Proud, autocratic patriarch and leader of the Christians in Alexandria; he plots and counterplots for the elimination of the Jews, the philosopher Hypatia, and all remaining polytheistic tendencies; his plans succeed but sow seeds of future violence among the Christians in Charles Kingsley's *Hypatia*.

Cyrus   Ancient conqueror; unable to trust himself in the presence of the beautiful captive Panthea, he entrusts her to the care of the virtuous Araspes in a parable told by Henry Clinton in Henry Brooke's *The Fool of Quality*.

D

Dowager Countess of D. Suitor to Harriet Byron on behalf of her twenty-five-year-old son, the Earl of D.; Harriet's inability to encourage the project awakens her consciousness of her love for Sir Charles Grandison in Samuel Richardson's *Sir Charles Grandison*.

Earl of D. Willing though unsuccessful aspirant to the hand of Harriet Byron; his entire suit is conducted by his mother, the Dowager Countess of D., in Samuel Richardson's *Sir Charles Grandison*.

Earl and Countess of D—— Aristocrats and Bedfordshire neighbors of the B——s; they are a "fashionable married couple" whose behavior toward each other is a foil to Pamela and Mr. B——'s behavior in Samuel Richardson's *Pamela, or Virtue Rewarded*.

Lady D—— Countess of B——'s sister; perceptive and benevolent, she tries to dissuade Henrietta Courteney from going into service and then places her with Mrs. Autumn and later with Miss Belmour in Charlotte Lennox's *Henrietta*.

Mr. D—— Young gentleman who earns £800 a year; he returns to his first love, Maria, only after an affair with Syrena Tricksy in Eliza Haywood's *Anti-Pamela: or, Feign'd Innocence Detected*.

Mrs. D—— Headmistress of an English girls' school in Brussels; she employs Frances Henri as a French teacher on Mrs. Wharton's advice in Charlotte Brontë's *The Professor*.

Mr. Dabb London provision dealer, who yields to his wife's request to take her nephew, Andrew Tacchi, as a clerk, and who dismisses him for drunkenness in Mark Rutherford's *Miriam's Schooling*.

Mrs. Dabb Wife of Mr. Dabb and sister of Giacomo Tacchi; she lives in London and reluctantly persuades her husband to employ Andrew Tacchi in Mark Rutherford's *Miriam's Schooling*.

Daniel Dabbs Good-humored proletarian friend of Richard Mutimer; he becomes alienated from him and Socialism and opens a pub in George Gissing's *Demos*.

Mrs. Dabby Deputy's wife who comes up short in Jeanie Deans's comparison of her with Queen Caroline in Sir Walter Scott's *The Heart of Midlothian*.

Percy Dacier Lord Dannisburgh's nephew, who falls in love with Diana Warwick but repudiates her to marry the heiress Constance Asper when Diana leaks his confidential news of upcoming political action to a newspaper in George Meredith's *Diana of the Crossways*.

Mr. Dacre Courtly, virtuous, astute, wealthy Catholic gentleman; he is the guardian of the young Duke of St. James during his minority and father of May Dacre in Benjamin Disraeli's *The Young Duke*.

Arundel Dacre Serious career diplomat, who is cousin to May Dacre and heir to all the Dacre property; he is engaged to Miss Dacre but ends up marrying Lady Caroline St. Maurice in Benjamin Disraeli's *The Young Duke*.

May Dacre The beautiful, lively, intelligent, generous, conscientious daughter of the Catholic guardian of the Duke of St. James; she eventually marries the duke in Benjamin Disraeli's *The Young Duke*.

Dagley A farmer, Arthur Brooke's insolent tenant in George Eliot's *Middlemarch*.

Richard Dagworthy Brutal, overbearing mill owner who tries to force Emily Hood to marry him by threatening to have her father arrested for theft in George Gissing's *A Life's Morning*.

Solomon Daisy Parish clerk of Chigwell, who entertains the patrons of the Maypole Inn with a strange experience he had on the night Reuben Haredale died in Charles Dickens's *Barnaby Rudge*.

Grandfather (grandsire) Dale Grandfather of Black Andie Dale; he takes young Andie fishing in the "Tale of Todd Lapraik" in Robert Louis Stevenson's *Catriona*.

Black Andie Dale Swarthy Scottish lowlander and gamekeeper, who supervises David Balfour's kidnapping to the highlands and becomes his friend after David saves his life in Robert Louis Stevenson's *Catriona*.

Captain Bernard Dale Nephew and heir of Christopher Dale, the squire of Allington; he is rejected by his cousin Bell Dale in Anthony Trollope's *The Small House at Allington*. He marries Emily Dunstable in *The Last Chronicle of Barset*.

Charles Dale Benevolent clergyman and friend of William Hazeldean; he assists Leonard Fairfield and reveals the truth about his identity to Audley Egerton in Edward Bulwer-Lytton's *"My Novel," by Pisistratus Caxton*.

Christopher Dale Squire of Allington; he becomes resentful with disappointment when his niece, Bell, refuses to marry his heir, Captain Bernard Dale, in Anthony Trollope's *The Small House at Allington*. He appears in *The Last Chronicle of Barset*.

Isabella (Bell) Dale   Mary Dale's elder daughter, who is in love with Dr. James Crofts of Guestwick; she disappoints her uncle, Christopher Dale, by not marrying his heir in Anthony Trollope's *The Small House at Allington*.

Laetitia Dale   Sentimental, unrequited lover of the callous Sir Willoughby Patterne; their positions are reversed when, after recognizing his true colors, she agrees to a loveless marriage of convenience to the jilted Willoughby in George Meredith's *The Egoist*.

Lilian (Lily) Dale   Mary Dale's younger daughter; obstinate and proud though good-tempered and loving, she will not marry her worthy suitor, Johnny Eames, once she has been jilted by Adolphus Crosbie in Anthony Trollope's *The Small House at Allington*. She vows to remain a spinster, rejecting Eames for a last time in *The Last Chronicle of Barset*.

Mary Dale   High-minded widow of the youngest brother of Christopher Dale, who dislikes but respects her; he allows her to occupy a modest house on his estate; her life is devoted to her daughters, Bell and Lily, in Anthony Trollope's *The Small House at Allington*. She gives refuge to Grace Crawley during the stolen-cheque controversy in *The Last Chronicle of Barset*.

Colonel Orlando Dale   Languid, whist-playing father of Bernard and brother-in-law of Lord de Guest in Anthony Trollope's *The Small House at Allington*.

Tam Dale   Father of Scottish lowlander Black Andie Dale; devilish and ungodly in his youth, he later becomes honest and the victim of warlock Todd Lapraik's black magic in Robert Louis Stevenson's *Catriona*.

Malcolm, Lord Dalgarno   Only son of the Earl of Huntinglen; he befriends Nigel Olifaunt to the ruin of his reputation, employs Andrew Skurliewhitter to steal Nigel's property, is forced by the king to marry Lady Hermione, and is murdered by Captain Colepepper while fleeing with Nelly Christie to Scotland in Sir Walter Scott's *The Fortunes of Nigel*.

Dugald Dalgetty of Drumthwacket   Mercenary serving as a major under Montrose and formerly a ritt-master in the army of Gustavus Adolphus, a position he recalls quite often; his military view of honor does not allow him to betray Montrose while a prisoner in Argyle's castle, from which he eventually escapes in Sir Walter Scott's *A Legend of Montrose*.

Olivier Dalibard   French scholar who corrupts his son, Gabriel Varney, and his pupil, Lucretia Clavering, with such success that they coldly betray him to political enemies in Edward Bulwer-Lytton's *Lucretia*.

Dalica   Kinswoman of Charoba; she succeeds her as Queen of Egypt in the appended romance "The History of Charoba, Queen of Egypt" in Clara Reeve's *The Progress of Romance*.

Dallach   Escaped thrall of the Dusky Men; he is rescued by Face-of-god and after hostilities becomes alderman of Rose-dale in William Morris's *The Roots of the Mountains*.

Dalmaine   Member of Parliament who takes a harshly practical view of the problems of the poor, marries an attractive young woman, and bullies her in George Gissing's *Thyrza*.

Adeline Dalrymple   Beautiful married neighbor of the Kirklands; she is the first innocent love of Christopher Kirkland in Mrs. Lynn Linton's *The Autobiography of Christopher Kirkland*.

Dowager Viscountess Dalrymple   Noble family connection much courted by Sir Walter Elliot and his eldest daughter, Elizabeth, in Jane Austen's *Persuasion*.

Conway Dalrymple   Fashionable artist, who paints a portrait of Clara Van Siever and marries her in Anthony Trollope's *The Last Chronicle of Barset*.

Marriott Dalrymple   Charming, sensitive father of Julie Le Breton in Mrs. Humphry Ward's *Lady Rose's Daughter*.

J. Daly   Unscrupulous attorney engaged by Barry Lynch to swindle Anty Lynch out of her fortune in Anthony Trollope's *The Kellys and the O'Kellys*.

Tom (Black Daly) Daly   Imposing master of the Galway hounds known for his fierce black whiskers and hatred for all those who would interfere with the hunt in Anthony Trollope's *The Landleaguers*.

General Thomas Dalzell   The Duke of Monmouth's chief lieutenant, infamous for military cruelty; he argues against leniency for Henry Morton in Sir Walter Scott's *Old Mortality*.

Tommy Damer   Sailor and beloved brother of Eleanor Tirrel; he is stabbed when her jealous husband mistakes him for a lover in Henry Brooke's *The Fool of Quality*.

Mrs. Eustace Damerel   Matron who is secretly the mother of the Lord children and seeks to guide them in George Gissing's *In the Year of Jubilee*.

Jane Dampier   Aunt of John Dampier; she takes Elizabeth Gilmour from her grim Parisian home to convalesce at the English seaside in Anne Thackeray Ritchie's *The Story of Elizabeth*.

John Dampier Worldly bachelor who, while idling away time in Paris, attaches the affections of both Caroline Gilmour and her daughter, Elizabeth; he ultimately marries the latter in Anne Thackeray Ritchie's *The Story of Elizabeth*.

Will Dampier Brother of John Dampier; he first mistrusts Elizabeth Gilmour but eventually befriends her in Anne Thackeray Ritchie's *The Story of Elizabeth*.

Lord Damplin Nobleman who proposes, unsuccessfully, to Arabella Bloomville instead of attending a boxing master in William Beckford's *Modern Novel Writing; or, the Elegant Enthusiast*.

Suke Damson Village girl who had a pre-marital affair with Dr. Edred Fitzpiers; though she is now unimportant to him, she cannot forget him; the man-trap set by her jealous husband, Tim Tang, accidentally assists in the reunion of Fitzpiers and his wife, Grace Melbury, in Thomas Hardy's *The Woodlanders*.

Marquis de Damville Father-in-law of Reginald de St. Leon and patron of culture; his house was frequented by Marot, Rabelais, Erasmus, and Scaliger in William Godwin's *St. Leon*.

Marguerite de Damville Beautiful and accomplished girl who studies drawing with Leonardo da Vinci and literature with Clement Marot; as Reginald de St. Leon's wife she bears him four children and, until her death, tirelessly seeks to save her husband from his vices in William Godwin's *St. Leon*.

Dan of Arimathea Wealthy fishmonger and widower, who is devoted to his son Joseph and pleased with Joseph's scholarship and with his willingness to join in partnership; a Pharisee, he forbids Joseph's following Jesus in George Moore's *The Brook Kerith*.

Dan of the Howlet-hirst Provincial gallant and a friendly member of the Halidome in Sir Walter Scott's *The Monastery*. A vassal of the Monastery of St. Mary's, he becomes a Protestant and participates in a masquerade which mocks the monastery in *The Abbot*.

Sir Paul Danbury Second to the malicious Lord Mahogany in a farcical duel with Don Pedro de Gonzales in William Beckford's *Modern Novel Writing; or, the Elegant Enthusiast*.

Miss Danby Daughter of John Danby, whose plot to have his brother murdered was foiled by Sir Charles Grandison; subsequently the executor and legatee of the uncle's estate, Sir Charles divides it among Miss Danby and her brothers, facilitating her marriage in Samuel Richardson's *Sir Charles Grandison*.

Mr. Danby Benevolent friend of Sir Charles Grandison, who saves his life from an attack by killers hired by his villainous brother; on his death, he leaves his property to Sir Charles instead of to his brother's sons and daughter, but Sir Charles magnanimously divides it among them in Samuel Richardson's *Sir Charles Grandison*.

Edward Danby Mr. Danby's younger nephew, apprenticed to a wine merchant; his brother and sister and Sir Charles Grandison are offended by his mercantile assessment of his marriage prospects, but Sir Charles treats him as generously as them in Samuel Richardson's *Sir Charles Grandison*.

Sir Isaac Danby Old fop who still believes himself a young dandy; he is chosen by Lady Meadows to be Henrietta Courteney's husband but is spurned by the heroine in Charlotte Lennox's *Henrietta*.

John Danby Mr. Danby's vicious brother, who greedily plots his murder though Mr. Danby has benevolently educated his children; the crime is foiled and exposed through the opportune interference of Sir Charles Grandison in Samuel Richardson's *Sir Charles Grandison*.

Thomas Danby Mr. Danby's elder nephew, apprenticed to a West-India merchant; Sir Charles Grandison's generosity facilitates his becoming a partner and his marrying his master's niece in Samuel Richardson's *Sir Charles Grandison*.

Superior Dance Supervisor of the revenue officers who come to the rescue of Jim Hawkins and his mother and put the pirates at the Admiral Benbow Inn to flight, killing Pew; he takes Jim to Squire Trelawney's house in Robert Louis Stevenson's *Treasure Island*.

Frederic Dancer Wealthy Irishman who cohabits with Carola Bennet for some time after she has been exploited as a prostitute in Thomas Amory's *The Life of John Buncle, Esq.*

William Dane A friend of Silas Marner in their youth; he steals money from a dead church member and frames Marner for the crime in the town of Lantern Yard in George Eliot's *Silas Marner*.

Paul Dangerfield (Charles Archer) Mysterious businessman, who comes to Chapelizod highly touted by Lord Castlemallard; with Aunt Becky Chattesworth's consent, he tries to court Gertrude Chattesworth but is unsuccessful; after an assault which leaves Dr. Barney Sturk in a coma and after indulging in bribery, perjury, and deceit to cover all his previous crimes, he is revealed as Charles Archer, the man who killed Beauclerc and then testified that Lord Dunoran was guilty; he dies in prison before he can be hanged in J. Sheridan Le Fanu's *The House by the Churchyard.*

Lord Danglecourt　Peer who takes Pompey from the Milliner in Francis Coventry's *The History of Pompey the Little.*

Daniells　A hand on the *Norah Creina* in Robert Louis Stevenson's *The Wrecker.*

Lord Dannisburgh　An elderly cabinet member; his innocent and intellectually based friendship with Diana Warwick leads her husband to sue for divorce in George Meredith's *Diana of the Crossways.*

Lucy Danton　Mother of Amelia (de Gonzales); rejected by her family when she married an Irish baron, she resides in Spain but returns to England to die; she succumbs when gout settles in her head in William Beckford's *Modern Novel Writing; or, the Elegant Enthusiast.*

Grace Danver　Actress who throws acid in the face of Clara Hewett, a rival who has replaced her in George Gissing's *The Nether World.*

Mr. Danvers　Manager of Austin Ruthyn's estate in J. Sheridan Le Fanu's *Uncle Silas.*

Mr. Danvers　Father confessor to Lady Meadows; he tries to seduce Henrietta Courteney and then turns on her; he encourages Lady Meadows's attempts to force the heroine to marry Sir Isaac Danby, then to have her imprisoned in a convent; he is eventually caught with Lady Meadows's maid and dismissed in Charlotte Lennox's *Henrietta.*

Julian Danvers　Disinherited son of Arthur Danvers, Lord Alton, and his Greek wife; he is, according to the bargain struck between his uncle, Richard (Lord Alton), and the servant Cloudesley, brought up in Italy as Cloudesley's son; while his foster father is away in Ireland, Julian escapes the supervision of Borromeo to join St. Elmo's robber band and is subsequently captured, imprisoned, and then released owing to the intervention of William Meadows in William Godwin's *Cloudesley.*

Soliman Ben Daoud　Sufferer in the palace of Eblis and a wise ruler of the earth before Adam; the story of his journey to the subterranean palace is similar to Vathek's in William Beckford's *Vathek.*

Lady Darby　Lady who was brought to Chapelizod to be buried; when digging her grave, the sexton finds the skull of Barney Sturk, precipitating the telling of the story of his murder to the narrator and his uncle Charles in J. Sheridan Le Fanu's *The House by the Churchyard.*

Car Darch　A strong, vulgar village woman, nicknamed The Queen of Spades, and a former lover of Alec Stoke-D'Urberville; drunk and jealous of his interest in Tess Durbeyfield, she proposes to fight Tess; Stoke-D'Urberville's timely rescue of Tess gives him his hoped-for opportunity to seduce her in Thomas Hardy's *Tess of the D'Urbervilles.*

Nancy Darch　Car's sister, nicknamed the Queen of Diamonds, in Thomas Hardy's *Tess of the D'Urbervilles.*

Mrs. Darcy　Eccentric sister of Squire Wendover; her strange ways develop into madness in Mrs. Humphry Ward's *Robert Elsmere.*

Fitzwilliam Darcy　Clever and handsome friend and houseguest of Mr. Bingley; his youthful inheritance of wealth has reinforced his pride and reserve; his love for Elizabeth Bennet impels him to change his behavior after she refuses his first proposal of marriage in Jane Austen's *Pride and Prejudice.*

Georgiana Darcy　Mr. Darcy's shy, accomplished younger sister, whom he and Mr. Bingley's sisters would like to see married to Bingley; her earlier foiled elopement with Wickham has been kept secret; she welcomes Elizabeth Bennet as sister at the end of Jane Austen's *Pride and Prejudice.*

William Dare　Captain DeStancy's illegitimate son, a diabolical photographer, who plots to marry his father to the rich Paula Power so that he may insure his own financial security; ruthless and amoral, he represents the modern, technologically dangerous man who is able to deceive and ruin people through manipulating photographic images in Thomas Hardy's *A Laodicean.*

Dare-not-lie　One of the good people of Vanity Fair introduced to Christiana and her party by Mnason in John Bunyan's *The Pilgrim's Progress From this World to That Which Is to Come.*

Mrs. Dareville　Member of snobbish English society who pokes fun at the Clonbronys' Irish heritage in Maria Edgeworth's *The Absentee.*

Saunders Darlet　Irascible villager of Kinross; he opposes paying Dr. Luke Lundin in Sir Walter Scott's *The Abbot.*

Sir George Darlington　Friend of Colonel and Lady Maria Lambert in William Beckford's *Modern Novel Writing; or, the Elegant Enthusiast.*

Count Darlowitz Passionate aristocrat, who is intent on his own gratification; he pursues his best friend's wife, even though reason tells him the path leads only to destruction in Charlotte Dacre's *The Passions*.

Amelia Darlowitz Venetian countess who represents the "ideal" woman, selfless and forgiving; she miscarries her child and dies in anguish over her husband's infidelity in Charlotte Dacre's *The Passions*.

Charles Darnay See Charles St. Evrémonde.

Lucie Darnay Daughter of Charles Darnay and Lucie Manette; Madame Defarge wants her dead in Charles Dickens's *A Tale of Two Cities*.

Mrs. Darnel Mother of Aurelia Darnel; she approves of Sir Launcelot and blesses his courtship of her daughter just before dying in Tobias Smollett's *The Adventures of Sir Launcelot Greaves*.

Anthony Darnel Uncle and guardian of Aurelia Darnel; defeated for Parliament by Sir Everhard Greaves, he prevents Aurelia from seeing Sir Launcelot Greaves and fights a duel with Sir Launcelot; he loses his guardianship of Aurelia when he suffers a stroke in Tobias Smollett's *The Adventures of Sir Launcelot Greaves*.

Aurelia Darnel (Miss Meadows) Young woman beloved of Sir Launcelot Greaves; she suffers imprisonment, kidnapping, and other hardships on the road from York to London; intended by her uncle to marry Squire Philip Sycamore, she wishes to marry Sir Launcelot, is rescued by him in a London madhouse, and is married to him at the end in Tobias Smollett's *The Adventures of Sir Launcelot Greaves*.

Dicky Darnell Mr. Brownjohn's half brother, who succeeds in kidnapping Medora Glenmorris but is ineffectual in his efforts to force her to marry him in Charlotte Smith's *The Young Philosopher*.

Frances Darnford Primary correspondent in this epistolary work; she is unable to accept Lady A—'s request to serve as governess for her daughters but responds by sending Lady A— a series of letters detailing the proper education for young women; she supports a firmly moral and domestically oriented education, along the way advocating strict separation of classes, the reinstatement of sumptuary law, and continuation of the African slave trade in Clara Reeve's *Plans of Education*.

Henry Darnford Gallant yet sensitive aristocrat, who intercedes on behalf of Maria Venables; he is hunted by her estranged husband and his attorney; later, as a fellow inmate in a corrupt private madhouse, he becomes Maria's confidant, lover, and true "husband" in Mary Wollstonecraft's *Maria; or The Wrongs of Woman*.

Mary (Polly) Darnford Pamela Andrews's disappointed rival for Mr. B——'s matrimonial intentions; she becomes a close friend and important correspondent of Pamela; she rejects the boorish, silly Mr. Murray on solid principles and finally marries Sir William G—— but dies in labor with her fourth child in Samuel Richardson's *Pamela, or Virtue Rewarded*.

Nancy Darnford Ill-natured sister of Mary Darnford; she thoughtlessly accepts Mr. Murray's proposal only to find the marriage cross-grained in Samuel Richardson's *Pamela, or Virtue Rewarded*.

Sir Simon Darnford Cantankerous, self-indulgent aristocrat and Lincolnshire neighbor of Mr. B——; he warns B—— of Mr. Williams's plan to free Pamela Andrews; he is no match for Pamela's charm and perspicacity; he is one of the correspondents in Samuel Richardson's *Pamela, or Virtue Rewarded*.

Mr. Darnley Sophia's father; a gentleman, he squanders his fortune, marries a beautiful and expensive wife, and dies, leaving his family in poverty in Charlotte Lennox's *Sophia*.

Mrs. Darnley Sophia's mother; having spoiled her older daughter, Harriot, and having been willing to "sell" both daughters' honor for the gifts of their noble suitors, she is punished when Harriot, as wealthy mistress to Lord L—, refuses to help her out of poverty in Charlotte Lennox's *Sophia*.

Harriot Darnley Sophia Darnley's older sister, more obviously though less truly beautiful; vain, supercilious, and expensive, she attracts seducers rather than honorable lovers and eventually becomes mistress to Lord L—, loses her beauty to jaundice, and winds up unhappily married to a peruke maker turned ensign in Charlotte Lennox's *Sophia*.

Sophia Darnley Mr. Darnley's younger daughter, whose subtler qualities attract Sir Charles Stanley away from her sister; she deserves to marry him but, because of her poverty, doubts his honorable intentions, treats him coldly, and leads him to doubt her love; eventually she wins him through quiet persistence, with Mr. Herbert's help, in Charlotte Lennox's *Sophia*.

Laird of Darnlinvarach See Angus M'Aulay.

Miss Darrell Pretty, shallow girl, who briefly attracts Harry Ormond; he quickly sees her pettiness in Maria Edgeworth's *Ormond*.

Guy Darrell   Wealthy landowner, whose obsession with his family honor and grief over the loss of Caroline Montfort have blighted his life in Edward Bulwer-Lytton's *What Will He Do With It? by Pisistratus Caxton.*

Matilda Darrell   Secretive daughter of Guy Darrell; she elopes with Jasper Losely in Edward Bulwer-Lytton's *What Will He Do With It? by Pisistratus Caxton.*

Philip Darrell   Middle-class friend and Oxford schoolmate of William Ashe; he betrays Ashe by tacitly permitting Lady Kitty Ashe to publish a book that will ruin Ashe's career in Mrs. Humphry Ward's *The Marriage of William Ashe.*

Thames Darrell   Adopted son of Owen Wood; he prospers in the Wood household, survives a plot by his uncle, Sir Rowland Trenchard, to have him murdered, escapes overseas, and returns to find he is of noble birth and to marry Wood's daughter, Winifred, in William Harrison Ainsworth's *Jack Sheppard.*

Rosa Dantle Dartle   Slight, dark woman who lives with Mrs. Steerforth; she is disfigured by a scar on her lip caused by a hammer thrown at her by James Steerforth when a child; she is obsessively in love with Steerforth and hates Emily Peggotty because of Steerforth's attraction to her; she tries to punish Emily after she returns to London in Charles Dickens's *The Personal History of David Copperfield.*

Alice Darvil   Luke Darvil's innocent daughter, whose love for Ernest Maltravers never wavers, despite the birth and death of her illegitimate daughter and her unconsummated marriage to Richard Templeton (Lord Vargrave) in Edward Bulwer-Lytton's *Ernest Maltravers.* As the widowed Lady Vargrave she raises Evelyn Templeton as her own daughter and is at last reunited with Maltravers in *Alice.*

Luke Darvil   Alice Darvil's criminal father, also known as Jack Walters; a violent, trouble-making ruffian, he dies suddenly of apoplexy in Edward Bulwer-Lytton's *Ernest Maltravers.*

Lady Dashfort   Conniving Englishwoman who, with her daughter's compliance, schemes to make Lord Colambre fall in love with and marry her daughter, Lady Isabella, in Maria Edgeworth's *The Absentee.*

Miss Dashwood   Superintendent of nursing in the London hospital where Miriam Tacchi is an apprentice; she decides Miriam can never qualify as a nurse in Mark Rutherford's *Miriam's Schooling.*

Elinor Dashwood   Heroine who embodies the "sense" of the title; she views her sister Marianne's excessive romantic sensibility with distress; loving Edward Ferrars, she must suffer the impertinent confidence of his secret betrothed, Lucy Steele; steadfast of heart as well as clear-sighted in attention to duty, Elinor is eventually rewarded by marrying Edward in Jane Austen's *Sense and Sensibility.*

Fanny Ferrars Dashwood   Wife of John Dashwood and a selfish and unfeeling sister to Edward Ferrars in Jane Austen's *Sense and Sensibility.*

Sir George Dashwood   General in the British army and father of Lucy Dashwood; he endeavors unsuccessfully to contest Godfrey O'Malley's seat in Parliament and is insultingly prevented from buying the O'Malley estates but is reconciled to Charles O'Malley, who saves him from a French firing squad, in Charles Lever's *Charles O'Malley.*

Harry Dashwood   Only child of John and Fanny Dashwood; in his interests the Norwood estate has unnecessarily enriched his parents at the expense of his step-grandmother, Mrs. Henry Dashwood, and her daughters in Jane Austen's *Sense and Sensibility.*

Mrs. Henry Dashwood   Widowed mother of Elinor, Marianne, and Margaret Dashwood; she exhibits much romantic sensibility in Jane Austen's *Sense and Sensibility.*

John Dashwood   Elder half brother of the Dashwood sisters; having inherited the family estate, he is easily persuaded by his wife to disregard his promise to his dying father of generosity to his sisters and stepmother in Jane Austen's *Sense and Sensibility.*

Lucy Dashwood   Daughter of Sir George Dashwood; her life is saved by Charles O'Malley, who falls in love with her in Charles Lever's *Charles O'Malley.*

Margaret Dashwood   At fourteen, the youngest of the three Dashwood sisters in Jane Austen's *Sense and Sensibility.*

Marianne Dashwood   Heroine who embodies the "sensibility" of the title; she falls in love with the handsome but dissolute John Willoughby, who disappoints her; her despair makes her gravely ill, but she survives to learn sense and to marry Colonel Brandon in Jane Austen's *Sense and Sensibility.*

Secundra Dass   Devoted Hindu servant of the Master (James Durie); she spies out Alison (Graeme) and Henry Durie's American destination, supports the Master by goldsmithing, and conspires with him to bury him in a state of suspended animation for his third apparent death; she is unable to restore him to more than a flickering of life, however, in Robert Louis Stevenson's *The Master of Ballantrae: A Winter's Tale.*

Dick Datchery   A mysterious figure who appears, apparently in disguise; he gets Princess Puffer, the opium dealer, to identify John Jasper as one of her clients in Charles Dickens's *The Mystery of Edwin Drood*.

Mr. Daubeny   Parliamentary gladiator and leader of the Conservative party whose success owes more to tactical skills than principles in Anthony Trollope's *Phineas Finn*. He outmaneuvres the Liberals by introducing a bill to disestablish the Church in *Phineas Redux*. His inability to form a government causes the (younger) Duke of Omnium to become leader in *The Prime Minister*.

Daughter   Honourable young widow without support or friends; she falls under the protection of the Matron and finds her long-lost father in Charles Johnstone's *Chrysal: or, The Adventures of a Guinea*.

Daughter of Charity Supporter Number Eight   A daughter who takes all her father's possessions and then accuses him of an impious passion in Charles Johnstone's *Chrysal: or, The Adventures of a Guinea*.

Daughter of Eusebius   Intelligent but not beautiful girl who is at a dangerous age, runs away with the Nominee to the Mock Monastery, and ends her days as a common prostitute in Charles Johnstone's *Chrysal: or, The Adventures of a Guinea*.

Mrs. Davenport   Friend of the Bartons and widow of Ben Davenport in Elizabeth Gaskell's *Mary Barton*.

Ben Davenport   Mill worker and friend of John Barton; his death and the deaths of his children from poverty increase John Barton's anger over conditions in Elizabeth Gaskell's *Mary Barton*.

Barbara, Lady Davers   Aristocrat and sister of Mr. B——; she first insults and physically threatens his servant-class wife Pamela Andrews, whose virtue and letters finally win her esteem; thereafter she accepts Pamela as a sister and becomes her staunch defender, especially against her brother's transgressions, in Samuel Richardson's *Pamela, or Virtue Rewarded*.

David   A gravedigger in the village where Nell Trent and her grandfather eventually reside in Charles Dickens's *The Old Curiosity Shop*.

David (Wilkins)   A son of Peter Wilkins and Youwarkee in Robert Paltock's *The Life and Adventures of Peter Wilkins*.

Davie of Stenhouse   One of Hobbie (Halbert) Elliot's friends; he helps rescue Grace Armstrong in Sir Walter Scott's *The Black Dwarf*.

Dr. Davies   Bachelor clergyman who is the object of Anne Steele's pursuit and the subject of much of her conversation in Jane Austen's *Sense and Sensibility*.

Mr. Davies   Ginevra Fanshawe's rich brother-in-law, who is older than her father in Charlotte Brontë's *Villette*.

Mrs. Davies   Susan Merton's aunt, a practical housekeeper, who helps Susan nurse Francis Eden back to health at the prison in Charles Reade's *It Is Never Too Late to Mend*.

Augusta Davies   Ginevra Fanshawe's beautiful elder sister, who made a match with a rich old gentleman in Charlotte Brontë's *Villette*.

Danvers Davies (Mr. Danby)   Profligate nephew of Sir Matthew Davies; he is disinherited by his virtuous uncle; after his reformation they are reconciled in S. J. Pratt's *Shenstone-Green*.

Captain John Davies (Captain Brown)   Former American sea captain, who loses his command through drunkenness and becomes a beachcomber in the South Sea islands; he turns to drinking aboard his next command, the *Farallone*, which he pirates from course; he plans the robbery of the gentleman recluse and pearl trader William John Attwater in Robert Louis Stevenson's *The Ebb-Tide: A Trio and a Quartette*.

Sir Matthew Davies (Mr. Seabrooke)   Gentleman of wealth and virtue who poses as the indigent Seabrooke in order to measure the success of the utopian Shenstone-Green; he oversees its conversion to a viable community; he rescinds his disinheritence of his nephew in S. J. Pratt's *Shenstone-Green*.

Alice Davilow   Half sister of Gwendolen Harleth in George Eliot's *Daniel Deronda*.

Bertha Davilow   Half sister of Gwendolen Harleth and a whisperer in Goerge Eliot's *Daniel Deronda*.

Fanny Davilow   Middle-aged, indecisive, twice-widowed woman; her first marriage produced the beautiful Gwendolen Harleth and her second, four weak-minded girls in George Eliot's *Daniel Deronda*.

Fanny Davilow (the younger)   Half sister of Gwendolen Harleth and a whisperer in George Eliot's *Daniel Deronda*.

Isabel Davilow   Half sister of Gwendolen Harleth and a listener in George Eliot's *Daniel Deronda*.

Mr. Davis   The Ecclestone physician who publicly supports Ruth Hilton and takes her illegitimate son Leonard as his apprentice shortly before her fatal illness, revealing his own illegitimacy, in Elizabeth Gaskell's *Ruth*.

Mrs. Davis Landlady of the Cat and Whistle public house; she tries to inveigle Charley Tudor into marrying Norah Geraghty in Anthony Trollope's *The Three Clerks*.

Esther Davis Vain, treacherous servant girl from Fanny Hill's home village; she first entices Fanny to London and then abruptly abandons her there in John Cleland's *Memoirs of a Woman of Pleasure*.

Davy Dawdle Counselor and companion to Squire Philip Sycamore; he suggests the scheme to imprison Sir Launcelot Greaves in a madhouse; he flees to the Continent with Sycamore in Tobias Smollett's *The Adventures of Sir Launcelot Greaves*.

Jack Dawkins (Artful Dodger) Fagin's head pickpocket, who befriends Oliver Twist north of London and brings him to Fagin's house; he is arrested for theft and transported in Charles Dickens's *Oliver Twist*.

Dawson Serious-minded friend of Ernest Pontifex at Cambridge; he is pleased at Ernest's devotion in religion in Samuel Butler's *The Way of All Flesh*.

Dawson Ne'er-do-well and confederate of Thomas Thornton in the murder-robbery of Sir John Tyrrell; tracked down by Henry Pelham, he gives testimony which clears Sir Reginald Glanville of the murder in Edward Bulwer-Lytton's *Pelham*.

Mr. Dawson Elderly physician called in to treat Marian Halcombe when she is suddenly taken ill; he takes exception to Count Fosco's amateur interference in the patient's treatment and is adroitly steered away from the case in Wilkie Collins's *The Woman in White*.

'Lias Dawson Deranged visionary, who befriends the young Grieve orphans, Louie and David, in Mrs. Humphry Ward's *The History of David Grieve*.

Margaret Dawson 'Lias Dawson's wife, who shelters and feeds the young David Grieve in Mrs. Humphry Ward's *The History of David Grieve*.

Margaret Dawson Central character, who recounts her youth as one of Lady Ludlow's ''young gentlewomen'' in Elizabeth Gaskell's *My Lady Ludlow*.

Mr. Day Scottish farmer, neighbor and toady to Lord Senton; he is received into county society ''on sufferance'' in George Moore's *A Modern Lover*.

Mrs. Day Stepmother of Fancy and wife of Geoffrey Day, who staunchly endures her comically deranged behavior in Thomas Hardy's *Under the Greenwood Tree*.

Fancy Day Pretty, guileless young schoolmistress and organist of the instrument which supplants the parish choir; admired by three variously qualified suitors, she marries Dick Dewey at the end of Thomas Hardy's *Under the Greenwood Tree*.

Geoffrey Day A landowner's agent and Fancy's father, ambitious for her social advancement; her calculated pretense of languishing tricks him into abandoning his support of Fred Shiner's courtship and consenting to her marrying Dick Dewey in Thomas Hardy's *Under the Greenwood Tree*.

Sally Day Dark, lean far-west South Sea native, who serves as good-natured crew member and friend to Robert Herrick aboard the pirated schooner *Farallone* in Robert Louis Stevenson's *The Ebb-Tide: A Trio and a Quartette*.

Peter Dealtry Proprietor of the Spotted Dog at Grassdale in Edward Bulwer-Lytton's *Eugene Aram*.

Dean A lawyer with an office in the same building as Harry Bellairs in Robert Louis Stevenson's *The Wrecker*.

Ellen (Nelly) Dean Loyal, garrulous servant; she goes from Wuthering Heights with Catherine Earnshaw to Thrushcross Grange upon Catherine's marriage to Edgar Linton, and later at Wuthering Heights she is Heathcliff's housekeeper; she narrates to Mr. Lockwood the story of the Earnshaw and Linton families in Emily Brontë's *Wuthering Heights*.

Ulick Dean Music critic and an admirer of Mr. Innes; he composes an opera with a role for Evelyn Innes; he counters Owen Asher's atheism with spiritual beliefs in Celtic-Rosicrucianism; he becomes Evelyn's lover and proposes marriage in George Moore's *Evelyn Innes*. His interest in the opera and his charm appeal to her even after she has entered the convent in *Sister Teresa*.

Mr. Deane Lucy Deane's father; he is a businessman who rises quickly to wealth; he helps his nephew, Tom Tulliver, to get a warehouse job and eventually to possess the mill on the Floss in George Eliot's *The Mill on the Floss*.

Lucy Deane The pretty and mild-mannered girl who makes her cousin Maggie Tulliver seem naughty by comparison; years later, Maggie visits the Deanes, and Lucy's suitor, Stephen Guest, becomes enamored of her, but Lucy remains faithful and forgiving in George Eliot's *The Mill on the Floss*.

Susan Dodson Deane The third sister of Mrs. Tulliver and the mother of Lucy; she was thought to have married a man beneath her family's standards in George Eliot's *The Mill on the Floss*.

Thomas Deane   Harriet Byron's godfather in Samuel Richardson's *Sir Charles Grandison*.

David (Douce Davie) Deans   Jeanie and Effie Deans's stern father; a Cameronian, he is deeply religious and morally rigid; he disowns Effie when he discovers that she is pregnant in Sir Walter Scott's *The Heart of Midlothian*.

Euphemia (Effie) Deans (Lady Staunton)   Jeanie Deans's younger half sister; beautiful and spoiled, she becomes pregnant by Geordie Robertson (George Staunton); when her child disappears, she is tried for murder and sentenced to hang; pardoned through Jeanie's efforts, she marries George and becomes Lady Staunton; she is generous to Jeanie's family and remains with them after George is killed by the Whistler in Sir Walter Scott's *The Heart of Midlothian*.

Jeanie Deans   Honest and generous half sister of Effie Deans; she refuses to lie for Effie, yet walks to London to obtain a pardon for her; her devotion captures Queen Caroline and John, Duke of Argyle; she marries Reuben Butler and lives comfortably through the largesse of Lady Staunton (Effie) and of Argyle in Sir Walter Scott's *The Heart of Midlothian*.

Rebecca Deans   David Deans's second wife and Effie's mother, who tries to bring about a match between Jeanie and the young Laird of Dumbiedikes in Sir Walter Scott's *The Heart of Midlothian*.

Death   Emperor presiding over a court including Charles XII of Sweden, Alexander, and Caligula, all of whom contributed many subjects (corpses) to his reign in the Palace of Death in Henry Fielding's *A Journey From This World to the Next*.

Deb   Servant of Hiram Yorke in Charlotte Brontë's *Shirley*.

Captain Jack de Baron   Dashing Coldstream Guards officer; pleasure-loving and mercenary, he devotes himself to flirtations and believes himself in love with Lady George Germain; he is finally captured in marriage by Augusta Mildmay in Anthony Trollope's *Is He Popenjoy?*.

General Sir Thomas De Boots, K. C. B.   Calvary officer who served in India; he is Barnes Newcome's fellow club member in William Makepeace Thackeray's *The Newcomes*.

Lady Debarry   Sir Maximus Debarry's wife in George Eliot's *Felix Holt, the Radical*.

Augustus Debarry   Clergyman brother of Sir Maximus Debarry and like him an arch-Tory in George Eliot's *Felix Holt, the Radical*.

Harriet Debarry   The Debarrys' eldest daughter in George Eliot's *Felix Holt, the Radical*.

Sir Maximus Debarry   The wealthy owner of Treby Manor and an arch-Tory; although he refuses to associate with the Transome family when Harold Transome declares himself to be of the Radical party, he petitions Parliament to have Felix Holt released from prison in George Eliot's *Felix Holt, the Radical*.

Philip Debarry   Tory candidate for Parliament running against the Radical Harold Transome in George Eliot's *Felix Holt, the Radical*.

Selina Debarry   A Debarry daughter in George Eliot's *Felix Holt, the Radical*.

Deborah Debbitch   Governess of Alice Bridgenorth and Julian Peveril; she serves as an intermediary between Alice and Julian on the Isle of Man in Sir Walter Scott's *Peveril of the Peak*.

Deborah   Scullery maid who drunkenly describes her enthusiastic participation in Methodist services in Richard Graves's *The Spiritual Quixote*.

Deborah   Arabella's servant, bribed by Sir George Bellmour to spy on her mistress; she reveals his plot to Charlotte Glanville, thus bringing on the violent climax in Charlotte Lennox's *The Female Quixote*.

Anne de Bourgh   Pale, sickly, and insipid daughter of the arrogant Lady Catherine de Bourgh in Jane Austen's *Pride and Prejudice*.

Lady Catherine de Bourgh   Overbearing aunt of Mr. Darcy and patroness of Mr. Collins; she wishes Darcy to marry her insipid daughter, is horrified to hear a report of his interest in Elizabeth Bennet, and unwittingly gives him the courage to propose a second time in Jane Austen's *Pride and Prejudice*.

Decius   Scholarly kinsman of Basil in George Gissing's *Veranilda*.

Earl de Courcy   Gouty head of the de Courcy family; proud and ill-tempered, he hates in varying degrees his wife and children in Anthony Trollope's *The Small House at Allington*. He appears in *Doctor Thorne*.

Lady Alexandrina de Courcy   Handsome, vain, cold-hearted daughter of an earl; twice disappointed in engagements broken over marriage-settlement problems, she accepts the proposal of Adolphus Crosbie; soon after the wedding she leaves him to live with her mother in Baden-Baden in Anthony Trollope's *The Small House at Allington*. She appears briefly in *Barchester Towers* and in *Doctor Thorne*. Her death contributes to Crosbie's financial distress in *The Last Chronicle of Barset*.

Lady Amelia de Courcy   An earl's daughter mentioned in Anthony Trollope's *Barchester Towers*. Her rank qualifies her as matrimonial consultant to her cousin Augusta Gresham; she persuades Augusta that the social inferiority of Mortimer Gazebee makes him unacceptable; later she marries him herself in *Doctor Thorne*. As Lady Amelia Gazebee she is officious in advising and directing Adolphus Crosbie in *The Small House at Allington*.

George de Courcy   Spendthrift second son of the Earl de Courcy; he becomes parsimonious on marrying a low-born heiress and sponges on his family in Anthony Trollope's *The Small House at Allington*. He appears briefly in *Barchester Towers* and in *Doctor Thorne*. He serves on the bench dealing with Josiah Crawley's case in *The Last Chronicle of Barset*.

Mrs. George de Courcy   Coal merchant's daughter, whose money makes up for her low birth in Anthony Trollope's *The Small House at Allington*.

John de Courcy   Third son of the Earl de Courcy; an extravagant wastrel, he is a burden to his father in Anthony Trollope's *The Small House at Allington*. He appears in *Barchester Towers* and in *Doctor Thorne*.

Lady Margaretta de Courcy   Favorite daughter of Countess de Courcy, whom she resembles except in having no beauty; she accompanies her mother to Baden-Baden in Anthony Trollope's *The Small House at Allington*. She appears in *Barchester Towers* and in *Doctor Thorne*.

Rosina, Countess de Courcy   Wife of the earl; she is always scheming on behalf of her large, impecunious family in Anthony Trollope's *The Small House at Allington*. She urges her nephew, Frank Gresham, to pay court to the wealthy Martha Dunsable in *Dr. Thorne*. She appears in *Barchester Towers*.

Lady Rosina de Courcy   Proud, pious second daughter of the Earl de Courcy in Anthony Trollope's *The Small House at Allington*. She appears in *Barchester Towers*. She is the last of the family to remain in Barsetshire, living alone in a small cottage, much respected, especially by the (younger) Duke of Omnium, in *The Prime Minister*.

Honoria, Lady Dedlock   Cold, haughty, and beautiful wife of Sir Leicester Dedlock; she is under investigation by Mr. Tulkinghorn because she seems to have a secret past; the secret is revealed to be the birth, before her

marriage, of her illegitimate daughter, Esther Summerson; fearing exposure and rejection, she flees her husband after Tulkinghorn's murder and dies at the dreadful paupers' graveyard where her lover is buried in Charles Dickens's *Bleak House*.

Sir Leicester Dedlock   Baronet of an old family; proud and chivalrous, he represents the country's decaying aristocracy; he devotedly loves his wife even after she runs away in Charles Dickens's *Bleak House*.

Volumnia Dedlock   A "young lady (of sixty)" who is cousin to Sir Leicester Dedlock and frequently visits Chesney Wold in Charles Dickens's *Bleak House*.

Mr. Deedles   Banker whose suicide is deemed morally acceptable in contrast to suicides of indigent citizens in Charles Dickens's *The Chimes*.

Baron of Deepdale   Enemy of Sir Medard; he besieges the men of Eastcheaping; he is captured by Sir Medard, Osberne Wulfsson, and Stephen the Eater in William Morris's *The Sundering Flood*.

Jack Deepley   Silly young gentleman in William Beckford's *Modern Novel Writing; or, the Elegant Enthusiast*.

Ernest Defarge   Keeper of a wine shop in Paris and an important figure in the French revolutionary movement based in the suburb of St. Antoine; he often assumes the name of Jacques Four and is a friend of Dr. Alexander Manette in Charles Dickens's *A Tale of Two Cities*.

Thérèse Defarge   Wife of Ernest Defarge; her sister is murdered by the Marquis St. Evrémonde; most militant of the revolutionists, she vows vengeance on all the St. Evrémondes; her fierce knitting is a code for guillotined aristocrats in Charles Dickens's *A Tale of Two Cities*.

Degraded Clergyman   The author who writes all of Hunchback's pamphlets, letters, religious tracts, and sermons in Charles Johnstone's *Chrysal: or, The Adventures of a Guinea*.

Lady Julia de Guest   Sister of Lord de Guest, whose house she manages; a fellow guest at Courcy Castle, she works hard but unsuccessfully to keep Adolphus Crosbie true to Lily Dale in Anthony Trollope's *The Small House at Allington*. She tries to comfort Johnny Eames when Lily refuses his marriage offer in *The Last Chronicle of Barset*.

Theodore, Earl de Guest   Bachelor peer dedicated to his estate and livestock who bestows a legacy on Johnny Eames for saving him from a bull in Anthony Trollope's *The Small House at Allington*.

Frederick DeHorn   A Swedish nobleman's illegitimate

son, who poses as the legitimate heir; he persuades Angelica Kauffmann into a clandestine marriage in Anne Thackeray Ritchie's *Miss Angel*.

Lady Delacour   Belinda Portman's sophisticated, witty, dissipated friend, who believes herself to be dying of a self-inflicted wound; jaded with her life and the high society she is so popular in, and estranged from her husband and daughter, she recovers from her wound, is reconciled to her husband and daughter with Belinda's encouragement, and helps to unite Belinda with Clarence Hervey in Maria Edgeworth's *Belinda*.

Lord Delacour   Drunken, jealous husband of Lady Delacour; with Belinda Portman's help he is reformed and reconciled to his wife and daughter in Maria Edgeworth's *Belinda*.

Helena Delacour   Young daughter of Lord and Lady Delacour; she is reared with another family but is later happily reunited with her parents in Maria Edgeworth's *Belinda*.

Margaret Delacour   Stern, passionate aunt of Lord Delacour; she dislikes Lady Delacour but is eventually reconciled to her through the intervention of Belinda Portman in Maria Edgeworth's *Belinda*.

Jacob Delafield   Quiet, sincere aristocrat, whose strong moral sense leads him to reform Julie Le Breton's social attitudes when they marry; he becomes the Duke of Chudleigh after the deaths of his cousin and uncle in Mrs. Humphry Ward's *Lady Rose's Daughter*.

Geoffrey Delamayn   Blackguard athlete, who seduces Anne Silvester and abandons her, sending a friend, Arnold Brinkworth, with his promises of marriage; later he wins the love of the wealthy widow Mrs. Glenarm; his unscrupulous attempts to free himself from any impediment from Anne have a directly contrary effect; he therefore determines to get rid of her by unprovable murder; having forced her to accompany him to an isolated cottage, he dies while trying to smother her: incapacitated by stroke, he is strangled by his insane accomplice, Hester Dethridge, in Wilkie Collins's *Man and Wife*.

Lady Augusta Delamere   Younger sister of Frederick Delamere; she allies herself with him against parental disapproval of marriage to Emmeline Mobray; later, as Lady Westerhaven, she takes Emmeline under her protection during travels through Switzerland and France in Charlotte Smith's *Emmeline: The Orphan of the Castle*.

Frederic Delamere   Fiery and willful son of Lord and Lady Montreville; by way of courtship, he pursues, harasses, and abducts Emmeline Mobray in spite of her scruples and the opposition of his parents; although pro-

tected by her against violence triggered by jealousy, he challenges and is killed by Bellozane, the lover of his sister, Frances Crofts, in Charlotte Smith's *Emmeline: The Orphan of the Castle*.

Roger Delane   Upper-class Cambridge graduate and divorced husband of Rachel Henderson; he murders her because of his physical and moral depravity and desire for revenge in Mrs. Humphry Ward's *Harvest*.

Colonel Delaney   Stiff-necked husband of Lady Rose Chantrey, whom he will not divorce when she leaves him for another man in Mrs. Humphry Ward's *Lady Rose's Daughter*.

Poll Delaney   Character who sells eggs in Chapelizod in J. Sheridan Le Fanu's *The House by the Churchyard*.

Ernest De la Poer   Katharine Umfraville's cousin who shares her childhood love of imaginative play and eventually becomes her husband in Charlotte Yonge's *Countess Kate* He is Robina Underwood's employer in *The Pillars of the House*.

Captain Delaserre   Henry Bertram's Swiss friend and correspondent; their letters relate much of Henry's history in Sir Walter Scott's *Guy Mannering*.

F. J. de la Tour   Robert Lovelace's traveling valet and second for the duel between Lovelace and Clarissa Harlowe's cousin, Colonel Morden, in Samuel Richardson's *Clarissa: or, The History of a Young Lady*.

Elise Delaunay   French painter who is loved by David Grieve during his sojourn in France; she is unwilling to give up her painting to marry him in Mrs. Humphry Ward's *The History of David Grieve*.

Delia   A very childish coquette in Eliza Haywood's *Life's Progress Through the Passions: or, the Adventures of Natura*.

Delia   Character who recounts the history of Lydia in Sarah Fielding's *Familiar Letters between the Principal Characters of David Simple and Some Others*.

Olympia della Anzasca   Rival of Megalena de Metastasio for Wolfstein's affections; she is driven to suicide over her unrequited love for Wolfstein in Percy Bysshe Shelley's *St. Irvyne*.

Henry della Campo   Murdered member of a family rival to Mazzini ancestors; the Marquis de Mazzini claims that his ghost haunts the Mazzini castle in Ann Radcliffe's *A Sicilian Romance*.

Ranieri della Faggiuola   Uguccione's cowardly son,

who becomes governor of Lucca and a deceitful pretender to the hand of Euthanasia dei Adimari; he stupidly takes Castruccio dei Antelminelli prisoner, causing open revolt in Lucca in Mary Shelley's *Valperga*.

Uguccione della Faggiuola   Exiled Italian soldier hired by Pisa for protection; unscrupulous and dishonorable, he breaks his agreement with Castruccio dei Antelminelli in Mary Shelley's *Valperga*.

Marquis della Fazelli   Dance partner of Emilia de Mazzini at a ball held by the Marquis de Mazzini in Ann Radcliffe's *A Sicilian Romance*.

Marchesa della Porretta   Mother of several grown children, including Lady Clementina della Porretta; devoted to her daughter, she is at a loss in dealing with the problems surrounding Clementina's love for the "heretic," Sir Charles Grandison, and therefore allows Clementina to fall into malicious hands in Samuel Richardson's *Sir Charles Grandison*.

Marchese della Porretta   Wealthy Italian nobleman and father of Lady Clementina della Porretta, whom he treats harshly in hopes of curing her passion for Sir Charles Grandison in Samuel Richardson's *Sir Charles Grandison*.

Lady Clementina della Porretta   A beautiful Catholic maiden of noble birth who has fallen into a deep depression; her parents recall Sir Charles Grandison, a past suitor who was rejected because of religious differences, being now willing to accept his status in an attempt to cure their daughter; as she recovers, she grows unwilling to disappoint her parents with marriage to a heretic, and Sir Charles is free to be with Harriet Byron; he later confirms his lifetime friendship with Clementina in Samuel Richardson's *Sir Charles Grandison*.

Giacomo della Porretta   The Marchese's eldest son, called "the General"; he is enraged at the affront to his family when Sir Charles Grandison cannot accept the conditions for his marriage to Lady Clementina della Porretta in Samuel Richardson's *Sir Charles Grandison*.

Jeronymo della Porretta   Devoted friend of Sir Charles Grandison, whose rescue of him from assassins leads to Sir Charles's intimacy in the Porretta household and to Clementina della Porretta's dangerous attachment to Sir Charles; Jeronymo remains an advocate of their marriage, though religious differences prove irreconcilable, in Samuel Richardson's *Sir Charles Grandison*.

Messer Tadeo della Ventura   Italian merchant who hosts Benedetto Pepi and Castruccio dei Antelminelli in Mary Shelley's *Valpergia*.

Lady Dellwyn (Charlotte Lucum)   Woman who is corrupted by her exposure to London; she agrees to marry Lord Dellwyn, commits adultery with Lord Clermont, is divorced by her husband, and is rejected by her family and society in Sarah Fielding's *The History of the Countess of Dellwyn*.

Lord Dellwyn   Decrepit, diseased aristocrat who marries the young Miss Lucum, grows to hate her as she reveals her contempt for him, and then divorces her after arranging evidence of her adultery in Sarah Fielding's *The History of the Countess of Dellwyn*.

Colonel Delmont   Father of Adolphus and George Delmont; outraged by his uncle Lord Castledane's second marriage, he breaks with him and requires that his children do the same in Charlotte Smith's *The Young Philosopher*.

Adolphus Delmont   George Delmont's older brother, an army officer and heir to an earldom until his great-uncle Lord Castledanes's September-May marriage disappoints his expectations; exhausting his resources and George's to pay gambling debts, he marries Martha Goldthorp for her £50,000; when his infant cousins die and he becomes Lord Castledanes, he regrets having limited his fortune by his marriage in Charlotte Smith's *The Young Philosopher*.

Caroline Delmont   The elder of George Delmont's two sisters and her aunt Mrs. Crewkherne's favorite; she marries a man of substance in Charlotte Smith's *The Young Philosopher*.

George Delmont   Hero, whose early education at home on principles derived from Rousseau, reinforced by his independent reading, commits him to the exercise of reason; he becomes engaged to Medora Glenmorris, fails to secure her claim against her grandfather's estate, risks his own property to cover his brother's gambling debts, and after his marriage takes up residence in America to escape the corruption that permeates English society in Charlotte Smith's *The Young Philosopher*.

Louisa Delmont   The younger of George Delmont's two sisters; she marries Mr. Sydenham in Charlotte Smith's *The Young Philosopher*.

Sir Henry Delmore   Model of prudential benevolence in S. J. Pratt's *Pupil of Pleasure*.

Bernardo Del Nero   Godfather of Romola de' Bardi; he is executed for plotting the return of the Medici family to Florence in George Eliot's *Romola*.

Catherine Deloraine   Daughter of Deloraine and his first wife, Emilia Fitzcharles; she sacrifices everything to accompany her father on his flight from the law following the murder of William; driven to extremity, she throws herself on the mercy of Travers, who is leading the search for Deloraine, and who grants him a reprieve in exile; she retires to live in Holland near her father and marries Thornton, her father's protector and devoted friend, in William Godwin's *Deloraine*.

Charles, Lord Deloraine   Sensible marquis, who becomes the second husband of Charles Egremont's mother, Lady Marney, in Benjamin Disraeli's *Sybil*.

Emilia Fitzcharles Deloraine   Beautiful and charming wife of Deloraine and mother of Catherine Deloraine; she dies as a result of a miscarriage in William Godwin's *Deloraine*.

P. Deloraine   An arch-romantic outcast from human society; a modern Cain, he offers this work as a confidential memoir, which describes how from birth to forty years of age he enjoyed all the privileges of a member of the ruling class; elected to Parliament at age twenty-two, he later serves as ambassador from the English court to various governments on the Continent; his fortunes change with the death of his exemplary first wife, the former Emilia Fitzcharles; he becomes ill and, during his convalescence in the north, meets and then marries the hauntingly beautiful Margaret Borradale; he keeps secret the news that William, her true love, who is presumed lost at sea, has miraculously survived; returning home one day from a journey and discovering Margaret and William together, he flies into a rage and kills him; Margaret dies from a stroke; he flees to the Continent with his devoted daughter, Catherine; he is betrayed to pursuit but is finally allowed to accept permanent exile in Holland in William Godwin's *Deloraine*.

Augusta Delvile   Wife to Compton Delvile and mother of Mortimer; she persuades Cecilia Beverley to break her engagement with Mortimer by telling her what the family stands to lose; she bursts a blood vessel in her anger over her son's engagement and goes to the Continent for her health after she is reconciled to the marriage of her son with Cecilia in Frances Burney's *Cecilia*.

Compton Delvile   A trustee of Cecilia Beverley's estate; he is proud of his family ancestry and violently opposes his son's desire to marry Cecilia in Frances Burney's *Cecilia*.

Jonathan Delvile   Healthy, lecherous gentleman who tricks Diana Stern into debt, then prison, so that she is within his power; he suffocates from swollen glands in Henry Brooke's *The Fool of Quality*.

Mortimer Delvile   Son of Compton and Augusta Devile; he loves Cecilia Beverley but misinterprets her rela-

tionships with other men, particularly Mr. Belfield; in defiance of his parents he offers her marriage but is abandoned by Cecilia at the altar during their first marriage ceremony; he finally succeeds in marrying her with his mother's blessing and then with his father's begrudging approval in Frances Burney's *Cecilia*.

Mrs. De Malthe   Affected woman of rank whose ambitions are to be accepted by the unimpressed great and to be known as a woman of learning in William Beckford's *Modern Novel Writing; or, The Elegant Enthusiast*.

Demariste   Young Greek Christian slave who is martyred in Rome with her lover Charmides in the story by the Reverend Theophilus Cardew in Mark Rutherford's *Catharine Furze*.

Demas   Son of Abraham; at the Hill Lucre he tries to tempt Christian and Hopeful to dig at his silver mine; they refuse, but By-ends and his friends are seduced and disappear there in John Bunyan's *The Pilgrim's Progress From this World to That Which Is to Come*.

Demetrius   Gossipy politician of Constantinople in Sir Walter Scott's *Count Robert of Paris*.

Clara Demijohn   Niece of Jemima Demijohn, with whom she lives in Holloway; courted by Samuel Crocker, she finally chooses Daniel Tribbledale as the steadier husband in Anthony Trollope's *Marion Fay*.

Jemima Demijohn   Busybody neighbor of the Fays in Holloway; she writes anonymously to the Marchioness of Kingsbury reporting that Lord Hampstead is pursuing Marion Fay in Anthony Trollope's *Marion Fay*.

Lady Demolines   Languid mother of Madalina; her title makes her useful as a dinner guest of Dobbs Broughton; with a policeman's help, Johnny Eames escapes her conspiracy to bully him into marriage with Madalina in Anthony Trollope's *The Last Chronicle of Barset*.

Madalina Demolines   Fashionable husband hunter who tries to attract and then to entrap Johnny Eames; she successfully allures Peter Bangles in Anthony Trollope's *The Last Chronicle of Barset*.

The Demon   Jockey for the Barfield family who undergoes extreme physical treatment to keep his correct weight but remains good-natured in George Moore's *Esther Waters*.

Monsieur DeMontaigne   Literary friend of Ernest Maltravers; he tries to control his mad brother-in-law, Castruccio Caesarini, in Edward Bulwer-Lytton's *Ernest Maltravers* and in *Alice*.

Teresa DeMontaigne   Sister of Castruccio Caesarini, wife to DeMontaigne, and friend to Ernest Maltravers in Edward Bulwer-Lytton's *Ernest Maltravers* and in *Alice*.

George Demple   Student at Salem House school in Charles Dickens's *The Personal History of David Copperfield*.

Mr. Dempster   Scots tutor to George and Harry Warrington and good friend of the Warrington family in William Makepeace Thackeray's *The Virginians*.

Thomas de Multon (Thomas de Vaux, Lord of Gilsland)   English baron who is the faithful guard of King Richard in Sir Walter Scott's *The Talisman*.

Ruth Denbigh   See Ruth Hilton.

Charles Dengate   Businessman who unexpectedly pays Maurice Hilliard the money owed to his dead father in George Gissing's *Eve's Ransom*.

Edmund (Longford) Denham   A sick, weak student of Redlaw; he respects Redlaw very much and is invigorated by studying; Milly Swidger nurses him in Charles Dickens's *The Haunted Man and the Ghost's Bargain*.

Jenny Denham   Ward of Dr. Shrapnel; she nurses Nevil Beauchamp during an illness, marries him, and becomes pregnant; he drowns soon after the marriage in George Meredith's *Beauchamp's Career*.

Dr. Denholm   Local minister who marries Walter Walkinshaw to Betty Bodle and later comforts Claud Walkinshaw when he confesses to the sin of pride in John Galt's *The Entail*.

Mr. Denman   Butler at the Carthew estate and a stamp collector; his stamps give Loudon Dodd a clue to Norris Carthew's French hideaways in Robert Louis Stevenson's *The Wrecker*.

Lord Denmeath   Uncle and guardian of Lady Aurora Granville; he acts to prevent Juliet Granville from discovering her relationship with his family and tries to force her to return to France in Frances Burney's *The Wanderer*.

Denner   Faithful maid of Arabella Transome in George Eliot's *Felix Holt, the Radical*.

Frederick Dennis   Mr. Marshal's Chartist friend, who debates Chartist ideas with Baruch Cohen and Clara Hopgood in Mark Rutherford's *Clara Hopgood*.

Ned Dennis   Public hangman, who enjoys his occupation and takes an active role in the Gordon riots; he is a coward when hanged himself for his actions in Charles Dickens's *Barnaby Rudge*.

Charles Dennison   School friend of Matthew Bramble and father of George Dennison; he recognizes Matthew as Matthew Loyd, leading to the discovery that Matthew is the father of Humphry Clinker in Tobias Smollett's *The Expedition of Humphry Clinker*.

Jenny Dennison   Lady Margaret Bellenden's servant, who tries to help Henry Morton escape Francis Stewart, Sergeant Bothwell, and who marries Cutty Headrigg in Sir Walter Scott's *Old Mortality*.

George Dennison (Wilson)   Charles Dennison's son, who has left his home and school to stroll about the country disguised as a player; he has tried to court Liddy Melford as "Wilson," and he is allowed to marry her when his true identity is discovered in Tobias Smollett's *The Expedition of Humphry Clinker*.

Mr. Denny   George Wickham's friend, also a young army officer, in Jane Austen's *Pride and Prejudice*.

George Denny   Middle-class Labour-party Member of Parliament who reveals Harry Wharton's bribe-taking to the press in Mrs. Humphry Ward's *Marcella*.

Colonel Dent   One of the house guests at Thornfield Hall who arrive for Mr. Rochester's bout of entertaining in Charlotte Brontë's *Jane Eyre*.

Mrs. Dent   Colonel Dent's ladylike wife, who, unlike most of Mr. Rochester's other house guests, shows consideration for the governess, Jane Eyre, in Charlotte Brontë's *Jane Eyre*.

Mrs. Dent   Parishioner of Father O'Grady; she has taken in Rose Leicester, helping her find music pupils in George Moore's *The Lake*.

Lady Dently   Character who discovers a familial relationship to Mrs. Bilson, pays the Bilsons' debts, and on her death leaves them the fortune of £4,000 a year which allows them to retire to the country in Sarah Fielding's *The History of the Countess of Dellwyn*.

Mr. Denyer   Traveling man who tries desperately to support his family in cheap lodgings in Naples by attempts at business in various parts of the world and then dies of yellow fever in George Gissing's *The Emancipated*.

Mrs. Denyer   Mother of three girls who is eager for them to marry because she fails to receive support from her absent husband; she is left an impoverished widow in George Gissing's *The Emancipated*.

Barbara Denyer   Oldest daughter of Mrs. Denyer; she marries Mr. Musselwhite in George Gissing's *The Emancipated*.

Madeline Denyer   Second daughter of Mrs. Denyer; she breaks off her engagement to the penniless artist Clifford Marsh and then agrees to marry him when he consents to go into his stepfather's business; when she is crippled by a fall, Marsh leaves her, and she later dies in George Gissing's *The Emancipated.*

Zillah Denyer   Mrs. Denyer's youngest daughter, an ineffective and unhappy student of history who becomes religious and tends her crippled sister in George Gissing's *The Emancipated.*

Denys   Burgundian arbalestier, whose motto is "le diable est mort"; he becomes Gerard's protector and comrade until impressed into the army of the Bastard of Burgundy; mustered out, he locates Margaret Brandt and is named master of the Gouda almshouse; finally he returns to Burgundy on a small military pension, inherits a considerable sum from a relative, and lives on in comfort in Charles Reade's *The Cloister and the Hearth.*

Deodatus   Basil's servant, who decides to remain at the Abbey of Cassino in George Gissing's *Veranilda.*

Derba   Old wise-woman who, unlike her fellow townsmen, welcomes and protects Curdie Peterson when he enters Gwyntystorm in George MacDonald's *The Princess and Curdie.*

Earl of Derby   Supporter of the Duke of Norfolk's plan to free the pregnant Mary, Queen of Scots in Sophia Lee's *The Recess.*

Charlotte de la Tremouille, Countess of Derby   Catholic queen of the Isle of Man; she is wanted by the government for her execution of William Christian, is protected by Lady Peveril, and sends Julian Peveril to London for help when she is implicated in the Popish Plot in Sir Walter Scott's *Peveril of the Peak.*

Philip, Earl of Derby   Son of Charlotte de la Tremouille, Countess of Derby, and Julian Peveril's young companion, who is bored with life on the Isle of Man; he yearns to return to London, where he can gamble and enjoy himself; he disappoints his mother with his feckless life in Sir Walter Scott's *Peveril of the Peak.*

Lord Derford   Son of Lord Ernolf; he is pushed by his father and others unsuccessfully to court Cecilia Beverley for her wealth in Frances Burney's *Cecilia.*

Daniel Deronda   Sir Hugo Mallinger's handsome ward, raised without knowledge of his parents; he falls in love with a Jewish woman, Mirah Lapidoth, whom he saves from suicide; when he meets his mother, Princess Leonora Halm-Eberstein, he learns that he is also Jewish; he and Mirah marry and leave for Israel with her brother, Ezra Mordecai Lapidoth, in George Eliot's *Daniel Deronda.*

Louise Derrick   Young woman who moves into lodgings and involves Clarence and Emmeline Mumford, her hosts, in her family quarrels and love affairs in George Gissing's *The Paying Guest.*

Tom Derrick   Quartermaster to Captain Clement Cleveland's pirate crew in Sir Walter Scott's *The Pirate.*

Benjamin Derriman   Aged, comically pathetic farmersquire, who constantly and sensibly fears his nephew's cheating him out of his money; he leaves his estate to Anne Garland when he dies in Thomas Hardy's *The Trumpet-Major.*

Festus Derriman   Benjamin Derriman's boastful, dishonest, and greedy nephew, who pursues the pretty Anne Garland; aware of his character, she rejects him; he later marries Matilda Johnson, a woman of ill repute, in order to spite Anne and under the mistaken impression that John Loveday cares for her; he is constantly trying to cheat his grandfather out of his money, but is properly rewarded when, upon the old man's death, Anne Garland inherits the estate in Thomas Hardy's *The Trumpet-Major.*

Mr. Derrydown   (caricature of Sir Walter Scott) Countryside traveler who studies poetry and peasantry in Thomas Love Peacock's *Melincourt.*

Philip Derval   Landowner learned in the occult; he is murdered by the agency of Louis Grayle in Edward Bulwer-Lytton's *A Strange Story.*

Dr. Derwent   Irene Derwent's father, a pathologist who follows humane principles in his research in George Gissing's *The Crown of Life.*

Eustace Derwent   Irene Derwent's brother, an Oxford graduate and law student who marries a wealthy widow in George Gissing's *The Crown of Life.*

Irene Derwent   Witty and convivial girl who regrets her engagement to a model Englishman and ultimately realizes that she loves Piers Otway in George Gissing's *The Crown of Life.*

Colonel Desborough   Soldier and brother-in-law of Oliver Cromwell; he is one of the Parliamentary commissioners sent to take possession of Woodstock in Sir Walter Scott's *Woodstock.*

Lucy Desborough   Farmer Giles Blaize's niece; she and Richard Feverel meet accidentally and fall in love, but must marry secretly because of Sir Austin Feverel's opposition; her faithfulness disproves Sir Austin's belief that women are an "ordeal" for men; she dies because of the impediments Sir Austin's system has placed between her and Richard in George Meredith's *The Ordeal of Richard Feverel.*

Jean Desmarais   Valet to Morton Devereux and spy for the Abbe Julian Montreuil; he forges the will of William Devereux in Edward Bulwer-Lytton's *Devereux.*

Gabrielle Desmarets   Jasper Losely's French mistress, who plots to impose Sophy on Guy Darrell as his granddaughter in Edward Bulwer-Lytton's *What Will He Do With It? by Pisistratus Caxton.*

Clara, Dowager Countess of Desmond   Grand, proud owner of an impoverished estate; she falls in love with Owen Fitzgerald only to find he loves her daughter, Lady Clara Desmond; finally she lays bare her heart and becomes a recluse in Anthony Trollope's *Castle Richmond.*

Lady Clara Desmond   Unhappy rival of her mother for the love of Owen Fitzgerald; she finds happiness at last with Herbert Fitzgerald in Anthony Trollope's *Castle Richmond.*

James Desmond   Treacherous Irishman who murders several Englishmen in their beds to demonstrate his allegiance to the Spaniards in Charles Kingsley's *Westward Ho!.*

Lionel Desmond   A Jacobin sympathizer who visits France in 1790 in part to distance himself from Geraldine Verney, the married woman he loves; while abroad, he has an affair with Josephine de Boisbelle and fathers an illegitimate child; returning to England, he assists and protects Geraldine; after her husband dies he looks forward to marriage with her in Charlotte Smith's *Desmond.*

Patrick, Earl of Desmond   The Dowager Countess of Desmond's son, a schoolboy at Eton; he hero worships Owen Fitzgerald but draws the line at Owen's wish to marry his sister in Anthony Trollope's *Castle Richmond.*

Giant Despair   Owner of Doubting Castle; he imprisons Christian and Hopeful, attempting to make them despair and commit suicide; he is killed by Great-heart in John Bunyan's *The Pilgrim's Progress From this World to That Which Is to Come.*

Despondency   Traveler rescued with his daughter Much-afraid from the Castle of Despair by Christiana and her party in John Bunyan's *The Pilgrim's Progress From this World to That Which Is to Come.*

Monsieur Dessein   Owner of the hotel in Calais where Yorick meets Madame de L*** in Laurence Sterne's *A Sentimental Journey through France and Italy.*

Captain DeStancy   Paula Power's irresponsible and immoral suitor, who courts her mainly for her money and beauty; father of the illegitimate William Dare, he allows himself to be blackmailed by his son and forced into conspiring against his rival, George Somerset, in Thomas Hardy's *A Laodicean.*

Charlotte DeStancy   Meek, quiet young woman who is the best friend of Paula Power and who lives with her in the DeStancy castle; secretly in love with George Somerset, Paula's suitor, she uncovers the plot waged against him by William Dare and Captain DeStancy and succeeds in restoring the faithful Somerset to Paula's good favor in Thomas Hardy's *A Laodicean.*

Lord de Terrier   Tory Prime Minister who succeeds Lord Brock in Anthony Trollope's *Framley Parsonage.* He leads his party in *Phineas Finn.* He has given up the leadership to Mr. Daubeny in *Phineas Redux.*

Hester Limbrick Dethridge   Industrious and skilled cook, a servant in the Lundie household; she has been mute ever since she succeeded in the undetected locked-room murder of her abusive husband; she becomes Geoffrey Delamayn's landlady and is blackmailed by him into helping him murder Anne Silvester in a locked room; she goes berserk, strangling him while he is incapacitated by stroke in the murder attempt, and is incarcerated in a madhouse in Wilkie Collins's *Man and Wife.*

Joel Dethridge   Abusive, drunken, worthless husband, from whom Hester cannot escape, though he costs her job after job; though rarely employed, he is a skilled paper-hanger and plasterer, and Hester learns from him the technique she uses to smother him in a locked room in Wilkie Collins's *Man and Wife.*

Madame DeTracy   Sister of Catherine George's employers; her estate in Normandy provides the backdrop for Anne Thackeray Ritchie's *The Village on the Cliff.*

Mr. Deuceace   A confederate of Major Loder in William Makepeace Thackeray's *Vanity Fair.*

Mr. De Verdon   Wealthy European businessman, who takes the family name of his wife, Lady Mary De Verdon, when he marries; he is dominated by her; his will does not exclude his younger daughter, Laura Glenmorris, and her daughter, Medora, but Lady Mary and her financial advisers keep them from their inheritance in Charlotte Smith's *The Young Philosopher.*

Guilielmina De Verdon   Elder daughter of Lady Mary De Verdon and so much her mother's favorite that her sister, Laura (Glenmorris), is neglected and almost portionless; she marries the rich Mr. Cardonnel and dies, leaving her daughter, Mary, to her mother's care in Charlotte Smith's *The Young Philosopher*.

Lady Mary De Verdon Mother of two daughters; the family wealth and all her attention are devoted to the elder; her indifference to the younger, Laura, turns to hatred when Laura, forcibly separated from her suitor, elopes with him; her repudiation of Laura remains obdurate in Charlotte Smith's *The Young Philosopher*.

De Vere Pious chaplain to the Earl of Somerset; he cares for the dying Matilda in Sophia Lee's *The Recess*.

Guy Deverell Son of Lady Alice Redcliffe; he is killed by Sir Jeckyl Marlowe in an unfair duel witnessed only by Herbert Strangways (Varbarriere), whose sister he had secretly married; he is father of the young man who goes by the name Guy Strangways in J. Sheridan Le Fanu's *Guy Deverell*.

Guy Deverell (the younger) See Guy Strangways.

Countess Devereux Morton Devereux's mother, whose coldness blights his character in Edward Bulwer-Lytton's *Devereux*.

Aubrey Devereux Youngest brother of Morton Devereux; he falls under the spell of the Abbe Julian Montreuil and murders Isora D'Alvarez; he ends his days in Italy as the mad Hermit of the Well in Edward Bulwer-Lytton's *Devereux*.

Gerald Devereux Younger twin brother of Morton Devereux; he is falsely suspected by his brother of embezzling the estate of William Devereux; he is blackmailed by Jean Desmarais in Edward Bulwer-Lytton's *Devereux*.

Morton Devereux Son of an English adventurer ennobled by Louis XIV; he grows up in an atmosphere of Jacobite intrigues and is deceived by his brother Aubrey Devereux and the Abbe Julian Montreuil; he weds Isora D'Alvarez in Edward Bulwer-Lytton's *Devereux*.

Captain Richard Devereux Dashing, handsome, intelligent, but somewhat rakish young member of the Royal Irish Artillery; he is in love with Lilias Walsingham, who, although she loves him, refuses him because of his reputation; he is forced to leave Chapelizod by his aunt, but returns when they quarrel; he grieves over Lily's death and tries to reform in J. Sheridan Le Fanu's *The House by the Churchyard*.

William Devereux Wealthy, good-natured landowner and uncle of Morton, Gerald, and Aubrey Devereux in Edward Bulwer-Lytton's *Devereux*.

The Devil A rather charming fast-talk artist; he lurks about Cologne, combats Monk Gregory, and with his horrible smell renders Cologne unfit for a visit from the Kaiser, leading Farina to invent eau de cologne in George Meredith's *Farina*.

Devilsdust Intelligent but melancholy orphan, who survives a miserable childhood working in factories to become a labor union activist in Benjamin Disraeli's *Sybil*.

Earl of Devonshire Rejected suitor of Queen Elizabeth; Leicester frees him from captivity in Sophia Lee's *The Recess*.

Reuben Dewey Dick Dewey's father and spokesman for the parish choir in their protest over being supplanted by the church organ in Thomas Hardy's *Under the Greenwood Tree*.

Richard (Dick) Dewey Young, carefree tranter (carter) and violinist for the parish choir; his devoted courtship of Fancy Day ends in their marriage under a large tree in Thomas Hardy's *Under the Greenwood Tree*.

William Dewey Father of Reuben and grandfather of Dick Dewey; as leader of the parish choir, he is distressed when they are supplanted by an organ in Thomas Hardy's *Under the Greenwood Tree*.

Mr. De Wit German friend who introduces Henry Clinton, disguised as a tutor, to the beautiful but mysterious Louisa D'Aubigny (later Clinton) and her mother in Henry Brooke's *The Fool of Quality*.

Miserrimus Dexter Mentally diseased megalomaniac, born without legs, who lives in a house adorned with skulls, and who tyrannizes over his grotesque servant; the rejected suitor of Sara Macallan and a guest in the Macallan house at the time of her death, he knows the secret of her poisoning; he feeds Valeria Macallan's conviction that the poisoner was Mrs. Beauly in Wilkie Collins's *The Law and the Lady*.

Evan Dhu of Lochiel (Lochiel) Capable Highland chieftain, who settles a dispute among his colleagues by persuading them that Montrose is the best man to command them in Sir Walter Scott's *A Legend of Montrose*.

Diamond The coach horse for whom Diamond the child is named in George MacDonald's *At the Back of the North Wind*.

Diamond (the child) Spontaneous poet of inspired nonsense verse; considered God's baby, silly, and not right in the head by some, he is seen as profound in metaphysics by the narrator; he is taken on several night journeys by North Wind and to the country at the back of the North Wind when seriously ill; when his father falls ill, he drives the cab to support the family; although befriended by the philanthropic Mr. Raymond, he dies in George MacDonald's *At the Back of the North Wind*.

Diamond   Sir Halbert Glendinning's favorite falcon in Sir Walter Scott's *The Abbot*.

Lady Diana (Aunt Dumpy)   Least attractive but nicest of the sisters of Lady Eudocia Wallingham; she marries a doctor who becomes famous; she continues her close relationship with Mariana and Beatrice Brooks in Caroline Norton's *Lost and Saved*.

Mr. Dibdin   Writer of "Who Hasn't Heard of a Jolly Young Waterman," a song adapted for the Brick Lane Branch of the United Grand Junction Ebeneezer Temperance Association in Charles Dickens's *The Posthumous Papers of the Pickwick Club*.

Dick   Small boy who had been Oliver Twist's friend and playmate in the branch workhouse in Charles Dickens's *Oliver Twist*.

Good-natured Dick   Idiot boy who sells flowers and who, when seduced on a whim by Fanny Hill's colleague Louisa, proves a priapic prodigy in John Cleland's *Memoirs of a Woman of Pleasure*.

Mr. Dick   See Richard Babley.

Dickie of the Dingle   Cautious old borderer and elder of the Elliot clan; he attempts to calm Hobbie (Halbert) Elliot when Grace Armstrong is abducted in Sir Walter Scott's *The Black Dwarf*.

Dickieson   Treacherous countryside neighbor to the younger Gilbert Elliot; he acts as guide to the vagabond robbers, who beat and eventually kill but fail to rob Elliot in Robert Louis Stevenson's *Weir of Hermiston: An Unfinished Romance*.

Aunt Dickinson   Ephraim Mackellar's aunt, who paid his fees at the University of Edinburgh in Robert Louis Stevenson's *The Master of Ballantrae: A Winter's Tale*.

Mr. Dickson   The valet of Lord Danglecourt in Francis Coventry's *The History of Pompey the Little*.

Charles Dickson   Thomas Dickson's son; a brave follower of Sir James Douglas, he is killed by Sir John de Walton in Sir Walter Scott's *Castle Dangerous*.

Thomas Dickson   Stern father of Charles Dickson and faithful follower of Sir James Douglas; although he hates the English, he is forced to host a portion of their garrison in Sir Walter Scott's *Castle Dangerous*.

Beau Didapper   Effeminate rake and friend of Lady Booby; he attempts to rape Fanny Goodwill and then to bribe her into becoming his mistress in Henry Fielding's *The History of the Adventures of Mr. Joseph Andrews and of his Friend Mr. Abraham Adams*.

Dr. Didapper   Divine who praises William Pitt with unconscious irony in William Beckford's *Azemia*.

Elise Didon   Voluble maidservant of Madame Melmotte; she acts as go-between for Marie Melmotte and Sir Felix Carbury and is called upon to assist their elopement plans in Anthony Trollope's *The Way We Live Now*.

Neversay Die   Tory legal oracle and friend of Henry Harcourt; George Bertram half-heartedly studies law under his tutelage in Anthony Trollope's *The Bertrams*. Herbert Fitzgerald studies under him in *Castle Richmond*. He is consulted over the legality of Sir Roger Scatcherd's will in *Doctor Thorne*.

Diego   Comic servant who rushes in with his fellow servant, Jaquez, to give an incoherent report of a supernatural visitation they have witnessed in Horace Walpole's *The Castle of Otranto*.

Diffidence   Wife of Giant Despair; she advises him to persuade Christian and Hopeful to commit suicide; she is killed by Honest in John Bunyan's *The Pilgrim's Progress From this World to That Which Is to Come*.

Dr. Digby   Headmaster at Graham Bretton's school in Charlotte Brontë's *Villette*.

Helen Digby   Orphan who is rescued from destitution by Leonard Fairfield; she becomes the ward of Harley L'Estrange but ultimately marries Fairfield in Edward Bulwer-Lytton's *"My Novel," by Pisistratus Caxton*.

Mr. Diggs   Surgeon who treats the wounds of Clarissa Harlowe's brother James after his duel with Robert Lovelace in Samuel Richardson's *Clarissa: or, The History of a Young Lady*.

Joseph Diggs   Vulgar and malicious proprietor of his father's supply shop; he abuses the poor factory workers who are his customers in Benjamin Disraeli's *Sybil*.

Dijon   Portly Frenchman, Loudon Dodd's fellow student, who designs clocks and lends Dodd a corner of his studio in Robert Louis Stevenson's *The Wrecker*.

Dilara   Jealous Sultana, whose letter detailing the presence of Nouronihar in Vathek's train brings Princess Carathis in a rage to Vathek; her absence in the capital allows a revolt to begin in William Beckford's *Vathek*.

Mrs. Dilber   Laundress who raids the deceased Ebenezer Scrooge's lodgings for goods to pawn in Charles Dickens's *A Christmas Carol.*

Dr. Dillon (Black Dillon)   Surgeon from London known for both his skill and his depraved life-style; Paul Dangerfield tries to bribe him into killing Dr. Barney Sturk under the pretense of operating to bring him out of the coma, but Dillon performs a trepan successfully, awakening Sturk long enough for him to identify his murderer in J. Sheridan Le Fanu's *The House by the Churchyard.*

Major Dillon   A friend of Captain Anderson in Samuel Richardson's *Sir Charles Grandison.*

Dinah   Alice's cat, to which Alice's thoughts and conversations occasionally refer, though she does not share Alice's adventures in Lewis Carroll's *Alice's Adventures in Wonderland* and in *Through the Looking-glass.*

Dinah   Tristram Shandy's great aunt who "was married and got with child by the coachman" to the chagrin of the family; she dies and leaves Tristram's father £1,000 in Laurence Sterne's *The Life and Opinions of Tristram Shandy, Gentleman.*

Professor Dingo   Botanist and the second of Mrs. Bayham Badger's often-mentioned late husbands in Charles Dickens's *Bleak House.*

Davie Dingwall   Calculating provincial attorney, who becomes Sir William Ashton's agent and acts against the Ravenswood family in Sir Walter Scott's *The Bride of Lammermoor.*

Ailie Dinmont   Rustic but hospitable wife of Dandie Dinmont in Sir Walter Scott's *Guy Mannering.*

Dandie Dinmont   Rustic, brave, stubborn, and kind-hearted Scottish store-farmer; a generous husband and loving father, he is also a devoted friend to Henry Bertram; he is proud of his breed of terriers, the "Mustards and Peppers," in Sir Walter Scott's *Guy Mannering.*

Diogenes   Michael Agelastes's Negro slave, who picks up philosophical quirks; the philospher trusts him to carry out many of his unscrupulous plans in Sir Walter Scott's *Count Robert of Paris.*

Dirk   Lookout for the pirates' attack on the Admiral Benbow Inn; he deserts Pew in Robert Louis Stevenson's *Treasure Island.*

Discretion   A virgin of the Palace Beautiful in John Bunyan's *The Pilgrim's Progress From this World to That Which Is to Come.*

Disguised Gentleman   A young man "bubbled" out of his money at a horse race; he disguises himself as a common traveler in order to pursue a beautiful young country girl in Charles Johnstone's *Chrysal: or, The Adventures of a Guinea.*

Dissuava   King of Ceylon's emissary, who tricks Robert Knox and others into coming on shore and holds them prisoner in Daniel Defoe's *The Life, Adventures, and Pyracies of the Famous Captain Singleton.*

Dick Distich   Poet who is confined to the London madhouse in which Sir Launcelot Greaves is imprisoned in Tobias Smollett's *The Adventures of Sir Launcelot Greaves.*

Distressed Father   Son of a good family with no money who becomes an army officer and suffers the pains of poverty because of bureaucratic difficulties in Charles Johnstone's *Chrysal: or, The Adventures of a Guinea.*

Distressed Parents   Starving couple who will not eat bread acquired by vice and infamy; they are saved from despair by the benevolence of the Author in Charles Johnstone's *Chrysal: or, The Adventures of a Guinea.*

Distressed Young Woman   A wretched and starving girl who buys bread for her family in Charles Johnstone's *Chrysal: or, The Adventures of a Guinea.*

Colonel Diver   Editor of the *New York Rowdy Journal,* a publication of dubious ethics and popular appeal; he is the younger Martin Chuzzlewit's first acquaintance in America in Charles Dickens's *The Life and Adventures of Martin Chuzzlewit.*

Tom Diver   Arthur Pendennis's neighbor at Shepherd's Inn who has a scheme to retrieve sunken treasure in William Makepeace Thackeray's *The History of Pendennis.*

Mr. Dix   Landowner unsuccessfully sued by Edward Tulliver in George Eliot's *The Mill on the Floss.*

Dixon   The faithful but crusty old servant of the Hale family, who moves with them to the north while retaining her southern sense of superiority in Elizabeth Gaskell's *North and South.*

Dixon   Richard Vere's stupid manservant; he accompanies Isabella Vere and her father on their walk prior to her abduction in Sir Walter Scott's *The Black Dwarf.*

Mr. Dixon   Husband of the daughter of Jane Fairfax's guardian; Emma Woodhouse confides to Frank Churchill her suspicion of a dangerous attraction between

Dixon and Jane, but Frank does not refute the charge in Jane Austen's *Emma*.

Mrs. Dixon   Colonel Campbell's daughter, with whom Jane Fairfax has been reared almost as a sister; her parents' visit to her in Ireland after her marriage occasions Jane's return to Mrs. Bates's home in Highbury in Jane Austen's *Emma*.

Sebastian Dixon   Violinist uncle of Sir Guy Morville and an inveterate gambler; his debts occasion misunderstanding between Sir Guy and his guardian, Mr. Edmonstone, in Charlotte Yonge's *The Heir of Redclyffe*.

Mrs. Doasyouwouldbedoneby   See Queen of the Fairies.

Montgomerie Dobbes   Close friend of Adolphus Crosbie and best man at his wedding in Anthony Trollope's *The Small House at Allington*.

Reginald Dobbes   Sports fanatic and sharer with Lord Popplecourt of the shooting at Crummie-Toddie; he is a tyrant in requiring commitment to the sport of killing birds and detests Mrs. Montacute Jones of the neighboring estate Killancodlem in Anthony Trollope's *The Duke's Children*.

Maudge Dobbie   The Walkinshaw family nurse who raises Claud Walkinshaw and instills in him the desire to recover his family's lost estate in John Galt's *The Entail*.

Captain William Dobbin   Loyal friend of George Osborne; selflessly in love with the gentle Amelia Sedley, he persuades Osborne to flout his father's dishonorable command by keeping his promise to marry her; Dobbin woos her after Osborne's death and finally wins her in William Makepeace Thackeray's *Vanity Fair*.

Jane Dobbin   Child of Amelia Sedley (Osborne) Dobbin and William Dobbin in William Makepeace Thackeray's *Vanity Fair*.

Captain Dobbs   Drunken pilot in Butaritari who tells Captain Joe Wicks about the wreck of the *Leslie* in Robert Louis Stevenson's *The Wrecker*.

Mrs. Dobson   Bedfordshire housewife whose dairy farm provides the local gentry with breakfast after morning rides in Samuel Richardson's *Pamela, or Virtue Rewarded*.

Goodman Gaffer Dobson   Tenant farmer and the kindly foster father of Master Harry Clinton; he nurtures the boy's natural goodness in Henry Brooke's *The Fool of Quality*.

Nurse Kate Dobson   Wife of Goodman Dobson and the loving foster mother of Master Harry Clinton; she nurtures the boy's natural goodness in Henry Brooke's *The Fool of Quality*.

Mrs. Docimer   Warm-hearted sister-in-law of Imogene Docimer; she does her best to offset her husband's attempts to prevent the match between Imogene and Frank Houston in Anthony Trollope's *Ayala's Angel*.

Imogene Docimer   High-principled cousin of Frank Houston; she meets his cynical arguments on marrying for money with scorn; when he returns to her after trying to marry Gertrude Tringle, she accepts him as her husband, and they agree to live by hard work and a cradle filled annually in Anthony Trollope's *Ayala's Angel*.

Mudbury Docimer   Inveterate opponent of Frank Houston's self-interested courtship of his sister Imogene in Anthony Trollope's *Ayala's Angel*.

Miriam Dockwrath   Mild wife of Samuel; she tries to mitigate his hatred of Lady Mason in Anthony Trollope's *Orley Farm*.

Samuel Dockwrath   Conniving lawyer, who becomes angry when Lucius Mason cancels his lease and finds evidence to resurrect an accusation of forgery against Lady Mason regarding a codicil to the will of her late husband leaving the Orley Farm estate to Lucius Mason in Anthony Trollope's *Orley Farm*.

Doctor   English traveler who considers himself to be a poet; he often quarrels with his friend, the painter Mr. Pallet; he meets Perry Pickle in Paris, gives a Roman banquet much to the disgust of his guests in Paris, and accompanies Perry on many of his Continental adventures; he fights a duel with Pallet fomented by Perry, and he rejoins Pallet to separate from Perry in Rotterdam in Tobias Smollett's *The Adventures of Peregrine Pickle*.

Doctor   Grub Street hack writer, who wins Chrysal at the gaming tables and is deeply in debt; he takes Chrysal to his first coffee house in Charles Johnstone's *Chrysal: or, The Adventures of a Guinea*.

Doctor   Miss Tippitt's physician, who attends Andrew Tacchi and helps Miriam Tacchi get an apprenticeship for nursing in a London hospital in Mark Rutherford's *Miriam's Schooling*.

Doctor——   Clergyman whose arguments finally bring the seriously ill Arabella to her senses; he grants that the romance world may have advantages over reality, but shows that these books are untrue, morally dangerous, and aesthetically flawed in Charlotte Lennox's *The Female Quixote*.

Doctor of Obstetrics Physician called to take care of an injured pregnant cat; he kills the cat in a disappointed rage in Charles Johnstone's *Chrysal: or, The Adventures of a Guinea.*

Captain David Dodd Sea captain who survives a pirate attack and a hurricane, enters an asylum where he is rescued from fire by his son, and totally loses his memory until resuscitated from a supposed death by a fly sting in Charles Reade's *Hard Cash.*

Edward Dodd Son of David and Lucy Dodd; he fails at Exeter but wins the Henley boat race; in his father's absence he becomes a fireman and head of his family, losing his sweetheart Jane Hardie by death but receiving £14,000 inheritance from her father in Charles Reade's *Hard Cash.*

James K. (Big Head) Dodd Successful real estate entrepreneur, who wants his son, Loudon Dodd, to inherit his joy of business; he dies penniless as Loudon finishes his art studies in Paris in Robert Louis Stevenson's *The Wrecker.*

Jane (Jeannie) Dodd Loudon Dodd's Scottish mother and the favorite child of her father, Alexander Loudon, who treats her son well for her sake in Robert Louis Stevenson's *The Wrecker.*

Julia Dodd Daughter of David and Lucy Dodd; she is betrothed to Alfred Hardie, for whom she waits in vain at the altar; she becomes a district visitor for her church but is finally united with Alfred in Charles Reade's *Hard Cash.*

Loudon (Dromedary) Dodd Reluctant business student, erstwhile sculptor and painter, convivial picnicker, and eventual entrepreneur and bankrupt; he is the steadfast but sometimes foolhardy gentleman who traces out the secret of the *Flying Scud*'s wreck in Robert Louis Stevenson's *The Wrecker.*

Lucy Fountain Dodd Her husband's and children's beloved companion, the perfect lady, who turns to dressmaking in adversity in Charles Reade's *Hard Cash.*

Franklin Dodge Jim Pinkerton's boss when Pinkerton works as a clerk after bankruptcy in Robert Louis Stevenson's *The Wrecker.*

Dodo Initiater of the caucus-race, following the failure of the Mouse to dry the creatures after their swim in the pool of tears; it also requires Alice to distribute presents and ceremoniously bestows on her her own thimble in Lewis Carroll's *Alice's Adventures in Wonderland.*

Johnny Dods Weaver who first shelters Robert Colwan, then beats him and drives him out as the devil in James Hogg's *The Private Memoirs and Confessions of a Justified Sinner.*

Meg Dods Owner of an inn once the property of the Mowbray family; she befriends Francis Tyrrell and Peregrine Touchwood and tends the dying Clara Mowbray in Sir Walter Scott's *St. Ronan's Well.*

Nans Dods Weaver's wife, who defends Robert Colwan from her husband's suspicions that he is the devil in James Hogg's *The Private Memoirs and Confessions of a Justified Sinner.*

Mr. Dodson Portly and stern-looking sharpster lawyer, who is a partner of Mr. Fogg and is employed by Martha Bardell in her breach-of-promise suit against Samuel Pickwick in Charles Dickens's *The Posthumous Papers of the Pickwick Club.*

Dogger Revenue officer with whom Jim Hawkins rides to Squire Trelawney's house in Robert Louis Stevenson's *Treasure Island.*

Doig Fat, plain, little man who is the private hand of Prestongrange, Lord Advocate of Scotland, in Robert Louis Stevenson's *Catriona.*

Corney Dolan Illegal poteen maker at Drumleesh; he gives temporary sanctuary to Thady Macdermot after Thady murders Captain Ussher in Anthony Trollope's *The Macdermots of Ballycloran.*

Captain Doleful Nondescript opportunist, who becomes master of ceremonies at Handley Cross and provides introductions for the rich; he sues John Jorrocks over the death of a horse in Robert Surtees's *Handley Cross.*

Thomas Doleman Robert Lovelace's libertine friend, who is directed to find lodgings for Clarissa Harlowe in London in Samuel Richardson's *Clarissa: or, The History of a Young Lady.*

Princess Dolgoruki Patron who requests a portrait of her lapdog; the commission leads to a split between Sucrewasser and Insignificanti, occasioned by an argument over the merits of blue and red in William Beckford's *Biographical Memoirs of Extraordinary Painters.*

Sergius Dolgorouki Leading member of a prominent boyar family; he is persecuted and then executed by John Ernest Biren, Duke of Courland, who fears him as a rival to his power in William Godwin's *Cloudesley.*

Mr. Dolloby Owner of a second-hand shop where David Copperfield sells his waistcoat on the way to

Dover in Charles Dickens's *The Personal History of David Copperfield.*

Dolly Rawdon and Becky (Sharp) Crawley's London housekeeper, who is adept at fending off dunning tradesmen in William Makepeace Thackeray's *Vanity Fair.*

Dolly Housekeeper for Jonathan Burge in George Eliot's *Adam Bede.*

Dolores A rebellious student at Mme. Beck's school, to control whom Lucy Snowe has to use severe measures in Charlotte Brontë's *Villette.*

Mr. Dolphin London theater manager who hires Miss Fotheringay (Emily Costigan) in William Makepeace Thackeray's *The History of Pendennis.*

Lord Doltimore Dim but wealthy young peer, who marries Caroline Merton through the machinations of her lover, Lumley Ferrers, in Edward Bulwer-Lytton's *Alice.*

Fanny Dombey Paul Dombey's first wife, who married him for convenience after her hope for happiness was gone; she dies after giving birth to little Paul in Charles Dickens's *Dombey and Son.*

Florence Dombey Little Paul Dombey's pretty older sister, who longs for her father's withheld love; instead, he is jealous of the love she evokes from little Paul and from Edith (Granger), her stepmother, and grows to hate her; finally rejected by him, she flees to Solomon Gills's shop; she marries Walter Gay and is eventually reunited with her father in Charles Dickens's *Dombey and Son.*

Paul Dombey Stern and pompous wealthy merchant, who invests all his ambition and emotion in his son, Paul, whom he expects to carry on the tradition of Dombey and Son; neglecting his daughter Florence even after Paul's death, he marries Edith Granger, who deserts him; in the end, bankrupt and alone, he is awakened to Florence's love in Charles Dickens's *Dombey and Son.*

Paul (Little Paul) Dombey Son of the elder Paul Dombey; his birth represents the continuation of the Dombey line, but he is small and sickly and dies at the age of six in Charles Dickens's *Dombey and Son.*

Dominick Footman at Belmont in J. Sheridan Le Fanu's *The House by the Churchyard.*

Donacha dhu na Dunaigh (Black Duncan the Mischievous) Highland outlaw who buys the Whistler, the illegitimate son of Effie Deans and George Staunton, as an infant; he dies in the attack upon Staunton in Sir Walter Scott's *The Heart of Midlothian.*

Donald An old family servant to the M'Aulays in Sir Walter Scott's *A Legend of Montrose.*

Old Donald The elderly, observant manservant of Glenfern Castle in Susan Ferrier's *Marriage.*

Mr. Doncastle Wealthy acquaintance of Ethelberta Petherwin; he is not disturbed that his excellent butler, Chickerel, waited on his guest Mrs. Petherwin without appearing to recognize her in Thomas Hardy's *The Hand of Ethelberta.*

Mrs. Doncastle Mr. Doncastle's wife, who thinks the butler Chickerel should be dismissed for not reacting to his daughter's presence among the dinner guests in Thomas Hardy's *The Hand of Ethelberta.*

Captain Donellan Hunting crony and frequent guest of Owen Fitzgerald in Anthony Trollope's *Castle Richmond.*

Mr. Donn Arabella's father, who assists her the second time she tricks Jude Fawley into marriage in Thomas Hardy's *Jude the Obscure.*

Arabella Donn Jude Fawley's coarse, calculating wife, who tricks Jude into marrying her and then leaves him to seek wealth in Australia; she returns, leaving Jude with a boy she claims is his, and marries a second time; after the death of her second husband, she tricks Jude into marrying her again; she nurses the dying Jude but brings him no comfort; it is her intensely physical nature that makes her the antithesis of Jude's second lover, the intellectual and frail Sue Bridehead, in Thomas Hardy's *Jude the Obscure.*

Henry Donne See Henry Bellingham.

Joseph Donne Self-satisfied Whinbury curate, who unsuccessfully courts Shirley Keedlar before making a more suitable match at the novel's end in Charlotte Brontë's *Shirley.*

Squire Donnithorne The cold, rich old man who loves no one, including his grandson, Arthur; his unfairness towards his tenant farmers is reflected in Mrs. Poyser's spirited attack on his personal and public behavior in George Eliot's *Adam Bede.*

Arthur Donnithorne The elegant, impulsive grandson of Squire Donnithorne and the heir to his large estate; he deflowers Hetty Sorrel and leaves to join the army before knowing that she is pregnant; he returns just in time to have Hetty's sentence of execution commuted to transportation; he leaves Hayslope again, returning many years later, appearing tired, sick, and unhappy in George Eliot's *Adam Bede.*

Lydia Donnithorne Squire Donnithorne's daughter, whose few appearances in society lower than her own clearly show her contempt for the lower classes in George Eliot's *Adam Bede*.

Miss Donny One of the mistresses at the boarding school Esther Summerson attended in Charles Dickens's *Bleak House*.

Michael Donovan Seaman and husband of Jane Holt in Charles Reade's *Foul Play*.

Major Donthorne Resort owner who provides Walter Hartright with information linking Philip Fairlie and Mrs. Catherick in Wilkie Collins's *The Woman in White*.

Colonel Dick Doocey Retired colonel, courtly and agreeable, who is a houseguest at Marlowe in J. Sheridan Le Fanu's *Guy Deverell*.

Carver Doone Leader of the Doones; barbaric, cruel, uneducated, and disrespectful, he is the first Doone leader with no gentility and no comprehension of social rules; the actual murderer of John Ridd's father, he hates John Ridd; Lorna Doone bravely resists the Doone clan's efforts to marry her to Carver in R. D. Blackmore's *Lorna Doone*.

Sir Ensor Doone Carver Doone's father, loved by Lorna Doone; he gives his dying blessing to her marriage to John Ridd in R. D. Blackmore's *Lorna Doone*.

Lorna Doone (Dugal) Beautiful, noble, graceful woman trapped by her upbringing; a gentle, complex creature, she loves John Ridd and his family despite the Doone family's prejudices against the Ridds; she turns out to be an heiress, Lady Dugal, who was captured as a small child by the Doones in R. D. Blackmore's *Lorna Doone*.

His Adiposity Baron Doppelgeist Bearer of the letter from Fairyland that asks the Warden to serve as Elfinking; he is a military hero and a very fat gourmand; asked to review Uggug's "accomplishments," he finds Uggug has filled his room with frogs and leaves in a huff in Lewis Carroll's *Sylvie and Bruno*.

Cecily Doran Young woman of advanced views and education; she runs away with and marries the unreliable Reuben Elgar, finds herself in an unhappy marriage, and loses both her child and her husband in George Gissing's *The Emancipated*.

Lord Dorchester Aristocratic libertine who kidnaps Ophelia from her aunt's retreat in Wales, learns the value of female virtue, and finally marries the heroine in Sarah Fielding's *The History of Ophelia*.

Dorilaus Guardian for Horatio and Louisa; a bachelor and a "man of steady resolutions," he thinks he is in love with Louisa but then learns he is her father in Eliza Haywood's *The Fortunate Foundlings*.

Dorina Wary Tuscan peasant, in whose cottage Emily St. Aubert is confined in Ann Radcliffe's *The Mysteries of Udolpho*.

La petite de Doriodot Mlle. Reuter's young pupil who is taken home one night by Frances Henri, indicating Frances's lowly status in Charlotte Brontë's *The Professor*.

Countess of Dorking Lady Clara Pulleyn's mother, who assists the earl in misdirecting Lady Clara's matrimonial affairs in William Makepeace Thackeray's *The Newcomes*.

Earl of Dorking Impoverished nobleman who separates his daughter, Lady Clara Pulleyn, from her first love and presses her into marriage with the wealthy Barnes Newcome in William Makepeace Thackeray's *The Newcomes*.

Rumford Dorking Squire who devotes himself to hunting, to the disgust of his wife, who loathes the country, in Sarah Fielding's *The History of Ophelia*.

Mme. La Baronne de Dorlodot Colonel de Hamal's aunt, who uses her influence to get him admitted to the school fête in Charlotte Brontë's *Villette*.

Ayala Dormer Vivacious, highly romantic younger sister of Lucy; after her parents have died, she lives with Sir Thomas Tringle, whose son Tom begs her to marry him; she dreams of the beau ideal, an angel of light, and finds him eventually in Jonathan Stubbs in Anthony Trollope's *Ayala's Angel*.

Egbert Dormer Impecunious artist who dies, leaving his daughters, Lucy and Ayala, dependent on his late wife's brother and sister, Reginald Dosett and Lady Tringle, in Anthony Trollope's *Ayala's Angel*.

Lucy Dormer Elder sister of Ayala and equally romantic about love and marriage; after her parents have died, she lives with her uncle, Reginald Dosett; when the girls switch homes, she meets and falls in love with Isadore Hamel, a sculptor, whom she marries in Anthony Trollope's *Ayala's Angel*.

Dormina Clarinau's elderly maid, who keeps watch over Calista, and whose heavy sleeping facilitates the affair between Calista and Philander in Aphra Behn's *Love Letters Between a Nobleman and His Sister*.

Dormouse Creature whose tendency to sleep renders

it indifferent to the abuse of the Mad Hatter and the March Hare; during the mad tea party it is roused to tell a story of three little girls who live in a treacle well; it appears at the trial of the Knave of Hearts in Lewis Carroll's *Alice's Adventures in Wonderland.*

Laird of Dornock　　Sullen Scotsman who procures King James's permission to detain both Ellinor and the woman he desires, Lady Southampton, in Sophia Lee's *The Recess.*

Dorothea　　Melancholy servant hired by Felicia, who is now married to Lucius Manly; Dorothea is discovered to be a gentlewoman raised as a Catholic and fleeing religious bigotry at home; she agrees to examine Catholic doctrines with an open mind, after which she converts to Protestantism in Mary Collyer's *Felicia to Charlotte.*

Dorothee　　Elderly housekeeper of Chateau-le-Blanc, who shows Emily St. Aubert the room where the Marchioness de Villeroi died in Ann Radcliffe's *The Mysteries of Udolpho.*

Dorriforth　　See Dorriforth, Lord Elmwood.

Mrs. Dorrit　　William Dorrit's wife, who died in the Marshalsea debtors' prison when their daughter Amy was eight in Charles Dickens's *Little Dorrit.*

Amy (Little Dorrit) Dorrit　　Self-sacrificing "daughter of the Marshalsea"; born in prison, she looks after and supports her father, brother, and sister by working as a seamstress for Mrs. Clennam; she is bewildered by the new wealthy life of her family when their luck changes; she loves and eventually marries Arthur Clennam in Charles Dickens's *Little Dorrit.*

Edward (Tip) Dorrit　　Amy's lazy, indolent older brother, who is unable to pursue any profession at length and eventually dies in the Marshalsea debtors' prison in Charles Dickens's *Little Dorrit.*

Fanny Dorrit　　Amy's selfish and capricious older sister, who dances in a theater; she lives with their uncle Frederick Dorrit; after the Dorrits become wealthy, she marries Edmund Sparkler mainly to defy and humiliate his mother, Mrs. Merdle, in Charles Dickens's *Little Dorrit.*

Frederick Dorrit　　William Dorrit's elderly, feeble-minded brother, who long ago supported Arthur Clennam's mother while she was pregnant; he plays clarinet in the orchestra of the theater where Fanny Dorrit dances, travels with the Dorrits after they become wealthy, and dies shortly after William's death in Charles Dickens's *Little Dorrit.*

William Dorrit　　"Father of the Marshalsea" and now proud of this title; he was imprisoned for debt in the Marshalsea as a young husband and father; he grows dependent upon his daughter Amy to support and minister to him while selfishly ignoring her service; he inherits an estate in Charles Dickens's *Little Dorrit.*

Mademoiselle Dorville　　Wealthy Martinique heiress about whom it is rumored to Julia de Roubigné that Savillon is engaged in Henry Mackenzie's *Julia de Roubigné.*

Margaret Dosett　　Puritanical wife of Reginald; she is depressed by economies enforced upon them by having to make a home for his niece, Lucy Dormer, in Anthony Trollope's *Ayala's Angel.*

Reginald Dosett　　Hard-working Admiralty clerk living in humble circumstances; he generously gives a home to his niece, Lucy Dormer, after her parents' deaths in Anthony Trollope's *Ayala's Angel.*

Douban　　Adept physician and elderly royal slave in Sir Walter Scott's *Count Robert of Paris.*

Gustavus Douce　　Absconding joint trustee of the fortune left to Evelyn Templeton; he tricks Lumley Ferrers in Edward Bulwer-Lytton's *Alice.*

Dougal　　Rob Roy MacGregor's loyal and devoted agent; though possessing an appearance of savage stupidity, he is actually shrewd and gentle; he cunningly leads Captain Thornton's men into an ambush and rescues Francis Osbaldistone and Bailie (Nicol) Jarvie in Sir Walter Scott's *Rob Roy.*

Laird Douglas　　Henry Douglas's practical Scottish father, master of Glenfern Castle, and target of his sisters' and daughters' schemes and advice in Susan Ferrier's *Marriage.*

Mrs. Douglas　　Wife of Tam Douglas, the innkeeper of Ancrum, in James Hogg's *The Private Memoirs and Confessions of a Justified Sinner.*

Adelaide Julia Douglas　　The elder twin daughter of Henry and Lady Juliana Douglas; she is spoiled by her mother and her uncle, Frederick, Lord Lindore, in Susan Ferrier's *Marriage.*

Alicia ("Alice") Malcolm Douglas　　The wise and refined half-Scottish and half-English wife of Archibald Douglas; she becomes foster mother to Mary Douglas and mother to Norman Douglas in Susan Ferrier's *Marriage.*

Archibald Douglas　　A son of Laird Douglas and brother of Henry Douglas; he marries Alicia Malcolm and rears the unwanted twin daughter of Henry and Lady Juliana Douglas in Susan Ferrier's *Marriage*.

Archibald, Earl of Douglas   Father-in-law of the Duke of Rothsay; he orders the executions of John Ramorny, Henbane Dwining, and Bonthron for their murder of the prince (The Duke of Rothsay), and he sends Catherine Glover to Marjory Douglas for protection in Sir Walter Scott's *The Fair Maid of Perth*.

Babby Douglas   One of Henry Douglas's five younger uneducated and unmarried sisters, who live in Glenfern with their father and three spinster aunts in Susan Ferrier's *Marriage*.

Becky Douglas   One of Henry Douglas's five younger uneducated and unmarried sisters, who live in Glenfern with their father and three spinster aunts in Susan Ferrier's *Marriage*.

Beenie Douglas   One of Henry Douglas's five younger uneducated and unmarried sisters, who live in Glenfern with their father and three spinster aunts in Susan Ferrier's *Marriage*.

Belle Douglas   One of Henry Douglas's five younger uneducated and unmarried sisters, who live in Glenfern with their father and three spinster aunts in Susan Ferrier's *Marriage*.

Betty Douglas   One of Henry Douglas's five younger, uneducated and unmarried sisters, who live in Glenfern with their father and three spinster aunts in Susan Ferrier's *Marriage*.

Edward Douglas   The son of Henry and Lady Juliana Douglas and the brother of Mary and Adelaide Douglas; he is reared by his mother and his uncle, Frederick, Lord Lindore, and eventually becomes the spouse of his cousin Emily Lindore in Susan Ferrier's *Marriage*.

George Douglas   Seneschal of Lochleven Castle and the handsome grandson of the Lady of Lochleven (Margaret Erskine); he is fiercely loyal to Queen Mary of Scotland and assists her escape before being fatally wounded at Langside in Sir Walter Scott's *The Abbot*.

Gertrude Douglas   Sir Reginald Glanville's beloved deceased mistress; beautiful and sensitive but not Glanville's social equal, she eloped with him; during an absence caused by his mother's illness and then his own, she went mad after being raped by Sir John Tyrrell; located and cared for by Glanville, she died without recovering her sanity in Edward Bulwer-Lytton's *Pelham*.

Grizzy Douglas   The mild-mannered middle spinster

sister of Laird Douglas; she valiantly tries to please all parties at all times in Susan Ferrier's *Marriage*.

Henry (Harry) Douglas   The ill-fated son of Laird Douglas; he marries Lady Juliana, becomes the father of Adelaide, Mary, and Edward Douglas, becomes heavily indebted, and spends his last days in India as a soldier in Susan Ferrier's *Marriage*.

Ivy Douglas   John Douglas's curiously unfeeling apparent widow in Arthur Conan Doyle's *The Valley of Fear*.

Sir James Douglas (The Black Douglas, The Knight of the Tomb)   An associate of Robert the Bruce; he is dedicated to winning back his castle, eventually succeeding after capturing Lady Augusta de Berkely; he sometimes rides as the Knight of the Tomb, wearing armor painted to resemble a skeleton in Sir Walter Scott's *Castle Dangerous*.

Joan (Jacky) Douglas   The matriarchal eldest spinster sister of Laird Douglas; she runs Glenfern Castle and the lives of the people resident in it in Susan Ferrier's *Marriage*.

John Douglas   Former gold miner and former Pinkerton detective, also known as Birdy Edwards and John McMurdo; he appears to have been murdered in Arthur Conan Doyle's *The Valley of Fear*.

Lady Juliana Douglas   The spoiled, extravagant daughter of the Earl of Courtland; she elopes with soldier Henry Douglas against her father's wishes; mother of Mary, Adelaide, and Edward Douglas, she is a manipulating socialite in London and Bath in Susan Ferrier's *Marriage*.

Marjory Douglas   Wife of the Duke of Rothsay; she is ignored by the prince (her husband); she accepts Catherine Glover as her protected guest after the murder of Rothsay in Sir Walter Scott's *The Fair Maid of Perth*.

Mary Douglas   The younger twin daughter of Henry and Lady Juliana Douglas; reared by Archibald and Alicia Douglas, she eventually becomes the wife of Colonel Charles Lennox in Susan Ferrier's *Marriage*.

Nicky Douglas   The youngest spinster sister of Laird Douglas; she lives in Glenfern Castle in Susan Ferrier's *Marriage*.

Norman Douglas   The only child borne to Archibald and Alicia Douglas; he is brought up without incident, despite the constant advice of his aunts and great-aunts in Susan Ferrier's *Marriage*.

Tam Douglas   Innkeeper of Ancrum; his house is attacked by Gil-martin and fiends battling for possession of Robert Colwan; he turns Colwan out in James Hogg's *The Private Memoirs and Confessions of a Justified Sinner.*

Tibby Douglas   Daughter of Tam Douglas, the innkeeper of Ancrum, in James Hogg's *The Private Memoirs and Confessions of a Justified Sinner.*

DouLache   A cunning and jealous lover who spreads rumors about the Baroness de Tortillee; he is an unscrupulous villain in Eliza Haywood's *The Injur'd Husband; or, the Mistaken Resentment.*

Lady Blessingbourne, Duchess of Dounderdale   A parody of aristocratic snobbery in S. J. Pratt's *Tutor of Truth.*

Lord Blessingbourne, Duke of Dounderdale   A parody of aristocratic snobbery in S. J. Pratt's *Tutor of Truth.*

Herman Dousterswivel   German mining engineer, who uses magic during a visit to the ruins of St. Ruth's Priory to swindle money from Sir Arthur Wardour, is exposed as a fraud by Oldbuck (Jonathan Oldenbuck), and is punished with a mocking trick by Edie Ochiltree and Steenie Mucklebackit in Sir Walter Scott's *The Antiquary.*

Thomas Dove   Acerbic learned counsel employed by Samuel Camperdown to explore legal niceties concerning ownership of the diamonds Lady Eustace claims are hers by gift; his opinion is equivocal and brings Mr. Camperdown no comfort in Anthony Trollope's *The Eustace Diamonds.*

Gerard Dow   Dutch painter celebrated for his rendering of minute detail; he becomes the teacher of Jeremy Watersouchy; he emphasizes detail and minute methodological rituals in William Beckford's *Biographical Memoirs of Extraordinary Painters.*

Olly Dowden   A broom maker and a female voice of rural wisdom on Egdon Heath in Thomas Hardy's *The Return of the Native.*

Mr. Dowler   Outwardly fierce but inwardly cowardly gentleman, whom Samuel Pickwick and friends meet on the way to Bath, and who later threatens Nathaniel Winkle over an incident with his wife in Charles Dickens's *The Posthumous Papers of the Pickwick Club.*

Mrs. Dowler   Pretty wife of Mr. Dowler; she is accidentally involved in an unfortunate incident with Nathaniel Winkle in Charles Dickens's *The Posthumous Papers of the Pickwick Club.*

Lawyer Dowling   Self-serving lawyer to Squire Western, Squire Allworthy, and Master Blifil; he pressures witnesses to testify against Tom Jones at Blifil's instigation but quickly unmasks Bilfil when Allworthy threatens him with unemployment in Henry Fielding's *The History of Tom Jones.*

Jemmy Downes   Coarse, drunken, abusive tailor, who sets up the sweatshop in which Alton Locke finds Billy Porter and Mike Kelly; finally, destroyed by gin, he drowns in the cesspool which, exuding deadly vapors, also kills his family in Charles Kingsley's *Alton Locke.*

Sir Harry Downeton   Gentleman who reports to Clarissa Harlowe's friend Anna Howe and her mother information detrimental to the character of Clarissa's despised suitor Roger Solmes; although his report validates Clarissa's antipathy toward Solmes, Downeton prefers to support the Harlowes' right of parental authority in Samuel Richardson's *Clarissa: or, The History of a Young Lady.*

Dr. Downie   Thinker in Ordinary to the Royal Family, Professor of Logomachy, and perhaps the most subtle dialectician in Erewhon; he is skeptical about Sunchildism; he aids in Jack Higgs's escape in Samuel Butler's *Erewhon Revisited Twenty Years Later.*

Charles Downs   A leading Muskegon businessman who "bit the dust" in Robert Louis Stevenson's *The Wrecker.*

Dr. Downward   Abortionist quack who invents a new role for himself as Doctor le Doux, running a private sanatorium for the care of the mentally disturbed while attempting to avoid the laws governing such institutions; he colludes with Lydia Gwilt in her diabolical murder attempt on Allan Armadale in Wilkie Collins's *Armadale.*

Daniel Doyce   Engineer and inventor, who cannot get his invention patented by the Circumlocution Office; he owns a factory in the Bleeding Heart Yard, takes Arthur Clennam into partnership, travels abroad to sell his invention, and releases Arthur from the Marshalsea prison by paying his debt in Charles Dickens's *Little Dorrit.*

Count Dracula   Aristocratic vampire, who leaves his home in Transylvania and tries to establish himself in London but is chased and ultimately killed by a small band of Englishmen in Bram Stoker's *Dracula.*

Sir Francis Drake   Leicester's friend, who imprisons Williams on his ship in Sophia Lee's *The Recess.* He is a courtier and Plymouth mariner, who takes Amyas Leigh to sea, and who fights in the Battle of the Armada in Charles Kingsley's *Westward Ho!.*

Sophia Drake   Cross-grained head housekeeper at St. Crux, the home of Admiral Bartram; she reports to George Bartram on the misdeeds of a servant, who is

Magdalen Vanstone in disguise, in Wilkie Collins's *No Name*.

Mr. Draper London lawyer, agent for Madam Esmond and her half-sister, the Baroness Bernstein (Beatrix Esmond), in William Makepeace Thackeray's *The Virginians*.

Theobald Draper Seemingly virtuous but actually dissolute tempter of the hero Benignus; he dies in a duel in S. J. Pratt's *Liberal Opinions upon Animals, Man, and Providence*.

Captain Drayton Handsome though somewhat egotistical young man, a houseguest at Marlowe; he attempts with Sir Jeckyl Marlowe's approval to court Beatrix Marlowe but is unsuccessful in J. Sheridan Le Fanu's *Guy Deverell*.

Enoch J. Drebber Principal Elder of the Church of Latter Day Saints (Mormons) and the widowed husband of Lucy Ferrier; he is a murder victim in Arthur Conan Doyle's *A Study in Scarlet*.

John Thomas Drew Man rescued by Nevil Beauchamp in the Crimean War in George Meredith's *Beauchamp's Career*.

Driver Paulus Plydell's clerk, who never allows his drunkenness to interfere with his efficiency in Sir Walter Scott's *Guy Mannering*.

Driver Passer-by who finds the body of Robert Colwan hanging from a hayrick in James Hogg's *The Private Memoirs and Confessions of a Justified Sinner*.

Mr. Driver Man who runs the post office in the village near Brandon Hall in J. Sheridan Le Fanu's *Wylder's Hand*.

Anne Driver Woman who helps her father run the post office in the village near Brandon Hall in J. Sheridan Le Fanu's *Wylder's Hand*.

Adele Dronsart Mlle. Reuter's Belgian pupil, who looks fresh and sturdy, but whose attitude and expression are "Gorgon-like," explaining her lack of friends in Charlotte Brontë's *The Professor*.

Tronda Dronsdaughter Barbara Yellowley's servant, whose half-starved condition is due to her mistress's economies in Sir Walter Scott's *The Pirate*.

Edwin Drood John Jasper's nephew, who is engaged to Rosa Bud, whom he calls Pussy; their engagement is broken off, perhaps precipitating his disappearance either through murder or his own will; he despises Neville Landless on racial and aristocratic grounds; Drood is part of the complicated, *doppelganger* motif that exists among himself, John Jasper, and Neville in Charles Dickens's unfin *The Mystery of Edwin Drood*.

Sir Orlando Drought Consistent old Tory in Anthony Trollope's *Phineas Redux*. He becomes leader of the House in the (younger) Duke of Omnium's coalition government; he opposes the duke by insisting on expenditure on gunboats as government policy; he resigns, hoping to wreck the unstable coalition in *The Prime Minister*. He appears in *The Way We Live Now*.

Lady Drum Eccentric, elderly Irish dowager, who is moved by the sight of the Hoggarty diamond to claim kinship with Samuel Titmarsh, thus bringing him temporary prosperity in William Makepeace Thackeray's *The History of Samuel Titmarsh and the Great Hoggarty Diamond*.

Bentley Drummle The gentleman Estella decides to marry in her effort to fulfill Miss Havisham's desire for revenge on the male sex; he and Pip Pirrip actively despise each other in Charles Dickens's *Great Expectations*.

Captain Drummond Selfish parasite who attaches himself first to Sir Harry Cleveland and then to Lord Dellwyn, to whom he reveals Lady Dellwyn's adultery in Sarah Fielding's *The History of the Countess of Dellwyn*.

Catriona (MacGregor) Drummond Beautiful, brave, and spirited daughter of the unscrupulous highland clansman James More MacGregor; she breaks her father out of prison and falls in love with and marries David Balfour in Robert Louis Stevenson's *Catriona*.

Lord Drummond Cabinet colleague of the (younger) Duke of Omnium; he is denied the Garter and is volubly displeased in Anthony Trollope's *The Prime Minister*. He becomes Prime Minister, has a falling out with his leader in the House, Sir Timothy Beeswax, and is forced to resign in *The Duke's Children*. He is a guest at Mistletoe in *The American Senator*.

Thomas Drummond Friend of young George Colwan; he quarrels slightly with him and is falsely convicted of his subsequent murder in James Hogg's *The Private Memoirs and Confessions of a Justified Sinner*.

Will Drybone The "Man in Black," an elderly gentleman who befriends Lien Chi Altangi in Westminster Abbey and guides him around London; he exemplifies autumnal love gone sour in a cynical episode at the end of Oliver Goldsmith's *The Citizen of the World*.

Jasper Dryfesdale Baleful and suspicious elderly steward at Lochleven Castle; though devoted to the Douglas family, he hates Romanism and Queen Mary of Scotland

and so tries to poison her; he is afterwards killed by Henry Seyton in Sir Walter Scott's *The Abbot.*

Drysdale Indolent undergraduate of St. Ambrose's College, Oxford, who reforms and brings about the denouement in Thomas Hughes's *Tom Brown at Oxford.*

Dubbley Constable Daniel Grummer's Officer of Justice, who participates in the arrest of Samuel Pickwick and his friends at Ipswich in Charles Dickens's *The Posthumous Papers of the Pickwick Club.*

Dubois Second comic in Dick Lennox's acting company; small, ugly, and the laughingstock of the company, he likes to talk of his experiences in France in George Moore's *A Mummer's Wife.*

Mr. Du Boung Local brewer with sufficient wealth to contest the Silverbridge seat in Parliament against Arthur Fletcher; Du Boung loses in Anthony Trollope's *The Prime Minister* In another election he steps down in favor of Lord Silverbridge in *The Duke's Children.*

Monsieur Dubourg Agent for the mercantile firm Osbaldistone and Tresham and father of Clement in Sir Walter Scott's *Rob Roy.*

Clement Dubourg Efficient clerk employed by the mercantile firm Osbaldistone and Tresham; Francis Osbaldistone compares unfavorably with him in Sir Walter Scott's *Rob Roy.*

Nugent Dubourg Identical twin brother of Oscar Dubourg; he seeks to win Lucilla Finch for himself, knowing of her engagement to his brother, by representing himself to her as Oscar when her sight is temporarily restored; his elopement with her is foiled by Madame Pratolungo in Wilkie Collins's *Poor Miss Finch.*

Oscar Dubourg Young gentleman of means whose pastime is the crafting of gold and silver vessels; he resides alone in the isolated village of Dimchurch following a near-conviction on a false criminal charge; he and the blind Lucilla Finch fall mutually in love; to cure the severe epilepsy that follows a head injury caused by robbers he takes silver nitrate, which turns his skin dark blue; afraid to reveal the truth to his beloved, he leaves when her sight has been temporarily restored, inadvertently allowing his twin brother to impersonate him; through Madame Pratolungo's efforts he returns and is restored to Lucilla in Wilkie Collins's *Poor Miss Finch.*

Duchess An ill-tempered mother tending her baby in her kitchen when Alice first encounters her; she flings the baby to Alice when she goes to play croquet with the Queen of Hearts; at a later meeting she lards her conver-

sation with irrelevant homilies and is disagreeably cozy to Alice in Lewis Carroll's *Alice's Adventures in Wonderland.*

Duchess Married woman who has had an affair with Don Alonzo; she conspires with Grizalinda to ruin Arminda's reputation for the purpose of regaining the affections of Don Alonzo, in which she is successful until Lewis Augustus Albertus convinces her to repent in Penelope Aubin's *The Life and Adventures of the Lady Lucy.*

Duck Disputatious creature from the pool of tears; she interrupts the Mouse's "dry" history in Lewis Carroll's *Alice's Adventures in Wonderland.*

Lady Duckle Older woman Owen Asher hires to chaperon Evelyn Innes; she knows high society in George Moore's *Evelyn Innes.*

Ellis Duckworth (The Black Arrow, John Amend-All) Outlaw robbed of his lands and blamed for Sir Harry Shelton's murder by the real murderer, Sir Daniel Brackley; he leads a band of merry men intent on revenge and plunder, protects Dick Shelton for his father's sake, and kills Nick Appleyard and Brackley; he uses the alias John Amend-All on all Black Arrow's messages in Robert Louis Stevenson's *The Black Arrow: A Tale of Two Roses.*

Dudley Artist and companion to Henry Bertram through England and Scotland in Sir Walter Scott's *Guy Mannering.*

Amy Robsart Dudley Sir Hugh Robsart's daughter and wife of Robert Dudley, Earl of Leicester, whose political ambitions as Queen Elizabeth's favorite depend on his keeping his marriage secret; Amy remains hidden at Cumnor-Place until she fears that Richard Varney is trying to poison her; she flees to her husband at Kenilworth, but, persuaded by Varney that she has been unfaithful to him, he sends her back to Cumnor-Place in the care of Varney, who dupes him into consenting to her death; having placed Amy in a chamber at the threshold of which is a trap door, Varney imitates Leicester's whistle, and Amy, rushing out, falls to her death almost as rescue arrives in Sir Walter Scott's *Kenilworth.*

Miss Dudley Elderly invalid whom Mike Fletcher sincerely admires; her death augments his ennui and despair in George Moore's *Mike Fletcher.*

Duessa Spokeswoman for The Cry, a group representative of error in all its forms; she leads the chorus of howls which greets Portia's attempt to narrate a story of good rewarded and evil punished in Sarah Fielding's *The Cry.*

Mr. Duff Bow Street runner who investigates the attempted burglary at Mrs. Maylie's house in Charles Dickens's *Oliver Twist*.

Jamie Duff   Idiot employed by the undertaker; he attends all funerals in Edinburgh in Sir Walter Scott's *Guy Mannering*.

Herbert Duffian   Priest responsible for the conversion to Catholicism of Louisa Harrington, the Countess de Saldar, in George Meredith's *Evan Harrington*.

Duke   Lecherous nobleman, whose favor Captain Wappingshot hopes to cultivate by giving him the captive Azemia; he tries to recapture the young Turk after she is spirited away from his household in William Beckford's *Azemia*.

Duke of --   Father of the Marquis of -- and employer of Charles Courteney; he opposes his son's marriage to Henrietta Courteney until she manages to scrape up a dowry of twenty thousand pounds; he values Charles's loyalty in refusing to promote this advantageous match for his sister until the terms are met in Charlotte Lennox's *Henrietta*.

Lady Dumbello   See Griselda Grantly.

Gustavus, Lord Dumbello (later Marquis of Hartletop)   Nitwit aristocrat, who marries Griselda Grantly in Anthony Trollope's *Framley Parsonage*. He rewards her with an emerald necklace after she relieves his anxiety over tittletattle of her supposed liaison with Plantagenet Palliser in *The Small House at Allington*. He appears briefly in *The Last Chronicle of Barset*.

Young Laird of Dumbiedikes   Awkward clod, who worships Jeanie Deans from afar and generally lets his kindness overrule his selfishness in Sir Walter Scott's *The Heart of Midlothian*.

Mr. Dumkin   Famous batter of the All-Muggleton cricket club in Charles Dickens's *The Posthumous Papers of the Pickwick Club*.

Dummie Dummaker   Pickpocket and friend of Margery Lobkin in Edward Bulwer-Lytton's *Paul Clifford*.

Dr. Dummerar   Anglican Vicar of Martindale, reinstated by Sir Geoffrey Peveril at the time of the Restoration, in Sir Walter Scott's *Peveril of the Peak*.

Dumple   Dandie Dinmont's beloved pony in Sir Walter Scott's *Guy Mannering*.

Neil (of the Tom) Duncan   Red-headed servant of and spy for James More MacGregor and his daughter,

Catriona Drummond, in Robert Louis Stevenson's *Catriona*.

Duncan of Knockdunder   High-tempered protector of Knocktarlities, the estate of John, Duke of Argyle; he is generally kindly and combines both the Lowlands and Highlands in his dress in Sir Walter Scott's *The Heart of Midlothian*.

Lieutenant Hector Duncansby   Gangly young Scottish swordsman with a speech impediment; at the contrivance of David Balfour's enemies, he insults David in order to engage him in a duel and kill him in Robert Louis Stevenson's *Catriona*.

Bessie Duncombe   Publicist for women's rights; she neglects her own children but behaves valiantly as fire and then a typhoid epidemic rage in the nearby town in Charlotte Yonge's *The Three Brides*.

Dungaree   South-Sea-native crew member aboard the schooner *Farallone*; he is so named by Captain John Davies because he wears blue dungarees in Robert Louis Stevenson's *The Ebb-Tide: A Trio and a Quartette*.

Lord Dungory   Aristocratic old roué, who is father of three daughters and ignores them all; he is attached to Mrs. Barton in George Moore's *A Drama in Muslin*.

Agnes Dunk   Daughter of the cruel Old Dunk, who confines her until John Buncle rescues her; apparently dead of a fever, she is buried but revives and marries her would-be dissector, Dr. Stanvil; she finally marries Buncle when Dr. Stanvil dies suddenly; she dies of smallpox within a few years of marriage in Thomas Amory's *The Life of John Buncle, Esq*.

Old Dunk   Cruel, miserly father of Agnes Dunk; he holds her against her will until John Buncle rescues her; he dies later in Thomas Amory's *The Life of John Buncle, Esq*.

Dr. Ginery Dunkle   A shrill boy and the poetical spokesman of the delegation welcoming Elijah Pogram in Charles Dickens's *The Life and Adventures of Martin Chuzzlewit*.

Mr. Dunkley   Wealthy Irish gentleman and John Buncle's contemporary at Trinity College, Dublin; he is a good-humored philosopher; he meets his future wife, Alcmena Cox, at the Harrogate dance Buncle attends in Thomas Amory's *The Life of John Buncle, Esq*.

Dunlop   Respectful but vigilant guard of the imprisoned Matilda and (younger) Mary in Sophia Lee's *The Recess*.

Onesiphorus (Siph) Dunn Irish man about town delegated to be Lily Dale's escort when she rides in Rotten Row in Anthony Trollope's *The Last Chronicle of Barset*.

Michael Dunne Clever prisoner who helps Moriarty Carroll escape from prison in Maria Edgeworth's *Ormond*.

Count de Dunois A champion of France, beloved by the people and esteemed by Louis XI; he assists in attempting to stop Isabelle de Croye from leaving France in Sir Walter Scott's *Quentin Durward*.

Viscount Dunoran Mervyn's father, wrongly accused of the murder of Beauclerc and convicted on the evidence of Charles Archer (Paul Dangerfield), the actual murderer; he kills himself while in prison awaiting hanging in J. Sheridan Le Fanu's *The House by the Churchyard*.

Betty Dunshaughlin Housekeeper for Cornelius O'Shane in Maria Edgeworth's *Ormond*.

Tommy Dunshaughlin Studious, hardworking young man of lower-class birth, befriended by Harry Ormond; Ormond's concern for the boy's education greatly increases Florence Annaly's esteem for Ormond and contributes to his finally marrying her in Maria Edgeworth's *Ormond*.

Emily Dunstable Cousin of Martha (Dunstable) Thorne; Susan Grantly has ambitions for her marriage to Henry Grantly, opposing his choice of Grace Crawley; Emily becomes Lily Dale's friend and eventually marries Lily's cousin Bernard Dale in Anthony Trollope's *The Last Chronicle of Barset*.

Martha Dunstable Outspoken, good-humored, sensible, no-longer-young heiress to a fortune from patent medicine; she is pursued by the Hon. George de Courcy and by Gustavus Moffat, and she admonishes Frank Gresham for proposing to her for her money in Anthony Trollope's *Doctor Thorne*. She makes a happy marriage to Dr. Thorne in *Framley Parsonage*. She is Emily Dunstable's cousin and hostess in *The Last Chronicle of Barset*.

Emma, Lady Dunstane Diana Warwick's best friend and Sir Lukin Dustane's wife, an intellectual invalid whose ill health keeps Diana from an almost certainly disastrous liaison with Percy Dacier in George Meredith's *Diana of the Crossways*.

Sir Lukin Dunstane Husband of Diana Merion's best friend, Emma Dunstane; he helps to precipitate Diana into a loveless marriage with Augustus Warwick by attempting to seduce her while she is visiting Emma in George Meredith's *Diana of the Crossways*.

Mrs. Dunster Honest farmer's wife who recognizes the perfidy of the Orgueils toward the Simples but is unable to offset it in Sarah Fielding's *David Simple. Volume the Last*.

Dupin Rich Parisian who fathered Pauline (Caillaud) in 1790 upon the poor Victorine and deserted her at his father's insistence in Mark Rutherford's *The Revolution In Tanner's Lane*.

Chevalier Dupont Pugnacious young French nobleman, who insults the honor of Charles de St. Leon with insinuations concerning his father's mysterious rise from poverty in William Godwin's *St. Leon*.

Colney Durance Friend and opposite to Victor Radnor; his pessimism and satirical wit illuminate Victor's conventional and ill-founded optimism in George Meredith's *One of Our Conquerors*.

Genevieve Durant Bewitching Frenchwoman, who is loved hopelessly by Gilbert Kendal; after his death she marries Ulick O'More in Charlotte Yonge's *The Young Step-Mother*.

Abraham Durbeyfield Tess's young brother in Thomas Hardy's *Tess of the D'Urbervilles*.

Eliza-Louisa (Liza-Lu) Durbeyfield Tess's younger sister who waits with Angel Clare while Tess is executed for the murder of Alec Stoke-D'Urberville in Thomas Hardy's *Tess of the D'Urbervilles*.

Hope Durbeyfield One of Tess's young sisters in Thomas Hardy's *Tess of the D'Urbervilles*.

Joan Durbeyfield Well-meaning but misguided mother of Tess; she encourages her daughter to present herself to Alec Stoke-D'Urberville, a presumed relative, in hopes that he will help them financially; a former beauty herself, she advises Tess to play upon her good looks; her opportunistic counsel is useless to the innocent, high-minded, proud Tess in Thomas Hardy's *Tess of the D'Urbervilles*.

John Durbeyfield Tess's father, a carter whose shiftlessness increases when he learns he is descended from an ancient family; later, his death drives Tess to maintain her mother and siblings by accepting the protection of Alec Stoke-D'Urberville in Thomas Hardy's *Tess of the D'Urbervilles*.

Modesty Durbeyfield One of Tess's young sisters in Thomas Hardy's *Tess of the D'Urbervilles*.

Tess Durbeyfield Beautiful, high-minded, proud, courageous country girl, who is seduced by the rich Alec Stoke-D'Urberville, has an illegitimate child who soon dies, and goes to work on a dairy farm where she meets

Angel Clare, whom she marries; when she reveals the facts about her seduction, he cannot bear his changed perception of her, and they separate; despondent, in need, and to provide sustenance for her mother and siblings after her father's death, she allows herself to become Stoke-D'Urberville's mistress; when, too late, Clare returns for her, she kills Stoke-D'Urberville out of desperation and escapes with Clare but is soon caught and executed for her crime in Thomas Hardy's *Tess of the D'Urbervilles*.

Durdles Writer of witty epitaphs on tombs; he discusses his practice with John Jasper one evening in the Cloisterham Cathedral churchyard in Charles Dickens's *The Mystery of Edwin Drood*.

Alexander Durie Son of Alison (Graeme) and Henry Durie, who dotes on him just as old Lord Durrisdeer doted on the Master (James Durie) in Robert Louis Stevenson's *The Master of Ballantrae: A Winter's Tale*.

Henry Durie See Henry, Lord Durrisdeer.

Katharine Durie Daughter of Allison (Graeme) and Henry Durie in Robert Louis Stevenson's *The Master of Ballantrae: A Winter's Tale*.

James Durie (Mr. Bally, Master of Ballantrae) Profligate, fascinating, sinister elder son of Lord Durrisdeer and Henry Durie's brother and Alison Graeme's intended; he is believed dead after the Battle of Culloden and again after he, as "Mr. Bally," is wounded by Henry in a duel; his pact with his brother and his three returns from the dead destroy the lives of tenants of Durrisdeer in Robert Louis Stevenson's *The Master of Ballantrae: A Winter's Tale*.

Duncan Duroch Donald Bean Lean's lieutenant, who helps rescue Edward Waverly from jail and then guides him to Doune Castle in Sir Walter Scott's *Waverly*.

Lord Durrisdeer Doting, deluded eighth lord of Durrisdeer, who never quite accepts his younger son, Henry Durie, nor loses his love for his elder son, James Durie (the Master), in Robert Louis Stevenson's *The Master of Ballantrae: A Winter's Tale*.

Alison Graeme, Lady Durrisdeer Durie kinswoman, an orphan and an heiress; betrothed to the Master (James Durie), she weds his brother, Henry Durie, after his reported death at the Battle of Culloden; she is mother of Katharine and Alexander; her devotion to James and initial blindness about Henry contribute to the accumulating distress in Robert Louis Stevenson's *The Master of Ballantrae: A Winter's Tale*.

Henry, Lord Durrisdeer Honest, capable second son

of Lord Durrisdeer; left at home to tend the estates after the falsely reported death of his brother the Master (James Durie), he marries his brother's betrothed, Alison Graeme; after years of torment at his brother's hands—in part the result of his mistaken belief that he has killed his brother in a duel—Henry finds his brother on the point of a third "resurrection"; the brothers die almost simultaneously in Robert Louis Stevenson's *The Master of Ballantrae: A Winter's Tale*.

Quentin Durward Bold and chivalrous archer of the Scottish Guard; he leaves Scotland to seek his fortune in France, where he gains Louis XI's favor; entrusted with the ladies of Croye, he extricates them from numerous hazards and falls in love with Isabelle de Croye in Sir Walter Scott's *Quentin Durward*.

Algernon Dusautoy Bullying, wealthy would-be artist who marries Lucy Kendal and forces her to accompany him to Italy amid distressing family circumstances in Charlotte Yonge's *The Young Step-Mother*.

Dutton Servant who is hired by Jery Melford; he prides himself on his clothing and manners and competes with Humphry Clinker for the affections of Winifrid Jenkins; he elopes with a woman with money in Tobias Smollett's *The Expedition of Humphry Clinker*.

Dutton Shabby archer, who is set by Richard of Gloucester to watch Dick Shelton during battle and stab him if he is faithless in Robert Louis Stevenson's *The Black Arrow: A Tale of Two Roses*.

Dutton Pirate and mutineer on Teach's *Sarah*; he guides the Master (James Durie) out of the swamp only to be stabbed by him in Robert Louis Stevenson's *The Master of Ballantrae: A Winter's Tale*.

Jim Dutton Former servant of the Lake family; bearing a striking resemblance to Mark Wylder, he is paid by Stanley Lake to travel abroad, sending forged letters from various locations; eventually he becomes suspicious of Lake's actions and writes to the attorney Josiah Larkin, but returns and is mollified by Lake; he reports his actions and suspicions after Lake's accident in J. Sheridan Le Fanu's *Wylder's Hand*.

Madame Duval French grandmother of Evelina Anville Belmont; she journeys to England to take charge of Evelina but fails to make Sir John Belmont acknowledge Evelina as his daughter; she is subjected to insults and practical jokes by Captain Mirvan; she notifies Evelina she is to be her heir in Frances Burney's *Evelina*.

Denis Duval Youthful hero and narrator of the novel; he grows up in humble circumstances and is involved unwittingly in his grandfather's smuggling expeditions and the intrigues of the Chevalier de la Motte; he incurs the dangerous enmity of Joseph Weston but is clearly destined for success and a happy marriage to his childhood sweetheart Agnes de Saverne in William Makepeace Thackeray's unfin *Denis Duval*.

Jacque Duval   Varbarriere's servant, who is willing to do unethical tasks for money in J. Sheridan Le Fanu's *Guy Deverell*.

Peter Duval   Rascally and cowardly grandfather of Denis Duval; a refugee French Protestant, he supplements his income as a wig-maker and hairdresser by smuggling goods from France in William Makepeace Thackeray's *Denis Duval*.

Ursule Duval   Brave, bad-tempered mother of Denis Duval, whom she chastises but also protects, as she does her childhood friend and foster sister Clarisse, now the Comtesse de Saverne in William Makepeace Thackeray's *Denis Duval*.

Philip Duvergois   Faithful valet of Henry Lambert in William Beckford's *Modern Novel Writing; or, the Elegant Enthusiast*.

Lady Dorothy Dwadle   Lady of rank and an amiable hostess in William Beckford's *Azemia*.

Dwarf   Distressed opera goer, whose view is blocked by a tall, corpulent German; Yorick regards the incident as an example of the need for mercy toward the unfortunate in Laurence Sterne's *A Sentimental Journey through France and Italy*.

Dwarf   Noisy, evil, spiteful servant of the Lady; he spies on the Maid and Walter Golden, who slays him in William Morris's *The Wood beyond the World*.

Henbane Dwining   Apothecary who treats John Ramorny for his mutilated hand and conspires with Ramorny in the kidnapping and murder of the Duke of Rothsay; he gives Catherine Glover his gold just before

he is hanged by Archibald, Earl of Douglas, in Sir Walter Scott's *The Fair Maid of Perth*.

Dykes   A gamekeeper at Knowl who helps protect Maud Ruthyn from a coach of rough intruders (one of whom is her cruel cousin, Dudley Ruthyn) in J. Sheridan Le Fanu's *Uncle Silas*.

Lord Dymchurch   Thoughtful aristocrat of moderate means; he decides to retire to his small estate after he is rejected by May Tomalin in George Gissing's *Our Friend the Charlatan*.

Felix Dymes   Conceited composer in love with Alma Frothingham; he manages her concert appearance in George Gissing's *The Whirlpool*.

Colonel Dymond   Kindly, middle-aged husband of Susanna Dymond; he fails to satisfy her intellectual or emotional needs in Anne Thackeray Ritchie's *Mrs. Dymond*.

Jo Dymond   Son of Colonel Dymond in Anne Thackeray Ritchie's *Mrs. Dymond*.

Susanna Dymond   Young woman from the Lake District; at her grandfather's death she goes to live with her mother and the despicable Irish journalist she has married; for self-preservation Susanna marries Colonel Dymond, but his death frees her to realize her own values in a marriage with the artist Max du Parc in Anne Thackeray Ritchie's *Mrs. Dymond*.

Temperance (Tempy) Dymond   Daughter of Colonel Dymond by his first wife; she resents the domestic tyranny of her elderly aunts and is loyal to Susanna Dymond in Anne Thackeray Ritchie's *Mrs. Dymond*.

Oliver Dynevor   Catharine Frost's son, who spends thirty-four years in Peru working to win back his mother's estate, only to find his triumph hollow in Charlotte Yonge's *Dynevor Terrace*.

E

Jemy (James) E Moll Flanders's fourth husband, who deceives her into thinking he is wealthy; he himself finds he was deceived when he learns that Moll has no money; they separate because they are poor, and when he later lands in prison for robbery, Moll arranges to have him transported with her to Virginia in Daniel Defoe's *The Fortunes and Misfortunes of the Famous Moll Flanders*.

Mr. E–– A wealthy, married gentleman who becomes enamored of Serena Tricksy and courts her at an auction where he makes her an expensive present in Eliza Haywood's *Anti-Pamela: or, Feign'd Innocence Detected*.

Mrs. E–– Cunning wife of Mr. E––; she manipulates another jealous wife into having Syrena Tricksy arrested as a prostitute in Eliza Haywood's *Anti-Pamela: or, Feign'd Innocence Detected*.

Mr. Eadie Lowland Presbyterian minister of a lower social class and a more skeptical tradition concerning foreknowledge; he is married to the Highlander Mrs. Eadie; he educates Charles Walkinshaw's son James in John Galt's *The Entail*.

Mrs. Eadie Highland lady who possesses the second sight, befriends Charles Walkinshaw's wife and family, and correctly predicts their future in connection with her own in John Galt's *The Entail*.

Eadwyn Monk of Saint Mary's Priory who sees the ghost of Reginald de Folville, reports to the prior, and then dies mysteriously in Ann Radcliffe's *Gaston de Blondeville*.

Solomon Eagle An "enthusiast," who proclaims that the plague is a judgment upon the city of London while walking through the streets naked and with a pan of burning charcoal on his head in Daniel Defoe's *A Journal of the Plague Year*.

Lord Eaglesham Principal landowner of the Dalmailing region and a benevolent landlord; he patronizes the Malcolm family, helps improve the parish, and is shot by Mungo Argyle in John Galt's *Annals of the Parish*.

Eaglet Bird whose impudence to the Dodo brings an appreciative response from the other creatures after the swim in the pool of tears in Lewis Carroll's *Alice's Adventures in Wonderland*.

John Eames Scapegrace civil-service clerk hopelessly in love with Lily Dale; he thrashes Adolphus Crosbie for jilting her; he saves Lord de Guest from a bull and becomes his legatee in Anthony Trollope's *The Small House at Allington*. His susceptibility to feminine attraction does not affect his love for Lily but is a factor in her final rejection of him in *The Last Chronicle of Barset*.

Lady Eardham Imperious and strong-willed wife of Sir George; she is dedicated to finding suitable husbands for her three daughters; when Ralph Newton, heir to Newton Priory, shows interest in her second daughter, Augusta, she makes sure he is well and truly captured in Anthony Trollope's *Ralph the Heir*.

Augusta (Gus) Eardham Second daughter of Sir George; her mother leaves no stone unturned to ensure that she marries Ralph Newton, heir to Newton Priory, in Anthony Trollope's *Ralph the Heir*.

Sir George Eardham Gouty and ill-tempered father of Augusta and two other dowerless daughters, for all of whom husbands have to be found in Anthony Trollope's *Ralph the Heir*.

Earl of Earlybird Zealous campaigner for improved conditions of labor in housing and education, chosen by the (younger) Duke of Omnium to become Knight of the Garter in Anthony Trollope's *The Prime Minister*.

Patrick Earnscliff Brave and generous border laird, much admired by his ruder neighbors, and a good friend of Hobbie (Halbert) Elliot; though he is Isabella Vere's lover, her father will not allow them to marry because of a distant feud between the families in Sir Walter Scott's *The Black Dwarf*.

Mr. Earnshaw Prosperous yeoman, owner of Wuthering Heights, and father of Catherine and Hindley; his inexplicable action in bringing back from a trip to Liverpool the boy Heathcliff sets up the tragedy in Emily Brontë's *Wuthering Heights*.

Catherine Earnshaw Spoiled and willful sister of Hindley; she loves Heathcliff but marries Edgar Linton, making a match that brings about much unhappiness when Heathcliff returns; she dies after giving birth to a daughter, Catherine, in Emily Brontë's *Wuthering Heights*.

Frances Earnshaw Wife of Hindley; her death of consumption shortly after the birth of Hareton brings about her husband's moral decline in Emily Brontë's *Wuthering Heights*.

Hareton Earnshaw Last of the Earnshaws, who, in spite of losing both his parents at an early age and receiving brutal treatment at the hands of Heathcliff, is destined for a share of happiness in his marriage to Catherine Linton in Emily Brontë's *Wuthering Heights*.

Hindley Earnshaw   Son of Mr. Earnshaw; as a boy he is jealous of Heathcliff and torments him; he deteriorates after the death of his wife and dies disgraced and degraded by Heathcliff in Emily Brontë's *Wuthering Heights*.

John Earwaker   Sensible journalist and friend of Godwin Peak; he writes for a paper that advocates Conservative views at odds with his own but gains a better position and acts as adviser to Peak and Malkin in George Gissing's *Born in Exile*.

Harry (Scud) East   Scapegrace companion of Tom Brown at Rugby School in Thomas Hughes's *Tom Brown's Schooldays*. He becomes an army officer, is courtmartialled for helping Harry Winburn, and emigrates to New Zealand in *Tom Brown at Oxford*.

Mr. Easthupp   Cocky purser's steward, who fights a ridiculous duel with Mr. Biggs and Jack Easy in Captain Frederick Marryat's *Mr. Midshipman Easy*.

Mrs. Easy   Foolish wife of Nicodemus Easy; bearing Jack Easy late in life, she treats him with absurd indulgence in Captain Frederick Marryat's *Mr. Midshipman Easy*.

John (Jack, "Equality Jack") Easy   A bright teenager, who discovers the absurdity of the egalitarian ideas dear to his father, Nicodemus, while serving as a midshipman under Captain Wilson; he marries Agnes de Rebiera in Captain Frederick Marryat's *Mr. Midshipman Easy*.

Nicodemus Easy   Jack's father, a rich Hampshire landowner, whose ideas of equality are shown to be absurd, and who is killed in a phrenological machine of his own invention in Captain Frederick Marryat's *Mr. Midshipman Easy*.

Dr. Easyman   Personal physician to Martha Dunstable; he is always in poor health, and she looks after him in Anthony Trollope's *Doctor Thorne*. He also appears in *Framley Parsonage*.

Mr. Eaton   Principal landowner in the town of Eastthorp in 1840 and a customer of Mr. Furze in Mark Rutherford's *Catharine Furze*.

Carl Eberson   William de La Marck's handsome illegitimate son, treasured by his father in Sir Walter Scott's *Quentin Durward*.

Eblis   Prince of the infernal powers who resembles a tarnished angel of light; his votaries spend eternity with their hands over hearts enveloped in flames in William Beckford's *Vathek*.

Mrs. Eccles   Milliner and procuress in whose house the runaway Henrietta Courteney first finds lodgings in Charlotte Lennox's *Henrietta*.

Robert Armstrong Eccles   Rhoda Fleming's beloved, estranged from her for refusing to believe that her sister Dahlia has retained her honor in an affair; he goes in search of Dahlia and her wealthy seducer; he is unable to prevent his enemy, Nic Sedgett, from marrying Dahlia; after the marriage proves invalid, he marries Rhoda in George Meredith's *Rhoda Fleming*.

Mrs. Echo   Lady D—'s servant; she advises Henrietta Courteney to flatter Mrs. Autumn in Charlotte Lennox's *Henrietta*.

Tom Eckerthy   Farmer and cricket fan, who sees Harry Richmond in his flight from Rippenger's school and notifies Squire Beltham in George Meredith's *The Adventures of Harry Richmond*.

(Lord Destrier) Marquis of Edbury   Rake who seduces Mabel Sweetwinter and makes her his mistress; he becomes engaged to Janet Ilchester, who believes she can reform him, but he is lost at sea while pursuing Mabel in George Meredith's *The Adventures of Harry Richmond*.

Mrs. Ede   Interfering mother of Ralph Ede; piously condemning worldly activities, she is fond of her daughter-in-law, Kate, but sharp-tongued; she is indignant at their taking in a lodger from the theater in George Moore's *A Mummer's Wife*.

Kate D'Arcy Ede   Working-class wife in the Five Towns and manager of the sewing in her husband's dress shop; charmed by their lodger, Dick Lennox, proprietor of a traveling acting troupe, she leaves her pious home to join Dick and the mummers; madly enjoying the excitement, she becomes a singer and star of the company, but hard times bring poverty, childbirth, and drunkenness; jealous and lonely, she becomes unmanageable and dies from alcoholism in George Moore's *A Mummer's Wife*.

Ralph Ede   An invalid, self-centered and ambitious for his dressmaking shop; although fond of his wife, Kate, he does not pursue her when she elopes with Dick Lennox; he marries Miss Herder, Kate's assistant, in George Moore's *A Mummer's Wife*.

Francis Eden   Saintly, courageous clergyman, who, as the village's part-time pastor for three months, shows Susan how to overcome her grief at George Fielding's absence; he becomes chaplain of a jail in which the "new" separate-silent-system is being cruelly misused until he proves the crimes to a representative of the Home Office; he redeems many sinners, among them Tom Robinson in Charles Reade's *It Is Never Too Late to Mend*.

Edinburgh innkeeper   Keeper of the Black Bull of Norway; he is instrumental in escalating the first quarrel of the Colwan brothers into a factious riot in James Hogg's *The Private Memoirs and Confessions of a Justified Sinner.*

Edinburgh jailor   Scots-speaker who accuses Robert Colwan of hypocrisy and madness when the latter is jailed and tries to convert him in James Hogg's *The Private Memoirs and Confessions of a Justified Sinner.*

Editor   Rationalistic skeptic, who finds the memoirs of Robert Colwan in a suicide's grave and prefaces them with his own researched account in James Hogg's *The Private Memoirs and Confessions of a Justified Sinner.*

Editor   Man about town who discovers the manuscript (in pieces) in a Whitechapel chandler's shop in Charles Johnstone's *Chrysal: or, The Adventures of a Guinea.*

Mrs. Edlin   Widow who serves as "counselor" to Sue Bridehead in her confusion over her feelings for Jude Fawley and Richard Phillotson; although highly sympathetic to Jude and Sue's plight, she represents an older generation that scorns what she perceives as a trend toward avoiding marriage and commitment in Thomas Hardy's *Jude the Obscure.*

Mr. Edmonstone   Good-natured guardian of Sir Guy Morville; he is easily convinced by his nephew Philip Morville that Sir Guy has been gambling but is ultimately shown the truth in Charlotte Yonge's *The Heir of Redclyffe.*

Mrs. Edmonstone   Warmhearted, loving wife of Sir Guy Morville's guardian; she becomes Sir Guy's confidante and advisor in Charlotte Yonge's *The Heir of Redclyffe.*

Amabel (Amy) Edmonstone   Cousin of Sir Guy Morville; her character deepens during their engagement and marriage and her early widowhood until she becomes the moral center of the Edmonstone family in Charlotte Yonge's *The Heir of Redclyffe.*

Charles Edmonstone   Crippled, satiric son of Guy Morville's guardian; he is rescued from self-pity and uselessness by Sir Guy's influence in Charlotte Yonge's *The Heir of Redclyffe.*

Charlotte Edmonstone   Youngest and cleverest of the children of Sir Guy Morville's guardian in Charlotte Yonge's *The Heir of Redclyffe.*

Laura Edmonstone   Eldest daughter of Sir Guy Morville's guardian; she agrees to a secret engagement with her cousin Philip Morville and undergoes grievous

emotional and mental suffering before they can marry in Charlotte Yonge's *The Heir of Redclyffe.*

Edmund   Guard who helps Osbert escape the evil Malcolm's castle in Ann Radcliffe's *The Castles of Athlin and Dunbayne.*

Prince Edmund   Younger son of Henry III in Ann Radcliffe's *Gaston de Blondeville.*

Edmunds   Wicked, abusive husband and father in "The Convict's Return," told by the clergyman at Manor Farm, Dingley Dell, in Charles Dickens's *The Posthumous Papers of the Pickwick Club.*

John Edmunds   Son of Edmunds and title character of "The Convict's Return," told by the clergyman at Manor Farm, Dingley Dell, in Charles Dickens's *The Posthumous Papers of the Pickwick Club.*

Edric   Guard who helps Alleyn (Philip) to escape Castle Dunbayne and who joins Osbert's forces in Ann Radcliffe's *The Castles of Athlin and Dunbayne.*

Edric   Hereward's Saxon attendant in Sir Walter Scott's *Count Robert of Paris.*

Edward   The Marquis of–-'s well-mannered gardener, whom Arabella mistakes for a disguised nobleman and intended rapist; he proves his low birth to everyone but Arabella by stealing carp from the fish pond in Charlotte Lennox's *The Female Quixote.*

Edward   Vicious and indulgent aristocrat, who neglects and later harasses his invalid wife and arranges a loveless marriage for his daughter, Mary, before his violent death from a riding accident in Mary Wollstonecraft's *Mary, A Fiction.*

Prince Edward   Eldest son of Henry III; he believes Gaston de Blondeville is guilty of murdering Reginald de Folville in Ann Radcliffe's *Gaston de Blondeville.*

Edward of Caernarvon (King Edward II)   Weak English king, who uses the young Castruccio dei Antelminelli to restore an exiled friend to his court in Mary Shelley's *Valperga.*

Edward the Confessor (King Edward III)   N o r m a n king of England whom Julian the Apostate, in his incarnation as an English minister of state, brings to power; his weak character makes him an easy victim for unscrupulous politicians in Henry Fielding's *A Journey From This World to the Next.*

Edwards   Harley's elderly former neighbor, who was forced off his land and pressed into the army; Harley rescues him and his two grandchildren from poverty in Henry Mackenzie's *The Man of Feeling.*

Miss Edwards   Poor apprentice at Miss Monflathers's girls' school; kind to Nell Trent after the scolding by Miss Monflathers, she is shamed for her kindness; she is later watched by Nell with envy when her sister comes to visit in Charles Dickens's *The Old Curiosity Shop.*

Birdy Edwards   See John Douglas.

George Edwards   Proud but essentially honorable hero; a native of the plantations to which his grandfather was transported and where the family prospered, he is sent to his uncle, Jeremy Edwards, in London because his father wants to detach him from July Wentworth, whom he loves; he yields to the temptations of the London underworld but is opportunely rescued by the appearance of July, whom he marries; they return to the plantations, where he finds he has inherited his father's wealth in John Hill's *The Adventures of Mr. George Edwards, a Creole.*

Jack Edwards   Edwards's deceased son, who had been saved from the pressmen by his father and who has left his children to Edwards's care in Henry Mackenzie's *The Man of Feeling.*

Jeremy Edwards   Avaricious, corrupt half brother of Thomas Edwards and father of the illegitimate Ruth, whom he has retained as housekeeper and mistress; he plots to do away with his nephew, George Edwards, in order to inherit Thomas's fortune in John Hill's *The Adventures of Mr. George Edwards, a Creole.*

Ruth [Edwards]   Mistress of Jeremy Edwards and, unknown to her, his illegitimate daughter in John Hill's *The Adventures of George Edwards, a Creole.*

Thomas Edwards   Father of the hero, George, and half brother of Jeremy in John Hill's *The Adventures of Mr. George Edwards, a Creole.*

Tom Edwards   Lady Bellaston's friend, who fabricates Tom Jones's death while dueling to show Lord Fellamar Sophia Western's love for Tom in Henry Fielding's *The History of Tom Jones.*

Violet Effingham   Orphaned heiress of independent leanings much loved by Lord Chiltern and simultaneously courted by Lord Fawn and Mr. Appledom; because Phineas Finn is interested in marrying her, Chiltern wings him in a duel; although his violent temper frightens her, Violet is ultimately moved by Chiltern's constancy and passion, and she accepts him in Anthony Trollope's *Phineas Finn.* As Lady Chiltern, she follows the escapades of Lady Eustace in *The Eustace Diamonds.* She mitigates her husband's wrath over Plantagenet Palliser's neglect of the coverts and remains Phineas Finn's loyal friend during his trial for murder in *Phineas Redux.* She is a guest at Lord Mistletoe's in *The American Senator.*

Audley Egerton   Half brother of Squire William Hazeldean; he advances the career of his kinsman Randal Leslie and keeps the secret of his marriage to Leonora Avenel from his friend and rival Harley L'Estrange in Edward Bulwer-Lytton's *"My Novel," by Pisistratus Caxton.*

Egger   A Swiss who teaches at Dr. Tootle's school and becomes a friend of Osmond Waymark in George Gissing's *The Unclassed.*

Captain Egglane   Lord Fellamar's servant; he challenges Squire Western to duel after Western rejects Fellamar's proposal to Sophia Western in Henry Fielding's *The History of Tom Jones.*

Mr. Eggleston   Next heir after Cecilia Beverley; he assumes control of the estate after Cecilia's marriage in Frances Burney's *Cecilia.*

Lady Charlotte Eglett   Strong-willed and adoring sister of Lord Ormont; she brings Matey Weyburn back into Lady Ormont's life by hiring him as her brother's secretary in George Meredith's *Lord Ormont and his Aminta.*

Pomponius Ego   Author whose overinflated rhetoric leads John Jorrocks to consider him an authority on fox hunting in Robert Surtees's *Handley Cross.*

Charles Egremont   Second son of Lady Marney and the late Lord Marney; he sheds his aristocratic prejudices against the working-class poor after learning of their deplorable condition from Walter Gerard and his daughter, Sybil, whom he finally marries; as a Member of Parliament he persuades the aristocracy to take responsibility for improving the condition of the poor in Benjamin Disraeli's *Sybil.*

Walter Egremont   Wealthy young idealist, who tries to educate workers and becomes infatuated with the working-class girl Thyrza Trent, although she is engaged to another man; he is ultimately persuaded that her reeducation has made her too good for him, and he marries a woman of his own class in George Gissing's *Thyrza.*

Lady Elburne   Rose Jocelyn's grandmother; she tames her independently minded granddaughter in George Meredith's *Evan Harrington.*

Lord Elcho   Commander of the Covenanters; he is beaten at Tippermuir in Sir Walter Scott's *A Legend of Montrose.*

Elder Brother   Merchant who is the elder brother of

the narrator (H.F.) and who has recently returned from Lisbon; the narrator watches over his house while he and his family live away from the city in Daniel Defoe's *A Journal of the Plague Year*.

Elder Brother   Older son of the rich matron who takes Moll Flanders into her household; he seduces Moll and then gets rid of her by arranging to have her marry his younger brother in Daniel Defoe's *The Fortunes and Misfortunes of the Famous Moll Flanders*.

Hubert Eldon   Young aristocrat of bitterly anti-Socialist convictions; he is disinherited by lack of a will but then inherits after all and, to restore the environment, closes down the factory that has been built in his town in George Gissing's *Demos*.

Mrs. Eldridge   London landlady who, taking advantage of Harriet Wilkins's presence in her home, takes the opportunity to praise Sir Thomas Sindall to her and present him with opportunities to seduce her in Henry Mackenzie's *The Man of the World*.

Eleanor   Widowed sister of Henry III now married to the duplicitous Simon de Montfort and member of the royal entourage in Ann Radcliffe's *Gaston de Blondeville*.

Queen Eleanor   French wife of Henry III; she is attended by Lady Barbara, wife of Gaston de Blondeville, in Ann Radcliffe's *Gaston de Blondeville*.

Elenor   English girl who is Ferdinand's first victim in England, seduced by him after meeting him in a carriage to London; she loses her sanity and is put in Bethlem when he abandons her; she recovers her mind, discovers Ferdinand desperate in prison, accompanies him on his wanderings, and nurses him to recovery in Tobias Smollett's *The Adventures of Ferdinand Count Fathom*.

Elfhild   Osberne Wulfsson's beloved, who is separated from him by a torrent and, with Anna the Carline, seeks him southward when he goes to war in William Morris's *The Sundering Flood*.

Elfin-king   See Warden.

Mrs. Elford   Hugh Trevor's aunt, who becomes moody and fretful in her unhappy second marriage, to the generous Mr. W. Elford, in Thomas Holcroft's *The Adventures of Hugh Trevor*.

W. Elford   Generous and loving man who marries Hugh Trevor's aunt, conceives a great affection for young Hugh, leaves his wife, and returns at the end of the novel to be Hugh's benefactor in Thomas Holcroft's *The Adventures of Hugh Trevor*.

Reuben Elgar   Dissolute brother of Miriam Baske; he proposes to the underaged Cecily Doran in the ruins of Pompeii, marries her against the wishes of her guardians, and becomes involved in a scandal that ruins the marriage in George Gissing's *The Emancipated*.

Elias   Trader in silk, brown holland, and leather, married to Catherine, and the father of nine children; he turns Gerard over to a burgomaster to keep him true to his clerical vocation; later he is reconciled to Gerard, Margaret, and their son; he and his wife move to Rotterdam in Charles Reade's *The Cloister and the Hearth*.

Eliza   The addressee of Yorick's letters and the object of his occasional idealized flights of passion in Laurence Sterne's *A Sentimental Journey through France and Italy*.

Eliza   Overdelicate, languid, and sickly lady of leisure, whose affectation and weak constitution lead her to neglect her daughter, Mary, who forgives her on her deathbed in Mary Wollstonecraft's *Mary, A Fiction*.

Eliza   Skillful cook for the Reverend Mr. Helstone in Charlotte Brontë's *Shirley*.

Queen Elizabeth   Queen of England, for whose favor Thomas Ratcliffe, Earl of Sussex, and Robert Dudley, Earl of Leicester, are rivals; though she refuses to marry Leicester for reasons of policy, she is in love with him, and her wrath at finding him already married almost costs him his life in Sir Walter Scott's *Kenilworth*. She proposes marriage to Lord Leicester and has Mary, Queen of Scots executed after learning that Leicester has secretly wed Matilda and that Matilda and Ellinor are Mary's daughters; her rage over the negotiations between the Earl of Essex (2) and King James for the release of Ellinor precipitates Essex's execution in Sophia Lee's *The Recess*.

Ellen   Vibrant young woman of the year 2090 whose natural manners and oneness with nature embody for William Guest the life of the new age in William Morris's *News from Nowhere*.

Ellen   Poverty-stricken, pockmarked girl dying in a garret, supported by her sister Lizzy and befriended by the compassionate Sandy Mackaye in Charles Kingsley's *Alton Locke*.

Ellen   Maid to Sidney Bidulph; she is discharged for receiving a letter from Mr. Faulkland's servant against Lady Bidulph's wishes in Frances Sheridan's *Memoirs of Miss Sidney Bidulph*.

Ellen   Very beautiful servant to Theobald and Christina Pontifex; she is dismissed from service when she becomes pregnant; later the wife of Ernest, by whom she has two children, she becomes an alcoholic; the marriage ends with Ernest's discovery that she is a bigamist in Samuel Butler's *The Way of All Flesh*.

Eleanor Staunton, Lady Ellerton   Idealistic, well-educated heiress, niece of Dean Winnstay; she marries Lord Ellerton; initially disliked by Alton Locke, though she is sympathetic toward him, she becomes an active proponent of Christian socialism after her husband's death and, nursing Alton through his fever, converts him to her beliefs in Charles Kingsley's *Alton Locke*.

Lynedale, Lord Ellerton   High-minded aristocrat, to whom George Locke toadies at Cambridge, and who behaves generously toward Alton Locke, recognizing his potential; he is thrown from his horse and killed soon after his marriage to the adoring Eleanor Staunton in Charles Kingsley's *Alton Locke*.

George Ellesborough   Yale graduate and forester; he is a captain in the American army stationed in England's countryside; he loves Rachel Henderson but loses her when she is murdered by her former husband in Mrs. Humphry Ward's *Harvest*.

Ellesmere   Successful gamester who wins possession of the house and belongings of Angelo D'Albini and later restores them on his death in Charlotte Dacre's *The Libertine*.

Mistress Ellesmere   Lady Peveril's housekeeper, who kept Charlotte de la Tremouille, the Countess of Derby, in hiding at the castle of the Peverils in Sir Walter Scott's *Peveril of the Peak*.

Ellinor   Twin sister of Matilda and daughter of Mary, Queen of Scots; her passion for the Earl of Essex (2) prompts Queen Elizabeth to marry her to Lord Arlington (1); she flees to Essex in Ireland and plans to rejoin him in England but lapses into permanent insanity after hearing of his execution in Sophia Lee's *The Recess*.

Elliot   Enthusiastic and talented English tutor of Julian Danvers; he instills in him a love of learning and a high regard for English culture in William Godwin's *Cloudesley*.

Mrs. Elliot   Kindly grandmother of the Elliot household; she is pious with a touch of superstition in Sir Walter Scott's *The Black Dwarf*.

Andrew (Dand, Dandie) Elliot   Dextrous but undisciplined shepherd; he is brother to Christina Elliot and is the youngest of the "Four Black Brothers"; his outrageous spirit and gifted minor verse make him a sought-after local bard in Robert Louis Stevenson's *Weir of Hermiston: An Unfinished Romance*.

Anne Elliot   Selfless, high-principled, and refined twenty-seven-year-old heroine, who was persuaded eight years earlier to break her engagement to Captain Frederick Wentworth, whom she still loves; she encounters him again, regains her bloom and beauty, and is finally reunited with him in Jane Austen's *Persuasion*.

Annot Elliot   Sister of Hobbie (Halbert) Elliot in Sir Walter Scott's *The Black Dwarf*.

Christina Elliot   Dark and lovely youngest daughter of Gilbert Elliot, the son; she is sister to the "Four Black Brothers"; she falls in love with Archibald Weir, an estate lord, in Robert Louis Stevenson's *Weir of Hermiston: An Unfinished Romance*.

Clement (Clem) Elliot   Wealthy and corpulent middle-class Glasgow businessman; he is brother to Christina Elliot and is the third eldest of the "Four Black Brothers" in Robert Louis Stevenson's *Weir of Hermiston: An Unfinished Romance*.

Elizabeth Elliot   Eldest of the three Elliot sisters; cold, proud, and vain, she would like to marry the one man she deems suitable, her father's heir, William Elliot; he disappoints her twice in Jane Austen's *Persuasion*.

Gilbert Elliot   Smuggler, pious disciplinarian, and father of housekeeper Kirstie Elliot in Robert Louis Stevenson's *Weir of Hermiston: An Unfinished Romance*.

Gilbert Elliot (the son)   Farmer of Cauldstaneslap; he is the half-brother of Kirstie Elliot and father of Christina and the "Four Black Brothers"; he dies from the attack of highway robbers in Robert Louis Stevenson's *Weir of Hermiston: An Unfinished Romance*.

Gilbert (Gib) Elliot   Scottish weaver and revolutionary turned schismatic evangelist; he is brother to Christina Elliot and is the second eldest of the "Four Black Brothers" in Robert Louis Stevenson's *Weir of Hermiston: An Unfinished Romance*.

Halbert (Hobbie of the Heugh-foot) Elliot   Substantial Scottish farmer, who is well loved by his family and by Grace Armstrong, his betrothed; blunt, courageous, and shrewd, he enjoys outdoor sports and acts kindly towards Elshender the Recluse (Sir Edward Mauley), earning his friendship and aid, as well as his gold as a wedding gift, in Sir Walter Scott's *The Black Dwarf*.

Harry Elliot   Brother of Hobbie (Halbert) Elliot in Sir Walter Scott's *The Black Dwarf*.

Jean Elliot   Sister of Hobbie (Halbert) Elliot in Sir Walter Scott's *The Black Dwarf*.

John Elliot Brother of Hobbie (Halbert) Elliot in Sir Walter Scott's *The Black Dwarf.*

Kirstie Elliot Capable, healthy, and unmarried housekeeper of the Hermiston estate, sister of a minor but landed farmer, and distant cousin to Mrs. Weir; devoted to Mrs. Weir and her son Archibald, she is jealous of her niece, Christina Elliot, with whom Archibald later falls in love in Robert Louis Stevenson's *Weir of Hermiston: An Unfinished Romance.*

Lilias Elliot Sister of Hobbie (Halbert) Elliot in Sir Walter Scott's *The Black Dwarf.*

Robert (Hob) Elliot Decent and prudent Scottish laird of Cauldestaneslap and church elder; he is brother to Christina Elliot and is the eldest of the "Four Black Brothers" in Robert Louis Stevenson's *Weir of Hermiston: An Unfinished Romance.*

Sir Walter Elliot Widower father of Anne Elliot and her sisters; a handsome baronet, he is vain both of his appearance and his title; his debts force him to rent his estate to Admiral Croft, setting the stage for Anne Elliot's reunion with Captain Wentworth in Jane Austen's *Persuasion.*

William Elliot The heir presumptive of Sir Walter Elliot and the object of Elizabeth Elliot's matrimonial hopes; he behaved insultingly to both at the time of his marriage, years earlier, to a lowbred woman of fortune; now a childless widower, he renews acquaintance with the Elliots, being fearful that Mrs. Clay will marry Sir Walter and produce an heir to the title; he is attracted to Anne Elliot but after her engagement to Captain Wentworth he secures Mrs. Clay by establishing her as his mistress in Jane Austen's *Persuasion.*

Edith Ellis Daughter of Ralph Ellis and pupil of Rose Leicester in George Moore's *The Lake.*

Eliza Ellis Enoch Ellis's flirtatious, self-serving daughter, who attempts to trap Hugh Trevor into a marriage proposal in Thomas Holcroft's *The Adventures of Hugh Trevor.*

Enoch Ellis Vain, servile London cleric, who introduces Hugh Trevor to important persons in the city and who later acts as agent for the bishop in Thomas Holcroft's *The Adventures of Hugh Trevor.*

Ralph Ellis Poet-scholar who hires Rose Leicester as a tutor for his daughter, Edith, then as his secretary; his enlarging her knowledge and outlook arouses the jealousy of Father Oliver Gogarty, who fears he is undermining Rose's faith and morals in George Moore's *The Lake.*

Mrs. Ellison Bawd to the Noble Lord; she houses the Booth family and tries to effect Amelia's ruin using the same scheme that worked on Molly Bennet in Henry Fielding's *Amelia.*

Dorriforth, Lord Elmwood Young and handsome but stubborn Catholic priest, who is granted a papal dispensation from his vows of celibacy in order to marry and keep the title of Elmwood in a Catholic family; despite their religious differences, he is wed to his Protestant ward, Miss Milner, by Sandford; her adultery causes their separation and his disowning their daughter, Matilda, with whom he is finally reunited in Elizabeth Inchbald's *A Simple Story.*

Elmy Honest justice who hears the case brought by Geoffrey Prickle against Captain Samuel Crowe and Sir Launcelot Greaves in Tobias Smollett's *The Adventures of Sir Launcelot Greaves.*

Elphin Fisherman son of Gwythno Garanhir and his successor as king of Caredigon (Wales); his kingdom is too poor to attract enemies until Maelgon, resentful of Elphin's claims for his wife's virtue, imprisons him in Thomas Love Peacock's *The Misfortunes of Elphin.*

Elqidia Sister to the Abbess and a member of Le Convent de Riche Dames; she loves Natura but loses him through the machinations of her sister in Eliza Haywood's *Life's Progress Through the Passions: or, the Adventures of Natura.*

Elshender See Edward Mauley.

Mowbray Elsmere Robert Elsmere's cousin, to whom he owes the living of Murewell in Mrs. Humphry Ward's *Robert Elsmere.*

Robert Elsmere Liberal, idealist Rector of Murewell; he marries Catherine Leyburn, loses his faith, embraces a works-oriented Unitarianism, and dies of cancer in Mrs. Humphry Ward's *Robert Elsmere.*

Augusta Hawkins Elton Disagreeable, self-satisfied, and ill-bred daughter of a tradesman and possessor of a modest fortune; she marries Mr. Elton after his disappointment with Emma Woodhouse; she attempts to patronize Emma and others in Jane Austen's *Emma.*

Philip Elton Conceited clergyman whom Emma Woodhouse fancies in love with Harriet Smith, though he is really, with unsuspected self-interest, courting herself; at her rejection he becomes spiteful and marries a wealthy tradesman's daughter in Jane Austen's *Emma.*

Sarah Elton Evelyn Templeton's former wet-nurse, who reveals Evelyn's parentage to Ernest Maltravers, removing his horrifying conviction that he has been court-ing his own daughter in Edward Bulwer-Lytton's *Alice*.

Rosamund Elvan   Attractive girl who breaks her en-gagement to Norbert Franks and is loved by Will Warburton while trying to support herself as an artist; she marries Franks when she discovers that Will has be-come a grocer in George Gissing's *Will Warburton*.

Dr. Elweys   Village doctor who pronounces Austin Ruthyn dead in J. Sheridan Le Fanu's *Uncle Silas*.

Emanthe   Placentia's woman servant in Eliza Haywood's *Philidore and Placentia; or, L'Amour trop delicat*.

Emanuel   Mr. Mortimer's major domo and the orga-nizer of the slave uprising that aborts Mortimer's plans to wed Matilda; he generously protects Matilda in Sophia Lee's *The Recess*.

Josef Emanuel   M. Paul Emanuel's less forceful half brother, a well-known pianist in Charlotte Brontë's *Vill-ette*.

Paul Carl David Emanuel   A visiting teacher of litera-ture at the school of his cousin, Mme. Beck; he first rec-ommends that Lucy Snowe be hired; he and Lucy fall in love, but his family commitments require him to leave her for three years; on the return voyage it is unlikely that his ship survives a storm at sea in Charlotte Brontë's *Villette*.

Emanuella   Bright and intellectually curious heroine, who enters Pourclairs after her disastrous affair with Emilius; she has a baby by Emilius and dies in Eliza Haywood's *The Rash Resolve; or, the Untimely Discovery*.

Emilia   The hermit's wife's sister, seduced and, later, poisoned by him when her pregnancy threatens exposure in Penelope Aubin's *The Life and Adventures of the Lady Lucy*.

Emilius   Man who is in love with Emanuella but is eas-ily swayed by rumors and abandons her in Eliza Haywood's *The Rash Resolve; or, the Untimely Discovery*.

Joseph Emilius (Mealyus)   A Bohemian Jew who has changed his name and a charismatic, popular London preacher with a knack for making churchgoing pleasant; when Lizzie Eustace has exhausted her list of suitors, she marries him in Anthony Trollope's *The Eustace Diamonds*. She leaves him with an ample settlement for his mainte-nance, but her friend Mr. Bonteen is looking for proof he has a prior wife still living in Prague; though he is finally understood to have been the murderer of Bon-teen, he is not brought to trial for that crime; he is con-victed of bigamy and sent to prison in *Phineas Redux*.

Emily   Blonde, blue-eyed friend and fellow prostitute of Fanny Hill; she began life as a runaway, lost her virginity to a ploughboy, and lapsed into prostitution at Mrs. Cole's, but ultimately returns to her penitent parents in John Cleland's *Memoirs of a Woman of Pleasure*.

Little Em'ly   See Emily Peggotty.

Emma   Maidservant at Manor Farm, Dingley Dell, in Charles Dickens's *The Posthumous Papers of the Pickwick Club*.

Emperor   See Sub-Warden.

Empress   See My Lady.

Martha Endell   Friend of Emily Peggotty from Yarmouth; she becomes a prostitute; she finds Emily and shelters her and later emigrates with the Peggottys in Charles Dickens's *The Personal History of David Copperfield*.

Emily Enderby   Mother of Maud; she attempts suicide after her husband's desertion and remains mentally dis-turbed after she is rejoined by her husband and child in George Gissing's *The Unclassed*.

Mrs. Enderby   Elderly and docile mother of Philip En-derby and Priscilla Rowland; she is used as a pawn in her daughter's manipulative display of power in Harriet Martineau's *Deerbrook*.

Maud Enderby   Ida Starr's friend, a governess at Dr. Tootle's school who is engaged to Osmond Waymark but refuses to marry because she is afraid she will prove to have inherited her mother's madness in George Gissing's *The Unclassed*.

Paul Enderby   Father of Maud; he steals money en-trusted to him, deserts his family, rejoins them after ten years, and is eventually arrested in George Gissing's *The Unclassed*.

Philip Enderby   Son of Mrs. Enderby and brother of Priscilla Rowland; he is nearly separated from his be-loved Margaret Ibbotson by his sister's jealous machina-tions in Harriet Martineau's *Deerbrook*.

Richard Enfield   Reputable gentleman, distant rela-tive, friend, and walking companion to the lawyer Mr. Utterson in Robert Louis Stevenson's *The Strange Case of Dr. Jekyll and Mr. Hyde*.

Engelbrecht   Sentinel at the Varangian barracks in Sir Walter Scott's *Count Robert of Paris*.

Captain England   Pirate with whom Long John Silver

and his parrot sailed before joining Flint in Robert Louis Stevenson's *Treasure Island.*

English Captain   Commander of a vessel whose crew has mutinied; he is helped by Robinson Crusoe and Friday to retake his ship in Daniel Defoe's *The Life and Strange Surprizing Adventures of Robinson Crusoe of York, Mariner.*

English General   Aristocrat of captious and unquiet disposition; accused of cowardice in the face of the enemy, he goes to court to vindicate his character in Charles Johnstone's *Chrysal: or, the Adventures of a Guinea.*

Englishman   Well-bred, middle-aged man, who lives naked among the natives of Africa and engages in the ivory trade; he accompanies Captain Singleton's group in their trip across Africa in Daniel Defoe's *The Life, Adventures, and Pyracies of the Famous Captain Singleton.*

English Tar   Trustworthy, modest, and true man, who is freed by the Inquisitor to assist with the escape of Pheron and Ilissa in Charles Johnstone's *Chrysal: or, The Adventures of a Guinea.*

Mrs. Enville   Blacksmith's wife, who is frustrated in her feelings of superiority toward Dorothy Tugwell by Jeremiah Tugwell's returning home with some money in Richard Graves's *The Spiritual Quixote.*

Envy   One of three men who give evidence against Faithful and Christian at their trial at Vanity Fair in John Bunyan's *The Pilgrim's Progress From this World to That Which Is to Come.*

Eojaeu   King of Ijaveo and father of Eovaai; he is a master of science in Eliza Haywood's *Adventures of Eovaai, Princess of Ijaveo.*

Eovaai   Princess brought up in statecraft; she has few women companions and has not been conditioned to pursue usual female goals; she becomes queen of Ijaveo at fifteen years of age; initially she listens to Ochihatou, but soon perceives her mistake; she must put down a rebellion but ultimately becomes a good ruler in Eliza Haywood's *Adventures of Eovaai, Princess of Ijaveo.*

(Count Delzenburg) Prince Ernest of Eppenweld-Sarkeld   Friend and patron of Richmond Roy and father of Princess Ottilia; he opposes Roy's plans for Harry Richmond and the Princess to be married in George Meredith's *The Adventures of Harry Richmond.*

(Wilhelmina Frederina Hedwig, Countess of Delzenburg) Princess Ottilia of Eppenweld-Sarkeld   Beautiful, idealistic, somewhat ethereal daughter of the German Prince Ernest; Harry Richmond loves and wants to marry her, but she realizes that Janet Ilchester is better suited to him and helps arrange their marriage in George Meredith's *The Adventures of Harry Richmond.*

Eppie (Cass, Marner, Winthrop)   The unacknowledged daughter of Godfrey Cass and his opium-addict wife, Molly; baby Eppie crawls to Silas Marner's house when her mother dies; in Marner's heart, she acts as a substitute for his stolen gold; she later marries Aaron Winthrop and they both take care of Marner in George Eliot's *Silas Marner.*

Erasmus   Son of Gerard and Margaret Brandt; he is destined for greatness in Charles Reade's *The Cloister and the Hearth.*

Sweyn Erickson   Disreputable fisherman, expert at extortion and argument in Sir Walter Scott's *The Pirate.*

Barrington Erle   Party hack and private secretary to William Mildmay and the Whig administration; his constant theme is party loyalty; he warns Phineas Finn against independent action over rotten boroughs in Anthony Trollope's *Phineas Finn.* He is enraged by Finn's shillyshalling over the Church disestablishment issue in *Phineas Redux.* He is a guest of the Pallisers in *The Eustace Diamonds.* He appears in *The Duke's Children.*

Madame d' Ermand   Milliner who is supposed to have been rescued from the monastery and set up in the millinery business by Natura in Eliza Haywood's *Life's Progress Through the Passions: or, the Adventures of Natura.*

Ermengarde   French actress and companion of Clotilde; she entertains Lord Monmouth after his separation from his wife, Lucretia (Colonna), in Benjamin Disraeli's *Coningsby; or, The New Generation.*

Lady Ermengarde   Saxon aunt of Sir Raymond Berenger; she subjects Eveline Berenger, who stays with her when traveling, to nightmarish ritual in Sir Walter Scott's *The Betrothed.*

Ermyntrude   Daughter of Lady Winterbourne in Mrs. Humphry Ward's *Marcella.*

Erne of the Sea Eagles   Chief of the Ravagers; captor of the Hostage of the Rose, he restores her to Hallblithe of the Raven on the Isle of Ransom in William Morris's *The Story of the Glittering Plain.*

Alan Ernescliffe   Naval lieutenant who engages himself to Margaret May, dies in the Loyalty Islands, and leaves a legacy to complete the church at Cocksmoor in Charlotte Yonge's *The Daisy Chain.*

Hector Ernescliffe   Younger brother of Alan

Ernescliffe; he is incorporated into the May family in Charlotte Yonge's *The Daisy Chain*. He marries Blanche May in *The Trial*.

Ernest of Otranto   Prince Tancred's handsome and courteous Italian page in Sir Walter Scott's *Count Robert of Paris*.

Lord Ernolf   Aristocrat who unsuccessfully courts Cecilia Beverley on behalf of his son Lord Derford in Frances Burney's *Cecilia*.

Constance Vernon, Countess of Erpingham   Widow who had renounced Percy Godolphin because of misguided ambition but is finally reunited with him in Edward Bulwer-Lytton's *Godolphin*.

Mr. Erskine   Celebrated Scottish divine in Sir Walter Scott's *Guy Mannering*.

Erskine, Sheriff of Perth   Cool and even-tempered associate of Prestongrange, Lord Advocate of Scotland, in the prosecution of the Appin murder case in Robert Louis Stevenson's *Catriona*.

Mr. Escot   "Deteriorationist," who expresses the belief that the world is headed for ruin; he successfully courts Cephalis Cranium in Thomas Love Peacock's *Headlong Hall*.

Frank Escott   Irish heir to Lord Mount Rorke's title and school friend of Willy Brookes, who invites him to spend a summer's idyll in an artist's studio on the Brookes estate; he falls in love with Maggie Brookes, but their marriage plans fall through because of Mr. Brookes's mercenary approach to the marriage settlement and because of his attentions to his model, barmaid Lizzie Baker, in George Moore's *Spring Days*. In London he shares living quarters with Mike Fletcher and edits a magazine; he persuades Lizzie Baker to marry him, thereby losing his inheritance; nevertheless, he remains happily married, the envy of Mike in *Mike Fletcher*.

Mr. Esdale   Respected military surgeon, who had been imprisoned by Prince Hyder Ali Khan Bahauder and is strongly opposed to Dr. Adam Hartley's attempting to free Menie Gray in Sir Walter Scott's *The Surgeon's Daughter*.

Mr. Eshton   A magistrate who has Mr. Rochester as a house guest and then repays the compliment by taking his family with him to Thornfield in Charlotte Brontë's *Jane Eyre*.

Mrs. Eshton   Well-preserved wife of Mr. Eshton; they have three daughters in Charlotte Brontë's *Jane Eyre*.

Amy Eshton   Lively but child-like eldest daughter of the Eshtons in Charlotte Brontë's *Jane Eyre*.

Louisa Eshton   Second daughter of the Eshtons, more elegant than her elder sister in Charlotte Brontë's *Jane Eyre*.

Lord Eskdale   Lord Monmouth's influential friend, whose political sagacity and strength of character are contrasted with the opportunism and frivolity of characters such as Tadpole and Taper in Benjamin Disraeli's *Coningsby; or, The New Generation*. The trusted friend and adviser to the Duke of Bellamont, he helps to arrange Tancred, Lord Montacute's introduction into society; he assists the duke's schemes to dissuade Tancred from his intention to tour the Holy Land in *Tancred; or, The New Crusade*.

Lord Esmond   Eldest son of Eugene, Earl of Castlewood in William Makepeace Thackeray's *The Virginians*.

Lady Beatrix Esmond   Beautiful daughter of the fourth Viscount Castlewood; Henry Esmond faithfully loves her in spite of her many flirtations, near-engagements, and terminated engagements; her romantic adventures culminate in an escapade with the Chevalier de St. George (the "Old Pretender"), whom she follows to France, returning years later to marry Tom Tusher in William Makepeace Thackeray's *The History of Henry Esmond*. She is the elderly, worldly widow of both Bishop Tusher and the Baron Bernstein; she successively takes to Harry and George Warrington because they resemble their grandfather, Henry Esmond, in *The Virginians*.

Captain Charles Esmond   Younger son of Eugene, Earl of Castlewood in William Makepeace Thackeray's *The Virginians*.

Lady Dorothea Esmond   Daughter of Edward, Earl and Marquis of Castlewood, and heir to his property; she marries Henry Poyns and is ancestress of the Viscounts Castlewood in William Makepeace Thackeray's *The History of Henry Esmond*.

Lady Fanny Esmond   Frivolous younger half sister of Eugene, Earl of Castlewood; she treats Harry Warrington disdainfully in William Makepeace Thackeray's *The Virginians*.

Francis Esmond   Third son of the first Viscount Castlewood; in holy orders, he dies defending Castlewood, the family seat, in 1647; his son, Francis, becomes the fourth Viscount Castlewood in William Makepeace Thackeray's *The History of Henry Esmond*.

Henry Esmond   Noble hero who, brought up as the illegitimate son of the third Viscount Castlewood, is treated kindly by the fourth viscount and his wife; he goes to Cambridge, fights in Europe, quixotically conceals the legitimacy of his birth after it has been revealed to him, and in spite of his much-tried love for Lady Beatrix Esmond marries her widowed mother and emigrates to America in William Makepeace Thackeray's *The History of Henry Esmond.* He is grandfather to George and Harry Warrington in *The Virginians.*

Henry Poyns Esmond Lady Dorothea's husband; he was a page in her family's household before his marriage, when he took the Esmond family name; his son, Francis, becomes first Viscount Castlewood in William Makepeace Thackeray's *The History of Henry Esmond.*

Lady Maria Esmond Middle-aged elder sister of Eugene, Earl of Castlewood; she becomes engaged to Harry Warrington; though his love cools, she does not release him from his engagement until he is supplanted as heir to his mother's property by the arrival of his elder twin brother, George, believed dead in America; she marries the actor Hagan and is thrown off by her family in William Makepeace Thackeray's *The Virginians.*

Rachel Esmond (Madam Esmond, Mrs. Warrington) Daughter of Henry Esmond and his wife Rachel (Viscountess Castlewood); married and widowed, she is called by choice "Madam Esmond"; she is a haughty, aristocratic Tory, who tries to rule her sons, George and Harry Warrington, opposes their marriages, and is estranged from them in William Makepeace Thackeray's *The Virginians.*

Colonel Thomas Esmond Second son of the first Viscount Castlewood, brother of the second, and father of the third; a colonel in the army of King Charles I, he later joins Cromwell in William Makepeace Thackeray's *The History of Henry Esmond.*

William Esmond Drunken younger half brother of Eugene, Earl of Castlewood; he pursues George and Harry Warrington to America and dies a disgraceful death as a spy in William Makepeace Thackeray's *The Virginians.*

Esora Elderly family servant, who heals Jesus with her balsams and helps Joseph of Arimathea conceal Jesus until he is able to join the Essenes in the mountains in George Moore's *The Brook Kerith.*

Lord and Lady Esquart Diana Warwick's happily married friends with whom she travels after her divorce suit is settled in George Meredith's *Diana of the Crossways.*

Lady Essex Peevish daughter of Sir Frederick Walsingham; she marries Sir Philip Sidney and, wid-

owed, the Earl of Essex (2); both husbands despise her in Sophia Lee's *The Recess.*

Sir Walter Devereux, Earl of Essex (1) Queen Elizabeth's commander of forces in Ireland; he marries the daughter of Sir Patrick Lineric in Sophia Lee's *The Recess.*

Earl of Essex (2) Accomplished soldier and favorite of Queen Elizabeth; his marriage to Sir Philip Sidney's widow follows his erroneous belief that his beloved Ellinor has willingly deserted him, and his execution is largely the result of Elizabeth's discovery of his negotiations with King James for Ellinor's release in Sophia Lee's *The Recess.*

Estella Miss Havisham's adopted daughter, educated to torture men with her beauty and femininity but never to fall in love with them; she is revealed to be the daughter of Abel Magwitch and Mr. Jaggers's housekeeper, Molly; Pip Pirrip is hopelessly in love with her despite her scorn in Charles Dickens's *Great Expectations.*

Marguerite, Madame d'Estrees Outrageously fast-living mother of Lady Kitty Ashe; an Irish heiress, born Margaret Fitzgerald, she is twice widowed, her first husband having been Lady Kitty's father, Lord Blackwater; her salons are frequented by artistic and literary society; she marries her long-time companion, Markham Warington, for financial security in Mrs. Humphrey Ward's *The Marriage of William Ashe.*

Mrs. Etoff Lady Bellaston's maid, whose reports of Tom Jones's handsomeness pique the lady's curiosity in Henry Fielding's *The History of Tom Jones.*

Eudaemon Little Alexandrian porter and philosopher, enamored of Hypatia; he befriends Philammon and offers him lodgings in his house, where Miriam secretly rents an apartment; he tries with Philammon to save Hypatia in Charles Kingsley's *Hypatia.*

Eudocia Servant girl of Irene Colocotroni; she marries Cloudesley and conspires with her husband and Richard Danvers (Lord Alton) to raise the disinherited Julian Danvers as if he were her own son in William Godwin's *Cloudesley.*

Eugenius Undefined confidant of Yorick and the narrator and a pragmatist and raissonneur in Laurence Sterne's *The Life and Opinions of Tristram Shandy, Gentleman.* He is mentioned as Yorick's intimate friend in *A Sentimental Journey through France and Italy.*

Eulalie Mlle. Reuter's handsome pupil, who has acquired only a rudimentary education after six years at school in Charlotte Brontë's *The Professor.*

Euodius A comrade and well-wisher of Victoria's father, Majoricus, in Charles Kingsley's *Hypatia*.

Euphrasia Primary interlocutor, who defends Romances, arguing that they may be as meritorious and as useful as Epics; after defending and categorizing Romances and singling out those of special merit and moral value, she proceeds to do the same for Novels in Clara Reeve's *The Progress of Romance*.

European Lady Widow of an English naval officer; she is lost in the forest and is found by the Indian Sovereign; she marries the Army Chaplain in Charles Johnstone's *Chrysal: or, The Adventures of a Guinea*.

Dona Eusebia Wife whom Kenneth Carmichael Ross, Sir Douglas Ross's nephew, brings from Italy; she becomes dissatisfied and bored, fights with her husband, and finally leaves in Caroline Norton's *Old Sir Douglas*.

Eusebius Friend of Nominee to the Mock Monastery; his vanity in his ability to reform people through conversation opens the door for the seduction of his beloved daughter in Charles Johnstone's *Chrysal: or, The Adventures of a Guinea*.

Father Eustace Efficient sub-prior, and then abbot, of the Monastery of St. Mary's of Kennaquhair; sent to advise Abbot Boniface, he succeeds his incompetent predecessor and uses his courage and tact to guide the monastery through the turmoils of the Reformation relatively unscathed in Sir Walter Scott's *The Monastery* and in *The Abbot*.

Sir Florian Eustace Wealthy baronet with a Scottish estate who falls in love with Lizzie Greystock; he dies within a year of the marriage, leaving her well provided for in her own right and mother of an heir to extensive property in Anthony Trollope's *The Eustace Diamonds*.

John Eustace Kindly, fair-minded, sensible brother of the late Sir Florian; he extends his generous view of human motives even to his mercenary sister-in-law, Lizzie Eustace, in Anthony Trollope's *The Eustace Diamonds*.

Lizzie Greystock, Lady Eustace Hard-hearted gold digger, who, after her husband's death, secretes a Eustace-family diamond necklace worth £10,000 and pretends it has been stolen; she entices Lord Fawn, flirts with Frank Greystock, and throws herself at her ideal romantic lover, Lord George de Bruce Carruthers; in the end, her character exposed in the aftermath of a second, successful robbery of the necklace, she settles for a spurious but popular London preacher, Mr. Emilius, in Anthony Trollope's *The Eustace Diamonds*. Having left her husband, she is taken up by the Bonteens, who set out to prove Mr. Emilius a bigamist in *Phineas Redux*. Ferdinand

Lopez tries to involve her in a business venture and in an elopement in *The Prime Minister*. She appears briefly in *The Duke's Children*.

Orlando Eustace Passionate bridegroom, who murders his wife, Belinda Coote, after arguing with her over the merits of her sister Maria's painted fan; he is shot and killed in a struggle with constable John Mansel in Thomas Amory's *The Life of John Buncle, Esq*.

Eutropius Prime minister whose henchman seduces Julian the Apostate, now freed during his incarnation as a slave, into betraying his benefactor, Timasius; he rewards Julian by having him executed in Henry Fielding's *A Journey From This World to the Next*.

William Maxwell, Lord Evandale Young royalist nobleman, who successfully pleads for Henry Morton's life, and whose own life is saved from the Cameronians by Morton; after Morton's exile he becomes engaged to Edith Bellenden; he is killed by Burley (John Balfour) after an ambush directed by Basil Olifant in Sir Walter Scott's *Old Mortality*.

Evangelist Christian's director to the gate through which he must pass to begin his journey; he advises and comforts Christian along the way in John Bunyan's *The Pilgrim's Progress From this World to That Which Is to Come*.

Evans English elephant hunter in Africa; a collector of Kaffir tales, he relates to Allan Quatermain the legend of King Solomon's mines in H. Rider Haggard's *King Solomon's Mines*.

Mr. Evans Miss Coleman's gentleman, who, when brought into her father's firm as a junior partner, influences Mr. Coleman to make unwise and shady investments; after being lost at sea, he is reunited with the Colemans in George MacDonald's *At the Back of the North Wind*.

Gregory Evans Editor of the Carmarthen *Herald* who attacks Henry Jones in several articles concerning his claims to be heir to the Llanfere estate, thereby forcing Jones to bring a libel action; Nicholas Apjohn, the estate lawyer, is therefore empowered to have matters brought into the open in Anthony Trollope's *Cousin Henry*.

Jack Evans Prison turnkey who is changed from a dutiful follower of the cruel jail governor to Francis Eden's helper and a friend of the prisoners in Charles Reade's *It Is Never Too Late to Mend*.

Morgan (Father Parsons) Evans Rascally Jesuit priest, who stays with Eustace Leigh and his father, pretending to be a Welshman; he plots against Queen Elizabeth and marries Don Guzman de Soto to Rose Salterne in Charles Kingsley's *Westward Ho!*.

Richard Evans   Student of Mr. Marton in his second teaching position in Charles Dickens's *The Old Curiosity Shop*.

Eve   Second wife of Adam, created to take Lilith's place; with her husband, she watches over the House of the Dead, to which all of her children must come in George MacDonald's *Lilith*.

Evelyn   Younger son of Lionel Verney and Perdita in Mary Shelley's *The Last Man*.

Mr. Evelyn   A wealthy, honest botanist, who provides financial support that allows Hugh Trevor to pursue a Parliamentary career in Thomas Holcroft's *The Adventures of Hugh Trevor*.

Colonel Markham Everard   Parliamentary soldier; the nephew of Henry Lee, he loves Alice Lee and persuades Oliver Cromwell to return Woodstock Lodge to the Lees; he challenges Charles II to a duel when the king in disguise as Louis Kerneguy attempts to seduce Alice Lee; he is arrested by Cromwell when he refuses to betray Albert Lee and the king; he marries Alice in Sir Walter Scott's *Woodstock*.

Bathsheba Everdene   Willful, spirited heroine who inherits a farm and decides to manage it herself; loved by three men, she unwisely chooses the shallow, deceptive Sergeant Frank Troy, only to discover that he married her for her looks and money; after Troy is killed by Bathsheba's obsessive suitor John Boldwood, she learns the value of Gabriel Oak's love for her and eventually marries him in Thomas Hardy's *Far from the Madding Crowd*.

Augustus, Lord Everingham   Husband of Lady Everingham and a principled Whig politician, who supports the New Poor Law and leads a labor union in Benjamin Disraeli's *Coningsby; or, The New Generation*.

Isabel, Lady Everingham   Clever and charming married daughter of the Duke of Beaumanoir and friend of Harry Coningsby, whom she introduces to aristocratic society in Benjamin Disraeli's *Coningsby; or, The New Generation*.

Evelyn Evremonde   Wife sheltered by the Jocelyns from her deranged husband in George Meredith's *Evan Harrington*.

Captain Lawson Evremonde   The mentally deranged husband of Evelyn; he receives a letter forged by Louisa

Harrington, Countess of Saldar, informing him his wife is at Beckley in George Meredith's *Evan Harrington*.

Ewan of Brigglands   Capable Highlander in charge of the captured Rob Roy MacGregor; on the way to prison, the outlaw convinces Ewan to free him in Sir Walter Scott's *Rob Roy*.

Antony (Nanty) Ewart   Smuggler and ship's captain, who transports the kidnapped Darsie Latimer (Arthur Redgauntlet) into Cumberland and is shot by Cristal Nixon for threatening to inform Hugh Redgauntlet of Nixon's treachery but kills Nixon before he dies himself in Sir Walter Scott's *Redgauntlet*.

Ewdwyn   Monk of Saint Mary's Priory who dies before he can testify to the burial of Reginald de Folville in Ann Radcliffe's *Gaston de Blondeville*.

Exciseman   Frequenter of the Black Bear in Sir Walter Scott's *Rob Roy*.

Exciseman   Traveler on the wagon who seizes the Ale-Wife's bottle until he knows whether the duty has been paid in Charles Johnstone's *Chrysal: or, The Adventures of a Guinea*.

Exilius   A Sardinian, an excellent soldier, and the titular hero of Jane Barker's *Exilius; or, The Banish'd Roman*.

Experience   One of four Shepherds who show Christian and Hopeful, and later Christiana and her party, the hills of Error, Caution, and Clear, and advise them on their journey in John Bunyan's *The Pilgrim's Progress From this World to That Which Is to Come*.

Baron d' Eyrac   Natura's benefactor, who gets him a place in the army and gives him money in Eliza Haywood's *Life's Progress Through the Passions: or, the Adventures of Natura*.

Jane Eyre   Orphan who is brought up by her uncle's tyrannical widow, Mrs. Reed, before she is sent to Lowood School, where she becomes a teacher after six years; she takes a position as governess to the ward of Mr. Rochester, with whom she falls in love; she agrees to marry him, but the ceremony is halted, and to avoid becoming his mistress, Jane flees to a remote town, where she teaches school and lives with a family who have befriended her and turn out to be her cousins; she is finally reuinted with the widowed Mr. Rochester in Charlotte Brontë's *Jane Eyre*.

John Eyre   Jane's wealthy uncle, a wine merchant in the West Indies; he sends a solicitor to warn Jane of the existence of Rochester's mad wife; he also leaves his fortune to her in Charlotte Brontë's *Jane Eyre*.

F

Lady F—— A married woman whose "intrigue" with Arthur Huntingdon is perceived by him as the beginning of his corruption in Anne Brontë's *The Tenant of Wildfell Hall*.

Lord F—— A married nobleman, a charming dancer, and one of the two principal admirers of Rosalie Murray at her coming-out ball; his wife is annoyed with him for his conduct in Anne Brontë's *Agnes Grey*.

Gabriel Faa Gypsy nephew of Meg Merriles; he assists her in restoring Henry Bertram to his inheritance in Sir Walter Scott's *Guy Mannering*.

Julius Faber Elderly physician, who cedes his practice to Allen Fenwick in Edward Bulwer-Lytton's *A Strange Story*.

Don Fabin Friend of Emanuella in Eliza Haywood's *The Rash Resolve; or, the Untimely Discovery*.

Don Fabio A gentleman of Florence and an indulgent father to his only son, Aurelian; he has contracted for Aurelian's marriage in order to end a long-standing feud in William Congreve's *Incognita*.

Fabius Brother of Clelia and husband of Scipiana in Jane Barker's *Exilius; or, The Banish'd Roman*.

Signor Fabroni A young Venetian nobleman of high rank, whom Arthur Danvers, Lord Alton challenges to a duel because of insulting remarks he makes concerning the behavior of the Greeks in the recently concluded war; in the subsequent swordfight he kills his English foe in William Godwin's *Cloudesley*.

(Gold-mane) Face-of-god Warrior of Burgdale who makes contact with Kindred of the Wolf in Shadowy Vale and, as War-leader, assists them to reclaim Silver-dale from the Dusky Men (Huns); he marries Sun-beam in William Morris's *The Roots of the Mountains*.

Samuel Faddle Friend of Tom Tringle and fellow club crony; he takes Tom's challenge to a duel to Jonathan Stubbs and is snubbed for his pains in Anthony Trollope's *Ayala's Angel*.

Fadge An editor hated by Alfred Yule; Jasper Milvain succeeds him as editor and as object of hatred in George Gissing's *New Grub Street*.

Captain Jack Fagan Witness of the duel between Redmond Barry and Captain Quin and later Barry's patron in the army in William Makepeace Thackeray's *The Luck of Barry Lyndon*.

Nicholas Faggot Justice Foxley's law clerk, who reviews the laws broken by Hugh Redgauntlet when Peter Peebles identifies him in Sir Walter Scott's *Redgauntlet*.

Annie Ridd Faggus John Ridd's younger sister, who is also his closest friend and understands him better than anyone else; she is a wonderful cook, very pretty, a good, kind person, and the pride of the county; she is wife of Tom Faggus in R. D. Blackmore's *Lorna Doone*.

Tom Faggus John Ridd's cousin, a rebel and a legendary highwayman turned cattleman; Tom is intelligent, always a gentleman, and well liked by the nobility; he respects and likes John, even though they clash at times in R. D. Blackmore's *Lorna Doone*.

Fagin Red-haired, villainous-looking, shriveled old Jew, who operates a thievery ring made up of boys; he takes in Oliver Twist to make him part of the ring and trains him in the art of picking pockets; he also works with Monks (Edward Leeford) to find Oliver after the boy is taken away; he is finally hanged in Charles Dickens's *Oliver Twist*.

Mr. Fairbrother Effie Deans's counselor during her trial in Sir Walter Scott's *The Heart of Midlothian*.

Alice Fairfax A kindly, cheerful relative of Mr. Rochester; she keeps house for him at Thornfield Hall and becomes a companion for Jane Eyre in Charlotte Brontë's *Jane Eyre*.

Guy Fairfax Intimate and correspondent of Coke Clifton; he assists Coke in his attempt to ruin Anna St. Ives and Frank Henley in Thomas Holcroft's *Anna St. Ives*.

Isabella Fairfax Poor but beautiful gleaner who marries a squire in an anecdote told by a farmer in Richard Graves's *The Spiritual Quixote*.

Jane Fairfax Lovely, elegant, and accomplished niece of Miss Bates; an orphan without fortune, though reared by the well-off Campbell family, she has been educated to earn her living as a governess; she is secretly engaged to Frank Churchill and is tormented by his pseudo-courtship of Emma Woodhouse in Jane Austen's *Emma*.

Sir Thomas Fairfax Roundhead military leader who is fearless and strict in discipline; he is elected general of the army after the New Model Army is introduced in Daniel Defoe's *Memoirs of a Cavalier*.

Mr. Fairfield Dr. Harrison's friend, a sober, sensible

squire, who is running against Colonel Trompington for mayor in Henry Fielding's *Amelia*.

Jane Fairfield   Leonora Avenel's sister, who has raised Leonard Fairfield as her own son in Edward Bulwer-Lytton's *"My Novel," by Pisistratus Caxton*.

Leonard Fairfield   Writer of genius who has been raised as the son of plain country folk but is revealed as the son of Leonora Avenel and Audley Egerton; he marries Helen Digby in Edward Bulwer-Lytton's *"My Novel," by Pisistratus Caxton*.

Margery Fairfield   Wife of a deer poacher and smuggler; she lives in the New Forest, provides lodgings for Juliet Granville during her flight, and marries Ambroise after her husband is hanged in Frances Burney's *The Wanderer*.

William Fairfield   Kind but not very wise curate of the parish at Knowl; he speaks highly of Silas Ruthyn to his ward, Maud Ruthyn, in J. Sheridan Le Fanu's *Uncle Silas*.

Alan Fairford   Young Scottish barrister, who receives his first brief, flees the court to search for his friend Darsie Latimer (Arthur Redgauntlet), and finds himself a prisoner of Jacobite rebels in Sir Walter Scott's *Redgauntlet*.

Alexander (Saunders) Fairford   Scottish barrister and father of Alan; he is relieved that Darsie Latimer (Arthur Redgauntlet) is out of his house and anxious that Alan succeed at the bar in Sir Walter Scott's *Redgauntlet* .

Mr. Fairlawn   Elderly master of the Hitchin Hunt who confronts Mr. Harkaway's team at the Cumberlow Green meet in Anthony Trollope's *Mr. Scarborough's Family*.

Mr. Fairlie   Publisher, primarily of religious works; Ruth Pontifex's brother-in-law, he takes George Pontifex on as apprentice and makes George his heir in Samuel Butler's *The Way of All Flesh*.

Frederick Fairlie   Selfish hypochondriac owner of Limmeridge House in Cumberland who insists that his niece marry Sir Percival Glyde; the baronet ill-treats her, confining her in an asylum, and Fairlie refuses to acknowledge her, insisting that she is an imposter named Anne Catherick, whom she closely resembles; he is forced at last to recognize her as his heir in Wilkie Collins's *The Woman in White*.

Laura Fairlie   Charming, ingenuous ward and niece of Frederick Fairlie and half sister to both Marian Halcombe and the illegitimate Anne Catherick, her double; she is married to Sir Percival Glyde, who plots with Count Fosco to seize her fortune; drugged, she is dressed in Anne's clothes and incarcerated in an asylum from which

Marian Halcombe rescues her; after Glyde's death she marries Walter Hartright in Wilkie Collins's *The Woman in White*.

Philip Fairlie   The late father of Laura, Lady Glyde and, following an affair with Mrs. Catherick, of Anne Catherick in Wilkie Collins's *The Woman in White*.

Mr. Fairman   Henry Fairman's uncle, who employs Frederic Vaughan and shuns Bryan Perdue because of his gambling in Thomas Holcroft's *The Memoirs of Bryan Perdue*.

Henry Fairman   Bryan Perdue's kind and virtuous schoolmate, who later becomes a lawyer and represents Bryan in his forgery trial in Thomas Holcroft's *The Memoirs of Bryan Perdue*.

Marianne Fairman   Henry Fairman's young and virtuous wife in Thomas Holcroft's *The Memoirs of Bryan Perdue*.

Mr. Fairscribe   Lawyer and friend of Mr. Croftangery; he suggests the story of his relative, Menie Gray, as interesting material for his friend's book in Sir Walter Scott's *The Surgeon's Daughter*.

Kate Fairscribe   Youngest daughter of Mr. Fairscribe; she relates the story of Menie Gray to Mr. Croftangery in Sir Walter Scott's *The Surgeon's Daughter*.

Andrew Fairservice   A prejudiced Scotch Presbyterian and Sir Hildebrand Osbaldistone's lazy gardener, who becomes Francis Osbaldistone's servant; his shrewdness and sense of humor are counterbalanced by his cowardliness and dishonesty; discharged by Francis, he refuses to leave, continuing to argue with and advise his master in Sir Walter Scott's *Rob Roy*.

Charlotte (Charlie) Fairstairs   Young friend of Mrs. Greenow at Yarmouth; through her planning, Charlotte is provided with a husband, Samuel Cheesacre, in Anthony Trollope's *Can You Forgive Her?*.

Richard Fairthorn   Guy Darrell's companion, who is marvelously gifted with the flute; he attempts to prevent the marriage of Sophy and Lionel Haughton in Edward Bulwer-Lytton's *What Will He Do With It? by Pisistratus Caxton*.

Earl of Fairville   Nobleman who marries the daughter of the Marquis of Mushroom and dies dancing a hornpipe in William Beckford's *Modern Novel Writing; or, the Elegant Enthusiast*.

Wilhelmina, Countess of Fairville   Dowager, vain of her interior decorating skills; she discovers herself to be the mother of Arabella Bloomville; her lost daughter's identity is confirmed by a strawberry mark in William Beckford's *Modern Novel Writing; or, the Elegant Enthusiast*.

Timothy Fairway　Lighthearted furze cutter and voice of rural wisdom on Egdon Heath in Thomas Hardy's *The Return of the Native*.

Faithful　Christian's fellow pilgrim from the City of Destruction; he meets Christian after emerging from the Valley of the Shadow of Death; he tells Christian of events in the City and travels with him to Vanity Fair, where he is burned at the stake in John Bunyan's *The Pilgrim's Progress From this World to That Which Is to Come*.

Admiral Fakenham　Henrietta (Fakenham) Kirby's father, much taken with Carinthia Kirby, Henrietta's sister-in-law; he is delighted when Carinthia marries Lord Fleetwood; when she is deserted by her new husband, he attempts to protect her despite his ill-health in George Meredith's *The Amazing Marriage*.

Lieutenant Fakenham　Pompous officer in Redmond Barry's regiment; his illness in Germany provides an escape for Barry, who adopts his identity in William Makepeace Thackeray's *The Luck of Barry Lyndon*.

Henrietta Fakenham　Admiral Fakenham's daughter, who marries Chillon Kirby rather than wealthy Lord Fleetwood but misses the life in wealthy society denied her by Kirby's poverty; in narrowly escaping seduction by Lord Brailstone she suffers a scar to her beauty that proves a blessing to her and to her sister-in-law, Carinthia (Kirby), in George Meredith's *The Amazing Marriage*.

Emir Fakreddin　Pious, devoted father of the exquisite Nouronihar; he tries to prevent Vathek from marrying her by feigning the deaths of his daughter and Gulchenrouz; she escapes and joins Vathek in William Beckford's *Vathek*.

Emir Fakredeen　A prince of Lebanon, foster brother of Eva Besso, and companion to Tancred, Lord Montacute; he is a boisterous and ambitious Syrian, whose unscrupulous schemes for independence cause turmoil during Tancred's visit in Benjamin Disraeli's *Tancred; or, The New Crusade*.

Mr. Falconer　Quarrelsome and stupid Laird of Balmawhapple; he joins Prince Charles Stuart's cavalry and escorts Edward Waverly to Holyrood Palace in Sir Walter Scott's *Waverly*.

Algernon Falconer　(caricature of Percy Bysshe Shelley) Figure of romantic high-mindedness; he first lives in Platonic felicity with seven "vestal virgin" sisters; later he marries Morgana Gryll in Thomas Love Peacock's *Gryll Grange*.

Falieri　Youthful conspirator against Doge Andreas; he is trapped and exposed by Abellino/Flodoardo (Count Rosalvo) in Matthew Lewis's *The Bravo of Venice*.

Ferdinando Falkland　A squire and Caleb Williams's employer; he is known for his great chivalry and kindness and is revered in his town, but it is his love of his untarnished reputation that leads him to commit crimes against Barnabas Tyrrel, the Hawkinses, and finally Caleb Williams; he finally admits to his crimes, but it is too late, and Caleb's life is destroyed in William Godwin's *Caleb Williams*.

Captain John (Rupert) Falkner　Aristocratic Indian cavalry officer, whose foolhardy abduction of his lover, Alithea Neville, results in her accidental death and his guilt and despair; the nurturing love of his adopted daughter, Elizabeth Raby, and a public confession assuage his misery in Mary Shelley's *Falkner*.

Douglas, Lord Falloden　Aristocratic, proud Oxford scholar, who loses his fortune through his father's financial dealings; he nearly loses the love of Lady Connie Bledlow through his own insensitivity to the feelings of others, but he learns his lesson and all ends well in Mrs. Humphry Ward's *Lady Connie*.

Downe Falvey　Eminent harpist, who plays at Terelah O Crohane's home during John Buncle's visit in Thomas Amory's *The Life of John Buncle, Esq.*

Fan　Ebenezer Scrooge's younger sister, who persuades her harsh father to allow Ebenezer's return home from school, and whose tenderheartedness is reincarnated in her son Fred in Charles Dickens's *A Christmas Carol*.

Violet Fane　Lady Madeline Trevor's beautiful, consumptive cousin, who dies just after Vivian Grey declares his love to her, a tragedy which sends him wandering throughout Germany and Austria in Benjamin Disraeli's *Vivian Grey*.

Mr. Fang　Magistrate who hears Mr. Brownlow's case against Oliver Twist after the boy is mistakenly arrested for picking Mr. Brownlow's pocket in Charles Dickens's *Oliver Twist*.

Fanny　Mr. Helstone's servant at Briarfield Rectory in Charlotte Brontë's *Shirley*.

Miss Fanny　Lady to whom Conny Keyber dedicates his novel in Henry Fielding's *An Apology for the Life of Mrs. Shamela Andrews*.

Captain Fanshawe　Ginevra's father, a gentleman and an officer on half-pay in Charlotte Brontë's *Villette*.

Catherine Fanshaw Friend of Emilia Fitzcharles Deloraine; she serves as nanny and surrogate mother to her namesake, Catherine Deloraine, during the extended absence of the parents following the child's birth in William Godwin's *Deloraine*.

Ginevra Fanshawe A pretty but vain pupil at Mme. Beck's school who meets Lucy Snowe on the ferry crossing; she encouraged Dr. John Bretton but elopes with Alfred de Hamal in Charlotte Brontë's *Villette*.

Mrs. Farebrother The Reverend Camden Farebrother's mother, who still lives with her son; she constantly gives advice on every subject in George Eliot's *Middlemarch*.

Camden Farebrother Kindly and popular Vicar of St. Botolph's and Rector of Lowick, who develops a friendship with Dr. Lydgate; he has a bad habit of gambling at cards; after Edward Casaubon's death, he moves with his family to Lowick Manor at the request of Dorothea (Brooke); although he is love with Mary Garth, he delivers Fred Vincy's proposal in George Eliot's *Middlemarch*.

Winifred Farebrother Spinster sister of the Reverend Camden Farebrother; she lives with him in George Eliot's *Middlemarch*.

Donald Farfrae Michael Henchard's young, talented, and good-hearted friend and business manager; after they quarrel, he becomes Henchard's business rival, and his fortunes rise as Henchard's decline; he succeeds Henchard as mayor and marries Henchard's former lover, Lucetta Le Sueur; after her death he marries Henchard's stepdaughter in Thomas Hardy's *The Mayor of Casterbridge*.

Farina Poor youth who, despite his refusal to join the White Rose Club, is dedicated to Margarita Groschen; his loyalty to her is made evident, and when he invents eau de cologne so that Kaiser Heinrich may enter the city despite the smell that the devil has left in the city, the Kaiser awards Farina Margarita's hand in George Meredith's *Farina*.

Marquis of Farintosh Grandest suitor of Ethel Newcome, whom in spite of his colorless stupidity she nearly marries in William Makepeace Thackeray's *The Newcomes*. He is mentioned in *The Adventures of Philip on His Way through the World*.

Farmer Owner of Hunter's farm; he directs the narrator, Sylvie, and Bruno to his house; he relates the story of Willie, an alcoholic, in Lewis Carroll's *Sylvie and Bruno Concluded*.

Farmer Rich and kind son of a servant to Lady Lucy's

family, whom he provides with shelter after their castle has been plundered in Penelope Aubin's *The Life and Adventures of the Lady Lucy*.

Farmer Man to whom Hugh Trevor is first apprenticed; he beats and abuses his animals, family, and Hugh despite his benevolent intentions in Thomas Holcroft's *The Adventures of Hugh Trevor*.

Walter Farquhar Mr. Bradshaw's partner, betrothed to and later husband of Jemima Bradshaw; his tolerance and good sense provide solutions to the problems involving Richard Bradshaw; he also works to reconcile Mr. Bradshaw and the Benson household in Elizabeth Gaskell's *Ruth*.

Mary Collet Farrar Daughter of Nicholas Farrar and known as one of the "Nuns of Gidding"; she is admired by John Inglesant and dies in a convent in Paris in J. Henry Shorthouse's *John Inglesant, A Romance*.

Nicholas Farrar Founder of the "Protestant Nunnery" at Gidding and father of Mary Collet Farrar; he is a writer and translator of devotional books in J. Henry Shorthouse's *John Inglesant, A Romance*.

Major Farrel Irish officer in the Austrian army who befriends Renaldo de Melvil; he helps rescue Renaldo's sister and marries her in Tobias Smollett's *The Adventures of Ferdinand Count Fathom*.

Lady Selina Farrell Middle-aged, rich daughter of a peer; she marries Harry Wharton in Mrs. Humphry Ward's *Marcella*.

Grace Farren Scrupulous housewife of William Farren and mother of several children in Charlotte Brontë's *Shirley*.

William Farren A Yorkshireman and member of Barraclough's group who has genuine concern for the welfare of the workers and is therefore treated more leniently when the revolt is quelled in Charlotte Brontë's *Shirley*.

Didymus Farrow Basketmaker in Cowfold and a widower aged thirty; he marries Miriam Tacchi after she abandons her nursing apprenticeship; he helps her learn astronomy in Mark Rutherford's *Miriam's Schooling*.

Father of the Young Beauty A wise man who visits the Rake and requests that he no longer visit the Young Beauty as they are separated from any possible marriage by fortune, family, and religion in Charles Johnstone's *Chrysal: or, The Adventures of a Guinea*.

Father Time The uncannily perceptive and despondent child of Jude Fawley and Arabella Donn; he hangs himself and his half brother and sister when he learns from his stepmother, Sue Bridehead, of the family's poverty, leaving a note that explains "Done because we are too menny" in Thomas Hardy's *Jude the Obscure.*

Isabella Fatherlans   Daughter of a penniless laird; she marries Claud Walkinshaw's son Charles; Claud uses this marriage (which he forbade) as an excuse to disinherit his son in John Galt's *The Entail.*

Fatout   French valet of Mr. Listless in Thomas Love Peacock's *Nightmare Abbey.*

Orlando Faulkland   Chivalrous suitor of Sidney Bidulph and best friend of Sir George Bidulph; through multiple misunderstandings, especially his entanglements with Miss Burchell and ultimately his own death in Holland (a possible suicide), he is kept forever apart from his beloved in Frances Sheridan's *Memoirs of Miss Sidney Bidulph.*

Orlando Jefferis Faulkland   Son of Miss Burchell and Orlando Faulkland; Sidney Bidulph Arnold entrusts him to Mr. Price after Mr. Faulkland's death in Frances Sheridan's *Memoirs of Miss Sidney Bidulph.*

Mephistopheles (Mesty) Faust   Freed slave, allegedly originally an African prince and now serving in the Royal Navy, who becomes the devoted servant of Jack Easy in Captain Frederick Marryat's *Mr. Midshipman Easy.*

Fausta   Emperor Zeno's mistress, with whom Julian the Apostate, in his incarnation as a general, conspires to confer various military appointments on those courtiers who can bribe the highest in Henry Fielding's *A Journey From This World to the Next.*

Faustina   The beautiful, scandalous wife of the Roman Emperor Marcus Aurelius; she is also known for her benevolence in establishing the first Roman orphanages in Walter Pater's *Marius the Epicurean.*

Faustus   Young deacon who routs the Ausurians at Myrsinitis with their leader's sword in Charles Kingsley's *Hypatia.*

Drusilla Fawley   Stern but goodhearted great-aunt who solely raised her orphaned nephew, Jude Fawley, in Thomas Hardy's *Jude the Obscure.*

Jude Fawley   Stonemason whose lifelong ambition is to become a scholar in the university city of Christminster; he errs in marrying the sensual Arabella Donn and then in living out of wedlock with his cousin, Sue Bridehead; both women desert him, leaving Jude brokenhearted, his

romantic and intellectual aspirations unrealized in Thomas Hardy's *Jude the Obscure.*

Fawn   Creature that accompanies Alice out of the wood where things have no names; when each has regained identity, it runs away in alarm in Lewis Carroll's *Through the Looking-Glass.*

Lady Fawn   Bemused mother of Lord Fawn, Mrs. Hittaway, and seven younger daughters; she employs Lucy Morris as governess and tries to obstruct Frank Greystock's vacillating courtship of Lucy, who resents the interference but loves Lady Fawn for her concern and affection in Anthony Trollope's *The Eustace Diamonds.*

Frederick, Viscount Fawn   Vacuous and timid nobleman who serves in minor governmental offices without distinction; having seven unmarried sisters, he courts the heiress Violet Effingham in Anthony Trollope's *Phineas Finn.* Vamped by the rich widow Lizzie Eustace, he proposes and then extricates himself from the engagement with great difficulty in *The Eustace Diamonds.* He thinks of marriage to Marie Goesler as solution to his financial woes; his evidence against Phineas Finn, central to the Bonteen murder case, breaks down on cross-examination to his great humiliation in *Phineas Redux.* He appears briefly in *The Prime Minister.*

Mr. Fax   (caricature of Thomas Robert Malthus) Economist who continually extols the virtues of population control in Thomas Love Peacock's *Melincourt.*

Marion Fay   Devoted daughter of Zachary; loved by Lord Hampstead, she persistently rejects his love because she knows she is dying of consumption; realizing she loves him, she bravely advises him to take a voyage and, still renouncing him, she dies in Anthony Trollope's *Marion Fay.*

Zachary Fay   Senior clerk of a city firm of commision agents; a Quaker, he lives by a doctrine of absolute truth; a widower, he lives in Holloway with his adoring only child, Marion, in Anthony Trollope's *Marion Fay.*

Euphane Fea   Elderly sibyl who keeps house at Burgh Westra in Sir Walter Scott's *The Pirate.*

Fearing   Man from the town of Stupidity; his fear and consequent delay and suffering are described by Greatheart in John Bunyan's *The Pilgrim's Progress From this World to That Which Is to Come.*

John Featherhead   Sir Kittlecourt's successful opponent, elected to Parliament by friends of the new administration in Sir Walter Scott's *Guy Mannering.*

Mr. Feathernest   (caricature of Robert Southey)

Trader of his conscience for a place on the exchange in Thomas Love Peacock's *Melincourt*.

Jonah Featherstone   A brother of Peter Featherstone; his hopes of inheritance are disappointed in George Eliot's *Middlemarch*.

Peter Featherstone   The rich old uncle of Fred and Rosamond Vincy; he is tended on his deathbed by Mary Garth and surrounded by greedy relatives, whom he delights in tormenting by not discussing the particulars of his will in George Eliot's *Middlemarch*.

Solomon Featherstone   Peter Featherstone's brother; he is awaiting Peter's death even though he believes that Peter has left the bulk of his fortune to Mary Garth; later, he causes the tenant farmers to join the protest against the railroad in George Eliot's *Middlemarch*.

Feeble-mind   Pilgrim rescued by Great-heart from the giant Slay-good; with Ready-to-halt he joins Christiana and her party in John Bunyan's *The Pilgrim's Progress From this World to That Which Is to Come*.

Mr. Feeder, B.A.   Dr. Blimber's assistant at the school; he grinds learning into the boys, turning them into misanthropes; he marries Cornelia Blimber in Charles Dickens's *Dombey and Son*.

Alfred Feeder, M.A.   Mr. Feeder's clergyman brother; he officiates at the wedding of Mr. Feeder and Cornelia Blimber in Charles Dickens's *Dombey and Son*.

Lord Feenix (Cousin Feenix)   Elderly aristocrat, who is a nephew of Mrs. Skewton; he lends his protection to Edith (Granger) Dombey after she deserts her husband, Paul Dombey, in Charles Dickens's *Dombey and Son*.

Felbamko   Violent, unpopular nephew and presumed heir of Oniwheske; he is slain in self-defense by Peter Wilkins in Robert Paltock's *The Life and Adventures of Peter Wilkins*.

Felicia   Young London woman who corresponds with a friend at home; she discovers the virtues of living in the country; her hand is sought by two admirers, which poses problems of picking the right husband and resolving a conflict between her love for a man and her duty to her father; as Lucius Manly's wife, she copes with the discovery that her husband has an illegitimate child and learns the dangers of judging only from appearances in Mary Collyer's *Felicia to Charlotte*.

Felicia's Cousin   Rakish young squire not improved by his European travels; he pretends to have reformed in hopes of marrying Marilla Manly, but she is not fooled;

he reverts to his usual behavior until a brush with death causes sincere reform in Mary Collyer's *Felicia to Charlotte*.

Felix   Trusted servant of Basil in George Gissing's *Veranilda*.

Lord Fellamar   Gullible nobleman enamored of Sophia Western; he attempts to follow Lady Bellaston's suggestions first to ravish Sophia Western, then to get rid of his rival, Tom Jones, by having him abducted into a ship's service in Henry Fielding's *The History of Tom Jones*.

Herbert Fellingham   A clever, intelligent journalist, suitor of Annette Smith; he finally wins her hand after Martin Tinman's numerous faults become apparent to her father in George Meredith's *The House on The Beach*.

Duke of the Fellowship of the Dry Tree   Massive leader, who helps Ralph escape from the Burg of the Four Friths; later he insanely haunts the cave where the Lady of Abundance was killed; he attacks Ursula and is slain by Ralph and Richard in William Morris's *The Well at the World's End*.

Mr. Felton   Prisoner who guides Sir Launcelot Greaves through London debtors' prison and tells the story of Captain and Mrs. Clewline in Tobias Smollett's *The Adventures of Sir Launcelot Greaves*.

Dartrey Fenellan   A widower, the overseer of Victor Radnor's finances; a non-conformist, he is rejected as a possible marriage prospect for Nesta by Victor, but eventually he and Nesta, who have a natural attraction for each other as independent spirits, fall in love and marry in George Meredith's *One of Our Conquerors*.

John Fenne   Foe of Sir Daniel Brackley; he watches Till River ferry to prevent any of his men crossing, shoots Dick Shelton's horse, and capsizes the ferry in Robert Louis Stevenson's *The Black Arrow: A Tale of Two Roses*.

Miss Fennimore   Scholarly, demanding governess to the Fulmort sisters; she is converted from agnosticism to Christianity in Charlotte Yonge's *Hopes and Fears*.

Ann Fentham   Wife of Richard Fentham and friend of Lady Isabella Thynne; she becomes involved in a harmless romantic intrigue in J. Henry Shorthouse's *John Inglesant, A Romance*.

Richard Fentham   Gentleman from Oxford and husband of Ann Fentham; a member of the Prince's Council, he is in great trust with King Charles I in J. Henry Shorthouse's *John Inglesant, A Romance*.

Fenton   Country lawyer and a friend of Fillet; he helps

Sir Launcelot Greaves deal with Justice Gobble in Tobias Smollett's *The Adventures of Sir Launcelot Greaves*.

Miss Fenton   Beautiful but boring heiress, whose temperament contrasts with that of the vivacious and independent Miss Milner; Dorriforth proposes to her but leaves her to enter a nunnery and marries Miss Milner in Elizabeth Inchbald's *A Simple Story*.

Mr. Fenton   See Henry Clinton.

Mrs. Fenton   Innkeeper who, with her customers, comically embarrasses some of Gudetown's "respectable" citizens in John Galt's *The Provost*.

Allen Fenwick   Young physician, who represents the image of the intellect; he falls under the influence of Louis Grayle and marries Lilian Ashleigh in Edward Bulwer-Lytton's *A Strange Story*.

Frank Fenwick   Zealous, good humored vicar, who works to prove that Sam Brattle did not murder Farmer Trumbull; by not evicting the Brattle family he falls afoul of the Marquis of Trowbridge, who has a Methodist chapel built at the vicarage gates to spite Fenwick; he helps trace Carry Brattle and bring her home in Anthony Trollope's *The Vicar of Bullhampton*.

Janet Fenwick   Efficient, capable parson's wife committed to parish work; she tries unsuccessfully to bring about a marriage between her friend Mary Lowther and the squire, Harry Gilmore, in Anthony Trollope's *The Vicar of Bullhampton*.

Richard Fenwick   Harriet Byron's adoring rejected suitor, whose former conquests of women make him unacceptable to her in Samuel Richardson's *Sir Charles Grandison*.

Ferdinand   Correspondent with Theodosius on the subject of wit and judgment in Sarah Fielding's *Familiar Letters between the Principal Characters of David Simple and Some Others*.

Ferdinand   Virtuous twin of Cordelia and the beloved of Portia; following his father's rejection of him, at the instigation of his brother Oliver, he seeks his fortune in Barbados and returns wealthy to marry Portia in Sarah Fielding's *The Cry*.

Ferdinand (Ferdinand Count Fathom, Grieve)   Bastard child of an English camp follower; he seduces many women in various schemes to defraud people from Vienna to London; he flees Paris with Don Diego de Zelos's jewels, is arrested in England as the son of the Stuart Pretender, defrauds and debauches in his disguise as a music master and a physician, and is imprisoned when he cannot raise money to pay legal expenses; rescued by Renaldo de Melvil, he deceives Renaldo into a separation from Monimia (Serafina de Zelos); he marries Sarah Muddy for her fortune, is sued by Sarah for bigamy, returns to prison, is released and nursed to health by Elenor, and receives forgiveness from all when he repents in Tobias Smollett's *The Adventures of Ferdinand Count Fathom*. He is the apothecary Grieve, who has a daughter named Seraphina Melvilia in *The Expedition of Humphry Clinker*.

Princess Ferdinanda Joanna Maria   Child who fears touching Aldrovandus Magnus's realistic rendering of Moses's burning bush, making her the first to recognize the painter's merits in William Beckford's *Biographical Memoirs of Extraordinary Painters*.

Fergusano   Scots sorcerer consulted by Hermione; he provides her with a love potion for Prince Cesario and counsels Cesario to marry her; he and Hermione attempt to manipulate the prince's campaign against the king for their own ambitions in Aphra Behn's *Love Letters Between a Nobleman and His Sister*.

Ferguson   Henry Lambert's military friend, who assists with the preparation of a ghostly banquet in a ruined abbey in William Beckford's *Modern Novel Writing; or, the Elegant Enthusiast*.

Mrs. Fergusson   Irish teacher at Swanley, the agricultural college where Rachel Henderson received her training in Mrs. Humphry Ward's *Harvest*.

Esther Fergusson   Mrs. Barton's sister, who ran away with an army officer; abandoned and now a prostitute rejected by her family, she warns Jem Wilson about Harry Carson and provides the clue that tells Mary Barton her father is the real murderer in Elizabeth Gaskell's *Mary Barton*.

Agatha, Lady Fermor   Lord Fermor's wife and Lord Henry Wotton's aunt; she is involved in charities and gives inane dinner parties in Oscar Wilde's *The Picture of Dorian Gray*.

Arabella Fermor   Young, self-proclaimed coquette in Quebec with her father; the chief letter writer of the novel, she has a pragmatic outlook on both the necessity for advantageous arranged marriage and the desirability of marriage by choice in Frances Brooke's *The History of Emily Montague*.

George, Lord Fermor   Lord Henry Wotton's uncle, who defends traditional aristocratic privileges and tells Lord Henry the story of Dorian Gray's beautiful mother to help Lord Henry understand Dorian's past in Oscar Wilde's *The Picture of Dorian Gray*.

Captain William Fermor Arabella's father, an English military officer commissioned to observe and report on conditions of economics, politics, religion, and language in the colony of Quebec in Frances Brooke's *The History of Emily Montague*.

Lilian (Lilly) Fern Nine-year-old niece of Will Fern; she wins the affection of Trotty Veck and his daughter Meg in Charles Dickens's *The Chimes*.

Will Fern Plainspoken countryman, whose poverty and desire to provide for his young niece lead him to seek better employment and thus to incur the ill will of local potentates Sir Joseph Bowley and Alderman Cute in Charles Dickens's *The Chimes*.

Mrs. Ferrars Proud, selfish, bad-tempered mother of Edward and Robert Ferrars and Fanny Dashwood; she disinherits Edward when she hears of his engagement to Lucy Steele in Jane Austen's *Sense and Sensibility*.

Edward Ferrars Mrs. Ferrars's elder son and brother to Fanny Dashwood; he loves Elinor Dashwood but finds himself disinherited when his youthful secret engagement to Lucy Steele is revealed; believing in Lucy's affection, he honorably keeps to his engagement but is happily released to marry Elinor when Lucy jilts him in Jane Austen's *Sense and Sensibility*.

Endymion Ferrars Patient, malleable son of the ruined William Ferrars; he begins his career with a junior government clerkship; he eventually marries Lady Montfort and rises to become Prime Minister largely through the efforts of the women in his life in Benjamin Disraeli's *Endymion*.

Maurice Ferrars Robust clergyman brother of Albinia Kendal; he advises her and helps to invigorate her husband, Edmund Kendal, in Charlotte Yonge's *The Young Step-Mother*.

Myra Ferrars Twin sister of Endymion Ferrars; she is devoted to her brother and marries Lord Roehampton (whom she later grows to love) so as to further Endymion's career; she marries Prince (later King) Florestan when Roehampton dies in Benjamin Disraeli's *Endymion*.

Robert Ferrars Self-consequential younger brother of Edward Ferrars and Fanny Dashwood; he marries Lucy Steele after Edward is disinherited by their mother for his engagement to Lucy in Jane Austen's *Sense and Sensibility*.

William Ferrars Father of twins Endymion and Myra; an undersecretary of state and said to be a rising political star, he is left in penury by his father's death; his political career ruined, he commits suicide in despair in Benjamin Disraeli's *Endymion*.

Bratti Ferravecchi Rag merchant who buys a ring from Tito Melema in George Eliot's *Romola*.

Lumley Ferrers Wholly unscrupulous, politically ambitious nephew of Richard Templeton; he separates Ernest Maltravers from Florence Lascelles; he becomes Lord Vargrave and contemplates marriage to the lovely child-heiress Evelyn Templeton in Edward Bulwer-Lytton's *Ernest Maltravers*. He manipulates his lover, Caroline Merton, and attempts to marry Evelyn until her fortune has been lost by Gustavus Douce; he seems to have weathered his bad luck just as he is murdered by Castruccio Caesarini in *Alice*.

Ferret Misanthropist who has been a political hack writer; he quarrels with Sir Launcelot Greaves at the Black Lion Inn and swears false charges against Sir Launcelot; he insults local politicians while pretending to sell an elixir of life; he disguises himself as the London astrologist Albumazar; he confesses his kinship with Captain Samuel Crowe and is rewarded for revealing that Crowe has an estate coming to him in Tobias Smollett's *The Adventures of Sir Launcelot Greaves*.

John Ferrier Member of the Church of Latter Day Saints and father of Lucy Ferrier; he is killed while trying to escape from Salt Lake City in Arthur Conan Doyle's *A Study in Scarlet*.

Lucy Ferrier Adopted daughter of John Ferrier; she dies a month after her marriage to Enoch Drebber in Arthur Conan Doyle's *A Study in Scarlet*.

Count of Ferroll (characterization of Bismarck) German ambassador and minister with whom Endymion Ferrars has sensitive negotiations in Benjamin Disraeli's *Endymion*.

Hugh Ferryman Till River ferryman, who ferries John Matcham (Joan Sedley) and Dick Shelton across the river until he is startled by John Fenne and the ferry capsizes in Robert Louis Stevenson's *The Black Arrow: A Tale of Two Roses*.

Vizier Feshnavat Father of Noorna bin Noorka; she frees him from captivity at the hands of Princess Goorelka and assists him in rising to the position of Chief Vizier under Shagpat, whom he secretly opposes in George Meredith's *The Shaving of Shagpat*.

Mr. de Fessac Soldier with whom Colonel Francis Burke had a drunken adventure in India in Robert Louis Stevenson's *The Master of Ballantrae: A Winter's Tale*.

Monsieur de Feuillade   Noble young ship's captain, who is shipwrecked with Ardelisa de Vinevil and her friends on Delos; he falls in love with Violetta but must wait until Osmin has died before she can honorably marry him; he learns that his uncle has died, leaving him a fortune and the title of Marquis de Rochemont; he marries Violetta and they accompany Ardelisa de Vinevil back to France in Penelope Aubin's *The Strange Adventures of the Count de Vinevil and His Family*.

Lady Feverel   Mother of Richard, wife of Sir Austin, and a woman of great beauty; she runs off with Sir Austin's friend, the artist Denzil Somers, leading Sir Austin to his distrust of women in George Meredith's *The Ordeal of Richard Feverel*.

Sir Austin Feverel   Richard's father; after his beautiful wife runs off with his best friend, he decides to raise his son according to a system that will keep him from sexual temptation and build heroic virtues, but when Richard marries Lucy Desborough, Sir Austin becomes estranged from his son, leading to grief in George Meredith's *The Ordeal of Richard Feverel*.

Richard Doria Feverel   Son of Sir Austin Feverel, by whom he is reared according to a system intended to keep him from sexual temptation and to encourage heroic virtues; he marries Lucy Desborough, whom Sir Austin refuses to recognize as his daughter-in-law, and leaves home and comes to know "the world" from which Sir Austin's system had shielded him in George Meredith's *The Ordeal of Richard Feverel*.

Mademoiselle Feydeau   Inquisitive boarder at the St. Clair convent in Ann Radcliffe's *The Mysteries of Udolpho*.

Mr. Fezziwig   Benevolent and jolly merchant, under whom young Ebenezer Scrooge was apprenticed; he held joyous Christmas celebrations for his employees in Charles Dickens's *A Christmas Carol*.

Mrs. Fezziwig   Wife of Fezziwig, the benevolent merchant; she shares her husband's jollity as dance partner and a merry celebrator of the Christmas season in Charles Dickens's *A Christmas Carol*.

Major Fiasco   Lugubrious, lonely colleague of Adolphus Crosbie at the General Committee in Anthony Trollope's *The Small House at Allington*.

Mrs. Fibbitson   Neighbor of Mrs. Mell; her appearance is that of a bundle of clothes in a chair by the fire in Charles Dickens's *The Personal History of David Copperfield*.

Mr. Fiche   Lord Steyne's confidential man, who warns Becky (Sharp) Crawley away from Rome when she has become abhorrent to his lordship in William Makepeace Thackeray's *Vanity Fair*.

Fielding ("Captain")   Cavalier's Oxford friend of good family but low fortune; he travels with the Cavalier, joins the Swedish army, and is wounded in battle in Daniel Defoe's *Memoirs of a Cavalier*.

Mr. Fielding   Christian gentleman whose son was kidnapped at a young age; his offer to adopt Neddy is rejected by Henry Clinton, but he turns out to be Ned's father; God's intervention is believed responsible for reuniting Ned with his parents in Henry Brooke's *The Fool of Quality*.

Mrs. Fielding   Kindly wife of Mr. Fielding; she suggests they adopt Neddy and is the one to discover the identifying scar on Ned's neck in Henry Brooke's *The Fool of Quality*.

Mrs. Fielding   Mother of May Fielding; she has arranged a pecuniary match for her daughter with the much older Mr. Tackleton in Charles Dickens's *The Cricket on the Hearth*.

Edward Fielding   Hardworking rector of a neighboring parish of Clavering; he marries Harry Clavering's sister Mary in Anthony Trollope's *The Claverings*.

Edward (Neddy or Ned) Fielding   Beggar child befriended by young Harry Clinton; he is given to mischievous practical jokes that temporarily ruin at least one man; he is discovered to be the kidnapped son of the Fieldings in Henry Brooke's *The Fool of Quality*.

George Fielding   Honest, kindly Berkshire farmer, who cannot make his small farm profitable and so is unable to wed his cousin, Susan Merton, until he returns from Australia, where he has many adventures and finds gold with the help of Tom Robinson in Charles Reade's *It Is Never Too Late to Mend*.

May Fielding   Sweetheart of Edward Plummer; she is engaged to marry the much older "domestic ogre" Mr. Tackleton but narrowly escapes to marry her long-lost love in Charles Dickens's *The Cricket on the Hearth*.

William Fielding   George Fielding's younger brother, who wants to run the farm and is given the chance while George is away but gets into trouble through the scheming of John Meadows in Charles Reade's *It is Never Too Late to Mend*.

Thomas Fierce   Member of Jonathan Wild's gang who refuses to give Wild his loot and is convicted and hanged on trumped-up charges in Henry Fielding's *The Life of Mr. Jonathan Wild the Great*.

Fiery Face John Westlock's charwoman, through whose self-interested, angry disapproval the betrothal of Westlock and Ruth Pinch is presented in Charles Dickens's *The Life and Adventures of Martin Chuzzlewit*.

Filby Captain Edward Strong's friend, whose many careers have included acting and preaching in William Makepeace Thackeray's *The History of Pendennis*.

Mrs. Filch Former cook to Sir William and Lady Forester; she was dismissed because she played favorites with the recipients of Lady Forester's charity in Richard Graves's *The Spiritual Quixote*.

Mr. Filer Political economist who reduces every aspect of life to a "mathematical certainty" and numerical average in Charles Dickens's *The Chimes*.

Fille de Chambre Madame de R****'s young chambermaid, who raises Yorick's passion at the Hotel de Modene in Paris; however, he leads his "conquest" to the hotel gate, leaving her with a kiss and her virtue in Laurence Sterne's *A Sentimental Journey through France and Italy*.

Mr. Fillet Country surgeon who travels with Thomas Clarke and Captain Samuel Crowe when they meet Sir Launcelot Greaves; he gives Crowe instructions in becoming a knight and conspires to frighten Crowe in the chapel in Tobias Smollett's *The Adventures of Sir Launcelot Greaves*.

Dr. Fillgrave Reactionary physician bitterly opposed to Dr. Thorne's more progressive medical practices in Anthony Trollope's *Doctor Thorne*. He appears briefly in *Barchester Towers*. He attends the dying Mr. Harding in *The Last Chronicle of Barset*.

Fillide Jealous mistress of Clarence Glyndon; she schemes with Jean Nicot to have Viola Pisani executed during the Reign of Terror in Edward Bulwer-Lytton's *Zanoni*.

Fillpot Publican who uses fireworks to disrupt an assembly of abolitionist Methodists and who causes the eviction of his Methodist neighbor, Tom Keen, in Richard Graves's *The Spiritual Quixote*.

Mr. Fillygrove Clerk in Mr. Sumelin's bank; he runs away to marry Sumelin's daughter, Harriet, but finds himself lusting after Miss Wavel in Robert Bage's *Hermsprong*.

Mr. Filmer Dishonest steward of Sir Thomas Grandison's Irish estate; he brings a young Irish beauty, Miss Obrien, to England for the purpose of establishing her as Sir Thomas's mistress in Samuel Richardson's *Sir Charles Grandison*.

Marchese Filosanto Elder brother of Andrea Filosanto; he gives advice and assistance to Reginald de St. Leon during his early period of residence in Italy in William Godwin's *St. Leon*.

Andrea Filosanto Younger brother of the Marchese Filosanto of Pisa; having fallen victim to mountain bandits, he is rescued by Reginald de St. Leon and his servant Hector in William Godwin's *St. Leon*.

Mr. Finch Country clergyman and father, by his first wife, of Lucilla Finch, and by his second of fourteen younger children; a pompous man of insignificant appearance and impressive voice, he intervenes to restore Oscar Dubourg to Lucilla for mercenary reasons: Oscar has kept his fortune, whereas Nugent Dubourg has squandered his; Mr. Finch becomes a bishop in a distant colony in Wilkie Collins's *Poor Miss Finch*.

Mrs. Finch The vacant but sympathetic friend and visitor of the newly widowed Lady Matilda Sufton in Susan Ferrier's *Marriage*.

Amelia Finch Mr. Finch's second wife, the mother of fourteen children; always damp and semi-dressed and carrying a novel and a nursing infant, she loses a half hour each morning and never finds it again in Wilkie Collins's *Poor Miss Finch*.

Lucilla Finch A country clergyman's daughter, blind since infancy, who is repelled by intimations of dark colors around her; she falls in love with Oscar Dubourg; her sight temporarily restored, she allows herself to be deceived by Nugent Dubourg's impersonating Oscar; reunited with Oscar and again blind, she refuses further treatment in Wilkie Collins's *Poor Miss Finch*.

Selina (Jinks) Finch Three-year-old half sister of Lucilla Finch; always wandering about alone, she discovers the reconnoitering robbers and, subsequently, the wounded Oscar Dubourg in Wilkie Collins's *Poor Miss Finch*.

Flora Finching Fat, verbose, silly, but kind-hearted widowed daughter of Mr. Casby; she was once the pretty and slim sweetheart of Arthur Clennam; she recommends Amy Dorrit as seamstress to Mrs. Clennam and hires Amy to do needlework in Charles Dickens's *Little Dorrit*.

Mr. F's (Finching's) Aunt The aunt of Flora Finching's late husband and his "legacy" to the widow; she lives with Flora and Christopher Casby, has a habit of bursting out with irrelevant statements, and evinces antipathy toward Arthur Clennam in Charles Dickens's *Little Dorrit*.

Isabella Lawrence, Mrs. Finchley Friend of Aminta

(Lady Ormont) after Lord Ormont's failure to bring her into society; Mrs. Finchley's husband has attempted and failed to divorce her, and she now runs in the fast set in George Meredith's *Lord Ormont and his Aminta*.

Sir Frederick Fineer Suitor to Betsy Thoughtless; he is overwhelming with his romantic rhetoric, a true "Orlando Furioso" in love; he is Charles Trueworth's valet de chambre in Eliza Haywood's *The History of Miss Betsy Thoughtless*.

Dr. Malachi Finn Successful physician in County Clare who has mixed feelings when called upon to support the Parliamentary career of his son, Phineas, in Anthony Trollope's *Phineas Finn*.

Phineas Finn Handsome, personable, ambitious Irish politician, whose election to Parliament involves him in high society; he temporarily forgets his Irish sweetheart, Mary Flood Jones, and falls in love with Lady Laura Standish; after she refuses him to wed the rich landowner Robert Kennedy, he courts Violet Effingham, and his rival, Lord Chiltern, wounds him in a duel; Madame Max Goesler, who has fallen in love with him, offers him her hand and fortune to support his political career, but he has already committed himself to marry Mary Jones; he returns to Ireland in Anthony Trollope's *Phineas Finn*. After his wife's death he is again in Parliament; Lady Laura Kennedy renews her interest in his career, arousing her husband's animosity towards him; upon the death of Mr. Bonteen he is accused of murder, tried and acquitted; he marries Madame Goesler in *Phineas Redux*. He is a valuable political ally of the Duke of Omnium (Plantagenet Palliser) and serves as Secretary to Ireland in *The Prime Minister*. He appears as friend of the Palliser family in *The Duke's Children*.

Mrs. Phineas Finn See Marie (Madame Max) Goesler.

Mr. Finney Meddling Barchester attorney, who urges John Bold to investigate misuse of almshouse charity in Anthony Trollope's *The Warden*. As "Finnie" he appears briefly in *Barchester Towers*. He acts as attorney for Louis Scatcherd in *Doctor Thorne*.

Jack Finucane Irish journalist and the devoted friend of Captain and Mrs. Shandon in William Makepeace Thackeray's *The History of Pendennis*. He is Mrs. Shandon's second husband in *The Adventures of Philip on His Way through the World*.

Mr. Fips Lawyer who mysteriously offers Tom Pinch employment in Charles Dickens's *The Life and Adventures of Martin Chuzzlewit*.

Fireblood Young member of Jonathan Wild's gang who cheats and cuckolds Jonathan Wild; his testimony

against Wild gets the great man hanged in Henry Fielding's *The Life of Mr. Jonathan Wild the Great*.

Lady Firebrace Sir Vavasour Firebrace's gossiping wife, whom Mr. Tadpole and Mr. Taper manipulate for their own political ends in Benjamin Disraeli's *Sybil*.

Sir Vavasour Firebrace Pompous and corrupt companion of George, Lord Marney; he bribes Baptiste Hatton to use his political influence to make him a baron in Benjamin Disraeli's *Sybil*.

Mrs. Firkin Miss Matilda Crawley's lady's maid; she is jealous of Becky Sharp in William Makepeace Thackeray's *Vanity Fair*.

Brand Firmin George Firmin's father, a handsome, hot-tempered duellist when young; he is mentioned as having quarreled with his son in William Makepeace Thackeray's *The Adventures of Philip on His Way through the World*.

Dr. George Brand Firmin Fashionable medical doctor, whose suave manner and distinguished appearance conceal his disreputable past and financial waywardness; he is forced to flee to America, where he continues to belittle and to prey upon his son until he dies of yellow fever in William Makepeace Thackeray's *The Adventures of Philip on His Way through the World*.

Laura Carolina Firmin Eldest child of Philip and Charlotte (Baynes) Firmin in William Makepeace Thackeray's *The Adventures of Philip on His Way through the World*.

Louisa Ringwood Firmin Faded, sickly, boring, kind woman, ill-treated by her husband, Dr. Firmin, with whom she eloped when a young heiress; Philip, her only child, is defrauded by his father of the fortune he inherits from her in William Makepeace Thackeray's *The Adventures of Philip on His Way through the World*.

Philip Firmin Warmhearted, generous, but quarrelsome hero, whose father spends his inheritance, forcing him to earn his living as a barrister and journalist; he improvidently marries Charlotte Baynes on a small income; his hot temper jeopardizes his livelihood, but his courage and some good luck sustain him in William Makepeace Thackeray's *The Adventures of Philip on His Way through the World*.

First Minister of State Honest and idealistic man, who exemplifies all the positive qualities of a public servant in Charles Johnstone's *Chrysal, or, The Adventures of a Guinea*.

Mr. Fish Confidential secretary to Sir Joseph Bowley;

he is a Member of Parliament in Charles Dickens's *The Chimes*.

Selina Fish   Bigoted roommate of Madge Hopgood at Brighton; she distrusts Madge's religious leanings in Mark Rutherford's *Clara Hopgood*.

Fish Footman   Servant to the Queen of Hearts; he brings the Duchess an invitation to play croquet in Lewis Carroll's *Alice's Adventures in Wonderland*.

Jim (Jem) Fisher   Young clerk in a London office who is a friend of Richard in Thomas Hughes's *The Scouring of the White Horse*.

Sally Fisher   Friend and roommate of Ida Starr; she marries Osmond Waymark's friend Philip O'Gree in George Gissing's *The Unclassed*.

Fisherwoman   Woman who carries Pompey to a coffee-house near the Temple and sells him for a dram of brandy in Francis Coventry's *The History of Pompey the Little*.

Hamilton K. Fisker   Shady promoter of a company to sell shares in the South Central Pacific and Mexican Railway; he involves Paul Montague on the board, of which Augustus Melmotte becomes chairman; the scheme crashes, but the unscrupulous Fisker determines to maintain the American end of the operation; he persuades Marie Melmotte to travel with him to San Francisco, where they marry in Anthony Trollope's *The Way We Live Now*.

Fitchew   Odd-jobbing handyman in Cowfold, whose illiterate religious skepticism fascinates Miriam Tacchi in Mark Rutherford's *Miriam's Schooling*.

Mrs. Fitz-Adam   Sister of Mr. Hoggins and barely accepted as a member of genteel Cranford society in Elizabeth Gaskell's *Cranford*.

Albert Fitzallen   Apothecary's assistant in Clapham district; he falls in love with Felix Graham's protegée, Mary Snow, and marries her in Anthony Trollope's *Orley Farm*.

Lord Fitz-Allen   The vain and wealthy uncle of Anna St. Ives; he encourages her match with Coke Clifton in Thomas Holcroft's *Anna St. Ives*.

Lord Fitz-Booby   Superficial noble, who gossips about the political scene in Benjamin Disraeli's *Coningsby; or, The New Generation*.

Captain Fitzchrome   Poor but honest soldier, whose romantic constancy overcomes Lady Clarinda

Bossnowl's decision to marry for money rather than love in Thomas Love Peacock's *Crotchet Castle*.

Major Fitz-David   Friend of Eustace Macallan and an acquaintance of Mr. Starkweather; he provides Valeria Macallan with documents of Macallan's trial for murder; a cheerful womanizer, he finally marries Miss Hoighty, a young, vulgar protegée, in Wilkie Collins's *The Law and the Lady*.

George Fitz-Edward   Friend of both Frederic Delamere and George Godolphin and a charming but unprincipled libertine until he seduces Lady Adelina Trelawny, to whom he then remains devoted in Charlotte Smith's *Emmeline: The Orphan of the Castle*.

Fitzeustace   Sensitive, romantic hero and lover of Eloise de St. Irvyne in Percy Bysshe Shelley's *St. Irvyne*.

Fitzgarden   Angelo D'Albini's aristocratic friend, who finds him and Gabrielle di Montmorency at the point of starvation and brings news of their renewed fortune in Charlotte Dacre's *The Libertine*.

Captain Fitzgerald   Irish officer with the English garrison at Quebec; his sensibility combines the best of masculine and feminine traits; chosen by Arabella Fermor, he marries her before they return to England in Frances Brooke's *The History of Emily Montague*.

Burgo Fitzgerald   Handsome, well-connected, worthless, and penniless nephew of Lady Monk; he is mentioned as the disappointed, inappropriate suitor of the heiress Lady Glencora MacCluskie in Anthony Trollope's *The Small House at Allington*. Living without conscience and assisted by the mischief-making Lady Monk, Burgo tempts the married Lady Glencora Palliser to the brink of an elopement and infidelity; in despair at his failure, he wanders around Europe, a dissipated, desolate figure, until Plantagenet Palliser, Lady Glencora's husband, rescues him in Basle, pays his debts, and arranges a pension for him in Anthony Trollope's *Can You Forgive Her?*.

Emmelina Fitzgerald   Younger daughter of Sir Thomas Fitzgerald and bridesmaid of Lady Clara Desmond in Anthony Trollope's *Castle Richmond*.

Herbert Fitzgerald   Modest and likeable son and heir of Sir Thomas Fitzgerald; his succession to the title is jeopardized by Matthew Mollett's evidence that his parents' marriage was illegal; he helps victims of the potato famine in County Cork and finally marries Lady Clara Desmond in Anthony Trollope's *Castle Richmond*.

Letty Fitzgerald   Sir Thomas's staunch Protestant sister, forever preaching against Catholics and Puseyites and for pride in lineage in Anthony Trollope's *Castle Richmond*.

Mary Fitzgerald Elder daughter of Sir Thomas Fitzgerald and bridesmaid of Lady Clara Desmond in Anthony Trollope's *Castle Richmond*.

Mary Wainwright, Lady Fitzgerald Unfortunate wife of Sir Thomas Fitzgerald; a poor clergyman's beautiful daughter, married young to the unscrupulous swindler Matthew Mollett, who deserted her and was presumed dead, she is the unwitting agent of the misfortunes in the family resulting from Mollett's blackmail of Sir Thomas in Anthony Trollope's *Castle Richmond*.

Owen Fitzgerald Bachelor neighbor of the Dowager Countess of Desmond, whose love for him makes her a rival of her own daughter, Lady Clara Desmond; when he loses Lady Clara to Herbert Fitzgerald he quits Ireland to shoot big game in Africa; he would have inherited the Castle Richmond property had Sir Thomas's marriage been proved illegal in Anthony Trollope's *Castle Richmond*.

Sir Thomas Fitzgerald Wealthy Irish owner of the Castle Richmond property, blackmailed by Matthew Mollett, who claims that Sir Thomas is illegally married to Mary Wainwright, Mollett's own wife of many years past; after Sir Thomas dies it is discovered that the Fitzgerald marriage was legal because Mollett had bigamously married Mary in Anthony Trollope's *Castle Richmond*.

Aspasia Fitzgibbon Acid-tongued, affluent sister of Lawrence Fitzgibbon; her policy is to do anything for her improvident brother but supply him with money; nevertheless, when she learns of Phineas Finn's scrape she pays the bill he unwisely signed for her brother in Anthony Trollope's *Phineas Finn*.

Lawrence Fitzgibbon Affable but cynical politician, who befriends Phineas Finn and guides him in the ways of the House of Commons but persuades Phineas to sign for a loan he has no intention of repaying in Anthony Trollope's *Phineas Finn*. He stands by Phineas during his misfortunes in *Phineas Redux*. He appears briefly in *The Eustace Diamonds* and in *The Prime Minister*.

Dr. Fitzgibbons Irish physician and father of Julia, John Buncle's seventh wife; his son is saved by Buncle in a sword-fight in Thomas Amory's *The Life of John Buncle, Esq.*

Julia Fitzgibbons Daughter of the Irish Dr. Fitzgibbons and John Buncle's seventh wife; she dies of drowning after ten months of marriage in Thomas Amory's *The Life of John Buncle, Esq.*

Sir Loghlin Fitzgibbons Old Irish knight in Thomas Amory's *The Life of John Buncle, Esq.*

Captain Fitzjames A navy captain, who marries Diana Rivers in Charlotte Brontë's *Jane Eyre*.

Louis Fitzjocelyn Pure-hearted but fickle son of the Earl of Ormersfield; he develops strength of character through religious discipline and the love of his cousin, Mary Ponsonby, in Charlotte Yonge's *Dynevor Terrace*.

James Fitzmaurice Irishman who, despite his sworn allegiance to Queen Elizabeth, conspires with Nick Saunders against her in Charles Kingsley's *Westward Ho!*.

William Fitz-Osborne Bold, impudent politician, whose support of the poor draws from Julian the Apostate, in his incarnation as an English alderman, a public expression of approval; the Archbishop of Canterbury arrests Fitz-Osborne and hangs him in chains in Henry Fielding's *A Journey From This World to the Next*.

Fitzowen Parliamentary candidate who solicits Matthew Bramble for his vote in Tobias Smollett's *The Expedition of Humphry Clinker*.

Baron Fitz-Owen Noble brother-in-law of Sir Walter Lovel; he acquires Lovel Castle and befriends Edmund Lovel until the jealousy of his kinsmen forces him to send Edmund away in Clara Reeve's *The Old English Baron*.

Lady Emma Fitz-Owen Only daughter of Baron Fitz-Owen; she is pursued by her cousin Richard Wenlock, who turns against Edmund Lovel when he sees that she secretly admires Edmund; Edmund marries her when he finally proves he is of noble birth in Clara Reeve's *The Old English Baron*.

Robert Fitz-Owen Baron Fitz-Owen's eldest son, who is turned against Edmund Lovel by his jealous cousins in Clara Reeve's *The Old English Baron*.

William Fitz-Owen Youngest son of Baron Fitz-Owen; he recognizes Edmund Lovel's true merit and is the only one of the baron's kinsmen to remain true to Edmund in Clara Reeve's *The Old English Baron*.

Brian Fitzpatrick Irish fortune hunter, who marries Sophia Western's cousin, Harriet; he squanders her fortune, pursues her across England, and then takes up with Jenny Jones Waters in Henry Fielding's *The History of Tom Jones*.

Harriet Fitzpatrick Sophia Western's cousin, who was disowned when she married Brian Fitzpatrick without family consent; his mercenary motives devastate her and her dowry; she becomes mistress of the Irish peer who shelters her in Henry Fielding's *The History of Tom Jones.*

Edred Fitzpiers Ambitious physician, who marries Grace Melbury but soon proves unfaithful to her by having an affair with the beautiful, wealthy Felice Charmond; he leaves Grace to follow Charmond, and when she is killed, he returns to Grace, professing repentance; the two are reunited, although there are hints that his reform is dubious in Thomas Hardy's *The Woodlanders.*

Earl of Fitz-pompey Tory, anti-Catholic uncle of the young Duke of St. James; he hopes the young duke will marry his daughter, Lady Caroline St. Maurice, and thus further enhance his social position in Benjamin Disraeli's *The Young Duke.*

Mrs. Fitzsimmons Highway robbery victim who, aided by Redmond Barry, later assists her husband, Captain Fitzsimmons, in fleecing him in William Makepeace Thackeray's *The Luck of Barry Lyndon.*

Captain Fitzgerald Fitzsimmons Dishonest Dublin swindler, who with his wife ruins Redmond Barry in William Makepeace Thackeray's *The Luck of Barry Lyndon.*

Mr. Fitz-Solanum Irish Member of Parliament, who is unaware of the irony in his praise of William Pitt in William Beckford's *Azemia.*

Lady Alicia Fitzurse Waldemar Fitzurse's daughter, a court beauty and favorite of Prince John; Desdichado (Ivanhoe) slights her by choosing Lady Rowena as the queen of the tournament in Sir Walter Scott's *Ivanhoe.*

Waldemar Fitzurse Ambitious Norman courtier; he is Prince John's oldest and most important follower; he attempts to assassinate King Richard in Sir Walter Scott's *Ivanhoe.*

Lady Joan Fitz-Warene Lord De Mowbray's wealthy sister, whom Charles Egremont's older brother orders him to marry; when Charles refuses, the brothers become permanently estranged in Benjamin Disraeli's *Sybil.*

Lady Maud Fitz-Warene Lady Joan Fitz-Warene's arrogant sister, who condescendingly tries to introduce Sybil Gerard to high society in Benjamin Disraeli's *Sybil.*

Colonel Fitzwilliam Cousin of Mr. Darcy and nephew of Lady Catherine de Bourgh; though he is not a serious suitor of Elizabeth Bennet, his admiration of her reinforces Mr. Darcy's; he reveals to Elizabeth Mr. Darcy's complicity in separating Jane Bennet from Mr. Bingley in Jane Austen's *Pride and Prejudice.*

Horatio Fizkin The Buff Party's candidate to Parliament from Eatanswill, who runs against Samuel Slumkey in Charles Dickens's *The Posthumous Papers of the Pickwick Club.*

Don Bolaro Fizzgig Spanish grandee in an anecdote related by Alfred Jingle in Charles Dickens's *The Posthumous Papers of the Pickwick Club.*

Donna Christina Fizzgig A Spanish grandee's daughter, who dies for love of Alfred Jingle in an anecdote related by Jingle in Charles Dickens's *The Posthumous Papers of the Pickwick Club.*

General Fladdock Snobbish American military officer, who exposes young Martin Chuzzlewit as a steerage passenger and thus unworthy of American "high" society in Charles Dickens's *The Life and Adventures of Martin Chuzzlewit.*

Solomon Flamborough Loquacious farmer and a neighbor of the Primrose family; one of his daughters becomes engaged to Moses Primrose in Oliver Goldsmith's *The Vicar of Wakefield.*

Rose Flammock Wilkin Flammock's daughter, who is maid in waiting to Eveline Berenger; she advises Eveline to marry Damian de Lacy rather than Hugo de Lacy in Sir Walter Scott's *The Betrothed.*

Wilkin Flammock Flemish weaver who serves as guardian of Garde Doloreuse Castle for Raymond Berenger during Gwenwyn's siege; he negotiates with King Henry II during his siege of Eveline Berenger's castle in Sir Walter Scott's *The Betrothed.*

Moll (Mary) Flanders (Mrs. Betty, Lady Cleave, Gabriel Spencer) Former criminal who narrates the story of her life; born in Newgate Prison, she eventually is married seven times (once to her own brother); after a long career as a petty thief, she is imprisoned and, after repenting, transported to Virginia, where she becomes wealthy before returning again to England in Daniel Defoe's *The Fortunes and Misfortunes of the Famous Moll Flanders.*

Joe Flannelly Builder of the Ballycloran mansion; he becomes an enemy of the Macdermots after failing to persuade Larry Macdermot to marry his daughter in Anthony Trollope's *The Macdermots of Ballycloran.*

Wilkins Flasher Stockbroker who invests Tony Weller's inheritance from his late wife, Susan, when he wishes to resume his life as a coachman in Charles Dickens's *The Posthumous Papers of the Pickwick Club.*

Flashman Pampered, self-indulgent, seventeen-year-old bully, who is humbled by Tom Brown and later expelled from Rugby School in Thomas Hughes's *Tom Brown's Schooldays*.

Mrs. Flather Mother of Emma Flather in Robert Surtees's *Hillingdon Hall*.

Emma Flather A model of propriety who lives with her widowed mother next to John Jorrocks; she believes that James, Marquis of Bray is in love with her in Robert Surtees's *Hillingdon Hall*.

Flavian A poor yet brilliant student, whose tuition at Pisa is paid for by an unknown benefactor; tutor to Marius at Pisa, he is also an aspiring poet, who wishes to reestablish Latin as the dominant language of poetry in Walter Pater's *Marius the Epicurean*.

Flavius Anicius Maximus Roman senator, uncle of Basil and father of Aurelia; his will makes Basil his trustee and Aurelia his main heiress in George Gissing's *Veranilda*.

Hugh Flaxman Worldly aristocrat who marries Rose Leyburn in Mrs. Humphry Ward's *Robert Elsmere*.

Olivia Q. Fleabody Bespectacled, ardent advocate of women's issues; she wrests control of the Rights of Women Institute in the Marylebone Road from Baroness Banmann and grows rich from admission charges to the hall in Anthony Trollope's *Is He Popenjoy?*.

(Fascination) Fledgeby Awkward, small-eyed bill-broker, who is the invisible head of Pubsey and Co.; he bargains with Alfred Lammle to marry Georgiana Podsnap in exchange for forgiving Lammle's debts, tightens the strings on his debtors, and is bested by Lammle and Jenny Wren (Fanny Cleaver) in Charles Dickens's *Our Mutual Friend*.

Mr. Fleeceall John Jorrocks's secretary, who keeps the accounts concerning the foxhounds in Robert Surtees's *Handley Cross*.

Sir Matthew Fleet Richard May's former fellow student, who has become an important practitioner in London; his skill and his moral values are inferior to Dr. May's in Charlotte Yonge's *The Daisy Chain* and in *The Trial*.

Ambrose Fleetwood Grandfather of Casimir Fleetwood; he raises the orphaned William Ruffigny in his household and treats him like his own son in William Godwin's *Fleetwood*.

Casimir Fleetwood Misanthropic, dissolute, world-weary "new man of feeling," who travels about Europe in search of experiences which will reconcile him to life;

his narrative is a record of his errors and an act of penitence and humiliation in William Godwin's *Fleetwood*.

Casimir Fleetwood (the elder) Widowed father of Casimir Fleetwood; having withdrawn from society, he educates his son in the bosom of nature and remains indifferent to life among men in William Godwin's *Fleetwood*.

Edward Russet, Earl of Fleetwood Henrietta Fakenham's rejected suitor; he impulsively proposes to Carinthia Kirby, the sister of his rival, Chillon Kirby; ashamed of her social status, he maintains only a legal relationship with her, then idealizes her as a natural woman; he dies still unreconciled to her and incapable of understanding her as a multi-faceted woman rather than a symbol in George Meredith's *The Amazing Marriage*.

Livia, Countess Fleetwood Young widow of the late Earl of Fleetwood, stepmother of Lord Fleetwood, and cousin of Henrietta Fakenham; she marries a young earl in George Meredith's *The Amazing Marriage*.

Mary Macneil Fleetwood Wife of Casimir Fleetwood; her generous and loving spirit temporarily reconciles her misanthropic husband to life in William Godwin's *Fleetwood*.

Archdeacon Fleming Clergyman to whom Meg Murdockson makes her dying confession in Sir Walter Scott's *The Heart of Midlothian*.

Baron Fleming Father of Contarini Fleming; the wealthy and powerful foreign minister of a northern European kingdom, he lost his Italian family, power, and fortune, but regained position and wealth by hard work in the service of others in Benjamin Disraeli's *Contarini Fleming*.

Friar Fleming Eldest brother of the three Flemings at Ulubrae; he marries John Buncle to four of his wives and provides Charlotte (Melmoth) Buncle's coffin in Thomas Amory's *The Life of John Buncle, Esq.*

Lieutenant Fleming Son of Orlando Somerive's comrade in America; he marries Selina Somerive in Charlotte Smith's *The Old Manor House*.

Mrs. Fleming Widow of Orlando Somerive's comrade in America; she gives protection to Monimia Morysine; her son marries Selina Somerive in Charlotte Smith's *The Old Manor House*.

Agnes Fleming Mother of Oliver Twist and sister of Rose Maylie; she dies shortly after Oliver is born; she had been seduced by Edwin Leeford, who was already married, in Charles Dickens's *Oliver Twist*.

Contarini Fleming The eldest son of Baron Fleming and only child of the Baron's first marriage; he is conscious of possessing great powers and is unable to decide between the contemplative literary life and the life of a man of action and affairs as the appropriate outlet for his greatness in Benjamin Disraeli's *Contarini Fleming*.

Dahlia Fleming A simple country girl who goes to London, is seduced by wealthy Edward Blancove, and then deserted; her sister Rhoda Fleming forces her to marry a scoundrel rather than the repentant Edward; despairing, Dahlia attempts suicide; although the marriage proves invalid, her will to live is broken, and she refuses Blancove and dies soon after in George Meredith's *Rhoda Fleming*.

Jemmy Fleming Youngest of the Fleming brothers; he farms at Ulubrae, where a group of formerly wealthy men have formed a reclusive philosophical society in Thomas Amory's *The Life of John Buncle, Esq.*

Sir Malcolm Fleming Handsome follower of Robert the Bruce and Sir James Douglas's friend; he is faithless to his betrothed, Lady Margaret de Hautlieu, after she is disfigured; subsequently, she saves his life and they marry in Sir Walter Scott's *Castle Dangerous*.

Lady Mary Fleming Formal and uninteresting tire-woman to Queen Mary of Scotland and her companion in captivity; she accompanies the queen to England in Sir Walter Scott's *The Abbot*.

Rhoda Fleming Stern daughter of a Kentish farmer; she rejects her suitor Robert Armstrong Eccles because he doubts her sister Dahlia's honor; when she discovers Dahlia *is* besmirched she insists Dahlia throw away the promise of marital happiness for pride and honor; Rhoda chooses the same fate for herself; however, wealthy Algernon Blancove gives Rhoda up, and she marries Eccles in George Meredith's *Rhoda Fleming*.

Tom Fleming Close friend of John Buncle and Catholic farmer of Ulubrae, a small, reclusive society of twenty men; he is converted to Protestantism by Buncle and dies of a fever in Thomas Amory's *The Life of John Buncle, Esq.*

Mr. Fletcher Town butcher at Silverbridge to whom Josiah Crawley pays the cheque he is then accused of having stolen in Anthony Trollope's *The Last Chronicle of Barset*.

Mrs. Fletcher Aristocratic, loving mother of John and Arthur; her dearest wish is realized when her Arthur is finally married to the widowed Emily Lopez in Anthony Trollope's *The Prime Minister*.

Antonia Fletcher Companion of Azora Burcot and member of the self-sufficient female republic of Burcot Lodge; she is learned in mathematics, theology, music, and needlework in Thomas Amory's *The Life of John Buncle, Esq.*

Arthur Fletcher Young paragon of an outstanding Hertfordshire family vainly in love with Emily Wharton, who rejects him to marry Ferdinand Lopez; to his further dismay, he finds Lopez is his rival in the Silverbridge election; after Lopez commits suicide, he renews his suit and Emily accepts him in Anthony Trollope's *The Prime Minister*.

Dick Fletcher John Bunce's burly colleague in piracy in Sir Walter Scott's *The Pirate*.

John Fletcher Wealthy squire and man of property in Herefordshire and cousin of Sir Alured Wharton's elder daughter, who conspires with him to bring the widowed Emily Lopez and Arthur Fletcher together in Anthony Trollope's *The Prime Minister*.

Mike Fletcher Modern aesthete and Don Juan, who is a poet and writer for Frank Escott's *Pilgrim*; son of a shepherd on Escott's estate, now an envied man about town, he pleases both men and women; a chameleon-like character who dramatizes himself and yields to every passion, he is overcome with ennui and commits suicide in George Moore's *Mike Fletcher*.

Sandie Fletcher Fisherman who shoots the dancing apparition of Todd Lapraik in Black Andie Dale's "Tale of Todd Lapraik" in Robert Louis Stevenson's *Catriona*.

Mr. Flick Junior partner in a law firm which figures in the court case over Earl Lovel's supposedly bigamous marriage; he tries to promote a match between the young earl, Frederick, and Lady Anna Lovel in Anthony Trollope's *Lady Anna*.

Flimnap Lord High Treasurer and chief minister to the Emperor of Lilliput; he intrigues against Lemuel Gulliver and advocates his death in Jonathan Swift's *Travels into Several Remote Nations of the World. In Four Parts. By Lemuel Gulliver*.

Mrs. Flimnap Wife of the Lord High Treasurer of Lilliput, who accuses her of adultery with Lemuel Gulliver in Jonathan Swift's *Travels into Several Remote Nations of the World. In Four Parts. By Lemuel Gulliver*.

Alfred Flinders Disreputable half brother of Dolores Mohun's dead mother; he presumes on this distant relationship and on her unhappiness to defraud Dolores in Charlotte Yonge's *The Two Sides of the Shield*.

Affery Flintwich Maid and housekeeper of Mrs.

Clennam and wife of Jeremiah Flintwich; she is intimidated and bullied by her mistress and husband but still remains a friend to Arthur Clennam; she hears strange noises in the house which scare her in Charles Dickens's *Little Dorrit*.

Ephraim Flintwich Jeremiah's identical twin brother, who looked after Arthur Clennam's mother long ago in Charles Dickens's *Little Dorrit*.

Jeremiah Flintwich Mrs. Clennam's old, twisted, and bad-tempered manservant, who has some power over her because of their conspiracy over Arthur Clennam's true mother; he goes into partnership with Mrs. Clennam, is cruel to his wife, and runs off with the business strongbox after the house collapses in Charles Dickens's *Little Dorrit*.

Lord Flippant Neighbor of the Moreland estate and a typical member of the gentry who has no trouble speaking nonsense in Henry Brooke's *The Fool of Quality*.

Miss Flite Elderly suitor in Chancery and a friend of Gridley; she attends Chancery daily and keeps caged birds in her room in Charles Dickens's *Bleak House*.

Widow Flockhart Fergus MacIvor and Edward Waverly's male-crazy landlady in Edinburgh in Sir Walter Scott's *Waverly*.

Flodoardo See Count Rosalvo.

Flopson Nurse to the Pocket children, whose mother is more interested in reading about peerages than in taking care of the family in Charles Dickens's *Great Expectations*.

Flora Antonia de las Cisternas's maid, who suspects Ambrosio's designs on her mistress in Matthew Lewis's *The Monk*.

Lady Flora Lord Muirfell's attractive daughter, who tries to speak to the reclusive Archibald Weir; at one time, he watches and covets her from afar in Robert Louis Stevenson's *Weir of Hermiston: An Unfinished Romance*.

Mademoiselle (La Petite) Flora Villebecque's ethereal stepdaughter, who turns out to be Lord Monmouth's illegitimate daughter; she bequeaths the fortune she inherits from Lord Monmouth to Harry Coningsby when she dies in Benjamin Disraeli's *Coningsby; or, The New Generation*.

Comte de Florac Young officer with the French forces in Quebec and George Esmond Warrington's acquaintance in *The Virginians*. He is much older and a music teacher in London, exiled by the French Revolution, when he marries Léonore de Blois; he returns to France

and recovers part of his fortune under Napoleon in William Makepeace Thackeray's *The Newcomes*.

Léonore de Blois, Comtesse de Florac Daughter of the young Tom Newcome's French tutor, the Chevalier de Blois; she innocently loves and affectionately remembers Colonel Newcome even after she has married the Comte de Florac in William Makepeace Thackeray's *The Newcomes*.

Paul, Vicomte de Florac Mildly dissolute son of Colonel Newcome's first love; he befriends Clive Newcome in England and on the Continent; he becomes reconciled to his rich English wife after he inherits the title of Prince de Moncontour in William Makepeace Thackeray's *The Newcomes*.

Vicomtesse de Florac Older woman, formerly Miss Higg, whom Paul, Vicomte de Florac married for her money; long estranged, they are reconciled when he becomes Prince de Moncontour in William Makepeace Thackeray's *The Newcomes*.

Grand Duchess of Florence Patroness and protector of Lauretta Capece in J. Henry Shorthouse's *John Inglesant, A Romance*.

Prince Florestan (alias Colonel Albert) (characterization of Prince Louis Napoleon, later Napoleon III) Prince who becomes King Florestan of France and marries Myra Ferrars after Lord Roehampton dies in Benjamin Disraeli's *Endymion*.

Florio Italian who marries Olga Hannaford in George Gissing's *The Crown of Life*.

Mr. Flosky (caricature of Samuel Taylor Coleridge) A poet-philosopher who sustains his reputation by answering questions in language beyond human comprehension in Thomas Love Peacock's *Nightmare Abbey*.

Guy Flouncey A wealthy sportsman, whose most distinguished accomplishment is his marriage to a young and stunningly beautiful wife in Benjamin Disraeli's *Coningsby; or, The New Generation*.

Mrs. Guy Flouncey Flirtatious and fashionable wife of Guy Flouncey; her many male admirers provoke the envy of other aristocratic ladies in Benjamin Disraeli's *Coningsby; or, The New Generation*.

Sir Robert Floyer Foolish London fop who, encouraged by Mr. Harrel, courts Cecilia Beverley despite her discouragements; he wounds Mr. Belfield in a duel for Cecilia in Frances Burney's *Cecilia*.

Maria Fluart Caroline Campinet's friend, who pretends to love Lord Grondale and who helps Caroline escape her betrothal to Sir Philip Chestrum in Robert Bage's *Hermsprong*.

Lady Fanny Flurry   Friend of Mrs. Booby; she invites her to play cards and teases her about being envious of her former lover's wife in Richard Graves's *The Spiritual Quixote*.

Prudentia Flutter   Naive correspondent of Lucy Rural; she unquestioningly accepts the corruptions of urban life in Sarah Fielding's *Familiar Letters between the Principal Characters of David Simple and Some Others*.

Luckie Flyter   Hostess of the Glasgow inn where Francis Osbaldistone rooms while in that city in Sir Walter Scott's *Rob Roy*.

Horace Fogey   Barnes Newcome's fellow club member in William Makepeace Thackeray's *The Newcomes*. He is mentioned in *Vanity Fair* and in *The History of Pendennis*.

Mr. Fogg   Small, elderly sharpster lawyer, who is a partner of Mr. Dodson and is employed by Martha Bardell in her breach of promise suit against Samuel Pickwick in Charles Dickens's *The Posthumous Papers of the Pickwick Club*.

Elizabeth Foker   Hermann Foker's wife; widowed, she marries the Reverend Mr. Sampson in William Makepeace Thackeray's *The Virginians*.

Henry (Harry) Foker   Son of a wealthy brewer and grandson of an earl; he is a school friend of Arthur Pendennis, to whom he introduces Miss Fotheringay (Emily Costigan); betrothed to his cousin, Lady Ann Milton, he falls in love with and nearly marries Blanche Amory in William Makepeace Thackeray's *The History of Pendennis*. He appears in *The Adventures of Philip on His Way through the World*.

Hermann Foker   Kindly London brewer, who befriends George and Theo (Lambert) Warrington in need in William Makepeace Thackeray's *The Virginians*. His great-grandson is Henry (Harry) Foker in *The History of Pendennis*.

Lady Agnes Foker   Lord Rosherville's sister and wife of a wealthy brewer; she dotes on her son Henry in William Makepeace Thackeray's *The History of Pendennis*.

Mr. Folair   Pantomimist in the Crummles Theatrical Company, who feels that his talents are not recognized with sufficient billing and roles in Charles Dickens's *The Life and Adventures of Nicholas Nickleby*.

(Regulus) Folk-might   Brother of Sun-beam and Chieftain of the Kindred of the Wolf living in Shadowy Vale until, with the aid of the men of Burgdale, they regain control of Silver-dale from the Dusky Men (Huns); he marries the Bride in William Morris's *The Roots of the Mountains*.

Dr. Folliot   Robustious clergyman, who uses a strong pair of lungs to inveigh against the Industrial Revolution and Lord Brougham's "March of Mind" in Thomas Love Peacock's *Crotchet Castle*.

Reginald de Folville   Hugh Woodreeve's kinsman, who is slain in Arden forest; his ghost appears at Henry III's court to accuse Gaston de Blondeville of murder; finally he strikes Blondeville dead at a tournament in Ann Radcliffe's *Gaston de Blondeville*.

Ludovico de Fondi   Ghibelline nobleman who gives Castruccio dei Antelminelli an update on Euthanasia dei Adimari upon his return to Lucca in Mary Shelley's *Valperga*.

Lord Fondville   Wealthy and titled but extravagant and foppish suitor of first Lady Julia Belmont and then Miss Westbrook, whom he marries inconsiderately soon after the tragic deaths of Julia and Henry Mandeville in Frances Brooke's *The History of Lady Julia Mandeville*.

Charles Fontaine   Pompous but kindly middle-aged mayor of Petitport; he marries Catherine George in Anne Thackeray Ritchie's *The Village on the Cliff*.

Toto Fontaine   Son of Charles Fontaine; he makes his home with Catherine George after his father is drowned in Anne Thackeray Ritchie's *The Village on the Cliff*.

(Dickie) Lord Fontenoy   Conservative party leader who befriends and sponsors Sir George Tressady in Mrs. Humphry Ward's *Sir George Tressady*.

Captain Fooks   Horse-riding, gambling friend of Ralph Newton, heir to Newton Priory, in Anthony Trollope's *Ralph the Heir*.

Ford   Man who, along with twelve other people traveling through the countryside, encounters the three men from Wapping in Daniel Defoe's *A Journal of the Plague Year*.

Miss Ford   Performer of the introduction of Amelia de Gonzales to the dashing Captain Beville, who is killed by Amelia's jealous husband in William Beckford's *Modern Novel Writing; or, the Elegant Enthusiast*.

Betty Ford   One of the nine pupils of Mrs. Teachum's school; she learns by the novel's end what constitutes proper female behavior in Sarah Fielding's *The Governess*.

Georgiana Ford Merthyr Powys's devoted half sister, incapable of romantic love; despite her jealousy she nurses Emilia Belloni in George Meredith's *Emilia in England*. She follows her brother to Italy, and with Emilia—renamed Vittoria Campa—nurses his wounds and those of Captain Gambier; the two become engaged, though she had earlier rejected him in *Vittoria*.

Montague Ford Actor-manager who produces and acts in Hubert Price's play *Divorce* twice; he urges Hubert to finish *The Gipsy* in George Moore's *Vain Fortune*.

Mr. Fordham Mysterious and aristocratic admirer and eventual husband of Lady Western; his name is taken as an alias by Colonel Mildmay in Margaret Oliphant's *Salem Chapel*.

Mr. Fordyce Vicar and friend who ministers to the physical and psychological needs of the Penrhyn family in Caroline Norton's *Stuart of Dunleath*.

Emma Fordyce Sweet, quiet daughter of Mr. Fordyce and wife of Godfrey Marsden, who controls her; she is kind to Eleanor Raymond in Caroline Norton's *Stuart of Dunleath*.

Laura Forest Wealthy, middle-aged eccentric with classical interests; she lives on a spiritual plane; she wishes to produce plays and agrees to underwrite Montgomery's opera; though her interest in Dick Lennox is Platonic, she arouses Kate Ede's jealousy in George Moore's *A Mummer's Wife*.

Lady Forester Gentlewoman who, despite an atheistic upbringing, subscribes to "mystical" variations of Anglicanism and provides food and schooling for the local poor in Richard Graves's *The Spiritual Quixote*.

Mr. Forester Ferdinando Falkland's elder half-brother, who takes a liking to Caleb Williams, and to whom Caleb turns when he wishes to leave Falkland's service; when evidence that Caleb has committed a crime is discovered, Mr. Forester is horrified and urges putting Caleb in jail; he believes Falkland to be too soft-hearted in William Godwin's *Caleb Williams*.

Arthur Forester Young and pious but penniless and shy doctor who loves Lady Muriel Orme; he is a spokesman for Victorian virtues and ideologies; news of Lady Muriel's engagement results in his decision to leave for India; he is the counterpart of Bruno in Lewis Carroll's *Sylvie and Bruno*. The bridegroom of Lady Muriel, he leaves immediately to help victims of a plague and is presumed dead but is finally rescued by Eric Lindon in *Sylvie and Bruno Concluded*.

Kitty Forester Younger sister of Sir William Forester and facilitator of polite conversation in Richard Graves's *The Spiritual Quixote*.

Sylvan Forester (portrait of Percy Bysshe Shelley) Romantic figure who blends ideas of chivalry with those of liberal reform; he marries Anthelia Melincourt in Thomas Love Peacock's *Melincourt*.

Sir William Forester Wealthy landowner and perpetual host; Geoffry Wildgoose and Jeremiah Tugwell stay at his home and converse with his friends in Richard Graves's *The Spiritual Quixote*.

Clare Forey Richard Feverel's quiet, unhappily married cousin; she loves and is devoted to Richard, who, unaware of her love, tells her that death is preferable to a loveless marriage, thus prompting her suicide in George Meredith's *The Ordeal of Richard Feverel*.

Formalist Traveler who, along with Hypocrisy, gets into the highway by climbing over the Wall of Salvation rather than entering through the wicket-gate; he avoids the Hill of Difficulty and takes the way of Danger in John Bunyan's *The Pilgrim's Progress From this World to That Which Is to Come*.

Mr. Forrest Barchester bank manager, who gently warns Mark Robarts against financial dealings with Nathaniel Sowerby in Anthony Trollope's *Framley Parsonage*.

Mrs. Forrester One of the group of ladies who form genteel Cranford society in Elizabeth Gaskell's *Cranford*.

Sir Arthur Forrester Witness to the secret wedding of Mary, Queen of Scots and the Duke of Norfolk in Sophia Lee's *The Recess*.

Kattie Forrester Plain-speaking, sensible sweetheart of the doting Reverend Montagu Blake in Anthony Trollope's *An Old Man's Love*.

Colonel Forster Commander of a militia quartered in the neighborhood of the Bennets; its removal to Brighton causes despair in Kitty Bennet—and in Lydia Bennet until she is invited along as Mrs. Forster's guest in Jane Austen's *Pride and Prejudice*.

Harriet Forster Colonel Forster's young wife and Lydia Bennet's intimate friend, from whose residence Lydia elopes with George Wickham in Jane Austen's *Pride and Prejudice*.

John Forster Literary critic and rival of Christopher Kirkland for the rights to the biography of Walter Savage Landor in Mrs. Lynn Linton's *The Autobiography of Christopher Kirkland*.

Mrs. Fortescue   A friend of Lady Betty Lawrence and the source of Anna Howe's knowledge about Robert Lovelace in Samuel Richardson's *Clarissa: or, The History of a Young Lady*.

Hugh Fortescue   Younger brother of a large family and member of the Brotherhood of the Rose in Charles Kingsley's *Westward Ho!*.

Selina Fortescue   A sea captain's daughter, who marries Richard Danvers (Lord Alton); she and all her children tragically die in an epidemic, leaving her husband without an heir in William Godwin's *Cloudesley*.

Drummond Forth   Snob who sneers at Evan Harrington when he suspects his humble origins in George Meredith's *Evan Harrington*.

William de Fortibus   British nobleman who leads the challenging forces at Henry III's tournament in Ann Radcliffe's *Gaston de Blondeville*.

Miss Forward   Betsy Thoughtless's school friend who is a coquette and encourages a flirtation with Master Sparkish; Charles Trueworth thinks she is a prostitute in Eliza Haywood's *The History of Miss Betsy Thoughtless*.

Foscario   A wealthy fop, who is Philander's rival for Sylvia at Bellfont; when Sylvia's parents discover her affair with Philander, they attempt to force her to marry Foscario, and he wounds Philander in a duel in Aphra Behn's *Love Letters Between a Nobleman and His Sister*.

Count Fosco   Seemingly amiable Italian rogue, fond of his white mice and pet cockatoo; he masterminds the plot to secure Laura (Fairlie), Lady Glyde's fortune on behalf of her husband, Sir Percival Glyde; he connives in the kidnapping of Laura and her incarceration while her double, Anne Catherick, is buried under her name; he matches wits with the redoubtable Marian Halcombe; he is murdered by Italian conspirators in Wilkie Collins's *The Woman in White*.

Eleanor Fairlie, Countess Fosco   Aunt of Laura Fairlie; she is boastfully proud of her husband, Count Fosco, but utterly cowed by his overpowering personality in Wilkie Collins's *The Woman in White*.

Miss Foster   Daughter of a banker in Eastthorp; she offers some employment to Mike and Tom Catchpole to help them through their economic crisis in Mark Rutherford's *Catharine Furze*.

Mr. Foster   "Perfectabilian," who expresses the belief in the continual progress of mankind in Thomas Love Peacock's *Headlong Hall*.

Anthony Foster   Amy Robsart Dudley's sour and miserly warden at Cumnor-Place; he is tortured by conscience and religious superstitions, but his religious scruples cannot overcome his greed, and he serves Richard Varney while believing himself damned for doing so; his affections and his hope for salvation rest on his innocent daughter, Janet; years after his disappearance, his skeleton is found in a secret treasure room in Cumnor-Place in Sir Walter Scott's *Kenilworth*.

Charlie Foster of Tinning Beck (Charlie Cheat-the-Woodie)   Willie Graeme's confederate, who keeps Grace Armstrong after her abduction in Sir Walter Scott's *The Black Dwarf*.

Janet Foster   Anthony Foster's beloved and virtuous daughter and heir; she serves Amy Rosart Dudley faithfully at Cumnor-Place; she eventually marries Wayland Smith in Sir Walter Scott's *Kenilworth*.

Jeremiah Foster   One of the two Quaker businessmen who employ Philip Hepburn; his particular interest in Sylvia (Robson) and her baby supports Sylvia through the tragedy of her marriage in Elizabeth Gaskell's *Sylvia's Lovers*.

John Foster   One of the two Quaker businessmen who employ Philip Hepburn and later counsel and guide Sylvia (Robson) and Philip as tragic events overtake them in Elizabeth Gaskell's *Sylvia's Lovers*.

Sir John Foster   Warden of the West Marches of England; he is a borderer who declares war against the Monastery of St. Mary's for harboring Piercie Shafton in Sir Walter Scott's *The Monastery*.

Lucy Foster   Naive American girl, who succumbs to the beauty of Italy while maintaining the beliefs of Puritan New England; she finds love and happiness with Edward Manisty, a haughty and rich aristocrat in Mrs. Humphry Ward's *Eleanor*.

Mr. Fothergill   Zealous land manager for the (old) Duke of Omnium; he has to press his friend Nathaniel Sowerby for mortgage payments owed to the duke in Anthony Trollope's *Framley Parsonage*. He quarrels with Lord Chiltern over fox hunting and retires in *Phineas Redux*. He appears briefly in *Doctor Thorne*, in *The Small House at Allington*, and in *The Last Chronicle of Barset*.

Helen Fotheringham   Self-sacrificing sister of Percy Fotheringham and bride-elect of John Martindale; she serves as a guide to Violet Martindale in Charlotte Yonge's *Heartsease*.

Percy Fotheringham   Explorer and author, whose

stormy love affair with Theodora Martindale ends happily in Charlotte Yonge's *Heartsease*.

Foulata   Fair young woman of the Kukuana tribe, saved by Allan Quatermain from sacrificial death; she falls in love with John Good while nursing him back to health; she is killed attempting to prevent Gagool from sealing the Englishmen in the caves of King Solomon's mines in H. Rider Haggard's *King Solomon's Mines*.

Old Foulon   Man hanged by a mob during the French Revolution because he had told the starving people to eat grass in Charles Dickens's *A Tale of Two Cities*.

Augustina Fountain   Catholic sister of Alan Helbeck; she returns to her brother's home on the death of her Protestant husband in Mrs. Humphry Ward's *Helbeck of Bannisdale*.

Laura Fountain   Protestant stepdaughter of Alan Helbeck's sister; Laura falls in love with Helbeck, a deeply religious Catholic; when Laura is unable to reconcile her religious beliefs and her love for Helbeck, she commits suicide in Mrs. Humphry Ward's *Helbeck of Bannisdale*.

Steven Fountain   Deceased Cambridge don, whose agnostic, humanistic beliefs shape his daughter Laura's approach to life in Mrs. Humphry Ward's *Helbeck of Bannisdale*.

Monsieur de Fountain   Cousin of Monsieur de Feuillade; he brings news to Venice that his cousin has inherited the title and wealth of the Marquis de Rochemont; he captains the ship that carries Ardelisa de Vinevil safely from Venice to France in Penelope Aubin's *The Strange Adventures of the Count de Vinevil and His Family*.

Billy Fowler   Big, dissipated smuggling partner of Sharpe; he smuggles for adventure in Robert Louis Stevenson's *The Wrecker*.

James Fowler   Nephew of Sir Rowland Meredith and Harriet Byron's abject suitor in Samuel Richardson's *Sir Charles Grandison*.

Miss Fox   Cousin and companion to Juliet Berrisfort in Thomas Amory's *The Life of John Buncle, Esq.*

Mrs. Fox   A conniving and hypocritical socialite introduced to Miss Grizzy Douglas during a trip to Bath with Lord and Lady Maclaughlan in Susan Ferrier's *Marriage*.

Imoinda Fox   John Buncle's childhood love from Galway, Ireland, where they danced together; Buncle meets her briefly at Miss Wolf's in Clankford, Yorkshire, in Thomas Amory's *The Life of John Buncle, Esq.*

Fox the Red of the Hrossings   A spy for the Gothic Markmen; he penetrates the camp of the invading Romans in William Morris's *A Tale of the House of the Wolfings*.

Lord Foxham   Gallant guardian of Joan Sedley and an enemy of Sir Daniel Brackley; wounded in a raid, he gives Dick Shelton papers to deliver to Richard of Gloucester; he arranges the marriages of Dick and Joan and of Alicia Risingham and Joan's former betrothed John Hamley in Robert Louis Stevenson's *The Black Arrow: A Tale of Two Roses*.

Squire Foxley   English justice of the peace who hears the appeal of Darsie Latimer (Arthur Redgauntlet) for release from the guardianship of Hugh Redgauntlet in Sir Walter Scott's *Redgauntlet*.

Sister Frances   Talkative nun in the St. Clair convent, who gives Emily St. Aubert information about the mysterious Sister Agnes in Ann Radcliffe's *The Mysteries of Udolpho*.

Father Francis   Household chaplain to the Catholic Mr. Leigh in Charles Kingsley's *Westward Ho!*.

Father Francis   Shipwrecked missionary living as hermit in Turkey; he helps Ardelisa de Vinevil elude Mahomet, then leaves Constantinople with her but is shipwrecked on the island of Delos; he helps Violetta through her moral dilemma; he goes with Ardelisa and Violetta to Venice and then on to France, where, at Ardelisa's request, he tests Longueville's love for her before they are reunited, then lives out his years as their priest in Penelope Aubin's *The Strange Adventures of the Count de Vinevil and His Family*.

King Francis   Sovereign of France; his apollonian beauty and battlefield prowess inspire the fifteen-year-old Reginald de St. Leon, and in whose service Reginald first tastes the glory of victory and the ignominy and bitterness of defeat in William Godwin's *St. Leon*.

Mr. Francis   A radical philosopher who befriends and instructs Emma Courtney in Mary Hays's *Memoirs of Emma Courtney*.

Lady Sarah Francis   Stern but loving aunt, who raises Dorothea and George Vanborough while their parents are in India in Anne Thackeray Ritchie's *Old Kensington*.

Frank   Mr. Arnold's servant, who shamefully and sorrowfully visits Sidney Bidulph Arnold after her estrangement from her husband in Frances Sheridan's *Memoirs of Miss Sidney Bidulph*.

Frank   Miss Marchmont's betrothed, who dies before their marriage in Charlotte Brontë's *Villette*.

Mr. Frank   Faithful domestic in the household of Mr. Fenton (Henry Clinton) in Henry Brooke's *The Fool of Quality*.

Alphonse Frankenstein   Respected public servant of Geneva, father of Victor Frankenstein; he dies grieving for his murdered family members in Mary Shelley's *Frankenstein; or, The Modern Prometheus*.

Caroline Beaufort Frankenstein   Mother of Victor Frankenstein and wife of Alphonse; she terms Victor's adopted sister, Elizabeth Lavenza, "a pretty present" for Victor in Mary Shelley's *Frankenstein; or, The Modern Prometheus*.

Ernest Frankenstein   Victor Frankenstein's younger brother, whose military career is hindered by Victor's absence from the family; he is the only Frankenstein to survive the revenge of the demon in Mary Shelley's *Frankenstein; or, The Modern Prometheus*.

Victor Frankenstein   Brilliant Genevan chemist and anatomist, who endows a being of immense proportions with life and then, horrified at its hideousness, shuns it, abdicating his responsibility totally, and thus is doomed by the being's revenge to suffer the murders of his friend and family members in Mary Shelley's *Frankenstein; or, The Modern Prometheus*.

William Frankenstein   Victor Frankenstein's younger brother, who, as a small child, is strangled by Frankenstein's demon in Mary Shelley's *Frankenstein; or, The Modern Prometheus*.

Frankenstein's Being   The unnamed creature or "demon," a gigantic, hideous, synthetic man to which Victor Frankenstein gives life; eavesdropping on conversations of a French family, he learns language and the value of love and companionship, only to be utterly rejected by all, including his creator, on whom he revenges himself by many murders in Mary Shelley's *Frankenstein; or, The Modern Prometheus*.

Frankland   Litigious neighbor of the Baskerville family and father of Laura Lyons in Arthur Conan Doyle's *The Hound of the Baskervilles*.

Lady Barbara Frankland   Niece of Lady Kendover; she takes lessons in the harp from Juliet Granville until removed out of social snobbery; she is engaged to Lord Melbury at the end in Frances Burney's *The Wanderer*.

Norbert Franks   Will Warburton's friend, an artist who becomes rich and successful as a painter of society women after Rosamund Elvan breaks her engagement to him; he eventually marries her in George Gissing's *Will Warburton*.

Phillip Franks   Hugh Trevor's servant, who Hugh mistakenly thinks stole ten pounds and who serves Olivia Mowbray both before and after her marriage in Thomas Holcroft's *The Adventures of Hugh Trevor*.

Simon Fraser, Master of Lovat   Ugly and malevolent Scottish Highland chief of the clan Fraser; he abandons his loyalties to the Highlanders by becoming the advocate-depute in the Appin murder case; he attempts to have David Balfour killed in Robert Louis Stevenson's *Catriona*.

Frazer   Painter of the Modern school, not a financial success; he exhibits at the Academy but is unimpressed by Lewis Seymour in George Moore's *A Modern Lover*.

Ellen Frazer   Mrs. Eadie's adopted daughter who was raised with Charles Walkinshaw's children and marries his son James in John Galt's *The Entail*.

Fred   Ebenezer Scrooge's nephew, son of his tender-hearted sister, Fan; he invites Scrooge to dine every Christmas despite Scrooge's persistent refusals and is a devout believer in keeping Christmas in Charles Dickens's *A Christmas Carol*.

Mrs. Fred   Dimpled wife of Fred in Charles Dickens's *A Christmas Carol*.

Mme. Frederic   A Frenchwoman who looks after Adèle Varens after her mother abandons her and before Mr. Rochester becomes her guardian in Charlotte Brontë's *Jane Eyre*.

Frederick   Handsome lord, who is a cousin of Lewis Augustus Albertus; he falls in love with Albertus's wife, Lady Lucy, whose friend Henrietta disguises herself as Lucy and carries on an affair with Frederick until Albertus finds a letter Henrietta has forged and murders him in Penelope Aubin's *The Life and Adventures of the Lady Lucy*.

Michael (Mickey) Free   Uninhibited but faithful Irish servant of Charles O'Malley in Charles Lever's *Charles O'Malley*.

Harriot Freke   Lady Delacour's spiteful, false friend, who leads her into much mischief in the name of "frolic"; it is through her prodding that Lady Delacour duels and subsequently wounds herself in Maria Edgeworth's *Belinda*.

Mrs. French   Dispirited mother of two husband-hunting daughters, Camilla and Arabella; she agonizes over the vacillating attentions and intentions of the Reverend Thomas Gibson towards them; ultimately she negotiates the truce by which he is secured in Anthony Trollope's *He Knew He Was Right*.

Arabella French   Elder of a pair of aging Exeter belles; her right of possession in the Reverend Thomas Gibson has for years been challenged by her sister, Camilla, but she is at last successful in Anthony Trollope's *He Knew He Was Right*.

Beatrice French   Vulgar, half-educated girl, who nevertheless begins a successful dress shop and befriends and employs Nancy Lord in George Gissing's *In the Year of Jubilee*.

Camilla French   Younger sister of Arabella; she enjoys for a time an engagement with the Reverend Thomas Gibson until her triumph and greed rouse him to rebellion; thwarted, she threatens murder in her rage in Anthony Trollope's *He Knew He Was Right*.

Fanny French   Vulgar, brainless girl who pretends to refinement; she has a scandalous affair with the disreputable Mankelow but later persuades Horace Lord, to whom she was formerly engaged, to marry her in George Gissing's *In the Year of Jubilee*.

Margaret French   Middle-class friend and secretary of Lady Kitty Ashe in Mrs. Humphrey Ward's *The Marriage of William Ashe*.

French Captain   Captain of a privateer vessel which overtakes Colonel Jack's ship while Jack is on his way back to England; he holds Jack for ransom but is tricked and doesn't receive it in Daniel Defoe's *The History and the Remarkable Life of the Truly Honourable Colonel Jacques, Commonly Call'd Col. Jack*.

French Captain   Debonaire young captain, who becomes more familiar with Yorick's female companion in a moment than Yorick has become after many cautious inquiries, thus providing a lesson in spontaneity and initiative in Laurence Sterne's *A Sentimental Journey through France and Italy*.

"French governour"   An exiled French heretic, who tutors Oroonoko in language and European manners in Aphra Behn's *Oroonoko*.

French Officer   Old military man who, while sitting beside Yorick at the opera, comes to the aid of a dwarf whose view is blocked by a tall, discourteous German in Laurence Sterne's *A Sentimental Journey through France and Italy*.

Captain Freny   A highwayman who robs Mrs. Fitzsimmons in William Makepeace Thackeray's *The Luck of Barry Lyndon*.

James Frere   Pseudo-preacher, who marries Alice Ross in secret without telling her about his criminal past; he helps in the plot to separate Sir Douglas and Gertrude Ross; he repents and dies before he is caught by the law for his crimes in Caroline Norton's *Old Sir Douglas*.

Henny Frett   One of the nine pupils of Mrs. Teachum's school; her mentor's gentle instruction cures Henny's vice, malice, in Sarah Fielding's *The Governess*.

Frewen   Young man of literary ambitions, who is at Oxford with Casimir Fleetwood; he plays an important role in Morrison's elaborately staged hoax which ridicules the unfortunate poet, Withers, and results in his suicide in William Godwin's *Fleetwood*.

Madame Fribsby   Romantically minded milliner at Clavering whom it turns out Colonel Altamont married as Johnny Armstrong before he married Miss Snell (now Lady Clavering) as J. Amory in William Makepeace Thackeray's *The History of Pendennis*.

Friday   Native whom Robinson Crusoe saves and names; he becomes Crusoe's servant and companion and is eventually converted to Christianity; he and Crusoe rescue other men who are taken to the island by natives, and he later returns to England with Crusoe in Daniel Defoe's *The Life and Strange Surprizing Adventures of Robinson Crusoe of York, Mariner*.

Friday's Father   Native who, like his son, is captured by an opposing tribe and brought to Robinson Crusoe's island to be killed and eaten; he is rescued by Friday and Crusoe in Daniel Defoe's *The Life and Strange Surprizing Adventures of Robinson Crusoe of York, Mariner*.

Dr. Friedland   Cambridge don and friend of Laura Fountain's father in Mrs. Humphry Ward's *Helbeck of Bannisdale*.

Molly Friedland   Laura Fountain's friend from her Cambridge days in Mrs. Humphry Ward's *Helbeck of Bannisdale*.

Dolly Friendly   One of the nine pupils of Mrs. Teachum's school; she recites the "Story of Caelia and Chloe" in Sarah Fielding's *The Governess*.

Jack Friendly   Thomas Heartfree's apprentice, who sticks by his afflicted master until the court frees him; he marries Nance Heartfree in Henry Fielding's *The Life of Mr. Jonathan Wild the Great*.

Daughter Frippery   The Fripperys' only child, who has not one natural gesture or motion in Francis Coventry's *The History of Pompey the Little*.

Lady Frippery   A would-be lady of fashion and the accomplished spouse of Sir Thomas Frippery; having been something of a beauty in her youth, she retains her youthful airs and manners in Francis Coventry's *The History of Pompey the Little*.

Sir Thomas Frippery   A vain knight, who held a little post in Queen Anne's court, and who spends his small fortune in the attempt to live like a man of consequence in Francis Coventry's *The History of Pompey the Little*.

Frog Doorman   Creature who kicks Queen Alice's door so that Alice may enter for the coronation feast in Lewis Carroll's *Through the Looking-Glass*.

Frog Footman   Servant who attends the door at the Duchess's house and receives the invitation for the Duchess to play croquet with the Queen of Hearts; he debates with Alice over entering the house in Lewis Carroll's *Alice's Adventures in Wonderland*.

Mr. Froggatt   Bookseller and country newspaper publisher, who employs Felix Underwood and eventually takes him into partnership in Charlotte Yonge's *The Pillars of the House*.

Earl of Frolicsfun   Deceased uncle of Henry Lambert; he passes to Henry the title of the ancient Barony of Laughable in William Beckford's *Modern Novel Writing; or, the Elegant Enthusiast*.

Sir Reginald Front-de-Boeuf   Brutal baron who holds Ivanhoe's barony by permission of Prince John; he dies horribly when his castle of Torquilstone is besieged to free his captives in Sir Walter Scott's *Ivanhoe*.

Frosch   James Morgan's successor as valet to Major Pendennis in William Makepeace Thackeray's *The History of Pendennis*.

Catharine (Aunt Kitty) Frost   Noble old woman, who has supported first her children and then her grandchildren by preparing boys for public school in Charlotte Yonge's *Dynevor Terrace*.

Clara (Giraffe) Frost   Young sister of James Frost; she becomes first the heir and then the caretaker of her uncle, Oliver Dynevor, in Charlotte Yonge's *Dynevor Terrace*.

James Frost   Cousin and advocate of Louis Fitzjocelyn; he fails as a schoolmaster but succeeds as a tender parent to his four daughters in Charlotte Yonge's *Dynevor Terrace*.

Froth   One of Amoranda's suitors, who wants only her money and is ready to abduct her and dishonor her to get it in Mary Davys's *The Reform'd Coquet*.

Maximilian, Lord Froth   Bryan Perdue's dull-witted schoolmate and fellow gambler, who accuses Bryan of gambling and has him dismissed from school in Thomas Holcroft's *The Memoirs of Bryan Perdue*.

Mrs. Frothingham   Mother of Alma; when her husband's business fails and he shoots himself, she insists on paying restitution to the investors who have lost their money in George Gissing's *The Whirlpool*.

Alma Frothingham   Young woman who, after marrying Harvey Rolfe and living in the country, begins a career as a professional violinist against her husband's wishes, becomes involved with a lover, and ultimately commits suicide in George Gissing's *The Whirlpool*.

Bennet Frothingham   Alma's father, who commits suicide when his firm fails in George Gissing's *The Whirlpool*.

Fry   Prison turnkey who keeps a methodical record of everything that happens in the jail, faithfully follows Hawes's instructions, and is unable to judge the immoral results in Charles Reade's *It Is Never Too Late to Mend*.

Amos (Haymoss) Fry   Garrulous rustic in Thomas Hardy's *Two on a Tower*.

John Fry   Emissary sent to fetch John Ridd from school; reaching home, they discover that Ridd's father has been murdered by the Doones in R. D. Blackmore's *Lorna Doone*.

Mr. Fudge   Bookseller whose description of forthcoming books unintentionally satirizes the literary tastes of the age in Oliver Goldsmith's *The Citizen of the World*.

Joshua Fullalove   American whaling skipper, Methodist parson, engineer, inventor, and money-maker, who rescues the *Agra* by a makeshift rudder, carries a line to the French shore, and testifies in behalf of Alfred Hardie in court in Charles Reade's *Hard Cash*. He first reports Robert Penfold's bird-borne requests for help, harpoons the whale that supplies oil for Robert's escape, and buys the location of Godsend Island for cash and a fifty-fifty partnership in *Foul Play*.

Phoebe Fulmort   Wealthy young neighbor of Honora Charlecote; she protects her sisters from the dissipated life of her older brothers and is ultimately rewarded by marriage to the Canadian Humfrey Charlecote, Honora Charlecote's heir, in Charlotte Yonge's *Hopes and Fears*.

Robert Fulmort   Neglected son of a wealthy distiller;

as a child he falls under the influence of Honora Charlecote, takes orders, and rejects Lucilla Sandbrook for her flightiness in Charlotte Yonge's *Hopes and Fears*. He is a founder of a mission in London in *The Pillars of the House*.

Fum Hoam   President of the Peking Ceremonial Academy of China and correspondent of Lien Chi Altangi in Oliver Goldsmith's *The Citizen of the World*.

Pepin de Fumier   French abbé, who meets Ferdinand in Paris, joins in the visit to a brothel, and is the victim of a brawl in Tobias Smollett's *The Adventures of Ferdinand Count Fathom*.

Mr. Furley   Owner of the mortgage on Edward Tulliver's land; he transfers it to John Wakem in George Eliot's *The Mill on the Floss*.

Kitty Furnival   Devoted wife of the London barrister Thomas Furnival; she is bitterly hurt and resentful when he appears to have fallen for his client Lady Mason in Anthony Trollope's *Orley Farm*.

Sophia Furnival   Handsome, shallow, complacent daughter of Thomas Furnival; she allows herself to drift into an engagement with Lucius Mason, but when he relinquishes his estate she extricates herself ruthlessly from the relationship in Anthony Trollope's *Orley Farm*.

Thomas Furnival   Successful, middle-aged London barrister, who is engaged in Lady Mason's defence in the case of the forged codicil; his affection for her arouses his wife's jealousy and clouds his judgment in Anthony Trollope's *Orley Farm*.

Mr. Furze   Largest ironmonger in Eastthorp in 1840; he rebuilds in a fashionable part of his town after his home-shop burns; he is tricked by his wife into dismissing Tom Catchpole in Mark Rutherford's *Catharine Furze*.

Mrs. Furze   Wife of Mr. Furze and daughter of a Cambridge draper; she is socially ambitious for her daughter, Catharine; she plots to fire Tom Catchpole and drive him away from Catharine in Mark Rutherford's *Catharine Furze*.

Catharine Furze   Daughter of Mr. and Mr. Furze and aged nineteen in 1840; she rejects Tom Catchpole as a husband because she is in love with the married Reverend Theophilus Cardew; she sacrifices her love to save Cardew's reputation before she dies in Mark Rutherford's *Catharine Furze*.

G

Lord G——   A married nobleman and one of two principal admirers of Rosalie Murray at her coming-out ball in Anne Brontë's *Agnes Grey*.

Lord G.   Patient suitor, then husband, of Charlotte Grandison; witty and high-spirited, she ridicules and resists him until motherhood makes her happily submissive in Samuel Richardson's *Sir Charles Grandison*.

Harriet G.   Infant daughter of Charlotte (Grandison), Lady G., and Lord G.; she is named in honor of Harriet Byron in Samuel Richardson's *Sir Charles Grandison*.

J. G.   Peter Wilkins's opportunistic stepfather and the sole beneficiary of Alice Wilkins's will in Robert Paltock's *The Life and Adventures of Peter Wilkins*.

Julia and Georgiana G——   Pupils of Frances (Henri) Crimsworth's school to whom she shows no favoritism even though they are the daughters of an English baronet in Charlotte Brontë's *The Professor*.

Sir William G——   Gentleman who marries Mary Darnford in Samuel Richardson's *Pamela, or Virtue Rewarded*.

Gabble   Political lecturer who uses attacks on the government for self-aggrandizement; his motives are criticized by Lord Charles Oakley in William Beckford's *Modern Novel Writing; or, the Elegant Enthusiast*.

Théophile Gabelle   Postmaster and tax gatherer on the estate of the Marquis St. Évrémonde; because of his letter begging Charles Darnay's assistance when he is seized by the revolutionists, Darnay returns to France, where he is denounced as an aristocrat in Charles Dickens's *A Tale of Two Cities*.

Bethlem Gabor   Gloomy, mysterious, savage misanthrope; he is the protector turned jailer of Reginald de St. Leon (known as Chattilon), whom he forces to produce massive quantities of gold with the aid of the philosopher's stone; he perishes in the seige of his castle led, coincidentally, by St. Leon's son Charles de St. Leon (known as the Chevalier de Damville) in William Godwin's *St. Leon*.

Gabriel   Aged servant at Kenilworth in Sophia Lee's *The Recess*.

Clement Gabriel   A serious painter of scenes of poverty who feels contempt for his friend Bernard Kingcote because he lacks purpose, but enables him to find an occupation by giving him the bookshop left after his father dies in George Gissing's *Isabel Clarendon*.

Gabriella   French friend of Juliet Granville; she flees revolutionary France to England, mourns the death of her young son, and works with Juliet in a London shop to survive while her husband is away in France in Frances Burney's *The Wanderer*.

Gaddi   Camel driver who becomes Joseph of Arimathea's business partner in George Moore's *The Brook Kerith*.

Gadsi   Governor of the country of Mount Alkoe both before and after its colonization by Peter Wilkins and Georigetti in Robert Paltock's *The Life and Adventures of Peter Wilkins*.

Mr. Gager   Intelligent young detective, who challenges his colleague, Mr. Bunfit, in the mystery of Lady Eustace's stolen diamonds; testimony provided by Patience Crabstick proves his theories correct, and he marries her in Anthony Trollope's *The Eustace Diamonds*.

Gagool   Vulture-like prophetess, who has lived for countless generations among the Kukuanas; through fear and magic, she exercises political control over the kings, including Twala; she is killed by a stone gate she herself set in motion in H. Rider Haggard's *King Solomon's Mines*.

Mr. Gainsborough   Whig and a self-made man who, despite pressure from his family to vote for the Whig candidate as promised, is persuaded by the charm of Helen Molesworth to cast his deciding vote in favor of Aubrey Bohun in Benjamin Disraeli's *A Year at Hartlebury; or, The Election*.

Jean Gaisling   Captain Armour's sister, who was hanged in public for murdering her illegitimate child in John Galt's *The Provost*.

Gaius   Innkeeper who serves Christiana and her party a banquet and promotes the marriages of Matthew to Mercy and his own daughter Phebe to James in John Bunyan's *The Pilgrim's Progress From this World to That Which Is to Come*.

Major Duncan Galbraith   Amiable Laird of Garschattachin and officer in the Lennox Militia; he is Bailie (Nicol) Jarvie's debtor and possesses Jacobite inclinations in Sir Walter Scott's *Rob Roy*.

Mrs. Gale   Mr. Donne's Yorkshire landlady, who is appalled by his uncivil manner in Charlotte Brontë's *Shirley*.

Abraham Gale   Son of Mrs. Gale in Charlotte Brontë's *Shirley*.

John Gale   A small clothier and an indulgent landlord for the curate Mr. Donne in Charlotte Brontë's *Shirley*.

Margaret Gale   Fellow servant who befriends Esther Waters at the Barfields' estate; she comes to London when the estate breaks up and has a chance meeting with Esther; she has become a prostitute in George Moore's *Esther Waters*.

Galen   Roman physician who influences the young Marius in Walter Pater's *Marius the Epicurean*.

Mynheer Van Galgebrook   A Dutchman who early foretells Jack Sheppard's death on the gallows; he works for Jonathan Wild but finally turns against him in William Harrison Ainsworth's *Jack Sheppard*.

Monsieur de Galgenstein   Officer who impresses Redmond Barry into the Prussian army after he deserts from the English army in William Makepeace Thackeray's *The Luck of Barry Lyndon*.

Miss Galindo   Shrewd and slightly eccentric lady, who is asked by Lady Ludlow to assist her steward; her story reflects the changing social scene in Elizabeth Gaskell's *My Lady Ludlow*.

Tom Gallagher   Wealthy Irish gentleman and John Buncle's contemporary at Trinity College, Dublin; he is handsome, a good storyteller, and the father of nineteen well-provided-for daughters in Thomas Amory's *The Life of John Buncle, Esq.*

Jack Gallaspy   Wealthy Irish gentleman and John Buncle's contemporary at Trinity College, Dublin; he is generous and even-tempered, though he smokes, drinks, and womanizes in Thomas Amory's *The Life of John Buncle, Esq.*

Galliard   Montamour's brother in Eliza Haywood's *The Injur'd Husband; or, the Mistaken Resentment*.

Mr. Gallilee   Mrs. Gallilee's second husband, father of Maria and Zoe; a kind, apparently foolish man very much dominated by his wife, he rebels at last and quietly removes his daughters to their uncle Lord Northlake's estate in Scotland in Wilkie Collins's *Heart and Science*.

Maria Graywell Gallilee   Widowed mother of Ovid Vere and now wife of Mr. Gallilee; a greedy, heartless woman of great vitality and vanity, she has taken up science in order to excel her "inferior" sister, Lady Northlake, whom she envies; she hopes to acquire a fortune by destroying the marriage prospects of her niece and ward, Carmina Graywell; temporarily insane after her plots are frustrated, she recovers to devote herself entirely to science in Wilkie Collins's *Heart and Science*.

Maria Gallilee   Mrs. Gallilee's elder daughter, a prim, industrious, unloving child, who occasionally acts as her mother's spy in Wilkie Collins's *Heart and Science*.

Zoe (Zo) Gallilee   Hoydenish, supposedly stupid younger daughter of Mrs. Gallilee; it is she who writes the letter that brings Ovid Vere home to cure Carmina Graywell; she is the only person for whom Dr. Benjulia feels affection in Wilkie Collins's *Heart and Science*.

Mr. Gallstone   Stern old man who monopolizes conversations and criticizes Azemia's naivete in William Beckford's *Azemia*.

Luke Gamble   Attorney consulted by Dr. Toole and the Nutters when Mary Matchwell claims to be Charles Nutter's wife; he helps prove she committed bigamy and therefore was never really married to Nutter in J. Sheridan Le Fanu's *The House by the Churchyard*.

Gambler Number One   Older, self-made businessman, who is made a peer and gambles instead of looking after business in Charles Johnstone's *Chrysal: or, The Adventures of a Guinea*.

Gambler Number Two   Unskilled but compulsive gambler, who has lost everything and is deeply in debt in Charles Johnstone's *Chrysal: or, The Adventures of a Guinea*.

Gambler Number Three   Senior military officer, who gains rank through seniority, not talent, and who is a great collector of art in Charles Johnstone's *Chrysal: or, The Adventures of a Guinea*.

Gambler Number Four   Aristocrat who is the best breeches-maker of his time; his passion to make breeches gets him into many difficulties in Charles Johnstone's *Chrysal: or, The Adventures of a Guinea*.

Gambler Number Five (Virtuoso)   An obsessive collector of the anomalous frolics of nature who is tricked into buying a horned cock in Charles Johnstone's *Chrysal: or, The Adventures of a Guinea*.

Gambler Number Six   Well-born man with many natural abilities; he justifies his gambling as a type of charity in Charles Johnstone's *Chrysal: or, The Adventures of a Guinea*.

Gambler Number Seven   Younger son who inherited money from his rich, miserly, cruel, vindictive father and who gambles the money away in Charles Johnstone's *Chrysal: or, The Adventures of a Guinea*.

"The Game Chicken"   Boxing instructor and general

assistant to Mr. Toots in Charles Dickens's *Dombey and Son*.

Mr. Gamfield   Fierce chimney sweep, who wishes to have Oliver Twist for an apprentice in Charles Dickens's *Oliver Twist*.

Mr. Gammon   A genial commercial salesman, who becomes involved in intrigue when he joins the search for a man he believes is related to his employer in George Gissing's *The Town Traveller*.

Sarah (Sairey) Gamp   Garrulous and alcoholic professional nurse, midwife, and layer-out of the dead; she delivers many comic speeches of self-praise, quoting the words of her unseen friend Mrs. Harris in Charles Dickens's *The Life and Adventures of Martin Chuzzlewit*.

Mr. Gander   Border at Todgers's and second in seniority to Mr. Jinkins in Charles Dickens's *The Life and Adventures of Martin Chuzzlewit*.

Professor Gandish   Cockney painter, head of the academy where Clive Newcome and J. J. Ridley study in William Makepeace Thackeray's *The Newcomes*.

Charles Gandish   Professor Gandish's son in William Makepeace Thackeray's *The Newcomes*.

Gandolf, King of Utterbol   Ruler from whom Ursula escapes in company with Ralph; he is slain by Bull Shockhead in William Morris's *The Well at the World's End*.

James Gann   Good-natured, lazy inebriate, called "Captain" in honor of his invented tales of military prowess; he lives with his daughter, Caroline Brandon, in William Makepeace Thackeray's *The Adventures of Philip on His Way through the World*.

Gwythno Garanhir   Sixth-century king of Caredigon (Wales); he is given to hunting, feasting, and playing the harp in Thomas Love Peacock's *The Misfortunes of Elphin*.

Mr. Garbets   Tragedian and friend of Captain Jack Costigan in William Makepeace Thackeray's *The History of Pendennis*.

Don Garcia de Pimentesia de Carravalla   Captain of the Portuguese vessel on which the old pilot and young Bob Singleton sail; he orders Bob to be left on an island after Bob participates in an unsuccessful mutiny attempt in Daniel Defoe's *The Life, Adventures, and Pyracies of the Famous Captain Singleton*.

Gardener   Scarecrow-like man; he sings and dances constantly and appears to be crazy, but his songs provide transitions in the plot; he helps Sylvie and Bruno escape through the garden gate to see their father in Lewis Carroll's *Sylvie and Bruno*. He is the assistant who brings in the Professor's specimens at Uggug's birthday banquet in *Sylvie and Bruno Concluded*.

Colonel Gardiner   Commanding officer of Edward Waverly's regiment; he is greatly admired by Edward until he brings charges of desertion and high treason against him in Sir Walter Scott's *Waverly*.

Mrs. Gardiner   Amiable, intelligent, and well-bred wife of the uncle of Jane and Elizabeth Bennet; her letter to Elizabeth reveals the role of Mr. Darcy in effecting the marriage of Wickham and Lydia Bennet in Jane Austen's *Pride and Prejudice*.

Edward Gardiner   Respectable, well-bred businessman and brother of Mrs. Bennet; he and his wife take Elizabeth Bennet on a pleasure trip which includes a tour of Mr. Darcy's estate; Darcy's courteous behavior at their unexpected meeting accelerates Elizabeth's change of heart in Jane Austen's *Pride and Prejudice*.

Georgina Gardner   Friend of Theodora Martindale; she has made a mercenary marriage but continues to encourage the attentions of her dissolute cousin, Mark Gardner, in Charlotte Yonge's *Heartsease*.

Mark Gardner   Vicious young man who cheats at gambling and imposes on naive Emma Brandon in Charlotte Yonge's *Heartsease*.

Joe Gargery   A blacksmith and the kind, decent husband of Pip Pirrip's harridan sister; he is ruled mercilessly by his wife; though he is the only kindly influence in Pip's childhood, when Pip becomes a gentleman he spurns Joe because of his lack of gentlemanly manners; Joe forgives Pip for his scorn and looks after him when he is ill in Charles Dickens's *Great Expectations*.

Mrs. Joe Gargery   Pip Pirrip's sister, who hits him upon the smallest provocation; bitter, hateful, and ungenerous by nature, she becomes the victim of Dolge Orlick's attack, which kills her after a period of paralysis in Charles Dickens's *Great Expectations*.

Mr. Garland   Little, fat, placid-faced gentleman, who employs Kit Nubbles and becomes his benefactor; he works to clear Kit of any wrongdoing and assists in the search for Little Nell in Charles Dickens's *The Old Curiosity Shop*.

Mrs. Garland   Plump and placid wife of Mr. Garland and mother of Abel in Charles Dickens's *The Old Curiosity Shop*.

Abel Garland   Quiet and reserved son, who lives at home with his parents and works for Mr. Witherden in Charles Dickens's *The Old Curiosity Shop*.

Anne Garland   Heroine loved by John and Bob Loveday and sought also by the braggart Festus Derriman; she unwisely chooses the Loveday brother who loves her the least; although she is an intelligent and good-natured young woman, she lacks the insight and depth of character that would have directed her to the more devoted, constant brother in Thomas Hardy's *The Trumpet-Major*.

Martha Garland   Widow of a landscape painter and Anne Garland's mother; sociable and unaspiring, she marries Miller Loveday, father of John and Bob, in Thomas Hardy's *The Trumpet-Major*.

Maria Campinet Garnet   Aunt of Lord Grondale and great-aunt of Caroline Campinet; she rescues Gregory Glen from a suicidal leap; she is mother figure to Charles Hermsprong in Robert Bage's *Hermsprong*.

Dennis Garraghty   Dishonest brother of Nicholas Garraghty in Maria Edgeworth's *The Absentee*.

Nicholas Garraghty   Corrupt agent in charge of collecting rents from Clonbrony (a town in Lord Clonbrony's Irish estate); he is exposed by Lord Colambre and fired in Maria Edgeworth's *The Absentee*.

Madame De Garré   Woman who cares for Bernardo when he becomes lost and is taken ill; she accuses him of breaking a marriage contract with her daughter when he recovers and attempts to leave her home in Sarah Scott's *The History of Cornelia*.

Mademoiselle De Garré   Thirty-year-old daughter of Madame De Garré; she obtains Bernardo's signature by deceit and uses it to forge a marriage contract in Sarah Scott's *The History of Cornelia*.

Mary Garrett   A pupil at Jane Eyre's school in Morton, who must tend her ill mother in Charlotte Brontë's *Jane Eyre*.

Peter Garstin   A mine owner who is a Liberal candidate for Parliament in George Eliot's *Felix Holt, the Radical*.

Alfred Garth   Caleb Garth's son who intends to become an engineer; the money saved for his education must be used to pay Fred Vincy's debts in George Eliot's *Middlemarch*.

Ben Garth   Active son of Caleb Garth in George Eliot's *Middlemarch*.

Caleb Garth   The man who trusts Fred Vincy so much that he signs a note of debt for him, an act which nearly destroys the Garth family financially when Fred does not pay the loan back; when he is given his old job back on Arthur Brooke's estate, Caleb allows Fred Vincy to work for him in George Eliot's *Middlemarch*.

Christy Garth   Caleb Garth's scholarly eldest son, who becomes a tutor in George Eliot's *Middlemarch*.

Harriet Garth   Loyal governess of Norah and Magdalen Vanstone; her love for both her charges remains unchanged throughout the circumstances which deny them parentage and fortune in Wilkie Collins's *No Name*.

Letty Garth   Younger daughter of Caleb Garth in George Eliot's *Middlemarch*.

Mary Garth   Daughter of Caleb Garth; she nurses the dying Peter Featherstone and refuses his offer to leave her his fortune; she marries her childhood sweetheart Fred Vincy in George Eliot's *Middlemarch*.

Susan Garth   A good wife and mother, who is very angry when Fred Vincy is unable to repay a loan cosigned by her husband, Caleb, in George Eliot's *Middlemarch*.

Anna Gascoigne   Gwendolen Harleth's sweet-tempered cousin, who becomes quite concerned when she realizes that her brother, Rex, is romantically interested in the cold-hearted Gwendolen in George Eliot's *Daniel Deronda*.

Edward (Ned) Gascoigne   Adventurous midshipman serving on H.M.S. *Harpy*; he becomes boon companion of Jack Easy in Captain Frederick Marryat's *Mr. Midshipman Easy*.

Henry Gascoigne   Rector of Pennicote, near Offende; Gwendolen Harleth's uncle, he has been very prosperous and involved with high society; he encourages Gwendolen to marry Henleigh Mallinger Grandcourt in George Eliot's *Daniel Deronda*.

Nancy Gascoigne   Wife of the Reverend Henry Gascoigne, sister of Fanny Davilow, and aunt of Gwendolen Harleth; she is interested in maintaining a position in society in George Eliot's *Daniel Deronda*.

Rex Gascoigne   Gentle son of the Reverend Henry Gascoigne; he falls in love with his cousin Gwendolen Harleth and wishes to leave Oxford to remain near her; even when he is thrown from a horse, Gwendolen remains unconcerned for his welfare in George Eliot's *Daniel Deronda*.

Mr. Gashford   Lord George Gordon's villainous secretary, who uses Lord George in an attempt to seduce Emma Haredale but is foiled by Edward Chester and Joe Willet; Gashford deserts Gordon during the riots, becomes a government spy, and poisons himself in an obscure inn in Charles Dickens's *Barnaby Rudge*.

Gaspard Assassin who kills the Marquis St. Evrémonde in his bed, after the marquis's coach killed his child; he is hanged for his crime in Charles Dickens's *A Tale of Two Cities*.

Dr. Gaster A cleric and an expert on the art of stuffing a turkey; he is a guest of Squire Headlong in Thomas Love Peacock's *Headlong Hall*.

Robert Gates John Brough's faithful porter, who invests all his wages in the Independent West Diddlesex Fire and Life Insurance Co.; he remains loyal to Brough until he is ruined in William Makepeace Thackeray's *The History of Samuel Titmarsh and the Great Hoggarty Diamond*.

Lord Gaunt Eldest son of the Marquis of Steyne, with whom he is on bad terms in William Makepeace Thackeray's *Vanity Fair*. He has become Lord Steyne in *The Newcomes*.

Lady Blanche Thistlewood, Lady Gaunt Daughter of the impecunious Earl of Bareacres and wife of Lord Steyne's eldest son; her father-in-law holds her in contempt because she is childless in William Makepeace Thackeray's *Vanity Fair*.

Lady George Gaunt A banker's daughter and wife of the second son of the Marquis of Steyne; though she has provided money and borne children, the Gaunts hold her in contempt in William Makepeace Thackeray's *Vanity Fair*.

Lord George Gaunt The Marquis of Steyne's second son, whose rising career in the diplomatic service is cut short by his inherited insanity in William Makepeace Thackeray's *Vanity Fair*.

Plantagenet Gaunt Idiot son of Lord George Gaunt; he is mentioned in William Makepeace Thackeray's *Vanity Fair*.

Adela Gauntlet Devoted friend of Caroline Waddington and beloved of Arthur Wilkinson, whom she eventually marries in Anthony Trollope's *The Bertrams*.

Emilia Gauntlet Beautiful young woman who is loved and courted by Perry Pickle; often embarrassed by him, she resists him when he attempts an assault on her virtue and is alienated but finally agrees to marry him after

many years of waiting for his return to virtue in Tobias Smollett's *The Adventures of Peregrine Pickle*.

Godfrey Gauntlet Soldier who is the brother of Emilia Gauntlet; he overcomes hostility to Perry Pickle and becomes his friend; he learns his father was a friend of Commodore Trunnion; he receives financial assistance from Perry, whose influence advances his military career; he marries Miss Sophy and helps Perry when he is in the Fleet in Tobias Smollett's *The Adventures of Peregrine Pickle*.

Penelope Gauntlet Maiden aunt of Adela Gauntlet; she lives at Littlebath and is friendly with Mary Baker in Anthony Trollope's *The Bertrams*.

Pierce Gavan Friend at Trinity College, Dublin; John Buncle meets him on a ship to England; he falls overboard but is thrown back, despite his irreligion, while the morally upright Charles Henley is drowned in Thomas Amory's *The Life of John Buncle, Esq.*

Piers Gavaston Insolvent friend of Edward II of England; disliked by the English barons, he is exiled and later restored to court in Mary Shelley's *Valperga*.

Bob Gawffaw A former rural schoolmate and friend of Archibald Douglas; he gallantly entertains Archibald and Mary Douglas on their trip to London in Susan Ferrier's *Marriage*.

May Gawffaw The pretentious and slovenly wife of Bob Gawffaw in Susan Ferrier's *Marriage*.

Jeremy Gawky Schoolmate whose life Roderick Random saved; he assists in the punishment of the schoolmaster, betrays Roderick to the tricks of his cousins, flees Roderick's revenge, reappears as an army lieutenant and lodger in rooms of the apothecary Lavement in London, and marries Lavement's daughter in Tobias Smollett's *The Adventures of Roderick Random*.

Lucian Gay Nicholas Rigby's witty protégé, whose lack of a personal fortune enables Rigby to manipulate him in Benjamin Disraeli's *Coningsby; or, The New Generation*.

Walter Gay Cheerful, merry boy, who works for Dombey and Son and is the nephew of Solomon Gills; he rescues Florence Dombey when she is lost and dreams of marrying her some day but is sent to the West Indies; he is believed to have drowned in a shipwreck, but he returns and marries Florence in Charles Dickens's *Dombey and Son*.

Gayland Impudent suitor whom Betsy Thoughtless scorns; not to be outdone, he seduces Flora Mellasin in Eliza Haywood's *The History of Miss Betsy Thoughtless*.

Mortimer Gazebee   Junior partner in a powerful London firm of solicitors who becomes Member of Parliament for Barchester and marries Lady Amelia de Courcy in Anthony Trollope's *Doctor Thorne*. As "Gagebee" he presses Nathaniel Sowerby for mortgage payments in *Framley Parsonage*. He draws up the marriage settlement on behalf of Lady Alexandrina de Courcy in *The Small House at Allington*.

Mr. Gebbie   Scottish merchant and husband to Mrs. Gebbie and guardian of Catriona Drummond during her passage to Leyden, Holland, in Robert Louis Stevenson's *Catriona*.

Mrs. Gebbie   Scottish merchant's seasick wife, who acts as invalid guardian to Catriona Drummond during her passage to Leyden, Holland, in Robert Louis Stevenson's *Catriona*.

Gebirus   Giant who wishes either to marry or to conquer Charoba; he is repeatedly put off by her and is finally defeated and poisoned by Charoba in the appended romance "The History of Charoba, Queen of Egypt" in Clara Reeve's *The Progress of Romance*.

Gecko   Svengali's nervous, shabby companion, who is a master of the violin; Svengali and Gecko are constantly together until the two argue over Trilby O'Ferrall and break relations with each other permanently in George Du Maurier's *Trilby*.

Joshua Geddes   Quaker fisherman who befriends Darsie Latimer (Arthur Redgauntlet), is assaulted by Hugh Redgauntlet's men as they are kidnapping Darsie, and is taken prisoner in England when he searches for Darsie in Sir Walter Scott's *Redgauntlet*.

Rachel Geddes   Sister of Joshua; she persuades her brother to let Darsie Latimer (Arthur Redgauntlet) join him in defense of his fishing stations in Sir Walter Scott's *Redgauntlet*.

Albert, Count of Geierstein   Swiss count and brother of Arthur Biederman; he is reunited with his daughter, Anne; disguised as a priest and monk, he spies on Charles, Duke of Burgundy; he blesses the marriage of Arthur de Vere and Anne; he dies in the battle when the duke is killed in Sir Walter Scott's *Anne of Geierstein*.

Anne of Geierstein   Daughter of an exiled Swiss count; she has lived with her uncle for seven years before being reunited with her father; she is rumored to have inherited magical powers from her sorceress mother; she helps Arthur Philipson (Arthur de Vere) escape prison and marries him in Sir Walter Scott's *Anne of Geierstein*.

Peterkin Geislaer   Hermann Pavillon's lieutenant and confidant, free with his advice to the syndic of Liège in Sir Walter Scott's *Quentin Durward*.

David (Davie) Gellatley   A storyteller who plays the Baron of Bradwardine's fool; he protects his master from royal dragoons in Sir Walter Scott's *Waverly*.

Old Janet Gellatley   David Gellatley's mother, who is thought to be a witch; she nurses Edward Waverly back to health and hides the Baron of Bradwardine after the war in Sir Walter Scott's *Waverly*.

General   Old man who advanced in the army through the assistance of Captain Standard's father; he is tricked into helping Captain Standard by William in Charles Johnstone's *Chrysal: or, The Adventures of a Guinea*.

General   A good officer, who is anxious to prove himself worthy of command, and who is caught between his inclination to reward for merit and the tradition which rewards according to seniority and interest in Charles Johnstone's *Chrysal: or, The Adventures of a Guinea*.

General   A friend of the King of Bulgaria; he saves Theodora from a fate worse than death in Charles Johnstone's *Chrysal: or, The Adventures of a Guinea*.

General in America   A proud and avaricious man, who holds the army in place, and who puts an embargo on all shipping in order to enrich himself in Charles Johnstone's *Chrysal: or, The Adventures of a Guinea*.

Mrs. General   Stiff, opinionless, but proper lady, who is hired by William Dorrit as a chaperon and mentor to his daughters, and who perhaps plots to marry her employer in Charles Dickens's *Little Dorrit*.

Muscovite General   Father of Zara; he captures Count de Beaumont in war and treats him as a friend until the count refuses Zara, whereupon the General has him imprisoned in Penelope Aubin's *The Life of Madam de Beaumont*.

Lady Gentle   Vain and turbulent wife of Mr. Gentle in Henry Brooke's *The Fool of Quality*.

Mr. Gentle   Henpecked neighbor of the Moreland estate; he represses his good sense in Henry Brooke's *The Fool of Quality*.

Gentleman   Unnamed man who promises Parson Adams favors and riches but delivers nothing in Henry Fielding's *The History of the Adventures of Mr. Joseph Andrews and of his Friend Mr. Abraham Adams*.

Gentleman of Bath   Moll Flanders's friend and, later, lover; after recovering from a lengthy illness, he repents of having had an affair with her and abandons her in Daniel Defoe's *The Fortunes and Misfortunes of the Famous Moll Flanders.*

Gentleman of Chance   Hibernian who supports himself royally on his winnings at the race track and on his exploits as a highwayman in Charles Johnstone's *Chrysal: or, The Adventures of a Guinea.*

Gentleman in Coffee-house   Defender of the government in a dispute with the Coffee-house Orator in Francis Coventry's *The History of Pompey the Little.*

Gentleman Draper   Moll Flanders's unprincipled second husband, who spends money extravagantly and is put into debtor's prison; he later escapes to France, telling Moll to consider him dead in Daniel Defoe's *The Fortunes and Misfortunes of the Famous Moll Flanders.*

Gentleman of the Esculapian Art   The physician who attends Mrs. Qualmsick in Francis Coventry's *The History of Pompey the Little.*

Gentleman of Honor   Player of a trick on the Wife of Charity Supporter Number Six in order to convince the lady that Sunday is not an acceptable day for parties in Charles Johnstone's *Chrysal; or, The Adventures of a Guinea.*

Gentlewoman   Rich matron who takes Moll Flanders into her household after Moll's "Mistress Nurse" dies; she does not want her younger son (Robin) to marry Moll; she and her husband raise Robin and Moll's two children after Robin's death in Daniel Defoe's *The Fortunes and Misfortunes of the Famous Moll Flanders.*

North Country Gentlewoman   Jemy E.'s ex-lover, who helps him to deceive Moll Flanders into marrying him, believing that Moll has money in Daniel Defoe's *The Fortunes and Misfortunes of the Famous Moll Flanders.*

Captain Geoff   Ruthless commander of the pirate crew during Captain Clement Cleveland's absence; petulant and resentful, he leads a rebellious faction and is hanged for piracy in Sir Walter Scott's *The Pirate.*

Geoffrey of the Dry Tree   Discoverer that the Lady of Abundance is the vanished queen of the Land of the Tower; he brings her from the house of the sorceress to her castle of Abundance in William Morris's *The Well at the World's End.*

George   Cavalier's footman, who gathers a large amount of booty during the battle between King Gustavus Adolphus and Count Tilly in Daniel Defoe's *Memoirs of a Cavalier.*

George   Man who works for Mrs. Jarley, the owner of the waxwork collection, in Charles Dickens's *The Old Curiosity Shop.*

George   Mr. Weller's friend who is going to court for debt in Charles Dickens's *The Posthumous Papers of the Pickwick Club.*

Blind George   Observer of dock life who tries to use his knowledge for self gain; he blinds Dan Ogle with lime in Arthur Morrison's *The Hole in the Wall.*

King George II   King whose throne, from which Prince Charles Stuart's grandfather, King James II, was ousted, is the object of the revolt in Sir Walter Scott's *Waverly.* John, Duke of Argyle is attached to his court in *The Heart of Midlothian.*

King [George III]   Monarch whom Anne Garland encounters by chance just after the Battle of Trafalgar; her charming anxiety for sailor Bob Loveday contributes much to the "luck" of his promotion from the ranks to lieutenant in Thomas Hardy's *The Trumpet-Major.*

Trooper George   See George Rouncewell.

Mr. George   Butler to Sir William Forester; he becomes jealous of the attention Mrs. Molly pays Geoffry Wildgoose in Richard Graves's *The Spiritual Quixote.*

Mrs. George   Friend of Mrs. Jiniwin, who has tea with her in Charles Dickens's *The Old Curiosity Shop.*

Catherine George   Naive young governess to the Butler family; her adoration of her employer's nephew, Richard Butler, leads to her exile in Normandy; she marries Charles Fontaine in Anne Thackeray Ritchie's *The Village on the Cliff.*

Essper George   A resourceful conjurer and Vivian Grey's devoted servant, who frequently rescues his master during his romantic travels but dies during a storm at the conclusion of Benjamin Disraeli's *Vivian Grey.*

Miss Georgiana   Annual birthday visitor to Miss Havisham; she flatters her in the hope of inheriting money in Charles Dickens's *Great Expectations.*

Georgina   Aristocratic, red-haired woman loved by Owen Asher before he meets Evelyn Innes in George Moore's *Evelyn Innes.*

Georigetti   Benign, malleable king of Normnbdsgrsutt whose domain is defended and considerably expanded by Peter Wilkins in Robert Paltock's *The Life and Adventures of Peter Wilkins.*

Norah Geraghty   Pretty Irish barmaid, with whom

Charley Tudor becomes briefly involved in Anthony Trollope's *The Three Clerks*.

Major Neville, Lord Geraldin Young stranger who travels under the assumed name William Lovel from Edinburgh to Fairport with Oldbuck (Jonathan Oldenbuck), keeps secret his illegitimate birth and his army commission, courts Isabel Wardour, saves Sir Arthur Wardour from drowning, fights a duel with Hector M'Intyre, and discovers he is the legitimate son of William, Lord Geraldin, Earl of Glenallan in Sir Walter Scott's *The Antiquary*.

Sir Francis Geraldine Choleric baronet, who, wishing to marry to spite his cousin, becomes engaged to Cecilia Holt; resentful when she jilts him, he nurses a grievance and, after her marriage to George Western, he tells the husband of their prior relationship, egged on by Francesca Altifiorla, to whom he becomes engaged and whom he then jilts in Anthony Trollope's *Kept in the Dark*.

Captain Walter Geraldine Affable cousin of the tyrannical baronet Sir Francis Geraldine; he marries Miss Tremenhere, who had jilted George Western in Anthony Trollope's *Kept in the Dark*.

Gerard Elias's son, destined for the church, who falls in love with Margaret Brandt, escapes to Rome to make his fortune as copyist-illustrator, receives forged news of Margaret's demise, and turns to a life of debauchery; rescued from a suicide attempt in the Tiber and nursed back to health by Jerome, at Margaret's instigation he becomes vicar of Gouda; his son becomes the great Erasmus in Charles Reade's *The Cloister and the Hearth*.

Gerard of the Clee Yeoman who with his sons conveys Birdalone from Greenford to the City of the Five Crafts in William Morris's *The Water of the Wondrous Isles*.

Lady Gerard Lady Juliana Douglas's friend, a London socialite who advises and criticizes the London social scene in Susan Ferrier's *Marriage*.

Constantine Gérard A member of an old business family ruined by the French Revolution and father of Hortense Gérard Moore in Charlotte Brontë's *Shirley*.

Sybil Gerard Walter Gerard's beautiful and deeply religious daughter, whose prejudice against the English aristocracy is dissipated by her growing love of Charles Egremont, whom she marries, and her own experience of the corruption within the Chartist labor movement in Benjamin Disraeli's *Sybil*.

Walter Gerard Noble leader of the Chartist labor movement and rightful heir to the Marney estates; George, Lord Marney and Baptiste Hatton have conspired to deprive him of his patrimony; he is killed by Lord Marney's troops while leading a group of peaceful marchers at the conclusion of Benjamin Disraeli's *Sybil*.

Mrs. Gerkin Pleasant housekeeper in the Winyard household in William Beckford's *Azemia*.

Lady Amelia Germain Youngest sister of the Marquis of Brotherton; she is devoted to church attendance in Anthony Trollope's *Is He Popenjoy?*.

Lord George Germain High-principled younger brother of the unpleasant Marquis of Brotherton; he is prodded by his father-in-law, Dean Lovelace, to make inquiries as to the legitimacy of Popenjoy, the Marquis's son and heir; the child's death makes further investigation unnecessary, and the newborn son of Lord George becomes the heir to the title and estate in Anthony Trollope's *Is He Popenjoy?*.

Mary Lovelace, Lady George Germain High-spirited, cheerful wife of Lord George Germain and much-loved daughter of Henry Lovelace, Dean of Brotherton; she is criticized as frivolous by her well-meaning sisters-in-law and insulted by her malicious brother-in-law, the Marquis of Brotherton; at last her husband becomes marquis, she becomes marchioness, and her baby son Lord Popenjoy in Anthony Trollope's *Is He Popenjoy?*.

Lady Sarah Germain Most austere and rigorous in church attendance of the four pious sisters of the Marquis of Brotherton; she is untiring in parish affairs and good works in Anthony Trollope's *Is He Popenjoy?*.

Lady Susanna Germain Zealous churchgoer second only to her sister, Lady Sarah, in her piety; she is much given to admonishing her sister-in-law Lady George Germain, daughter of the dean of Brotherton Cathedral, Henry Lovelace, in Anthony Trollope's *Is He Popenjoy?*.

German General Commander of British troops; he wins battles despite his English officers in Charles Johnstone's *Chrysal: or, The Adventures of a Guinea*.

Mr. Gerrarde Mrs. Gerrarde's brother, who is intimate with the Widow Arnold; he is revealed as the secret witness in her case for the Arnold estate and is presumably the father of her child in Frances Sheridan's *Memoirs of Miss Sidney Bidulph*.

Mrs. Gerrarde Widow of Captain Gerrarde and Miss Burchell's aunt; she devises an intrigue with Mr. Arnold, leading Orlando Faulkland to entice her out of the country and into a marriage to Monsieur Pivet, from whom she flees to be a nobleman's mistress in Frances Sheridan's *Memoirs of Miss Sidney Bidulph*.

Gertrude Beautiful young lady from Namur, who begs Lewis Augustus Albertus to spare her from his soldiers; she becomes his mistress, bears him three children, begs him to marry her when his colonel pursues her, but gives in to the colonel when Albertus refuses; convinced by Albertus to live virtuously when he becomes a hermit, she stays with a kindly couple until she dies a few years later in Penelope Aubin's *The Life and Adventures of the Lady Lucy.*

Fray Gerundio Witness to the burning of Frank Leigh and Rose Salterne; he is hanged in retribution by Amyas Leigh in Charles Kingsley's *Westward Ho!.*

Monna Ghita Cruel mother of Tessa Melema in George Eliot's *Romola.*

Ghost of Christmas Past The first Christmas spirit who appears to Ebenezer Scrooge, garbed in white with haloed head and physically resembling both a child and an old man, to take Scrooge on a tour of scenes from his past life in Charles Dickens's *A Christmas Carol.*

Ghost of Christmas Present A jolly giant and the second ghost who visits Ebenezer Scrooge; he first appears among the decorations and feast foods of Christmas, then takes Scrooge to see how others, including his nephew Fred and clerk Bob Cratchit, keep the Christmas spirit in Charles Dickens's *A Christmas Carol.*

Ghost of Christmas Yet To Come Spirit shrouded in black and with only one hand visible that remains silent as it pays its ghostly visitation to Ebenezer Scrooge, showing him grisly scenes of the aftermath of his own death in Charles Dickens's *A Christmas Carol.*

Giacinta Mr. Rochester's second mistress, an Italian with a violent temper, of whom he tires in three months; the fact of his inconstancy is not lost on Jane Eyre in Charlotte Brontë's *Jane Eyre.*

Giacinta Vittoria Campa's loyal maid in George Meredith's *Vittoria.*

Giovanni Gianni Captain of *Principe Umberto,* the ship that rescues Jack Higgs and Arowhena Nosnibor; the reader is to refer to him for the truth of Higgs's story in Samuel Butler's *Erewhon.*

The Giaour Ugly, monster-like visitor to Vathek's kingdom; his promises of inestimable riches, unlimited power, and access to forbidden knowledge if the prince will deny his god and commit blood sacrifices launch Vathek on a pilgrimage to the palace of subterranean fire in William Beckford's *Vathek.*

John Gibbet Thief and thief-taker in Charles Johnstone's *Chrysal: or, The Adventures of a Guinea.*

Captain Gibbon Suitor to Olive Barton, belatedly acceptable in her mother's eyes as a replacement for Captain Hibbert; Olive is not interested in him in George Moore's *A Drama in Muslin.*

Mr. Gibbons Farmer and William Gibbons's father in Charlotte Lennox's *Sophia.*

Mrs. Gibbons William Gibbons's aunt and godmother; proud of her false and rigid "good breeding," she takes offense at Mrs. Lawson's raillery and forbids the match between Dolly Lawson and William in Charlotte Lennox's *Sophia.*

Martha (Patty) Gibbons Pretty Berkshire lass, with whom Tom Brown flirts when she works as a barmaid in the Choughs public house in Oxford; she marries Harry Winburn in Thomas Hughes's *Tom Brown at Oxford.*

William Gibbons Farmer's son, educated as a gentleman by his aunt, though he prefers to marry Dolly Lawson and farm; talking to Sophia Darnley about his romantic difficulties, he is seen by Sir Charles Stanley and mistaken for a rival for Sophia in Charlotte Lennox's *Sophia.*

Lord Giblet Helpless victim of Mrs. Montacute Jones's scheme to marry him off to Olivia Green in Anthony Trollope's *Is He Popenjoy?.*

Mr. Gibson The widowed Hollingford medical practitioner, whose position and character give him admission to all levels of local society; he marries to provide a mother for his daughter, Molly, in Elizabeth Gaskell's *Wives and Daughters.*

Mr. Gibson Mrs. Reed's brother, who settles the affairs after her death and takes Georgiana, her middle child, to live with him in London in Charlotte Brontë's *Jane Eyre.*

Mrs. Gibson Mr. Gibson's wife, who takes the Reed daughters into society when they come to visit her in Charlotte Brontë's *Jane Eyre.*

Mrs. Gibson Molly's stepmother and Cynthia Kirkpatrick's mother; former governess to the Cumnor family, she is well-meaning but affected and snobbish in Elizabeth Gaskell's *Wives and Daughters.*

Janet (Jenny) Gibson Orphan taken in as a companion for Margaret Bertram; she receives a £100 settlement, then moves in with the Dinmonts in Sir Walter Scott's *Guy Mannering*.

Molly Gibson   Central character, who grows from child to young woman; her relationships with all elements of the Hollingford community influence and are influenced by individual and social change and values in Elizabeth Gaskell's *Wives and Daughters*.

Thomas Gibson   Minor canon of Exeter Cathedral whose only charm is the potent one of his bachelor status; he acts on Jemima Stanbury's financially sweetened offer of her niece Dorothy Stanbury, whose refusal has the effect of wearing down his long-established resistance to the French sisters; he becomes engaged to Camilla but marries Arabella in Anthony Trollope's *He Knew He Was Right*.

Katchen Giesslinger   Tyrolean servant who helps Vittoria Campa and Angelo Guidascarpi escape from Captain Weisspreiss when they flee from Milan in George Meredith's *Vittoria*.

Mr. Gifford   Waspish writer of poor satirical verse, whose asperity is partly responsible for the death of Lucina Howard in William Beckford's *Modern Novel Writing; or, the Elegant Enthusiast*.

Mrs. Gifford   Beautiful, animated sister of Ambrose Fleetwood; after a turbulent career of adultery centered in Bath, "the very focus of artificial society," she retires to a small town in Northern Wales and marries Mr. Kenrick in William Godwin's *Fleetwood*.

Mrs. Gifford   Ill-tempered mistress whom Lord W. wishes to be rid of, but without paying the bonus such action would require by written agreement; his nephew, Sir Charles Grandison, solves the problem by agreeing to make the payments himself in Samuel Richardson's *Sir Charles Grandison*.

Gigantilla   The duchess, an ambitious, power-mad woman with a reputation for cruelty; she will do anything for control, but at the end she is exiled and powerless in Eliza Haywood's *The Perplex'd Dutchess; or, Treachery Rewarded*.

Adrian Gilbert   Brother of Sir Humphrey Gilbert; he is devastated to hear from Amyas Leigh the fate of the ship *The Squirrel* and of his brother's death; he is ruined by the failure of the expedition in Charles Kingsley's *Westward Ho!*.

Sir Humphrey Gilbert   Bosom friend of Sir Richard Grenvile and half brother of Sir Walter Raleigh; he plans a colony as a halfway house between England and the Indies, sails in *The Squirrel*, and perishes in Charles Kingsley's *Westward Ho!*.

Mark Gilbert   Confederate of Simon Tappertit; he becomes a member of the 'Prentices Knights' in Charles Dickens's *Barnaby Rudge*.

Cordelia Gilchrist   Roman Catholic friend whom Christopher Kirkland must give up when their religious beliefs become irreconcilable in Mrs. Lynn Linton's *The Autobiography of Christopher Kirkland*.

Giles   A stupid and malicious dwarf with a huge voice and immense strength in his upper body; he goes to the ducal court, where he requests the vicarage of Gouda for his brother Gerard in Charles Reade's *The Cloister and the Hearth*.

Giles   Gentle but very old butler at Bartram-Haugh; he is unaware of the plot against Maud Ruthyn in J. Sheridan Le Fanu's *Uncle Silas*.

Giles   Apprentice to the cooper Guilbert Girder in Sir Walter Scott's *The Bride of Lammermoor*.

Giles   Leader of the Shepherd contingent in the battle of Upmeads in William Morris's *The Well at the World's End*.

Father Giles   Elderly parish priest at Headford, County Galway, out of sympathy with his firebrand curate, Father Brosnan, and opposed to the terrorism in the community in Anthony Trollope's *The Landleaguers*.

Mr. Giles   Banker who informs Hammel Clement that a stop payment has been put on large bank note given him by his father in Henry Brooke's *The Fool of Quality*.

Mr. Giles   Butler and steward in Mrs. Maylie's household; he shoots Oliver Twist after he breaks into the house in Charles Dickens's *Oliver Twist*.

Putney Giles   Lawyer and man of business who handles Lothair's affairs; he is the voice of disinterested reason in dealing with the practical matters in Lothair's life in Benjamin Disraeli's *Lothair*.

Mrs. Gill   Housekeeper at the Keeldar home, who gradually becomes loyal to Shirley Keeldar in Charlotte Brontë's *Shirley*.

Mrs. Gill   Mother of six; her punctuality in childbirth is the admiration of her husband and a gratification to her attendant, Sarah Gamp, in Charles Dickens's *The Life and Adventures of Martin Chuzzlewit*.

Gillespie   Old clergyman from Donegal who attends

the secret burial of the coffin Mervyn brings to Chapelizod in J. Sheridan Le Fanu's *The House by the Churchyard.*

Dame Gillian   Servant in the household of Eveline Berenger; she allows Randal de Lacy to enter the Castle in disguise in Sir Walter Scott's *The Betrothed.*

Gillies   Thirteen-year-old prisoner, flogged and otherwise abused, who makes a false attempt at suicide, in Charles Reade's *It Is Never Too Late to Mend.*

Bessy Gillies   Maid to Arabella Logan; she refuses to incriminate Bell Calvert in distrust of the evidence of senses and memory in James Hogg's *The Private Memoirs and Confessions of a Justified Sinner.*

Gilliman   Kidnapping rogue who has Colonel Jack and Captain Jack sent to Virginia in Daniel Defoe's *The History and the Remarkable Life of the Truly Honourable Colonel Jacques, Commonly Call'd Col. Jack.*

George Gillingham   Schoolmaster and longtime friend of Richard Phillotson, to whom he recommends severity in the treatment of Phillotson's wife, Sue (Bridehead), in Thomas Hardy's *Jude the Obscure.*

Solomon (Sol) Gills   Ship's-instrument maker who lives with his nephew, Walter Gay; he shelters Florence Dombey when she is lost; he is nearly bankrupt but is saved through Paul Dombey; he searches for Walter, who is believed to be drowned at sea in Charles Dickens's *Dombey and Son.*

Gil-martin   Mysterious stranger with uncanny powers; he first appears to Robert Colwan on the day of his assurance of election, becomes his constant companion, tempting him to murder and other crimes as champion of the cause of Christ, and finally hounds his victim to suicide in James Hogg's *The Private Memoirs and Confessions of a Justified Sinner.*

Harry Gilmore   Genial Squire of Bullhampton, who opposes the Marquis of Trowbridge over the latter's demand that the miller Jacob Brattle be evicted because Brattle's son faces a murder charge; Harry loves Mary Lowther and is devastated when, having been persuaded to accept him, she has a change of heart; he generously releases her from their engagement in Anthony Trollope's *The Vicar of Bullhampton.*

Vincent Gilmore   Trusted family lawyer of Frederick Fairlie; he draws up the marriage settlement on behalf of Fairlie's niece, Laura, when she is to marry Sir Percival Glyde in Wilkie Collins's *The Woman in White.*

Caroline Gilmour   Youthful, pleasure-seeking mother of Elizabeth Gilmour; she is her daughter's rival for the affections of John Dampier; she marries the French Pasteur Tourneur in Anne Thackeray Ritchie's *The Story of Elizabeth.*

Elizabeth Gilmour   Young woman of frivolous education; she suffers first from the coldness of her mother, Caroline Gilmour, and then from the oppressive atmosphere of the dismal household of Caroline's second husband; she marries John Dampier in Anne Thackeray Ritchie's *The Story of Elizabeth.*

Mr. Gimble   Picture-dealer friend of Valentine Blyth in Wilkie Collins's *Hide and Seek.*

Jack Gines   Thief who nearly kills Caleb Williams after Caleb's escape from jail; he blames Caleb for his expulsion from the gang and becomes an enemy, following Caleb to London; as a result of his actions, Caleb is recaptured; Ferdinando Falkland later hires Gines to stalk Caleb and destroy his reputation wherever he goes in William Godwin's *Caleb Williams.*

Ginotti   Brigand who betrays the secret hideout of Leonardo di Loredani in Charlotte Dacre's *Zofloya; or, The Moor.*

Ginotti (Frederic de Nempere)   Bandit who holds a secret over Wolfstein and pursues him relentlessly; as Frederic de Nempere, he captures Eloise de St. Irvyne in Percy Bysshe Shelley's *St. Irvyne.*

Signor Giotto   Signora Bianchi's relative, who occasionally chaperones Vincentio di Vivaldi and Ellena Rosalba in Ann Radcliffe's *The Italian.*

Giovanni   Servant of the di Bruno family, who testifies to the Inquisition that he witnessed the attempt by Father Schedoni (Ferando di Bruno) to assassinate Olivia di Bruno in Ann Radcliffe's *The Italian.*

Gipsy   Reader of Pamela Andrews's palm while she is imprisoned on Mr. B——'s Lincolnshire estate; she is taken by Pamela to be a secret messenger from her supporters with a warning against the plots and intrigues of Mr. B——'s seduction in Samuel Richardson's *Pamela, or Virtue Rewarded.*

Mrs. Girder   Guilbert Girder's wife and Luckie Lightbody's daughter in Sir Walter Scott's *The Bride of Lammermoor.*

Guilbert Girder   Obstinate and opinionated but skilled artisan and cooper to the queen's stores in Sir Walter Scott's *The Bride of Lammermoor.*

Giuseppe   Julian Danvers's devoted tutor, distinguished by a vivacious personality in William Godwin's *Cloudesley*.

Peggy Givan Bride selected by Claud Walkinshaw for his son George; she gives birth to twin daughters instead of the male heir Claud wants in John Galt's *The Entail*.

Madame Glück German landlady of the lodging house in Naples where many of the characters stay in George Gissing's *The Emancipated*.

Lord Glamorgan Irish nobleman who sends John Inglesant with promises of aid to the royal garrison at Chester commanded by Lord Biron in J. Henry Shorthouse's *John Inglesant, A Romance*.

Bob Glamour Customer at the Six Jolly Fellowship Porters who helps to revive Roger Riderhood in Charles Dickens's *Our Mutual Friend*.

Charles Owen Glandore Mr. Lluelling's cousin and heir, a debauchee who wants him dead without issue; left in charge of the estate when Lluelling goes to France, he lusts after Belinda Lluelling and abducts her but is killed by highwaymen before he can ravish her in Penelope Aubin's *The Life of Madam de Beaumont*.

Glanlepze African with whom Peter Wilkins escapes from slavery in Angola; his cleverness and homely wisdom make a considerable impression on Peter in Robert Paltock's *The Life and Adventures of Peter Wilkins*.

Sir Charles Glanville Charles Glanville's father, Arabella's uncle; a plainspoken man, he is alternately incensed, puzzled, and concerned by his niece's occasionally mad-sounding speech in Charlotte Lennox's *The Female Quixote*.

Charles Glanville Arabella's cousin; the favorite and would-be son-in-law of the Marquis of –-, he loves Arabella but is exasperated by her folly and her demands for worship; he becomes a romance hero by fighting Sir George Bellmour on her behalf; he ultimately accepts the ''cured'' heroine's humble apologies in Charlotte Lennox's *The Female Quixote*.

Charlotte Glanville Charles Glanville's sister, an average girl, vain and ignorant; her observance of the normal rules of female conduct is in contrast to both the immodesty of the romance heroine and the false modesty of the fashionable woman; she loves and eventually marries the reluctant Sir George Bellmour in Charlotte Lennox's *The Female Quixote*.

Ellen Glanville Sir Reginald Glanville's beautiful, cultivated, animated sister; Henry Pelham makes a happy marriage with her at the end of Edward Bulwer-Lytton's *Pelham*.

Louis Glanville Viviette Constantine's overbearing and opportunistic brother, who helps promote her marriage to Bishop Helmsdale in Thomas Hardy's *Two on a Tower*.

Sir Reginald Glanville Closest school friend of Henry Pelham; he is a baronet who loses his health to grief after the tragic death of his mistress, Gertrude Douglas, and obsessively pursues his revenge against her rapist, Sir John Tyrrell; exonerated of the crime of murdering Tyrrell, thanks to Pelham's detection, he dies contented when his sister and Pelham are wed in Edward Bulwer-Lytton's *Pelham*.

Glascock Hostler to Beauclerc; he is killed by Charles Archer (Paul Dangerfield) when he tries to blackmail Archer with his knowledge of the murder of Beauclerc in J. Sheridan Le Fanu's *The House by the Churchyard*.

Charles Glascock Wealthy heir to a title who falls in love with his friend Louis Trevelyan's sister-in-law Nora Rowley; he recovers from her rejection to fall in love with and marry the American Caroline Spalding; on the death of his father he becomes Lord Peterborough in Anthony Trollope's *He Knew He Was Right*.

Lydia Glasher Dark-haired beauty, who left her husband to become Henleigh Mallinger Grandcourt's mistress; she tries to stop Gwendolen Harleth from marrying Grandcourt because she wants Grandcourt to acknowledge legally the four children he has fathered in George Eliot's *Daniel Deronda*.

Mrs. Glass Gossipy tobacco dealer and Jeanie Deans's distant kinswoman; she is Jeanie's kind hostess in London in Sir Walter Scott's *The Heart of Midlothian*.

Adrian Glastonbury Gentle, wise, scholarly Roman Catholic priest, friend and former tutor of Sir Ratcliffe Armine; he is also tutor of Ferdinand Armine and pays for the young man's army commission when Sir Ratcliffe's resources are not sufficient in Benjamin Disraeli's *Henrietta Temple: A Love Story*.

Catherine Glatz Servant and coconspirator with Pietro Mondovi to blackmail Countess Zulmer in Charlotte Dacre's *The Passions*.

Glaucus Young Athenian who loves Ione; he is falsely accused by Arbaces of the murder of Apaecides in Edward Bulwer-Lytton's *The Last Days of Pompeii*.

Eustace Glazzard A man of artistic tastes and abilities who is given to gambling; he becomes jealous of the success of his old schoolfellow, Denzil Quarrier, and tries to wreck his Parliamentary campaign by exposing his false marriage; Glazzard marries a wealthy woman and ultimately confesses his betrayal in George Gissing's *Denzil Quarrier*.

William Glazzard   Brother of Eustace and a country gentleman prominent in the town where the election occurs in George Gissing's *Denzil Quarrier*.

Sir Charles Gleed   Slow-witted fellow student of Casimir Fleetwood at Oxford; he surfaces in Paris as an *elegant*, who is admired as a man of breeding, amusement, and fashion, and who introduces Fleetwood to Parisian society in William Godwin's *Fleetwood*.

Mr. Glegg   The retired wealthy wool merchant who works in his garden and humors his wife's ill-temper; he is "a lovable skinflint" in George Eliot's *The Mill on the Floss*.

Jane Dodson Glegg   The richest of all of Bessie Tulliver's sisters; she holds a note on Mr. Tulliver's property, and he borrows money to repay the debt after a quarrel with her; she believes in rigid adherence to the Dodson family code, which means formal social correctness in George Eliot's *The Mill on the Floss*.

Gregory Glen (Grooby)   Gregory Grooby's illegitimate son, who migrates to the village of Grondale; he is one of Charles Hermsprong's closest friends and the narrator of Robert Bage's *Hermsprong*.

William, Earl of Glenallan   Moody old Catholic recluse, who suffers from memories of incestuous love and guilt, having been led to believe that his wife was his sister; she had taken her own life after the birth of her son; he is released from his suffering by the confessions of Elspeth Mucklebackit, and discovers that William Lovel is his legitimate son in Sir Walter Scott's *The Antiquary*.

David Keith Carnegie, Lord Glenalmond   Tall, thin, and aristocratic lawyer and Lord Hermiston's acquaintance, who draws out his son, Archibald Weir, and becomes his cautious mentor and friend in Robert Louis Stevenson's *Weir of Hermiston: An Unfinished Romance*.

Mrs. Glenarm   A friend of the Delamayn family and a rich widow, who falls in love with Geoffrey Delamayn; her declaration of fidelity motivates his attempt to murder Anne Silvester; after his death Mrs. Glenarm converts to Roman Catholicism and joins a sisterhood in Wilkie Collins's *Man and Wife*.

Edward Glendinning (Ambrosius)   Elspeth Glendinning's youngest son, a promising student and ardent

suitor for Mary Avenel's love; because Mary chooses his brother, Halbert, Edward grows to hate Halbert and rejoices at his supposed death; rejected by Mary, he sorrowfully enters the monastery to become a monk in Sir Walter Scott's *The Monastery*. Called Ambrosius, he is secretly elected abbot but is forced into hiding when the election is annulled by the government; he acts as counselor for Queen Mary of Scotland in *The Abbot*.

Elspeth Glendinning   Mother of Halbert and Edward Glendinning and the widow of a vassal of the monastery; her rustic demeanor disguises her quick-wittedness; generous and kind, she gladly shares her residence, the Tower of Glendearg, with Lady Alice Avenel and Mary Avenel in Sir Walter Scott's *The Monastery*.

Halbert Glendinning   Elspeth Glendinning's eldest son; dark and handsome, with an attachment to adventure, he loves Mary Avenel, though he despairs of ever winning her; he often consults the White Lady, whose guidance leads him to become a Protestant and join the army of James Stuart, Earl of Murray, in Sir Walter Scott's *The Monastery*. He is Sir Halbert Glendinning and husband of Mary Avenel; favored by the Earl of Murray, now Regent of Scotland, he is often absent on political and military matters in *The Abbot*.

Chief of Glengarry (M'Dougal of Lorne)   Highlander in Montrose's army in Sir Walter Scott's *A Legend of Montrose*.

Lord Glenkindie   Short, large-bodied, and malicious senator of the College of Justice; he informs Lord Hermiston that his son, Archibald Weir, has indiscreetly denounced Hermiston's sentence to hang Duncan Jopp in Robert Louis Stevenson's *Weir of Hermiston: An Unfinished Romance*.

Lady Glenlivat   The Marquis of Farintosh's mother; her resurrection from the dead goes unremarked in William Makepeace Thackeray's *The Newcomes*.

Lady Glenmire   Down-to-earth widow and sister-in-law of the Hon. Mrs. Jamieson; she is at first the innocent agent through whom Mrs. Jamieson snubs her old friends; she is herself dropped by Mrs. Jamieson when she shocks Cranford society by marrying the medical practitioner Mr. Hoggins in Elizabeth Gaskell's *Cranford*.

Glenmorris   Heir to an impoverished Scottish estate, to which he returns after trying a career in commerce and eloping with Laura De Verdon; kidnapped by pirates, he returns again to find his wife and land held by his cousin, the Laird of Kilbrodie; reunited, he and his wife emigrate to America to escape the oppression of a rapacious society in Charlotte Smith's *The Young Philosopher*.

Laura De Verdon Glenmorris Lady Mary De Verdon's younger, neglected daughter, disowned when she elopes with Glenmorris; her husband's abduction by pirates places her in the dangerous hands of his kinsman and heir; the murder of her newborn son is thwarted by the infant's natural death; her escape and reunion with Glenmorris precede their emigration to America and her subsequent return with a daughter, Medora, to claim an inheritance; Medora's kidnapping leads to Laura's temporary insanity before the family are reunited and return to America in Charlotte Smith's *The Young Philosopher*.

Medora Glenmorris Daughter of Laura de Verdon Glenmorris; raised in America and educated by her mother on principles derived from Rousseau, she becomes engaged to George Delmont but is kidnapped in a plot to obtain her inheritance by forced marriage through the agency of an unscrupulous lawyer; she escapes and demonstrates self-possession and fortitude in negotiating hazards on the road toward London; she marries Delmont, and the couple join her parents in America in Charlotte Smith's *The Young Philosopher*.

Nigel Olifaunt, Lord Glenvarloch Destitute earl, whose estates are mortgaged, who pleads with King James I for restitution, and who compromises his reputation when he gambles in the company of Lord Dalgarno; he hides himself in Alsatia to avoid arrest, kills one of the murderers of his host Trapbois, is imprisoned in the Tower for a suspected attack on the king, and recovers his Scottish estate after his marriage to Margaret Ramsay in Sir Walter Scott's *The Fortunes of Nigel*.

Mr. Glibly London newspaper critic who describes—with heavy irony—various Londoners at the opera to Hugh Trevor and who later works as agent for the Earl of Idford in Thomas Holcroft's *The Adventures of Hugh Trevor*.

Bob Gliddery Pot-boy at the Six Jolly Fellowship Porters who helps rescue Roger Riderhood from the river in Charles Dickens's *Our Mutual Friend*.

Lucy Glitters A former entertainer of the Astley Royal Amphitheater; she is a houseguest of Lady Scattercash and marries Soapey Sponge in Robert Surtees's *Mr. Sponge's Sporting Tour*.

Captain Glomax Energetic rider who is Master of Hounds for the Rufford hunt and therefore a great man in the county in Anthony Trollope's *The American Senator*. He is succeeded as Master of Hounds by Sir Harry Albury in *Ayala's Angel*. He is again said to be retiring from the hunt in *The Duke's Children*.

Guilbert Glossin Lawyer for Godfrey Bertram; in order to facilitate his illegal scheme to get possession of the Bertram estate, he is responsible for Henry Bertram's kidnapping; imprisoned for these crimes, he is strangled by a fellow inmate in Sir Walter Scott's *Guy Mannering*.

Catherine (Katie) Glover Simon Glover's daughter, who is courted for her beauty by the Duke of Rothsay, Conochar, and Henry Smith; she flees persecution as a religious heretic; she marries Henry Smith in Sir Walter Scott's *The Fair Maid of Perth*.

Hans Glover Gertrude Pavillon's good-natured and devoted lover, who serves as guide to Isabelle de Croye and Quentin Durward in Sir Walter Scott's *Quentin Durward*.

Simon Glover Aged Scottish burgess, who takes his name from his craft as a glover; he wishes his daughter to marry Henry Smith; he flees to the Highlands to escape persecution for association with a heretic priest but makes peace with the Church in Sir Walter Scott's *The Fair Maid of Perth*.

Lady Glowrowrum Elderly gossip, who vigilantly chaperones her nieces, Clara and Maddie Groatsettar, in Sir Walter Scott's *The Pirate*.

Scythrop Glowry (caricature of the young Percy Bysshe Shelley) Christopher Glowry's son, whose two passions are for reforming the world and drinking Madeira; he is torn between love for the vivacious Marionetta O'Carroll and the solemn Stella (Celinda Toobad) in Thomas Love Peacock's *Nightmare Abbey*.

Christopher Glowry Melancholy owner of Nightmare Abbey and father of Scythrop in Thomas Love Peacock's *Nightmare Abbey*.

Glubb Old man who wheels little Paul Dombey's chariot along the beach in Brighton in Charles Dickens's *Dombey and Son*.

King of Glubbdubdrib Magician who summons ghosts from the dead for use as servants or for the entertainment and edification of his guest Lemuel Gulliver in Jonathan Swift's *Travels into Several Remote Nations of the World. In Four Parts. By Lemuel Gulliver.*

Glumdalclitch Lemuel Gulliver's "little nurse," the young daughter of a farmer in Brobdingnag; she accompanies Gulliver to court to take care of him in Jonathan Swift's *Travels into Several Remote Nations of the World. In Four Parts. By Lemuel Gulliver.*

Sir Percival Glyde Mean-spirited villain, who marries Laura Fairlie for her fortune; aided by the sinister Count Fosco, he embarks on a plan to incarcerate her in an asylum while he passes off her double, Anne Catherick, conveniently dead, as the deceased Lady Glyde; trying to destroy his own birth records, he is burnt to death in Wilkie Collins's *The Woman in White*.

Adela Glyndon Clarence Glyndon's sister, who fatally participates in her brother's distress over the failure of his apprenticeship to the adept, Mejnour, in Edward Bulwer-Lytton's *Zanoni*.

Clarence Glyndon Idealistic artist, who fails to become an initiate of the brotherhood of the Chaldeans; he represents unsustained aspiration, and his memoirs form the text of Edward Bulwer-Lytton's *Zanoni*.

Mrs. Glynn Woman who visits Lily Walsingham and then Dr. Walsingham to tell them—falsely—that Richard Devereux had promised to marry her daughter Nan, prompting Lily to refuse Devereux's proposal in J. Sheridan Le Fanu's *The House by the Churchyard*.

Nan Glynn Beautiful, lively young woman from Palmerston who attends the Royal Irish Artillery party; she loves Captain Richard Devereux faithfully, although she is heartbroken because he loves Lily Walsingham in J. Sherian Le Fanu's *The House by the Churchyard*.

Dr. Gmelin German philosopher who converts Helen Norman to Positivism in George Gissing's *Workers in the Dawn*.

Gnat Creature Alice encounters in the railway carriage as she begins her chessboard journey; it converses with Alice concerning the usefulness of naming insects and shows her several looking-glass insects which resemble the literal translations of their names in Lewis Carroll's *Through the Looking-Glass*.

Dan Goarly Curmudgeonly farmer suspected of poisoning foxes, which causes great outcry in Dillsborough among the fox-hunting gentry; Elias Gotobed's championing of him adds to the popular outrage in Anthony Trollope's *The American Senator*.

Justice Gobble Wicked man who uses his office to punish his enemies and is frightened into giving up his office by Sir Launcelot Greaves in Tobias Smollett's *The Adventures of Sir Launcelot Greaves*.

Mrs. Gobble Justice Gobble's wife, who was the cause of tragedy for Dorothy Oakley in Tobias Smollett's *The Adventures of Sir Launcelot Greaves*.

Captain Goby Rosey Mackenzie's godfather, who admires Mrs. Mackenzie in William Makepeace Thackeray's *The Newcomes*.

Mr. Goddard Apothecary who attends Clarissa

Harlowe in her decline in Samuel Richardson's *Clarissa: or, The History of a Young Lady*.

Mrs. Goddard Head of the school where Harriet Smith boards; she occasionally partakes of Mr. Woodhouse's over-solicitous hospitality in Jane Austen's *Emma*.

Dolly Goddard Chorus girl and friend of Lucy Leslie; she most resents Kate Ede's rise in Dick Lennox's acting company in George Moore's *A Mummer's Wife*.

Elias Goddedaal Gigantic, musical Swedish mate of the *Flying Scud*; he kills Richard Hemstead, breaks Mac's arm, and is shot by Norris Carthew, who takes his place only to disappear in San Francisco in Robert Louis Stevenson's *The Wrecker*.

Goddess of Fortune Envious and deformed spirit, who dispenses fortunes to the souls about to return to another human life in Henry Fielding's *A Journey From This World to the Next*.

Goderic Goth warrior and a particular friend of Amalric the Amal in Charles Kingsley's *Hypatia*.

Godfrey Duke of Bouillon and Lower Lorraine; a respected and efficient leader of the crusade, he becomes the King of Jerusalem in Sir Walter Scott's *Count Robert of Paris*.

Sally Godfrey (Wrightson) Young girl seduced by the rake Mr. B—— several years before he attempts to seduce Pamela Andrews; posing as a widow, she emigrated to Jamaica and married; her illegitimate daughter, Sally Goodwin, is supported financially by Mr. B—— and brought into the family home by Pamela in Samuel Richardson's *Pamela, or Virtue Rewarded*.

George Godolphin A naval officer who loves and finally marries Emmeline Mobray; he demonstrates manly restraint by curbing his resentment of George Fitz-Edward, who fathered his sister's illegitimate child, short of a duel and by sparing Emmeline sure knowledge of his feelings until persuaded she returns them in Charlotte Smith's *Emmeline: The Orphan of the Castle*.

Percy Godolphin Wealthy man who dabbles in the arts and in the occult; he is the lover of Fanny Millinger and of Lucilla Volktman and husband of Constance Vernon (Countess of Erpingham) in Edward Bulwer-Lytton's *Godolphin*.

Sir Godrick of Longshaw Man who enlists Osberne Wulfsson and his men to aid the guilds of lesser crafts in expelling the tyrannous king from the City of the Sundering Flood; later he becomes Burgreve of the City in William Morris's *The Sundering Flood*.

Marie (Madame Max) Goesler Dynamic Viennese widow and ornament of society; her charms excite the old Duke of Omnium, much to the anxiety of Lady Glencora Palliser; by refusing the Duke's offer of marriage, Marie Goesler begins a lifelong friendship with Lady Glencora, though her love for Phineas Finn has in fact directed her; having become betrothed in Ireland, Finn must decline her offer of money and marriage, which would enable him to follow his political career in Anthony Trollope's *Phineas Finn*. She amuses the old Duke of Omnium with accounts of Lizzie Eustaces's escapades in *The Eustace Diamonds*. She stands by Finn when he is accused of murder, and by her ingenuity evidence is uncovered which leads to his acquittal, after which they marry in *Phineas Redux*. She is for a time repudiated by the (younger) Duke of Omnium because of his misunderstanding of her role in Lady Mary Palliser's romance with Frank Tregear in *The Duke's Children*.

Hermann Goetze Manager of the opera company; he engages Evelyn Innes and Louise Helbrun in George Moore's *Evelyn Innes*.

Goffe One of Sir Daniel Brackley's trumpeters; he covers a consultation between Bennet Hatch and Sir Oliver Oates in Robert Louis Stevenson's *The Black Arrow: A Tale of Two Roses*.

Eliza Gogarty Favorite sister of Oliver Gogarty; she understands his vocation as a priest since she intends to become a nun, predicting accurately that she will become Abbess of Tinnick Convent in George Moore's *The Lake*.

Father Oliver Gogarty Sensitive young Irish priest, who is sure of his vocation but deeply convinced of his wrong in publicly condemning the schoolmistress and organist Rose Leicester, whose company and conversation he enjoys; he corresponds with her after she leaves, and her ideas lead to his break for freedom in George Moore's *The Lake*.

James Gogarty Oliver Gogarty's brother, who goes to America and succeeds well enough to provide an organ for Oliver's parish church in George Moore's *The Lake*.

Mary Gogarty Younger sister of Oliver Gogarty; failing in several enterprises, she becomes a nun in her sister's convent but finds it awkward and becomes a complainer in George Moore's *The Lake*.

Queen of Goldburg Enamored ruler, who disappears after Ralph leaves Goldburg in William Morris's *The Well at the World's End*.

Bartholomew Golden Rich merchant of Langton on Holm by the sea; he is father of Walter (Golden Walter) in William Morris's *The Wood beyond the World*.

Walter (Golden Walter) Golden Discoverer of the Wood Beyond the World, which is ruled by a heartless, sensual enchantress (the Lady); he flees with her thrall (the Maid) to Stark-wall, where they rule as king and queen in William Morris's *The Wood beyond the World*.

Mr. Golding Virtuous man and successful London merchant to whom Henry Clinton is apprenticed; he makes Clinton a partner and becomes Clinton's father-in-law; he dies from excessive grief and bequeaths immense wealth to his son-in-law in Henry Brooke's *The Fool of Quality*.

Arthur Golding Orphan boy who is brought up by a kindly printer; he studies with an artist, hesitates between art and social reform, and contracts an unhappy marriage with an alcoholic wife (Carrie Mitchell); he then falls in love with the educated, middle-class Helen Norman and ends by committing suicide in George Gissing's *Workers in the Dawn*.

Johanetta Golding A girl of questionable virtue; she impersonates Robert Lovelace's cousin, Charlotte Montague, in his kidnapping of Clarissa Harlowe in Samuel Richardson's *Clarissa: or, The History of a Young Lady*.

Matilda (Matty) Golding Plain and devout daughter of Mr. Golding; she becomes the loving wife of Henry Clinton; a faithful Christian to the end, she dies as the result of a miscarriage brought on by an emotional shock in Henry Brooke's *The Fool of Quality*.

Martha Goldthorp Dr. Winslow's ward, whose fortune is £50,000; traveling, she suffers a broken arm in an accident which George Delmont's intervention prevents from being worse and recuperates in his household; she falls in love with him but is disappointed at his continued indifference; her marriage to his elder brother is unhappy because his title is no compensation for his indifference in Charlotte Smith's *The Young Philosopher*.

Laurence Goldthred A mercer and frequenter of Giles Gosling's Black Bear in Sir Walter Scott's *Kenilworth*.

Clementina Golightly Heiress daughter of Mrs. Valentine Scott; as trustee of her fortune, Alaric Tudor misappropriates funds in Anthony Trollope's *The Three Clerks*.

Gomez Half-breed guide and bearer hired by the expedition that Professor Challenger leads to the region of dinosaurs; he later betrays them in Arthur Conan Doyle's *The Lost World*.

Cardinal Gonzaga Cynical conspirator against Doge Andreas; he is trapped and exposed by Abellino/Flodoardo (Count Rosalvo) in Matthew Lewis's *The Bravo of Venice*.

Amelia de Gonzales Arabella Bloomville's friend, who enters the narrative as a fair stranger with a melancholy story; she is followed to England by her husband; her indiscretion leads to the death of a gallant officer; she dies after accidentally eating contaminated celery at her husband's banquet in William Beckford's *Modern Novel Writing; or, the Elegant Enthusiast*.

Don Pedro de Gonzales Spanish aristocrat who elopes with the English girl Amelia; she abandons her husband to return to England with her ill mother; he follows her to England, fights a farcical duel with Lord Mahogany, and accidentally poisons himself and several guests who eat the contaminated celery he serves at a banquet in William Beckford's *Modern Novel Writing; or, the Elegant Enthusiast*.

Captain John (Bougwan) Good Short, dark, stout, and bemonocled former naval officer, who accompanies Allan Quatermain and Sir Henry Curtis on two expeditions into Africa; the first is in search of King Solomon's mines and Henry's lost brother in H. Rider Haggard's *King Solomon's Mines*. The second expedition is to find a rumored white race, the Zu-Vendi, in *Allan Quatermain*.

Good old Genius Old man whose sole occupation is the protection of children, to whom he gives eternal childhood; he saves the fifty children Vathek sacrificed to the Giaour and rescues Gulchenrouz from Princess Carathis's assassination attempt in William Beckford's *Vathek*.

Good Poor Woman Foster parent for Roxana and the brewer's children; she tries to get the brewer's sister to help raise the children, but succeeds only in persuading other family members to help support them financially in Daniel Defoe's *The Fortunate Mistress*.

Fanny Goodall (Countess of Maitland, Marchioness D'Aubigny Young cousin who loves Henry Clinton; her well-meaning parents obstruct a serious relationship; she is persuaded to marry Count Maitland, a man she learns to admire; after his death she marries Lewis D'Aubigny and becomes Clinton's sister-in-law in Henry Brooke's *The Fool of Quality*.

Dr. John Goodenough Physician who attends the ill Arthur Pendennis in London in William Makepeace Thackeray's *The History of Pendennis*. He is a kindly doctor whose gruffness and good heart are in contrast to Dr. George Firmin's in *The Adventures of Philip on His Way through the World*.

Dr. Samuel Goodman Betsy Thoughtless's guardian in Eliza Haywood's *The History of Miss Betsy Thoughtless*.

Father Goodriche Catholic priest who baptizes Richard Middlemas in Sir Walter Scott's *The Surgeon's Daughter*.

Alfred Goodricke Medical practitioner who signs Lady Glyde's death certificate not knowing that the dead woman is Anne Catherick in Wilkie Collins's *The Woman in White*.

Mr. Goodville Charitable man who tries unsuccessfully to find Hammel Clement work in London; he also tries to establish a home for reforming prostitutes in Henry Brooke's *The Fool of Quality*.

Frances (Fanny) Goodwill Joseph Andrews's betrothed, whose beauty makes her the object of unsavory plans and attacks as she travels home with Joseph and Parson Adams; the news that she is sister to Pamela and Joseph nearly scuttles her plans to marry the latter in Henry Fielding's *The History of the Adventures of Mr. Joseph Andrews and of his Friend Mr. Abraham Adams*.

Good-will Keeper of the wicket-gate who lets Christian through and points him the way to Mount Zion; he also helps Christiana and Mercy in John Bunyan's *The Pilgrim's Progress From this World to That Which Is to Come*.

Earl Goodwin Julian the Apostate's incarnation as an English minister of state to Edward the Confessor in Henry Fielding's *A Journey From This World to the Next*.

Editha Goodwin Earl Goodwin's daughter, whose forced marriage to Edward the Confessor elevates her opinion of herself and endangers her life because of the hatred Edward bears her father in Henry Fielding's *A Journey From This World to the Next*.

Sally Goodwin Illegitimate daughter of Mr. B—— and Sally Godfrey; she is later championed and accepted into his home by his wife, Pamela (Andrews), in Samuel Richardson's *Pamela, or Virtue Rewarded*.

Swane Goodwin Earl Goodwin's son, whose barbarous behavior prompts his banishment from England; his father blackmails Edward the Confessor into finally pardoning him in Henry Fielding's *A Journey From This World to the Next*.

Mr. Goodworth Mrs. Thorpe's father, who criticizes his son-in-law's child-rearing unsuccessfully in Wilkie Collins's *Hide and Seek*.

Princess Goorelka Sorceress, enemy of Noorna bin Noorka; her beauty comes at the expense of Noorna until

Shibli Bagarag uproots the Lily of the Enchanted Sea, restoring Noorna's beauty and making Goorelka again ugly; she fights as a scorpion on the side of Karaz when Shibli attempts to shave Shagpat in George Meredith's *The Shaving of Shagpat*.

Melinda Goosetrap London heiress who encourages Roderick Random in his courtship until she discovers he has no property; she finally marries Narcissa's brother, the Squire, in Tobias Smollett's *The Adventures of Roderick Random*.

Sophie Gordeloup Scheming sister of Count Pateroff; she is vaguely connected with the Russian embassy and allegedly a spy; she has small success in her chief object: to extort money from Lady Ongar; repudiated, she retreats to Boulogne accompanied by Captain Boodle in Anthony Trollope's *The Claverings*.

Captain Gordon Scottish officer who flirts with Mrs. Cullpepper, good-naturedly opposes Geoffry Wildgoose's assertion that all plays should be outlawed, and later tricks Wildgoose and Jeremiah Tugwell into thinking they are on a ship to Ireland when they are actually traveling to Wales in Richard Graves's *The Spiritual Quixote*.

Father Gordon Amateur in charge of music in St. Joseph's, where Mr. Innes wishes to reintroduce the plain chant in George Moore's *Evelyn Innes*.

Major Gordon Suitor of long standing who marries Jessie Brown after the deaths of her father and elder sister in Elizabeth Gaskell's *Cranford*.

Adam Gordon Friend of young George Colwan; he tries unsuccessfully to aid him in evading the shadowy company of Robert Colwan in James Hogg's *The Private Memoirs and Confessions of a Justified Sinner*.

Alexander Gordon (Lord Aberdeen) Bryan Perdue's schoolmate and friend, who shuns Bryan because of his gambling and later purchases the Jamaican Hammond estate, which is managed by Bryan, in Thomas Holcroft's *The Memoirs of Bryan Perdue*.

Emma Gordon Tightrope dancer in Sleary's Circus; she marries a cheesemonger in Charles Dickens's *Hard Times*.

Lord George Gordon Fierce Protestant who opposes the Catholic Relief Act; in his name the Gordon rioters sack Roman Catholic homes and churches in July 1780, and he is held for high treason but acquitted in Charles Dickens's *Barnaby Rudge*.

John Gordon Successful prospector for diamonds in South Africa; he returns to England only to find his sweetheart, Mary Lawrie, engaged to her guardian, William Whittlestaff; the older man frees her to marry John in Anthony Trollope's *An Old Man's Love*.

Mr. Goren A tailor who was a fellow apprentice with the Great Mel Harrington; after the Great Mel dies, he helps Evan Harrington with the Harringtons' tailor shop in George Meredith's *Evan Harrington*.

Sir Appulby Gorges Attorney, chief among a group of mean and corrupt parasites enriched by prolonged litigation; his machinations keep Medora Glenmorris, whom he is supposed to represent, from claiming her inheritance in Charlotte Smith's *The Young Philosopher*.

Mr. Gosford Farmer, friend, and customer of Mr. Furze in Mark Rutherford's *Catharine Furze*.

Giles Gosling Hospitable Cumnor innkeeper, landlord of the Black Bear in Sir Walter Scott's *Kenilworth*.

Mr. Gosport London gentlemen who explains the supercilious and voluble classes of people to Cecilia Beverley in Frances Burney's *Cecilia*.

Gossett Midshipman who is bullied by Vigors until Jack Easy intervenes in Captain Frederick Marryat's *Mr. Midshipman Easy*.

Lady Gosstre The social superior of the Poles; she delights the Pole sisters by inviting them, along with Emilia Belloni, to dinner in George Meredith's *Emilia in England*.

Mr. Gotobed Constable who conveys William Booth before Justice Jonathan Thrasher, accusing him of beating the watchman and breaking his lantern in Henry Fielding's *Amelia*.

Elias Gotobed Cigar-chewing Republican Senator from Mikewa much given to unsparing criticism of British ways and institutions; his frankness at a public lecture in London rouses anger, and he beats a hasty retreat; returning home, he thunders against his own country and extols things British in Anthony Trollope's *The American Senator*. He is American Ambassador to the Court of St. James in *The Duke's Children*.

Goton The cuisinière, a Flemish cook at Mme. Beck's school in Charlotte Brontë's *Villette*.

Ellen Gough Shop assistant valued by Joanna Grice; her lack of sympathy for Mary Grice's predicament results in her dismissal by Joshua Grice in Wilkie Collins's *Hide and Seek*.

May Gould Next to Alice Barton, the cleverest of the

five graduating debutantes; she loves Fred Scully, who loves horses; she loses out in the marriage market and remains friends with Alice Barton in George Moore's *A Drama in Muslin*.

Ailsie Gourlay   Hideous old sibyl employed by Lady Ashton to nurse Lucy Ashton and help break her engagement to Edgar Ravenswood; her mysterious tales succeed in unsettling Lucy's mind in Sir Walter Scott's *The Bride of Lammermoor*.

Governess   Bryan Perdue's foreign governess and his father's lover, who teaches Bryan a variety of vices in Thomas Holcroft's *The Memoirs of Bryan Perdue*.

Governor   Bryan Perdue's Irish governor (tutor), a well-bred, educated gentleman and Catholic priest, who encourages Bryan to forsake gambling in Thomas Holcroft's *The Memoirs of Bryan Perdue*.

Mrs. Gowan   Former beauty and mother of Henry Gowan; she condescends to the Meagleses and refers to her son as a "poor boy" for marrying Minnie Meagles, although the marriage settles her son's debts and gives him an income in Charles Dickens's *Little Dorrit*.

Henry Gowan   Handsome, supercilious, and cruel young artist connected with the upper-class Barnacles and Stiltstalkings; he marries Minnie Meagles, refers to himself as "disappointed" for not receiving the income he thought he was entitled to, and belittles all his acquaintances with an affable manner in Charles Dickens's *Little Dorrit*.

Mrs. Gower   Old and blind tenant of Mrs. Jupp; Ernest Pontifex, as clergyman, tries to help her in Samuel Butler's *The Way of All Flesh*.

Andy Gowran   Steward manager of the Eustace estate in Scotland; he stays on, although he loathes his new mistress, Lizzie Eustace, in order to protect the ancestral home from her depredations in Anthony Trollope's *The Eustace Diamonds*.

Grace   A woman who is named after Grace Nugent; she marries Brian O'Neill in Maria Edgeworth's *The Absentee*.

Grace   Mnason's daughter who marries Samuel in John Bunyan's *The Pilgrim's Progress From this World to That Which Is to Come*.

Grace   Landlady's maid who is caught in the act with the puppet master's Merry Andrew and occasions the embarrassment of all for various reasons in Henry Fielding's *The History of Tom Jones*.

Mrs. Gradgrind   Feeble, bewildered wife of Thomas Gradgrind in Charles Dickens's *Hard Times*.

Adam Smith Gradgrind   One of Thomas Gradgrind's force-educated younger children in Charles Dickens's *Hard Times*.

Jane Gradgrind   Unhappy victim of utilitarian education and Thomas Gradgrind's youngest child in Charles Dickens's *Hard Times*.

Louisa Gradgrind   Thomas Gradgrind's daughter who is trained in utilitarian philosophy, marries Josiah Bounderby without feeling love, nearly runs off with James Harthouse, undergoes an emotional and mental breakdown, and is finally restored to health in Charles Dickens's *Hard Times*.

Malthus Gradgrind   One of Thomas Gradgrind's force-educated younger children in Charles Dickens's *Hard Times*.

Thomas Gradgrind   Practical-minded hardware merchant and staunch advocate of utilitarian philosophy; he influences the local school to employ this philosophy and insists that his own children adhere strictly to their utilitarian training in Charles Dickens's *Hard Times*.

Tom Gradgrind   Thomas Gradgrind's son who, disillusioned with his utilitarian upbringing, becomes dissolute and dishonest in Charles Dickens's *Hard Times*.

Grady   Complaining pirate and mutineer on Teach's *Sarah*; he drowns in a swamp in Robert Louis Stevenson's *The Master of Ballantrae: A Winter's Tale*.

Mrs. Graeme   An old hag, who is the mother and accomplice of the robber Westburnflat (Willie Graeme) in Sir Walter Scott's *The Black Dwarf*.

Alison Graeme   See Lady Durrisdeer.

Magdalen Graeme (Mother Nichneven)   Roland Graeme's devoted grandmother; haughty and majestic, she is a devout Catholic driven slightly insane by her fanaticism; conspiring for the escape of Queen Mary of Scotland, she assumes the guise of Mother Nichneven and foils Jasper Dryfesdale's assassination attempt by selling him a harmless drug in Sir Walter Scott's *The Abbot*.

Roland Graeme   Magdalen Graeme's haughty, brave grandson; he is the pampered page of the Lady of Avenel (Mary Avenel) before becoming the page of Queen Mary of Scotland and effecting her escape; upon discovering he is the legitimate child of Julian Avenel and Catherine Graeme's secret marriage, he returns to Avenel Castle in Sir Walter Scott's *The Abbot*.

Willie Graeme (The Red Reiver of Westburnflat)
Border robber who destroys Hobbie (Halbert) Elliot's home and kidnaps Grace Armstrong for revenge; as Mr. Vere's Jacobite emissary, he abducts Isabella Vere so that Vere can accuse Patrick Earnscliff of the crime and be rid of him in Sir Walter Scott's *The Black Dwarf*.

Lady Aphrodite Grafton　Beautiful daughter of an earl and wife of the vicious Sir Lucius Grafton; she becomes mistress of the Duke of St. James in Benjamin Disraeli's *The Young Duke*.

Sir Lucius Grafton　Licentious baronet, the cruel and brutal husband of Lady Aphrodite Grafton; he develops an obsession for May Dacre and ends up dueling with both the Duke of St. James and Arundel Dacre in Benjamin Disraeli's *The Young Duke*.

Felix Graham　Energetic, idealistic lawyer, who tries to groom Mary Snow as his ideal wife; when she falls in love with Albert Fitzallen he is much relieved, since he wants to marry Madeline Staveley; he also assists in Lady Mason's trial but with a troubled uncertainty about her innocence in Anthony Trollope's *Orley Farm*.

Helen Graham　See Helen Lawrence Huntingdon.

James Graham　See Marquis of Montrose.

Lord Graham　Scottish nobleman and friend of Lord Clifford; he hosts the joust between Sir Philip Harclay and Sir Walter Lovel in Clara Reeve's *The Old English Baron*.

Mr. Graham　Gentleman philosopher whom Geoffry Wildgoose first sees fighting a butcher who has beaten a horse; he later tells Wildgoose about his ill-fated romance with Ophelia in Richard Graves's *The Spiritual Quixote*.

Mary Graham　Seventeen-year-old paid companion to Martin Chuzzlewit; her purity and lack of avarice remain uncorrupted by Chuzzlewit's wealth and his relatives' greed and assist the reformation of his selfishness; she devotedly loves young Martin Chuzzlewit, and withstands Seth Pecksniff's amorous extortion in Charles Dickens's *The Life and Adventures of Martin Chuzzlewit*.

Colonel Grahame (Grahame of Claverhouse, Claverhouse, Viscount Dundee)　Officer in King James's army who tries Henry Morton for treason, leads the forces defeated by Cameronian rebels, and vows revenge for the killing of his nephew, Cornet Richard Grahame; later as Viscount Dundee he leads Jacobite Highlanders against King William and is mortally wounded in battle in Sir Walter Scott's *Old Mortality*.

Cornet Richard Grahame　Nephew of Colonel Gra-hame; he is killed by Burley (John Balfour) after he delivers an ultimatum to the rebels, although he is protected by a flag of truce in Sir Walter Scott's *Old Mortality*.

Gilbert Grail　Workingman of frustrated intellectual tastes; he responds eagerly to an educational program brought to his neighborhood by a reformer, Walter Egremont, and loses his betrothed, Thyrza Trent, to this benefactor in George Gissing's *Thyrza*.

Mr. Grainger　James Steerforth's friend who dines with David Copperfield in London in Charles Dickens's *The Personal History of David Copperfield*.

Mr. Grame　Steward to the one baronet in the area, Sir Philip Nunnely, in Charlotte Brontë's *Shirley*.

Mr. Granby　Well-connected suitor to Rosamond Oliver; she marries him after St. John Rivers decides she would not make a suitable missionary's wife in Charlotte Brontë's *Jane Eyre*.

Sir Frederic Granby　Grandfather of Mr. Granby; his estate falls to his grandson in Charlotte Brontë's *Jane Eyre*.

Grand Domestic　Emperor Alexius Comnenus's prime minister in Sir Walter Scott's *Count Robert of Paris*.

Henleigh Mallinger Grandcourt　Nephew and heir of Sir Hugo Mallinger; although the father of Lydia Glasher's four illegitimate children, he marries Gwendolen Harleth and treats her cruelly in an attempt to break her spirit; he drowns on a boating excursion in George Eliot's *Daniel Deronda*.

Lord Granderville　Father of Lady Helen Seely and diplomat to Russia and America; although opposed to his daughter's marriage to Lewis Seymour, he is more kindly disposed than is his wife in George Moore's *A Modern Lover*.

Henrietta, Lady Granderville　Lady Helen Seely's mother, who lives abroad with her diplomat husband; she is violently opposed to Lady Helen's marriage to Lewis Seymour in George Moore's *A Modern Lover*.

Grandfather　Grandfather of Ellen; he lives on Runnymede Island in the River Thames and yearns for the return of the Victorian period in William Morris's *News from Nowhere*.

Cardinal Grandison　One of Lothair's two guardians; he was friend and former tutor of Lothair's father and converted to the Roman Catholic church soon after Lothair was orphaned; he wants Lothair to convert and bring his vast fortune to the service of the Catholic cause in England in Benjamin Disraeli's *Lothair.*

Lady Grandison   Lovely and loving wife of the often absent and unfaithful Sir Thomas Grandison and mother of (Sir) Charles, Caroline (Lady L.), and Charlotte; her death follows the shock of her husband's injury in a duel and leads to her husband's more open licentiousness in Samuel Richardson's *Sir Charles Grandison.*

Lord Grandison   Wealthy grandfather of Ferdinand Armine; he leaves his entire fortune to his granddaughter, Katherine Grandison, in Benjamin Disraeli's *Henrietta Temple: A Love Story.*

Mr. Grandison   Gentleman farmer and "near relation of Sir Charles Grandison"; he takes on Mr. Rivers as a tenant farmer in Richard Graves's *The Spiritual Quixote.*

Sir Charles Grandison   Unvaryingly wise and magnanimous young baronet, handsome and independent; courageous whenever necessary, rescuing even his enemies from assassins and liberating Harriet Byron from her abductor, he eloquently and persuasively defends his refusal to duel on numerous occasions; an enemy to licentious behavior and himself virginal, he causes unrest only through his attractiveness to women: the violent Lady Olivia, the oversensitive and emotionally delicate Lady Clementina della Porretta, the young, adoring Emily Jervois, and Harriet, the much-courted, virtuous, and sensible heroine, whom he eventually marries, in Samuel Richardson's *Sir Charles Grandison.*

Charlotte Grandison (Lady G.)   High-spirited, affectionate, witty, and often unwise younger sister of Sir Charles Grandison; she is rescued by his assistance from a rash romantic commitment to Captain Anderson; she marries Lord G., to whom she is unable to subjugate herself until motherhood tames her in Samuel Richardson's *Sir Charles Grandison.*

Eleanor Grandison   Unmarried Methodist sister of Sir Thomas Grandison; she is attracted to Dr. Bartlett in Samuel Richardson's *Sir Charles Grandison.*

Everard Grandison   Foppish, extravagant cousin of Sir Charles Grandison; he pays suit to Harriet Byron but without much expectation of success; he eventually succeeds in restoring his fortunes through marriage in Samuel Richardson's *Sir Charles Grandison.*

Katherine Grandison   Mild, pretty cousin of Ferdinand Armine and granddaughter of Lord Grandison; she inherits Lord Grandison's entire fortune, falls in love with Ferdinand Armine and pays his debts, and later releases him from his promise to marry her; she finally marries

Lord Montford in Benjamin Disraeli's *Henrietta Temple: A Love Story.*

Sir Thomas Grandison   Baronet and father of (Sir) Charles, Caroline (Lady L.), and Charlotte Grandison; he is extravagant and arrogant, an absent and philandering husband, and, though generous to his son, a stingy, contemptuous tyrant to his daughters, especially following the death of his wife; his death, occurring as he is contracting to maintain a third mistress, liberates his daughters and gives scope to his son's judicious magnanimity in Samuel Richardson's *Sir Charles Grandison.*

Graneangowl   Poetically verbose, vain Covenanter, who serves as Argyle's chaplain in Sir Walter Scott's *A Legend of Montrose.*

Anthony Granger   Prosperous tanner and Giffard Homley's employer and eventual father-in-law in Henry Brooke's *The Fool of Quality.*

Edith Granger   Handsome and willful daughter of Mrs. Skewton; she was manipulated by her mother into a disastrous first marriage; she later marries the elder Paul Dombey, defying him throughout the marriage; she eventually runs away with James Carker, ruining herself and Carker in Charles Dickens's *Dombey and Son.*

Dr. Grant   Gourmand clergyman to whom the Mansfield living devolves upon the death of Mrs. Norris's husband (the extravagance of Tom Bertram having made the sale necessary); his death allows the living to be restored to Edmund Bertram at the end of Jane Austen's *Mansfield Park.*

Miss Grant   Sister of William Grant (Prestongrange), Lord Advocate of Scotland, and stately aunt to his three beautiful but haughty daughters in Robert Louis Stevenson's *Catriona.*

Mrs. Grant   Agreeable, good-natured wife of Dr. Grant and elder half sister of Mary and Henry Crawford; she delights in their extended stays with her and, not being unprincipled herself, is unsuspicious of their mischief in Jane Austen's *Mansfield Park.*

The younger Misses Grant   The two pretty but snobbish younger sisters of Barbara Grant and daughters of Prestongrange, Lord Advocate of Scotland, in Robert Louis Stevenson's *Catriona.*

Barbara Grant   The consummate beauty and eldest daughter of Prestongrange, Lord Advocate of Scotland; she acts as a faithful but playful confidante and friend to David Balfour and Catriona Drummond in Robert Louis Stevenson's *Catriona.*

Bertha, Lady Grant Kindly widowed sister of George Western; her mediation in the quarrel between her brother and his wife, Cecilia (Holt), brings about a reconciliation in Anthony Trollope's *Kept in the Dark*.

Bishop Grantly Beloved Bishop of Barchester, whose son, Theophilus, is married to Mr. Harding's daughter, Susan, in Anthony Trollope's *The Warden*. His death brings the Proudies to Barchester in *Barchester Towers*.

Charles James Grantly Archdeacon Grantly's eldest son, who is at university and mindful of his status in Anthony Trollope's *The Warden*. He is married and a busy London preacher in *The Last Chronicle of Barset*.

Edith Grantly Major Henry Grantly's young daughter in Anthony Trollope's *The Last Chronicle of Barset*.

Florinda Grantly Elder daughter of Archdeacon Grantly; she assists in Sunday schools in Anthony Trollope's *The Warden* and in *Barchester Towers*. Her death is mentioned in *The Small House at Allington*.

Griselda Grantly (Lady Dumbello; Marchioness of Hartletop) Archdeacon Grantly's daughter, who distributes buns to deserving children in Anthony Trollope's *The Warden*. She gives promise of beauty in *Barchester Towers*. Her mother wishes her to marry Lord Lufton, but she is more ambitious and accepts Lord Dumbello in *Framley Parsonage*. As the cold-hearted, classic beauty Lady Dumbello, she attracts Plantagenet Palliser's guarded attentions and disappoints society by dismissing them in *The Small House at Allington*. As the Marchioness of Hartletop (in mourning for her father-in-law) she contrasts with the passionate Lady Glencora Palliser in *Can You Forgive Her?*. Consulted, she recommends that her father withdraw her brother Henry's income should he persist in courting Grace Crawley; she becomes a mother in *The Last Chronicle of Barset*. She is a patroness of the Negro Soldiers' Orphan Bazaar in *Miss Mackenzie*.

Major Henry Grantly A young widower retired from active and honored service in India to property provided by his father; Archdeacon Grantly's favorite son, he successfully resists his father's objections to his marriage to Grace Crawley, the daughter of an impoverished and beleaguered curate in Anthony Trollope's *The Last Chronicle of Barset*. He is mentioned as a boy in *The Warden* and as an army officer in *Barchester Towers*.

Samuel Grantly Youngest son of Archdeacon Grantly; known to the family as "Soapy," he appears briefly in Anthony Trollope's *The Warden* and in *Barchester Towers*. He is mentioned as entering university in *The Last Chronicle of Barset*.

Susan Grantly Tactful wife of Archdeacon Grantly and elder daughter of Mr. Harding; she skilfully counsels her husband in Anthony Trollope's *The Warden* and in *Barchester Towers*. She also appears in *Doctor Thorne*, in *Framley Parsonage*, in *The Small House at Allington*, and in *The Last Chronicle of Barset*.

Theophilus Grantly High Church Rector of Plumstead Episcopi and Archdeacon of Barchester, who fights the case brought by Mr. Bold concerning abuse of almshouse charity brought against his father-in-law, Mr. Harding, in Anthony Trollope's *The Warden*. He battles with Low Church Bishop Proudie and Mr. Slope in *Barchester Towers*. He suffers at his son's insistence on loving Grace Crawley; he calls on Grace to bully her but is won by her gentle high-mindedness in *The Last Chronicle of Barset*. He appears in *Framley Parsonage*, in *The Small House at Allington*, and in *Doctor Thorne*.

Juliet (Ellis) Granville The Stranger, who flees from Revolutionary France to England; she is forced into an illegal marriage with a French official wanting money from her English family; she is assisted and loved by Albert Harleigh, flees from London to other places in England, including Salisbury and Stonehenge, to escape capture and return to France, and learns she is an heir of the Granville family just before she is married to Albert in Frances Burney's *The Wanderer*.

Lady Aurora Granville Sixteen-year-old half sister of Juliet Granville; she befriends Juliet when neither knows of their relationship; she is prevented by her uncle from communication with Juliet for most of the story in Frances Burney's *The Wanderer*.

M. Grascour Earnest member of the Belgian Foreign Office; he falls in love with Florence Mountjoy while she is staying at the British Legation in Brussels in Anthony Trollope's *Mr. Scarborough's Family*.

Lord Grasslough Graceless, impecunious aristocrat crony of Adolphus Longestaffe at the Beargarden Club; he tries to attract Marie Melmotte, but she rejects him in Anthony Trollope's *The Way We Live Now*. He is an unsuitable acquaintance of Lord Silverbridge in *The Duke's Children*.

Grave Assistant at Snap's gaming table; he restores his losses at dice by picking other players' pockets in Henry Fielding's *The Life of Mr. Jonathan Wild the Great*.

Miss Grave-Airs Snobbish young woman on the stagecoach journey who prudishly objects to any elaboration of the love scenes in the story of Leonora in Henry Fielding's *The History of the Adventures of Mr. Joseph Andrews and of his Friend Mr. Abraham Adams*.

Mr. Graves   Assistant to Dr. MacTurk, the local physician, in Charlotte Brontë's *Shirley*.

Mrs. Graves   Owner of a milliner shop rescued from a rapist by Hammel Clement, who is shot during the fracas; she tends him while he recovers and invites him to move in; her daughter Arabella becomes Hammel's wife in Henry Brooke's *The Fool of Quality*.

Gray   Undergraduate of St. Ambrose's College, Oxford, who becomes a parson in the East End of London in Thomas Hughes's *Tom Brown at Oxford*.

Mr. Gray   Scrupulous, outspoken legal adviser of George Western; he is directed by his client to offer an allowance to Western's wife, Cecilia (Holt), when their marriage breaks down; he does his best to reconcile them in Anthony Trollope's *Kept in the Dark*.

Mr. Gray   Young and enthusiastic reforming clergyman, who wins the respect and helps change the attitudes of Lady Ludlow in Elizabeth Gaskell's *My Lady Ludlow*.

Abraham Gray   Carpenter's mate on the *Hispaniola*; he joins the loyal party when Captain Smollett calls him; he kills Job Anderson and ultimately buys part of a ship with his share of treasure in Robert Louis Stevenson's *Treasure Island*.

Dorian Gray   Extremely handsome man who remains handsome and ageless while a changing portrait of him reveals the evil changes in his soul; he is corrupted by the decadent philosophy of Lord Henry Wotton and descends into unspeakable moral degradation and evil as he ruins men and woman and commits murders in Oscar Wilde's *The Picture of Dorian Gray*.

Dr. Gideon Gray   Unselfish surgeon, who delivers Richard Middlemas and becomes his devoted guardian; honest and hardworking, he takes no payment for raising and training Richard, and maintains ties with the boy's grandfather in the hope that one day Richard will be recognized in Sir Walter Scott's *The Surgeon's Daughter*.

Jean Gray   Dr. Gideon Gray's simple but good-natured wife, who dies giving birth to their only child, Menie Gray, in Sir Walter Scott's *The Surgeon's Daughter*.

Marion (Menie) Gray   Beautiful, affectionate daughter of Dr. Gray; she loves Richard Middlemas from childhood on; upon her father's death, she becomes a relative's drudge before traveling to India at Middlemas's request; rescued by Adam Hartley after Middlemas attempts to place her in a seraglio, she returns to England and devotes her life to charitable deeds in Sir Walter Scott's *The Surgeon's Daughter*.

Mr. Graybody   Disciple and companion of President John Neverbend; he supports the compulsory euthanasia program advocated by the president and becomes curator of the college where candidates for disposal will spend their final year in Anthony Trollope's *The Fixed Period*.

Ambrose Graye   Architect who in his youth loved a woman who mysteriously rejected him; he marries another and has a son, Owen, and a daughter, named Cytherea after his lost love; his wife dies, and he dies in an accident in Thomas Hardy's *Desperate Remedies*.

Cytherea Graye   Beautiful young woman whose father's death compels her to take a position as a lady's maid; her employer, Miss Aldclyffe, promotes her marriage to the steward Aeneas Manston, assisted by the fact that Cytherea's beloved, Edward Springrove, has been long engaged to marry his cousin; news of the cousin's elopement comes just too late to prevent Cytherea's marriage, but information that Manston's first wife lives drives her at once from her husband; after his death she hears Miss Aldclyffe's dying admission that Manston was her son, marries Springrove, and inherits the Aldclyffe property in Thomas Hardy's *Desperate Remedies*.

Owen Graye   Young, orphaned architect and brother of Cytherea Graye; his salary prohibits him from supporting Cytherea, compelling her to take a position with a wealthy woman; Owen's period of invalidism and need partly motivates Cytherea's marriage to Aeneas Manston; when Manston is suspected of lying about his first wife's whereabouts, Owen investigates and helps to save his sister from what would have been an unhappy marriage in Thomas Hardy's *Desperate Remedies*.

Louis (Margrave) Grayle   Wicked amateur of the occult; he murders Haroun of Aleppo and pursues Lilian Ashleigh; he dies in his attempt to obtain the elixir of life in Edward Bulwer-Lytton's *A Strange Story*.

Mr. and Mrs. Grayper   Neighbors of David Copperfield and his mother at Blunderstone Rookery in Charles Dickens's *The Personal History of David Copperfield*.

Carmina Graywell   Lovely, sensitive, talented niece and ward of Mrs. Gallilee; she falls happily in love with Ovid Vere; in his absence she is tormented into a serious nervous disease by her aunt, and the illness is aggravated by the inappropriate treatment of Mr. Null; Vere returns in time to cure her and becomes her husband in Wilkie Collins's *Heart and Science*.

Robert Graywell   An Englishman of fortune and a gifted painter, who has lived his adult life in Italy; a widower, he dies, leaving the care of his only child, Carmina, to his sister Mrs. Gallilee, whom he erroneously trusts because he has repeatedly paid her debts in Wilkie Collins's *Heart and Science*.

Frederick the Great   King of Prussia, for whom Redmond Barry is sent to spy on the Chevalier de Balibari (Cornelius Barry) in William Makepeace Thackeray's *The Luck of Barry Lyndon*.

Great Shadow (Prince of the Power of the Air)   Lilith's consort and power of evil; he passes over the Lovers (Little ones), initiating them into fear and sorrow in George MacDonald's *Lilith*.

Great-heart   Servant of the Interpreter; he leads Christiana and her party on their journey to the House Beautiful; he leaves and returns to lead them on to the Celestial City; he kills Giant Despair, Grim Bloody-man, Maul, and Slay-good in John Bunyan's *The Pilgrim's Progress From this World to That Which Is to Come*.

Mr. Greaves   Worldly adviser to the naive hero Benignus in S. J. Pratt's *Liberal Opinions upon Animals, Man, and Providence*.

Mrs. Greaves   A respectable servant, who leaves Grassdale Manor after Arthur Huntingdon deteriorates while living on his own in Anne Brontë's *The Tenant of Wildfell Hall*.

Sir Everhard Greaves   Baronet, the late father of Sir Launcelot; his defeat of Anthony Darnel in election to Parliament created the enmity which has formed the obstacle to his son's romance in Tobias Smollett's *The Adventures of Sir Launcelot Greaves*.

Sir Launcelot Greaves   Baronet; wearing armor in his role as defender of justice, he travels the road from York to London doing deeds of chivalry and pursuing his beloved, Aurelia Darnel, along the way; he duels with Anthony Darnel and later with Squire Philip Sycamore, is briefly imprisoned on account of Ferret, tours a London debtors' prison searching for Aurelia, is imprisoned in a private London madhouse, and marries Aurelia after rescuing her from the same madhouse in Tobias Smollett's *The Adventures of Sir Launcelot Greaves*.

Captain Green   Fatherly captain of the *British Maria*, on which Nares shipped as mate in 1874 for Australia in Robert Louis Stevenson's *The Wrecker*.

Captain Green   Racing crony of Major Tifto; he connives in Tifto's nobbling of a horse in Anthony Trollope's *The Duke's Children*.

Dame Green   Nurse of the infant Evelina Anville Belmont; she persuades Sir John Belmont her own baby is

his daughter; she is exposed by Mrs. Clinton in Frances Burney's *Evelina*.

Mr. Green   The one of Rosalie Murray's suitors whom she considers "most stupid" of her choices in Anne Brontë's *Agnes Grey*.

Mr. Green   Investigator hired for the Dodds by Dr. Sampson; he goes to extraordinary lengths to restore the missing money, to locate the missing clerk, and to set Alfred Hardie and David Dodd free from Drayton House asylum in Charles Reade's *Hard Cash*.

Mrs. Adolphus Green   Put-upon wife of the Groby curate; she teaches music to Joseph Mason's daughters and is recompensed with useless, damaged, ugly, cheap metal furniture by Mrs. Mason in Anthony Trollope's *Orley Farm*.

Anthony Green   Rustic whose marriage to Christiana is promoted by Lady Constantine in Thomas Hardy's *Two on a Tower*.

Christiana Green   Servant whose special loyalty Lady Constantine has purchased by insisting on Anthony Green's marriage to her in Thomas Hardy's *Two on a Tower*.

Jane Green   One of Mr. Green's two sisters and a friend of Rosalie Murray in Anne Brontë's *Agnes Grey*.

John Green   Church clerk who is present during the interruption of the wedding between Mr. Rochester and Jane Eyre in Charlotte Brontë's *Jane Eyre*.

Joseph Green   London attorney and friend of Will Belton; he also manages the affairs of Mr. Amedroz in Anthony Trollope's *The Belton Estate*.

Mounser Green   Distinguished linguist and valued member of the Foreign Office who is made Ambassador to Patagonia; when John Morton dies, he marries Arabella Trefoil in Anthony Trollope's *The American Senator*.

Olivia Green   Docile and compliant daughter of Mrs. Patmore Green; she marries Lord Giblet in Anthony Trollope's *Is He Popenjoy?*.

Mrs. Patmore Green   Close friend of Mrs. Montacute Jones and mother of Olivia Green, whom both women scheme to marry off to Lord Giblet in Anthony Trollope's *Is He Popenjoy?*.

Polly Green (Miss Belmont)   Daughter of Dame Green; she is raised as his daughter by Sir John Belmont;

she is married to his son Macartney after the truth of her parentage is revealed in Frances Burney's *Evelina*.

Sally Green   Tough, fighting woman in the Leary gang who scalps Nora Walsh and injures Hannah Perrott in Arthur Morrison's *A Child of the Jago*.

Susan Green   A sister of Mr. Green; she and her sister, Jane, are friends of Rosalie Murray in Anne Brontë's *Agnes Grey*.

Tom Green   See Joe Willett.

Will Green   Prominent yeoman of Kent; he welcomes the Scholar to his village, where John Ball encourages resistance to the King's soldiers during Wat Tyler's Rebellion in William Morris's *A Dream of John Ball*.

Greenacre   A figure of impoverished gentility who rises to prosperity by assisting in the intrigues of the debilitated Lord Polperro in George Gissing's *The Town Traveller*.

Henry (Harry) Greenacre   Young farmer who is thrown from his horse during the Ullathorne sports in Anthony Trollope's *Barchester Towers*.

Gilbert Greenleaf   Veteran archer at Castle Douglas, who is bitter over his lack of advancement in Sir Walter Scott's *Castle Dangerous*.

Arabella Greenow   Buxom widowed aunt of Alice Vavasor; comfortably placed with a fortune from her late husband, she enjoys the attentions of a steady farmer, Samuel Cheesacre, and the raffish Captain Bellfield, and chooses the latter as a more exciting husband in Anthony Trollope's *Can You Forgive Her?*.

Kit Greensheve   One of Ellis Duckworth's men; he and Will Lawless find Dick Shelton after his escape from Moat House; he keeps watch on the wall at the cottage where Sir Daniel Brackley has Joan Sedley imprisoned in Robert Louis Stevenson's *The Black Arrow: A Tale of Two Roses*.

Thomas Greenwood   Evil-minded chaplain of the Kingsbury family; he conspires with the Marchioness against her stepchildren, Lady Frances Trafford and Lord Hampstead, even planning to murder the latter; he so antagonizes the Marquis of Kingsbury that he is dismissed in Anthony Trollope's *Marion Fay*.

W. Rutherford Gregg   Alexander Loudon's Edinburgh lawyer, who changes Alexander's will at his request; his letter informs Loudon Dodd of his grandfather's death and his inheritance in Robert Louis Stevenson's *The Wrecker*.

Gregory   King Peter's son who becomes a monk in Saint Mary's Abbey in William Morris's *The Well at the World's End*.

Gregory   Foreman of the packers at Murdstone and Grinby in Charles Dickens's *The Personal History of David Copperfield*.

Dr. Gregory   Celebrated physician, whose clients include the Weir family; he tells Archibald Weir about the concern his father, Lord Hermiston, felt for him when he was a child near death in Robert Louis Stevenson's *Weir of Hermiston: An Unfinished Romance*.

Father Gregory (The Monk)   Falsely humble monk who overcomes the Devil by resisting his temptations; he becomes unpopular in his home of Cologne when the Devil leaves behind his horrible smell in the city as he returns to the underworld in George Meredith's *Farina*.

Mr. Gregsbury   Member of Parliament who hires Nicholas Nickleby as his secretary but dismisses him when Nicholas will not take shorthand in Charles Dickens's *The Life and Adventures of Nicholas Nickleby*.

Harry Gregson   Young urchin secretly educated by Mr. Horner; with the help of money left him by Mr. Horner, he becomes a schoolmaster and ultimately vicar of Hanbury; his career demonstrates social change in Elizabeth Gaskell's *My Lady Ludlow*.

Job Gregson   Harry Gregson's father, a poacher whose wrongful arrest first leads Lady Ludlow to a knowledge of the underside of social conditions in Elizabeth Gaskell's *My Lady Ludlow*.

Tobias Gregson   Scotland Yard detective, colleague of Lestrade in Arthur Conan Doyle's *A Study in Scarlet*.

Mrs. Greme   Housekeeper on Lord M—'s Herefordshire estate; at Robert Lovelace's instigation, she writes a letter to Clarissa Harlowe which defends Lovelace's character and intentions in Samuel Richardson's *Clarissa: or, The History of a Young Lady*.

Emile Grenat   French schoolmate of Matey Wayburn; his friendship illustrates Matey's breadth of sympathy; Emile has also given up ambitions for a military career and becomes a fellow school teacher with Matey in George Meredith's *Lord Ormont and his Aminta*.

Lord Alfred Grendall   Whist-playing drone, who allows himself to drift into becoming a lackey to Augustus Melmotte and one of the board of directors behind the nonexistent American railroad in Anthony Trollope's *The Way We Live Now*.

Robert de Grendon   Knight defeated unfairly by Gaston de Blondeville in Henry III's tournament in Ann Radcliffe's *Gaston de Blondeville*.

Lady Grenvile   Beautiful wife of Sir Richard and close friend of Mrs. Leigh in Charles Kingsley's *Westward Ho!*.

Sir Richard Grenvile   High-minded nobleman, who is the godfather and mentor of Amyas Leigh after the death of his father, and who advises Amyas against going to sea with the ill-fated John Oxenham; he later offers hospitality to Don Guzman de Soto in Charles Kingsley's *Westward Ho!*.

Mr. Gresham   Great orator and Mr. Daubeny's foe; he leads the Liberal party with energy and tact, evolving progressive policies for the times; when Phineas Finn resigns his seat on a principle, Gresham appoints him Poor Law inspector in Ireland in Anthony Trollope's *Phineas Finn*. He becomes Prime Minister in *Phineas Redux*. He appears in *The Eustace Diamonds* and in *The Prime Minister*.

Lady Arabella Gresham   Sister of the Earl de Courcy and therefore entitled to domineer over her commoner husband and almost everyone else; she tries to force her son Frank into a wealthy marriage for the sake of the Greshamsbury estate in Anthony Trollope's *Doctor Thorne*.

Augusta Gresham   Eldest daughter of Francis and Lady Arabella Gresham; she is betrothed to Gustavus Moffat, who jilts her to court an heiress; later, having consulted her cousin Lady Amelia de Courcy about Mortimer Gazebee's marriage proposal, she regretfully accepts Lady Amelia's advice to reject him as a social unequal; she is subsequently a visitor at the home of Lady Amelia Gazebee in Anthony Trollope's *Doctor Thorne*.

Beatrice Gresham   Frank Gresham's favorite sister, to whom he confides his love for Mary Thorne; she marries the Reverend Caleb Oriel in Anthony Trollope's *Doctor Thorne*.

Francis (Frank) Gresham   Handsome eldest son of Francis and Lady Arabella Gresham; an eligible bachelor, he is expected to save the Greshamsbury estate by marrying a fortune; he vacillates but is true to his love for Mary Thorne, whom he eventually marries in Anthony Trollope's *Doctor Thorne*. He persuades Arthur Fletcher to run for Parliament in *The Prime Minister*. He appears briefly in *Framley Parsonage* and in *The Last Chronicle of Barset*.

Francis Newbold Gresham   Country squire, whose property has become burdened with debt, and an ineffectual Member of Parliament; he and his wife, the domi-neering sister of an earl, have a large family in Anthony Trollope's *Doctor Thorne*.

George Gresham   Aristocratic classmate responsible for corrupting Jack, Man of the Hill; he encourages friends to overextend themselves financially, contributing to their ruin in Henry Fielding's *The History of Tom Jones*.

Gilbert Gresham   An artist and the father of Maud Gresham; he teaches Arthur Golding and falls in love with Helen Norman in George Gissing's *Workers in the Dawn*.

Maud Gresham   Daughter of Gilbert Gresham; she marries John Waghorn and has an adulterous affair with Augustus Whiffle in George Gissing's *Workers in the Dawn*.

Lord Alfred Gresley   Minor government official, who is eminently suitable as husband for Emily Hotspur in the eyes of her father, Sir Harry, in Anthony Trollope's *Sir Harry Hotspur of Humblethwaite*.

Dr. Greville   Benevolent, rational Anglican clergyman, who persuades Geoffry Wildgoose to give up his roving Methodist ministry, and who arranges Wildgoose's marriage to Julia Townsend in Richard Graves's *The Spiritual Quixote*.

Mrs. Greville   Wife of Dr. Greville; her illicit reading of a letter from Geoffry Wildgoose to Julia Townsend leads to the Grevilles' approval of the relationship; she later charges Mrs. Sarsenet with partial responsibility for Julia's ill-treatment by her stepmother in Richard Graves's *The Spiritual Quixote*.

John Greville   High-spirited, devoted suitor to Harriet Byron; his rakish past makes him unacceptable to her; he is the immediate suspect in her abduction, thanks to Sir Hargrave Pollexfen's suggestions, in Samuel Richardson's *Sir Charles Grandison*.

Marquis de Grevres   Distinguished guest of the Montagus, who comes directly from France and the court of Louis XIV, and who brings fresh news of the exile King Charles in William Godwin's *Mandeville*.

Hiram Grewgious   Rosa Bud's guardian, who is dutiful about Rosa's intentions to marry Edwin Drood; he accepts Rosa into his house after she flees from John Jasper's declaration of love for her in Charles Dickens's *The Mystery of Edwin Drood*.

Earl Grex   Selfish peer whose ancient property is in decay, who has squandered his daughter's fortune as well as his own, and who is rarely on speaking terms with his son; he is openly and insultingly impatient for the marriage of his daughter, Lady Mabel, and is incensed when the gambling debts of his son, Lord Percival, further threaten his precarious financial situation in Anthony Trollope's *The Duke's Children*.

Lady Mabel Grex   Discontented cousin of Frank Tregear, whom she loves but has rejected for prudential reasons; intent on marrying well, she decides on Lord Silverbridge but cannot bring forth the requisite encouragement when her opportunity comes; his sudden and increasing passion for Isabel Boncassen drives her to a desperate and unmaidenly declaration of love, but she is unsuccessful; she salves her pride by telling him the truth: that she has loved Frank all along in Anthony Trollope's *The Duke's Children*.

Lord Percival Grex   Unscrupulous gambler and spendthrift, who sees his father only when signing documents which provide money at the expense of the property in Anthony Trollope's *The Duke's Children*.

Aunt Grey   Kind sister of Richard Grey; she erroneously recommends Mrs. Bloomfield as a worthy person to employ Agnes Grey as governess in Anne Brontë's *Agnes Grey*.

Lord Grey   Lord deputy of Ireland who evades responsibility in the campaign against the Spaniards, handing it to an annoyed Sir Walter Raleigh in Charles Kingsley's *Westward Ho!*.

Lord Grey   Favorite of the Cecils and enemy of the Earl of Essex (2) and Lord Southampton in Sophia Lee's *The Recess*.

Lord Grey   Prime minister and leader of the Whig party who is ousted from office in Benjamin Disraeli's *Coningsby; or, The New Generation*.

Mr. Grey   Dissenter, business partner of Mr. Rowland, and husband of the socially competitive Mrs. Grey; his kind invitation to the recently orphaned nieces Hester and Margaret Ibbotson changes the community of Deerbrook in Harriet Martineau's *Deerbrook*.

Mrs. Grey   Wife of Mr. Grey, mother of four, and dissenter; she competes with her neighbors the Rowlands for status in the village of Deerbrook in Harriet Martineau's *Deerbrook*.

Mrs. Grey   Blanche and Mary Ingram's former governess who was too insensitive to notice their insults in Charlotte Brontë's *Jane Eyre*.

Agnes Grey   Gentle, determined daughter of Richard Grey; she successively becomes a governess in two families; having failed to influence the children in the first household, she has greater success in her second position;

she meets and eventually marries the earnest curate (later vicar) Mr. Weston in Anne Brontë's *Agnes Grey*.

Alice Grey   Daughter of a rich squire; she leaves behind her fortune when she marries Richard Grey; she becomes the more industrious and self-sufficient the more trying the circumstances in Anne Brontë's *Agnes Grey*.

Alice Grey (Blind Alice)   The last retainer of the house of Ravenswood, a family she has served most of her life; she is remarkably clear-sighted despite her handicap in Sir Walter Scott's *The Bride of Lammermoor*.

Dorothy (Dolly) Grey   Spirited spinster daughter of John Grey; she lives with and is devoted to her widowed father, who makes a habit of private consultation with her as to his clients' affairs; she refuses to make a marriage of convenience with his practical partner, Mr. Barry, in Anthony Trollope's *Mr. Scarborough's Family*.

Fanny Grey   Twin daughter of the Greys; with her sister Mary she brings a higher sense of charity into the family, thanks to the instruction of her esteemed teacher Maria Young in Harriet Martineau's *Deerbrook*.

Henry Grey   Upper-class idealist and Oxford scholar, who is the advisor and mentor of Robert Elsmere throughout the latter's life in Mrs. Humphry Ward's *Robert Elsmere*.

Horace Grey   Vivian Grey's contemplative father, who urges his son to devote himself to moral and humanitarian concerns instead of the quest for political power in Benjamin Disraeli's *Vivian Grey*.

John Grey   Bemused, high-minded attorney and moral opposite of the intriguer, John Scarborough, whom he tries to counsel, although he is usually in the dark over his client's legal and domestic chicanery; knowing that his reputation is inevitably tainted by Scarborough's manipulations, he retires from his law practice in Anthony Trollope's *Mr. Scarborough's Family*.

John Grey   Worthy and gentle, widely respected Member of Parliament for Silverbridge; his love for Alice Vavasor leads him to supply money secretly to defray her cousin George Vavasor's election expenses; his devotion is rewarded when Alice marries him in Anthony Trollope's *Can You Forgive Her?*. He appears in *Phineas Finn*, in *The Eustace Diamonds*, and in *The Prime Minister*.

Lucia de Grey   Beloved and finally wife of the hero, Captain Carlisle, in S. J. Pratt's *Tutor of Truth*.

Mary Grey   One of the Greys' twin daughters; with her sister Fanny she brings a higher sense of charity into the family, thanks to the instruction of her esteemed teacher Maria Young in Harriet Martineau's *Deerbrook*.

Mary Grey   Capable older sister of Agnes; she later marries a respectable clergyman, Mr. Richardson, in Anne Brontë's *Agnes Grey*.

Richard Grey   Agnes's father, a clergyman, who, in marrying Alice, caused her to be disinherited by her father; he loses his capital in a rash investment and dies full of self-reproach in Anne Brontë's *Agnes Grey*.

Sophia Grey   Heiress with £50,000 who marries John Willoughby; spiteful and ill-tempered, she dictates the cruelty of his rejection of Marianne Dashwood in Jane Austen's *Sense and Sensibility*.

Sophia Grey   Sixteen-year-old eldest daughter in the Grey family; her hysteria on the night the villagers attack the Hopes' house prevents Mr. Grey from offering any assistance; she eventually marries the immature surgeon Mr. Walcot in Harriet Martineau's *Deerbrook*.

Sydney Grey   Young son of the Greys who delights in fishing and romping in Harriet Martineau's *Deerbrook*.

Vivian Grey   Talented and principled protagonist, who leaves England to escape the tragic consequences of his early political career only to become enmeshed in the political intrigue of the Austrian court and two tragic love affairs, after which he barely survives a torrential storm, which leaves him in a perilous state at the conclusion of Benjamin Disraeli's *Vivian Grey*.

Mr. Greystock   Amiable father of Frank and Dean of Bobsborough Cathedral; he thinks it ill that a man should marry for money but well that his son should go where money is and therefore hopes for Frank's marriage with Lizzie Eustace in Anthony Trollope's *The Eustace Diamonds*.

Mrs. Greystock   Frank's doting mother, who rather prefers that her son marry Lady Eustace, with her rank and fortune, than pledge himself to a mere governess, Lucy Morris, in Anthony Trollope's *The Eustace Diamonds*.

Ellinor Greystock   Adoring sister of Frank and close friend of Lucy Morris; she speaks up to her parents on Lucy's behalf when they urge the need for Frank to marry for money and rank in Anthony Trollope's *The Eustace Diamonds*.

Frank Greystock   Only son of Dean Greystock of Bobsborough Cathedral and a Member of Parliament; charmed by his wicked cousin, Lizzie Eustace, and tempted by her rank and fortune, he comes close to abandoning Lucy Morris, but he comes to his senses and asks

Lucy to marry him in Anthony Trollope's *The Eustace Diamonds*.

Joanna Grice   Shopkeeper so alive to the shame of her niece's love affair that she secretly appropriates and burns unopened the young man's letters after his departure and, knowing her brother means to bring his daughter and her child home if he finds them, sends him looking in the wrong direction in Wilkie Collins's *Hide and Seek*.

Joshua Grice   A shopkeeper, the loving father of Mary (his son Mat having run off to America); his search for Mary after her disappearance is doomed because his sister, Joanna, has sent him in the wrong direction; he dies without finding her in Wilkie Collins's *Hide and Seek*.

Mary (Madonna) Grice   A pretty, winsome, cheerful young woman and a deaf mute; since the age of ten, when she was rescued from an abusive circus master by the painter Valentine Blyth, she has lived as the Blyths' adopted daughter; she is called Madonna because of her resemblance to Raphael's madonnas; searching for his lost niece, Mat Grice finds her and pursues the mystery of her paternity in Wilkie Collins's *Hide and Seek*.

Mat (Marksman) Grice   An explorer and gold prospector returned from the Americas, where he was scalped by Indians; a cheerful, skull-capped ruffian, he is relentlessly determined to track down his niece and the identity of her mother's seducer; though successful, he proves magnanimous rather than revengeful in Wilkie Collins's *Hide and Seek*.

Arthur Gride   Elderly miser, who agrees to forgive Walter Bray his debts if he can marry his daughter, Madeline Bray, for whom he has long lusted; he also has documents unknown to the Brays which prove that Madeline is an heiress in Charles Dickens's *The Life and Adventures of Nicholas Nickleby*.

Mr. Gridley   Angry old man from Shropshire, who is a neighbor of the Necketts and Miss Flite's friend; he has been enmeshed in a Chancery case for years, but when a warrant is put out for his arrest, he flees to the shooting gallery of Trooper George (Rouncewell), where he dies, in Charles Dickens's *Bleak House*.

Mr. Grieve   See Ferdinand.

David Grieve   Freethinking bookseller and printer of Manchester; after a harsh childhood he rises to become a prosperous merchant; he loves the French Elise Delaunay but marries Lucy Purcell, who dies of cancer; his self-education leads him ultimately to reject secularism for independence in his philosophical and scientific thought in Mrs. Humphry Ward's *The History of David Grieve*.

Hannah Grieve Cruel, pennypinching aunt by marriage who raises the Grieve children, Louie and David, grudgingly in Mrs. Humphry Ward's *The History of David Grieve*.

Louie Grieve Fey sister of David Grieve; while in France she models for Jules Montjoie's statue the Maenad; she marries and supports the alcoholic artist because of her child in Mrs. Humphry Ward's *The History of David Grieve*.

Reuben Grieve Farmer uncle who raises the orphaned Louie and David Grieve; he is powerless to prevent his wife, Hannah, from abusing the children in Mrs. Humprhy Ward's *The History of David Grieve*.

Seraphina Melvilia Grieve Daughter of an apothecary; she accompanies the Count (Renaldo de Melvil) and Countess (Serafina de Zelos) de Melville to Edinburgh in Tobias Smollett's *The Expedition of Humphry Clinker*.

Mr. Griffenbottom Conservative running mate of Sir Thomas Underwood in the Percycross election and holder of the seat, thoroughly cynical about political expediency in Anthony Trollope's *Ralph the Heir*.

Mrs. Griffith Housekeeper to Indefer Jones; she believes that Jones, master of Llanfere estate, executed a final will not known to the family in Anthony Trollope's *Cousin Henry*.

John Griffith Tenant farmer of the late Indefer Jones; he believes at first that Henry Jones is rightful heir of Llanfere estate where his wife is housekeeper but grows suspicious of some wrongdoing on Henry's part in Anthony Trollope's *Cousin Henry*.

Miss Griffon The insignificant but highly idolized authoress at a tea Nancy Shaw Bluemits gives for Miss Grizzy Douglas and Mary Douglas in Susan Ferrier's *Marriage*.

Adolphus Griggs Vulgar and vain guest of the Tappitts; his attention causes Rachel Ray some embarrassment and arouses jealousy among some ladies present in Anthony Trollope's *Rachel Ray*.

Monsieur Grillade The head cook and target of Dr. Redgill's discerning taste at the Beech Park residence of Frederick, Lord Lindore and Lady Juliana Douglas in Susan Ferrier's *Marriage*.

Grim Bloody-man Adversary who backs the lions at the foot of the Hill of Difficulty; he tries to stop the pilgrims and is killed by Great-heart in John Bunyan's *The Pilgrim's Progress From this World to That Which Is to Come*.

Grimes Boorish and uncouth lad of twenty, selected by Barnabas Tyrrel to be Emily Melville's husband in William Godwin's *Caleb Williams*.

Mr. Grimes Coarse, brutal, drunken master chimney sweep, employer of Tom; he is punished in kind by Mrs. Bedonebyasyoudid and finally repents in Charles Kingsley's *The Water-Babies*.

Mrs. Grimes Dan Ogle's sister, who plots with him against Captain Nat Kemp to get Lewis Marr's money away from the captain in Arthur Morrison's *The Hole in the Wall*.

Jacob Grimes Sleazy proprietor of the public house which George Vavasor uses as a constituency office in his bid for Parliament in Anthony Trollope's *Can You Forgive Her?*.

Margaret Grimes Arabella Bloomville's faithful servant and friend since Arabella's childhood in William Beckford's *Modern Novel Writing; or, the Elegant Enthusiast*.

Grimsby The most base and corrupt of Arthur Huntingdon's friends; he does not marry and finally dies in a drunken brawl in Anne Brontë's *The Tenant of Wildfell Hall*.

Monsieur Grimseld Shriveled, prematurely old Swiss, who has Reginald de St. Leon imprisoned for returning to Switzerland, and who tries to defraud him of property rightfully owed to him in William Godwin's *St. Leon*.

Mr. Grimshaw Evil squire, who murders his first wife, their baby, and her brother and nearly kills Eleanor, his second wife; he is eventually executed for the murders in a ghost story interpolated into the narrative of William Beckford's *Azemia*.

Anne Lilburne Grimshaw Also called Gertrude, the first young wife of the evil Mr. Grimshaw, who murders her, her baby, and her brother; her ghost helps the second Mrs. Grimshaw escape in a ghost story interpolated into the narrative of William Beckford's *Azemia*.

Eleanor Grimshaw Daughter of wealthy London tradespeople who thought to advance themselves through connection with a squire, the murderous Mr. Grimshaw; she nearly dies, but is saved by her girlhood sweetheart; they marry in a ghost story interpolated into the narrative of William Beckford's *Azemia*.

Lady Grimston Lady Bidulph's austere old friend, at whose residence, Grimston Hall, Sidney Bidulph meets and marries Mr. Arnold, a distant Grimston relation; she dies leaving her whole fortune to charity, not to either of her daughters, in Frances Sheridan's *Memoirs of Miss Sidney Bidulph*.

Miss Grimston   Favorite daughter of Lady Grimston; she resembles her mother in temperament and marries an equally temperamental baronet, whose argument with his mother-in-law leads to his wife's estrangement from her mother in Frances Sheridan's *Memoirs of Miss Sidney Bidulph*.

Abel Grimston   Attorney to Austin Ruthyn; he presides at the reading of Austin's will in J. Sheridan Le Fanu's *Uncle Silas*.

Mr. Grimwig   Mr. Brownlow's stout, gruff friend, who leads him into believing that Oliver Twist is a bad lot after all in Charles Dickens's *Oliver Twist*.

Mr. Grinder   Honest shopowner, who gives Dicky Perrott a job; however, Aaron Weech tricks him into believing Dicky is stealing from him, so he fires Dicky in Arthur Morrison's *A Child of the Jago*.

Mr. Grinder   Manager and drum player in a traveling company, the other two members of which walk on stilts; he meets Nell Trent and her grandfather while they travel with Tom Codlin and Harris Short in Charles Dickens's *The Old Curiosity Shop*.

Grip   Barnaby Rudge's tame raven and his constant companion in Charles Dickens's *Barnaby Rudge*.

Biddy Gripewell   Heiress to a London pawnbroker; she becomes the object of Roderick Random's courtship after his affair with Melinda Goosetrap in Tobias Smollett's *The Adventures of Roderick Random*.

Gregory Griskin   Anglican cleric, conversationalist, and gourmand, who generally espouses "custom" over rigid rules, but who has broken with his cousin Mr. Rivers over Rivers's choice of a wife; he is eventually persuaded by Geoffry Wildgoose to reconcile with Rivers in Richard Graves's *The Spiritual Quixote*.

Lady Griskin   London lady of fashion who tries to help Ralph Barton court Liddy Melford in Tobias Smollett's *The Expedition of Humphry Clinker*.

Grizalinda   Arminda's waiting-woman, who betrays her mistress by allowing Constantine to hide in Arminda's bedroom and then joins with the Duchess to spread false rumors in Penelope Aubin's *The Life and Adventures of the Lady Lucy*.

Miss Grizel   Prim and acid Edinburgh seamstress, who is contemptuous of Effie Deans in discussions with friends in Sir Walter Scott's *The Heart of Midlothian*.

Mrs. Grizzle   Gamaliel Pickle's sister, who manages his household for him until his marriage; she pursues Commodore Trunnion until she succeeds in marrying him, marries Jack Hatchway after the death of the Commodore, and dies herself, leaving Hatchway a widower in Tobias Smollett's *The Adventures of Peregrine Pickle*.

Clara Groatsettar   Heiress who, like her sister Maddie, is vigilantly chaperoned by her gossipy aunt, Lady Glowrowrum, in Sir Walter Scott's *The Pirate*.

Maddie Groatsettar   Heiress who, like her sister Clara, is vigilantly chaperoned by her gossipy aunt, Lady Glowrowrum, in Sir Walter Scott's *The Pirate*.

Farmer Groby   Owner of Flintcomb-Ash farm, where Tess (Durbeyfield) and Marian are laborers; Tess is indifferent to his brutality because it is not sexually threatening in Thomas Hardy's *Tess of the D'Urbervilles*.

Thomas Groffin   Juryman for the prosecution in Martha Bardell's breach-of-promise suit against Samuel Pickwick in Charles Dickens's *The Posthumous Papers of the Pickwick Club*.

Mr. Grogram   Penrith attorney who reads Squire Vavasor's will in which George Vavasor is passed over in Anthony Trollope's *Can You Forgive Her?*.

Sir Gregory Grogram   Great Whig advocate who, as Attorney General, leads the prosecution against Phineas Finn, on trial for the murder of Mr. Bonteen in Anthony Trollope's *Phineas Redux*. He is an uneasy member of a coalition government in *The Prime Minister*.

Henry Campinet, Lord Grondale   Aristocrat of the village of Grondale who flaunts his status; he is father of Caroline Campinet and nephew of Maria Garnet; his despising the common people and his attempt to make Caroline marry Sir Philip Chestrum make him Charles Hermsprong's bitter enemy in Robert Bage's *Hermsprong*.

Gregory Grooby   Father of the illegitimate Gregory Glen in Robert Bage's *Hermsprong*.

Gottlieb Groschen   Rich merchant, father of Margarita; his wealth does not protect his daughter from Werner and his men; he dislikes the "poor youth" Farina, his daughter's favored suitor and (with Guy the Goshawk) rescuer, but consents to their marriage when Kaiser Heinrich takes up Farina's case in George Meredith's *Farina*.

Lisbeth Groschen   Spinster aunt of Margarita Groschen; she tells her niece romantic and gloom-filled stories and is mistakenly taken to Werner's Eck, where she is held for ransom until she is belatedly freed by Guy the

Goshawk and Schwartz Thier in George Meredith's *Farina*.

Margarita Groschen   Beautiful object of the White Rose Club's ardor; she prefers Farina, who rescues her from Schwarz Thier and Werner, who had captured and imprisoned her; she eventually marries Farina in George Meredith's *Farina*.

Joseph Groschut   Chaplain to the Bishop of Brotherton and bitter enemy of the dean, Henry Lovelace; he leaks gossip about the dean's hunting to the press but is transferred to a remote parish in Anthony Trollope's *Is He Popenjoy?*.

Herr Grosse   Gluttonous German oculist introduced by Nugent Dubourg; he temporarily restores Lucilla Finch's sight in Wilkie Collins's *Poor Miss Finch*.

Cardinal Grossocavallo   Patron who introduces Og of Basan to the pope, who commissions two well-received paintings on Christian themes in William Beckford's *Biographical Memoirs of Extraordinary Painters*.

Adelina, Lady Grosville   Rigidly religious aunt of Lady Kitty Ashe; she scorns association with the fast artistic set known as "The Archangels" in Mrs. Humphry Ward's *The Marriage of William Ashe*.

William, Lord Grosville   Gouty aristocrat, who enjoys being a power behind the political scene at his country house in Mrs. Humphry Ward's *The Marriage of William Ashe*.

Colonel Hugh Grove   Officer in the Royalist army, who, along with Colonel Penruddock, surrenders to the insurgents on what he wrongly assumes are terms of quarter, and who is subsequently beheaded at Exeter in William Godwin's *Mandeville*.

Mr. Grovelgrub   Venal clergyman, tutor, and henchman to villainous Lord Anophel Achthar in Thomas Love Peacock's *Melincourt*.

James (Jem) Groves   Landlord of the Valiant Soldier, the public house where Nell Trent's grandfather gambles and loses all of the money Nell earned in Charles Dickens's *The Old Curiosity Shop*.

Miss Groves   Young woman, unrestrained as a child, seduced and ruined by Mr. L—, and secretly married in the end to a relative of her servant; she is mistaken by Arabella for an innocent romance heroine in Charlotte Lennox's *The Female Quixote*.

Gabriel Grub   Misanthropic sexton and grave digger, who undergoes a moral transformation in "The Story of the Goblins Who Stole a Sexton," told by Mrs. Wardle in Charles Dickens's *The Posthumous Papers of the Pickwick Club*.

Miss Gruchette   Occupant of a lavish cottage on Lord Mountclere's property and known as "Lady Mountclere"; the discovery of the cottage by the newly married Lady Mountclere (Ethelberta Petherwin) precipitates her aborted attempt to run away; Lord Mountclere assures her that "Lady Mountclere" will not return in Thomas Hardy's *The Hand of Ethelberta*.

Mrs. Grudden   Actress of small parts in the Vincent Crummles Theatrical Company in Charles Dickens's *The Life and Adventures of Nicholas Nickleby*.

John Grueby   Lord George Gordon's loyal servant, who attempts to protect him from the consequences of the violence of the Gordon rioters in Charles Dickens's *Barnaby Rudge*.

Gillespie Grumach   See Marquis of Argyle.

Daniel Grummer   Constable who arrests Samuel Pickwick and Tracy Tupman in Ipswich in Charles Dickens's *The Posthumous Papers of the Pickwick Club*.

Abraham Grundle   First love of Eva Crasweller when she was sixteen; the son of her father's partner in the wool trade, he supports the law of Britannula requiring euthanasia at age sixty-eight because he wishes to acquire her father's property in Anthony Trollope's *The Fixed Period*.

Mr. Grundy   One of the regulars at the Magpie and Stump; she refuses to sing in Charles Dickens's *The Posthumous Papers of the Pickwick Club*.

Miss Gryce   A teacher at Lowood School with whom Jane Eyre shares her bed and who keeps Jane awake with her snoring in Charlotte Brontë's *Jane Eyre*.

Morgana Gryll   Niece of Squire Gryll; she marries Algernon Falconer in Thomas Love Peacock's *Gryll Grange*.

Squire Gryll   Bachelor host and uncle of Morgana Gryll in Thomas Love Peacock's *Gryll Grange*.

Gryphon   Creature that speaks in lower-class dialect; it introduces Alice to the Mock Turtle and demonstrates the Lobster-Quadrille in Lewis Carroll's *Alice's Adventures in Wonderland*.

Cavaliere di Guardino   Lauretta Capece's brother, a wicked villain who betrays his sister and dies a pauper of leprosy and the plague in J. Henry Shorthouse's *John Inglesant, A Romance*.

Philip Guarine   Hugo de Lacy's squire, who protects his lord during their years on the Crusade in Sir Walter Scott's *The Betrothed*.

Golbasto Momaren Evlame Gurdilo Shefin Mully Ully Gue   Emperor of Lilliput in Jonathan Swift's *Travels into Several Remote Nations of the World. In Four Parts. By Lemuel Gulliver*.

Andrew Guelph   Fifteenth-century disciple of Aldrovandus Magnus but more sedate and interested in wealth than his friend Og of Basan; he is admired for the exactness of the plants in his paintings, for his renderings of peasant life, and especially for his moonlight in William Beckford's *Biographical Memoirs of Extraordinary Painters*.

Lady Guenevere   The woman for whose reputation Bertie Cecil sacrifices himself by not challenging the accusation of forgery against him in Ouida's *Under Two Flags*.

Guenevra   Dwarf who is Queen Berengaria's slave and Nectabanus's wife in Sir Walter Scott's *The Talisman*.

Contessa Guerrini   Reclusive aristocrat, who mourns the death of her son in the Italian battles; she becomes the confidante of Eleanor Burgoyne and Lucy Foster in their self-imposed exile at Torre Amiata in Mrs. Humphry Ward's *Eleanor*.

Mr. Guest   Expert critic of handwriting and head clerk and confidant to the attorney Mr. Utterson; he identifies similarities between Dr. Henry Jekyll's and Edward Hyde's writing in Robert Louis Stevenson's *The Strange Case of Dr. Jekyll and Mr. Hyde*.

Stephen Guest   Lucy Deane's suitor, who becomes smitten by Maggie Tulliver; on a boat ride, he tries to persuade Maggie to run away with him; she declines, but they drift too far in the water, and her reputation is ruined when they spend the night on the boat in George Eliot's *The Mill on the Floss*.

William Guest   (persona of William Morris) Nineteenth-century man who is granted his wish to see a day after the Socialist revolution that has transformed England by 2090 from a land of commercial exploitation to one of neighborly cooperation; he is tutored on the revolution by Old Hammond and accompanies Richard and Clara Hammond and Ellen on a river trip to Kelmscott in William Morris's *News from Nowhere*.

Angelo Guidascarpi   Clelia Guidascarpi's brother, who kills Paul von Lenkenstein, an Austrian, for his involvement with her; he dies in a failed uprising with Carlo Ammiani in George Meredith's *Vittoria*.

Clelia Guidascarpi   Angelo and Rinaldo Guidascarpi's sister, who commits suicide after a clandestine alliance with the Austrian Count Paul von Lenkenstein; he is then murdered by her brothers in George Meredith's *Vittoria*.

Rinaldo Guidascarpi   Clelia Guidascarpi's brother; responsible for the death of Clelia and her lover, Count Paul von Lenkenstein, he is rescued from execution by the Austrians by death at the hand of Rossellina Rizzo in George Meredith's *Vittoria*.

Adeline de Guides   Acquaintance who has a passion for one of Amelia de Gonzales's admirers in William Beckford's *Modern Novel Writing; or, the Elegant Enthusiast*.

Arrigo de Guinigi   Son of Francesco de Guinigi; a member of the Italian Emperor Henry's court, he acts as messenger between Castruccio dei Antelminelli and Euthanasia dei Adimari and is dearly loved by Castruccio as brother or son in Mary Shelley's *Valperga*.

Francesco de Guinigi   A military peasant and father of Arrigo de Guinigi; Ruggieri dei Antelminelli entrusts his son Castruccio to his care; he supports the seventeen-year-old Castruccio for a year in the Euganean hills in Mary Shelley's *Valperga*.

Leodino de Guinigi   Italian knight who is refused a command in Castruccio dei Antelminelli's army; he organizes the Guelph party in Lucca and is executed for conspiracy in Mary Shelley's *Valperga*.

Gulchenrouz   Ali Hassan's effeminate son, betrothed to Nouronihar; his innocence and boyish charm are rewarded with eternal childhood in William Beckford's *Vathek*.

Betty Gulliver   Wife whom Lemuel Gulliver loathes as a Yahoo when he is forcibly repatriated from Houyhnhnmland in Jonathan Swift's *Travels into Several Remote Nations of the World. In Four Parts. By Lemuel Gulliver*.

Lemuel Gulliver   Ship's surgeon whose final four voyages take him to Lilliput; to Brobdingnag; to Laputa, Balnibarbi, Glubbdubdrib, Luggnagg, and Japan; and to the country of the Houyhnhnms in Jonathan Swift's *Travels into Several Remote Nations of the World. In Four Parts. By Lemuel Gulliver*.

Mr. and Mrs. Gulpidge   Couple present at the Waterbrooks' dinner party in Charles Dickens's *The Personal History of David Copperfield*.

Gumbo   Harry Warrington's accomplished Negro slave and valet, who attends him in England, creating a sensation in the servants' hall; when Harry returns to America, he remains in England as George Warrington's servant and, given his freedom, marries Molly in William Makepeace Thackeray's *The Virginians*.

Mrs. Gummidge   Widow of a former partner of Daniel Peggotty and later Mr. Peggotty's housekeeper; she emigrates to Australia with him and Emily Peggotty in Charles Dickens's *The Personal History of David Copperfield*.

Gunman   Guide for the group led by Captain Singleton; he amazes the natives by shooting and killing a leopard in Daniel Defoe's *The Life, Adventures, and Pyracies of the Famous Captain Singleton*.

Ben Gunn   Former member of Flint's crew; having persuaded some fellow sailors into a mapless and fruitless search for the treasure, he was marooned on Treasure Island for three years before Jim Hawkins finds him; in his solitary exile he found and moved Flint's treasure; he helps Dr. Livesey outwit the pirates; he remains fearful of Long John Silver in Robert Louis Stevenson's *Treasure Island*.

Mr. Gunnery   Godwin Peak's geology tutor, who leaves his specimens and instruments to Peak in his will in George Gissing's *Born in Exile*.

Mr. Gunter   A guest at Bob Sawyer's party who quarrels with Mr. Noddy in Charles Dickens's *The Posthumous Papers of the Pickwick Club*.

William Guppy   Clerk for Kenge and Carboy who meets Esther Summerson in London, falls in love with her, works to discover information about her parentage with the help of Tony Jobling, notices the resemblance between Lady Dedlock and Esther, and is rejected in his marriage proposal in Charles Dickens's *Bleak House*.

Dr. Gurgoyle   Writer of "The Physics of Vicarious Existence" and also "Being Structures on Certain Heresies Concerning a Future State that have been engrafted on the Sunchild's teaching," arguing the superiority of the Sunchild's after-life in myth to his real life in Samuel Butler's *Erewhon Revisited Twenty Years Later*.

Gurta   Crone and sorceress whose pupil Juba becomes but whose claim of control over him he scorns in John Henry Newman's *Callista*.

Gurth   Cedric's loyal swineherd and good friend of Wamba the Fool; he helps besiege Torquilstone Castle and is given his freedom in Sir Walter Scott's *Ivanhoe*.

Miss Gushing   Spinster member of Caleb Oriel's congregation; when he becomes engaged to Beatrice Gresham, she becomes a Methodist and is later mentioned as Mrs. Rantaway in Anthony Trollope's *Doctor Thorne*.

Gustave   A pupil at the school next to Mme. Beck's in Charlotte Brontë's *Villette*.

Gustavus   Dalgetty's handsome and intelligent horse, named for the mercenary's much-admired former employer in Sir Walter Scott's *A Legend of Montrose*.

Gustavus Adolphus   Prince of Sweden called Gustavus the Victorious; he is Dalgetty's previous employer in Sir Walter Scott's *A Legend of Montrose*. He is the king of Sweden whose army defeats that led by Count Tilly; he engages the Cavalier in his service and frequently relies on him for military advice in Daniel Defoe's *Memoirs of a Cavalier*.

Johnny Guthrie   One of Louis XI's Scottish Guard archers who save Quentin Durward from hanging in Sir Walter Scott's *Quentin Durward*.

Guy   Sexton who finds a chest containing the manuscript relating Gaston de Blondeville's story in Ann Radcliffe's *Gaston de Blondeville*.

Octavius (Gooseberry) Guy   Messenger boy employed by Mr. Bruff, the lawyer; he gives important evidence to Sergeant Cuff concerning the way Mr. Luker passed to a bearded sailor a package which turns out to be a stolen diamond in Wilkie Collins's *The Moonstone. A Romance*.

Guy (the Goshawk)   Stout, good-hearted English soldier in the service of the Kaiser; he befriends Farina and rescues Margarita Groschen; he is captured in Werner's Eck but ultimately defeats Werner in George Meredith's *Farina*.

Bertrand Guyot   Brave Gascon soldier, who is killed while defending the ladies of Croye from William de La Marck's attack in Sir Walter Scott's *Quentin Durward*.

Don Guzman   Wealthy gentleman whose false will leads to the near destruction of the Walberg family in Charles Maturin's *Melmoth the Wanderer*.

Don Alphonso Guzman   Young Spanish nobleman who braves the English lines to save the life of the woman he loves; he marries her in Charles Johnstone's *Chrysal: or, The Adventures of a Guinea*.

Don Pedro Guzman   Noble father of Don Alphonso; he disowns his son because of Don Alphonso's love of Olivia and is killed in battle in Charles Johnstone's *Chrysal: or, The Adventures of a Guinea*.

Rosita Guzman   Adolescent Limenian girl, who becomes Robert Ponsonby's second wife in discreditable circumstances and after his death runs off with his dishonest clerk in Charlotte Yonge's *Dynevor Terrace*.

Gwenwyn Welsh prince, who wishes to marry Eveline Berenger; rejected, he slays her father, Raymond Berenger, and is killed by Hugo de Lacy while attacking the Castle of Garde Doloureuse in Sir Walter Scott's *The Betrothed*.

Gwenyvar King Arthur's queen; the problem of her abduction by Melvar is resolved by Taliesin with the diplomacy of threat and by Seithenyn with the diplomacy of wine in Thomas Love Peacock's *The Misfortunes of Elphin*.

Lydia Gwilt Red-haired temptress intent on gaining Allan Armadale's fortune; she makes Ozias Midwinter fall in love with her and marries him; her fiendish plan for the perfect murder involving poison gas in a sealed chamber at a sanatorium misfires, and she turns the fatal machinery on herself in Wilkie Collins's *Armadale*.

Mrs. Gwyllim Housekeeper at Brambleton Hall and the correspondent to whom Tabitha Bramble gives instructions for maintaining the household during the expedition in Tobias Smollett's *The Expedition of Humphry Clinker*.

Maelgon Gwyneth Sixth-century king whose realm borders Elphin's; outwitted by Taliesin in his plots against Angharad, he imprisons Elphin in Thomas Love Peacock's *The Misfortunes of Elphin*.

Miss Gwynn Writing and ciphering governess at the girls' boarding school at Westgate House in Charles Dickens's *The Posthumous Papers of the Pickwick Club*.

Donica Gwynn Sir Jeckyl Marlowe's housekeeper, who was once his father's mistress and thus knows of the secret passage; she leaves to serve Lady Alice Redcliffe; she confirms Varbarriere's suspicions of the secret passage to Sir Jeckyl's room; she goes abroad with Lady Jane Lennox in J. Sheridan Le Fanu's *Guy Deverell*.

Dr. Gwynne Master of Lazarus College, Oxford, and friend of Archdeacon Grantly and Francis Arabin; through his effort the deanship of Barchester Cathedral is offered to Mr. Harding in Anthony Trollope's *Barchester Towers*.

H

Jackey (John), Lord H——   Dissolute, stupid nephew-in-law of Lady Davers, in whose household he resides; his presence is the ostensible reason for Mr. B——'s refusal to allow Pamela (Andrews) B—— to move to his sister's household; later his dalliance with Pamela's maid is interrupted by Pamela; he eventually makes an unfortunate marriage with a woman of questionable repute in Samuel Richardson's *Pamela, or Virtue Rewarded*.

Mr. H——   Handsome, wealthy aristocrat, who keeps Fanny Hill in high style as his mistress for a long period before they fall out in John Cleland's *Memoirs of a Woman of Pleasure*.

Dr. H——   Physician who attends Clarissa in her decline in Samuel Richardson's *Clarissa: or, The History of a Young Lady*.

Gifted Gilfillan Habakkuk   Cameronian leader of the small military party which escorts Edward Waverly to Sterling Castle in Sir Walter Scott's *Waverly*.

Habundia   Supernatural wood-mother who aids Birdalone to mature while living with the Witch-Wife and helps her in later crises in William Morris's *The Water of the Wondrous Isles*.

Anthony Hackbut   Dahlia and Rhoda Fleming's miserly uncle, who works in a bank, where he steals a large sum of money which Rhoda convinces him to give to her in order to pay Nic Sedgett to marry the seduced Dahlia in George Meredith's *Rhoda Fleming*.

Tommy Hadden   Dissolute, affable young gentleman, who meets Norris Carthew in Sydney, ships on the *Currency Lass*, and assumes John Hardy's identity in Robert Louis Stevenson's *The Wrecker*.

Mrs. Hadoway   Widow of a clergyman; she rents rooms to William Lovel in Fairport in Sir Walter Scott's *The Antiquary*.

Hagan (Mr. Geoghegan)   Handsome, dashing Irish actor, who marries Lady Maria Esmond, gives up the stage, becomes a clergyman, and goes to America, where he is a loyalist during the War of Independence in William Makepeace Thackeray's *The Virginians*.

Hagar   Servant of Charoba; she is given to Sarah as recompense for Totis's near-seduction of Sarah in the appended romance "The History of Charoba, Queen of Egypt" in Clara Reeve's *The Progress of Romance*.

Archibald von Hagenbach   A German noble who is a governor of a city loyal to Charles, Duke of Burgundy; he is executed by the Swiss at the encouragement of Count Albert of Geierstein (in disguise as a priest); his death is the cause of Burgundy's invasion of Swiss cantons in Sir Walter Scott's *Anne of Geierstein*.

Dr. Haggage   Mrs. Dorrit's medical attendant during the birth of Amy in the Marshalsea prison in Charles Dickens's *Little Dorrit*.

Haigha   See March Hare.

Lord Hair-Trigger   Lady Charlotte Hair-Trigger's brother and the impoverished friend of Bryan Perdue's father in Thomas Holcroft's *The Memoirs of Bryan Perdue*.

Lady Charlotte Hair-Trigger   Bryan Perdue's virtuous, honorable mother; of Milesian heritage, she died when he was six years old in Thomas Holcroft's *The Memoirs of Bryan Perdue*.

Halafamai   Genie of Truth and Mercy, who helps Eovaai by revealing Ochihatou in Eliza Haywood's *Adventures of Eovaai, Princess of Ijaveo*.

Marian Halcombe   Intelligent and resourceful half sister of Laura Fairlie and pupil of Walter Hartright, the drawing master; she proves a brave antagonist to Count Fosco and Sir Percival Glyde in their schemes to gain Laura's fortune after her marriage to Glyde; she arranges Laura's escape from an asylum where the villains have incarcerated her in Wilkie Collins's *The Woman in White*.

Claud Halcro   Delightful and sprightly old bard, whose circuitous stories never reach their point; boastful of his youthful meeting with "Glorious John" Dryden, he entertains the Zetlanders with his minstrel's talents in Sir Walter Scott's *The Pirate*.

Mr. Hale   The vicar of a picturesque rural parish in the south of England; his decision to resign because of doubts and to move to the industrial northern city of Milton changes his family's life in Elizabeth Gaskell's *North and South*.

Mrs. Hale   The ailing, nostalgic, and genteel wife of Mr. Hale; she dies in Elizabeth Gaskell's *North and South*.

Frederick Hale   Margaret's brother, in exile after leading a mutiny against a vicious navy captain; his secret return, undisclosed identity, and involvement in the death of George Leonards lead to major complications in Elizabeth Gaskell's *North and South*.

Margaret Hale   Genteel daughter of a rural vicar in the south of England; she has to adjust to the manners and conditions of a northern industrial town when her father moves his family in Elizabeth Gaskell's *North and South*.

Halford The friend to whom Gilbert Markham writes his long epistle and who marries Rose Markham in Anne Brontë's *The Tenant of Wildfell Hall*.

Colonel Halkett A conservative who disapproves of Nevil Beauchamp's radicalism; he succeeds in marrying his daughter Cecilia, in love with Beauchamp, to Blackburn Tuckham in George Meredith's *Beauchamp's Career*.

Cecilia Halkett Colonel Halkett's daughter who, despite her conservatism, falls in love with the radical Nevil Beauchamp; his loyalties to Dr. Shrapnel and to a hapless Frenchwoman lead her to marry Blackburn Tuckham in George Meredith's *Beauchamp's Career*.

Mr. Hall Neighbor and friend of William Whittlestaff and squire of Alresford; his daughters assist at the wedding of Montagu Blake in Anthony Trollope's *An Old Man's Love*.

Sir Christopher Hall Saxon knight from Cumraik serving in Montrose's army in Sir Walter Scott's *A Legend of Montrose*.

Cyril Hall The frank, scholarly Vicar of Nunnely, who is both a practical and spiritual adviser in Charlotte Brontë's *Shirley*.

Margaret Hall A kindly old maid, who spends much of her time doing genuine good works for the poor in Charlotte Brontë's *Shirley*.

Pearson Hall Shirley Keeldar's family solicitor, who is related to Cyril Hall in Charlotte Brontë's *Shirley*.

(Tadpole) Hall Scapegrace companion of Tom Brown at Rugby School in Thomas Hughes's *Tom Brown's Schooldays*.

Hallblithe of the Raven Young tribesman of Northern Europe who seeks his betrothed, the Hostage of the Rose, in the Isle of Ransom and the Land of the Glittering Plain; he regains her with the aid of Puny Fox in William Morris's *The Story of the Glittering Plain*.

Hall-face Warrior brother of Face-of-god in William Morris's *The Roots of the Mountains*.

Edward Hallin Cambridge don, labor economist, and friend of Aldous Raeburn; although a Liberal, he leads and instructs the thought of his friend in Mrs. Humphry Ward's *Marcella*. He continues to influence the social and political ideas of Lord and Lady Maxwell (Raeburn and Marcella Boyce), who name their son in his honor in *Sir George Tressady*.

Hall-Sun Young daughter of Wood-Sun and Thiodolf; she has charge of the ever-burning lamp in the great hall of the Wolfings; she foresees future events and commands Hrosshild to organize maidens to report on the movements of the Romans in William Morris's *A Tale of the House of the Wolfings*.

Basil Hallward Aesthete painter of Dorian Gray's "essence" in the infamous, haunting portrait; he is in love with Dorian and tries to exert a good moral influence on Dorian, but Dorian murders him in Oscar Wilde's *The Picture of Dorian Gray*.

Hall-ward Leader of the House of the Steer and father of the Bride in William Morris's *The Roots of the Mountains*.

Hallycarnie Youwarkee's sister in Robert Paltock's *The Life and Adventures of Peter Wilkins*.

Hallycarnie (Wilkins) Second daughter of Peter Wilkins and Youwarkee; she is adopted by Jahamel in Robert Paltock's *The Life and Adventures of Peter Wilkins*.

Princess Leonora Halm-Eberstein Daniel Deronda's mother, who gave him to Sir Hugo Mallinger to raise as his nephew because she did not want her child to be aware of his Jewish origin in George Eliot's *Daniel Deronda*.

Peter Halsey Elderly, common laborer at Great End Farm; he fears the farm's ghost in Mrs. Humphry Ward's *Harvest*.

Halsi *Gawry* (flying woman) who disguises herself as a *glumm* (flying man) and wins the flying competition organized by Peter Wilkins in Robert Paltock's *The Life and Adventures of Peter Wilkins*.

Alfred Fanshawe de Bassompierre de Hamal Son of Ginevra (Fanshawe) and Alfred de Hamal in Charlotte Brontë's *Villette*.

Colonel Alfred, Count de Hamal Suitor of Ginevra Fanshawe; he bests Dr. John Bretton by eloping with and marrying her; he and she are equally superficial in Charlotte Brontë's *Villette*.

Isadore Hamel Dilettante sculptor, who falls in love with Lucy Dormer and is too proud to accept handouts from Sir Thomas Tringle, her uncle; his principles intact, he marries Lucy and Sir Thomas acts munificently towards his niece in Anthony Trollope's *Ayala's Angel*.

Hamet-beig Azemia's prosperous father, a high-rank-ing noble in Constantinople; he betroths Azemia to Oglow Muley, a wealthy merchant, in William Beckford's *Azemia*.

Duke of Hamilton   Scottish nobleman and widower, whose proposal satisfies Lady Beatrix Esmond's ambitions; he kills and is killed by Lord Mohun in a duel just before his marriage is to take place in William Makepeace Thackeray's *The History of Henry Esmond*.

Claudia Hamilton   Wealthy, talented, and beautiful niece of Christopher Kirkland; she makes her home with him for four years in Mrs. Lynn Linton's *The Autobiography of Christopher Kirkland*.

Mrs. Hamley   The gentle, ailing wife of Squire Hamley; she brings Molly Gibson into the Hamley household as a young friend before her death in Elizabeth Gaskell's *Wives and Daughters*.

Squire Hamley   An archetypal Tory of the old school; his resistance to changing ideas causes family estrangement before he can recognize his error in Elizabeth Gaskell's *Wives and Daughters*.

Aimee Hamley   The French, Roman Catholic former servant girl who marries Osborne Hamley in Elizabeth Gaskell's *Wives and Daughters*.

John Hamley   Courtly kinsman of Lord Foxham and Joan Sedley's betrothed; he marries Alicia Risingham in Robert Louis Stevenson's *The Black Arrow: A Tale of Two Roses*.

Osborne Hamley   The delicate heir of Squire Hamley; his secret marriage (known to Molly Gibson) and his illness and death lead to social and emotional complications in Elizabeth Gaskell's *Wives and Daughters*.

Roger Hamley   Younger son of Squire Hamley; he falls in love with Cynthia Kirkpatrick before finally realizing that he loves Molly Gibson; he also represents the emerging role of science in the world of Elizabeth Gaskell's *Wives and Daughters*.

Mr. Hammerdown   The auctioneer at the sale of the Sedleys' household goods in William Makepeace Thackeray's *Vanity Fair*.

Claus Hammerlein   Rude and drunken ironworker, who participates in the revolt at Liège and calls for the bishop's head in Sir Walter Scott's *Quentin Durward*.

Captain Hammersley   Sinister rival to Charles O'Malley for the affection of Lucy Dashwood; he is killed at the Battle of Waterloo in Charles Lever's *Charles O'Malley*.

Hammond   Mate on Teach's *Sarah*; he has one of three keys to treasure in Robert Louis Stevenson's *The Master of Ballantrae: A Winter's Tale*.

Mr. Hammond   Mr. Rivers's friend, who urges him to marry Charlotte Woodville immediately and is himself attracted to her in Richard Graves's *The Spiritual Quixote*.

Mrs. Hammond   Mrs. Jakeman's sister, to whose house Emily Melville flees after her imprisonment, and from whose care Emily is taken to jail in William Godwin's *Caleb Williams*.

Old Hammond   Possible descendant of William Guest and great-grandfather of Richard Hammond; from his residence in the British Museum he describes to William Guest the Socialist revolution of the twentieth century and the new order of society in William Morris's *News from Nowhere*.

Clara Hammond   Estranged wife of Richard Hammond; she is reconciled to him by Old Hammond in William Morris's *News from Nowhere*.

Henry Hammond   Emma Corbett's betrothed, who fights for the British in America; he dies of sorrow when he discovers that Emma is mortally ill from the poison she sucked from his arrow wound in S. J. Pratt's *Emma Corbett*.

Richard (Dick) Hammond   Young Thames boatman of 2090; he introduces William Guest to his great-grandfather Old Hammond and later rows with Guest, Clara Hammond, and Ellen to Kelmscott in William Morris's *News from Nowhere*.

Ane Hammorgaw   Friend of Andrew Fairservice; he is a solemn Glasgow precentor in Sir Walter Scott's *Rob Roy*.

Josiah Hampole   Neighbor of Charles Mandeville's paternal uncle, Audley Mandeville, and a vulgar and conceited supporter of Cromwell; he permits himself to be used by the dishonest attorney Holloway, who schemes to bilk Audley of his property in William Godwin's *Mandeville*.

Lord Hampstead   Eldest son of the Marquis of Kingsbury; he is disliked and resented by his stepmother, the Marchioness; he is annoyed when his friend, George Roden, aspires to the hand of his sister, Lady Frances Trafford, although he wishes to marry the commoner Marion Fay; when Marion, dying, refuses him, he is left with his only keepsake of her, the poker she had touched in his drawing room, in Anthony Trollope's *Marion Fay*.

J. Hand   Actor hired by Arthur Wardlaw to makes a false confession to Helen Rolleston that he forged the note of demand which jailed Robert Penfold in Charles Reade's *Foul Play*.

Handassah Young Gypsy woman attendant upon Sybil Lovel and later Eleanor Mowbray in William Harrison Ainsworth's *Rookwood*.

Harry Handcock Halfhearted suitor of Margaret Mackenzie in her youth; when her brother dies and she inherits a fortune, his ardor becomes overwhelming, and she rejects him in Anthony Trollope's *Miss Mackenzie*.

Israel Hands Wily coxswain of the *Hispaniola* and Flint's exgunner; Jim Hawkins overhears him plotting with Long John Silver and Dick Johnson; he kills the pirate O'Brien and tries to outwit "Captain" Jim aboard the *Hispaniola*; he slightly wounds Jim, who shoots him dead in Robert Louis Stevenson's *Treasure Island*.

Mrs. Hannaford Matron who leaves her uncongenial husband, loves an unworthy man who victimizes her, and dies in George Gissing's *The Crown of Life*.

Lee Hannaford Disagreeable science teacher and inventor of armaments who accuses his innocent wife of infidelity in George Gissing's *The Crown of Life*.

Olga Hannaford Boheman girl with a minor talent for art and an undependable husband-to-be; she ultimately rejects him and marries an Italian friend in George Gissing's *The Crown of Life*.

Hannah "Gammer" Martin's servant in Thomas Hardy's *Two on a Tower*.

Hannah The Rivers family's servant, who suspects Jane Eyre's motives when she asks for food at the door, but who is won over by Jane's candor in Charlotte Brontë's *Jane Eyre*.

Mrs. Hannah Amiable servant in the house of Mr. Fenton (Henry Clinton); she teaches young Harry Clinton and Ned (Fielding) reading and helps with a practical joke in Henry Brooke's *The Fool of Quality*.

Hannibal A soldier (later general) in Jane Barker's *Exilius; or, The Banish'd Roman*.

Hansi Korean wife of Choang; three days after his death she is about to remarry, despite having promised him eternal fidelity, but dies of shame when he returns to life in a parable told by Lien Chi Altangi in Oliver Goldsmith's *The Citizen of the World*.

Mr. Hanson Lawyer who sorts out the affairs of Nicoemdus Easy and helps his son, Jack Easy, in Captain Frederick Marryat's *Mr. Midshipman Easy*.

Sir Abraham Haphazard Formidable lawyer and Attorney General consulted by Mr. Harding in the Hiram's Hospital controversy in Anthony Trollope's *The Warden*. He also appears in *Doctor Thorne*.

Hob Happer Shrewd and wealthy convent miller and Mysie Happer's father in Sir Walter Scott's *The Monastery*.

Mysie Happer Lovely, merry daughter of Hob Happer, the wealthy convent miller; though Elspeth Glendinning wants her eldest son, Halbert, to marry Mysie, she falls in love with Sir Piercie Shafton; after she helps Sir Piercie escape from the Tower, they marry and go into political exile in Sir Walter Scott's *The Monastery*.

Mills Happerton Trading partner in Hunky and Sons and one of Ferdinand Lopez's dubious business associates; he and his wife attend the Robys' dinner party in Anthony Trollope's *The Prime Minister*.

Jenny Harberton Woman farmhand at Great End Farm during the First World War in Mrs. Humphry Ward's *Harvest*.

Fabian Harbothel Sir Aymer de Valence's squire; quick to anger and to judge, he is hated by Gilbert Greenleaf in Sir Walter Scott's *Castle Dangerous*.

Sir Philip Harclay Aristocrat who befriends Edmund and helps him prove his true parentage; his defeat of Sir Walter Lovel in a tourney compels Sir Walter's confession and clears the way for Edmund's accession to his family estate in Clara Reeve's *The Old English Baron*.

Mr. Harcourt Eusebia's father, who initially encourages the Athanasian beliefs in his daughter; he dies twelve years before Eusebia of the plague during their travels abroad in Thomas Amory's *The Life of John Buncle, Esq.*

Caroline Waddington, Lady Harcourt Headstrong Juno long determined on a wealthy match; she rejects George Bertram and marries Sir Henry Harcourt, who tries to force her to obtain money from her grandfather, the elder George Bertram; some time after Harcourt's suicide she marries George Bertram in Anthony Trollope's *The Bertrams*.

Eusebia Harcourt Beautiful, educated, and young foundress of a small reclusive Protestant society in Richmondshire; her talents include painting, music, and languages, and her religious discussions with John Buncle convince her to repudiate the Athanasian Creed in Thomas Amory's *The Life of John Buncle, Esq.*

Sir Henry Harcourt Highly intelligent barrister who rises to Solicitor General; he tries to force his wife to extort money from her grandfather to maintain his lifestyle; his marriage fails, and he commits suicide in Anthony Trollope's *The Bertrams.*

Hardcastle   Violent ruffian, who tries to seize Wethermel but is killed in a duel with Osberne Wulfsson in William Morris's *The Sundering Flood.*

Sir Freestone Hardgrave   Avaricious aristocrat; the benevolence of others prevents his greed from destroying Mrs. Graves and Giffard Homely in Henry Brooke's *The Fool of Quality.*

Alfred Hardie   Son of Richard Hardie, who has him abducted on the eve of his marriage into a lunatic asylum in order to avoid paying him the trust funds Richard has already dipped into; Alfred receives £3,000 damages from the uncle who signed him in and inherits £60,000 from a father who now (insanely) considers himself bankrupt in Charles Reade's *Hard Cash.*

Jane Hardie   Sister of Alfred; Dr. Sampson calls her the "virgin martyr," and indeed she dies of wounds inflicted by an insane victim of her father's criminal bankruptcy in Charles Reade's *Hard Cash.*

Richard Hardie   Former suitor of Lucy Fountain (Dodd); he embezzles from his own firm, robs the trust funds of his children, Alfred and Jane, incarcerates his own son in an asylum for life to cover his thefts, and drives Captain Dodd insane by refusing to acknowledge the Captain's £14,000 deposit; he ends up his son's pensioner, thinking he is bankrupt in Charles Reade's *Hard Cash.*

John Harding   Brilliant but cynical novelist from London, in Dublin to write on the social season; he shows Alice Barton that her intelligence can be as satisfying as the marriage game the debutantes play; he finds a publisher for her but resists a romantic attraction in George Moore's *A Drama in Muslin.* He becomes the confidant to Sir Owen Asher in *Evelyn Innes.* He continues the role of confidant but refuses an offer to travel to the Middle East with Asher in *Sister Teresa.* He is one of the group of artists and writers who discuss the modern art movements in the bars, at the Royal Academy, and in Frank Escott's room in *A Modern Lover.* He is invited by Laura Forest to attend a rehearsal of her opera in *A Mummer's Wife.* He joins Frank Escott, Mike Fletcher, and Lady Helen Seely on a visit to Mount Rorke in *Spring Days.* He argues with John Norton on philosophy and architecture; along with Norton, Escott, and Fletcher he discovers the suicide of Lady Helen after one of their parties in *Mike Fletcher.* He is a respected critic in *Vain Fortune.*

Eleanor Harding   Septimus Harding's spirited daughter, torn between devotion to her father and love of John Bold, whom she eventually marries in Anthony Trollope's *The Warden.* As a propertied widow she is courted by Mr. Slope and Bertie Stanhope but marries Francis Arabin in *Barchester Towers.* Mrs. Arabin's inopportune foreign travel brings Josiah Crawley to the brink of calamity in *The Last Chronicle of Barset.* She also appears in *Doctor Thorne* and in *Framley Parsonage.*

Septimus Harding   Clergyman and warden of Hiram's Hospital almshouse, beloved for his gentleness and respected for his principles; accused of an abuse of charity funds, he becomes convinced he is receiving more money than he is morally entitled to and resigns, annoying his embattled supporters in Anthony Trollope's *The Warden.* He is again a pawn in church politics when his son-in-law Archdeacon Grantly battles with Bishop Proudie in *Barchester Towers.* He appears briefly in *Framley Parsonage,* in *The Small House at Allington,* and in *Doctor Thorne.* His death occurs in *The Last Chronicle of Barset.*

Miss Hardingham   Barnabas Tyrrel's favorite among the women of the town; she scorns him at a dance in favor of Ferdinando Falkland, adding to Tyrrel's paranoia in William Godwin's *Caleb Williams.*

Sir Gregory Hardlines   Chief clerk in Weights and Measures Office who proposes competitive examinations for entrants to Civil Service in Anthony Trollope's *The Three Clerks.*

Miss Hardman   Mrs. Hardman's daughter, who sees governesses as a necessary commodity to be used at her own discretion in Charlotte Brontë's *Shirley.*

Mrs. Hardman   Early employer of Mrs. Pryor (Agnes Helstone); she suggests that humility is the most appropriate manner for governesses to adopt in Charlotte Brontë's *Shirley.*

Mr. Hardy   Assistant to the Commissioner; he advises Mr. Secretary of the raid on the London Radical Club just before the Secretary is assassinated in Mark Rutherford's *The Revolution In Tanner's Lane.*

Abel Hardy   One of the bedesmen in Hiram's Hospital; he becomes discontented when he hears about possible abuse of almshouse charity in Anthony Trollope's *The Warden.*

John Hardy   English *Flying Scud* sailor caught in the sail after he is shot; his identity is assumed by Tommy Hadden in Robert Louis Stevenson's *The Wrecker.*

John (Jack) Hardy   A poor but talented student, who works his way through St. Ambrose's College, Oxford, as a "servitor," impresses Tom Brown both as an oarsman and an exponent of "muscular Christianity," becomes fellow of the college, and finally marries Tom's cousin, Katie Winter, in Thomas Hughes's *Tom Brown at Oxford.*

Michael Hardy   Deceased leader of the hunt; his death has created a void in Robert Surtees's *Handley Cross.*

Kitty Hare   Charming, joyful, seventeen-year-old daughter of William Hare; she spends much time with their neighbor Lizzie Norton; in love with Lizzie's son, John, she becomes engaged to him and is planning marriage when she is brutally attacked and raped by a tramp; she becomes insane and commits suicide in George Moore's *A Mere Accident.*

William Hare   Widower and Protestant clergyman, who was a childhood friend of Lizzie Norton and is now her neighbor; he enjoys theological discussions with Lizzie's son, John; he is devoted to his daughter, Kitty, and pleased with her planned marriage to John in George Moore's *A Mere Accident.*

Emma Haredale   Daughter of the murdered Reuben and niece of Geoffrey Haredale; her marriage to Edward Chester is initially thwarted because of mutual family animosity; she is captured during the Gordon riots and must endure Gashford's attempts to seduce her before she is rescued by Edward in Charles Dickens's *Barnaby Rudge.*

Geoffrey Haredale   Emma Haredale's uncle, who is suspected of killing his brother Reuben until he proves that the steward Rudge committed the murder for his master's money in Charles Dickens's *Barnaby Rudge.*

Reuben Haredale   Emma's father, murdered for his money by his steward, Rudge; Geoffrey Haredale, Reuben's brother, is suspected of the crime in Charles Dickens's *Barnaby Rudge.*

Harelip   Prince of the goblins; he plots to kidnap little Princess Irene and marry her; like his father and mother, he hates the king and his subjects for expelling the goblins from the upper world in George MacDonald's *The Princess and the Goblin.*

John Harewood   Military engineer, who wins Wilmet Underwood, marries her under romantic circumstances in Egypt, and proves an ideal husband and devoted in-law in Charlotte Yonge's *The Pillars of the House.* He appears in *The Long Vacation.*

William Harewood   Clerical half brother of John Harewood; he succeeds as a writer on social and religious issues, marries Robina Underwood, and follows Clement Underwood as Vicar of Vale Leston in Charlotte Yonge's *The Pillars of the House.*

Mr. Harford   Old-style Tory and a clergyman of Baslehurst; he supports Butler Cornbury in his bid to represent the town at Westminster; he cherishes a healthy animosity towards Samuel Prong, the sanctimonious evangelical vicar of the neighbouring parish, in Anthony Trollope's *Rachel Ray.*

Mrs. Hargrave   A grasping, pretentious woman, whose sole aim is to marry her daughters, Milicent and Esther, to wealthy suitors; she indulges her son, Walter, in Anne Brontë's *The Tenant of Wildfell Hall.*

Sir Charles Hargrave   Rakish Lincolnshire aristocrat, who unknowingly interrupts Pamela (Andrews) and Mr. B——'s first dinner and evening together just after they are married, and whose lewd comments at a later dinner party embarrass Pamela in Samuel Richardson's *Pamela, or Virtue Rewarded.*

Esther Hargrave   The youngest of the Hargrave family; her spirit and independence of mind finally win her a husband (Frederick Lawrence) worthy of her integrity in Anne Brontë's *The Tenant of Wildfell Hall.*

Milicent Hargrave   A pretty but timid friend of Helen Huntingdon and cousin of Annabella Wilmot; she marries Ralph Hattersley and, though for a time tormented by his dissipation, lives happily with him once he reforms in Anne Brontë's *The Tenant of Wildfell Hall.*

Walter Hargrave   Friend and neighbor of Arthur Huntingdon; he pursues Helen Huntingdon when Arthur neglects her and abandons his intrigue only when Helen feels compelled to threaten violence in Anne Brontë's *The Tenant of Wildfell Hall.*

Mr. Harkaway   Bluff, unmarried Master of Hounds of the Cumberlow Green Hunt who lives for horses and hounds in Anthony Trollope's *Mr. Scarborough's Family.*

Jonathan Harker   Young lawyer who travels to Transylvania to help Count Dracula purchase a house in London and who subsequently helps to defeat the count in Bram Stoker's *Dracula.*

Wilhelmina (Mina) Murray Harker   Wife of Jonathan Harker and a friend of Lucy Westenra; she, like Lucy, is threatened with vampirism; she is instrumental in Count Dracula's defeat in Bram Stoker's *Dracula.*

Albert Harleigh   English gentleman who is courteous to the Stranger on the boat from France; he is pursued by Elinor Joddrel but loves the Stranger, Juliet Granville, and offers to negotiate her release from the French marriage; he marries her in the end in Frances Burney's *The Wanderer.*

Gwendolen Harleth   Beautiful, selfish girl, who marries the rich Henleigh Mallinger Grandcourt to avoid becoming a governess even though his mistress, Lydia Glasher, begs her not to marry him for the sake of his four illegitimate children; because Grandcourt becomes a cruel, dominating husband, she seeks comfort from his attractive acquaintance, Daniel Deronda, especially after the death by drowning of her husband; feelings of guilt over her husband and disappointment at Deronda's preference for Mirah Lapidoth cause her to resolve to reform her selfish nature in George Eliot's *Daniel Deronda*.

Harley   Tenderhearted hero, who earns the sobriquet "The Man of Feeling"; after a trip to London, where he is much buffeted by the corruptions of the world, Harley returns to his country home to lead a life of benevolent action, halted by his untimely death in Henry Mackenzie's *The Man of Feeling*.

Mrs. Harley   Widowed mother of Augustus; she befriends Emma Courtney, constantly praising Augustus and his virtues, until Emma falls in love before she meets him in Mary Hays's *Memoirs of Emma Courtney*.

Adrian Harley   Cynical older cousin and tutor of Richard Feverel; entrusted by Sir Austin Feverel with overseeing Richard, he is often more concerned with satisfying his love of good food than with satisfying Sir Austin's desires in George Meredith's *The Ordeal of Richard Feverel*.

Augustus Harley   Mysterious beloved of Emma Courtney; he refuses her repeated proposals because he is already secretly married; he dies after an accident, despite Emma's competent medical aid in Mary Hays's *Memoirs of Emma Courtney*.

Augustus Harley (the younger)   Son of Augustus Harley's secret marriage; he is raised by Emma Courtney; after his first (unrequited) love marries another, Emma sends him long letters analyzing the influences on her own life, thus writing Mary Hays's *Memoirs of Emma Courtney*.

Harlokin   Rebel prince of western Normnbdsgrsutt who initiates a plot to overthrow Georigetti; he is slain by Peter Wilkins in Robert Paltock's *The Life and Adventures of Peter Wilkins*.

Anthony Harlowe   Clarissa Harlowe's younger unmarried uncle, who joins with her parents in persecuting her; the threat of a forced marriage while under virtual house arrest at his estate precipitates Clarissa's flight with Robert Lovelace in Samuel Richardson's *Clarissa: or, The History of a Young Lady*.

Arabella Harlowe   The spiteful, envious sister of Clarissa; lacking the charm, beauty, and graciousness of her younger sister, she is instrumental in turning her parents against Clarissa in Samuel Richardson's *Clarissa: or, The History of a Young Lady*.

Charlotte Harlowe   Clarissa's mother, whose desire to help her daughter is hindered by her meekness and subordinate position in the family in Samuel Richardson's *Clarissa: or, The History of a Young Lady*.

Clarissa (Clary) Harlowe   An eighteen-year-old gentlewoman, whose refusal to marry the man her father chooses for her leads to her kidnapping and rape by Robert Lovelace; she refuses Lovelace's later offer of marriage, and her shame and her family's refusal to forgive her bring about her decline and death; her story is told in her correspondence, in which she also uses the pseudonyms Miss Laetitia Beaumont, Mrs. Harriot Lucas, Mrs. Rachel Clark, Mrs. Mary Atkins, and Mrs. Dorothy Salcomb, in Samuel Richardson's *Clarissa: or, The History of a Young Lady*.

James Harlowe   Wealthy, imperious merchant, who, out of greed, arranges a marriage between his daughter Clarissa and Roger Solmes, whom the girl despises and is forced to leave home to escape; afterward, Harlowe illegally withholds Clarissa's inheritance and refuses all forms of negotiation and reconciliation with her in Samuel Richardson's *Clarissa: or, The History of a Young Lady*.

James Harlowe (the younger)   The imperious, fierce, ill-tempered brother of Clarissa and the main architect in creating and then maintaining his parents' antipathy to Robert Lovelace and in pressing Roger Solmes's suit of Clarissa in Samuel Richardson's *Clarissa: or, The History of a Young Lady*.

John Harlowe   Elder unmarried uncle of Clarissa Harlowe; he joins her parents in their persecution of her; he blames her education and literacy for her refusal to accept the family's choice of husband for her in Samuel Richardson's *Clarissa: or, The History of a Young Lady*.

Aunt Harman   Anna Howe's aunt, whose ill health keeps Anna from attending her friend Clarissa Harlowe during her decline in London in Samuel Richardson's *Clarissa: or, The History of a Young Lady*.

John Harmon (Julius Handford, John Rokesmith)   Central character thought to be murdered by drowning; he lets the mistake continue, boards with the Wilfers under an assumed name, works as a secretary for the Boffins, proposes to Bella Wilfer and eventually marries her, and at the end reveals his identity in Charles Dickens's *Our Mutual Friend*.

Johnny Harmon   Betty Higden's baby grandson, who is so named by Mrs. Boffin; she wishes to adopt him in place of John Harmon, but he dies before he can be adopted in Charles Dickens's *Our Mutual Friend*.

Louis Harmon   Upper-class painter, dilettante, and frequenter of the salons of Mme. d'Estrees in London and Venice in Mrs. Humphry Ward's *The Marriage of William Ashe*.

Haroun of Aleppo   Benevolent Syrian sage, who is murdered by Louis Grayle in his pursuit of the elixir of life in Edward Bulwer-Lytton's *A Strange Story*.

Harpax   A Centurion of the Immortals; he is a thief and conspirator in Sir Walter Scott's *Count Robert of Paris*.

Alderman Harper   Character who, fifteen years before Mervyn moves into Tiled House, refused to go through with a lease from Lord Castlemallard on it because of the strange occurrences his daughter and son-in-law, the Prossers, experienced while staying there in J. Sheridan Le Fanu's *The House by the Churchyard*.

Mr. Harrel   One of Cecilia Beverley's three trustees; he allows her to live with his family after the death of her guardian and plots to make money from Sir Robert Floyer for arranging a marriage with Cecilia; having borrowed money and run up debts, he commits suicide in a public place in Frances Burney's *Cecilia*.

Priscilla Harrel   Wife of one of Cecilia Beverley's trustees; once Cecilia's playmate and school fellow, she is as spendthrift as her husband; she lives as Cecilia's companion after Harrel's suicide in Frances Burney's *Cecilia*.

Mrs. Harridan   Innkeeper and procuress who extorts money from Roderick Random with threats of prosecution for theft in Tobias Smollett's *The Adventures of Roderick Random*.

Harriet   Petite, dark-eyed friend and collegue of Fanny Hill; raised an orphan and raped by a neighbor boy at a swimming hole, she plied the prostitute's trade at Mrs. Cole's before setting up as mistress to a baronet in John Cleland's *Memoirs of a Woman of Pleasure*.

Harriet   Character created by Henry Clinton to illustrate how women acquire the defects of fashionable society in Henry Brooke's *The Fool of Quality*.

Evan Harrington   Son of a tailor, suited to the upper class by talent and inclination; he foils the plans of his scheming sisters to marry him to wealthy Rose Jocelyn by taking the responsibility for a letter forged to humiliate his rival; when his innocence in the matter is revealed to Rose, the two marry and Harrington becomes a gentleman in George Meredith's *Evan Harrington*.

Sir Jasper Harrington   Uncle of Mr. Ireton; he urges his nephew to marry someone to keep their property in the family; he offers marriage to Juliet Granville and helps her escape Salisbury in Frances Burney's *The Wanderer*.

Melchisedec (The Great Mel) Harrington   Evan's father, a tailor who socializes with the nobility and romances their wives; he dies, saddling Evan with great debts in George Meredith's *Evan Harrington*.

Harriot   A prostitute with whom Natura is in love in Eliza Haywood's *Life's Progress Through the Passions: or, the Adventures of Natura*.

Lady Harriot   Charlotte's London friend, who receives the only letter written by Charlotte in Mary Collyer's *Felicia to Charlotte*.

Captain Harris   American Indian trader and adventurer hired by Henry Durie to accompany the Master (James Durie) into the wilderness on his treasure search and presumably to murder him there in Robert Louis Stevenson's *The Master of Ballantrae: A Winter's Tale*.

Captain Harris   Shipmate of Captain Singleton while on a voyage to Cadiz; he encourages Singleton to join a mutiny attempt, which fails; he joins Wilmot in becoming a pirate; his ship is later taken by the English, and he dies before being brought back to England for trial in Daniel Defoe's *The Life, Adventures, and Pyracies of the Famous Captain Singleton*.

Mr. Harris   Bath greengrocer in Charles Dickens's *The Posthumous Papers of the Pickwick Club*.

Mrs. Harris   Sarah Gamp's respectable and admiring patron and friend, who appears constantly in Mrs. Gamp's conversation, but who has never been seen in Charles Dickens's *The Life and Adventures of Martin Chuzzlewit*.

Mrs. Harris   Bedfordshire midwife who attends Pamela (Andrews) B—— during her first childbirth in Samuel Richardson's *Pamela, or Virtue Rewarded*.

Mrs. Harris   Amelia and Betty Harris's mother; she censures Amelia's love match with William Booth but is ultimately reconciled to the union; she makes Amelia her heir in Henry Fielding's *Amelia*.

Betty Harris   Amelia Booth's scheming sister in Henry Fielding's *Amelia*.

Howel Harris   Disciple of John Wesley; he engages a town hall for Geoffry Wildgoose in Richard Graves's *The Spiritual Quixote*.

Timotheus (Tim) Harris Innkeeper of the Red Lion Inn where Joseph Andrews shelters from a hailstorm in Henry Fielding's *The History of the Adventures of Mr. Joseph Andrews and of his Friend Mr. Abraham Adams.*

Harrison Old steward who serves Lady Margaret Bellenden at Tillietudlem in Sir Walter Scott's *Old Mortality.*

General Harrison Brutal and stupid soldier, who is one of the Parliamentary commissioners sent to take possession of Woodstock in Sir Walter Scott's *Woodstock.*

Dr. R. Harrison Generous and compassionate clergyman, who supports the Booths and time after time rescues William Booth from the consequences of his folly in Henry Fielding's *Amelia.*

Harry Underling vociferously ordered by Long John Silver in pursuit of Black Dog, whom Jim Hawkins has spotted at the Spy Glass tavern in Robert Louis Stevenson's *Treasure Island.*

Harry Husband of Peggy; he is rescued from debt by the generous Frank Henley in Thomas Holcroft's *Anna St. Ives.*

Hart of Highcliff Valiant warrior and "man of good counsel"; he is wounded in the battle of Silver-stead; he marries Bow-may in William Morris's *The Roots of the Mountains.*

Mr. Hart London tailor who contests the Parliamentary constituency of Baslehurst and loses to Butler Cornbury in Anthony Trollope's *Rachel Ray.*

Mrs. Hart Wife of Lord Leicester's steward at Kenilworth in Sophia Lee's *The Recess.*

Abraham Hart Jocose self-styled attorney, in fact a moneylender, to whom George Hotspur owes considerable sums in Anthony Trollope's *Sir Harry Hotspur of Humblethwaite.*

Samuel Hart Predatory money-lender, who tracks Mountjoy Scarborough to Monte Carlo in Anthony Trollope's *Mr. Scarborough's Family.*

James Harthouse Gentleman and political dilettante, who uses young Tom Gradgrind and tries to seduce Louisa (Gradgrind) Bounderby; he is finally defeated by Sissy Jupe in Charles Dickens's *Hard Times.*

Lady Harthover Wife of Sir John Harthover and mother of Ellie; she takes Ellie to the seaside in Charles Kingsley's *The Water-Babies.*

Ellie Harthover Beautiful, white-skinned little girl, down whose chimney Tom falls, and whose terrified screams result in Tom's flight; she is taken by the fairies and assists in Tom's moral education before they both return to the world in Charles Kingsley's *The Water-Babies.*

Sir John Harthover Genial squire, whose chimneys Tom is cleaning when he falls into Ellie Harthover's bedroom; he initiates an unsuccessful search for Tom when he disappears in Charles Kingsley's *The Water-Babies.*

Mr. Hartlepod Ambitious secretary of a mining venture in Guatemala willing to take on Ferdinand Lopez if he buys shares in the company in Anthony Trollope's *The Prime Minister.*

Marchioness of Hartletop Lord Dumbello's mother, of whose worldliness Lady Lufton disapproves; the scandal of her liason with the (old) Duke of Omnium is mentioned in Anthony Trollope's *Framley Parsonage.* She is alluded to by the duke in his reprimand of Plantagenet Palliser's attentions to Lady Dumbello (Griselda Grantly) in *The Small House at Allington.* As the Dowager Marchioness she is mentioned in *Phineas Finn.* She is refused admittance by Lady Glencora Palliser to the dying duke's bedside in *Phineas Redux.*

Mr. Hartley Virginia St. Pierre's father, who after much searching is finally united with his daughter through the aid of Clarence Hervey in Maria Edgeworth's *Belinda.*

Dr. Adam Hartley Bright, athletic student of Dr. Gideon Gray and an unsuccessful suitor for Menie Gray's love; after rescuing and then helping Richard Middlemas, he travels to India as a military doctor; he saves Menie from the seraglio and dies shortly thereafter of a tropical disease in Sir Walter Scott's *The Surgeon's Daughter.*

Michael Hartley The Antinomian weaver, a drunkard and possibly crazed, who shoots Robert Moore as an example of a tyrant in Charlotte Brontë's *Shirley.*

Mayor Hartopp Kindly mayor of Gatesboro; he believes the accusations of Jasper Losely against William Waife but finally exonerates him in Edward Bulwer-Lytton's *What Will He Do With It? by Pisistratus Caxton.*

Walter Hartright Upright drawing master, who tutors Laura Fairlie and Marian Halcombe; he falls in love with Laura, but, hearing that she must marry Sir Percival Glyde, he departs to Central America; he returns home in time to assist Marian in rescuing Laura from the diabolical schemes of her husband and Count Fosco; after Glyde's death he is able to marry Laura in Wilkie Collins's *The Woman in White.*

Erminia Harvey   Mr. Buxton's ward and a wealthy heiress; he is disappointed in his hope that she will marry his son in Elizabeth Gaskell's *The Moorland Cottage.*

Captain Harville   Friend of Captain Wentworth; he has been settled with his wife and children in lodgings at Lyme since his service wound two years earlier; Louisa Musgrove convalesces in the Harville home after her injury; his disappointment at Captain Benwick's infidelity to his dead sister is confided to the sympathetic Anne Elliot; overhearing them, Wentworth is moved to renew his proposal in Jane Austen's *Persuasion.*

Mrs. Harville   Captain Harville's warm-hearted and hospitable wife; she nurses the injured Louisa Musgrove in Jane Austen's *Persuasion.*

Hasem   Slave of Nourjahad and director of his household during his master's first sleep; he is reported dead after Nourjahad's second sleep; he reappears disguised as the prime vizier in the court of Schemerzad in Frances Sheridan's *The History of Nourjahad.*

Ali Hassan   Brother of Emir Fakreddin and Gulchenrouz's father in William Beckford's *Vathek.*

Hastie   Member of Captain Harris's gang who had studied for the church; he attends the Master (James Durie) in his last illness in Robert Louis Stevenson's *The Master of Ballantrae: A Winter's Tale.*

Alison Hastie   Innkeeper's charitable young daughter, who risks her countymen's wrath by ferrying Alan Breck Stewart and David Balfour across the river to Queensferry, where David may safely seek aid and advice in Robert Louis Stevenson's *Kidnapped.* She is named and rewarded by David in *Catriona.*

Bell Hastings   Niece of Lady Anne Wilmot's deceased husband and the inheritor of Lady Anne's income, should she remarry; Bell's coming forward makes it possible to resettle the jointure terms so that Lady Anne is free to marry again; Bell is admired by Lord Melvin, to whom she is happily united in Frances Brooke's *The History of Lady Julia Mandeville.*

George Hastings   Bailiff of Great End Farm; he supports Rachel Henderson's modern ideas on farming in Mrs. Humphry Ward's *Harvest.*

Bennet Hatch   Gruff retainer of Sir Daniel Brackley, bailiff, and the burner of Brimstone; he tells Dick Shelton how to get out through a secret passageway and raises an alarm when he discovers Dick in the woods in Robert Louis Stevenson's *The Black Arrow: A Tale of Two Roses.*

Goody Hatch   Bennet Hatch's wife, who teases Dick Shelton about not knowing John Matcham (Joan Sedley) is a woman; she tells Joan how to find Dick's room in Robert Louis Stevenson's *The Black Arrow: A Tale of Two Roses.*

Jack Hatchway   Retired naval lieutenant who served under Commodore Trunnion, lost a leg in battle, and is a great practical joker; he lives with the commodore and marries the commodore's widow; he cares for the estate in Perry Pickle's absence and insists on remaining near the Fleet until Perry leaves in Tobias Smollett's *The Adventures of Peregrine Pickle.*

Lord Hate-good   Judge at Vanity Fair who condemns Faithful to death and Christian to imprisonment for their adherence to religion in John Bunyan's *The Pilgrim's Progress From this World to That Which Is to Come.*

Duke of Hatfield   Secretary of Benevolence (colonial secretary) in the British Government; he sends Sir Ferdinando Brown to the South Pacific island of Britannula to be president in place of John Neverbend in Anthony Trollope's *The Fixed Period.*

Mr. Hatfield   Vain, fashionable Rector of Horton, who is attracted to and then spurned by Rosalie Murray and who ignores Agnes Grey in Anne Brontë's *Agnes Grey.*

Hatta   See Mad Hatter.

Dirk Hatteraick (Jans Janson)   Smuggler involved in Francis Kennedy's murder and Henry Bertram's kidnapping; he murders Meg Merriles because she turns him in, and he strangles Guilbert Glossin before hanging himself in Sir Walter Scott's *Guy Mannering.*

Helen Hattersley   Daughter of Milicent (Hargrave) and Ralph Hattersley, and Helen Huntingdon's namesake; she grows up to marry Helen Huntingdon's son, Arthur, in Anne Brontë's *The Tenant of Wildfell Hall.*

Ralph Hattersley   One of Arthur Huntingdon's friends; he finally gives up his drinking and gambling several years after his marriage to Milicent Hargrave; he becomes a successful horse breeder after he reforms in Anne Brontë's *The Tenant of Wildfell Hall.*

Ralph Hattersley (the younger)   Stalwart eldest son of Ralph Hattersley in Anne Brontë's *The Tenant of Wildfell Hall.*

Baptiste Hatton   Politically powerful politician and attorney who conspires with George, Lord Marney to deprive Walter Gerard of his estate, but who, having fallen in love with Sybil Gerard, restores the documents which prove her claim to the estate after her father has been killed in Benjamin Disraeli's *Sybil.*

Simon Hatton (Bishop of Wodgate) Baptiste Hatton's crude brother and brutal overseer of the Wodgate Mill; he leads a rapacious mob across the Lancashire countryside and dies in a fire while pillaging Marney Abbey in Benjamin Disraeli's *Sybil.*

Jessica Haughton Lionel Haughton's mother, who is nearly imposed on by Jasper Losely in Edward Bulwer-Lytton's *What Will He Do With It? by Pisistratus Caxton.*

Lionel Haughton Guy Darrell's kinsman, who wins his affections and those of Sophy in Edward Bulwer-Lytton's *What Will He Do With It? by Pisistratus Caxton.*

Count d' Hauteville The Marquis de Montfleuri's uncle, who defends hereditary titles and privilege, but whose neglected estate in Normandy, a stronghold of royalist resistance, represents reprehensible exploitation of property in Charlotte Smith's *Desmond.*

Lady Amaldina Hauteville Eldest daughter of Lord Persiflage; she condescends to Lady Frances Trafford for loving an official in the Post Office; marrying, after many delays, the Marquis of Llwddythlw, she boasts there is so much in a name in Anthony Trollope's *Marion Fay.*

Lady Margaret de Hautlieu (Sister Ursula) A novice at the Abbey of Saint Bride; she is Lady Augusta de Berkely's friend and the betrothed of Sir Malcolm Fleming; disfigured while attempting an escape, she loses her beauty and her lover; when Sir Malcolm is in peril, she saves his life, thereby regaining his love in Sir Walter Scott's *Castle Dangerous.*

Madame de Hautville Countess Zulmer's former governess, who first advises her only to use and not to love any man but later repents her teaching in Charlotte Dacre's *The Passions.*

Havens Gentlemanly English trader in Marquesas and the friend to whom Loudon Dodd tells his story in Robert Louis Stevenson's *The Wrecker.*

James Havill The imitative, talentless architect who competes with the younger, gifted George Somerset for position as head architect of the De Stancy castle restoration; blackmailed by William Dare, who knows Havill secretly stole Somerset's ideas, Havill agrees to help Dare in his plot to undo Somerset in Thomas Hardy's *A Laodicean.*

Miss Havisham Reclusive lady, who was left standing at the church door by Compeyson on their wedding day; she has stopped the clocks, kept the wedding breakfast, and worn her wedding gown for years; she prides herself on her broken heart; she brings up the adopted Estella to inflict vengeance on men but later repents when she sees how Pip Pirrip's love for Estella resembles her own frustrated love; she dies after her dress catches fire in Charles Dickens's *Great Expectations.*

Arthur Havisham Miss Havisham's half-brother, through whom she became involved with the swindler Compeyson, in Charles Dickens's *Great Expectations.*

Mr. Hawbury Kindly medical practitioner, who tries to interpret Allan Armadale's disturbing dreams about drowning and a mysterious woman to allay fears of impending doom in Wilkie Collins's *Armadale.*

Captain Hawdon (Nemo) Lady Dedlock's lover in their youth and Esther Summerson's father; he ends up as a law-writer for Mr. Snagsby under the name Nemo, and dies of an opium overdose in Charles Dickens's *Bleak House.*

Mr. Hawes Sadistic governor of the jail in which Tom Robinson is a prisoner and Francis Eden the chaplain until his villainy and the hypocrisy of his supporting "justices" is exposed to a representative of the Home Office in Charles Reade's *It Is Never Too Late to Mend.*

Sir Mulbery Hawk Fashionable gentleman, who attempts to seduce and ruin Kate Nickleby with the help of her uncle Ralph Nickleby; Nicholas Nickleby thrashes him when he learns of the plot in Charles Dickens's *The Life and Adventures of Nicholas Nickleby.*

Gideon Hawke Clergyman and speaker, whose handsome and charismatic person gives impact to what he says; he changes Ernest Pontifex's feelings about religion in Samuel Butler's *The Way of All Flesh.*

Dickon (Pegtop) Hawkes Rough, cruel miller, who is the employee of Silas Ruthyn and father of Meg Hawkes; he conspires to help Dudley Ruthyn and Silas in the attempt to kill Maud Ruthyn; his role is never revealed, but he is later convicted of an old crime and reveals the whereabouts of Madame de la Rougierre's body in J. Sheridan Le Fanu's *Uncle Silas.*

Meg (Beauty) Hawkes Rough but good-hearted daughter of the evil Dickon Hawkes; she befriends Maud Ruthyn after Maud visits her when she is sick; she helps save her from Silas and Dudley Ruthyn; she marries Tom Brice and, with Maud's aid, buys a farm in Australia in J. Sheridan Le Fanu's *Uncle Silas.*

Francis Hawkesworth Gentleman of good property who endures a long engagement to Eleanor Mohun so that she may bring up her sisters in Charlotte Yonge's *Scenes and Characters.*

Hawkins Elderly pirate and boatswain in Sir Walter Scott's *The Pirate*.

Lady Hawkins Wife of Sir John Hawkins; she dies broken with sorrow for her husband's sins as a slave trader and her son's early death in Charles Kingsley's *Westward Ho!*.

Mr. Hawkins Chaplain of H.M.S. *Aurora*; he can never resist the temptation of taking part in the fighting in Captain Frederick Marryat's *Mr. Midshipman Easy*.

Mr. Hawkins Owner of the Admiral Benbow Inn and Jim's father; cowed by Billy Bones, he dies on the evening that Bones gets Jim to bring him rum in Robert Louis Stevenson's *Treasure Island*.

Mrs. Hawkins Jim Hawkins's mother, who runs Admiral Benbow Inn; her determination to get from Bones's effects the exact amount of the money due her delays her departure and puts her and Jim in a dangerous situation in Robert Louis Stevenson's *Treasure Island*.

Benjamin Hawkins A freeholder and tenant of Barnabas Tyrrel, who takes a liking to Hawkins's son, Leonard; because Hawkins refuses to allow Leonard to come into service with Tyrrel, the Hawkinses are harassed and Leonard ultimately jailed; Hawkins frees his son, and the family disappears; when Tyrrel is found dead, Hawkins and his son are executed for the crime in William Godwin's *Caleb Williams*.

Jim Hawkins The narrator and the son of the proprietors of the Admiral Benbow Inn, where Billy Bones spends his violent last days; a resourceful and plucky boy, Jim acquires what proves to be a treasure map; he ships as cabinboy on the *Hispaniola*, fortuitously uncovers the mutineers' plot, discovers Ben Gunn on the island, and by guile and courage takes the ship away from the pirates in Robert Louis Stevenson's *Treasure Island*.

Sir John Hawkins Brave but obstinate and ruthless mariner and slave trader, who dies in the tropics in Charles Kingsley's *Westward Ho!*.

Leonard Hawkins Benjamin Hawkins's son; the father's refusal of Barnabas Tyrrel's offer to take Leonard into his service so enrages Tyrrel that he destroys the family in William Godwin's *Caleb Williams*.

Peter Hawkins Elderly lawyer, the employer and friend of Jonathan Harker in Bram Stoker's *Dracula*.

Sir Richard Hawkins Gallant captain and Euphuist, son of Sir John Hawkins; he is knighted and made a privy councillor, but he dies with his promise unfulfilled in Charles Kingsley's *Westward Ho!*.

Hawksley Lord Foxham's servant who recommends leaving the cottage before Sir Daniel Brackley's and Lord Shoreby's men arrive in Robert Louis Stevenson's *The Black Arrow: A Tale of Two Roses*.

Frank Hawley Local citizen who hears John Raffles discuss his connection with Mr. Bulstrode and demands, at a town meeting after Raffles has been killed, that Bulstrode confess to the murder in George Eliot's *Middlemarch*.

Colonel Hay Montrose's gallant friend in Sir Walter Scott's *A Legend of Montrose*.

Hay (Young Hay) of Romanes Tipsy Scottish country lord and uncouth neighbor to Archibald Weir in his residency as Lord of Hermiston in Robert Louis Stevenson's *Weir of Hermiston: An Unfinished Romance*.

Captain Hayes Skipper of *The Golden Hind*, which returns safely in Charles Kingsley's *Westward Ho!*.

Mr. Hayes Acting manager of Dick Lennox's company; he drinks and loses track of money in George Moore's *A Mummer's Wife*.

Bully Hayes Naval hero, perhaps a smuggler and pirate, discussed by the club men of Tai-o-hae's Cercle Internationale in Robert Louis Stevenson's *The Wrecker*.

Frank Hayston, Laird of Bucklaw A reckless, dissipated sportsman, who is saved from ruin by a timely legacy; as Lucy Ashton will not receive him, he leaves the matchmaking to Lady Ashton and Lady Blenkensop; surviving his bride's insane attack, he leaves Scotland a wiser and more sober man in Sir Walter Scott's *The Bride of Lammermoor*.

Charles Hayter A young clergyman, not yet in possession of a living, who loves his cousin Henrietta Musgrove; though he is an eldest son, the modesty of his father's estate makes him an unsuitable suitor in the opinion of Mary Elliot Musgrove; he prevails and is welcomed by the other Musgroves in Jane Austen's *Persuasion*.

John Hayward Under sexton (grave digger) and neighbor of the narrator's brother; he assists the narrator (H.F.) in stopping the looting of his brother's house in Daniel Defoe's *A Journal of the Plague Year*.

Hazael President of the Essene monastery where Jesus returns to continue sheepherding; Joseph of Arimathea accompanies him there in George Moore's *The Brook Kerith*.

Mr. Hazard Investor and friend of George Saville; he

employs Bryan Perdue and later accuses him of forgery in Thomas Holcroft's *The Memoirs of Bryan Perdue*.

Frank Hazeldean   Squire William Hazeldean's son, who lives extravagantly in London and is enamored of Beatrice de Negra in Edward Bulwer-Lytton's *"My Novel," by Pisistratus Caxton*.

Jemima Hazeldean   Squire William Hazeldean's niece, who marries Alphonso Riccabocca and gradually wins his deepest love in Edward Bulwer-Lytton's *"My Novel," by Pisistratus Caxton*.

William Hazeldean   Country squire whose decision to revive the use of stocks in the parish leads to complications which affect the lives of Leonard Fairfield and Randal Leslie in Edward Bulwer-Lytton's *"My Novel," by Pisistratus Caxton*.

Charles Hazzelwood   Son and heir of Sir Robert Hazzelwood; he remains Lucy Bertram's faithful and considerate lover despite her impoverished state; following his mistake in thinking Captain Vanbest Brown (Henry Bertram) an outlaw, he is wounded as they struggle; eventually Brown is identified as Bertram, and Charles weds Lucy in Sir Walter Scott's *Guy Mannering*.

Sir Robert Hazzelwood   Powerful, vindictive father of Charles Hazzelwood; he is exceedingly conscious of family honor and is a doting family man in Sir Walter Scott's *Guy Mannering*.

G. O. A. Head   Manchester mill owner, who encourages Harry Coningsby to visit Mr. Millbank's factory in Benjamin Disraeli's *Coningsby; or, The New Generation*.

Caprioletta Headlong   Squire Headlong's charming sister in Thomas Love Peacock's *Headlong Hall*.

Harry Headlong   Squire of Headlong Hall, a Welshman who, having allowed books to find their way into his house, wishes to surround himself with philosophers and men of taste in Thomas Love Peacock's *Headlong Hall*.

Cutty Headrigg   Plowman of Lady Margaret Bellenden's estate; he is put off her lands because his mother does not allow him to follow King James; he becomes a follower of Henry Morton, whom he protects; he is pardoned for his rebellion and marries Jenny Dennison in Sir Walter Scott's *Old Mortality*.

Mause Headrigg   Mother of Cutty and a fierce Cameronian Covenanter, whose zealotry keeps her and her son in trouble with Anglican and Catholic authorities in Sir Walter Scott's *Old Mortality*.

Bradley Headstone   Outwardly decent but inwardly repressed and fiery schoolmaster of working-class children and of Charley Hexam; he loves Lizzie Hexam with a passion that is literally deadly, as jealousy leads him to the attempted murder of Eugene Wrayburn in Charles Dickens's *Our Mutual Friend*.

Jem Hearn   Rustic lover of Matilda Jenkyns's maid, Martha, in Elizabeth Gaskell's *Cranford*.

Mrs. Heartfree   Loving wife of Thomas Heartfree; she naively leaves England with Jonathan Wild and the jewels, repulses Wild's and others' lustful overtures amidst adventures, and returns home to save Heartfree in Henry Fielding's *The Life of Mr. Jonathan Wild the Great*.

Nancy Heartfree   Thomas Heartfree's daughter, who comforts him while he is imprisoned; she later marries Jack Friendly in Henry Fielding's *The Life of Mr. Jonathan Wild the Great*.

Thomas Heartfree   Jonathan Wild's good-hearted former school friend, whom Wild tries to swindle out of costly jewels and his wife in Henry Fielding's *The Life of Mr. Jonathan Wild the Great*.

Mr. Heartless   Unethical neighbor whose part in a conspiracy to ruin Harry Ruth is disguised as financial help in Henry Brooke's *The Fool of Quality*.

King of Hearts   Ineffectual but not ill-tempered monarch, who pardons all those sentenced to death by the queen; only the Cheshire-cat's impudence attracts his sentence of execution—impossible to be carried out; he presides as judge at the trial of the Knave of Hearts in Lewis Carroll's *Alice's Adventures in Wonderland*.

Knave of Hearts   A member of the royal procession to the queen's croquet-ground; his trial on a charge of stealing tarts is the concluding episode of Lewis Carroll's *Alice's Adventures in Wonderland*.

Queen of Hearts   Tyrant whose wrath occasionally yields to flattery; her reiterated "Off with their heads" causes anxiety in her subjects but results in no executions in Lewis Carroll's *Alice's Adventures in Wonderland*.

Harriet Hearty   Good-hearted young woman, who inherits the winnings of a lottery ticket Wilson had once owned and bails him out of prison; they marry and retire to a quiet country life; she is Joseph Andrews's mother in Henry Fielding's *The History of the Adventures of Mr. Joseph Andrews and of his Friend Mr. Abraham Adams*.

Dr. Heath   "Good Christian" and physician friend of the narrator (H.F.); he advises him on the precautions that must be taken against the plague in Daniel Defoe's *A Journal of the Plague Year.*

Heathcliff Dynamic but savage hero of the story; thwarted in his love for Catherine Earnshaw, he takes a terrible revenge on those who have thwarted him and on their innocent descendants; he destroys his boyhood tormentor Hindley Earnshaw, marries and destroys Isabella Linton, and gets control of the Earnshaw and Linton properties; his wrath toward Hareton Earnshaw, whom he has degraded, abates before his death, partly because of Hareton's resemblance to Catherine in Emily Brontë's *Wuthering Heights.*

Linton Heathcliff Feeble, sickly, and spiteful son of Isabella Linton and Heathcliff; he is driven by his father into marriage with Catherine Linton shortly before his death in Emily Brontë's *Wuthering Heights.*

Colonel Heathcock Bumbling English aristocrat, who marries the conniving Lady Isabella in Maria Edgeworth's *The Absentee.*

Edgar Walton Heatherley Clergyman who guides Helen Norman in her charitable activities and whose proposal is accepted by Lucy Venning in George Gissing's *Workers in the Dawn.*

Alfred Heathfield Doctor Jeddler's ward, an idealistic man, who loves Marion Jeddler for many years but learns to love her sister Grace and marries her after Marion's apparent elopement; he becomes a village doctor in Charles Dickens's *The Battle of Life.*

Savile Heaton Former tutor of Kenneth Carmichael Ross and second husband of Margaret Carmichael Ross in Caroline Norton's *Old Sir Douglas.*

Captain Charles Heavyside Barnes Newcome's fellow clubmember in William Makepeace Thackeray's *The Newcomes.*

Cornet Hebbers Duplicitous soldier, who steals Fanny Matthews's heart through her vanity, ruins her, and then prompts her violent revenge when he marries Widow Carey in Henry Fielding's *Amelia.*

Mr. Heckletext A visiting minister; the discovery that he is the father of an illegitimate child in Dalmailing is an embarrassment to Micah Balwhidder in John Galt's *Annals of the Parish.*

Hector Faithful, virtuous, and brave servant of Reginald de St. Leon in William Godwin's *St. Leon.*

Harry Hedgerow Eldest of the seven suitors who marry the seven "vestal virgin" sisters in Thomas Love Peacock's *Gryll Grange.*

Mrs. Heep Mother of Uriah Heep; she is as devious and conniving as he in Charles Dickens's *The Personal History of David Copperfield.*

Uriah Heep Red-haired, thin, snake-like clerk to Mr. Wickfield; he claims to be "umble" but is a dishonest, scheming blackmailer; he gradually puts Mr. Wickfield under his power, runs Wickfield's law practice, ruins clients he dislikes, and aspires to the hand of Agnes Wickfield in Charles Dickens's *The Personal History of David Copperfield.*

Kaiser Heinrich Popular monarch whose plan to visit Cologne is thwarted by the smell the Devil has left behind, until Farina gives him a bottle of fragrance (eau de cologne) which overcomes the stench; in return for this service the Kaiser awards Farina the hand of Margarita Groschen in George Meredith's *Farina.*

Alan Helbeck Squire of Bannisdale of ancient Catholic stock; he is unable to compromise his religious beliefs despite his deep love for Laura Fountain in Mrs. Humphry Ward's *Helbeck of Bannisdale.*

Louise Helbrun Opera singer and friend of Evelyn Innes in George Moore's *Evelyn Innes.* She is Evelyn's only former friend to visit her in the convent in *Sister Teresa.*

Dick Heldar An orphan brought up harshly; he loves Maisie, the companion of his childhood, becomes a famous war artist for a newspaper syndicate, but loses his sight because of a war injury; after losing Maisie, and having his masterpiece painting destroyed, he makes his way out to war in the southern Soudan where he is mercifully killed in Rudyard Kipling's *The Light That Failed.*

Heliodora Wealthy and disreputable woman in love with Basil; she seeks to corrupt Bessas, the Greek commander of Rome; when he turns against her, she is arrested and her house is pillaged in George Gissing's *Veranilda.*

Dr. Cuthbert Helmsdale Middle-aged bishop and suitor of the young widow, Lady Constantine, who agrees to marry him out of desperation when she learns she is pregnant with the child of Swithin St. Cleeve, whose secret marriage to her had by happenstance proved invalid; the bishop is an unsympathetic husband but dies after a short time in Thomas Hardy's *Two on a Tower.*

Help Christian's helper out of the Slough of Despond in John Bunyan's *The Pilgrim's Progress From this World to That Which Is to Come.*

Dr. (Professor) Abraham Van Helsing Dutch teacher of Dr. John Seward; a medical doctor and an expert in vampire lore, he is called in to treat Lucy Westenra; he leads the young people in their fight against Dracula in Bram Stoker's *Dracula*.

Agnes Grey Helstone Shirley Keeldar's companion, known as Mrs. Pryor; she hides her real name for fear of reprisals from her drunken husband, James, but comes to the aid of her daughter and through her love gives Caroline Helstone the necessary will to live in Charlotte Brontë's *Shirley*.

Caroline Helstone A shy girl of eighteen, who is brought up by her uncle, and who falls in love with Robert Moore but almost pines away when he does not commit himself to her; she recovers with the love of her lost mother, known as Mrs. Pryor, and marries Moore in Charlotte Brontë's *Shirley*.

James Helstone Caroline's neglectful, drunken father, who dies when she is eight after mistreating his wife in Charlotte Brontë's *Shirley*.

Matthewson Helstone Rector of Briarfield; he is Caroline Helstone's taciturn uncle, who brings her up but has little empathy with the plight of women, many of whom are confined to lives of drudgery in Charlotte Brontë's *Shirley*.

Walsingham Hely Sentimental, romantically inclined attaché at the British embassy in Paris; his courtship of Charlotte Baynes is favored by her parents in William Makepeace Thackeray's *The Adventures of Philip on His Way through the World*.

Jean Hemmelinck Bohemian painter who saves Aldrovandus Magnus from a career in trade when he discovers the youth's talent; he accepts him as a student, guides his disciple at court, and dies from overeating in William Beckford's *Biographical Memoirs of Extraordinary Painters*.

Polly Hemp Unscrupulous street girl who befriends Carrie Mitchell in George Gissing's *Workers in the Dawn*.

Richard Hemstead Unemployed shopkeeper's assistant, who meets Norris Carthew in Australia, ships on the *Currency Lass*, and is killed by Goddedaal in Robert Louis Stevenson's *The Wrecker*.

Bernardo Henault Katterienna's brother, who falls in love with Isabella through the convent grate and convinces her to elope; he is believed killed in battle, and when he returns to the remarried Isabella after many years of enslavement, she kills him out of a sense of panic over her honor in Aphra Behn's *The History of the Nun*.

Michael Henchard The mayor, a proud, stubborn grain merchant, who marries a supposed widow with a daughter; a quarrel between him and his manager leads to business rivalry and his decline of fortune; his wife dies; the daughter marries his business rival; and he is publicly humiliated when it is revealed that he had drunkenly sold his wife and baby long ago to a sailor; the final blow occurs when he learns that the woman who he presumed was his daughter is the daughter of the sailor; Henchard dies a lonely, broken-hearted man in Thomas Hardy's *The Mayor of Casterbridge*.

Susan Henchard-Newson Supposed widow with a daughter; she marries Michael Henchard and dies; it is discovered that she was his wife eighteen years earlier and was drunkenly sold, with her baby, by him to a sailor, Richard Newson; believing Newson dead, she located and was reunited with Henchard in Thomas Hardy's *The Mayor of Casterbridge*.

Captain Henchman Kinsman and toady of Lord Farintosh in William Makepeace Thackeray's *The Newcomes*.

Mr. Henderland Benevolent, snuff-favoring preacher and traveling catechist who guides and gives David Balfour shelter and spiritual advice in Robert Louis Stevenson's *Kidnapped*. David rewards him with a generous pouch of snuff in *Catriona*.

Elias Henderson Calvinist chaplain at Lochleven Castle; he converts Roland Graeme to Protestantism and tries to convert Queen Mary of Scotland in Sir Walter Scott's *The Abbot*.

Rachel Henderson Middle-class clergyman's daughter, who educates herself as an agriculturalist and rents Great End Farm in Ipscombe; her alcoholic former husband murders her just as she is to marry George Ellesborough in Mrs. Humphry Ward's *Harvest*.

Mr. Henley Grandfather and guardian of Statia Henley, John Buncle's second wife; he tells the story of his son Charles and proposes that Buncle marry Statia in Thomas Amory's *The Life of John Buncle, Esq.*

Abimelech (Honest Aby) Henley Greedy, dishonest steward and gardener for Sir Arthur St. Ives; he pilfers Sir Arthur's funds and attempts to gain the estate by marrying his son, Frank, to Sir Arthur's daughter in Thomas Holcroft's *Anna St. Ives*.

Charles Henley (1) Father of Statia, John Buncle's second wife; he goes abroad, marries into a noble family, and after some years of study in retreat dies, having requested that his skeleton be left as a *memento mori* in Thomas Amory's *The Life of John Buncle, Esq.*

Charles Henley (2) Honest Christian merchant who drowns in a storm during John Buncle's trip from Dublin to England in May 1725 in Thomas Amory's *The Life of John Buncle, Esq.*

Frank Henley Noble, brave son of Sir Arthur St. Ives's dishonest steward; he repeatedly protects Anna St. Ives and her family from harm; he convinces his rival, Coke Clifton, to forsake vice; at the end of the novel, he is about to marry Anna in Thomas Holcroft's *Anna St. Ives*.

Robert Henley Dorothea Vanborough's rigid, priggish cousin and for a time her betrothed; he betrays her with Rhoda Parnell in Anne Thackeray Ritchie's *Old Kensington*.

Statia Henley John Buncle's second wife and daughter of Charles Henley of the Groves of Basil; she desires a single, celibate life, but Buncle persuades her otherwise, using the Abrahamic covenant; she dies of smallpox two years after her marriage in Thomas Amory's *The Life of John Buncle, Esq.*

Frances Evans Henri A quiet, serious, industrious student in William Crimsworth's class at Mlle. Reuter's school, who makes enough money to attend classes by mending lace; she later teaches French, then marries her professor, has a son, and moves to England, where she starts her own school in Charlotte Brontë's *The Professor*.

Julienne (Tante) Henri Frances Henri's aunt, who brings her up in Switzerland and moves to Belgium, where she dies; Frances is reunited with William Crimsworth at her gravesite in Charlotte Brontë's *The Professor*.

Henrietta Fair but false woman, who marries an elderly, wealthy knight but carries on an affair with Lord Lycidas, with whom she tries unsuccessfully to flee; reunited with Lycidas after her husband dies, she marries him after a year's penance; they go to Germany, where Henrietta pretends to be Lucy and has an affair with Frederick; she remains silent about Lucy's innocence and her own guilt until on her deathbed in Penelope Aubin's *The Life and Adventures of the Lady Lucy*.

Queen Henrietta Marie French-born, Catholic wife of Charles I of England; she enlists John Inglesant for the papists' cause in J. Henry Shorthouse's *John Inglesant, A Romance*.

Prince Henrik A handsome young man, who joins the Fransciscan order and changes his name to Francisco after his brother deprives him of his lover, marries her, and hires men to assassinate him; when Francisco refuses Miranda's attentions, she accuses him of rape; he is sentenced to death, languishes in prison, and is finally released in Aphra Behn's *The Fair Jilt*.

Henriquez Il Conte Berenza's brother, who disdains his brother's wife, Victoria (di Loredani), but cannot escape her passionate pursuit in Charlotte Dacre's *Zofloya; or, The Moor*.

Henry Brother of Kate and handsome suitor of Maria Lobbs in "A Tale of True Love," told by Sam Weller and written down by Samuel Pickwick in Charles Dickens's *The Posthumous Papers of the Pickwick Club*.

Henry Sensitive and cultivated gentleman of vestigial aristocracy; Mary meets and falls in love with him in Lisbon; after a short separation, his dramatic death in Mary's arms casts her into despair and ultimate resignation in Mary Wollstonecraft's *Mary, A Fiction*.

Henry, Prince of Wales Accomplished heir to the throne of King James; he falls in love with (the younger) Mary but dies, perhaps poisoned, before he can marry her in Sophia Lee's *The Recess*.

Emperor Henry Italian nobleman who serves as emperor for two years and tries unsuccessfully to unite the warring Guelph and Ghibelline parties; he degenerates into cruelty in Mary Shelley's *Valperga*.

King Henry II King of England, who lays siege to Eveline Berenger's castle, Garde Doloureuse, imprisons Eveline and Damian de Lacy, and releases them upon the return of Hugo de Lacy in Sir Walter Scott's *The Betrothed*.

King Henry III British monarch who sponsors the young knight Gaston de Blondeville in his marriage suit of Lady Barbara; he believes Blondeville is innocent of charges of theft and murder brought against him by Hugh Woodreeve and imprisons Woodreeve, only to be visited by the ghost of the murdered Reginald de Folville in Ann Radcliffe's *Gaston de Blondeville*.

King Henry VIII Splendid young king of England; his meeting with King Francis of France stimulates the fifteen-year-old Reginald de St. Leon's "passion for splendour and distinction" in William Godwin's *St. Leon*. He is the monarch who grants Richard Inglesant, great-grandfather of John Inglesant, the priory at Westacre for his part in the suppression of monasteries in England in J. Henry Shorthouse's *John Inglesant, A Romance*.

Maister Henry Henry III's court poet in Ann Radcliffe's *Gaston de Blondeville*.

Mr. Henry The strict new land agent, who prosecutes all who have cheated Mr. Buxton, including Edward Browne, in Elizabeth Gaskell's *The Moorland Cottage*.

Flora, Lady Henry   Old, blind hostess to society; her salons are crowded with the powerful people of the day; her companion, Julie Le Breton, outshines her as a hostess and provokes Lady Henry to revenge in Mrs. Humphry Ward's *Lady Rose's Daughter*.

Henslowe   Cruel agent of Squire Wendover; he is reformed by Robert Elsmere's social action in Mrs. Humphry Ward's *Robert Elsmere*.

Bella Hepburn   Baby daughter of Philip Hepburn's marriage to Sylvia Robson; he saves her from drowning when he returns unrecognized at the climax of Elizabeth Gaskell's *Sylvia's Lovers*.

Sir John Hepburn   Colonel of the Scottish regiment in the army of King Charles I; he becomes the Cavalier's friend and brings him to speak with the king regarding Count Tilly; he tries to get the Cavalier to join the Swedish army in Daniel Defoe's *Memoirs of a Cavalier*.

Philip Hepburn   Sylvia Robson's cousin, whose intense love for her leads to tragedy; his failure to pass on to her the message from her betrothed, Charley Kinraid, makes his own marriage to her possible; the subsequent discovery of his deception leads to his self-sacrifice in Elizabeth Gaskell's *Sylvia's Lovers*.

Her Grace   A woman of quality with financial interests in many arenas; she dispenses patronage and withholds information in order to improve her own financial position in Charles Johnstone's *Chrysal: or, The Adventures of a Guinea*.

Her Grace's Maid   Servant who uses her position to obtain favors and to take revenge in Charles Johnstone's *Chrysal: or, The Adventures of a Guinea*.

Heraclian   Sleek, ambitious Italian Count of Africa; he tries to overthrow Honorius, Emperor of Rome, but is routed at Ostia and flees to Carthage in Charles Kingsley's *Hypatia*.

Herald   A confidence man who creates coats of arms for the first generation of the newly rich and creates ancient artifacts for antiquarians in Charles Johnstone's *Chrysal: or, The Adventures of a Guinea*.

Mr. Herbert   Mr. Darnley's relation and family adviser; he helps protect Sophia Darnley from her rapacious mother and sister, lodges her with the respectable Lawsons, and intercedes with Sir Charles Stanley to bring about the happy ending in Charlotte Lennox's *Sophia*.

Mrs. Herbert   Woman, also called Mrs. Chesterton, who digs out an old manuscript containing a ghost story interpolated into William Beckford's *Azemia*.

Lady Annabel Herbert   Marmion Herbert's beautiful, well-born wife, whose bitterness at her husband's desertion and abhorrence of his radical views lead her to conceal his identity from their daughter, Venetia, whose failing health is restored by the reconciliation of her parents in Benjamin Disraeli's *Venetia*.

Henry Herbert   Sentimental merchant whom Savillon befriends in Martinique and who eventually receives Savillon's letters when he returns to Paris in Henry Mackenzie's *Julia de Roubigné*.

Marmion Herbert   (characterization of Percy Bysshe Shelley) Venetia's father and Lady Annabel's estranged husband; he recants his radical and heretical views and is reunited with his wife and daughter for a few months before he drowns in Benjamin Disraeli's *Venetia*.

Venetia Herbert   Sensitive daughter of the heretical and radical Marmion Herbert; the circumstances of his estrangement have been concealed from her by her mother; Venetia is loved by and marries Plantagenet, Lord Cadurcis, and after his death by drowning marries his cousin, George Cadurcis, in Benjamin Disraeli's *Venetia*.

Hercules   Hero ruined by owning fine clothes in a parable told by Henry Clinton; young Harry Clinton purposely destroys his expensive clothes to avoid this boy's fate in Henry Brooke's *The Fool of Quality*.

Miss Herder   Sewing assistant to Kate Ede in the dress shop of Kate's husband, Ralph Ede; a dresser at the theater, she is attracted to the stage carpenter; she talks Kate into attending the theater against Kate's principles; after Kate's elopement with Dick Lennox, she marries Kate's ex-husband in George Moore's *A Mummer's Wife*.

Lord Hereford   A guard of the imprisoned Mary, Queen of Scots in Sophia Lee's *The Recess*.

Hereward the Saxon   Handsome, courageous, and incorruptible member of the Varangian Guard; he is trusted by Emperor Alexius Comnenus and loved by his comrades; he is also a good friend of Robert of Paris, whom he follows to Palestine and whose influence regains him a portion of his English property in Sir Walter Scott's *Count Robert of Paris*.

George (Jingling Geordie) Heriot   Goldsmith for King James I and godfather of Margaret Ramsay; he helps Nigel Olifaunt secure the king's warrant for funds to redeem the mortgage on Nigel's Scottish estate in Sir Walter Scott's *The Fortunes of Nigel*.

Judith Heriot   George Heriot's sister, who keeps his

house for him and protects Lady Hermione from the public in Sir Walter Scott's *The Fortunes of Nigel.*

Heriulf Massive ancient warrior, who had fought the Huns and the Franks but defers to Otter in war-duke elections; he is killed in an attack on the Romans in William Morris's *A Tale of the House of the Wolfings.*

Prince Hermann Man who marries Princess Ottilia, with her father's consent, thus enabling her to escape Richmond Roy's attempt to have her marry Harry Richmond in George Meredith's *The Adventures of Harry Richmond.*

Signora Herminia Venetian lady whose miniature Emily St. Aubert sketches in Ann Radcliffe's *The Mysteries of Udolpho.*

Hermione Cesario's mistress, who desires fame and power and conspires with Fergusano to drive the love-sick Cesario into battle against the king of France in Aphra Behn's *Love Letters Between A Nobleman and His Sister.*

Lady Hermione Noble lady living in retreat at George Heriot's house, having been seduced by Lord Dalgarno in Spain; she provides money to Margaret Ramsay to help Nigel Olifaunt and is legally married to Dalgarno at the king's insistence in Sir Walter Scott's *The Fortunes of Nigel.*

Adam Weir, Lord Hermiston (Lord Justice-Clerk, Judge Hermiston, "Hanging Hermiston") The upright, dignified, and ruthlessly righteous and authoritarian Lord Advocate of Scotland; after receiving public insult from his humane and tender-hearted son, Archibald Weir, he prevents him from coming to the Bar and sentences him to a life as estate lord at Hermiston in Robert Louis Stevenson's *Weir of Hermiston: An Unfinished Romance.*

Hermit Sick man who appears at the farmer's house, where he tells his story to Lady Lucy and her mother: he fell in love with his wife's sister, Emilia, poisoned her suitor, Leander, seduced her, and then poisoned her when she became pregnant; remorse finally overtook him, and he has lived as a hermit for forty years in Penelope Aubin's *The Life and Adventures of the Lady Lucy.*

Charles Hermsprong (Campinet) American who challenges Lord Grondale's aristocratic attitude, does good deeds for common people, and woos Caroline Campinet; he is the true heir to the Campinet fortune and the Grondale barony in Robert Bage's *Hermsprong.*

John Herncastle Lady Verinder's brother, a ruthless professional soldier in the siege of Seringapatam who violated an Indian shrine by stealing a huge yellow diamond; he bequeathes the stone to his niece, Rachel Verinder, with strange consequences in Wilkie Collins's *The Moonstone. A Romance.*

Mrs. Herner Marchioness of Trente's poor cousin; she suffers constant humiliations as a result of her dependent status in Sarah Fielding's *The History of Ophelia.*

Walter Heroit Head boy at Rippenger's school, looked up to by the younger Harry Richmond; he becomes a seducer of women, including Kiomi, but he remains loyal to Harry and assists his marriage to Janet Ilchester by getting Lord Edbury aboard Captain Welsh's ship and out of the way in George Meredith's *The Adventures of Harry Richmond.*

Sir George Heron Knight of the Chip-chase and a border soldier in Sir Walter Scott's *The Monastery.*

Robert Herrick (Mr. Hay) Promising but failed Oxford graduate, who ends up a starving beachcomber in the South Sea islands; he reluctantly joins the other outcasts, Captain John Davies and Mr. Huish, on a schooner but breaks with them when they pirate it and attempt the robbery and murder of the gentleman pearl merchant William John Attwater in Robert Louis Stevenson's *The Ebb-Tide: A Trio and a Quartette.*

Lord Herries Queen Mary of Scotland's loyal but erring follower, who mistakenly advises her to flee to England in Sir Walter Scott's *The Abbot.*

Mr. Hervey Londoner, the first man to pay Arabella the attention she expects; led on by her encouraging dismissals to try for her favor, he is finally beaten by her servants for, as she believes, planning to abduct her in Charlotte Lennox's *The Female Quixote.*

Clarence Hervey Attractive, generous, brilliant bachelor and good friend of Lady Delacour; although attracted to Belinda Portman, he idealistically tries to fashion a "perfect" wife for himself out of a young girl he meets in the woods; he is saved from making an unhappy marriage with her and instead marries Belinda in Maria Edgeworth's *Belinda.*

Dolly Hervey Clarissa Harlowe's kindly cousin, who tries to warn Clarissa secretly of the family's various plans, and who inherits Clarissa's music books, harpsichord, and chamber organ in Samuel Richardson's *Clarissa: or, The History of a Young Lady.*

Dorothy Hervey Half sister of Clarissa Harlowe's mother; she is sympathetic to her niece Clarissa but is under obligation to her nephew James, Clarissa's brother, because he paid off a mortgage for her in Samuel Richardson's *Clarissa: or, The History of a Young Lady.*

Bob Hewett   Scapegrace son of an impoverished family; he mistreats his wife, is arrested for forging coins, and dies from a street injury soon afterward in George Gissing's *The Nether World*.

Clara Hewett   Independent-minded and ambitious girl of slum origins; she escapes by becoming an actress but is disfigured when a rival throws acid in her face; she marries but is restless and unhappy in later years in George Gissing's *The Nether World*.

John Hewett   Unemployed carpenter and father of a family who has failed in business and is in desperate poverty until helped by a friend; he searches for his daughter Clara, who has run away from home to become an actress, and finds her after she has been disfigured by a rival who has thrown vitriol in her face; his efforts to support his family fail, and he is left in poverty in George Gissing's *The Nether World*.

Maggie Hewett   Woman who was imprisoned for theft but has become the wife of a kindly but impoverished widower whose children she cares for in George Gissing's *The Nether World*.

Godfrey Bertram Hewit   Godfrey Bertram's illegitimate son; Guilbert Glossin tries to pass him off as Henry Bertram in Sir Walter Scott's *Guy Mannering*.

Gabriel Hewson   Parody scholar and owner of Sombre Hedges in S. J. Pratt's *Tutor of Truth*.

Henrietta Hewson   Wife of the recently enriched Henry Hewson; she is determined at any cost to become genteel in S. J. Pratt's *Tutor of Truth*.

Henry Hewson   Parody squire of Helter Skelter Hall in S. J. Pratt's *Tutor of Truth*.

Thomas Hewson   Robert Fitz-Owen's servant, who is made Robert's squire in preferment over Edmund Lovel, and who aids in various plots to discredit Edmund in Clara Reeve's *The Old English Baron*.

Charley Hexam   Lizzie Hexam's younger brother, who goes to school through her influence; he leaves home and eventually rejects Lizzie after she turns down Bradley Headstone's marriage proposal because he wishes to rise in the world and believes she is holding him back in Charles Dickens's *Our Mutual Friend*.

Jesse (Gaffer) Hexam   Father of Lizzie and Charley Hexam; he is a middle-aged, strong man, who earns his living by fishing dead bodies out of the Thames; he is suspected of murdering John Harmon; he drowns after being entangled in his rope in Charles Dickens's *Our Mutual Friend*.

Lizzie Hexam   Gaffer Hexam's pretty daughter, who is the uniting force behind the Hexam family, sending her brother Charley to school; she is like a magnet, drawing toward her both Bradley Headstone and Eugene Wrayburn, whom she loves; she rescues Eugene from drowning after the assault by Bradley, then marries him in Charles Dickens's *Our Mutual Friend*.

James Hexton   An ignorant, brutal businessman, who married Miss Arbour when she was nineteen and made her life so miserable she left him in Mark Rutherford's *The Autobiography of Mark Rutherford*.

George Heyling   Prisoner for debt at the Marshalsea, who later becomes rich and ruins his hard-hearted father-in-law in "The Old Man's Tale about the Queer Client," told by Jack Bamber in Charles Dickens's *The Posthumous Papers of the Pickwick Club*.

Mary Heyling   Wife of George Heyling; she dies in the Marshalsea in "The Old Man's Tale about the Queer Client," told by Jack Bamber in Charles Dickens's *The Posthumous Papers of the Pickwick Club*.

Reicht Heynes   Originally housekeeper to Margaret Van Eyck; she becomes housekeeper of the Gouda parsonage; at Margaret Brandt's suggestion she weds Luke Peterson and manages Margaret Brandt's Rotterdam shop in Charles Reade's *The Cloister and the Hearth*.

H.F.   Well-off saddler and bachelor, who decides to stay in London during the plague because he believes the "Divine Power" has willed that he should; as narrator, he provides a detailed account of the events, large and small, that take place before and after the plague in Daniel Defoe's *A Journal of the Plague Year*.

Captain Hibbert   Suitor of Olive Barton; he is frustrated by her mother's fixation on a title; he tries to elope with Olive but is thwarted by Mrs. Lawler; he goes off to India in George Moore's *A Drama in Muslin*.

Mr. Hickery   Wealthy repatriate to Gudetown from America; he becomes a thorn in the provost's side; he brings contentious "American argumentatives" to bear on local taxation in John Galt's *The Provost*.

Hickes   Husband of Denner and butler of Arabella Transome in George Eliot's *Felix Holt, the Radical*.

Charles Hickman   Gentleman and suitor of Anna Howe; he is sympathetic to and respectful of Clarissa Harlowe; he agrees to collect Clarissa's letters to Anna after Mrs. Howe forbids their correspondence in Samuel Richardson's *Clarissa: or, The History of a Young Lady*.

Hicks   Drunken shoemaker and member of Captain

Harris's gang who is the second scalped after the burial of the Master (James Durie) in Robert Louis Stevenson's *The Master of Ballantrae: A Winter's Tale.*

Hannah Hicks   Martha Honeyman's devoted servant in William Makepeace Thackeray's *The Newcomes.*

Lord Hide   Uncle of Madam de Beaumont and father of Mr. Hide; having fallen out of grace with the king, he lives under a false name until he meets Count de Beaumont in Ireland and discovers that his niece is alive in Penelope Aubin's *The Life of Madam de Beaumont.*

Mr. Hide   Accomplished young gentleman, who meets Belinda Lleulling when she is brought to his house after highwaymen have killed Glandore; he falls in love with her but acts honorably when he hears she is married; he grieves until he meets her stepsister, Isabella, whom he marries, in Penelope Aubin's *The Life of Madam de Beaumont.*

(Hieracus) Hierax   Christian who is taken and tortured in Alexandria, sparking off a riot in Charles Kingsley's *Hypatia.*

Elizabeth (Betty) Higden   Spirited old woman, who lives with her grandson and the orphan Sloppy and minds two little children; she leaves her home after her grandson dies so that Sloppy can live with the Boffins, and would literally rather die than go to the workhouse in Charles Dickens's *Our Mutual Friend.*

Samuel Higg   Brother of the Vicomtesse de Florac and a wealthy neighbor of Sir Barnes Newcome, who treats him with much consideration until he defeats Sir Barnes in a Parliamentary election in William Makepeace Thackeray's *The Newcomes.*

Dr. Higgins   Doctor from Slowton who is called in by Dr. Pratt to help save Sir Jeckyl Marlowe but cannot do so in J. Sheridan Le Fanu's *Guy Deverell.*

Mrs. Higgins   Embarrassingly vulgar and quarrelsome mother of Louise Derrick in George Gissing's *The Paying Guest.*

The Misses Higgins   Three sisters whose mother keeps a tavern; "academical" misses from Cambridge, they are admirers of Williams in Francis Coventry's *The History of Pompey the Little.*

Bessy Higgins   Nicholas Higgins's daughter, who suffers and dies from unhealthy factory life; Margaret Hale's concern for her leads Margaret into contact with and understanding of the lives of mill workers in Elizabeth Gaskell's *North and South.*

George Higgins   A villager in Horton whom the rector, Mr. Hatfield, would like to frighten out of his evening walks on the Sabbath in Anne Brontë's *Agnes Grey.*

Mary Higgins   Younger sister of Bessy; she is rescued from factory work by becoming a maid to Margaret Hale in Elizabeth Gaskell's *North and South.*

Nicholas Higgins   Factory worker and union leader; his friendship with Margaret Hale assists his significance in the social and industrial relationships of Elizabeth Gaskell's *North and South.*

Mr. Higgs   Ex-butler of the Carthew estate; he now runs Carthew Arms, where Loudon Dodd stays in Robert Louis Stevenson's *The Wrecker.*

Mrs. Higgs   Ex-lady's maid who runs the Carthew Arms with her husband in Robert Louis Stevenson's *The Wrecker.*

Agnes Higgs   Frowsy-headed daughter of a former butler and a former lady's maid; she accuses Loudon Dodd of stealing her stamp in Robert Louis Stevenson's *The Wrecker.*

Jack Higgs   The narrator, a middle-class Englishman who, seeking his fortune as a sheep rancher in a carefully vague location, accidentally discovers the unknown country Erewhon; his adventures there end with his elopement and escape with Arowhena Nosnibor in a hot-air balloon; he is unnamed in Samuel Butler's *Erewhon.* Older, he returns to Erewhon after the death of Arowhena and discovers an illegitimate son, George Strong, whom he loves; he discovers he is the model for Sunchild; he dies on his return to England in Samuel Butler's *Erewhon Revisited Twenty Years Later.*

John Higgs   Son of Jack Higgs and Arowhena Nosnibor; he is fluent in Erewhonian and in English; his notes for this book are responsible for its publication ten years after his father's death; he makes his own visit to Erewhon in Samuel Butler's *Erewhon Revisited Twenty Years Later.*

Three Highlanders   Three rugged, unkempt, and superstitious Gaelic-speaking men, who are David Balfour's captors and attendants in his kidnapping to the Scottish highlands in Robert Louis Stevenson's *Catriona.*

Highway Man   A thief captured by his intended victim, the Turnham-Green Gentleman; he escapes because the Justice convinces everyone that he is a gentleman who has lost his wits in Charles Johnstone's *Chrysal: or, The Adventures of a Guinea.*

Hilarius Refectioner at the Monastery of St. Mary's in Sir Walter Scott's *The Monastery*.

Mr. Hilary Uncle of Marionetta O'Carroll and the only character not afflicted with romantic black bile and melancholy in Thomas Love Peacock's *Nightmare Abbey*.

Mr. Hilary Attorney and relation to Mr. Evelyn; he introduces Hugh Trevor to Counsellor Ventilate in Thomas Holcroft's *The Adventures of Hugh Trevor*.

Duke Jacob Hildebrod Lord of misrule and protector of liberties in Alsatia; he advises Nigel Olifaunt to marry Martha Trapbois in Sir Walter Scott's *The Fortunes of Nigel*.

Frederick Hildy Orlando Faulkland's honest servant, whose letter from Ireland includes news that Mrs. Faulkland (formerly Miss Burchell) survived the shooting in Frances Sheridan's *Memoirs of Miss Sidney Bidulph*.

Fanny Hill The sole heiress of a tailor; an "academical" miss from Cambridge, she is an admirer of Williams in Francis Coventry's *The History of Pompey the Little*.

Frances (Fanny) Hill Bright, beautiful heroine-prostitute, who in her maturity narrates, in epistolary style, how she first came to London an innocent, orphaned country girl, was lured into prostitution, survived and eventually enjoyed a series of sexual encounters, matured, grew rich, and retired; she finally marries and has a family with her long-lost first love, Charles O——, in John Cleland's *Memoirs of a Woman of Pleasure*.

Mrs. Hill Wife of a dying carpenter; she receives help from Cecilia Beverley after Mr. Harrel refuses to pay his debt to her husband in Frances Burney's *Cecilia*.

English Hillario A vain young fop who, while making his tour of Europe, enters into an intrigue with the Courtesan of Bologna and takes Pompey to England as a sign of the Courtesan's lasting affection in Francis Coventry's *The History of Pompey the Little*.

Mr. Hillary Gentlemanly young poet, who criticizes supporters of the Pitt government in William Beckford's *Azemia*.

Tom Hillary Foppish, crooked clerk of Mr. Lawford; he becomes an unscrupulous recruiter for the East India Company and betrays Richard Middlemas in Sir Walter Scott's *The Surgeon's Daughter*.

Emily Hilliard Widowed sister-in-law of Maurice Hilliard; her second marriage turns out badly in George Gissing's *Eve's Ransom*.

Maurice Hilliard Young man infatuated with Eve Madeley; he uses a sum of money he has unexpectedly received to take her to Paris so that she can recover from an unhappy love affair, but he never succeeds in winning her love and is deceived as she marries his wealthy friend in George Gissing's *Eve's Ransom*.

Tom Hills Huntsman hired by John Jorrocks; his hounds are more apt to go for a hare than a fox in Robert Surtees's *Jorrocks's Jaunts and Jollities*.

Mr. Hilton An Academician who engages in the art discussions; he is one of the medievalists in George Moore's *A Modern Lover*.

Leonard Hilton Son of Ruth Hilton and Henry Bellingham; his self-esteem is shattered when he finds out he is illegitimate and people know about it; he learns to be proud of his mother and is taken on as apprentice to Mr. Davis, the Ecclestone physician, in Elizabeth Gaskell's *Ruth*.

Ruth Hilton The orphaned girl apprenticed to a dressmaker and seduced and then abandoned while pregnant by Henry Bellingham; sheltered by the Bensons and presented to Ecclestone as the widowed Mrs. Denbigh, she is again in difficulty when the deception is discovered and when Bellingham reappears in her life; her conduct as a nurse during a cholera epidemic changes public opinion; she dies from cholera caught while she is nursing Bellingham in Elizabeth Gaskell's *Ruth*.

Mrs. Hilyard Poor seamstress who turns out to be the wife of Colonel Mildmay, whom she tries melodramatically to murder in Margaret Oliphant's *Salem Chapel*.

Hind in border hamlet Poor widower who shelters Robert Colwan and whose house is protected by a power superior to that of the fiends seeking Colwan in James Hogg's *The Private Memoirs and Confessions of a Justified Sinner*.

Mr. Hintman Profligate, self-appointed guardian of Louisa Mancel; he suggests a compromising trip into the country but dies providentially before Louisa must give him her reply in Sarah Scott's *A Description of Millenium Hall*.

Adelaide Hinton Independent young country woman, long engaged to .her cousin, Edward Springrove; she elopes with Farmer Bollens in Thomas Hardy's *Desperate Remedies*.

Miss Hinxworth Talented member of a singing and dancing company who had been "carried off" by the renowned Irish dancing-master O'Regan; she meets John

Buncle at Oliver Wincup's country dance in Thomas Amory's *The Life of John Buncle, Esq.*

Mr. Hippesley Brother-in-law to Sir Francis Geraldine and Dean of Exeter Cathedral; he conducts the wedding ceremony between George Western and Cecilia Holt in Anthony Trollope's *Kept in the Dark.*

Hippolita Long-suffering wife of Manfred, Prince of Otranto; she is faithful to the end despite his villainy and cold rejection of her; she eventually accompanies him into religious seclusion after his ruin in Horace Walpole's *The Castle of Otranto.*

Hippolito di Saviolina Spanish gentleman who travels with his friend Aurelian to Florence; at a masked ball he is mistaken for Don Lorenzo and is approached by Leonora, with whom he falls instantly in love; learning that Aurelian has assumed his identity, he fears that the two beauties will think one man is courting both; he presents himself to Leonora as Aurelian and clandestinely marries her in that guise in William Congreve's *Incognita.*

Clara Hittaway Eldest of Lady Fawn's eight daughters; she opposes a match between her brother, Lord Fawn, and the dangerous Lizzie Eustace in Anthony Trollope's *The Eustace Diamonds.*

Orlando Hittaway Government official and brother-in-law of Lord Fawn; he spends his time agonizing over Lizzie Eustace's escapades and Fawn's entanglement with her in Anthony Trollope's *The Eustace Diamonds.*

Claudius Hobart Recluse of Wardrew, who withdraws from society after he loses his estate and wife-to-be, and whose manuscript on Christian Deism is posthumously printed by John Buncle in Thomas Amory's *The Life of John Buncle, Esq.*

Hobbes Royalist and supporter of Charles I and the Church of England; he strongly dissuades John Inglesant's tendencies toward Catholicism in J. Henry Shorthouse's *John Inglesant, A Romance.*

Dr. Hobbler Convivial Jacobite clergyman, who is to conduct the marriage ceremony of Isabella Vere and Sir Frederick Langley in Sir Walter Scott's *The Black Dwarf.*

Mr. Hobson Widower with two children and chaplain to Lord Rosherville, with whose daughter he elopes in William Makepeace Thackeray's *The History of Pendennis.*

Mr. Hobson London borough man who lets rooms to the Belfields; he is a witness to the suicide of Harrel in Frances Burney's *Cecilia.*

Mr. Hobson The third man from whom Agnes Grey's father borrows over his means in Anne Brontë's *Agnes Grey.*

Captain Clarence Hoby Captain Goby's friend, who admires Rosy Mackenzie in William Makepeace Thackeray's *The Newcomes.*

Mr. and Mrs. Hocking Mrs. Carter's cousins, who open their house in Liverpool for the Colemans after Zachariah Coleman's release from the workhouse infirmary in Mark Rutherford's *The Revolution In Tanner's Lane.*

Hodges Prison turnkey who follows Hawes's instructions until he is sickened by the death of gentle Joseph in Charles Reade's *It Is Never Too Late to Mend.*

Joe Hodges Henry Bertram's shrewd and kindly landlord, who chooses not to tell of Henry's lake crossings in Sir Walter Scott's *Guy Mannering.*

Miss Hodgins Local woman whose gossip nearly forces Hammel Clement to part from Mrs. Graves and his soon-to-be wife, Anabella Graves, in Henry Brooke's *The Fool of Quality.*

Mrs. Hogg Landlady for the exasperating curate Malone in Charlotte Brontë's *Shirley.*

Mrs. Hogg Lieutenant Puddock's landlady in J. Sheridan Le Fanu's *The House by the Churchyard.*

James Hogg Author of a letter to *Blackwood's Magazine* telling of the exhumation of a mysterious suicide's body in James Hogg's *The Private Memoirs and Confessions of a Justified Sinner.*

Susan Hoggarty Rich widowed aunt and patroness of Samuel Titmarsh; her gift to him of the Hoggarty diamond at first seems to bring good fortune but proves to bring disaster in William Makepeace Thackeray's *The History of Samuel Titmarsh and the Great Hoggarty Diamond.*

Giles Hoggett Brickmaker at Hoggle End who counsels doggedness to Mr. Crawley in the affair of the stolen cheque in Anthony Trollope's *The Last Chronicle of Barset.*

Mr. Hoggins The town's medical practitioner, reckoned too unrefined for society by the genteel ladies in Elizabeth Gaskell's *Cranford.*

Princess von Hohenweiss Enchanted princess in the independent story contained within the novel; she is loved and freed by Cosmo von Wehrstahl in George MacDonald's *Phantastes.*

Miss Hoighty A cheerful, vulgar, untalented girl,

whose musical career is supported and promoted by Major Fitz-David; she becomes Mrs. Fitz-David in Wilkie Collins's *The Law and the Lady*.

Thomas Holbrook   Man who in his youth was not considered a good enough match for Matilda Jenkyns; she meets him again when he is old in Elizabeth Gaskell's *Cranford*.

Mr. Delamayn, Lord Holchester   Able, honorable, cynical solicitor, who makes the discovery that the Vanborough marriage is invalid; he becomes a successful barrister and Member of Parliament; envy over his rise to the House of Lords on being named Baron Holchester motivates John Vanborough's suicide; he is father of Julian and Geoffrey Delamayn in Wilkie Collins's *Man and Wife*.

Julian Delamayn, Lord Holchester   Upright elder son, who inherits his father's property as well as the title Baron Holchester; persuaded by Sir Patrick Lundie of the danger to Anne Silvester's life, he offers his brother, Geoffrey Delamayn, a substantial income to allow Anne a legal separation; planning to free himself by murder and then to marry a larger fortune, Geoffrey refuses in Wilkie Collins's *Man and Wife*.

Mr. Holdenough   Canon and High Church member of the Brotherton Cathedral chapter whose lineage gives him as much power in the community as the dean, Henry Lovelace; he joins the dean in opposing the baleful presence of the Marquis of Brotherton in Anthony Trollope's *Is He Popenjoy?*.

Lady Alice Germain, Mrs. Holdenough   The Marquis of Brotherton's sister, married to an influential canon and regarded as worldly by her sisters in Anthony Trollope's *Is He Popenjoy?*.

Nehemiah Holdenough   Presbyterian minister who is removed from his pulpit by the Independent Joseph Tomkins; he feels guilty for the supposed death of Joseph Albany in Sir Walter Scott's *Woodstock*.

Charles Holdorsen   Swedish second mate of the *Flying Scud*; reported drowned, he was really shot in the face by Norris Carthew in Robert Louis Stevenson's *The Wrecker*.

Edward Holdsworth   Railway engineer, who speaks of his love for Phillis Holman to her cousin Paul Manning but not to herself; his love is transient, and he marries another woman soon after he leaves; he is the man of the new age, whose impact on Phillis and her family and whose later departure end the sense of idyllic life in Elizabeth Gaskell's *Cousin Phillis*.

Jane Holdsworth   Mary Grice's friend, dismissed from

her job as "disreputable" by the shopkeeper Joanna Grice; a letter from her to Mary provides Mat Grice with a lead in discovering the identity of Mary's seducer in Wilkie Collins's *Hide and Seek*.

Hold-the-world   One of three friends of By-ends; he uses religion for selfish and worldly ends in John Bunyan's *The Pilgrim's Progress From this World to That Which Is to Come*.

Erasmus Holiday   A country pedagogue, full of learned bombast, who helps prepare the revels at Kenilworth in Sir Walter Scott's *Kenilworth*.

Lord Hollingford   Scientist son of Lord and Lady Cumnor; he promotes Roger Hamley's career in Elizabeth Gaskell's *Wives and Daughters*.

Mr. Hollow   Unethical neighbor whose part in a conspiracy to ruin Harry Ruth is disguised as financial help in Henry Brooke's *The Fool of Quality*.

Holloway   Uncle of Mallison, who joins him in an attempt to swindle Audley Mandeville in William Godwin's *Mandeville*.

Ludwig Horace Holly   Extremely ugly, intelligent Cambridge professor, narrator of a tale describing the quest into the unexplored African interior with his adoptive son, Leo Vincey, to find She and the Pillar of Life; his learned commentaries and doubting eye-witness accounts lend verisimilitude to H. Rider Haggard's *She*.

Mrs. Holman   The wife of the Reverend Holman; she is the motherly domestic figure in the quiet routine of Hope Farm in Elizabeth Gaskell's *Cousin Phillis*.

Ebenezer Holman   A clergyman, farmer, and scholar and father of Phillis; he has created a pastoral idyll around his farm that is shattered when his daughter falls in love in Elizabeth Gaskell's *Cousin Phillis*.

Phillis Holman   The young girl, sheltered by pastoral life and her father's influence, who changes from girl to woman when she falls in love with Edward Holdsworth; she remains an innocent young woman, but her emotional peace is destroyed at the end of Elizabeth Gaskell's *Cousin Phillis*.

Betty Holmes   A villager in Horton whom the rector, Mr. Hatfield, would like to frighten out of her thirty-year habit of smoking a pipe in Anne Brontë's *Agnes Grey*.

Sherlock Holmes   Scientist of deduction, who shares rooms with John Watson; he solves the mystery of the violent deaths of Enoch Drebber and Joseph Stangerson in Arthur Conan Doyle's *A Study in Scarlet*. He defends to

Watson his use of cocaine as a refuge from intellectual boredom and solves the mystery of Mary Morstan's father's disappearance in *The Sign of Four*. For a time engaged in on-site investigation, incognito, while supposed in London, he solves the mystery of the renewal of the ancient Baskerville curse amid the dangerous moors of Devonshire in *The Hound of the Baskervilles*. He solves the case of the apparent murder of an American, John Douglas, at Birlstone Manor in *The Valley of Fear*.

Arthur Holmwood (later Lord Godalming) Lucy Westenra's betrothed and one of the men who defeat Dracula in Bram Stoker's *Dracula*.

Mr. Holt A tailor who beats his wife and lives in Mrs. Jupp's building; he is to be Ernest's first real attempt at "teaching Christ" but proves too intimidating in Samuel Butler's *The Way of All Flesh*.

Mr. Holt An Academician who dislikes Lewis Seymour's paintings; he yields to Seymour's bribe in which Holt promotes Seymour for the Academy vacancy in exchange for Lady Helen (Seely) Seymour's social recognition of Mrs. Holt in George Moore's *A Modern Lover*.

Mrs. Holt Former model and now wife of Mr. Holt; she is not accepted by society until Lewis Seymour schemes to exchange his wife's patronage of her for an Academy vote for himself; she is charming in her own right in George Moore's *A Modern Lover*.

Mrs. Holt The widowed mother of Felix Holt; she is forced into greater poverty when her son high-mindedly discontinues the patent-medicine business created by her husband; she is later supported by her son in George Eliot's *Felix Holt, the Radical*.

Cecilia Holt Overscrupulous, conscientious girl, who, realizing that her betrothed, Sir Francis Geraldine, is marrying to spite his cousin, incurs his wrath by breaking the engagement; she falls in love with George Western; when he tells her he was once jilted, she cannot bear to confess a similar guilt; after the marriage, when the truth comes out, Western is callous and resentful, but mediation by Lady Grant brings about the couple's reconciliation in Anthony Trollope's *Kept in the Dark*.

Felix Holt A young, well-educated intellectual of Radical politics; he becomes a poor watchmaker in order to fight for the common people; he is a working-class hero prosecuted for his involvement in the Election Day riot, which results in the death of a constable; he is saved from prison by the impassioned plea of Esther Lyon, whom he eventually weds in George Eliot's *Felix Holt, the Radical*.

Felix Holt (the younger) Eldest child of Felix and Esther (Lyon) Holt in George Eliot's *Felix Holt, the Radical*.

Father Henry Holt Jesuit priest who befriends Henry Esmond in his youth and again in Europe, where he gives Esmond information about his mother; he is an unsuccessful Jacobite conspirator in William Makepeace Thackeray's *The History of Henry Esmond*.

Jack Holt Arthur Pendennis's neighbor at Shepherd's Inn who has a scheme for smuggling tobacco in William Makepeace Thackeray's *The History of Pendennis*.

Jane Holt Helen Rolleston's maid aboard the *Proserpine*; she is the wife of seaman Michael Donovan in Charles Reade's *Foul Play*.

Holy-man One of the good people of Vanity Fair introduced to Christiana and her party by Mnason in John Bunyan's *The Pilgrim's Progress From this World to That Which Is to Come*.

Mr. Home (later M. Home de Bassompierre) Doting, possessive father, who leaves his daughter, Paulina, under the care of Mrs. Bretton and later inherits a French title and a fortune in Charlotte Brontë's *Villette*.

Ginevra Home Superficial wife of Mr. Home and mother of Paulina; her aloofness from her husband and her early death have reinforced his bond to his daughter in Charlotte Brontë's *Villette*.

Paulina Mary Home (later Home de Bassompierre) Quaint child, who becomes friendly with John Graham Bretton during her stay with the Brettons; when she develops into a modest, graceful woman, he makes a fortunate union by overcoming her father's possessiveness in Charlotte Brontë's *Villette*.

Giffard Homely Second son of a farmer; saved from the machinations of the avaricious aristocrat Sir Freestone Hardgrave by Henry Clinton, he is discovered to have been the stranger who once saved Clinton from drowning in Henry Brooke's *The Fool of Quality*.

Peggy Granger Homely A tanner's pious daughter, who becomes Giffard Homely's wife in Henry Brooke's *The Fool of Quality*.

Homer Epic poet whose soul the author encounters in Elysium in Henry Fielding's *A Journey From This World to the Next*.

Harriet Homespun Wife of Horace Homespun; she is seduced by the rake Sedley in S. J. Pratt's *Pupil of Pleasure*.

Horace Homespun Virtuous clergyman cuckolded by his vain wife in S. J. Pratt's *Pupil of Pleasure*.

Mrs. Hominy Strong-minded American philosopher

and authoress, also known as "Mother of the Modern Gracchi," who tortures her listeners with her high-flown intellectual discourse in Charles Dickens's *The Life and Adventures of Martin Chuzzlewit.*

Lord Honain   Physician to the caliph and brother of the high priest Jabaster; he has forsaken the spiritual cause of his captive people for the earthly rewards of service to the caliph in Benjamin Disraeli's *The Wondrous Tale of Alroy.*

Honest   Old man from the town of Stupidity; he joins Christiana's party and tells the story of Self-will; he kills Diffidence in John Bunyan's *The Pilgrim's Progress From this World to That Which Is to Come.*

Charles Honeyman   Brother-in-law of Colonel Newcome, to whom he causes some distress because, though a fashionable preacher, he has a propensity to fall into debt in William Makepeace Thackeray's *The Newcomes.*

Martha Honeyman   Maternal aunt of Clive Newcome and landlady in Brighton to his cousins; she sees through the pretensions of her brother, Charles Honeyman, in William Makepeace Thackeray's *The Newcomes.*

Luke Honeythunder   Guardian of Neville and Helena Landless; he calls himself a philanthrophist but is indifferent to the fate of his wards when Neville is accused by John Jasper of murdering his nephew; he upbraids Canon Crisparkle for defending Neville in Charles Dickens's *The Mystery of Edwin Drood.*

Honorius   Roman emperor who remains undefeated by Heraclian in Charles Kingsley's *Hypatia.*

Mr. Honyman   Cautious local lawyer who acts for Mr. Tappitt, the brewer, of Baslehurst in Devon in the conflict over Luke Rowan's claim to management and the production of better beer in Anthony Trollope's *Rachel Ray.*

Mrs. Hood   Mother of Emily Hood; she lives a hard life on her husband's small income, is alienated from her educated daughter, and dies soon after her husband, leaving her daughter an orphan in George Gissing's *A Life's Morning.*

Emily Hood   Governess from a dreary industrial town who is engaged to her employer's son, Wilfrid Athel; her father's cruel employer tries to force her to marry him, but she resists; she breaks off her engagement when she learns of her father's disgrace and suicide, loses her mother, and is tragically left alone for six years until she again meets William and marries him in George Gissing's *A Life's Morning.*

James Hood   Father of Emily Hood; he falls into a trap by stealing money from his employer, who is in love with his daughter; he is dismissed and kills himself in George Gissing's *A Life's Morning.*

Sabrina Hooky   A vain and worldly successor to Nanse Banks as schoolmistress in John Galt's *Annals of the Parish.*

Alice Hooper   Elder daughter of Dr. Ewen Hooper; she finally marries the Oxford mathematician Herbert Pryce in Mrs. Humphry Ward's *Lady Connie.*

Dr. Ewen Hooper   Hard-working scholar, whose financial burdens are lightened by his aristocratic and rich niece, Lady Connie Bledlow, in Mrs. Humphry Ward's *Lady Connie.*

Nora Hooper   Young, scholarly cousin of Lady Connie Bledlow; she takes on the burden of running the Hooper household in Oxford in Mrs. Humphry Ward's *Lady Connie.*

Edward Hope   Village surgeon, whose professional reputation is destroyed by malicious rumors of gravesnatching after he casts an unpopular vote; he marries the sister of the woman he loves because he has inadvertently won her heart and feels responsible for her happiness, but his dutifulness and patience enable him to make his marriage happy and to win back the community's respect in Harriet Martineau's *Deerbrook.*

Jefferson Hope   Former hunter, trapper, and prospector from California, who works as cab driver in London in pursuit of his prey in Arthur Conan Doyle's *A Study in Scarlet.*

Hopeful   Resident of Vanity Fair who joins Christian after Faithful's execution; he helps Christian and is helped by him during the journey to the Celestial City, where he is welcomed along with Christian; his conversations with Christian help to clarify doctrine in John Bunyan's *The Pilgrim's Progress From this World to That Which Is to Come.*

Mrs. Hopgood   Widow of a London banker who settled in the village of Fenmarket and mother of Clara and Madge Hopgood; she is an intimate friend of her daughters in Mark Rutherford's *Clara Hopgood.*

Clara Hopgood   Twenty-five-year-old daughter of Mrs. Hopgood in 1844; having gone to school in Germany, she clerks in a London bookstore, where she meets Baruch Cohen; she begins to love him but chooses to devote herself to the cause of Italian independence and loses her life in the service of Mazzini's followers in Mark Rutherford's *Clara Hopgood.*

Young Clara (Hopgood)   Madge Hopgood's daughter by Frank Palmer; she asks about her Aunt Clara (Hopgood) when she is ten years old in Mark Rutherford's *Clara Hopgood*.

Madge Hopgood   Twenty-year-old sister of Clara Hopgood; she attended school in Brighton before going to Germany like Clara; she is attracted to Frank Palmer and bears him a child but refuses to marry him; she finally marries Baruch Cohen instead in Mark Rutherford's *Clara Hopgood*.

Captain Hopkins   Prisoner for debt in the King's Bench prison; he lends a knife and fork to Mr. Micawber in Charles Dickens's *The Personal History of David Copperfield*.

Mr. Hopkins   Curmudgeonly head gardener at Allington who feuds with the farm bailiff over stable manure in Anthony Trollope's *The Small House at Allington*.

Mr. and Mrs. Hopkins   Mr. and Mrs. Furze's neighbors who take them in after the fire in Mark Rutherford's *Catharine Furze*.

The Misses Hopkins   Daughters of Captain Hopkins; they are with him in the King's Bench prison in Charles Dickens's *The Personal History of David Copperfield*.

Mrs. Hopkins   Captain Hopkins's wife, a "very dirty lady," also a resident of the King's Bench prison in Charles Dickens's *The Personal History of David Copperfield*.

Mrs. Hopkins   Housekeeper at Bragton Hall and devoted servant of the Morton family in Anthony Trollope's *The American Senator*.

Jack Hopkins   Medical student present at Ben Allen and Bob Sawyer's drinking party to which Samuel Pickwick is invited in Charles Dickens's *The Posthumous Papers of the Pickwick Club*.

Mrs. Hopper   Inefficient part-time housekeeper of Will Warburton's lodgings in George Gissing's *Will Warburton*.

Horatio   Ward (actually, son) of Dorilaus; he becomes a soldier who fights in the famous siege of Ingolstadt; he is taken prisoner by the Baron de la Valiers and then by the Russians; he finally marries Charlotta in Eliza Haywood's *The Fortunate Foundlings*.

Horatio   Lothario's friend, who pretends to avenge Miss Johnson against Lothario but seduces her instead in Tobias Smollett's *The Adventures of Roderick Random*.

Horatio   Leonora's jilted lover, who wounds Bellarmine in a duel; he never recovers from rejection in Henry

Fielding's *The History of the Adventures of Mr. Joseph Andrews and of his Friend Mr. Abraham Adams*.

General Horlock   Mild-mannered military man, who has retired from India and is dominated by Mrs. Horlock, whose many dogs he deplores in George Moore's *Spring Days*.

Mrs. Horlock   Respected neighbor of the Brookes family who has many pets and visits the new people in the villas in George Moore's *Spring Days*.

Gustavus Horn   Colonel in the service of King Gustavus Adolphus of Sweden; he leads the king's forces in battle against the Germans in Daniel Defoe's *Memoirs of a Cavalier*.

Mr. Hornbeck   English traveler who meets Perry Pickle on the way to Paris, mistreats his wife, and recaptures her from Perry with the help of the British ambassador in Tobias Smollett's *The Adventures of Peregrine Pickle*.

Deborah Hornbeck   Married woman who meets Perry Pickle while traveling with her husband from Calais to Paris, yields to Perry's desire, flees to him for help in Paris, and is recaptured by her husband in Tobias Smollett's *The Adventures of Peregrine Pickle*.

Mr. Horner   The old-fashioned, reserved steward of Hanbury Court, who secretly trains Harry Gregson as a clerk in Elizabeth Gaskell's *My Lady Ludlow*.

Mr. Horrock   Friend of Mr. Bambridge in George Eliot's *Middlemarch*.

Horrocks   Sir Pitt Crawley's butler in William Makepeace Thackeray's *Vanity Fair*.

Betsy Horrocks   Daughter of the butler to Sir Pitt Crawley, whose mistress she becomes; Mrs. Bute Crawley interferes to deprive her of any pecuniary advantage in William Makepeace Thackeray's *Vanity Fair*.

Mr. Horsball   Manager of the Moonbeam Public House; Ralph Newton, the heir to Newton Priory, owes him money; the members of the local hunt carouse in Horsball's establishment in Anthony Trollope's *Ralph the Heir*.

Zillah Horsfall   The imposing nurse, a dragon, assigned by Dr. MacTurk to attend Robert Moore; she obeys the doctor's orders implicitly in Charlotte Brontë's *Shirley*.

Conrade Horst   Favorite soldier in William de La Marck's employ; he is cruel and daring in Sir Walter Scott's *Quentin Durward*.

Hortense Lady Dedlock's French maid, who, jealous of the new favorite, Rosa, quits her service and aids Mr. Tulkinghorn in his investigation of Lady Dedlock; she murders Mr. Tulkinghorn and sends letters implicating Lady Dedlock to the police in Charles Dickens's *Bleak House.*

Hortense A mischievous pupil of Mlle. Reuter; she makes up in vivacity for what she lacks in good sense in Charlotte Brontë's *The Professor.*

Hortensius Conservative interlocutor, who defends Epic as superior to Romance; as a result of the case presented by Euphrasia, he gradually comes to recognize the value and merit of some Romances in Clara Reeve's *The Progress of Romance.*

Mrs. Horton Housekeeper to Dorriforth, Lord Elmwood in Elizabeth Inchbald's *A Simple Story.*

Polly Horton A former mistress of Robert Lovelace, now a madam in the London brothel where he lodges the unsuspecting Clarissa Harlowe; she is a conspirator in his deception of Clarissa in Samuel Richardson's *Clarissa: or, The History of a Young Lady.*

Captain Hoseason Cruel and sober captain of the Scottish brig *Covenant*; paid by David Balfour's uncle, Ebenezer, he agrees to kidnap David with the intention of selling him into slavery in the American colonies in Robert Louis Stevenson's *Kidnapped.* He is named but rejected as a possible aid in securing Alan Breck Stewart's clandestine passage to France in *Catriona.*

Gus Hoskins Faithful friend of Samuel Titmarsh, whom he supports through thick and thin; he marries Winnie Titmarsh in William Makepeace Thackeray's *The History of Samuel Titmarsh and the Great Hoggarty Diamond.*

Hostage of the Rose Beloved of Hallblithe of the Raven and the object of his search after sea rovers capture her in William Morris's *The Story of the Glittering Plain.*

Lady Elizabeth Hotspur Timid wife of Sir Harry; she is constantly mediating between her daughter, Emily, who refuses to believe her cousin, George Hotspur, is a villain, and her stubborn husband, who forbids the cousins to marry in Anthony Trollope's *Sir Harry Hotspur of Humblethwaite.*

Emily Hotspur Beloved, strong-willed daughter of Sir Harry, who wishes she could be his heir to prevent his estate's falling into the hands of her worthless cousin, George; she succumbs to George's wooing and stubbornly refuses to think him capable of wrongdoing; when her father forbids the marriage, she goes into a decline and dies in Anthony Trollope's *Sir Harry Hotspur of Humblethwaite.*

George Hotspur Worthless heir to the baronetcy of Sir Harry Hotspur; charming but unprincipled and deeply in debt, he woos his cousin, Emily Hotspur, so that he can gain the Cumberland estate to go with the title of the Hotspur family; his plan fails, and he marries Lucy Morton, an actress who has been supporting him, in Anthony Trollope's *Sir Harry Hotspur of Humblethwaite.*

Sir Harry Hotspur Highly respected Cumberland landowner of ancient lineage grieved by the death of his only son; he must leave his title to a distant cousin, George Hotspur, although he longs for his daughter, Emily, to inherit his estate; when the worthless George wins Emily's love, Sir Harry forbids the match; after her death he is left with no descendant in Anthony Trollope's *Sir Harry Hotspur of Humblethwaite.*

Adelaide de Baron Houghton Vivacious and mischief-making distant relative of the Germain family; having once rejected Lord George Germain to marry for money, she amuses herself by trying to revive his affection and by throwing the raffish Jack de Baron into the company of Lady George Germain in Anthony Trollope's *Is He Popenjoy?.*

Hetta Houghton Wealthy, unmarried sister of Jeffrey; she lives alone in London and is much admired for her spirited independence in Anthony Trollope's *Is He Popenjoy?.*

Humphrey Houghton Tenant under Edward Waverly's care; his dying in battle reminds Edward of his neglected responsibilities in Sir Walter Scott's *Waverly.*

Jeffrey Houghton Wealthy, elderly gambler, whom Adelaide de Baron married for an income in Anthony Trollope's *Is He Popenjoy?.*

Hound-under-Greenbury Leader of the Shepherds in the Silver-dale campaign in William Morris's *The Roots of the Mountains.*

Mrs. Housekeeper Colonel Jack's first wife, whom he divorces because of her profligate behavior and infidelity, but whom he later remarries after she is transported to Virginia as a criminal in Daniel Defoe's *The History and the Remarkable Life of the Truly Honourable Colonel Jacques, Commonly Call'd Col. Jack.*

Richard Houseman Eugene Aram's kinsman, who involves him in the robbery and murder of Geoffrey Lester and many years later gives evidence against him to save his own life in Edward Bulwer-Lytton's *Eugene Aram.*

Frank Houston Idle, mercenary suitor of Gertrude Tringle; when he learns she will have no dowry from her father, Sir Thomas, he leaves her and returns to his first love, Imogene Docimer, in Anthony Trollope's *Ayala's Angel*.

Rosina Houston Fond aunt of Frank Houston; she believes that truth in love is everything and gives Frank the money to marry Imogene Docimer in Anthony Trollope's *Ayala's Angel*.

Lady Howard Friend of Arthur Villars; she invites Evelina Anville Belmont to visit her and accompany her granddaughter to London in Frances Burney's *Evelina*.

Mr. Howard Secretary to Lord Vargrave (Lumley Ferrers) and the only person to feel grief at his death in Edward Bulwer-Lytton's *Alice*.

Mr. Howard Mrs. Howard's nineteen-year-old son, whose love for Sophia Darnley enrages his mother and leads to the heroine's dismissal in Charlotte Lennox's *Sophia*.

Mrs. Howard Hypocritical philanthropist who takes Sophia Darnley as companion and tries to marry her off to Mr. Barton; when her own son falls in love with Sophia, she dismisses her and tries to ruin her reputation in Charlotte Lennox's *Sophia*.

Emily Howard Devoted friend of Lady Julia Belmont and occasionally the recipient of her correspondence in Frances Brooke's *The History of Lady Julia Mandeville*.

Lucinda Howard Arabella Bloomville's friend, who secretly loves Mr. Squares; she is seduced by a handsome young man she discovers sleeping in a bed of daisies; she dies overcome by her delicate nerves when she observes the severe demeanor of her beloved Mr. Squares and Mr. Gifford in William Beckford's *Modern Novel Writing; or, the Elegant Enthusiast*.

Mrs. Howder Gossipy Edinburgh saleswoman, who discusses Effie Deans's trial with her friends in Sir Walter Scott's *The Heart of Midlothian*.

Anna ("Nancy") Howe The chief correspondent and closest friend of Clarissa Harlowe; her outspoken defense of Clarissa and condemnations of Annabella and James Harlowe and Roger Solmes frequently anger Clarissa's family and inadvertently exacerbate the estrangement; she endeavors to help Clarissa discover Lovelace's intentions, but he intercepts crucial letters from her to Clarissa in Samuel Richardson's *Clarissa: or, The History of a Young Lady*.

Annabella Howe Widowed mother of Clarissa Harlowe's closest confidante and correspondent, Anna Howe, and an occasional correspondent with Clarissa; her plans for Anna's marriage counterpoint those of the Harlowes for Clarissa in Samuel Richardson's *Clarissa: or, The History of a Young Lady*.

Mrs. Howel Guardian of Lady Aurora Granville; the cousin of Lord Denmeath, she acts to prevent communication between Aurora and Juliet Granville; she unsuccessfully tries to arrest Juliet for theft in Frances Burney's *The Wanderer*.

Mrs. Howell Deerbrook village shop owner, who snubs Hester (Ibbotson) Hope when her husband, Edward Hope, casts an unpopular vote in Harriet Martineau's *Deerbrook*.

Joseph Howell Baron Fitz-Owen's old servant, who befriends Edmund Lovel and helps him uncover and prove his true lineage in Clara Reeve's *The Old English Baron*.

Melchisedech Howler Dissenting, ranting minister, whose church Mrs. MacStinger attends in Charles Dickens's *Dombey and Son*.

Hrosshild Valiant young woman of the Wolfings; Hall-Sun puts him in command of ten maidens who spy on the Romans in William Morris's *A Tale of the House of the Wolfings*.

Mr. Hubble Wheelwright and acquaintance of Joe Gargery; he and his wife join in the humiliation of Pip Pirrip at the Christmas dinner with "moral goads" in Charles Dickens's *Great Expectations*.

Hubert Expert Norman archer, who competes with Locksley (Robin Hood) in the tournament at Ashby in Sir Walter Scott's *Ivanhoe*.

Reuben Huckabuck John Ridd's Uncle Ben, a shrewd, mysterious businessman who is considered callous and is rich but does not like the Ridds in his own way in R. D. Blackmore's *Lorna Doone*.

Ruth Huckabuck John Ridd's cousin, a tiny, shy, sweet, well-mannered lady who wins the hearts of the Ridds in R. D. Blackmore's *Lorna Doone*.

Lud Hudibras Mighty monarch of the ancient British featured in "The True Legend of Prince Bladud," recounted by Samuel Pickwick in Charles Dickens's *The Posthumous Papers of the Pickwick Club*.

Mrs. Hudson Sherlock Holmes's and John H. Watson's long-suffering landlady, who is introduced in Arthur Conan Doyle's *The Sign of Four*.

Sir Geoffrey Hudson   Dwarf soldier, who served the king, is a cell mate of Julian Peveril in the Tower, and leaps from a fiddle case to report the plotting of the Duke of Buckingham to the king in Sir Walter Scott's *Peveril of the Peak*.

Captain Hiram Hudson   The *Proserpine*'s skipper, who has a long history of scuttled ships; he goes down with his ship, dead drunk, in Charles Reade's *Foul Play*.

Izz Huett   Milkmaid at Richard Crick's dairy who falls in love with Angel Clare; she agrees to his impulsive offer to take her to Brazil, but he withdraws it when she admits that his wife, Tess (Durbeyfield), would be equally ready to die for him; later informed of Clare's offer, Tess despairs of his loving her enough to return in Thomas Hardy's *Tess of the D'Urbervilles*.

Hugh   Gracious younger brother of the Laird of Dornock in Sophia Lee's *The Recess*.

Hugh   Sir John Chester's illegitimate son, who works at the Maypole Inn and likes only his dog and Barnaby Rudge, though he pursues Dolly Varden; he participates in the Gordon riots and is hanged after Gabriel Varden's intercession on his behalf fails with Chester in Charles Dickens's *Barnaby Rudge*.

Hugh   King Peter's son who leaves the forces of the Abbot at Higham to join the army of his brother Ralph in William Morris's *The Well at the World's End*.

Sir Hugh   The Green Knight, who helps to rescue the three imprisoned damsels; he marries Viridis in William Morris's *The Water of the Wondrous Isles*.

Mr. Hughes   Prison chaplain with whom Ernest Pontifex first discusses rationalism in Samuel Butler's *The Way of All Flesh*.

Mrs. Hughes   Thurstan Benson's sympathetic Welsh landlady, who helps him to help Ruth Hilton in Elizabeth Gaskell's *Ruth*.

Mr. Huish (Whish, Hay, Tomkins, the clerk)   Vile, cunning, and unscrupulous cockney clerk turned sickly beachcomber in the South Sea islands; the basest of the three desperate outcasts, he fails horribly in his attempt to murder and rob the pearl merchant William John Attwater on a secluded island in Robert Louis Stevenson's *The Ebb-Tide: A Trio and a Quartette*.

Mrs. Hulme   Atheist and elderly hostess to the cognoscenti of literary and intellectual London in Mrs. Lynn Linton's *The Autobiography of Christopher Kirkland*.

Mrs. HumDrum   Dowager who helped Yram when she was pregnant with Jack Higgs's child and who is now Yram's primary confidante; she aids in Higgs's escape in Samuel Butler's *Erewhon Revisited Twenty Years Later*.

Anthony Humm   President of the Brick Lane Branch of the United Grand Junction Ebeneezer Temperance Association, where Mr. Stiggins preaches and Martha Bardell attends services in Charles Dickens's *The Posthumous Papers of the Pickwick Club*.

Humphrey   A furze cutter and a voice of rural commentary in Thomas Hardy's *The Return of the Native*.

Humphrey (the elder)   Moll Flanders's third husband, whom she marries without knowing they have the same mother; she deceives him into marrying her by leading him to think she is wealthy, but when he discovers that she is not, they move to his Virginia plantation, where she learns of his true relation to her; she leaves him and returns to England in Daniel Defoe's *The Fortunes and Misfortunes of the Famous Moll Flanders*.

Humphrey   Moll Flanders's son who is born to her of her marriage to her brother; he becomes a prosperous plantation owner in Virginia and helps care for Moll when she returns to Virginia in Daniel Defoe's *The Fortunes and Misfortunes of the Famous Moll Flanders*.

Humphrey   One of Sir Daniel Brackley's men killed in battle at Risingham in Robert Louis Stevenson's *The Black Arrow: A Tale of Two Roses*.

Master Humphrey   Opening narrator, who meets Nell Trent in the London streets and accompanies her to her home in Charles Dickens's *The Old Curiosity Shop*.

Mr. Humphries   Eastthorp builder who spreads gossip that Tom Catchpole is a thief in Mark Rutherford's *Catharine Furze*.

Humpty Dumpty   Vain and arrogant of manner, a development of the nursery-rhyme character; his conversation with Alice, in which he claims the right to make words mean whatever he likes, advances the examination of names as meaning or arbitrary signs; he explicates "Jabberwocky" for Alice in Lewis Carroll's *Through the Looking-Glass*.

Hunchback   High-priest of Conventicle, who is a roaring hypocrite and explains the mystery of his ministry in Charles Johnstone's *Chrysal: or, The Adventures of a Guinea*.

Mrs. Hunfleet   Carola Bennet's miserly aunt, who exploits Carola and sells her to Cantalupe for prostitution in Thomas Amory's *The Life of John Buncle, Esq.*

Gladys Hungerton   Young woman for whose sake Ned

Malone accompanies Professor Challenger to South America; she later forsakes him for William Potts in Arthur Conan Doyle's *The Lost World*.

Hunsden Yorke Hunsden   A mill owner and an unorthodox character, whose iconoclastic ways influence William Crimsworth by inciting Crimsworth to leave his employment with his brother, Edward, and by recommending him for a teaching post in Brussels; he keeps in touch, eventually retiring near the Crimsworths in England in Charlotte Brontë's *The Professor*.

Hunt   Captain Boldwig's head gardener, who finds Samuel Pickwick asleep in a wheelbarrow in Charles Dickens's *The Posthumous Papers of the Pickwick Club*.

Arabella Hunt   Mrs. Miller's young, widowed neighbor, who offers Tom Jones a secure future by proposing marriage, a temptation Tom gallantly refuses in Henry Fielding's *The History of Tom Jones*.

Charles Hunt   Father of Elizabeth Hunt and owner of a small estate in County Kildare, Ireland; he dies before he can ensure a good marriage for her or leave an inheritance in Thomas Amory's *The Life of John Buncle, Esq.*

Elizabeth Hunt   Daughter of Charles Hunt; ruined by a man who promises marriage but leaves her pregnant, she becomes destitute and ostracized and suffers a miscarriage and breast cancer; John Buncle provides her a funeral in Thomas Amory's *The Life of John Buncle, Esq.*

Tufton Hunt   Rascally clergyman, who officiated at the fraudulent marriage of "Dr. Brandon" (Dr. Firmin) and Caroline Brandon; he later blackmails Firmin in William Makepeace Thackeray's *The Adventures of Philip on His Way through the World*.

Lady Hunter   Wife of local potentate Sir William Hunter; she is attracted by the excitement surrounding the villagers' attack on the surgeon Mr. Hope's house; she revels in her husband's popularity and helps to emphasize the irresponsibility of the upper class in local governance in Harriet Martineau's *Deerbrook*.

The Misses Hunter   Daughters of Mr. and Mrs. Leo Hunter; they are girlishly attired to make their mother seem younger in Charles Dickens's *The Posthumous Papers of the Pickwick Club*.

John Hunter   Calm, competent servant of Squire Trelawney; a good rower, he conveys supplies to the stockade, guards it, and helps Captain Smollett run up the colors; his chest is crushed during a pirate attack in Robert Louis Stevenson's *Treasure Island*.

Leo Hunter   Proud husband of Mrs. Leo Hunter in Charles Dickens's *The Posthumous Papers of the Pickwick Club*.

Mrs. Leo Hunter   Aesthetic leader and poetess of Eatanswill, who wrote "Ode to an Expiring Frog" and held a fancy-dress breakfast at The Den in Charles Dickens's *The Posthumous Papers of the Pickwick Club*.

Sir William Hunter   Egotistical and irresponsible magistrate and leading citizen of Deerbrook; he is incensed when the surgeon Mr. Hope votes differently from him and does nothing to protect Hope from the villagers' growing superstitious distrust stemming from rumors that Hope has been grave-snatching in Harriet Martineau's *Deerbrook*.

Earl of Huntingdon   British nobleman who reluctantly allows his daughter, Lady Barbara, to marry Gaston de Blondeville in Ann Radcliffe's *Gaston de Blondeville*.

Lady Huntingdon   British noblewoman who reluctantly allows her daughter, Lady Barbara, to marry Gaston de Blondeville in Ann Radcliffe's *Gaston de Blondeville*.

Lord Huntingdon   One of Mary, Queen of Scots's guards in prison in Sophia Lee's *The Recess*.

Arthur Huntingdon   Handsome, charming, but indulgent and irresponsible man, who marries Helen Lawrence and becomes progressively more debauched until she feels compelled to leave him; he is prone to adultery, gambling, and especially drinking, which hastens his death after a fall while hunting in Anne Brontë's *The Tenant of Wildfell Hall*.

Arthur Huntingdon (the younger)   Boy known as Arthur Graham; he is the only child of Helen and Arthur Huntingdon; his father's overindulgence of him is one of the problems behind Helen's flight from Grassdale Manor in Anne Brontë's *The Tenant of Wildfell Hall*.

Helen Lawrence Huntingdon   Beautiful, headstrong sister of Frederick Lawrence; she marries Arthur Huntingdon with the intention of reforming his selfish habits, but after she realizes the hopelessness of that task, she flees with her son into hiding at Wildfell Hall, where she is known as Helen Graham; she returns to her husband only to attend him in his illness; she finally marries the gentleman farmer Gilbert Markham in Anne Brontë's *The Tenant of Wildfell Hall*.

Earl of Huntinglen   Father of Lord Dalgarno; he introduces Nigel Olifaunt to the king and puts Nigel in the company of his son; he deplores his son's evil conduct in Sir Walter Scott's *The Fortunes of Nigel*.

David, Earl of Huntington and Prince Royal of Scotland (Sir Kenneth, Knight of the Couchant Leopard) Valiant hero who joins King Richard's Crusade in the Holy Land in disguise as the knight Sir Kenneth; having disgraced himself while guarding Richard's standard, he redeems himself in disguise as the Nubian Zohuak; he is engaged to marry Lady Edith Plantagenet after his identity is disclosed in Sir Walter Scott's *The Talisman.*

Marquis of Huntley Chief of the Gordons in Sir Walter Scott's *A Legend of Montrose.*

Mr. Huntley Miss Wingman's unreliable husband in Eliza Haywood's *The History of Jemmy and Jenny Jessamy.*

Araminta (Minta) Hurd Wife of Jim Hurd, poacher; she is befriended and helped financially by Marcella Boyce in Mrs. Humphry Ward's *Marcella.*

Jim Hurd Dwarf poacher who, when caught, kills the keeper, George Westall; he is hanged despite the intervention of Marcella Boyce and others who attempt to abolish the cruel punishment for poaching in Mrs. Humphry Ward's *Marcella.*

Mr. Hurst Lethargic member of Mr. Bingley's household and the husband of Bingley's sister Louisa in Jane Austen's *Pride and Prejudice.*

Harriet Hurst Nursemaid and later maid to Paulina Home in Charlotte Brontë's *Villette.*

Joseph (Joe) Hurst Sturdy young Berkshire yeoman farmer, brother of Lucy; he invites Richard to come to Elm Close Farm in Thomas Hughes's *The Scouring of the White Horse.*

Louisa Hurst Mr. Bingley's married sister, who treats his home as her own in Jane Austen's *Pride and Prejudice.*

Lucy Hurst Joseph's pretty sister, with whom Richard falls in love in Thomas Hughes's *The Scouring of the White Horse.*

Winifred Hurtle Beautiful, passionate, determined American widow with a dubious past; she pursues Paul Montague after he has promised to marry her; when he extricates himself from the relationship, she contemplates shooting him but forgives him; troubling rumors that her abusive husband still lives turn out to have substance in Anthony Trollope's *The Way We Live Now.*

Hutton Lady Henry's conniving butler in Mrs. Humphry Ward's *Lady Rose's Daughter.*

Samuel Huxter A medical student, son of the Claver-ing apothecary, who marries Fanny Bolton in William Makepeace Thackeray's *The History of Pendennis.*

Edward Hyde See Dr. Henry Jekyll.

Prince Hyder Ali Khan Bahauder (Scheik Hali) Usurper of Mysore; he grants Adam Hartley's request to free Menie Gray, though it means humiliating his son; as Scheik Hali, an old fakir, he advises Hartley concerning Menie Gray's plight in Sir Walter Scott's *The Surgeon's Daughter.*

Baron d' Hymbercourt The Duke of Burgundy's marechal du camp, or quartermaster-general, in Sir Walter Scott's *Quentin Durward.*

Hyndman Envious and observant usher of the Council Chamber at Holyrood; James Stuart, Earl of Murray and Regent of Scotland, advises him to disguise his intelligence in Sir Walter Scott's *The Abbot.*

Hypatia Balthazar's beautiful bride-to-be, whose martyrdom by the Christians causes him to lament the loss of her engagement ring in Henry Fielding's *A Journey From This World to the Next.*

Hypatia Beautiful, chaste, golden-haired philosopher, teacher, and polytheist, who becomes engaged to the prefect Orestes after his promise, which he breaks, to champion her beliefs; finally, distraught and doubting her own creed, she is captured en route to her farewell lecture and dismembered by Cyril's monks in Charles Kingsley's *Hypatia.*

Girzy Hypel "The leddy Grippy," Claud Walkinshaw's unloved wife; she is a comic obstacle to Claud's plans concerning the entail and is instrumental in returning the estate to Charles Walkinshaw's family, its rightful inheritors, in John Galt's *The Entail.*

Malachi Hypel Girzy's father, owner of the Plealands estate; he is a coarse laird as much given to futile manipulation as is Claud Walkinshaw in John Galt's *The Entail.*

Hypocorisma Spoiled, petulant young slave to Orestes in Charles Kingsley's *Hypatia.*

Hypocrisy Traveler who, along with Formalist, gets into the highway by climbing over the Wall of Salvation rather than entering through the wicket-gate; he avoids the Hill of Difficulty and takes the way of Destruction in John Bunyan's *The Pilgrim's Progress From this World to That Which Is to Come.*

I

I. K. Cavalier's son, whose memorandum concerning the finding of the Cavalier's manuscript appears in the preface of Daniel Defoe's *Memoirs of a Cavalier*.

Hester Ibbotson Extremely handsome and proud sister of the milder, wiser Margaret; she struggles to overcome her innate discontent and jealousy, demonstrating courage and resilience throughout the professional adversity of her husband, the village surgeon Edward Hope, in Harriet Martineau's *Deerbrook*.

Margaret Ibbotson Luminously faithful and wise sister to the tempestuous and more beautiful Hester; her devotion to her troubled sister and her unselfish friendship with the crippled Maria Young inspire those who know her and win the love of Philip Enderby in Harriet Martineau's *Deerbrook*.

Earl of Idford (Lord Sad-dog) Hugh Trevor's corrupt schoolmate, who employs Hugh to write political letters under the pen name Themistocles, and who later conspires to ruin Hugh's political career in Thomas Holcroft's *The Adventures of Hugh Trevor*.

Idris Beautiful daughter of the late King of England, sister of Adrian, and wife of Lionel Verney; she is the anxious, loving mother of Albert and Evelyn in Mary Shelley's *The Last Man*.

Ignorance Traveler who tries to get to the Celestial City without taking the long road followed by Christian; he is sent to hell because of his ignorance of "justifying righteousness" in John Bunyan's *The Pilgrim's Progress From this World to That Which Is to Come*.

Ignosi See Umbopa.

Mr. Carysbroke, Lord Ilbury Noble, kind trustee of Maud Ruthyn's estate; he meets her on several occasions, particularly at Lady Knollys's houseparty; later he and Maud are happily married in J. Sheridan Le Fanu's *Uncle Silas*.

Janet Ilchester Practical, sympathetic daughter of Sir Roderick Ilchester; Squire Beltham plans to have her marry Harry Richmond, but her plain, practical nature does not appeal to Harry, and it is not until after many setbacks that Janet, Squire Beltham's heir, and Harry are married in George Meredith's *The Adventures of Harry Richmond*.

Sir Robert Ilchester Janet Ilchester's father in George Meredith's *The Adventures of Harry Richmond*.

Lucy Ilderton Isabella Vere's friend and cousin, a romantic young beauty, who treats the Black Dwarf (Sir Edward Mauley) as a novelty and favors Patrick Earnscliff as Isabella's lover in Sir Walter Scott's *The Black Dwarf*.

Nancy Ilderton Lucy Ilderton's younger, timid sister in Sir Walter Scott's *The Black Dwarf*.

Miss Ilex Spinster of independent means and opinions; she advises Morgana Gryll on marriage in Thomas Love Peacock's *Gryll Grange*.

Ilissa Young and beautiful girl, who threatens to kill herself unless she can see her father, Pheron; she promises to return the Inquisitor's love if he can reunite her with her father in Charles Johnstone's *Chrysal: or, The Adventures of a Guinea*.

Ill-favored ones Men who try to seduce Christiana and Mercy in John Bunyan's *The Pilgrim's Progress From this World to That Which Is to Come*.

Imlac Philosopher and poet who leads Rasselas on a trip to the Nile and instructs him concerning the vanity of human wishes in Samuel Johnson's *The History of Rasselas, Prince of Abissinia*.

Imoinda Oroonoko's lover, who is taken by the king of Coramantien as one of his wives and sold into slavery when she is discovered with Oroonoko; reunited with Oroonoko under slavery, she is pregnant when he stages his rebellion; he decides he must kill her to prevent her mistreatment at the hands of whites in Aphra Behn's *Oroonoko*.

Imotu The late king of Kukuanaland and father of Ignosi (Umbopa); he was murdered by his brother, the usurper Twala, in H. Rider Haggard's *King Solomon's Mines*.

Incognita See Juliana.

Indian Sovereign European living with the Indians; a determined and enterprising sovereign, he comes to the American General to discuss the stalled army and the arts of war in Charles Johnstone's *Chrysal: or, The Adventures of a Guinea*.

Christopher (Kit) Ines A prize-fighter patronized by Lord Fleetwood; he loses his sweetheart, Madge Winch, when he places money above right to become Fleetwood's henchman in George Meredith's *The Amazing Marriage*.

Infadoos Tough warrior and the younger half brother of the unlawful king of Kukuanaland, Twala; he joins the rightful heir Ignosi (Umbopa); with Allan Quatermain and his English party he helps overthrow Twala and put Ignosi on the Kukuana throne in H. Rider Haggard's *King Solomon's Mines*.

Ingenious Painter   Painter of Italian-style counterfeits; he sells them to Gambler Number Three and then publicly admits that the paintings are fakes in Charles Johnstone's *Chrysal: or, The Adventures of a Guinea*.

Fergus Ingleby   Scheming wretch who assumes the name of Allan Armadale to secure a fortune; he meets a watery death locked in the cabin of a sinking yacht in Wilkie Collins's *Armadale*.

Eustace Inglesant   Twin brother of John Inglesant and courtier to King Charles I; he marries a wealthy landowner, Lady Cardiff, and is murdered by an Italian, Malvoti, in J. Henry Shorthouse's *John Inglesant, A Romance*.

John (Il Cavaliere di San Giorgio) Inglesant   Courtier and messenger in the service of King Charles I; he is trained by Jesuits to be liaison between Church of England and papist factions in England and narrowly escapes execution for treason; he seeks revenge for the murder of his twin brother; he becomes involved in papal elections; he returns to England a confirmed supporter of the Church of England in J. Henry Shorthouse's *John Inglesant, A Romance*.

Richard Inglesant   John Inglesant's great-grandfather, granted the Priory at Westacre by Henry VIII for his part in the suppression of monasteries in England in J. Henry Shorthouse's *John Inglesant, A Romance*.

Squire Inglewood   Northumbrian justice and converted Jacobite; a kindly old bachelor, he holds a paternal regard for Diana Vernon and dismisses Francis Osbaldistone's charge on her account in Sir Walter Scott's *Rob Roy*.

Sergeant Inglis   Soldier under the command of Colonel John Grahame; he is left to assist Major Miles Bellenden in the defense of Tillietudlem in Sir Walter Scott's *Old Mortality*.

Dowager Baroness Ingram   Haughty mother of Lord Ingram, Blanche, and Mary; she instills in her children the same insupportable pride in Charlotte Brontë's *Jane Eyre*.

Blanche Ingram   Baroness Ingram's elder daughter, a tall, Grecian beauty, to whom Mr. Rochester pays court for the purpose of exciting Jane Eyre's jealousy in Charlotte Brontë's *Jane Eyre*.

Mary Ingram   Baroness Ingram's younger daughter,

milder and less spirited than her elder sister in Charlotte Brontë's *Jane Eyre*.

Theodore, Lord Ingram   Baroness Ingram's handsome but apathetic son, who indicates an interest in Amy Eshton in Charlotte Brontë's *Jane Eyre*.

Mr. Innes   Dreamer and "propagandist of old-time music and its instruments"; he sacrifices his daughter, Evelyn, to his own musical preferences; he loves her but fills his life with his hobby in George Moore's *Evelyn Innes*. Invited to Rome by the Pope for his music, he dies there in *Sister Teresa*.

Evelyn Innes   Gifted only daughter of musicians; under the aegis of Sir Owen Asher, she elopes to Paris and becomes a famous singer; her six-year liason with Asher leaves her with feelings of guilt, increased when she becomes the lover of Ulick Dean; she decides to become a nun, dismissing both lovers; influenced by Monsignor Mostyn, she makes a convent retreat after singing a concert to aid the Sisters in George Moore's *Evelyn Innes*. The death of her father and memories of her wordly life cloud her vision, but she takes the vows and after some adjustment finds peace in *Sister Teresa*.

Frank Innes   Handsome, superficial, self-serving, and manipulative college acquaintance of Archibald Weir; while a guest at his estate, Innes schemes to discover Weir's secretive meetings with Christina Elliot in Robert Louis Stevenson's *Weir of Hermiston: An Unfinished Romance*.

Innocent   Damsel at the door of the House of the Interpreter in Part 2 of John Bunyan's *The Pilgrim's Progress From this World to That Which Is to Come*.

Inquisitor   Inquisition official who conducts the trial against Father Schedoni (Ferando di Bruno) and condemns him to die in Ann Radcliffe's *The Italian*.

Inquisitor   Official who loves Ilissa to such a degree that he plans the escape of Ilissa and her father, Pheron, in Charles Johnstone's *Chrysal: or, The Adventures of a Guinea*.

Insignificanti   Successful Italian painter of the mid-sixteenth century; because of his wealth, Sucrewasser's parents order their son to become his disciple in William Beckford's *Biographical Memoirs of Extraordinary Painters*.

Mr. Inspector   Calm and reclusive night-inspector in the Limehouse police station; he is in charge of discovering the murderer of John Harmon in Charles Dickens's *Our Mutual Friend*.

Interpreter   Resident in the House of the Interpreter; he teaches Christian through pictures and allegories depicting spiritual truth; he also teaches Christiana and her party in John Bunyan's *The Pilgrim's Progress From this World to That Which Is to Come.*

Inverashalloch Allan Iverach's companion and Rob Roy MacGregor's enemy, whom Francis Osbaldistone and Bailie (Nicol) Jarvie fight with in the inn at Clachan of Aberfoil in Sir Walter Scott's *Rob Roy.*

Ione Neapolitan musician born in Greece; the ward of Arbaces, she is beloved by Glaucus and saved from death during the volcanic eruption by Nydia in Edward Bulwer-Lytton's *The Last Days of Pompeii.*

Iphanissa Woman whose antipathy to blank verse and adoration of sonnets make her a literary enemy of the Reverend Solomon Sheeppen, who detests sonnets and writes absurd blank verse in William Beckford's *Azemia.*

Mr. Ireland Man whose discovery of a trunk full of original Shakespearean manuscripts, love letters, and a deed of gift nearly makes an impression on Arabella (Bloomville) Lambert in William Beckford's *Modern Novel Writing; or, the Elegant Enthusiast.*

Empress Irene Elderly, dignified wife of Alexius Comnenus; she wields a strong influence over the emperor and adores her talented daughter, Anna Comnena, in Sir Walter Scott's *Count Robert of Paris.*

Princess Irene (Old Mother Wotherwop) Great-great-grandmother of little Princess Irene; her powers allow her to change her human forms; she watches over her granddaughter and Curdie Peterson and gives little Irene a ball of thread (like spun glass) that she uses to save Curdie from the goblins in George MacDonald's *The Princess and the Goblin.* She gives Curdie the power to tell men's characters by the feel of their hands and sends him to save the king in *The Princess and Curdie.*

Princess Irene Eight-year-old princess who, with her great-great-grandmother's ball of thread, saves Curdie Peterson from the goblins in George MacDonald's *The Princess and the Goblin.* She helps Curdie restore her father to health and defeat the court traitors; she marries Curdie when they are grown and rules a prosperous and happy kingdom in *The Princess and Curdie.*

Mr. Ireton English gentleman who escapes from France on the boat which transports the Stranger, Juliet Granville; he is engaged to marry Selina Joddrell; urged by his bachelor uncle to marry for an estate, he breaks with Selina, flirts with the Stranger, Juliet, and considers courting Elinor Joddrel in Frances Burney's *The Wanderer.*

Mrs. Ireton Mother of Mr. Ireton; she escapes with

him from Revolutionary France in Frances Burney's *The Wanderer.*

Irish Lord Lady Lucy's noble father, killed in the attack on his castle by a German regiment in Penelope Aubin's *The Life and Adventures of the Lady Lucy.*

Irish Peer Unnamed nobleman who helps Harriet Fitzpatrick escape from her husband; together, he and Lord Fellamar convince Fitzpatrick to divorce Harriet; she becomes his mistress in Henry Fielding's *The History of Tom Jones.*

Iron-face Alderman of Burgdale and deft weapon smith; he is father of Face-of-god and Hallface in William Morris's *The Roots of the Mountains.*

Mrs. Irons Colonel Newcome's cook and housekeeper; she is at odds with Mrs. Mackenzie in William Makepeace Thackeray's *The Newcomes.*

Mrs. Irons Suspicious wife of Zekiel Irons, who she believes carries on affairs with other women; she often laments to Captain Richard Devereux, their lodger, in J. Sheridan Le Fanu's *The House by the Churchyard.*

Zekiel Irons Seemingly sinister, reserved town clerk of Chapelizod, whose friendship and collusion Paul Dangerfield tries to win; Irons visits Mervyn and tells him the truth of Beauclerc's death and Lord Dunoran's innocence, but refuses to unmask the real murderer; he leaves Chapelizod but later returns and is bribed by Dangerfield into testifying that Charles Nutter attacked Dr. Barney Sturk, but decides to tell the truth and testifies that Dangerfield is Charles Archer and that he killed Beauclerc and Sturk in J. Sheridan Le Fanu's *The House by the Churchyard.*

Griselda Ursula Ironside Spinster descended from an ancient family; a boarder in the Wildcodger household, she temporarily instructs Azemia but eventually conspires with Mrs. Wildcodger to remove the captive to the custody of Mrs. Blandford in William Beckford's *Azemia.*

Irton Ambitious lover proposed by Queen Elizabeth and Lord Burleigh for Rose Cecil, who spurns him, in Sophia Lee's *The Recess.*

Hannah Irwin (Annie Heggie) Clara Mowbray's cousin, who was a witness to her mock marriage to Valentine Bulmer, was seduced and abandoned by Bulmer, and confesses her past before she dies in Sir Walter Scott's *St. Ronan's Well.*

Mrs. Irwine The stately, beautiful, aristocratic mother of the Reverend Adolphus Irwine; she lives in the comfort of old and threadbare opulence with her three children in George Eliot's *Adam Bede*.

Adolphus Irwine   The convivial and not overspiritual Rector of Boxton, Vicar of Hayslope, and Vicar of Blythe, who smooths over Arthur Donnithorne's near confession of his lust for Hetty Sorrel, and thereby loses his chance to forestall tragedy in George Eliot's *Adam Bede*.

Anne Irwine   Adolphus Irwine's sister who has been an invalid cared for by her sister, Kate, for fifteen years in George Eliot's *Adam Bede*.

Kate Irwine   Adolphus Irwine's sister who has been nursing their headache-prone sister, Anne, for fifteen years in George Eliot's *Adam Bede*.

Isaac of York   Wealthy but miserly Jew, whose greed is balanced by his love for his daughter, Rebecca, in Sir Walter Scott's *Ivanhoe*.

Lady Isabel   One of Queen Eleanor's attendants in Ann Radcliffe's *Gaston de Blondeville*.

Isabella   A beautiful, witty, and pious nun, who breaks her vows in order to marry Bernardo Henault; she marries Villenoys after Bernardo is presumed dead and smothers Bernardo when he reappears years later; she tells Villenoys that Bernardo died naturally, but, fearing that he will always resent her for her unlawful remarriage, she sews the sack containing Bernardo's body to Villenoy's shirt, causing him to drown when he throws the body into the river in Aphra Behn's *The History of the Nun*.

Isabella   Victimized heroine pursued by the villainous Manfred, Prince of Otranto; she escapes his clutches to marry Theodore, the rightful heir to Otranto, in Horace Walpole's *The Castle of Otranto*.

Isabella   Lovely and kind daughter of the Count de Beaumont's second wife; she accompanies her stepfather to England, where she meets Mr. Hide, whom she marries, in Penelope Aubin's *The Life of Madam de Beaumont*.

Lady Isabella   Lady Dashfort's daughter who tries to con Lord Colambre into marrying her in Maria Edgeworth's *The Absentee*.

Isabelle   Center of a series of love triangles which end tragically; she retires to a convent after recounting her tale of woe to Cynthia in Sarah Fielding's *The Adventures of David Simple in Search of a Faithful Friend*.

Isabelle   A pupil at Mme. Beck's school who says bluntly that Lucy Snowe should be burnt as a heretic or else she will burn in hell in Charlotte Brontë's *Villette*.

Isabelle of Bourbon   Canoness of Triers and the Bishop of Liège's sister in Sir Walter Scott's *Quentin Durward*.

Isabinda   Woman who endures a series of unsatisfactory suitors for her hand until she meets in the country a gentleman she esteems in Sarah Fielding's *Familiar Letters between the Principal Characters of David Simple and Some Others*.

Isidor   Cowardly Belgian servant to Joseph Sedley in William Makepeace Thackeray's *Vanity Fair*.

Isidore   Plain-speaking abbot admired by the priest Hieracus (Hierax) in Charles Kingsley's *Hypatia*.

Ismael (Muly, Moely)   Moor whom Robinson Crusoe tricks into helping with his escape from slavery; Crusoe tosses him overboard while on a fishing outing for his master in Daniel Defoe's *The Life and Strange Surprizing Adventures of Robinson Crusoe of York, Mariner*.

Ismail the Infidel   Daring Moslem soldier and robber of the Immortal Guard in Sir Walter Scott's *Count Robert of Paris*.

Ismenus   Slave of Hannibal, who—believing him to be a rival for Clarenthia—imprisons him in Jane Barker's *Exilius; or, The Banish'd Roman*.

Countess Violetta (D'Asolo) D'Isorella   Carlo Ammiani's first love; she interferes in his relationship with Vittoria Campa and in his involvement in revolutionary activity, and finally contributes to his death by betraying him to the Austrians in George Meredith's *Vittoria*.

Wilfred of Ivanhoe (Desdichado)   Noble young Saxon knight who is disinherited by his father, Cedric the Saxon, because he loves Lady Rowena; he follows King Richard to Palestine; as Desdichado (The Disinherited) he becomes champion of the tournament at Ashby; he rescues Rebecca from the Templars before marrying Rowena with Cedric's blessing in Sir Walter Scott's *Ivanhoe*.

Allan Iverach   Inverashalloch's friend and one of Rob Roy MacGregor's enemies, whom Francis Osbaldistone and Bailie Jarvie fight with in the inn at Clachan of Aberfoil in Sir Walter Scott's *Rob Roy*.

Duc d' Ivry   Young-looking old French nobleman; he marries a woman forty-five years younger than himself and is disappointed that his only child is a girl; the Comte de Florac inherits his title in William Makepeace Thackeray's *The Newcomes*.

Duchesse d' Ivry   Immoral relative of the Florac family; her attempted seduction of Lord Kew nearly brings about his death in William Makepeace Thackeray's *The Newcomes.*

Antoinette d' Ivry   Neglected young daughter of the Duc and Duchesse; her father places her in the care of the Comtesse de Florac in William Makepeace Thackeray's *The Newcomes.*

Dick Ivy   London poet, who is an acquaintance of Jery Melford, and who is recently out of the Fleet in Tobias Smollett's *The Expedition of Humphry Clinker.*

J

Jabaster High priest, who teaches and later counsels Alroy during the "holy war" against the occupying Turks in Benjamin Disraeli's *The Wondrous Tale of Alroy*.

Jabberwocky A dragon-like monster, slain by the beamish boy in a poem Alice finds in the looking-glass drawing-room in Lewis Carroll's *Through the Looking-Glass*.

Joan Jablinouski Wife of Aldrovandus Magnus and a present from Duke Podebrac in William Beckford's *Biographical Memoirs of Extraordinary Painters*.

Jock Jabos Postilion at the Gordon Arms; he mistakenly tells Henry Bertram that Julia Mannering is to marry Charles Hazzelwood; as a boy, he had guided Guy Mannering to the Bertram household in Sir Walter Scott's *Guy Mannering*.

Donna Jacinta Widow who has to sell herself to get money in Eliza Haywood's *The Rash Resolve; or, the Untimely Discovery*.

Jacintha Antonia and Elvira de las Cisternas's landlady, whose credulousness assists Ambrosio in making Antonia his prisoner in Matthew Lewis's *The Monk*.

Jack Sentinel guarding Ensign Northerton; he mistakes Tom Jones for a ghost and is accused of allowing Northerton to escape in Henry Fielding's *The History of Tom Jones*.

Jack Young buck at Vauxhall who harasses Amelia Booth despite the presence of Dr. Harrison and his friends in Henry Fielding's *Amelia*.

Jack Disabled British soldier whose tragic life story exemplifies the manifold hardships and intrepidity of the poor in an account by Lien Chi Altangi in Oliver Goldsmith's *The Citizen of the World*.

Jack One of Ellis Duckworth's men; he warns Dick Shelton about sailing the *Good Hope* in a storm when he is set to guard her in Robert Louis Stevenson's *The Black Arrow: A Tale of Two Roses*.

Jack (Man of the Hill) Elderly recluse whom Tom Jones rescues from robbers; he relays his history—a tale of corruption, redemption, and ultimate disillusionment, which prompts his withdrawal from society in Henry Fielding's *The History of Tom Jones*.

Black Jack See John McGinty.

Captain Jack ("horrid Jack") Eldest of the three Jack boys raised by Colonel Jack's nurse and the only one who is her actual son; he is sly and revengeful and becomes a kidnapper in Daniel Defoe's *The History and the Remarkable Life of the Truly Honourable Colonel Jacques, Commonly Call'd Col. Jack*.

Colonel Jack (John, Colonel Jacque, Monsieur Charnot, Monsieur Charnock) Supposed son of a gentleman; he is raised by a nurse and, when she dies, becomes a street thief and pickpocket until he is transported to Virginia; there he goes from servant to plantation owner and later marries five times, fights bravely in the wars, and finally becomes a pentitent in Daniel Defoe's *The History and the Remarkable Life of the Truly Honourable Colonel Jacques, Commonly Call'd Col. Jack*.

Colonel Jack's Second Wife Italian woman whom Colonel Jack marries while in the military; he is convinced she is unfaithful, and he leaves her to return to England in Daniel Defoe's *The History and the Remarkable Life of the Truly Honourable Colonel Jacques, Commonly Call'd Col. Jack*.

Colonel Jack's Third Wife Ship captain's widow, who becomes a slave to alcohol after marrying Colonel Jack; she twice commits adultery with another ship captain while drunk and finally commits suicide in Daniel Defoe's *The History and the Remarkable Life of the Truly Honourable Colonel Jacques, Commonly Call'd Col. Jack*.

Chaffing Jack Sly, eccentric informant, who assists Stephen Morley and Walter Gerard in their attempt to locate Baptiste Hatton so that they can recover Gerard's inheritance in Benjamin Disraeli's *Sybil*.

Long Jack Grizzly-chinned, long-lipped Galway fisherman on the cod-fishing boat that rescues Harvey Cheyne in Rudyard Kipling's *"Captains Courageous": A Story of the Grand Banks*.

Major Anthony Jack Youngest of the three Jack boys raised by Colonel Jack's nurse; he is a merry and facetious thief, who is finally broken on the wheel for robbery in France in Daniel Defoe's *The History and the Remarkable Life of the Truly Honourable Colonel Jacques, Commonly Call'd Col. Jack*.

Mrs. Jacks Proper but flirtatious wife of John Jacks in George Gissing's *The Crown of Life*.

Arnold Jacks Egotistic patriot, politician, and empire enthusiast who is rejected by his bride-to-be in George Gissing's *The Crown of Life*.

John Jacks Conscientious member of Parliament who

is skeptical of British nationalism in George Gissing's *The Crown of Life*.

Major Jackson Old military-style gentleman who lives in Gylingden; he acts as Stanley Lake's second in the duel with Sir Harry Bracton in J. Sheridan Le Fanu's *Wylder's Hand*.

Mr. Jackson Domestic tutor of the Brother of the Little Girl; he is a coxcomb and prefers to flatter his benefactors rather than to educate his charge in Francis Coventry's *The History of Pompey the Little*.

Mr. Jackson Cowardly clergyman, to whom Eleanor Grimshaw appeals for help in a ghost story interpolated into the narrative of William Beckford's *Azemia*.

Mr. Jackson Employee of Dodson and Fogg in Charles Dickens's *The Posthumous Papers of the Pickwick Club*.

Mr. Jackson The first man with whom Agnes Grey's father overextends his credit in Anne Brontë's *Agnes Grey*.

John Jackson Fellow job applicant, who explains to Roderick Random how to qualify for the position of navy surgeon's mate, reveals Staytape's real business, borrows money from Roderick in London, tries to trick surgeons' examiners and is briefly imprisoned, is discovered by Roderick in the Marshalsea for debts made by his wife, and introduces the poet Melopoyn to Roderick in Tobias Smollett's *The Adventures of Roderick Random*.

Polly Jackson A baker's daughter, who is an "academical" miss from Cambridge, and who is an admirer of Williams in Francis Coventry's *The History of Pompey the Little*.

Thomas Jackson A villager in Horton whom the rector, Mr. Hatfield, would like to exhort because of his hope of a resurrection on the last day in Anne Brontë's *Agnes Grey*.

Jacky Australian aborigine whom George Fielding rescues from a shark and who then befriends George in many ways without accepting "the white man's strange ways," in Charles Reade's *It Is Never Too Late to Mend*.

Jacob A man close at hand when Eliza Millward tells Gilbert Markham that Helen Huntingdon is about to remarry in Anne Brontë's *The Tenant of Wildfell Hall*.

Madame Jacob Grim, widowed sister of Pasteur Tourneur; she makes Elizabeth Gilmour's life a misery in Anne Thackeray Ritchie's *The Story of Elizabeth*.

Mrs. Jacox The mother of Bella Jacox, the young girl Malkin intends for his wife; she erroneously believes that she is herself the object of his matrimonial intentions in George Gissing's *Born in Exile*.

Bella Jacox Young girl whom Malkin trains as his future wife and ultimately marries in George Gissing's *Born in Exile*.

Martha Jacquelot Cousin and companion of John Buncle's fifth wife, Miss Turner of Skelsmore-Vale; she paints, plays the fiddle, and is witty; later she marries and moves to London in Thomas Amory's *The Life of John Buncle, Esq*.

Jacques Servant to Phillippe de Montalt; he informs Theodore Peyron of Montalt's plan to seduce Adeline in Ann Radcliffe's *The Romance of the Forest*.

Jacques One Revolutionist and associate of Ernest Defarge in Charles Dickens's *A Tale of Two Cities*.

Jacques Two Revolutionist and associate of Ernest Defarge in Charles Dickens's *A Tale of Two Cities*.

Jacques Three Revolutionist and associate of Ernest Defarge in Charles Dickens's *A Tale of Two Cities*.

Jacques Four See Ernest Defarge.

Jacques Five A road-mender and one of the *jacquerie* who travel under the same name in order to avoid detection in pre-revolutionary France in Charles Dickens's *A Tale of Two Cities*.

Mr. Jaggers The lawyer who acts for Abel Magwitch as Pip Pirrip's guardian and writes out the drafts of money that Pip thinks Miss Havisham has given him; Jaggers is also responsible for Estella's adoption by Miss Havisham and employs Molly, Estella's mother and Magwitch's former lover, in Charles Dickens's *Great Expectations*.

Jahamel Sister of Georigetti in Robert Paltock's *The Life and Adventures of Peter Wilkins*.

Mrs. Jakeman Head housekeeper for Barnabas Tyrrel and friend and instructress to Emily Melville; she is sent on a journey so that she is not available to help Emily during her marriage crisis in William Godwin's *Caleb Williams*.

Mrs. Jakin Bob Jakin's oversized mother in George Eliot's *The Mill on the Floss*.

Bob Jakin Tom Tulliver's childhood acquaintance, who later becomes a clever packman and involves Tom Tulliver in his business; Bob and his mother allow Maggie Tulliver to live in their home after her disgrace in George Eliot's *The Mill on the Floss*.

Prissy Jakin Bob Jakin's dainty wife in George Eliot's *The Mill on the Floss*.

Mary Jalland Bernard Kingcote's sister, left impoverished when her husband dies; Kingcote is forced to come back to London to support her in George Gissing's *Isabel Clarendon*.

Jamella Persecuted heroine, who is first abducted by Clodius, then captured by a male siren in Jane Barker's *Exilius; or, The Banish'd Roman*.

James Guard who deserts Malcolm's forces and enlists his brother Edmund in a plan to rescue Osbert from Castle Dunbayne in Ann Radcliffe's *The Castles of Athlin and Dunbayne*.

James Mr. Armstrong's gardener, who scorns Mrs. Bullen's criticisms of the vicar's astronomy in Mark Rutherford's *Miriam's Schooling*.

James Youngest son of Christian and Christiana; he marries Phebe, daughter of Gaius, in John Bunyan's *The Pilgrim's Progress From this World to That Which Is to Come*.

James Old servant of Matilda and Ellinor in Sophia Lee's *The Recess*.

Captain James Naval officer chosen by Lady Ludlow to succeed Mr. Horner as steward; he marries Miss Brooke in Elizabeth Gaskell's *My Lady Ludlow*.

King James James VI of Scotland and later James I of England; he is the corrupt and hypocritical monarch who imprisons his half sister Matilda and her daughter, Mary, in Sophia Lee's *The Recess*. He is the clownish king of Great Britain; he orders Nigel Olifaunt imprisoned when he thinks Nigel is trying to kill him, spies on Nigel in prison with Margaret Ramsay, orders Lord Dalgarno to marry Lady Hermione, and approves the marriage of Nigel and Margaret Ramsay when he discovers she is of noble background in Sir Walter Scott's *The Fortunes of Nigel*.

Mr. James Devoted servant in the household of Henry Clinton in Henry Brooke's *The Fool of Quality*.

Jenny Bath James Impoverished sister of Colonel Bath; she marries Colonel James to become a fine lady; vanity dims her friendship with Amelia Booth in Henry Fielding's *Amelia*.

Robert (Bob) James Wealthy colonel whose patronage and friendship support the Booths; in undertaking his pursuit of Fanny Matthews he uses the pen name Damon; his desire for Amelia Booth motivates and ultimately damages his friendship with William Booth in Henry Fielding's *Amelia*.

Mrs. Jamieson The snobbish and self-centered self-appointed leader of genteel society in Cranford after Deborah Jenkyns's death in Elizabeth Gaskell's *Cranford*.

Bet Jamieson Housekeeper and nurse in the Gray household, who entertains Richard Middlemas with romantic accounts of his parentage in Sir Walter Scott's *The Surgeon's Daughter*.

Jamoan Leader of an enemy army; he is captured by Oroonoko and becomes his devoted follower in Aphra Behn's *Oroonoko*.

Jane Servant of Mr. and Mrs. Pott of Eatanswill in Charles Dickens's *The Posthumous Papers of the Pickwick Club*.

Jane Maidservant at Manor Farm, Dingley Dell, in Charles Dickens's *The Posthumous Papers of the Pickwick Club*.

Jane Maid who lies in bed with her mistress's friend while her mistress goes to other customers in Charles Johnstone's *Chrysal: or, The Adventures of a Guinea*.

Jane (Little Jane) Martin Tinman's underpaid servant, who salvages from his flooded house the letter that exposes his betrayal of Smith (Ribstone) in George Meredith's *The House on the Beach*.

Janet Pretty maid of Betsey Trotwood in Charles Dickens's *The Personal History of David Copperfield*.

Emperor of Japan Ruler who suspects that Lemuel Gulliver, because he requests exemption from trampling on a crucifix, is not Dutch in Jonathan Swift's *Travels into Several Remote Nations of the World. In Four Parts. By Lemuel Gulliver*.

Victoire Jaquêtanàpe Dapper Frenchman, who marries Clementina Golightly for her fortune in Anthony Trollope's *The Three Clerks*.

Jaques The faithful servant who tries to save Clement de Crequy in Elizabeth Gaskell's *My Lady Ludlow*.

Jaquez Comic servant who, with his fellow servant, Diego, rushes in to give an incoherent report of a supernatural visitation they have witnessed in Horace Walpole's *The Castle of Otranto*.

Mrs. Jarley Stout, kindhearted owner of "Mrs. Jarley's

Waxworks," who hires Nell Trent to show the waxworks to customers and lets Nell's grandfather stay also in Charles Dickens's *The Old Curiosity Shop*.

John Jarndyce   Guardian to Ada Clare, Richard Carstone, and Esther Summerson; he is kindly and generous, trying to undo the harm of the Chancery suit Jarndyce and Jarndyce; he wishes to marry Esther but instead arranges to have her marry the man she loves, Allan Woodcourt, in Charles Dickens's *Bleak House*.

Tom Jarndyce   Former suitor in the Jarndyce and Jarndyce case, who eventually blew his brains out, leaving Bleak House to John Jarndyce in Charles Dickens's *Bleak House*.

Nicol Jarvie (Bailie Jarvie)   Rotund Glasgow bailie and merchant and an honorable businessman; a strongheaded kinsman of Rob Roy MacGregor, he accompanies Francis Osbaldistone on a dangerous Highland mission for the firm of Osbaldistone and Tresham, for whom he acts as Glasgow agent in Sir Walter Scott's *Rob Roy*.

Jasper   Elderly plowman at Glendearg in Sir Walter Scott's *The Monastery*.

John Jasper   Music teacher by day in Cloisterham, where he also acts as choirmaster in the cathedral; by night he often travels to Princess Puffer's opium den in London, where he smokes and dreams (ambiguously) of killing his nephew and marrying Rosa Bud in Charles Dickens's *The Mystery of Edwin Drood*.

Charles Jawleyford   Gentleman who invites Soapey Sponge to his house, assuming him to be wealthy; he has great difficulty getting Sponge to leave when he finds out that Sponge is penniless in Robert Surtees's *Mr. Sponge's Sporting Tour*.

Jeanette   Woodcutter's daughter, who becomes the caretaker of the mad Julia Wiemar in Charlotte Dacre's *The Passions*.

Mr. Jeans   Adolphus and George Delmont's private tutor at Eton who condemns George's philanthropic instincts; his departure as Adolphus's traveling companion abroad liberates George's education in Charlotte Smith's *The Young Philosopher*.

Dr. Jeddler   A man whose philosophy of the world is shattered because his house is no longer happy after his daughter Marion's departure; the old battleground where he lives symbolizes his own battle for happiness in Charles Dickens's *The Battle of Life*.

Grace Jeddler   Doctor Jeddler's selfless, retiring elder daughter, who mothers her younger sister, Marion, loves her family, and is loved in return; she secretly loves Alfred Heathfield, and after her sister leaves, apparently having eloped with Michael Warden, she marries Heathfield in Charles Dickens's *The Battle of Life*.

Marion Jeddler   Devoted younger sister of Grace Jeddler and a complex character; loved by both Alfred Heathfield and Michael Warden, she runs away when Warden leaves, simulating an elopement, in order to facilitate her sister's love for Heathfield; after living with her spinster aunt, she returns and marries Michael Warden in Charles Dickens's *The Battle of Life*.

Martha Jeddler   Doctor Jeddler's unmarried sister, with whom Marion Jeddler lives while she is believed to have run away with Michael Warden in Charles Dickens's *The Battle of Life*.

Captain Henry Jekyl   Friend and confidant of the usurping Earl of Etherington (Valentine Bulmer); he serves as mediator between Etherington and Francis Tyrrel in Sir Walter Scott's *St. Ronan's Well*.

Mrs. Jekyll   The housekeeper who gossips ill-naturedly of Flora Macfuss Pullens's methods of housekeeping in Susan Ferrier's *Marriage*.

Dr. Henry Jekyll   Brilliant scientist, medical man, and philanthropic gentleman led to dangerous and ingenious experimentation which periodically liberates his troubling moral duality by transforming him into an evil alter ego—the pale, dwarfish Edward Hyde, who tramples over a child and clubs Sir Danvers Carew to death; although Dr. Jekyll makes Hyde his heir by will, when he is finally unable to restore his original personality, he kills himself in the person of Hyde in Robert Louis Stevenson's *The Strange Case of Dr. Jekyll and Mr. Hyde*.

Mr. Jellyby   Mrs. Jellyby's mild, bald, silent, and despairing spouse, who eventually goes bankrupt in Charles Dickens's *Bleak House*.

Mrs. Jellyby   Philanthropic woman dedicated to missions in Borioboola-Gha but neglectful of her family and household, which is in shambles, in Charles Dickens's *Bleak House*.

Caroline (Caddy) Jellyby   Oldest daughter of the Jellybys; she is her mother's resentful secretary, tries to mother her siblings, and eventually marries Prince Turveydrop in Charles Dickens's *Bleak House*.

Peepy Jellyby   Younger Jellyby child who is constantly in physical danger in Charles Dickens's *Bleak House*.

Conkey Jem   Ferryman with a huge nose; he is killed

while betraying Dick Turpin in William Harrison Ainsworth's *Rookwood*.

Jemima   Oppressed and misanthropic ex-prostitute and outcast, who serves as ambivalent caretaker in a private madhouse and is restored by Maria Venable's example to sensibility and benevolence in Mary Wollstonecraft's *Maria; or The Wrongs of Woman*.

Jemima   Sister of Polly Toodle; she looks after Mr. Toodle and Polly's children while Polly is a wet nurse to the infant Paul Dombey in Charles Dickens's *Dombey and Son*.

Jemmy (Wilkins)   A son of Peter Wilkins and Youwarkee in Robert Paltock's *The Life and Adventures of Peter Wilkins*.

Jenkins   Clergyman who is awarded a living by Sir Launcelot Greaves in Tobias Smollett's *The Adventures of Sir Launcelot Greaves*.

Rose Jenkins   Villager and recipient of Henry Clinton's charity; she praises the man's benevolence to the Fieldings in Henry Brooke's *The Fool of Quality*.

Winifrid Jenkins   Maidservant of Liddy Melford; she flirts with Humphry Clinker and with Dutton until Dutton runs off with another; she then marries Humphry Clinker, though he is discovered to belong to another social class in Tobias Smollett's *The Expedition of Humphry Clinker*.

Jenkinson   Messenger in the Circumlocution Office in Charles Dickens's *Little Dorrit*.

Mr. Jenkinson   "Status-quo-ite," who expresses the belief that the world stays much the same in Thomas Love Peacock's *Headlong Hall*.

Mrs. Jenkinson   Miss de Bourgh's companion in Jane Austen's *Pride and Prejudice*.

Ephram Jenkinson   Reformed con man encountered by Dr. Charles Primrose in prison; he formerly victimized both Primrose and Moses Primrose but ultimately saves the Primrose family by being the instrument whereby the wicked Squire Thornhill is exposed in Oliver Goldsmith's *The Vicar of Wakefield*.

Jacquetta Agenta Martiana Jenks   Fictional author of *Azemia*, her first novel, which she hopes is innocuous enough to earn the praise of readers and reviewers; she devotes one chapter to her philosophy of novel writing and another to thanking critics in advance for the praise she expects to receive in William Beckford's *Azemia*.

Deborah Jenkyns   Elder sister of Matilda Jenkyns, whom she dominates; as daughter of the rector, she is a recognized social arbiter until her death in Elizabeth Gaskell's *Cranford*.

Matilda (Miss Matty) Jenkyns   The gentle and unaffected younger sister of Deborah Jenkyns; having rejected a suitor in her youth in order to stay with her mother, she finds the responsibility for herself difficult after the death of her sister, Deborah, in Elizabeth Gaskell's *Cranford*.

Peter Jenkyns   The long-lost brother of Matilda Jenkyns; he is finally reunited with her in Elizabeth Gaskell's *Cranford*.

Lieutenant Jenna   Austrian officer; he quarrels with Wilfrid Pole in George Meredith's *Vittoria*.

Mrs. Jennett   Amiable keeper of a boarding house in Henry Brooke's *The Fool of Quality*.

Sukey Jennett   One of the nine pupils of Mrs. Teachum's school; she learns to control her passionate nature in Sarah Fielding's *The Governess*.

Jennings   Henry Lambert's military friend, who assists with the preparation of a ghostly banquet in a ruined abbey in William Beckford's *Modern Novel Writing; or, the Elegant Enthusiast*.

Jennings   Tutor who undertakes to manage Perry Pickle at boarding school and leaves when he learns the master has spied on him in Tobias Smollett's *The Adventures of Peregrine Pickle*.

Mrs. Jennings   Good-hearted, vulgar, match-making widow of a wealthy tradesman; she is the mother of Charlotte Palmer and Lady Middleton; she befriends Elinor and Marianne Dashwood and takes them to London with her; her unfailing but sometimes comically over-solicitous kindness wins Elinor's affection in Jane Austen's *Sense and Sensibility*.

Ezra Jennings   Eccentric, solitary medical assistant to Mr. Candy in the village of Frizinghall; long addicted to opium, he exerts strange fascination over Franklin Blake; by an ingenious opium experiment, he unlocks the mystery concerning Blake and a stolen yellow diamond in Wilkie Collins's *The Moonstone. A Romance*.

Jack Jennings   Impoverished London boy whom Harry Bolton helps in Henry Mackenzie's *The Man of the World*.

Margaret Jennings   Granddaughter of Job Legh and friend of Mary Barton; she gradually goes blind; she becomes a well-known singer and marries Will Wilson in Elizabeth Gaskell's *Mary Barton*.

Jenny Sensible servant to young Mr. Miles in Australia; she befriends fellow servant Tom Robinson and becomes his wife on his return to Australia; she understands his restless nature and travels with him in Charles Reade's *It Is Never Too Late to Mend*.

Jenny Tristram Shandy's female friend, or possibly daughter, though his coy insistence that she is neither his wife nor his mistress seems too much protested; she is frequently alluded to as a kind of feminine ideal in Laurence Sterne's *The Life and Opinions of Tristram Shandy, Gentleman*.

Jenny Passenger in a wagon to London; she makes Isaac Rapine pay for raping her in Tobias Smollett's *The Adventures of Roderick Random*.

Jenny A brickmaker's wife whose baby dies; she keeps the handkerchief Esther Summerson lays on the baby and later gives it to Lady Dedlock; she exchanges clothing with the fleeing Lady Dedlock in Charles Dickens's *Bleak House*.

Jenny Amoranda's maidservant in Mary Davys's *The Reform'd Coquet*.

Miss Jenny An "academical" miss from a coffee-house, who is an admirer of Williams in Francis Coventry's *The History of Pompey the Little*.

Mr. Jephson Kinsman of the Anneslys, who tries to guide Billy Annesly and finally informs his father of his slipping from virtue in Henry Mackenzie's *The Man of the World*.

Young Jeremy Hero of a silly poem written by the Reverend Solomon Sheeppen, who thinks blank verse is merely the absence of rhyme in William Beckford's *Azemia*.

Mrs. Jermyn Matthew Jermyn's socially aspiring wife in George Eliot's *Felix Holt, the Radical*.

Louisa Jermyn Daughter of Matthew Jermyn; she takes French lessons from Esther Lyon in George Eliot's *Felix Holt, the Radical*.

Matthew Jermyn The wealthy, underhanded lawyer who has been cheating the Transome family for years, even though he once loved Arabella Transome and is father to her second son, the apparent heir, in George Eliot's *Felix Holt, the Radical*.

Jerome Abbot of the Convent of Saint Bride and an English ally; he is venerable and influential but loves money and his little comforts in Sir Walter Scott's *Castle Dangerous*.

Fra Jerome Giant Dominican friar, who helps Gerard to land from a shipwreck and later nurses him back to health in a Roman monastery; he sends the Princess Claelia Cesarini to Loretto on a pilgrimage of penitence; as new prior to the Dominican convent at Gouda, he renews fellowship with Gerard, who has come there to die; Jerome dies a mitred abbot but alone, revered, and unloved in Charles Reade's *The Cloister and the Hearth*.

Monsieur Jerome Mysterious "concierge" of the castle on the Rhine who offers Deloraine and Catherine, his daughter, refuge—at a price—and then betrays them to the pursuing Travers in William Godwin's *Deloraine*.

Father Jerome (Count of Falconara) Priest who aids the victimized heroine and is finally revealed to be the father of Theodore, the rightful heir to Otranto, in Horace Walpole's *The Castle of Otranto*.

Friar Jeronimo Deceitful friar, who betrays Vincentio de Vivaldi in his plan to smuggle Ellena Rosalba from the San Stefano convent in Ann Radcliffe's *The Italian*.

Jerry Gardener whom Harry Bolton employs to protect Lucy Sindall and spy on Sir Thomas Sindall when he learns of Sindall's advances towards Lucy in Henry Mackenzie's *The Man of the World*.

Jerry Manager of a troupe of dancing dogs, who meets Nell Trent, her grandfather, Tom Codlin, and Harris Short in an inn in Charles Dickens's *The Old Curiosity Shop*.

Miss Jervis Kind, loving, but proper governess, who accompanies Elizabeth Raby and John Falkner on their travels in Mary Shelley's *Falkner*.

Mrs. Jervis Housekeeper on Mr. B——'s Bedfordshire estate; she befriends and protects Pamela Andrews from their master's attempts at seduction, incurring his wrath and her consequent loss of position, to which she is ultimately restored upon Pamela's intercession in Samuel Richardson's *Pamela, or Virtue Rewarded*.

Lucretia Jervis Squire John Booby's maidservant who, following orders, arranges a chance for him to ravish Shamela Andrews; she is part of Booby's servants' conspiracy to extract a comfortable settlement for Shamela in Henry Fielding's *An Apology for the Life of Mrs. Shamela Andrews*.

Emily Jervois Sir Charles Grandison's ward, who only gradually recognizes what Harriet Byron long suspects: that her gratitude and admiration mask deep feelings of romantic love; she behaves sensibly upon his marriage to Harriet; her returning the love of the "second Sir Charles," his virtuous young friend Sir Edward Beauchamp, is anticipated at the end of Samuel Richardson's *Sir Charles Grandison.*

Jemmy Jessamy   Honest hero, who works at being a good man for Jenny in Eliza Haywood's *The History of Jemmy and Jenny Jessamy.*

Jenny Jessamy   Liberated heroine, who allows Jemmy Jessamy to sow all his wild oats before she marries him in Eliza Haywood's *The History of Jemmy and Jenny Jessamy.*

Jesuit   Corrupt churchman, who demands gold and a son from the Peruvian as payment for forgiveness, and who easily forgives an Army Commander for heinous crimes in Charles Johnstone's *Chrysal: or, the Adventures of a Guinea.*

Jesuit from Peru   Cleric who explains the role of Jesuits as international conspirators who sow dissension between people and their governments, and who tries, unsuccessfully, to overthrow the King of Portugal in Charles Johnstone's *Chrysal: or, The Adventures of a Guinea.*

Jesus of Nazareth   Essene with a message that convinces many, including Joseph of Arimathea; he is crucified and put in Joseph's tomb, then cured secretly; he returns to the Essene monastery to manage the sheep, convinced that he has sinned in claiming he was the Messiah in George Moore's *The Brook Kerith.*

Felix Jethway   Youth unintentionally encouraged by Elfride Swancourt; rebuffed trying to kiss her, he languishes; his mother blames Elfride for his death and destroys Henry Knight's faith in her in Thomas Hardy's *A Pair of Blue Eyes.*

Gertrude Jethway   A poor widow who blames Elfride Swancourt for the death of her son and, just before her death in the fall of the undermined church tower, sends Henry Knight a letter which causes him to break with Elfride in Thomas Hardy's *A Pair of Blue Eyes.*

Mr. Jetsome   Young man, endangered by drink, who manages Dorlcote Mill for John Wakem after Edward Tulliver's death in George Eliot's *The Mill on the Floss.*

The Jew   Provider of early art instruction to Og of Basan and Andrew Guelph in William Beckford's *Biographical Memoirs of Extraordinary Painters.*

Jewish Butcher   Peddler and miser who cheats his customers and takes part in the "sacrifice of the Passover" in Charles Johnstone's *Chrysal: or, The Adventures of a Guinea.*

Jewish Jeweller   Merchant who at first attempts to buy jewels from Roxana, but then, believing them to be stolen, tries to have Roxana arrested and prosecuted in Daniel Defoe's *The Fortunate Mistress.*

Mrs. Jewkes   Housekeeper on Mr. B——'s Lincolnshire estate; she acts as jailer and veritable procuress when Pamela Andrews is abducted on Mr. B——'s orders; she is persuaded to piety by Pamela's forgiveness and mercy after Pamela marries Mr. B——; she then lives worthily until her early death in Samuel Richardson's *Pamela, or Virtue Rewarded.*

Nancy (Nanny) Jewkes   John Booby's servant in Lincolnshire who suspects Shamela Andrews's true nature; she recommends Booby to Shamela, then holds Shamela's arm when Booby attempts to rape her in Henry Fielding's *An Apology for the Life of Mrs. Shamela Andrews.*

Jim   Hunter, guide, and servant of George Curtis; he loses directions for King Solomon's mines and looses a boulder on George Curtis's leg; they are forced to spend two years at an oasis until Sir Henry Curtis rescues them in H. Rider Haggard's *King Solomon's Mines.*

Cripple Jim   Nanny's street friend, who is brought into Mr. Raymond's household along with Nanny and Diamond's family in George MacDonald's *At the Back of the North Wind.*

Alfred Jingle (Charles Fitz-Marshall)   Rascally theatrical itinerant, who dupes Samuel Pickwick and his friends, elopes with Rachael Wardle, and eventually ends up in the Fleet prison and is rescued by Pickwick in Charles Dickens's *The Posthumous Papers of the Pickwick Club.*

Mrs. Jiniwin   Shrewish mother of Betsy Quilp; she lives with the Quilps, quarrels with Daniel Quilp, and nags her daughter in Charles Dickens's *The Old Curiosity Shop.*

Mr. Jinkins   A bookkeeper, the oldest and acknowledged first of the boarders at Todgers's; his claim to Mercy Pecksniff's attention makes him the object of Augustus Moddle's maudlin hatred in Charles Dickens's *The Life and Adventures of Martin Chuzzlewit.*

Mr. Jinkins   Deceitful beau of a widow who owns an inn in "The Bagman's Tale," told by a one-eyed bagman in Charles Dickens's *The Posthumous Papers of the Pickwick Club.*

Mr. Jinks   Shabby clerk and adviser to George Nupkins in Charles Dickens's *The Posthumous Papers of the Pickwick Club.*

Jo Ragged boy in Tom-All-Alone's who sweeps the crossing; he testifies at the inquest on Nemo's death; he is befriended by Mr. Snagsby but is chased out of London; dying of fever, he is aided by Charley Neckett and Esther Summerson, who become successively ill in Charles Dickens's *Bleak House*.

Princess Joan Louis XI's timid and deformed youngest daughter; though she loves the Duke of Orleans, to whom she is betrothed, he loathes her in Sir Walter Scott's *Quentin Durward*.

Job Respectable, round-faced, matter-of-fact male attendant, hired by Ludwig Horace Holly for his adopted son, Leo Vincey; he accompanies Holly and Leo on their quest to the interior of Africa; he dies of terror after the dreadful transformation and death of She in H. Rider Haggard's *She*.

John Jobling Unscrupulous consulting physician to the Anglo-Bengalee Disinterested Loan and Life Assurance Company in Charles Dickens's *The Life and Adventures of Martin Chuzzlewit*.

Tony Jobling (Mr. Weevle) Mr. Guppy's seedy friend, who lodges in the room where Nemo died in order to help Guppy find papers related to Captain Hawdon, Lady Dedlock, and Esther Summerson in Charles Dickens's *Bleak House*.

Joseph Jobson Squire Inglewood's enthusiastic clerk, whose illegal activities get him dismissed from the list of attorneys in Sir Walter Scott's *Rob Roy*.

Emily, Lady Jocelyn Rose's unconventional mother; she acts justly toward Evan Harrington in George Meredith's *Evan Harrington*.

Sir Franks Jocelyn Rose's father in George Meredith's *Evan Harrington*.

Harry Jocelyn Rose's brother, in disgrace for fathering an illegitimate baby; after other mishaps, he agrees to marry his child's mother in George Meredith's *Evan Harrington*.

Rose Jocelyn Wealthy young lady who overcomes her aversion to tradesmen to fall in love with Evan Harrington, a tailor's son; the two are almost separated by a plot to discredit his rival, but Rose discovers his innocence and the two marry in George Meredith's *Evan Harrington*.

Slounging Jock David MacGuffog's assistant at the jail; he helps to capture Jans Janson (Dirk Hatteraick) in Sir Walter Scott's *Guy Mannering*.

Elinor Joddrel Niece of Mrs. Maple; she is in love with Albert Harleigh and tries to commit suicide twice because he will not return her love; she is persuaded by Albert to abandon suicide for religion in Frances Burney's *The Wanderer*.

Selina Joddrel Fourteen-year-old sister of Elinor Joddrel; she is betrothed to Ireton; hypocritical in her friendship with the Stranger, Juliet Granville, she snubs Juliet for a socially superior life in the end in Frances Burney's *The Wanderer*.

Joe The fat boy who works for Mr. Wardle and who either eats or falls asleep in Charles Dickens's *The Posthumous Papers of the Pickwick Club*.

Joe Working man at the river wharf who fetches Walter Gay to attend to the lost Florence Dombey in Charles Dickens's *Dombey and Son*.

Old Joe Pawnbroker and dealer in rags and bones who appears in one of the scenes in the visitation of the Ghost of Christmas Yet to Come; he receives goods stolen from the deceased Ebenezer Scrooge in Charles Dickens's *A Christmas Carol*.

Joey Wagon driver who picks up Roderick Random and Hugh Strap on their way to London in Tobias Smollett's *The Adventures of Roderick Random*.

Grand Duke of Johannisberg Revolting leader of a group of German wine-drinking nobles, from whom Vivian Grey and Essper George barely escape in Benjamin Disraeli's *Vivian Grey*.

John One of Arthur Huntingdon's servants in Anne Brontë's *The Tenant of Wildfell Hall*.

John London chop-house waiter, who is rescued from despair at his wife's alcoholism by M'Kay and Mark Rutherford when they turn his attention to the needs of his son, Tom, in Mark Rutherford's *Mark Rutherford's Deliverance*.

John Coachman from the north country and formerly driver for Theobald Pontifex; he is the probable first husband of Ellen and father of her baby; when Ernest Pontifex gives Ellen everything in his pocket upon her expulsion and Theobald threatens him, John receives Ernest's gratitude by defending Ernest and warning Theobald not to hurt him in Samuel Butler's *The Way of All Flesh*.

John Alcoholic juggler of "The Stroller's Tale," related by Dismal Jemmy (Trotter) in Charles Dickens's *The Posthumous Papers of the Pickwick Club*.

John Servant at the Keeldar home in Charlotte Brontë's *Shirley*.

John   Mr. Rochester's taciturn coachman, who accompanies Mr. Rochester to Ferndean after the fire at Thornfield Hall in Charlotte Brontë's *Jane Eyre*.

John   Manservant in the Booby household who recognizes and rescues Fanny Goodwill from her abductor in Henry Fielding's *The History of the Adventures of Mr. Joseph Andrews and of his Friend Mr. Abraham Adams*.

John   Unemployed worker with whom Florence Dombey speaks, noticing his devotion to his sullen and ill daughter, Martha, in Charles Dickens's *Dombey and Son*.

John   Amiable footman in the household of Lord Clinton in Henry Brooke's *The Fool of Quality*.

John (Captain John)   Bisquit-maker, former soldier, and brother of Thomas; he joins his brother and Richard the joiner in leaving Wapping; he is chosen leader of the small band of travelers going to Epping who live in huts on the outskirts of villages in Daniel Defoe's *A Journal of the Plague Year*.

Corporal John   Loudon Dodd's American painter friend, who is present at Genius of Muskegon's judging in Robert Louis Stevenson's *The Wrecker*.

Prince John   Brother and adversary of Prince Richard in Sir Walter Scott's *The Betrothed*. He is King Richard's traitorous brother, who plots to usurp his kingdom while Richard is in Palestine in *Ivanhoe*.

John-of-Mally's-of-Hannah's-of-Deb's   One of the suitors of Sarah, servant of Robert and Hortense Moore in Charlotte Brontë's *Shirley*.

John of Moidart   Captain of Clan Roland, serving in Montrose's army in Sir Walter Scott's *A Legend of Montrose*.

Johnny   One of the pirates who desert Pew in their flight after the raid on the Admiral Benbow Inn in Robert Louis Stevenson's *Treasure Island*.

Johnny   Young cousin to the schoolmaster Mr. Selkirk; he demonstrates Selkirk's pedagogy by jumping around and shouting Latin pronouns in Richard Graves's *The Spiritual Quixote*.

John Paul   Servant at Durrisdeer loyal to the master (James Durie); he usually carries Jessie Brown's pension; he is dismissed by Henry Durie for admitting the Master when he returns from India in Robert Louis Stevenson's *The Master of Ballantrae: A Winter's Tale*.

Johnson   Pupil at Dr. Blimber's boarding school in Charles Dickens's *Dombey and Son*.

Johnson   Inarticulate third officer of the *Gleaner*; he sails with Captain Nares and Loudon Dodd on the *Norah Creina* in Robert Louis Stevenson's *The Wrecker*.

Captain Johnson   Young army officer who recounts to Geoffry Wildgoose his botched attempt to help a married Parisian woman, Lady Ruelle, escape to England; he later allows a young Englishwoman to convert him to Methodism in Richard Graves's *The Spiritual Quixote*.

Miss Johnson   Fanny Matthews's rival for William Booth's attention in Henry Fielding's *Amelia*.

Miss Johnson   Young woman successively debauched by Lothario and Horatio in Tobias Smollett's *The Adventures of Roderick Random*.

Mr. Johnson   A family lawyer hired by Matthew Jermyn to stir the tavern men towards voting for the Radical political candidate; his words have more effect on the men than he intends, and the men begin to riot in George Eliot's *Felix Holt, the Radical*.

Mr. Johnson   Proprietor of Johnson's hotel; he gives the lawyer Josiah Larkin information on the movements of Rachel and Stanley Lake at the time of Mark Wylder's disappearance in J. Sheridan Le Fanu's *Wylder's Hand*.

Anthony Johnson   Shopkeeper whose silks Moll Flanders steals; when she is caught, she is finally sent to Newgate, and her criminal career ends in Daniel Defoe's *The Fortunes and Misfortunes of the Famous Moll Flanders*.

Dick Johnson   Young hand corrupted by Long John Silver as Jim Hawkins listens in the apple barrel; later he superstitiously regrets cutting his Bible in order to give Silver the black spot; he and another pirate are marooned with Morgan at the end of Robert Louis Stevenson's *Treasure Island*.

Henry (Golden Dustman) Johnson   Dustman and writer of reactionary novels; his love of showy dress amuses Richard Hammond in William Morris's *News from Nowhere*.

Isabel Johnson   Chambermaid of Roxana after Amy is fired; she completes the account of Roxana's life after Roxana's death in Daniel Defoe's *The Fortunate Mistress*.

Matilda Johnson   Conniving woman who arrives as the betrothed of Bob Loveday; she leaves him when the immoral nature of her character is discovered by Bob's brother; she returns later in the novel as the bride-to-be of Festus Derriman, another conniving and greedy character; she and Festus meanly betray Bob's whereabouts to the press-men before the Battle of Trafalgar in Thomas Hardy's *The Trumpet-Major*.

Nanny Johnson   Young woman who rejects David Simple for a wealthier suitor from whom she catches "spotted fever" and dies in Sarah Fielding's *The Adventures of David Simple in Search of a Faithful Friend.*

Roger Johnson   King of the Newgate thieves; Jonathan Wild deposes him in Henry Fielding's *The Life of Mr. Jonathan Wild the Great.*

Sir William Johnson   Resident of Albany who lets Henry Durie and Ephram Mackellar accompany him on a diplomatic errand to Indians; he investigates the burial of the Master (James Durie) in Robert Louis Stevenson's *The Master of Ballantrae: A Winter's Tale.*

Johnstone   Young fisherman who carries messages between Julia Mannering and Henry Bertram in Sir Walter Scott's *Guy Mannering.*

Agnes and Catherine Johnstone   Pupils at Lowood School who incite Mr. Brocklehurst's wrath by wearing two clean frocks in one week in Charlotte Brontë's *Jane Eyre.*

Peggie Johnstone   Laundry maid at Woodburne; she assists her brother in the correspondence between Julia Mannering and Henry Bertram in Sir Walter Scott's *Guy Mannering.*

William Johnstone   Old fisherman, father of Peggie and Johnstone in Sir Walter Scott's *Guy Mannering.*

Joceline Joliffe   Under-keeper for Henry Lee of Woodstock Park; he kills Joseph Tomkins and helps Phoebe Mayflower bury him in Sir Walter Scott's *Woodstock.*

Dr. Jolks   Pompous but not unkind medical man, who cares for Silas Ruthyn at Bartram-Haugh and hints to his ward and niece, Maud Ruthyn, that Silas is addicted to opium and laudanum in J. Sheridan Le Fanu's *Uncle Silas.*

Mrs. Joll   Stout London landlady, who helps Miriam Tacchi nurse her brother, Andrew, during his critical illness in Mark Rutherford's *Miriam's Schooling.*

Mr. Jolliffe   Pockmarked, one-eyed master's mate serving on H.M.S. *Harpy*; until wounded in fight, he befriends Jack Easy in Captain Frederick Marryat's *Mr. Midshipman Easy.*

Colonel Jolly   Neighbor of the Moreland estate who forces himself to be merry in company in Henry Brooke's *The Fool of Quality.*

Jacob Jolter   Tutor hired by Commodore Trunnion to govern Perry Pickle when he goes to Winchester; he becomes a constant companion to the young man, though he is frequently the victim of Perry's pranks; he remains at the estate of the commodore after Trunnion's death in Tobias Smollett's *The Adventures of Peregrine Pickle.*

Jonathan   Mr. Pottle's valet, who defends Pottle's beliefs against Geoffry Wildgoose's by means of a fistfight with Jeremiah Tugwell in Richard Graves's *The Spiritual Quixote.*

Jones   Maid to Beatrix Marlowe in J. Sheridan Le Fanu's *Guy Deverell.*

Chaplain Jones   Francis Eden's predecessor, who protests Hawes's cruelty but resigns rather than fight for the prisoners' rights in Charles Reade's *It Is Never Too Late to Mend.*

Lady Jones   Wealthy widow of the Lincolnshire neighborhood; she refuses the Reverend Williams's request to allow Pamela Andrews to take refuge with her should Pamela be able to escape from imprisonment on Mr. B——'s Lincolnshire estate; later she becomes a cordial acquaintance of Pamela in Samuel Richardson's *Pamela, or Virtue Rewarded.*

Master Jones   David Copperfield's fellow pupil at Dr. Strong's school in Charles Dickens's *The Personal History of David Copperfield.*

Mr. Jones   A bookseller in Paternoster Row by whom Lucy Snowe is impressed in Charlotte Brontë's *Villette.*

Mr. Jones   Butcher of Deerbrook; he retains faith in the surgeon Edward Hope during his professional crisis in Harriet Martineau's *Deerbrook.*

Mrs. Jones   Rapacious landlady and procuress, who forces Fanny Hill, then bereft and penniless, to become mistress to Mr. H—— in John Cleland's *Memoirs of a Woman of Pleasure.*

Mrs. Jones   Will Wilson's landlady, who helps Mary Barton in her search for Will Wilson in Elizabeth Gaskell's *Mary Barton.*

Mrs. Jones   Jovial innkeeper of the Plough Inn, where Sir Jeckyl Marlowe stops on his way to his estate, in J. Sheridan Le Fanu's *Guy Deverell.*

Ada Jones   Charming elder sister of Edith; she helps nurse Captain Clayton back to health after he has been shot in Anthony Trollope's *The Landleaguers.*

Athelney Jones   Scotland Yard detective who receives the official credit for solving the mystery in Arthur Conan Doyle's *The Sign of Four.*

Charley Jones Mrs. Jones's son, who helps Mary Barton reach Will Wilson's ship as it sails in Elizabeth Gaskell's *Mary Barton.*

Edith Jones Modest, agreeable daughter of Philip Jones; she is so convinced of her lack of appeal that she assumes Captain Clayton is interested in Ada, her sister; she at last realizes he loves her in Anthony Trollope's *The Landleaguers.*

Florian Jones Timid ten-year-old son of Philip Jones; terrorists bind him to secrecy over their actions against the Galway landlords; he is eventually murdered in Anthony Trollope's *The Landleaguers.*

Frank Jones Upright son of Philip Jones of County Galway; when family income is curtailed, he breaks off his engagement with Rachel O'Mahony, the opera singer; when she loses her voice, he returns to her in Anthony Trollope's *The Landleaguers.*

George Jones Customer at the Six Jolly Fellowship Porters in Charles Dickens's *Our Mutual Friend.*

Henry Jones Weak, pathetic nephew of Indefer Jones, whose Carmarthen estate he covets; discovering in the library a will naming his cousin Isabel Brodrick as heir, Henry suppresses the information; the knowledge preys on his mind, making him ill; when the truth comes out, he leaves Wales a broken man, friendless and ostracized in Anthony Trollope's *Cousin Henry.*

Indefer Jones Childless owner of Llanfere in Carmarthenshire; although he prefers his niece Isabel Brodrick, he feels bound to leave his estate to a Jones; unable to decide, he leaves several wills, the last naming Isabel; the will is lost and for a time Henry Jones inherits until the last will turns up in Anthony Trollope's *Cousin Henry.*

Jenny Jones Servant girl punished for bearing and abandoning the infant, Tom Jones, found in Squire Allworthy's bed; later, as Mrs. Waters, she is rescued by Tom from a murderer, precipitating a brief affair; his apparent guilt of incest is shocking to Tom and others, but Mrs. Waters reveals to Squire Allworthy Tom Jones's true parentage in Henry Fielding's *The History of Tom Jones.*

John Paul Jones American naval commander with whose ship the *Serapis,* on which Denis Duval is a sailor, would become engaged in the unfinished portion of William Makepeace Thackeray's *Denis Duval.*

Lady Maria Jones Narrator to Arabella (Bloomville) Lambert of a melancholy story about her marriage to a fortune hunter, whom she discovers in bed with a kept mistress masquerading as her friend in William Beckford's *Modern Novel Writing; or, the Elegant Enthusiast.*

Mary (Molly) Jones Brambleton Hall friend and workmate of Winifrid Jenkins; she is Winifred's confidential correspondent in Tobias Smollett's *The Expedition of Humphry Clinker.*

Lady Mary Jones An orphan who grows up in the home of her coquettish aunt, Lady Sheerness; she nearly elopes with a married man, is later propositioned by Lord Robert St. George, and eventually joins the women at Millenium Hall in Sarah Scott's *A Description of Millenium Hall.*

Mary Flood Jones Long-suffering Irish sweetheart of Phineas Finn; he leaves her in Ireland while he pursues his Parliamentary career in London, but her loyalty is rewarded when he comes home to marry her in Anthony Trollope's *Phineas Finn.* She has died in childbirth in *Phineas Redux.*

Mrs. Montacute Jones Jolly and gregarious hostess much in society and fond of parties; she is protective of Lady George Germain in Anthony Trollope's *Is He Popenjoy?.* She entertains the Boncassens; the luxury of Killancodlem, her country estate in Scotland, is held in contempt by her sportsman neighbor, Reginald Dobbes, at Crummie-Toddie in *The Duke's Children.*

Philip Jones Widower Protestant landowner, master of the Ballintubber and Morony estates in County Galway; he is victimized by terrorism in which he fears his son Florian is involved in Anthony Trollope's *The Landleaguers.*

Septimus Jones Toadying friend of Augustus Scarborough; he gives his encouragement to Augustus's devious strategies over the family property; his presence is an irritant to Mr. Scarborough in Anthony Trollope's *Mr. Scarborough's Family.*

Thomas (Tom) Jones Essentially generous and good-natured young foundling, whom Squire Allworthy rears as his own; he is in fact the son of Bridget Allworthy (later Mrs. Blifil) and Mr. Summer, who dies before Tom's birth; Tom's high spirits and kind heart get him into numerous scrapes, but his love for Sophia Western culminates in banishment from Allworthy's house; Tom is restored to favor when a series of coincidences reveal his good heart as well as his parentage; Sophia forgives Tom his infidelities and, following her father's command as well as her own inclination, marries him in Henry Fielding's *The History of Tom Jones.*

Jacob (Job) Jonson Traveling thief, a man of two boasted virtues: perseverance and ingenuity; a victim of his skill as a pickpocket, Henry Pelham recognizes him and uses him as an assistant in the pursuit of Dawson and Thomas Thorton in Edward Bulwer-Lytton's *Pelham*.

Joo Drawer at Robin's inn who, terrified of the sentinel's story about Tom Jones's ghost, refuses to answer Tom's ringing bell in Henry Fielding's *The History of Tom Jones*.

Jopp Michael Henchard's former employee who was snubbed by Lucetta Le Sueur; in retaliation he destroys her reputation by exposing her old love affair with Henchard in Thomas Hardy's *The Mayor of Casterbridge*.

Duncan Jopp Cowardly, vicious, and pathetic criminal Lord Hermston sentences to death; Archibald Weir, Hermiston's son, witnesses the hanging and denounces his father's judgment in Robert Louis Stevenson's *Weir of Hermiston: An Unfinished Romance*.

Jacob Jopson Man who hides Edward Waverly from the English soldiers near Penrith and then helps him reach London safely in Sir Walter Scott's *Waverly*.

Mr. Joram Coffin maker in Mr. Omer's shop; he marries Minnie Omer in Charles Dickens's *The Personal History of David Copperfield*.

Sir John Joram Eminent barrister who defends John Caldigate on a charge of bigamy and succeeds in securing a pardon after his client has served time in prison in Anthony Trollope's *John Caldigate*.

Joe Joram Son of the coffin maker Mr. Joram and Minnie Omer Joram in Charles Dickens's *The Personal History of David Copperfield*.

Minnie Joram Daughter of Mr. Joram, the coffin maker, and Minnie Omer Joram in Charles Dickens's *The Personal History of David Copperfield*.

Minnie Omer Joram Daughter of Mr. Omer; she works in her father's shop and later marries his assistant Mr. Joram in Charles Dickens's *The Personal History of David Copperfield*.

Mr. Jorkins Unseen partner of Francis Spenlow and a man of mythical ruthlessness, to which Mr. Spenlow refers all refused favors in Charles Dickens's *The Personal History of David Copperfield*.

Belinda Jorrocks Beautiful and charming niece of John and Julia Jorrocks; she is courted by Captain Doleful in Robert Surtees's *Handley Cross*.

John Jorrocks Friendly, affluent Cockney grocer who rises in the world; his main interests are in eating and fox hunting in Robert Surtees's *Jorrocks's Jaunts and Jollities*. He comes to Handley Cross to revive fox hunting in *Handley Cross*. He purchases an estate and is elected to Parliament in *Hillingdon Hall*.

Julia Jorrocks Wife of John Jorrocks; he calls her his worser half; she looks so different in her many extravagant dresses that Jorrocks often fails to recognize her in Robert Surtees's *Jorrocks's Jaunts and Jollities*, in *Handley Cross*, and in *Hillingdon Hall*.

Jorworth Welsh soldier who negotiates for Gwenwyn with Wilkin Flammock to surrender Eveline Berenger's castle in Sir Walter Scott's *The Betrothed*.

Father Jos Priest and drinking companion of Cornelius O'Shane in Maria Edgeworth's *Ormond*.

Fra Jose Conniving priest who manipulates Clara di Aliaga and Fernan di Aliaga in order to strengthen his own conjectures and establish his own power in Charles Maturin's *Melmoth the Wanderer*.

Joseph Diamond's father, a coachman who loses his position in Mr. Coleman's financial ruin, sets up as a cabby, becomes Mr. Raymond's coachman, and moves with his family to The Mound in George MacDonald's *At the Back of the North Wind*.

Joseph Faithful and brave servant of the Vinevils; he helps Ardelisa de Vinevil elude her pursuers and is shipwrecked with her on Delos; they finally make their way back to France, where he marries Nanetta, Ardelisa's maid, in Penelope Aubin's *The Strange Adventures of the Count de Vinevil and His Family*.

Joseph Servant at the boarding house where Clarissa Harlowe dies; he is frightened by Robert Lovelace's bravado in Samuel Richardson's *Clarissa: or, The History of a Young Lady*.

Joseph Third son of Christian and Christiana; he marries Martha, daughter of Mnason, in John Bunyan's *The Pilgrim's Progress From this World to That Which Is to Come*.

Joseph Dourly religious if slightly hypocritical servant at Wuthering Heights, who remains its sole inhabitant at the end of the story in Emily Brontë's *Wuthering Heights*.

Joseph A servant at Horton Lodge and frequent companion to Matilda Murray, who prefers his outdoor activities to her lessons in Anne Brontë's *Agnes Grey*.

Joseph Gentle prison inmate, whose death turns the turnkey Hodge against Hawes's sadistic methods in Charles Reade's *It Is Never Too Late to Mend*.

Joseph of Arimathea Rich young Pharisee, who is converted to Jesus despite his father's objections; he is not made a disciple by Jesus as he won't leave his ailing father; he begs permission of Pilate to bury Jesus after the crucifixion; he hides the ailing Jesus until he is cured and can return to the Essene monastery; leaving Jesus there, he continues to Jerusalem and his own reported death by Zealots in George Moore's *The Brook Kerith*.

Father Joseph Very holy Franciscan friar who dreams of Lady Lucy lying wounded in the forest, takes her to a convent, where she is restored to health, and brings her news of her family for several years afterward; much later, he becomes friends with Augustus the Hermit (Lewis Augustus Albertus) and is instrumental in reuniting him and the Lady Lucy in Penelope Aubin's *The Life and Adventures of the Lady Lucy*.

Mme. Joubert Blanche and Mary Ingram's former governess who was quickly exasperated by their taunts in Charlotte Brontë's *Jane Eyre*.

Joe Jowl One of the gamblers who play cards with Nell Trent's grandfather in Charles Dickens's *The Old Curiosity Shop*.

Mr. Joyce Rector who persuades Martha Peckover to part with "Madonna" (Grice) and who is unintimidated by the blustering Mr. Jubber in Wilkie Collins's *Hide and Seek*.

Richard Joyce Squire Trelawney's polite, timid valet; he loads stores, guards the stockade, and is shot through the head by pirates in Robert Louis Stevenson's *Treasure Island*.

Monsieur de Joyeuxe French merchant and friend of the Vinevils; he mistakenly believes Ardelisa de Vinevile dead along with her father after Mahomet's attack and tells Count de Longueville so; he returns to France when the sultan is deposed in Penelope Aubin's *The Strange Adventures of the Count de Vinevil and His Family*.

Juba Mr. Vincent's West-Indian servant, who fiercely defends his master; his name is given to Mr. Vincent's dog in Maria Edgeworth's *Belinda*.

Juba Agellius's brother, who accepts the Christian ideas of creation but proclaims his own freedom and scorns Agellius's piety; he becomes a pupil of the sorceress Gurta while still claiming mastery of himself; terrified by her, he recognizes that he cannot escape servitude to himself and goes mad; contact with the body of the martyred Callista changes his madness to placid idiocy; years later he regains his wits, accepts baptism, and dies in John Henry Newman's *Callista*.

Mr. Jubber Cruel master of a traveling circus, one of the advertised attractions of which is a child deaf-mute ("Madonna" Grice); he blusters but is ineffectual in reclaiming her from Valentine Blyth in Wilkie Collins's *Hide and Seek*.

Jucundus Uncle of Agellius and Juba; he is a well-to-do dealer in amulets and images of classical and barbarian devotion; despite his hatred of Christianity, he does his best to protect Agellius and Callista from the persecutors of Christians in John Henry Newman's *Callista*.

Judge Dispenser of Erewhonian justice, who is benign in appearance and deemed kind and wise, yet who rules inhumanely in three cases that Jack Higgs observes in Samuel Butler's *Erewhon*.

Judith Abused black wife of Eudaemon; a fanatic Christian, she interferes with Miriam's plot against Hypatia by appearing at a crucial moment and waving a crucifix at the drugged Philammon in Charles Kingsley's *Hypatia*.

Judith Brave and loyal Irish wetnurse of Charles Mandeville; she saves him from the massacre of Englishmen which takes place at the time of the rebellion of 1614, and she delivers her charge into the reliable hands of the Reverend Hilkiah Bradford in William Godwin's *Mandeville*.

Mr. Juffles A noted preacher, whom Dora Warrington marries in William Makepeace Thackeray's *The Virginians*.

Mrs. Jukes Paul Dangerfield's housekeeper, who is shocked to discover her master's true character in J. Sheridan Le Fanu's *The House by the Churchyard*.

Julia Wealthy Pompeiian who loves Glaucus and schemes with Arbaces to obtain a love potion from the Saga in Edward Bulwer-Lytton's *The Last Days of Pompeii*.

Julia Friend of Cornelia and Lucinda De La Roche; she shares Cornelia's income when a dissolute brother spends her settlement; eventually she marries Mr. De Rone in Sarah Scott's *The History of Cornelia*.

Countess Julia Verezzi's virtuous and innocent lover, who is ultimately murdered by the jealous Matilda di Laurentini in Percy Bysshe Shelley's *Zastrozzi*.

Donna Julia Donna Jacinta's cousin, who is in love with Emilius in Eliza Haywood's *The Rash Resolve; or, the Untimely Discovery*.

Julian Last pagan emperor of Rome, worshipped and cited as an ideal by Hypatia in Charles Kingsley's *Hypatia*.

Julian the Apostate   Spirit whose narration of his twenty-three different incarnations before he was allowed to enter Elysium comprises the middle half of Henry Fielding's *A Journey From This World to the Next*.

Christopher Julian   Poor composer, who loves heroine Ethelberta Petherwin but is refused by her because of his poverty; he finally marries her younger sister, Picotee Chickerel, in Thomas Hardy's *The Hand of Ethelberta*.

Faith Julian   Quiet, plain, and gentle sister of Christopher Julian in Thomas Hardy's *The Hand of Ethelberta*.

Juliana (Incognita)   Noble daughter of the Marquis of Viterbo; she is betrothed to Aurelian in order to end the feud between their families; she takes the name Incognita because she knows that "Hippolito" (in reality, Aurelian), to whom she is attracted, is a friend of Aurelian, to whom she is promised in marriage; disguised as a boy, she flees to a monastery and is rescued from her trusted guide's attack by the opportunely present, unsuspecting Aurelian; in the presence of both fathers, each discovers the fortunate true identity of the other at the end of William Congreve's *Incognita*.

Juliet   Aristocratic girl who loves a commoner she cannot marry and who solitarily nurses and later grieves for her plague-stricken family in Mary Shelley's *The Last Man*.

Julio   Father of Pompey and canine companion to an Italian nobleman in Francis Coventry's *The History of Pompey the Little*.

Julius Caesar   Hero whose spirit the author encounters in Elysium in Henry Fielding's *A Journey From This World to the Next*.

Jerry Juniper   Ladies' man, gambler, and agile acrobat in William Harrison Ainsworth's *Rookwood*.

Richard Juniper   Flashy horse trainer at Newmarket; he holds a promissory note from Mountjoy Scarborough but cannot document the sum he actually advanced; his offer of marriage to Amelia Carroll is contingent on a dowry which John Grey does not meet in Anthony Trollope's *Mr. Scarborough's Family*.

Jagd Junker   Devoted servant to the Prince of Lilliput and the keeper of his hunting hounds in Benjamin Disraeli's *Vivian Grey*.

Signor Jupe   Sissy Jupe's father, who performs with his dog, Merrylegs, in Mr. Sleary's circus, and who disappears in Charles Dickens's *Hard Times*.

Cecilia (Sissy) Jupe   Student in Thomas Gradgrind's school; she resists utilitarian training; she stays with the Gradgrinds, teaching them about beauty and feelings, and finally saves Louisa from ruin in Charles Dickens's *Hard Times*.

Mrs. Jupp   Ernest Pontifex's first landlady; she befriends Ernest and later receives a small allowance from him in Samuel Butler's *The Way of All Flesh*.

Justice   Venial man who is more concerned with appearances and acquiring money than with justice; he is the head of thief-takers (promised protection for information) in Charles Johnstone's *Chrysal: or, The Adventures of a Guinea*.

Justine-Marie   First bride-elect of Paul Emanuel but separated from him by her family; she dies after becoming a nun in Charlotte Brontë's *Villette*.

Justinian II   Emperor over whom Julian the Apostate, in his incarnation as a monk, gains great influence; Julian claims responsibility for the cruelties which finally get Justinian deposed in Henry Fielding's *A Journey From This World to the Next*.

K

Mr. Kags   Returned transport, who hides with Toby Crackit and Tom Chitling in Jacob's Island after the murder of Nancy in Charles Dickens's *Oliver Twist*.

Kahabuke (Chowbuk)   Bibulous old native, a shearer of sheep, who deserts Higgs after leading him partway to Erewhon; he falsely reports her son's death to Higgs's mother and claims the finding of the Erewhonians for himself; he casts aspersions on Higgs's book in Samuel Butler's *Erewhon*. As Bishop Kahabuka he is head of the Christian Mission to Erewhemos and delivers a letter to John Higgs urging him to come to the Erewhonians' aid in *Erewhon Revisited Twenty Years Later*.

Joe Kaiser   A leading Muskegon businessman who "bit the dust" in Robert Louis Stevenson's *The Wrecker*.

Kallikrates   Egyptian priest of Isis, husband of Princess Amenartas, and lover of She, who murders him when he refuses to abandon his wife; his body is preserved in perfect condition for two thousand years while She, living beneath the ruins of the ancient city Kôr, awaits the arrival of his reincarnation, Leo Vincey, in H. Rider Haggard's *She*.

Joseph Kalonymos   Banker from whom Daniel Deronda learns about some of his heritage in George Eliot's *Daniel Deronda*.

Mr. Kantwise   Shifty-eyed commercial traveler and friend of Mr. Moulder; he sells trashy collapsible steel furniture to Mrs. Mason of Groby Park and passes the time with Moulder debating the famous forgery case in Anthony Trollope's *Orley Farm*.

Karaz   Evil genie at first under the control of Noorna bin Noorka; he becomes free because of Shibli Bagarag's vanity and attempts to thwart Noorna and Shibli in their quest to shave Shagpat in George Meredith's *The Shaving of Shagpat*.

Irma (La Lazzerolla) Di Karski   An Italian opera singer who makes a great deal of mischief for her rival, Vittoria Campa, in George Meredith's *Vittoria*.

Kate   Pretty cousin of Maria Lobbs in "A Tale of True Love," told by Sam Weller and written down by Samuel Pickwick in Charles Dickens's *The Posthumous Papers of the Pickwick Club*.

Kate   Orphan girl staying at Sir Barnet Skettles's home while Florence Dombey is there; she asks her aunt questions about Florence in Charles Dickens's *Dombey and Son*.

Dame Katherine   Wife to Clement in William Morris's *The Well at the World's End*.

Sister Katterienna   Bernardo's sister, who is Isabella's friend in the convent; she was forced to become a nun when her love for her father's page was discovered in Aphra Behn's *The History of the Nun*.

Katty   Servant at the Sturks' who assists Dr. Dillon in the operation on Dr. Barney Sturk in J. Sheridan Le Fanu's *The House by the Churchyard*.

Angelica Kauffmann   Artist of German descent; she struggles between the claims of music and painting; aided by Sir Joshua Reynolds, she becomes a success in London; she succumbs to the false count, Frederick DeHorn, and after many years of unhappiness marries Antonio Zucchi in Anne Thackeray Ritchie's *Miss Angel*.

Johann Josef Kauffmann   Mediocre artist, who trains and supports the greater talents of his daughter, Angelica, in Anne Thackeray Ritchie's *Miss Angel*.

Dr. Kawdle   Husband of Aurelia Darnel's kinswoman; he becomes Aurelia's legal guardian after her uncle's stroke in Tobias Smollett's *The Adventures of Sir Launcelot Greaves*.

Mrs. Kawdle   Aurelia Darnel's cousin, who helps Sir Launcelot Greaves rescue Aurelia from the madhouse in Tobias Smollett's *The Adventures of Sir Launcelot Greaves*.

Jean Kay   Scottish widow whom Robin Oig kidnapped and supposedly forced into marriage; having met her, Catriona Drummond believes she was more manipulative than reports of the kidnapping suggested in Robert Louis Stevenson's *Catriona*.

Captain Kedgick   Landlord of the National Hotel; his expectation of his countrymen's antagonism to Mark Tapley's and young Martin Chuzzlewit's return alive is accurate, but the antagonism is dissipated in the general enthusiasm for Elijah Pogram in Charles Dickens's *The Life and Adventures of Martin Chuzzlewit*.

Hyacinth Keegan   Treacherous attorney, who schemes with Thady Macdermot's manager, Pat Brady, to gain Ballycloran estate in Anthony Trollope's *The Macdermots of Ballycloran*.

Sally Keegan   Daughter of Joe Flannelly; after Larry Macdermot refuses to marry her, she becomes the wife of Hyacinth Keegan in Anthony Trollope's *The Macdermots of Ballycloran*.

Charles Cave Keeldar   Shirley's father, who dies before she becomes a legal adult in Charlotte Brontë's *Shirley*.

Shirley Keeldar   Beautiful, young, and brave heiress, who runs her own estate; she is proposed to by Robert Moore but rejects him because she is in love with his brother, Louis, whom she marries against the wishes of her worldly relatives, the Sympsons, in Charlotte Brontë's *Shirley*.

Mrs. Keeler   Dalcastle widow; she accuses Robert Colwan of seducing her daughter and is in revenge fraudulently deprived of her property in James Hogg's *The Private Memoirs and Confessions of a Justified Sinner*.

Mr. Keelevin   Benevolent lawyer who tries in vain to deter Claud Walkinshaw from disinheriting his eldest son in John Galt's *The Entail*.

Mr. Keelevine   Town clerk of Gudetown whose instinct for power and superior knowledge of law initially make James Pawkie, the provost, feel threatened in John Galt's *The Provost*.

Tom Keen   Kindly barber, who gives Geoffry Wildgoose and Jeremiah Tugwell lodgings and becomes a local Methodist leader; his anti-Methodist neighbor, Fillpot, later causes his eviction that results in his brief career as a highway robber in Richard Graves's *The Spiritual Quixote*.

Mr. Keene   Unscrupulous journalist, who unsuccessfully courts the sister of the newly enriched Richard Mutimer in George Gissing's *Demos*.

Keeper of Mock Monastery Member Number Three   Well-born, rich, and debauched woman, who replaces her old lover with the Servant Lover in Charles Johnstone's *Chrysal: or, The Adventures of a Guinea*.

Mr. Keg   An ex-smuggler appointed to the borough council through provost James Pawkie's influence; he is easily manipulated by Pawkie in John Galt's *The Provost*.

Lord Keith   Elderly widower and chief of his clan; he marries Bessie Keith, is neglected by her, and dies soon after the birth of their son in Charlotte Yonge's *The Clever Woman of the Family*.

Alick Keith   Much-decorated officer and nephew of Mr. Clare; he admires Rachel Curtis for her ideals and her honesty and rescues her from social ostracism by proposing in Charlotte Yonge's *The Clever Woman of the Family*.

Colin Keith   Devoted suitor of Ermine Williams and

advisor to Lady Temple in Charlotte Yonge's *The Clever Woman of the Family*.

Elizabeth (Bessie) Keith   Fascinating but duplicitous sister of Alick Keith; she marries her elderly cousin Lord Keith because she is deeply in debt; she dies in childbirth in Charlotte Yonge's *The Clever Woman of the Family*.

Lovely Kelland   Abused child lacemaker with a love of learning; she is cruelly used by the adventurer Mauleverer and dies of diphtheria after having been wrongly cared for by Rachel Curtis in Charlotte Yonge's *The Clever Woman of the Family*.

John Kelly   Attorney's clerk and brother of Martin in Anthony Trollope's *The Kellys and the O'Kellys*.

Martin Kelly   Tenant farmer and distant relative of Francis O'Kelly, Lord Ballindine; attracted by Anty Lynch's fortune, he marries her for love in Anthony Trollope's *The Kellys and the O'Kellys*.

Mary Kelly   Mother of John and Martin; she tries to save Anty Lynch from the murderous plots of her brother in Anthony Trollope's *The Kellys and the O'Kellys*.

Michael (Mike) Kelly   Passionate, scatter-brained Irish tailor, brother of Crossthwaite's wife, Katie; he is rescued by Alton Locke from servitude in Jemmy Downes's sweatshop and becomes a Chartist leader in Charles Kingsley's *Alton Locke*.

Dr. Kelman   King's physician and tool of the conspirators; he weakens the king by feeding him poisoned food and wine in George MacDonald's *The Princess and Curdie*.

Keltie   Landlord of the change-house at Keiry Craigs, where the courier John Auchtermuchty loiters in Sir Walter Scott's *The Abbot*.

Nathaniel Kemp (Captain Nat)   Tough, salty proprietor of the Hole in the Wall pub and grandfather of Stephen; he has been involved in buying stolen goods and other activities outside the law, but his love for Stephen causes him to mend his ways in Arthur Morrison's *The Hole in the Wall*.

Stephen Kemp   Grandson of Captain Nat Kemp and narrator of much of the novel; he is left in the care of his grandfather when his mother dies and his father is killed; he observes the crime and low life around the docks, and is instrumental in influencing his grandfather to mend his ways in Arthur Morrison's *The Hole in the Wall*.

Albinia Ferrars Kendal   Admirable second wife of Edmund Kendal; her idealistic visions of her role soon conflict with the realities of her difficult stepchildren and her husband's melancholy in Charlotte Yonge's *The Young Step-Mother*.

Edmund Kendal Scholar in Indian languages; he marries Albinia Ferrars Kendal and is brought by her to a sense of his parental and social responsibilities in Charlotte Yonge's *The Young Step-Mother*.

Gilbert Kendal Weak-natured son of Edmund Kendal; he redeems himself from moral failure by dying of wounds received during a heroic action in the Charge of the Light Brigade in Charlotte Yonge's *The Young Step-Mother*.

Lucy Kendal Shallow daughter of Edmund Kendal; she matures only after her marriage to the domineering Algernon Dusautoy in Charlotte Yonge's *The Young Step-Mother*.

Maurice Kendal Son of Edmund and Albinia Kendal; he is exposed to moral danger by his half brother, Gilbert, in Charlotte Yonge's *The Young Step-Mother*.

Sophia Kendal Thoughtful, reserved daughter of Edmund Kendall; she comes to appreciate her stepmother, Albinia Kendal, and is disappointed in love in Charlotte Yonge's *The Young Step-Mother*.

Lady Kendover Provincial English lady who hires Juliet Granville to teach the harp to her niece, Lady Barbara Frankland, in Frances Burney's *The Wanderer*.

Mr. Kendrew John Vanborough's old friend, an unprepossessing, honorable man secretly in love with Vanborough's wife, Anne ("Mrs." Silvester); he witnesses Vanborough's cruel dismissal of her and their daughter and denounces him in Wilkie Collins's *Man and Wife*.

Mr. (Conversation) Kenge Important attorney, who represents John Jarndyce in arranging the guardianship of Esther Summerson, Ada Clare, and Richard Carstone in Charles Dickens's *Bleak House*.

Dr. Kenn Rector of St. Ogg's; he hires Maggie Tulliver as governess to his children but forces her to leave when rumors persist that he will marry Maggie, who has been labeled a "fallen woman" in George Eliot's *The Mill on the Floss*.

Mrs. Kenn Wife of the Reverend Dr. Kenn; she runs a charity bazaar in George Eliot's *The Mill on the Floss*.

John Kenneby Slow-witted brother of Mrs. Moulder; his witnessing of wills involving the Orley Farm estate makes him a key witness in Lady Mary Mason's trial, in which he endures devastating cross-examination; he

courts and marries Mrs. Smiley in Anthony Trollope's *Orley Farm*.

Francis Kennedy Revenue officer whose murder by smugglers results in Henry Bertram's kidnapping by the same men in Sir Walter Scott's *Guy Mannering*.

Lady Laura Standish, Mrs. Kennedy Energetic, intellectual daughter of Lord Brentford and sister of Lord Chiltern; resentful of being outside the political sphere although intensely concerned with issues, she compensates by backing Phineas Finn's career; she marries Robert Kennedy and suffers from his violent temper and jealousy; realizing she loves Finn, she grows more wretched and decides to leave her husband in Anthony Trollope's *Phineas Finn*. After Finn's arrest on a murder charge, she is desolate, vowing to go to him against all standards of propriety; a wealthy woman after Kennedy's death, she becomes increasingly more isolated and melancholy in *Phineas Redux*.

Robert Kennedy Millionaire landowner and Scottish Member of Parliament; although she loves Phineas Finn, Lady Laura Standish marries Kennedy and soon suffers from his tyranny; she leaves him in Anthony Trollope's *Phineas Finn*. Thinking Finn is to blame for her desertion, he tries unsuccessfully to shoot him, and he finally goes mad before dying in *Phineas Redux*.

Kenneth Untamed grandson of Randal MacEagh; he acts as guide for Montrose's army in Sir Walter Scott's *A Legend of Montrose*.

Sir Kenneth See David, Earl of Huntington.

Mr. Kenrick Modest Welsh surgeon, who is much admired by all for the humane and liberal style in which he practices his profession, but whose marriage to the former Mrs. Gifford leads to disaster; he is ruined by her lavish taste and dissolute manners in William Godwin's *Fleetwood*.

Edward Kenrick Son of Mrs. Gifford and her second husband; he is the exact opposite of his brooding half brother: a sincere, good-natured, high-spirited army officer; he is unaware of Gifford Kenrick's attempts to defraud him of his estate in William Godwin's *Fleetwood*.

Gifford Kenrick Darkly handsome illegitimate son of Mrs. Gifford; he is adopted by her second husband, Mr. Kenrick; unloved by his mother and rejected by his dead stepfather's relatives, he is shrewd, hypocritical, and filled with resentment at his condition in William Godwin's *Fleetwood*.

Mr. Kenwigs A lodger with Newman Noggs; Nicholas Nickleby teaches his three daughters French; he has one son named Lillyvick after his wife's uncle, who promises to bestow fortunes on the daughters in Charles Dickens's *The Life and Adventures of Nicholas Nickleby.*

Morleena Kenwigs Eldest daughter of the Kenwigses in Charles Dickens's *The Life and Adventures of Nicholas Nickleby.*

Susan Kenwigs Niece of Mr. Lillyvick; she hopes he will leave his money to her three daughters and goes to great lengths to propitiate him in Charles Dickens's *The Life and Adventures of Nicholas Nickleby.*

Keppoch Highland chief in Montrose's army in Sir Walter Scott's *A Legend of Montrose.*

Kester Loyal farmhand of Daniel Robson and faithful friend to Robson's daughter, Sylvia, after Daniel's death in Elizabeth Gaskell's *Sylvia's Lovers.*

Mr. Ketch Hangman who executes Thomas Fierce in Henry Fielding's *The Life of Mr. Jonathan Wild the Great.*

La Fayette Kettle Intrusive, pompous secretary of the Watertoast Association of United Sympathisers, an anti-British, pro-slavery organization encountered in America by Mark Tapley and young Martin Chuzzlewit in Charles Dickens's *The Life and Adventures of Martin Chuzzlewit.*

Baptist Kettleby Publican and "Master of the Mint," a safe haven for criminals, first in Southwark and later in Wapping, in William Harrison Ainsworth's *Jack Sheppard.*

Gabriel Kettledrummle Zealous preacher and leader of Cameronian rebels, who is killed fighting the army of King James in Sir Walter Scott's *Old Mortality.*

Frank, Earl of Kew Good-tempered, dissolute aristocrat, whose grandmother plans his marriage to his cousin, Ethel Newcome; after being rejected by her and wounded in a duel with Castillonnes, instigated by the Duchesse d'Ivry, he marries Lady Henrietta Pulleyn in William Makepeace Thackeray's *The Newcomes.*

Louisa Joanna Gaunt, Dowager Countess of Kew Imperious mother of Lady Ann Newcome; she is grimly determined to marry her granddaughter Ethel Newcome to her grandson Lord Kew in William Makepeace Thackeray's *The Newcomes.* She is sister of the Marquis of Steyne of *Vanity Fair.*

Conny Keyber (parody of Conyers Middleton) Fictitious author of the novel in Henry Fielding's *An Apology for the Life of Mrs. Shamela Andrews.*

Mr. Keypstick Principal master of the boarding school to which Perry Pickle is sent; he is the victim of the boy's practical joking in Tobias Smollett's *The Adventures of Peregrine Pickle.*

Jacob Kibble Fellow passenger of John Harmon on a ship to England; he is witness of Harmon's identity in Charles Dickens's *Our Mutual Friend.*

Mr. Kibbock Lizy's father and a successful experimenter in farming methods in John Galt's *Annals of the Parish.*

Lizy Kibbock Agricultural improver and Micah Balwhidder's second wife; she turns his manse into "a factory of butter and cheese" in John Galt's *Annals of the Parish.*

Young Captain Kid Gunner aboard Wilmot's pirate vessel in Daniel Defoe's *The Life, Adventures, and Pyracies of the Famous Captain Singleton.*

Master Kidderminster (Cupid) An impish performer in Sleary's circus in Charles Dickens's *Hard Times.*

Mrs. Kidgebury Charwoman for David and Dora Copperfield in Charles Dickens's *The Personal History of David Copperfield.*

Ladie of Kilbrodie Witch-like Scotswoman; she imprisons her kinsman Glenmorris's supposed widow, who is pregnant, in order to thwart, by murder if necessary, any interference in the succession of the modest Glenmorris property to her son, the Laird of Kilbrodie, in Charlotte Smith's *The Young Philosopher.*

Laird of Kilbrodie Glenmorris's grotesque and violent kinsman, whose designs on the supposed widow Laura Glenmorris include forced marriage; he pursues her relentlessly after her escape and loses a hand by amputation after a duel with Lord Macarden in Charlotte Smith's *The Young Philosopher.*

Adolphus, Lord Kilcullen Heartless roué, who willingly obeys his father in seeking to marry the heiress Fanny Wyndham in Anthony Trollope's *The Kellys and the O'Kellys.*

Mr. Kilfuddy Presbyterian minister who warns Claud Walkinshaw that his plan to disinherit his son Charles is derived from sinful motives in John Galt's *The Entail.*

Amelia Kiljoy Lady Lyndon's friend, an heiress whom Redmond Barry abducts and forces to marry Ulick Brady in William Makepeace Thackeray's *The Luck of Barry Lyndon.*

Lord Kilkee   Only son of the Earl of Callonby; he becomes the friend of Harry Lorrequer in Charles Lever's *The Confessions of Harry Lorrequer.*

Dr. Killdarby   A physician who treats Lady Tempest and discusses philosophy with Lady Sophister in Francis Coventry's *The History of Pompey the Little.*

Lord and Lady Killpatrick   Examples of the worst of Irish nobility in Maria Edgeworth's *The Absentee.*

Kim   Born Kimball O'Hara, the orphaned son of an Irish soldier; brought up in Lahore, India, at the age of fourteen he becomes the disciple of a Tibetan lama and the friend of an Afghan horse trader who spies for the British; after some years at an English school, he joins the "Great Game" of intrigue; working for the British, he foils the plans of two Russian spies and matures to be a man in Rudyard Kipling's *Kim.*

King   Princess Irene's father, whose rule and health are jeopardized by treasonable conspirators who include his court physician; the invasion is defeated by Curdie Peterson, and the king is restored to health in George MacDonald's *The Princess and Curdie.*

King   Absolute monarch, who uses his armies as a source of revenue, and who lives in ostentation to conceal his poverty in Charles Johnstone's *Chrysal: or, The Adventures of a Guinea.*

King of Bulgaria   Temperate, benevolent, prudent, and rational monarch, who leads and cares for his country and his army in Charles Johnstone's *Chrysal: or, The Adventures of a Guinea.*

King of the Celestial City   God, who welcomes Christian and Hopeful into the Celestial City, having helped them along the way in John Bunyan's *The Pilgrim's Progress From this World to That Which Is to Come.*

King of Gypsies   Nomad who shows Tom Jones the Gypsy notion of punishment based on shame when Partridge finds himself caught with another man's wife in Henry Fielding's *The History of Tom Jones.*

King of the Kingdom of the Tower   Ruler who sustains a prolonged war against his son in William Morris's *The Well at the World's End.*

Son of the King of the Kingdom of the Tower   Husband of the Lady of Abundance; he dies after his war with the king his father in William Morris's *The Well at the World's End.*

King of the Land   Undying King of the Glittering Plain; he wishes Hallblithe to marry his daughter in William Morris's *The Story of the Glittering Plain.*

King's Daughter   Royal damsel who falls in love with the picture of Hallblithe of the Raven in an illuminated manuscript volume in William Morris's *The Story of the Glittering Plain.*

King's Son   Current lover of the Lady; he lusts after the unwilling Maid, whose magic power leads to his destruction in William Morris's *The Wood beyond the World.*

King-Spirit   Soul who, having drawn the lot of king in his next life, responds to the other souls' jeers by describing his resolution to be a good and well-loved king in Henry Fielding's *A Journey From This World to the Next.*

Jemmy King   Famous Irish attorney, who is also a debauchee, in Thomas Amory's *The Life of John Buncle, Esq.*

Mrs. King   Landlady for William Crimsworth in the town of X——, England, while he is working for his brother Edward in Charlotte Brontë's *The Professor.*

Bernard Kingcote   Former medical student, who retires to a cottage in the country where he wins the love of the wealthy Isabel Clarendon; however, he is forced to go back to London to live with his widowed sister, grows bitter as he feels he is too poor to marry, becomes seriously ill, and becomes alienated from Isabel; he ultimately finds happiness by running a bookshop in his native town of Norwich in George Gissing's *Isabel Clarendon.*

Marquis of Kingsbury   Reticent nobleman with a domineering second wife; when he learns of her conspiracy against the children of his first marriage, he reasserts his authority in Anthony Trollope's *Marion Fay.*

Clara, Marchioness of Kingsbury   Wicked stepmother of Lady Frances Trafford and Lord Hampstead; she plots with the family chaplain, Thomas Greenwood, to make their lives unpleasant and alienate them from their father, the Marquis; her schemes unmasked, she has to submit to her husband's authority in Anthony Trollope's *Marion Fay.*

Charley Kinraid   The press-ganged betrothed of Sylvia Robson; he is later, after becoming a naval officer, rescued in battle by Philip Hepburn, who had let Sylvia believe him to be dead; his dash and physical attraction contrast with Philip's less colorful character in Elizabeth Gaskell's *Sylvia's Lovers.*

Kint   One of two earnest but soulless Flemish ushers who supervise the pupils and for whom the headmaster, M. Pelet, has only contempt in Charlotte Brontë's *The Professor.*

Mme. Kint   Mme. Beck's mother in Charlotte Brontë's *Villette*.

Victor Kint   Mme. Beck's brother in Charlotte Brontë's *Villette*.

Kiomi   Gypsy girl who assists Harry Richmond during his flight from Rippenger's school; she reappears later in the novel as a beautiful and exotic young woman in George Meredith's *The Adventures of Harry Richmond*.

Carinthia Jane Kirby   A naive, German-born English girl, who marries wealthy Lord Fleetwood after an evening's acquaintance; while she grows in maturity and devotes herself to her son and her brother, he can only idealize her as the essence of nature or scorn her as a social inferior; after her husband's death, she marries Owain Wythan in George Meredith's *The Amazing Marriage*.

Chillon Switzer John Kirby   Henrietta Fakeham's suitor, who is succesful over his rival, Lord Fleetwood; his marriage to this beautiful woman is made difficult by his poverty resulting from his uncle's miserliness in George Meredith's *The Amazing Marriage*.

Captain John Peter Avason (the Old Buccaneer) Kirby   Hardy old captain who runs away with the soon-to-be-widowed, youthful Countess of Cressett; the couple have two children, Chillon and Carinthia, in George Meredith's *The Amazing Marriage*.

Kirkaldy, Laird of Grange   An outstanding soldier in the Regent Murray's army at Langside in Sir Walter Scott's *The Abbot*.

Captain Kirke   Sea captain who returns from a voyage and finds Magdalen Vanstone broken in health and spirits, occupying dingy London lodgings; he nurses her back to health and marries her in Wilkie Collins's *No Name*.

Christopher Kirkland   Upper-class professional journalist and novelist, who writes about the literary and intellectual society of London in the latter part of the nineteenth century in Mrs. Lynn Linton's *The Autobiography of Christopher Kirkland*.

Godfrey Kirkland   Beloved elder brother of Christopher, for whom he embodies heroic qualities in Mrs. Lynn Linton's *The Autobiography of Christopher Kirkland*.

Cynthia Kirkpatrick   The beautiful and willful stepsister of Molly Gibson; her conduct is largely the result of thoughtless upbringing by Mrs. Gibson; Roger Hamley falls in love with her, and she conceals a youthful indiscretion with Mr. Preston while entangling Molly in her attempts to recover old letters in Elizabeth Gaskell's *Wives and Daughters*.

William Kirkup   Retired captain who sells Captain Joe Wicks his papers and his name to sail under in Robert Louis Stevenson's *The Wrecker*.

Sidney Kirkwood   Sensitive and intelligent worker in a jeweler's shop; he falls in love with a girl who, he learns, will inherit a fortune, but he does not feel that he can assume the responsibility for the philanthropic work attached to the inheritance; instead he marries another woman and eventually finds that he must support the family of her impoverished father in George Gissing's *The Nether World*.

Andrew Kirlay   Druggist who testified that Eustace Macallan purchased poison in the murder trial that precedes the opening of Wilkie Collins's *The Law and the Lady*.

Mr. Kirwin   Irish magistrate who, marking his reaction, makes Frankenstein view the body of Henry Clerval, but thereafter treats him kindly in Mary Shelley's *Frankenstein; or, The Modern Prometheus*.

The Kitchner   Timorous servant at the Monastery of St. Mary's in Sir Walter Scott's *The Monastery*.

Mr. Kite   Shabby artist whose appearance arouses the opposition of the mother of the girl he proposes to marry in George Gissing's *The Crown of Life*.

Miss Kitt   Guest at Dora Spenlow's birthday party, where she sat by David Copperfield in Charles Dickens's *The Personal History of David Copperfield*.

Sir Thomas Kittlecourt   Member of Parliament in the old administration; he is set against Godfrey Bertram after Godfrey votes for a kinsman in Sir Walter Scott's *Guy Mannering*.

Klepper   Hayraddin Maugrabin's faithful and beloved horse, bestowed on Quentin Durward in Sir Walter Scott's *Quentin Durward*.

Julius Klesmer   Intense German-Jewish music teacher, who is the first man not charmed by Gwendolen Harleth; he marries the heiress, Catherine Arrowpoint, against her parents' wishes, and they live happily together in George Eliot's *Daniel Deronda*.

Miss Knag   Madame Mantalini's forewoman in her dressmaking shop, who resents Kate Nickleby's favored position in Madame Mantalini's affections; she later owns the shop when Alfred Mantalini's debts force a sale in Charles Dickens's *The Life and Adventures of Nicholas Nickleby*.

William Kneebone Vain, philandering woollen-draper, friend of Owen Wood—and his wife—and Jacobite sympathiser in William Harrison Ainsworth's *Jack Sheppard*.

Alice Knevett Kittenish young woman, who is admired by Felix Underwood but engages herself to his brother Edgar; she jilts Edgar to marry M. Tanneguy, a Frenchman, and prompts her husband to challenge Edgar to a fatal duel in Charlotte Yonge's *The Pillars of the House*.

Knight Wealthy old aristocrat, whom Henrietta marries in spite of her love for another; he is betrayed by her and killed by robbers when he goes after her and her lover in Penelope Aubin's *The Life and Adventures of the Lady Lucy*.

Knight of Malta Confidence man who duped the citizens of Canterbury into believing he was what his name implied in William Harrison Ainsworth's *Rookwood*.

Mr. Knight Prudent friend of Charles Courteney; he gives Henrietta Courteney sanctuary in Paris when she leaves Miss Belmour's service in Charlotte Lennox's *Henrietta*.

Mrs. Knight Friendly wife of Mr. Knight; she welcomes Henrietta Courteney into her home in Charlotte Lennox's *Henrietta*.

Henry (Harry) Knight Essayist and Elfride Swancourt's betrothed; though convinced he is an excellent judge of feminine nature, he naively hopes for absolute purity in a woman; informed with malicious exaggeration that he was not her first love, he breaks the engagement; having arrived at an understanding of her naivete and innocence, he returns to find that she has married and died in Thomas Hardy's *A Pair of Blue Eyes*.

George Knightly Wealthy, respectable bachelor and long-time friend and mentor of Emma Woodhouse; he alone criticizes her meddling in others' affairs; he comes to recognize that he has long admired and loved her; he and Emma marry at the end of Jane Austen's *Emma*.

Isabella Knightly Elder sister of Emma Woodhouse; she is pretty, amiable, and overcareful of the health of her five children; she is married to Mr. Knightly's younger brother, John, and resides in London in Jane Austen's *Emma*.

John Knightly London barrister and husband of Emma Woodhouse's elder sister, Isabella; as sensible but not so good-humored as his elder brother, George, he

keeps Emma alert to indications of exasperation with his father-in-law when he visits Hartfield in Jane Austen's *Emma*.

Mrs. Knolly Woman to whose house Anna Howe tells Clarissa Harlowe to direct her letters after Mrs. Howe forbids her daughter's correspondence with Clarissa in Samuel Richardson's *Clarissa: or, The History of a Young Lady*.

Lady Monica Knollys Energetic, kind cousin of Austin Ruthyn; she befriends Maud Ruthyn and tries to warn her father against Mme. de la Rougierre; she disapproves of Silas Ruthyn's guardianship of Maud; she invites Maud and her cousin Milly Ruthyn to a houseparty at Elverston, where they meet many good friends; Maud flees to Lady Knollys when Silas and Dudley Ruthyn attempt to murder her in J. Sheridan Le Fanu's *Uncle Silas*.

Knowledge One of four Shepherds who show Christian and Hopeful, and later Christiana and her party, the hills of Error, Caution, and Clear, and advise them on their journey in John Bunyan's *The Pilgrim's Progress From this World to That Which Is to Come*.

Mr. Knox The Marquis of Brotherton's harassed man of business in Anthony Trollope's *Is He Popenjoy?*.

Robert Knox English commander of an East India ship which is shipwrecked off the coast of Ceylon; he is tricked into coming ashore by the dissuava of the king of Ceylon and dies in captivity there in Daniel Defoe's *The Life, Adventures, and Pyracies of the Famous Captain Singleton*.

Robert Knox (the younger) Commander's son, who goes ashore at Ceylon with his father and is also held captive; he escapes after nineteen years in Daniel Defoe's *The Life, Adventures, and Pyracies of the Famous Captain Singleton*.

Baron Julius von Konigstein Corrupt nobleman, whose failure to protect Lady Madeline Trevor's cousin from unscrupulous gamblers resulted in his suicide, and whom Vivian Gray and Essper George expose when he attempts to cheat Lady Madeline's brother, Albert St. George, in Benjamin Disraeli's *Vivian Grey*.

Korolevitch Russian who befriends Piers Otway in George Gissing's *The Crown of Life*.

Aurelia Koslow A German-Russian pupil of Mlle. Reuter's school, who has only ignorance to show for her twelve years of schooling but who fancies herself a coquette in Charlotte Brontë's *The Professor*.

Mr. Krempe Uncouth and conceited professor of natural history at the University of Ingolstadt; he shows contempt for Victor Frankenstein's study of ancient scientists in Mary Shelley's *Frankenstein; or, The Modern Prometheus*.

Mr. Krook Cadaverous old man, who keeps a rag-and-bone shop around the corner from Chancery and is Miss Flite's landlord; he collects papers and other objects, possesses Lady Dedlock's letters to Captain Hawdon and the true will in Jarndyce and Jarndyce, and dies of spontaneous combustion in Charles Dickens's *Bleak House*.

Miss Kybes Elderly, sentimental guest at the Hunt Ball; she later corresponds with the narrator of the story, Charles de Cresseron, telling him of the results of the duel between Stanley Lake and Sir Harry Bracton and of the marriage between Lake and Dorcas Brandon in J. Sheridan Le Fanu's *Wylder's Hand*.

William Kyrle Self-possessed, undemonstrative junior partner to the Fairlie family lawyer, Vincent Gilmore; he secretly brings word to Marian Halcombe that a document Sir Percival Glyde wants his wife to sign would enable him to swindle her of a fortune in Wilkie Collins's *The Woman in White*.

L

Duke of L––   The Earl of Courtland's choice of a prominent and rich spouse for his daughter, Lady Juliana (Douglas), in Susan Ferrier's *Marriage*.

Lady L––   Lord L––'s wife, who ignores his affair with Syrena Tricksy in Eliza Haywood's *Anti-Pamela: or, Feign'd Innocence Detected*.

Lord L––   Nobleman who has a passionate affair with Syrena Tricksy in Eliza Haywood's *Anti-Pamela: or, Feign'd Innocence Detected*.

Lord L––   Young nobleman used by Harriot Darnley to make Sir Charles Stanley jealous; he takes her as mistress, becomes disgusted with her when she boasts that she is his wife, and casts her off to make an advantageous marriage in Charlotte Lennox's *Sophia*.

Lord L.   Sir Charles Grandison's friend, who pays a visit to Sir Thomas Grandison and falls in love with his elder daughter, Caroline; Lord L.'s generosity in dowering his sisters is a factor in the resentment of Sir Thomas, who intends to give Caroline and Charlotte nothing; Lord L. weds Caroline after Sir Thomas's opportunely prompt illness and death in Samuel Richardson's *Sir Charles Grandison*.

Madame de L*   Young woman of status; she quickly wins the affections of Yorick, but despite an exchange of intimate feelings and letters she parts from him in Laurence Sterne's *A Sentimental Journey through France and Italy*.

Mr. L––   Seducer of Miss Groves; he gets her pregnant twice, abandons her, takes the one child who lives, and boasts of his conquest in Charlotte Lennox's *The Female Quixote*.

Mr. L––   Abductor of Syrena Tricksy; he wants to make her his mistress, but Syrena gets him arrested for rape in Eliza Haywood's *Anti-Pamela: or, Feign'd Innocence Detected*.

Caroline (Grandison), Lady L.   The elder of Sir Charles Grandison's sisters; her joy in the suit of the unexceptionable and devoted Lord L. is resented by her tyrannical father, who puts an end to it and threatens both daughters with penury and expulsion if her opposition to him persists; his illness and speedy death make the happy marriage possible in Samuel Richardson's *Sir Charles Grandison*.

King of Labassecour   A small man in his fifties whose face shows signs of melancholia in Charlotte Brontë's *Villette*.

Queen of Labassecour   A mild, graceful young woman, mother of a prince in Charlotte Brontë's *Villette*.

La Branche   A vain coxcomb who is a careless lover and indiscreet in Eliza Haywood's *The Injur'd Husband; or, the Mistaken Resentment*.

Mr. Lacey   Undersecretary from the Home Office, who is quickly convinced that Francis Eden has just cause to call for an investigation of the prison in Charles Reade's *It Is Never Too Late to Mend*.

Lord Lackington   Usually kind father, who repents the harshness he showed to his dead daughter, Lady Rose Chantrey, and welcomes Julie Le Breton, his granddaughter, into the family in Mrs. Humphry Ward's *Lady Rose's Daughter*.

Countess Lacleur   Parisian hostess whose parties Valancourt frequents during his separation from Emily St. Aubert in Ann Radcliffe's *The Mysteries of Udolpho*.

Vincent Lacour   Handsome and irresponsible suitor of the heiress Ada Warren, who accepts him after a first refusal; he postpones marriage when he suspects that she will not inherit her father's fortune, rejects her entirely, and marries someone else after he comes into the title and property left by his father's death in George Gissing's *Isabel Clarendon*.

Miss LaCreevy   Friend and landlady of the Nicklebys when they first come to London; she draws miniatures and marries Tim Linkinwater in Charles Dickens's *The Life and Adventures of Nicholas Nickleby*.

Firmian Lactantius   Impudent, intelligent, handsome boy taken up by Arnobius after he has been harshly treated in school in John Henry Newman's *Callista*.

Will Ladislaw   Second cousin of Edward Casaubon; he originally dislikes Dorothea Brooke but eventually moves to Middlemarch and works for her uncle just to be near her; after Casaubon dies suddenly, Will marries Dorothea despite a codicil to Casaubon's will which states that all of her inheritance will be lost if they marry in George Eliot's *Middlemarch*.

Lady   Visitor to the Owens' house who, the brothers discover, prays only when she is observed; her hypocrisy in foregoing prayer when she believes the boys to be asleep leads to skepticism on the part of John in Samuel Butler's *The Fair Haven*.

Lady   Cruel sorceress, who rules the Wood Beyond the

World; she wishes to replace the King's Son with Walter Golden as her lover but is defeated by the Maid in William Morris's *The Wood beyond the World*.

Lady——   A lady of quality who owns a female lap-dog and wishes to breed her with Pompey in Francis Coventry's *The History of Pompey the Little*.

Lady Behind the Bar   Owner of the coffee-house, who buys Pompey from the Fisherwoman in Francis Coventry's *The History of Pompey the Little*.

Lady in white   Apparition who warns Robert Colwan against the sin of murdering his brother in James Hogg's *The Private Memoirs and Confessions of a Justified Sinner*.

Lady of Abundance   Beautiful, ageless woman, who had achieved the well and endured years of good and bad fortune; she became the lover of Ralph but is murdered by the Knight of the Sun in William Morris's *The Well at the World's End*.

Lady of Fashion   Beautiful woman of obscure birth who is sold to a procuress by her very poor parents, is educated by and marries the old Reformed Debauchee; following the death of her husband, she is taken to the law by his relatives and loses everything in Charles Johnstone's *Chrysal: or, The Adventures of a Guinea*.

Lady of Fashion   A dupe to hypocritical zeal; she is not blinded to the entertainments frequented by persons of her sex and rank in Charles Johnstone's *Chrysal: or, The Adventures of a Guinea*.

Lady of Large Fortune   Capricious woman who takes a liking to the Disguised Gentleman despite his not having pretended any regard for her and who gives him all her money for a promise of marriage in Charles Johnstone's *Chrysal: or, The Adventures of a Guinea*.

Lady of Quality   Anonymous lady who meets Perry Pickle in London; she helps the needy, tells the long story of her rebellious life against her husband, and reappears to offer money and help to Perry when he is in the Fleet in Tobias Smollett's *The Adventures of Peregrine Pickle*.

Lady of Quality   Child of fortune, who rises to her present position in society by means which ruin others in Charles Johnstone's *Chrysal: or, The Adventures of a Guinea*.

Lady's Maid   Gentlewoman, Lady Tempest's maid, who, although she dislikes dogs, is given the tasks of washing, brushing, and combing Pompey; she then persecutes the little dog because he is a favorite in Francis Coventry's *The History of Pompey the Little*.

Mr. Ladywell   Painter and a suitor of heroine Ethelberta Petherwin in Thomas Hardy's *The Hand of Ethelberta*.

Laetitia   A neighboring yeoman's daughter, whom Natura was going to marry but doesn't marry in Eliza Haywood's *Life's Progress Through the Passions: or, the Adventures of Natura*.

Lafance   Physician who saves Theodore Peyron's life after a swordfight with Phillippe de Montalt in Ann Radcliffe's *The Romance of the Forest*.

Baptiste La Fere (Le Limosin)   Emmeline Mobray's father's valet, whom she meets by chance on a road in France and from whom she learns of provisions made by her father before he died to document her claim to his estate in Charlotte Smith's *Emmeline: The Orphan of the Castle*.

La Fleur   Yorick's sociable, affectionate, and loyal servant, whose resourcefulness provides him with a timely letter to avoid a social *faux pas* with Madame de L*** in Laurence Sterne's *A Sentimental Journey through France and Italy*.

Rachel Lake   Beautiful, animated, kind, and brave sister of Stanley Lake and cousin to Dorcas Brandon; she lives in a quiet cottage near Brandon Hall; she is tortured by her knowledge of her brother's crimes but coerced by him into keeping secret his murder of Mark Wylder; she loves and is loved by Lord Chelford but refuses to marry him while keeping Stanley's secret; she travels abroad with Dorcas after Stanley's death in J. Sheridan Le Fanu's *Wylder's Hand*.

Captain Stanley Lake   Unscrupulous, selfish, manipulative brother of Rachel Lake and cousin of Mark Wylder; having come to try to stop the marriage of Mark and Dorcas Brandon, he kills Mark Wylder and conceals the body, then forces his sister to help him pretend Mark has gone abroad; he succeeds in marrying Dorcas after being badly wounded in a duel with Sir Harry Bracton over her; as he is planning to run for county elections, he is thrown by his horse when it comes upon the hand of Wylder, which the rain has uncovered; he continues trying to lie about Wylder's murder until a few hours before he dies, when he confesses to Lord Chelford in J. Sheridan Le Fanu's *Wylder's Hand*.

Lallio   First king of Normnbdsgrsutt and builder of the great city of Brandleguarp in Robert Paltock's *The Life and Adventures of Peter Wilkins*.

Mr. Lally   Irishman with whom Colonel Francis Burke was going to India in Robert Louis Stevenson's *The Master of Ballantrae: A Winter's Tale*.

Madame La Luc Arnand La Luc's sister, who acts as housekeeper and village apothecary; she treats Adeline's fever upon her arrival in Savoy in Ann Radcliffe's *The Romance of the Forest*.

Arnand La Luc Elderly clergyman of sensibility, who shelters Adeline in Savoy; he nearly dies of consumption during his son Theodore Peyron's imprisonment; he is restored to health upon Theodore's release and marriage to Adeline in Ann Radcliffe's *The Romance of the Forest*.

Clara La Luc Impulsive daughter of Arnand La Luc; she befriends Adeline and falls in love with Monsieur Verneuil in Ann Radcliffe's *The Romance of the Forest*.

Mlle. la Malle A pupil at Mme. Beck's school who interrupts M. Paul Emanuel's class with her piano lesson in Charlotte Brontë's *Villette*.

William de La Marck (Wild Boar of Ardennes) A dissolute and brutal baron, excommunicated by the pope for his many crimes; coveting the wealthy Isabelle de Croye, he joins in the revolt of the Liègeois and orders the Bishop of Liège's murder before being killed in battle in Sir Walter Scott's *Quentin Durward*.

Mr. Lamb Orlando Faulkland's old servant, who assists Faulkland in carrying Mrs. Gerrarde and her maid out of England for the ostensible purpose of elopement in Frances Sheridan's *Memoirs of Miss Sidney Bidulph*.

Mrs. Lamb Wife of Mr. Lamb, Orlando Faulkland's servant; she keeps an eye on Mrs. Gerrarde and her maid in Frances Sheridan's *Memoirs of Miss Sidney Bidulph*.

Charity Lamb Nursery maid to Tom Brown before he goes to Rugby School in Thomas Hughes's *Tom Brown's Schooldays*.

Colonel Lambert Henry Lambert's father, distinguished for having sat through several sessions of Parliament without taking a bribe in William Beckford's *Modern Novel Writing; or, the Elegant Enthusiast*.

Charles Lambert Schoolboy son of Colonel Lambert in William Makepeace Thackeray's *The Virginians*.

Esther Lambert Tireless social reformer and women's rights advocate, who, after the death of her husband, Joshua, marries Christopher Kirkland; their marriage is a failure, and they separate but remain good friends in Mrs. Lynn Linton's *The Autobiography of Christopher Kirkland*.

Henry Lambert Courageous son of Colonel and Lady Maria Lambert; he praises William Pitt and the government for its excellence; after being lost on the Guinea coast, he returns only to leave again in a jealous rage; he is eventually reunited with his beloved, Arabella Bloomville, and inherits wealth and the title Lord Laughable in William Beckford's *Modern Novel Writing; or, the Elegant Enthusiast*.

Hester (Hetty) Lambert Vivacious younger daughter of Colonel Lambert; she disguises her love for Harry Warrington; she refuses all offers of marriage, even Harry's when he proposes to her years later, having become a widower in William Makepeace Thackeray's *The Virginians*.

Jack Lambert Priggish clergyman, the eldest son of Colonel Lambert; he is joined by his wife in jealousy of the Warrington brothers in William Makepeace Thackeray's *The Virginians*.

Mrs. Jack Lambert Vulgar, voluble wife of Jack Lambert in William Makepeace Thackeray's *The Virginians*.

Joshua Lambert Dreamy, unworldly artist in poor health; he is a friend of Christopher Kirkland in Mrs. Lynn Linton's *The Autobiography of Christopher Kirkland*.

Lucy Lambert Younger sister of Theo and Hetty Lambert in William Makepeace Thackeray's *The Virginians*.

Lady Maria Lambert Mother of Henry Lambert in William Beckford's *Modern Novel Writing; or, the Elegant Enthusiast*.

Colonel Martin Lambert Military man who in spite of his daughters' involvement with the Warrington brothers is their good friend; he is appointed Governor of Jamaica in William Makepeace Thackeray's *The Virginians*.

Mary Lambert Madam Esmond's old schoolmate, now married to Colonel Lambert; she is a kindly matron, who looks after Harry Warrington after he falls from his horse; she remains a good friend of the family in William Makepeace Thackeray's *The Virginians*.

Theodosia (Theo) Lambert Thoughtful elder daughter of Colonel Lambert; in spite of difficulties contrived by Madam Esmond and others she becomes the cheerful, loving wife of George Warrington in William Makepeace Thackeray's *The Virginians*.

Tommy Lambert Son born to Arabella Bloomville Lambert six months after her marriage to Henry Lambert; the child is drowned but miraculously revives a few hours later in William Beckford's *Modern Novel Writing; or, the Elegant Enthusiast*.

Michael Lambourne Giles Gosling's nephew, an unscrupulous rogue and soldier of fortune, who becomes

Richard Varney's henchman; Varney kills him when Lambourne's ambitions threaten his own in Sir Walter Scott's *Kenilworth*.

Lady Lambton   An elderly woman who invites Louisa Mancel to live with her but whose pride makes her object to her grandson's love for Louisa in Sarah Scott's *A Description of Millenium Hall*.

Edward Lambton   Lady Lambton's grandson, who falls in love with Louisa Mancel and is fatally wounded when he responds to rejection by going off to war in Sarah Scott's *A Description of Millenium Hall*.

Madam la Mer   Ferdinand's London landlady, who conspires with him to seduce Monimia (Serafina de Zelos) in Tobias Smollett's *The Adventures of Ferdinand Count Fathom*.

Nancy Lammeter   The woman courted and married by Godfrey Cass; when she and her husband are unable to produce children, they unsuccessfully attempt to claim and adopt Eppie in George Eliot's *Silas Marner*.

Priscilla Lammeter   The outspoken feminist sister of Nancy Lammeter; she never marries, preferring to care for her father and supervise their farm in George Eliot's *Silas Marner*.

Alfred Lammle   Bullying, conniving, mature young man, who has a mysterious trade in shares but no real income; he marries Sophronia Akersham thinking she is wealthy; learning the truth, he conspires with her against others to augment their income in Charles Dickens's *Our Mutual Friend*.

Sophronia Akersham Lammle   Mature young woman who marries Alfred Lammle thinking he is wealthy; she conspires unsuccessfully with him to marry Georgiana Podsnap to Fascination Fledgeby, then succeeds in getting Mr. Boffin to fire John Harmon in Charles Dickens's *Our Mutual Friend*.

Mr. Lamont   Conceited son of the narrator's friend; his skeptical questions prompt the Millenium Hall ladies to explain their philosophies in Sarah Scott's *A Description of Millenium Hall*.

Constance de La Mott   Kind but weak-willed gentlewoman who acquiesces to her husband's plan to surrender the innocent Adeline to the evil Phillippe, Marquis de Montalt in Ann Radcliffe's *The Romance of the Forest*.

Louis de La Mott   French officer who falls in love with Adeline during her stay with his parents, befriends Theodore Peyron during his imprisonment, and is responsible for Adeline's discovering her true parentage in Ann Radcliffe's *The Romance of the Forest*.

Pierre de La Mott   French gentleman of weak character, who loses his fortune gambling, flees Paris, and reluctantly rescues Adeline from assassins; he settles in an abandoned abbey and conspires with Phillippe, Marquis de Montalt in his plans to seduce and then murder Adeline; he releases Adeline and flees Montalt only to be captured, imprisoned, and tried in Paris; he is ultimately banished from France in Ann Radcliffe's *The Romance of the Forest*.

Chevalier de la Motte   Ill-fated friend of the Comte de Saverne, with whose wife he flees to England; he subsequently kills the count in a duel before embarking on a career of smuggling and espionage; he is a generous friend to the count's orphan daughter, Agnes, in William Makepeace Thackeray's *Denis Duval*.

Duchess of Lanark   Guest of Sir Stephen and Eleanor (Raymond) Pehrhyn; she learns from Eleanor not to flirt and to appreciate her husband, the duke, in Caroline Norton's *Stuart of Dunleath*.

Duke of Lanark   Character who shows all the good characteristics of aristocracy; he loves his wife and is unhappy about her flirting, enjoys cleverness and good conversation, understands Eleanor Raymond's tragedy, and tries to help in Caroline Norton's *Stuart of Dunleath*.

Landlady   Unnamed proprietor of Upton Inn who fears Jenny Waters's half-naked appearance will ruin her inn's fine reputation in Henry Fielding's *The History of Tom Jones*.

Landlady   Unnamed woman who accepts a bribe, allowing Ensign Northerton to escape after assaulting Tom Jones in Henry Fielding's *The History of Tom Jones*.

Helena Landless   Celonese orphan, twin sister of Neville Landless; she and Rosa Bud become friends in a sisterly way after Neville is suspected of murdering Edwin Drood in Charles Dickens's *The Mystery of Edwin Drood*.

Neville Landless   Celonese orphan, twin brother of Helena Landless and pupil of Septimus Crisparkle; his fight with Edwin Drood after Edwin has attacked his race and character makes him a prime suspect in Edwin's disappearance; Crisparkle attempts to help Neville control his temper in Charles Dickens's *The Mystery of Edwin Drood*.

Landlord   Unnamed proprietor of Upton Inn who joins his wife in assaulting Tom Jones because they object to Jenny Waters's appearance in Henry Fielding's *The History of Tom Jones*.

Landlord Proprietor of an alehouse who nearly reconsiders letting Parson Adams depart without paying his bill because of their ridiculous argument in Henry Fielding's *The History of the Adventures of Mr. Joseph Andrews and of his Friend Mr. Abraham Adams.*

Landlord Jeweler who is also the landlord of the house where Roxana and the brewer live; he becomes unusually kind toward Roxana after learning of her hardships; after she becomes his mistress, he travels with her to France, where he is robbed and murdered, leaving Roxana with a substantial fortune in Daniel Defoe's *The Fortunate Mistress.*

Landlord of the Gleed's Nest Honest but parsimonious man, who feels compelled to establish the truth in Sir Walter Scott's *The Monastery.*

Landlord's Daughter The idol of the inn who gives Chrysal to a circulating library in Charles Johnstone's *Chrysal: or, The Adventures of a Guinea.*

Walter Savage Landor Writer and literary lion of London; he is the "noblest man of his generation" for Christopher Kirkland, who calls him "Father" in Mrs. Lynn Linton's *The Autobiography of Christopher Kirkland.*

Mrs. Landseer Loyalist housewife, who gives refuge to Sir Joseph Wagstaff, and who plays along with Charles Mandeville's scheme to fool Captain Unton Croke into mistaking Sir Joseph for Mr. Landseer, a committed Roundhead, in William Godwin's *Mandeville.*

Mrs. Lane Member of the Unitarian congregation where Mark Rutherford preaches after being driven from the Independent chapel; the only one to befriend him, she impresses him with her moral strength and independent spirit in Mark Rutherford's *The Autobiography of Mark Rutherford.*

Kitty Lane Character who sells eggs in Chapelizod in J. Sheridan Le Fanu's *The House by the Churchyard.*

Padre Lanfranco Beatrice's confessor, who prepares her for the convent by dispelling her belief in the power of evil in Mary Shelley's *Valperga.*

Lady Langdale Member of snobbish English society who pokes fun at the Clonbronys' Irish heritage in Maria Edgeworth's *The Absentee.*

Thomas Langdale Distiller who loses his house and business on Holborn Hill during the Gordon riots in Charles Dickens's *Barnaby Rudge.*

Baron von Langen Husband of Gwendolen Harleth's hostess in Leubronn in George Eliot's *Daniel Deronda.*

Baroness von Langen Gwendolen Harleth's hostess in Leubronn in George Eliot's *Daniel Deronda.*

Edward Langham Brilliant Oxford scholar, who secretly loves Rose Leyburn for her beauty and the beauty of her violin playing in Mrs. Humphry Ward's *Robert Elsmere.*

Sir Marmaduke Langland Cavalier general who is forced to take refuge on the Isle of Man after King Charles I's forces are defeated in Daniel Defoe's *Memoirs of a Cavalier.*

Edmund Langley Gentleman of private means who learns that Louis Reed, the young man he meets in Greece, is his son; ultimately he persuades his former sweetheart, Lady Revill, who has become the young man's guardian, to marry him in George Gissing's *Sleeping Fires.*

Sir Frederick Langley Fortune hunter who agrees to participate in Richard Vere's Jacobite schemes in exchange for his daughter Isabella's hand in Sir Walter Scott's *The Black Dwarf.*

Lady Langly Amiable lady of fashion who dies from eating contaminated celery in William Beckford's *Modern Novel Writing; or, the Elegant Enthusiast.*

Mrs. Langston Mrs. Darnford's friend who is instrumental in putting Lady A— in touch with Mrs. Darnford in Clara Reeve's *Plans of Education.*

Languish Young spark who pays some slight attention to Mrs. Autumn and thus furnishes her with an imaginary intrigue with which to torment her husband in Charlotte Lennox's *Henrietta.*

Mr. Langweilig The German Moravian minister who preaches at the Bible Society meeting in Charlotte Brontë's *Shirley.*

Betty Lanshaw Micah Balwhidder's distant cousin and first wife; she dies after a few years of marriage in John Galt's *Annals of the Parish.*

Miss Lant Charity worker in the slums whose soup kitchen threatens to fail when the poor refuse to accept the changes she has made in George Gissing's *The Nether World.*

Mrs. Lant A woman who knows the secrets of adulterous love affairs and adopts the pseudonym Maskell in George Gissing's *The Whirlpool.*

Dr. Hastie Lanyon Ruddy-faced medical man and mutual friend of Dr. Henry Jekyll and his lawyer Mr. Utterson; critical of Jekyll's scientific heresies, he ages quickly and dies after discovering Jekyll's secret in Robert Louis Stevenson's *The Strange Case of Dr. Jekyll and Mr. Hyde.*

Mr. Lapidoth   Mirah Lapidoth's father, an unsuccessful actor who deserted his children; they eventually forgive him in George Eliot's *Daniel Deronda.*

Ezra Mordecai Lapidoth   Mirah's consumptive older brother, who is a Jewish religious enthusiast and wants to impart his knowledge to Daniel Deronda in George Eliot's *Daniel Deronda.*

Mirah Lapidoth   Dark, pretty Jewish girl, who runs away from her abusive, alcoholic father to look for the mother and brother she loved in her childhood; she is saved from suicide by Daniel Deronda, whom she later marries in George Eliot's *Daniel Deronda.*

Todd Lapraik   Old, fat, and unholy weaver and former soldier, who, losing a position of status to Tam Dale, sells his soul and becomes a haunted and hunting warlock in Black Andie Dale's "Tale of Todd Lapraik" in Robert Louis Stevenson's *Catriona.*

Lord Larborough   Man who informs Ophelia of Lord Dorchester's illicit desire for her in order to further his own intended seduction in Sarah Fielding's *The History of Ophelia.*

Mrs. Larcher   Edwin Larcher's gossiping wife in George Eliot's *Middlemarch.*

Edwin Larcher   A Middlemarch businessman in George Eliot's *Middlemarch.*

Larcom   Butler at Brandon Hall; he reports to the lawyer Josiah Larkin on the movements of the inhabitants; when Mark Wylder's corpse is found, he claims to have recently seen Wylder alive but actually saw Jim Dutton in J. Sheridan Le Fanu's *Wylder's Hand.*

Miss Lardner   Early romantic interest of Harry Ormond; her shallow character eventually stands revealed and teaches him a lesson about human nature in Maria Edgeworth's *Ormond.*

Miss Lardner   Cousin of one of Anna Howe's friends; she recognizes Clarissa Harlowe at St. James Church, discovers that the house where Clarissa is living is really a brothel, and informs Anna Howe in Samuel Richardson's *Clarissa: or, The History of a Young Lady.*

Tabitha Lark   Young, pretty, rural maiden, who becomes a successful student of music in London; she will perhaps bring consolation to Swithin St. Cleeve at the end of Thomas Hardy's *Two on a Tower.*

Larkey Boy   A boxer who defeated the Game Chicken in Charles Dickens's *Dombey and Son.*

Josiah Larkin   Unscrupulous, hypocritically pious lawyer to William Wylder and Stanley Lake; he blackmails Lake into turning over part of the Brandon estate to him and manipulates William Wylder under the guise of helping him resolve his debts but is prevented by Lord Chelford and Rachel Lake from taking his inheritance; he is discredited and disbarred by the revelations at the end of J. Sheridan Le Fanu's *Wylder's Hand.*

Miss Larkins   Pretty woman of thirty in Canterbury with whom the young David Copperfield is infatuated and dances a waltz in Charles Dickens's *The Personal History of David Copperfield.*

Mr. Larkins   Father of Miss Larkins and her sisters in Canterbury in Charles Dickens's *The Personal History of David Copperfield.*

Mr. Larkins   Edward Overton's tailor, who says that Ernest Pontifex's plan to work as a tailor in someone's shop is all wrong: no one will hire a gentleman for such a position for fear that he will upset the other workers in Samuel Butler's *The Way of All Flesh.*

Madame De La Roche   Ill-tempered woman, who engages Cornelia as instructor for her youngest daughter and jails her stepson Bernardo to prevent his marriage to Cornelia in Sarah Scott's *The History of Cornelia.*

Henrietta De La Roche   Madame De La Roche's eldest daughter, who, intent on marrying Bernardo, tricks him into revealing his secret devotion to Cornelia and deceives Cornelia into thinking Bernardo is unfaithful in Sarah Scott's *The History of Cornelia.*

Lucinda De La Roche   Madame De La Roche's youngest daughter, who is sent to a convent when her mother discovers she has facilitated meetings between Bernardo and Cornelia in Sarah Scott's *The History of Cornelia.*

Miss Larolles   London gossip who is considered leader of the voluble class; she offends and embarrasses Cecilia Beverley in Frances Burney's *Cecilia.*

Mme. de la Rougierre   Governess to Maud Ruthyn; alternately ingratiating and cruel, she appears to be evil embodied to her young charge at Knowl; at Bartram-Haugh she becomes an accomplice of Silas and Dudley Ruthyn in their plot to kill Maud but is killed herself in J. Sheridan Le Fanu's *Uncle Silas.*

Lady Louisa Larpent   Sister of Lord Orville; she journeys to Bristol to be courted by Lord Merton and snubs

Evelina Anville Belmont until Evelina is reconciled with her father in Frances Burney's *Evelina*.

Count La Ruse   Noble but immoral gentleman, who joins Jonathan Wild in swindling Thomas Heartfree; Theodosia Snap's lover, he also courts Mrs. Heartfree in Africa in Henry Fielding's *The Life of Mr. Jonathan Wild the Great*.

Lascaris   Citizen of Constantinople in Sir Walter Scott's *Count Robert of Paris*.

Lady Florence Lascelles   Heiress daughter of Lord Saxingham; her love is rewarded by betrothal to Ernest Maltravers; the intrigues of her other rival suitors, Lumley Ferrers and Castruccio Caesarini, precipitate her decline and death in Edward Bulwer-Lytton's *Ernest Maltravers*.

Antonia de las Cisternas   Beautiful, innocent, impoverished daughter of Elvira de la Cisternas; after Elvira's murder, cut off from her father's family, unaware of Lorenzo de Medina's love, she falls victim to Abbot Ambrosio, who feigns her death and rapes and murders her in a sepulchre, later discovering that she was his sister in Matthew Lewis's *The Monk*.

Beatrice de las Cisternas (Bleeding Nun)   Licentious nun, murdered long ago; as the Bleeding Nun ghost, she haunts Raymond de las Cisternas and foils Agnes de Medina's escape from Lindenberg in Matthew Lewis's *The Monk*.

Elvira (Dalfa) de las Cisternas   Antonia's lowborn but noble-spirited mother; murdered by Abbot Ambrosio (later identified as her son) while preventing Antonia's rape, she reappears as a ghost to predict Antonia's death in Matthew Lewis's *The Monk*.

Raymond, Marquis de las Cisternas   Lover of Agnes de Medina in his travel guise as Alphonso d'Alvarada and father of her child; he twice fails to rescue Agnes (from Lindenberg Castle and the Convent of St. Clare) and falls ill believing her dead but marries her when she is freed by Lorenzo de Medina in Matthew Lewis's *The Monk*.

Mrs. Lashmar   Dyce Lashmar's mother, an authoritarian matron who is oppressively ambitious for her son in George Gissing's *Our Friend the Charlatan*.

Dyce Lashmar   Ambitious and conceited young man, who runs for Parliament under false pretenses, preaching a theory he has stolen from a French thinker; he becomes involved with both Constance Bride and May Tomalin in his pursuit of a wealthy wife and ultimately marries Iris Woolstan, who loses most of her income in George Gissing's *Our Friend the Charlatan*.

Philip Lashmar   Dyce Lashmar's father, a liberal Anglican clergyman disappointed in the failures of Christianity in George Gissing's *Our Friend the Charlatan*.

Lasmeel   Intelligent and inquisitive young man, whom Peter Wilkins educates, and who helps Peter translate the Bible into the language of Normnbdsgrsutt in Robert Paltock's *The Life and Adventures of Peter Wilkins*.

La Sourbe   A devoted supporter of the Baroness de Tortillee, although he is old and diseased in Eliza Haywood's *The Injur'd Husband; or, the Mistaken Resentment*.

Lasune   Good-hearted former nurse to both Savillon and Julia de Roubigné; her house serves as a meeting place for the unhappy pair in Henry Mackenzie's *Julia de Roubigné*.

Mrs. Latch   The cook who supervises Esther Waters but only gradually warms to her; although ambitious for her son, William, she protects Esther after William seduces her; she is angry over William's elopement with Peggy Barfield in George Moore's *Esther Waters*.

Jackie Latch   Son of Esther Waters and William Latch, reared by a nurse, Mrs. Lewis, but watched carefully by Esther; he joins Esther and William after their marriage and lives with them above the pub; after William's death he enlists in the army; he is a satisfaction to his mother in George Moore's *Esther Waters*.

William Latch   Handsome son of the cook; angered at Esther Waters's refusal to marry him after he seduces her, he elopes with Peggy Barfield to an unhappy marriage but finally marries Esther and gives her and their son a decent home and happiness with his pub, until illegal gambling ruins him in George Moore's *Esther Waters*.

Mr. Latherum   Diminutive Jacobite barber who frequents the Black Bear in Sir Walter Scott's *Rob Roy*.

Lady Latimer   Aged attendant of Queen Elizabeth in Sophia Lee's *The Recess*.

Arthur Latimer   Shy but enthusiastic clergyman; he succeeds his father as rector at Hartlebury and shares Helen Molesworth's genuine interest in helping the poor in Benjamin Disraeli's *A Year at Hartlebury; or, The Election*.

Darsie Latimer   See Sir Arthur Redgauntlet.

Latoni   Servant of Il Conte Berenza; he stabs the Moor Zofloya, pushes him into the water, and then suddenly dies of fever in Charlotte Dacre's *Zofloya; or, The Moor*.

Archbishop Laud   Archbishop of Canterbury during the reign of Charles I; he is beheaded for his involvement with papists in J. Henry Shorthouse's *John Inglesant, A Romance*.

Laura   A woman of great accomplishments; she becomes a friend and mother figure to Caleb Williams while he lives in Wales; she discovers (through Gines) Caleb's crime, rebukes him, and asks him never to visit her family again; he is devastated in William Godwin's *Caleb Williams*.

Laura   Lady Clementina della Porretta's maid in Samuel Richardson's *Sir Charles Grandison*.

Laura   Anna St. Ives's maid, who, though usually faithful to Anna, assists Coke Clifton in his scheme to ruin Anna in Thomas Holcroft's *Anna St. Ives*.

Laura   Niece of the evil Scottish baron Malcolm; she is held captive in Dunbayne; she falls in love with Osbert and upon Malcolm's death marries Osbert in Ann Radcliffe's *The Castles of Athlin and Dunbayne*.

Madame Laure   A French actress once loved by Dr. Tertius Lydgate; the discovery that she had killed her husband caused his resolution against romantic entanglements, which gives way to Rosamond Vincy in George Eliot's *Middlemarch*.

Father Laurence   Monk, as pious as he was brave when a soldier, and a relative of Don Pedro de Gonzales; he officiates at Don Pedro's marriage to Amelia in William Beckford's *Modern Novel Writing; or, the Elegant Enthusiast*.

Tom Laurence (Tom Tuck, Tyburn-Tom)   Brutal and sulky highwayman, who testifies against his associates to help himself in Sir Walter Scott's *The Heart of Midlothian*.

Matilda di Laurentini   Beautiful but jealous aristocrat, who schemes with Zastrozzi to win Verezzi's love and who finally kills her rival, the Countess Julia, in Percy Bysshe Shelley's *Zastrozzi*.

Lausanne   Servant/secretary/confidant of Baron Fleming and later of Contarini Fleming in Benjamin Disraeli's *Contarini Fleming*.

Maria (Pierre) de Lausanne   Niece of a French woman of fashion; disguised as Pierre, she helps young Harry Clinton escape the clutches of her aunt, Madame Maintenon; she dies when she selflessly intercepts a robber's ball intended for her beloved Harry Clinton in Henry Brooke's *The Fool of Quality*.

Baron de la Valiers   French nobleman who acts as a patron to his prisoner, Horatio; he introduces Horatio to

the establishment of the exiled English King James II and frees him unransomed in Eliza Haywood's *The Fortunate Foundlings*.

Mr. Lavement   French apothecary, who employs Roderick Random as a journeyman in London in Tobias Smollett's *The Adventures of Roderick Random*.

Elizabeth Lavenza   Beautiful, aristocratic Milanese, who is adopted by the Frankensteins; she becomes Victor Frankenstein's bride and is tragically murdered by his demon in Mary Shelley's *Frankenstein; or, The Modern Prometheus*.

Lavinia   Coquette who briefly helps Mr. Graham forget his broken engagement to the virtuous Ophelia in Richard Graves's *The Spiritual Quixote*.

Lavinia   Object of much attention from persistent suitors after she inherits a fortune in Sarah Fielding's *Familiar Letters between the Principal Characters of David Simple and Some Others*.

La Voisin   French peasant in whose cottage Monsieur St. Aubert dies in Ann Radcliffe's *The Mysteries of Udolpho*.

Jenny Law   Servant girl accused by Lucius Manly of seducing him in his sleep; her handkerchief, found in Lucius's bed, was actually left by Prudilla Stevens in Mary Collyer's *Felicia to Charlotte*.

Mr. Lawford   Town clerk who serves as joint trustee with Dr. Gideon Gray for Richard Middlemas in Sir Walter Scott's *The Surgeon's Daughter*.

Mrs. Lawler   Disreputable neighbor of the Barton family; she is spurned by society but liked by the men; she prevents Olive Barton's eloping with Captain Hibbert, injuring Olive in a quarrel over him in George Moore's *A Drama in Muslin*.

Colonel Lawless   Aspiring lover to Lady Delacour, who uses him to make her husband jealous; when he is killed by Lord Delacour in a duel, Lady Delacour feels great remorse and blames herself for his death in Maria Edgeworth's *Belinda*.

Will Lawless   Roguish forester, ex-Gray Friar, ex-sailor, thief, and cook for Ellis Duckworth; he steals and sails the ship in the cottage raid, hides Dick Shelton in his underground den and disguises him as a friar, and ends his life as Brother Honestus in Robert Louis Stevenson's *The Black Arrow: A Tale of Two Roses*.

Sir Frederick Lawnly   Villain who finally succeeds in seducing Lady Elmwood (formerly Miss Milner); he is severely scarred in a subsequent duel with Dorriforth, Lord Elmwood in Elizabeth Inchbald's *A Simple Story*.

Lady Betty Lawrence   Half sister to Robert Lovelace's uncle; Lovelace kidnaps Clarissa Harlowe by arranging an impersonation of her; once the family learns of his treatment of Clarissa, Lady Betty insists that Lovelace marry Clarissa and urges Clarissa to accept him in respectful letters in Samuel Richardson's *Clarissa: or, The History of a Young Lady*.

Frederick Lawrence   Well-bred, taciturn brother of Helen Huntingdon and a friend of Gilbert Markham; he does little to further Markham's friendship with Helen and quietly marries Esther Hargrave in Anne Brontë's *The Tenant of Wildfell Hall*.

Sir John Lawrence   Lord Mayor of London who, along with the aldermen, issues orders concerning the measures to be taken to control the plague in Daniel Defoe's *A Journal of the Plague Year*.

Mary Lawrie   Reserved but strong-minded orphan, who allows herself to become engaged to her guardian, William Whittlestaff, out of gratitude for his kindness; in reality she loves John Gordon, who reappears with a fortune from diamond prospecting in South Africa; her guardian releases her from her promise, and she marries John in Anthony Trollope's *An Old Man's Love*.

Mr. Lawson   Country curate paid by Mr. Herbert to take Sophia Darnley in when Sir Charles Stanley's attentions take a suspicious turn in Charlotte Lennox's *Sophia*.

Mrs. Lawson   Sensible and polite wife of the curate Mr. Lawson; her ridicule of old Mrs. Gibbons leads that lady to break the engagement of Dolly Lawson and William Gibbons in Charlotte Lennox's *Sophia*.

Dolly Lawson   The curate's daughter, an innocent country girl, who becomes Sophia Darnley's friend and confidante; she loves William Gibbons but is prevented from marrying him by the objections of his aunt until Sophia makes peace between the families in Charlotte Lennox's *Sophia*.

Fanny Lawson   Sister of Dolly Lawson in Charlotte Lennox's *Sophia*.

Terry Lax   Cold-blooded assassin in Galway, responsible for several killings and outbreaks of violence; he is responsible for the murder of Florian Jones in Anthony Trollope's *The Landleaguers*.

Ferdinand Laxley   Evan Harrington's aristocratic and arrogant rival for Rose Jocelyn; he loses her to Harrington when she discovers Harrington's innocence in a plot

designed to discredit Laxley in George Meredith's *Evan Harrington*.

Mr. Leach   Overworked solicitor, who is forced by lack of money to deny his family their pleasures in George Gissing's *The Whirlpool*.

Sally Leadbitter   Seamstress at Miss Simmons's shop, who encourages Mary Barton to accept the advances of Harry Carson in Elizabeth Gaskell's *Mary Barton*.

Leah   Servant at Thornfield Hall who is aware of the existence of the madwoman in the attic but not of her identity in Charlotte Brontë's *Jane Eyre*.

Mrs. Leake   Deaf old lady with a biting tongue; her grand house and carriage give her some pride of place among the ladies of Littlebath society in Anthony Trollope's *The Bertrams*.

Leander   Emilia's suitor, poisoned by her jealous brother-in-law in Penelope Aubin's *The Life and Adventures of the Lady Lucy*.

Leander   A deacon of the Catholic church; he is trusted by Petronilla and sympathetic to the Gothic cause; he is the source of the conspiracy to abduct Aurelia and Veranilda in George Gissing's *Veranilda*.

Billy Leary   Leader of the Leary gang and noted for his toughness; Josh Perrott gains the respect of the Jago when he beats Billy in a fight in Arthur Morrison's *A Child of the Jago*.

Peter Leather   Groom to Soapey Sponge in Robert Surtees's *Mr. Sponge's Sporting Tour*.

Sir Richard Leatherham   Able Solicitor-General, who leads for the prosecution in Lady Mason's trial in Anthony Trollope's *Orley Farm*.

Robert Leaven   Mrs. Reed's compassionate coachman at Gateshead, who marries Bessie Lee and has three children in Charlotte Brontë's *Jane Eyre*.

Le Blanc   Faithful and talkative servant of the de Roubigné family in Henry Mackenzie's *Julia de Roubigné*.

Julie Le Breton   Illegitimate daughter of Lady Rose Chantrey; she becomes the companion of Lady Henry; Julie's intelligence and her manipulative skills as an aristocratic hostess rival those of Lady Henry, thereby provoking a quarrel; the protection of Jacob Delafield and later her marriage to him save her reputation in Mrs. Humphry Ward's *Lady Rose's Daughter*.

Mademoiselle Lebrun   Governess of the Hobson Newcome children in William Makepeace Thackeray's *The Newcomes*.

Lebruno Performer who plays Count Orso in the opera *Camilla*, wearing the Austrian colors to emphasize the Italian nationalism of the opera in George Meredith's *Vittoria*.

Lord Lechmore Unethical guardian of William Thornhill; he helps a greedy aristocrat steal the farm of honest Giffard Homely in Henry Brooke's *The Fool of Quality*.

Pierre Le Choux Frenchman with a superior method of growing asparagus referred to in William Beckford's *Azemia*.

Virginie Lecount Noel Vanstone's cunning French housekeeper, eager to acquire his money; always shrewd and resourceful, she tries unsuccessfully to thwart Magdalen Vanstone's attempt to marry her employer and then persuades him to change his will in Wilkie Collins's *No Name*.

Miss "Led" Ledbrook Member of the Vincent Crummles Theatrical Company in Charles Dickens's *The Life and Adventures of Nicholas Nickleby*.

M. Ledru The music-master, a married man of almost fifty, whom Mlle. Reuter does not trust among her pupils in Charlotte Brontë's *The Professor*.

Annette Ledru Frenchwoman who, with her infant daughter, was rescued from destitution by Rufus Lyon, who became her husband; she dies, leaving Esther to be brought up as Lyon's own child in George Eliot's *Felix Holt, the Radical*.

Leonie Ledru A quick-witted pupil of Mlle. Reuter's school, who places second in a composition contest in Charlotte Brontë's *The Professor*.

Colonel Albert Lee A soldier, the son of Henry Lee; he conceals King Charles II from Cromwell at Woodstock and arranges for Charles's escape; he dies fighting for the king in Sir Walter Scott's *Woodstock*.

Alice Lee Henry Lee's daughter, who loves Markham Everard; she is courted by King Charles II disguised as Louis Kerneguy and accompanies Charles when he escapes England; she marries Markham Everard in Sir Walter Scott's *Woodstock*.

Bessie Lee Sympathetic maid at Gateshead, the only member in the Reed household who cares for Jane Eyre; she visits Jane at Lowood before Jane leaves to become a governess in Charlotte Brontë's *Jane Eyre*.

Sir Henry Lee The Ranger of Woodstock, an old knight loyal to Stuart monarchs; his house is used by King Charles II to hide from Oliver Cromwell in Sir Walter Scott's *Woodstock*.

Edwin Leeford Father of Oliver Twist and Edward Leeford (Monks); he had seduced Oliver's mother, Agnes Fleming, and died before he could make any reparation in Charles Dickens's *Oliver Twist*.

Edward Leeford (Monks) Elder, epileptic half brother of Oliver Twist, he bargains with Fagin to remove Oliver, the legatee under their father's will, in Charles Dickens's *Oliver Twist*.

Miss Leeson London gossip who is considered leader of the supercilious class; she offends and embarrasses Cecilia Beverley in Frances Burney's *Cecilia*.

Le Fever Dying, poverty-stricken soldier befriended by Toby Shandy, who takes charge of his young son after his pathetic death in an episode illustrative of Toby's selfless generosity and military sodality in Laurence Sterne's *The Life and Opinions of Tristram Shandy, Gentleman*.

Mr. Le Frank Untalented, unattractive, vile music master to the Gallilee children; Mrs. Gallilee's plot to use him to compromise Carmina Graywell, breaking up her romance with Ovid Vere, is scotched by Carmina's ridicule of his musicianship; he becomes her enemy, spying on her for Mrs. Gallilee with some success; Teresa puts an end to his investigations, smashing his hand in the process in Wilkie Collins's *Heart and Science*.

Ferdinand Lefroy Absconding first husband of Ella Peacocke; believing him dead, she marries the Reverend Henry Peacocke only to have Lefroy reappear to destroy her happiness in her second marriage; he dies shortly thereafter in San Francisco in Anthony Trollope's *Dr. Wortle's School*.

Robert Lefroy Rascally brother of Ferdinand, the ex-husband of Ella, who is now married to the Reverend Henry Peacocke; pretending his brother still lives, Robert tries to blackmail the Peacockes until evidence of Ferdinand's death confounds his scheme in Anthony Trollope's *Dr. Wortle's School*.

George Legard Dazzling young officer, who is aided by Ernest Maltravers and wins Evelyn Templeton in Edward Bulwer-Lytton's *Alice*.

Sir Leger The man presumed to have run off with Lady Lindore, the socialite wife of Frederick, Lord Lindore, in Susan Ferrier's *Marriage*.

Job Legh Mill worker with a reputation as a biologist;

he mediates with John Carson after John Barton confesses to the murder of Carson's son, Harry, in Elizabeth Gaskell's *Mary Barton*.

Legouve Parisian member of the French Revolutionary Committee of Public Safety, with whom Victorine lives; he abandons her when she secures Dupin's release from prison in Mark Rutherford's *The Revolution In Tanner's Lane*.

M. Le Guardien The prostitute Elizabeth Sparkle's pimp in John Hill's *The Adventures of Mr. George Edwards, a Creole*.

Lady Leicester Daughter of Sir Patrick Lineric; she weds the Earl of Essex (1) and conducts a tempestuous liaison with Lord Leicester; after Essex's death she secretly weds Leicester and is impregnated by her brother, with whom she is poisoned when their plan to kill Leicester fails in Sophia Lee's *The Recess*.

Lady Leicester See Amy Robsart Dudley.

Robert Dudley, Earl of Leicester Ambitious leader of a court faction and a favorite of Queen Elizabeth, whose jealousy makes politic his keeping secret his marriage to Amy Robsart (Dudley); his villainous and duplicitious Master of Horse, Richard Varney, works on his ambition to become king and persuades him that Amy has been unfaithful; Varney disregards his order rescinding his acquiescence in Amy's death; he is punished only by personal remorse, a temporary loss of court favor, and reduced ambition in Sir Walter Scott's *Kenilworth*. He attempts to wed Mary, Queen of Scots and has an adulterous liaison and a sordid marriage with the wife of the Earl of Essex (1) before secretly marrying Matilda; he flees England with Matilda to escape Queen Elizabeth's displeasure but is murdered by Elizabeth's men at Rouen in Sophia Lee's *The Recess*.

Rose Leicester Attractive schoolmistress, who becomes pregnant and is denounced from the pulpit by Father Oliver Gogarty; after she leaves, she enjoys the excitement of her life in London and her work as a scholarly researcher; she carries on a lively correspondence with Father Oliver and inspires him to make a break for freedom in George Moore's *The Lake*.

Mr. Leigh Catholic gentleman, father of Eustace and uncle of Frank and Amyas Leigh; he plots, somewhat reluctantly, with the Jesuits in Charles Kingsley's *Westward Ho!*.

Mrs. Leigh Selfless, loving, and devoutly Protestant widowed mother of Frank and Amyas Leigh; she welcomes Ayacanora as a daughter in Charles Kingsley's *Westward Ho!*.

Mrs. Leigh A former schoolmate of Lucy Snowe; she is improved by marriage and motherhood but forgets Lucy in Charlotte Brontë's *Villette*.

Amyas Leigh Gentleman, mariner, and member of the Brotherhood of the Rose whose adventures take him to Ireland and the New World; he vows to revenge Rose Salterne's death in the Inquisition, pursues Don Guzman de Soto, and is blinded in the battle against the Spanish Armada, finally returning to Ayacanora in Charles Kingsley's *Westward Ho!*.

Eustace Leigh Catholic cousin of Amyas and Frank; he plots with the Jesuits against Queen Elizabeth and is rejected by Rose Salterne; he later threatens to turn Rose over to the Inquisition if she will not leave Don Guzman de Soto for him; he escapes reprisal and disappears in Charles Kingsley's *Westward Ho!*.

Frank Leigh Scholar, courtier, brother of Amyas, and founder of the Brotherhood of the Rose; he tries with Amyas to rescue Rose Salterne from Don Guzman de Soto but is captured by Guzman's men and tortured and burned at the stake by the Inquisitors in Charles Kingsley's *Westward Ho!*.

Mr. Leighton Clergyman at the church attended by the Maxwells, Helen Huntingdon's aunt and uncle, in Anne Brontë's *The Tenant of Wildfell Hall*.

Janet Leighton Former classmate of Rachel Henderson at Swanley Agricultural College and her companion at Great End Farm in Mrs. Humphry Ward's *Harvest*.

Joseph Leman Servant in the Harlowe household and paid informer of Robert Lovelace; he is responsible for supplying the family with false information from Lovelace which hardens their hearts against Clarissa; his letter to Lovelace about Colonel Morden's private threats precipitates Lovelace's challenge to Morden and their duel in Samuel Richardson's *Clarissa: or, The History of a Young Lady*.

Graf (Count Adalbert) Commendatore von Lenkenstein The head of the von Lenkenstein family; he directs the search for Angelo Guidascarpi in George Meredith's *Vittoria*.

Countess Anna von Lenkenstein Count Paul von Lenkenstein's sister, an Austrian aristocrat who hates Vittoria Campa because of her relationship with his killer, Angelo Guidascarpi; her scheming results in her beloved Captain Wiesspriess's death in George Meredith's *Vittoria*.

Count Karl von Lenkenstein Honorable Austrian leader of the soldiers who capture Rinaldo Guidascarpi and escort Vittoria Campa and Pericles after her kidnapping in George Meredith's *Vittoria*.

Countess Lena von Lenkenstein   Once Carlo Ammiani's sweetheart, now that of Wilfrid Pole; she is more reasonable in her treatment of Carlo and Vittoria Campa than is her sister Anna in George Meredith's *Vittoria*.

Count Paul von Lenkenstein   Austrian killed by the brothers of Clelia Guidascarpi, his lover, in George Meredith's *Vittoria*.

Rachel Lennard   Miss Rayland's housekeeper and Monimia Morysine's aunt; she virtually imprisons her niece lest Orlando Somerive's attentions trigger Miss Rayland's resentment; she is later similarly confined by her husband, Roker; her fears that he will have her declared insane prompt her to help Orlando recover the will she has hidden in Charlotte Smith's *The Old Manor House*.

General Lennox   Imperious and dim-witted but kindly old soldier with a young wife, who he discovers is having an affair with Sir Jeckyl Marlowe; he seriously wounds Sir Jeckyl and separates from his wife in J. Sheridan Le Fanu's *Guy Deverell*.

Mrs. Lennox   The elderly, bereaved, and blind London widow befriended by Mary Douglas; she dies before the marriage of Colonel Charles Lennox and Mary Douglas in Susan Ferrier's *Marriage*.

Colonel Charles Lennox   Mrs. Lennox's only surviving child, who eventually becomes the well-suited spouse of Mary Douglas in Susan Ferrier's *Marriage*.

Captain Cosmo Lennox   Man who marries Edith Shaw and introduces his brother Henry to Margaret Hale in Elizabeth Gaskell's *North and South*.

Dick Lennox   Popular boss of a traveling acting company; he falls in love with Kate Ede and persuades her to leave her husband Ralph and elope with him; he develops her voice and acting ability and marries her when he learns she is pregnant; friendly to all and attracted to Laura Forest for her wealth, he arouses Kate's jealousy; he is unable to cope with Kate's drunken fury in George Moore's *A Mummer's Wife*.

Henry Lennox   A lawyer and the brother of Captain Lennox; he proposes to Margaret Hale; he also advises her brother, Frederick, in Elizabeth Gaskell's *North and South*.

Lady Jane Lennox   Willful young wife of General Lennox; she is much admired as a society beauty; she resumes an old affair with Sir Jeckyl Marlowe while a houseguest at Marlowe; after Lennox discovers them and

wounds Sir Jeckyl, she spends the rest of her life on the Continent in J. Sheridan Le Fanu's *Guy Deverell*.

Mrs. Lenville   Wife of Thomas Lenville and a member of the Vincent Crummles Theatrical Company; she sympathizes with him when Nicholas Nickleby knocks him down after an insult in Charles Dickens's *The Life and Adventures of Nicholas Nickleby*.

Thomas Lenville   Actor of tragic roles in the Vincent Crummles Theatrical Company in Charles Dickens's *The Life and Adventures of Nicholas Nickleby*.

Leonard   Character in Dick Adams's story who relies on his friend Paul to mediate petty quarrels with his wife in Henry Fielding's *The History of the Adventures of Mr. Joseph Andrews and of his Friend Mr. Abraham Adams*.

Sir Leonard   Chaplain at the Castle of the Quest, where he advances the education of Birdalone in William Morris's *The Water of the Wondrous Isles*.

George Leonards   Malcontent ex-sailor, now railway worker, who recognizes Frederick Hale; his death after a push leads to problems for Margaret Hale in Elizabeth Gaskell's *North and South*.

Leonella   Old aunt of Antonia de las Cisternas; she is comically in love with youthful Lorenzo de Medina; she marries an opportunistic apothecary in Matthew Lewis's *The Monk*.

Leonidas of Sparta   First soul with whom the author's soul converses upon arriving in Elysium in Henry Fielding's *A Journey From This World to the Next*.

Leonora   Noble daughter of Don Mario; she meets and falls in love with a man whom she first mistakes for her cousin Don Lorenzo and then believes to be Aurelian, promised to her friend Juliana; in desperation she marries him secretly and then happily discovers his true identity as Hippolito in William Congreve's *Incognita*.

Leonora   Heroine of the stagecoach story who jilted her faithful Horatio for the dashing Bellarmine and was jilted in turn in Henry Fielding's *The History of the Adventures of Mr. Joseph Andrews and of his Friend Mr. Abraham Adams*.

Leontia   Subject of Cynthia's letter to Camilla (Simple); her husband Leontine envies her superior intelligence in Sarah Fielding's *Familiar Letters between the Principal Characters of David Simple and Some Others*.

Archduke Leopold, Grand Duke of Austria   A leader of Christian forces on Crusade and a rival of King Richard in Sir Walter Scott's *The Talisman*.

Lepel   Chaplain of a prison in the North of England and a friend of Francis Eden; he only superficially understands prisoners in Charles Reade's *It Is Never Too Late to Mend*.

Lepra   Eldest of the three genteel but ugly daughters of Maladie Alamode; her name is translated as "leprosy"; she causes her mother's heartache by denying their relationship in Henry Fielding's *A Journey From This World to the Next*.

Miss Leroy (Mrs. Butts)   Eccentric daughter of Old Leroy; she has unusual religious beliefs and amazes her neighbors when she marries George Butts, so ordinary and her opposite, and bears him a son, Clement, in Mark Rutherford's *Mark Rutherford's Deliverance*.

Old Leroy   A French soldier held prisoner in England during the wars with Revolutionary France, who settles permanently in England and raises his daughter, Miss Leroy, in Mark Rutherford's *Mark Rutherford's Deliverance*.

Lesley   Soldier and Captain M'Intyre's friend, who serves as his second in the duel with William Lovel in Sir Walter Scott's *The Antiquary*.

Mrs. Leslie   Elderly, devoted friend of Lady Vargrave (Alice Darvil); she is a custodian of the secret of the parentage of Evelyn Cameron (Templeton) in Edward Bulwer-Lytton's *Alice*.

Juliet Leslie   Daughter of impoverished gentry; her chance of a happy marriage to Frank Hazeldean in unintentionally blasted by the intrigues of her brother, Randal Leslie, in Edward Bulwer-Lytton's *"My Novel," by Pisistratus Caxton*.

Lucy Leslie   Star in the acting company and mistress of Dick Lennox until he meets Kate Ede; she is Kate's best friend in the company, though Kate is frequently jealous of her in George Moore's *A Mummer's Wife*.

Sir Ludovich Leslie   Dalgetty's military teacher while in Germany with Gustavus Adolphus's army in Sir Walter Scott's *A Legend of Montrose*.

Ralph Leslie   Enemy of Lord Seyton in Sir Walter Scott's *The Abbot*.

Randal Leslie   Poor kinsman of Audley Egerton; he repays the educational and political benefits he has received by plotting with Baron Levy to defeat Egerton in a Parliamentary election and have him imprisoned for debt in Edward Bulwer-Lytton's *"My Novel," by Pisistratus Caxton*.

Ludovic Lesly (Le Balafré)   Archer of the Scottish Guard and Quentin Durward's uncle; indifferent to human suffering, he nonetheless refuses to be an assassin; he relinquishes his right to Isabelle de Croye to Quentin; he is called Le Balafré ("the scarred") because of a hideous scar on his face in Sir Walter Scott's *Quentin Durward*.

Le Songe   A pimp for DouLache and a staunch villain in Eliza Haywood's *The Injur'd Husband; or, the Mistaken Resentment*.

Mrs. Lessingham   Aunt and companion of Cecily Doran; she believes in a broader education for women but becomes disillusioned with her theories when Cecily runs away and marries an irresponsible husband in George Gissing's *The Emancipated*.

Ellinor Lester   Younger daughter of Rowland Lester and sister of Madeline Lester; she ultimately marries her cousin, Walter Lester, in Edward Bulwer-Lytton's *Eugene Aram*.

Geoffrey Lester   Wanderer who abandons his family and assumes the name Daniel Clarke; his disappearance leads to a search which reveals that he was killed by Eugene Aram in Edward Bulwer-Lytton's *Eugene Aram*.

Madeline Lester   Rowland Lester's elder daughter, whose beauty, purity, and learning win Eugene Aram in Edward Bulwer-Lytton's *Eugene Aram*.

Rowland Lester   Brother of Geoffrey and father of Ellinor and Madeline Lester; he remains loyal to Eugene Aram even after Aram is charged with the murder of Geoffrey Lester in Edward Bulwer-Lytton's *Eugene Aram*.

Walter Lester   Geoffrey Lester's son, who is raised by his uncle, Rowland Lester, and loves his cousin Madeline Lester; he collects the evidence which condemns Eugene Aram in Edward Bulwer-Lytton's *Eugene Aram*.

Lestrade   Scotland Yard police detective who is acknowledged by Sherlock Holmes as quick and energetic but conventional—with Inspector Tobias Gregson "the pick of a bad lot"; he and Gregson receive the official credit for the solution in Arthur Conan Doyle's *A Study in Scarlet*. Holmes sends for him to assist in the denouement of *The Hound of the Baskervilles*.

Harley L'Estrange   Heir to an earldom; he has squandered his youth in mourning Leonora Avenel; in middle age he resolves the difficulties of her son, Leonard Fairfield, saves Audley Egerton and Alphonso Riccabocca from the machinations of Randal Leslie, and marries Violante Riccabocca in Edward Bulwer-Lytton's *"My Novel," by Pisistratus Caxton*.

Lucetta Le Sueur   Beautiful, lonely lover of Michael Henchard; as Lucetta Templeman, she moves to

Casterbridge in hopes that Henchard will marry her, but, meeting Donald Farfrae, she changes course and marries him instead; when her former relationship with Henchard is exposed, however, she is publicly disgraced and dies of a miscarriage in Thomas Hardy's *The Mayor of Casterbridge.*

Le Val Lord Leicester's devoted and watchful valet in Sophia Lee's *The Recess.*

Gryphard, Lord Levellier Miserly "woman-scorner," who helps to manipulate his niece, Carinthia Kirby, into marrying Lord Fleetwood and withholds an inheritance from his nephew, Chillon Kirby, in George Meredith's *The Amazing Marriage.*

Frank Leven Student at Eton and aristocratic friend of Aldous Raeburn; he marries Betty Macdonald in Mrs. Humphry Ward's *Marcella.* As Member of Parliament and Sir Frank Levin he yearns to return to his estates to live the life of a country squire in *Sir George Tressady.*

Mr. Leverre A widower with a young son; a bygone Jersey lover of Marcia Bencomb, he persuades her to marry him when she is left impoverished after her father's death; after his death she rears the boy in Thomas Hardy's *The Well-Beloved.*

Henri Leverre Marcia Bencomb's step-son, who elopes with Avice Pierston, forestalling Avice's marriage to Jocelyn Pierston in Thomas Hardy's *The Well-Beloved.*

Isaac Levi Elderly Oriental Jew, who is evicted from his longtime home by John Meadows; he becomes Meadows's nemesis, following George Fielding to Australia and returning to England to expose Meadows on his intended wedding day in Charles Read's *It Is Never Too Late to Mend.*

Dr. Levitt Rector of Deerbrook in Harriet Martineau's *Deerbrook.*

Frank Levitt Tall, thin outlaw, who maintains a restraining influence over his companions, Tom Laurence and Meg Murdockson, in Sir Walter Scott's *The Heart of Midlothian.*

Mr. Levy Clerk to George Vavasor, who sends him to extort money from Alice Vavasor for election expenses in Anthony Trollope's *Can You Forgive Her?.*

Baron Levy Sinister moneylender, whose rejection by Leonora Avenel drove him to blast her happiness; he entangles Randall Leslie in plots against Audley Egerton and Harley L'Estrange in Edward Bulwer-Lytton's *"My Novel," by Pisistratus Caxton.*

Maurice Lewellyn Closest friend of the Brooks family; he loves Mariana, but she rejects his proposal; he meets Beatrice Brooks when she is working and starving and helps Beatrice and her child; he marries Helen Wallingham, best friend of Beatrice, in Caroline Norton's *Lost and Saved.*

Dr. Lewen An elderly divine, whose conversations with the young Clarissa Harlowe develop her religious education in Samuel Richardson's *Clarissa: or, The History of a Young Lady.*

Mrs. Lewis Kind nurse who, in contrast to the baby-farmer, Mrs. Spires, takes good care of Jackie Latch for several years; she gives sanctuary to Esther Waters when she is unemployed in George Moore's *Esther Waters.*

Dr. Richard Lewis Friend with whom Matthew Bramble corresponds while on his expedition in Tobias Smollett's *The Expedition of Humphry Clinker.*

Mr. Lewsome A London doctor's assistant who becomes indebted to Jonas Chuzzlewit and provides him with lethal drugs; delirious with fever, Lewsome raves of the crime to his nurses, Sarah Gamp and Betsy Prig; he confesses to John Westlock in Charles Dickens's *The Life and Adventures of Martin Chuzzlewit.*

Agnes Leyburn Plain sister of Catherine in Mrs. Humphry Ward's *Robert Elsmere.*

Catherine Leyburn Puritanical, saintly daughter of a clergyman; she marries Robert Elsmere and has difficulty in accepting his loss of faith in Mrs. Humphry Ward's *Robert Elsmere.*

Rose Leyburn Beautiful, musically talented sister of Catherine; she finally marries Hugh Flaxman in Mrs. Humphry Ward's *Robert Elsmere.*

Antonio de Leyva Governor and tireless defender of the city of Pavia, which is besieged by the army of King Francis in William Godwin's *St. Leon.*

Tristan L'Hermite Provost-marshal of the royal household; a sullen and sinister hangman, he is a favorite of Louis XI in Sir Walter Scott's *Quentin Durward.*

Liberia A celebrated lady of the town who is addicted to cards and loses a lot of money; she sells her body to Jemmy Jessamy, among others, in an effort to pay her debts without her father's knowledge in Eliza Haywood's *The History of Jemmy and Jenny Jessamy.*

Robert Lickpan Rustic whose anecdotes of local history include references to King Charles the Third and

King Charles the Fourth in Thomas Hardy's *A Pair of Blue Eyes*.

Lien Chi Altangi   Chinaman visiting in London; his descriptive letters to Far Eastern associates are the vehicle of satire in Oliver Goldsmith's *The Citizen of the World*.

Lieutenant   Good man who is distressed because his reward for forty years of service in the Navy is poverty and contempt in Charles Johnstone's *Chrysal: or, The Adventures of a Guinea*.

Lieutenant   Honest soldier who recognizes Tom Jones's breeding and ensures that he receives fair treatment after Ensign Northerton assaults him in Henry Fielding's *The History of Tom Jones*.

Lieutenant-Colonel of Fort St. George   Richard Middlemas's priggish commanding officer, whom Richard kills in a duel in Sir Walter Scott's *The Surgeon's Daughter*.

Luckie Lightbody   Mrs. Girder's mother and Caleb Balderson's friend; she protects her daughter when Mr. Girder threatens her in Sir Walter Scott's *The Bride of Lammermoor*.

Janet Lightoheel   Godfrey Bertram's mistress and the mother of his illegitimate son, Godfrey Bertram Hewit, in Sir Walter Scott's *Guy Mannering*.

Mortimer Lightwood   Eugene Wrayburn's indolent solicitor friend, who attends the Veneering dinner parties regularly and has a law practice with no clients except the Boffins in Charles Dickens's *Our Mutual Friend*.

Lilith (Princess of Bulika)   Vampiric and disobedient first wife of Adam; after bearing the child Lona, she consorted with the Great Shadow, who made her the Queen of Hell; she fears children since a prophecy has predicted that her own daughter will destroy her; she transforms herself into a spotted leopardess to kill children born in Bulika; in her left hand she holds the water of the kingdom, thereby turning it into a wasteland; she kills her daughter in George MacDonald's *Lilith*.

Lilla   Noblewoman engaged to Henriquez; her innocence and beauty make her the victim of Victoria di Loredani in Charlotte Dacre's *Zofloya; or, The Moor*.

Prince of Lilliput   Foolish but good-hearted prince, whom Vivian Grey saves from a wild boar and assists in his political negotiations to regain his lands in Benjamin Disraeli's *Vivian Grey*.

William Lilly   Guy Mannering's old tutor, who taught him astrology in Sir Walter Scott's *Guy Mannering*.

Mr. Lillyvick   Collector of water rates, who bullies the Kenwigses by threatening to cut their three daughters out of his will when they displease him; he betrays them by marrying an actress, Henrietta Petowker, but returns to the Kenwigs family when Henrietta abandons him to return to the stage in Charles Dickens's *The Life and Adventures of Nicholas Nickleby*.

Mr. Limbkins   Chairman of the parish authorities, whose jurisdiction includes the workhouse where Oliver Twist was born in Charles Dickens's *Oliver Twist*.

Reuben Limbrick   Anti-social, intruder-phobic brother of Hester Dethridge; dying, he leaves her the isolated, fortified house Geoffrey Delamayn rents for his athletic training and retains as a convenient prison for Anne Silvester and suitable site for her murder in Wilkie Collins's *Man and Wife*.

Madame De Limon   Madame Du Maine's jealous daughter, who, with her husband, conspires with Monsieur De Rhíe in the kidnapping and imprisonment of Cornelia in Sarah Scott's *The History of Cornelia*.

Monsieur De Limon   Madame Du Maine's jealous son-in-law, who, with his wife, conspires with Monsieur De Rhíe in the kidnapping and imprisonment of Cornelia in Sarah Scott's *The History of Cornelia*.

Lina   Hideously ugly animal, who was once probably a woman who is atoning and improving former bad behavior; she is Curdie Peterson's faithful and courageous companion, sent by old Princess Irene, in George MacDonald's *The Princess and Curdie*.

Lindamira   Censorious prude, who leads Leonora's friends to snub her when she visits the wounded Bellarmine too freely in Henry Fielding's *The History of the Adventures of Mr. Joseph Andrews and of his Friend Mr. Abraham Adams*.

Lindamira   Lydia's beautiful sister, who is preferred by their parents in Sarah Fielding's *Familiar Letters between the Principal Characters of David Simple and Some Others*.

Lady Marion Lindell   Eldest sister of the Marquis of Worthing and a widow; as chaperon to Lady Helen Seely, she is unprepared for Lady Helen's insistence on marrying Lewis Seymour in George Moore's *A Modern Lover*.

Otto, Baron Lindenberg   Ancestor of the current baron and murderer of Beatrice de las Cisternas, the Bleeding Nun, in Matthew Lewis's *The Monk*.

Rodolpha, Baroness Lindenberg   Vengeful aunt who hastens Agnes de Medina's entry into a convent because she was rejected by Agnes's lover, Alphonso d'Alvereda (Raymond, Marquis de la Cisternas), in Matthew Lewis's *The Monk*.

Lindesay   One of Louis XI's Scottish Guard archers who save Quentin Durward from hanging in Sir Walter Scott's *Quentin Durward*.

Lord Lindesay   Rude and haughty commissioner sent by the Scottish privy council to force Queen Mary to abdicate; after brutishly bruising her with his gauntlet, he begs her forgiveness in Sir Walter Scott's *The Abbot*.

Eric Lindon   Handsome and brave soldier who lacks religious faith; he is Lady Muriel Orme's cousin and becomes her betrothed; he saves Bruno from being hit by a train in Lewis Carroll's *Sylvie and Bruno*. Lady Muriel's betrothed, he is unworthy because of religious doubts; he releases her from her commitment and departs but later returns, having begun to accept God; he saves Arthur Forester's life and restores him to Lady Muriel in *Sylvie and Bruno Concluded*.

Lord Lindore   The only son of Frederick, Lord Lindore and Lady Lindore; he is brother to Lady Emily Lindore and lover and second husband of Adelaide Douglas in Susan Ferrier's *Marriage*.

Lady Lindore   The wife of Frederick, Lord Lindore and sister-in-law of Lady Juliana Douglas; she runs off with Sir Leger when her children, Lady Emily and Lord Lindore, are very young in Susan Ferrier's *Marriage*.

Lady Emily Lindore   The only daughter of Frederick, Lord Lindore and Lady Lindore; she is reared by Frederick and his sister, Lady Juliana Douglas, and becomes the best friend of her cousin Mary Douglas in Susan Ferrier's *Marriage*.

Frederick, Lord Lindore   The only son of the Earl of Courtland and brother of Lady Juliana Douglas; he becomes Earl of Courtland after his father's death; he is father of Lady Emily Lindore and Lord Lindore in Susan Ferrier's *Marriage*.

Mr. Lindsay   Courageous Member of Parliament, who acts promptly in the Porteous riot in Sir Walter Scott's *The Heart of Midlothian*.

Mr. Lineric   Brother and lover of Lady Leicester, with whom he is poisoned when their plan to kill Leicester fails in Sophia Lee's *The Recess*.

Sir Patrick Lineric   Irish father of Mr. Lineric and Lady Leicester and brother-in-law of the Earl of Arundel in Sophia Lee's *The Recess*.

John Lingon   Arabella Transome's clergyman brother, who helps his nephew, Harold Transome, in politics in George Eliot's *Felix Holt, the Radical*.

Miss Linkinwater   Sister of Tim Linkinwater in Charles Dickens's *The Life and Adventures of Nicholas Nickleby*.

Tim Linkinwater   Chief clerk and long-time employee of the Cheeryble brothers; he teaches Nicholas Nickleby about the business; he marries Miss La Creevy in Charles Dickens's *The Life and Adventures of Nicholas Nickleby*.

Laurie Linklater   Royal cook, who helps Richie Moniplies and Nigel Olifaunt gain admission to King James I in Sir Walter Scott's *The Fortunes of Nigel*.

Lawyer Linkum   Dalcastle attorney who forges a grant, ostensibly by Robert Colwan's order, to assist him in the ruin of Mrs. Keeler and her daughter in James Hogg's *The Private Memoirs and Confessions of a Justified Sinner*.

Penelope, Lady Linlithgow   Parsimonious but duty-conscious aunt with whom Lizzie Greystock lives in London until marriage to Sir Florian Eustace makes her patronage and friendship unnecessary; out of duty she provides a temporary home also for Lucy Morris, who earns her affection in Anthony Trollope's *The Eustace Diamonds*.

Tom Linnet   Popular, good-natured houseguest at Marlowe; he is addicted to sentiment but is a practical joker in J. Sheridan Le Fanu's *Guy Deverell*.

Linton   Robert Colwan's fellow lodger in Edinburgh who introduces him to James Watson, the printer, in James Hogg's *The Private Memoirs and Confessions of a Justified Sinner*.

Catherine Linton   Attractive daughter of Edgar Linton and Catherine Earnshaw; she is forced into an unhappy and unnatural match to Linton Heathcliff but recovers to educate, love, and finally marry Hareton Earnshaw in Emily Brontë's *Wuthering Heights*.

Edgar Linton   Rich and conventionally handsome owner of Thrushcross Grange, who marries Catherine Earnshaw and brings up their daughter with a patient dignity that is no match for Heathcliff's revenge in Emily Brontë's *Wuthering Heights*.

Isabella Linton   Edgar Linton's romantic and silly sister, whom Heathcliff marries to further his vengeance; her infatuation with Heathcliff soon turns into fear and hatred after her marriage when she discovers his true nature in Emily Brontë's *Wuthering Heights*.

Lion Creature developed from the traditional nursery rhyme; after his fight with the Unicorn for the White King's crown, he instructs Alice to serve the plumcake backwards in Lewis Carroll's *Through the Looking-Glass*.

Lionel Brother of Mary, the heroine; he tries to prevent her marriage because he is lonely and needs her company; there are suggestions of "psychological" incest in Caroline Norton's *The Wife and Woman's Reward*.

Lisbia Monsieur de Maintenon's former servant, kidnapped in Wales by robbers who later abduct Belinda Lluelling, Maintenon's granddaughter; they escape together in Penelope Aubin's *The Life of Madam de Beaumont*.

Sir Charles Lisdale Character who retires to Wales under assumed identity, falls in love, discovers true happiness, and reveals to his surprised bride-to-be that he is not poor but extremely wealthy in Sarah Fielding's *The History of Ophelia*.

Lisette Literate servant of the de Roubignés; she writes to Julia de Roubigné's friend Maria de Roncilles when her mistress is unable to write in Henry Mackenzie's *Julia de Roubigné*.

Lieutenant Obadiah Lismahago Veteran of American wars who wins Tabitha Bramble with his accounts of his shocking experiences as a captive of Miami Indians; he is the victim of a practical joke by Thomas Bullford, on whom he gets his revenge in Tobias Smollett's *The Expedition of Humphry Clinker*.

Isaac List A gambler at the Valiant Soldier public house, who gambles with Nell Trent's grandfather in Charles Dickens's *The Old Curiosity Shop*.

Mr. Listless Young man who devotes his life to doing nothing whatever but becomes a rival to Scythrop Glowry in Thomas Love Peacock's *Nightmare Abbey*.

Mr. Liston A handsome, serious man, who is interested in the ancient Egyptians and unaware that his wife flirts with the young men in George Moore's *A Modern Lover*.

Littimer James Steerforth's valet, who surrounds himself with a great air of respectability; he assists his master in the seduction of Emily Peggotty; she spurns his degrading offer of marriage to her after Steerforth abandons her in Charles Dickens's *The Personal History of David Copperfield*.

Little Daylight Princess in the fairy tale told by Mr. Raymond to the children in the hospital; cursed at birth by an old witch to sleep all day and grow old with the waning moon, she is freed when, in her anile phase, she is kissed by a prince in George MacDonald's *At the Back of the North Wind*.

Little Girl The daughter of a middle-class merchant; she finds Pompey, takes him home, and then cruelly tortures and neglects him in Francis Coventry's *The History of Pompey the Little*.

Little Girl's Aunt Maiden lady and sister of the Father of the Little Girl; she delivers Pompey from the hands of the little tyrants by taking him home in Francis Coventry's *The History of Pompey the Little*.

Little Girl's Brother Spoiled and indulged favorite, who is educated at home by a tutor because it is "genteel" to educate young gentlemen at home in Francis Coventry's *The History of Pompey the Little*.

Little Girl's Father A rich merchant's son, who gives up business and retires to enter society in Francis Coventry's *The History of Pompey the Little*.

Little Girl's Mother Pale, unhealthy, and consumptive woman, who is out of place in society, but who is anxious to be accepted as a woman of fashion in Francis Coventry's *The History of Pompey the Little*.

Little Son of Honour The son whom Roxana has by the Prince of —— in Daniel Defoe's *The Fortunate Mistress*.

Little-faith Hero of a story told by Christian; he is robbed by three men, but his faith, though little, aids him in John Bunyan's *The Pilgrim's Progress From this World to That Which Is to Come*.

Bailie Littlejohn Crusty magistrate, who interrogates Edie Ochiltree on the charge of assault against Herman Dousterswivel and releases Edie into the custody of Oldbuck (Jonathan Oldenbuck) in Sir Walter Scott's *The Antiquary*.

Lively Small man who operates as a fence in Charles Dickens's *Oliver Twist*.

Tobias Liversedge Denzil Quarrier's brother-in-law, a Liberal, who urges Quarrier to run for Parliament in George Gissing's *Denzil Quarrier*.

Dr. David Livesey Shrewd physician, who warns Billy Bones about rum, looks after Jim Hawkins, outwits the pirates, and makes a deal with Long John Silver in Robert Louis Stevenson's *Treasure Island*.

Livia Wicked stepmother of Valentine and Camilla (Simple); she falsely charges them with incest; her deathbed confession of her machinations against them leads to their reconciliation with their father in Sarah Fielding's *The Adventures of David Simple in Search of a Faithful Friend.*

Signora Livona   Venetian mistress of the evil Montoni in Ann Radcliffe's *The Mysteries of Udolpho.*

Liz   Brickmaker's wife who is a friend of Jenny and nurses Jo when he has fever in Charles Dickens's *Bleak House.*

Lizzy   Young pieceworker forced into prostitution in order to support her dying sister, Ellen; she is befriended by Sandy Mackaye and ultimately rehabilitated by Lady Ellerton in Charles Kingsley's *Alton Locke.*

Alithea Llansoy   Ward of the cruel lawyer Old Cock; she escapes his clutches with the aid of John Buncle and his servant, Soto O'Fin, and takes refuge at Buncle's retreat, Orton Lodge, until Old Cock's death in Thomas Amory's *The Life of John Buncle, Esq.*

Dr. Lloyd   Inadequate physician, who attracts wealthy patients but is ruined by his rivalry with Allen Fenwick in Edward Bulwer-Lytton's *A Strange Story.*

Mr. Lloyd   An apothecary who treats Jane Eyre at the Reed residence and suggests that she be sent away to school because he can sense her mistreatment by the family in Charlotte Brontë's *Jane Eyre.*

Gwynnie Lloyd (Westhall)   Working girl, model for the artist Lewis Seymour in his poverty; forgotten when he moves to higher society, she is not recognized by him when she later becomes maid to Lady Helen (Seely) Seymour in George Moore's *A Modern Lover.*

Mr. Lluelling   Kind Welsh gentleman with a handsome estate; he falls in love with and marries Madam de Beaumont's daughter, Belinda; fulfilling a pledge, he searches for and finds Count de Beaumont in France; they are forced to land in Ireland on their way back to Wales, which they finally reach only to discover that Belinda has been kidnapped; after a search, she is found and reunited with Lluelling in Penelope Aubin's *The Life of Madam de Beaumont.*

Belinda Lluelling   Madam de Beaumont's beautiful, virtuous daughter, who marries Mr. Lluelling; she is abducted by Mr. Glandore, who is killed by highwaymen before he can ravish her; she takes refuge with Mr. Hide, who loves her but respects her virtue and sends her home; stopped by robbers, she is saved by a fisherman, who reunites her with her family in Penelope Aubin's *The Life of Madam de Beaumont.*

Marquis of Llwddythlw   Dedicated Member of Parliament, who constantly pleads pressure of work to post-

pone his marriage to Lady Amaldina Hauteville in Anthony Trollope's *Marion Fay.*

Lo   Young Gy (woman) who loves the elder son of Aph-Lin and is persuaded to confess her affection by his mother, Bra, in Edward Bulwer-Lytton's *The Coming Race.*

Mr. Loadsworth   A legal counselor involved in the scheme to keep Medora Glenmorris from getting her inheritance in Charlotte Smith's *The Young Philosopher.*

Old Lobbs   Prosperous saddler with a beautiful daughter in "A Tale of True Love," told by Sam Weller and written down by Samuel Pickwick in Charles Dickens's *The Posthumous Papers of the Pickwick Club.*

Maria Lobbs   Beautiful daughter of Old Lobbs and beloved by Nathaniel Pipkin in "A Tale of True Love," told by Sam Weller and written down by Samuel Pickwick in Charles Dickens's *The Posthumous Papers of the Pickwick Club.*

Margery Lobkin   Drunken foster mother of Paul Clifford in Edward Bulwer-Lytton's *Paul Clifford.*

Margaret Erskine, Lady of Lochleven   The petulant wife of Sir William Douglas and Queen Mary of Scotland's vigilant keeper; as mistress of James V, she conceived James Stuart, now Earl of Murray and Regent of Scotland; deeply ashamed of her former unchastity, she eagerly embraces the austere tenets of Protestantism in Sir Walter Scott's *The Abbot.*

Sir William Douglas, Lord of Lochleven   Margaret Erskine's long-suffering husband; Queen Mary of Scotland is held captive in his castle in Sir Walter Scott's *The Abbot.*

Lockard   Sir William Ashton's confidential servant in Sir Walter Scott's *The Bride of Lammermoor.*

Mr. Locke   Uncle of Alton Locke; a prosperous grocer and father of Alton's unpleasant cousin, George, he arranges for the young Alton to start work as a tailor in Charles Kingsley's *Alton Locke.*

Mrs. Locke   Alton Locke's widowed mother, who enables her son to receive a minimal education; a fanatic Baptist and a stern disciplinarian, she turns young Alton out of the house when he becomes skeptical and defiant in Charles Kingsley's *Alton Locke.*

Alton Locke   Sickly Cockney tailor, self-educated poet, and Chartist, the narrator of the novel; befriended by Sandy Mackaye and Dean Winnstay, he falls in love with the dean's daughter, Lillian; influenced by the dean's niece, Eleanor (Lady Ellerton), who nurses him through a fever, he finally turns Christian socialist and dies en route to America in Charles Kingsley's *Alton Locke*.

George Locke   Cousin, enemy, and rival in love of Alton Locke; ambitious and self-serving, he uses and betrays his cousin; he becomes a clergyman and marries Lillian Winnstay, finally perishing from typhus supposedly caught from an infected coat made in a sweatshop in Charles Kingsley's *Alton Locke*.

Susan Locke   Alton Locke's sister, who grows up to be a fanatic Baptist like her mother and marries the hypocritical preacher Mr. Wiglinton in Charles Kingsley's *Alton Locke*.

Patty Lockit   One of the nine pupils of Mrs. Teachum's school; she learns of the potentially dire effects of envy in Sarah Fielding's *The Governess*.

Mr. Lockwood   The primary first-person narrator, the conventional outsider who comes as tenant of Thrushcross Grange and to whom Nelly Dean narrates the story of the Lintons and the Earnshaws in Emily Brontë's *Wuthering Heights*.

Jack Lockwood   Faithful servant to Henry Esmond in William Makepeace Thackeray's *The History of Henry Esmond*. He is the aged porter at Castlewood in *The Virginians*.

Miss Lockyer   A gentlewoman ruined by Robert Lovelace before he ruins Clarissa Harlowe in Samuel Richardson's *Clarissa: or, The History of a Young Lady*.

Major Loder   A disreputable gambler, who is an ally of Becky Sharp in her decline in William Makepeace Thackeray's *Vanity Fair*. He is a follower of the Duchesse d'Ivry in *The Newcomes*.

Lodovico   Teresa's husband, who is hired by Princess Claelia Cesarini to assassinate Gerard; when Gerard begs him to do so and throws himself into the Tiber River, Lodovico rescues him and turns him over to Fra Jerome in Charles Reade's *The Cloister and the Hearth*.

Dan Loftus   Erudite young scholar, somewhat meek but kindly; he is hired to travel the Continent as tutor to Richard Devereux's cousin; he returns to Chapelizod just after Lilias Walsingham's death to comfort her father, Dr. Walsingham; he serves as Walsingham's curate until the rector's death, then becomes personal chaplain to the young Lord Dunoran (Mervyn) and Gertrude Chattesworth in J. Sheridan Le Fanu's *The House by the Churchyard*.

Lord Lofty   An admirer of Amoranda; he is very vain;

he is an imposter and seduces Altemira in Mary Davys's *The Reform'd Coquet*.

Arabella Logan   Mistress of the elder George Colwan; she seeks evidence against Lady Dalcastle (Rabina Colwan) and Robert Colwan for the murder of their son and brother, the younger George Colwan, in James Hogg's *The Private Memoirs and Confessions of a Justified Sinner*.

The Logothe   Chancellor of the empire in Sir Walter Scott's *Count Robert of Paris*.

Rummun Loll   Dishonest founder of the Bundelcund Bank, the demise of which bankrupts Colonel Newcome and many others in William Makepeace Thackeray's *The Newcomes*.

Adrian (Daddy) Lomax   Freethinking secularist of Manchester; he runs the "Parlour," a popular vegetarian restaurant and meeting place for Freethinkers; he befriends David Grieve and shapes his education in Mrs. Humphry Ward's *The History of David Grieve*.

Dora Lomax   Daughter of Adrian Lomax; she rejects his freethinking secularism to become a devoted member of and worker for the Church of England in Mrs. Humphry Ward's *The History of David Grieve*.

Larquis de Lomelli   Neapolitan relative whose illness calls Hippolitus de Vereza away from Mazzini castle and whose death makes Vereza heir to a small fortune in Ann Radcliffe's *A Sicilian Romance*.

Lomellino   Aged counselor to Doge Andreas; he knows that Count Rosalvo is Abellino/Flodoardo and assists his entrapment of the conspirators in Matthew Lewis's *The Bravo of Venice*.

Lord de Lomene   Nobleman at Henry III's court in Ann Radcliffe's *Gaston de Blondeville*.

Lona   Daughter of Lilith; largest of the Lovers (Little Ones), she is regarded by all the others as their mother; Vane falls in love with her; she is killed by her mother in George MacDonald's *Lilith*.

Adolphus Longestaffe   Extravagant squire, proud of his estates and of his idleness but forced by lack of funds to associate with upstart entrepreneurs, especially Augustus Melmotte, to whom he eagerly gives up the title deeds for one of his country houses in exchange for promises of payment, with disastrous results in Anthony Trollope's *The Way We Live Now*.

Adolphus (Dolly) Longestaffe   Dim-witted member of the Beargarden Club frequently at odds with his father over his spendthrift ways; after his father loses one of the entailed family properties, he puts his affairs into the hands of the lawyer Squercum in Anthony Trollope's *The Way We Live Now*. His infatuation with Isabel Boncassen takes him by surprise; she is insulted by his persistent courtship in *The Duke's Children*.

Georgiana Longestaffe　　Strong-minded, too-long-un-married younger daughter of Adolphus Longestaffe; angered by her father's economies curtailing her social round, she redoubles her efforts to find a rich husband; she breaks her engagement with Ezekiel Brehgert when he loses money in Augustus Melmotte's business swindles and ends up in a desperate elopement with a country curate in Anthony Trollope's *The Way We Live Now*.

Lady Pomona Longestaffe　　Greedy consort of the squire of Caversham; she prides herself on the grandeur of their establishment and schemes unsuccessfully for years to get her daughters, Sophia and Georgiana, rich husbands in the London marriage market in Anthony Trollope's *The Way We Live Now*.

Sophia Longestaffe　　Unalluring elder daughter of Adolphus Longestaffe; her mother's efforts to secure a rich husband for her come to nothing and she settles, with smug complacency maddening to her still-unmarried sister, for the brainless George Whitstable of Toodlum Hall in Anthony Trollope's *The Way We Live Now*.

Edward Longfield　　Gentleman's son working as a servant for Lord Stivers; his testimony clears Arabella Clement of murder and robbery charges; befriended by the Clements, he is eventually rewarded with a schoolmaster's position by Henry Clinton in Henry Brooke's *The Fool of Quality*.

Douglas B. Longhurst　　San Francisco tycoon, head of the wrecker ring, and friend of Dr. Urquart; he lends Norris Carthew money in Robert Louis Stevenson's *The Wrecker*.

Mr. Longman　　Longtime, faithful steward of Mr. B——'s Bedfordshire estate and friend to Pamela Andrews in her early tribulations in Samuel Richardson's *Pamela, or Virtue Rewarded*.

Nicholas Long-shanks　　Warden of the High House at Upmeads; his men cut off Ralph's fleeing foes in the final battle in William Morris's *The Well at the World's End*.

Sir Lords Longstop　　Enthusiastic member of the British touring side in the epic encounter with cricketers of the host island Britannula in Anthony Trollope's *The Fixed Period*.

Count de Longueville　　Noble ward of Count de Vinevil; he marries Ardelisa de Vinevil just before they attempt to flee Turkey but is swept out to sea before she can join him; he believes her dead and sets sail for France, where he retires into an abbey until he and Ardelisa are happily reunited in Penelope Aubin's *The Strange Adventures of the Count de Vinevil and His Family*.

Lonquillez　　Faithful servant of Count Louis de Montauban; he spies on Julia de Roubigné for his master in Henry Mackenzie's *Julia de Roubigné*.

Figgins Lonsford　　Son of a lord and schoolmate, though never an acquaintance, of Ernest Pontifex; envisioned as the friend of Ernest and the husband of her daughter, he is the object of Christina Pontifex's aspirations in Samuel Butler's *The Way of All Flesh*.

Dr. Looby　　Physician who is displaced by the fraudulent Ferdinand in Tobias Smollett's *The Adventures of Ferdinand Count Fathom*.

Mr. Lookaloft　　Tenant farmer at Ullathorne in Anthony Trollope's *The Warden*.

Mrs. Lookaloft　　Snobbish wife of a Ullathorne tenant farmer; she intrudes with her daughters into Miss Thorne's drawing room at the Ullathorne party in Anthony Trollope's *Barchester Towers*.

Lootie　　Pet name of Princess Irene's nurse, who disbelieves the child's story about her visit with her great-great-grandmother in George MacDonald's *The Princess and the Goblin*.

Emily Wharton Lopez　　Stubborn only daughter of Abel Wharton; she distresses her father by marrying the adventurer Ferdinand Lopez; his attempts to use her to extract money from her wealthy father for his dubious business ventures cause her great misery; his suicide crushes her spirit, but she is at last won by the persistent kindness and love of Arthur Fletcher in Anthony Trollope's *The Prime Minister*.

Ferdinand Lopez　　Personable scoundrel of mysterious background; he marries Emily Wharton and tries to further his dubious business ventures by scrounging from her wealthy father; he inveigles the support of the Duchess of Omnium in his unsuccessful bid for Parliament; his financial affairs desperate, he commits suicide by jumping in front of a train in Anthony Trollope's *The Prime Minister*.

Lord——　　Gentleman who is the supposed nephew of the Matron, but who is, in reality, the father of the girl who has been procured for him in Charles Johnstone's *Chrysal: or, The Adventures of a Guinea*.

Lord——　　Roxana's lover; she grows tired of him and

finally provokes him into leaving her in Daniel Defoe's *The Fortunate Mistress*.

Lord High Chancellor   The godlike figure who presides over the Court of Chancery in Charles Dickens's *Bleak House*.

Horace Lord   Immature, dandified brother of Nancy; he insists on marrying Fanny French, to whom he has been engaged, even after she has had a scandalous affair with another man in George Gissing's *In the Year of Jubilee*.

Nancy Lord   Educated, restless middle-class girl, who must conceal her marriage to Lionel Tarrant or lose her inheritance according to her father's will; she becomes alienated from her irresponsible husband and gives birth secretly, but the marriage becomes known and she is forced to support herself for a time in George Gissing's *In the Year of Jubilee*.

Stephen Lord   Distant, blunt-speaking, autocratic father, whose will provides that his children must marry late or lose their inheritances in George Gissing's *In the Year of Jubilee*.

Marchese di Loredani   Venetian nobleman who is betrayed by his wife, Laurina, and killed by her lover, Count Ardolph, in Charlotte Dacre's *Zofloya; or, The Moor*.

Laurina di Loredani   Marchese di Loredani's vain wife, who is seduced away from her husband and two children by Count Ardolph in Charlotte Dacre's *Zofloya; or, The Moor*.

Leonardo di Loredani   Young nobleman, Marchese di Loredani's son, who tries to escape his mother's notoriety, and who falls victim to a jealous older woman; he later becomes leader of the banditti in Charlotte Dacre's *Zofloya; or, The Moor*.

Victoria di Loredani   Proud young noblewoman, whose love of Henriquez, brother of her husband, leads her to murder and the compromise of her soul in Charlotte Dacre's *Zofloya; or, The Moor*.

Don Lorenzo   Don Mario's nephew who is dying in a convent of his wounds; his identifiable costume is worn by Hippolito to the ball; his last rites are the cause of an open door between Don Mario's garden and the convent, enabling Hippolito to approach and then to marry Leonora in William Congreve's *Incognita*.

Father Lorenzo   Old Franciscan monk, whose begging provokes Yorick's criticism, but whose forgiving nature and eventual death elicit a tender eulogy from Yorick in Laurence Sterne's *A Sentimental Journey through France and Italy*.

Mr. Lorimer   Debauched youth who travels in Europe, sends his father a letter he has plagiarized from Sir Charles Grandison as evidence of his virtue, and has his governor, Dr. Bartlett, imprisoned in Athens by the Turkish authorities; he dies in Rome in Samuel Richardson's *Sir Charles Grandison*.

Lorimier   Sir Duncan's servant sent to tend Dalgetty in Sir Walter Scott's *A Legend of Montrose*.

Amalia, Mrs. Felix Lorraine   Duplicitous sister-in-law of the Marquess of Carabas; she spreads malicious lies, which damage Vivian Grey's political career, and tries to poison him to keep him from revealing her declaration of love to Frederick Cleveland in Benjamin Disraeli's *Vivian Grey*.

Sir Guy Lorrequer   Wealthy, childless uncle of both Harry Lorrequer and Harry's cousin, Guy Lorrequer, in Charles Lever's *The Confessions of Harry Lorrequer*.

Guy Lorrequer   Nephew of Sir Guy Lorrequer and unsuccessful aspirant for the affection of Lady Jane Callonby in Charles Lever's *The Confessions of Harry Lorrequer*.

Harry Lorrequer   High-spirited young army subaltern, who succeeds in winning the love of Lady Jane Callonby after numerous scrapes and adventures in Charles Lever's *The Confessions of Harry Lorrequer*.

Mariana Lorrimore   Young half sister of Colonel Delmont's wife; she marries the elderly Lord Castledanes and is soon left a widow with two young sons; the children do not live many years in Charlotte Smith's *The Young Philosopher*.

Jarvis Lorry   Clerk at Tellson's Bank in London and Paris and close friend of the Manettes; he helps them escape the French Reign of Terror in Charles Dickens's *A Tale of Two Cities*.

Lory   Self-important creature from the pool of tears in Lewis Carroll's *Alice's Adventures in Wonderland*.

Mr. Losberne   Eccentric bachelor surgeon, who tends Oliver Twist at Mrs. Maylie's after he is shot and attends Rose Maylie during her illness in Charles Dickens's *Oliver Twist*.

John Loscombe   Assiduous solicitor employed by Magdalen Vanstone to urge executors of Admiral Bartram's estate to search for a secret trust in her late husband's will in Wilkie Collins's *No Name*.

Jasper Losely   Criminal son of William Waife and lover of Gabrielle Desmarets; he is finally subdued by

Arabella Crane in Edward Bulwer-Lytton's *What Will He Do With It? by Pisistratus Caxton*.

William Losely See William Waife.

Lothair Serious-minded and impulsive youth, heir to great fortune and estates, who is torn among three influences: Church of England, Roman Catholicism, and revolutionary liberalism, each of which is represented by an attractive woman (Lady Corisande Brentham, Clare Arundel, and Theodora Campian, respectively) in Benjamin Disraeli's *Lothair*.

Lothaire Cruel son of King Louis of France; he breaks his promises to Duke Richard of Normandy in Charlotte Yonge's *The Little Duke*.

Lothario Young man who ravishes Miss Johnson and abandons her to his friend Horatio in Tobias Smollett's *The Adventures of Roderick Random*.

Adam Loudon Stiff, wealthy, retired Edinburgh grocer; his proposal that his penniless nephew, Loudon Dodd, take a job in his warehouse is opposed by his father, Alexander Loudon, in Robert Louis Stevenson's *The Wrecker*.

Alexander (Ecky) Loudon Cantankerous stonemason, Loudon Dodd's grandfather; he likes Dodd and leaves him nearly £17,000 in Robert Louis Stevenson's *The Wrecker*.

Louis Young singer and retainer at Avenel Castle in Sir Walter Scott's *The Monastery*.

King Louis Tenth-century king of France; he makes Duke Richard of Normandy a ward of his court but really a prisoner until he is freed by the daring plan of Osmond de Centeville in Charlotte Yonge's *The Little Duke*.

Prince Louis of Bourbon, Bishop of Liège The Duke of Burgundy's beloved brother-in-law, a luxury-loving old man and generous ruler; a French-inspired Liègeois revolt led by William de La Marck results in his murder and the ransacking of his castle in Sir Walter Scott's *Quentin Durward*.

Louis XI, King of France Ruthless and avaricious monarch who humiliates his nobility by raising low-born peasants to exalted ranks and amuses himself by assuming the disguise of Maître Pierre and mingling with the people; he kindles the Liègeois revolt and is imprisoned by the Duke of Burgundy in Sir Walter Scott's *Quentin Durward*.

Louisa Unhappy maid of Magdalen Vanstone; she reveals that she has a child born out of wedlock; her mis-

tress agrees to help her if she teaches her the duties of a parlor maid to further her scheme of recovering a lost inheritance by assuming Louisa's name and role in Admiral Bartram's household in Wilkie Collins's *No Name*.

Louisa Widowed sister-in-law of the evil Scottish baron Malcolm; she is held captive by Malcolm for control of her land and money; released upon Malcolm's death, she is reunited with her long-lost son Philip in Ann Radcliffe's *The Castles of Athlin and Dunbayne*.

Louisa Olive-skinned, brunette prostitute, the most capricious and high-spirited of Fanny Hill's colleagues at Mrs. Coles's; having eagerly given up her virginity at thirteen, she became a professional, seduced the retarded "Good-natured Dick," and abruptly disappeared abroad with an inamorato in John Cleland's *Memoirs of a Woman of Pleasure*.

Louisa Dorilaus's ward (actually, daughter), who runs away from his advances and goes to work for a jealous milliner; she is lavishly befriended by Melanthe, until the Count de Bellfleur's attentions make Melanthe jealous; she falls in love with du Plessis and marries him in Eliza Haywood's *The Fortunate Foundlings*.

Princess Louisa Maria Teresa The exiled King James II's daughter, attended by Charlotta de Palfoy in Eliza Haywood's *The Fortunate Foundlings*.

Louise Glee-maiden who is protected by Henry Smith and who becomes Catherine Glover's companion during their captivity by John Ramorny in Sir Walter Scott's *The Fair Maid of Perth*.

Laird of Louponheight An awkward "booby," who admires Menie Gray, causing Richard Middlemas and Adam Hartley to begin pursuing her in Sir Walter Scott's *The Surgeon's Daughter*.

Mr. Loveday Miller at Overcombe Mill and father of John and Bob; he marries Martha Garland in order not to waste the extensive housecleaning done for the reception of Matilda Johnson in Thomas Hardy's *The Trumpet-Major*.

John Loveday Trumpet-major during the Napoleonic wars who falls deeply and selflessly in love with Anne Garland, the daughter of the woman who marries his widowed father; after Anne rejects him in favor of his sailor brother, Bob, he strives to promote her happiness by assisting his brother's suit; successful, he goes off to die in battle in Thomas Hardy's *The Trumpet-Major*.

Robert (Bob) Loveday John Loveday's jovial, good-natured, though inconstant brother, a sailor who returns to his coastal village with Matilda Johnson, his betrothed;

when her history is known to him, he quickly transfers his affection to Anne Garland, the woman with whom his brother is in love, eventually winning her from John, although he is the less devoted of the two, in Thomas Hardy's *The Trumpet-Major*.

Mr. Lovegrove Very amiable man in love with Lady Speck in Eliza Haywood's *The History of Jemmy and Jenny Jessamy*.

Sir Basil Loveit Friend of Miss Forward and a suitor to Betsy Thoughtless in Eliza Haywood's *The History of Miss Betsy Thoughtless*.

Harriet Loveit An object of Charles Trueworth's pursuit in Eliza Haywood's *The History of Miss Betsy Thoughtless*.

Earl Lovel Lustful, vindictive peer, who abandons his wife, Josephine, claiming soon after their wedding that their marriage is void because he has a wife still living in Italy in Anthony Trollope's *Lady Anna*.

Mr. Lovel London fop who is sometimes a companion of Lord Orville and who is attacked by a monkey in a practical joke played by Captain Mirvan in Frances Burney's *Evelina*.

Lady Anna (Murray) Lovel Strong-minded daughter of Josephine Murray, Countess Lovel; when the machinations of her father, the old earl, place her legitimacy in doubt, she falls in love with Daniel Thwaite, son of the tailor who has spent his fortune in defense of her and her mother; when her fortunes are restored, she refuses to give Daniel up despite her mother's insistence; the couple marry and emigrate to Australia in Anthony Trollope's *Lady Anna*.

Barbara Lovel Queen of the Gypsies; having failed to marry her granddaughter, Sybil, to Luke Rookwood, she arranges for his death by poisoning and dies herself beneath a gibbet on which hang the bodies of her two sons in William Harrison Ainsworth's *Rookwood*.

Charles Lovel A clergyman and the affectionate uncle of Frederick Lovel, the young earl; he thinks it inappropriate that Frederick marry Lady Anna Lovel in Anthony Trollope's *Lady Anna*.

Edmund Lovel Rightful heir to the Lovel estate; he is taken in by peasants when his mother is driven from her castle; he is befriended by William Fitz-Owen and raised in the Fitz-Owen family until he discovers his true parentage; he is recognized by all as a paragon of virtue, morality, and decorum in Clara Reeve's *The Old English Baron*.

Frederick Lovel Decent and fair-minded nephew of the cruel Earl Lovel and heir to the title; he falls in love with Lady Anna Lovel, but she refuses him; she later divides her fortune with him in Anthony Trollope's *Lady Anna*.

Jane Lovel Patient wife of the Reverend Charles Lovel; she cares for Lady Anna Lovel and does all she can to promote a match between her and Frederick, the young Earl Lovel, in Anthony Trollope's *Lady Anna*.

Josephine Murray, Countess Lovel Wretched, proud victim of the wicked Lord Lovel; she is informed by him soon after marrying him that he already has another wife; befriended by a tailor, Thomas Thwaite, she brings up her daughter, Lady Anna, determined to prove her legitimacy; when Anna wishes to marry the tailor's son, Daniel, though sought in marriage by Frederick Lovel, she tries to kill Daniel; she ends up a recluse in Cumberland giving charity to the poor in Anthony Trollope's *Lady Anna*.

Julia Lovel Wise, strong-minded aunt of Frederick Lovel; she sympathizes with Lady Anna Lovel's wretchedness when her mother abandons her in Anthony Trollope's *Lady Anna*.

Minnie Lovel Younger daughter of the Reverend Charles Lovel; she is bridesmaid to Lady Anna Lovel when she marries Daniel Thwaite in Anthony Trollope's *Lady Anna*.

Sybil Lovel Beautiful Gypsy granddaughter of Barbara Lovel; at first loved by but later rejected by Luke (Bradley) Rookwood, she kills herself out of despair in William Harrison Ainsworth's *Rookwood*.

Sir Walter Lovel Wicked aristocrat who murders the rightful owners of the Lovel property and usurps their estate, which he sells to Baron Fitz-Owen when he is plagued by the accusing ghosts of his victims; after defeat in combat he confesses his guilt, surrenders his property, and goes into exile in Clara Reeve's *The Old English Baron*.

William Lovel See Major Neville, Lord Geraldin.

Henry Lovelace Socially ambitious Dean of Brotherton Cathedral and father of Mary (Lady George Germain); he promotes inquiry into the legitimacy of the son of the obnoxious Marquis of Brotherton, seeking thereby to secure heirship and inheritance to his son-in-law, Lord George Germain, brother of the marquis, in Anthony Trollope's *Is He Popenjoy?*.

Robert (Bob, Bobby) Lovelace Vain, presumptuous, and clever libertine, who isolates Clarissa Harlowe from her family's affections to effect her escape with him and finally manages to kidnap, drug, and rape her; he offers her marriage, which she spurns, and he dies of wounds incurred in a duel with her cousin Colonel Morden; he uses the pseudonyms Colonel Barrows, Robert Huntingford, and Captain Sloane and is one of the correspondents whose letters tell the story in Samuel Richardson's *Clarissa: or, The History of a Young Lady.*

Harry Lovell   Margaret Lovell's first husband, killed fighting a duel to please her in George Meredith's *Rhoda Fleming.*

Margaret (Peggy) Lovell   Woman widowed by her ability to incite men to duel; she is surrounded by men, including Algernon and Edward Blancove; Major Waring prompts her to a more responsible mode of behavior in George Meredith's *Rhoda Fleming.*

Miss Lovely   Beautiful neighbor of the Moreland estate; she inspires virtue and sense in others with her silence in Henry Brooke's *The Fool of Quality.*

Lovers (Little Ones)   Multitude of parentless children who cannot grow up and fear to grow up; they are befriended by Vane, who unintentionally keeps them from growing; they must learn to cry, to experience the fears and sorrows of maturity; they find mothers in the House of the Dead after failing to find them in Bulika in George MacDonald's *Lilith.*

Love-saint   One of the good people of Vanity Fair introduced to Christiana and her party by Mnason in John Bunyan's *The Pilgrim's Progress From this World to That Which Is to Come.*

Mrs. Lovick   Widow and lodger, whose kindness and integrity ease Clarissa Harlowe's final days; she becomes John Belford's housekeeper and reads Clarissa's letters to him for his improvement in Samuel Richardson's *Clarissa: or, The History of a Young Lady.*

Mr. Low   London barrister with whom Phineas Finn read law prior to running for Parliament; he counsels Phineas against a political career in Anthony Trollope's *Phineas Finn.* He urges Phineas to return to political life after his ordeals in *Phineas Redux.*

Georgiana Low   A barrister's submissive wife; she parrots his opinions to Phineas Finn on the dangerous career Finn is undertaking by entering politics before earning the right by professional achievement in Anthony Trollope's *Phineas Finn.* She is disappointed when he seems shattered after his trial for murder in *Phineas Redux.*

Will H. Low   Addressee of the letter which is the epilogue of Robert Louis Stevenson's *The Wrecker.*

Lady Lowborough   A plain woman noted for her genuine good sense; she becomes the second wife of Lord Lowborough, marrying him after he divorces Annabella Wilmot, in Anne Brontë's *The Tenant of Wildfell Hall.*

Lord Lowborough   The most desperate of Arthur Huntingdon's dissolute friends, given to excesses of both indulgences and repentances; he marries and divorces Annabella Wilmot in Anne Brontë's *The Tenant of Wildfell Hall.*

Annabella Lowborough   Daughter of Annabella (Wilmot) and Lord Lowborough; she is brought up by the second Lady Lowborough in Anne Brontë's *The Tenant of Wildfell Hall.*

Oliver Lowe   Stern, shrewd magistrate; at first taken in by Paul Dangerfield, he leads the arrest when Dangerfield's true identity is discovered in J. Sheridan Le Fanu's *The House by the Churchyard.*

Reginald Lowestoffe   Young gentleman of the Temple; he finds Nigel Olifaunt a place of hiding in the sanctuary of Alsatia, witnesses the delivery of gold to Andrew Skurliewhitter, and rides with Richie Moniplies to intercept Lord Dalgarno in flight to Scotland in Sir Walter Scott's *The Fortunes of Nigel.*

Mr. Lowten   Mr. Perker's puffy-faced clerk, who likes to sing comic songs in Charles Dickens's *The Posthumous Papers of the Pickwick Club.*

Mr. Lowther   Surgeon taken to Italy by Sir Charles Grandison to treat Jeronymo della Porretta's long unhealed injury in Samuel Richardson's *Sir Charles Grandison.*

Mary Lowther   Graceful, grey-eyed cousin and former betrothed of Walter Marrable and close friend of the Fenwicks; Harry Gilmore, the squire, loves her but releases her from their engagement so that she can marry Walter after his improved fortunes make it feasible in Anthony Trollope's *The Vicar of Bullhampton.*

Loyalty's Reward   A horse given to Dalgetty by Montrose after his escape from Argyle's castle in Sir Walter Scott's *A Legend of Montrose.*

Mr. L—t of C—d   Advocate who accompanies the Editor in an expedition to dig up the suicide's grave in James Hogg's *The Private Memoirs and Confessions of a Justified Sinner.*

Lady Lucas   Mother of Charlotte and neighbor to the Bennets in Jane Austen's *Pride and Prejudice.*

Charlotte Lucas   Elizabeth Bennet's practical-minded,

plain friend, whose unromantic view of marriage is in contrast to Elizabeth's belief in the necessity for affection; she marries William Collins out of a "pure and disinterested desire for an establishment" in Jane Austen's *Pride and Prejudice*.

Sir Christopher Lucas Gentleman whose base designs on a country girl result in the death of her parents and her becoming a prostitute and a pickpocket; his fury at his servant William Wilson's treachery in warning her family makes it impossible for Wilson to find honorable employment in Samuel Richardson's *Sir Charles Grandison*.

Maria Lucas Sir William's daughter who accompanies him and Elizabeth Bennet on a visit to the lately married Charlotte (Lucas) Collins in Jane Austen's *Pride and Prejudice*.

Solomon Lucas Owner of a costume shop in Eatanswill in Charles Dickens's *The Posthumous Papers of the Pickwick Club*.

Sir William Lucas Charlotte's father, a tradesman whose knighthood has made him both conceited and obsequious in Jane Austen's *Pride and Prejudice*.

Lucia A raven-haired beauty, whose portrait in miniature Yorke Hunsden shows to both Frances Henri and William Crimsworth and then compares to Frances's pale colouring in Charlotte Brontë's *The Professor*.

Romara Luciani Milanese revolutionary close to Carlo Ammiani in George Meredith's *Vittoria*.

Lucilius Eutropius's servant, who befriends Julian the Apostate, now freed during his incarnation as a slave, after determining Julian is corruptible in Henry Fielding's *A Journey From This World to the Next*.

Lucius Verus Younger brother of the Roman Emperor Marcus Aurelius and an extravagant aesthete; his manners worry the people of Rome because of their similarity to those of the late Emperor Nero in Walter Pater's *Marius the Epicurean*.

Mr. Lucum Unscrupulous politician who tricks his daughter into marrying Lord Dellwyn in order to further his own ambition for power and wealth in Sarah Fielding's *The History of the Countess of Dellwyn*.

Lucy Arabella's maid, a female Sancho Panza; she is too simple to be the romantic confidante her mistress wants; she is the go-between in Arabella's adventures and the failed narrator of her history in Charlotte Lennox's *The Female Quixote*.

Lady Lucy Beautiful, virtuous, accomplished daughter

of an Irish lord; she marries Lewis Augustus Albertus and goes to Germany to live; falsely accused of having an affair with her husband's cousin, she is stabbed by her husband and left to die in a forest; found by a friar who takes her to a convent, she gives birth to a son; she lives there until reunited with Albertus eighteen years later in Penelope Aubin's *The Life and Adventures of the Lady Lucy*.

Lady Lucy's Mother Wise, kind mother of Lady Lucy; she pleads with Lewis Augustus Albertus, chief of the invading soldiers, to spare her honor and that of her daughter; when Lucy marries Albertus, she goes to Germany with them and raises Lucy's daughters when Albertus breaks up the family; she is reunited with her daughter in the end in Penelope Aubin's *The Life and Adventures of the Lady Lucy*.

Miss Lucy Neighboring unmarried woman who has a baby; she is a target of Prudilla Stevens's unwarranted, malicious gossip in Mary Collyer's *Felicia to Charlotte*.

Lady Ludlow The benevolent and aristocratic autocrat of Hanbury Court; the events that lead her to understand and become part of changing social attitudes, in contrast to the violence of the French Revolution, form the theme and story line of Elizabeth Gaskell's *My Lady Ludlow*.

Helena Ludolfski Intimate friend of Isabella Scherbatoff; her father is opposed to her liaison with Isabella's brother, Alexis, in William Godwin's *Cloudesley*.

Ludovico Courageous servant, who falls in love with Annette in the Castle di Udolpho; he rescues Emily St. Aubert from imprisonment in Udolpho only to disappear mysteriously from the Chateau-le-Blanc; he helps to rescue Blanche de Villefort and her party from mountain bandits; he marries Annette and becomes steward of the St. Aubert estate in Ann Radcliffe's *The Mysteries of Udolpho*.

Mr. Luffey Top bowler of the Dingley Dell cricket club in Charles Dickens's *The Posthumous Papers of the Pickwick Club*.

Lady Lufton Kind, opinionated widow of a baron; she cannot understand Lucy Robarts's attraction for her son, Lord Lufton; she is eventually won by Lucy's selflessness in Anthony Trollope's *Framley Parsonage*. She supports the Crawleys in the investigation of a stolen cheque in *The Last Chronicle of Barset*.

Ludovic, Lord Lufton Young baron and intimate friend of Mark Robarts; he is determined to marry Lucy Robarts despite his mother's wish that he choose a woman of higher rank and more imposing personal style in Anthony Trollope's *Framley Parsonage*. He is constrained to pursue the investigation into the theft of a cheque in *The Last Chronicle of Barset*.

Emperor of Luggnagg   Ruler who must be approached with extraordinary subservience in Jonathan Swift's *Travels into Several Remote Nations of the World. In Four Parts. By Lemuel Gulliver.*

Septimus Luker   Vulgar, cringing usurer, who has charge of the stolen yellow diamond for a while; he ensures its safety by placing it in a bank strong room and then passes it to the disguised Godfrey Ablewhite in Wilkie Collins's *The Moonstone. A Romance.*

Clod Lumpewitz   University professor who writes an epitaph comparing Aldrovandus Magnus with Alexander the Great in William Beckford's *Biographical Memoirs of Extraordinary Painters.*

Blanche Lundie   Daughter of Sir Thomas Lundie; she is brought up almost as a younger sister to Anne Silvester, who becomes her governess; Blanche's happy marriage to Arnold Brinkworth is threatened by a fraudulent charge of bigamy against him in Wilkie Collins's *Man and Wife.*

Blanche, Lady Lundie   Friend from childhood of Anne, "Mrs." Silvester; she fulfills her pledge to educate Anne Silvester to become a governess, but her death deprives the younger Anne of a necessary friend in Wilkie Collins's *Man and Wife.*

Julia, Lady Lundie   Widowed stepmother of Blanche Lundie and employer of the governess Anne Silvester, whom she dislikes; she relishes the accusation that Blanche's marriage to Arnold Brinkworth is invalidated by his supposed "Scotch marriage" to Anne; she is ultimately devastated upon becoming "the Dowager Lady Lundie" when Anne, marrying Sir Patrick, becomes Lady Lundie in Wilkie Collins's *Man and Wife.*

Sir Patrick Lundie   A "young" old man, active and responsible, and a wily Scots lawyer who has inherited the family title and property on the death of his brother, Sir Thomas; he assists Anne Silvester and Arnold Brinkworth in thwarting the attempts of the blackguard Geoffrey Delamayn to prove that they are man and wife by "Scotch marriage," even though he recognizes that the contrary proof endangers Anne's life; his forced rescue of Anne is rendered unnecessary by Geoffrey's death; Sir Patrick marries Anne in Wilkie Collins's *Man and Wife.*

Sir Thomas Lundie   Baronet and husband of Blanche, Lady Lundie; he dies after his second marriage, leaving his daughter, Blanche, and Anne Silvester under the supervision of an unloving, self-serving, foolish woman in Wilkie Collins's *Man and Wife.*

Dr. Luke Lundin   The pompous chamberlain of Sir William Douglas, Lord of Lochleven, at Kinross in Sir Walter Scott's *The Abbot.*

Duke de Luovo   Cruel, politically ambitious nobleman infatuated with Julia de Mazzini; he schemes with the Marquis de Mazzini to force Julia to marry him; upon her escape, he chases her across the Sicilian countryside in Ann Radcliffe's *A Sicilian Romance.*

Riccardo de Luovo   Renegade son of the Duke de Luovo; he is captain of the Sicilian bandits who capture the duke in Ann Radcliffe's *A Sicilian Romance.*

Maria Lupex   Loud ex-actress, who lodges at Mrs. Roper's boardinghouse and flirts with the young men in Anthony Trollope's *The Small House at Allington.*

Orson Lupex   Scene-painter husband of Maria; he becomes jealous when his wife flirts with Joseph Cradell in Anthony Trollope's *The Small House at Allington.*

Mrs. Lupin   Comely and charitable landlady of the Blue Dragon Inn near Salisbury, who eventually marries Mark Tapley in Charles Dickens's *The Life and Adventures of Martin Chuzzlewit.*

Mr. Lupton   Older companion of Lord Silverbridge; he is well known in all fashionable circles and careful as to the dyeing of his whiskers; he warns Silverbridge about betting too much on his horse, Prime Minister, in Anthony Trollope's *The Duke's Children.*

Mrs. Lupton   Stout mamma to Sarah Martha; both of them attend Edward Crimsworth's birthday party and dance in Charlotte Brontë's *The Professor.*

Sarah Martha Lupton   Well-formed, dashing young woman, a guest at Edward Crimsworth's birthday dance, who is attended during the evening by Yorke Hunsden in Charlotte Brontë's *The Professor.*

Mr. Lurgan   Healer of jewels, practiced in the occult, and a master of the manners and fashions of the many peoples of India; he trains Kim in the art of disguise in Rudyard Kipling's *Kim.*

Thomas Carnmer Lush   Henleigh Mallinger Grandcourt's travelling companion and servant in all his dirty dealings; he induces Lydia Glasher's vain attempt to dissuade Gwendolen Harleth from marrying Grandcourt in George Eliot's *Daniel Deronda.*

Lieutenant Lütterloh   German spy and conspirator with the Chevalier de la Motte in William Makepeace Thackeray's *Denis Duval.*

Mr. Luttridge   Husband of Mrs. Luttridge; while running for election, he is caricatured by Lady Delacour, leading to a duel between Lady Delacour and Mrs. Luttridge in Maria Edgeworth's *Belinda*.

Mrs. Luttridge   "Odious" enemy and constant competitor of Lady Delacour, who winds up in a duel with her; she operates a dishonest gaming table and causes Mr. Vincent to lose his fortune in Maria Edgeworth's *Belinda*.

Anabella Luttridge   Mrs. Luttridge's niece, who flirts with Mr. Vincent until he loses his fortune at her aunt's home in Maria Edgeworth's *Belinda*.

Lady Luxellian   Lord Luxellian's wife and mother of two little girls; the children assist in their father's courtship of Elfride Swancourt after he is widowed in Thomas Hardy's *A Pair of Blue Eyes*.

Spenser Hugo, Lord Luxellian   A handsome peer with two children; widowed, he courts the suffering Elfride Swancourt after she has been deserted by her betrothed, Henry Knight, in Thomas Hardy's *A Pair of Blue Eyes*.

Mr. L—w   Man who accompanies the Editor in an expedition to dig up the suicide's grave in James Hogg's *The Private Memoirs and Confessions of a Justified Sinner*.

Lord Lycidas   Good-hearted but impetuous nephew of Lady Lucy's mother; he arrives wounded at the farmer's house and relates his history to his aunt and Lady Lucy: loving Henrietta, who jilted him to marry a wealthy old knight, he ran away with her and was pursued and wounded by the knight; reunited with the widowed Henrietta and married after a year's penance, he travels to Germany with her, Lady Lucy, and Lewis Augustus Albertus, but she betrays him by having an affair with Frederick in Penelope Aubin's *The Life and Adventures of the Lady Lucy*.

Lyddy   Faithful maid of Rufus Lyon in George Eliot's *Felix Holt, the Radical*.

Captain Lydgate   Dr. Lydgate's cousin, who comes to visit him and Rosamond (Vincy), his pregnant wife; Captain Lydgate takes Rosamond horseback riding, which causes her baby to be born fatally prematurely in George Eliot's *Middlemarch*.

Sir Godwin Lydgate   Dr. Tertius Lydgate's distinguished cousin; he rejects Rosamond (Vincy) Lydgate's appeals for money in George Eliot's *Middlemarch*.

Dr. Tertius Lydgate   New physician in town; he is determined not to become involved with women after having discovered that an actress he wanted to marry had

killed her husband; unfortunately, he cannot resist the charms of the mayor's beautiful daughter, Rosamond Vincy, a woman whose obsession with material goods as status symbols causes his bankruptcy; he is cleared by Dorothea Brooke from a possible murder charge in the opium overdose of John Ruffles in George Eliot's *Middlemarch*.

Lydia   Ugly sister of the beautiful Lindamira; she is loathed by her parents because of her appearance; she runs away from home and is reunited with her sister only after their parents' deaths in Sarah Fielding's *Familiar Letters between the Principal Characters of David Simple and Some Others*.

Lydiard   Friend of Dr. Shrapnel, Mrs. Wardour-Devereux, and Nevil Beauchamp in George Meredith's *Beauchamp's Career*.

Annot Lyle   Beautiful, musical daughter of Sir Duncan Campbell; kidnapped by Randal MacEagh while an infant, she becomes a captive of Allan M'Aulay and remembers nothing of her origins; though M'Aulay and the Earl of Menteith both love her, she marries Menteith after her true identity is discovered in Sir Walter Scott's *A Legend of Montrose*.

Eustace Lyle   Shy but clever Roman Catholic friend of Lord and Lady Everingham and the richest commoner in England; though politically neutral, he shares Harry Coningsby's desire to discover a "great political truth" which would transcend the squabbling of the Whigs and the Tories in Benjamin Disraeli's *Coningsby; or, The New Generation*.

Barry Lynch   Villainous brother of Anty Lynch; he plots her death in order to be sole possessor of the family fortune in Anthony Trollope's *The Kellys and the O'Kellys*.

Anastasia (Anty) Lynch   Wretched target of her brother's plot to steal her share of the family fortune; she is wooed and won by Martin Kelly in Anthony Trollope's *The Kellys and the O'Kellys*.

Barry Lyndon   See Redmond Barry.

Bryan Lyndon   Barry and Lady Lyndon's over-indulged son, who dies from a fall from his horse in William Makepeace Thackeray's *The Luck of Barry Lyndon*.

Sir Charles Lyndon   Lady Lyndon's cousin and first husband, a cynical, worn-out, crippled roué whose evidently imminent death alerts Redmond Barry to profitable courtship in William Makepeace Thackeray's *The Luck of Barry Lyndon*.

Honoria, Countess of Lyndon   Foolish, romantic, and

self-romanticizing heiress to a title as well as fortune and estates; her elderly husband's precarious health motivates Redmond Barry's courtship; she is ill-treated and confined as mad by her second husband, Barry, after the death of their son; eventually she is freed from his control, though her fortune is much depleted in William Makepeace Thackeray's *The Luck of Barry Lyndon*.

Roger Lyndon　Lady Lyndon's ancestor, whose acquisition of the Barrys' ancestral Irish property provides (Redmond) Barry Lyndon with justification for re-squandering it in William Makepeace Thackeray's *The Luck of Barry Lyndon*.

Lady Lynn　Sir George's proud wife, who associates with Baroness Ingram in Charlotte Brontë's *Jane Eyre*.

Frederick Lynn　Debonair son of Sir George and brother of Henry in Charlotte Brontë's *Jane Eyre*.

Sir George Lynn　One of Mr. Rochester's house guests, elected to Parliament for Millcote in Charlotte Brontë's *Jane Eyre*.

Henry Lynn　Debonair son of Sir George; he and his brother, Frederick, are interested in some of the ladies staying at Thornfield Hall in Charlotte Brontë's *Jane Eyre*.

Esther Lyon　Educated, sensitive, poetic girl raised as Rufus Lyon's daughter; her real father was Maurice Christian Bycliff, the heir of the Transome estates; her love for Felix Holt softens her into renouncing her wealth and embracing poverty along with a life of helping common people in George Eliot's *Felix Holt, the Radical*.

Rufus Lyon　The poor minister of the Independent Chapel who rescued the destitute Frenchwoman Annette Ledru, married her, and reared her daughter, Esther, as his own; he learns that Esther's real father was heir to the Transome estate; he befriends Felix Holt and sympathizes with the Radical party in George Eliot's *Felix Holt, the Radical*.

Laura Lyons　Deserted wife, daughter of Frankland, and friend and neighbor of the late Sir Charles Baskerville in Arthur Conan Doyle's *The Hound of the Baskervilles*.

Lysander　One of many brave young men; he is loved by Clarenthia in Jane Barker's *Exilius; or, The Banish'd Roman*.

Lysimachus　Timorous designer and conspirator in Sir Walter Scott's *Count Robert of Paris*.

Lysimachus　Correspondent with Cratander on the subject of the significance of criticism, specifically in relation to Shakespeare, in Sarah Fielding's *Familiar Letters between the Principal Characters of David Simple and Some Others*.

Dr. Lyster　Physician who tends to Mrs. Delvile during her illness in Frances Burney's *Cecilia*.

Mary Lyster　Rich spinster cousin of William Ashe; her romance with the scoundrel Geoffrey Cliffe is dashed by Lady Kitty Ashe; her hatred leads to Lady Kitty's downfall and death in Mrs. Humphry Ward's *The Marriage of William Ashe*.

M

Dr. M Bedfordshire physician who treats Pamela (Andrews) and baby William for smallpox in Samuel Richardson's *Pamela, or Virtue Rewarded.*

Lord M– Robert Lovelace's uncle, who exhorts Lovelace to marry Clarissa Harlowe once he learns of Lovelace's vile treatment of her and coolly deflects Lovelace's and Morden's heated tempers in their first interview, thereby delaying their duel in Samuel Richardson's *Clarissa: or, The History of a Young Lady.*

Mabel Beautiful sister of the Laird of Dornock; she becomes mistress to King James in Sophia Lee's *The Recess.*

Mabel A servant in the Sinclair brothel; Clarissa Harlowe uses her clothes to escape her imprisonment there in Samuel Richardson's *Clarissa: or, The History of a Young Lady.*

Miss Mabel Betsy Thoughtless's laundrywoman in Eliza Haywood's *The History of Miss Betsy Thoughtless.*

Mrs. Maberly Garrulous and good-natured cousin of the Blunkets and like them a houseguest at Marlowe in J. Sheridan Le Fanu's *Guy Deverell.*

Mac Pugnacious Scotch/Irish boatswain of the *Leslie* who ships on the *Currency Lass*; he kills Captain Jacob Trent, starting a fight on the *Flying Scud* in Robert Louis Stevenson's *The Wrecker.*

Lady MacAdam One of the older aristocracy whose cultivated secularity offends Micah Balwhidder; she instructs Kate Malcolm in aristocratic "accomplishments" but is incensed when her son marries Kate in John Galt's *Annals of the Parish.*

Laird MacAdam Lady MacAdam's son, who defies her opposition to his marrying her companion Kate Malcolm in John Galt's *Annals of the Parish.*

Mrs. Macallan Eustace Macallan's mother, whose accidental introduction proves to his wife Valeria that he has married her under an assumed name; the two women gradually become friends and allies in Wilkie Collins's *The Law and the Lady.*

Eustace Macallan Scottish gentleman whose reputation and happiness have been destroyed by the "Scotch Verdict" of *not proven* in his trial for the murder of his first wife, Sara; he leaves his second wife, Valeria, whom he has married as Woodville, because he cannot bear her

knowledge of his past; when she has solved the mystery they are happily reunited in Wilkie Collins's *The Law and the Lady.*

Sara Macallan Eustace Macallan's late wife, for whose death by arsenic poisoning he was tried; he had married her, a plain woman he could not care for, because of her self-endangering passion for him and after the marriage of his beloved, Helena Beauly, in Wilkie Collins's *The Law and the Lady.*

Valeria Brinton, Mrs. Eustace Macallan (also Woodville) Resourceful young woman, who learns after her marriage to Eustace Woodville that he is Eustace Macallan, tried but not convicted of the poisoning of his first wife; she sets out to prove her husband innocent, saving his character from the stain of the "Scotch Verdict" of *not proven* and their marriage from the estrangement caused by her discovery of his history in Wilkie Collins's *The Law and the Lady.*

Jeanie MacAlpine Pale, nervous hostess of the inn at Clachan of Aberfoil, who passes Francis Osbaldistone a note from Rob Roy MacGregor in Sir Walter Scott's *Rob Roy.*

Eachin MacAnaleister Rob Roy MacGregor's powerful lieutenant in Sir Walter Scott's *Rob Roy.*

Lord Macarden Glenmorris's friend who gives aid to his presumed widow Laura Glenmorris and proposes marriage to her; he is wounded in a duel with the Laird of Kilbrodie in Charlotte Smith's *The Young Philosopher.*

Mr. Macartney Impoverished Scottish poet who lodges in Mr. Branghton's London house; he is saved from suicide or a life of crime by Evelina Anville Belmont, and he discovers he is Evelina's brother in Frances Burney's *Evelina.*

Mr. MacBorrowdale Representative of the best of Scottish mental, moral, and political philosophy in Thomas Love Peacock's *Gryll Grange.*

Ephraim Macbriar Young Cameronian preacher, who is a firebrand leader of the rebels and refuses to reveal the whereabouts of Burley (John Balfour) when he is tortured before his execution in Sir Walter Scott's *Old Mortality.*

Mrs. MacCandlish Hostess of the Gordon Arms at Kippletrengan in Sir Walter Scott's *Guy Mannering.*

Mr. MacCasquil of Drumquag Heir-expectant of Margaret Bertram's property; his hopes are founded on a distant relationship and a shared church pew in Sir Walter Scott's *Guy Mannering.*

John Breck Maccoll Savage-looking and illiterate Scottish Highland tenant of the Appin Stewarts; he finds Alan Breck Stewart in the woods and carries a secret message from him to James Stewart in Robert Louis Stevenson's *Kidnapped*.

Evan Dhu Maccombich Fergus MacIvor's loyal lieutenant, who likes Edward Waverly and warns him of treachery; captured with Fergus, he chooses death at his side rather than proclaiming for King George in Sir Walter Scott's *Waverly*.

Macconochie Servant at Durrisdeer who confides in Ephram Mackellar; he delivers a letter from Alison (Graeme) to the Master (James Durie) at Carlisle with Prince Charles in Robert Louis Stevenson's *The Master of Ballantrae: A Winter's Tale*.

Ebenezer Mac Crotchet Retired stockbroker, a Scot, who invites eccentric philosophers to his house in Thomas Love Peacock's *Crotchet Castle*.

Euphemia (Feemy) Macdermot Sister of Thady Macdermot; she is seduced by Captain Myles Ussher and dies of remorse and shame in Anthony Trollope's *The Macdermots of Ballycloran*.

Lawrence (Larry) Macdermot Father of Thady and Feemy and owner of the run-down Ballycloran estate in Anthony Trollope's *The Macdermots of Ballycloran*.

Thady Macdermot Impoverished Irish landowner, who murders his sister's seducer and is hanged in Anthony Trollope's *The Macdermots of Ballycloran*.

Alec MacDonald A Scottish detective from Scotland Yard and one of the few official policemen who defer to Sherlock Holmes; he gets credit (perhaps as a reward) for solving the crime in Arthur Conan Doyle's *The Valley of Fear*.

Betty Macdonald Pretty young girl, whose loyalty and cheerfulness warm her friends, the Maxwells and the Boyces, in Mrs. Humphry Ward's *Marcella*. As Lady Leven she relinquishes her political ambitions for her husband in *Sir George Tressady*.

Randal MacEagh Kenneth's grandfather and chief of a band of Highland outlaws called "Children of the Mist"; their crimes, which include the kidnapping of Annot Lyle, bring upon them the enmity of Menteith, the Campbells, and the M'Aulays in Sir Walter Scott's *A Legend of Montrose*.

Phelim Mac Fane Highwayman who serves as accomplice to Mr. Webb; he is a gambler who assists Coke Clifton in his scheme to ruin Anna St. Ives and Frank Henley in Thomas Holcroft's *Anna St. Ives*.

Lady Macfarren Sir Stephen Penrhyn's widowed sister; she dislikes Eleanor Raymond and does not approve of her marriage to Sir Stephen; she treats Eleanor with dishonesty and disdain in Caroline Norton's *Stuart of Dunleath*.

Mr. MacFin Member of the firm of MacVittie, MacFin and Co. in Sir Walter Scott's *Rob Roy*.

Macglashan Laird Douglas's neighbor who kindly wills his farm to the Laird's son, Henry Douglas, to provide him with means of support after he is disinherited by his guardian in Susan Ferrier's *Marriage*.

MacGregor of Bohaldie Chieftain of the MacGregor clan who lives in exile in Paris; he provides for Catriona Drummond, giving her away in marriage to David Balfour after her father has dishonored himself in Robert Louis Stevenson's *Catriona*.

Hamish (James) MacGregor Rob Roy's eldest son and a handsome youth in Sir Walter Scott's *Rob Roy*.

Helen MacGregor (Helen Campbell) Rob Roy's stately wife, an arresting, middle-aged woman devoted to her husband and family; her bitterness against the English is due to their persecution of the MacGregor family; she leads the ambush on Captain Thornton's troops; the MacGregors use the adopted name of Campbell in Sir Walter Scott's *Rob Roy*.

James More (Drummond) MacGregor Deceitful and fallen Jacobite from the outlawed MacGregor clan and father to Catriona Drummond; imprisoned on a dubious charge, he is freed by Catriona; he arranges for David Balfour's kidnapping, extorts money from him, and attempts to betray him and Alan Breck Stewart in Robert Louis Stevenson's *Catriona*.

Rob Roy MacGregor (Robert Campbell, Robert the Red) Beloved Jacobite chieftain of the MacGregor clan; he is under the protection of the Duke of Argyle; politically sympathetic with Diana Vernon, he rescues Francis Osbaldistone many times by her direction; a renowned outlaw, he adopts the name of Campbell in Sir Walter Scott's *Rob Roy*.

Peter MacGrowler Tipsy Scottish man of letters; he tutors Paul Clifford and later betrays him in Edward Bulwer-Lytton's *Paul Clifford*.

Mrs. MacGuffog Jailor MacGuffog's wife, a robust woman capable of maintaining discipline when her husband is away from the jail in Sir Walter Scott's *Guy Mannering*.

David MacGuffog   Thief-taker and warden of the jail at Portanferry where Henry Bertram is imprisoned in Sir Walter Scott's *Guy Mannering*.

Niccolò Machiavelli   Young Florentine of intellect and imagination in George Eliot's *Romola*.

Mrs. MacHugh   Gossiping, whist-playing friend of Jemima Stanbury; she enjoys the setbacks to Miss Stanbury's interference in young people's lives and loves in Anthony Trollope's *He Knew He Was Right*.

Robert Macintosh   One of the four Scottish counsels to James Stewart, alleged murderer of Colin Ray Campbell in Robert Louis Stevenson's *Catriona*.

Fergus MacIvor   Vich Ian Vohr of Glennaquoich, brave and cocky Highland leader of the MacIvor clan; fiercely loyal to Prince Charles Stuart, he befriends Edward Waverly and hopes he will marry his sister, Flora; it is Fergus who introduces Waverly to the prince and encourages him to defend the Cause in Sir Walter Scott's *Waverly*.

Flora MacIvor   Fergus's beautiful and high-spirited sister and Rose Bradwardine's best friend; she rejects Edward Waverly's ardent proposal, saving her passion for the Cause; upon her brother's death, she enters a convent in Sir Walter Scott's *Waverly*.

Saunders (Sandy) Mackaye   Intelligent, kindly, dialect-speaking bookseller, who befriends Alton Locke, teaching him to teach himself and taking him in after his mother throws him out; although he supports the Chartists, he ultimately considers them too extreme and refuses to sign their petition in Charles Kingsley's *Alton Locke*.

Ephraim (Square Toes) Mackellar   The narrator, a meddling bachelor steward of Durrisdeer loyal to Henry Durie; he comes to understand Alison (Graeme) and is captivated by the Master (James Durie) in Robert Louis Stevenson's *The Master of Ballantrae: A Winter's Tale*.

Colonel Mackenzie   One of Captain Anderson's friends and intermediaries with whom Sir Charles Grandison deals in Samuel Richardson's *Sir Charles Grandison*.

Mr. Mackenzie   Grey-haired, kindly Scottish missionary who runs the mission station "The Highlands" on the Tana River; he returns to England after the kidnapping and near death of his daughter at the hands of Masai tribesmen in H. Rider Haggard's *Allan Quatermain*.

Mrs. Mackenzie   Charming and refined wife of the Reverend Mackenzie; she lives with her husband and daughter in the mission station on the Tana River in H. Rider Haggard's *Allan Quatermain*.

Mrs. Mackenzie   Rosey Mackenzie's mother, a seemingly good-natured widow, who turns out to be in adversity a shrewish mother-in-law to Clive Newcome in William Makepeace Thackeray's *The Newcomes*.

Clara Mackenzie   Wife of the younger Walter Mackenzie; sympathetic to his cousin Margaret Mackenzie, she urges John Ball to renew his marriage proposal to Margaret and eventually arranges with her husband for the bride to be married from her Cavendish Square home in Anthony Trollope's *Miss Mackenzie*.

Flossie (Waterlily) Mackenzie   Young, pretty, headstrong daughter of the Reverend Mackenzie; she is kidnapped by Masai warriors and rescued by Allan Quatermain and his party during a bloody battle in H. Rider Haggard's *Allan Quatermain*.

Josey Mackenzie   Rosey Mackenzie's religious-minded sister, who lives in Scotland with her grandmother in William Makepeace Thackeray's *The Newcomes*.

Margaret Mackenzie   Thin, ungainly spinster, neither beautiful nor clever; released from nursing her sickly brother in London, she finds her freedom with a legacy in Littlebath in the west of England; she is pursued by the Reverend Maguire, who wants money for his church, and by Samuel Rubb, whose business needs capital; she marries her cousin, John Ball, who turns out to be the true inheritor of the Mackenzie fortune in Anthony Trollope's *Miss Mackenzie*.

Rosa (Rosey) Mackenzie   Affectionate but weak-willed daughter of Mrs. Mackenzie; she dies a few years after her marriage to Clive Newcome in William Makepeace Thackeray's *The Newcomes*.

Sarah Mackenzie   Malicious, embittered wife of Thomas; she becomes angry when the fortune she believes ought to have come to her husband is left to Margaret Mackenzie and is ungrateful when her sister-in-law undertakes to care for and educate her daughter Susanna in Anthony Trollope's *Miss Mackenzie*.

Susanna Mackenzie   One of Thomas Mackenzie's seven children; a bright-eyed teenager, she comes to live with her aunt, Margaret Mackenzie, at the Paragon, Littlebath, and to attend private school; she becomes a great comfort to Margaret during her squabbles within the community in Anthony Trollope's *Miss Mackenzie*.

Thomas Mackenzie   Elder brother of Margaret and an

unsuccessful businessman who had used his inheritance to go into partnership with the Rubb family; he puts her into difficulty by dubious loan arrangements carried on by his partner, Samuel Rubb; when he dies, leaving his wife Sarah and seven children, Margaret promises to save them from want in Anthony Trollope's *Miss Mackenzie.*

Walter Mackenzie (the elder) Sickly brother of Thomas and Margaret; he leaves his portion of the money he and Thomas inherited from Jonathan Ball to Margaret when he dies in Anthony Trollope's *Miss Mackenzie.*

Walter Mackenzie (the younger) Margaret Mackenzie's cousin and generous friend; he and his wife arrange for her marriage to John Ball from their home in Cavendish Square in Anthony Trollope's *Miss Mackenzie.*

Duncan Mackiegh Blind but dangerous traveling catechist, who has a reputation for highway robbery, and who pretends to guide young David Balfour's path in Robert Louis Stevenson's *Kidnapped.*

Sir Ulic Mackilligut Irish knight, who escapes Tabitha Bramble's pursuit at Bath in Tobias Smollett's *The Expedition of Humphry Clinker.*

Major Mackintosh Painstaking head of the London police; he patiently tracks down the mystery of the diamonds and persuades Lizzie Eustace to tell the truth about their disappearance in Anthony Trollope's *The Eustace Diamonds.* He investigates the Bonteen murder in *Phineas Redux.*

Mrs. Mackirk Lord Macarden's sister and the mother of six; jealous of her brother's interest in Laura Glenmorris, she betrays her to the Laird of Kilbrodie and ejects her as the cause of Macarden's death when Kilbrodie wounds him in a duel; recovering, Macarden separates himself from his sister in Charlotte Smith's *The Young Philosopher.*

Mackitchinson Innkeeper who serves fish to travelers on the coach from Queensbury to Edinburgh in Sir Walter Scott's *The Antiquary.*

Macklachlan Irish cavalier at the Upton Inn who answers Jenny Waters's shrieks to find his friend Brian Fitzpatrick in her room searching for his wife in Henry Fielding's *The History of Tom Jones.*

Mr. Mackshane Surgeon who replaces Atkins on the *Thunder;* he causes the deaths of several sick sailors on orders of the captain and shows his cowardice during a battle in Jamaica in Tobias Smollett's *The Adventures of Roderick Random.*

Duncan (Dhu) Maclaren Lover of music and the Scottish Highlander host to David Balfour when David lies ill and bedridden during his fugitive flight with Alan Breck Stewart in Robert Louis Stevenson's *Kidnapped.*

Mrs. Maclaren Wife to Duncan Dhu Maclaren and hostess to David Balfour; she is greatly honored to have David and Alan Breck Stewart as her secret guests in Robert Louis Stevenson's *Kidnapped.*

Lady Maclaughlan The locally influential wife of Sampson, Lord Maclaughlan and the favorite visitor at Glenfern Castle of the spinster sisters, Jacky, Grizzy, and Nicky Douglas, in Susan Ferrier's *Marriage.*

Sampson, Lord Maclaughlan The infirm but influential best friend of Laird Douglas and husband of Lady Maclaughlan in Susan Ferrier's *Marriage.*

Mac Laurel Dialect-spouting Scot, Squire Headlong's guest in Thomas Love Peacock's *Headlong Hall.*

Luckie Macleary Widow innkeeper at Tully-Veolan, where Edward Waverly gets into a brawl with Balmawhapple in Sir Walter Scott's *Waverly.*

Major Macleaver Prisoner with Ferdinand in London; he fights a smoke-duel with Captain Goliah Minikin in Tobias Smollett's *The Adventures of Ferdinand Count Fathom.*

Lady Macleod Narrow-minded, censorious relative of the Vavasors; she lives frugally over a stable yard so that she can maintain an appearance of wealth and still move in society in Anthony Trollope's *Can You Forgive Her?.*

Mrs. Macleuchar Old lady who dispenses tickets for the coach from Queensbury to Edinburgh in Sir Walter Scott's *The Antiquary.*

Bessie Maclure Old woman who tells Henry Morton where to find Burley (John Balfour) when Morton returns from exile in Sir Walter Scott's *Old Mortality.*

Mr. MacMorlan Kindly and sensible sheriff-substitute, who tries to help Lucy Bertram while responsible for the sale of Ellangowan in Sir Walter Scott's *Guy Mannering.*

Mrs. MacMorlan Ladylike wife of the sheriff-substitute in Sir Walter Scott's *Guy Mannering.*

Patey Macmorland Ten-year-old brother of Tam Macmorland; he entertains Mackellar with gossip while guiding him to Durrisdeer in Robert Louis Stevenson's *The Master of Ballantrae: A Winter's Tale.*

Tam Macmorland A tenant's son who fought with the Master (James Durie); he brings news of the Battle of

Culloden and spreads rumors of Henry Durie's disloyalty in Robert Louis Stevenson's *The Master of Ballantrae: A Winter's Tale*.

Miss Macnamara   Shallow young woman in London society, who has a short attention span and a rambunctious monkey for a pet in William Beckford's *Modern Novel Writing; or, the Elegant Enthusiast*.

Mrs. Macnamara   Cunning, somewhat foolish mother of Magnolia; she is blackmailed by the evil fortune-teller Mary Matchwell when she turns to her for help in finding a husband; Matchwell uses her to gain entrance into the Nutter household in J. Sheridan Le Fanu's *The House by the Churchyard*.

Magnolia Macnamara   Sometimes spiteful, sometimes kind young woman from Chapelizod; she is the sweetheart of Lieutenant O'Flaherty, whom she later marries, and a friend to Mrs. Sturk during her troubles in J. Sheridan Le Fanu's *The House by the Churchyard*.

Patrick Mac Neale   A Hibernian poet and joke-teller who, as Bryan Perdue's schoolmate, writes verses about gambling which result in Bryan's dismissal from school in Thomas Holcroft's *The Memoirs of Bryan Perdue*.

Mr. Macneil   Wordly, cultured resident of the Lake District, who is prized by the inhabitants of Windermere as a man of honor, good sense, and aphoristic wisdom; an erstwhile acquaintance of Jean-Jacques Rousseau, he becomes a loyal friend of Casimir Fleetwood and encourages the development of affection between Fleetwood and his daughter, Mary; leaving Mary behind in England with Fleetwood, he and his wife and other daughters are lost at sea in William Godwin's *Fleetwood*.

Dr. MacNuffery   Medical man and nutritionist for the British cricket team visiting the island of Britannula; he keeps close watch on what the players eat and drink before the epic match in Anthony Trollope's *The Fixed Period*.

Julia Macnulty   Harried and patronized paid companion of Lizzie Eustace; she is much given to reading romantic novels; she fantasizes that Mr. Emilius is in love with her and is quietly heartbroken at his union with Lizzie Eustace in Anthony Trollope's *The Eustace Diamonds*.

Clancy Macpherson   Imperious, eccentric, and card-loving chief of the clan Vourich; a former leader in the Great Rebellion, he offers the hospitality of his hideaway to David Balfour and Alan Breck Stewart in Robert Louis Stevenson's *Kidnapped*.

Mr. MacQuedy   "Son of a demonstration," who re-

duces all human emotion to principles of political economy in Thomas Love Peacock's *Crotchet Castle*.

Pate Macready   Scottish peddler and distant relative of Andrew Fairservice in Sir Walter Scott's *Rob Roy*.

Violet Macshake   Archibald Douglas's old and doddering aunt, now residing in Leith, Scotland, who gives Mary Douglas a pair of diamond earrings in Susan Ferrier's *Marriage*.

Mrs. MacStinger   Sharp widow, who is Captain Cuttle's landlady and keeps an eye on him; she marries John Bunsby in Charles Dickens's *Dombey and Son*.

Alexander MacStinger   Young son of Mrs. MacStinger and favorite of Captain Cuttle in Charles Dickens's *Dombey and Son*.

Charles (Chowley) MacStinger   Son of Mrs. MacStinger in Charles Dickens's *Dombey and Son*.

Juliana MacStinger   Daughter of Mrs. MacStinger and the image of her mother in Charles Dickens's *Dombey and Son*.

Dr. MacTurk   The most skillful local physician; he attends Robert Moore and has a son, Dr. MacTurk, who is a replica of himself in Charlotte Brontë's *Shirley*.

Dr. MacTurk (the younger)   Son of Dr. MacTurk and a replica of his father in Charlotte Brontë's *Shirley*.

Captain Hector MacTurk   Highland soldier on half pay; he arbitrates quarrels among the social leaders at St. Ronan's Well; he accompanies Sir Bingo Binks to an abortive duel with Francis Tyrrel and accompanies John Mowbray when he flees after killing the Earl of Etherington (Valentine Bulmer) in Sir Walter Scott's *St. Ronan's Well*.

Mr. MacVittie   Principal member of the firm of MacVittie, MacFin and Co.; Glasgow agents for the firm of Osbaldistone and Tresham, they dishonorably withdraw their support when the English house encounters hardship in Sir Walter Scott's *Rob Roy*.

Duncan Macwheeble   Baron of Bradwardine's baron-bailie; he follows his master into battle and regains his estate for the baron in Sir Walter Scott's *Waverly*.

Major MacWhirter   Mrs. Baynes's brother-in-law, who joins his wife in taking Charlotte Baynes's part against her parents in William Makepeace Thackeray's *The Adventures of Philip on His Way through the World*.

Emily MacWhirter   Mrs. Baynes's sister, who joins

her husband to befriend Charlotte Baynes and Philip Firmin in William Makepeace Thackeray's *The Adventures of Philip on His Way through the World.*

Madame la Marquise　Aristocrat whose jewels are stolen by Angelo D'Albini's son Felix in Charlotte Dacre's *The Libertine.*

Maddelina　Kindly daughter of Tuscan peasants, Dorina and Marco, in whose cottage Emily St. Aubert is confined in Ann Radcliffe's *The Mysteries of Udolpho.*

Dr. Madden　Father of six girls; he is killed in a carriage accident and leaves his family in poverty at the beginning of George Gissing's *The Odd Women.*

Alice Madden　Impoverished gentlewoman, who shares a single room with her alcoholic sister, Virginia, in George Gissing's *The Odd Women.*

Monica Madden　Pretty but unstable girl, who contracts an unhappy marriage to Edmund Widdowson in order to escape drudgery in a draper's shop; she is discovered visiting her lover, Bevis, by her jealous husband; she leaves him and dies in childbirth in George Gissing's *The Odd Women.*

Virginia Madden　Impoverished gentlewoman, who shares a single room with her sister Alice and becomes an alcoholic in George Gissing's *The Odd Women.*

Eve Madeley　Educated young working woman, who accepts Maurice Hilliard's offer to pay for a long visit to Paris so that she can recover from her breakup with a married man; she deceitfully lets Hilliard make love to her while she falls in love with and eventually marries his wealthier friend, Robert Narramore, in George Gissing's *Eve's Ransom.*

Mad Hatter　Guest at the mad tea party, at which he parodies Victorian etiquette and academia, and witness at the trial of the Knave of Hearts in Lewis Carroll's *Alice's Adventures in Wonderland.* Released from prison, he appears as Hatta, the White King's messenger, in *Through the Looking Glass.*

Thomas Madison　Humbly born protegé of Louis Fitzjocelyn and lover of Charlotte Arnold; he prevents the total collapse of the Dynevor and Ponsonby fortunes in Peru in Charlotte Yonge's *Dynevor Terrace.*

Madwoman　Deranged young lady Harley meets on a visit to London; she was driven to distraction by the loss of her lover in Henry Mackenzie's *The Man of Feeling.*

Gertrude Maes　Henry Esmond's mother, who married Captain Thomas Esmond (later the third Viscount Castlewood) not long before the birth of her son; deserted, she joins a convent and becomes Soeur Marie Madeleine in William Makepeace Thackeray's *The History of Henry Esmond.*

Lady Maffei　Lady Olivia's aunt and companion in Samuel Richardson's *Sir Charles Grandison.*

"Musty" Mag　Dan Ogle's friend, who tries to help him when he is being hunted for murder in Arthur Morrison's *The Hole in the Wall.*

Magdalena　Monsieur de Maintenon's former servant, kidnapped in Wales by robbers who later abduct Belinda Lluelling, Maintenon's granddaughter; they escape together in Penelope Aubin's *The Life of Madam de Beaumont.*

Magfreda　Female disciple of the heretic Wilhemina of Bohemia; she is burned as a heretic in Mary Shelley's *Valperga.*

Mick Maggot　Hard-drinking miner, who guides the inexperienced prospectors John Caldigate and Dick Shand in their search for gold in Anthony Trollope's *John Caldigate.*

Polly Maggot　Woman of Amazonian size successively mistress to Jack Sheppard, William Kneebone, and Sheppard again in William Harrison Ainsworth's *Jack Sheppard.*

Maggy　Bald woman who calls herself a ten-year-old child and accompanies Amy Dorrit in her walks, calling her "Little Mother," in Charles Dickens's *Little Dorrit.*

Magistrate　Official who takes money from the Matron in order to let her go, but instead takes her to the Justice in Charles Johnstone's *Chrysal: or, The Adventures of a Guinea.*

Colonel Magle　Cowardly officer who will not risk interfering with the Porteous riot in Sir Walter Scott's *The Heart of Midlothian.*

Anthony Aldrovandus Magnus　Fifteenth-century Bohemian painter, among the first to develop oil painting; he becomes famous for his tints and realistic renderings; he dies from grief when all the kingdom's canvas is destroyed in a warehouse fire in William Beckford's *Biographical Memoirs of Extraordinary Painters.*

Peter Magnus　Sharp-nosed, red-haired acquaintance of Samuel Pickwick; he travels to Ipswich to court the lady in curlpapers in Charles Dickens's *The Posthumous Papers of the Pickwick Club.*

Baron de Magny　Honorable nobleman disgraced by

the behavior of his grandson, the Chevalier de Magny; he provides his grandson with money to escape from the police which is gambled away and with poison to escape the shame of execution in William Makepeace Thackeray's *The Luck of Barry Lyndon*.

Chevalier de Magny   Princess Olivia's lover, a weak and cowardly gambler; he commits suicide by poison just as he is to be executed in William Makepeace Thackeray's *The Luck of Barry Lyndon*.

Major Magruder   Intemperate chairman of a committee of inquiry; he grills Sir Marmaduke Rowley on his conduct of affairs in the Mandarin Islands in Anthony Trollope's *He Knew He Was Right*.

Mr. Magruin   Moneylender who supplies cash both to Burgo Fitzgerald and to George Vavasor in Anthony Trollope's *Can You Forgive Her?*.

Jeremiah Maguire   Canting curate with a pronounced squint; he pursues Margaret Mackenzie for her money so that he can set up an independent church; hearing that she is to marry the cousin to whom her inheritance has passed, he suspects conspiracy and writes articles to a Christian journal; his intervention fails, and he marries Miss Colza in Anthony Trollope's *Miss Mackenzie*.

Abel Magwitch (Provis, Campbell)   Escaped convict who frightens Pip Pirrip in the churchyard but remembers Pip's kindness when he is transported to Australia (New South Wales); he becomes a successful sheepfarmer and, as an unknown benefactor, arranges with Mr. Jaggers to make Pip a gentleman; when Magwitch returns to England to see what he has made of Pip, he is identified for the police by Compeyson and dies in an attempt to escape in Charles Dickens's *Great Expectations*.

Mahaina   Dipsomaniac and friend of the Nosnibors; unable to do her calisthenics, she pretends to illness due to immorality in Samuel Butler's *Erewhon*.

Lord Mahogany   Wicked nobleman, husband of the Marchioness of Oakley and father of Lord Charles Oakley; he attempts the rape of Amelia, fights a farcical duel with Don Pedro de Gonzales, and murders his paramour La Contessa Negri with poisoned sweetmeats; she murders him with poisoned wine in William Beckford's *Modern Novel Writing; or, the Elegant Enthusiast*.

Mahomet   Lustful chief officer in the sultan's army; desiring Ardelisa de Vinevil, he attacks her house and kills the Count de Vinevil but discovers that Ardelisa has already fled; he continues to pursue her until he is forced to leave the country with the army in Penelope Aubin's *The Strange Adventures of the Count de Vinevil and His Family*.

Captain Mahoney   Half-pay Irish officer and purported brother (actually, lover) of the Widow Townsend, Julia Townsend's stepmother; having left his own wife and children, he colludes with the widow in an effort to wed Julia or her sister Lucia and the accompanying fortune in Richard Graves's *The Spiritual Quixote*.

Mrs. Mahoney   Wife of Captain Mahoney; he has left her and their children on the prospect of marrying one of the Townsend sisters, and Geoffry Wildgoose helps her to find him in Richard Graves's *The Spiritual Quixote*.

Patrick Mahoney   Rowdy friend of Father Roach; he volunteers to act as Charles Nutter's second in the thwarted duel with Lieutenant O'Flaherty in J. Sheridan Le Fanu's *The House by the Churchyard*.

Maid   Thrall of the Lady; she is in love with Walter Golden; with magic she compasses the death of the Lady and the King's Son and flees with Walter to Stark-wall in William Morris's *The Wood beyond the World*.

Maid   Bell Western's snobbish maid, who fights with Honour Blackmore and gets her fired; the ensuing uproar diverts attention from Sophia's escape in Henry Fielding's *The History of Tom Jones*.

Maid of the Alder   Vampiric tree-woman with a smothering web of hair, who feeds on the love of men; she seduces Sir Percival and later, in the semblance of the marble lady, Anodos in George MacDonald's *Phantastes*.

Maidservant   Elderly servant of Jack, Man of the Hill; she reluctantly shelters Tom Jones and Partridge on a cold winter's night in Henry Fielding's *The History of Tom Jones*.

Maid-servant   The only eyewitness to Edward Hyde's murder of Sir Danvers Carew in Robert Louis Stevenson's *The Strange Case of Dr. Jekyll and Mr. Hyde*.

Mrs. Mailsetter   Wife of the Fairport postmaster; she allows her friends to examine the mail, is a source of gossip, and loses her post in Sir Walter Scott's *The Antiquary*.

Mr. Main   Heroic elder brother of Patty and Harry Main; he wins permission to marry his childhood sweetheart by restoring her to health through his superior surgical skill and tenderness rather than by being heir to a large fortune in Frances Sheridan's *Memoirs of Miss Sidney Bidulph*.

Harry Main   Sweet-tempered brother of Patty and young Mr. Main; he is employed as a linen draper in the Strand and marries Miss Price in Frances Sheridan's *Memoirs of Miss Sidney Bidulph*.

Patty Main Worthy servant and occasional amanuensis of Sidney Bidulph Arnold; she remains a faithful friend to her former mistress although enfranchised on the day of her brother Harry's marriage; she marries a gentleman of large estate during the first ten-year period of Sidney's retirement to the country in Frances Sheridan's *Memoirs of Miss Sidney Bidulph*.

Madame Du Maine Wealthy woman who employs Cornelia as companion after being estranged from her children and grandchildren; she eventually convinces Cornelia to accept a settlement in Sarah Scott's *The History of Cornelia*.

Madame Maintenon French woman of fashion; she abducts young Harry Clinton in a seduction attempt and imprisons him, but he escapes with the assistance of her niece, Maria de Lausanne, in Henry Brooke's *The Fool of Quality*.

Monsieur de Maintenon Governor of Normandy and father of Count de Beaumont and Katherine; he disapproves of his son's marriage to a Protestant and separates them; he has Madam de Beaumont imprisoned when she returns to France to look for her husband; he dies while his son is a prisoner in Muscovy in Penelope Aubin's *The Life of Madam de Beaumont*.

Katherine de Maintenon Daughter of Monsieur de Maintenon, sister of Count de Beaumont, and best friend of Belinda (later Madam de Beaumont) at their convent, which they flee so that Belinda can marry Katherine's brother and Katherine can marry the Colonel de Alancon; she dies a year after Madam de Beaumont's exile to England in Penelope Aubin's *The Life of Madam de Beaumont*.

Mr. Mainwaring Epicurean rector at Dillsborough who frequently dines in society, leaving his religious chores to his curate in Anthony Trollope's *The American Senator*.

Helen Mainwaring Daughter of Susan Mivers and William Mainwaring; she narrowly escapes death by poisoning at the hands of her aunt, Lucretia Clavering; she marries Percival St. John in Edward Bulwer-Lytton's *Lucretia*.

William Mainwaring Weak and reluctant suitor of Lucretia Clavering; he marries Susan Mivers and is later led by Lucretia to mismanage funds at the bank in which he is a partner in Edward Bulwer-Lytton's *Lucretia*.

Maisie A heartless charmer, who grows up with Dick Heldar; she strives to be an artist but does not recognize that she does not have talent; she selfishly throws away Dick's love in Rudyard Kipling's *The Light That Failed*.

Earl of Maitland Decent aristocrat who marries Fanny Goodall; he mistakes Henry Clinton for his wife's paramour and dies from a fever occasioned by the belief that his wife loves another more than him in Henry Brooke's *The Fool of Quality*.

Major Maitland English soldier who invites Zachariah Coleman to join the radical London political club of which he is a leader in 1814; he is killed during the march of Manchester Blanketeers in 1817 in Mark Rutherford's *The Revolution In Tanner's Lane*.

Miss Maitland A fellow tenant of Ernest Pontifex at Mrs. Jupp's; she is mistakenly believed by Ernest to be a prostitute; when he attempts to minister to her, she believes she is in danger and runs to a policeman, resulting in Ernest's arrest and imprisonment for six months in Samuel Butler's *The Way of All Flesh*.

Majoricus Christian prefect of a defeated legion and father of Victoria; he is found wounded and is cared for by Raphael Aben-Ezra; religious differences result in the friends' separation, but Marjoricus, Victoria, and Raphael meet again at Synesius's house in Charles Kingsley's *Hypatia*.

Mr. (Ugly) Makins John Buncle's contemporary at Trinity College, Dublin; though not wealthy, he is musically talented, and though monocular, he is very handsome; he is a zealous Unitarian in Thomas Amory's *The Life of John Buncle, Esq*.

Maladie Alamode Lady Disease (venereal disease), responsible for the author's death; his soul must visit her before leaving the City of Disease on his way to the next world in Henry Fielding's *A Journey From This World to the Next*.

Sir Mungo Malagrowther Court jester and former king's whipping boy; he delivers King James's sentence of punishment to Nigel Olifaunt in the Tower in Sir Walter Scott's *The Fortunes of Nigel*.

Malcolm Warlike Scottish baron, who imprisons his sister-in-law and niece, Louisa and Laura, for control of their money and lands; he holds the avenging Osbert for ransom of his sister Mary's hand in marriage; he attacks Castle Athlin only to be mortally wounded by Osbert; he repents on his deathbed and reveals the whereabouts of his nephew Philip in Ann Radcliffe's *The Castles of Athlin and Dunbayne*.

Mrs. Malcolm Exemplary widow of a Clyde shipmaster; fallen on hard times, she regards her children's social successes as an earthly reward for piety and endurance of hardship in John Galt's *Annals of the Parish*.

Charles Malcolm Mrs. Malcolm's eldest son; he begins his career as a cabin boy, rises to the rank of midshipman in the Royal Navy, and is killed in 1782 in battle with the French in John Galt's *Annals of the Parish.*

Duncan Malcolm The deceased Scottish grandfather of Alicia Malcolm Douglas in Susan Ferrier's *Marriage.*

Effie Malcolm Mrs. Malcolm's second daughter; she marries an aristocratic friend of her brother Charles in John Galt's *Annals of the Parish.*

Kate Malcolm Mrs. Malcolm's eldest daughter and a companion to Lady MacAdam; she falls in love with and marries Laird MacAdam, despite his mother's objection in John Galt's *Annals of the Parish.*

Robert Malcolm Mrs. Malcolm's second son, first a common sailor like his brother Charles; eventually he becomes captain of a ship, marries a wealthy merchant's daughter, and becomes a shipowner in John Galt's *Annals of the Parish.*

William (Willie) Malcolm Mrs. Malcolm's youngest son; he attends Glasgow University through Lord Eaglesham's patronage and becomes a Presbyterian minister and author of "A Volume of Moral Essays" in John Galt's *Annals of the Parish.*

Mr. Maldon Lady Audley's father, who keeps little George, the son of his daughter's marriage to George Talboys, in secret; he is kind but drinks too much in Mary Elizabeth Braddon's *Lady Audley's Secret.*

Jack Maldon Handsome, confident, but shallow cousin of Annie Strong; he has a selfish affection for her, serves as a cadet in India, and returns to England in Charles Dickens's *The Personal History of David Copperfield.*

Maleck Trustworthy *lask* (slave) who is freed at Peter Wilkins's request, and who becomes Peter's attendant and interpreter in Robert Paltock's *The Life and Adventures of Peter Wilkins.*

Mrs. Maleverer Lady of rank in London society in William Beckford's *Modern Novel Writing; or, the Elegant Enthusiast.*

Duke of Malfy Nobleman infatuated with Gigantilla and blind to all her plottings; he kills Philamont, his supposed rival, in Eliza Haywood's *The Perplex'd Dutchess; or, Treachery Rewarded.*

Michael (Father) de Malinos Popular Spanish priest and author of *La Guida Spirituale*; he is imprisoned for heresy in Rome in J. Henry Shorthouse's *John Inglesant, a Romance.*

Malkin Impetuous and unstable young politician and traveler; he forms the plan of training a young girl, Bella Jacox, to be his wife when she comes of marriageable age; he becomes comically involved with her mother and has to escape to New Zealand, but he ultimately marries Bella in George Gissing's *Born in Exile.*

Thomas Malkin Brother of Malkin; he appears at a crucial moment to help Malkin escape an unwise engagement by taking him to New Zealand in George Gissing's *Born in Exile.*

Mr. Mallard Elderly, sleek clerk of Serjeant Snubbins in Charles Dickens's *The Posthumous Papers of the Pickwick Club.*

Ambrose (Brosey) Mallard One of Lord Fleetwood's "Ixionides"; his suicide, resulting from gambling losses and jealousy of Countess Fleetwood's attentions, reveals the frivolity of society to Lord Fleetwood in George Meredith's *The Amazing Marriage.*

Ross Mallard Artist who is made a guardian of the orphaned Cecily Doran, loves her without hope, and tries to delay her marriage to the unworthy Reuben Elgar; he ultimately marries the changed Miriam Baske in George Gissing's *The Emancipated.*

Sir Hugo Mallinger Wealthy guardian of Daniel Deronda; he kindly raises the son of a Jewish woman, Leonora Halm-Eberstein, as his nephew; he remains attached to Deronda although he disapproves of Deronda's acknowledging his Jewish heredity in George Eliot's *Daniel Deronda.*

Louise, Lady Mallinger Sir Hugo Mallinger's wife, who is unable to produce a son and heir for her husband; they have three young daughters in George Eliot's *Daniel Deronda.*

Mallison Cruel, sallow-complexioned school-fellow of Charles Mandeville; he possesses an acerbic wit and takes pleasure in causing others mental pain; disturbingly, he is found to be in league with his uncle, Holloway, in defrauding Audley Mandeville in William Godwin's *Mandeville.*

Simon Malmesbury Owner of Brimstone, which was burned by Bennet Hatch on Sir Daniel Brackley's orders in Robert Louis Stevenson's *The Black Arrow: A Tale of Two Roses.*

Edward (Ned) Malone Newspaperman who accompanies Professor Challenger and Lord John Roxton to South America; he is narrator of Arthur Conan Doyle's *The Lost World.*

Peter Augustus Malone　Arrogant and quarrelsome Briarfield curate, who unsuccessfully woos both Caroline Helstone and Shirley Keeldar in Charlotte Brontë's *Shirley*.

Maloney　Steward of Mowbray Castle and an uncouth womanizer, who gets Lord Montreville's consent to marry Emmeline Mobray; she finds the offer offensive and refuses in Charlotte Smith's *Emmeline: The Orphan of the Castle*.

Archy M'Alpin　Old Scotsman and retired soldier, who is taken as Jery Melford's servant to replace Dutton in Tobias Smollett's *The Expedition of Humphry Clinker*.

Baron Maltby　Judge in the trial of Lady Mason in Anthony Trollope's *Orley Farm*.

Ernest Maltravers　Wealthy man of letters; he does not know of the birth and death of his daughter by his early lost love, Alice Darvil; he seeks his ideal woman in the short-lived Lady Florence Lascelles in Edward Bulwer-Lytton's *Ernest Maltravers*. Successfully courting Evelyn Templeton, he is falsely informed by Lumley Ferrers that she is his daughter; he is reunited with Alice in *Alice*.

Mrs. Maltrever　Woman who takes in Lucinda Howard and introduces her to London society in William Beckford's *Modern Novel Writing; or, the Elegant Enthusiast*.

Count Malvesi　One of Lady Pisani's lovers, most highly favored by her father; Ferdinando Falkland enables Malvesi and Lady Pisani to work out their differences without a loss of honor to either man; this episode is later related by Laura as proof of Falkland's goodness and Caleb Williams's villainy in William Godwin's *Caleb Williams*.

Madonna Marchesana, Viscountess di Malvezzi　Sister of Bishop Marsilio of Ferrara in Mary Shelley's *Valperga*.

Albert Malvoisin　Unprincipled Templar who conspires against King Richard; a friend of Brian de Bois-Guilbert, he tries to persuade him to renounce Rebecca in Sir Walter Scott's *Ivanhoe*.

Sir Philip Malvoisin　Prince John's adherent, who is vanquished by Desdichado (Ivanhoe) in the tournament at Ashby and is executed for treason with his brother, Albert, in Sir Walter Scott's *Ivanhoe*.

Malvoti　Murderer of John Inglesant's twin brother, Eustace; he becomes a martyr after losing his eyesight in Naples during the plague in J. Henry Shorthouse's *John Inglesant, A Romance*.

Joshua Manasseh　Wealthy London Jew, who lends money to Renaldo de Melvil to help him return to Hungary, and who helps Renaldo discover Monimia (Serafina de Zelos); he helps Don Diego de Zelos recover his honor in Tobias Smollett's *The Adventures of Ferdinand Count Fathom*.

Louisa Mancel　An apparent orphan whose guardian, Mr. Hintman, has dishonorable intentions toward her; when Lady Lambton opposes a match between her and Edward Lambton, she becomes a servant to Mrs. Thornby, who is discovered to be her long-lost mother; Louisa founds Millenium Hall with Mrs. Morgan (formerly Miss Melvyn) in Sarah Scott's *A Description of Millenium Hall*.

Sir Marmaduke Manchet　Pastry cook knighted for his support of the Pitt government in William Beckford's *Azemia*.

Sir Peter Mancrudy　Eminent Exeter physician, who treats Jemima Stanbury when she falls ill in Anthony Trollope's *He Knew He Was Right*.

Mandana　Beloved, beautiful maiden in Nourjahad's seraglio; she is falsely reported by Hasem to have died delivering Nourjahad's son; she is given as wife to Nourjahad by Schemzeddin in exchange for performing as the guardian genius who grants Nourjahad's secret wishes in Frances Sheridan's *The History of Nourjahad*.

Commodore Mandeville　Tyrannical parent and much-decorated explorer and military hero, who thwarts the intentions of his son, Audley, to marry Amelia Montfort in William Godwin's *Mandeville*.

Audley Mandeville　Uncle of Charles Mandeville; he is persecuted and manipulated in early life by his father, the Commodore Mandeville, and he nearly falls victim to a swindle masterminded by Holloway and his nephew, Mallison, in William Godwin's *Mandeville*.

Charles Mandeville　Young man who as a child was saved from the 1641 Irish uprising in which his parents died by his resourceful wetnurse, Judith; educated at Winchester and Oxford, he briefly serves the Royalist cause; thwarted in his ambition to become Secretary to Sir Joseph Wagstaff by his school-fellow, Lionel Clifford, and vilified back at Oxford by his other school-fellow, Mallison, he suffers alienation from his fellow students, which hastens the development of his misanthropy, a persistent element in his personality relieved only in the company of his beloved sister, Henrietta; enraged when he receives word that Henrietta and Clifford are to be wed, he hires mercenaries to ambush Clifford, Henrietta, and their party; in the fight that follows Charles receives a disfiguring wound, which permanently distorts his mouth to a hideous grimace and objectifies his disgust for mankind in William Godwin's *Mandeville*.

Dorothy Mandeville   Devout, colorless maiden sister of Commodore Mandeville; she takes over his household at the death of his wife in William Godwin's *Mandeville*.

Henrietta Mandeville   Graceful, talented sister of Charles Mandeville; they are affectionately attached, though she grows up separated from him in William Godwin's *Mandeville*.

Henry Mandeville   Young descendant of the first Earl of Belmont; of modest fortune and good education, he is morally and politically responsible but has a passionate temper; his betrothal to Lady Julia Belmont remains uncertain because of complex jointure arrangements by the well-meaning Belmont and Mandeville parents; he is killed dueling with Lord Melvin, whom he mistakenly believes to be Lady Julia's favored suitor in Frances Brooke's *The History of Lady Julia Mandeville*.

Colonel John Mandeville   Father of Henry and a descendant of the first Earl of Belmont; of modest fortune, he is concerned with the education of his son in matters of ethics and the state; his search for the "good" life independent of economic or political interest prompts him to delay revealing to Henry his inheritance from the Belmonts in Frances Brooke's *The History of Lady Julia Mandeville*.

Lady Julia Mandeville   See Lady Julia Belmont.

Fior de Mandragola   Witch of the forest near Lucca, a Paterin, who reacquaints Beatrice with the power of evil, and who poisons her with henbane in Mary Shelley's *Valperga*.

Mr. Mandrake   Henpecked husband of Mrs. Mandrake in William Beckford's *Modern Novel Writing; or, the Elegant Enthusiast*.

Mrs. Mandrake   Imperious woman of quality, a formerly celebrated beauty, who feigns indifference to the charms of Arabella (Bloomville) Lambert in William Beckford's *Modern Novel Writing; or, the Elegant Enthusiast*.

Dr. Alexander Manette   Paris physician imprisoned for many years in the Bastille because he protested the rape and murder of a French lower-class woman, Madame Defarge's sister, by the brothers St. Évrémonde; his diary kept during imprisonment provides details about their involvement in the murder and, ironically, convicts Charles Darnay, his son-in-law, in Charles Dickens's *A Tale of Two Cities*.

Lucie Manette   Daughter of Dr. Alexander Manette;

she sees her father for the first time when he is released from the Bastille; in love with Charles Darnay and courted by Sydney Carton, she marries Darnay and has a daughter; Carton gives up his life out of love for Lucie by replacing her husband in prison in Charles Dickens's *A Tale of Two Cities*.

Manfred (Prince of Otranto)   Unprincipled despot and unrightful inheritor of Otranto; he rejects his wife, Hippolita, to pursue Isabella, his son's betrothed, but is ultimately deposed and driven into religious seclusion in Horace Walpole's *The Castle of Otranto*.

Paolo Manfrone   Advisor to Doge Andreas; his murder is feigned in the plan of Flodoardo/Abellino (Count Rosalvo) to ensnare the conspirators in Matthew Lewis's *The Bravo of Venice*.

Sarah Matilda Mangles   Coarse young woman whom Dudley Ruthyn has secretly married; she arrives to confront Maud Ruthyn when she hears Dudley is courting her in J. Sheridan Le Fanu's *Uncle Silas*.

Alice Manisty   Eccentric and eventually mad sister of Edward Manisty; while staying at the Villa Barberini, she attacks Lucy Foster in Mrs. Humphry Ward's *Eleanor*.

Edward Manisty   Haughty aristocrat who selfishly uses his cousin Eleanor Burgoyne as secretary while he writes a book on the history of the Catholic church in Italy; he falls in love with Lucy Foster, a young American visitor; their love plunges Eleanor into a fatal decline in health in Mrs. Humphry Ward's *Eleanor*.

Pattie Manisty   Aunt of Edward Manisty; she is the chatelaine of his rented house, Villa Barberini, in the hills north of Rome in Mrs. Humphry Ward's *Eleanor*.

Mankelow   Wealthy, good-looking, predatory man, who runs off with the irresponsible Fanny French in George Gissing's *In the Year of Jubilee*.

Sir Robert Manley   Suitor to Jenny Jessamy in Eliza Haywood's *The History of Jemmy and Jenny Jessamy*.

Mr. Manly   Lucius's father, a squire of modest property, nearly ruined financially by his vices; he is rescued by a dutiful Lucius; Felicia's father's gift of a small estate causes him to reform; he eventually inherits a large fortune from a brother in Mary Collyer's *Felicia to Charlotte*.

Lucius Manly   Pious country gentleman possessed of a small estate; he wins Felicia's admiration and love with his sincere manners, his love of God, his philosophy, and his generosity, rather than with the manners and the flattery typical of fashionable gentlemen; he is discovered to have fathered an illegitimate child but is forgiven because the fault does not lie entirely with him; he is also the ideal landlord in Mary Collyer's *Felicia to Charlotte*.

Marilla Manly   Sister of Lucius Manly and confidante of Felicia; she rejects a dissembling reformed rake with a fortune and marries a clergyman whose want of fortune is compensated for by an excess of virtue in Mary Collyer's *Felicia to Charlotte*.

Sophronia Manly   Mother of Lucius Manly and a well-bred country woman, who agrees to rear her son's illegitimate child in Mary Collyer's *Felicia to Charlotte*.

Miss Mann   A selfless old maid, who has spent her life nursing others, and who becomes an example for Caroline Helstone in Charlotte Brontë's *Shirley*.

Mrs. Mann   Supervisor of the branch workhouse where Oliver Twist and other orphaned children live; she mistreats the children and keeps them short of food in Charles Dickens's *Oliver Twist*.

Colonel Guy Mannering   Wealthy, retired English officer and a dignified scholar, who enjoys astrology; on the night of Henry Bertram's birth he predicts that danger will come to Henry in his fifth, ninth, and twenty-first years; he generously supports Lucy Bertram and Dominie Sampson when Lucy has been orphaned; he vehemently disapproves of Henry Bertram because of a misunderstanding early in their acquaintance and so proves a formidable barrier to Henry and Julia Mannering's romance in Sir Walter Scott's *Guy Mannering*.

Julia Mannering   Beloved daughter and only child of Colonel Mannering; she is beautiful as well as brilliant, witty, and dramatic; self-possessed, she perseveres in her romance with Henry Bertram and eventually succeeds in Sir Walter Scott's *Guy Mannering*.

Sophie Wellwood Mannering   Guy Mannering's wife and Julia Mannering's mother; she is a spiteful, shallow woman who turns Julia against her father and betrays her husband in Sir Walter Scott's *Guy Mannering*.

Lady Manning   Henrietta Courteney's first guardian, a wealthy but low-born widow and friend to Henrietta's mother; she treats Henrietta superciliously and throws her out when she refuses to marry the old schoolmaster Mr. Vellum in Charlotte Lennox's *Henrietta*.

Miss Manning   Daughter to Lady Manning; low-born, ugly, ill-natured, and spoiled, she is taught to consider herself a great prize on the marriage market because of her fortune in Charlotte Lennox's *Henrietta*.

Mr. Manning   Self-taught engineer and father of Paul; he is an industrial counterpart to the rural Mr. Holman,

with whom he becomes friends in Elizabeth Gaskell's *Cousin Phillis*.

Sir Geoffrey Manning   Owner of the land on which Mr. Wardle and the Pickwickians hunt in Charles Dickens's *The Posthumous Papers of the Pickwick Club*.

Paul Manning   The narrator, a youthful railway engineer and cousin of Phillis Holman; he introduces Edward Holdsworth to her; his telling her of Holdsworth's love is well meant but ultimately adds to her unhappiness in Elizabeth Gaskell's *Cousin Phillis*.

Robert Mannion   Curiously impassive, handsome, intelligent business manager for Mr. Sherwin; of mysterious antecedents, he blames his family tragedy on Basil's father, and revenge partly motivates his corruption of Margaret Sherwin, whom he holds in contempt while he secretly woos her; attacked and horribly disfigured by Basil, he vows revenge and has begun a successful hounding of Basil when he dies accidentally in Cornwall in Wilkie Collins's *Basil: A Story of Modern Life*.

Manon   Serving girl in "The Fair Star," who warns Gerard and Denys of danger and notifies both soldiers and police in Charles Reade's *The Cloister and the Hearth*.

John Mansel   Constable who, in attempting to apprehend Orlando Eustace for murdering his wife, is shot and killed in a struggle in Thomas Amory's *The Life of John Buncle, Esq.*

Lady Mansfield   Perceptive mother of Lord Bottom; she realizes that some people mistake young Harry Clinton's natural manners for those of a fool in Henry Brooke's *The Fool of Quality*.

Lord Mansfield   Humble aristocrat; his insolent son, Lord Bottom, is beaten up by young Harry Clinton, who becomes aware of his own faults as a result of the incident in Henry Brooke's *The Fool of Quality*.

Miss Mansfield   Gentlewoman apparently destined for spinsterhood because the family wealth has been lost through the chicanery of a steward; Sir Charles Grandison arranges her marriage to his uncle, Lord W., in Samuel Richardson's *Sir Charles Grandison*.

Louisa Mansfield   Daughter of Lord Mansfield in Henry Brooke's *The Fool of Quality*.

Aeneas Manston   Cytherea Bradleigh Aldclyffe's steward, who falls in love with Cytherea Graye and marries her after the presumed death of his first wife; news that she survived the fire causes Cytherea Graye to leave him; though still loving Cytherea, he advertises for and is apparently reunited with his first wife, but Edward

Springrove's and Owen Graye's investigations prove that the woman is not the same wife but Manston's assistant in a deception; apprehended after being observed moving his first wife's body, he kills himself in jail; freed to remarry, Cytherea Graye also discovers that Manston was Miss Aldclyffe's natural son in Thomas Hardy's *Desperate Remedies*.

Eunice Rondley Manston   Wife of Aeneas Manston; an American actress, she has been on her own and using the name Rondley until she decides to claim her position as his wife; presumed to have died in the fire which destroyed the Three Tranters inn, she confronts her husband and is killed by him when he strikes her; he hides her body and fakes evidence to perpetuate the belief that she died in the fire in Thomas Hardy's *Desperate Remedies*.

Madame Mantalini   Owner of a dressmaking establishment, who is ruined by her profligate husband, Alfred, in Charles Dickens's *The Life and Adventures of Nicholas Nickleby*.

Alfred Mantalini   Extravagant and idle husband, who lives off his indulgent wife's dressmaking business and destroys it with his debts; his characteristic expression is "demd"; he ends up in prison in Charles Dickens's *The Life and Adventures of Nicholas Nickleby*.

Mantilla   Don Francisco di Aliaga's proposed husband for his daughter Isidora (Immalee) di Aliaga in Charles Maturin's *Melmoth the Wanderer*.

Manuel   A Portuguese fisherman who rescues Harvey Cheyne after he has fallen from the ocean liner and takes him to the cod-fishing boat *We're Here* in Rudyard Kipling's *"Captains Courageous": A Story of the Grand Banks*.

Captain Manuel   Cuban whom Lydia Gwilt married after murdering her first husband; years later at the opera she sees him among the chorus; she tries to use him in ridding herself of Allan Armadale, but her plan misfires in Wilkie Collins's *Armadale*.

Don Manuel   Venetian nobleman and ship's captain, father of Violetta; he finds her and Ardelisa de Vinevil shipwrecked on the island of Delos and carries them safely back to Venice in Penelope Aubin's *The Strange Adventures of the Count de Vinevil and His Family*.

Mr. Manylodes   Sly promoter of a Cornish tin mine who bribes Alaric Tudor with shares to report back favorably to the government on the mine in Anthony Trollope's *The Three Clerks*.

Mrs. Maple   Aunt of Elinor and Selina Joddrel; she is rude to the Stranger, Juliet Granville, on the boat escaping

France; she continues to insult Juliet when she resides in her house at Lewes in Frances Burney's *The Wanderer*.

Mara (Cat-Woman, Mother of Sorrows)   Daughter of Adam and Eve; she watches over the House of Bitterness and protects children in the form of a white leopardess; she shows Lilith her true self in George MacDonald's *Lilith*.

Marble Lady (White Lady)   Sir Percival's wife; freed from her enchantment by Anodos's song, she is pursued by Anodos, who wants to possess her, in George MacDonald's *Phantastes*.

Marcelline   Mrs. Gallilee's personal maid, sent to spy on Carmina Graywell; she behaves honorably to Carmina; she assists Mr. Gallilee in assembling clothing for the Gallilee children's surreptitious visit to Scotland in Wilkie Collins's *Heart and Science*.

Marcellus   A gallant and a womanizer, who has an affair with Clelia and is supposed to marry Jemella in Jane Barker's *Exilius; or, The Banish'd Roman*.

Lord March   Dissipated young nobleman with whom Harry Warrington associates in William Makepeace Thackeray's *The Virginians*.

March Hare   Host for the mad tea party, at which he parodies Victorian etiquette and academia, and interrupter of evidence at the trial of the Knave of Hearts in Lewis Carroll's *Alice's Adventures in Wonderland*. As Haigha, the White King's messenger, he exhibits "Anglo-Saxon attitudes" (awkward gestures) in *Through the Looking Glass*.

The Marchioness   Small, neglected girl, who is the housemaid for the Brasses; she lives in the cellar, is kept hungry, is befriended by Dick Swiveller, nurses Dick when he is ill, and reveals what she has overheard about the conspiracy to frame Kit Nubbles; she marries Dick, who has had her educated in Charles Dickens's *The Old Curiosity Shop*.

Mr. Marchmont   Maria Marchmont's cousin and heir, who belatedly sends money to Lucy Snowe, probably in compliance with Miss Marchmont's original instructions in Charlotte Brontë's *Villette*.

Maria Marchmont   A wealthy, crippled woman, who employs Lucy Snowe as a lady's companion; she is patient but stern because of her twenty-year-long affliction; her death sends Lucy again in search of employment in Charlotte Brontë's *Villette*.

Matilda Marchmont   Julia Mannering's correspondent

from school; their letters serve to provide much of Julia's history in Sir Walter Scott's *Guy Mannering*.

Marcia (Andrea)   Pietro Vanucci's color-grinder, a handsome boy who attends the party on the Tiber as a stunning woman, but forgets feminine decorum when he aids in the hunt for the frantic Gerard in Charles Reade's *The Cloister and the Hearth*.

Marcian   Armorer to Robert of Paris in Sir Walter Scott's *Count Robert of Paris*.

Marcian   Basil's duplicitous friend, neurotic and secretly envious, who takes part in the plot to abduct Veranilda, tries to keep Basil and Veranilda apart, and is ultimately slain by Basil in George Gissing's *Veranilda*.

Marco   Surly Tuscan peasant, in whose cottage Emily St. Aubert is confined by Montoni in Ann Radcliffe's *The Mysteries of Udolpho*.

Marco   Antonio dei Adimari's servant, who guides the exiled Ghibelline Castruccio de Antelminelli to Euthanasia dei Adimari's palace in Guelph Florence in Mary Shelley's *Valperga*.

Don Marco   Rescuer and liberater of Emanuella; he acts against his father's orders in Eliza Haywood's *The Rash Resolve; or, the Untimely Discovery*.

Marcus   Monk who cares for the sick Basil in the abbey of Cassino in George Gissing's *Veranilda*.

Marcus Aurelius   The emperor of Rome and the employer, friend, and advisor of Marius; he is admired by the people of Rome for both his political and religious leadership in Walter Pater's *Marius the Epicurean*.

Marcus Cornelius Fronto   Counselor to the Roman Emperor Marcus Aurelius and the leading Sophist of the time in Walter Pater's *Marius the Epicurean*.

Edward Gibbon Mardon   Compositor for a local newspaper in the town of Mark Rutherford's first chapel; he welcomes Mark as a guest in his house to discuss religion though he is an atheist himself, and he shows courage in the face of death after being attacked by a mob during a political riot in Mark Rutherford's *The Autobiography of Mark Rutherford*.

Mary Mardon   Edward Mardon's daughter, who keeps his house; she befriends Mark Rutherford, though she refuses his proposal of marriage when he falls in love watching her nurse her ailing father; she dies from a cold caught at her father's funeral in Mark Rutherford's *The Autobiography of Mark Rutherford*.

Ralph Mareschal   Richard Vere's cousin and his guest at the time of Isabella's abduction; he insists on questioning Patrick Earnscliff about her and on searching towards the tower of Westburnflat (Willie Graeme); later he marries Lucy Ilderton in Sir Walter Scott's *The Black Dwarf*.

Mr. Marfelt   Gentleman whose son Hammel Clement is engaged to tutor; the promise of gainful employment vanishes when the boy dies in Henry Brooke's *The Fool of Quality*.

Margaret   Servant to Mr. Innes and his daughter, Evelyn, in their Dulwich house in George Moore's *Evelyn Innes*.

Lady Margaret   Wife of David Stuart after the death of Eleanor (Raymond) Penrhyn in Caroline Norton's *Stuart of Dunleath*.

Mrs. Margaret (Moggy)   Middle-aged, plain country woman, who becomes Colonel Jack's fourth wife; she dies after a fall while pregnant in Daniel Defoe's *The History and the Remarkable Life of the Truly Honourable Colonel Jacques, Commonly Call'd Col. Jack*.

Margaret of Anjou   Widow of the English King Henry VI; in exile in Europe, she commissions John de Vere to negotiate for her with the Duke of Burgundy and dies while she is negotiating with her own father to ally himself with Burgundy in Sir Walter Scott's *Anne of Geierstein*.

Sister Margaritone   Grim nun, who acts as Ellena Rosalba's jailor in the San Stafano convent in Ann Radcliffe's *The Italian*.

Margery   Rachel Lake's young servant at Redman's Farm in J. Sheridan Le Fanu's *Wylder's Hand*.

Dame Margery   Housekeeper to Lady Leicester, after whose death she strangles herself in Sophia Lee's *The Recess*.

Mrs. Margery   Elderly maiden aunt with whom the orphaned Harley lives in Henry Mackenzie's *The Man of Feeling*.

Margrave   See Louis Grayle.

Viscount Margrave   Rich nobleman and attempted seducer of Matilda in Elizabeth Inchbald's *A Simple Story*.

Marguerite   Reluctant wife of the murderous bandit Baptiste; she kills him to save Alphonso d'Alvarada (Raymond de la Cisternas) and Rodolpha, Baroness Lindenberg in Matthew Lewis's *The Monk*.

Maria   Beautiful woman with a pathetic history, encountered by Tristram Shandy during his travels in Italy; she was driven mad by the treachery of a curate who forbade her wedding, evidently out of jealousy, in Laurence Sterne's *The Life and Opinions of Tristram Shandy, Gentleman*. Her poignant affection for a little goat evokes Yorick's sentimentalism in *A Sentimental Journey through France and Italy*.

Maria   Heiress who tries unsuccessfully to force Natura into marrying her in Eliza Haywood's *Life's Progress Through the Passions: or, the Adventures of Natura*.

Maria   Madam de Beaumont's faithful servant, a native of England and formerly a servant to her mistress's mother; she stays with Madam de Beaumont in the cave in Wales for fourteen years in Penelope Aubin's *The Life of Madam de Beaumont*.

Maria   Monsieur De Rhíe's servant, who helps in Cornelia's escape, is later seduced by De Rhíe, and bears his child in Sarah Scott's *The History of Cornelia*.

Maria   Faithful first love of Mr. D–; grief and suspense at his unfaithfulness with Syrena Tricksy send her into convulsions and fever; he returns to her repentant, but, saying she can live neither with nor without him, she dies in Eliza Haywood's *Anti-Pamela: or, Feign'd Innocence Detected*.

Maria   Queen Eleanor's French poet in Ann Radcliffe's *Gaston de Blondeville*.

Maria   Mrs. Cork's London maid, who pities Frank Palmer and helps him find where Madge Hopgood has moved after her ejection in Mark Rutherford's *Clara Hopgood*.

Maria Helen   Woman writer celebrated throughout Europe for the impartiality of her writings and her rational love of liberty in William Beckford's *Modern Novel Writing; or, the Elegant Enthusiast*.

Marian   The stoutest and least comely of the milkmaids at Richard Crick's dairy who all fall in love with Angel Clare; upon his marriage to Tess Durbeyfield she takes to drink, loses her job, and becomes a farm laborer; later she tries to aid Tess but is ineffectual in Thomas Hardy's *Tess of the D'Urbervilles*.

Mariana   Daughter of Leonora Aldi and ward of Captain Brooks; virtuous and chaste, she remains unmarried in order to follow her religious inclinations; she loves her half sister and half brother, Beatrice and Owen Brooks, in Caroline Norton's *Lost and Saved*.

Marquis Marinelli   Suitor of Cornelia de Vereza; she

chooses to become a nun rather than accept his proposal in Ann Radcliffe's *A Sicilian Romance*.

Guilia Marini   Luigi Marini's wife; she takes care of Emilia Belloni in London after Wilfrid Pole renounces Emilia in George Meredith's *Emilia in England*.

Luigi Marini   An Italian patriot living in London; he keeps Mr. Belloni from taking Emilia Belloni back to Italy, and with his wife nurses her in George Meredith's *Emilia in England*.

Don Mario   Noble father of Leonora; coming upon his daughter at the last moment of her clandestine marriage rites, he is persuaded to accept as son-in-law the noble Aurelian, soon discovering him to be in fact the equally noble Hippolito in William Congreve's *Incognita*.

Maritornes   Housemaid to Mr. Graham in Richard Graves's *The Spiritual Quixote*.

Marius   A devout young man of a poetical temper; he first attends school at Pisa, later is employed by the Roman Emperor Marcus Aurelius, and finally dies a Christian martyr; he is a believer in moderation and in the philosophy that the body should be a medium of reception for experience, both physical and spiritual, in Walter Pater's *Marius the Epicurean*.

Sir Mark (Blue Knight)   Man who shelters Elfhild and Anna the Carline in his castle, Brookside, until he is killed in battle in William Morris's *The Sundering Flood*.

Mr. Markham   Friend of James Steerforth; he dines with David Copperfield in London in Charles Dickens's *The Personal History of David Copperfield*.

Mr. Markham   Gilbert Markham's father, a gentleman farmer who wants his eldest son to continue working the farm in Anne Brontë's *The Tenant of Wildfell Hall*.

Mrs. Markham   Protective mother of Gilbert Markham; she is strict with her daughter, Rose, but lax with her sons, Gilbert and Fergus, and opposes Gilbert's attraction to Helen Huntingdon in Anne Brontë's *The Tenant of Wildfell Hall*.

Fergus Markham   Gilbert's younger brother; he makes fun of Gilbert's romances and cares little for the work on the farm until he falls in love and wants to make himself worthy of his beloved in Anne Brontë's *The Tenant of Wildfell Hall*.

Gilbert Markham   Elder son of a gentleman farmer; he flirts with Eliza Millward, the vicar's daughter, but then falls in love with Helen "Graham" (Huntingdon) and is given her journal to read; after several false starts, he marries Helen following Arthur Huntingdon's death and years later writes a long letter to Halford narrating the entire history in Anne Brontë's *The Tenant of Wildfell Hall*.

John Markham Cousin of Robert and William Fitz-Owen; he aids in the conspiracy to discredit Edmund Lovel in Clara Reeve's *The Old English Baron*.

Rose Markham Gilbert's even-tempered sister, whose loyalty is torn between her brother and her friends when the scandal erupts surrounding Helen "Graham" (Huntingdon); she marries Gilbert's friend Halford in Anne Brontë's *The Tenant of Wildfell Hall*.

Mrs. Markleham (Old Soldier) Sharp-eyed mother of Annie Strong; she lives with her daughter and son-in-law and perpetuates the suspicion that there is illicit affection between Annie Strong and her cousin Jack Maldon in Charles Dickens's *The Personal History of David Copperfield*.

Luke Marks Husband of Phoebe Marks; he blackmails Lady Audley and buys his own tavern with the money; he dies as a result of a fire set by Lady Audley in Mary Elizabeth Braddon's *Lady Audley's Secret*.

Phoebe Marks Lady Audley's personal maid; she leaks stories about her mistress to her husband, Luke Marks, and is involved in blackmailing her in Mary Elizabeth Braddon's *Lady Audley's Secret*.

Duke of Marlborough Commander-in-chief of the English army; he is a man of godlike calm and godlike reputation but capable of the meanest acts in William Makepeace Thackeray's *The History of Henry Esmond*.

Jacob Marley Ebenezer Scrooge's business partner in life; Marley's fettered ghost appears horrifically to warn Scrooge about the consequences of selfishness and greed in Charles Dickens's *A Christmas Carol*.

Lady Harriet Marlow Fictional author of William Beckford's *Modern Novel Writing; or, the Elegant Enthusiast*. She is the recipient of a dedication by Jacquetta Agenta Martiana Jenks, the fictional author of *Azemia*.

Beatrix Marlowe Beautiful and kind daughter of Sir Jeckyl Marlowe; innocent of her father's past schemes, she falls in love with Guy Strangways during the houseparty; they are separated after Sir Jeckyl dies but are later reunited and married through the auspices of Lady Alice Redcliffe, who convinces Varbarriere to agree in J. Sheridan Le Fanu's *Guy Deverell*.

E. Marlowe A friend of Jenny Jessamy; she constantly fights with her husband, though during their courtship she was very kind to him in Eliza Haywood's *The History of Jemmy and Jenny Jessamy*.

Gertrude Marlowe Illegitimate daughter of Lord Scroope (1); she unknowingly marries her brother, Anthony Colville; she becomes the loving guardian of Matilda and Ellinor in Sophia Lee's *The Recess*.

Sir Jeckyl Marlowe Baronet who, as a young man, killed Guy Deverell in an unfair duel and stole the paper that proved Marlowe belongs to the Deverells; his affair with Lady Jane Lennox is revealed to her husband by Varbarriere, who, as Herbert Strangways, was the only witness to the duel; Lennox inflicts a wound that leads to Jeckyl's death in J. Sheridan Le Fanu's *Guy Deverell*.

Silas Marner A linen weaver, who loses faith in his best friend, his betrothed, church, and God in his youth when he is framed for a robbery in Lantern Yard; he moves to an isolated area in Ravenloe, where he hoards gold coins until they are stolen from him; the gold's place in his heart is replaced by the love he feels for an orphan girl, Eppie, whom he raises as a daughter in George Eliot's *Silas Marner*.

Lady Marney Charles Egremont's mother and a distinguished stateswoman, who frequently intercedes in political affairs on her son's behalf in Benjamin Disraeli's *Sybil*.

Mrs. Marney Middle-aged woman Caleb Williams meets in London; she acts as Caleb's literary agent; arrested for aiding Caleb, she is released because of the intervention of her noble relative in William Godwin's *Caleb Williams*.

Arabella, Lady Marney Magnanimous but submissive wife of George, Lord Marney and sister-in-law of Charles Egremont, with whom she was in love before her mother forced her to marry Lord Marney because he instead of his brother would inherit the family fortune in Benjamin Disraeli's *Sybil*.

George, Lord Marney Charles Egremont's arrogant older brother, who has maintained his title by unscrupulous means and whose contempt for the working class estranges him from Charles; finally he dies at the hands of an angry mob of workers in Benjamin Disraeli's *Sybil*.

Count di Maro Roman nobleman who helps the Marchese di Vivaldi gain access to Inquisition officials during Vincentio di Vivaldi's incarceration in Ann Radcliffe's *The Italian*.

Captain Maroon Horse-chanter whose suit against Edward (Tip) Dorrit leads to Tip's incarceration in the

Marshalsea debtors' prison in Charles Dickens's *Little Dorrit*.

Marquis An officer of the Guard du Corps whom Colonel Jack accuses of being too familiar with his second wife; he engages in a duel with Jack, but neither is killed in Daniel Defoe's *The History and the Remarkable Life of the Truly Honourable Colonel Jacques, Commonly Call'd Col. Jack*.

Marquis of —- Banished courtier, Arabella's father, who accidentally causes her quixotism by raising her in seclusion; he desires, but would not force, Arabella to marry Glanville; he dies early in the first volume, leaving her to her delusions in Charlotte Lennox's *The Female Quixote*.

Marquis of —- (Mr. Melvil) Young nobleman traveling with Charles Courteney; he almost dies for love of Henrietta Courteney and tries to persuade her into a clandestine marriage, which both she and her brother oppose as a breach of filial duty in Charlotte Lennox's *Henrietta*.

Lewis Marr Henry Viney's estranged shipping partner, who is robbed and stabbed to death by Dan Ogle in Arthur Morrison's *The Hole in the Wall*.

Colonel Marrable Affable, unscrupulous brother of Sir Gregory; he confirms all bad opinions by cheating his son, Walter, of his estate in Anthony Trollope's *The Vicar of Bullhampton*.

Sir Gregory Marrable Elderly baronet, father of the invalid Gregory and uncle of Walter, who becomes his heir; he is twice disappointed in his plans for Edith Brownlow in Anthony Trollope's *The Vicar of Bullhampton*.

Gregory Marrable Sickly, studious, antiquarian cousin of Walter Marrable; his early death makes Walter the heir of Dunripple Park in Anthony Trollope's *The Vicar of Bullhampton*.

John Marrable Clergyman brother of Sir Gregory; he works behind the scenes to further a match between Mary Lowther and Harry Gilmore in hopes that with Mary out of the way Walter Marrable, who loves her, will turn to Edith Brownlow and make a wealthy match for the good of the Marrable family in Anthony Trollope's *The Vicar of Bullhampton*.

Sarah Marrable Sprightly aunt of Mary Lowther; she fervently hopes her niece will marry the local squire Harry Gilmore in Anthony Trollope's *The Vicar of Bullhampton*.

Captain Walter Marrable Dark-featured army officer who is cheated of his fortune by his own father; home from India, he falls in love with his second cousin, Mary Lowther; the death of a cousin makes him heir to an estate, and he marries Mary in Anthony Trollope's *The Vicar of Bullhampton*.

Marriott Lady Delacour's maid, who for a long time is the only one who knows the Lady's secret; she is manipulative but genuinely fond of her employer in Maria Edgeworth's *Belinda*.

Captain Marsden Rigid and controlling first husband of Clara, Lady Raymond; he leaves her with no money and a son, Godfrey Marsden, to raise in Caroline Norton's *Stuart of Dunleath*.

Godfrey Marsden Elder child of Clara, Lady Raymond and much like his late father, Captain Marsden, in belief and attitudes; he disapproves of Eleanor Raymond's freedom and sensitivity; he is intolerant yet honest in Caroline Norton's *Stuart of Dunleath*.

Judith Marsett "Fallen woman" who enlightens Nesta Radnor about the way of the world and is brought back to the path of righteousness (and marriage) by her in George Meredith's *One of Our Conquerers*.

Clifford Marsh Young man engaged to Madeline Denyer; he persuades her to renew their engagement by agreeing to leave art and go to work in his stepfather's business but drops her after she becomes an invalid and instead marries into a wealthy family in George Gissing's *The Emancipated*.

Miss Marshall Young, snobbish lady of the country estate of Mains and a neighbor to Archibald Weir of Hermiston in Robert Louis Stevenson's *Weir of Hermiston: An Unfinished Romance*.

Mr. Marshall Bookish London cabinetmaker and Mrs. Caffyn's son-in-law, who dabbles in Chartist politics; he makes rooms available for the Hopgoods after their ejection by Mrs. Cook in Mark Rutherford's *Clara Hopgood*.

Sarah Caffyn Marshall Wife of Mr. Marshall and daughter of Mrs. Caffyn; she objects to her husband's Chartist politics and dislikes London living in Mark Rutherford's *Clara Hopgood*.

Bishop Marsilio of Ferrara Virtuous and loving brother of Viscountess di Malvezzi of Ferrara; he urges Magfreda to recant her heresy and later adopts her daughter, Beatrice, in Mary Shelley's *Valperga*.

Mrs. Marston Austere but kind housekeeper at Brandon Hall when the narrator of the story, Charles de Cresseron, and Dorcas Brandon were children in J. Sheridan Le Fanu's *Wylder's Hand*.

Sarah Marstone   Pretentious woman who dresses in her own version of the Pre-Raphaelite style; she alienates Emma Brandon from her mother, encourages the schemes of Mark Gardner, and becomes a Roman Catholic in Charlotte Yonge's *Heartsease.*

Martha   Elderly, superstitious housekeeper at Osbaldistone Hall, who occasionally acts as duenna for Francis Osbaldistone and Diana Vernon in Sir Walter Scott's *Rob Roy.*

Martha   Old workhouse woman who nurses Old Sally in Charles Dickens's *Oliver Twist.*

Martha   Servant girl so severely persecuted by Mrs. Cross that she runs amok in George Gissing's *Will Warburton.*

Martha   Compassionate old woman, who rules the village of Little Marlow, and who courageously nurses its plague-stricken inhabitants in Mary Shelley's *The Last Man.*

Martha   Servant with whose assistance Lady Dalcastle (Rabina Colwan) confronts her husband, George Colwan, and Arabella Logan in James Hogg's *The Private Memoirs and Confessions of a Justified Sinner.*

Martha   Servant to Mrs. Bretton in Charlotte Brontë's *Villette.*

Martha   Matilda Jenkyns's blunt and devoted servant, whose plan preserves the home for her financially straitened mistress in Elizabeth Gaskell's *Cranford.*

Martha   Sullen, ill, but beloved daughter of John, an unemployed workingman whom Florence Dombey meets during her stay with the Skettleses in Charles Dickens's *Dombey and Son.*

Martha   Mnason's daughter who marries Joseph in John Bunyan's *The Pilgrim's Progress From this World to That Which Is to Come.*

Martha   Trusted servant of Jemima Stanbury; loyal and dutiful, she nevertheless sees through, softens, and manipulates her mistress, always to Miss Stanbury's ultimate advantage in Anthony Trollope's *He Knew He Was Right.*

Martha   Housekeeper; she grew up during the time of the novel's setting and compares past to present in Charlotte Brontë's *Shirley.*

Martha   Diamond's mother, who resembles North Wind in George MacDonald's *At the Back of the North Wind.*

Marthon (Rizpah)   Gypsy waiting-woman to the ladies of Croye, and Louis XI's agent; she is called Rizpah by her own people in Sir Walter Scott's *Quentin Durward.*

Jacques Martigny   Thief hired by Phillippe de Montalt to ambush his half-brother Henry de Montalt in Ann Radcliffe's *The Romance of the Forest.*

(Madman) Martin   A boy with an interest in chemistry and natural history who becomes the friend of George Arthur and Tom Brown in Thomas Hughes's *Tom Brown's Schooldays.*

Colonel Martin   One of Captain Anderson's friends with whom Sir Charles Grandison negotiates for his younger sister's release from a rash commitment in Samuel Richardson's *Sir Charles Grandison.*

Dr. Martin   The physician who delivered Ernest Pontifex; after Theobald Pontifex's death, he tells Ernest that Theobald was beloved in Samuel Butler's *The Way of All Flesh.*

Mr. Martin   Surly servant to the aunt of Ben and Arabella Allen in Charles Dickens's *The Posthumous Papers of the Pickwick Club.*

Mrs. Martin   A Fenmarket banker's widow, socially superior to the Hopgoods; she invites Madge Hopgood and Frank Palmer to play in a scene from *The Tempest* in Mark Rutherford's *Clara Hopgood.*

Squire Martin   Bedfordshire aristocrat whose loose morals are said to be an unfortunate model for his servants and other squires in Samuel Richardson's *Pamela, or Virtue Rewarded.*

Betsy Martin   Charwoman converted to temperance, mentioned in the "Report of the Committee of the United Grand Junction Ebeneezer Temperance Association" in Charles Dickens's *The Posthumous Papers of the Pickwick Club.*

Bob Martin   A sexton in Chapelizod in 1767; he helps with the secret burial of the coffin Mervyn brings to Chapelizod in J. Sheridan Le Fanu's *The House by the Churchyard.*

Edward Martin   Highwayman who is guilty of many robberies; he asks for a place in the service of Matthew Bramble and is helped by Matthew to find a new life for himself in Tobias Smollett's *The Expedition of Humphry Clinker.*

Elizabeth Martin   Harriet Smith's schoolmate and friend and one of Robert Martin's two sisters in Jane Austen's *Emma.*

Mrs. Giles ("Gammer") Martin   A countrywoman at whose house choristers meet for practice; her daughter's marriage above her social station to a curate resulted in the now orphaned Swithin St. Cleeve; he is residing with his grandmother and struggles not to be disdainful of local manners in Thomas Hardy's *Two on a Tower*.

Jack Martin   The bagman's uncle, hero of the story "The Bagman's Uncle" in Charles Dickens's *The Posthumous Papers of the Pickwick Club*.

Lucy Martin   Pretty, poor girl of the Windsor neighborhood; she must marry a Dachet innkeeper to provide for her bedridden mother and thereby sacrifices marriage to her true love in Mary Shelley's *The Last Man*.

Robert Martin   Sturdy, respectable young farmer, whose proposal of marriage is declined by Harriet Smith at Emma Woodhouse's instigation; he eventually marries Harriet in Jane Austen's *Emma*.

Sally Martin (Mrs. Sinclair)   Robert Lovelace's former mistress, now a madam in the London brothel where he lodges the unknowing Clarissa Harlowe and, posing as a genteel widow, a conspirator in his deception of Clarissa in Samuel Richardson's *Clarissa: or, The History of a Young Lady*.

Tom Martin   Butcher imprisoned for debt in the Fleet prison; Samuel Pickwick is assigned to share his room in Charles Dickens's *The Posthumous Papers of the Pickwick Club*.

Lord Martindale   Upright but distant father of John, Arthur, and Theodora Martindale; he is thawed by the influence of his daughter-in-law, Violet Martindale, in Charlotte Yonge's *Heartsease*.

Anna, Lady Martindale   Mother-in-law of Violet Martindale; she has been kept at a distance from her children by her domineering aunt, Theodora Nesbit, but is humanized by Violet's influence in Charlotte Yonge's *Heartsease*.

Arthur Martindale   Handsome, careless officer in the Queen's Lifeguards; he marries sixteen-year-old Violet Moss, treats her thoughtlessly, and squanders his money on racing but is reformed through redemptive illness in Charlotte Yonge's *Heartsease*.

John Martindale   Consumptive eldest son of Lord Martindale; he sacrifices his betrothed, Helen Fotheringham, to the needs of her grandparents and guides Violet Martindale in Charlotte Yonge's *Heartsease*.

John (Johnnie) Martindale   Fragile eldest son of Violet and Arthur Martindale; his timid mother asserts her-

self on his behalf; he inherits his aunt Theodora Nesbit's fortune in Charlotte Yonge's *Heartsease*.

Theodora Martindale   Proud sister-in-law of Violet Martindale, to whom she is at first contemptuous but from whom she ultimately learns humility; she marries Percy Fotheringham in Charlotte Yonge's *Heartsease*.

Violet Martindale   Mr. Moss's daughter and Arthur Martindale's young wife, who begins as the despised intruder but becomes the moral center of the entire Martindale family in Charlotte Yonge's *Heartsease*.

Major Bob Martingale   A friend of Captain Rawdon Crawley and an admirer of Becky (Sharp) Crawley in William Makepeace Thackeray's *Vanity Fair*.

Galeotti Martivalle   Louis XI's shrewd and influential astrologer; a pompous charlatan, who dislikes his monarch intensely, he agrees to misread the stars for Cardinal Balue in order to betray Louis in Sir Walter Scott's *Quentin Durward*.

Mr. Marton   A schoolmaster who befriends Nell Trent and her grandfather twice during their travels and finds them a place to live and an occupation in the village where he has his second teaching position in Charles Dickens's *The Old Curiosity Shop*.

Father Marty   Parish priest and friend of Mrs. O'Hara; he encourages the friendship between Kate O'Hara and Fred Neville and does all he can to force Fred to marry her in Anthony Trollope's *An Eye for an Eye*.

Fra Salvestro Maruffi   Dominican friar who aids Romola de' Bardi in George Eliot's *Romola*.

Marullo   Greek soldier and poet and husband of Alessandra Scala in George Eliot's *Romola*.

Teddy Marvin   Captain of the Coal and Iron Police, tool of the capitalists, and antagonist of John McGinty and the Scowrers in Arthur Conan Doyle's *The Valley of Fear*.

Mrs. Marwood (Good Mrs. Brown)   Ugly, old, poverty-stricken woman, who kidnaps the lost Florence Dombey and exchanges her clothing for rags; her daughter is Alice Marwood in Charles Dickens's *Dombey and Son*.

Alice Marwood (Alice Brown)   Mrs. Marwood's hardened daughter, who had been convicted and transported; she is James Carker's discarded mistress and Paul Dombey's illegitimate first cousin; she returns to England after ten years in Charles Dickens's *Dombey and Son*.

Mary Highly sensitive and pious daughter of dissipated aristocracy; she provides care for the sick and relief for the poor, causing her to vacillate between "enthusiastic devotion" and crushing despair in Mary Wollstonecraft's *Mary, A Fiction*.

Mary W. Elford's servant, who is stabbed by her lover and rescued by young Hugh Trevor, and who later acts as servant to Lydia Wilmot in Thomas Holcroft's *The Adventures of Hugh Trevor*.

Mary Mr. Rochester's cook at Thornfield Hall, who marries the coachman, John, and goes with him to help look after Mr. Rochester at Ferndean Manor in Charlotte Brontë's *Jane Eyre*.

Mary Maidservant at Manor Farm, Dingley Dell, in Charles Dickens's *The Posthumous Papers of the Pickwick Club*.

Mary Pretty housemaid of the Nupkinses and later a maid of Arabella Allen and sweetheart of Sam Weller in Charles Dickens's *The Posthumous Papers of the Pickwick Club*.

Mary Daughter of a Scottish earl murdered by Malcolm; she falls in love with the peasant Alleyn but agrees to surrender herself to Malcolm as ransom for her brother Osbert's life; upon Osbert's escape, she refuses to marry the Swiss Count de Santmorin; she is kidnapped by Santmorin but rescued by Osbert and Alleyn, who is discovered to be Philip of Dunbayne; she is betrothed to Philip in Ann Radcliffe's *The Castles of Athlin and Dunbayne*.

Mary Intelligent, self-educated heroine, who struggles for independence; she defies convention in her relationship with the hero, Clavering, and marries Clavering in a happy ending in Caroline Norton's *The Wife and Woman's Reward*.

Mary (Stuart or Stewart), Queen of Scots Tragic figure who is beset by enemies, deserted and betrayed by an ambitious half brother, and mistakenly advised by friends; nonetheless, she remains merry in prison, with a royal bearing and a biting wit in Sir Walter Scott's *The Abbot*. She secretly gives birth to Matilda and Ellinor after a clandestine marriage to the Duke of Norfolk; her execution follows Queen Elizabeth's discovery of the existence of her offspring in Sophia Lee's *The Recess*. She is a devious, imprisoned queen, who is reunited with Cecily Talbot, her daughter by the Earl of Bothwell, shortly before her execution in Charlotte Yonge's *Unknown to History*.

Mary (the younger) Daughter of Lord Leicester and Matilda; she is secretly engaged to Prince Henry but is in love with the Earl of Somerset, with whom she conducts an illicit correspondence until poisoned by the design of the Countess of Somerset in Sophia Lee's *The Recess*.

Aunt Mary James Brookes's talkative, sympathetic sister, sent for when the daughters are getting out of hand in George Moore's *Spring Days*.

Lady Mary Daughter of Henry VIII's first wife; she is befriended by Anna Boleyn, who reports Mary's statements against her father as coming from the queen and thereby hastens the king's decision to divorce her in Henry Fielding's *A Journey From This World to the Next*.

Mary Anne Miss Peecher's favorite student, who assists her in the household in Charles Dickens's *Our Mutual Friend*.

Mary Anne Maid of David and Dora Copperfield when they were first married in Charles Dickens's *The Personal History of David Copperfield*.

Mr. Marybone Member of Jonathan Wild's gang who will rob but not murder his victim; Wild has him impeached and executed in Henry Fielding's *The Life of Mr. Jonathan Wild the Great*.

Lord Marylebone Member of the British party defeated in an epic cricket match against the host country of Britannula in Anthony Trollope's *The Fixed Period*.

Sister Mary John Organist at the convent; she is thrilled to meet Evelyn Innes and to share Evelyn's understanding of music when Evelyn makes a retreat at the convent in George Moore's *Evelyn Innes*. Recognizing her physical attraction to Evelyn, she transfers to a French convent after Evelyn takes the veil in *Sister Teresa*.

Dr. Masham Marmion Herbert's tutor at Oxford and Lady Annabel Herbert's steadfast friend and adviser, who attempts to console her for Marmion's desertion in Benjamin Disraeli's *Venetia*.

Mrs. Masham Flint-hearted hanger-on of the wealthy and privileged, heartily disliked by Lady Glencora Palliser, whose husband, Plantagenet, encourages the lady as his wife's companion; she warns Plantagenet about Glencora's relationship with Burgo Fitzgerald; she later marries Mr. Bott in Anthony Trollope's *Can You Forgive Her?*.

Will Maskery A wheelwright and a Methodist in George Eliot's *Adam Bede*.

Maso Bardo de' Bardi's old servant, loyal to Romola de' Bardi in George Eliot's *Romola*.

Mrs. Mason   The dressmaker who employs the orphaned Ruth Hilton; she sees Ruth out late with Henry Bellingham, an encounter that leads to Ruth's dismissal and eventual seduction by the opportunist Bellingham in Elizabeth Gaskell's *Ruth*.

Mrs. Mason   Personal servant to Lady Alice Redcliffe in J. Sheridan Le Fanu's *Guy Deverell*.

Antoinetta Mason   Jonas Mason's mad Créole wife, whose insanity is passed to her children in Charlotte Brontë's *Jane Eyre*.

Diana Mason   Parsimonious wife of Joseph Mason of Groby Park; her passion is economy and her frugality notorious in Anthony Trollope's *Orley Farm*.

Elizabeth Mason   Laboring-class Protestant cousin of Laura Fountain; her fundamentalist beliefs shape her dealings with Laura in Mrs. Humphry Ward's *Helbeck of Bannisdale*.

Hubert Mason   Laboring-class cousin of Laura Fountain; she encourages him to publish his songs and succeed in business in Mrs. Humphry Ward's *Helbeck of Bannisdale*.

Jonas Mason   A rich merchant of the West Indies and friend of Mr. Rochester's father; he agrees to give his daughter, Bertha, a dowry of £30,000 to marry Edward Rochester in Charlotte Brontë's *Jane Eyre*.

Joseph Mason   Hard-hearted, grasping owner of Groby Park; he schemes to gain possession of Orley Farm, left in his late father's will to his half brother, Lucius; he tries to prove that his stepmother, Lady Mason, forged the codicil to the will depriving him of the estate in Anthony Trollope's *Orley Farm*.

Lucius Mason   Honorable, opinionated son of Lady Mason; he believes in his mother's innocence in the matter of a forged codicil to a will which made him heir to an estate but learns at last that although acquitted, she had been guilty; he also woos Sophia Furnival unsuccessfully; he voluntarily relinquishes the property to his half brother and emigrates to Australia in Anthony Trollope's *Orley Farm*.

Mary, Lady Mason   Melancholy and resolute mother of Lucius, on whose behalf she had forged a codicil to her dying husband's will conferring Orley Farm estate to her son; the much-beloved neighbor of Sir Peregrine Orme, she stands trial with great courage on a charge of forgery and is acquitted through the brilliance of her counsels, one of whom, Thomas Furnival, is half in love with her; she refuses Sir Peregrine's offer of marriage and ends her days in seclusion in Germany in Anthony Trollope's *Orley Farm*.

Richard Mason   Brother of Mr. Rochester's mad wife, Bertha; his concern for his sister results only in her attacking him; he comes later to interrupt the wedding which would have resulted in Mr. Rochester's bigamy in Charlotte Brontë's *Jane Eyre*.

Sarah Mason   Humble nurse and relative of Colonel Newcome, who befriends her unashamedly in wealth and poverty in William Makepeace Thackeray's *The Newcomes*.

Rose Massey   Struggling actress capable of becoming great; aware of her talent, she keeps her mind on her life role, not getting emotionally involved with Hubert Price in George Moore's *Vain Fortune*.

Bartle Massey   The lame, misogynistic old teacher who has Adam Bede among his adult students; while he berates all human females, he is tenderly considerate of his dog, Vixen, and her new puppies; he stays in Stoniton to comfort Adam during Hetty Sorrel's trial in George Eliot's *Adam Bede*.

Masson   Acquaintance of Loudon Dodd's student days in Paris; he had the studio in Barbizon where Norris Carthew now lives in Robert Louis Stevenson's *The Wrecker*.

Master   Owner of the plantation at which Colonel Jack is sold into servitude; he is impressed with Jack's honesty and the story of his life and makes him an overseer; later he helps Jack establish his own plantation in Daniel Defoe's *The History and the Remarkable Life of the Truly Honourable Colonel Jacques, Commonly Call'd Col. Jack*.

Miss Masters   Benjamin Cohen's young friend, who is saved from drowning by him in Mark Rutherford's *Clara Hopgood*.

Mrs. Masters   Odious second wife of Gregory Masters; born the daughter of an ironmonger, she has taken to hating the gentry; she tries to force her stepdaughter Mary to marry Lawrence Twentyman in Anthony Trollope's *The American Senator*.

Gregory Masters   Kindly attorney at Dillsborough who manages the Morton family's business affairs; he is much beset by his wife's interference and constant attacks on the gentry in Anthony Trollope's *The American Senator*.

Kate Masters   Younger sister of Mary; she is devoted to Lawrence Twentyman because he let her ride his pony when she was a child; they grow closer and seem likely to marry in Anthony Trollope's *The American Senator*. As Mrs. Twentyman she appears briefly in *Ayala's Angel*.

Mary Masters   Childhood companion of Reginald Morton, whom she has always loved; persecuted by her stepmother, who tries to force her to marry Larry Twentyman, she rebels and finally marries Reginald in Anthony Trollope's *The American Senator*.

Mastiff Guard at the entrance of Dogland; he takes Sylvie and Bruno to meet the King of Dogland in Lewis Carroll's *Sylvie and Bruno*.

Mat One of several gamblers at the Valiant Soldier public house who gamble with Nell Trent's grandfather in Charles Dickens's *The Old Curiosity Shop*.

Mary Matchwell Evil fortune-teller and purported matchmaker, who blackmails Mrs. Macnamara and, when Charles Nutter is missing, claims to be the real Mrs. Nutter and tries to force Sally Nutter out of her house; she is foiled when Nutter and Luke Gamble produce evidence she was already married when she went through the ceremony with Nutter in J. Sheridan Le Fanu's *The House by the Churchyard*.

Mathilde A pupil at Mme. Beck's school in Charlotte Brontë's *Villette*.

Mathilde de -- A pupil of Frances (Henri) Crimsworth's school to whom no favoritism is shown even though she is the heiress of a Belgian count in Charlotte Brontë's *The Professor*.

Matilda Twin sister of Ellinor and daughter of Mary, Queen of Scots; she secretly weds Lord Leicester, flees with him to France, and is abducted to Jamaica; she returns to England and is imprisoned after being falsely rumored to have poisoned Prince Henry in Sophia Lee's *The Recess*.

Matilda Innocent daughter of Manfred, Prince of Otranto; she is fatally stabbed by her father when he mistakes her for Isabella in Horace Walpole's *The Castle of Otranto*.

Matilda Daughter of Dorriforth, Lord Elmwood and Lady Elmwood (formerly Miss Milner); beautiful and well educated, she is disowned by her father because of her mother's infidelity; her attempted rape by Viscount Margrave reunites father and daughter; she marries Henry Rushbrook in Elizabeth Inchbald's *A Simple Story*.

Matilda Dying woman who reveals to Dorilaus that their youthful passion resulted in the twins, Louisa and Horatio, who were as infants mysteriously entrusted to his guardianship in Eliza Haywood's *The Fortunate Foundlings*.

Matilda The Earl of Athlin's kind-hearted widow, who is subject to mental breakdowns; she urges her daughter Mary to marry the Swiss Count de Santmorin rather than indulge the love of the peasant Alleyn (Philip) in Ann Radcliffe's *The Castles of Athlin and Dunbayne*.

Aunt Matilda Mrs. Furze's maiden sister, to whom Catharine Furze refuses to go when her mother suggests it in Mark Rutherford's *Catharine Furze*.

The Misses Matinters Single and singular sisters who live in Bath in Charles Dickens's *The Posthumous Papers of the Pickwick Club*.

Rosine Matou Cheery portress at Mme. Beck's school who Lucy mistakenly believes has bewitched Dr. John Bretton in Charlotte Brontë's *Villette*.

Matron Vicious old prostitute, who expands her business interests to include houses, sale and hire of clothes, and procuring, until she attempts to sell a daughter to her father in Charles Johnstone's *Chrysal: or, The Adventures of a Guinea*.

Miss Matson Milliner who rents Juliet Granville rooms and gives her temporary employment as a seamstress in Frances Burney's *The Wanderer*.

Mattakesa Woman who lusts after Horatio when he is a prisoner in Russia in Eliza Haywood's *The Fortunate Foundlings*.

Marie Estelle (Stella) Matteau Actress mother of Mademoiselle Flora and mistress of Lord Monmouth; she marries Villebecque after her husband deserts her in Benjamin Disraeli's *Coningsby; or, The New Generation*.

Matteo Strong and crafty leader of the Venetian bravos; he is outwitted and killed by Abellino (Count Rosalvo) in Matthew Lewis's *The Bravo of Venice*.

Mr. Matterson Curate and widower with five children; hoping to get a cheap upper servant, he marries the impudent and expensive Amelia Carroll in Anthony Trollope's *Mr. Scarborough's Family*.

Mr. Matthews Vain father of Fanny Matthews; he befriends the flattering Cornet Hebbers, introduces him to his daughters, and dies brokenhearted when Hebbers elopes with Fanny in Henry Fielding's *Amelia*.

Mr. Matthews Handsome dancing partner of Mary Fleetwood at the dance in Barmouth; he creates discord between Mary and her irritable older husband, Casimir, in William Godwin's *Fleetwood*.

Betty Matthews Fanny Matthews's sister, a gifted harpsichordist, whom Fanny tries to emulate at Cornet Hebbers's prompting but then grows to hate in Henry Fielding's *Amelia*.

Frances (Fanny) Matthews Beautiful young woman formerly enamored of William Booth; enraged at her lover Cornet Hebbers's marriage to a richer woman, she stabs him and is arrested; she seduces Booth in prison and then maligns him to his patron, Bob James, in Henry Fielding's *Amelia*.

Matthias Essene interpreter of Scriptures and an Aramaic scholar in George Moore's *The Brook Kerith*.

Mattie Bailie (Nicol) Jarvie's young, attractive serving woman, whom he eventually marries in Sir Walter Scott's *Rob Roy*.

Lemuel Mattocks Sexton who digs the grave for Lady Darby and finds the skull of Barney Sturk in J. Sheridan Le Fanu's *The House by the Churchyard*.

Ralph Mattocks Steward of Anthony Darnel; he sends the timely letter reporting Darnel's stroke in Tobias Smollett's *The Adventures of Sir Launcelot Greaves*.

Hayraddin Maugrabin (Rouge Sanglier) The African Moor, a Gypsy fortune-teller, whom Quentin Durward tries to save; Louis XI employs him to betray Isabelle de Croye to William de La Marck; he impersonates the herald Rouge Sanglier in the Duke of Burgundy's court and is hanged as a spy in Sir Walter Scott's *Quentin Durward*.

Zamet Maugrabin Hayraddin Maugrabin's brother; he acts as Louis XI's agent in persuading the ladies of Croye to flee to France; he attempts to cross the king by dealing with the Duke of Burgundy and is hanged as a traitor in Sir Walter Scott's *Quentin Durward*.

Maul Giant in the Valley of the Shadow of Death who uses sophistry to try to ruin the pilgrims; he is killed by Great-heart in John Bunyan's *The Pilgrim's Progress From this World to That Which Is to Come*.

Allan M'Aulay Brother of the Laird of Darnlinvarach, serving in Montrose's army; though intelligent and well respected by his tribe, he is touched by bouts of prophetic insanity; jealousy over Annot Lyle causes him to stab his good friend, Menteith, after which he disappears into the mist in Sir Walter Scott's *A Legend of Montrose*.

Angus M'Aulay Laird of Darnlinvarach and Allan M'Aulay's brother; courageous and daring, he serves in Montrose's army in Sir Walter Scott's *A Legend of Montrose*.

Gerard Maule Carefree, amiable drone, whose spineless inactivity irritates Adelaide Palliser, who loves him; Marie Goesler enables them to marry in Anthony

Trollope's *Phineas Redux*. He and his wife are guests of Lord Chiltern in *The Duke's Children*.

Maurice Maule Hedonistic, self-centred father of Gerard; he courts Marie Goesler with effusive gallantry and without success; he is reluctantly prevailed upon to turn over the unused, dilapidated Maule Abbey to his son in Anthony Trollope's *Phineas Redux*.

Lord Mauleverer Aging gourmand, who is the rival of Paul Clifford for the love of Lucy Brandon in Edward Bulwer-Lytton's *Paul Clifford*.

Mr. Mauleverer Adventurer who disguises himself as a clergyman and imposes on Rachel Curtis with a scheme to help the exploited child lacemakers in Charlotte Yonge's *The Clever Woman of the Family*.

Sir Edward Mauley (Elshender the Recluse, The Black Dwarf, Canny Elshie, The Wise-Wight of Mucklestane Moor) An educated, wealthy noble, who decides his deformity separates him from others; he becomes a bitter, taciturn hermit but does respond to kindness and so befriends Hobbie (Halbert) Elliot and Isabella Vere in Sir Walter Scott's *The Black Dwarf*.

Old Maunders A man who kept twenty-three giants, as told by Mr. Vuffin in Charles Dickens's *The Old Curiosity Shop*.

Sir Walter Mauny Emissary to citizens of Calais from the victorious British army in a parable told by Charles Meekly in Henry Brooke's *The Fool of Quality*.

Marquise of Maure Lucy Bentham's Parisian friend, who is attracted to Lewis Seymour and causes jealousy in George Moore's *A Modern Lover*.

Mauregas Usurper who agreed to pay the Moors a tribute of one hundred virgins a year; Julian the Apostate, in his incarnation as a Spanish king, decides to break the agreement in Henry Fielding's *A Journey From This World to the Next*.

Maurice Ferdinand's servant, who accompanies him from France to England; he conspires with a lawyer and Ratchcali to rob Ferdinand while he is in prison in Tobias Smollett's *The Adventures of Ferdinand Count Fathom*.

Captain Maurice Mrs. Darnford's acquaintance, who puts his daughter, Charlotte Brady, and his would-be betrothed, Madame di Soranzo, into Mrs. Darnford's care, for which he rewards her generously in Clara Reeve's *Plans of Education*.

Monsieur Mauron Monsieur Verneuil's friend, who invites Adeline and the La Luc family to stay at his chateau in Languedoc in Ann Radcliffe's *The Romance of the Forest.*

Colin Mavis   Clerk in Mr. Cayenne's weaving mill who publishes a book of poems, thus connecting Dalmailing with the "republic of letters" in John Galt's *Annals of the Parish.*

Messrs. Maw   Chemists to whom Dr. Henry Jekyll writes for the special drug which allows him to transform into the pale, deformed Edward Hyde and back again in Robert Louis Stevenson's *The Strange Case of Dr. Jekyll and Mr. Hyde.*

Mr. Mawmsey   A Middlemarch grocer in George Eliot's *Middlemarch.*

Mrs. Mawmsey   The grocer's gossiping wife in George Eliot's *Middlemarch.*

James Maxley   Miser who never pays Dr. Sampson and is defrauded by Richard Hardie; after his wife dies of angina, he goes to the almshouse, but then, in an insane rage, savagely attacks Jane Hardie and Julia Dodd, who has come to her friend's rescue, in Charles Reade's *Hard Cash.*

Lady Maxwell   See Marcella Boyce.

Lord Maxwell   Landowner and grandfather of Aldous Raeburn, his heir; the refusal of both to assist Marcella Boyce in her attempt to save the life of Jim Hurd disturbs her in Mrs. Humphry Ward's *Marcella.*

Lord Maxwell (the younger)   See Aldous Raeburn.

Mr. Maxwell   Helen Huntingdon's kindly uncle, who is indulgent toward her and leaves her his extensive property at Staningley Hall in Anne Brontë's *The Tenant of Wildfell Hall.*

Hallin Maxwell   Charming young son of Aldous Raeburn, Lord Maxwell and Lady Maxwell (Marcella Boyce); he is named for their deceased economist friend and teacher Edward Hallin in Mrs. Humphry Ward's *Sir George Tressady.*

Margaret (Peggy) Maxwell   Helen Huntingdon's strict but kindhearted aunt, who disapproves of Helen's marriage to Arthur Huntingdon; she makes her home with Helen and Gilbert Markham after they marry in Anne Brontë's *The Tenant of Wildfell Hall.*

Pater Maxwell of Summertrees (Pate-in-Peril)   Jacobite conspirator who is introduced to Alan Fairford by William Crosbie and writes a letter of introduction to Hugh Redgauntlet for Alan in Sir Walter Scott's *Redgauntlet.*

Captain May   Man who kills Adolphus Morsfield in a duel probably orchestrated by Lord Ormont in George Meredith's *Lord Ormont and his Aminta.*

Aubry May   Delicate, clever son of Dr. Richard May in Charlotte Yonge's *The Daisy Chain.* He befriends Leonard Ward and correctly refuses to believe that Ward murdered his uncle in *The Trial.*

Blanche May   Flirtatious daughter of Dr. Richard May; she is courted in childhood by Hector Ernescliffe in Charlotte Yonge's *The Daisy Chain.* She makes an early and happy marriage with him in *The Trial.*

Ethel May   Impetuous, intellectual daughter of the widowed Dr. Richard May; she helps bring up her youngest brothers and sisters and is instrumental in establishing a church in the desolate village of Cocksmoor in Charlotte Yonge's *The Daisy Chain.* She is venerated by Leonard Ward in *The Trial.* She appears in *The Pillars of the House* and in *The Long Vacation.*

Flora May   Worldly but scrupulous daughter of Dr. Richard May; she marries dull George Rivers and languishes after the death of her baby daughter Leonora in Charlotte Yonge's *The Daisy Chain.* Recovered, she does her duty unremittingly thereafter in *The Trial* and in *The Pillars of the House.*

Gertrude (Daisy) May   Youngest, motherless child of Dr. Richard May; her hard, satirical nature is softened by love for her sister Ethel in Charlotte Yonge's *The Daisy Chain.* Her admiration for the Underwood family leads to her marriage with Lancelot Underwood in *The Pillars of the House.* She appears in *The Trial* and in *The Long Vacation.*

Harry May   Sailor son of Dr. Richard May; he accompanies Alan Ernescliffe to the Loyalty Islands in Charlotte Yonge's *The Daisy Chain.* He marries Phyllis Mohun and settles in New Zealand in *Beechcroft at Rockstone.* He appears in *The Trial.*

Margaret May   Eldest daughter of Dr. Richard May; she is crippled in a driving accident; her engagement to Alan Ernescliffe ends with his death; she dies shortly thereafter in Charlotte Yonge's *The Daisy Chain.*

Margaret, Mrs. Richard May   Industrious, beloved mother of the eleven May children; she dies in a carriage accident for which her husband is largely to blame in Charlotte Yonge's *The Daisy Chain.*

Mary May   Daughter of Dr. Richard May in Charlotte

Yonge's *The Daisy Chain*. She befriends Averil Ward and marries Charles Cheviot, headmaster of the school at Market Stoneborough in *The Trial*.

Norman May   Brilliant son of Dr. Richard May; he wins high honors at Oxford but, doubting his ability to resist the drive of unworthy ambition, forgoes a political career to undertake mission work in New Zealand in Charlotte Yonge's *The Daisy Chain*. He appears in *The Long Vacation*.

Richard May   Physician and father of eleven who, widowed, must learn to be both father and mother to his children in Charlotte Yonge's *The Daisy Chain*. He appears in *The Trial*, in *The Pillars of the House*, and briefly in *The Long Vacation*.

Richard (Dickie) May   Precocious son of Meta (Rivers) and Norman May; he is sent from New Zealand to attend the Stoneborough School and comforts Leonard Ward after Leonard's release from prison in Charlotte Yonge's *The Trial*.

Richard (Ritchie) May   Eldest of Dr. Richard May's eleven children; he suffers by being compared to his brilliant brother, Norman, but ultimately enjoys success as rector of the church at Cocksmoor in Charlotte Yonge's *The Daisy Chain* and in *The Trial*.

Thomas May   Dirty, dishonest schoolboy son of Dr. Richard May; he matures into a skillful physician more interested in research than in patients in Charlotte Yonge's *The Daisy Chain*. He vindicates Leonard Ward's innocence and marries Ward's sister Averil in *The Trial*. He appears in *The Pillars of the House*.

Mr. Maybold   Good-looking village vicar and one of Fancy Day's three suitors; his gratifying proposal briefly deflects her constancy to Dick Dewey, but not her affection; his sympathy mollifies the parish choir members, who have been supplanted by the new church organ in Thomas Hardy's *Under the Greenwood Tree*.

Duchess of Mayfair   Imperious aunt of Arabella Trefoil; she is strongly opposed to her niece's pursuit of Lord Rufford; during the house party at Mistletoe, Arabella assures her that Rufford has proposed in Anthony Trollope's *The American Senator*.

Duke of Mayfair   Brother of Lord Augustus Trefoil; he has an enormous country seat at Mistletoe; here the country set assemble and Arabella Trefoil, his niece, launches her campaign to attract Lord Rufford in Anthony Trollope's *The American Senator*.

Phoebe Mayflower   Servant in the household of the Lees; she helps Joceline Joliffe and Joseph Tomkins

frighten the Parliamentary commissioners, and she marries Joliffe in Sir Walter Scott's *Woodstock*.

Mrs. Maylie   Adoptive aunt of Rose Maylie; she takes Oliver Twist in and nurses him when he suffers a gunshot wound during an aborted burglary attempt in Charles Dickens's *Oliver Twist*.

Harry Maylie   Handsome son of Mrs. Maylie; he loves Rose Maylie but is at first refused by Rose because she is poor and has no family; he quits his profession, becomes a clergyman, and marries Rose in Charles Dickens's *Oliver Twist*.

Rose Fleming Maylie   Sister of Agnes Fleming; she lives under the care of Mrs. Maylie, her adoptive aunt; beloved of Harry Maylie, she at first refuses to marry him because she is poor and has a blight on her name, but eventually accepts him in Charles Dickens's *Oliver Twist*.

Mrs. Maynard   The narrator's cousin, who lives at Millenium Hall and relates the histories of its foremost ladies in Sarah Scott's *A Description of Millenium Hall*.

Old Mazey   One-time seafaring man who keeps company with Admiral Bartram and amuses himself making model ships; he finds Magdalen Vanstone burgling the admiral's house but lets her disappear without reporting her in Wilkie Collins's *No Name*.

Mazzini   Forty-year-old Italian patriot, who is in exile in London; he accepts Clara Hopgood's offer of service in Italy in Mark Rutherford's *Clara Hopgood*.

Marquis de Mazzini   Cruel Sicilian marquis, who imprisons his wife in a cave beneath the castle in order to marry Maria de Vellorno; he schemes to marry his daughter Julia to the Duke de Luovo; he imprisons his son, Ferdinand, in a dungeon for helping Julia to escape; ultimately he is poisoned by Maria and dies in Ann Radcliffe's *A Sicilian Romance*.

Emilia de Mazzini   Mild-tempered eldest daughter of the Marquis de Mazzini in Ann Radcliffe's *A Sicilian Romance*.

Ferdinand de Mazzini   Only son of the Marquis de Mazzini; he champions Hippolitus de Vereza's suit to marry his sister, Julia de Mazzini; after a failed escape attempt, he is imprisoned in a dungeon by the Marquis; he escapes from the castle and rescues Julia from the Saint Augustin monastery, only to be captured by bandits and recaptured by the Marquis; ultimately he witnesses his father's death and is reunited with his mother and sisters in Ann Radcliffe's *A Sicilian Romance*.

Julia de Mazzini   Spirited daughter of the Marquis de

Mazzini; she falls in love with Hippolitus de Vereza and resists her father's scheme to marry her to the Duke de Louvo; fleeing the castle, she seeks refuge in the Saint Augustin monastery, escaping the monastery only to be captured by bandits; she hides in a cave beneath the castle, where she discovers her long-lost mother; ultimately she marries Hippolitus de Vereza in Ann Radcliffe's *A Sicilian Romance*.

John T. M'Brady   One of Muskegon's biggest operators; he fled to Canada with a creditor's money in Robert Louis Stevenson's *The Wrecker*.

Mr. M'Buffer   Corrupt Member of Parliament, whose resignation enables Undecimus Scott to obtain a seat in Anthony Trollope's *The Three Clerks*.

Sandy McAllister, the Laird of Cockpen   A pleasant, demonstrative man, whom Trilby O'Ferrall finds to be a good confidant and supportive friend; his concern for friends and praise for their talents show his paternal instincts; his romantic paintings provide irony in George Du Maurier's *Trilby*.

McArdle   Crusty old news editor who is Ned Malone's superior in Arthur Conan Doyle's *The Lost World*.

Mamie McBride   Jim Pinkerton's loyal bride, who had been his algebra tutor; she accuses Loudon Dodd of treachery in Robert Louis Stevenson's *The Wrecker*.

Father Bernard McCarthy   Catholic priest of Drumbarrow parish; he scorns the Reverend Townsend's policy of buying converts with soup during the terrible famine in Ireland in Anthony Trollope's *Castle Richmond*.

Dr. McCombie   Edinburgh physician who attends Alexander Loudon in his last illness in Robert Louis Stevenson's *The Wrecker*.

Patrick McDonald (M'Donald)   A smuggler employed in one of Robert Lovelace's impersonations to deceive Clarissa Harlowe; he uses the pseudonym Tomlinson; expelled from Dublin University for forgery, he dies in jail of wounds received in a theft in Samuel Richardson's *Clarissa: or, The History of a Young Lady*.

McGibbon   Scot who wants to make his money by blackmailing a rich man in Robert Louis Stevenson's *The Wrecker*.

McGill   Schoolboy whose academic success incites fellow student Robert Colwan to false accusations and who is beaten and expelled as a result in James Hogg's *The Private Memoirs and Confessions of a Justified Sinner*.

John McGinty   Formidable man, also known as Black

Jack, hanged for his role as boss of the Scowrers, a murderous secret organization that figures importantly in Arthur Conan Doyle's *The Valley of Fear*.

Denis McGovery   Blacksmith at Drumsna who marries Pat Brady's sister, Mary, in Anthony Trollope's *The Macdermots of Ballycloran*.

Mary McGovery   Pat Brady's sister, the tall, jolly wife of Denis McGovery; she is the close friend to whom Feemy Macdermot confides her pregnancy in Anthony Trollope's *The Macdermots of Ballycloran*.

Annie McGrath   Neighborhood girl Oliver Gogarty has considered marrying; her relatives in America could provide money for his early dreams to revive industry in Tinnick; her attractions are not as strong as his religious calling in George Moore's *The Lake*.

Father John McGrath   Kindly parish priest of Drumsna; he tries to save Feemy Macdermot from Captain Ussher's seduction and stands by Thady Macdermot at his trial in Anthony Trollope's *The Macdermots of Ballycloran*.

Darby McGraw   The last pirate Flint called to before he died; Ben Gunn calls his name to frighten the pirates in Robert Louis Stevenson's *Treasure Island*.

Mr. M'Choakumchild   Schoolmaster in Thomas Gradgrind's school; he fills the "little pitchers" (students) with facts and will not tolerate any demonstration of fancy in Charles Dickens's *Hard Times*.

Tony McKeon   Jovial farmer, who works zealously to save Thady Macdermot from the gallows in Anthony Trollope's *The Macdermots of Ballycloran*.

McManus   Groom at Durrisdeer who is beaten by Henry Durie in his agony over the second disappearance of the Master (James Durie) in Robert Louis Stevenson's *The Master of Ballantrae: A Winter's Tale*.

James McMull   Scot who marries Rhoda Swartz in William Makepeace Thackeray's *Vanity Fair*.

John McMurdo   See John Douglas.

Captain McMurtrie   Captain of the *Nonesuch*, in which Ephraim Mackellar, the Master (James Durie), and Secundra Dass travel from Glasgow to New York in Robert Louis Stevenson's *The Master of Ballantrae: A Winter's Tale*.

Mrs. M'Crule   See Miss Black.

Alister (Alexander) M'Donnell (Colkitto)   Brave but

foolhardy chief serving in Montrose's army; a kinsman of the Earl of Antrim, he is in charge of the Irish troops fighting in Scotland; a weapons master, he lacks military experience, often losing Montrose precious ground in Sir Walter Scott's *A Legend of Montrose*.

M'Dougal of Lorne   See Chief of Glengarry.

Duncan M'Drone   The officiating minister of Norman Douglas's baptism in Susan Ferrier's *Marriage*.

Mr. Mead   Victim of the highway robbery for which Humphry Clinker is falsely imprisoned in Tobias Smollett's *The Expedition of Humphry Clinker*.

Lady Meadows   Henrietta Courteney's aunt; under instruction of her Catholic confessor, Mr. Danvers, she tries to imprison the heroine in a convent and then, when Henrietta escapes, considers her disgraced and transfers her estate to Henrietta's brother in Charlotte Lennox's *Henrietta*.

Mr. Meadows   London man of fashion who is head of the insensiblists and who unsuccessfully courts Cecilia Beverley in Frances Burney's *Cecilia*.

Mrs. Meadows   John's mother, a pious woman, who disapproves of her son's materialism but is loyal to him when he needs her, even going to Australia with him in Charles Reade's *It Is Never Too Late to Mend*.

John Meadows   Middle-aged unscrupulous broker, who tries to take Susan Merton away from George Fielding but is finally deported to Australia in Charles Reade's *It Is Never Too Late to Mend*.

Maria Meadows   Querulous spinster sister-in-law of Edmund Kendal's first wife; she irritates his second wife but unexpectedly marries an old suitor in Charlotte Yonge's *The Young Step-Mother*.

William Meadows   Picaresque adventurer who, upon his father's death, is sent to sea; his travels take him from his native Britain to Russia where, after a stint on the faculty of the University of St. Petersburg, he enters the service of John Ernest Biren, confidential advisor to the Czarina Anne; his intimacy with Isabella Scherbatoff, Biren's niece, incurs the displeasure of his erstwhile employer, and he must flee to England; there he is summoned to the estate of Richard Danvers, Lord Alton; after hearing Meadows describe his ordeal in Russia, Danvers confides in him the story of his life: how years ago he stole his nephew Julian's inheritance; he sends Meadows to Italy to find him and make amends in William Godwin's *Cloudesley*.

Mr. Meager   Drunken husband of a lodginghouse keeper and owner of a pawned greatcoat, which the lodger Mr. Emilius could have worn to murder Mr. Bonteen in Anthony Trollope's *Phineas Redux*.

Mrs. Meager   Hard-working lodginghouse keeper in Northumberland Street with whom Mr. Emilus lodges after the break with Lizzie Eustace; Maria Goesler spends money and effort in pursuing Mrs. Meager's evidence linking him to the Bonteen murder in Anthony Trollope's *Phineas Redux*.

Mr. Meagles   Retired banker/gentleman traveling with his family; he meets Arthur Clennam in Marseilles and assists him in becoming a partner to Daniel Doyce; his love of the prestige of titled families lets him tolerate the unhappy marriage of his daughter to Henry Gowan in Charles Dickens's *Little Dorrit*.

Mrs. Meagles   Pleasant wife of Mr. Meagles in Charles Dickens's *Little Dorrit*.

Minnie (Pet) Meagles   Beautiful daughter of Mr. and Mrs. Meagles; she is futilely loved by Arthur Clennam but marries Henry Gowan and loves him devotedly despite his unkindness; she meets Amy Dorrit and her family in the Swiss Alps in Charles Dickens's *Little Dorrit*.

"Mealy Potatoes"   A boy who works at Murdstone and Grinby and has a mealy, pale complexion in Charles Dickens's *The Personal History of David Copperfield*.

Mrs. Measure   Mantua-maker, Mrs. Willis's cousin; she procures Henrietta Courteney her first position, that of maid to Jenny Cordwain in Charlotte Lennox's *Henrietta*.

Mecos   A rich Roman who discovers Turpius in bed with his wife in Jane Barker's *Exilius; or, The Banish'd Roman*.

Sir Medard   Knight who leads the men of Eastcheaping along with Osberne Wolfsson and his Dalesmen against the Baron of Deepdale in William Morris's *The Sundering Flood*.

Giovanni de' Medici   Younger brother of Piero de' Medici; he becomes Pope Leo X in George Eliot's *Romola*.

Piero de' Medici   Ineffectual ruler of Florence after his father's death in 1492 in George Eliot's *Romola*.

Duke de Medina   Humane aristocrat, who reconciles his nephew Lorenzo to the love of Virginia de Villa Franca after Antonia de la Cisternas's rape and murder in Matthew Lewis's *The Monk*.

Agnes de Medina   Spirited young noblewoman, who fails to escape her guardian with Raymond de las Cisternas and reluctantly enters the Convent of St. Clare; Agnes's pregnancy discovered, Mother St. Agatha feigns her death and imprisons her in the vaults; released by her brother, Lorenzo, she marries Raymond in Matthew Lewis's *The Monk*.

Gaston de Medina   Father of Agnes and Lorenzo; he rescues Alphonso d'Alvarada (Raymond, Marquis de la Cisternas) from assassins and reveals Agnes's whereabouts in Matthew Lewis's *The Monk*.

Inesilla de Medina   Agnes and Lorenzo's mother, who promises Agnes as a nun in return for a healthy pregnancy in Matthew Lewis's *The Monk*.

Lorenzo de Medina   Noble who loves Antonia de las Cisternas; bringing the Inquisition against Mother St. Agatha, the Prioress of St. Clare, for apparently murdering his sister, he finds Agnes de Medina confined and sees Antonia die of wounds inflicted by Abbot Ambrosio; he eventually marries Virginia de Villa Franca in Matthew Lewis's *The Monk*.

Mr. Medlar   Independently wealthy man about town, who meets Roderick Random in London and introduces him to Dr. Wagtail in Tobias Smollett's *The Adventures of Roderick Random*.

Mrs. Medlicott   The housekeeper who also helps to supervise the "young gentlewomen" maintained at Hanbury Court in Elizabeth Gaskell's *My Lady Ludlow*.

Count Medole   Revolutionary whose postponement of the Milanese uprising because of his suspicion of Vittoria Campa incites Carlo Ammiani's anger in George Meredith's *Vittoria*.

Countess Medole   Wife of the Milanese revolutionary and lover of Austrian Prince Radocky in George Meredith's *Vittoria*.

Charles Meekly   Gentleman and friend of Lord Clinton; a duel causes him to become a pious Christian, so that he is able to answer Lord Clinton's inquiries regarding Christianity; he has a plan to increase trade with a canal system in England in Henry Brooke's *The Fool of Quality*.

Saunders Meiklewham   Attorney who manages the financial affairs of young John Mowbray in Sir Walter Scott's *St. Ronan's Well*.

Mein Herr   A mysterious foreigner and a friend of Lady Muriel Orme; he explains the customs of a world he has visited and the efforts of this world to emulate Victorian England without great success; he closely resembles the Professor of Outland in Lewis Carroll's *Sylvie and Bruno Concluded*.

Mejnour   A sage who, except for Zanoni, is the only person to possess the wisdom of the brotherhood of the Chaldeans; he tutors Clarence Glyndon in Edward Bulwer-Lytton's *Zanoni*.

Melanghel   Daughter of Elphin and Angharad in Thomas Love Peacock's *The Misfortunes of Elphin*.

Melantha   Wealthy, devious, and passionate woman who introduces Portia to Nicanor's family; she pursues and then marries Oliver because she erroneously believes Portia loves him in Sarah Fielding's *The Cry*.

Melanthe   Young widow of quality but "no slave to reputation"; she takes Louisa as a companion on her European travels but becomes jealously self-deceived about Louisa when the Count de Bellfleur, having successfully wooed herself, pursues Louisa in Eliza Haywood's *The Fortunate Foundlings*.

Lord Melbury   Eighteen-year-old brother of Lady Aurora Granville; he tries to seduce the Stranger, Juliet Granville; later, having learned she is his half sister, he offers to assist her in rescue from her French marriage in Frances Burney's *The Wanderer*.

George Melbury   Grace's domineering father, a timber merchant, who intends to make amends for stealing a friend's bride-to-be years ago by marrying his daughter to the friend's son, Giles Winterborne; after Giles loses his lands, however, Melbury encourages Grace to marry Dr. Edred Fitzpiers; love and tragedy enable Grace to shed her father's domination in Thomas Hardy's *The Woodlanders*.

Grace Melbury   Young heroine who, having just finished her education and travels, returns to her hometown only to feel misplaced; her concern for social status prompts her to reject the marriage proposal of the worthy Giles Winterborne for marriage to the physician Edred Fitzpiers, but when Fitzpiers proves unfaithful, Grace leaves him with the help of Giles; Giles's death completes her emotional maturity; she mourns him faithfully for months until Fitzpiers returns begging forgiveness; Grace acquiesces and they are reunited in Thomas Hardy's *The Woodlanders*.

Blanche de Melcy   Most handsome and most vicious pupil at Mme. Beck's school in Charlotte Brontë's *Villette*.

Lillo Melema   The son of Tito Melema and Tessa; he is found lost in the streets by Romola de' Bardi, who takes him home and thereby meets her husband's "other wife" in George Eliot's *Romola.*

Ninna Melema Baby daughter of Tito Melema and Tessa in George Eliot's *Romola.*

Tessa Melema Simple peasant girl who assumes that her marriage ceremony with Tito Melema is legal; she is the mother of Tito's two children and, at the end, all three live with, and are cared for by, Romola de' Bardi in George Eliot's *Romola.*

Tito Melema Handsome, penniless young Greek, who arrives full of ambition in Florence in 1492; he pretends to marry Tessa and has two children by her, even though he is actually married to Romola de' Bardi; his abandoned benefactor, Baldassare Calvo, strangles him for revenge in George Eliot's *Romola.*

Countess Melespini Virtuous married woman with whom Henry Mandeville imagined himself in love before meeting Lady Julia Belmont in Frances Brooke's *The History of Lady Julia Mandeville.*

Jery Melford Matthew Bramble's young nephew, who is relieved to hear from Sir Watkin Phillips that a certain Oxford girl is not pregnant; he opposes Wilson's courtship of his sister on the grounds of Wilson's inferior social class but relents when "Wilson" is discovered to be George Dennison, the son of Matthew Bramble's good friend; he has his eye on Letty Willis at the end of Tobias Smollett's *The Expedition of Humphry Clinker.*

Lydia (Liddy) Melford Matthew Bramble's niece, who is courted by others though she is in love with "Wilson"; her brother finally allows her to accept Wilson when he is discovered to be George Dennison in Tobias Smollett's *The Expedition of Humphry Clinker.*

Anthelia Melincourt Independent young woman brought up amidst beauties of nature; she expresses romantic liberal opinions and marries Sylvan Forester in Thomas Love Peacock's *Melincourt.*

Melinda Sylvia's maid at Bellfont; she attempts to protect her mistress from suspicion by pretending that the letters she carries to Philander's man, Alexis, are actually her own in Aphra Behn's *Love Letters Between a Nobleman and His Sister.*

Mrs. Mell Old mother of Charles Mell; she lives in an almshouse in London in Charles Dickens's *The Personal History of David Copperfield.*

Charles (Charley) Mell Humble schoolmaster at Salem House; he takes David Copperfield to the school; he is sacked after Mr. Creakle finds out through James Steerforth that his mother lives in an almshouse; he becomes successful after emigrating to Australia in Charles Dickens's *The Personal History of David Copperfield.*

Lady Mellasin Dr. Samuel Goodman's wife, who is very much given to venting her spleen in Eliza Haywood's *The History of Miss Betsy Thoughtless.*

Flora Mellasin A very vain coquette, who has an affair with Gayland and a baby with Mr. Wildly; she is jealous and tries to break up all relationships in Eliza Haywood's *The History of Miss Betsy Thoughtless.*

Sophia Mellerby Tall, graceful member of an ancient English family; she is judged by Lady Scroope to be the suitable future wife of her protégé, Fred Neville; his brother, Jack, falls in love with her and, after Fred's death, marries her in Anthony Trollope's *An Eye for an Eye.*

Mellifont Gentleman suitor Felicia rejects because he has too much of fashionable society about him, though he turns out to be a decent man; he marries the virtuous Amelia in Mary Collyer's *Felicia to Charlotte.*

Ramirez de Mello Officer of the Inquision who apprehends Abbott Ambrosio and Mother St. Agatha, the Prioress of St. Clare, in Matthew Lewis's *The Monk.*

Sebastian Mello Impeccably dressed quack doctor, a competitor of Roger Swizzle; he surruptitiously doses his own spring with medicinal salts in Robert Surtees's *Handley Cross.*

Miss Melman A coquette who captivates Mr. Alworth and after marriage spends all her time on her appearance and her admirers in Sarah Scott's *A Description of Millenium Hall.*

Mrs. Melmoth Ideally suited wife of a kindly sea-captain; she is maternal aunt to Emma Courtney and fosters her from birth to age eighteen, teaching her family affection, in Mary Hays's *Memoirs of Emma Courtney.*

Mrs. Melmoth Distant relative of Emily Montague, who resides with her in Montreal; she is determined that the arranged marriage with Sir George Clayton take place despite Emily's changed disposition toward him and her love for Ed. Rivers in Frances Brooke's *The History of Emily Montague.*

Charlotte Melmoth First wife of John Buncle; he meets her on a ship by saving her from exposure and drowning; she meets Buncle later at Stanemore, where he proposes marriage; after two years of marriage she dies of fever in Thomas Amory's *The Life of John Buncle, Esq.*

John Melmoth   An Irishman who inherits his uncle's estate; while searching his uncle's possessions, he discovers a manuscript that tells of John's ancestor, Melmoth the Wanderer; later, Alonzo Monçada, a shipwrecked Spaniard, relates his encounters with Melmoth the Wanderer to John; one night, the tormented soul of the Wanderer appears to John and tells him that he has unsuccessfully completed his 150 year pilgrimage to secure souls for Satan; the same night, John hears odd noises, and the next morning, his kinsman is gone in Charles Maturin's *Melmoth the Wanderer*.

John (the Wanderer) Melmoth   A seventeenth-century ancestor of the younger John Melmoth; Melmoth the Wanderer is fated to roam the earth for 150 years; during this time, his goal is to seduce souls for Satan, but he is unsuccessful; he returns to Ireland at the novel's conclusion and ends his life by leaping, or being hurled, over a cliff in Charles Maturin's *Melmoth the Wanderer*.

Madame Melmotte   Browbeaten wife of Augustus Melmotte and Marie Melmotte's stepmother; by spending prodigiously her financier husband's ill-gotten gains she helps him in his rise to social eminence; after his suicide she marries his confidential secretary, Herr Croll, and moves to New York in Anthony Trollope's *The Way We Live Now*.

Augustus Melmotte   Monumentally swindling capitalist of Grosvenor Square; his financial empire includes a dubious railway scheme in America with a board of directors he systematically dupes; he rises in society to entertain the Emperor of China, and he is elected Member for Westminster to the House of Commons; on the brink of prosecution for forgery, he takes prussic acid in Anthony Trollope's *The Way We Live Now*.

Marie Melmotte   Augustus Melmotte's downtrodden daughter, whose legitimacy is obscure; her father wishes to crown and maintain his success in England by marrying her to a title; she shows her spirit when she chooses to elope with Sir Felix Carbury, having stolen money from her father; Carbury fails to keep their appointment, but she rallies and defies her father by refusing to release to him money that he put in her name for reasons of safety; after his suicide she goes to America, there to marry the American entrepreneur Hamilton K. Fisker in Anthony Trollope's *The Way We Live Now*.

Mr. Melopoyn   Ragged poet and playwright, who meets Roderick Random in the Marshalsea, where he is imprisoned for debt, and tells Roderick his woeful tale of a literary man's search for patrons in Tobias Smollett's *The Adventures of Roderick Random*.

Harry Meltham   Rosalie Murray's favorite admirer,

but a younger son who will not fall heir to his father's estate in Anne Brontë's *Agnes Grey*.

Sir Hugh Meltham   Father of Harry; he attends Rosalie Murray's coming-out ball in Anne Brontë's *Agnes Grey*.

Mr. Melton   A gentleman of highest fashion and a great favorite in society whose social adroitness intimidates the young and naive Harry Coningsby in Benjamin Disraeli's *Coningsby; or, The New Generation*.

Melvar   Elphin's neighboring king, who believes that his right to Queen Gwenyvar has been established by his power to abduct her in Thomas Love Peacock's *The Misfortunes of Elphin*.

Count Melvil   Hungarian soldier who keeps Ferdinand's mother until her death and takes Ferdinand into his protection in Tobias Smollett's *The Adventures of Ferdinand Count Fathom*.

Mademoiselle de Melvil   Count Melvil's daughter, who inspires love in Ferdinand while he lives in Presburg; imprisoned in a nunnery by her stepfather, Count Trebasi, she is rescued by her brother, Renaldo de Melvil, to whom she reveals the perfidies of Ferdinand; she marries Major Farrel in Tobias Smollett's *The Adventures of Ferdinand Count Fathom*.

Renaldo de Melvil   Son of Count Melvil; he befriends and trusts Ferdinand, who cheats and robs him and alienates and separates his beloved Monima (Serafina de Zelos) from him; he believes she has died on account of Ferdinand; he visits her tomb in England, discovers her alive, marries her, and forgives Ferdinand in Tobias Smollett's *The Adventures of Ferdinand Count Fathom*. As Count de Melville, he discovers Ferdinand under the name of Grieve in *The Expedition of Humphry Clinker*.

Mr. Melvill   Eulogist at Clarissa Harlowe's funeral in Samuel Richardson's *Clarissa: or, The History of a Young Lady*.

Melville   Scottish ambassador to England in Sophia Lee's *The Recess*.

Major Melville   Acting sheriff in Cairnvreckan; he arrests Edward Waverly for killing the smith John Mucklewrath in Sir Walter Scott's *Waverly*.

Emily Melville   Barnabas Tyrrel's orphan cousin, who falls in love with Ferdinando Falkland; as punishment for her perfidy, Emily is imprisoned and told she must marry Grimes; aided in an "escape" and nearly raped by her would-be groom, she is removed to safety; a few days later she dies in jail, where she has been taken while ill on a charge of not repaying her debt for seventeen years' living expenses in William Godwin's *Caleb Williams*.

Sir Robert Melville   The eldest and most experienced of the three commissioners sent by the Scottish privy council to force the abdication of Queen Mary of Scotland; he is instructed by Queen Mary's half brother, James Stuart, Earl of Murray and Regent of Scotland, to act as a mediator and calming influence in Sir Walter Scott's *The Abbot*.

Miss Melvilleson   Lady of musical ability who sings at the Sol's Arms in Cook's Court in Charles Dickens's *Bleak House*.

Lord Melvin   Wealthy and aristocratic guest at Belmont, suspected by Henry Mandeville of vying for and obtaining Lady Julia Belmont's hand; he meets Henry's passionate challenge to duel and kills him in Frances Brooke's *The History of Lady Julia Mandeville*.

Lady Melvyn   Mother of Miss Melvyn; she assists Sir Charles Melvyn in forcing their daughter to marry Mr. Morgan by accusing her of an affair with a farmer's son in Sarah Scott's *A Description of Millenium Hall*.

Miss Melvyn (Mrs. Morgan)   Honest, patient, and high-principled friend of Louisa Mancel; her forced marriage to Mr. Morgan separates her from Louisa; reunited after his death, the friends set up a philanthropic community in Sarah Scott's *A Description of Millenium Hall*.

Sir Charles Melvyn   Father of Miss Melvyn; with Lady Melvyn, he forces their daughter to marry Mr. Morgan by accusing her of an affair with a farmer's son in Sarah Scott's *A Description of Millenium Hall*.

Hans Memling   Pupil of Jan and Margaret Van Eyck; he carries the letter from Margaret Brandt to tell Gerard of Duke Philip's pardon; unwittingly he carries a forged letter claiming that Margaret Brandt has died in the arms of Margaret Van Eyck in Charles Reade's *The Cloister and the Hearth*.

Memmo   Weak-willed and timid conspirator against Doge Andreas; he publicly confirms the accusations of Flodoardo/Abellino (Count Rosalvo) against the conspirators in Matthew Lewis's *The Bravo of Venice*.

Abraham (Nab) Mendez   Dwarfish Jew and bodyguard to Jonathan Wild in William Harrison Ainsworth's *Jack Sheppard*.

Don Pedro de Mendez   Portuguese captain of the ship which rescues Lemuel Gulliver after he has left the country of the Houyhnhnms and escaped from the savage natives of New Holland; he treats Gulliver with kindness, takes him into his home in Lisbon, and persuades him to return to his own family in England in Jonathan Swift's *Travels into Several Remote Nations of the World. In Four Parts. By Lemuel Gulliver*.

Don Pedro de Mendoza   Young Spanish nobleman who wins Donna Corina's affections from Don Fernando de Cardiole, who then has him killed in Penelope Aubin's *The Strange Adventures of the Count de Vinevil and His Family*.

John Mengs   Landlord who forces John Philipson (John de Vere) to carouse with his guests and in whose inn Philipson is put on trial by Count Albert of Geierstein's secret society in Sir Walter Scott's *Anne of Geierstein*.

Menlove   Flighty servant of Lady Petherwin and later at the Doncastles'; Ethelberta Petherwin's brother Joey Chickerel becomes enamored of her and reveals to her Ethelberta's identity in Thomas Hardy's *The Hand of Ethelberta*.

Captain Mennell   A pander in one of Robert Lovelace's intrigues to seduce Clarissa Harlowe in Samuel Richardson's *Clarissa: or, The History of a Young Lady*.

Chevalier de Menon   Husband of Madame de Menon and friend to Orlando; after killing Orlando in an argument, he enters battle out of remorse and is himself killed in Ann Radcliffe's *A Sicilian Romance*.

Madame de Menon   Intelligent, gentle governess to Emilia and Julia de Mazzini, former companion to Louisa Bernini, and widow of Chevalier de Menon; she hides Julia from the Marquis de Mazzini in the Saint Augustin monastery only to be betrayed by the abbot; ultimately she is reunited with the Mazzini family and restored her fortune in Ann Radcliffe's *A Sicilian Romance*.

Earl of Menteith   Montrose's gallant young kinsman and Allan M'Aulay's good friend; an accomplished and chivalrous soldier, he often serves as peacemaker; he is in love with Annot Lyle and gladly marries her when it is discovered she is of noble parentage in Sir Walter Scott's *A Legend of Montrose*.

Mephistopheles   Vicious robber and a pal of Brutus; he kills the dog Carlo and tries to kill Tom Robinson and George Fielding in Charles Reade's *It Is Never Too Late to Mend*.

Merat   French maid who serves Evelyn Innes in Paris and then in her singing career in London in George Moore's *Evelyn Innes*. She hopes Evelyn will leave the convent so that she can again serve her in *Sister Teresa*.

Solomon Merceda   A Portuguese Jew and moneylender,

who is a conspirator in Sir Hargrave Pollexfen's plot to kidnap Harriet Byron; Sir Charles Grandison later saves his life in Samuel Richardson's *Sir Charles Grandison*.

The Mercer Shopkeeper who attempts suicide after his affair with Syrena Tricksy; his wife forgives him in Eliza Haywood's *Anti-Pamela: or, Feign'd Innocence Detected*.

Merchant Tradesman who sells valuable merchandises to the Auctioneer so that he can stand for election and remake his fortune by accepting bribes in Charles Johnstone's *Chrysal: or, The Adventures of a Guinea*.

Mercury Silk-waistcoated gentleman, who advises the soul of the newly dead author to hasten to catch the stagecoach for his journey to the other world in Henry Fielding's *A Journey From This World to the Next*.

Mercy Young neighbor of Christiana; she accompanies Christiana on the pilgrimage, revealing a gentle, charitable nature; she marries Matthew, Christiana's eldest son, in John Bunyan's *The Pilgrim's Progress From this World to That Which Is to Come*.

Mr. Merdle Immensely rich financier, who is actually a swindler and thief; although idolized by England's institutions and high society, he is dull and uncouth; he causes thousands of people to lose money through investing in his projects and commits suicide when he is about to be exposed in Charles Dickens's *Little Dorrit*.

Mrs. Merdle Mr. Merdle's handsome, cold wife, referred to as "the Bosom"; she is mother of Edmund Sparkler by her first husband; she frequently expresses regret that society is not "Natural" as a way to excuse her cold-heartedness in Charles Dickens's *Little Dorrit*.

Sir Meredith Welsh knight who serves as the Earl of Pembroke's messenger to Sir John de Walton in Sir Walter Scott's *Castle Dangerous*.

Sir George Meredith Husband of Lord Lufton's sister, Justinia, in Anthony Trollope's *Framley Parsonage*.

Justinia, Lady Meredith Daughter of Lady Lufton; she is a close friend of Fanny Monsell, who marries Mark Robarts in Anthony Trollope's *Framley Parsonage*.

Michael Meredith Joker and the man of mirth in the social circle of St. Ronan's Well in Sir Walter Scott's *St. Ronan's Well*.

Sir Rowland Meredith Prosperous, self-important Welsh knight, a middle-aged bachelor; examining Harriet Byron's suitability as a proposed bride for his nephew, James Fowler, he is much taken with her himself in Samuel Richardson's *Sir Charles Grandison*.

Hilda Meres Lively and clever younger sister of Rhoda in George Gissing's *Isabel Clarendon*.

Rhoda Meres Friend of Ada Warren; she falls in love with the man courting Ada and is rejected in George Gissing's *Isabel Clarendon*.

Thomas Meres Former secretary of Isabel Clarendon's husband; he comes to her for help after his employer's death, then becomes a hard-working author and editor; he educates Ada Warren and tells her that Isabel was mistreated by her husband in George Gissing's *Isabel Clarendon*.

Madam Merian Mid-seventeenth-century Dutch painter praised by Jeremy Watersouchy for the propriety of her nudes in William Beckford's *Biographical Memoirs of Extraordinary Painters*.

Duke of Merioneth Indolent nobleman reputedly the richest man in England and father of the Marquis of Llwddythlw in Anthony Trollope's *Marion Fay*.

Kit Merle Prophetic shoemaker who befriends William Waife and Sophy in Edward Bulwer-Lytton's *What Will He Do With It? by Pisistratus Caxton*.

Mrs. Merrick Lord Grondale's sister-in-law, who raises Caroline after Lady Grondale dies in Robert Bage's *Hermsprong*.

Gillian Merrifield Daughter of Sir Jasper and Lilias (Mohun) Merrifield; she clashes with her cousin Dolores Mohun in Charlotte Yonge's *The Two Sides of the Shield*. She imprudently attaches the affections of Alexis White in *Beechcroft at Rockstone*. She attends an Oxford woman's college and becomes engaged in *The Long Vacation*.

Sir Jasper Merrifield Military hero and husband of Lilias Mohun; he is injured while on duty in Ceylon and on his return must disentangle the difficulties in which his daughter Gillian has become entwined in Charlotte Yonge's *Beechcroft at Rockstone*. He appears in *The Long Vacation*.

Maria (Mysie) Merrifield Daughter of Sir Jasper and Lilias (Mohun) Merrifield; she befriends her cousin Dolores Mohun in Charlotte Yonge's *The Two Sides of the Shield*. She is sought for adoption by her uncle, the Marquess of Rotherwood, in *Beechcroft at Rockstone*. She appears in *The Long Vacation*.

Phyllis Merrifield Eldest daughter of Sir Jasper and Lilias (Mohun) Merrifield; she marries Bernard Underwood in Charlotte Yonge's *Beechcroft at Rockstone*.

Valetta Merrifield Daughter of Sir Jasper and Lilias

(Mohun) Merrifield; her weak character leads her into serious scrapes in Charlotte Yonge's *The Two Sides of the Shield*. She also appears in *Beechcroft at Rockstone* and in *The Long Vacation*.

Wilfred Merrifield Malicious son of Sir Jasper and Lilias (Mohun) Merrifield; he torments his cousin Dolores Mohun in Charlotte Yonge's *The Two Sides of the Shield*. He appears in *Beechcroft at Rockstone* and in *The Long Vacation*.

Meg Merriles Henry Bertram's Gypsy nurse and a commanding figure, who is venerated by her tribe and held in superstitious awe by others; devoted to Henry, she remains aware of all his movements and is killed while trying to restore him to his rights in Sir Walter Scott's *Guy Mannering*.

Mr. Merriman Quiet solicitor to Sir Percival Glyde; in response to the baronet's financial difficulties, he is called in to draw up a document requiring the signature of Glyde's wife, Laura (Fairlie); she refuses to sign in Wilkie Collins's *The Woman in White*.

Merrival Eccentric astronomer, frequent visitor to Windsor, who is so preoccupied with astronomical theories that he neglects his family; they subsequently are overcome by plague, and he goes mad from grief in Mary Shelley's *The Last Man*.

Miss Merry Governess of Fanny Davilow's four daughters in George Eliot's *Daniel Deronda*.

George Merry Tall pirate with yellow eyes who wants to depose Long John Silver and become captain himself; he is shot at the treasure site and finished off by Silver in Robert Louis Stevenson's *Treasure Island*.

Merry Andrew Clown who reveals the puppet master's sinful desire for Sophia Western, providing Tom Jones with information about her journey in Henry Fielding's *The History of Tom Jones*.

Merrylegs Signor Jupe's performing dog in Charles Dickens's *Hard Times*.

Dr. Merton Family physician in constant attendance upon John Scarborough at Tretton Park; he comes to admire his dying patient's courage in Anthony Trollope's *Mr. Scarborough's Family*.

Lord Merton Young Bristol aristocrat who is coarse and sometimes drunk; he is reforming himself to court Lady Louisa Larpent in Frances Burney's *Evelina*.

Mr. Merton Father of Susan and uncle of George and William Fielding; he is a man easily influenced by John

Meadows and persuaded by Clinton to make bad investments in Charles Reade's *It Is Never Too Late to Mend*.

Mrs. Merton Mrs. Leslie's daughter and Caroline Merton's mother; she acts as hostess to Evelyn Templeton in Edward Bulwer-Lytton's *Alice*.

Caroline Merton Socially ambitious daughter of Charles Merton; she marries Lord Doltimore to advance the interests of her lover, Lumley Ferrers, and to further his marriage to Evelyn Templeton; her infidelity becomes known to her husband, who leaves her; she becomes addicted to laudanum in Edward Bulwer-Lytton's *Alice*.

Charles Merton Worldly clergyman and father of Caroline Merton in Edward Bulwer-Lytton's *Alice*.

Hetty Merton Innocent village girl with whom Dorian Gray carries on a "harmless" flirtation; though Dorian prides himself that he has resisted the temptation to seduce her, Lord Henry Wotton explains to Dorian that she is ruined nonetheless because she will not be content with someone from her own class in Oscar Wilde's *The Picture of Dorian Gray*.

Susan Merton Pretty, virtuous cousin of George and William Fielding; she is faithful to George, her betrothed, until John Meadows persuades her that George has married another and that her father needs Meadows's money to rescue him from debt; she is saved from marriage to Meadows by Tom Robinson and George's return and by Levi's timely evidence in Charles Reade's *It Is Never Too Late to Mend*.

Mordaunt Mertoun Basil (Vaughan) Mertoun's handsome and athletic son; sensing his father's lack of affection, he seeks the company of Minna and Brenda Troil, which enrages Captain Clement Cleveland, who loves Minna and fears a rival; estranged from the Troil household, he discovers he loves Brenda, and they later marry in Sir Walter Scott's *The Pirate*.

Thomas Mervale Worldly friend of Clarence Glyndon; he represents convention in Edward Bulwer-Lytton's *Zanoni*.

Mr. Mervyn Tall, handsome, melancholy young man, who moves to Chapelizod and inhabits Tiled House, becoming a mystery to the townspeople; he loves Gertrude Chattesworth, to whom he is secretly engaged while trying to clear the name of his father, Lord Dunoran; when Paul Dangerfield's guilt is revealed, Mervyn's title and property are restored, and he marries Gertrude in J. Sheridan Le Fanu's *The House by the Churchyard*.

Mrs. Mervyn Mr. Mervyn's wife, who gains temporary custody of Julia Mannering in Sir Walter Scott's *Guy Mannering*.

Arthur Mervyn Childhood friend of Colonel Mannering; he is now fat and good-humored, entertaining others with his stories of the high life he once lived, in Sir Walter Scott's *Guy Mannering*.

Messenger Spy who goes to Germany but first applies to Her Grace for messages and information in Charles Johnstone's *Chrysal: or, The Adventures of a Guinea*.

Mr. Metaphor Poet who is a member of the London College of Authors, which Perry Pickle joins, in Tobias Smollett's *The Adventures of Peregrine Pickle*.

Megalena de Metastasio High-spirited young woman captured by bandits; she is helped to escape by Wolfstein and falls jealously and possessively in love with him in Percy Bysshe Shelley's *St. Irvyne*.

Methodist Preacher Traveler on the wagon who speaks of religion and temperance while eating more than anyone else and gloating over the Servant-Maid in Charles Johnstone's *Chrysal: or, The Adventures of a Guinea*.

Dr. Meyrick Kindly physician of Wendover in Mrs. Humphry Ward's *Robert Elsmere*.

Mrs. Meyrick Hans Meyrick's kind mother, who allows Mirah Lapidoth to recuperate in her home in George Eliot's *Daniel Deronda*.

Amy Meyrick Second daughter of Mrs. Meyrick in George Eliot's *Daniel Deronda*.

Hans Meyrick Daniel Deronda's friend at Eton; Deronda helps him win a Cambridge scholarship; he falls in love with Mirah Lapidoth but is rejected by her in George Eliot's *Daniel Deronda*.

Kate Meyrick Oldest daughter of Mrs. Meyrick in George Eliot's *Daniel Deronda*.

Mab Meyrick The musically talented youngest daughter of Mrs. Meyrick in George Eliot's *Daniel Deronda*.

Paulina Mezzotetto Beautiful lower-class woman, who acts at the direction of her adopted sister Oriana to seduce Angelo D'Albini in Charlotte Dacre's *The Libertine*.

Mr. M'Fittoch Dancing master who draws attention to the Laird of Louponheight's infatuation for Menie Gray while pointing out his mistakes to Richard Middlemas in Sir Walter Scott's *The Surgeon's Daughter*.

Duncan M'Free A poor tenant of Glenfern Castle, dis-

covered jailed in Leith, Scotland, by Archibald and Mary Douglas on their trip to London in Susan Ferrier's *Marriage*.

Mr. M'Gabbery Garrulous tourist on the expedition to the Holy Land; he bores Caroline Waddington by his amorous attentions in Anthony Trollope's *The Bertrams*.

Captain M'Gramm Fellow traveler with Major Biffin; their shipboard romances are scuttled when the two ladies flirt with Arthur Wilkinson and George Bertram in Anthony Trollope's *The Bertrams*.

Emma Micawber Thin, faded wife of Wilkins Micawber; she is resolutely attached to him despite his failure to provide for the family; she is always nursing a baby when David Copperfield sees her in Charles Dickens's *The Personal History of David Copperfield*.

Emma Micawber (the younger) Wilkins and Emma Micawber's daughter, aged three when David Copperfield boards with the family in Charles Dickens's *The Personal History of David Copperfield*.

Wilkins Micawber Affable, optimistic, grandiloquent, disastrously impecunious man, with whose family David Copperfield boards while working at Murdstone and Grinby; he is continually falling into debt and changing jobs; he passes time in the King's Bench prison, is instrumental in the unmasking of Uriah Heep, and in the end emigrates to Australia in Charles Dickens's *The Personal History of David Copperfield*.

(Master) Wilkins Micawber Wilkins and Emma Micawber's eldest child, aged four when David Copperfield boards with the family in Charles Dickens's *The Personal History of David Copperfield*.

Michael Servant and driver for the St. Aubert family on the trip to Languedoc, during which Monsieur St. Aubert dies in Ann Radcliffe's *The Mysteries of Udolpho*.

Eliza Michelson Credulous housekeeper in the service of Sir Percival Glyde at Blackwater Park; she is sent to Torquay to prevent her seeing how Marian Halcombe is hidden in another bedroom during her illness in Wilkie Collins's *The Woman in White*.

Thomas Micklethwaite Mathematics lecturer, who has to wait seventeen years before he can afford to marry in George Gissing's *The Odd Women*.

Micklewhimmen Scots lawyer who joins the expedition, saves Tabitha Bramble from a fire, and escapes her matrimonial pursuit in Tobias Smollett's *The Expedition of Humphry Clinker*.

Richard (Dick) Middlemas   Illegitimate son of Richard Tresham and Zilia Monçada; he is raised and trained by Dr. Gideon Gray; he becomes an unsavory character, who causes his mother's death from shock and kills his commanding officer in a duel; he attempts to place Menie Gray in a seraglio before being executed by Prince Hyder Ali Khan Bahauder in Sir Walter Scott's *The Surgeon's Daughter*.

Dr. Middleton   Father of Clara Middleton, the reluctant betrothed of Sir Willoughby Patterne, to whom he allies himself because Willoughby gives him some fine old wine in George Meredith's *The Egoist*.

Lady Middleton   Wife of Sir John Middleton and elder daughter of Mrs. Jennings; dull, cold, and proper, she is interested in nothing but her spoiled children in Jane Austen's *Sense and Sensibility*.

Mr. Middleton   The Reverend Henry Gascoigne's curate, who falls victim to Gwendolen Harleth's cold charm in George Eliot's *Daniel Deronda*.

Annamaria Middleton   Three-year-old child, one of Sir John and Lady Middleton's four spoiled children; the necessity for not disappointing her expectation of a filla-gree basket allows Elinor Dashwood opportunity for a private conversation with Lucy Steele in Jane Austen's *Sense and Sensibility*.

Clara Middleton   Sir Willoughby Patterne's betrothed, who wants to break her engagement when she overcomes romantic illusions to realize he is a selfish, chauvinistic egoist; she is finally freed to marry Willoughby's penniless but unselfish cousin Vernon Whitford only by learning that while refusing to release her, Willoughby proposed to Laetitia Dale in George Meredith's *The Egoist*.

Dr. G. Middleton   Medical practitioner who saves Jack Easy from being spoiled by the absurd ideas of his father, Nicodemus Easy, in Captain Frederick Marryat's *Mr. Midshipman Easy*.

Sir John Middleton   Sportsman and a genial host, somewhat foolish in manner; he provides his widowed cousin, Mrs. Dashwood, and her daughters with a cottage and with society and generous friendship in Jane Austen's *Sense and Sensibility*.

John Middleton   The eldest of Sir John and Lady Middleton's four spoiled children in Jane Austen's *Sense and Sensibility*.

William Middleton   Second son of Sir John and Lady Middleton; his and Harry Dashwood's comparative heights are a matter of character-revealing dispute in Jane Austen's *Sense and Sensibility*.

Margaret, Lady Midlothian   Busybody relative of Alice Vavasor; she is loudly critical of her conduct until Lady Glencora Palliser befriends Alice; she allows her daughters to be in the wedding party when Alice marries John Grey in Anthony Trollope's *Can You Forgive Her?*.

Ozias Midwinter   Dark-skinned, temperamental son of Allan Wrentmore and alter ego of Allan Armadale, with whom he forges a strange friendship based on ancient family feuds and centered on the machinations of a former governess, Lydia Gwilt; he marries her and almost becomes victim to her plot to secure the Armadale fortune in Wilkie Collins's *Armadale*.

Francis Van Cuyck de Mierhop   Mid-seventeenth-century Dutch painter noted for his realistic renderings of food; he persuades Jeremy Watersouchy's father to let his son study under the celebrated painter Gerard Dow in William Beckford's *Biographical Memoirs of Extraordinary Painters*.

Mieris   Mid-seventeenth-century Dutch painter who is praised by Jeremy Watersouchy in William Beckford's *Biographical Memoirs of Extraordinary Painters*.

Mrs. Miff   Pew opener at the Dombeys' church in Charles Dickens's *Dombey and Son*.

Miss Miggs   Martha Varden's maid, who has an eye for Simon Tappertit and is furious when he favors Dolly Varden; she aids her mistress in tormenting Gabriel Varden and ends up as a warden in a women's prison in Charles Dickens's *Barnaby Rudge*.

Mike   Mr. Jaggers's client, known for his informing or "peaching" on criminals in Charles Dickens's *Great Expectations*.

Milborough   Angelo D'Albini's servant and Felix D'Albini's nurse, who seduces both father and son away from Gabrielle di Montmorency and finally ends up chained in a madhouse in Charlotte Dacre's *The Libertine*.

Dowager Countess of Milborough   Louis Trevelyan's old friend, who warns him of Colonel Osborne's attentions to his wife and urges him repeatedly to take her to Naples in Anthony Trollope's *He Knew He Was Right*.

Colonel Mildmay   Half brother of Lady Western; his harsh treatment of his wife, known as Mrs. Hilyard, his attempted abduction of his daughter, and his attempted seduction of Susan Vincent are punished when his wife nearly murders him in Margaret Oliphant's *Salem Chapel*.

Alice Mildmay   Beautiful daughter of Colonel Mildmay and Mrs. Hilyard; she appears to be almost an idiot, but under the care of Susan Vincent she is miraculously cured in Margaret Oliphant's *Salem Chapel*.

Augusta (Gus) Mildmay   Sweet-natured, gentle, tender-hearted woman unlucky in love and desperately working to get a husband; she falls for Jack de Baron and clings to him resolutely until he marries her in Anthony Trollope's *Is He Popenjoy?*.

William Mildmay   Veteran leader of the Liberals who is related to all the great Whig families; almost worn out in public service, he resigns when his government is defeated in Anthony Trollope's *Phineas Finn*. His example as an old Whig moderate is referred to in *Phineas Redux*. He is often mentioned in *The Prime Minister*.

M'Ilduy   Chief of the Camerons and guide to Montrose; he provides the intelligence used to trap Argyle at Inverlochy in Sir Walter Scott's *A Legend of Montrose*.

Miles   Good-natured young gentleman, who is master of Jenny and Tom Robinson and cheerfully becomes their servant after he has lost his money in Charles Reade's *It Is Never Too Late to Mend*.

Marmaduke Milestone   Celebrated picturesque gardener, who espouses theories of landscape gardening in Thomas Love Peacock's *Headlong Hall*.

Mr. Millbank   Prosperous, middle-class Manchester mill owner, who embodies the virtues of a "natural aristocracy"; he forbids his daughter to marry Harry Coningsby because of his hatred of Coningsby's grandfather, Lord Monmouth, in Benjamin Disraeli's *Coningsby; or, The New Generation*.

Edith Millbank   Beautiful daughter of Mr. Millbank and sister of Oswald Millbank; she eventually marries Harry Coningsby, thereby establishing an alliance between the aristocracy and the middle class in Benjamin Disraeli's *Coningsby; or, The New Generation*.

Oswald Millbank   Mr. Millbank's stalwart son, whom Harry Coningsby rescues from drowning, thereby initiating a devoted friendship which signifies an alliance between the aristocracy and the middle class in Benjamin Disraeli's *Coningsby; or, The New Generation*.

Millepois   Chief cook at Gatherum Castle who brings new styles of cooking to the Duchess of Omnium's household in Anthony Trollope's *The Prime Minister*.

Miller   Coxswain of the rowing eight of St. Ambrose's College, Oxford, in Thomas Hughes's *Tom Brown at Oxford*.

Miss Miller   An under-teacher at Lowood School in charge of Jane Eyre when she first arrives in Charlotte Brontë's *Jane Eyre*.

Mr. Miller   Hardheaded man with a face like a pippin, who is a guest at Manor Farm, Dingley Dell, in Charles Dickens's *The Posthumous Papers of the Pickwick Club*.

Mrs. Miller   Tom Jones's London landlady, who has many opportunities of recognizing his generous nature; she is instrumental in restoring him to Squire Allworthy's good opinion in Henry Fielding's *The History of Tom Jones*.

Betty (Betsy) Miller   Younger daughter of Mrs. Miller and sister to Nancy; she grieves for Nancy's imminent ruin in Henry Fielding's *The History of Tom Jones*.

Harry Miller   Second-rate newspaperman, who wrote Loudon Dodd's San Francisco lecture on Parisian student life in Robert Louis Stevenson's *The Wrecker*.

Nancy (Nanny) Miller   Eldest daughter of Mrs. Miller; she finds herself pregnant and abandoned by Jack Nightingale when his father decides to arrange another match for him; Tom Jones intercedes, bringing about their happy marriage in Henry Fielding's *The History of Tom Jones*.

Sheriff Thomas Miller   One of the four Scottish counsels to James Stewart, alleged murderer of Colin Ray Campbell; he is quick-witted and ready to use David Balfour's testimony to political advantage in Stewart's trial in Robert Louis Stevenson's *Catriona*.

Millers   Servant in the Pocket household who specializes in rounding up the children in Charles Dickens's *Great Expectations*.

Lady Millicent   Charming, oversentimental young widow, who briefly captivates Harry Ormond in Maria Edgeworth's *Ormond*.

Milliner   A country gentleman's proud daughter; after a life of disappointment, she settles down with a rich keeper who leaves her enough money to set up a milliner's shop in London in Francis Coventry's *The History of Pompey the Little*.

Fanny Millinger   Young woman who becomes attached to Percy Godolphin in Edward Bulwer-Lytton's *Godolphin*.

Mr. Mills   Father of Julia Mills; he always seems to be an inconvenience in Julia's attempts to further the courtship of David Copperfield and Dora Spenlow in Charles Dickens's *The Personal History of David Copperfield*.

Julia Mills   Bosom friend of Dora Spenlow; wise and

benign at the age of twenty, she assists David in his court-ship of Dora in Charles Dickens's *The Personal History of David Copperfield*.

Eliza Millward Younger daughter of the Vicar of Lindenhope; she bewitches Gilbert Markham and, be-cause she feels betrayed when he shifts his attachment to Helen Huntingdon, does what she can to fuel the scandal surrounding Helen in Anne Brontë's *The Tenant of Wildfell Hall*.

Mary Millward Quiet eldest daughter of the Vicar of Lindenhope; she acts as family housekeeper, avoids lis-tening to scandal, and marries Richard Wilson when he becomes her father's curate in Anne Brontë's *The Tenant of Wildfell Hall*.

Michael Millward Robust Vicar of Lindenhope, who is so set in his attitudes and prejudices that he believes the fabrications about Helen Huntingdon in Anne Brontë's *The Tenant of Wildfell Hall*.

Miss Milner Beautiful, flirtatious, improperly educated heroine, who marries her Catholic guardian, Dorriforth, Lord Elmwood, but commits adultery with Sir Frederick Lawnly; separated from her husband, she dies, leaving her daughter, Matilda, in the care of Miss Woodley in Elizabeth Inchbald's *A Simple Story*.

Milrookit, Laird of Dirdumwhamle Husband of Claud Walkinshaw's only daughter, Margaret, and father of Walkinshaw Milrookit in John Galt's *The Entail*.

Walkinshaw Milrookit Son of Claud Walkinshaw's daughter Margaret; he marries George Walkinshaw's daughter Robina; they try unsuccessfully to claim the Walkinshaw estate after George Walkinshaw's untimely death in John Galt's *The Entail*.

Major Milroy Eleanor's dreamy and absent-minded fa-ther, absorbed in his invention of a replica of the Stras-bourg clock in Wilkie Collins's *Armadale*.

Mrs. Milroy Permanent-invalid wife of Major Milroy and mother of Eleanor; her constant grumbling is gener-ally disregarded in the household in Wilkie Collins's *Armadale*.

Eleanor (Neelie) Milroy Sixteen-year-old sweetheart of Allan Armadale; her father unwisely engages Lydia Gwilt as her governess; she eventually marries Allan in Wilkie Collins's *Armadale*.

Lady Ann Milton Daughter of Lord Rosherville; her betrothal to her first cousin Henry Foker is ended by her elopement with Mr. Hobson in William Makepeace Thackeray's *The History of Pendennis*.

John Milton Poet whose soul the author encounters in Elysium in Henry Fielding's *A Journey From This World to the Next*.

Dora Milvain Jasper Milvain's sister, who learns to write children's stories and later marries Whelpdale against her brother's wishes in George Gissing's *New Grub Street*.

Jasper Milvain Mercenary journalist, who is engaged to Marian Yule when she becomes an heiress but parts from her when her inheritance falls through; he marries Edwin Reardon's widow and becomes highly successful as a writer and editor in George Gissing's *New Grub Street*.

Maud Milvain Jasper Milvain's sister, who learns to write children's books and marries a prosperous writer her brother disapproves of in George Gissing's *New Grub Street*.

Frank Milvey Long-suffering, kind-hearted minister, who finds an orphan for the Boffins, conducts the funeral service for Betty Higden, and marries Eugene Wrayburn and Lizzie Hexam in Charles Dickens's *Our Mutual Friend*.

Margaretta Milvey Pretty, loyal wife of Frank Milvey in Charles Dickens's *Our Mutual Friend*.

Dr. Minchin A Middlemarch physician in George Eliot's *Middlemarch*.

Mindrack Satanic presence, the corporality of which Peter Wilkins disproves in Robert Paltock's *The Life and Adventures of Peter Wilkins*.

Frances Minerva Plain, unloved, observant governess to the Gallilee children; hopelessly and secretly in love with Ovid Vere, she is jealous of Carmina Graywell; her better nature and her natural affection for Carmina tri-umph to make her Carmina's friend and trustworthy ad-viser in Wilkie Collins's *Heart and Science*.

Captain Goliah Minikin Fellow prisoner with Ferdi-nand; he fights an unusual duel with Major Macleaver in Tobias Smollett's *The Adventures of Ferdinand Count Fathom*.

Minister Counselor to Moll Flanders while she is in Newgate Prison; he helps bring about her repentance and manages to get her sentence reduced from hanging to transportation to the colonies in Daniel Defoe's *The For-tunes and Misfortunes of the Famous Moll Flanders*.

Minnie Maid in Brussels for William and Frances (Henri) Crimsworth in Charlotte Brontë's *The Professor*.

Judge Minos Keeper of the gate to Elysium who ques-tions souls seeking entrance; he waves them in, redirects them to Hell, or returns them to earth for another incarnation and chance to enter Elysium in Henry Fielding's *A Journey From This World to the Next*.

Hector M'Intyre Army captain and nephew of Oldbuck (Jonathan Oldenbuck); he has a violent temper and insults William Lovel, who wounds him in a duel in Sir Walter Scott's *The Antiquary*.

Maria M'Intyre Niece of Oldbuck (Jonathan Oldenbuck); she suffers his mocking abuse of women and helps to run his household in Sir Walter Scott's *The Antiquary*.

Count Alcibiades de Mirabel Worldly, good-hearted dandy, who is a friend of Ferdinand Armine and helps Ferdinand when he gets into difficulty with his debts in Benjamin Disraeli's *Henrietta Temple: A Love Story*.

Sir Charles Mirabel Wealthy, ailing, aged former diplomat, who becomes infatuated with Miss Fotheringay (Emily Costigan) and marries her in William Makepeace Thackeray's *The History of Pendennis*.

Miranda A beautiful and selfish woman who falls in love with a Fransciscan priest and accuses him of rape when he refuses her attentions; she later marries Prince Tarquin, lives with him upon her sister's money, and plots to murder her sister to obtain her fortune in Aphra Behn's *The Fair Jilt*.

Miret A bad-tempered bookseller and supplier of Mme. Beck's books who is courteous to Lucy Snowe in Charlotte Brontë's *Villette*.

Miriam Elderly Jewish crone, slave dealer, money lender, sorceress, and mother figure to Pelagia; she wields enormous power in Alexandria, plots against all non-Jews, and finally confesses to Raphael Aben-Ezra that she is his mother before dying on his shoulder from a wound inflicted by Smid in Charles Kingsley's *Hypatia*.

Alcide Mirobolant Ridiculous French chef of the Claverings who aspires to the love of Blanche Amory in William Makepeace Thackeray's *The History of Pendennis*.

Mrs. Mirror Neighbor of the Moreland estate who has faults typical of people of fashion in Henry Brooke's *The Fool of Quality*.

Captain Mirvan Coarse sailor husband of Mrs. Mirvan; he returns home after seven years' absence; he subjects Madame Duval to insults and practical jokes in Frances Burney's *Evelina*.

Mrs. Mirvan Daughter of Lady Howard; she takes Evelina Anville Belmont as a companion of her daughter Maria to London in Frances Burney's *Evelina*.

Maria (Moll) Mirvan Daughter of Captain and Mrs. Mirvan; she is Evelina Anville Belmont's traveling companion in London in Frances Burney's *Evelina*.

Misanthropist Embittered bachelor whose loathing for mankind, the result of a series of betrayals, teaches Harley a lesson in Henry Mackenzie's *The Man of Feeling*.

Miser Father who disinherited his eldest son for providing the expensive medical aid which saved his own life instead of the cheap medical care he had demanded in Charles Johnstone's *Chrysal: or, The Adventures of a Guinea*.

Miss Miskin Assistant and bosom friend to shopkeeper Mrs. Howell; she refuses to enter her bedchamber, even at Mrs. Howell's dying request, and is quick to change the name on the shop after her employer's death in Harriet Martineau's *Deerbrook*.

Lord Mistletoe The Duke of Mayfair's son; he is reluctantly dragged in to support the case against Lord Rufford for breach of promise made by his cousin Arabella Trefoil in Anthony Trollope's *The American Senator*.

Mistress Nurse Moll Flanders's guardian, who raises Moll from about the age of three; she teaches housekeeping and sewing to orphans in order to help them go out to service when old enough; she dies when Moll is fourteen in Daniel Defoe's *The Fortunes and Misfortunes of the Famous Moll Flanders*.

Mistress of Disguised Gentleman A woman of ugly appearance and base temper who demands money and who holds great power over the Disguised Gentleman in Charles Johnstone's *Chrysal: or, The Adventures of a Guinea*.

Mistrust Timorous's companion in fleeing the lions away from the Celestial City in John Bunyan's *The Pilgrim's Progress From this World to That Which Is to Come*.

Carrie Mitchell Poor girl who is rescued from the streets and marries Arthur Golding but reverts to her former habits, becomes a drunkard, and wrecks their marriage in George Gissing's *Workers in the Dawn*.

Madame Miteau Widowed milliner in reduced circumstances; she employs Cornelia in Paris and is obliged to her for the rescue and reorganization of her business in Sarah Scott's *The History of Cornelia*.

Susan Mivers Half sister of Lucretia Clavering, wife of William Mainwaring, and mother of Helen Mainwaring in Edward Bulwer-Lytton's *Lucretia*.

Mr. Mivins (the Zephyr) Dancing and singing cell mate of Samuel Pickwick in the Fleet debtors' prison in Charles Dickens's *The Posthumous Papers of the Pickwick Club*.

Joe Mixet Dapper, loquacious friend of John Crumb, who relies too heavily on Mixet's aid in his courtship to suit Ruby Ruggles in Anthony Trollope's *The Way We Live Now*.

Mixit Jacobite apothecary and frequenter of the Black Bear in Sir Walter Scott's *Rob Roy*.

M'Kay Like Mark Rutherford, a London Parliamentary reporter for country newspapers; he joins Mark on Sundays listening to popular preachers for entertainment; having a passionate desire to reform, he opens a non-sectarian mission to rescue people in despair in Mark Rutherford's *Mark Rutherford's Deliverance*.

Mrs. M'Kay M'Kay's wife, whose opinions echo those of her husband; she is much pitied by Mark Rutherford, who thinks M'Kay mistreats her, until her serious illness makes him appreciate her just before she dies in Mark Rutherford's *Mark Rutherford's Deliverance*.

Sir Hector M'Lean Highland chief serving under Montrose in Sir Walter Scott's *A Legend of Montrose*.

Andrew M'Lucre The Dean of Guild in Gudetown and chief political rival of provost James Pawkie; he is more openly venal than provost Pawkie and thus more susceptible to public criticism in John Galt's *The Provost*.

Mnason Host to Christiana and her party in Vanity Fair; he marries his daughter Grace to Samuel and his daughter Martha to Joseph in John Bunyan's *The Pilgrim's Progress From this World to That Which Is to Come*.

Prince Stanilas Moanatini Native prince, who is going to inspect a mountain landslide as Loudon Dodd's ship arrives in Robert Louis Stevenson's *The Wrecker*.

Mrs. Mobbs Miss Leroy's neighbor, who is horrified at Miss Leroy's practice of fresh-air living and daily bathing in Mark Rutherford's *Mark Rutherford's Deliverance*.

Richard Mobray Libertine friend of Robert Lovelace in Samuel Richardson's *Clarissa: or, The History of a Young Lady*.

Mock Monastery Member Well-educated man, who in his youth had every reason and opportunity to patronize the arts and sciences, but whose inclination to vanity allows him to procure the life of a successful literary parasite in Charles Johnstone's *Chrysal: or, The Adventures of a Guinea*.

Mock Monastery Member Number Three Man of obscure origins who gains vast amounts of money by prostituting himself to an old, very rich woman and by using his friends in government in Charles Johnstone's *Chrysal: or, The Adventures of a Guinea*.

Mock Turtle Mournful creature that relates the history of its education; with the Gryphon it demonstrates the Lobster-Quadrille in Lewis Carroll's *Alice's Adventures in Wonderland*.

Augustus Moddle The passive, melancholy youngest gentleman resident in Mrs. Todgers's boarding house; his passion for Mercy Pecksniff is expressed in jealousy of Mr. Jinkins until she marries Jonas Chuzzlewit, whereupon he gives himself over to mourning; his weakness in becoming engaged to Charity Pecksniff does not survive the tyranny of her wedding preparations in Charles Dickens's *The Life and Adventures of Martin Chuzzlewit*.

Signora di Modena Mercenary relative who locks Victoria di Loredani in her chamber to break her proud spirit in Charlotte Dacre's *Zofloya; or, The Moor*.

Gustavus Moffat Augusta Gresham's betrothed, who breaks off his engagement to pursue the wealthy Martha Dunstable and is thrashed by Frank Gresham in Anthony Trollope's *Doctor Thorne*.

Aileen Moffatt Ethereally beautiful cousin of Julie Le Breton; she nearly dies of grief when Harry Warkworth dies in Africa in Mrs. Humphry Ward's *Lady Rose's Daughter*.

Blanche Moffatt Foolish aunt of Julie Le Breton; she encourages the fortune-hunting Harry Warkworth to court her daughter, Aileen, in Mrs. Humphry Ward's *Lady Rose's Daughter*.

Mr. Moggs Well-known bootmaker of Bond Street much in demand by society; he detests the radical political views of his son, Ontario, worships capital, and hates trade unions in Anthony Trollope's *Ralph the Heir*.

Luke Moggs Head miller at Dorlcote Mill; he explains to Maggie Tulliver why all her brother's long-eared rabbits are dead in George Eliot's *The Mill on the Floss*.

Ontario Moggs Boot-maker's son and tribune of the people with oratorical gifts; at odds with his father's worship of capital and hatred of unions, he contests an election on labor rights without success; his integrity wins the hand of Polly Neefit in Anthony Trollope's *Ralph the Heir*.

Mohammed Arab trader and steersman, who accompanies Ludwig Horace Holly and Leo Vincey by sea and river on their journey into Africa; his murder by the Amahagger is avenged by the Englishmen in a bloody and horrible altercation in H. Rider Haggard's *She*.

Lord Mohun Wicked gambler and duellist, who is responsible for the death of the fourth Viscount Castlewood; Henry Esmond survives a duel with him; his duel with the Duke of Hamilton is fatal to both in William Makepeace Thackeray's *The History of Henry Esmond*.

Mr. Mohun Ineffectual, widowed father of twelve children who lives on his secluded estate, Beechcroft, in Charlotte Yonge's *Scenes and Characters*.

Adeline Mohun Youngest daughter of Mr. Mohun of Beechcroft in Charlotte Yonge's *Scenes and Characters*. After years of luxurious invalidism she marries parvenu quarry owner James White in *Beechcroft at Rockstone*. She appears in *The Long Vacation*.

Claude Mohun Clergyman son of Mr. Mohun of Beechcroft; he steadies and advises his romantic younger sister, Lilias, in Charlotte Yonge's *Scenes and Characters*.

Dolores Mohun Only child of Maurice Mohun; she is sent to stay with the large family of her Aunt Lilias (Mohun) Merrifield and is eventually won over by them in Charlotte Yonge's *The Two Sides of the Shield*. As a young woman she becomes engaged to Gerald Underwood in *The Long Vacation*.

Eleanor Mohun Eldest daughter of Mr. Mohun of Beechcroft; she delays her own marriage to Francis Hawkesworth to bring up her younger sisters but alienates them by her cold, repressive manner in Charlotte Yonge's *Scenes and Characters*.

Emily Mohun Indolent daughter of Mr. Mohun of Beechcroft; her lack of self-discipline vitiates her attempts to manage her younger sisters after the marriage of her sister Eleanor in Charlotte Yonge's *Scenes and Characters*.

Jane Mohun Sharp, inquisitive daughter of Mr. Mohun of Beechcroft in Charlotte Yonge's *Scenes and Characters*. She matures into an archetypal British spinster and church worker in *Beechcroft at Rockstone* and in *The Long Vacation*.

Lilias Mohun Daughter of Mr. Mohun of Beechcroft; she overcomes her flightiness with the help of her brother Claude; she marries military hero Sir Jasper Merrifield in Charlotte Yonge's *Scenes and Characters*. Despite becoming an exemplary mother to her own dozen children, she cannot quite live down her girlhood reputation as "silly Lilly" in *The Two Sides of the Shield*, in *Beechcroft at Rockstone*, and in *The Long Vacation*.

Maurice Mohun Son of Mr. Mohun of Beechcroft; he alienates his family over his scientific interests in Charlotte Yonge's *Scenes and Characters*. Upon the death of his wife he leaves his daughter, Dolores, in England with his sister Lilias Merrifield to take up a post in Australia in *The Two Sides of the Shield*.

Phyllis (Honest Phyl) Mohun Daughter of Mr. Mohun of Beechcroft; her charm and truthful character win her the love of Henry May in Charlotte Yonge's *Scenes and Characters*. She appears in *Beechcroft at Rockstone*.

Reginald Mohun Son of Mr. Mohun of Beechcroft; as a retired military officer and bachelor he often comes to the aid of his sisters Lilias and Jane in Charlotte Yonge's *Scenes and Characters*. He also appears in *The Two Sides of the Shield*, in *Beechcroft at Rockstone* and in *The Long Vacation*.

William Mohun Eldest son of Mr. Mohun of Beechcroft; his marriage to a motherly, capable woman solves the domestic difficulties of his widowed father in Charlotte Yonge's *Scenes and Characters*.

Mr. Mole Philanthropist and philosopher; his anti-Christian arguments temporarily shake young Harry Clinton's faith in Henry Brooke's *The Fool of Quality*.

Mr. Molesworth Country squire in Hartlebury and father of Helen Molesworth; he is an honest but intellectually limited Tory supporter in Benjamin Disraeli's *A Year at Hartlebury; or, The Election*.

Helen Molesworth Beautiful, sensitive daughter of Mr. Molesworth; she falls in love with Aubrey Bohun and is his most effective campaigner in the election at Fanchester; she later discovers he is an unprincipled man in Benjamin Disraeli's *A Year at Hartlebury; or, The Election*.

Blear-eyed Moll Disreputable prostitute and fellow prisoner who verbally abuses William Booth because he can't buy her some gin in Henry Fielding's *Amelia*.

Abraham ("Aby") Mollett Villainous, mustachioed son of Matthew Mollett, and a worse rogue than his father; he has matrimonial designs on Emmeline Fitzgerald and adds to her father's torment in Anthony Trollope's *Castle Richmond*.

Mary Mollett Haggard and long-suffering abandoned wife of Matthew Mollett; Mr. Prendergast's discovery of her alive proves Matthew Mollett's marriage to Mary Wainwright (Lady Fitzgerald) illegal and clears the Fitzgerald children of illegitimacy in Anthony Trollope's *Castle Richmond*.

Mary Mollett (Swan) Matthew Mollett's daughter by his legal wife, whom he deserted; she has taken the name

Swan and supports herself and her mother by sewing in Anthony Trollope's *Castle Richmond.*

Matthew Mollett   Cunning scoundrel, who blackmails Sir Thomas Fitzgerald, claiming that Sir Thomas's marriage is illegal, Lady Fitzgerald being Mollett's own wife; his plans are thwarted by Mr. Prendergast's discovery that Mollett himself had committed bigamy when he married Mary Wainwright (Lady Fitzgerald) in Anthony Trollope's *Castle Richmond.*

Mrs. Molloy   Woman who runs the public house in Chapelizod in J. Sheridan Le Fanu's *The House by the Churchyard.*

Molly   Mr. Jaggers's housekeeper since his successful defense of her on a murder charge; she is revealed to be Estella's mother; she has large, powerful hands and a scarred wrist in Charles Dickens's *Great Expectations.*

Molly   Mrs. Poyser's maid who bears her mistress's cutting, sarcastic remarks in George Eliot's *Adam Bede.*

Molly   Lambert family servant who marries Gumbo and becomes George and Theo (Lambert) Warrington's devoted servant in William Makepeace Thackeray's *The Virginians.*

Mrs. Molly   Flirtatious maid to Lady Forester and reader of Samuel Richardson's *Pamela*; Geoffry Wildgoose imagines her to be seducing him in Richard Graves's *The Spiritual Quixote.*

Mr. Momson   Squire and father of a boy in Dr. Wortle's school; he supports Dr. Wortle's loyalty to the Peacockes in Anthony Trollope's *Dr. Wortle's School.*

Lady Margaret Momson   First cousin to Mrs. Stantiloup and one of the women who gossip about the marital status of two staff members at Dr. Wortle's academy in Anthony Trollope's *Dr. Wortle's School.*

Momus   Famous ballad-singer, who is in league with Hunchback to increase the ministry by attacking the clergy and religion in Charles Johnstone's *Chrysal: or, The Adventures of a Guinea.*

Alonzo de Monçada   A Spaniard who is shipwrecked near John Melmoth's estate; he met Melmoth the Wanderer while imprisoned during the Spanish Inquisition; the Wanderer offered Alonzo freedom in exchange for Monçada's soul; Alonzo later escapes from the prison on his own in Charles Maturin's *Melmoth the Wanderer.*

Juan de Monçada   Brother of Alonzo de Monçada; he is killed while helping Alonzo escape the Spanish Inquisition in Charles Maturin's *Melmoth the Wanderer.*

Matthias de Monçada   Zilia de Monçada's father, a severe and haughty Portuguese Jew, who uses the power of his wealth to separate Zilia from her son, Richard Middlemas, in Sir Walter Scott's *The Surgeon's Daughter.*

Zilia de Monçada (Middlemas, Witherington)   Daughter of Matthias de Monçada and mother of Richard Middlemas; a fragile beauty, she is seduced by Richard Tresham; while in Scotland for Richard's birth she assumes the name Middlemas; after she marries Tresham, she takes the name he is using, Witherington; the shock of seeing her son kills her in Sir Walter Scott's *The Surgeon's Daughter.*

Mr. Monaghan   Wealthy Irish gentleman and John Buncle's contemporary at Trinity College, Dublin; he has read many books but knows human nature; he meets Antiope Pearson at the Harrogate dance Buncle attends and later marries her in Thomas Amory's *The Life of John Buncle, Esq.*

Prince Monaldeschi   Neapolitan who obliges Count Rosalvo to disguise himself as Abellino/Flodoardo by stealing his lands and blackening his name; apparently murdered by Abellino, he is actually killed honorably by Rosalvo in a duel in Matthew Lewis's *The Bravo of Venice.*

André Moncharmont   Swiss business partner of Piers Otway in George Gissing's *The Crown of Life.*

Mr. Monckton   Wealthy neighbor of Cecilia Beverley's guardian; he despises his wife, secretly plots to acquire Cecilia's wealth by marrying her when his wife dies, and is wounded in a duel with Mortimer Delvile in Frances Burney's *Cecilia.*

Lady Margaret Monckton   Cold-spirited, jealous wife of Mr. Monckton; she refuses to oblige him and die in Frances Burney's *Cecilia.*

Avery Moncton   Gentleman and scholar who lives near London and is driven to a reclusive life by an adulterous wife; he chooses the single life despite John Buncle's protestations in Thomas Amory's *The Life of John Buncle, Esq.*

Pietro Mondovi   Blackmailer and later murderer of Countess Zulmer in Charlotte Dacre's *The Passions.*

Money-Love   One of three friends of By-ends; he uses religion for selfish and worldly ends in John Bunyan's *The Pilgrim's Progress From this World to That Which Is to Come.*

Miss Monflathers   Snobbish headmistress of the town's most prestigious girls' boarding and day school; she scolds and belittles Nell Trent in front of her pupils for being a "waxwork girl" in Charles Dickens's *The Old Curiosity Shop.*

Lord Mongrober   British aristocrat, fat and red-faced, who graces society by constantly dining out but never entertains; he attends the Robys' dinner party in Anthony Trollope's *The Prime Minister.*

Lady Monk   Handsome, worthless old aunt of the handsome, worthless Burgo Fitzgerald; she encourages his pursuit of Lady Glencora Palliser and provides funds for the planned elopement in Anthony Trollope's *Can You Forgive Her?.*

Sir Cosmo Monk   Aging Liberal Member of Parliament and husband of Burgo Fitzgerald's aunt; he is strongly opposed to his wife's indulgence of her nephew in Anthony Trollope's *Can You Forgive Her?.*

Geoffrey Monk   Student at Oxford who is commissioned to compile the journals left by John Inglesant and thus becomes the narrator in J. Henry Shorthouse's *John Inglesant, A Romance.*

Joshua Monk   Experienced senior radical politician, to whom Phineas Finn gives his allegiance and from whom he learns the business of governing and public service in Anthony Trollope's *Phineas Finn.* He testifies on behalf of Finn in *Phineas Redux.* He serves in a coalition government in *The Prime Minister.* He successfully persuades the (younger) Duke of Omnium to return to political life in *The Duke's Children.*

Monsieur Monluc   Gallant, handsome agent of the court of France; Reginald de St. Leon, while imprisoned in Constance, vainly seeks help from him in William Godwin's *St. Leon.*

Duke of Monmouth   Commander of Scottish armies loyal to King James II; he defeats the Cameronian rebels and orders the exile of Henry Morton to Holland in Sir Walter Scott's *Old Mortality.*

Lord Monmouth   Ostentatiously wealthy and epicurean marquess and grandfather of Harry Coningsby; he sees his grandson as a "brilliant tool" to maintain his own political power; he bequeaths his fortune to his illegitimate daughter, Flora, disinheriting Coningsby in Benjamin Disraeli's *Coningsby; or, The New Generation.*

Monna Lisa   Deaf old woman servant to Tessa Melema in George Eliot's *Romola.*

Sir Damask Monogram   Contractor's son of great wealth now courted by people of rank; his wife is Georgiana Longestaffe's old friend, the former Julia Triplex, in

Anthony Trollope's *The Way We Live Now.* He attends a dinner party at the Robys' in *The Prime Minister.*

Julia Triplex, Lady Monogram   Longtime friend of Georgiana Longestaffe; her marriage gives her rank and fortune and the power to snub and insult Georgiana for associating with the Melmottes in Anthony Trollope's *The Way We Live Now.* She attends a dinner party at the Robys' in *The Prime Minister.*

Richie Monoplies   Servant of Nigel Olifaunt; he kills Captain Colepepper, discovers the location of the mortgage and returns it to his master, and marries Martha Trapbois as his reward for killing her father's murderer in Sir Walter Scott's *The Fortunes of Nigel.*

Major Monsoon   Self-indulgent gourmand and plundering opportunist in the British army during the Napoleonic Wars in Charles Lever's *Charles O'Malley.*

Tancred, Lord Montacute   Son and heir of the Duke of Bellamont; he is concerned about England's spiritual condition and is not satisfied with the options for amelioration available, so he decides to undertake a "Quest" to the Holy Land in a search for spiritual peace in Benjamin Disraeli's *Tancred; or, The New Crusade.*

Edward Montagu   Handsome, sweet-tempered, and gallant young man, whose estate borders on that of the Willises; a stalwart in the cause of the Restoration, he is killed in the attack on the Dutch East India ships in the port of Bergen, Norway, in William Godwin's *Mandeville.*

Ralph Montagu   A true and valued friend to Charles and Henrietta Mandeville; contemplative and sober, he is no less estimable than his active and fiery brother, Edward, in William Godwin's *Mandeville.*

Mr. Montague   An impulsive young medical man who marries Emma Courtney, making her his assistant, and becomes jealous of her platonic love for Augustus Harley; he seduces the nursemaid Rachel, induces Rachel's miscarriage, strangles the premature infant, and shoots himself in Mary Hays's *Memoirs of Emma Courtney.*

Charlotte Montague   Gentlewoman and cousin of Robert Lovelace, who uses her name to reassure Clarissa of the propriety of her escape with Lovelace; ultimately she marries the reformed John Belford in Samuel Richardson's *Clarissa: or, The History of a Young Lady.*

Emily Montague   Young, supposedly orphaned friend of Arabella Fermor; she lives in Montreal with a distant relative; having broken an advantageous betrothal to George Clayton, made by her deceased guardian, she marries Ed. Rivers by choice after they return to England; she discovers Rivers to be the bridegroom selected for her by her father, Colonel Willmott, long believed dead in Frances Brooke's *The History of Emily Montague.*

Martha (Patty, Patsey) Montague   Robert Lovelace's retiring cousin in Samuel Richardson's *Clarissa: or, The History of a Young Lady.*

Paul Montague   Young businessman who arrives home from California and is drawn into investing in Hamilton K. Fisker's South Central Pacific and Mexican Railway; the project is a swindle and Paul extricates himself from the board; his involvement with Winifred Hurtle, who has pursued him from California, threatens his relationship with Hetta Carbury, whom he marries at last in Anthony Trollope's *The Way We Live Now.*

Tigg Montague   See Montague Tigg.

Henry, Marquis de Montalt   French nobleman who is robbed, imprisoned in an abbey, and finally killed by his half brother Phillippe de Montalt in order to obtain his title and fortune; later he is discovered to be Adeline's father in Ann Radcliffe's *The Romance of the Forest.*

Phillippe, Marquis de Montalt   Evil nobleman who blackmails Pierre de La Mott into helping him seduce, then murder the innocent Adeline; he is responsible for Theodore Peyron's death sentence; he is discovered to be Adeline's half uncle and her father's assassin; ultimately he commits suicide in Ann Radcliffe's *The Romance of the Forest.*

Montamour   Ingenue who is not bitter or jealous when she learns of Beuclair's affair; she disguises herself as the Chevalier Vrayment in Eliza Haywood's *The Injur'd Husband; or, the Mistaken Resentment.*

Count Louis de Montauban   The de Roubignés' stern neighbor, who falls in love with and marries the beautiful Julia de Roubigné, only to murder her in a jealous frenzy in Henry Mackenzie's *Julia de Roubigné.*

Lord Monteagle   Whig husband of Gertrude, Lady Monteagle; his discovery of his wife's affair with Plantagenet, Lord Cadurcis results in a duel in which Lord Monteagle is wounded in Benjamin Disraeli's *Venetia.*

Gertrude, Lady Monteagle   Lord Monteagle's celebrated, witty, and socially eminent wife, whose jealous passion for Plantagent Cadurcis leads her to reveal their affair to her husband in Benjamin Disraeli's *Venetia.*

Sir Philip de Montenay   Elderly seneschal of Douglas Castle in Sir Walter Scott's *Castle Dangerous.*

Conrade Mont-Fitchit   Confidant of the Grand Master

(Lucas Beaumanoir) and a bigoted Preceptor of the Order of the Templars; he is one of the knights to try Rebecca for sorcery in Sir Walter Scott's *Ivanhoe.*

Marquis de Montfleuri   A French aristocrat and "revolutionist," whose estate is a model of contemporary agricultural and social planning and whose liberal principles extend to Lionel Desmond, whom he does not fight when told of the liaison between Desmond and his sister, Josephine de Boisbelle; he marries Fanny Waverly, and will therefore be Desmond's brother-in-law in Charlotte Smith's *Desmond.*

Lord Montford   Rival of Ferdinand Armine for Henrietta Temple; his elegance and sensitivity in wooing her are a contrast to Ferdinand's intensity, and he is partially successful; he finally marries Katherine Grandison in Benjamin Disraeli's *Henrietta Temple: A Love Story.*

Lady Montfort   Society hostess who adopts Endymion Ferrars as her special protégé; she works hard to advance his career and marries him when her husband dies in Benjamin Disraeli's *Endymion.*

Marquess of Montfort   Impassive head of the house of Vipont and husband of Caroline Montfort in Edward Bulwer-Lytton's *What Will He Do With It? by Pisistratus Caxton.*

Amelia Montfort   Beloved cousin of Audley Mandeville; because of Commodore Mandeville's objections to her low birth, she is barred from marrying him; instead, she is married off to Lieutenant Jack Thomson and dies in childbirth in William Godwin's *Mandeville.*

Caroline Montfort   Exquisite widow of the Marquess of Montfort; she has been parted from Guy Darrell by the machinations of Jasper Losely in Edward Bulwer-Lytton's *What Will He Do With It? by Pisistratus Caxton.*

Simon de Montfort   Duplicitous nobleman married to Henry III's widowed sister and a combatant in a tournament held at Henry's court in Ann Radcliffe's *Gaston de Blondeville.*

Montgomery   Thin, unattractive conductor, composer, and pianist of Dick Lennox's traveling acting company; deeply in love with Kate Ede, who likes him as a friend, he is unfortunate in love as well as professionally; he is loyal and helpful to Kate and Dick in George Moore's *A Mummer's Wife.*

George Montgomery   Music-hall comic singer, thirty years old, with whom Andrew Tacchi meets to drink whiskey in London; Miriam becomes infatuated with him; he dies in her arms during her apprenticeship as a nurse in Mark Rutherford's *Miriam's Schooling.*

Guy Monthermer　Norman knight who delivers King Henry II's demands to Eveline Berenger for the surrender of Damian de Lacy in Sir Walter Scott's *The Betrothed.*

Jules Montjoie　Dissolute French Bohemian artist, who is coerced by David Grieve into marrying his sister, Louie, in Mrs. Humphry Ward's *The History of David Grieve.*

Adelaide Marie de Montmorence　Daughter of the French ambassador to England; to her Matilda narrates the story of her life in Sophia Lee's *The Recess.*

Montmorency　Misanthropic French gentleman, who moves to the wilds, educates and isolates his daughter Gabrielle to keep her virtuous, and on failing succumbs to melancholia in Charlotte Dacre's *The Libertine.*

Gabrielle di Montmorency (D'Albini)　Aristocratic innocent raised in the wilds; seduced and abandoned, she disguises herself as the page Eugene to follow her lover; once reunited with him, she endures many hardships including the loss of her children; she is married on her deathbed in Charlotte Dacre's *The Libertine.*

Signor Montoni　Murderous Italian gentleman, who loses his fortune gambling, marries Madame Cheron for her money, and confines her and her niece, Emily St. Aubert, in the Castle di Udolpho in an attempt to extort land from her; he uses Udolpho as a fortress for mercenaries until attacked by government forces; ultimately he dies in prison in Ann Radcliffe's *The Mysteries of Udolpho.*

Julian Montreuil　Jesuit confessor and abbe, who creates emnity among the Devereux brothers and is killed by Morton Devereux in Edward Bulwer-Lytton's *Devereux.*

Adela Montreville (Queen of Sheba)　Powerful Amazon, who betrays her lover, Richard Middlemas, when he hesitates in giving Menie Gray to Prince Tippoo Saib in Sir Walter Scott's *The Surgeon's Daughter.*

Eleonore, Lady Montreville　Mother whose indulgence has made her son, Frederic Delamere, selfish, headstrong, and reckless and her elder daughter, Lady Frances Crofts, disdainful, unprincipled, and shameless in Charlotte Smith's *Emmeline: The Orphan of the Castle.*

Frederic, Lord Montreville　A younger son who succeeds to the Mowbray estate, marries for wealth and a title, and wields power in business and politics; avaricious and arrogant, he begrudges his brother's orphaned (and presumed illegitimate) child, Emmeline Mobray, her small allowance and conspires with Sir Richard Crofts to keep his son, Frederic Delamere, from marrying her in Charlotte Smith's *Emmeline: The Orphan of the Castle.*

Duke of Montrose　Descendant of James Graham, the Marquis of Montrose, and highly placed in the government; he arrests Rob Roy McGregor in Sir Walter Scott's *Rob Roy.*

Marquis of Montrose (James Graham)　Commander of the Royalist forces in the Highlands and the hated enemy of the Marquis of Argyle; average-looking but possessing extraordinary charisma, he successfully unites the various Highland factions to form his army; he assumes the alias Anderson while traveling *incognito* in Sir Walter Scott's *A Legend of Montrose.*

Conrade, Marquis of Montserrat　Christian soldier who is jealous of King Richard; he conspires with the grand master, Giles Amaury, to divide the Christian forces; he is wounded in trial by combat with Sir Kenneth as Richard's champion and is murdered by the grand master in Sir Walter Scott's *The Talisman.*

Major Moody　Industrious card player who ekes out a modest living from fellow club members; playing at Captain Vignolles's, he is content with his small profit in hand from Mountjoy Scarborough in Anthony Trollope's *Mr. Scarborough's Family.*

Mr. Mool　The Gallilee family lawyer; a shy man of kindness and good sense, he sees through and helps to frustrate the schemes of Mrs. Gallilee; at his advice, Mr. Gallilee removes his daughters by stealth from their mother's influence in Wilkie Collins's *Heart and Science.*

Mooney　Feebleminded beadle of Chancery Lane, who is the authority the Cook's Court residents turn to when Nemo's body is found in Charles Dickens's *Bleak House.*

Teddy Mooney　Cabdriver in County Galway who loses his business in the boycott of the gentry; turning against the conspirators, he supplies evidence to convict Terry Lax of murdering Florian Jones in Anthony Trollope's *The Landleaguers.*

Martin Moonface　Celebrated Chancery lawyer, who accuses John Jorrocks of unlawful assembly and inciting a riot because of Jorrocks's zealous fox hunting in Robert Surtees's *Handley Cross.*

Saunders Moonshine　Devout smuggler who is religiously active at home and criminally active at sea in Sir Walter Scott's *The Bride of Lammermoor.*

Moore　Barber of Chapelizod, called in to assist Dr. Dillon to trepan Dr. Barney Sturk in J. Sheridan Le Fanu's *The House by the Churchyard.*

Mrs. Moore　Woman who runs the boardinghouse in Hampstead where Clarissa Harlowe flees after her first escape from Robert Lovelace; charmed and bribed by Lovelace, she betrays Clarissa in Samuel Richardson's *Clarissa: or, The History of a Young Lady.*

Hortense Moore   Sister of the younger Robert and Louis; she thinks highly of herself, remains wedded to her Flemish traditions, and tutors Caroline Helstone in Charlotte Brontë's *Shirley.*

Hortense Gérard Moore   Member of the Antwerp Gérard family, wife of the elder Robert Moore, and mother of Robert, Louis, and Hortense Moore in Charlotte Brontë's *Shirley.*

Louis Gérard Moore   Quiet, sensitive tutor, brother to Robert and Hortense; he teaches Henry Sympson and also Shirley Keeldar, with whom he falls in love; after many difficulties he finally marries her in Charlotte Brontë's *Shirley.*

Robert Moore   Father of Hortense, Louis, and Robert; he passes on his family debts to Robert in Charlotte Brontë's *Shirley.*

Robert Gérard Moore   Mill owner, who loses his foreign market as a result of the Napoleonic wars, gets caught in the battle to mechanize, and is shot and wounded by a worker; he does not have the time or finances to pay court to Caroline Helstone but instead proposes to Shirley Keeldar; he is finally united with Caroline when he recognizes her moral worth in Charlotte Brontë's *Shirley.*

Sylvia Moorhouse   Friend and confidante of Sidwell Warricombe in George Gissing's *Born in Exile.*

Mopsa   An ancient tabby cat, a descendant of the famous Puss that Wore Boots and a civil companion of the Maiden Aunt; she becomes a good friend to Pompey in Francis Coventry's *The History of Pompey the Little.*

Morakanabad   Vathek's prime vizir, whose son Vathek thought he had sacrificed to the Giaour; although faithful, the vizir recognizes the faults of his prince in William Beckford's *Vathek.*

Father Moran   Associate of Father Oliver Gogarty; after Father Oliver has helped him in a crisis, he seems miraculously to recognize Father Oliver's night of crisis and tries to help him in George Moore's *The Lake.*

Tim Moran   Townsperson present when the sexton of Chapelizod finds an old skull while digging a grave for Lady Darby in J. Sheridan Le Fanu's *The House by the Churchyard.*

Count Morano   Venetian nobleman who falls in love

with Emily St. Aubert at the encouragement of her evil guardian Montoni; he argues with Montoni and is severely wounded in an attempt to kidnap Emily from the Castle di Udolpho in Ann Radcliffe's *The Mysteries of Udolpho.*

George Mordaunt   Henry Mandeville's friend and the chief recipient of his letters in Frances Brooke's *The History of Lady Julia Mandeville.*

Mordecai   Elderly Jew in whose house Reginald de St. Leon finds refuge after escaping the procession of victims of the Spanish Inquisition, who are being led to an auto-da-fe in William Godwin's *St. Leon.*

Vanni Mordecastelli   Italian nobleman, governor of Lucca in Castruccio dei Antelminelli's absence; he squelches the conspiracy to overthrow Castruccio by casting its members into prison in Mary Shelley's *Valperga.*

Colonel William Morden   Cousin of Clarissa Harlowe and trustee of her estate; living in Italy, he arrives in England too late to help Clarissa physically, financially, or morally; after her death, he mortally wounds her seducer, Robert Lovelace, in a duel in Samuel Richardson's *Clarissa: or, The History of a Young Lady.*

Mr. Mordicai   Corrupt Jewish money lender who torments the Clonbronys in Maria Edgeworth's *The Absentee.*

Brother Mordlin   Adapter of songs and member of the Brick Lane Branch of the United Grand Junction Ebeneezer Temperance Association, where Mr. Stiggins preaches and Martha Bardell attends services in Charles Dickens's *The Posthumous Papers of the Pickwick Club.*

Dr. More   Royalist and Christian Platonist who becomes spiritual advisor to Lady Cardiff in J. Henry Shorthouse's *John Inglesant, A Romance.*

Adam More   Sir Daniel Brackley's candidate for high constable of Kettley in Robert Louis Stevenson's *The Black Arrow: A Tale of Two Roses.*

M'Callum More   See Marquis of Argyle.

Vich Alister More   Highland chief in Montrose's army and representative of the Lord of the Isles in Sir Walter Scott's *A Legend of Montrose.*

Sir Marmaduke Morecombe   Perpetual member of Mr. Mildmay's Liberal cabinet; as Lord Mount Thistle he becomes Chancellor of the Duchy of Lancaster; he rarely speaks on any issue in Anthony Trollope's *Phineas Finn.*

Richard Clinton, first Earl of Moreland   Gentleman

raised to the peerage by James I; he has two sons: the elder and the heir, Richard, given the conventional education of a nobleman, and Henry, apprenticed to a London merchant, in Henry Brooke's *The Fool of Quality*.

Richard Clinton, second Earl of Moreland Nobleman basically decent but a victim of his aristocratic upbringing; he also has two sons: Richard, a copy of his father, and Harry, reared by peasant foster parents until he is kidnapped by his wise and well-meaning uncle in Henry Brooke's *The Fool of Quality*.

Richard (Dicky) Clinton, third Earl of Moreland A victim of typical aristocratic upbringing; he considers his unaffected younger brother Harry a fool; he dies young, leaving the property and title to Harry in Henry Brooke's *The Fool of Quality*.

Abbe Morellet Frank, honest man, who introduces Harry Ormond to a group of literary men in France because he wants Ormond to see that there is more than dissipation among the men and women of upper French society; the exposure to this group is beneficial to Ormond in Maria Edgeworth's *Ormond*.

Miss Moreton Vain, weak girl; she runs away from her friends to live with Harriot Freke, who leads her into much mischief in Maria Edgeworth's *Belinda*.

Mr. Moreton Respectable clergyman, who earns Harriot Freke's ire when he disapproves of her influence over his cousin, Miss Moreton; he is hired by Lady Delacour to be her chaplain in Maria Edgeworth's *Belinda*.

Mr. Moreton Successor to Mr. Fothergill as land agent and business manager of the (younger) Duke of Omnium; he is charged with informing the Silverbridge electorate that each must vote according to conscience in Anthony Trollope's *The Prime Minister*. He pays Lord Silverbridge's debts for the duke in *The Duke's Children*.

Sir Humphry Moreton Miserly owner of Kenilworth after the death of Lord Leicester in Sophia Lee's *The Recess*.

Dudley Morewood Confidence trickster, who poses as Harry Lorrequer's cousin, Guy Lorrequer, in Paris in Charles Lever's *The Confessions of Harry Lorrequer*.

Mr. Morfin Cheerful, elderly bachelor who works at Paul Dombey's firm and plays the cello; he loves Harriet Carker and eventually marries her in Charles Dickens's *Dombey and Son*.

Morfinn the Minstrel Gandolf's wily servant, who betrays Ralph to his master in William Morris's *The Well at the World's End*.

Judge Morgan Welshman and forty-niner, who runs up the bidding on the *Flying Scud* in Robert Louis Stevenson's *The Wrecker*.

Mr. Morgan Welshman and surgeon's first mate on the *Thunder*; he suffers imprisonment with Roderick Random on complaints by Mackshane and is finally discovered married to the widow of an apothecary in Canterbury in Tobias Smollett's *The Adventures of Roderick Random*. He meets Peregrine Pickle with his friends on their way to Dover in Tobias Smollett's *The Adventures of Peregrine Pickle*.

Mr. Morgan Elderly miser and alcoholic, who marries Miss Melvyn and mistreats her but discovers her worth shortly before his fatal paralysis; he leaves her the estate that becomes Millenium Hall in Sarah Scott's *A Description of Millenium Hall*.

James Morgan Major Pendennis's shrewd valet, who has amassed a small fortune; his attempt to capitalize on information about Colonel Altamont results in his dismissal in William Makepeace Thackeray's *The History of Pendennis*.

Jenny Morgan Woman who runs the Welsh inn where Henry Bellingham falls ill while staying with Ruth Hilton; she has some pity for Ruth but is under pressure from the money and snobbish morality of Bellingham's mother in Elizabeth Gaskell's *Ruth*.

Jessica Morgan Unstable girl and admirer of Samuel Barmby; she pursues useless studies, has a breakdown as a result, and discloses Nancy Lord's secret marriage in George Gissing's *In the Year of Jubilee*.

Susanna Morgan Mr. Morgan's bitter, much-jilted sister, who, repulsive in physical appearance and manner, contrives with her brother to oppress his wife, the former Miss Melvyn, in Sarah Scott's *A Description of Millenium Hall*.

Tom Morgan Old pirate observed drinking with Black Dog at the Spy Glass; on Treasure Island he wants to kill Jim Hawkins, who has blundered into the pirates' lair; he is marooned on the island with Dick Johnson and another pirate at the end of Robert Louis Stevenson's *Treasure Island*.

Morgana Leader of the gypsy band joined by Plantagenet, Lord Cadurcis when he runs away from home; she helps return Plantagenet to his mother in Benjamin Disraeli's *Venetia*.

Evan (Father Campian) Morgans Jesuit priest, a rascal who stays with Eustace Leigh and his father, pretending to be a Welshman, and plots against Queen Elizabeth in Charles Kingsley's *Westward Ho!*.

Professor Moriarty   Criminal mastermind whose unexpected appearance interrupts "Fred Porlock's" coded communication to Sherlock Holmes in Arthur Conan Doyle's *The Valley of Fear*.

Jean Morin   Madame Babette's nephew, also referred to as Victor; he is infatuated with Virginie de Crequy and betrays her lover Clement de Crequy to the French Revolution in Elizabeth Gaskell's *My Lady Ludlow*.

Madame Moritz   French widow, mother of Justine Moritz; she dislikes and mistreats her daughter but allows her to live with the Frankensteins in Mary Shelley's *Frankenstein; or, The Modern Prometheus*.

Justine Moritz   Loyal and trusted family servant of the Frankensteins; weakly defended by Victor Frankenstein, she is executed unjustly for the murder of William Frankenstein in Mary Shelley's *Frankenstein; or, The Modern Prometheus*.

Monsieur Morlaix   A Frenchman whom Deloraine knew long ago in Paris; he and his daughter are also living as exiles in Bruges; his open and ingenuous nature is a reproach to Deloraine's guilty conscience in William Godwin's *Deloraine*.

Mr. Morland   Catherine's father, a prosperous clergyman and father of ten children in Jane Austen's *Northanger Abbey*.

Mrs. Morland   Busy, affectionate mother of Catherine and nine other children in Jane Austen's *Northanger Abbey*.

Catherine Morland   A prosperous clergyman's daughter, whose fondness for romantic fiction leads her into foolish suspicions; guileless, affectionate, and transparent of feeling, she wins the affection of the clever Henry Tilney in Jane Austen's *Northanger Abbey*.

Cecilia (Cissy) Morland   Frank Palmer's cousin, who marries him after he has been rejected by Madge Hopgood, and who does not know he has a daughter in Mark Rutherford's *Clara Hopgood*.

James Morland   Catherine's elder brother, who becomes infatuated with and, for a time, engaged to Isabella Thorpe in Jane Austen's *Northanger Abbey*.

Alban Morley   Guy Darrell's old friend, who undertakes the worldly education of Lionel Haughton in Edward Bulwer-Lytton's *What Will He Do With It? by Pisistratus Caxton*.

George Morley   Clergyman who is cured of a speech impediment by William Waife and reconciles Guy Darrell to the marriage of Sophy and Lionel Haughton in Edward Bulwer-Lytton's *What Will He Do With It? by Pisistratus Caxton*.

Stephen Morley   Visionary radical and friend of Walter Gerard; his passionate but concealed love for Gerard's daughter, Sybil, drives him to attempt to kill Charles Egremont, a rival suitor, and to betray Gerard himself so that he can blackmail Sybil into marrying him; Morley is killed while trying to recover the documents which prove Gerard's claim to the Marney estate in Benjamin Disraeli's *Sybil*.

Dennis Morolt   Norman squire who dies in battle with his master, Raymond Berenger, in Sir Walter Scott's *The Betrothed*.

Mr. Morphew   Canadian physician at whose request Ovid Vere attends a dying scientist; the compassionate act leads to Vere's discovery of the diagnosis and cure of a disease of the nervous system in Wilkie Collins's *Heart and Science*.

Cecil Morphew   Man who raises money through shady deals, opens a photography shop in partnership with Harvey Rolfe, and is rejected by his betrothed because of an earlier love affair in George Gissing's *The Whirlpool*.

Mr. Morrice   A young lawyer who has an accident at the masquerade party, is insensible to insult, and hopelessly pursues Cecilia Beverley from Suffolk to London in Frances Burney's *Cecilia*.

Morris   Faithful woman servant of Margaret and Hester Ibbotson; she is reluctant to leave their service even when they face penury in Harriet Martineau's *Deerbrook*.

Mr. Morris   Timorous revenue officer who, as Rashleigh Osbaldistone's agent, wrongly accuses Francis Osbaldistone of robbery and is instrumental in Rob Roy MacGregor's arrest; sent as a hostage for the outlaw's safety, he is executed by Helen MacGregor in Sir Walter Scott's *Rob Roy*.

Mrs. Morris   Miss Groves's maid; she is surprised by Arabella's impertinent curiosity about her mistress but disloyal enough to reveal her secrets in Charlotte Lennox's *The Female Quixote*.

Dan Morris   Brickmaker of Hogglestock who cashes the cheque that causes so much misery for Josiah Crawley in Anthony Trollope's *The Last Chronicle of Barset*.

Dinah Morris   An orphan raised in a bleak mill town; she becomes a Methodist preacher full of simple and loving expression; she aids all she encounters, especially Hetty Sorrel, her cousin, whom she stays with in prison until her confession and conversion are completed; eventually, Dinah marries Adam Bede, and they raise a family together in George Eliot's *Adam Bede*.

Jack Morris   Harry Warrington's acquaintance, a man who likes to associate with the nobility and toadies to Lord March in William Makepeace Thackeray's *The Virginians*.

Lucy Morris   Energetic and high-principled governess in Lady Fawn's household; she loves Frank Greystock and endures his flirtation with Lizzie Eustace until he comes to his senses and asks her to be his wife in Anthony Trollope's *The Eustace Diamonds*.

Quincey P. Morris   Texan who is an unsuccessful suitor of Lucy Westenra and a friend of Jack Seward and Arthur Holmwood; he dies helping to kill Dracula in Bram Stoker's *Dracula*.

Morrison   Fellow student of Casimir Fleetwood at Oxford and mastermind of the scheme to "honor" the poet Withers with a dinner at which praises turn to jeers in William Godwin's *Fleetwood*.

Susan Morrison   A tenant farmer's daughter, who, by impersonating Lady Betty Lawrence's maid, helps Robert Lovelace kidnap Clarissa Harlowe in Samuel Richardson's *Clarissa: or, The History of a Young Lady*.

Adolphus Morsfield   Rich young man who courts Lady Ormont after her husband fails to introduce her into proper society; he is killed by Captain May in a duel which may have been orchestrated by the jealous Lord Ormont in George Meredith's *Lord Ormont and his Aminta*.

Mary Morstan   Governess who asks Sherlock Holmes and John H. Watson for help in locating her missing father; she becomes Mrs. John Watson at the conclusion of Arthur Conan Doyle's *The Sign of Four*.

Alberick Mortemar (Theodorick of Engaddi)   Hermit known by the Arabs as the Hamako; once a Christian knight, he spends his life alone in the Palestinian deserts as penitence for the death of his beloved; he misinterprets his vision of Sir Kenneth's engagement to Lady Edith Plantagenet in Sir Walter Scott's *The Talisman*.

General Lord Mortimer   Deceased husband of Margaret, Lady Mortimer and one-time adherent to Philip II of Spain in Sophia Lee's *The Recess*.

Mr. Mortimer   Lawyer defending Mr. Cutts on a charge of arson; he hears and dismisses Miriam Tacchi's

perjured testimony in Mark Rutherford's *Miriam's Schooling*.

Mr. Mortimer   Fanny Mortimer's husband, who stabs to death Sedley, the rapist of his wife, but is acquitted of murder in S. J. Pratt's *Pupil of Pleasure*.

Mr. Mortimer   Villainous youngest son of Lord and Lady Mortimer and a powerful landowner in Jamaica; he abducts Matilda and attempts to force her into marriage in Sophia Lee's *The Recess*.

Ann Mortimer   Sister of Sir Roger Mortimer; unmarried, she presides over the Mortimer estate in Charles Maturin's *Melmoth the Wanderer*.

Elinor Mortimer   Granddaughter of Sir Roger Mortimer; she is left at the altar by John Sandal, her cousin, because of a stipulation in Sir Roger's will which entitled her to no more than £5000 if she marries Sandal in Charles Maturin's *Melmoth the Wanderer*.

Fanny Mortimer   Consumptive daughter of Sir Henry Delmore; she is raped by the villain Sedley in S. J. Pratt's *Pupil of Pleasure*.

James Mortimer   Physician, surgeon, medical scholar, and personal friend of the late Sir Charles Baskerville; he first brings the case to the attention of Sherlock Holmes in Arthur Conan Doyle's *The Hound of the Baskervilles*.

Joe Mortimer   Heavy lead in Dick Lennox's acting company; he is sarcastic and unpleasant but loyal in George Moore's *A Mummer's Wife*.

Margaret Mortimer   Beautiful granddaughter of Sir Roger Mortimer and heiress to the Mortimer estate; she later marries John Sandal even though it was Sandal who left Elinor Mortimer, Margaret's sister, at the altar in Charles Maturin's *Melmoth the Wanderer*.

Margaret, Lady Mortimer   Ostensible friend to the Stuart cause who betrays Lord Leicester to Queen Elizabeth and assists in the abduction of Matilda in Sophia Lee's *The Recess*.

Sir Roger Mortimer   Vigorous defender of the Reformers during the rule of Edward; his descendants are tormented by the Wanderer in Charles Maturin's *Melmoth the Wanderer*.

Mortlock   Edinburgh undertaker at Margaret Bertram's funeral in Sir Walter Scott's *Guy Mannering*.

Miss Morton   A peer's daughter and an heiress with a fortune of £30,000; Mrs. Ferrars perceives her as an acceptable wife for Edward Ferrars or—after Edward's engagement to Lucy Steele is made public—for Robert Ferrars in Jane Austen's *Sense and Sensibility*.

Mr. Morton   Scottish clergyman who uses Donald Bean Lean's confession to clear Edward Waverly of criminal charges in Sir Walter Scott's *Waverly*.

Basil Morton   Businessman of scholarly tastes who lives a quiet country life in George Gissing's *The Whirlpool*.

Henry Morton   Son of a Scottish hero; he competes with Lord Evandale (William Maxwell) for the love of Edith Bellenden; he becomes a prisoner of the forces of King James II because he helped Burley (John Balfour) escape; his life is saved by Lord Evandale upon Edith's plea; he becomes a leader of the rebels and is exiled to Holland for his rebellion; he returns with King William of Orange and marries Edith after the death of Evandale in Sir Walter Scott's *Old Mortality*.

James Douglas, Earl of Morton   Proud and ambitious noble, whose dark and suspicious mood hones his bitter tongue in Sir Walter Scott's *The Monastery*. A prominent member of the Scottish privy council, he is a bitter antagonist of Queen Mary of Scotland and a general of the army at Langside in *The Abbot*.

John Morton   Prominent landlord and squire of Bragton who is engaged to the cold and worldly Arabella Trefoil; although she runs after Lord Rufford, Morton forgives her, leaving her, at his death, a substantial legacy in Anthony Trollope's *The American Senator*.

Lucy Morton   Shrewd and successful actress, who counsels and supports the feckless George Hotspur; she advises him to renounce claims to his cousin, Emily Hotspur, for an allowance and settlement of his debts and agrees to marry him in Anthony Trollope's *Sir Harry Hotspur of Humblethwaite*.

Ralph Morton   Squire of Milnwood and Henry Morton's miserly uncle, who tries to bribe Francis Stewart, Sergeant Bothwell to prevent the arrest of Henry in Sir Walter Scott's *Old Mortality*.

Reginald Morton   Quiet, bookish owner of Hoppet Hall who inherits Bragton Hall after the death of John Morton, his cousin; he disapproves of a likely match between Mary Masters and Larry Twentyman and finally marries her himself in Anthony Trollope's *The American Senator*.

Johnnie Mortsheugh   Fiddler and grave digger in Sir Walter Scott's *The Bride of Lammermoor*.

Sir Guy Morville   Baronet of Redclyffe, who over-comes his inherited violent temper through Tractarian devotional practices and the love of his cousin Amy Edmonstone, and who dies on his honeymoon of a fever caught while nursing his cousin Philip Morville in Charlotte Yonge's *The Heir of Redclyffe*.

Phillip Morville   Older cousin of Sir Guy Morville; driven by social and sexual jealousy he unsuccessfully attempts to undermine Sir Guy in the eyes of his guardian, Mr. Edmonstone; he unwittingly causes Sir Guy's death; bowed with remorse, he inherits the Redclyffe estate in Charlotte Yonge's *The Heir of Redclyffe*.

Monimia Morysine   Orphaned niece of Rachel Lennard; raised as an upper servant but secretly educated by Orlando Somerive, she is apprenticed to a dressmaker after refusing the lucrative proposals of a libertine, from whom she is protected by Mrs. Fleming until Orlando finds and marries her, after which she briefly and secretly contributes to their support by doing needlework in Charlotte Smith's *The Old Manor House*.

Moses   Punisher of Faithful for his "secret inclining" to Adam the First in John Bunyan's *The Pilgrim's Progress From this World to That Which Is to Come*.

Dr. Alwin Mosgrave   Physician who specializes in the treatment of mental diseases; he is instrumental in helping Robert Audley commit Lucy Audley to a *Maison de Santeé* in Belgium in Mary Elizabeth Braddon's *Lady Audley's Secret*.

Mr. Moss   Unsuccessful farmer and husband of Gritty Moss in George Eliot's *The Mill on the Floss*.

Mr. Moss   Unscrupulous attorney and agent for Lord St. Erme; he is despised by his son-in-law, Arthur Martindale, in Charlotte Yonge's *Heartsease*.

Gritty Moss   The kind-hearted, poor sister of Mr. Tulliver; she treats Maggie as one of her own children; her husband borrowed money from her brother, who wants it back but cannot bring himself to ruin his sister in George Eliot's *The Mill on the Floss*.

Mahomet M. Moss   Swindling impresario and music teacher from America; he promotes the operatic career of Rachel O'Mahony and wants her to become his mistress in Anthony Trollope's *The Landleaguers*.

Monsignor Mostyn   Music expert who, with Mr. Innes and Ulick Dean, restores the old Catholic music to St. Joseph's; he invites Evelyn Innes to sing a concert to raise money for the convent; he exerts a spiritual power over Evelyn, becoming her confessor in George Moore's *Evelyn Innes*. He becomes the counter-balance to the worldly attractions of Owen Asher and Ulick Dean, advising Evelyn and officiating when she takes the convent vows in *Sister Teresa.*

Motavakel   Vathek's brother, who leads a revolt in the capital city when Vathek and Princess Carathis are away in William Beckford's *Vathek.*

Mother Brimstone   Old woman of loose morals; she uses religion to line her purse and to satisfy her vices in Charles Johnstone's *Chrysal: or, The Adventures of a Guinea.*

Mother Midnight (Mrs. B——,"the governess")   Woman with whom Moll Flanders boards when pregnant with Jemy E.'s child; she is a midwife who convinces her pregnant guests to become prostitutes after they have their babies; later she becomes a pawnbroker and helps Moll dispose of stolen goods, but she eventually becomes a penitent in Daniel Defoe's *The Fortunes and Misfortunes of the Famous Moll Flanders.*

Monsieur Motteville   Parisian investor who loses St. Aubert's fortune in Ann Radcliffe's *The Mysteries of Udolpho.*

Mouchat   Black slave on the Virginia plantation to whom Colonel Jack (as overseer) shows mercy; he acts heroically in Jack's aid and becomes his servant in Daniel Defoe's *The History and the Remarkable Life of the Truly Honourable Colonel Jacques, Commonly Call'd Col. Jack.*

Al Mouhateddin   Religious emissary to Mecca; he watches with horror as Vathek defiles a religious relic brought from the holy city in William Beckford's *Vathek.*

The Misses Mould   Partridge-plump daughters of Mr. Mould; they resemble the puffy-cheeked angels in their father's undertaking establishment in Charles Dickens's *The Life and Adventures of Martin Chuzzlewit.*

Mr. Mould   Undertaker who arranges Anthony Chuzzlewit's lavish funeral, and professional friend of Mrs. Gamp in Charles Dickens's *The Life and Adventures of Martin Chuzzlewit.*

Mrs. Mould   Plump, cheerful wife of the undertaker in Charles Dickens's *The Life and Adventures of Martin Chuzzlewit.*

Mr. Moulder   Obese commercial traveler who rules the roost over other salesmen in discussions of the forgery case involving Lady Mason in Anthony Trollope's *Orley Farm.*

Mary Anne Moulder   Childless wife of the huge Moulder; she spends her life feeding him and sewing back the buttons on his shirts; she engineers the marriage of

her brother, John Kenneby, to Mrs. Smiley in Anthony Trollope's *Orley Farm.*

Charlotte Moulin   The most prosperous of Ethelberta Petherwin's kindred; she keeps a hotel in Rouen, France, in Thomas Hardy's *The Hand of Ethelberta.*

Moullant   Peasant laborer enlisted by Monsieur De Rhíe's servant Maria to help Cornelia escape De Rhíe in Sarah Scott's *The History of Cornelia.*

Bella Mount   Attractive, disreputable woman whom Richard Feverel attempts to save from her wicked ways; she ends up seducing the would-be hero during his separation from Lucy Desborough in George Meredith's *The Ordeal of Richard Feverel.*

Lord Mount Rorke   Frank Escott's uncle, who is kind to Frank on his visit home; he is not entirely sympathetic to Frank's proposed marriage to Maggie Brookes in George Moore's *Spring Days.*

Mr. Mountain   American Indian trader and member of Captain Harris's gang; his account of his adventure in the wilderness is used by Ephraim Mackellar in Robert Louis Stevenson's *The Master of Ballantrae: A Winter's Tale.*

Mrs. Mountain   Faithful, affectionate companion of Madam Esmond in spite of frequent differences between them in William Makepeace Thackeray's *The Virginians.*

Fanny Mountain   Pretty but unamiable childhood friend of Harry Warrington; he marries her in opposition to his mother's wishes and is directed by her, especially in serving with George Washington in the War of Independence in William Makepeace Thackeray's *The Virginians.*

Alfred Mountchesney   Gallant nobleman, whose heroism while protecting Sybil Gerard from the riotous mob helps convince her that she has misjudged the character of the upper classes in Benjamin Disraeli's *Sybil.*

Mr. Mountclere   Lord Mountclere's brother; he accompanies Ethelberta Petherwin's brother Sol Chickerel in an unsuccessful effort to stop the marriage of Ethelberta and Lord Mountclere in Thomas Hardy's *The Hand of Ethelberta.*

Viscount Mountclere   Aged, wealthy, and disreputable suitor of the young widow, Ethelberta Petherwin; though a philanderer and a jealous tyrant, he is free of snobbery; the discovery of her servant-class family does not deter him, and he assists their careers after his marriage in Thomas Hardy's *The Hand of Ethelberta.*

Lord Mountfalcon   Aristocrat who pays Bella Mount

to divert Richard Feverel in London so that he may attempt to seduce Lucy (Desborough) on the Isle of Wight; when Mountfalcon's designs on Lucy become known to him, Richard provokes a duel in which Mountfalcon wounds him in George Meredith's *The Ordeal of Richard Feverel*.

Mountford   Gentleman tutor to young Sedley in one of the interpolated tales in Henry Mackenzie's *The Man of Feeling*.

Chevalier Mountfort   Gallant who helps save Eloise de St. Irvyne from Frederic de Nempere (Ginotti) in Percy Bysshe Shelley's *St. Irvyne*.

Lady Mountjoy   Overbearing wife of Sir Magnus; she relishes her social superiority as wife of the British minister in Brussels in Anthony Trollope's *Mr. Scarborough's Family*.

Florence Mountjoy   Generous, unselfish, and firm-minded daughter of widowed Sarah Mountjoy; despite her mother's ardent wish that she marry Captain Mountjoy Scarborough, she remains steadfast to her love of Harry Annesley, overcoming all obstacles to marry him in Anthony Trollope's *Mr. Scarborough's Family*.

Sir Magnus Mountjoy   Portly British minister in Brussels and uncle of Florence Mountjoy; when her mother tries to separate Florence from Harry Annesley, she takes her to stay with Sir Magnus in Anthony Trollope's *Mr. Scarborough's Family*.

Sarah Mountjoy   Obdurate widowed mother of Florence; she does all she can to separate her daughter from her true love, Harry Annesley, and to persuade her to marry the profligate Captain Mountjoy Scarborough in Anthony Trollope's *Mr. Scarborough's Family*.

Squire Mountmeadow   Pompous magistrate, who advises Dr. Masham of the legal steps to be taken to recover Plantagenet, Lord Cadurcis after he has run off with the gypsies in Benjamin Disraeli's *Venetia*.

Mouse   Creature encountered by Alice while swimming in the pool of tears; it unsuccessfully attempts to "dry" the assembled dripping creatures by reciting British history; after the caucus-race it tells the tail-shaped tale that presages the trial that concludes Lewis Carroll's *Alice's Adventures in Wonderland*.

Citizen Moutard   Commander of the French merchant ship conveying Azemia to Marseilles; the ship is captured by the British warship *Amputator*, commanded by Captain Josiah Wappingshot, in William Beckford's *Azemia*.

Lord De Mowbray   Arrogant nobleman and compan-

ion of George, Lord Marney; his condescending behavior to Sybil Gerard and insensitivity to the plight of the working classes epitomize the aristocracy's failure to improve the condition of England in Benjamin Disraeli's *Sybil*.

Major Mowbray   Son of Mrs. Mowbray and brother of Eleanor Mowbray in William Harrison Ainsworth's *Rookwood*.

Squire (Magog) Mowbray   Father of Olivia and Hector; he is despised by the rector in Thomas Holcroft's *The Adventures of Hugh Trevor*.

Clara Mowbray   Sister of the squire of St. Ronan's; she loves Francis Tyrrell and thought she had married him earlier, but learned she had been betrayed by Valentine Bulmer disguised as Tyrrell; she refuses to make the marriage to Bulmer legitimate and dies without a happy union in Sir Walter Scott's *St. Ronan's Well*.

Eleanor Mowbray   Daughter of Eleanor Rookwood Mobray; she falls in love with her cousin, Ranulph Rookwood, and marries him, having coincidentally discovered she is heir to the Rookwood estates in William Harrison Ainsworth's *Rookwood*.

Eleanor Rookwood Mowbray   Formerly Eleanor Rookwood, the estranged daughter of Sir Reginald Rookwood by his first wife, Eleanor, Lady Rookwood, and mother of a daughter also named Eleanor; she returns with her family to Rookwood Place on the death of Sir Piers Rookwood in William Harrison Ainsworth's *Rookwood*.

Emmeline Mowbray   Orphan raised by servants under the protection of her uncle, Lord Montreville, and thought to be illegitimate; she endures the imperious, lachrymose, and frenzied importunities of his son, Frederick Delamere, who courts her against his parents' wishes and hers, until in Godolphin she finds the respect for her judgment, integrity, and candor not accorded by her own family in Charlotte Smith's *Emmeline: The Orphan of the Castle*.

Hector Mowbray   Squire Mowbray's rich eldest son; he is alternately an antagonist and a friend to Hugh Trevor in Thomas Holcroft's *The Adventures of Hugh Trevor*.

John Mowbray   Young squire of St. Ronan's who is desperate for money; he gambles with the usurper Lord Etherington (Valentine Bulmer), agrees to persuade his sister Clara to marry Etherington, and kills Etherington in a duel when he learns the truth of Clara's mock marriage in Sir Walter Scott's *St. Ronan's Well*.

Olivia Mowbray   Noble, beautiful, and young daughter of the squire; after being convinced of Hugh Trevor's honest character, she finally becomes Olivia Trevor in Thomas Holcroft's *The Adventures of Hugh Trevor*.

William de Mowbray   Fat, fun-loving knight in Henry III's court in Ann Radcliffe's *Gaston de Blondeville*.

Miss Mowcher   Dwarf who is a hairdresser and manicurist; she has James Steerforth for a client along with others from the upper class; she tries to assist in tracing Emily Peggotty after Emily runs off with Steerforth and is instrumental in the arrest of Steerforth's valet, Littimer, after he turns criminal in Charles Dickens's *The Personal History of David Copperfield*.

Christian Moxey   Scientific friend of Godwin Peak; for many years he remains infatuated with a married woman; rejected by her after her husband's death, he marries his cousin Janet Moxey in George Gissing's *Born in Exile*.

Janet Moxey   Cousin of Christian and Marcella Moxey; she becomes a doctor and is engaged to Christian when he recovers from his infatuation with another woman in George Gissing's *Born in Exile*.

Marcella Moxey   Intellectual and emancipated girl, who feels an unrequited affection for Godwin Peak, generously resists betraying him, and makes him her heir when she dies in George Gissing's *Born in Exile*.

Mr. Moy   Geoffrey Delamayn's attorney, who presents the evidence for the "Scotch marriage" of Anne Silvester and Arnold Brinkworth; when the evidence in refuted by the testimony of Delamayn's own letter, he breaks with his client in Wilkie Collins's *Man and Wife*.

Mr. Moylan   Lawyer and willing accomplice of Barry Lynch in the plot to cheat Anty Lynch of her fortune in Anthony Trollope's *The Kellys and the O'Kellys*.

Jabesh M'Ruen   Moneylender who haunts Charley Tudor for repayment of loans in Anthony Trollope's *The Three Clerks*.

Much-afraid   Daughter of Despondency in John Bunyan's *The Pilgrim's Progress From this World to That Which Is to Come*.

Lord Muchross   Elegant and dissipated companion to Lord Snowdown in George Moore's *Mike Fletcher*.

Elspeth Mucklebackit   Aged mother of Saunders Mucklebackit; she confesses her complicity in the trick to deceive William, Earl of Glenallan into believing he had committed incest and dies after she repeats the confession to Oldbuck (Jonathan Oldenbuck) in Sir Walter Scott's *The Antiquary*.

Maggie Mucklebackit   Wife of Saunders and mother of Steenie; she sells fish at high prices to Oldbuck (Jonathan Oldenbuck) and grieves over the death of her son in Sir Walter Scott's *The Antiquary*.

Saunders Mucklebackit   Old fisherman and smuggler, who helps pull Isabel Wardour and her father, Sir Arthur Wardour, to safety after they are saved from drowning by Edie Ochiltree and William Lovel in Sir Walter Scott's *The Antiquary*.

(Steenie) Mucklebackit   Oldest son of Saunders; he courts Jenny Rintherout, helps Edie Ochiltree trick Herman Dousterswivel, and drowns while fishing with his father; his funeral is the occasion for confession by his grandmother to the Earl of Glenallan in Sir Walter Scott's *The Antiquary*.

Mr. Mucklewheel   A hosier who is manipulated by James Pawkie into persuading the borough council to celebrate his retirement with a "piece of plate" and a "vote of thanks" in John Galt's *The Provost*.

Mrs. Mucklewrath   The smith's wife, who goads her husband into attacking Edward Waverly in Sir Walter Scott's *Waverly*.

Habakkuk Mucklewrath   Fiery preacher to Cameronian rebels, who is insane from his captivity by government authorities; he utters a dying prophecy of doom against Colonel John Grahame in Sir Walter Scott's *Old Mortality*.

John Mucklewrath   Cairnvreckan smith, whom Edward Waverly kills in Sir Walter Scott's *Waverly*.

Mrs. Mudbury   Susannah Sanders's neighbor, who is a witness in Martha Bardell's breach-of-promise suit against Samuel Pickwick in Charles Dickens's *The Posthumous Papers of the Pickwick Club*.

Sarah Muddy   Young widow with a fortune; she marries Ferdinand in London, leaves him, and sues him for bigamy in Tobias Smollett's *The Adventures of Ferdinand Count Fathom*.

Mrs. Mugford   Vulgar, kind wife of Frederick Mugford; concerned for Philip Firmin, she orders her husband to restore him to his former position in William Makepeace Thackeray's *The Adventures of Philip on His Way through the World*.

Frederick Mugford   Proprietor of the *Pall Mall Gazette*; his vulgarity causes Philip Firmin to quarrel with him, but his good nature comes to Philip's rescue in William Makepeace Thackeray's *The Adventures of Philip on His Way through the World*.

Heinrich Muhler   A young German merchant, who is engaged to M. Paul Emanuel's goddaughter, Justine-Marie Sauveur, in Charlotte Brontë's *Villette*.

Lord Muirfell   Father of Lady Flora in Robert Louis Stevenson's *Weir of Hermiston: An Unfinished Romance*.

Oglow Muley   Sometimes known as Muley Oglow, a wealthy Constantinople merchant expected to be Azemia's future husband in William Beckford's *Azemia*.

Marmaduke Muleygrubs   Local magistrate so corrupt that he takes tradesmen who are out of work and threatens to lock them up for vagrancy if they refuse to crush the stones that he sells to surveyors; John Jorrocks arranges a fox hunt for him in Robert Surtees's *Handley Cross*.

Amelie Mullenberg   One of the eldest and most turbulent pupils learning sewing under Frances Henri's direction at Mlle. Reuter's school in Charlotte Brontë's *The Professor*.

Cora Muller   Young woman who befriends Averil Ward during her exile in the United States in Charlotte Yonge's *The Trial*.

Professor Mullet   Professor of Education in America, who writes pamphlets signed "Suturb" (Brutus reversed) in Charles Dickens's *The Life and Adventures of Martin Chuzzlewit*.

Mr. Mullins   Gentleman who makes an unsuccessful proposal of marriage to Clarissa Harlowe on the encouragement of her brother, James, in Samuel Richardson's *Clarissa: or, The History of a Young Lady*.

Jack Mullins   Customer at the Six Jolly Fellowship Porters in Charles Dickens's *Our Mutual Friend*.

Mrs. Mulready   Widow owner of Mohill Shebeen, a village pub where locals plot against Captain Ussher in Anthony Trollope's *The Macdermots of Ballycloran*.

Michael Mumblazen   Sir Hugh Robsart's confidant, a master of heraldry who always speaks in heraldic metaphors in Sir Walter Scott's *Kenilworth*.

Mr. Mumbray   Prominent citizen of a provincial town who decides to run for Parliament on the Conservative ticket but is beaten by the incumbent candidate in George Gissing's *Denzil Quarrier*.

Serena Mumbray   Unstable young woman of means who accepts Eustace Glazzard's proposal and, after some hesitation, marries him in George Gissing's *Denzil Quarrier*.

Clarence Mumford   Man who regrets taking in a young woman of lower social position as a lodger in George Gissing's *The Paying Guest*.

Emmeline Mumford   Lady who takes in a girl of lower social position as a lodger and comes to regret it when her love affairs create turmoil and nearly burn the house down in George Gissing's *The Paying Guest*.

Tib Mumps   Landlady of the alehouse where Dandie Dinmont stops; she is in league with robbers and sets him up for a burglary in Sir Walter Scott's *Guy Mannering*.

Mr. Munden   Betsy Thoughtless's tyrannical and despotic husband, who keeps a mistress after his marriage in Eliza Haywood's *The History of Miss Betsy Thoughtless*.

Mundungus   (parody of Dr. Samuel Sharp)   Smelfungus's traveling companion, who also possesses a jaundiced view of the world in Laurence Sterne's *A Sentimental Journey through France and Italy*.

Lord Munodi   Former Governor of Lagado; he entertains Lemuel Gulliver and arranges for him to see the Grand Academy of Projectors in Lagado in Jonathan Swift's *Travels into Several Remote Nations of the World. In Four Parts. By Lemuel Gulliver*.

Murdoch ("Philistine")   The able-bodied manservant of Sampson, Lord Maclaughlan; he must carry Sampson wherever he needs to go in Susan Ferrier's *Marriage*.

Martin Murdoch   Scottish teacher of mathematics who teaches Maria Spence "fluxions," a form of calculus, in Thomas Amory's *The Life of John Buncle, Esq*.

Meg Murdockson   An old hag who hates Effie Deans because Geordie Robertson (George Staunton) loves her instead of Meg's daughter, Madge Wildfire, whom he also seduced; as Effie Deans's midwife, she tries to destroy the child, convinces Effie that the baby is dead, and testifies that Effie killed the child; she later confesses and is hanged as a witch in Sir Walter Scott's *The Heart of Midlothian*.

Clara Copperfield Murdstone   David Copperfield's widowed mother, who is childlike and indulges her boy; she marries Edward Murdstone, who is cruel to her and David; she dies, along with her new baby, while David is away at school in Charles Dickens's *The Personal History of David Copperfield*.

Edward Murdstone   Stepfather of David Copperfield; he is stern to his wife, whose property he legally appropriates; he is cruel and harsh to David and casts him off after the death of David's mother in Charles Dickens's *The Personal History of David Copperfield*.

Jane Murdstone Metallic, harsh sister of Edward Murdstone; she lives with him and Clara Copperfield after their marriage and rules over Clara, taking over the housekeeping; she is cruel to David; later she is Dora Spenlow's companion in Charles Dickens's *The Personal History of David Copperfield*.

Fred Murgatroyd A worker at Robert Moore's mill who is tied up by machine breakers and discovers that their leader is Barraclough, his rival for Sarah, the Moores' servant in Charlotte Brontë's *Shirley*.

Count Muriani Guest at a ball held by the Marquis de Mazzini; he encourages Hippolitus de Vereza's attentions to Julia de Mazzini in Ann Radcliffe's *A Sicilian Romance*.

Marquis Muriani Nobleman who mistakenly captures Julia de Mazzini in his attempt to find his own runaway daughter in Ann Radcliffe's *A Sicilian Romance*.

Mr. Murphy Crooked attorney to the unsuspecting Dr. Harrison; he finds himself undone when Robinson confesses about the forged will that disinherited Amelia Booth; he is hanged in Henry Fielding's *Amelia*.

Catherine Murphy Housekeeper for Father Peter and Father Oliver Gogarty in George Moore's *The Lake*.

Paddy (Little Beau) Murphy Famous Member of Parliament; though he is also known for his dancing ability, John Buncle deems himself a better dancer in Thomas Amory's *The Life of John Buncle, Esq*.

Patsy Murphy Old villager who tells the history and legends of Irish families to Father Oliver Gogarty and his associate Father Moran in George Moore's *The Lake*.

Mr. Murray Boorish, indelicate, tippling gentleman, who first courts Polly Darnford and then her sister Nancy without distinguishing between them in Samuel Richardson's *Pamela, or Virtue Rewarded*.

Mr. Murray Blustering country squire and owner of Horton Lodge; his self-indulgence leads to gout in Anne Brontë's *Agnes Grey*.

Mrs. Murray Handsome wife of Mr. Murray; her indulgence of her children makes it difficult for Agnes to exert her own authority while teaching them in Anne Brontë's *Agnes Grey*.

Charles Murray Youngest child of the Murrays; his maliciousness makes him impossible for Agnes to control, so he goes to school having acquired little knowledge in Anne Brontë's *Agnes Grey*.

Sir David Murray Prince Henry's friend and confidant, who encourages Matilda to flee from King James in Sophia Lee's *The Recess*.

James Stuart, Earl of Murray Ambitious leader of the Protestant faction in Scotland and the illegitimate son of James V; he favors Halbert Glendinning, who serves under him, and whom he invests with Mary Avenel's estates after the two marry in Sir Walter Scott's *The Monastery*. As Regent of Scotland he attempts to restrict the violence directed toward his half sister, Queen Mary, in *The Abbot*.

John Murray Elder son whose roughness makes him unteachable by Agnes Grey; he is sent to school during the first year in Anne Brontë's *Agnes Grey*.

Mary Murray Grandmother of Loudon Dodd and second wife of Alexander Loudon; they visit her grave before Dodd returns to America in Robert Louis Stevenson's *The Wrecker*.

Matilda Murray A "veritable hoyden," the younger daughter of the family; she prefers larking outside to doing her lessons with Agnes Grey, who has little influence in amending her wild manners in Anne Brontë's *Agnes Grey*.

Rosalie Murray Beautiful elder daughter of the Murrays, pleasant but vain and shallow, who attracts suitors only to drop them when she tires of the sport; she becomes Lady Ashby when she marries the despicable Sir Thomas Ashby and has a child for whom she cares as little as a lapdog in Anne Brontë's *Agnes Grey*.

Edna Murrell Musically gifted village schoolmistress, whom the younger Owen Sandbrook marries on impulse; she is deserted by him and dies soon after bearing their son in Charlotte Yonge's *Hopes and Fears*.

Mr. Murthwaite Intrepid explorer thoroughly versed in Indian lore; he explains to Rachel Verinder that the huge diamond she wears may be a Hindoo religious object and a source of danger to her; when the diamond is stolen, he helps in its recovery and witnesses its having been restored to its rightful place in the forehead of the Moon-god in India in Wilkie Collins's *The Moonstone. A Romance*.

Muscula A light woman of Rome whom Heliodora conspires to have murdered in George Gissing's *Veranilda*.

Sir Giles Musgrave Saxon knight from Cumraik serving in Montrose's army in Sir Walter Scott's *A Legend of Montrose*.

Mrs. Musgrove Wife to one Charles Musgrove, mother of another, and grandmother of a third; she is a fond though inelegant parent of many children; her desire to hear news of her deceased sailor son brings Captain Frederick Wentworth into contact with Anne Elliot again in Jane Austen's *Persuasion*.

Charles Musgrove (the elder)   Country squire and father-in-law of Mary Elliot Musgrove; his estate, Uppercross, is the scene of Anne Elliot's renewed acquaintance with Captain Wentworth in Jane Austen's *Persuasion*.

Charles Musgrove   Heir to Uppercross estate, where he has his own house; he is a good son and an affectionate brother; husband of Anne Elliot's sister Mary following his rejection by Anne, he is often at odds with his fretful wife; he is kindhearted and addicted to sport in Jane Austen's *Persuasion*.

Charles Musgrove (the youngest)   Elder child of Charles and Mary Musgrove; his injury provides Anne Elliot with excuse to delay her reintroduction to Captain Wentworth in Jane Austen's *Persuasion*.

Henrietta Musgrove   Eldest daughter of the elder Charles Musgrove and, like her sister Louisa, somewhat infatuated with Captain Wentworth; she instead marries her cousin Charles Hayter in Jane Austen's *Persuasion*.

Louisa Musgrove   Vivacious and headstrong second daughter of the elder Charles Musgrove; she shares Captain Wentworth's attentions with her sister until Henrietta's engagement seems to leave the field clear for her; however, in her convalescence from a serious head injury she becomes engaged to Captain Benwick in Jane Austen's *Persuasion*.

Mary Elliot Musgrove   Youngest of the three Elliot sisters, wife to Charles Musgrove, and mother of two little boys; she is always imagining that she is being neglected; she invites Anne Elliot on a visit, where Anne again meets Captain Wentworth in Jane Austen's *Persuasion*.

Walter Musgrove   Younger child of Charles and Mary Musgrove in Jane Austen's *Persuasion*.

Marquis of Mushroom   Father of Wilhelmina, Countess of Fairville; he enjoys playing leapfrog with his children in William Beckford's *Modern Novel Writing; or, the Elegant Enthusiast*.

Augustus Musselboro   Objectionable, shady businessman, who is Dobbs Broughton's partner in money swindles in Anthony Trollope's *The Last Chronicle of Barset*.

Mr. Musselwhite   Disgraced Englishman who is forced to live idly in Italy while supported by his relatives; when his allowance is increased he is able to marry Barbara Denyer in George Gissing's *The Emancipated*.

Baba Mustapha   Uncle of Shibli Bagarag and chief barber to the Court of Persia; he assists his nephew in the shaving of Shagpat, and, for his assistance, is named King of Oolb by Shibli in George Meredith's *The Shaving of Shagpat*.

Lord Mutanhed   Richest and most eligible young man in Bath but also very stupid in Charles Dickens's *The Posthumous Papers of the Pickwick Club*.

Mrs. Mutimer   Richard Mutimer's working-class mother, who is contemptuous of the wealth he inherits and refuses to change her ways in George Gissing's *Demos*.

Alice Mutimer   Young working-class woman, who becomes lazy and idle after her brother comes into a fortune; against her brother's will she marries a man who bullies her and who is ultimately found to have another wife and family in George Gissing's *Demos*.

Arry Mutimer   Richard Mutimer's dissolute young brother, who refuses to work after his brother comes into a fortune and is eventually jailed for theft in George Gissing's *Demos*.

Richard Mutimer   Working-class union leader, who inherits a fortune and builds an industrial plant, using its profits to further Socialist principles; he abandons his working-class sweetheart and marries a middle-class girl, but then loses his fortune and his factory, falls into disgrace, and is killed when a Socialist meeting turns to a riot in George Gissing's *Demos*.

Muzzle   Footman to George Nupkins in Charles Dickens's *The Posthumous Papers of the Pickwick Club*.

Muzzled-Abi   Governor of Oglow Muley's harem; he is ordered to fetch Azemia to Marseilles, where his master is detained by business in William Beckford's *Azemia*.

M'Vourigh   Highland chief in Montrose's army in Sir Walter Scott's *A Legend of Montrose*.

My Lady (Tabby, Lovey)   Wife of the Sub-Warden and mother of Uggug; she helps her husband to usurp the Warden and gain the authority of Outland for her husband and her son; she is oblivious to the meaning of her own words in Lewis Carroll's *Sylvie and Bruno*. Empress of Outland, she finally repents her misdeeds in *Sylvie and Bruno Concluded*.

My Lord   Nobleman who is also a jockey and who throws a race in Charles Johnstone's *Chrysal: or, The Adventures of a Guinea*.

Alice Myers   Arthur Huntingdon's mistress, who

comes to Grassdale under the guise of little Arthur's governess, but who leaves Huntingdon before his final illness in Anne Brontë's *The Tenant of Wildfell Hall.*

John Myner   English art student who advises Loudon Dodd to invite his father to Paris; he is later brutally honest with Dodd when he wants a loan in Robert Louis Stevenson's *The Wrecker.*

Myrtilla   Sylvia's sister and Philander's wife, whose love for Cesario provides Philander with an excuse for his own transgressions with Sylvia in Aphra Behn's *Love Letters Between a Nobleman and His Sister.*

Mysie   Faithful old Ravenswood servant in Sir Walter Scott's *The Bride of Lammermoor.*

Mysterious Old Gentleman   Anonymous character who tells Richard about the history of the Berkshire region in Thomas Hughes's *The Scouring of the White Horse.*

Moley Mystic   (caricature of Samuel Taylor Coleridge) Owner of Cimmerian Lodge; he continually resides in an intellectual fog of his own making in Thomas Love Peacock's *Melincourt.*

N

Augusta, Marchioness of N Noblewoman in love with Captain Carlisle; she follows him to England disguised as a boy in S. J. Pratt's *Tutor of Truth*.

Lady Frances N. Lady of wealth and high rank who admires (Sir) Charles Grandison and is proposed by her family to his father as a bride for him; Sir Charles breaks off the treaty with tact and without offense in Samuel Richardson's *Sir Charles Grandison*.

Pandora Nadasti Sweet, simple, and beautiful girl, whom Charles de St. Leon, using his mother's name de Damville, wishes to marry; she falls in love with Charles's father, who is using the alias D'Aubigny, and whose youthful appearance is attained with the aid of the philosopher's stone in William Godwin's *St. Leon*.

Mr. Nadgett Mysterious secret-inquiry agent in the service of Tigg Montague and London landlord of Tom Pinch in Charles Dickens's *The Life and Adventures of Martin Chuzzlewit*.

Mr. Nadin Chief Constable in Manchester, who arrests Zachariah Coleman during his visit with the condemned Jean Caillaud in Mark Rutherford's *The Revolution In Tanner's Lane*.

Major Nagen Austrian who schemes for Countess Anna von Lenkenstein; in exchange, she promises herself to him in George Meredith's *Vittoria*.

Naggitt *Glumm* (flying man) who places second in the flying competition organized by Peter Wilkins in Robert Paltock's *The Life and Adventures of Peter Wilkins*.

Mr. Nagle Brass founder who insists upon payment from Mr. Furze at the time of his bankruptcy in Mark Rutherford's *Catharine Furze*.

Mr. Naird Surgeon who cares for the suicidal and distraught Elinor Joddrel in Frances Burney's *The Wanderer*.

Mr. Namby Sheriff's deputy who takes Samuel Pickwick to the Fleet debtors' prison in Charles Dickens's *The Posthumous Papers of the Pickwick Club*.

Nan Cook at an inn; she mistakes Geoffry Wildgoose for her lover in a dark bedroom, disrobes, and is caught in the act by another guest, who in turn circulates the story in Richard Graves's *The Spiritual Quixote*.

Nan Mr. B——'s servant who acts as Pamela Andrews's jailer in Samuel Richardson's *Pamela, or Virtue Rewarded*.

Totty Nancarrow Lively and independent-minded working-class girl, under suspicion as a Catholic, who refuses an undependable lover and marries a reliable workingman, sharing her small inheritance with him in George Gissing's *Thyrza*.

Nance Tunstall townswoman Bennet Hatch questions about Nick Appleyard in Robert Louis Stevenson's *The Black Arrow: A Tale of Two Roses*.

Nancy Faithful old servant of the Brownes, who gives Maggie the affection she needs in Elizabeth Gaskell's *The Moorland Cottage*.

Nancy Prostitute who lives with Bill Sikes and works for Fagin; she pities Oliver Twist, tries to save him from Fagin, and is murdered by Bill Sikes in Charles Dickens's *Oliver Twist*.

Nancy (Nanny) Chambermaid Coquettish servant at Robin's inn who lusts after Tom Jones during his convalescence in Henry Fielding's *The History of Tom Jones*.

Mr. Nandy Mrs. Plornish's beloved and worn-out father, who lives in the workhouse, is patronized and referred to as "my pensioner" by William Dorrit, and unwittingly causes trouble for Amy Dorrit with her family when she accompanies him arm-in-arm to the Marshalsea prison in Charles Dickens's *Little Dorrit*.

Nanetta Faithful maid who brought up Ardelisa de Vinevil; she travels with the family to Turkey, remains loyal to Ardelisa in her flight from her pursuers, and is shipwrecked with her on Delos; she marries Joseph once they return to France in Penelope Aubin's *The Strange Adventures of the Count de Vinevil and His Family*.

Nanhoa (Queen of the Scarlet Dragons) Chosen bride of Prince Bonbennin bonbobbin-bonbobbinet; taking the shape of a blue cat, she saves him from a spell cast by Queen Barbacela in the shape of a white mouse, in an oriental fable told by Lien Chi Altangi in Oliver Goldsmith's *The Citizen of the World*.

Nanny Orphaned crossing-sweep, who is befriended by Diamond, falls ill, and is taken to the hospital by Mr. Raymond; she works as a nanny for Diamond's mother and moves with the family and Cripple Jim to Mr. Raymond's estate in George MacDonald's *At the Back of the North Wind*.

Narcissa Beautiful young heiress, who lives in Sussex with her drunken and tyrannic brother; she is pursued by the brutal Sir Timothy Thicket but marries Roderick Random against her brother's wishes in Tobias Smollett's *The Adventures of Roderick Random*.

Captain Nares Businesslike captain of the *Norah Criena* and former first mate of the *Gleaner*; he prefers loyalty to law in Robert Louis Stevenson's *The Wrecker*.

Miss Nares Village milliner in Harriet Martineau's *Deerbrook*.

Robert Narramore Prosperous though lazy friend of Maurice Hilliard; he is not aware that Hilliard loves Eve Madeley, whom Narramore makes love to and ultimately marries in George Gissing's *Eve's Ransom*.

Narrator An old man when he narrates a story told to him when he was fourteen and visiting his uncle Charles in Chapelizod; the story is of Mr. Mervyn, Paul Dangerfield, Barney Sturk, Charles Nutter, and the other townspeople of Chapelizod in 1767 in J. Sheridan Le Fanu's *The House by the Churchyard*.

Narrator Middle-aged man who has come from London to Elveston because of health problems to see an old friend, Dr. Arthur Forester; he becomes Arthur's confidant in matters of love and experiences trances and eerie episodes that transport him to Outland and Fairyland; he is the earthly companion of Sylvie and Bruno in Lewis Carroll's *Sylvie and Bruno*. He continues his relationship with the little fairies and helps Arthur win Lady Muriel Orme in *Sylvie and Bruno Concluded*.

Narse Royal slave in Sir Walter Scott's *Count Robert of Paris*.

Charles (Charley), Lord Naseby Rich aristocrat who is a student of social issues and is interested in setting up experimental workshops run along socialist lines in Mrs. Humphry Ward's *Sir George Tressady*.

Nasgig Intrepid and penetrating *lask* (slave), who earns his freedom and becomes a regional governor in Robert Paltock's *The Life and Adventures of Peter Wilkins*.

Richard Nash Master of Ceremonies at Bath; Harriet (Fitzpatrick) ignores his advice to shun Brian Fitzpatrick in Henry Fielding's *The History of Tom Jones*. An opponent of John Wesley's preaching practices, he disrupts a Methodist meeting with loud music in Richard Graves's *The Spiritual Quixote*.

Mr. Nasmyth An excellent clergyman, who marries Miss Temple, the headmistress of Lowood, and takes her to a distant home in Charlotte Brontë's *Jane Eyre*.

General Nasta Tall, middle-aged, black-bearded soldier, greatest Lord of the Zu-Vendi people; he starts a civil war after Queen Nyleptha denies him her hand in marriage; he is killed by Umslopogaas while attempting to storm the palace in H. Rider Haggard's *Allan Quatermain*.

Nathan Young, intelligent disciple of Isaac Levi; he assists in exposing John Meadows's villainy in Charles Reade's *It Is Never Too Late to Mend*.

The Native Ill-treated servant of Major Bagstock in Charles Dickens's *Dombey and Son*.

Natura Compassionate and curious hero, who is heir to a good estate but gets himself into debt; he is a man of spirit and honor in Eliza Haywood's *Life's Progress Through the Passions: or, the Adventures of Natura*.

Natura's Wife Shameless woman who sleeps with her brother-in-law in Eliza Haywood's *Life's Progress Through the Passions: or, the Adventures of Natura*.

Adolf Naumann German artist who sees Dorothea Brooke on her honeymoon and desires to capture her beauty on canvas; in order to be allowed to paint Dorothea, he flatters her husband, Edward Casaubon, by asking him to pose for the head of St. Thomas Aquinas in George Eliot's *Middlemarch*.

Neal Gentleman in attendance upon Argyle in Sir Walter Scott's *A Legend of Montrose*.

Mr. Neal Thin, taciturn Scots traveler at a German spa; he unwillingly hears Allan Wrentmore's dying confession, a tale of intrigue over wills and heirs involving the Armadales in Wilkie Collins's *Armadale*.

Vanbrugh Neal Cambridge don and former tutor of Edward Manisty; he is able to convince Manisty that his book on Italy promulgates Jesuitical superstitions in Mrs. Humphry Ward's *Eleanor*.

Mr. Nearthewinde Political agent for Gustavus Moffat in his unsuccessful contest against Sir Roger Scatcherd for the Barchester seat in Parliament in Anthony Trollope's *Doctor Thorne*.

Mr. Neckett (Coavins) The bailiff who arrests Harold Skimpole for debt and eventually dies, leaving three small children in Charles Dickens's *Bleak House*.

Charlotte (Charley) Neckett Mr. Neckett's eldest daughter, who looks after her younger siblings following her father's death and becomes Esther Summerson's maid in Charles Dickens's *Bleak House*.

Emma Neckett Eighteen-month-old child, who is supported by her older sister Charley in Charles Dickens's *Bleak House*.

Tom Neckett   Younger brother of Charley (Charlotte); around five years old, he minds his younger sister Emma while Charley is away working in Charles Dickens's *Bleak House*.

Nectabanus   Mischievous dwarf and Queen Berengaria's slave; he lures Sir Kenneth from his sentry post; sent by King Richard to Saladin as punishment, he witnesses the murder of Conrade, Marquis of Montserrat in Sir Walter Scott's *The Talisman*.

Uncle Ned (Taveeta, King of Islael)   Sympathetic native crew member aboard the *Farallone*; he tells Robert Herrick his tale of exile and suffering among the whites in Robert Louis Stevenson's *The Ebb-Tide: A Trio and a Quartette*.

Neddy   Friend of Mr. Roker in the Fleet debtors' prison in Charles Dickens's *The Posthumous Papers of the Pickwick Club*.

Mrs. Neefit   Socially ambitious wife of Thomas; having persuaded her husband to buy a villa in Hendon and provide her with a one-horse carriage, she is bored and restless, but she firmly supports her daughter, Polly, in her attachment to Ontario Moggs in Anthony Trollope's *Ralph the Heir*.

Maryanne (Polly) Neefit   Robust, strong-willed daughter of Thomas Neefit, the breeches-maker; despite her father's insistence that she marry Ralph Newton, heir to the estate of Newton Priory and heavily in his debt, she refuses to be sold, and marries her sweetheart, Ontario Moggs, in Anthony Trollope's *Ralph the Heir*.

Thomas Neefit   Stout, voluble breeches-maker with hectoring manners obsessed with marrying his daughter, Polly, into society; he orders her to marry Ralph Newton, the heir to Newton Priory, who owes him money; furious and saddened by her opposition, he finally relents in Anthony Trollope's *Ralph the Heir*.

Beatrice de Negra   Count di Peschiera's sister, who is beloved by Frank Hazeldean and forced by Count di Peschiera to further his schemes against the Riccabocca family in Edward Bulwer-Lytton's *"My Novel," by Pisistratus Caxton*.

La Contessa Negri   Lord Mahogany's paramour, whom he murders with poisoned sweetmeats as she poisons him with wine in William Beckford's *Modern Novel Writing; or, the Elegant Enthusiast*.

Alfred Neigh   Suitor of heroine Ethelberta Petherwin in Thomas Hardy's *The Hand of Ethelberta*.

Mrs. Neighborly   Friendly neighbor of Henry Clinton in Henry Brooke's *The Fool of Quality*.

Christopher Neilson   Lively old Glasgow surgeon, who tends to Francis Osbaldistone's wound after his fight with his cousin Rashleigh Osbaldistone in Sir Walter Scott's *Rob Roy*.

Nekayah   Sister of Rasselas; she accompanies him on his abortive search for human happiness in Samuel Johnson's *The History of Rasselas, Prince of Abissinia*.

Nello   The barber who befriends Tito Melema and helps him sell his jewels in George Eliot's *Romola*.

Nemo   See Captain Hawdon.

Monsieur Nemours   Lawyer who helps Pierre de La Mott flee his debtors in Paris and who later defends him in his trial in Ann Radcliffe's *The Romance of the Forest*.

Nerkes   Princess Carathis's Negress attendant, who forms love relationships with ghouls and enjoys romping in graveyards and other strange activities in William Beckford's *Vathek*.

Nero (His Majesty, Monarch of Dogland)   A Newfoundland, ruler of Dogland; he provides Sylvie and Bruno with a banquet and lodgings on their way to Fairyland; he escorts them to the boundaries of Dogland and plays fetch the stick with them in Lewis Carroll's *Sylvie and Bruno*. Nero, the dog at Hunter's farm, is made invisible by Sylvie and helps catch an apple thief in *Sylvie and Bruno Concluded*.

Madeline Stanhope, Signora Neroni   Beautiful, seductive, crippled younger daughter of the Reverend Vesey Stanhope; she has left an abusive husband to return to her parents' roof; she holds court from her couch to entrap admirers; she involves Mr. Slope in a flirtation which brings about his downfall in Anthony Trollope's *Barchester Towers*.

Paulo Neroni   False, worthless, abusive Italian husband, whom Madeline Stanhope Neroni has left in Anthony Trollope's *Barchester Towers*.

Theodora Nesbit   Lady Martindale's aunt, who has systematically thwarted Lady Martindale's intimacy with her children; she despises the wife of her nephew Arthur Martindale and attempts to leave a heritage of family discord by the terms of her will in Charlotte Yonge's *Heartsease*.

The Misses Nettingall   Heads of a girls' boarding school in Canterbury in Charles Dickens's *The Personal History of David Copperfield*.

Mr. Neuchatel   Wealthy banker and friend of Endymion Ferrars; he is an influential force in political affairs and is created Lord Hainault at the end of Benjamin Disraeli's *Endymion.*

Adriana Neuchatel   Daughter of Mr. Neuchatel; she falls in love with Endymion Ferrars and anonymously gives him £20,000 so that he can run for the House of Commons; she eventually marries Endymion's friend Mr. Waldershare in Benjamin Disraeli's *Endymion.*

Fidus Neverbend   Public servant of fierce integrity who with Alaric Tudor investigates government interests in Cornish tin mines in Anthony Trollope's *The Three Clerks.*

Jack Neverbend   Idealist son of the president of Britannula; he loves Eva Crasweller and on her behalf opposes his father's law that requires compulsory euthanasia for her father now that he is approaching the mandatory disposal age of sixty-eight in Anthony Trollope's *The Fixed Period.*

John Neverbend   President of an island near New Zealand; he decrees that all inhabitants must be prepared for euthanasia by entering a college at sixty-seven where they enjoy their creature comforts until their next birthday; when the British navy arrives, Neverbend yields, the law is repealed, and he goes into exile in Anthony Trollope's *The Fixed Period.*

Lactimel Neverbend   Snobbish, unmarried daughter of Fidus Neverbend; she toadies to the wealthy Mrs. Valentine Scott in Anthony Trollope's *The Three Clerks.*

Sarah Neverbend   Sensible wife of John Neverbend, the president of Britannula, an ex-British colony near New Zealand; she tries to persuade her husband to relax the compulsory euthanasia law he has established and encourages a match between her son, Jack, and Eva Crasweller in Anthony Trollope's *The Fixed Period.*

Ugolina Neverbend   Younger sister of Lactimel; she longs for romance in Anthony Trollope's *The Three Clerks.*

Neville   See George Curtis.

Mrs. Neville   Widowed mother of Fred and Jack; she is overwhelmed by the Earl of Scroope's generosity in naming Fred as his heir and cowed in the presence of the earl in Anthony Trollope's *An Eye for an Eye.*

Alithea Rivers Neville   A commoner whose uncouth father rejects her childhood friend John Falkner as her suitor in favor of Sir Boyvill Neville; she has a son, Gerald Neville; she accidentally drowns during Falkner's attempt to liberate her from her tyrannical husband in Mary Shelley's *Falkner.*

Sir Boyvill Neville   Haughty, morose baronet; he is a tyrannical husband to Alithea Rivers Neville and an insensitive father to Gerald, their son; convinced of his wife's infidelity after her disappearance, he divorces her and mistreats their son; he brings murder charges against John Falkner but later forgives him in Mary Shelley's *Falkner.*

Fred Neville   Selfish, weak-willed cavalry officer, who seduces Kate O'Hara and then refuses to marry her because to do so would go against the wishes of the Earl of Scroope, whose heir he is; thrown from a cliff by Kate's desperate mother, he is killed in Anthony Trollope's *An Eye for an Eye.*

Gerald Neville   Sullen but compassionate son of Sir Boyvill and Alithea Neville; his sole purpose is to discover the circumstances of his mother's disappearance and exonerate her; unaware of John Falkner's responsibility in the death of his mother, he nurses him and falls in love with his adopted daughter, Elizabeth Raby, in Mary Shelley's *Falkner.*

Jack Neville   Fred's younger brother; after Fred has seduced Kate O'Hara and made her pregnant, he urges him to marry her and take the consequences; after Fred dies, Jack becomes Earl of Scroope and marries Sophia Mellerby in Anthony Trollope's *An Eye for an Eye.*

Mr. Newcome   High Church clergyman who befriends Robert Elsmere even though he is opposed to Elsmere's philosophy in Mrs. Humphry Ward's *Robert Elsmere.*

Lady Ann Newcome   Affectionate if shallow daughter of Lady Kew and wife of Sir Brian Newcome; her six children include Barnes and Ethel in William Makepeace Thackeray's *The Newcomes.*

Barnes Newcome   Snobbish, self-satisfied, carefully immoral, heartless eldest son of Sir Brian and Lady Ann Newcome; he continually thwarts his cousin Clive; his ill treatment of his wife, Lady Clara (Pulleyn), drives her to elope in William Makepeace Thackeray's *The Newcomes.*

Barnes Newcome (the younger)   Son of Lady Clara (Pulleyn) and Barnes Newcome; Ethel Newcome devotes herself to his care after Lady Clara's elopement in William Makepeace Thackeray's *The Newcomes.*

Sir Brian Newcome   Elder twin brother of Hobson Newcome and half brother of Colonel Newcome; he is stately and pompous and a morally ineffective uncle to Clive and father to Ethel in William Makepeace Thackeray's *The Newcomes.*

Clara Newcome   Daughter of Lady Clara (Pulleyn) and Barnes Newcome; Ethel Newcome devotes herself to her care after Lady Clara's elopement in William Makepeace Thackeray's *The Newcomes*.

Clemency Newcome   Doctor Jeddler's charming, hefty, useful housekeeper, who is clumsy and simple, but so cheerful, organized, and outgoing that she is beloved; she ends up knowing more about life than she ever thought possible and marries Benjamin Britain in Charles Dickens's *The Battle of Life*.

Clive Newcome   Warm-hearted, lively, generous hero, whose ambitions to become a painter are supported by his father, Colonel Newcome; he is thwarted in his love for his cousin Ethel and unhappy in his marriage to Rosey Mackenzie; his marriage to Ethel is probable at the end of William Makepeace Thackeray's *The Newcomes*.

Emma Honeyman Casey Newcome   A silly widow, mistreated by her late husband; Colonel Tom Newcome marries her out of pity; she dies, having had one child, Clive, in William Makepeace Thackeray's *The Newcomes*.

Ethel Newcome   Unselfish and original heroine, who intends to make a brilliant, worldly marriage and rejects her cousin Clive Newcome; Lady Clara (Pulleyn) Newcome's elopement causes her to question her values; she breaks her engagement to Lord Farintosh to devote herself to Lady Clara's children; her marriage to the widowed Clive is anticipated at the end of William Makepeace Thackeray's *The Newcomes*.

Hobson Newcome   Sir Brian Newcome's twin brother and Colonel Newcome's half brother, a selfish, genial, shrewd banker in William Makepeace Thackeray's *The Newcomes*.

Maria Newcome   Hobson Newcome's wife, an aspiring hostess to the intelligentsia in William Makepeace Thackeray's *The Newcomes*.

Sophia Alethea Hobson Newcome   Pious second wife of Thomas Newcome and mother of (Sir) Brian and Hobson Newcome; she quarrels with her stepson, (Colonel) Tom Newcome, in his youth, but relents just before her death in William Makepeace Thackeray's *The Newcomes*.

Susan Newcome   First wife of Thomas Newcome; she dies after giving birth to her only child, Tom (later Colonel Newcome), in William Makepeace Thackeray's *The Newcomes*.

Thomas Newcome   Honest, thrifty weaver, who rises to partnership in the wealthy London house of Hobson Brothers, Cloth Factors; he has one son, (Colonel) Tom, by his first wife, Susan, and twin sons, (Sir) Brian and Hobson, by his second wife, Sophia Alethea Hobson, in William Makepeace Thackeray's *The Newcomes*.

Colonel Tom Newcome   Gallant Indian warrior, father of Clive Newcome and half brother of Brian and Hobson Newcome; he amasses and then loses a vast fortune; he behaves with chivalry, fortitude and naiveté in William Makepeace Thackeray's *The Newcomes*.

Tommy Newcome   Clive and Rosey Mackenzie Newcome's son, to whom Clive is devoted in William Makepeace Thackeray's *The Newcomes*.

Inspector Newcomer   Investigator from Scotland Yard brought by Mr. Utterson to Edward Hyde's household to query his servants about Hyde's whereabouts during the murder of Sir Danvers Carew in Robert Louis Stevenson's *The Strange Case of Dr. Jekyll and Mr. Hyde*.

Captain Newenden   Mrs. Glenarm's uncle, who has doubts as to Geoffry Delamayn's character and on her behalf attends the informal hearing of the "Scotch marriage" issue in Wilkie Collins's *Man and Wife*.

Mr. Newland   Ambitious law clerk, who tries to prove Geoffry Wildgoose and Jeremiah Tugwell guilty of stealing a horse but is overruled by the magistrate Mr. Aldworth in Richard Graves's *The Spiritual Quixote*.

Elizabeth-Jane Newson   Daughter of Michael Henchard's wife and believed by him to be his own child, born before he sold his wife to the sailor Richard Newson; she marries Henchard's business rival Donald Farfrae after the death of Lucetta Le Sueur; the final blow to Henchard is the discovery that Elizabeth-Jane is Newson's natural daughter in Thomas Hardy's *The Mayor of Casterbridge*.

Richard Newson   Kind-hearted sailor who years earlier purchased the drunken Michael Henchard's wife, Susan, and daughter; his happy life with Susan ended when he was presumed drowned; his return at the novel's end to reclaim Elizabeth-Jane, the girl Henchard thought his long-lost daughter, as his own natural child completes the destruction of Henchard's reputation and spirit in Thomas Hardy's *The Mayor of Casterbridge*.

Mr. Newthorpe   Annabel's convalescent father, an intellectual who oversees her education in George Gissing's *Thyrza*.

Annabel Newthorpe   Studious middle-class girl, who at first rejects Walter Egremont's proposal but suffers when she hears that he is in love with another woman and ultimately accepts him in George Gissing's *Thyrza*.

Gregory Newton   Proud owner of Newton Priory in

Hampshire; he dearly wishes to pass the estate to his natural son, Ralph, rather than to the legal heir, his nephew, also named Ralph; he is negotiating the reversion of the estate when he dies on the hunting field before the matter is resolved in Anthony Trollope's *Ralph the Heir*.

Gregory Newton (the younger) Rector of Newton Peele and the generous and high-principled younger brother of Ralph, the heir to Newton Priory; for many years he is devoted to Clarissa Underwood, whom he finally marries, in Anthony Trollope's *Ralph the Heir*.

Ralph Newton Much-loved illegitimate son of Squire Gregory Newton, who wishes to make him heir to Newton Priory but is prevented from doing so by entail; with the fortune his father has bequeathed him he buys a farm in Norfolk and is able to marry Mary Bonner in Anthony Trollope's *Ralph the Heir*.

Ralph Newton (the heir) Squire Gregory Newton's scapegrace nephew, the legal heir to Newton Priory; widely in debt, he makes up to Mary Bonner and is tempted into a mercenary marriage with Polly Neefit, the daughter of a breeches-maker to whom he owes money; his uncle's death relieves him of this match, and he marries Gus Eardham in Anthony Trollope's *Ralph the Heir*.

Nicanor Corrupt father of Oliver, Ferdinand, and Cordelia; he is victimized by his double in iniquity, Oliver, in Sarah Fielding's *The Cry*.

Nicanor (Protospathaire) The First Swordsman, or general-in-chief, of the imperial army; he is in opposition to Achilles Tatius in Sir Walter Scott's *Count Robert of Paris*.

Father Nicholas Prosaic and ancient monk, who wearies his fellow monks with descriptions of life with the preceding abbot; he collapses under the pressures of the Reformation in Sir Walter Scott's *The Monastery* and in *The Abbot*.

Master Nicholas of Wethermel Osberne Wulfsson's grandfather, who raised him after the death of his parents in William Morris's *The Sundering Flood*.

Samuel Nickem Hard-drinking clerk of Gregory Masters; he collects evidence against Goarly and Scrobby in the mystery of the poisoned foxes in Anthony Trollope's *The American Senator*.

Nickits Former owner of the estate Josiah Bounderby owns; Bounderby boastfully contrasts Nickits's fortunes to his own in Charles Dickens's *Hard Times*.

Mrs. Nickleby Foolishly optimistic mother of Nicholas

and Kate; she cannot understand why her brother-in-law mistreats her family, speaks in a wildly unconnected way, and naively thinks Sir Mulberry Hawk can help her daughter in Charles Dickens's *The Life and Adventures of Nicholas Nickleby*.

Kate Nickleby Heroine who works as a dressmaker for Madame Mantalini and is pursued by Sir Mulberry Hawk but rescued by her brother, Nicholas; her uncle, Ralph Nickleby, is willing to have her seduced in order to secure Lord Frederick Verisopht as a borrower in Charles Dickens's *The Life and Adventures of Nicholas Nickleby*.

Nicholas Nickleby Hero left penniless by his father's death; his uncle Ralph Nickleby finds work for him with Wackford Squeers at Dotheboys Hall in Yorkshire; outraged by Squeers's cruel treatment of the boys, who are starved and beaten, Nicholas beats Squeers with a whip; he later is an actor with the Vincent Crummles Theatrical Company, saves his sister Kate from Sir Mulberry Hawk's clutches, and is hired by the Cheeryble brothers; he marries Madeline Bray, whom he rescues from the lust of Arthur Gride in Charles Dickens's *The Life and Adventures of Nicholas Nickleby*.

Ralph Nickleby Unscrupulous money lender and uncle to Nicholas and Kate Nickleby; he resents having to provide for them and their mother; resentment of Nicholas turns into hatred when Nicholas assists Smike, Ralph's illegitimate son (warehoused at Dotheboys Hall), beats up Squeers, and batters Sir Mulberry Hawk who, with Ralph's help, was attempting to seduce Kate; he hangs himself when his plots are exposed in Charles Dickens's *The Life and Adventures of Nicholas Nickleby*.

Nicodemus Colorful figure, who is a follower of Jesus; he informs Joseph of Arimathea of events leading to Jesus's crucifixion in George Moore's *The Brook Kerith*.

Nicor Trusted minister to Georigetti; he is corrupted by the rebel Harlokin; he is reprieved by Peter Wilkins in Robert Paltock's *The Life and Adventures of Peter Wilkins*.

Jean Nicot Evil-minded painter, who represents the coming scourge of the French Revolution in Edward Bulwer-Lytton's *Zanoni*.

Lord Nidderdale Good-natured nincompoop cousin of the Duchess of Omnium; he becomes a director of the company selling shares in a nonexistent American railroad; the parentally favored aspirant to Marie Melmotte's fortune, he continues to act as her friend in spite of her refusal; he finds himself becoming fond of her too late, when the Melmotte scandal is breaking in Anthony Trollope's *The Way We Live Now*. He has married the daughter of Lady Cantrip, who consults him about Frank Tregear in *The Duke's Children*.

Mr. Niggards   Wealthy gentleman; his prosecution of a stolen loaf of bread enables Henry Clinton to save Giffard Homely from the machinations of an avaricious aristocrat in Henry Brooke's *The Fool of Quality*.

Mr. Nightingale   Curmudgeonly father of Jack Nightingale; Tom Jones and Squire Allworthy convince him to accept his son and his unendowered daughter-in-law, Nancy Miller, in Henry Fielding's *The History of Tom Jones*.

Uncle Nightingale   Jack Nightingale's hypocritical uncle, who salutes his nephew's marriage for love until he learns that the marriage has not yet taken place but is scheduled for the next day, whereupon he urges his nephew to escape; he rages against his own daughter's elopement in Henry Fielding's *The History of Tom Jones*.

Harriet Nightingale   Cousin to Jack Nightingale; she throws her father into an uproar by marrying a poor clergyman for love; the cousins' respective escapades assist each father's becoming reconciled to his own child in Henry Fielding's *The History of Tom Jones*.

Jack Nightingale   Friend of Tom Jones; he is a boarder at Mrs. Miller's and has made love to her daughter, Nancy; Jack reconsiders abandoning her under pressure from Tom; he marries her against his father's wishes in Henry Fielding's *The History of Tom Jones*.

Nina   Old peasant woman, who adopts Leonardo di Loredani in Charlotte Dacre's *Zofloya; or, The Moor*.

Miss Niphet   Young woman who marries Lord Curryfin in Thomas Love Peacock's *Gryll Grange*.

Susan Nipper   Dark, small maid of Florence Dombey; although quick-tempered and hasty, she is kind-hearted and loyal; she loses her position after scolding Paul Dombey about his treatment of Florence; she marries Mr. Toots in the end in Charles Dickens's *Dombey and Son*.

Cristal Nixon   Hugh Redgauntlet's manservant, who betrays his master and all the Jacobite rebels and is killed by Nanty Ewart in Sir Walter Scott's *Redgauntlet*.

John Nixon   Inventor of an elaborate musical clockwork, which entertains John Buncle during his stay at Miss Wolf's in Clankford, Yorkshire in Thomas Amory's *The Life of John Buncle, Esq*.

Noah O'Tim's   A machine breaker who is second in command under the leadership of Barraclough in Charlotte Brontë's *Shirley*.

Nobbs   Lady Constantine's coachman in Thomas Hardy's *Two on a Tower*.

Noble Lord   Unnamed peer whose plan to seduce Amelia Booth is foiled when Molly Bennet reveals his identical campaign of seduction that previously compromised herself in Henry Fielding's *Amelia*.

Noble Lord   First English master of Chrysal; he loses the coin at the gaming table in Charles Johnstone's *Chrysal: or, The Adventures of a Guinea*.

Noble Spaniard   Gallant and brave young man, who is so impressed by his treatment by the English that he promises to go and intercede for peace; he is killed by Spanish troops while under a flag of truce in Charles Johnstone's *Chrysal: or, The Adventures of a Guinea*.

Henrietta Noble   The Reverend Farebrother's aunt, who intervenes to reconcile Dorothea Brooke and Will Ladislaw in George Eliot's *Middlemarch*.

Will Noble   Printer and organizer of a workingmen's club in George Gissing's *Workers in the Dawn*.

Nobleman of the First Rank   A man of weak reason who is the object of the Widow of Great Distinction in Charles Johnstone's *Chrysal: or, The Adventures of a Guinea*.

Nobleman of the Track   Lord who pays his duty to the Prince and earns the Prince's disapproval for repeating gossip in Charles Johnstone's *Chrysal: or, The Adventures of a Guinea*.

Bishop of Nocera   Cleric and second son of the Marchese della Porretta; any compromise which would allow Sir Charles Grandison to marry his sister, Lady Clementina della Porretta, without conversion from his Church of England "heresy" is unacceptable to him in Samuel Richardson's *Sir Charles Grandison*.

Mr. Noddy   Scorbutic medical student, who picks a fight with Mr. Gunter at Bob Sawyer's party in Charles Dickens's *The Posthumous Papers of the Pickwick Club*.

Harriet Noel   John Buncle's first encounter, who, though indifferent to love, promises marriage to him; she is given to long theological debates with Buncle; at twenty-four she contracts smallpox and dies before marrying in Thomas Amory's *The Life of John Buncle, Esq*.

Newman Noggs   Ralph Nickleby's clerk, who hates himself for his weakness in being Nickleby's victim and agent; restored to self-respect by Nicholas Nickleby's example and need of him, Noggs helps Nicholas by informing him of his uncle's machinations against him and finds him a job teaching French to the Kenwigses' daughters in

Charles Dickens's *The Life and Adventures of Nicholas Nickleby*.

Nominee to the Mock Monastery   Aristocrat who is witty, charming, vain, and high-spirited and who plays a trick on the Monastery members by arranging for a baboon to come when the devil is called in Charles Johnstone's *Chrysal: or, The Adventures of a Guinea*.

Nominee to the Mock Monastery   Younger son, a captain who goes on half-pay at the outbreak of war, who is a cypher of fashion, and who debauches the daughter of his friend; he is accepted into the Mock Monastery in Charles Johnstone's *Chrysal: or, The Adventures of a Guinea*.

Noorna bin Noorka   Sorceress, assistant to, and the eventual bride of Shibli Bagarag; she is the daughter of the Vizier Feshnavat; although she appears to be a wrinkled old crone, by the end of the story her beauty has been restored to her in George Meredith's *The Shaving of Shagpat*.

Noot   A hermit and philosopher skilled in the secrets of nature; he lived in the hidden caverns of an extinct volcano and before his death taught She the secret of longevity in H. Rider Haggard's *She*.

Mr. Norbert   Prematurely jaded and debauched young gentleman, who pays 400 guineas for Fanny Hill's faked maidenhead and, despite near impotence, keeps her as his mistress before dying suddenly in John Cleland's *Memoirs of a Woman of Pleasure*.

Countess Christina Norbert   Object of the boy Contarini Fleming's romantic infatuation; years later, she influences his decision to give up the self-interest of political life in order to write literature that she inspires in Benjamin Disraeli's *Contarini Fleming*.

Duke of Norfolk   Man who falls in love with and secretly weds the captive Mary, Queen of Scots, by whom he fathers Matilda and Ellinor; he is detected in a plot to raise military support for Mary and is executed in Sophia Lee's *The Recess*.

Earl of Norfolk   Marshal of the field at Henry III's tournament, who confronts the ghost of Reginald de Folville in Ann Radcliffe's *Gaston de Blondeville*.

Norman   Forester at Ravenswood Castle in Sir Walter Scott's *The Bride of Lammermoor*.

Edward Norman   Kindly clergyman, father of Helen Norman; he cares for Arthur Golding after his father dies in George Gissing's *Workers in the Dawn*.

Helen Norman   Arthur Golding's lover and moral

guide; she educates herself about social problems and does charitable work but is never able to marry Golding in George Gissing's *Workers in the Dawn*.

Henry (Harry) Norman   Modest clerk balked of his love, Gertrude Woodward; he finds happiness at last with her sister, Linda, in Anthony Trollope's *The Three Clerks*.

Miss Norris   The prettier of Mr. Norris's two daughters, who, though an abolitionist, laughs at young Martin Chuzzlewit's sympathy for the "ridiculous" blacks in Charles Dickens's *The Life and Adventures of Martin Chuzzlewit*.

Mr. Norris   A well-traveled New York merchant, an abolitionist disdainful of Negroes, and a kinsman of Mr. Bevan; he makes his guest, young Martin Chuzzlewit, welcome until the revelation that Martin came to America as a steerage passenger in Charles Dickens's *The Life and Adventures of Martin Chuzzlewit*.

Mr. Norris Junior   Mr. Norris's son, a student, who "regularly corresponds with four members of the English peerage" in Charles Dickens's *The Life and Adventures of Martin Chuzzlewit*.

Mrs. Norris   The faded wife of Mr. Norris; she is a self-proclaimed egalitarian, who chats of her familiarity with English duchesses and finds her neighbors insufficiently genteel for her acquaintance in Charles Dickens's *The Life and Adventures of Martin Chuzzlewit*.

Mrs. Norris   Eldest sister of Lady Bertram and Mrs. Price; she is a penny-pinching busybody, who treats her niece Fanny Price with selfish unkindness but injudiciously spoils her Bertram nieces, especially Maria; Sir Thomas Bertram comes to dislike her officiousness in Jane Austen's *Mansfield Park*.

Norroy   Keeper of Henry III's arms in Ann Radcliffe's *Gaston de Blondeville*.

North Wind   God's agent, called variously Bad Fortune, Evil Chance, Ruin, and Death; appearing to Diamond as a beautiful woman with enveloping hair, she can change size; she takes Diamond on night journeys and, when he is seriously ill, to the country at her back, a beautiful, peaceful land; she maternally guides Diamond through life and death in George MacDonald's *At the Back of the North Wind*.

Ensign Northerton   Arrogant soldier, who slanders Sophia Western when Tom Jones toasts her, then assaults Tom with a bottle in Henry Fielding's *The History of Tom Jones*.

Lord Northlake Husband of Susan Graywell, Lady Northlake; according to his niece Zo Gallilee he "owns Scotland"; he receives her and her sister there when their father removes them from Mrs. Gallilee in Wilkie Collins's *Heart and Science*.

Susan Graywell, Lady Northlake Good-humored, kind sister of Robert Graywell and Mrs. Gallilee; envy of her brilliant marriage drives Mrs. Gallilee to extravagance, to science, and to cruel scheming in Wilkie Collins's *Heart and Science*.

Countess of Northumberland Exile to whom the Duke of Norfolk has sent money in Sophia Lee's *The Recess*.

Earl of Northumberland Supporter of the Duke of Norfolk's plan to free the pregnant Mary, Queen of Scots in Sophia Lee's *The Recess*.

Arthur Northway Estranged husband of Lilian Quarrier; he was arrested for forgery at the scene of his wedding and imprisoned; his attempt to blackmail the Quarriers just before the election drives Lilian to suicide in George Gissing's *Denzil Quarrier*.

Emperor Norton San Francisco madman, who thinks he is emperor of the two Americas and has appointed Jim Pinkerton a cabinet member in Robert Louis Stevenson's *The Wrecker*.

Farmer Norton Tenant farmer on Mr. B——'s estate, to whose cottage Pamela is taken the first night of her abduction in Samuel Richardson's *Pamela, or Virtue Rewarded*.

Lady Norton Sir Ulick O'Shane's niece, who comes to care for his home after he divorces his third wife, Lady O'Shane, in Maria Edgeworth's *Ormond*.

Mr. Norton London deputy marshal and a friend of Thomas Clarke; he escorts Sir Launcelot Greaves to the debtors' prison looking for Aurelia Darnel in Tobias Smollett's *The Adventures of Sir Launcelot Greaves*.

John Norton Heir to a Sussex estate; his mother wishes him to marry Kitty Hare; he decides on the priesthood, then on turning his estate into a monastery, then on marrying Kitty; upon her sudden death, he decides the world will be his monastery in George Moore's *A Mere Accident*. His strong moral conscience is evident in his philosophical discussions in *Mike Fletcher*.

Judith ("Goody") Norton Clarissa Harlowe's former governess, whose piety, kindness, and discretion helped to form Clarissa's morality; she endeavors to reconcile Clarissa and the other Harlowes, but the family refuse

her advice as prejudiced in Clarissa's favor; she is an occasional correspondent with Clarissa in Samuel Richardson's *Clarissa: or, The History of a Young Lady*.

Lizzie Norton Widowed mother of John; she is a sharp, determined woman, who wants John to marry and stay on the estate; she is a close friend of William Hare, the neighboring parson and father of Kitty in George Moore's *A Mere Accident*.

Lady Clementina Norwynne Arrogant daughter of an impoverished Scottish earl; she is the unloving wife of the elder William Norwynne and mother of the younger; she dies from the effects of a cold attributable to her body-baring fashionable dress in Elizabeth Inchbald's *Nature and Art*.

Henry Norwynne (the elder) The musically talented one of a pair of orphaned brothers without money or connections; he supports his brother, William, by working as a musician until a broken wrist prevents his playing the violin; neglected by the now-prosperous William, he leaves England with his son, Henry, and is shipwrecked on an island off the African coast; years later he is sought for and rescued by his son; they return to England to live in contented poverty in Elizabeth Inchbald's *Nature and Art*.

Mrs. Henry Norwynne Wife of the elder Henry Norwynne; she is despised by William and Lady Clementina Norwynne because she was a public singer; she does not long survive the birth of her only child, Henry, in Elizabeth Inchbald's *Nature and Art*.

Henry Norwynne (the younger) Only son of the fiddler Henry Norwynne; raised on a desert island, he returns to England to offer "innocent" critical perspective on social institutions; he discovers the abandoned infant of Agnes Primrose and is for a period reviled for his supposed complicity with Rebecca Rymer in begetting the child; he takes a long sea voyage to rescue his father from the island and returns to marry Rebecca in Elizabeth Inchbald's *Nature and Art*.

William Norwynne (the elder) The scholarly one of a pair of orphaned brothers without money or connections; the support of his musical brother Henry enables him to pursue his studies; rising to prosperity as a clergyman, he marries the well-connected Lady Clementina; governed always by selfish interests, he neglects his brother in need and spoils his son, William; he becomes a bishop; his brother and nephew, returning to England after many years, find his funeral in progress; he is spoken of with public praise and private contempt by everyone in Elizabeth Inchbald's *Nature and Art*.

William Norwynne (the younger) The foppish,

spoiled only son of William and Lady Clementina Norwynne; he seduces Agnes Primrose and abandons her, unaware that she is pregnant; he becomes a barrister and a justice and condemns Agnes to death for forgery without recognizing her; learning too late her identity and history, he seeks his son, only to learn that the youth has died of grief in Elizabeth Inchbald's *Nature and Art*.

Madam Nosebag   Gossipy army wife, who rides with Edward Waverly to London and later sounds the alarm when she realizes who he is in Sir Walter Scott's *Waverly*.

Mrs. Nosnibor   Very courteous wife of Senoj Nosnibor; she is a passionate defender of musical banks in Samuel Butler's *Erewhon*. She embraces Sunchildism and has visions in *Erewhon Revisited Twenty Years Later*.

Arowhena Nosnibor   Senoj Nosnibor's younger daughter, with whom Jack Higgs falls in love; she agrees to run away with him and leaves in a hot-air balloon; she gives birth to a son in England in Samuel Butler's *Erewhon*. Her death in England is a reason for Higgs's return to Erewhon in *Erewhon Revisited Twenty Years Later*.

Senoj Nosnibor   A leading citizen of Erewhon; he is an embezzler and a swindler dealt with sympathetically by Erewhonian society and harshly by straighteners in Samuel Butler's *Erewhon*. He embraces Sunchildism in *Erewhon Revisited Twenty Years Later*.

Zulora Nosnibor   Senoj Nosnibor's haughty elder daughter, whom Jack Higgs actively dislikes but is expected to marry in Samuel Butler's *Erewhon*. She never embraces Sunchildism and eventually has a separate residence from her parents in *Erewhon Revisited Twenty Years Later*.

Notary   Frustrated man who, after an argument with his wife, happens to be called from the street to record a man's will; Yorick's fragment ends before the notary hears the dying man's story in Laurence Sterne's *A Sentimental Journey through France and Italy*.

Earl of Nottingham   Enemy of the Earl of Essex (2) and Lord Southampton in Sophia Lee's *The Recess*.

Nourjahad   The favored but flawed rising star in Schemzeddin's court; his secret wishes for eternal life and inexhaustible riches discredit him; he is restored to favor and made first in power beside the Schemzeddin after the sultan's scheme leads him to renounce his wishes in Frances Sheridan's *The History of Nourjahad*.

Nourmahal   Sultana of Persia as wife of Schemzeddin; she is reported by Hasem to be the mother of the supposed Prince Schemerzad (Schemzeddin) in Frances Sheridan's *The History of Nourjahad*.

Nouronihar   Vain, grasping daughter of Emir Fakreddin; anxious to share in the treasures Vathek is seeking, she foils her father's plans to protect her, abandons Gulchenrouz in order to accompany the smitten prince, and is damned with him in William Beckford's *Vathek*.

Mr. Novit   Young Laird of Dumbiedikes's shrewd business manager, who presents a blustery facade in Sir Walter Scott's *The Heart of Midlothian*.

Lord No Zoo   Disputed noble ancestor of the Chuzzlewits, identified as his grandfather by the dying Toby Chuzzlewit in Charles Dickens's *The Life and Adventures of Martin Chuzzlewit*.

Mrs. Nubbles   Homely, hardworking, widowed mother of Kit Nubbles; she believes in her son's goodness and innocence in Charles Dickens's *The Old Curiosity Shop*.

Christopher (Kit) Nubbles   Nell Trent's clumsy but good-hearted friend, who worked for her grandfather; he becomes a servant in the Garland household but is framed by the Brasses and Daniel Quilp for theft; he becomes imprisoned but is cleared and eventually marries the servant girl Barbara in Charles Dickens's *The Old Curiosity Shop*.

Jacob Nubbles   One of Kit Nubbles's two brothers in Charles Dickens's *The Old Curiosity Shop*.

Mrs. Nugent   "Well-bred" widow of a Glasgow University professor; she becomes the third Mrs. Balwhidder in John Galt's *Annals of the Parish*.

Grace Nugent   Beautiful, kind, intelligent cousin and beloved of Lord Colambre; at first mistakenly believed to be illegitimate, she later is proven to be an heiress; she eventually weds Colambre in Maria Edgeworth's *The Absentee*.

Mr. Null   Incompetent physician, whose well-meant prescriptions aggravate Carmina Graywell's illness; able to cure her, Dr. Benjulia as consultant prefers only to voice approval of the treatment because he wishes to study her decline in Wilkie Collins's *Heart and Science*.

Antonio (Menassah-ben-Solomon) di Nunez   The son of the Jew Don Fernan di Nunez in Charles Maturin's *Melmoth the Wanderer*.

Fernan di Nunez   Jew who initially provides a haven for Alonzo Moncada from the Spanish Inquisition; Fernan di Nunez is himself taken by the Inquisitors; before he is secured, di Nunez leads Moncada to a secret chamber which allows Moncada to escape in Charles Maturin's *Melmoth the Wanderer*.

Maria (Rebekah-ben-Solomon) di Nunez The wife of the Jew Don Fernan di Nunez in Charles Maturin's *Melmoth the Wanderer*.

Rhoda Nunn Strong-minded feminist, who believes women should avoid marrying for economic reasons and learn to support themselves; nevertheless, she falls in love and plans to marry but cannot come to an agreement with her lover in George Gissing's *The Odd Women*.

Lady Nunnely Sir Philip's mother, who, supported by her daughters, dislikes Sir Philip's choice of a wife in Charlotte Brontë's *Shirley*.

Sir Philip Nunnely The only baronet in the area; his wealth and position are not enough to win Shirley Keeldar, who turns down his proposal of marriage in Charlotte Brontë's *Shirley*.

Johnny Nunsuch Child who is an accidental witness to events on Egdon Heath; his testimony about the death of Mrs. Yeobright causes Clym Yeobright to separate from his wife in Thomas Hardy's *The Return of the Native*.

Susan Nunsuch Johnny's superstitious mother, who believes Eustacia Vye to be a witch who has cast a spell on the boy; her own practice of black magic, the burning of an image of Eustacia, is simultaneous with Eustacia's drowning in Thomas Hardy's *The Return of the Native*.

Mrs. Nupkins Bewigged and majestic wife of George Nupkins in Charles Dickens's *The Posthumous Papers of the Pickwick Club*.

George Nupkins Mayor of Ipswich, who puts Samuel Pickwick in the stocks and is the employer of Mary, Sam Weller's sweetheart, in Charles Dickens's *The Posthumous Papers of the Pickwick Club*.

Henrietta Nupkins Haughty and ill-natured daughter of George and Mrs. Nupkins in Charles Dickens's *The Posthumous Papers of the Pickwick Club*.

Nurse Onetime servant in the household of Colonel Jack's parents; she is paid to raise him but dies when he is only ten in Daniel Defoe's *The History and the Remarkable Life of the Truly Honourable Colonel Jacques, Commonly Call'd Col. Jack*.

Nurse Charoba's nurse, an enchantress who conjures demons to frustrate the efforts of Gebirus to build a city to win the hand of Charoba in the appended romance "The History of Charoba, Queen of Egypt" in Clara Reeve's *The Progress of Romance*.

Nurse Scurrilous woman who, entrusted with the care of Lucy Sindall after her mother's death, eventually turns her over to Sir Thomas Sindall and reappears at the end to tell Sindall that Lucy is his daughter in Henry Mackenzie's *The Man of the World*.

Charles Nutter Solemn agent of Lord Castlemallard's Irish estates; he resents the arrival of Paul Dangerfield, who he feels is helping Dr. Barney Sturk challenge him for the agency; he disappears the same night Sturk is found near death from a beating in the woods and is believed guilty of the attack on Sturk until Dangerfield is uncovered as the true criminal; Nutter had left to gather evidence Mary Matchwell was not his true wife in J. Sheridan Le Fanu's *The House by the Churchyard*.

Sally Nutter Charles Nutter's good-natured wife, who is frightened by Mary Matchwell until she becomes sick in J. Sheridan Le Fanu's *The House by the Churchyard*.

Nydia Blind Grecian slave, who hopelessly loves Glaucus, serves him faithfully, and leads him and Ione to safety during the eruption of Mount Vesuvius in Edward Bulwer-Lytton's *The Last Days of Pompeii*.

Nyleptha Young, dazzlingly fair, golden-haired queen of the Zu-Vendis and twin sister of Sorais; she falls in love with Sir Henry Curtis and refuses a political marriage to General Nasta, causing a civil war; after their victory she marries Sir Henry and reigns with him as king-consort in H. Rider Haggard's *Allan Quatermain*.

O

Charles O—— Fanny Hill's handsome and virtuous first love, who, having suffered three years' separation from her and lost all contact, returns to England financially ruined but accidentally rediscovers and marries the now wealthy Fanny in John Cleland's *Memoirs of a Woman of Pleasure.*

Gabriel Oak Devoted admirer of Bathsheba Everdene; bad luck costs him his farm, and he becomes Bathsheba's faithful, trusted, and successful farm manager; he helplessly watches her marry the unworthy Frank Troy and, when Troy is killed, once again renews his proposal, realizing that the now wiser Bathsheba returns his love; his constancy is rewarded by her acceptance in Thomas Hardy's *Far from the Madding Crowd.*

Captain Oakhum Captain of the ship *Thunder*, who brutalizes his crew, including Roderick Random, in Tobias Smollett's *The Adventures of Roderick Random.*

Captain Oakley Handsome and elegant nephew of Lady Monica Knollys; something of a gambler and dandy, he flirts with Maud Ruthyn at Knowl and later sends her verses in J. Sheridan Le Fanu's *Uncle Silas.*

Marchioness of Oakley Lord Mahogany's malicious wife, who assists her husband in an attempted rape of Amelia de Gonzales, has Amelia kidnapped by ruffians, and is a casualty at Don Pedro de Gonzales's fatal banquet in William Beckford's *Modern Novel Writing; or, the Elegant Enthusiast.*

Lord Charles Oakley Son of the Marchioness of Oakley and Lord Mahogany and the admirer of Lucinda Howard; he accuses political commentator Gabble of hypocrisy and self-aggrandizement in William Beckford's *Modern Novel Writing; or, the Elegant Enthusiast.*

Dorothy Oakley Friend of Sir Launcelot Greaves's mother and once his nursemaid; nearly insane in jail because of her son's supposed death, she is rescued by Sir Launcelot, becomes Sir Launcelot's housekeeper, and marries Captain Samuel Crowe in Tobias Smollett's *The Adventures of Sir Launcelot Greaves.*

Greaves Oakley Son of Dorothy Oakley; pressed into army service by Mrs. Gobble, he returns from the dead to marry Susan Sedgemoor in Tobias Smollett's *The Adventures of Sir Launcelot Greaves.*

Lieutenant Sir Derby Oaks Arthur Pendennis's rival suitor for Miss Fotheringay (Emily Costigan) in William Makepeace Thackeray's *The History of Pendennis.*

Sir Oliver Oates Parson of Tunstall and the pawn of Sir Daniel Brackley; he unknowingly lured Sir Harry Shelton to his death; he helps Dick Shelton escape from Brackley only to betray him later in Robert Louis Stevenson's *The Black Arrow: A Tale of Two Roses.*

Titus Oates Protestant clergyman, who is the chief witness in the trial of the Peverils as accomplices in the Popish Plot, and who is laughed out of court in Sir Walter Scott's *Peveril of the Peak.*

Titus Oates Villain who baptized Jonathan Wild in Henry Fielding's *The Life of Mr. Jonathan Wild the Great.*

Sally Oats A woman in Ravenloe whom Silas Marner cures of heart problems by a mixture of herbs; by so doing he shows the town his talent for medicine in George Eliot's *Silas Marner.*

Obadiah Shandy family servant who clumsily knocks Dr. Slop into the mud and ties the doctor's bag with so many knots that he can hardly get his forceps out in time to assist in Tristram Shandy's delivery in Laurence Sterne's *The Life and Opinions of Tristram Shandy, Gentleman.*

Doad O'Bill A member of the Methodist congregation at the chapel of Briarmains, Hiram Yorke's residence in Charlotte Brontë's *Shirley.*

Miss Obrien Sixteen-year-old Irish beauty, whose mother connives with Sir Thomas Grandison's stewards in a lucrative contract which would make her his mistress; Sir Thomas's death before the signing of the contract gives scope to the magnanimity of his son, Sir Charles, who provides a dowry to facilitate her honorable marriage to a tradesman in Samuel Richardson's *Sir Charles Grandison.*

Mrs. Obrien Miss Obrien's mother, who hopes her daughter's beauty will enrich the family by attracting a rich gentleman to set her up in an establishment; she is disappointed when her daughter makes a happy marriage to a tradesman in Samuel Richardson's *Sir Charles Grandison.*

O'Brien Pirate with a red cap; given the job of guarding the *Hispaniola*, he is killed by his fellow watchman, Israel Hands, in a drunken brawl aboard the ship in Robert Louis Stevenson's *Treasure Island.*

Obsequiousness A native slave so named by William John Attwater; he commits some minor treacheries against Attwater and then blames another native; in retribution, he is shot by Attwater in Robert Louis Stevenson's *The Ebb-Tide: A Trio and a Quartette.*

Obstinate Christian's neighbor in the City of Destruction; he tries to persuade Christian to return, but fails and returns himself in John Bunyan's *The Pilgrim's Progress From this World to That Which Is to Come.*

Mr. O'Callaghan　Severe evangelical curate susceptible to tea and muffins; he is a guest of Miss Todd's in Anthony Trollope's *The Bertrams.*

Marionetta O'Carroll　Vivacious, flirtatious young woman, who consciously induces love and jealousy in Scythrop Glowry; she finally accepts the proposal of the dandy, Mr. Listless, in Thomas Love Peacock's *Nightmare Abbey.*

Ochihatou　Wicked, deformed, and ugly prime minister of Hypotosa; disguised as a vulture, he kidnaps and almost rapes Eovaai in Eliza Haywood's *Adventures of Eovaai, Princess of Ijaveo.*

Edie Ochiltree　Old "King's Bedesman," who enjoys his independence as a professional beggar, helps William Lovel rescue Isabel Wardour and her father, Sir Arthur, from drowning, helps Lovel in a trick to supply money to Sir Arthur, and is arrested for assaulting Herman Dousterswivel; he is rescued by Oldbuck (Jonathan Oldenbuck) and carries an identifying ring and letters from Elspeth Muckelbackit to the Earl of Glenallan (William, Lord Geraldin) in Sir Walter Scott's *The Antiquary.*

Captain O'Connor　Predecessor to Hawes as governor of the prison; a humane man who treats the prisoners with mercy, he is dismissed by the justices (inspectors) for a slight indiscretion in Charles Reade's *It Is Never Too Late to Mend.*

Terelah O Crohane　Old Irish gentleman of County Kerry, Ireland; he shows John Buncle traditional Irish hospitality; Buncle gets drunk and nearly drowns in a pit on this visit in Thomas Amory's *The Life of John Buncle, Esq.*

Octavia　The embodiment of "conscious virtue" and the narrative foil to Cleopatra's wickedness; she dies peacefully with the applause of the public and the love of her children in Sarah Fielding's *The Lives of Cleopatra and Octavia.*

Octavio　Young council member of the States of Holland; he befriends the exiled Philander and Sylvia and falls in love with Sylvia; Philander flees Holland and pursues another affair; Octavio's obsession with Sylvia results in the termination of his council membership and the accidental shooting of his uncle, Sebastian; suffering endless betrayals by Sylvia and a near fatal wound from Philander, he despairs and takes religious orders in Aphra Behn's *Love Letters Between a Nobleman and His Sister.*

Octavio　Cornelia's dissipated uncle and guardian, whose passion for Cornelia forces her to go into hiding, and who later attempts to prevent her marriage to Bernardo in Sarah Scott's *The History of Cornelia.*

Don Octavio　Fighter of a duel with Emilius in Eliza Haywood's *The Rash Resolve; or, the Untimely Discovery.*

Miss Oddly　Woman who succeeds Miss Sedate in George Edwards's affections in John Hill's *The Adventures of Mr. George Edwards, a Creole.*

O'Donaghan　Sir Ulic Mackillgut's nephew, who is unable to succeed with his courtship of Liddy Melford at Bath in Tobias Smollett's *The Expedition of Humphry Clinker.*

Captain Odonnell　Irish officer, who courts Mrs. Lavement and her daughter, attacks Roderick Random in jealousy, and is humiliated by Roderick's revenge in Tobias Smollett's *The Adventures of Roderick Random.*

Auralia Margaretta (Peggy) O'Dowd　Wife of William Dobbin's commanding officer; she tries to marry her sister-in-law Glorvina O'Dowd to Dobbin in William Makepeace Thackeray's *Vanity Fair.*

Glorvina O'Dowd　Major O'Dowd's sister, who hopes to marry Captain William Dobbin in William Makepeace Thackeray's *Vanity Fair.*

Major (later General) Sir Michael O'Dowd　Captain William Dobbin's commanding officer, capable in battle but dominated by his wife at home in William Makepeace Thackeray's *Vanity Fair.*

Mr. O'Dwyer　Father of Fanny and joint owner with his brother, Mick, of the Kanturk Hotel, Cork, in Anthony Trollope's *Castle Richmond.*

Fanny O'Dwyer　Father Bernard McCarthy's niece, barmaid of the Kanturk Hotel in Cork; Aby Mollett carries on a flirtation with her in Anthony Trollope's *Castle Richmond.*

Mick O'Dwyer　Joint owner with his brother of the Kanturk Hotel, Cork, frequented by Aby Mollett in Anthony Trollope's *Castle Richmond.*

Oeros　Father of Adelhu and king of Hypotosa; by means of a poisoned magic feather he is rendered the helpless tool of Ochihatou in Eliza Haywood's *Adventures of Eovaai, Princess of Ijaveo.*

Mademoiselle O'Faley　Half-French, half-Irish aunt of Dora O'Shane; she delights in all things French and succeeds in bringing together Dora and Black Connal; when

Dora and Connal marry, she moves to Paris with them, her happiness complete, in Maria Edgeworth's *Ormond*.

Sir Terence O'Fay Fat, jolly, Falstaff-like character who tries to keep the Clonbronys out of financial trouble in Maria Edgeworth's *The Absentee*.

Trilby O'Ferrall A charming artist's model, whose kindness and beauty entrance men; independent, simple, and trusting, she is admired by many painters as a model but admired by the world as a very talented singer, La Svengali; having undergone traumatic changes during her short life, she dies at the end of George Du Maurier's *Trilby*.

Officer of the Troop Man who raids the Passover services and finds his son in Charles Johnstone's *Chrysal: or, The Adventures of a Guinea*.

Soto O'Fin John Buncle's principal "squire" or servant, who provides food and, on one occasion, a successful plan to rescue Martha Tilston and Alithea Llansoy from the miserly lawyer Old Cock in Thomas Amory's *The Life of John Buncle, Esq.*

Lieutenant Hyacinth (Fireworker) O'Flaherty Exuberant, touchy new member of the Royal Irish Artillery; he almost fights a duel with Charles Nutter, who he mistakenly believes makes jokes about O'Flaherty's baldness and toupee; he marries Magnolia Macnamara in J. Sheridan Le Fanu's *The House by the Churchyard*.

Terence (Terry) O'Flaherty Irish watchman sympathetic to Thames Darrell in William Harrison Ainsworth's *Jack Sheppard*.

Thomas O'Flaherty Army acquaintance of Harry Lorrequer; he is cashiered from his regiment and eventually becomes engaged to Emily Bingham in Charles Lever's *The Confessions of Harry Lorrequer*.

Mr. O'Flynn Coarse, bombastic editor of the workers' journal *The Weekly Warwhoop* who rewrites Alton Locke's articles, producing writing so biased that Alton confronts him and resigns; O'Flynn then attacks Alton and his poems in print in Charles Kingsley's *Alton Locke*.

Og of Basan Aldrovandus Magnus's wandering disciple, admired for the wild grandeur of his landscapes and for the expressions on the faces of living subjects, including fish; his brief encounter with a maid from Tivoli leads to her suicide and his guilt; the resulting torment influences his work until he falls from a cliff during a storm in William Beckford's *Biographical Memoirs of Extraordinary Painters*.

William Ogden Methodist who helps Zachariah Cole-man find work and join the political club in Manchester in 1815; he is imprisoned after the march of Blanketeers in Mark Rutherford's *The Revolution In Tanner's Lane*.

John Ogilby Translator of Professor Clod Lumpewitz's Latin epitaph to Aldrovandus Magnus in William Beckford's *Biographical Memoirs of Extraordinary Painters*.

Mrs. Ogilvy (Lady Allardyce) Crotchety, grim, but devoted cousin, guardian and nurse to Catriona Drummond in Robert Louis Stevenson's *Catriona*.

Dan Ogle Friend of Musty Mag and murderer of Lewis Marr; he is blinded with lime by Blind George and is burned to death in the fire that burns down the Hole in the Wall in Arthur Morrison's *The Hole in the Wall*.

Father O'Grady London priest who writes to Father Oliver Gogarty to inform him about Rose Leicester to relieve his assumed worry as to her fate in George Moore's *The Lake*.

Miss O'Grady Antoinette d'Ivry's governess in William Makepeace Thackeray's *The Newcomes*.

Mrs. O'Grady Gossip who comes to Father Oliver Gogarty to report Rose Leicester's rumored pregnancy in George Moore's *The Lake*.

Lady Ogram Temperamental, wealthy old invalid with an interest in social reform and politics; he supports Dyce Lashmar's candidacy for Parliament and tries to force him to marry Constance Bride in George Gissing's *Our Friend the Charlatan*.

Philip O'Gree An amusing Irishman, who teaches at Dr. Tootle's school but leaves it to open a shop and marry Sally Fisher in George Gissing's *The Unclassed*.

Mr. O'Halaghan Bryan Perdue's father's Irish cousin, who wrote a book on the arts and sciences in Thomas Holcroft's *The Memoirs of Bryan Perdue*.

Count O'Halloran Eccentric Irish landowner who aids Lord Colambre in finding the truth about Grace Nugent's parentage in Maria Edgeworth's *The Absentee*.

Captain O'Hara Drunken father of Kate; having abandoned his wife and daughter and done time in France, he reappears in Ireland; hearing of Fred Neville's affair with his daughter, Kate, he scrounges an annual allowance from the Nevilles in return for his second disappearance in Anthony Trollope's *An Eye for an Eye*.

Major O'Hara Blustering husband of the heiress Emily Jervois's widowed mother; when he accompanies her on a visit to force access to her daughter, his rank and marital status are held in equal suspicion by Sir Charles Grandison; the latter is discovered to be real in Samuel Richardson's *Sir Charles Grandison*.

Mrs. O'Hara A lady who, like Mrs. Crafton, is renowned for her grotto, second only to Harriet Noel's in Thomas Amory's *The Life of John Buncle, Esq.*

Mrs. O'Hara Mother of Kate; distraught by Fred Neville's refusal to marry Kate after making her pregnant, she hurls Fred from the cliffs of Moher and kills him; she ends her days in a lunatic asylum in Anthony Trollope's *An Eye for an Eye*.

Helen Jervois O'Hara Mother of Emily Jervois; left only a modest allowance by her late husband because of her licentiousness, she hopes to reclaim her daughter, now Sir Charles Grandison's ward, and so share in Emily's large fortune; Sir Charles treats her with clearheaded justice and unsentimental kindness in Samuel Richardson's *Sir Charles Grandison*.

Kate O'Hara Gentle, trusting, raven-haired daughter of Mrs. O'Hara of Ardkill Cottage, County Clare; she is seduced by Fred Neville, who refuses to marry her when she is pregnant; her illegitimate child dies, and she seeks out her father in France after Fred's death in Anthony Trollope's *An Eye for an Eye*.

Robin Oig Haughty and nervy outlaw son of Rob Roy; he visits but snubs David Balfour in his illness at the Maclarens and proves the superior musician in a piping contest with Alan Breck Stewart in Robert Louis Stevenson's *Kidnapped*. He is a distant cousin to Catriona Drummond in *Catriona*.

Mr. O'Keefe John Buncle's contemporary at Trinity College, Dublin, a descendant of Irish kings, and a sensible, generous man of genteel and useful learning in Thomas Amory's *The Life of John Buncle, Esq.*

Old Acquaintance Frenchman of poor parents; his rise in the world is marked by vice, disguise, duplicity, hypocrisy, and betrayal in Charles Johnstone's *Chrysal: or, The Adventures of a Guinea*.

Old Colonel Honest old soldier, who tolerates no questions concerning his honor and who gets the best of Her Grace and her Agent in Charles Johnstone's *Chrysal: or, The Adventures of a Guinea*.

Old Doctor Uncle of Maria Spence, John Buncle's fourth wife, and an old clergyman whom Buncle meets at Cleator and who discusses the dangers of Jacobitism and the benefits of Hanoverian succession in Thomas Amory's *The Life of John Buncle, Esq.*

Old Dutchman Elderly Dutch gentleman from whom David Balfour obtains credit and lodgings in Leyden, Holland, and who is suspicious of Catriona Drummond's guise as David's sister in Robert Louis Stevenson's *Catriona*.

Old Dutchman Native of Holland who lives in Ceylon and serves the king there; he tries to persuade Captain Singleton and his crew to come ashore when their ship is run aground off the coast of that country in Daniel Defoe's *The Life, Adventures, and Pyracies of the Famous Captain Singleton*.

Griselda (Grizzel) Oldenbuck Maiden sister of Oldbuck (Jonathan Oldenbuck); she impatiently looks after his house for him in Sir Walter Scott's *The Antiquary*.

Jonathan (Oldbuck) Oldenbuck Sixty-year-old antiquary, who is an attorney though he never practiced the law; he befriends William Lovel traveling from Edinburgh to Fairport, decides Lovel is a poet, and exposes the fraud of Herman Dousterswivel against Sir Arthur Wardour; he had loved Lovel's mother when he was young, though he affects to be a misogynist; he assists the Earl of Glenallan (William, Lord Geraldin) in discovering that Lovel is the earl's son in Sir Walter Scott's *The Antiquary*.

Maria Oldershaw Beautician and procurer, who counsels Lydia Gwilt to entrap Allan Armadale into marriage so that she can obtain his fortune; she connives in Gwilt's ingenious plot to murder Armadale in Wilkie Collins's *Armadale*.

Mr. Oldeschole Secretary of the Internal Navigation Office who examines Charley Tudor for a post in Anthony Trollope's *The Three Clerks*.

Mr. Oldfield The elderly, wealthy suitor whose age and ugliness cause Esther Hargrave to refuse his persistent offers of marriage in Anne Brontë's *The Tenant of Wildfell Hall*.

Mr. Oldfield Hospitable relative in whose house Amelia de Gonzales meets Miss Ford in William Beckford's *Modern Novel Writing; or, the Elegant Enthusiast*.

"Old General" Father of Imoinda and a seasoned warrior, who trains Oroonoko as a warrior; he dies in battle when he takes an arrow in his eye meant for Oroonoko in Aphra Behn's *Oroonoko*.

Old Gentleman A seemingly kindly cardsharp, who lures Harley into gambling away twelve pounds in Henry Mackenzie's *The Man of Feeling*.

Mrs. Oldham Widow and mother in straitened circumstances; she occupies one of Sir Thomas Grandison's country houses as his mistress and bears him two children; Sir Charles Grandison's magnanimity to her and continued support to her children are a tacit reprimand of his sisters' unkind treatment of her immediately after Sir Thomas's death in Samuel Richardson's *Sir Charles Grandison.*

Old Indian Chief   Man who adopts Billy Annesly as his son after torturing him to test his mettle in Henry Mackenzie's *The Man of the World.*

John Olding   A workingman who finds Hetty Sorel's dead baby and testifies against her in court in George Eliot's *Adam Bede.*

Old Man   Hermit who spends sixty years calculating the answers to absurd questions in William Beckford's *Modern Novel Writing; or, the Elegant Enthusiast.*

Old Man   Peasant who shows Henry Willoughton and Mr. Simpson the ruins of Kenilworth castle and then sells Willoughton the manuscript relating the story of Gaston de Blondeville in Ann Radcliffe's *Gaston de Blondeville.*

Old Pilot   Portuguese sailor under Don Garcia de Pimentesia de Carravalla; he takes young Bob Singleton under his care for about two years; he hires him out as a cabin boy but then threatens to take him before the inquisition as a heretic and beats him often in Daniel Defoe's *The Life, Adventures, and Pyracies of the Famous Captain Singleton.*

Old Woman   Maternal figure who lives in the cottage with four doors—past, present, future, and eternal; she sends Anodos to do something worth doing in George MacDonald's *Phantastes.*

Old Woman   Harridan housekeeper to a gang of thieves; because of the dismissal of her favorite, Jack Gines, from the gang, she attempts to kill Caleb Williams, then tries to turn him in, forcing Caleb to run away in William Godwin's *Caleb Williams.*

Arthur Fitzmaurice O'Leary   Eccentric traveler fleeing his wife; he involves Harry Lorrequer in a Paris riot in Charles Lever's *The Confessions of Harry Lorrequer.*

Basil Olifant   Traitorous turncoat cousin of the Bellendens, whose estate he gains possession of by joining the Cameronians; he orders the death of Lord Evandale (William Maxwell) and is himself killed by soldiers led by Henry Morton in Sir Walter Scott's *Old Mortality.*

Nigel Olifaunt   See Nigel Olifaunt, Lord Glenvarloch.

Olinthus   Fanatical Christian, who is responsible for the conversion of Apaecides in Edward Bulwer-Lytton's *The Last Days of Pompeii.*

Oliver   Cunning, avaricious son of Nicanor; he falls into a lingering disease after the failure of his attempts to ruin Ferdinand and Portia; his marriage to Melantha is a complete contrast to the ideal union of Ferdinand and Portia in Sarah Fielding's *The Cry.*

Oliver (Oliver Le Dain)   Louis XI's barber and counselor; an oily little sneak, he is a low-born favorite raised to an influential position; the court has given him the derogative nicknames of Oliver le Dain, le Mauvais, and le Diable in Sir Walter Scott's *Quentin Durward.*

Oliver, Q. C.   Lady Clara (Pulleyn) Newcome's counsel in the Newcome divorce case in William Makepeace Thackeray's *The Newcomes.*

J. Oliver   Perspicacious parson who collects Shamela Andrews's letters and publishes them to reveal the truth about (Samuel Richardson's) Pamela Andrews; these letters form Henry Fielding's *An Apology for the Life of Mrs. Shamela Andrews.*

Rosemond Oliver   Mr. Oliver's beautiful daughter, whose sincerity and simplicity do much to outweigh her lack of depth; she loves and is loved by St. John Rivers, who nevertheless shuns her, knowing she would be an unsuitable missionary's wife; she is consoled for the loss of St. John by Mr. Granby in Charlotte Brontë's *Jane Eyre.*

William Oliver   Wealthy owner of a needle factory in Morton Vale, who would like his daughter Rosamond to marry St. John Rivers in Charlotte Brontë's *Jane Eyre.*

Olivia   A rich merchant's daughter, who is the beloved of Don Alphonso Guzman; put into a convent by the Inquisition, she is rescued and married to Don Alphonso in Charles Johnstone's *Chrysal: or, The Adventures of a Guinea.*

Lady Olivia   An Italian beauty whose early wealth and unrestrained independence have injured her character; her ardent pursuit of Sir Charles Grandison becomes violent when she is rebuffed in Samuel Richardson's *Sir Charles Grandison.*

Princess Olivia   False, extravagant, charming young wife of Prince Victor of X—; she gives her lover, the Chevalier de Magny, a state jewel, which he pawns for money to lose by gambling; still obsessed with de Magny after his death, she is executed by her husband's order in William Makepeace Thackeray's *The Luck of Barry Lyndon.*

Madame de Olonne   Temperamental mistress of de

Coigney; his sister plots to get him to drop her and pursue Charlotta de Palfoy in Eliza Haywood's *The Fortunate Foundlings*.

Olympiodorus   Leader of a violent pagan mob in the time of the patriarch Theophilus in Charles Kingsley's *Hypatia*.

Gerald O'Mahony   American-Irish advocate of Home Rule; he objects to violent methods but sympathizes with the tenants' struggle in Anthony Trollope's *The Landleaguers*.

Rachel O'Mahony   American opera singer in London and daughter of Gerald O'Mahony; Philip Jones loves her, but his poverty keeps them apart; for a time she engages herself to Lord Castlewell, but she returns to Philip in Anthony Trollope's *The Landleaguers*.

Mr. O'Malley   Defence lawyer in Thady Macdermot's trial for murder in Anthony Trollope's *The Macdermots of Ballycloran*.

Charles O'Malley   Young Irishman who abandons his brief university studies to soldier in the Napoleonic Wars, inherits his uncle Godfrey O'Malley's encumbered Galway estate, and eventually marries Lucy Dashwood in Charles Lever's *Charles O'Malley*.

Godfrey O'Malley   Impoverished Member of Parliament for Galway and uncle and guardian of Charles O'Malley in Charles Lever's *Charles O'Malley*.

Mr. Omer   Draper, tailor, haberdasher, and funeral furnisher who made David Copperfield's mourning clothes and who apprentices Emily Peggotty to work for him in Charles Dickens's *The Personal History of David Copperfield*.

Gilbert Omit   Lawyer who tries to persuade Claud Walkinshaw against changing the entail to benefit Walter, his second son, rather than Charles, his eldest, in John Galt's *The Entail*.

Duchess of Omnium   See Lady Glencora MacCluskie Palliser.

Duke of Omnium (the Old Duke)   E n o r m o u s l y wealthy, haughty, debauched old bachelor, whose unapproachable manner brings him great esteem in Anthony Trollope's *Doctor Thorne* and in *Framley Parsonage*. He orders his nephew and heir, Plantagenet Palliser, to lose interest in Lady Dumbello in *The Small House at Allington*. He expresses his satisfaction at Lady Glencora Palliser's state of pregnancy in *Can You Forgive Her?*. He becomes infatuated with Marie Goesler, who refuses, first, his indirect offer to make her his mistress and, subsequently,

his direct offer to make her his wife, but remains his friend in *Phineas Finn*. He is kept amused by the controversies surrounding Lady Eustace in *The Eustace Diamonds*. He dies, attended by Lady Glencora and Mrs. Goesler, to whom he bequeaths a fortune in jewels in *Phineas Redux*.

Duke of Omnium (the younger)   See Plantagenet Palliser.

Ulick O'More   Irish cousin by marriage of Maurice Ferrars; he is beloved by Sophia Kendal but chooses Genevieve Durant in Charlotte Yonge's *The Young Stepmother*.

Onahal   An older wife of the king; she has charge of Imoinda but is enamoured of Aboan; in exchange for Aboan's favors, she allows Oroonoko to see Imoinda and consummate their relationship in Aphra Behn's *Oroonoko*.

Sir Phelim O'Neile   Dissembling leader of the Irish conspiracy, who takes Lord Caulfield prisoner in William Godwin's *Mandeville*.

Major O'Neill   Brother of Mrs. Macnamara and good friend of General Chattesworth; he is under Colonel Stafford in the chain of command of the Royal Irish Artillery in J. Sheridan Le Fanu's *The House by the Churchyard*.

Widow O'Neill   Tenant of the Clonbronys abused by Garraghty and forced out of her home; Lord Colambre stays with the O'Neills while investigating the Clonbrony estate in Maria Edgeworth's *The Absentee*.

Brian O'Neill   Son of the Widow O'Neill in Maria Edgeworth's *The Absentee*.

Lord Ongar   Debauched, tyrannical husband of Julia Brabazon, whom he grievously mistreats in their brief marriage until his sudden death in Anthony Trollope's *The Claverings*.

Julia Brabazon, Lady Ongar   The vain, mercenary daughter of a peer; she jilts Harry Clavering to marry the wealthy Lord Ongar; the marriage is unhappy and touched by scandal, but Lady Ongar is soon a widow; she tries to win back Harry, for a while coming between him and Florence Burton, to whom he is engaged; at last she congratulates Florence on her coming marriage on the spot at which she had rejected Harry two years previously in Anthony Trollope's *The Claverings*.

Oniwheske   Aged ruler of the kingdom of Norbon and father of the future Queen Stygee in Robert Paltock's *The Life and Adventures of Peter Wilkins*.

Ophelia   Virtuous clergyman's daughter, who is loved and lost by Mr. Graham; she dies after seeing Graham (who has been falsely informed that she has a drinking problem) with another woman in Richard Graves's *The Spiritual Quixote*.

Ophelia   Innocent orphan raised by an aunt in Wales; she is subjected to the persecutions of the rakish Lord Dorchester, to whom she is ultimately married after his reformation in Sarah Fielding's *The History of Ophelia*.

Dr. Opimian   Clergyman whose tastes are for a good library, a good dinner, a pleasant garden, and rural walks in Thomas Love Peacock's *Gryll Grange*.

General Ople   Retired officer, who fails to perceive the romance between his daughter and Lady Camper's nephew, Reginald Rolles, because he can think only of courting Lady Camper, who is forced to satirize him until he sees his foolishness, whereupon she marries him in George Meredith's *The Case of General Ople and Lady Camper*.

Elizabeth Ople   Attractive, obedient daughter of General Ople; she is the love and, eventually, the wife of Lady Camper's nephew, Reginald Rolles, in George Meredith's *The Case of General Ople and Lady Camper*.

Sir Lucius O'Prism   Dilettante painter and an opponent of Marmaduke Milestone's theories of the picturesque in Thomas Love Peacock's *Headlong Hall*.

Mr. Optimist   Chairman of the General Committee Office after Sir Raffle Buffle's departure to the Income Tax Office in Anthony Trollope's *The Small House at Allington*.

Sir Oran Haut-ton   Orangutan that gains a baronetcy and estate and is elected to Parliament in Thomas Love Peacock's *Melincourt*.

Lady Oranmore   Respected Irish woman whom Lord Colambre visits when traveling through Ireland; she teaches Colambre to be proud of his Irish heritage in Maria Edgeworth's *The Absentee*.

Lord Oranmore   Respected Irish nobleman and husband of Lady Oranmore in Maria Edgeworth's *The Absentee*.

Baillie Orde   Unaffectionate father of Lady Dalcastle (Rabina Colwan); when his newlywed daughter runs home, he cunningly "punishes" her husband in her person by beating her and locking her up; she is driven into returning to her husband in James Hogg's *The Private Memoirs and Confessions of a Justified Sinner*.

Rourk Oregan   Stupid man who challenges Roderick Random to a duel over Melinda Goosetrap, whom he has never met, in Tobias Smollett's *The Adventures of Roderick Random*.

Mr. O'Regan   Irish dancing master, whose memorable performance of the *Harlequin Sorcerer* is recalled by John Buncle because he finds O'Regan's lover, Miss Henxworth, at a country dance held by Oliver Wincup in Thomas Amory's *The Life of John Buncle, Esq.*

David (Dirty Dave) O'Regan   Mary Matchwell's accomplice, who claims to be a lawyer; he helps her force her way into Charles Nutter's house in J. Sheridan Le Fanu's *The House by the Churchyard*.

Orestes   Cunning, corrupt Prefect of Alexandria, betrothed to Hypatia; he plots to capitalize on Count Heraclian's plan to overthrow the Roman emperor to become emperor of an independent Africa; his plans fail, but he adapts himself to prevailing circumstances in Charles Kingsley's *Hypatia*.

Mr. and Mrs. Orgueil   Hypocritical and avaricious couple who through culpable thoughtlessness and cupidity contribute to the financial downfall and ultimately the deaths of David and Camilla Simple in Sarah Fielding's *David Simple. Volume the Last*.

Oriana   Angelo D'Albini's mistress, who plots to kill him, declares her love to Eugene, and seeks revenge when Eugene is revealed as Gabrielle di Montmorency in Charlotte Dacre's *The Libertine*.

Caleb Oriel   Rector of Greshamsbury much loved in the parish; he marries Frank Gresham's sister Beatrice in Anthony Trollope's *Doctor Thorne* He appears briefly in *The Last Chronicle of Barset*.

Patience Oriel   Sister of Caleb Oriel and early a rival to Mary Thorne for Frank Gresham's unsettled affections; later she serves as bridesmaid for Beatrice Gresham and for Mary Thorne in Anthony Trollope's *Doctor Thorne*.

Orkid Jim   Workman for Mr. Furze; hating Tom Catchpole, he plots with Mrs. Furze to drive Tom away; he confesses after Tom saves him from drowning, and he emigrates to America to become a preacher in Mark Rutherford's *Catharine Furze*.

Orkid Joe   Orkid Jim's brother, who assists Jim in setting a trap to accuse Tom Catchpole of theft in Mark Rutherford's *Catharine Furze*.

Orlando   Madame de Menon's brother and former suitor of Louisa Bernini; he is killed in an argument with his friend, Chevalier de Menon, in Ann Radcliffe's *A Sicilian Romance*.

Duke of Orleans   Heir to the French crown, and afterwards Louis XII; he is virtually a prisoner in the French court; though betrothed to the deformed Princess Joan, he is infatuated with Isabelle de Croye and endeavors to prevent her leaving France in Sir Walter Scott's *Quentin Durward*.

Dolge Orlick   Joe Gargery's apprentice blacksmith, who jealously hates Pip Pirrip; he beats Mrs. Joe so severely that after a period of speechlessness and paralysis she dies; after Pip has achieved his dismissal from a post at Miss Havisham's, he tries to kill Pip in Charles Dickens's *Great Expectations*.

Edith Orme   Close friend of Lady Mason and widow of Sir Peregrine Orme's only son; she comforts both Sir Peregrine and Lady Mason during the latter's long ordeal in Anthony Trollope's *Orley Farm*.

Kitty Orme   Harriet Byron's friend, whose being sister to one of her rejected suitors constrains their intimacy in Samuel Richardson's *Sir Charles Grandison*.

Lady Muriel Orme   Strongly religious daughter of the Earl of Ainslie; she loves Arthur Forester but is engaged to Eric Lindon, her cousin, and feels duty bound to him; she is the counterpart of Sylvie in Lewis Carroll's *Sylvie and Bruno*. Eric's bethrothed, she has doubts about his religious faith; released from her promise to marry him, she weds Arthur; she shares with the narrator an "eerie" episode with the fairies in *Sylvie and Bruno Concluded*.

Sir Peregrine Orme   Old-fashioned, high-principled baronet, whose love for Lady Mason makes him her staunchest defender in the forgery case brought against her; to shield her he asks her to marry him, but she honorably refuses in Anthony Trollope's *Orley Farm*.

Peregrine (Perry) Orme   Scapegrace grandson and heir of Sir Peregrine; he falls in love with Madeline Staveley, and when she at last vows to marry Felix Graham, he vows to hunt big game in Africa in Anthony Trollope's *Orley Farm*.

Robert Orme   Gentle, forlorn rejected suitor of Harriet Byron and brother of her friend Kitty Orme in Samuel Richardson's *Sir Charles Grandison*.

Earl of Ormersfield   Embittered widower who is mellowed by the dutifulness and love of his son, Louis Fitzjocelyn, in Charlotte Yonge's *Dynevor Terrace*.

Duke of Ormond   Catholic nobleman in the court of King Charles II; he urges the king to release the Peverils from the Tower in Sir Walter Scott's *Peveril of the Peak*.

Mrs. Ormond   Elderly, simple lady hired by Clarence

Hervey to care for Virginia St. Pierre; she unwittingly misinforms Virginia that Hervey will soon wed her, causing some mischief in Maria Edgeworth's *Belinda*.

Harry Ormond   Son of a friend of Sir Ulick O'Shane; he is taken and raised by O'Shane after his mother dies; uneducated and undisciplined, he lets his passionate temper lead him into various scrapes, but his generous nature and quick intelligence aid his development into an educated, cultured young man who becomes an asset to society in Maria Edgeworth's *Ormond*.

Duke of Ormonde   Jacobite nobleman in William Makepeace Thackeray's *The History of Henry Esmond*.

Mrs. Ormonde   Philanthropic widow who runs a home for poor children; she takes charge of the working-class girl Thyrza Trent, who has left home, and educates her in George Gissing's *Thyrza*.

Lord Ormont   Vain, disgraced general in the British army; his pride and scorn for the public that censured him lead him to fail to introduce his new wife, Aminta (Farrell), into society, casting doubt upon the legitimacy of their relationship and leading to the dissolution of the marriage in George Meredith's *Lord Ormont and his Aminta*.

Aminta (Browny) Farrell, Countess of Ormont   Intelligent, spirited young woman, who is mistreated by her husband, Lord Ormont, and who, refusing to settle for a loveless marriage to a famous man, eventually takes up with Matey Weyburn, who, despite his lack of fame, has a character that offers her suitable companionship in George Meredith's *Lord Ormont and his Aminta*.

Christina Ormsay   Sara Macallan's nurse, who testified in court that the Macallan marriage was unhappy in the murder trial that precedes the opening of Wilkie Collins's *The Law and the Lady*.

Mr. Ormsby   Millionaire friend of Lord Monmouth in Benjamin Disraeli's *Coningsby; or, The New Generation*.

Mrs. Ormsby   Mistress discovered in bed with the husband of Lady Maria Jones in William Beckford's *Modern Novel Writing; or, the Elegant Enthusiast*.

Prince Oroonoko   A great warrior and the only grandson of the King of Coramantien; he is deceived by a slave trader, captured, and taken to Surinam; he is reunited there with Imoinda and distinguishes himself among the whites by his bravery and strength, but is executed after he encourages an uprising among the slaves in Aphra Behn's *Oroonoko*.

Orpheus   One of the numerous souls of famous artists

whom the author encounters in Elysium in Henry Fielding's *A Journey From This World to the Next.*

Signor Orsino Vicious gambler, who assassinates an Italian nobleman, takes refuge in the Castle di Udolpho, and becomes a partner in Montoni's plan to use Udolpho as a fortress for mercenaries; ultimately he is executed for his crimes in Ann Radcliffe's *The Mysteries of Udolpho.*

John Orton Penitent man of wealth, who, after twenty years of debauchery, decides to reform by living as a hermit in the Stanemore mountains, and whose skeleton is found by Buncle with a note recording such a morally efficacious life story that Buncle decides to make Orton Lodge a summer retreat in Thomas Amory's *The Life of John Buncle, Esq.*

Lord Orville Young aristocrat who meets Evelina Anville Belmont at a dance in London, courts her, is jealous of others' attentions to her, and marries her when he learns her family history in Frances Burney's *Evelina.*

Francis (Frank) Osbaldistone William Osbaldistone's genteel son and Diana Vernon's ardent lover; an aversion to business results in his banishment to Osbaldistone Hall; a perilous Highland mission saves the family firm from ruin, providing reconciliation between father and son; Francis is narrator in Sir Walter Scott's *Rob Roy.*

Sir Hildebrand Osbaldistone Northumbrian Jacobite and father of six reckless sons; knighted by King James II, he lives in retirement because of his politics, which nearly impoverish him; kind and hospitable, he is left childless in old age and names his nephew, Francis Osbaldistone, his heir in Sir Walter Scott's *Rob Roy.*

John Osbaldistone Sir Hildebrand's licentious son, who excels at wrestling and gamekeeping; he is killed in the rebellion of 1715 in Sir Walter Scott's *Rob Roy.*

Perceival (Percy) Osbaldistone Sir Hildebrand's drunken eldest son, who dies during the rebellion of 1715 while engaged in an immense drinking wager in Sir Walter Scott's *Rob Roy.*

Rashleigh Osbaldistone Sir Hildebrand's scheming youngest son; educated for the priesthood, he is employed by his uncle and flees with the firm's substantial assets; disinherited for his betrayal of the Jacobite interests, he is the malicious rival of his cousin Francis Osbaldistone, whom he attempts to kill in Sir Walter Scott's *Rob Roy.*

Richard (Dickon) Osbaldistone Dissolute son of Sir Hildebrand Osbaldistone; he is a sportsman and gambler who breaks his neck falling from a horse in Sir Walter Scott's *Rob Roy.*

Thorncliff (Thornie) Osbaldistone Sir Hildebrand's favorite son and Diana Vernon's proposed future husband; a bully, he resents his cousin Francis Osbaldistone, and dies in a quarrel with a fellow Jacobite in Sir Walter Scott's *Rob Roy.*

Wilfred Osbaldistone Sir Hildebrand's imbecilic son, who is slain while fighting bravely during the rebellion of 1715 in Sir Walter Scott's *Rob Roy.*

William Osbaldistone Francis Osbaldistone's uncompromising father; a wealthy, powerful London merchant, he was disinherited as a youth and amassed his fortune unaided; his displeasure with his son causes a temporary estrangement, which ends when Francis saves the firm; his political sympathies lie with the government in Sir Walter Scott's *Rob Roy.*

Osbert Young Scottish nobleman who seeks revenge against Malcolm for the murder of his father, the Earl of Athlin; he is captured by Malcolm and held for the ransom of his sister Mary's hand in marriage; he falls in love with Malcolm's niece, Laura; he escapes Castle Dunbayne and mortally wounds Malcolm in the attack of Castle Athlin; he rescues Mary from Count de Santmorin and finally marries Laura in Ann Radcliffe's *The Castles of Athlin and Dunbayne.*

Miss Osborne Former best friend of Amelia Booth until the overturning chaise disfigures Amelia; she rejoices in Amelia's misfortune in Henry Fielding's *Amelia.*

Mr. Osborne Rich merchant and domestic tyrant, who in spite of his hostility to his son and his son's family is afraid of his son's and grandson's aristocratic airs in William Makepeace Thackeray's *Vanity Fair.*

Colonel Frederic Osborne Sir Marmaduke Rowley's old friend and Emily Trevelyan's godfather; his bachelorhood, manners, appearance, and reputation belie his age and status; Louis Trevelyan becomes progressively enraged by his attentions to Emily, and he enjoys the mischief in Anthony Trollope's *He Knew He Was Right.*

George Osborne Spoiled son of a rich father, who cuts him off when he marries his betrothed, Amelia Sedley, after her father's financial collapse; bored with the doting Amelia, he flirts with Becky (Sharp) Osborne just before his death at Waterloo in William Makepeace Thackeray's *Vanity Fair.*

George (Georgy) Osborne Spoiled but adored son of Amelia (Sedley) and the late George Osborne; he is the means of reconciling his mother to his father's family in William Makepeace Thackeray's *Vanity Fair.*

James Osborne   Cowardly American accomplice of John Falkner in the abduction of Alithea Neville; he later redeems himself by declaring Falkner's innocence in Mary Shelley's *Falkner*.

Jane Osborne   Mr. Osborne's elder, unmarried daughter, who meets Georgy Osborne and brings him to her father's attention in William Makepeace Thackeray's *Vanity Fair*.

Maria Osborne   Mr. Osborne's younger daughter, who marries the banker Fred Bullock; the Bullock family is jealous of the favor shown to Georgy Osborne in William Makepeace Thackeray's *Vanity Fair*.

Mr. Osgood   Cousin of John Belford; Robert Lovelace deceptively tells Clarissa Harlowe that her family should direct their letters for her to him in Samuel Richardson's *Clarissa: or, The History of a Young Lady*.

Lady O'Shane   Intolerant and jealous third wife of Sir Ulick O'Shane; hating her husband's son, Marcus, and his ward, Harry Ormond, as well as everything that is Irish, she is eventually put aside by O'Shane in Maria Edgeworth's *Ormond*.

Cornelius (King Corny) O'Shane   Sir Ulick O'Shane's cousin and gamekeeper, who is designated "King of the Black Islands"; he "educates" Ulick's ward, Harry Ormond, mostly through hunting and fishing excursions, and provides him an example of unpolished generosity, goodness, and unpretentiousness in contrast to the sophisticated and often calculating manner of his cousin, Sir Ulick, in Maria Edgeworth's *Ormond*.

Dora O'Shane   Cornelius O'Shane's pretty daughter, who attracts Harry Ormond but has been promised in marriage to White Connal; upon White's accidental death, she marries his brother, Black Connal, and, moving to Paris with him, becomes the toast of Parisian high society as well as one of the few virtuous married women in that society in Maria Edgeworth's *Ormond*.

Emmy Annaly O'Shane   Sir Ulick O'Shane's first wife; she dies childless, a victim of love and jealousy in Maria Edgeworth's *Ormond*.

Marcus O'Shane   Sir Ulick O'Shane's prejudiced, spiteful son, who is raised with his father's ward, Harry Ormond; despite his genteel upbringing, he is ill-mannered and jealous of his father's love for Ormond and runs up huge gambling debts early in life, causing his banishment from his native country in Maria Edgeworth's *Ormond*.

Lady Theodosia O'Shane   Second wife of Sir Ulick

O'Shane; married to him for fourteen years, she bears him a son and later dies in Maria Edgeworth's *Ormond*.

Sir Ulick O'Shane   Harry Ormond's shrewd guardian, who, although more fond of Ormond than of his own son, ambitiously favors his son regarding education, marriage, and fortune, to the detriment of Ormond's basic education; his love of luxury leads him to speculate foolishly with his own and Ormond's money, causing his downfall in Maria Edgeworth's *Ormond*.

General Osmin   Turkish general who abducts Violetta and lives with her for three years; then he abducts Ardelisa de Vinevil but, before he can ravish her, he is imprisoned by the sultan for being the bearer of bad news; he dies shortly thereafter in Penelope Aubin's *The Strange Adventures of the Count de Vinevil and His Family*.

Dr. Osmond   A consulting surgeon in Barkington; he testifies that Alfred Hardie, even though sane, has the "incubation of insanity" in Charles Reade's *Hard Cash*.

Osmund   Skillful veteran soldier in Sir Walter Scott's *Count Robert of Paris*.

Christoval, Conde d' Ossorio   Companion of Lorenzo de Medina in Matthew Lewis's *The Monk*.

Father Oswald   Priest of the Fitz-Owen family; he befriends Edmund Lovel and helps him to uncover and prove his true lineage in Clara Reeve's *The Old English Baron*.

Marie Osward   Intriguing messenger in Edward Bulwer-Lytton's *Devereux*.

Other Professor   Colleague of the Professor; he seems to read while in a deep sleep; he recites the poem "Peter and Paul" in an attempt to explain the difference between convenient and inconvenient to Sylvie and Bruno in Lewis Carroll's *Sylvie and Bruno*. He attends Uggug's birthday banquet, though he has been lost in a cupboard for several months, in *Sylvie and Bruno Concluded*.

Otter   Captain of the guard of Gandolf, King of Utterbol; he befriends Ralph and helps Bull Shockhead to replace Gandolf in William Morris's *The Well at the World's End*.

Otter of the Laxings   With Thiodolf, a chief leader of the Markmen against the Romans; he dies in a rash attack led by Arinbiorn in William Morris's *A Tale of the House of the Wolfings*.

Prince Otto   Nephew of Prince Ernest; he wounds

Harry Richmond in a duel in George Meredith's *The Adventures of Harry Richmond.*

Mrs. Otway Lady whose religious interests irritate her husband in George Gissing's *The Crown of Life.*

Alexander Otway Piers Otway's brother, a patriotic journalist, theatrical agent, and father of a disorderly family always in need of money in George Gissing's *The Crown of Life.*

Daniel Otway Piers Otway's brother, a spurious art expert and scoundrel who practices blackmail and sells private letters in George Gissing's *The Crown of Life.*

Jerome Otway Piers Otway's father, a libertarian in his youth; he becomes a Dante scholar and the father of three sons in George Gissing's *The Crown of Life.*

Piers Otway Young man who, distracted from his studies by an infatuation with Irene Derwent, becomes a merchant in Russia and a student of Russian culture but is brought back to England by his love for Irene, who after some years consents to marry him in George Gissing's *The Crown of Life.*

Nathaniel Outerman Hard-working tailor, to whom Charley Tudor owes money; the unpaid bill leads to Charley's apprehension for debt in Anthony Trollope's *The Three Clerks.*

Mrs. Outhouse Harassed rector's wife and sister of Sir Marmaduke Rowley; she reluctantly provides shelter for Emily Trevelyan, estranged from her husband, and for her other niece, Nora Rowley, in Anthony Trollope's *He Knew He Was Right.*

Oliphant Outhouse Hard-working, joyless Rector of St. Biddulph-in-the-East, a poor London parish; although reluctant to become involved in the Trevelyan marriage breakdown, he orders Bozzle, the private detective, out of his house when the man tries to take away Emily Trevelyan's child in Anthony Trollope's *He Knew He Was Right.*

Lance Outram Sir Geoffrey Peveril's park keeper, who courts Deborah Debbitch, is Mistress Ellesmere's nephew, and becomes Julian Peveril's servant and companion during the journey to London in Sir Walter Scott's *Peveril of the Peak.*

Sir Kennington Oval Distinguished member of the British cricketing team matched against the home team of Britannula; he annoys Jack Neverbend by flirting with Eva Crasweller in Anthony Trollope's *The Fixed Period.*

Edward Overton Playwright and narrator of the story; Ernest Pontifex's second godfather, he is friend to the Pontifex family for eighty years; in love with Alethea, Ernest's aunt, and appointed by her executor of Ernest's estate, he plays guardian angel to Ernest in Samuel Butler's *The Way of All Flesh.*

Owen Son of Bridget by Sir Stephen Penrhyn, whose admission of paternity provokes Eleanor (Raymond) to leave her husband, Sir Stephen; Owen is recognized as legitimate when Bridget marries Sir Stephen after Eleanor's death in Caroline Norton's *Stuart of Dunleath.*

Mr. Owen Loving father to John P. and William B.; he refuses to scold or punish his children, leaving that to his wife in Samuel Butler's *The Fair Haven.*

Mrs. Owen Mother of John P. and William B.; responsible for discipline, she is not loved as much as her husband; she wants her sons to be martyrs and believes in absolute literal accuracy of the Bible in Samuel Butler's *The Fair Haven.*

John Owen Student of Mr. Marton in his second teaching position in Charles Dickens's *The Old Curiosity Shop.*

John Pickard Owen Former skeptic, who writes his memoirs in order to answer those questions which cause people to turn away from Chrisitianity, setting up parallel arguments; when the work is completed, he falls into deep melancholy for four years and dies in Samuel Butler's *The Fair Haven.*

Joseph Owen Loyal head clerk of the mercantile firm Osbaldistone and Tresham; he is temporarily imprisoned for their debts before being bailed out by Bailie (Nicole) Jarvie; solemn and correct in his conduct, he is a conscientious worker and fond of Francis Osbaldistone in Sir Walter Scott's *Rob Roy.*

Robert Owen Social philosopher who converts Christopher Kirkland to his idea of the societal value of cooperative living in Mrs. Lynn Linton's *The Autobiography of Christopher Kirkland.*

William Owen Minor canon of Hereford Cathedral devoted to Isabel Brodrick; long separated from her by the controversy over who is the legal heir of Indefer Jones, he finally marries her and changes his name to Jones in accordance with old Indefer's wishes when Isabel is declared true heir to the estate in Anthony Trollope's *Cousin Henry.*

William Bickersteth Owen John Pickard Owen's younger brother, who is responsible for putting together the memoirs and for publishing them after his brother's death in Samuel Butler's *The Fair Haven.*

Lieutenant Oxbelly   Immensely portly and henpecked naval officer, who acts as master of the privateer Jack Easy commissions in Captain Frederick Marryat's *Mr. Midshipman Easy.*

John Oxenham   Greedy, hot-tempered mariner, who recruits a crew to sail to the New World and the South Seas in search of treasure, and who fathers the daughter of a Spanish lady, Dona de Xarate; his expedition runs into trouble, and he is hanged by the Spaniards in Charles Kingsley's *Westward Ho!.*

Lord Oxmington   Aristocrat who unknowingly insults Matthew Bramble and prefers to apologize rather than fight a duel in Tobias Smollett's *The Expedition of Humphry Clinker.*

P

R. P. Amanuensis of Peter Wilkins and author of Robert Paltock's *The Life and Adventures of Peter Wilkins*.

Father Pablos Physician who arranges the burial of the apparently dead Antonia de las Cisternas, thus unwittingly aiding Abbot Ambrosio in Matthew Lewis's *The Monk*.

Mr. Pabsby Salivating, devious Wesleyan minister who is expected to influence the wives of voters in the Percycross election in Anthony Trollope's *Ralph the Heir*.

Mr. Page Singer at the Hunt Ball in J. Sheridan Le Fanu's *Wylder's Hand*.

Mrs. Page Village confectioner who prepares supper and refreshments for the Hunt Ball in J. Sheridan Le Fanu's *Wylder's Hand*.

Mrs. Bruce Page Silly, garrulous society woman, who separates Vincent Lacour from Ada Warren by sending him an anonymous letter which says that Ada will not inherit her father's fortune in George Gissing's *Isabel Clarendon*.

Mr. Paley Successful student, who applies his intellect to the law, excluding all else, in William Makepeace Thackeray's *The History of Pendennis*.

Charlotta de Palfoy French noblewoman and heiress attendant on Princess Louisa Maria Teresa, daughter of the exiled English King James II in Eliza Haywood's *The Fortunate Foundlings*.

Layman Pallet English painter who travels with the Doctor and meets Perry Pickle while examining paintings in Paris; arrested wearing women's clothing, he fears he will be castrated as his punishment; he accompanies Perry on his Continental adventures and embarrasses all with his enthusiastic rapture at the tomb of Rubens in Antwerp; he fights a duel with the Doctor, fomented by Perry, and rejoins the Doctor to separate from Perry in Rotterdam in Tobias Smollett's *The Adventures of Peregrine Pickle*.

Captain Palliser English captain of the *Seahorse*; he writes to James More MacGregor in compliance with his plot to sell Alan Breck Stewart to the English in Robert Louis Stevenson's *Catriona*.

Adelaide Palliser Impecunious distant relative of Plantagenet Palliser; she loves Gerard Maule; they are able to marry when Marie Goesler endows her with the embarrassing fortune in jewels bequeathed by the old Duke of Omnium in Anthony Trollope's *Phineas Redux*. She and her husband are guests of Lord Chiltern in *The Duke's Children*.

Lord Gerald Palliser Younger brother of Lord Silverbridge and similarly a source of anxiety and disappointment to his father, the (younger) Duke of Omnium; he is sent down from Cambridge for attending the Derby without leave but is, with assurances of reform, enrolled at Oxford in Anthony Trollope's *The Duke's Children*. He is in line for a diplomatic post in *The American Senator*.

Lady Glencora MacCluskie Palliser (Duchess of Omnium) The young MacCluskie heiress whose arranged marriage to Plantagenet Palliser relieves his family's anxiety over Lady Dumbello and her family's anxiety over Burgo Fitzgerald in Anthony Trollope's *The Small House at Allington*. She becomes interested in John Eames's fortunes in *The Last Chronicle of Barset*. The adorable, lively impetuous wife of Plantagenet Palliser, she finds her early love for Burgo Fitzgerald rekindled, and she almost runs away with him because of her husband's seeming coldness in *Can You Forgive Her?*. Her concern for the inheritance of her children causes her to interfere when the old Duke of Omnium pays court to Marie Goesler in *Phineas Finn*. She is Marie's intimate friend and Phineas Finn's loyal supporter during his ordeal in *Phineas Redux*. Her patronage lends heart to Lady Eustace in *The Eustace Diamonds*. She mounts lavish house parties to help her husband, but her political indiscretions add to his burdens in *The Prime Minister*. After her death, the enthusiastic but clandestine encouragement she had bestowed on her daughter's love for Frank Tregear causes her husband more pain in *The Duke's Children*.

Jeffrey Palliser Plantagenet Palliser's cousin who would have been the heir had no son been born to Plantagenet and Lady Glencora in Anthony Trollope's *Can You Forgive Her?*.

Lady Mary Palliser Strong-willed daughter of the (younger) Duke of Omnium; with the encouragement of her romantic late mother she has secretly become engaged to an impecunious gentleman, Francis Tregear; her father forbids the match absolutely; at last persuaded, by observation and by Mrs. Finn's argument, of the unalterable nature of Mary's love, the duke blesses their union in Anthony Trollope's *The Duke's Children*.

Plantagenet Palliser (Duke of Omnium) Scrupulous, oversensitive, and self-doubting nephew of the old Duke; his serious infatuation for the married Lady Dumbello is cured by his arranged marriage to Lady Glencora MacCluskie in Anthony Trollope's *The Small House at Allington*. His dedication to his country's service is in conflict with his devotion to his wife; her reawakened feelings for

Burgo Fitzgerald cause him pain, but he declines to become Chancellor of the Exchequer in order to save his marriage in *Can You Forgive Her?*. He works diligently for the Liberal interest in *Phineas Finn*. After his uncle's death he succeeds to the dukedom but pursues his pet project of originating a new decimal currency in *Phineas Redux*. Buffeted by political swings, he tries to maintain a coalition government but has to face his personal failings as leader in *The Prime Minister*. He meets the opposing wills of his children in their own choices of marriage partners and finally returns to political life in *The Duke's Children*.

Palmer   Prison justice (inspector) who is dominated by Williams in approving Hawes's methods and accusations against Francis Eden in Charles Reade's *It Is Never Too Late to Mend*.

Mr. Palmer   London wholesale and manufacturing chemist, who is a wealthy member of the Broad Church movement in 1844, and who receives prominent men as his houseguests in Mark Rutherford's *Clara Hopgood*.

Charlotte Palmer   Mrs. Jennings's silly younger daughter; she laughs at everything, including her disagreeable husband in Jane Austen's *Sense and Sensibility*.

Constance Palmer   Married woman loved from afar by Christian Moxey; she rejects him when he approaches her after her husband's death in George Gissing's *Born in Exile*.

Frank Palmer   Mr. Palmer's twenty-five-year-old son, who visits Fenmarket on his father's business; his slight musical talent attracts the interest of Madge Hopgood; he falls in love with her and fathers her child but is rejected when he proposes that they marry; he finally marries his cousin Cecilia Morland in Mark Rutherford's *Clara Hopgood*.

Harriet Palmer   Prostitute who cheats Hugh Trevor of ten guineas and offers her services to Hector Mowbray and Lord Sad-dog (the Earl of Idford) at Oxford in Thomas Holcroft's *The Adventures of Hugh Trevor*.

Admiral Hawtry Palmer   Authoritarian, evangelical second husband of Philippa Palmer in Anne Thackeray Ritchie's *Old Kensington*.

Philippa Palmer   Indolent, frivolous mother of Dorothea and George Vanborough; she returns after many years spent in India; she fails to satisfy Dorothea's dream of affectionate sympathy in Anne Thackeray Ritchie's *Old Kensington*.

Thomas Palmer   Supercilious, disagreeable husband of Charlotte Palmer; he delights in refuting everything she says in Jane Austen's *Sense and Sensibility*.

Lord Ernest Palmet   A frivolous womanizer, who contributes to Everard Romfrey's decision to horsewhip Dr. Shrapnel in George Meredith's *Beauchamp's Career*.

Pambo   Wise abbot of the monastery of the Laura and confidant of Aufugus; he gives his blessing to Philammon and Aufugus when they leave for Alexandria in Charles Kingsley's *Hypatia*.

Mr. Pamphlet   Bookseller and business rival of Mr. Vellum; the Doctor sells them the same wares in Charles Johnstone's *Chrysal: or, The Adventures of a Guinea*.

Mme. Panache   Clever history teacher at Mme. Beck's school who battles with M. Paul Emanuel and is dismissed; afterwards he pities her and finds her another position in Charlotte Brontë's *Villette*.

Mr. Pancks   Rent collector for Christopher Casby in the Bleeding Heart Yard; he calls himself the "fortune-teller" and is instrumental in discovering William Dorrit's inheritance; he eventually exposes Mr. Casby as a hard-hearted, grasping landlord and humiliates him by cutting off his hair and hat brim in Charles Dickens's *Little Dorrit*.

Miss Pankey   Girl who resides at Mrs. Pipchin's boarding establishment with little Paul Dombey in Charles Dickens's *Dombey and Son*.

Mr. Panscope   (caricature of Samuel Taylor Coleridge) Squire Headlong's guest whose long-winded pronouncements are characterized by classical references and abstruse words; hating Mr. Escott, who openly ridicules him, he becomes in retaliation a rival suitor for Cephalis Cranium in Thomas Love Peacock's *Headlong Hall*.

Panthea   Captive whose beauty threatens the virtue of those who behold her in a parable told by Henry Clinton in Henry Brooke's *The Fool of Quality*.

Peter Paypaul Paperstamp   (caricature of William Wordsworth) Self-indulgent owner of Mainchance Villa in Thomas Love Peacock's *Melincourt*.

Paralytic Sibyl   Sinister crony of Ailsie Gourlay in Sir Walter Scott's *The Bride of Lammermoor*.

Madame du Parc   Mother of Max du Parc and owner of the pension in Neuilly near Paris where Susanna Dymond lodges with her mother's family in Anne Thackeray Ritchie's *Mrs. Dymond*.

Max du Parc   Artist and engraver, who is the center of a group of radical artisans during the Paris Commune; he becomes the second husband of Susanna Dymond in Anne Thackeray Ritchie's *Mrs. Dymond*.

Mrs. Pardiggle Formidable philanthropist with five sons, who demonstrates her charity by bullying the brickmakers into better behavior, making a great amount of noise but accomplishing little, in Charles Dickens's *Bleak House*.

Alfred Pardiggle Son of Mrs. Pardiggle in Charles Dickens's *Bleak House*.

Egbert Pardiggle Rebellious son of Mrs. Pardiggle in Charles Dickens's *Bleak House*.

Felix Pardiggle Son of Mrs. Pardiggle in Charles Dickens's *Bleak House*.

Francis Pardiggle Son of Mrs. Pardiggle in Charles Dicken's *Bleak House*.

O. A. Pardiggle Husband of Mrs. Pardiggle in Charles Dickens's *Bleak House*.

Osbert Pardiggle Son of Mrs. Pardiggle in Charles Dickens's *Bleak House*.

Lord Parham Egocentric, autocratic prime minister, who befriends William Ashe; conflict between their wives threatens their work together in Mrs. Humphry Ward's *The Marriage of William Ashe*.

Xanthippe, Lady Parham Middle-class, shrewish wife of the prime minister; she is offended at Lady Kitty Ashe's insolent behavior in Mrs. Humphry Ward's *The Marriage of William Ashe*.

Paris Beggar Older man who approaches only women for charity and whose surprising success is a mystery that captures Yorick's interest at his Paris hotel gate in Laurence Sterne's *A Sentimental Journey through France and Italy*.

Paris Shopkeeper Beautiful young woman who sells two pairs of gloves to Yorick while he takes her pulse; her husband's indifference to the incident leads Yorick to reflect on female social status in Laurence Sterne's *A Sentimental Journey through France and Italy*.

Christopher Parish Clerk who courts Polly Sparkes, reluctantly helps her trace her missing uncle, and ultimately wins her hand in George Gissing's *The Town Traveller*.

Theodore Parish Clerk in a railway company; he is much occupied with matters of health and infection in George Gissing's *The Town Traveller*.

Sextus (Sexty) Parker Crafty broker well known in Stock Exchange circles for shady dealings who associates with Ferdinand Lopez in business ventures; eventually he

is himself ruined after Lopez forges his signature to a bill in Anthony Trollope's *The Prime Minister*.

Mrs. Sextus Parker Vulgar, ultimately pathetic mother of five; she beseeches Ferdinand Lopez's widow, Emily, to rescue her family from want after her husband is ruined by Lopez's speculations; she becomes a permanent recipient of Abel Wharton's charity in Anthony Trollope's *The Prime Minister*.

Parkes Poor and simple maid to the Marchioness of Updown; she is fired by her employer for supporting Beatrice Brooks; she goes to live with Beatrice when she marries a marquis in Caroline Norton's *Lost and Saved*.

Phil Parkes Ranger and a Maypole Inn regular in Charles Dickens's *Barnaby Rudge*.

Mr. Parkhurst Benevolent clergyman and erstwhile guardian of the orphaned Gifford Kenrick; following the discovery of his young ward's scheme to rob him of his property, he sends him to sea in William Godwin's *Fleetwood*.

Lady Jane Parnell Well-connected woman who falls in love with John Vanborough, believing him to be a bachelor; their marriage does not bring him to the social and political heights he expects in Wilkie Collins's *Man and Wife*.

Rhoda Parnell Scheming friend of Dorothea Vanborough; she flirts with Dorothea's brother, George, and snares her betrothed, Robert Henley, in Anne Thackeray Ritchie's *Old Kensington*.

Parozzi Prominent nobleman, spurned suitor of Rosabella of Corfu, and a leader of the thwarted revolt against Doge Andreas in Matthew Lewis's *The Bravo of Venice*.

Will Parracombe Sailor and scapegrace recruited for the Brotherhood of the Rose by Will Cary; he turns savage, is recaptured by Amyas Leigh, and dies in camp in Charles Kingsley's *Westward Ho!*.

Archibald Parsons Lawyer of the hero Benignus in S. J. Pratt's *Liberal Opinions upon Animals, Man, and Providence*.

Fred Parsons Stationer's clerk attracted to Esther Waters while she is working for Miss Rice; he proposes and presents her to his Dissenting parents, but their prospects of a happy marriage end with William Latch's appearance in London; later, Fred does William a favor by warning him of his imminent arrest in George Moore's *Esther Waters*.

Mr. Partridge Superstitious schoolmaster unjustly

punished by Squire Allworthy for fathering Tom Jones; later, under the name Little Benjamin, he becomes a barber/surgeon; he attaches himself to Tom as an unpaid servant; though his gossip often causes ill treatment to Tom, his superstitious confidence in Tom's ultimate good fortune—and his own—is justified in Henry Fielding's *The History of Tom Jones.*

Anne Partridge Ill-favored, jealous wife of Mr. Partridge; her accusation that he fathered Tom Jones ruins them and causes her death in Henry Fielding's *The History of Tom Jones.*

Lucy Passmore White witch who helps Rose Salterne flee to Don Guzman de Soto; she escapes the Inquisition by turning Catholic and, finally found aboard a Spanish ship by Amyas Leigh, relates the fate of Rose and Frank Leigh before she dies in Charles Kingsley's *Westward Ho!.*

Willy Passmore Fisherman husband of Lucy, the witch; he helps the Jesuits and is carried off by them with his boat in Charles Kingsley's *Westward Ho!.*

Mr. Passnidge Mr. Murdstone's friend, whom Murdstone visits with David Copperfield in Charles Dickens's *The Personal History of David Copperfield.*

Mrs. Pastoureau Athanasias Pastoureau's dictatorial second wife, who treats the child Henry Esmond unkindly in William Makepeace Thackeray's *The History of Henry Esmond.*

Athanasias Pastoureau French refugee and silk weaver, who looks after Henry Esmond in his early years in William Makepeace Thackeray's *The History of Henry Esmond.*

George Pastoureau Athanasias Pastoureau's son; disappointed in his love for Gertrude Maes, he treats her little son, Henry Esmond, kindly in William Makepeace Thackeray's *The History of Henry Esmond.*

Pat The White Rabbit's Irish-dialect-speaking gardener in Lewis Carroll's *Alice's Adventures in Wonderland.*

Count Edouard Pateroff Sly and menacing brother of Sophie Gordeloup; he constantly pesters Lady Ongar to marry him, hinting that he possesses damaging information about her past and that he is acting according to her late husband's wishes in Anthony Trollope's *The Claverings.*

Robert Paterson Old Mortality, who wanders the Scottish countryside tending to monuments of the Cameronian martyrs of the seventeenth century, and whose anecdotes provide the story for Mr. Pattieson in Sir Walter Scott's *Old Mortality.*

Louise Path The pupil at Mlle. Reuter's school possessing the happiest disposition, but who has not been taught honesty in Charlotte Brontë's *The Professor.*

Gatty Patience Shrewish wife of Peter; she chastises him for passively accepting the abuse of others in Henry Brooke's *The Fool of Quality.*

Peter Patience London currier and clergyman's son; his philosophy teaches young Harry Clinton that anger is a sign of cowardice in Henry Brooke's *The Fool of Quality.*

Patrick Malcolm's servant, who is responsible for placing the infant Philip with a peasant couple; later he identifies Alleyn as Philip in Ann Radcliffe's *The Castles of Athlin and Dunbayne.*

Patrickson Sir Ulick O'Shane's "man of business," who gets Harry Ormond's signature on a power of attorney, thus giving O'Shane control over Ormond's money in Maria Edgeworth's *Ormond.*

Patron A man who gives the Clergyman the character he deserves in Charles Johnstone's *Chrysal: or, The Adventures of a Guinea.*

Crossjay Patterne Young relative of Sir Willoughby Patterne; his overhearing Sir Willoughby proposing to Laetitia Dale while he is engaged to Clara Middleton enables Clara to win her freedom in George Meredith's *The Egoist.*

Sir Willoughby Patterne The Egoist; he toys with Laetitia Dale's affections only to surprise her with his engagement to Clara Middleton; as he reveals his selfish, vindictive nature to Clara she realizes she cannot marry him and frees herself when Willoughby proposes to Laetitia, who agrees to a marriage of convenience in George Meredith's *The Egoist.*

Sir William Patterson Solicitor-General who sees a solution to the legal tangle brought about by the cynical Earl Lovel and his repudiation of his wife, Josephine, and her daughter, Anna, in a marriage between the old earl's nephew, Frederick, and Lady Anna Lovel in Anthony Trollope's *Lady Anna.*

Mr. Pattieson Schoolteacher whose meeting with Old Mortality (Robert Paterson) leads to his writing the narrative in Sir Walter Scott's *Old Mortality.*

Patty (Wilkins) Eldest daughter of Peter Wilkins and Youwarkee; she is adopted by Pendlehamby in Robert Paltock's *The Life and Adventures of Peter Wilkins.*

Mrs. Patullo   Lady Ashton's maid in Sir Walter Scott's *The Bride of Lammermoor.*

Paul   Hero in Dick Adams's story who finds himself scorned by husband and wife when asked to mediate their silly quarrels in Henry Fielding's *The History of the Adventures of Mr. Joseph Andrews and of his Friend Mr. Abraham Adams.*

Paul of Tarsus   Visitor to the monastery, who tells of his vision; meeting and talking with Jesus, he concludes that this Jesus cannot be the one of his vision and must be a madman in George Moore's *The Brook Kerith.*

Mona Paula   Spanish lady-in-waiting to Lady Hermione in Sir Walter Scott's *The Fortunes of Nigel.*

Paulo   Vincentio di Vivaldi's loyal and intrepid servant, who helps to rescue Ellena Rosalba from the San Stefano convent, only to be imprisoned with Vincentio by the Inquisition; he escapes to inform the Marchese di Vivaldi of Vincentio's plight; ultimately he is made steward of Vincentio's household in Ann Radcliffe's *The Italian.*

Paulo   Bandit who captures Julia de Mazzini and is then killed by Hippolitus de Vereza in Ann Radcliffe's *A Sicilian Romance.*

Mistress Pauncefort   Lady Annabel Herbert's kind and devoted servant, who cares for Lady Annabel's daughter Venetia in Benjamin Disraeli's *Venetia.*

Bramin Paupiah   Secretary of the English governor; he secretly deals with Richard Middlemas and attempts to stall Adam Hartley's rescue effort in Sir Walter Scott's *The Surgeon's Daughter.*

Gertrude (Trudchen) Pavillon   Fair and kindly daughter of Hermann Pavillon and Mother Mabel; she befriends Isabelle de Croye and Quentin Durward and plans their escape in Sir Walter Scott's *Quentin Durward.*

Hermann Pavillon   Portly and jovial syndic of Liège; wealthy and influential, he participates in the Liègeois revolt and then helps Isabelle de Croye and Quentin Durward to escape in Sir Walter Scott's *Quentin Durward.*

Mabel Pavillon ("Mother Mabel")   Hermann Pavillon's wife; aware of her position as the syndic's wife, she is sometimes a shrew but is generally kindly and good natured in Sir Walter Scott's *Quentin Durward.*

Mrs. Pawkie   Provost James Pawkie's wife, who enthusiastically supports his attempts to rise in the world, in John Galt's *The Provost.*

James Pawkie   The provost (mayor) of Gudetown; his autobiographical memoir *The Provost* is a Machiavellian handbook on the attainment and retainment of political power; it traces his rise to power, covers his years in office, and chronicles social change; his venality is covert but is his central motivating factor in John Galt's *The Provost.*

Major Pawkins   Dull-witted but rising New York politician, whose wife runs the boarding-house where young Martin Chuzzlewit first stays upon his arrival in America in Charles Dickens's *The Life and Adventures of Martin Chuzzlewit.*

Mrs. Pawkins   Keeper of the New York boarding house where Mark Tapley and young Martin Chuzzlewit encounter several of the most remarkable men in America in Charles Dickens's *The Life and Adventures of Martin Chuzzlewit.*

Dr. Payne   Man with the campstool, who attends the duel between Dr. Slammer and Nathaniel Winkle in Charles Dickens's *The Posthumous Papers of the Pickwick Club.*

Mary Paynham   A woman whose reputation has been attacked by society; she is befriended by Diana Warwick, whose portrait she paints, in George Meredith's *Diana of the Crossways.*

Jenny Peace   The eldest of the nine pupils of Mrs. Teachum's school; she reinforces the precepts of her beloved teacher in Sarah Fielding's *The Governess.*

Ada Peachey   Idle, slovenly, violent wife of Arthur and sister of the French girls in George Gissing's *In the Year of Jubilee.*

Arthur Peachey   Submissive, oppressed husband, who leaves his turbulent home, taking his little son with him, but then weakly returns to his wife in George Gissing's *In the Year of Jubilee.*

Ella Peacocke   Devoted American wife of Henry and assistant at Dr. Wortle's academy, where she is housemother; though the Peacockes left America because of the reappearance of her supposedly dead first husband, she is unprepared for the arrival of his blackmailing brother; her problems are resolved when the grave of her first husband is found in San Francisco in Anthony Trollope's *Dr. Wortle's School.*

Henry Peacocke   Scholar, clergyman, and the earnest, hardworking assistant master of Dr. Wortle's school; he married the deserted widow of Ferdinand Lefroy in America only to discover the man alive; starting afresh in England, they are haunted by Lefroy's brother, Robert, and are the targets of local gossip until Peacocke finds the original husband's grave; husband and wife remarry in Anthony Trollope's *Dr. Wortle's School.*

Peak   Sir John Chester's valet, who takes all of his master's money and valuables when Chester dies in Charles Dickens's *Barnaby Rudge.*

Andrew Peak   Vulgar uncle of Godwin Peak; his intention of opening a cheap restaurant opposite Godwin's college leads the youth to leave school in George Gissing's *Born in Exile.*

Charlotte Peak   Godwin Peak's sister, who is engaged to a local man Godwin finds dull and vulgar in George Gissing's *Born in Exile.*

Godwin Peak   A rebellious freethinker from a lower-middle-class family; he admires the distinction of the upper classes, pretends to be a believer, and prepares to become a clergyman in order to marry into a wealthy family; he is exposed, goes abroad, and dies in George Gissing's *Born in Exile.*

Oliver Peak   Brother of Godwin; he is impatient with Godwin's vulgar and trivial interests in George Gissing's *Born in Exile.*

Captain Pearson   Friend of Dr. Barnard and captain of the ship *Serapis,* on which Denis Duval embarks as a midshipman in William Makepeace Thackeray's *Denis Duval.*

Mr. Pearson   A mill owner, who, like Robert Moore, is having difficulty selling his cloth because of the wars in Charlotte Brontë's *Shirley.*

Mrs. Pearson   A new dressmaker in Ecclestone, who points out to Jemima Bradshaw that Mrs. Denbigh resembles the Ruth Hilton she knew in her former position in Elizabeth Gaskell's *Ruth.*

Ann Pearson   Mr. Pearson's daughter whose name is mentioned in conjunction with Robert Moore; her younger sisters are friends of Rose and Jessica Yorke in Charlotte Brontë's *Shirley.*

Antiope Pearson   Guest at a Harrogate dance, where she meets Mr. Monaghan, whom she later marries in Thomas Amory's *The Life of John Buncle, Esq.*

Gilbert Pearson   Parliamentary officer who is in charge of the assault ordered by Oliver Cromwell on Woodstock Lodge in Sir Walter Scott's *Woodstock.*

Mrs. Peckover   Prosperous and vulgar keeper of a slum lodging house in George Gissing's *The Nether World.*

Clem Peckover   Vulgar and brutal slum girl, who marries because she expects her husband to inherit a fortune; initially disappointed, she plans to have him murdered by her lover when the inheritance materializes, but he prevents this by deserting her in George Gissing's *The Nether World.*

Martha Peckover   Kind wife of a circus clown; she nurses the starving baby of a dying woman (Mary Grice) and then cares for the child as her own, even after an injury while performing has left the child ("Madonna" Grice) deaf and dumb; she is reluctantly persuaded to give the child to Valentine Blyth and remains an attentive friend in Wilkie Collins's *Hide and Seek.*

Charity (Cherry) Pecksniff   Mean-spirited elder daughter of Seth Pecksniff and envious sister of Mercy; disappointed and humiliated by Jonas Chuzzlewit's preference for Mercy, she is filled with hate for him and for her father, and is vindictive and unforgiving to the suffering Mercy; she is jilted by Augustus Moddle in Charles Dickens's *The Life and Adventures of Martin Chuzzlewit.*

Mercy (Merry) Pecksniff   Pretty, giddy, and capricious younger daughter of Seth Pecksniff; she suffers cruelly in her marriage to Jonas Chuzzlewit; in her redemptive misery she becomes a kind and loving friend to old Mr. Chuffey in Charles Dickens's *The Life and Adventures of Martin Chuzzlewit.*

Seth Pecksniff   Architect and teacher, father of Mercy and Charity, arch-hypocrite and supreme orator of moral cant; he steals architectural designs from his pupils, exploits the fidelity of his faithful employee Tom Pinch, attempts to win Mary Graham through extortion, and poses as the elder Martin Chuzzlewit's only disinterested and sincere relation in hopes of getting Chuzzlewit's money in Charles Dickens's *The Life and Adventures of Martin Chuzzlewit.*

Pedan the Prophet   Wild and fearsome man of God and prophet in Black Andie Dale's "Tale of Todd Lapraik" in Robert Louis Stevenson's *Catriona.*

Mr. Pedgift   Worldly lawyer and adviser to Allan Armadale; he emphasizes his legal opinions by telling gestures with pinches of snuff suspended for dramatic effect in Wilkie Collins's *Armadale.*

Mr. Pedgift (the younger)   Smart, perky assistant to his father in handling legal business for Allan Armadale; he helps manage the Norfolk Broads picnic party in Wilkie Collins's *Armadale.*

Pedlar   Former drummer (traveling salesman), who lends Parson Adams his last shilling; he tells how his wife switched the infants Fanny Goodwill and Joseph Andrews to reveal Fanny's parentage in Henry Fielding's *The History of the Adventures of Mr. Joseph Andrews and of his Friend Mr. Abraham Adams.*

Don Pedro   Emanuella's greedy guardian; he wants his son, Don Marco, to marry her so he can get the money; he imprisons Emanuella in Eliza Haywood's *The Rash Resolve; or, the Untimely Discovery.*

Pedro (Wilkins)   Helpful eldest son of Peter Wilkins and Youwarkee in Robert Paltock's *The Life and Adventures of Peter Wilkins.*

Lord Peebles   Kindly, rich, and foolish friend of the Penrhyn family in Caroline Norton's *Stuart of Dunleath.*

Peter Peebles   Impoverished madman, who has an endless lawsuit in the Scottish courts, is Alan Fairford's first client, and pursues Alan with a warrant when he leaves the court to search for Darsie Latimer (Arthur Redgauntlet) in Sir Walter Scott's *Redgauntlet.*

Miss Peecher   Small, neat, buxom mistress of a girls' school adjacent to Bradley Headstone's boys' school; she has a secret, unavailing love for Headstone in Charles Dickens's *Our Mutual Friend.*

Sir Robert Peel   Tory prime minister and leader of the Conservative party in Benjamin Disraeli's *Coningsby; or, The New Generation.*

John Peerybingle   Carrier and middle-aged husband of a young wife, Dot; despite his apparent dullness, he has a wise and generous heart, which is tested when he sees his wife in intimate conversation with a stranger in Charles Dickens's *The Cricket on the Hearth.*

Mary (Dot) Peerybingle   Pretty young wife of the much older John Peerybingle; observed by him in an apparently compromising situation, she is restored to her husband when her disguised male friend is revealed to be the long-lost lover of her friend May Fielding in Charles Dickens's *The Cricket on the Hearth.*

Clara Peggotty   Clara Copperfield's servant, who takes care of Clara's son, David, giving him affection after his mother's second marriage; she takes him with her to Yarmouth to visit her brother, Daniel Peggotty, and his family; she marries Mr. Barkis after Clara dies in Charles Dickens's *The Personal History of David Copperfield.*

Daniel (Dan'l) Peggotty   Fisherman who lives in a converted beached boat by the sea outside Yarmouth with his nephew Ham, niece Emily, and housekeeper Mrs. Gummidge; he searches for Emily all over Europe after she runs off with James Steerforth; he emigrates to Australia with Emily and Mrs. Gummidge after Ham's

death in Charles Dickens's *The Personal History of David Copperfield.*

Emily (Little Em'ly) Peggotty   Orphaned niece and adopted daughter of Daniel Peggotty; David Copperfield loves her when he is a boy and she is a little girl; she is engaged to her cousin, Ham Peggotty, when she grows up but leaves him to become James Steerforth's mistress in Charles Dickens's *The Personal History of David Copperfield.*

Ham Peggotty   Nephew of Clara Peggotty; like his uncle, Daniel Peggotty, he is a Yarmouth fisherman; he becomes engaged to Emily Peggotty; she breaks the engagement to elope with James Steerforth; rescuing passengers after a shipwreck, Ham drowns trying unsuccessfully to save Steerforth in Charles Dickens's *The Personal History of David Copperfield.*

Peggy   Poor sister of the old nurse of Maria (Venables); her financial struggles after her husband is killed at sea bring the small and uncharacteristic act of charity that erroneously elevates George Venables in Maria's eyes and engages the heroine's youthful fancy in Mary Wollstonecraft's *Maria; or The Wrongs of Woman.*

Peggy   Niece to Mrs. Clarke and sister to Mr. Webb in Thomas Holcroft's *Anna St. Ives.*

Hannah Pegham   Malicious, trusted servant of the evil Mr. Grimshaw in a ghost story interpolated into the narrative of William Beckford's *Azemia.*

Mrs. Pegler   Josiah Bounderby's poor mother, who finally exposes her son to be a blustering liar in Charles Dickens's *Hard Times.*

Pekuah   Princess Nekayah's favorite servant, who accompanies her on the search for nonexistent human happiness in Samuel Johnson's *The History of Rasselas, Prince of Abissinia.*

Pelagia   Beautiful dancer, rival of Hypatia, and devoted mistress of Amalric; bought and trained by Miriam, she performs in Orestes's circus, turns out to be Philammon's sister, and retires with him to the desert after Amalric's death to live in solitary penance in Charles Kingsley's *Hypatia.*

Mlle. Pelagie   A teacher at Mlle. Reuter's school who is common and ordinary in all respects in Charlotte Brontë's *The Professor.*

Pelagius   Powerful cleric sympathetic to the Greeks who advises Basil that there will be difficulties in fulfilling his aim of finding and marrying the Gothic princess Veranilda in George Gissing's *Veranilda.*

Mme. Pelet   M. Pelet's mother and the housekeeper of his school, who tests the waters to see if William Crimsworth would like to teach at Mlle. Reuter's school in Charlotte Brontë's *The Professor*.

Francois Pelet   Headmaster of a boys' school next to Mlle. Reuter's girls' school; engaged to Mlle. Zoraide Reuter, he employs William Crimsworth to teach English and Latin and becomes briefly jealous of Crimsworth as a rival; he marries Mlle. Reuter in Charlotte Brontë's *The Professor*.

Mr. Pelham   Henry Pelham's father and the extravagant, worldly younger son of an earl; his financial straits are periodically relieved by the deaths or generous impulses of family members in Edward Bulwer-Lytton's *Pelham*.

Lady Frances Pelham   Extravagant, impecunious daughter of a Scots peer and mother of Henry Pelham; her life centers around theatrical presentations of herself; she writes her son cheerful, worldly letters of unscrupulous advice for social advancement in Edward Bulwer-Lytton's *Pelham*.

Henry Pelham   Young man of fashion; he narrates the story of his moral and political education at the hands of his friends Lord Vincent, Sir Reginald Glanville, and the Countess of Roseville; his affection for Ellen and Reginald Glanville impels him to uncharacteristic action in tracking down Sir John Tyrrell's murderer in Edward Bulwer-Lytton's *Pelham*.

Dr. Pell   Renowned doctor who is called in from Dublin to treat Dr. Barney Sturk, but is unable to bring him out of his coma in J. Sheridan Le Fanu's *The House by the Churchyard*.

Solomon Pell   Attorney at Lincoln's Inn Fields hired by Tony Weller and Sam Weller to get Sam imprisoned for debt in the Fleet prison so he can remain with Samuel Pickwick in Charles Dickens's *The Posthumous Papers of the Pickwick Club*.

Mr. Pelter   Lawyer to Sir Jeckyl Marlowe; he drops a letter from Sir Jeckyl which says cruel, selfish things about Varbarriere, who finds it and decides to go through with the plans for revenge he has been on the verge of abandoning in J. Sheridan Le Fanu's *Guy Deverell*.

Lady Honoria Pemberton   A cousin of the Delviles; she encourages Lord Derford to court Cecilia Beverley and urges Cecilia to annul her marriage and turn to someone she does not love in Frances Burney's *Cecilia*.

Earl of Pembroke   Stern old warrior; he is Sir John de Walton's ally and Sir Aymer de Valence's uncle; he is defeated by Robert the Bruce at London Hill in Sir Walter Scott's *Castle Dangerous*.

Lady Pembroke   Attendant to Queen Elizabeth and sister of Sir Philip Sidney and Lady Arundel; she is a constant friend to Ellinor in Sophia Lee's *The Recess*.

Lord Pembroke   Husband of Lady Pembroke and supporter of the Duke of Norfolk's plan to free the pregnant Mary, Queen of Scots in Sophia Lee's *The Recess*.

Mr. Pembroke   Pompous but well-meaning tutor, who provides Edward Waverly with his erratic education in Sir Walter Scott's *Waverly*.

William Penberthy   Sailor and friend of Salvation Yeo; he stands by John Oxenham in Charles Kingsley's *Westward Ho!*.

Major Arthur Pendennis   Snobbish uncle of Arthur Pendennis, whose welfare he cares for in spite of his worldliness in William Makepeace Thackeray's *The History of Pendennis*. He also appears in *The Newcomes* and in *The Adventures of Philip on His Way through the World*.

Arthur Pendennis   Impetuous young man, who falls in love with an actress, fails his examinations at Oxbridge, earns his living as a journalist, and after falling in love with Blanche Amory and Fanny Bolton marries Laura Bell, his mother's ward who has long loved him, in William Makepeace Thackeray's *The History of Pendennis*. He returns as the narrator of *The Newcomes* and *The Adventures of Philip on His Way through the World*.

Helen Laura Bell, Mrs. Arthur Pendennis   The Reverend Francis Bell's orphaned daughter, later the ward of Helen Pendennis; she marries Arthur Pendennis in William Makepeace Thackeray's *The History of Pendennis*. Though priggish, she is a helpful friend to Colonel Newcome and Ethel Newcome in *The Newcomes* and to Philip and Charlotte (Baynes) Firman in *The Adventures of Philip on His Way through the World*.

Helen Thistlewood Pendennis   Saintly mother of Arthur Pendennis and guardian of his virtue; her discovery of a possible liaison between her son and Fanny Bolton brings about her premature death in William Makepeace Thackeray's *The History of Pendennis*.

John Pendennis   Surgeon who marries the much younger Helen Thistlewood, purchases a small estate, and dies when his son Arthur is sixteen in William Makepeace Thackeray's *The History of Pendennis*.

Katie Pender   Landlady's daughter whom Christopher Kirkland befriends and attempts to educate in Mrs. Lynn Linton's *The Autobiography of Christopher Kirkland*.

Pendlehamby *Colamb* (governor) of Arndrumnstake; he is Youwarkee's gracious and affectionate father, who is much loved by Peter Wilkins in Robert Paltock's *The Life and Adventures of Peter Wilkins.*

William Pendril Trusted lawyer of the Vanstone family; he breaks the news to Miss Garth that irregularities concerning Andrew Vanstone's marriage invalidate his will and leave his daughters, Norah and Magdalen, totally dependent on their uncle in Wilkie Collins's *No Name.*

Lady Penelope Penfeather Society leader who has spread the fame of the waters from St. Ronan's Well and whose gossip about the sexual ruin of Clara Mowbray drives John Mowbray to desperate measures in Sir Walter Scott's *St. Ronan's Well.*

David Penfold Gardener employed by Lady Sarah Francis; his daughter, Emma, makes a disastrous marriage with Frank Raban in Anne Thackeray Ritchie's *Old Kensington.*

Emma Penfold Young first wife of Frank Raban in Anne Thackeray Ritchie's *Old Kensington.*

Michael Penfold Robert Penfold's father, the cashier for Wardlaw and Company, who overcomes his natural timidity to help exonerate his son in Charles Reade's *Foul Play.*

Robert Penfold (James Seaton, John Hazel) Clergyman condemned to five years of penal servitude for a forgery he did not commit; as James Seaton he becomes gardener to General Rolleston in the colony; as John Hazel he saves the life of Helen Rolleston, the General's daughter; he is exonerated by her efforts; he marries her and, leaving the conduct of business to his father, Michael, returns to pastoral duties in the vale of Kent in Charles Reade's *Foul Play.*

Caroline Penge Heiress from Welsh coal mines selected by Lady Penwether to be a suitable wife for her brother, Lord Rufford, following his escape from Arabella Trefoil in Anthony Trollope's *The American Senator.* She appears briefly as Lady Rufford in *Ayala's Angel.*

Susan Penhale William's wife; she assists the reunion of Basil and his family in Wilkie Collins's *Basil: A Story of Modern Life.*

William Penhale Miner in Cornwall who assists Basil on the third occasion of his becoming incapacitated by an emotional crisis—this being caused by the accidental death of his enemy, Robert Mannion, in Wilkie Collins's *Basil: A Story of Modern Life.*

Penitent One of the good people of Vanity Fair introduced to Christiana and her party by Mnason in John Bunyan's *The Pilgrim's Progress From this World to That Which Is to Come.*

Mr. Pennywise A dying alderman, for whom the Methodist preacher Mr. Whitfield confidently prays but who "falls asleep" nonetheless in Richard Graves's *The Spiritual Quixote.*

Clephane Penrhyn Son of Sir Stephen and Eleanor (Raymond) Penrhyn; he is sensitive like his mother, but not a favorite of his father; he drowns, bravely telling his father to save his brother, Frederick, in Caroline Norton's *Stuart of Dunleath.*

Frederick Penrhyn A son of Sir Stephen and Eleanor (Raymond) Penrhyn; hearty and strong, he is liked by all and is his father's favorite; he drowns despite the attempts of Sir Stephen to save him in Caroline Norton's *Stuart of Dunleath.*

Sir Stephen Penrhyn Husband of Eleanor (Raymond) and the father of Clephane and Frederick; impetuous and jealous of Eleanor's obvious feeling for David Stuart, he takes Bridget as a mistress and has an illegitimate child, Owen; he abuses Eleanor in Caroline Norton's *Stuart of Dunleath.*

Colonel John Penruddock Royalist officer under the command of Sir Joseph Wagstaff; he is taken prisoner following the retreat from Salisbury and is beheaded at Exeter in William Godwin's *Mandeville.*

Nigel Penruddock Son of the vicar of Hurstley, where William Ferrars and his family were in "exile"; he is enthusiastically High Church and achieves a London post before converting to Roman Catholicism and returning to London as papal legate in Benjamin Disraeli's *Endymion.*

Mrs. Pentecost Doting mother of Samuel; she constantly harangues members of the Norfolk Broads picnic party about her son's health and welfare in Wilkie Collins's *Armadale.*

Samuel Pentecost Local curate who joins the Norfolk Broads picnic organized by Allan Armadale and suffers from overindulgence in Wilkie Collins's *Armadale.*

Lady Eleanor Penwether Sister of Lord Rufford; she steers Caroline Penge into his arms as a suitably rich wife and as insurance against fortune hunters in Anthony Trollope's *The American Senator.*

Sir George Penwether Brother-in-law of Lord Rufford; his counsels help Rufford escape from Arabella

Trefoil's clutches in Anthony Trollope's *The American Senator*.

Benedetto Pepi (Benedetto the Rich)   Cowardly Italian Guelph nobleman, who undertakes a usurious scheme to become Lord of Cremona, and whose unscrupulous behavior influences Castruccio dei Antelminelli in Mary Shelley's *Valperga*.

Pepper (The Avenger)   Pip Pirrip's servant in London, who dresses in outlandish livery, and who uses Pip's status as a gentlemen to run up bills in Charles Dickens's *Great Expectations*.

Fred Pepper   Expert in horseflesh and keen member of the set which congregates at the Moonbeam pub and encourages the gambling and indebtedness of Ralph Newton, the heir of Newton Priory, in Anthony Trollope's *Ralph the Heir*.

Mr. Peppermint   Widower with three children who marries Norah Geraghty in Anthony Trollope's *The Three Clerks*.

Dr. Parker Peps   Court physician, who attends Fanny Dombey at the birth of little Paul Dombey and pretends to confusion over the names of his aristocratic patients; he attends little Paul at his death in Charles Dickens's *Dombey and Son*.

Perch   Messenger at Paul Dombey's firm who prepares Dombey's office each morning and has a pregnant wife in Charles Dickens's *Dombey and Son*.

Mrs. Perch   Wife of the messenger Perch; she is present at the ceremony of Paul Dombey's second marriage in Charles Dickens's *Dombey and Son*.

Sir Percival   Knight errant, seduced by the Maid of the Alder; he must make his red, rusted armor shine by doing his duty once more; Anodos becomes his page and learns humility and love in George MacDonald's *Phantastes*.

Lady Anne Percival   Charming, good-natured wife of Henry Percival and a model of domestic tranquility and integrity in Maria Edgeworth's *Belinda*.

Henry Percival   Honorable ex-beau of Lady Delacour; he marries an amiable woman and becomes the picture of domestic bliss; he is the guardian of Mr. Vincent but refuses to vouch for Vincent's honor when Vincent turns to gaming in Maria Edgeworth's *Belinda*.

Lord Percy   Eldest son of the Earl of Northumberland; he loves Anna Boleyn but finds his engagement to her canceled after Henry VIII sees her and lusts after her in Henry Fielding's *A Journey From This World to the Next*.

Lord Alfred Percy   Junior officer aboard the British gunboat sent to re-annex the independent island of Britannula and depose its president, John Neverbend, in Anthony Trollope's *The Fixed Period*.

Perdita   A commoner, the reserved sister of Lionel Verney and the wife of Lord Raymond; she suffers anguish from her husband's infidelity but rushes to him when he is wounded and later commits suicide to join him in the grave in Mary Shelley's *The Last Man*.

Bryan Perdue   Alias of the otherwise nameless narrator who, after years of gambling, is imprisoned for debt, tried for forgery, and finally moves to Jamaica, where he manages a large sugar plantation and teaches the natives how to lead virtuous lives in Thomas Holcroft's *The Memoirs of Bryan Perdue*.

Bryan Perdue's father   An Irish man of fashion, an adulterer, and a gambler in Thomas Holcroft's *The Memoirs of Bryan Perdue*.

Bernardino Perfetti   Poet laureate of the Vatican and a renowned *improvisator*; originally from Siena, he is the uncle of Francesco Perfetti in William Godwin's *Cloudesley*.

Francesco Perfetti   Nephew of the poet laureate of the Vatican, Bernardino Perfetti; he is the loyal, trusted friend of Julian Danvers; the two young friends steal away from Verona and join the robber St. Elmo in his depredations on the rich; he leads an attack against a group of interlopers, which includes Cloudesley, in William Godwin's *Cloudesley*.

Antonio Agriopoulos Pericles   A Greek business associate of Samuel Pole; he discovers Emilia Belloni singing in a wood and wants to send her to Italy to study music; his attempt to seduce her when she loses her voice helps to precipitate her near death and the near financial ruin of the Poles in George Meredith's *Emilia in England*. He arranges to have her kidnapped to keep her from involvement in the cause for Italian liberation in *Vittoria*.

Perigen   Mythical brother to Philella, with whom he propagates a race of flying people in Normnbdsgrsutt in Robert Paltock's *The Life and Adventures of Peter Wilkins*.

Mrs. Periwinkle   Owner of a slop shop and housekeeper to the duke; she is the first person in England to assume custody of the captive Azemia in William Beckford's *Azemia*.

Sally Periwinkle   Aging, aspiring niece of Mrs. Periwinkle; long a pimp among the poor for the duke, she recaptures Azemia with the help of Mr. Perkly but loses her again, this time to poachers in William Beckford's *Azemia*.

Mr. Perker Small, elderly, wise lawyer, who assists Jem Wardle in buying off Alfred Jingle after the elopement with Rachael Wardle, and who counsels Samuel Pickwick in the breach-of-promise suit in Charles Dickens's *The Posthumous Papers of the Pickwick Club*.

Mrs. Perkins Resident in Cook's Court in Charles Dickens's *Bleak House*.

Peter Perkins Self-absorbed young gentleman, a longtime admirer of Arabella Bloomville; he aggressively pursues the new bride, who temporarily forgets she is married in William Beckford's *Modern Novel Writing; or, the Elegant Enthusiast*.

Courtney Perkly Unpleasant man who attaches himself to Mrs. Blandford; he is secretly the duke's agent and searching for Azemia, whom he eventually tricks into leaving the safety of Mrs. Blandford's house in William Beckford's *Azemia*.

Duchesse de Perpignan Self-defined "Byronic" woman, who becomes a lover of Henry Pelham in Paris; upon his announced departure, she attempts to arrange his death at the hands of a dueling-prone rival in Edward Bulwer-Lytton's *Pelham*.

Dicky Perrott Child who grows up in the tough East End slum called the Jago; he learns the ways of crime, turns temporarily straight under the influence of Father Sturt, and is finally stabbed to death in Arthur Morrison's *A Child of the Jago*.

Hannah Perrott Mother of Dicky and wife of Josh; she is beaten down by the harshness and violence of life in the Jago in Arthur Morrison's *A Child of the Jago*.

Josh Perrott Tough father of Dicky; he earns the respect of the Jago dwellers for his prowess in fighting, but he murders Aaron Weech and is sentenced to death by hanging in Arthur Morrison's *A Child of the Jago*.

Perry Geoffrey Delamayn's trainer for the race in the losing of which Delamayn exhibits his susceptibility to stroke in Wilkie Collins's *Man and Wife*.

Mr. Perry Highbury apothecary on whom Mr. Woodhouse relies in Jane Austen's *Emma*.

Perseus Warwick's Negro servant, who travels with Orlando Somerive in America and, escaping an ambush during which he believes Orlando has been killed, returns to erroneously report his death to the Somerive family in Charlotte Smith's *The Old Manor House*.

Lord Persiflage Worldly Secretary of State, who makes light of things in general and plays down his work in the cabinet in Anthony Trollope's *Marion Fay*.

Geraldine, Lady Persiflage Mother of Lady Amaldina Hauteville and sister of the Marchioness of Kingsbury; she is kindly disposed towards her sister's two stepchildren, Lord Hampstead and Lady Frances Trafford, much to the annoyance of the Marchioness in Anthony Trollope's *Marion Fay*.

Peruvian Chrysal's first owner, who steals the gold and presents it as a peace-offering during confession in Charles Johnstone's *Chrysal: or, The Adventures of a Guinea*.

Professor Pesca Diminutive Italian refugee friend of Walter Hartright and one-time political associate of Count Fosco; he secures Walter a post as drawing master to Laura Fairlie; Pesca informs on Fosco to an Italian secret society in Wilkie Collins's *The Woman in White*.

Count di Peschiera An Italian and Alphonso Riccabocca's devious kinsman, who betrayed him to the Austrians, forced him into exile, and years later attempts to marry his daughter, Violante Riccabocca, in Edward Bulwer-Lytton's *"My Novel," by Pisistratus Caxton*.

Peter Harley's faithful, honest servant, distinguished by a solitary lock of hair on either side of his head in Henry Mackenzie's *The Man of Feeling*. He also appears in *The Man of the World*.

Peter Loquacious servant to the La Mott family, whose attempt to help Adeline escape the abbey is thwarted; ultimately he escapes with Adeline to his native Savoy, where she is sheltered by the La Luc family in Ann Radcliffe's *The Romance of the Forest*.

Peter Bullying, unpleasant reader and henchman of Cyril the patriarch in Charles Kingsley's *Hypatia*.

Peter Servant who brings food to Ferdinand de Mazzini while he is imprisoned in a dungeon in Ann Radcliffe's *A Sicilian Romance*.

Peter Disagreeable bridge ward of the drawbridge of Brigton at Kennaquhair; he feuds with the monks of the Monastery St. Mary's over their tolls and laments his inability to extort tolls from the soldiers and feudal retainers in Sir Walter Scott's *The Monastery* and in *The Abbot*.

Peter the Hermit Influential but fanatical crusader in Sir Walter Scott's *Count Robert of Paris*.

Father Peter Priest who introduces his curate, Oliver Gogarty, to Rose Leicester, the new schoolmistress; he seems aware that she will cause trouble in the parish because of her beauty; he falls ill, and after his death is replaced by Oliver in George Moore's *The Lake.*

King Peter King of Upmeads and father of Blaise, Hugh, Gregory, and Ralph in William Morris's *The Well at the World's End.*

Mr. Peters Lincolnshire clergyman who, to protect his standing with Mr. B——, refuses the Reverend Williams's request to help Pamela escape her imprisonment on Mr. B——'s Lincolnshire estate; later, after reading Pamela's letters, he becomes one of her admirers in Samuel Richardson's *Pamela, or Virtue Rewarded.*

Curdie Peterson (later Prince Conrad) Twelve-year-old miner's son, who thwarts the goblins' plot to kidnap little Princess Irene and to flood the mines and is himself rescued by the princess in George MacDonald's *The Princess and the Goblin.* He saves the king and kingdom from the treasonable plot laid by the lord chamberlain, attorney-general, master of the horse, and the king's private secretary; he marries Princess Irene when they are grown and rules a prosperous and happy kingdom in *The Princess and Curdie.*

Joan Peterson Curdie's mother, whose character resembles that of old Princess Irene; she gives Curdie a ball of thread to prevent him from getting lost in the mines in George MacDonald's *The Princess and the Goblin.* She also appears in *The Princess and Curdie.*

Peter Peterson Curdie's father, a miner, who, leading the miners, defeats the goblins' attempt to flood the mines in George MacDonald's *The Princess and the Goblin.* He joins the king in a successful battle against the King of Borsagrass in *The Princess and Curdie.*

Luke Peterson Nineteen-year-old boy who carries Margaret Brandt's laundry baskets, thinking he is wooing her, but finally marries Reicht Heynes in Charles Reade's *The Cloister and the Hearth.*

John Pether Eccentric umbrella mender who befriends Arthur Golding in George Gissing's *Workers in the Dawn.*

Lady Petherwin Mother-in-law of the young widowed heroine Ethelberta Petherwin; the sudden death of her husband following her son's reconciles her to Ethelberta, and she plans to leave her well provided for, but she resents Ethelberta's published authorship and, dying, withdraws most of her property in Thomas Hardy's *The Hand of Ethelberta.*

Ethelberta Petherwin Handsome young widow, whose literary talent soon makes her famous among the upper class; she keeps hidden the fact that she is the daughter of servants and is courted by several gentlemen; she finally marries the aged and disreputable Lord Mountclere for financial security and triumphs over the resentment of his family and society to manage him and his household completely in Thomas Hardy's *The Hand of Ethelberta.*

Petit-André A short, stout, and merry hangman, Provost L'Hermite's assistant and Trois-Eschelles's colleague in Sir Walter Scott's *Quentin Durward.*

Henrietta Petowker Actress of the Theatre Royal, Drury Lane, and a friend of the Kenwigs family; after a special appearance with the Crummles company she marries Mr. Lillyvick but leaves him in Charles Dickens's *The Life and Adventures of Nicholas Nickleby.*

Wallachia Petrie Bluestocking American poet known as the Republican Browning; she is strongly critical of British institutions; she opposes Caroline Spalding's marriage to Charles Glascock in Anthony Trollope's *He Knew He Was Right.*

Petronilla Pious and severe aunt of Basil; he suspects her of kidnapping Aurelia and Veranilda in George Gissing's *Veranilda.*

Laird of Pettlechase A neighbor and friend of Laird Douglas in Susan Ferrier's *Marriage.*

Petty-fogger Somersetshire lawyer who slanders Tom Jones at the Bell Inn, turning his listeners against Tom in Henry Fielding's *The History of Tom Jones.*

Sir Geoffrey Peveril High Church cavalier who fought for King Charles I during the English civil wars, suffered during Cromwell's Protectorate, and rejoices at the Restoration in Sir Walter Scott's *Peveril of the Peak.*

Julian Peveril Son of Sir Geoffrey and Lady Peveril and a childhood companion of Alice Bridgenorth; he is imprisoned in Newgate and the Tower as an accomplice in the Popish Plot; acquitted at the trial, he is received by King Charles II; he marries Alice in Sir Walter Scott's *Peveril of the Peak.*

Margaret Stanley, Lady Peveril Wife of Sir Geoffrey and mother of Julian; she has raised the motherless Alice Bridgenorth with her son in Sir Walter Scott's *Peveril of the Peak.*

Pew Blind pirate, who sailed with Flint; he delivers the black spot to Billy Bones and leads the attack on the Admiral Benbow Inn; fleeing and abandoned by the others, he is trampled to death by a horse in Robert Louis Stevenson's *Treasure Island.*

Theodore Peyron Son of Arnand La Luc, and a French officer in Phillippe, Marquis de Montalt's regiment; he falls in love with Adeline and helps her to escape from Montalt; captured, he is tried for insubordination and sentenced to death; upon Montalt's trial, he is released and married to Adeline in Ann Radcliffe's *The Romance of the Forest*.

Phaortes Grecian admiral, who burns to death with his squadron because of mismanagement of Greek fire in Sir Walter Scott's *Count Robert of Paris*.

Pharamond Character who writes from London to his friend Cleomenes at Oxford on the subject of self-pride, using as an exemplary situation the response of a group of ladies to Pope's *Rape of the Lock* in Sarah Fielding's *Familiar Letters between the Principal Characters of David Simple and Some Others*.

Phebe Daughter of Gaius; she marries James in John Bunyan's *The Pilgrim's Progress From this World to That Which Is to Come*.

Pheron Native of Abissinia, a noble savage, who, proselytized by a Jesuit, travels to Europe to receive the blessings of the pope; brought to Lisbon because of his wealth, he is made a prisoner of the Holy Office because of his opinions in Charles Johnstone's *Chrysal: or, The Adventures of a Guinea*.

Philammon Beautiful, impetuous, intelligent young monk, who leaves the monastery of the Laura for Alexandria and falls under Hypatia's influence; he learns that he is Pelagia's brother and the slave of Arsenius (Aufugus); he finally tries to save Hypatia, reforms Pelagia, and returns to the Laura, becoming abbot, in Charles Kingsley's *Hypatia*.

Philamont Count of Lacedemon killed by the Duke of Malfy, who thinks he is having an affair with the duchess, Gigantilla, in Eliza Haywood's *The Perplex'd Dutchess; or, Treachery Rewarded*.

Philander Amorous brother-in-law to Sylvia and an accomplished liar who breaks all political and romantic vows; a self-interested member of the cabal against the king, he first seduces Sylvia and later Calista, loses both women, but ultimately gains the king's pardon, when, disenchanted with Cesario, he refuses to fight in his campaign in Aphra Behn's *Love Letters Between a Nobleman and His Sister*.

Philella Mythical sister to Perigen, with whom she propagates a race of flying people in Normnbdsgrsutt in Robert Paltock's *The Life and Adventures of Peter Wilkins*.

Philidore Hero, whose lack of wealth makes his love for Placentia hopeless; he disguises himself as her servant, Jacobin; forced to flee to Persia, he comes into a small fortune when his uncle dies; he ultimately finds and wins Placentia in Eliza Haywood's *Philidore and Placentia; or, L'Amour trop delicat*.

Philip Madam de Beaumont's faithful servant, who stays with her in a cave in Wales for fourteen years and helps her through many trials in Penelope Aubin's *The Life of Madam de Beaumont*.

(Alleyn) Philip Powerful young Scot, called Alleyn and reared by peasants; he befriends Osbert of Athlin and falls in love with Mary; he helps to lead an attack on Malcolm of Dunbayne but is captured and imprisoned; escaping from Castle Dunbayne, he rescues Mary from kidnappers and rescues Osbert from Dunbayne; he exiles himself from Mary, only to rescue her from the Count de Santmorin; discovered to be Philip of Dunbayne, nephew of Malcolm, he is betrothed to Mary in Ann Radcliffe's *The Castles of Athlin and Dunbayne*.

Duke Philip Duke of Burgundy, Earl of Holland, Count of Flanders; he is a fighter, a womanizer, and a patron of the arts in Charles Reade's *The Cloister and the Hearth*.

Father Philip Sacristan at the Monastery of St. Mary's; a ladies' man, he is nonetheless orthodox in his Catholicism and despairs of Lady Alice Avenel's heresy; upon seizing her Protestant Bible, he receives a rough dunking by the White Lady in Sir Walter Scott's *The Monastery*. He is the "mock" priest who performed the secret marriage of Julian Avenel and Catherine Graeme; his dying confession makes Roland Graeme heir to the Avenel estates in *The Abbot*.

King Philip King of France and a leader of Christian forces on Crusade; he is eager to return to Europe in Sir Walter Scott's *The Talisman*.

King Philip II Spanish monarch who wars with England in Sophia Lee's *The Recess*. He is a zealous supporter of the Inquisition; his return to his native land after seven years' absence in England and the Netherlands is celebrated by the auto-da-fe which Reginald de St. Leon only just escapes in William Godwin's *St. Leon*.

Mother Philippa Subprioress of The Passionist Sisters; she is competent, managerial, and instinctive in George Moore's *Evelyn Innes* and in *Sister Teresa*.

Laetitia Philips Daughter of a respectable family in Merionetshire and a new friend of Mary Fleetwood; she encourages Mary to go to the dance at Barmouth with Mr. Matthews in William Godwin's *Fleetwood*.

King Phillip le Bel King of France; he rewards Castruccio dei Antelminelli for bravery in battle in Mary Shelley's *Valperga*.

Mr. Phillips Country-town attorney and the husband of Mrs. Bennet's sister in Jane Austen's *Pride and Prejudice*.

Mrs. Phillips Mrs. Bennet's good-humored, inelegant sister, who married a country attorney; she is aunt of the five Bennet girls in Jane Austen's *Pride and Prejudice*.

Sir Watkin Phillips Oxford school friend of Jery Melford; he is Jery's confidential correspondent in Tobias Smollett's *The Expedition of Humphry Clinker*.

Richard Phillotson Aging, pitiable schoolmaster who marries the young Sue Bridehead and then, against his judgment and desires, allows her to run off with Jude Fawley; he welcomes her back when tragedy drives her from Jude in Thomas Hardy's *Jude the Obscure*.

Philometra A princess whom Exilius loves in Jane Barker's *Exilius; or, The Banish'd Roman*.

Phoebe Gracious youngest sister of the Laird of Dornock; she becomes the confidante of Ellinor and falls in love with Tracey in Sophia Lee's *The Recess*.

Phoebe Helena Beauly's maid at the time of Sara Macallan's death; she is later Lady Clarinda's maid in Wilkie Collins's *The Law and the Lady*.

Mr. Phoebus Painter and philosopher; he is part of Theodora Campian's revolutionary circle; he utters the famous remark that critics are "... men who have failed at literature and art" in Benjamin Disraeli's *Lothair*.

Mr. Phunky Nervous and timid lawyer, junior to Serjeant Snubbins; he is retained to represent Samuel Pickwick in court for the breach-of-promise suit in Charles Dickens's *The Posthumous Papers of the Pickwick Club*.

Phutatorius Acquaintance of Yorick the parson; he disrupts postprandial conversation when a hot chestnut accidentally falls into his breeches; he accuses Yorick of putting it there in Laurence Sterne's *The Life and Opinions of Tristram Shandy, Gentleman*.

Phyllis Mother of Pompey and canine companion to the celebrated Courtesan of Bologna in Francis Coventry's *The History of Pompey the Little*.

Laura Piaveni Energetic and passionate Italian patriot, who aids Vittoria Campa, Angelo Guidascarpi, and Merthyr Powys in George Meredith's *Vittoria*.

Gam (Gammy, Crookback) Pickle Second son of Gamaliel and Sally Pickle; he hates his elder brother, Perry; he is favored by his mother and is victimized by Perry's pranks; he refuses reconciliation with Perry after the death of their father in Tobias Smollett's *The Adventures of Peregrine Pickle*.

Gamaliel Pickle A London merchant's son, who retires to the country, marries, and fathers Peregrine; he joins his wife in hostility toward Peregrine; he dies intestate, and his property is claimed by Peregrine in Tobias Smollett's *The Adventures of Peregrine Pickle*.

Julia Pickle Sister of Perry and Gam; driven from her house by her mother for defending Perry, she goes to live with her aunt and Commodore Trunnion; she marries Mr. Clover in Tobias Smollett's *The Adventures of Peregrine Pickle*.

Peregrine (Perry) Pickle Young man whose mother hates him; he lives with his aunt's husband, Commodore Trunnion, enjoys practical jokes, attends Winchester and then Oxford, and falls in love with Emilia Gauntlet; he is sent on a tour of the Continent, where he seduces various women; he has other picaresque adventures there and in London before he seeks refuge in the Fleet when he is nearly bankrupt; he returns home after his father's death, taking possession of his property and marrying Emilia, in Tobias Smollett's *The Adventures of Peregrine Pickle*.

Sally Appleby Pickle Wife of Gamaliel; having had Mrs. Grizzle's help in marrying, she alienates Mrs. Grizzle after the marriage; she hates her first son, Peregrine, drives away her daughter, Julia, and dotes on her second son, Gam, in Tobias Smollett's *The Adventures of Peregrine Pickle*.

Pickthank One of three men who give evidence against Faithful and Christian at their trial at Vanity Fair in John Bunyan's *The Pilgrim's Progress From this World to That Which Is to Come*.

Samuel Pickwick General chairman of the Pickwick Club, a model of kindness and generosity, and the elderly, bespectacled, plump protagonist, who leads his three companions in quixotic adventures to Rochester, Eatanswill, Dingley Dell, and Bath; he becomes incarcerated in the Fleet prison in Charles Dickens's *The Posthumous Papers of the Pickwick Club*.

Sir Omicron Pie Eminent London surgeon, who attends the dying Bishop Grantly and is also called to treat Dean Trefoil in Anthony Trollope's *Barchester Towers*. He attends the dying Duke of Omnium in *Phineas Redux*. His expertise is also required in *Doctor Thorne*, in *The Small House at Allington*, in *The Bertrams*, and in *The Prime Minister*.

Pierre Queen Eleanor's minstrel, whose ballad relates a story dangerously similar to the murder of Reginald de Folville in Ann Radcliffe's *Gaston de Blondeville*.

Pierre Woodcutter who finds Julia Wiemar lying half dead in the snow and takes her to his hut to nurse her back to health in Charlotte Dacre's *The Passions*.

Flora Pierson Young seamstress for Miss Matson; she is befriended by Juliet Granville and is saved by Juliet from seduction by Sir Lyell Sycamore in Frances Burney's *The Wanderer*.

Colonel/General John Pierson An officer in the Austrian military and an uncle of the Poles; he gives Wilfrid Pole the idea of joining the Austrian service in George Meredith's *Emilia in England*. He refuses to help Wilfrid regain his lost army commission because he helped Angelo Guidascarpi escape in *Vittoria*.

Avice Pierston The daughter of Ann Avice (Caro) and Isaac Pierston; her widowed mother writes to Jocelyn Pierston because she wants him to fall in love with and marry young Avice; he perceives in her his "well-beloved" and is enthusiastic about the plan, but Avice Pierston, loving Henri Leverre, jilts the elderly Jocelyn by eloping; Jocelyn plans to use his fortune to provide for the young couple in Thomas Hardy's *The Well-Beloved*.

Isaac (Ike) Pierston Youth from the isolated peninsular society which also includes the Benscomb and Caro families; his relationship to Jocelyn Pierston is remote; having secretly married Ann Avice Caro, he is reunited with her through the assistance of Jocelyn Pierston; he proves an indifferent but not an unkind husband and dies when their daughter, Avice Pierston, has reached young womanhood in Thomas Hardy's *The Well-Beloved*.

Jocelyn Pierston Sculptor of talent and wealth whose emotional life is wasted because he transfers his affections from woman to woman in pursuit of the abstract, elusive "well-beloved," a woman who he believes is his kindred spirit; the principal objects of his shifting admiration are young women of three successive generations: Avice Caro, her daughter Ann Avice Caro, and granddaughter Avice Pierston; he also loves as a youth and marries, without love, in old age Marcia Bencomb; he finds that his artistic powers as well as his pursuit of the "well-beloved" have left him empty in Thomas Hardy's *The Well-Beloved*.

Pietrino Assassin who enables Abellino (Count Rosalvo) to join his band and thus bring them and the conspirators to justice in Matthew Lewis's *The Bravo of Venice*.

Piety One of three virgins of the Palace Beautiful who catechize Christian and later his sons; she shows them the house and its contents in John Bunyan's *The Pilgrim's Progress From this World to That Which Is to Come*.

Pigeon Nesting bird that addresses Alice as "serpent" after the elongation of her neck; Alice's admission that little girls eat eggs confirms the Pigeon's opinion in Lewis Carroll's *Alice's Adventures in Wonderland*.

Mr. Pigeon Main opponent of Arthur Vincent in the Salem congregation because he thinks the minister despises him and his family for their vulgarity in Margaret Oliphant's *Salem Chapel*.

James Pigg Huntsman hired by John Jorrocks to be keeper of the Handley Cross hounds; he develops a scheme to sell the fox hunters insurance in Robert Surtees's *Handley Cross*. He manages Hillingdon Hall when Jorocks is away in attendance at Parliament in *Hillingdon Hall*.

Jeremiah Pighills A worker at Robert Moore's mill, who is supposed to be a suitor of his servant Sarah in Charlotte Brontë's *Shirley*.

Matthew Pike Adroit and tactful old butler of Peter Prosper; he dreads his proposed new mistress, Miss Thoroughbung, in Anthony Trollope's *Mr. Scarborough's Family*.

Pilate Governor who is reluctant to condemn Jesus but does so to prevent insurrection; he permits Joseph of Arimathea to remove Jesus from the cross for private burial in George Moore's *The Brook Kerith*.

Mr. Pile Boot-maker and powerbroker among the citizens of Percycross; he loathes the very idea of purity of election; he tells Sir Thomas Underwood, the Conservative candidate, that if he wants the seat he will have to pay for it in Anthony Trollope's *Ralph the Heir*.

Dr. Pillule Physician who is replaced at Mme. Beck's by Dr. John Bretton in Charlotte Brontë's *Villette*.

Ruth Pinch Tom Pinch's sister, abused as a governess and rescued by her brother to become the domestic angel in his household and later to marry John Westlock in Charles Dickens's *The Life and Adventures of Martin Chuzzlewit*.

Tom Pinch Assistant to Seth Pecksniff and his most profound admirer until Pecksniff's hypocrisy and cruelty are shockingly revealed to him by Mary Graham; his modesty, loyalty, unselfishness, and kindness make him universally loved; he keeps secret his own self-denying love for Mary Graham in Charles Dickens's *The Life and Adventures of Martin Chuzzlewit*.

Nichola Pine-Avon   Handsome young widow whom Jocelyn Pierston meets in society and briefly perceives as the "well-beloved"; she is attracted to him, but he has lost interest; she marries his friend, the painter Alfred Somers in Thomas Hardy's *The Well-Beloved*.

Hester Pinhorn   Simple, illiterate cook in the service of Count Fosco; she is a witness at the death of Anne Catherick in Fosco's house, believing her to be Laura (Fairlie), Lady Glyde in Wilkie Collins's *The Woman in White*.

Pinkerton   Bragging, drunken Scot and member of Captain Harris's gang; he is the first scalped after the burial of the Master (James Durie) in Robert Louis Stevenson's *The Master of Ballantrae: A Winter's Tale*.

Pinkerton   Political opponent of Arthur Brook in the election for Parliament in George Eliot's *Middlemarch*.

Barbara Pinkerton   Formidable headmistress of the select school for young ladies where Amelia Sedley meets Becky Sharp; she dislikes Becky too much to make her the customary gift of Johnson's *Dictionary* in William Makepeace Thackeray's *Vanity Fair*.

Jemima Pinkerton   Good-natured sister of Barbara Pinkerton; her gift of Johnson's *Dictionary* to Becky Sharp meets with scant gratitude in William Makepeace Thackeray's *Vanity Fair*.

Jim (Broken-Stool) Pinkerton   Would-be gentleman, sometime newspaperman, irrepressible entrepreneur, and steadfast friend and supporter of Loudon Dodd; he buys the *Flying Scud* wreck with Dodd in Robert Louis Stevenson's *The Wrecker*.

Mr. Pinnick   Mrs. Gerrarde's servant, whom she calls "cousin"; he discloses to Sir George Bidulph much of Mrs. Gerrarde's past stratagems to obtain money in Frances Sheridan's *Memoirs of Miss Sidney Bidulph*.

Mr. Pip   Theatrical man, whose conversation is sprinkled with oaths and with references to noble acquaintances; he is a guest at the dinner Tigg Montague gives for Jonas Chuzzlewit in Charles Dickens's *The Life and Adventures of Martin Chuzzlewit*.

Mrs. Pipchin   Bitter old woman with a stooping figure and hooked nose; she keeps a select infantine boarding school in Brighton, where little Paul Dombey is sent with his sister Florence and Mrs. Wickam; she later becomes Mr. Dombey's housekeeper in Charles Dickens's *Dombey and Son*.

Mr. Pipe   Wine merchant who, with provost James Pawkie's help, raises a volunteer corps in 1793 ostensibly as a patriotic gesture; the enterprise offers "the honors of command" to Pipe and "the profits of contract" to Pawkie in John Galt's *The Provost*.

Piper   Blind man who goes door to door in London playing his pipe so that people will take him in each night in Daniel Defoe's *A Journal of the Plague Year*.

Anastasia Piper   Resident in Cook's Court in Charles Dickens's *Bleak House*.

Tom Pipes   Retired naval man who had been Commodore Trunnion's boatswain's mate and lives with the Commodore and runs his household; he writes a new note from Perry Pickle to Emilia Gauntlet that makes her think Perry is insane; he insists on accompanying Perry on many of his adventures on the Continent until he is dismissed in disgrace, and he rejoins Perry after his return to England in Tobias Smollett's *The Adventures of Peregrine Pickle*.

Mrs. Pipkin   Respectable lodginghouse keeper in London and aunt of Ruby Ruggles, who foolishly runs away from home to take a room with her aunt so that she can see Felix Carbury on the sly; Mrs. Hurtle also lodges with Mrs. Pipkin in Anthony Trollope's *The Way We Live Now*.

Nathaniel Pipkin   Parish clerk of a country village in "A Tale of True Love," told by Weller and written down by Samuel Pickwick in Charles Dickens's *The Posthumous Papers of the Pickwick Club*.

Count Alessandro Pippi   Card-playing crony of Redmond Barry and the Chevalier de Balibari (Cornelius Barry) in William Makepeace Thackeray's *The Luck of Barry Lyndon*.

Pirret   Skipper Arblaster's friend who convinces him to take Will Lawless and Dick Shelton to a pub where they can tell their story in Robert Louis Stevenson's *The Black Arrow: A Tale of Two Roses*.

Philip (Pip) Pirrip   Orphan brought up by his abusive sister, Mrs. Joe Gargery, and from boyhood in love with Estella, who taunts him for being low-bred and common; his visits to Miss Havisham's house make him dissatisfied with his station; provided with great expectations (money) from an unknown source, he believes his patron to be Miss Havisham, motivated by a wish to help him rise in the world and marry Estella; instead, she is interested in Pip only as a male object of her vengeance through Estella; Pip is greatly shocked to learn that Abel Magwitch, the convict he helped in the churchyard, is his benefactor; caring for Magwitch, Pip learns to value affection rather than affectation in Charles Dickens's *Great Expectations*.

Gaetano Pisani Neapolitan composer, who dies shortly after his daughter, Viola Pisani, makes a triumphant operatic debut in an opera of his own composition in Edward Bulwer-Lytton's *Zanoni*.

Lucretia, Lady Pisani Beautiful and haughty heiress, whose trifling with Count Malvesi's affections nearly leads to a duel between Malvesi and Ferdinando Falkland in William Godwin's *Caleb Williams*.

Viola Pisani Gaetano Pisani's daughter, for whom Zanoni sacrifices his mystic powers and ultimately his life; she represents human instinct in Edward Bulwer-Lytton's *Zanoni*.

Piso A wicked traitor, who is responsible for the rebellion and uprising in Rome; he wants to seduce the queen of Egypt in Jane Barker's *Exilius; or, The Banish'd Roman*.

Mr. Pittle Young, widely unpopular assistant minister of Gudetown who was appointed by provost James Pawkie for private family reasons in John Galt's *The Provost*.

Gabriel Pitwinnoch Solicitor who helps George Walkinshaw prove his brother Walter mentally incapable of managing the Walkinshaw estate of Kittlestonheugh and later conspires with Robina Walkinshaw and her husband Walkinshaw Milrookit in their attempt to obtain control of the estate in John Galt's *The Entail*.

Mr. Pivart A client of John Wakem; he is involved in the water rights dispute with Mr. Tulliver in George Eliot's *The Mill on the Floss*.

Monsieur Pivet Orlando Faulkland's valet de chambre, whom Faulkland appoints as interpreter for and would-be suitor to Mrs. Gerrarde; he marries her with the benefit of a financial settlement from Faulkland and finally rids himself of her by allowing her to go to Paris as mistress of a nobleman in Frances Sheridan's *Memoirs of Miss Sidney Bidulph*.

Placentia Heroine, whose pride interferes with her love for the impecunious Philidore; forced to run away, she has many adventures, including several near rapes, but is finally united with Philidore in Eliza Haywood's *Philidore and Placentia; or, L'Amour trop delicat*.

Mrs. Placket Proprietress of a coffeehouse who confesses to Geoffry Wildgoose that she is also a procuress in Richard Graves's *The Spiritual Quixote*.

Mr. Plan Borough council member whose idea for a new school is thwarted by James Pawkie, the provost, because it conflicts with a self-interested scheme of his own in John Galt's *The Provost*.

Lady Edith Plantagenet Lady in waiting to Queen Berengaria and a kinswoman of King Richard; she is loved by Sir Kenneth and is sought by the Saladin as a bride; she is betrothed to Sir Kenneth when his true identity is disclosed in Sir Walter Scott's *The Talisman*.

Mr. Platt Father of the destitute and plague-stricken Platt family; he confesses to Margaret Ibbotson before his death that it was he who, dressed as a woman, stole Margaret's turquoise ring, a keepsake from Philip Enderby; he returns the ring to her in Harriet Martineau's *Deerbrook*.

Tom Platt A fisherman, formerly with the navy, who works on the cod-fishing boat that rescues Harvey Cheyne in Rudyard Kipling's *"Captains Courageous": A Story of the Grand Banks*.

Mr. Playmore Lawyer who prepared the defense in Eustace Macallan's trial for the murder of his first wife; he assists and advises Valeria Macallan in her investigation; he believes the poisoner to be Miserrimus Dexter in Wilkie Collins's *The Law and the Lady*.

Lady Plealands Claud Walkinshaw's mother-in-law, a woman of sensibility who influences Charles Walkinshaw to adopt a romantically naive view of life, thus unintentionally making him an easier victim for his father in John Galt's *The Entail*.

M. du Plessis Virtuous young man, who brings unwelcome messages of love from the Count de Bellfleur to Louisa and falls in love with her himself; loving him, she rejects him because her misfortunes have deprived her of the appropriate social and financial equality, but he remains steadfast and they are at last united in Eliza Haywood's *The Fortunate Foundlings*.

Pliable Christian's companion as far as the Slough of Despond who then returns to the City of Destruction; he is despised by the people in John Bunyan's *The Pilgrim's Progress From this World to That Which Is to Come*.

Mr. Pliant Gamester who preys on George Edwards in John Hill's *The Adventures of Mr. George Edwards, a Creole*.

Mr. Plomacy Steward of Ullathorne Grant who runs the garden party given by the Thornes in Anthony Trollope's *Barchester Towers*.

Mr. Plornish Unemployed, kind-hearted plasterer, who lives with his family in the Bleeding Heart Yard; he put up a job notice for Amy Dorrit in his window which led to her employment with Mrs. Clennam; he shares his wife's pride in Mr. Nandy in Charles Dickens's *Little Dorrit*.

Sally Plornish   Kind-hearted and optimistic wife of Mr. Plornish and mother of many children; she names their home "Happy Cottage," is a friend of Amy Dorrit and Arthur Clennam, and is inordinately proud of the singing ability of her father, Mr. Nandy, in Charles Dickens's *Little Dorrit*.

Mr. Pluck   Gentleman friend of Sir Mulberry Hawk; he helps him flatter Mrs. Nickleby in Hawk's attempt to seduce Kate Nickleby in Charles Dickens's *The Life and Adventures of Nicholas Nickleby*.

Hector Pluck   Butcher; when losing a cudgel match, he stabs Giffard Homely in Henry Brooke's *The Fool of Quality*.

Peter Plumdamas   Gossipy Edinburgh grocer, whose discussions with friends provide commentary on Effie Deans's trial in Sir Walter Scott's *The Heart of Midlothian*.

Bertha Plummer   Caleb Plummer's blind daughter, who makes dolls, and who lives in a pleasant fantasy world created by her father to brighten her existence in Charles Dickens's *The Cricket on the Hearth*.

Caleb Plummer   Aged father to blind Bertha; he describes their meager home and harsh employer Tackleton in glowing terms to make Bertha's life happier, only to have his lies backfire when Bertha falls in love with Tackleton in Charles Dickens's *The Cricket on the Hearth*.

Edward Plummer   Caleb Plummer's long-lost son, who returns from "the golden South Americas" to save his childhood sweetheart from a loveless marriage in Charles Dickens's *The Cricket on the Hearth*.

Mrs. Plumstead   Village scold whose husband was reputed to have "died of exhaustion from his wife's voice" in Harriet Martineau's *Deerbrook*.

Paulus Plydell   Distinguished and witty Edinburgh lawyer and friend of Guy Mannering; having been sheriff at the time of Francis Kennedy's murder, he remains interested in Henry and Lucy Bertram in Sir Walter Scott's *Guy Mannering*.

Ned Plymdale   Selina Plymdale's son and an unsuccessful suitor to Rosamond Vincy in George Eliot's *Middlemarch*.

Selina Plymdale   A gossiping friend of the Vincys and the Bulstrodes in George Eliot's *Middlemarch*.

Belinda Pocket   Mother of Herbert Pocket; Pip Pirrip visits her household and finds it to be completely disorganized, with Mrs. Pocket more interested in reading about peerages than in taking care of her children in Charles Dickens's *Great Expectations*.

Herbert Pocket   Pip Pirrip's friend who shares his chambers in London and who aids Pip in learning social graces; Pip assists him by buying him a partnership in Clarriker and Co.; he marries Clara Barley in Charles Dickens's *Great Expectations*.

Matthew Pocket   Father of Herbert Pocket and a relative of Miss Havisham; he refuses to demean himself in pursuit of her money; at Pip Pirrip's urging, Miss Havisham leaves him £4,000 in Charles Dickens's *Great Expectations*.

Sarah Pocket   Miss Havisham's relative, who visits her every year on her birthday in the hopes of "feasting" upon Miss Havisham's will; she is left twenty-five pounds to buy pills in Charles Dickens's *Great Expectations*.

Mr. Podder   Famous batter of the All-Muggleton cricket club in Charles Dickens's *The Posthumous Papers of the Pickwick Club*.

George Podebrac   Bohemian duke and a generous patron of Aldrovandus Magnus in William Beckford's *Biographical Memoirs of Extraordinary Painters*.

Mrs. Podsnap   Mr. Podsnap's wife and female counterpart, who resembles a large rocking horse in Charles Dickens's *Our Mutual Friend*.

Georgiana Podsnap   Weak-eyed, intimidated, oppressed daughter of the Podsnaps; she is a victim of Podsnappery and nearly a victim of the Lammles' conspiracy to marry her to Fascination Fledgeby in Charles Dickens's *Our Mutual Friend*.

John Podsnap   Large, opinionated, insular, and narrow-minded middle-class businessman, who clears away social problems by refusing to notice them in Charles Dickens's *Our Mutual Friend*.

Poet Number One   A writer who sacrifices independence for well-being in Charles Johnstone's *Chrysal: or, The Adventures of a Guinea*.

Poet Number Two   Playwright who knows little about the "laws" of drama in Charles Johnstone's *Chrysal: or, The Adventures of a Guinea*.

Poet Number Three   Writer of plays which are improper for the stage and are not to the taste of the time in Charles Johnstone's *Chrysal: or, The Adventures of a Guinea.*

Poet Number Four   Playwright who depends upon passion and writes tragic plays which reflect only distress in poverty in Charles Johnstone's *Chrysal: or, The Adventures of a Guinea.*

Elijah Pogram   Member of Congress and political opportunist encountered by Martin Chuzzlewit and Mark Tapley in America in Charles Dickens's *The Life and Adventures of Martin Chuzzlewit.*

Miss Pole   Close friend of Matilda Jenkyns and a leading figure in the genteel society of Cranford ladies in Elizabeth Gaskell's *Cranford.*

Mrs. Pole   Sinister landlady who corrupts and victimizes Carrie Mitchell in George Gissing's *Workers in the Dawn.*

Adela Pole   The ambitious daughter of a merchant; she is both sentimental and scheming, juggling a number of suitors and courting Emilia Belloni for the social advantage to be gained by her lovely voice in George Meredith's *Emilia in England.* She reappears as Mrs. Sedley, the wife of a wealthy merchant, still meddling and flirting in *Vittoria.*

Arabella Pole   The youngest daughter of a merchant; she is interested in "mounting" socially and in "Nice Feelings" and "Fine Shades"; she helps attach the family to Emilia Belloni in order to benefit socially from her beautiful voice in George Meredith's *Emilia in England.*

Cornelia Pole   A sentimental social climber who befriends Emilia Belloni to benefit from her acclaim as a singer; when she fails to act concretely on her love for Purcell Barrett, he commits suicide in George Meredith's *Emilia in England.*

Horace Pole   Cynical confidant of Gertrude, Lady Monteagle and arch-critic of Planatagenet, Lord Cadurcis and his poetry in Benjamin Disraeli's *Venetia.*

Samuel Bolton Pole   An unprincipled London merchant with high hopes for his children's advantageous marriages; his own prospects center on Mrs. Martha Chump after he brings both of them to the brink of financial ruin with shady and shaky speculation in George Meredith's *Emilia in England.*

Wilfrid Pole   A sentimentalist who falls in love with Emilia Belloni; his involvement with Lady Charlotte Chillingsworth contributes to Emilia's breakdown; despite his desire to re-establish their relationship, she refuses him in George Meredith's *Emilia in England.* After

taking his uncle's last name, Pierson, and becoming an officer in the Austrian army, he compromises his position in the army by involving himself in the plight of Italian patriots including Emilia—renamed Vittoria Campa—with whom he is still in love, despite his engagement to an Austrian countess, Lena von Lenkenstein, in *Vittoria.*

Polemo of Rhodes   Celebrated oracular lecturer, called "the Bottomless"; the failure of his arguments with Callista angers and frightens him in John Henry Newman's *Callista.*

Politan   Alessandra Scala's rejected suitor in George Eliot's *Romola.*

Politician   Faithful, loyal, diligent, and successful servant of his king; he is disregarded and used to increase the power of others; he desires the restoration of his former power in Charles Johnstone's *Chrysal: or, The Adventures of a Guinea.*

Pigeony Poll   Jago woman who marries Kiddo Cook in Arthur Morrison's *A Child of the Jago.*

Sir Hargrave Pollexfen   The powerful but unscrupulous baronet who is astonished and enraged by Harriet Byron's persistent rejection of his marriage proposals; he has her kidnapped, attempts to marry her secretly, and tries to hold her hostage; he is foiled by Sir Charles Grandison; ultimately he repents and, dying, leaves his fortune to Harriet and Sir Charles in Samuel Richardson's *Sir Charles Grandison.*

Mr. Pollock   (the author's self portrait) Overweight literary gentleman, who rides fearlessly with the hunt at Edgehill in Anthony Trollope's *Can You Forgive Her?.*

Polly   Willie's wife; angry with Willie when he comes home, she hears his vow to stop drinking and is thankful to God; she is reconciled with her husband through the efforts of Sylvie and Bruno in Lewis Carroll's *Sylvie and Bruno Concluded.*

Polly   The ten-year-old youngest sister of Amelia; her quick mind makes her a pleasant companion to Felicia in Mary Collyer's *Felicia to Charlotte.*

Mr. Polonius   Fashionable jeweler to whom Samuel Titmarsh takes the Hoggarty diamond for resetting in William Makepeace Thackeray's *The History of Samuel Titmarsh and the Great Hoggarty Diamond.*

Lord Polperro   Polly Sparkes's uncle, a sickly gentleman who leaves his middle-class wife after coming into his title through the death of his brother and is the object of a search in George Gissing's *The Town Traveller.*

Mrs. Pomfret   A lady's maid at Donnithorne Chase in George Eliot's *Adam Bede*.

Pompey   The little Bologna lap-dog of great beauty and illustrious family who travels throughout England as the companion or the servant of people of all classes and temperaments in Francis Coventry's *The History of Pompey the Little*.

Miss Ponsonby   A Calvinistic evangelical woman of Irish background; she is headmistress of a school for girls in Abchurch, near Eastthorp, where Mrs. Furze sends her daughter, Catharine, in Mark Rutherford's *Catharine Furze*.

Adela Ponsonby   Younger sister of Miss Ponsonby; she teaches in their school for girls in Mark Rutherford's *Catharine Furze*.

Mary Ponsonby   Sensible, dutiful cousin of Louis Fitzjocelyn; she sacrifices her engagement to him to obey the commands of her father, Robert Ponsonby, but ultimately marries him in Peru in Charlotte Yonge's *Dynevor Terrace*.

Robert Ponsonby   Tyrannical, corrupt father of Mary Ponsonby; he holds Lord Ormersfield responsible for his marital disasters and obstructs his daughter Mary's marriage to Louis Fitzjocelyn in Charlotte Yonge's *Dynevor Terrace*.

Chevalier Du Pont   French officer who falls in love with Emily St. Aubert; later he is imprisoned in the Castle di Udolpho, from which he escapes with Emily, who continues to reject his suit in Ann Radcliffe's *The Mysteries of Udolpho*.

Alethea Pontifex   Ernest Pontifex's aunt and the only grandchild of the elder John Pontifex to have his sense of fun; pretty and affectionate, she is a good business-woman, who takes Ernest under her wing and makes him her heir in Samuel Butler's *The Way of All Flesh*.

Alice Pontifex   Ernest's daughter by Ellen; raised by the Rollinses, she marries Jack Rollins in Samuel Butler's *The Way of All Flesh*.

Charlotte Pontifex   Daughter of Christina and Theobald Pontifex and sister of Ernest and Joseph; she is plain and clever in Samuel Butler's *The Way of All Flesh*.

Christina Allaby Pontifex   Second daughter of Mr. Allaby; wife of Theobald Pontifex and mother of Ernest, she is even-tempered and indolently good-natured in Samuel Butler's *The Way of All Flesh*.

Eliza Pontifex   George Pontifex's oldest daughter; she receives £15,000 from her father in Samuel Butler's *The Way of All Flesh*.

Ernest Pontifex   Gentleman and hero of the story, godson of Edward Overton; a lover of music and intelligent, he lacks common sense; he is ordained as a clergyman at Cambridge but begins to doubt his faith; he serves six months in jail, marries unhappily, ends the marriage, and becomes an unsuccessful yet happy writer; he is heir to Alethea's fortune—£3500 a year in Samuel Butler's *The Way of All Flesh*.

George Pontifex   Son of the elder John, father of Theobald, grandfather of Ernest; a successful publisher, he has £1000 a year but is a bad father in Samuel Butler's *The Way of All Flesh*.

George Pontifex (the younger)   Ernest's son by Ellen; he lives with the Rollinses; when he is twenty-one, Ernest buys him a barge and a steamer in Samuel Butler's *The Way of All Flesh*.

John Pontifex (the elder)   Genial and able man, a carpenter by trade, but also a parish clerk, artist, musician, farmer, and organ builder; he is great-grandfather to Ernest Pontifex in Samuel Butler's *The Way of All Flesh*.

John Pontifex   George Pontifex's oldest son, well dressed, though perhaps too handsome; he gets on well with masters but not with peers; he is the only child to receive his father's approval and confidence in Samuel Butler's *The Way of All Flesh*.

Joseph Pontifex   Clergyman, brother of Ernest and son of Theobald and Christina; he dislikes his father and never gets along with Ernest in Samuel Butler's *The Way of All Flesh*.

Maria Pontifex   George Pontifex's second daughter; she receives £15,000 from her father in Samuel Butler's *The Way of All Flesh*.

Ruth Pontifex   Wife of the elder John Pontifex and, after fifteen years of marriage, the surprised mother of a son, George; she invites Edward Overton's family to tea on a regular basis in Samuel Butler's *The Way of All Flesh*.

Theobald Pontifex   Clergyman and second son of George Pontifex; husband of Christina Allaby, he is the first of George's sons to have a son—Ernest; reserved, shy, and indolent, he is the family scapegoat and a poor father to Ernest, Charlotte, and Joseph; loved by his community, he loves no one in Samuel Butler's *The Way of All Flesh*.

Mr. Pook   Enthusiastic trainer of Lord Silverbridge's

horse; while under his care, the horse is mysteriously nobbled in Anthony Trollope's *The Duke's Children*.

Poole   Elderly, well-dressed butler and chief servant of Dr. Henry Jekyll; he brings Mr. Utterson to the Jekyll household and ultimately to the dark discovery of Jekyll's death in Robert Louis Stevenson's *The Strange Case of Dr. Jekyll and Mr. Hyde*.

Adolphus (Dolly) Poole   Gambling associate of Jasper Losely; blackmailed by Losely, he is ultimately saved by the intervention of Arabella Crane in Edward Bulwer-Lytton's *What Will He Do With It? by Pisistratus Caxton*.

Grace Poole   Mr. Rochester's hired assistant, who looks after the madwoman, being aware of her real identity, and who has a weakness for gin which allows her prisoner to escape with dire consequences in Charlotte Brontë's *Jane Eyre*.

Lord Popenjoy   The Marquis of Brotherton's sickly half-Italian young son, if indeed his birth is legitimate; the question becomes moot after the death of the child in Anthony Trollope's *Is He Popenjoy?*.

Frederic Augustus Tallowax Germain, Lord Popenjoy   Baby son of Lord Germain, heir to the estates and title of the Marquis of Brotherton in Anthony Trollope's *Is He Popenjoy?*.

Lord Popplecourt   Vacuous owner of a large estate chosen by the (younger) Duke of Omnium to assist his daughter, Lady Mary Palliser, to recover from Frank Tregear; she emphatically refuses to consider him as future husband in Anthony Trollope's *The Duke's Children*.

Philomela Poppyseed   (caricature of Amelia Opie) Author of very moral and aristocratic novels in Thomas Love Peacock's *Headlong Hall*.

Margaret Porcher   Slovenly housemaid hired by Sir Percival Glyde to keep Marian Halcombe and Laura (Fairlie), Lady Glyde apart in Wilkie Collins's *The Woman in White*.

The Misses Porkenham   Daughters of the Porkenhams in Charles Dickens's *The Posthumous Papers of the Pickwick Club*.

Mr. Porkenham   Old acquaintance and "rival" of George Nupkins in Charles Dickens's *The Posthumous Papers of the Pickwick Club*.

Mrs. Porkenham   Bosom friend of the Nupkinses in Charles Dickens's *The Posthumous Papers of the Pickwick Club*.

Sidney Porkenham   Son of the Porkenhams and suitor of Henrietta Nupkins in Charles Dickens's *The Posthumous Papers of the Pickwick Club*.

Lord Porlock   The Earl de Courcy's eldest son and heir, utterly estranged from his father, to his mother's distress; he marries in order to disappoint the expectations of his younger brothers in Anthony Trollope's *The Small House at Allington*.

"Fred Porlock"   Alias of a person who works for Professor Moriarity and is one of Sherlock Holmes's informants, tipping him off about the events in Arthur Conan Doyle's *The Valley of Fear*.

Joseph Porta   Venetian painter celebrated for his knowledge of anatomy; he takes Blunderbussiana as a student when the young outlaw corrects the painter's anatomical renderings in William Beckford's *Biographical Memoirs of Extraordinary Painters*.

John Porteous   Brutal but effective captain of the Edinburgh City Guard; he is hanged by an angry mob after shooting into a crowd in Sir Walter Scott's *The Heart of Midlothian*.

Billy Porter   Farmer Porter's son, who is rescued from Jemmy Downes's sweatshop by his father and Alton Locke in Charles Kingsley's *Alton Locke*.

Bob (Woodenhouse Bob, Farmer) Porter   Good-natured farmer, who offers Alton Locke a ride to Cambridge and asks him to look for his tailor son Billy, finally coming to London and helping Alton find him in Charles Kingsley's *Alton Locke*.

Mary Porter   Friend of Katie Winter, with whom she visits Oxford, where she meets Tom Brown; she marries Tom Brown after complications caused by the attentions of the Hon. Piers St. Cloud in Thomas Hughes's *Tom Brown at Oxford*.

Portia   Principal witness before The Cry, Duessa, and Una; her account of the turbulent course of her love for Ferdinand with its ultimate resolution in marriage serves as the occasion for her more general pronouncements on a wide range of topics in Sarah Fielding's *The Cry*.

Lord Portland   King's favorite and an ally of Henry Clinton; he uses the law to help Giffard Homely regain wealth and property lost to a scheming aristocrat in Henry Brooke's *The Fool of Quality*.

Dr. Portman   Vicar of Clavering who disapproves of Arthur Pendennis's amours in William Makepeace Thackeray's *The History of Pendennis*.

Belinda Portman Charming, prudent, attractive young woman, who inspires Lady Delacour to quit her dissipated ways and be reconciled to her husband, Lord Delacour; Belinda later reunites the couple with their daughter, Helena; possessing great integrity and determined not to marry for fortune or convenience, Belinda rejects one suitor, Mr. Vincent, because of his gambling habits and marries her first love, Clarence Hervey, in Maria Edgeworth's *Belinda*.

Reverend Portpipe Clergyman who gives two reasons for drinking, either to cure thirst or to prevent it, in Thomas Love Peacock's *Melincourt*.

Portuguese Banker A Jewish professed Christian and the brother of Aminadab; he gives Chrysal to his nephew in Charles Johnstone's *Chrysal: or, The Adventures of a Guinea*.

Portuguese Captain Commander of the vessel which rescues Robinson Crusoe and Xury after their escape from slavery; he transports Crusoe to Brazil and keeps Xury as a cabin boy; years later, he meets Crusoe and gives a full account of his finances in Daniel Defoe's *The Life and Strange Surprizing Adventures of Robinson Crusoe of York, Mariner*.

Mr. Possitt Weakly, wretchedly overworked curate, who conducts the funeral service of the late Mrs. Winterfield in Anthony Trollope's *The Belton Estate*.

Mr. Postlecott Chief clerk to the Grundle sheep-farming concern in Britannula; he grows increasingly melancholy at the prospect of being deposited in a college to prepare for euthanasia at age sixty-eight under the laws promulgated by John Neverbend in Anthony Trollope's *The Fixed Period*.

Roger Potion Apothecary who ejects Roderick Random from his lodging after news of Bowling's misfortunes in Tobias Smollett's *The Adventures of Roderick Random*.

Mr. Pott Wealthy young man touring the Holy Land with his tutor, Mr. Cruse, in Anthony Trollope's *The Bertrams*.

Mr. Pott Contentious editor of the *Eatanswill Gazette*, who hosts Samuel Pickwick and Nathaniel Winkle and is henpecked by his wife in Charles Dickens's *The Posthumous Papers of the Pickwick Club*.

Mrs. Pott Mr. Pott's domineering wife, who strikes up a flirtation with Nathaniel Winkle in Charles Dickens's *The Posthumous Papers of the Pickwick Club*.

Abigail (Abbey) Potterson High-principled proprietress of the Six Jolly Fellowship Porters public house in Limehouse; she denies service to Gaffer Hexam and Roger Riderhood and is kind to Lizzie Hexam in Charles Dickens's *Our Mutual Friend*.

Job Potterson Steward on the ship on which John Harmon traveled to England and a witness of Harmon's identity in Charles Dickens's *Our Mutual Friend*.

Dr. Pottinger Friend of the Reverend Hilkiah Bradford; he is headmaster of Winchester when Charles Mandeville matriculates there in William Godwin's *Mandeville*.

Mr. Pottle "Orthodox" Anglican pastor and copious smoker, whom Geoffry Wildgoose meets in an alehouse; Pottle and Wildgoose have an argument about theology that leads to a fistfight between Jeremiah Tugwell and Pottle's valet, Jonathan, in Richard Graves's *The Spiritual Quixote*.

Chumley Potts One of Lord Fleetwood's "Ixionides," a group of hedonistic, idle young men who depend upon Fleetwood's generosity in George Meredith's *The Amazing Marriage*.

Tom Potts Reporter, later editor, of the *Newcome Independent*; he hates Barnes Newcome in William Makepeace Thackeray's *The Newcomes*.

Mr. Pottyphar First lieutenant of H.M.S. *Aurora*; he believes firmly in the virtue of Enouy's Universal Medicine in Captain Frederick Marryat's *Mr. Midshipman Easy*.

Captain de Potzdorff Officer in the Prussian army and nephew to the chief of police; he employs Redmond Barry as a spy until Barry's recognition of a suspect as his uncle causes his shift of allegiance and the captain's downfall in William Makepeace Thackeray's *The Luck of Barry Lyndon*.

Mr. Poulter Village schoolmaster who teaches Tom Tulliver to march with a sword and allows the boy to borrow the weapon with which he badly cuts his foot in George Eliot's *The Mill on the Floss*.

Peter Pounce Lady Booby's avaricious steward; lust prompts him to offer Fanny Goodwill a ride in the Booby carriage, but his pride settles for Parson Adams when she refuses in Henry Fielding's *The History of the Adventures of Mr. Joseph Andrews and of his Friend Mr. Abraham Adams*.

Thomas Poundage Dishonest and self-seeking steward of the Noble Lord in Charles Johnstone's *Chrysal: or, The Adventures of a Guinea*.

Peter Poundtext Moderate Presbyterian minister who stands by Henry Morton to oppose the radical violence of the Cameronians and dies in a battle of rebellion against the armies of King James II in Sir Walter Scott's *Old Mortality*.

Major Pountney   Effusive guest of the Duchess of Omnium at Gatherum Castle; he mightily offends the (younger) Duke by asking for the vacant parliamentary seat of Silverbridge and is asked to leave the house in Anthony Trollope's *The Prime Minister*.

Admiral Powel   English navy man who escapes Revolutionary France on the same boat as his niece Juliet Granville but does not know who she is until the end of the story; he helps her escape arrest and offers her a home in England before she agrees to marry Albert Harleigh in Frances Burney's *The Wanderer*.

Dr. Powell   Physician to Indefer Jones; he informs Nicholas Apjohn about the indecisive state of mind Jones was in during his last days, thus increasing the mystery concerning the old man's final will in Anthony Trollope's *Cousin Henry*.

Mr. Powell   Vicar who unwittingly causes Geoffry Wildgoose to leave home and the Anglican Church by arguing with him over the distinction between a window and a door; he later vouches for Wildgoose's character in a misunderstanding about a stolen horse in Richard Graves's *The Spiritual Quixote*.

Colonel Eustace Powell   Pious Protestant beheaded immediately before John Inglesant's intended execution in J. Henry Shorthouse's *John Inglesant, A Romance*.

(Bower, Brown) Power   Rascally Irishman, known by several names, who sells fake combustibles to the Chartists for use on April 10, 1848, in Charles Kingsley's *Alton Locke*.

Abner Power   Paula Power's scheming and heartless uncle, who attempts to manipulate his niece away from the man she loves, George Somerset, and into the arms of a man she does not love, Captain DeStancy, in Thomas Hardy's *A Laodicean*.

Fred Power   Professional soldier and close friend of Charles O'Malley; he marries Donna Inez da Silviero in Charles Lever's *Charles O'Malley*.

Paula Power   Young, willful, and repressively austere heroine courted by both George Somerset and Captain DeStancy in Thomas Hardy's *A Laodicean*.

Miss Powers   Elderly neighbor, daughter of a clergyman; her thankfulness that she did not soil her dress during a fall leads to a discussion about God's attention to trifles on earth in Mary Collyer's *Felicia to Charlotte*.

Lazarus Powheid   Venerable sexton of the kirk of Douglas; he is an expert on the history of the Douglas family in Sir Walter Scott's *Castle Dangerous*.

Robert Powney   Stationer who sends to the unnamed editor an order of pens wrapped in the manuscript that becomes Henry Fielding's *A Journey From This World to the Next*.

Merthyr Powys   Welsh partisan of Italian liberty; he is Sandra (Emilia) Belloni's true friend and lover; he rescues her from her father's designs and from suicide; although Sandra feels only friendship for him, she vows to grow to love him in George Meredith's *Emilia in England*. After being wounded fighting in Italy, he is nursed by Sandra—renamed Vittoria Campa—though she marries an Italian patriot, Ammiani; after Ammiani's death, Powys and Vittoria are together at the end of *Vittoria*.

Lord George Poynings   The Marquis of Tiptoff's younger son and rival to the successful Redmond Barry for the hand of Lady Lyndon; he eventually helps to ruin her husband in William Makepeace Thackeray's *The Luck of Barry Lyndon*.

Margaret Poyntz   Social leader who turns against Dr. Lloyd to his ruin in Edward Bulwer-Lytton's *A Strange Story*.

Charlotte ("Totty") Poyser   The three-year-old daughter of Mr. and Mrs. Poyser, who shows her soft side when she allows the child to misbehave without punishment; Totty is often cared for by Hetty Sorrel but much prefers the kindlier Dinah Morris in George Eliot's *Adam Bede*.

Martin Poyser (the elder)   The aged father of farmer Martin Poyser; he lives with his son's family at Hall Farm in George Eliot's *Adam Bede*.

Martin Poyser   The uncle of Dinah Morris and Hetty Sorrel; he is a prosperous dairy farmer at Hall Farm who is very jolly, except when his farm is threatened; he disowns Hetty after learning of her crime in George Eliot's *Adam Bede*.

Marty Poyser   Prosaic eldest son of the younger Martin Poyser in George Eliot's *Adam Bede*.

Rachel Poyser   Wife of the younger Martin Poyser and aunt of Dinah Morris and Hetty Sorrel; she is confident of her ability to verbally express herself, but her words wound; she is a perfectionist in everything and is so shamed by Hetty's behavior that she plans to move her husband away from Hall Farm in George Eliot's *Adam Bede*.

Tommy Poyser   Second son of the younger Martin Poyser; he is devoted to his mother in George Eliot's *Adam Bede*.

Madame Pratolungo   The narrator, a French-born widow of a republican agitator; she becomes Lucilla Finch's music teacher and companion; fiercely devoted, she thwarts the usurping Nugent Dubourg in Wilkie Collins's *Poor Miss Finch*.

Dr. Pratt   Medical practitioner from the village near Marlowe; at Sir Jeckyl Marlowe's request, he treats his wound in secret while telling the houseguests Sir Jeckyl suffers from gout in J. Sheridan Le Fanu's *Guy Deverell*.

Miss Pratt   Brighton headmistress who expels Madge Hopgood after parents' complaints in Mark Rutherford's *Clara Hopgood*.

Mr. Pratt   Scholar in whose house Edward Ferrars was privately educated before attending Oxford; Edward fell in love with Mr. Pratt's niece, Lucy Steele, while a resident and later a visitor there in Jane Austen's *Sense and Sensibility*.

Fowler Pratt   Friend and groomsman of Adolphus Crosbie at his wedding in Anthony Trollope's *The Small House at Allington*. He appears in *The Last Chronicle of Barset*.

Hannah Pratt   A Brighton headmistress's sister, who is in charge of household matters in Mark Rutherford's *Clara Hopgood*.

Pennsylvania Pratt   A Moravian preacher whose wife and children drowned in the Johnstown flood; he becomes half-witted and is befriended by the crew of the cod-fishing boat *We're Here* in Rudyard Kipling's *"Captains Courageous": A Story of the Grand Banks*.

Zoraya Prebel   Hungarian singer, who entices Edgar Underwood into marriage and deserts him and their infant son, Gerald, in Charlotte Yonge's *The Pillars of the House*. She deteriorates and is finally cared for at the end of her life by Gerald and his half sister, Ludmilla Schnetterling, in *The Long Vacation*.

Mr. Prendergast   Loyal London attorney of Sir Thomas Fitzgerald; he unravels Matthew Mollett's blackmail plot designed to invalidate Sir Thomas's marriage and make his children illegitimate in Anthony Trollope's *Castle Richmond*.

President of *** College, Oxford   Corrupt president of the college Hugh Trevor attends; influenced by the London bishop, he conspires to prevent Hugh's graduation in Thomas Holcroft's *The Adventures of Hugh Trevor*.

Mr. Preston   Land agent to the Cumnors; his attempts to force Cynthia Kirkpatrick to keep her youthful promise to marry him lead to complications for Molly Gibson in Elizabeth Gaskell's *Wives and Daughters*.

Edmund Preston   Haughty secretary of state, who is disagreeable to Samuel Titmarsh and later takes an improper interest in Mary Titmarsh in William Makepeace Thackeray's *The History of Samuel Titmarsh and the Great Hoggarty Diamond*.

Lady Jane Preston   Lady Drum's granddaughter and Edmund Preston's wife; she behaves with generous kindness to Samuel Titmarsh in William Makepeace Thackeray's *The History of Samuel Titmarsh and the Great Hoggarty Diamond*.

Prestongrange (William Grant), Lord Advocate of Scotland   High government prosecutor of the Scottish Highland murder of Colin Ray Campbell; he takes David Balfour under his wing but discourages and indirectly prevents his testimony exonerating the alleged murderer, James Stewart, in Robert Louis Stevenson's *Catriona*.

Presumption   One of three men Christian finds fettered and sleeping; he ignores Christian's warning and goes back to sleep in John Bunyan's *The Pilgrim's Progress From this World to That Which Is to Come*.

Mr. Prettyfat   Deputy surveyor of the wretched forest of Pinch-me-near; he employs John Jorrocks to capture an old fox who preys on the royal forest's poultry in Robert Surtees's *Handley Cross*.

Annabella Prettyman   The elder of two sisters, joint proprietors of a girls' school at Silverbridge at which Grace Crawley teaches; she is thin and prevented by ill health from leaving her roof but has a loving heart in Anthony Trollope's *The Last Chronicle of Barset*.

Anne Prettyman   The plump, healthy younger of a pair of kindly sisters who keep a girls' school at Silverbridge in Anthony Trollope's *The Last Chronicle of Barset*.

Lieutenant Price   Retired Marine officer residing in a crowded house in Portsmouth, and the impecunious husband of Mrs. Price and father of nine living children, including William and Fanny; his loud voice and coarse manners are distressing to Fanny in Jane Austen's *Mansfield Park*.

Miss Price   Mr. Price's destitute daughter, who sells artificial flowers while living with her wrongly jailed father after escaping the advances of young Mr. Ware; she marries Harry Main after Sidney Bidulph Arnold and Mr.

Warner act on the Prices' behalf in Frances Sheridan's *Memoirs of Miss Sidney Bidulph*.

Mr. Price   Clergyman and father of Miss Price; hired by the elder Mr. Ware to be his son's tutor, he is falsely jailed for refusing to surrender his daughter to young Mr. Ware; released from jail through Sidney Bidulph Arnold's and Mr. Warner's efforts, he is made educator of Master Orlando Jefferis Faulkland in Frances Sheridan's *Memoirs of Miss Sidney Bidulph*.

Mr. Price   Coarse, vulgar man of the world in the Fleet debtors' prison in Charles Dickens's *The Posthumous Papers of the Pickwick Club*.

Mr. Price   Gentleman farmer of Cross Hall House; his horse is involved in a brush with Adelaide Houghton's, causing her to dislocate her arm in Anthony Trollope's *Is He Popenjoy?*.

Betsey Price   The spoiled youngest of Lieutenant and Mrs. Price's many children in Jane Austen's *Mansfield Park*.

Fanny Price   Virtuous, modest, sensitive, and shy niece of Lady Bertram; reared from the age of nine with her elder cousins, the Bertram children, she loves Edmund, has a rival for his affections in Mary Crawford, and is herself wooed by Mary's brother, Henry; after an uncomfortable visit with her own family in Portsmouth, Fanny returns to gain Edmund's love in Jane Austen's *Mansfield Park*.

Frances Ward Price   Sister to Lady Bertram and Mrs. Norris, wife of Lieutenant Price, and the careworn, slatternly mother of Fanny, William, and seven other living children in Jane Austen's *Mansfield Park*.

Hubert Price   Promising young playwright with one success; struggling in poverty, he inherits an estate; unable to finish his new play, he finds needed criticism and conversation with Julia Bentham; unable to endure Emily Watson's infatuation with him and jealousy of Julia, he flees with Julia to London, where their marriage begins with unhappiness at the news of Emily's suicide; he fears that he will be unable to fulfill his role in life in George Moore's *Vain Fortune*.

John Price   Farmer of Stanemore who was John Buncle's classmate at Sheridan's school, Dublin; profligate when young, he is robbed by two whores in Paris; reformed by the Christian simplicity of his wife, he debates natural religion with Buncle in Thomas Amory's *The Life of John Buncle, Esq.*

Matilda ('Tilda) Price   Fanny Squeers's friend until the friendship is soured by her superiority in attracting men; she marries John Browdie and later comes to Fanny's aid in Charles Dickens's *The Life and Adventures of Nicholas Nickleby*.

Susan Price   Fanny's younger sister, whom she grows to love when she visits her parents' home after a ten-year absence; Susan accompanies Fanny back to Mansfield Park and becomes the indispensable niece after Fanny's marriage in Jane Austen's *Mansfield Park*.

William Price   Fanny's beloved elder brother, a midshipman, who gains his lieutenancy with Henry Crawford's assistance in Jane Austen's *Mansfield Park*.

Geoffrey Prickle   Quarrelsome farmer, who has tables turned against him while prosecuting Captain Samuel Crowe and Sir Launcelot Greaves in Tobias Smollett's *The Adventures of Sir Launcelot Greaves*.

Ritty Priddle   Milkmaid at Richard Crick's dairy who falls in love with Angel Clare; she attempts suicide by drowning when he marries Tess Durbeyfield but is revived in Thomas Hardy's *Tess of the D'Urbervilles*.

Betsey Prig   Bosom friend and fellow nurse of Mrs. Gamp until a falling-out over the existence or nonexistence of Mrs. Gamp's friend Mrs. Harris in Charles Dickens's *The Life and Adventures of Martin Chuzzlewit*.

Mr. Prigmore   Whig candidate in the Fanchester election who is defeated by Aubrey Bohun by the margin of a single vote in Benjamin Disraeli's *A Year at Hartlebury; or, The Election*.

Lord Prim   Neighbor of the Moreland estate who labors hard to be easy in conversation in Henry Brooke's *The Fool of Quality*.

Dorothea Ray Prime   Widowed elder daughter of Mrs. Ray; dedicated to the notion that cheerfulness is a sin, she allows herself to be wooed by the Reverend Samuel Prong, a sanctimonious clergyman; her love of power prompts her interference without success in the love of her sister, Rachel, for Luke Rowan; she remains grimfaced to the last in Anthony Trollope's *Rachel Ray*.

Agnes Primrose   Daughter of John and Hannah Primrose; a beautiful country girl, she is seduced and abandoned by the younger William Norwynne; she becomes a prostitute to support their illegitimate child and herself; apprehended for the crime of forgery, she is condemned to death by her own seducer, a justice, in Elizabeth Inchbald's *Nature and Art*.

Bill Primrose   One of the two youngest sons of Dr. Charles Primrose in Oliver Goldsmith's *The Vicar of Wakefield*.

Dr. Charles Primrose   Eternally optimistic, naive, pompous, and altogether good vicar, whose many Job-like misfortunes land him in debtors' prison, though all is restored to him in the end, in Oliver Goldsmith's *The Vicar of Wakefield.*

Deborah Primrose   Wife of the Reverend Dr. Charles Primrose; she is a silly and rather selfish woman with aspirations to gentility, though her husband nonetheless perceives in her the virtues of an Old Testament matriarch in Oliver Goldsmith's *The Vicar of Wakefield.*

Dick Primrose   One of the two youngest sons of Dr. Charles Primrose; he and Bill are sweet and faithful boys who comfort their father during his stay in debtors' prison in Oliver Goldsmith's *The Vicar of Wakefield.*

George Primrose   Eldest son of Dr. Charles Primrose; he challenges Squire Thornhill to a duel, for which he is sentenced to die, but he is saved and marries Arabella Wilmot in Oliver Goldsmith's *The Vicar of Wakefield.*

Hannah Primrose   Mother of Agnes Primrose; like her husband, John, she dies soon after learning of Agnes's unwed motherhood in Elizabeth Inchbald's *Nature and Art.*

John Primrose   Prudent, prosperous cottager and father of the beautiful Agnes Primrose; he does not long survive the shame of Agnes's unwed motherhood in Elizabeth Inchbald's *Nature and Art.*

Moses Primrose   Second son of Dr. Charles Primrose; something of a simpleton, he is cheated by con men at the fair where he has been sent to sell the family horse and returns with a gross of green spectacles in exchange in Oliver Goldsmith's *The Vicar of Wakefield.*

Olivia (Livy) Primrose   Elder daughter of Dr. Charles Primrose; she is seduced and abandoned by Squire Thornhill and nearly dies of the shock, but the supposedly sham marriage whereby he tricked her turns out to have been legal; at the end there is even a suggestion that the couple may one day be reconciled in Oliver Goldsmith's *The Vicar of Wakefield.*

Sophia (Sophy) Primrose   Younger daughter of Dr. Charles Primrose; a more subdued beauty than her sister Olivia, she is abducted by Squire Thornhill's minions as an encore to his seduction of Olivia but is rescued by Sir William Thornhill in his Mr. Burchell guise; she marries Sir William in Oliver Goldsmith's *The Vicar of Wakefield.*

Prince   Elderly horse essential to John Durbeyfield's business as a carter; Tess Durbeyfield's responsibility for its accidental death impels her to take employment at Mrs. Stoke-D'Urberville's poultry farm in Thomas Hardy's *Tess of the D'Urbervilles.*

Prince of ––   See Count de Clarac.

Princess of ––   Wife of the prince who has an affair with Roxana; her illness and death bring about the prince's repentance in Daniel Defoe's *The Fortunate Mistress.*

Pringle of Drumanno   Young, drunken country lord, neighbor to Archibald Weir of Hermiston and member of the local lords' social gathering, the "Tuesday Club," in Robert Louis Stevenson's *Weir of Hermiston: An Unfinished Romance.*

Miss Pringle   Snobbish country lady, sister to Pringle of Drumanno in Robert Louis Stevenson's *Weir of Hermiston: An Unfinished Romance.*

Prior of Dundrennan Abbey   Loyal friend of Queen Mary of Scotland in Sir Walter Scott's *The Abbot.*

Prior of Saint Mary's   False clergyman and accomplice in the murder of Reginald de Folville; he plots with Gaston de Blondeville to do away with Blondeville's accuser, Hugh Woodreeve; upon Blondeville's death, he urges Henry III to kill Woodreeve, only to die mysteriously himself in Ann Radcliffe's *Gaston de Blondeville.*

Priscilla   Slatternly maid of the Jellybys in Charles Dickens's *Bleak House.*

William Pritchard   Commander of the sloop-of-war *Shark,* which sinks Dirk Hatteraick's ship in Sir Walter Scott's *Guy Mannering.*

Samuel Pritchett   Loyal man of business to the elder George Bertram; he is disappointed in his small legacy when his employer dies in Anthony Trollope's *The Bertrams.*

Mr. Prodgers   Plainclothes policeman who is paid by the moneylender Tyrrwhit to find the whereabouts of Mountjoy Scarborough in Anthony Trollope's *Mr. Scarborough's Family.*

Professor   A teacher and inventor; he helps Sylvie and Bruno move from Outland to Fairyland and to the real world; he tutors Uggug but dislikes him in Lewis Carroll's *Sylvie and Bruno.* As court-physician he gives his long-awaited lecture on science at Uggug's birthday banquet; he catches Uggug after he has become a porcupine in *Sylvie and Bruno Concluded.*

Professor   Character who explains the baby formula which all infants must sign at birth and which clears parents of all responsibility in their having been born in Samuel Butler's *Erewhon.*

Professor of Botany Author of "The Rights of Vegetables," which is meant to show that man has to eat something and it may as well be animals; Erewhonians give up the abolition of meat in Samuel Butler's *Erewhon.*

Professor of Worldly Wisdom President of the Society for the Suppression of Useless Knowledge and for the Complete Obliteration of the Past in Samuel Butler's *Erewhon.*

Promlino Hired assassin who kills his master by mistake in Charlotte Dacre's *The Libertine.*

Samuel Prong Intolerant, severe vicar of a Baslehurst parish, lacking in breeding and with an eye to the main chance; he woos Mrs. Ray's widowed, elder daughter, Dorothea Prime, but when she becomes difficult over her fortune his ardour cools and they go their separate ways in Anthony Trollope's *Rachel Ray.*

Prophet Spokesman for vegetarianism, to which Erwhonians briefly adhere in Samuel Butler's *Erewhon.*

Dr. Prose Witty companion of Mrs. Blandford in William Beckford's *Azemia.*

Mr. Prosee Mr. Perker's eminent counsel and guest in Charles Dickens's *The Posthumous Papers of the Pickwick Club.*

Peter Prosper Petulant, self-important bachelor uncle of Harry Annesley, his designated heir; offended by Harry's neglect of himself, he tries to cut Harry out by marrying; the redoubtable economic feminism of his bride-elect, Matilda Thoroughbung, frightens him off in Anthony Trollope's *Mr. Scarborough's Family.*

Miss Pross Lucie Manette's maid, who is defiant in the best British manner; she prevents Madame Defarge from stopping the escape of Lucie and Charles Darnay during the Reign of Terror by shooting her in a hand-to-hand struggle in Charles Dickens's *A Tale of Two Cities.*

Solomon Pross Miss Pross's brother, who defrauded her; he is a spy who operates under the name John Barsad; Sydney Carton recognizes him as a prison turnkey in Paris and uses his knowledge to effect his self-sacrificing rescue of Charles Darnay in Charles Dickens's *A Tale of Two Cities.*

Mr. Prosser Alderman Harper's son-in-law; he and his wife are haunted by a mysterious hand and other strange occurrences while staying at Tiled House in J. Sheridan Le Fanu's *The House by the Churchyard.*

Mrs. Prosser Alderman Harper's daughter in J. Sheridan Le Fanu's *The House by the Churchyard.*

Prostitute Woman who gives to William the favors that she sells to others; she is kept by an impotent young aristocrat in Charles Johnstone's *Chrysal: or, The Adventures of a Guinea.*

Prostitute A woman who claims to have attempted to kill herself and poison her noble client in Charles Johnstone's *Chrysal: or, The Adventures of a Guinea.*

Peter Protocol Honorable and proper trustee of Margaret Bertram's property in Sir Walter Scott's *Guy Mannering.*

Magdalen (Maudie) Proudfute Widow of the murdered Oliver Proudfute; she chooses Henry Smith as her champion in a trial with the murderer Bonthron in Sir Walter Scott's *The Fair Maid of Perth.*

Oliver Proudfute Scottish bonnet maker who associates himself with Henry Smith during Henry's fight with John Romorny; mistaken for Henry, he is murdered by Bonthron in Sir Walter Scott's *The Fair Maid of Perth.*

Mrs. Proudie Tyrannical wife of the Bishop of Barchester; with Mr. Slope as her aide-de-camp she wages ecclesiastical war on Archdeacon Grantly in Anthony Trollope's *Barchester Towers.* She appears in *Framley Parsonage,* in *The Small House at Allington,* and in *Dr. Thorne.* She is defied by Josiah Crawley and mildly condemned by Dr. Tempest in her personal prosecution of the stolen-cheque issue, and she dies upright clutching the bedpost in *The Last Chronicle of Barset.*

Olivia Proudie Robust elder daughter of the bishop; she is highly scornful of Mr. Slope, who at one time sought her in marriage until it became clear that her father would not endow her with a fortune in Anthony Trollope's *Barchester Towers.* She sends the Grantlys a spiteful, anonymous letter hinting at Lord Dumbello's flight; she marries Tobias Tickler in *Framley Parsonage.*

Thomas Proudie Insignificant, weak-minded Bishop of Barchester, dominated by his wife and chaplain, Mr. Slope; he feebly opposes Archdeacon Grantly in Anthony Trollope's *Barchester Towers.* He appears in *Dr. Thorne,* in *The Small House at Allington,* and in *Framley Parsonage.* He chairs an ecclesiastical commission in *He Knew He Was Right.* He requires the Reverend Henry Clavering to give up hunting in *The Claverings.* He is at last freed from his wife's dominance by her death in *The Last Chronicle of Barset.*

Prudence One of three virgins of the Palace Beautiful who catechize Christian and later his sons; she shows them the house and its contents in John Bunyan's *The Pilgrim's Progress From this World to That Which Is to Come.*

Pruffle Servant to the scientific gentleman who lives next door to Arabella Allen's aunt in Bristol in Charles Dickens's *The Posthumous Papers of the Pickwick Club.*

Herbert Pryce Social-climbing Oxford mathematician, who finally marries Alice Hooper in Mrs. Humphry Ward's *Lady Connie.*

Sir Twickenham Pryme A Member of Parliament; he proposes to Cornelia Pole, whose love for Purcell Barrett causes her to hesitate; Cornelia's grief at Barrett's consequent suicide drives Pryme away, ending her sister Adela's attempts to attract his interests in George Meredith's *Emilia in England.*

Mr. Pryor The senior clergyman at the first church at which Ernest Pontifex works; a high churchman sympathetic to Rome, he has great influence over Ernest; he swindles Ernest out of his first inheritance in Samuel Butler's *The Way of All Flesh.*

Mrs. Pryor See Agnes Grey Helstone.

Professor Ptthmllnsprts Good-natured old Polish naturalist, fond of children, who teaches Ellie Harthover about marine life and catches Tom in a net but lets him go, denying that he is a water-baby, in Charles Kingsley's *The Water-Babies.*

Public Officer from the Navy Office Receiver of the bribe from the Captain of the English Man of War in Charles Johnstone's *Chrysal: or, The Adventures of a Guinea.*

Giannozzo Pucci Florentine aristocrat executed for his support of the Medici in George Eliot's *Romola.*

Miss Pucker Squint-eyed, malicious gossip in a sewing circle of religious zealots in the Devonshire town of Baslehurst, thoroughly under the thumb of the evangelical Dorothea Prime in Anthony Trollope's *Rachel Ray.*

Mr. Puddicombe Outspoken vicar in a neighboring parish to Bowick who has the knack of asking irritating questions of his friend, Jeffrey Wortle, concerning the controversy surrounding the Peacockes in Anthony Trollope's *Dr. Wortle's School.*

Mr. Puddlebrane Amateur cricketer and member of the British team which meets the host club of Britannula in a hard-fought contest in Anthony Trollope's *The Fixed Period.*

Mr. Puddleham Obsequious Primitive Methodist minister, on whose behalf the Marquis of Trowbridge builds a chapel in order to annoy Frank Fenwick in Anthony Trollope's *The Vicar of Bullhampton.*

Lieutenant Puddock Plump, sentimental, slightly absurd but truly good-hearted member of the Royal Irish Artillery; he wants to believe he is courting Gertrude Chattesworth, but he isn't taken seriously; he is happily united with Aunt Becky Chattesworth in the end in J. Sheridan Le Fanu's *The House by the Churchyard.*

John Puff (parody of Samuel Richardson) Author of a laudatory letter of self-congratulation in Henry Fielding's *An Apology for the Life of Mrs. Shamela Andrews.*

Princess Puffer Opium seller who supplies the drug to John Jasper in a den in the East End of London; she travels to Cloisterham on several occasions and identifies him as her client while he sings at the cathedral in Charles Dickens's *The Mystery of Edwin Drood.*

Lord Puffington Master of the Hanby hounds; he invites Soapey Sponge to his house, mistakenly believing him to be a wealthy sportswriter in Robert Surtees's *Mr. Sponge's Sporting Tour.*

Paridel Puffwell Undersecretary of state and the author of a panegyrical ode praising William Pitt but unaware of its ironic content in William Beckford's *Azemia.*

Mrs. Pugh Young, pretentious widow, who is courted by Henry Ward to the intense disgust of his sister Averil; the courtship ends when Leonard Ward is convicted of murder in Charlotte Yonge's *The Trial.*

Flora Macfuss Pullens The daughter of a former Scottish friend of the Laird Douglas family; she now resides in Bath and prides herself on being the most economical woman ever born in Susan Ferrier's *Marriage.*

Mr. Pullet A wealthy farmer, who does little beyond regulating the many types of medication taken by his hypochondriac wife, Sophy, and dispensing lozenges to the children in George Eliot's *The Mill on the Floss.*

Sophy Dodson Pullet Mrs. Tulliver's second sister, who is a hypochondriac; she is certain that she will die at any moment in George Eliot's *The Mill on the Floss.*

Lady Clara Pulleyn Unfortunate daughter of the penurious Lord Dorking; poverty separates her from her first love, Jack Belsize; propelled into marriage with the rich, scornful, neglectful, and cruel Barnes Newcome, she leaves her two children to elope with Jack, now Lord Highgate, in William Makepeace Thackeray's *The Newcomes.*

Lady Henrietta Pulleyn Lady Clara's younger sister,

who marries Lord Kew after his engagement with Ethel Newcome is broken off in William Makepeace Thackeray's *The Newcomes.*

Mr. Pumblechook   Joe Gargery's uncle, who torments Pip Pirrip with moral goading and reminds him to remember those who have brought him up; he later patronizes him when Pip comes into his fortune in Charles Dickens's *Great Expectations.*

Mr. Pummice   Local house painter who retouches Brandon Hall in preparation for the Hunt Ball in J. Sheridan Le Fanu's *Wylder's Hand.*

Puny Fox   Large sea rover, who brings Hallblithe of the Raven to the Isle of Ransom, unites him with his kidnapped lover, the Hostage of the Rose, and accompanies them to their home in Cleveland by the sea in William Morris's *The Story of the Glittering Plain.*

Puppet-master   Unnamed entertainer who has his harangue about his performances' good influence undercut by his Merry Andrew's immoral behavior in Henry Fielding's *The History of Tom Jones.*

Puppy   Though playful, a danger to Alice because of her greatly reduced size when she encounters him after escaping from the White Rabbit's house; she bravely exhausts him by playing a game with a stick in Lewis Carroll's *Alice's Adventures in Wonderland.*

Lucy Purcell   Sweet wife of David Grieve; she renounces her father's tyranny and harsh religion; she dies young in Mrs. Humphry Ward's *The History of David Grieve.*

Tom Purcell   Rigidly self-righteous Baptist bookseller and father of Lucy; he gives David Grieve his first chance in Mrs. Humphry Ward's *The History of David Grieve.*

Purdie   Ellenshaws farm worker sharing a loft with Robert Colwan while Gil-martin and fiends contend out-of-doors for possession of Colwan in James Hogg's *The Private Memoirs and Confessions of a Justified Sinner.*

Purser   Agent of the Captain of the English Man of War; he carries the captain's bribe to the Navy Office in Charles Johnstone's *Chrysal: or, The Adventures of a Guinea.*

Mr. Pyke   Gentleman friend and toady of Sir Mulberry Hawk in Charles Dickens's *The Life and Adventures of Nicholas Nickleby.*

Pym   Faithful servant of Arthur Donnithorne in George Eliot's *Adam Bede.*

George Pynsent   The Dowager Countess of Rockminster's grandson, who woos Laura Bell (later Pendennis) in William Makepeace Thackeray's *The History of Pendennis.*

Q

Madame de Q*** Apparently superficial woman, who is exaggeratedly impressed by Yorick's conversation during a supper at Count de B****'s home in Laurence Sterne's *A Sentimental Journey through France and Italy*.

Dr. Quackenboss Rosey Mackenzie Newcome's fashionable doctor in William Makepeace Thackeray's *The Newcomes*.

Mrs. Quackly Wealthy widow whose vanity causes her to court the acquaintance of the celebrated in William Beckford's *Azemia*.

Quaker Disappointed father whose bewailing of his daughter's marriage to a pauper sparks Tom Jones's anger and reproach in Henry Fielding's *The History of Tom Jones*.

Quaker Gentlewoman Landlady of Roxana and Amy after they move out of Kensington to live incognito; she becomes Roxana's companion and remains with her after she marries the Dutch merchant, but they part when Roxana and her husband leave to live in Holland in Daniel Defoe's *The Fortunate Mistress*.

Dr. Quentin Quakleben Medical man who has proclaimed the merits of the waters of St. Ronan's Well and is among the social leaders at its thriving inn in Sir Walter Scott's *St. Ronan's Well*.

Mr. Quale Mrs. Jellyby's loquacious, philanthropic friend, who would like to marry Caddy Jellyby in Charles Dickens's *Bleak House*.

Mr. Qualmsick A meek-spirited man, whose fortune is lavished on physician and apothecary bills in Francis Coventry's *The History of Pompey the Little*.

Mrs. Qualmsick A lady whose life is an uninterrupted series of invented illnesses and into whose house Pompey wanders following his escape from the Rymers in Francis Coventry's *The History of Pompey the Little*.

Young Qualmsick Son of the Qualmsicks; he goes to Cambridge and, unlike his parents, has a most violent appetite for pleasure in Francis Coventry's *The History of Pompey the Little*.

Quangrollart Governor of the criminal colony of Crashdoorpt; he is Youwarkee's brother and the first of her relatives to visit Peter Wilkins's grotto in Robert Paltock's *The Life and Adventures of Peter Wilkins*.

Quanko Sambo Faithful attendant to Colonel Sir Thomas Blazo in an anecdote related by Alfred Jingle in Charles Dickens's *The Posthumous Papers of the Pickwick Club*.

Denzil Quarrier A barrister, who is unable to make a legal union with Lilian, the woman he loves, because she has had a previous, unconsummated marriage; they pretend to have been married abroad; when Quarrier runs for Parliament, his wife's estranged husband is hired by a jealous friend to expose the false marriage, but the plot fails, and Quarrier is elected; Lilian is driven to suicide in George Gissing's *Denzil Quarrier*.

Lilian Quarrier Denzil Quarrier's apparent wife, who is unable to marry him legally because of her unconsummated previous marriage; she drowns herself when her estranged husband, Arthur Northway, threatens exposure in George Gissing's *Denzil Quarrier*.

Orlando Quartezzani Italian nobleman who supported Castruccio dei Antelminelli's rise to power in Lucca but who later conspires to overthrow him in Mary Shelley's *Valperga*.

Cavaliere Pagana Quartezzani Ally of Castruccio dei Antelminelli in the capture of Lucca; he becomes proconsul of Lucca with him but later joins a conspiracy to overthrow him in Mary Shelley's *Valperga*.

Ugo Quartezzani Italian nobleman who supported Castruccio dei Antelminelli's rise to power in Lucca and who becomes the chief conspirator in a plot to overthrow him in Mary Shelley's *Valperga*.

Allan (Hunter, Macumazahn) Quatermain Small, wiry hunter/trader, who narrates the tale of two journeys with John Good and Sir Henry Curtis into Africa; the first is to find King Solomon's mines and Sir Henry's lost brother in H. Rider Haggard's *King Solomon's Mines*. The second is to discover as lost white race, the Zu-Vendi, in *Allan Quatermain*.

Harry Quatermain Allan Quatermain's son, a medical student who dies of smallpox; his death initiates Allan Quatermain's journey to find the Zu-Vendi people in H. Rider Haggard's *Allan Quatermain*.

Mr. Quaverdale Clergyman's son who quarrels with his father and becomes a hack journalist notable for his filthy clothes and easy-going ways in Anthony Trollope's *Mr. Scarborough's Family*.

Queen Character who has Jack Higgs's clothing put upon a dummy so that it can be observed and preserved; excited about Higgs's hot-air balloon, she allows one to be built to his specifications in Samuel Butler's *Erewhon*.

Queen-Mother of France   Kinswoman of Charles I; she has the Cavalier and Fielding put into custody and then released after the uprising in Lyon in Daniel Defoe's *Memoirs of a Cavalier*.

Queen of the Fairies   Kindly fairy who appears in human form as an Irishwoman to Tom, arranges his metamorphosis into a water-baby, and supervises his moral reeducation; she adopts several personae: Mrs. Bedonebyasyoudid, an ugly fairy who teaches the water-babies and all mankind, including Grimes, the consequences of their actions; Mrs. Doasyouwouldbedoneby, a soft, pretty, motherly fairy who treats the water-babies with infinite gentleness; and Mother Carey, who lives in Peacepool and teaches Tom the wisdom of learning from experience, furnishing him with a dog and a pass to help him in his journey to the Other-end-of-Nowhere in Charles Kingsley's *The Water-Babies*.

Madame Quesnel   Emily St. Aubert's social-climbing aunt, whose distant connection to the evil Montoni leads to his introduction to the St. Aubert family in Ann Radcliffe's *The Mysteries of Udolpho*.

Monsieur Quesnel   Emily St. Aubert's social-climbing uncle, who mismanages her estate while she is confined in the Castle di Udolpho in Ann Radcliffe's *The Mysteries of Udolpho*.

Mrs. Quick   Housekeeper to the hypochondriac Mr. Slicer in Richard Graves's *The Spiritual Quixote*.

Richard Quickenham   Industrious member of the Chancery bar and brother-in-law of Frank Fenwick; on a brief holiday in Bullhampton he is consulted as to the legality of the actions by the Marquis of Trowbridge in allowing a chapel to be built on land opposite the vicarage gates in Anthony Trollope's *The Vicar of Bullhampton*.

Sir Valentine Quickset   Fox-hunting baronet, who opposes Isaac Vanderpelft for election to Parliament, and whose followers are insulted by Ferret in Tobias Smollett's *The Adventures of Sir Launcelot Greaves*.

Mr. Quid   Margaret Bertram's advantage-seeking kinsman, a coarse tobacconist who holds high hopes of profiting by his cousin's death in Sir Walter Scott's *Guy Mannering*.

Quilly   Officious *bash* (valet) assigned to Peter Wilkins by Georigetti in Robert Paltock's *The Life and Adventures of Peter Wilkins*.

Betsy Quilp   Daniel Quilp's mild, pretty wife, who is kept in constant terror by him in Charles Dickens's *The Old Curiosity Shop*.

Daniel Quilp   Villainous, money-lending dwarf; he enjoys torturing his wife and Sampson Brass; he pursues Nell Trent and her grandfather, is behind the plot to frame Kit Nubbles, and eventually drowns in Charles Dickens's *The Old Curiosity Shop*.

Captain Quin   Cowardly officer betrothed to Nora Brady; his duel with Redmond Barry is rigged to convince Barry he has killed Quin; Nora's brothers keep Quin to his promise of marriage in William Makepeace Thackeray's *The Luck of Barry Lyndon*.

Lady Mary Quin   Inquisitive spinster in County Clare; she alerts Lady Scroope to the local presence of Mrs. O'Hara and her young daughter, Kate, and continues to relay gossip about the girl and Fred Neville in Anthony Trollope's *An Eye for an Eye*.

Captain Redmond Quin   Son of Nora (Brady) and Captain Quin; Bryan Lyndon's tutor, he successfully plots Lady Lyndon's escape from her husband, Redmond Barry, in William Makepeace Thackeray's *The Luck of Barry Lyndon*.

Mary Quince   Kindly, faithful, elderly maid to Maud Ruthyn and the only one allowed to go to Bartram-Haugh with her in J. Sheridan Le Fanu's *Uncle Silas*.

Mr. Quinion   Friend of Mr. Murdstone and manager of the Murdstone and Grinby wine warehouse, where David Copperfield is put to work in Charles Dickens's *The Personal History of David Copperfield*.

James Quinn   Actor and epicurean, who is a friend of Matthew Bramble; he entertains Bramble's family at Bath in Tobias Smollett's *The Expedition of Humphry Clinker*.

Jason Quirk   Son of the family steward Thady Quirk; he begins as the estate clerk, moves up to accountant, and finally becomes the attorney who confiscates the land for debts in Maria Edgeworth's *Castle Rackrent*.

Judy Quirk   Thady Quirk's grandniece, who is considered for marriage by her landlord and then rejected; later, when he has lost his fortune, she rejects him; she makes an appropriate marriage to a huntsman in Maria Edgeworth's *Castle Rackrent*.

Ned Quirk   Baked-potato man who helps the young Arthur Golding in George Gissing's *Workers in the Dawn*.

Thady Quirk   Faithful family steward through four landlords at the estate; he is the narrator of their history and downfall in Maria Edgeworth's *Castle Rackrent*.

Lady Jane Quirp   Character created by Henry Clinton to illustrate his opinions on the validity of physiognomy as a science and to show how young women acquire the defects of fashionable society in Henry Brooke's *The Fool of Quality*.

Mr. Quisque A lawyer who aids Mr. Glibly, Mr. Ellis, and Hugh Trevor in preventing Hugh's pamphlet from being published in Thomas Holcroft's *The Adventures of Hugh Trevor*.

Mr. Quitam Frequenter of the Black Bear who, as an attorney hopeful of acquiring some office, supports the government in Sir Walter Scott's *Rob Roy*.

Mr. Quiverful Meek Vicar of Puddingdale, whose appointment as Warden of Hiram's Hospital after Mr. Harding's resignation occasions a crucial battle in the war for power that develops between Mrs. Proudie and Mr. Slope in Anthony Trollope's *Barchester Towers*. He serves on the commission examining the Crawley case in *The Last Chronicle of Barset*.

Letitia Quiverful Vicar's wife and mother of fourteen children, who strongly defends to Mrs. Proudie her husband's claim to be Warden of Hiram's Hospital in Anthony Trollope's *Barchester Towers*. She is mentioned in *Framley Parsonage*.

Lord Quiverwit Aristocrat who is introduced to Narcissa by her brother, is Roderick Random's chief rival for her hand, and is defeated in a duel with Roderick in Tobias Smollett's *The Adventures of Roderick Random*.

R

Lord R—— A womanizer in Eliza Haywood's *Anti-Pamela: or, Feign'd Innocence Detected*.

Frank Raban Complex scholar, who makes a disastrous youthful marriage to Emma Penfold but finally appreciates and wins Dorothea Vanborough in Anne Thackeray Ritchie's *Old Kensington*.

Queen Rabesqurat Evil Queen of the Enchanted Sea; she tempts Shibli Bagarag during his adventures and fights on the side of Shagpat while Shibli attempts to shave him; she is overcome by Shibli and the sword of Aklis in George Meredith's *The Shaving of Shagpat*.

Mrs. Raby Aristocratic aunt of Elizabeth Raby; she compassionately forgives her heretic brother, Edwin, and accepts his daughter into the family in Mary Shelley's *Falkner*.

Edwin Raby Elizabeth Raby's aristocratic father, disowned by his rich Catholic family because of his heretical beliefs in Mary Shelley's *Falkner*.

Elizabeth Raby The virtuous, beautiful daughter of Edwin Raby; orphaned as a child, she is adopted by John Falkner; she prevents Falkner's suicide and assuages his guilt with compassion and filial love; after his admission of complicity in his lover's death and his indictment for murder, she courageously visits him daily; she loves and marries Gerald Neville, son of her father's lover, Alithea Rivers Neville, in Mary Shelley's *Falkner*.

Mrs. Rachael (later Mrs. Chadband) Repressive, forbidding housekeeper to Miss Barbary; later, married to the Reverend Chadband, she reveals information about Esther Summerson's parentage to Mr. Guppy in Charles Dickens's *Bleak House*.

Rachel Good-hearted and loving friend of Stephen Blackpool and fellow worker in Josiah Bounderby's factory in Charles Dickens's *Hard Times*.

Rachel Mrs. Gerrarde's maid, who accompanies her mistress to France in Frances Sheridan's *Memoirs of Miss Sidney Bidulph*.

Rachel Kind, gentle grandmother of Joseph of Arimathea; she often understands Joseph better than his father does in George Moore's *The Brook Kerith*.

Rachel A nursemaid in the household of Mr. Montague; she is seduced by him and unknowingly takes his abortifacient drugs, but after his suicide is befriended by his wife, Emma (Courtney), in Mary Hays's *Memoirs of Emma Courtney*.

Rachel Wife of Robert the waterman; she is infected with the plague and cannot come near her husband in Daniel Defoe's *A Journal of the Plague Year*.

Rachel Helen Huntingdon's faithful lady's maid, who accompanies her and little Arthur on the flight to Wildfell Hall in Anne Brontë's *The Tenant of Wildfell Hall*.

Sir Conolly (Sir Condy) Rackrent Remote cousin and successor to Sir Kit Rackrent; he is a well-loved landlord, who chooses his wife by a coin toss, loses the castle to debts, and dies of fever brought on by drink in Maria Edgeworth's *Castle Rackrent*.

Isabella Moneygawl Rackrent Sir Conolly Rackrent's wife, whose marriage results in her disinheritance; she is a spendthrift who leaves her husband when debts accumulate in Maria Edgeworth's *Castle Rackrent*.

Jessica Rackrent Jewish wife of Sir Kit Rackrent; although she is locked in her room until her husband's death, she retains her separate property and diamond cross in Maria Edgeworth's *Castle Rackrent*.

Sir Kit Rackrent Sir Murtagh Rackrent's younger brother, a philandering husband who locks his Jewish wife in her room for seven years in a futile attempt to get her money; he dies in a duel in Maria Edgeworth's *Castle Rackrent*.

Sir Murtagh Rackrent Sir Patrick Rackrent's heir, a lawyer who always has his tenants in suits over livestock and property; he dies of a broken blood vessel in an argument with his wife in Maria Edgeworth's *Castle Rackrent*.

Sir Patrick (O'Shaughlin) Rackrent Hospitable gentleman who changes his surname and agrees to bear the arms of Rackrent in order to inherit the castle; his body is seized for debt in Maria Edgeworth's *Castle Rackrent*.

Stainsforth Radclyffe Percy Godolphin's friend, who helps to renew his failing marriage with Constance Vernon (Countess of Erpingham) in Edward Bulwer-Lytton's *Godolphin*.

Mr. Raddle Much-maligned husband of Mary Ann Raddle in Charles Dickens's *The Posthumous Papers of the Pickwick Club*.

Mary Ann Raddle Sister of Elizabeth Cluppins; she is a shrill landlady, who tries to collect rent from Ben Allen and Bob Sawyer in Charles Dickens's *The Posthumous Papers of the Pickwick Club*.

George Radfoot   Third mate of the ship on which John Harmon sailed to England; having used his resemblance to Harmon as a means to burglarize Harmon upon returning to London, he is drowned and mistakenly identified as Harmon in Charles Dickens's *Our Mutual Friend*.

Dandy Mick Radley   Carefree, intelligent ruffian, who joins Walter Gerard's trade union and assists Stephen Morley in his search for the documents which prove Gerard's claim to the Marney estate in Benjamin Disraeli's *Sybil*.

Nataly Radnor   Victor Radnor's apparent wife, who shares with him the guilt of living out of wedlock, which undermines her health and her relationship with their daughter, Nesta; Nataly learns from her suffering, and is capable of sympathy and honesty; she dies almost simultaneously with Victor's elderly legal wife in George Meredith's *One of Our Conquerers*.

Nesta Radnor   Attractive, intelligent, independent daughter of Victor and Nataly Radnor, who intend for her to marry Dudley Sowerby; after Sowerby breaks their engagement upon learning that Nesta is illegitimate, she falls in love with Dartrey Fenellan, whose love compensates her for her mother's death and her father's madness in George Meredith's *One of Our Conquerers*.

Victor Radnor   Handsome, successful, and intelligent, but also vain and self-deceiving businessman who abandons his wealthy, older wife, Mrs. Burman, in order to live with his true love, Nataly; when his egotism sours their relationship, he lives in fear that its illicit nature will be exposed until the deaths of both Mrs. Burman and Nataly lead him to madness in George Meredith's *One of Our Conquerers*.

Colonel Prince Louis Radocky   Austrian who narrowly escapes being captured visiting his Italian lover, Countess Medole, in George Meredith's *Vittoria*.

Otto Radowitz   Oxford musician whose Polish background causes trouble with Douglas Falloden and the Oxford "swells"; because his hand is permanently injured in a college fight, he must relinquish his ambitions to become a pianist in Mrs. Humphry Ward's *Lady Connie*.

Aldous Raeburn   Cambridge-educated heir to Lord Maxwell; he becomes an influential Member of Parliament and wins the hand of Marcella Boyce in Mrs. Humphry Ward's *Marcella*. He becomes Lord Maxwell; he endeavors to influence society through the passage of his Factory Bill, which will abolish sweatshops and regulate working conditions in *Sir George Tressady*.

Netta Raeburn   Spinster sister of Lord Maxwell; she keeps house for him at Maxwell Court in Mrs. Humphry Ward's *Marcella*.

Mrs. Raffarty   Nicholas Garraghty's affected, silly sister in Maria Edgeworth's *The Absentee*.

John Raffles   Joshua Rigg's red-faced stepfather, who visits at Stone Court hoping to grab some of Joshua's new wealth, although he had mistreated him as a child; he knows Nicholas Bulstrode's guilty secret and tells a few people before Bulstrode causes his death by allowing him to overdose on opium in George Eliot's *Middlemarch*.

I.O. Ragan   Priest in Georigetti's establishment in Robert Paltock's *The Life and Adventures of Peter Wilkins*.

Charles Raggles   Landlord in Curzon Street to Rawdon and Becky (Sharp) Crawley, who never pay him, in William Makepeace Thackeray's *Vanity Fair*.

John (Jack) Feversham Raikes   Evan Harrington's former schoolmate, who pretends to high status; he matures to marry Polly Wheedle and to attend to Evan's tailor shop in George Meredith's *Evan Harrington*.

Father Railston   Indulgent confessor to Evelyn Innes in her early years in George Moore's *Evelyn Innes*.

Jack Railton   Quaker who lives in Bows, near the Stanemore mountains, in Thomas Amory's *The Life of John Buncle, Esq.*

Roger Raine   Loyal publican of the Peveril Arms in Sir Walter Scott's *Peveril of the Peak*.

Rake   A young, rich aristocrat who is free of every restraint of principle and who is determined to ruin a young lady of uncommon beauty and merit, to whom he proposes marriage with the stipulation that it be kept secret from society in Charles Johnstone's *Chrysal: or, The Adventures of a Guinea*.

Rake   Bertie Cecil's faithful servant, killed while serving with Bertie in the Foreign Legion in Ouida's *Under Two Flags*.

Walter Raleigh   Ambitious, handsome young follower of Thomas Ratcliffe, Earl of Sussex; his action of spreading his rich cloak upon a miry spot in Queen Elizabeth's path results in his knighthood in Sir Walter Scott's *Kenilworth*. As Sir Walter Raleigh he is a soldier and courtier who fights in Ireland and rules in Munster before returning to court; although he plans to sail with the *Golden Hind* expedition, the queen requests that he remain behind in Charles Kingsley's *Westward Ho!*. He is a suitor to Ellinor, who detests him, in Sophia Lee's *The Recess*.

Ralph Profligate, worldly elder brother of Basil; having returned with a morganatic wife to England, he assists Basil by his practical management of Mr. Sherwin in Wilkie Collins's *Basil: A Story of Modern Life*.

Ralph One of John Buncle's servants; despite his agility, he falls into a river on the way to Richmondshire, the residence of Eusebia Harcourt, in Thomas Amory's *The Life of John Buncle, Esq.*

Ralph King Peter's son who becomes the lover of the Lady of Abundance and after her murder seeks the Well with Ursula; following many adventures he returns to defeat his foes at Upmeads and reigns there with Ursula in William Morris's *The Well at the World's End*.

Mr. Ram Owner of the bookshop where Ezra Mordecai Lapidoth works and meets Daniel Deronda in George Eliot's *Daniel Deronda*.

Ramgolam Mrs. Beresford's Hindu servant, who hides during the pirate attack on the *Agra* and tries to steal the wounded Captain Dodd's wallet, thinking it to be a powerful amulet in Charles Reade's *Hard Cash*.

Lén Ramon Parisian artist who painted Cigarette when she was a child and later falls in love with her, is rejected by her, and joins the French Foreign Legion; he dies of his battle wounds in Ouida's *Under Two Flags*.

Sir John Ramorny Scottish knight who is companion of the Duke of Rothsay; he loses his hand to Henry Smith while helping Rothsay try to kidnap Catherine Glover; he conspires with the Duke of Albany to murder Rothsay, and he is executed by Archibald, Earl of Douglas, for the deed in Sir Walter Scott's *The Fair Maid of Perth*.

Captain Rampan A womanizer who chases after unprotected young women, including Diana Merion; he, among others, propels her into a loveless marriage with Augustus Warwick in George Meredith's *Diana of the Crossways*.

David Ramsay Scottish watchmaker who helps Nigel Olifaunt gain access to King James I in Sir Walter Scott's *The Fortunes of Nigel*.

Margaret Ramsay David Ramsay's beautiful daughter; in love with Nigel Olifaunt, she disguises herself as a page to plead before King James I for Nigel's release from the Tower; the discovery of her noble descent makes her marriage to Nigel acceptable in Sir Walter Scott's *The Fortunes of Nigel*.

Mrs. Ramsden Housewife who has ordered some socks to be knit by Caroline Helstone for the charity "Jew Basket" in Charlotte Brontë's *Shirley*.

Timothy Ramsden The corn-factor at Royd Mill who attends the Whitsuntide gathering in Charlotte Brontë's *Shirley*.

Ramsey Debtor being sucked dry by Dodson and Fogg in an anecdote related by Mr. Wicks in Charles Dickens's *The Posthumous Papers of the Pickwick Club*.

John Rance Police constable who discovers the body of Enoch Drebber in Arthur Conan Doyle's *A Study in Scarlet*.

Mathilda Rancliffe Airy, cheerful, hypocritical London friend of Mary Macneil (later Fleetwood) in William Godwin's *Fleetwood*.

Annie Randall Wife of John Randall; she reveals to Esther Waters the poverty and unhappiness caused by her husband's gambling in George Moore's *Esther Waters*.

John (Leopold) Randall Barfield family butler, private servant to Arthur Barfield; a tipster on the horses and an adviser to jockeys, he is arrogant with his gambling knowledge and indifferent to his own family's poverty in George Moore's *Esther Waters*.

Roderick (Rory) Random Young man left with his hostile grandfather after the death of his mother; apprenticed to become a surgeon, he is a journeyman to a London apothecary; kidnapped by a press-gang and taken aboard the *Thunder*, he sails to Jamaica, becomes surgeon's mate on the *Lizard*, and barely survives shipwreck to land in England, where he falls in love with Narcissa; taken to France by smugglers, he joins a French army fighting in Germany, returns to London, and pursues various heiresses; he becomes the object of Lord Strutwell's homosexual lust; he joins his uncle on a ship for South America, where he discovers his lost father; he returns to Scotland with his new bride, Narcissa, in Tobias Smollett's *The Adventures of Roderick Random*.

Mr. Rankeillor Prudent lawyer to David Balfour; he hears David's tale of kidnapping and fugitive flight and advises him to be cautious about his Jacobite friends in Robert Louis Stevenson's *Kidnapped*. He aids David in acquiring his rightful estate in *Catriona*.

Joshua Rann The village shoemaker and parish clerk who tries to excite the Reverend Adolphus Irwine against the Methodist preaching of Dinah Morris in George Eliot's *Adam Bede*.

Tommy Rann Dicky Perrott's Jago playfellow, with

whom Dicky gets into mischief in Arthur Morrison's *A Child of the Jago.*

Ransome Ignorant, swearing, and abused cabin boy of the Scottish brig *Covenant*; he is duped into loyal service and continually beaten, eventually to his death, by chief mate Mr. Shuan in Robert Louis Stevenson's *Kidnapped.*

Raoul Dame Gillian's antipathetic husband, a huntsman who is wounded during the ambush by Randal de Lacy in Sir Walter Scott's *The Betrothed.*

Isaac Rapine Usurer who climbs into Miss Jenny's bed, is threatened with jail, and pays her for dropping charges in Tobias Smollett's *The Adventures of Roderick Random.*

Colonel Rappee Peacetime military officer and guest of Sir William Forester; he annoys the other guests, particularly Miss Sainthill and Geoffry Wildgoose, with stock attacks on religion in Richard Graves's *The Spiritual Quixote.*

Rasselas Prince of Abyssinia who leaves his home in the Happy Valley to gain experience and make the choice of life; he discovers that life is everywhere a state in which much is to be endured and little to be enjoyed, then returns to Abyssinia in Samuel Johnson's *The History of Rasselas, Prince of Abissinia.*

Ratchcali Tyrolese young man, who meets Ferdinand in Vienna, robs him while deserting the army, meets him again in London, and suggests the first of his many fraudulent disguises and schemes in London; Ratchcali reveals more of Ferdinand's perfidies to Reynaldo de Melvil when he is finally discovered a prisoner in irons in Tobias Smollett's *The Adventures of Ferdinand Count Fathom.*

Peter Ratcliff Lawyer who urges David Simple's prosecution of a suit in Chancery and then withdraws his offer of service to the family after the case is resolved against the Simples in Sarah Fielding's *The Adventures of David Simple in Search of a Faithful Friend.*

Hugh Ratcliffe Sir Edward Mauley's trusted friend and agent, who carries out the Dwarf's requests in Sir Walter Scott's *The Black Dwarf.*

James (Daddie Rat) Ratcliffe Inmate who rises to become captain of the Tolbooth and befriends Jeanie Deans in Sir Walter Scott's *The Heart of Midlothian.*

Mr. Ratler Liberal whip, who becomes Patronage Secretary in an administration led by Lord Mildmay in Anthony Trollope's *Phineas Finn.* He is disliked by Phineas, whose independence strikes the whip as disloyalty to the

party in *Phineas Redux.* As "Rattler" he continues to rally the party in *The Prime Minister.*

Jack Rattlin Sailor aboard the *Thunder* who befriends Roderick Random and who loses a hand during a battle in Jamaica in Tobias Smollett's *The Adventures of Roderick Random.*

Mr. Raunham Rector who helps Cytherea Graye, her brother Owen, and Edward Springrove solve the mystery behind Aeneas Manston and his wife's disappearance in Thomas Hardy's *Desperate Remedies.*

Raven A servant at Nightmare Abbey in Thomas Love Peacock's *Nightmare Abbey.*

Mr. Raven (Adam) Sexton of the House of the Dead; he awakens his children to new life by inviting them to sleep; he meets Vane in his library and attempts to guide him throughout the novel; he cuts off Lilith's left hand to restore the living waters and to allow her to sleep in George MacDonald's *Lilith.*

Lord Allan Ravenswood Edgar Ravenswood's father; he is an enemy of Sir William Ashton, whom he bitterly curses and is ruined by in Sir Walter Scott's *The Bride of Lammermoor.*

Edgar Ravenswood Dark, handsome heir of Lord Allan Ravenswood; he agrees to end the feud with Sir William Ashton after falling in love with Ashton's daughter, Lucy; after Lady Ashton disrupts the romance, he is unable to prevent Lucy from marrying Bucklaw (Frank Hayston); he disappears upon the moors after her funeral in Sir Walter Scott's *The Bride of Lammermoor.*

Roger Ravine Attorney who is victim of a practical joke against Commodore Trunnion in Tobias Smollett's *The Adventures of Peregrine Pickle.*

Rawley Handsome young officer invited to Ashwood to interest Emily Watson; he is unsuccessful in doing so in George Moore's *Vain Fortune.*

Miss Rawlins Spinster at the boardinghouse in Hampstead where Clarissa Harlowe first hides from Robert Lovelace; she is charmed by Lovelace into betraying Clarissa in Samuel Richardson's *Clarissa: or, The History of a Young Lady.*

Rawlinson Virtuous younger friend of Richard Annesly; he proposes to Harriet Annesly and later leaves his considerable fortune to Harry Bolton and Billy Annesly in Henry Mackenzie's *The Man of the World.*

Mrs. Ray Tender-hearted, widowed mother of Dorothea Prime and Rachel; her natural good spirits are much dampened by the evangelical severity of her elder daughter; this leads her to oppose a match between Luke Rowan and Rachel, but she is won over by Luke and blesses the union in Anthony Trollope's *Rachel Ray*.

Rachel Ray   Tall, fair-haired sweetheart of Luke Rowan, beset by the determination of her elder sister, Dorothea Prime, to keep them apart; always firm of purpose, even when her mother sides for a time with Dorothea, she marries Luke in Anthony Trollope's *Rachel Ray*.

Miss Rayland   The last of three unmarried sisters; she is characterized by pride in her ancestors; she makes Orlando Somerive her heir in a will that is destroyed; a copy hidden in the manor house by Rachel Lennard is later seized by Orlando in Charlotte Smith's *The Old Manor House*.

Raymond of Toulouse   Distinguished French nobleman and soldier, who joins the crusade in Sir Walter Scott's *Count Robert of Paris*.

Cousin Raymond   Husband of Camilla, a relative of Miss Havisham; he is disappointed in the results of his toadying to Miss Havisham in Charles Dickens's *Great Expectations*.

Lord Raymond   Perdita's noble husband, who chooses love over ambition; dissatisfied with domesticity, he becomes Lord Protector, takes a lover, resigns his public office, resumes a military career, and dies heroically in Mary Shelley's *The Last Man*.

Mr. Raymond   Captain of the gang of thieves; he finds Caleb Williams after his fight with Gines; he takes care of Caleb and refuses to turn him in for a reward in William Godwin's *Caleb Williams*.

Mr. Raymond   Philanthropist and poet, who befriends Diamond and his family and takes them, along with Nanny and Cripple Jim, to live with him at his estate, The Mound, in George MacDonald's *At the Back of the North Wind*.

Clara, Lady Raymond   Mother of the heroine, Eleanor Raymond; she is weak and dependent, yet a good wife; she is careless of the welfare of her children in Caroline Norton's *Stuart of Dunleath*.

Eleanor Raymond   Heroine, whom the reader meets as a child; she is mature, insightful, loving, pure, and virtuous; she marries Sir Stephen Penrhyn when she thinks David Stuart is dead, leaves her husband when he abuses her, and dies loving David in Caroline Norton's *Stuart of Dunleath*.

General Sir John Raymond   Second husband of

Clara, Lady Raymond and father of Eleanor; kind, considerate, and concerned for his wife, he dies as the result of illness contracted in India in Caroline Norton's *Stuart of Dunleath*.

Ready-to-halt   Pilgrim on crutches; he becomes Feeblemind's companion, giving him one of his crutches; he joins Christiana and her party in John Bunyan's *The Pilgrim's Progress From this World to That Which Is to Come*.

Amy Yule Reardon   Wife of Edwin Reardon, daughter of Alfred Yule, and cousin of Marian Yule; she urges her husband to regard his writing as a trade and refuses to share his poverty; she and Edwin are reconciled through the fatal illness of their child, Willie; after Edwin's death she marries the mercenary and successful Jasper Milvain in George Gissing's *New Grub Street*.

Edwin Reardon   A novelist of scholarly temperament who has lost his power to write after his first promising novels and struggles unsuccessfully to meet the demands of the literary market place; he parts from his wife and child, takes a position as a clerk, lives alone, grows ill, and eventually dies in George Gissing's *New Grub Street*.

Willie Reardon   Amy and Edwin Reardon's young son; he dies soon after his illness reconciles his parents in George Gissing's *New Grub Street*.

Rebecca   Brave and beautiful Jewess, the daughter of Isaac of York; gifted in the art of healing, she nurses Ivanhoe's wounds after no one will recognize him; she spurns Brian de Bois-Guilbert, though her acceptance would save her life; condemned to death for sorcery, she is rescued by Ivanhoe, whom she loves, in Sir Walter Scott's *Ivanhoe*.

Rebecca   Servant girl occasionally employed in the household of the evil Mr. Grimshaw in a ghost story interpolated into the narrative of William Beckford's *Azemia*.

Mrs. Rebecca   Margaret Bertram's favorite attendant, to whom she leaves £100 in Sir Walter Scott's *Guy Mannering*.

Agnes de Rebiera   Pretty young lady of Palermo; Jack Easy falls in love with her in Captain Frederick Marryat's *Mr. Midshipman Easy*.

Rector   Hugh Trevor's vain and spiteful maternal grandfather; he turns his back on his daughters when Red Knight   Ruffian who kills Sir Baudoin before being slain by Arthur in William Morris's *The Water of the Wondrous Isles*.

Lady Alice Redcliffe   Somewhat egotistical but good-hearted mother-in-law of Sir Jeckyl Marlowe, grandmother of Beatrix, and mother of the late Guy Deverell; she dislikes Sir Jeckyl but agrees to visit Marlowe, where she meets Varbarriere and Guy Strangways, who turns out to be her lost grandson; she becomes Beatrix Marlowe's guardian after Sir Jeckyl's death and manages to reunite her with Guy in J. Sheridan Le Fanu's *Guy Deverell*.

Red-coat of Waterless Captain of a reconnoitering band in the Silver-dale campaign in William Morris's *The Roots of the Mountains*.

Mr. Reddypalm Publican whose vote carries the Barchester election in favor of Sir Roger Scatcherd in Anthony Trollope's *Doctor Thorne*.

Sir Arthur Redgauntlet (Darsie Latimer) Young law student and friend of Alan Fairford; kidnapped by his uncle while taking a fishing holiday, he discovers his true identity as the son of a Jacobite martyred after the Rising of 1745; he refuses to compromise his patriotic loyalty in Sir Walter Scott's *Redgauntlet*.

Edward Hugh Redgauntlet (Mr. Herries of Birrenswork, Laird of the Lakes) Catholic uncle of Darsie Latimer (Arthur Redgauntlet); he kidnaps his nephew, aims to convert Darsie to the Jacobite cause, leads a conspiracy to place the Stuart Pretender on the British throne, and is released after he is captured with the Pretender in Sir Walter Scott's *Redgauntlet*.

Lilias Redgauntlet Arthur Redgauntlet's sister, who has been raised by Hugh Redgauntlet apart from her brother; she alerts Alan Fairford that Darsie Latimer (Arthur Redgauntlet) is in danger and finally marries Alan in Sir Walter Scott's *Redgauntlet*.

Sir Robert Redgauntlet Ancestor of Arthur and Hugh; he summons Steenie Steenson to hell for a receipt in Wandering Willie Steenson's tale in Sir Walter Scott's *Redgauntlet*.

Dr. Redgill The Beech Park family physician of Frederick, Lord Lindore and Lady Juliana Douglas; he stays on primarily because of the good, rich food served at Beech Park in Susan Ferrier's *Marriage*.

Cyrus Redgrave Wealthy and predatory bachelor, who is killed by a jealous husband in George Gissing's *The Whirlpool*.

Redhead Retainer of Gandolf, King of Utterbol; he helps Ralph to escape and to meet Ursula in William Morris's *The Well at the World's End*.

Charles Reding Protagonist, whose disillusionment

with his Anglo-Catholic religion leads to his conversion to Roman Catholicism in John Henry Newman's *Loss and Gain*.

Red King Chess piece who sleeps under a tree throughout the game; Alice is frustrated by the impossibility of disproving Tweedledee's argument that she exists only in his dream in Lewis Carroll's *Through the Looking-Glass*.

Red Knight Ruffian who kills Sir Baudoin before being slain by Arthur in William Morris's The Water of the Wondrous Isles.

Red Knight Chess piece who tries to take Alice prisoner but loses in battle with the White Knight in Lewis Carroll's *Through the Looking-Glass*.

Mr. Redlaw Lonely, depressed older man, whose scientific studies brought him happiness; he loved his sister very much and became a recluse when he lost her; with only his students and William and Milly Swidger to talk to, Redlaw is as barren and stark as the winter in Charles Dickens's *The Haunted Man and the Ghost's Bargain*.

Red Queen Chess piece who introduces Alice to the game; she explains the dimensions of the chess board world and gives Alice directions to the eighth square; she quizzes and lectures Queen Alice; at Alice's coronation feast she is seized and shaken by Alice, turning into the black kitten in Lewis Carroll's *Through the Looking-Glass*.

Tom Redruth Squire Trelawney's loyal gamekeeper, who holds the ship's cabin against the pirates while Richard Joyce and Dr. Livesey load supplies; he is shot dead during the first attack on the stockade in Robert Louis Stevenson's *Treasure Island*.

Beatrice Redwing Conventionally pious girl who becomes a concert singer; engaged to Wilfred Athel, she nobly releases him and accepts his marriage to Emily Hood in George Gissing's *A Life's Morning*.

Red-wolf Bearer of the banner of the Wolf; he is wounded in the battle of Silver-stead in William Morris's *The Roots of the Mountains*.

Thomas Redworth Faithful lover of Diana Merion (Warwick); he hesitates to propose to her until she has become engaged to Augustus Warwick; he remains her faithful friend and financial adviser, buying her family home when she is in debt, and marrying her after Warwick is dead and her lover Percy Dacier deserts her in George Meredith's *Diana of the Crossways*.

Edward Reed Country doctor with sympathy for the poor and without high social standing; Alice Barton marries him, and they establish a middle-class home in London in George Moore's *A Drama in Muslin*.

Eliza Reed   Jane Eyre's cousin and the eldest of the Reed children; she prefers her own society to that of others and eventually withdraws into a convent in Charlotte Brontë's *Jane Eyre*.

Georgiana Reed   The middle Reed child, as self-indulgent as her sister is ascetic, who loves fashionable society and finally marries a worn-out dandy in Charlotte Brontë's *Jane Eyre*.

John Reed   The youngest child, Mrs. Reed's favorite, who is violent in his early conduct with Jane, and whose lack of restraint runs him into debt and finally suicide in Charlotte Brontë's *Jane Eyre*.

Louis Reed   Young man who does not know that Edmund Langley, the man he meets in Greece, is his father and who dies before learning the truth in George Gissing's *Sleeping Fires*.

Sarah Gibson Reed   Jane Eyre's uncle's widow, who hates being saddled with the responsibility of bringing up her husband's relative and does much to make Jane miserable but confesses her sins to Jane on her deathbed in Charlotte Brontë's *Jane Eyre*.

Mrs. Reeves   Harriet Byron's cousin and hostess in London in Samuel Richardson's *Sir Charles Grandison*.

Archibald Reeves   Husband of Mrs. Reeves and Harriet Byron's host in London in Samuel Richardson's *Sir Charles Grandison*.

Reformed Debauchee   Well-born and well-educated but vicious man who educates and then marries a common whore and is disinherited by his family in Charles Johnstone's *Chrysal: or, The Adventures of a Guinea*.

Grand Duke of Reisenburg   Former ally of the Prince of Lilliput and ruler of the rival principality, who turns against him for political reasons and becomes his mortal enemy in Benjamin Disraeli's *Vivian Grey*.

Madame Carolina of Reisenburg   The Grand Duke of Reisenburg's charming but superficial wife, who affects the latest literary fashion, and whose attitudes epitomize the frivolity of the Austrian court in Benjamin Disraeli's *Vivian Grey*.

The Crown Prince of Reisenburg   Gloomy, grotesque son of the Grand Duke, stepson of Madame Carolina, and the betrothed of the Baroness Sybilla; he is unaware that the latter is paying a visit to his court in Benjamin Disraeli's *Vivian Grey*.

Reldresal   Principal Secretary of Private Affairs to the Emperor of Lilliput and second minister after Flimnap; Lemuel Gulliver trusts his friendship until he advocates severe penalties (though less severe than Flimnap's) against Gulliver when he is impeached in Jonathan Swift's *Travels into Several Remote Nations of the World. In Four Parts. By Lemuel Gulliver*.

Reliever   Rescuer of Christiana and Mercy from the Ill-favored ones in John Bunyan's *The Pilgrim's Progress From this World to That Which Is to Come*.

René   King of Sicily, a poet prince, who rules also in Provence and who negotiates with his daughter Margaret of Anjou to cede Provence to Charles, Duke of Burgundy, in Sir Walter Scott's *Anne of Geierstein*.

Renfield   Patient of Dr. Seward; he is completely dominated by Count Dracula, whom he admits to the sanitarium where the count's enemies have taken refuge, thus allowing Dracula to attack Mina Harker in Bram Stoker's *Dracula*.

Dr. Rerechild   Barchester physician whose patients include Eleanor Bold in Anthony Trollope's *Barchester Towers*. He attends Sir Roger Scatcherd's deathbed in *Doctor Thorne*.

Lord Reresby   Accepted suitor of Lucy Selby, who has rejected John Greville on Harriet Byron's advice in Samuel Richardson's *Sir Charles Grandison*.

Reuben   Keeper of Julius (Uncle Lorne) Brandon at Brandon Hall in J. Sheridan Le Fanu's *Wylder's Hand*.

Mme. Reuter   Mlle. Reuter's mother and housekeeper at her school, who contacts William Crimsworth through her friend Mme. Pelet about teaching English at the girls' school in Charlotte Brontë's *The Professor*.

Zoraide Reuter   Headmistress of a girls' school in Brussels, who is secretly engaged to M. Pelet, the headmaster next door, but who nevertheless succeeds in attracting William Crimsworth until he overhears a conversation which dampens his interest; she finally marries Pelet in Charlotte Brontë's *The Professor*.

Reverend Mother   Elderly, small, and delicate nun, who is probably of upper-class origin; she seems to have suffered and renounced worldly experience in George Moore's *Evelyn Innes*. Her death leaves Evelyn much less secure in *Sister Teresa*.

Lady Revill   Woman who becomes the guardian of Edmund Langley's illegitimate son, Louis Reed; she is reunited with Langley, her old lover, through the young man's troubles and death in George Gissing's *Sleeping Fires*.

John Rewcastle Jedburgh smuggler and Jacobite in Sir Walter Scott's *The Black Dwarf*.

Mr. Reynolds (the elder) Grace Nugent's paternal grandfather, who discovers that Grace is his legitimate granddaughter and makes her his sole heir in Maria Edgeworth's *The Absentee*.

Mr. Reynolds Grace Nugent's father, who dies before her birth but is legitimately married to Grace's mother, Miss St. Omar, in Maria Edgeworth's *The Absentee*.

Mrs. Reynolds Mr. Darcy's housekeeper; her extravagant praise of her master as she shows the house to Elizabeth Bennet and the Gardiners encourages Elizabeth's improving opinion of Darcy in Jane Austen's *Pride and Prejudice*.

Lady Emilia Reynolds Harriot Selvyn's mother, who, having vowed never to marry after her "misconduct" with her betrothed, brings her illegitimate daughter, Harriot, to live with her after the death of Mr. Selvyn, who raised her, and leaves her a fortune in Sarah Scott's *A Description of Millenium Hall*.

Joe Reynolds Tenant farmer of Larry Macdermot; he leads illegal makers of poteen in Anthony Trollope's *The Macdermots of Ballycloran*.

Sir Joshua Reynolds Leader of the British artistic establishment; he furthers the career of Angelica Kauffmann but rejects any romantic attachment in Anne Thackeray Ritchie's *Miss Angel*.

Monsieur De Rhie Monomaniacal gentleman, who kidnaps and imprisons Cornelia in his house with the intent of making her his lover in Sarah Scott's *The History of Cornelia*.

Rhün Son of Maelgon Gwyneth; pursuing Angharad and Melanghel, he is entrapped by Taliesin; his release is exchanged for that of Elphin in Thomas Love Peacock's *The Misfortunes of Elphin*.

Arthur Rhodes Would-be writer befriended by Diana Warwick; he proposes to her but is refused in George Meredith's *Diana of the Crossways*.

Dr. Rhubarb A physician who treats Lady Tempest in Francis Coventry's *The History of Pompey the Little*.

Mr. Rhymer A very poor poet, whose patron, Lord Danglecourt, gives him Pompey instead of money in Francis Coventry's *The History of Pompey the Little*.

Mrs. Rhymer Wife of the poet Rhymer; very close to lying-in, she is furious that her husband brings home a dog instead of money in Francis Coventry's *The History of Pompey the Little*.

Mr. Riach Short, red-headed second mate of the Scottish brig *Covenant*; when drunk, he is kind to kidnapped David Balfour and makes his life bearable in Robert Louis Stevenson's *Kidnapped*.

Riah Old, venerable Jewish man, who works for Fascination Fledgeby by posing as the hard-hearted head of Pubsey and Co.; he befriends Jenny Wren (Fanny Cleaver) and offers protection to Lizzie Hexam when she is pursued by Eugene Wrayburn in Charles Dickens's *Our Mutual Friend*.

Mr. Ribble Old consumptive chemist living near Nottingham; he gives John Buncle a long discourse, ranging from the separation of metals to disappearing or "sympathetic" ink; he warns Buncle of the consequences of immorality in Thomas Amory's *The Life of John Buncle, Esq.*

Philip (Van Dieman Smith) Ribstone Childhood friend of Martin Tinman; he returns to England a wealthy man after fleeing to Australia as an army deserter; he seeks to renew his old friendship but slowly realizes that Tinman is a cheap, vain social climber in George Meredith's *The House on the Beach*.

Alphonso Riccabocca Exiled Italian nobleman who lives simply in England as a scholar; he marries Jemima Hazeldean to provide a mother for his daughter, Violante Riccabocca, and is ultimately restored to his estates in Edward Bulwer-Lytton's *"My Novel," by Pisistratus Caxton*.

Violante Riccabocca Beautiful daughter of Alphonso Riccabocca; she is courted for selfish ends by Randal Leslie and Count di Peschiera but ultimately marries Harley L'Estrange in Edward Bulwer-Lytton's *"My Novel," by Pisistratus Caxton*.

Mademoiselle Ricci Notorious European actress and former mistress of Geoffrey Cliffe in Mrs. Humphry Ward's *The Marriage of William Ashe*.

Miss Rice An author who hires Esther Waters, providing her with more comfort and understanding than she has ever before encountered in London; she is concerned about Esther's illegitimate son, Jackie Latch, and interested in Esther's personal problems in George Moore's *Esther Waters*.

Richard Son of W. Elford's servant, Mary; he works as an apprentice in a printer's shop and helps prevent

Hugh Trevor's pamphlet from being published in Thomas Holcroft's *The Adventures of Hugh Trevor*.

Richard   Handsome young blacksmith engaged to marry Meg Veck in Charles Dickens's *The Chimes*.

Richard   Kindly and pious schoolmaster, whom Peter Wilkins makes his guardian after the death of his mother in Robert Paltock's *The Life and Adventures of Peter Wilkins*.

Richard   Arthur Huntingdon's coachman, who, in showing concern for the horses' welfare, incurs Arthur's wrath in Anne Brontë's *The Tenant of Wildfell Hall*.

Richard   Henry III's minstrel in Ann Radcliffe's *Gaston de Blondeville*.

Richard   Joiner who decides to leave Wapping with John and Thomas in Daniel Defoe's *A Journal of the Plague Year*.

Richard (Dick)   Young London clerk, who learns about local history and country ways when he spends his holidays in Berkshire in September 1857 and falls in love with Lucy Hurst in Thomas Hughes's *The Scouring of the White Horse*.

Richard (Dicky) (Wilkins)   Fifth and youngest son of Peter Wilkins and Youwarkee in Robert Paltock's *The Life and Adventures of Peter Wilkins*.

Richard of Gloucester (Crookback)   Brave, bloodthirsty, ambitious future King Richard III of England; he meets Dick Shelton in lieu of the Earl of Risingham, has Dick fight in the Battle of Shoreby, and knights him for his services; he offers Joan Sedley a rich marriage in Robert Louis Stevenson's *The Black Arrow: A Tale of Two Roses*.

Duke (Richard the Fearless) Richard of Normandy   Son of Duke William; he successfully defends his kingdom and forgives his father's murderer in Charlotte Yonge's *The Little Duke*.

(King) Richard (Plantagenet, Coeur de Lion, The Black Knight, Le Noir Faineant, Knight of the Fetterlock)   Hot-tempered prince who takes the Castle of Garde Douloureuse by assault; he is King Henry II's son and at odds with his brother, Prince John, in Sir Walter Scott's *The Betrothed*. King Richard I of England and leader of Christian forces in the Crusade to recapture Jerusalem from Saladin, he is healed by the talisman of Saladin, accepts Sir Kenneth as his champion in the quarrel with Conrade, Marquis of Montserrat, and blesses the engagement of Lady Edith to Sir Kenneth in *The Talisman*. Rightful king of England, he returns from Palestine at the height of his brother's conspiracy and must travel in disguise; as the Black Knight, he jousts at Ashby, besieges

Torquilstone Castle, and supports Ivanhoe at Templestowe before identifying himself in *Ivanhoe*.

Richard the Red   Squire to Blaise; he joins Ralph in Whitwall on his return from the Well and fights in the battle of Upmeads in William Morris's *The Well at the World's End*.

Mr. Richardson   A decent, wise clergyman, who marries Agnes's sister, Mary Grey, and provides her with a comfortable life in Anne Brontë's *Agnes Grey*.

Mr. Richmond   Young, sickly cousin of Ribble; though tall and handsome, he has become ill as a result of a wanton life in Thomas Amory's *The Life of John Buncle, Esq.*

Annabelle Richmond   Mary Cardonnel's friend and Sir Harry Richmond's virtuous daughter; recognizing Medora Glenmorris's danger from Sir Harry, she warns her and assists her flight in Charlotte Smith's *The Young Philosopher*.

Sir Harry Richmond   Landowner whose estate includes a private brothel and who pursues Medora Glenmorris in Charlotte Smith's *The Young Philosopher*.

Harry Richmond   Intelligent, romantic son of Richmond Roy raised mostly by his maternal grandfather, Squire Beltham; loyalty to his father alienates him from Beltham, and his romanticism makes Princess Ottilia more appealing to him than Janet Ilchester until he learns to integrate Beltham's practicality with the romanticism of his father in George Meredith's *The Adventures of Harry Richmond*.

Marion Richmond   Wife of Richmond Roy, daughter of Squire Beltham, and mother of Harry Richmond; she goes insane and dies while Harry is very young in George Meredith's *The Adventures of Harry Richmond*.

Mabel Rickets   Old Northumbrian woman who served as nurse to both William Osbaldistone and his son, Francis; it is she who told Francis of the history of the Osbaldistones in Sir Walter Scott's *Rob Roy*.

John Ridd   Intelligent, modest, honest, and semi-educated farmer whose father, a yeoman, was killed by the Doone family; John is respected for his strength, his wrestling, and his lineage; his love for Lorna Doone is stronger than family grudges in R. D. Blackmore's *Lorna Doone*.

Sarah Ridd   John's mother, a good, hard-working, pretty woman who loves John so much that she does not try to prevent John and Lorna Doone's love; Sarah is well-respected, loves her family, and has a deep sense of duty in R. D. Blackmore's *Lorna Doone.*

Pleasant Riderhood Swivel-eyed daughter of Roger Riderhood; she has a small, unlicensed pawnbroking shop in Limehouse; loved by Mr. Venus, she at first turns him down because he is an articulator of female skeletons in Charles Dickens's *Our Mutual Friend.*

Roger (Rogue) Riderhood Gaffer Hexam's hardened former partner, who earns his living on the river, often dishonestly; he accuses Gaffer Hexam of murdering John Harmon; he is rescued from drowning and is revived, but he later drowns in a fight with Bradley Headstone in Charles Dickens's *Our Mutual Friend.*

Ridley Personal servant to Austin Ruthyn in J. Sheridan Le Fanu's *Uncle Silas.*

Mrs. Ridley J. J.'s mother, a former housekeeper in William Makepeace Thackeray's *The Newcomes.*

John James ("J. J.") Ridley Sickly, talented boy, who becomes a successful painter, elected to the Royal Academy; he is Clive Newcome's lifelong friend and patron in time of difficulties in William Makepeace Thackeray's *The Newcomes.* He is a successful painter in *The Adventures of Philip on His Way through the World.*

Samuel Ridley J. J.'s father, valet and butler to Lord Todmorden in William Makepeace Thackeray's *The Newcomes.*

Niccolò Ridolfi Florentine aristocrat executed for his support of the Medici in George Eliot's *Romola.*

Ridolpho Merchant through whom the Duke of Norfolk negotiates the support of the Duke of Alva in Sophia Lee's *The Recess.*

Ridsley Criminal and lover of Bell Calvert; he witnesses the young George Colwan's murder and positively identifies Robert Colwan in James Hogg's *The Private Memoirs and Confessions of a Justified Sinner.*

Rifle Highwayman who flees from the inn where Roderick Random and Hugh Strap overhear him, and who wounds Strap in a fight in Tobias Smollett's *The Adventures of Roderick Random.*

M. Rigaud (Blandois/Lagnier) Villainous Frenchman imprisoned in Marseilles with Cavalleto and awaiting trial for murdering his wife; he conspires against Mrs. Clennam with Miss Wade's help and holds the iron box which contains information about Arthur Clennam's birth in Charles Dickens's *Little Dorrit.*

Nicholas Rigby Pompous and malicious factotum of Lord Monmouth; he schemes to gain control of Lord Monmouth's wealth, thus to deprive Harry Coningsby of his inheritance in Benjamin Disraeli's *Coningsby; or, The New Generation.*

Joshua Rigg A "frog-faced" man, who is left much of Peter Featherstone's money in the second will, and who sells Stone Court to Nicholas Bulstrode in George Eliot's *Middlemarch.*

Dr. Rile Physician, less efficient than Dr. MacTurk, who attends Caroline Helstone in Charlotte Brontë's *Shirley.*

Mr. Riley Elderly Englishman who refuses to kneel for prayer on the boat escaping from France in Frances Burney's *The Wanderer.*

Mr. Riley An auctioneer who advises Mr. Tulliver to send Tom Tulliver to Mr. Stelling's school, rather than admit that he has no knowledge on the subject of a boy's education in George Eliot's *The Mill on the Floss.*

Lottie Rilly Actress at the Strand and Mike Fletcher's abandoned lover; both she and their son are ignored by Mike until his decision to commit suicide, leaving them his money in George Moore's *Mike Fletcher.*

Patty Ringrose Eve Madeley's friend, who constantly changes her mind about marrying her lover; she keeps Maurice Hilliard informed about Eve in George Gissing's *Eve's Ransom.*

Franklin Ringwood Philip Ringwood's younger brother; Philip Firmin's poverty surprises him in William Makepeace Thackeray's *The Adventures of Philip on His Way through the World.*

Sir John Ringwood of Appleshaw The heir of the Earl of Ringwood's estates but not of the title, which he affects to scorn until he is himself elevated to the peerage; he belatedly assists Philip Firmin in William Makepeace Thackeray's *The Adventures of Philip on His Way through the World.*

Sir John Ringwood of Wingate (later Baron Ringwood) Father of John George, second Baron and first Earl of Ringwood in William Makepeace Thackeray's *The Adventures of Philip on His Way through the World.*

John George, second Baron and first Earl of Ringwood Crotchety great uncle of Philip Firmin, with whom he quarrels just before his death; his will leaving money to Philip is belatedly found in William Makepeace Thackeray's *The Adventures of Philip on His Way through the World.*

Philip Ringwood   Patronizing, dandified eldest son of Sir John Ringwood of Appleshaw; his attentions to Charlotte (Baynes) Firmin are resented by her husband, Philip Firmin, in William Makepeace Thackeray's *The Adventures of Philip on His Way through the World.*

Colonel Philip Ringwood   The Earl of Ringwood's late brother, father of Louisa Firmin and Maria Twysden in William Makepeace Thackeray's *The Adventures of Philip on His Way through the World.*

Jenny Rintherout   Servant of Oldbuck (Jonathan Oldenbuck); she loves Steenie Muckelbackit but overcomes her grief when he is drowned in Sir Walter Scott's *The Antiquary.*

Cardinal Rinucci   Brother of Pope Innocent X's nuncio; he convinces John Inglesant to leave a monastery and accompany him to Rome in J. Henry Shorthouse's *John Inglesant, A Romance.*

Alamanno Rinuccini   Scholar friend of Bardo de' Bardi and a suitor of Romola de' Bardi in George Eliot's *Romola.*

Lady Riot   Noblewoman who, in an ancedote related by Mr. Rouvell, makes a fool of the ambitious apothecary Mr. Calomel by awakening him late at night and taking him in his pajamas to a large party in Richard Graves's *The Spiritual Quixote.*

Mr. Rippenger   Headmaster of Harry Richmond's school; he favors Harry because he believes his father to be a prosperous gentlemen until months pass without payment from Harry's father in George Meredith's *The Adventures of Harry Richmond.*

Mr. Ripple   Undistinguished, attention-craving writer of paragraphs for a society paper; he serves as best man for Lewis Seymour in George Moore's *A Modern Lover.*

Earl of Risingham   Lancastrian gentleman and ally of Sir Daniel Brackley and Alicia's uncle; Dick Shelton throws himself on his mercy at Lord Shoreby's wedding; he frees Shelton and Will Lawless in Robert Louis Stevenson's *The Black Arrow: A Tale of Two Roses.*

Alicia Risingham   Provoking friend and bridesmaid of Joan Sedley and niece of the Earl of Risingham; she helps Joan see Dick Shelton at Lord Shoreby's house; she is rescued in the snow by Dick; she is engaged to John Hamley in Robert Louis Stevenson's *The Black Arrow: A Tale of Two Roses.*

Captain Rivers   The tyrannical, uncouth father of Alithea Rivers (later Neville); he disdainfully rejects John Falkner's plea to marry his daughter in Mary Shelley's *Falkner.*

Mr. Rivers   Father of St. John, Diana and Mary; he goes bankrupt, forcing his daughters to become governesses; his death is the reason the family has been temporarily reunited when Jane arrives at Morton in Charlotte Brontë's *Jane Eyre.*

Mr. Rivers   Geoffry Wildgoose's college friend, who gives him a detailed and reverent account of his courtship of Charlotte Woodville; after a period in which he depends on the generosity of wealthy friends, he becomes an Anglican clergyman and is reconciled with his estranged cousin Gregory Griskin in Richard Graves's *The Spiritual Quixote.*

Mrs. Rivers   The wise and affectionate mentor and foster mother to the orphaned John Falkner; she implants his hope of marrying her daughter Alithea Rivers (later Neville) in Mary Shelley's *Falkner.*

Diana Rivers   Jane Eyre's vibrant, strong-willed cousin, who, along with her sister, takes Jane in without being aware of their connection and works as a governess until Jane's legacy frees her to continue with her studies and to marry in Charlotte Brontë's *Jane Eyre.*

Colonel Ed. Rivers   A lieutenant colonel on half pay entitled to a land settlement after the Conquest; his sensibility combines the best of feminine and masculine attributes; he believes in marriage by choice between men and women of equal sensibility, and upon receipt of an inheritance he returns to England to marry Emily Montague in Frances Brooke's *The History of Emily Montague.*

George Rivers   Lumpish half brother of Meta Rivers; he marries Flora May and with her help achieves a seat in Parliament in Charlotte Yonge's *The Daisy Chain.* He appears in *The Trial* and briefly in *The Pillars of the House.*

Leonora Rivers   Infant daughter of Flora (May) and George Rivers; prematurely weaned, she dies of opium poisoning in Charlotte Yonge's *The Daisy Chain.*

Lucy Rivers   Colonel Ed. Rivers's younger sister, who marries his friend John Temple in Frances Brooke's *The History of Emily Montague.*

Margaret Rivers   Younger daughter of George and Flora (May) Rivers; neglected from birth because of her mother's guilt over the death of her first daughter, Leonora, she grows up to be physically and emotionally unstable in Charlotte Yonge's *The Daisy Chain.* She appears in *The Trial.*

Margaret (Meta) Rivers   Exquisite heiress, who gives

up her social position and marries Norman May in order to join him in mission work in New Zealand in Charlotte Yonge's *The Daisy Chain*. She appears in *The Long Vacation*.

Mary Rivers　Jane Eyre's milder cousin, who helps to revive Jane's interest in living and studying while she stays at Morton, and who marries a clergyman after receiving her portion of Jane's legacy in Charlotte Brontë's *Jane Eyre*.

St. John Rivers　Jane Eyre's cousin, a strong-willed clergyman at Morton who subverts all his other desires in order to follow his spiritual ambition to perform missionary work in India; his proposal of marriage to Jane, arising from his perception of her suitability for missionary work, does not tempt her because she recognizes that he could never love her in Charlotte Brontë's *Jane Eyre*.

Barto (The Miner, The Great Cat, The Eye of Italy) Rizzo　Italian revolutionist; his suspicion of Vittoria Campa's loyalty causes a revolt to be called off and his wife to stab her in George Meredith's *Vittoria*.

Rossellina Rizzo　Barto Rizzo's wife who, like her husband, is deeply suspicious of Vittoria Campa; she finally stabs her, blaming her for Barto's capture by the Austrians in George Meredith's *Vittoria*.

Father Roach　Dapper priest of the parish, who likes funny stories; he enjoys the duel while claiming to want to avert it; although poor himself, he is generous to Sally Nutter in her time of need; he also tries to help her against Mary Matchwell in J. Sheridan Le Fanu's *The House by the Churchyard*.

Roakes　A mill owner, who is prevented from selling cloth to America because of the war in Charlotte Brontë's *Shirley*.

Lucinda Roanoke　Eighteen-year-old, Junoesque American niece of Jane Carbuncle, who bullies her into an engagement with a sadistic baronet, Sir Griffin Tewett; on the wedding day she refuses to go through with the ceremony and descends into acute mental disorder in Anthony Trollope's *The Eustace Diamonds*.

Dr. Robarts　Father of Mark, Lucy, and five other children; though a prosperous Exeter physician he leaves at his death no fortune to relieve Mark of the debts he has rashly assumed in Anthony Trollope's *Framley Parsonage*.

Fanny Monsell Robarts　High-principled wife of Mark Robarts and staunch ally of Lucy, his youngest sister, in Anthony Trollope's *Framley Parsonage*.

Gerald Robarts　Mark's brother, promoted to captain in the Crimea in Anthony Trollope's *Framley Parsonage*.

Jane Robarts　The third of Mark's sisters; she goes to live with their sister Mrs. Crowdie of Creamclotted Hall until her marriage to the squire of Heavybed House in Anthony Trollope's *Framley Parsonage*.

John (Jack) Robarts　Youngest brother of Mark; he becomes clerk and secretary in the Petty Bag Office in Anthony Trollope's *Framley Parsonage*.

Lucy Robarts　Mark's energetic, intelligent youngest sister; loved by Lord Lufton, she will not marry him until accepted by his imperious mother, Lady Lufton; Lucy's selfless nursing of Mrs. Crawley wins Lady Lufton's approval in Anthony Trollope's *Framley Parsonage*. She never wavers in her belief in Josiah Crawley's innocence in the case of the stolen cheque in *The Last Chronicle of Barset*.

Mark Robarts　Vicar of Framley, who rashly allows himself to be persuaded to signs loans for the spendthrift squire Nathaniel Sowerby and comes close to ruin in Anthony Trollope's *Framley Parsonage*. He serves on the church commission in the Crawley case in *The Last Chronicle of Barset*.

Robert　Osbert's servant, who is paid by the Count de Santmorin to abduct Mary in Ann Radcliffe's *The Castles of Athlin and Dunbayne*.

Robert　Religious waterman, who pilots a boat on the Thames, and who is separated from his family because they have the plague; he remains on his boat and leaves food for them on the shore each day in Daniel Defoe's *A Journal of the Plague Year*.

Robert　Servant to the Marquis de Mazzini; he tells him of mysterious noises in the south wing of the castle in Ann Radcliffe's *A Sicilian Romance*.

Robert　Selfish and tyrannical elder brother of Maria Venables; he becomes a lawyer, then lords his family privilege over his siblings and begrudges Maria her favor with her rich uncle and protector in Mary Wollstonecraft's *Maria; or The Wrongs of Woman*.

Robert　A servant at Horton Lodge and frequent companion of Matilda Murray; she prefers his company outdoors to her schoolwork inside in Anne Brontë's *Agnes Grey*.

King Robert III (John Stewart)　King of Scotland during the last years of the fourteenth century; he is weak-minded but affectionate toward his son, the Duke of Rothsay; he accuses his brother, the Duke of Albany, of complicity in the murder of Rothsay in Sir Walter Scott's *The Fair Maid of Perth*.

King Robert of Naples　Head of the Guelph army at

Genoa; he is the target of Castruccio dei Antelminelli's unsuccessful murder plot in Mary Shelley's *Valperga*.

Count Robert of Paris　French crusader of the blood of Charlemagne, and a famous knight-errant; though haughty, he is also handsome and generous and so is a favorite of the army; while in Constantinople, he insults Emperor Alexius Comnenus, putting his and Brenhilda's lives in peril in Sir Walter Scott's *Count Robert of Paris*.

Captain Roberts　Naval officer whose takeover of the *Agra* from Captain Dodd institutes naval discipline; he grounds the ship on the French coastline when he is almost in harbor and jumps overboard in a life buoy in Charles Reade's *Hard Cash*.

Mr. Roberts　Sir Charles Glanville's steward, asked by young Charles Glanville to guard Arabella from Sir George Bellmour in Charlotte Lennox's *The Female Quixote*.

Robin　Young Colonel Jack's pickpocket comrade, who teaches Jack the trade in Daniel Defoe's *The History and the Remarkable Life of the Truly Honourable Colonel Jacques, Commonly Call'd Col. Jack*.

Robin　Landlord who, alienated by the guide's version of Tom Jones's history, sits up all night to ensure that Tom doesn't rob him in Henry Fielding's *The History of Tom Jones*.

Robin (Robert, Brother Robin)　Younger son of the rich matron who takes Moll Flanders into her household; having fallen in love with Moll, he convinces her to marry him with the help of his older brother (who had been Moll's first lover and who wants to be rid of her); he dies after five years of marriage with her in Daniel Defoe's *The Fortunes and Misfortunes of the Famous Moll Flanders*.

Lincolnshire Robin (Mr. Robert)　Coachman for Mr. B——'s Lincolnshire estate; he surreptitiously drives Pamela Andrews to the Lincolnshire estate when she thinks he is returning her to her parents in Samuel Richardson's *Pamela, or Virtue Rewarded*.

Robin Coachman　John Booby's coachman, who reveals information that helps Shamela Andrews and Mrs. Jervis refine their strategy against Booby in Henry Fielding's *An Apology for the Life of Mrs. Shamela Andrews*.

Robin Hood (Locksley)　Brave and generous leader of outlaws; his band is instrumental in freeing the Saxons from Torquilstone Castle; they also prevent King Richard's assassination; he competes as Locksley at the Ashby tournament in Sir Walter Scott's *Ivanhoe*.

Fanny Robin　Bathsheba Everdene's servant who is seduced and made pregnant by Sergeant Frank Troy, the man who subsequently marries Bathsheba; unaware of his marriage to her former employer, Fanny walks miles to find him and dies from exhaustion and a broken heart in Thomas Hardy's *Far from the Madding Crowd*.

Robinson　Atheistic gambler, who cheats William Booth of his last shilling in prison but later confesses his part in conspiring to disinherit Amelia Booth in Henry Fielding's *Amelia*.

Robinson　One of three mutineers; he turns against the English Captain but is eventually captured by the captain, Friday, and Robinson Crusoe in Daniel Defoe's *The Life and Strange Surprizing Adventures of Robinson Crusoe of York, Mariner*.

Mr. Robinson　Employee in the firm of Dombey and Son in Charles Dickens's *Dombey and Son*.

Tom Robinson (Lyon, Scott, Sinclair)　Clever thief who begins to reform under the sincere kindness of Francis Eden, relapses on his arrival in Australia, and earns an honest character befriending George Fielding and controlling the gold fields in Charles Reade's *It Is Never Too Late to Mend*.

Sir Hugh Robsart　An old country gentleman who knows more about hounds and horses than court and queen; devastated by grief at the disappearance of his daughter, Amy Robsart (Dudley), he gives her former suitor Edmund Tressilian the power to petition Queen Elizabeth on his behalf for Amy's safety and reputation; his death soon follows Amy's in Sir Walter Scott's *Kenilworth*.

Mr. Robson　Uncle of the Bloomfield children and brother of Mrs. Bloomfield; he treats the governess disdainfully and teaches the children a similar attitude in Anne Brontë's *Agnes Grey*.

Bell Robson　Sylvia's mother and the patient wife of Daniel; she is cared for by Sylvia and Philip Hepburn after Daniel's death in Elizabeth Gaskell's *Sylvia's Lovers*.

Daniel Robson　The father of Sylvia; his impetuous role in encouraging the burning of the press-gang headquarters leads to his being sentenced to be hanged in Elizabeth Gaskell's *Sylvia's Lovers*.

Sylvia Robson　The sensitive but willful farmer's daughter, who matures through the tragic events of the supposed death of her betrothed, Charley Kinraid, the execution of her father, and the bitter breakdown of her marriage to Philip Hepburn in Elizabeth Gaskell's *Sylvia's Lovers*.

Harriet Roby Inquisitive, meddling maternal aunt of Emily Wharton; she promotes Emily's disastrous marriage to Ferdinand Lopez; after his death Emily refuses to see her in Anthony Trollope's *The Prime Minister*.

Richard Roby Florid and indolent brother-in-law of Abel Wharton; he is addicted to hunting, billiards, and pigeon shooting and neglectful of his wife, Harriet, in Anthony Trollope's *The Prime Minister*.

Thomas Roby Staunch ally of Mr. Daubeny and opposite number of Mr. Ratler, rallying Tory support and likewise a party hack in Anthony Trollope's *Phineas Finn*. He is Patronage Secretary and chief whip in *Phineas Redux*. He is the elder half brother of Richard Roby; he vies with Ratler for office in a coalition government in *The Prime Minister*.

Lord Rochdale Father of Lord Melvin in Frances Brooke's *The History of Lady Julia Mandeville*.

Mr. Roche Tom Stern's angry father-in-law, who offers to pay Diana Stern's debts if she will abandon her father; the family reconciles in Henry Brooke's *The Fool of Quality*.

Dr. Joseph Albany Rochecliffe Anglican clergyman who plots the escape of King Charles II; he reveals his identity as a man Nehemiah Holdenough believed dead in Sir Walter Scott's *Woodstock*.

Count de Rochefoucault Madam de Beaumont's father, a French nobleman who married an English lady; he dies from grief shortly after his wife's death in Penelope Aubin's *The Life of Madam de Beaumont*.

Humphrey Rochely A wealthy, middle-aged banker, whom Emmeline Mobray meets at Mrs. Ashwood's house, and who solicits Lord Montreville's permission to marry her, a proposal Sir Richard Crofts then conveys as her only alternative to penury; Frederic Delamere, afraid she may capitulate, abducts her and starts for Scotland in Charlotte Smith's *Emmeline: The Orphan of the Castle*.

Rochemort Scoffing, pompous professor from M. Paul Emanuel's college; he suggests that Lucy Snowe's compositions are plagarized and forces her to take an examination in Charlotte Brontë's *Villette*.

Mme. des Roches French-Canadian widow and landowner, whose acquaintance Ed. Rivers makes in his attempts at land settlement, and whose mature charm temporarily infatuates him in Frances Brooke's *The History of Emily Montague*.

Bertha Antoinetta Mason Rochester Mr. Rochester's mad wife, whom he, ignorant of her heritage of insanity, married in the West Indies; secretly confined to a nurse's care in Thornfield Hall, she occasionally escapes to attempt injury and destruction; revelation of her existence interrupts Mr. Rochester's bigamous wedding to Jane Eyre; later she burns Thornfield to the ground and herself with it in Charlotte Brontë's *Jane Eyre*.

Edward Fairfax Rochester The younger son of a man so avaricious that he kept secret the familial madness of Edward's wealthy bride; Edward is now, following the deaths of his elder brother and father, owner of Thornfield Hall, where his mad wife is secretly tended, and where resides his ward, the daughter of a former mistress; after roaming about Europe, he comes home to fall in love with the child's governess, Jane Eyre; Charlotte Brontë's *Jane Eyre*.

Rowland Rochester Deceased elder brother of Edward in Charlotte Brontë's *Jane Eyre*.

Mr. Rochfort Shallow, false friend of Clarence Hervey; he stands by with Mr. St. George and does nothing while Hervey nearly drowns in Maria Edgeworth's *Belinda*.

Lord Rockingham (the Seraph) Future Duke of Lyonesse; a member of the elite English guard, he is a loyal friend of Bertie Cecil in Ouida's *Under Two Flags*.

Dowager Countess of Rockminster Helen Pendennis's kinswoman, who takes charge of Laura Bell after Mrs. Pendennis's death until Laura's marriage to Arthur Pendennis in William Makepeace Thackeray's *The History of Pendennis*. She is mentioned in *The Newcomes*.

Rockwood Hunting dog killed by Joseph Andrews after it attacks Parson Adams at its master's bidding in Henry Fielding's *The History of the Adventures of Mr. Joseph Andrews and of his Friend Mr. Abraham Adams*.

George Roden Post Office clerk in love with Lady Frances Trafford, sister of Lord Hampstead, who disapproves of the match on grounds of rank although he is George's friend; all difficulties are removed when George turns out to be impeccably blueblooded as the Duca de Crinola in Anthony Trollope's *Marion Fay*.

Mary Roden Abandoned wife of an Italian nobleman and mother of George; when her husband dies, George inherits the title of Duca di Crinola in Anthony Trollope's *Marion Fay*.

Willis Rodman Socialist and adviser to Richard Mutimer; he has abandoned a wife and children and bigamously marries Mutimer's sister Alice in George Gissing's *Demos*.

Mr. and Mrs. Rodney Friends of Endymion Ferrars's parents; they offer him lodgings when he comes to London to take up the clerkship arranged by his father in Benjamin Disraeli's *Endymion*.

Imogen Rodney Beautiful but uneducated daughter of Mr. and Mrs. Rodney; she becomes the "pupil" of Mr. Waldershare and learns her lessons so well that she marries into the nobility in Benjamin Disraeli's *Endymion*.

Jem Rodney The poor man incorrectly accused by Silas Marner of stealing his gold in George Eliot's *Silas Marner*.

Rodophil Sophia's suitor, who wants her only for her money in Eliza Haywood's *The History of Jemmy and Jenny Jessamy*.

Rodoric An owner of Julian the Apostate in his incarnation as a Roman slave; he orders Julian castrated after discovering him in bed with his wife in Henry Fielding's *A Journey From This World to the Next*.

Don Rodriguez Father of Roderick Random; discovered in South America, where he has become wealthy, he returns with Roderick and Tom Bowling to England; he provides money for Roderick to marry Narcissa, returns with Roderick and Hugh Strap to Scotland, and buys back the ancestral lands of his family in Tobias Smollett's *The Adventures of Roderick Random*.

Lord Roehampton (characterization of the third Viscount Palmerston). Foreign minister who marries Endymion Ferrars's sister, Myra, and helps advance Endymion's career in Benjamin Disraeli's *Endymion*.

Roger of the Rope-walk Member of the Fellowship of the Dry Tree; he helps Ralph to escape from the Burg of the Four Friths and takes him to the Castle of Abundance; later he becomes a hermit but joins Ralph in the battle of Upmeads in William Morris's *The Well at the World's End*.

Hannah Rogers A villager in Horton who has a disagreement with Nancy Brown, another villager, in Anne Brontë's *Agnes Grey*.

Mr. Rogers Lawyer used by Colonel James (as Damon) to free Fanny Matthews from prison and from her murder charge in Henry Fielding's *Amelia*.

Mrs. Rogers Genteel new boarder at Martha Bardell's, replacing Samuel Pickwick, and present when Mrs. Bardell is seized for nonpayment of debt in Charles Dickens's *The Posthumous Papers of the Pickwick Club*.

Roker Unscrupulous, avaricious man, who marries Rachel Lennard for the legacy she received from her employer, Miss Rayland; he keeps his wife virtually a prisoner; she fears he will have her declared insane in Charlotte Smith's *The Old Manor House*.

Tom Roker Stout turnkey of the Fleet debtors' prison in Charles Dickens's *The Posthumous Papers of the Pickwick Club*.

Neil Rolandson The old Ranzelman, a corrupt, greedy, and conceited magistrate in Sir Walter Scott's *The Pirate*.

Betty Rolfe Village farmhand at Great End Farm during the First World War in Mrs. Humphry Ward's *Harvest*.

Harvey Rolfe Bookish gentleman, who marries the unstable Alma Frothingham, tolerates her infidelity, and after her death finds solace in caring for his son in George Gissing's *The Whirlpool*.

Hughie Rolfe Little son of Harvey and Alma (Frothingham) Rolfe; he is neglected by his mother but cared for by his father in George Gissing's *The Whirlpool*.

Mr. Rolland Mealymouthed bishop who harries Dr. Wortle over keeping the Peacockes at his preparatory school when local gossip suggests some irregularity in their marital status in Anthony Trollope's *Dr. Wortle's School*.

Reginald Rolles Nephew of Lady Camper; he courts and marries the daughter of General Ople, Elizabeth Ople, in George Meredith's *The Case of General Ople and Lady Camper*.

General Sir Edward Rolleston Helen Rolleston's father; he is restored to full generalship through the influence of John Wardlaw; he searches for and finds his missing daughter on Godsend Island on the steam sloop *Springbok* in Charles Reade's *Foul Play*.

Helen Rolleston Rolleston's daughter, betrothed to Arthur Wardlaw; shipwrecked aboard the scuttled *Proserpine*, she survives on Godsend Island through the ministrations of the Reverend John Hazel (Robert Penfold) and vows to clear his name upon her return to England; she succeeds, after great difficulties, and marries her rescuer in Charles Reade's *Foul Play*.

Mr. and Mrs. Rollins A working-class couple with seven children, who live by the sea; Ernest Pontifex gives them one pound a week to take care of George and Alice, whom the Rollinses raise and love as their own in Samuel Butler's *The Way of All Flesh*.

Jack Rollins Bargeman who marries Alice Pontifex; her father, Ernest Pontifex, gives Jack a barge and steamer in Samuel Butler's *The Way of All Flesh*.

Mr. Rolliver Owner and proprietor of a local tavern frequented by Tess's father, John Durbeyfield, in Thomas Hardy's *Tess of the D'Urbervilles*.

Prince Marko Romaris Thin, fragile, loyal, and kind suitor of Clotilde Von Rüdiger; he realizes that Clotilde loves Sigismund Alvan and not him, but remains near her to assist her in any way possible; he stands as a substitute for Clotilde's father in the duel with Alvan, kills him, and weds Clotilde, but dies shortly thereafter in George Meredith's *The Tragic Comedians*.

Charley ("Facey") Romford A penniless gentleman who lives by his wits and is an avid rider to hounds in Robert Surtees's *Mr. Sponge's Sporting Tour*.

Everard Romfrey A Tory who deserts his nephew, Nevil Beauchamp, a Liberal Parliamentary candidate, and horsewhips Dr. Shrapnel, Beauchamp's mentor, but finally apologizes and reconciles with him in George Meredith's *Beauchamp's Career*.

Romney Starving artist friend of Loudon Dodd in Paris; he is present at Genius of Muskegon's judging in Robert Louis Stevenson's *The Wrecker*.

Arthur Ronalds Christopher Kirkland's brilliant friend, who dies young in Mrs. Lynn Linton's *The Autobiography of Christopher Kirkland*.

Maria de Roncilles Julia de Roubigné's epistolary intimate in Henry Mackenzie's *Julia de Roubigné*.

Mr. De Rone Benevolent but unchaste gentleman, who mistakes Cornelia for a prostitute, helps her escape from the brothel, falls in love with her but is rejected, and finally marries Cornelia's friend Julia in Sarah Scott's *The History of Cornelia*.

Roodhouse Radical rival of Richard Mutimer in the Socialist Union in George Gissing's *Demos*.

Nurse Rooke Attendant for both the invalid Mrs. Smith and Mrs. Wallis, a new mother whose husband is privy to William Elliot's motives; her gossip is a source of Anne Elliot's better knowledge of her cousin's infamy in Jane Austen's *Persuasion*.

Alan Rookwood The aged, embittered sexton of Rookwood Church; known as Peter Bradley, he is in fact Alan Rookwood, returned to seek revenge for the deaths of his wife and daughter and to effect the restitution of the Rookwood estates to his grandson, known as Luke Bradley; entombed alive, he dies in the family vault in William Harrison Ainsworth's *Rookwood*.

Eleanor, Lady Rookwood First wife of the dissipated Sir Reginald Rookwood; she dies giving birth to a daughter, Eleanor (later Mrs. Mowbray), after being struck by him in William Harrison Ainsworth's *Rookwood*.

Luke Rookwood Son of the secret marriage of Sir Piers Rookwood and Susan Rookwood (known as Susan Bradley) and grandson of Alan Rookwood (known as Peter Bradley); known as Luke Bradley and raised by Gypsies, he is apparently heir to Rookwood Place, but he dies by poisoning while he seeks to win his inheritance in William Harrison Ainsworth's *Rookwood*.

Maud D'Aubeny, Lady Rookwood The proud second wife of Sir Piers Rookwood and mother of Ranulph; she works to secure the Rookwood inheritance for her son but, buried alive in the tomb of her dead husband, dies in William Harrison Ainsworth's *Rookwood*.

Sir Piers Rookwood Knight of Rookwood Place, Yorkshire, and son of Sir Reginald Rookwood; he succeeds to the title on the death of his older brother; he marries first, in secret, Susan Bradley, by whom he has a son, Luke, and second, Maud D'Aubeny, by whom he has a son, Ranulph, in William Harrison Ainsworth's *Rookwood*.

Ranulph Rookwood Second son of Sir Piers Rookwood; he falls in love with Eleanor Mowbray; apparently superseded by his half brother, Luke, in his claim to the family estates, he inherits them through his marriage to Eleanor in William Harrison Ainsworth's *Rookwood*.

Sir Reginald Rookwood Knight of Rookwood Place, Yorkshire, and older brother of Alan Rookwood; three times married, he is the father of Eleanor (Mrs. Mowbray) by his first wife and of Piers by his third in William Harrison Ainsworth's *Rookwood*.

Susan Rookwood Though known as Susan Bradley, a Rookwood by birth and marriage; the daughter of Peter Bradley (really Alan Rookwood), she is secretly married to Sir Piers Rookwood, by whom she has a son, Luke Bradley; she is murdered by Father Checkley in William Harrison Ainsworth's *Rookwood*.

Terry Rooney Sly manservant of Barry Lynch; he monitors his master's affairs by dilligent eavesdropping in Anthony Trollope's *The Kellys and the O'Kellys*.

Mrs. Roper Owner of the boardinghouse in which Johnny Eames takes up lodgings and becomes entangled in a romance with Amelia Roper in Anthony Trollope's *The Small House at Allington*.

Amelia Roper   Flirtatious daughter of a boardinghouse keeper; she wheedles a declaration of love from Johnny Eames but eventually marries his colleague, Joseph Cradell, in Anthony Trollope's *The Small House at Allington*.

Bobby Roper   Dicky Perrott's nemesis; Dicky does several things against him, but Bobby gains revenge by stabbing Dicky to death in Arthur Morrison's *A Child of the Jago*.

Rosa   Shy young village maid, who becomes a favorite with Lady Dedlock, a surrogate for the daughter Lady Dedlock lost; eventually she marries Watt Rouncewell in Charles Dickens's *Bleak House*.

Rosabella of Corfu   Doge Andreas's beautiful, chaste niece, dubbed "The Bravo's Bride" when the seemingly villainous Abellino saves her life; the constant lover of Flodoardo, even when he reveals that he is Abellino, she marries him after he reveals his true identity (Count Rosalvo) in Matthew Lewis's *The Bravo of Venice*.

Rosabelle   Queen Mary of Scotland's beloved horse, which George Douglas abducts from the stables of James Douglas, Earl of Morton for Mary's escape from Lochleven Castle in Sir Walter Scott's *The Abbot*.

Ellena Rosalba   Orphaned Neapolitan gentlewoman, who falls in love with Vincentio de Vivaldi but is scorned by his family; abducted and imprisoned in the San Stefano convent at the orders of the Marchesa di Vivaldi, she is rescued by Vincentio, only to be recaptured by the evil Father Schedoni (Ferando di Bruno) in his attempt to assassinate her; Schedoni mistakenly believes she is his daughter and returns her to Naples, where she meets her long-lost mother; ultimately she marries Vincentio in Ann Radcliffe's *The Italian*.

Rosalie   Portress at Mlle. Reuter's school in Charlotte Brontë's *The Professor*.

Count Rosalvo   Neapolitan sent into hiding by the intrigues of his enemy, Prince Monaldeschi; disguised as both the fearsome bravo (assassin) Abellino and his nemesis, the heroic Flodoardo, he rids Venice of assassins and political conspirators, thus winning the doge's niece, Rosabella of Corfu, in Matthew Lewis's *The Bravo of Venice*.

Rosario   See Matilda de Villanegas.

Alice Rose   The mother of Hester and a strict, often disapproving support to Sylvia Robson in Elizabeth Gaskell's *Sylvia's Lovers*.

Hester Rose   The quiet shop colleague of Philip Hepburn, hopelessly in love with him and loved unavailingly in turn by his colleague William Coulson; her uncomplaining self-sacrifice supports the themes of Elizabeth Gaskell's *Sylvia's Lovers*.

Rosebel   Character who refuses to be educated as a governess though she has no money; she ends her life in dependency in Caroline Norton's *The Wife and Woman's Reward*.

Baron Rosendorf   Venetian aristocrat who sees women as they are and not as the ideals his male friends perceive; however, he also advocates their just treatment when male pride stands in the way of reason in Charlotte Dacre's *The Passions*.

Countess of Roseville   Beautiful young widow of wealth, to whom Henry Pelham is attracted, and who is devoted to Ellen and Sir Reginald Glanville in Edward Bulwer-Lytton's *Pelham*.

Earl of Rosherville   Nobleman who wants to repair the family fortunes through the marriage of his daughter, Lady Ann Milton, to his nephew Henry Foker in William Makepeace Thackeray's *The History of Pendennis*.

Rosig   Employee, friend, and traveling companion of Quangrollart in Robert Paltock's *The Life and Adventures of Peter Wilkins*.

Lady Ross   Second wife of Sir Neil Douglas Ross and mother of Alice Ross; she is jealous of and mistreats her husband's sons, Sir Douglas and Kenneth, and is responsible for Kenneth's wildness in Caroline Norton's *Old Sir Douglas*.

Alice Ross   Sir Douglas Ross's half sister, who hates Sir Douglas's wife, Gertrude, and resents her position as mistress of the household; she lies to cause trouble for Gertrude in Caroline Norton's *Old Sir Douglas*.

Dick Ross   Good-natured, amoral toady of George Western; he speaks out against Western's outrageous treatment of his wife, Cecilia (Holt), in Anthony Trollope's *Kept in the Dark*.

Sir Douglas Ross (Old Sir Douglas)   Kind hero of the novel; he is not old but is called so affectionately because of his responsible nature; he loves and marries Gertrude, but misunderstands her by thinking she loves another, thus perpetuating the tragedy of the novel; he returns to his wife and almost dies from misunderstanding in Caroline Norton's *Old Sir Douglas*.

Effie Ross   Child of Kenneth Carmichael Ross and Dona Eusebia; she is deserted by her mother and father but grows up to be the lovely girl who will be the bride of Neil Ross and mistress of the manor in Caroline Norton's *Old Sir Douglas*.

Euphemia Ross Alexander Loudon's first wife; he and Loudon Dodd visit her grave in Edinburgh in Robert Louis Stevenson's *The Wrecker*.

Gertrude Ross Daughter of Lady Skifton; unlike her mother, she is kind, honorable, and gentle; she keeps the truth of Kenneth Carmichael Ross's advances from her husband, Sir Douglas Ross, to spare him and thus ruins her life; she has a son, Neil; she pines for Sir Douglas Ross, until he returns to her in Caroline Norton's *Old Sir Douglas*.

Kenneth Ross Wild brother of Sir Douglas Ross and father of Kenneth Carmichael Ross; he is jealous of his brother, drinks, and becomes vicious; he makes a death-bed confession in Caroline Norton's *Old Sir Douglas*.

Kenneth Carmichael Ross Son of Kenneth Ross; he is wild, like his father; in love with Gertrude Ross, he is the main cause of the tragedy between Gertrude and Sir Douglas Ross, who believes his nephew when he pretends Gertrude has loved him; he is spoiled by Sir Douglas, who feels responsible for his fatherless nephew in Caroline Norton's *Old Sir Douglas*.

Margaret Carmichael Ross Wife and later widow of Kenneth Ross and mother of Kenneth Carmichael Ross; she brings up her son as well as she can and later marries again in Caroline Norton's *Old Sir Douglas*.

Neil Ross Son of Sir Douglas Ross and Gertrude Ross; named after Sir Douglas's father, he is as handsome and good as his father is in Caroline Norton's *Old Sir Douglas*.

Sir Neil Douglas Ross Father of Sir Douglas, Kenneth, and Alice Ross; he is important because of his influence on his sons in Caroline Norton's *Old Sir Douglas*.

Edith Rossall Wilfrid Athel's widowed aunt, who has two children and keeps house for Wilfrid and his father in George Gissing's *A Life's Morning*.

Henker Rothals Member of Werner's band; he initiates Shwartz Thier's accosting of Margarita Groschen, is bested in combat by Guy the Goshawk, tells Thier of Margarita's abduction by Warner, and tries to assist Guy in his rescue of Margarita before being wounded by a knife-throw from Werner in George Meredith's *Farina*.

Lord Rotherwood Cousin of Lilias Mohun Merrifield in Charlotte Yonge's *The Two Sides of the Shield*. He wishes to adopt Maria Merrifield in *Beechcroft at Rockstone*. He allows his son to marry Franceska Vanderkist in *The Long Vacation*.

Duke of Rothsay (David Stewart, Prince of Scotland) Son of King Robert III and heir to the throne of Scotland; he ignores his wife, Marjory Douglas, to pursue Catherine Glover, among others, and is implicated in the quarrel which ensues after his companion John Ramorny loses his hand in the fight with Henry Smith; he is murdered by Ramorny and Bonthron in a plot to clear the throne for the Duke of Albany in Sir Walter Scott's *The Fair Maid of Perth*.

Raoul, Marquis de Rouaillout Renée's husband, whose interest in her is aroused only when she is near Nevil Beauchamp in George Meredith's *Beauchamp's Career*.

Renée de Croisnel Rouaillout Nevil Beauchamp's first love, a Frenchwoman who jilts him but continues to undermine his personal and political happiness by summoning him to her side and fleeing to him from her husband in George Meredith's *Beauchamp's Career*.

Madame de Roubigné Julia's sainted mother, who dies of a fever, leaving her daughter without much-needed guidance and support in Henry Mackenzie's *Julia de Roubigné*.

Julia de Roubigné Melancholy heroine, whose correspondence traces the sad course of her life, from sudden impoverishment, to the exile of her lifelong sweetheart because of financial difficulties, to her arranged marriage to the jealous Count Louis de Montauban and death at his hands, in Henry Mackenzie's *Julia de Roubigné*.

Pierre de Roubigné Julia's brooding father, who has lost his fortune in a lawsuit and therefore seeks a financially advantageous marriage for his daughter in Henry Mackenzie's *Julia de Roubigné*.

Madam de Rouchefoucault Madam de Beaumont's mother, an English lady who married a French nobleman; despite the objections of her husband's relatives, she raises her daughter as a Protestant; she dies when her daughter is ten in Penelope Aubin's *The Life of Madam de Beaumont*.

Monsieur de Rouille Wise and lively cousin of Count Louis de Montauban; he befriends Julia de Roubigné in Henry Mackenzie's *Julia de Roubigné*.

Mr. Rouncewell Mrs. Rouncewell's oldest son, a prominent ironmaster, Member of Parliament, and the father of Watt Rouncewell in Charles Dickens's *Bleak House*.

Mrs. Rouncewell Handsome, stately housekeeper for the Dedlocks at Chesney Wold, who has great loyalty to the Dedlock family and the aristocracy in Charles Dickens's *Bleak House*.

George (Trooper George) Rouncewell Mrs. Rouncewell's younger son, who joined the military when young and served under Captain Hawdon; he now owns a shooting gallery in Leicester Square, is suspected and imprisoned by Inspector Bucket for the murder of Tulkinghorn, and is reconciled with his mother in Charles Dickens's *Bleak House*.

Watt Rouncewell Mrs. Rouncewell's grandson, who visits Chesney Wold and falls in love with a village girl, Rosa, who works at the estate in Charles Dickens's *Bleak House*.

Miss Rouncy Emily Costigan's friend, who writes her letters for her in William Makepeace Thackeray's *The History of Pendennis*.

Matthew (Mat) Round Bright young lawyer, whose firm Round and Crook acts for Joseph Mason in Lady Mason's trial in Anthony Trollope's *Orley Farm*.

Richard Round Semi-retired senior partner in the law firm of Round and Crook; much of the business has passed to the sharper practices of his son, Matthew, in Anthony Trollope's *Orley Farm*.

Antony Roundhand Chief clerk and then actuary to the West Diddlesex Fire and Life Insurance Co.; he is married to a snob in William Makepeace Thackeray's *The History of Samuel Titmarsh and the Great Hoggarty Diamond*.

Milly Roundhand Anthony Roundhand's vulgar wife, who takes Samuel Titmarsh up when she understands him to have aristocratic relations in William Makepeace Thackeray's *The History of Samuel Titmarsh and the Great Hoggarty Diamond*.

Hadgi Rourk Swiss valet who accompanies Perry Pickle on Continental adventures; he acquires his name from the part he plays in Cadwallader Crabtree's soothsayer scheme; he seduces and regrets marrying the beggar girl bought by Perry in Tobias Smollett's *The Adventures of Peregrine Pickle*.

Mrs. Rouse A member of the ladies' group which sews for the "Jew Basket" in Charlotte Brontë's *Shirley*.

Nancy Rouse General Rolleston's kitchen maid, Joseph Wylie's sweetheart; she will marry only if her swain brings £2,000 to establish a rooming house offering board and laundry service; she finally marries her penitent wooer and purchases a house by loan from Michael Penfold in Charles Reade's *Foul Play*.

Mr. Rouvell ("Beau Rueful") Social-climbing wit at Bath, who ridicules Geoffry Wildgoose in front of people he wishes to impress, but who later confides to Wildgoose that he plans to take holy orders in Richard Graves's *The Spiritual Quixote*.

Mrs. Rowan Opionated mother of Luke; she opposes his marriage to Rachel Ray on the ground of her humble background but eventually overcomes her snobbish pride and blesses the union in Anthony Trollope's *Rachel Ray*.

Luke Rowan Energetic nephew of one of the founders of the Baslehurst brewery; he is ambitious to become a partner and is dedicated to improving the beer; he falls in love with Rachel Ray, finally wins her, and becomes a partner in the brewing company in Anthony Trollope's *Rachel Ray*.

Mary Rowan Mrs. Rowan's lively daughter, in whose honor the Tappitts give a ball; she welcomes the romance blossoming between her brother, Luke, and Rachel Ray in Anthony Trollope's *Rachel Ray*.

Lady Rowena Beautiful Saxon heiress; she is Cedric's ward and a descendant of Alfred the Great; though betrothed to Athelstane, she loves Ivanhoe, whom she eventually marries in Sir Walter Scott's *Ivanhoe*.

Mr. Rowland Business partner of Mr. Grey and husband of scheming and deceitful Priscilla Rowland; he is placed in an embarrassing position when he learns his wife's malicious lies have discredited Edward Hope's medical practice; he prefers to offer Hope money to relocate rather than to confront his wife in Harriet Martineau's *Deerbrook*.

Mr. Rowland Officer who arrests Clarissa Harlowe on the false charge of debt and in whose miserable lodging in High Holburn she is incarcerated in Samuel Richardson's *Clarissa: or, The History of a Young Lady*.

Mrs. Rowland Kind and civil wife of the officer who arrests and incarcerates Clarissa Harlowe for debt in Samuel Richardson's *Clarissa: or, The History of a Young Lady*.

Serjeant Rowland Counsel for Sir Barnes Newcome in his divorce case in William Makepeace Thackeray's *The Newcomes*.

George Rowland Overprotected young son of Priscilla Rowland in Harriet Martineau's *Deerbrook*.

John Rowland Steward on Deloraine's estate and eyewitness to William's murder in William Godwin's *Deloraine*.

Matilda Rowland   Foolish and vain young daughter of the Rowlands; her death is the occasion of an apology from her mother to the surgeon Edward Hope in Harriet Martineau's *Deerbrook*.

Priscilla Rowland   A jealous sister and nagging wife; selfish, manipulative, and deceitful, she craves to control family and neighbors, which leads her to interfere with the engagement of her brother, Philip Enderby, to remove her mother from all contact with friends, and to destroy Edward Hope's medical practice with lies about grave-snatching and malpractice in Harriet Martineau's *Deerbrook*.

Bessie, Lady Rowley   Wife of Sir Marmaduke, governor of the Mandarin Islands, and mother of eight daughters, for whose establishment she is anxious; the apparent triumph of Emily's marriage turns to disaster, but she is equally distressed at Nora's refusal of Mr. Glascock in Anthony Trollope's *He Knew He Was Right*.

Sir Marmaduke Rowley   Governor of the Mandarin Islands and father of Emily, the wife of Louis Trevelyan, of Nora, and of six younger daughters; his and Lady Rowley's looked-for visit to England, arranged by Colonel Osborne, brings little relief to Emily in Anthony Trollope's *He Knew He Was Right*.

Nora Rowley   Emily Trevelyan's sister and companion in England; she cannot bring herself to accept the advantageous proposal of the Honourable Charles Glascock because she loves Hugh Stanbury in Anthony Trollope's *He Knew He Was Right*.

Roxana (Susan, Mlle. Beleau, Countess de Wintselsheim, "la belle veufeu de Poictou")   Daughter of French Protestants who is brought up in England, and who marries a brewer who abandons her; she describes her life of prosperous intrigues, illicit affairs, social prominence, and eventual poverty (and imprisonment for debt) in Daniel Defoe's *The Fortunate Mistress*.

Lord John Roxton   Explorer, adventurer, and hunter who joins the Challenger expedition and befriends Ned Malone in Arthur Conan Doyle's *The Lost World*.

Richmond (Roy Richmond, Augustus Fitz-George Frederick William Richmond Guelph) Roy   Charming, adventurous, irresponsible father of Harry Richmond; he takes his son from the stability of his dead wife's family and exposes him to the world; he dies when his attempt to light up Riversley Grange in honor of Harry and Janet (Ilchester) causes it to burn down in George Meredith's *The Adventures of Harry Richmond*.

Viscount Royallieu   Nobleman who dislikes his second son, Bertie Cecil, because he perceives a resemblance to his wife's lover in Ouida's *Under Two Flags*.

Samuel Rubb   Smooth-talking tradesman in oilcloth manufacturing; he cheats Margaret Mackenzie into advancing a large sum in a dubious mortgage arrangement; he apologizes, falls in love with her, and asks her to marry him in Anthony Trollope's *Miss Mackenzie*.

Mrs. Rubelle   Uncommunicative foreign nurse brought in by Count Fosco to nurse Marian Halcombe and assist in the conspiracy under which Fosco and Sir Percival Glyde aim to separate Marian from her half sister, Laura (Fairlie), Lady Glyde, and gain a fortune in Wilkie Collins's *The Woman in White*.

Mr. Rubrick   The Baron of Bradwardine's loyal chaplain, who appeals to King George II for the baron's pardon and marries Rose Bradwardine to Edward Waverly in Sir Walter Scott's *Waverly*.

Bernardo Rucellai   Wealthy Florentine who has Baldassare Calvo arrested after Calvo accuses Tito Melema in George Eliot's *Romola*.

Mr. Ruddles   Liberal-party local organizer, who handles Phineas Finn's campaign in the Tankerville election in Anthony Trollope's *Phineas Redux*.

Rudge   Reuben Haredale's steward, who kills Haredale for money but disguises the body so that people think it is himself; he lives a secret existence, appearing occasionally to demand money from his wife; exposed by Geoffrey Haredale, he is hanged for the crime in Charles Dickens's *Barnaby Rudge*.

Mr. Rudge   Grocer, smuggler, and landlord to Denis Duval in Rye; he falsely accuses him of theft in William Makepeace Thackeray's *Denis Duval*.

Mr. Rudge   Student of the law who, along with Mr. Trottman, introduces Hugh Trevor to legal absurdities in Thomas Holcroft's *The Adventures of Hugh Trevor*.

Barnaby Rudge   Idiot son of the steward Rudge; he is duped by the Gordon rioters and almost hanged for his role in the riots; he is distinguished for his love of a pet raven that is constantly with him in Charles Dickens's *Barnaby Rudge*.

Mary Rudge   Barnaby Rudge's mother, who lives in fear of Rudge, her husband, who threatens her; Gabriel Varden hides her when she suspects that Rudge will visit in Charles Dickens's *Barnaby Rudge*.

Sukey Rudge   Ugly daughter of Mr. Rudge and enemy to Denis Duval, whom she accuses of theft and attacks when he is found innocent in William Makepeace Thackeray's *Denis Duval.*

General von Rüdiger Father of Clotilde; he actively opposes the marriage of the "dirty Jew," Sigismund Alvan, to his daughter and sees to it that the two do not meet again in George Meredith's *The Tragic Comedians.*

Clotilde von Rüdiger A witty, coquetteish, well-born young woman with whom Sigismund Alvan falls in love; she is unable to resist her family's pressure to renounce Alvan, even though she, in some way, still loves him; her irresolution leads to Alvan's death in George Meredith's *The Tragic Comedians.*

Lotte von Rüdiger Sister of Clotilde; she opposes Clotilde's marriage to Sigismund Alvan because it would lessen her own ability to marry well in George Meredith's *The Tragic Comedians.*

Rudolph of Donnerhugel Swiss soldier who is a cousin of the Biederman family; he wishes to marry Anne of Geierstein; he leads the Swiss in battle against Charles, Duke of Burgundy, and is killed in a fight with Arthur de Vere in Sir Walter Scott's *Anne of Geierstein.*

Lady Ruelle Married Parisian gentlewoman, who asks Captain Johnson to help her escape to London; her lack of a passport gets both of them into trouble in Richard Graves's *The Spiritual Quixote.*

William Ruffigny Foster son of Ambrose Fleetwood and an inhabitant of the Swiss alps; his character reflects the qualities of his native country—independence, moderation, and good sense; he attempts to save Casimir Fleetwood from his dissipations in William Godwin's *Fleetwood.*

Lord Rufford Great landowner in Dillsborough chiefly dedicated to hunting; his flirtation with Arabella Trefoil enables her to claim he has asked her to marry him, and her mother charges him with breach of promise; after much difficulty he extricates himself and marries Caroline Penge from sheer weariness in Anthony Trollope's *The American Senator.* He appears briefly in *Ayala's Angel.*

Miss Rugg Mr. Rugg's daughter, who is distinguished in Pentonville through being successful in a breach-of-promise suit against a baker in Charles Dickens's *Little Dorrit.*

Mr. Rugg General agent and accountant, who is Mr. Panck's landlord, assists in recovering the Dorrits' inheritance, and assists Arthur Clennam in paying off the creditors' bills after Doyce and Clennam becomes bankrupt in Charles Dickens's *Little Dorrit.*

Mr. Ruggles Agent for country wool growers in the town of Gladstonopolis in the ex-British colony of Britannula; a friend of President Neverbend, he neither supports nor opposes the law on compulsory euthanasia at age sixty-eight in Anthony Trollope's *The Fixed Period.*

Daniel Ruggles Cantankerous grandfather of Ruby and small-farmer tenant of Roger Carbury; he frets over Ruby's infatuation with Sir Felix Carbury in Anthony Trollope's *The Way We Live Now.*

Ruby Ruggles Daniel Ruggles's pretty, honest, but susceptible granddaughter; though engaged to John Crumb she is flattered by the attention of Sir Felix Carbury and briefly becomes an overworked helper in her aunt's lodginghouse in order to be near him in London; John thrashes Sir Felix, whose bad intentions have become obvious, and persuades her to marry him in Anthony Trollope's *The Way We Live Now.*

Michael Rumball Pet-shop keeper who befriends the young Arthur Golding in George Gissing's *Workers in the Dawn.*

Mr. Rumsey Methodical, quiet, but highly efficient lawyer to Varbarriere in J. Sheridan Le Fanu's *Guy Deverell.*

John Runce Ardent member of the Rufford hunt who denounces Elias Gotobed for criticizing fox-hunting in Anthony Trollope's *The American Senator.*

Mr. Runciman Cheerful landlord of the Bush Inn and moving spirit in the Dillsborough Club of local gentry; he is much given to extolling the joys of fox-hunting in Anthony Trollope's *The American Senator.*

Prince Rupert Undisciplined Loyalist general who, being eager to chase the enemy, stubbornly refuses the Cavalier's counsel not to stay on the offensive after taking York; his subsequent defeat at York becomes the turning point in the war in Daniel Defoe's *Memoirs of a Cavalier.*

Rupil London surgeon hired by Cecilia Beverley to care for Mr. Belfield in Frances Burney's *Cecilia.*

Lucy Rural Correspondent of Prudentia Flutter; she extols the innocent happiness of rural life in Sarah Fielding's *Familiar Letters between the Principal Characters of David Simple and Some Others.*

Henry Rushbrook Disowned nephew of Dorriforth, Lord Elmwood, with whom he is eventually reunited; he marries Matilda, Dorriforth's daughter, in Elizabeth Inchbald's *A Simple Story.*

Mrs. Rushworth A self-important widow who lives

with her equally stupid son, who has inherited a large estate; she soon quarrels with her disrespectful daughter-in-law, Maria (Bertram), in Jane Austen's *Mansfield Park*.

James Rushworth   Ignorant, stupid, and awkward young man, who recently inherited a large estate near Mansfield Park; he marries Maria Bertram, knowing she prefers Henry Crawford; they are divorced after her adulterous elopement at the end of Jane Austen's *Mansfield Park*.

Mrs. Rusk   Loyal housekeeper at Knowl and a faithful friend to Maud Ruthyn; she distrusts Mme. de la Rougierre in J. Sheridan Le Fanu's *Uncle Silas*.

Lady Russell   The widowed adviser and much-loved confidante of Anne Elliot; she persuaded the young Anne to break her engagement to Captain Wentworth and even now prefers the insinuating William Elliot as husband for Anne in Jane Austen's *Persuasion*.

John Edward Russet   The son of Carinthia (Kirby) and Lord Fleetwood; his birth further estranges his parents, as Carinthia fears Fleetwood wants to steal him from the wife he considers his inferior in George Meredith's *The Amazing Marriage*.

Mr. Ruth   Volatile eldest son of a baron; he almost succeeds in ruining his younger brother before he suffocates from rising choler in Henry Brooke's *The Fool of Quality*.

Belinda Ruth   Niece of Harry Ruth; she anonymously conveys money stolen from her father to her uncle's desperate family; she flees her father's brandished sword in Henry Brooke's *The Fool of Quality*.

Harry Ruth   Second son of a baron; unjustly imprisoned for debt, he is rescued by the Christian charity of Henry Clinton exercised through young Harry Clinton in Henry Brooke's *The Fool of Quality*.

Miss Rutherford   Schoolmistress who dismisses Ida Starr when she learns that her mother is disreputable in George Gissing's *The Unclassed*.

Mark Rutherford   Calvinist minister, born 1830, who loses his faith preaching in an Independent chapel and then in a Unitarian chapel before becoming a publisher's assistant in London on the way to Parliamentary journalism in Mark Rutherford's *The Autobiography of Mark Rutherford*. He is insecure until he marries Ellen Butts after many years of separation in *Mark Rutherford's Deliverance*.

Lord William Ruthven   One of three commissioners sent by the Scottish privy council to force Queen Mary of Scotland to abdicate; a celebrated soldier and states-

man, he terrorizes Mary with his pitiless and unyielding severity in Sir Walter Scott's *The Abbot*.

Austin Ruthyn   Wealthy recluse and widower, a Swedenborgian who devotes his time to scientific and literary studies; although aloof, he loves his daughter, Maud; he dies having appointed several friends as trustees for his estate and having placed his daughter under the guardianship of his brother, Silas, in J. Sheridan Le Fanu's *Uncle Silas*.

Dudley (Dud) Ruthyn   Maud Ruthyn's cousin, son of Silas; a rough, cruel man, he tries to marry Maud for her money until it is revealed that he is already married to Sarah Mangles; at his father's instigation, he attempts to kill Maud but kills Mme. de la Rougierre by mistake and then disappears in J. Sheridan Le Fanu's *Uncle Silas*.

Maud Ruthyn   Narrator-heroine, who tells of her experiences as a young, sensitive girl who becomes a wealthy heiress and is placed under the guardianship of her Uncle Silas Ruthyn when her father dies; she is tricked into being made a prisoner after refusing to marry her cousin Dudley Ruthyn, who with her uncle tries to murder her but fails; later she marries Lord Ilbury in J. Sheridan Le Fanu's *Uncle Silas*.

Millicent (Milly) Ruthyn   Daughter of Silas Ruthyn and cousin of Maud Ruthyn; a loud, unrefined, but good-tempered girl, who befriends Maud and whom Maud polishes, she is sent off to Paris while Silas and Dudley Ruthyn plot against Maud; she eventually marries Sprigge Biddlepen in J. Sheridan Le Fanu's *Uncle Silas*.

Silas Ruthyn   Uncle of Maud Ruthyn; in his youth he was accused of killing a man to whom he owed a great deal of money; supposedly reformed and a religious recluse, he is appointed his wealthy niece's guardian; after he fails to coerce her into marrying his son, Dudley, he attempts to murder her; he commits suicide when he fails in J. Sheridan Le Fanu's *Uncle Silas*.

Stephen Rutland   Companion and co-prisoner with the younger Robert Knox on Ceylon; he too escapes after nineteen years of captivity in Daniel Defoe's *The Life, Adventures, and Pyracies of the Famous Captain Singleton*.

Archie (Gaffer) Rutledge   Constable of the county; he incurs Joseph Jobson's wrath by calling him a pettifogger while acting as a witness in Francis Osbaldistone's case in Sir Walter Scott's *Rob Roy*.

Rutter   Dwarfish spy for Lord Shoreby; he finds a tassel from Dick Shelton's clothing; he is killed by Dick when Will Lawless gives away Dick's hiding place in Robert Louis Stevenson's *The Black Arrow: A Tale of Two Roses*.

Colonel Ryde   Commander in charge of the barracks where Robert Moore finds soldiers to protect his mill in Charlotte Brontë's *Shirley*.

Widow Rye   Dependable woman who washes the linen of the sick during the fever epidemic in Harriet Martineau's *Deerbrook*.

Ryland   Lord Raymond's political adversary, who believes England should remain a republic, and who serves as Lord Protector but, panicked by the virulence of the plague, resigns his post in Mary Shelley's *The Last Man*.

Jack Ryland   Friend of Tom, the Editor; he lives a simple, happy life and was a good friend of the Anneslys in Henry Mackenzie's *The Man of the World*.

Miss Rymer   The eldest and handsomest of Rebecca Rymer's pretty elder sisters; her beauty, being of face and form, vanishes as the years pass, unlike Rebecca's beauty of mind in Elizabeth Inchbald's *Nature and Art*.

Rebecca Rymer   A country curate's youngest and least pretty daughter; she loves and is loved by the younger Henry Norwyne; compassionately accepting the charge of a foundling, she is disgraced and reviled until it is discovered that the infant is Agnes Primrose's; she waits for Henry many years while he searches for his father; returning, he finds her beauty undiminished because it is beauty of the mind; they marry and live in contented poverty with the elder Henry Norwynne in Elizabeth Inchbald's *Nature and Art*.

S

Mr. S—— False, self-interested, and glib "friend," whom George Venables encourages to proposition his wife, Maria, in return for a loan, finalizing her decision to move out and disown the marriage in Mary Wollstonecraft's *Maria; or The Wrongs of Woman.*

Lady Anne S. Wealthy, agreeable daughter of an earl; she is the sister-in-law hoped for by Charlotte Grandison until supplanted in Charlotte's affection by Harriet Byron in Samuel Richardson's *Sir Charles Grandison.*

Robert S. Right-minded servant, who tries to help Lucy Sindall escape from her guardian but is foiled by him in Henry Mackenzie's *The Man of the World.*

Sabina Distinguished lady who rescues Julian the Apostate in his incarnation as a fiddler after a former patron casts him off; her celebrated physicians cause the fiddler's untimely demise in Henry Fielding's *A Journey From This World to the Next.*

Mr. Sackbut Curate who is tutor of Gam Pickle; he is driven away from a fight with Perry Pickle in Tobias Smollett's *The Adventures of Peregrine Pickle.*

Mrs. Saddletree Efficient, kindly businesswoman, who takes in Effie Deans as a shopgirl in Sir Walter Scott's *The Heart of Midlothian.*

Bartoline Saddletree Edinburgh saddler and would-be lawyer, who lets his wife run the business so he can haunt the courts in Sir Walter Scott's *The Heart of Midlothian.*

Sadhu Sing Gallant mercenary, whose bride is killed by a tiger; he never leaves the spot of her death and ages prematurely in Sir Walter Scott's *The Surgeon's Daughter.*

Safie Lovely Christian Arab woman, lover of Felix De Lacey; their overheard French lessons provide Frankenstein's being a basic education in the language in Mary Shelley's *Frankenstein; or, The Modern Prometheus.*

Saga The Witch of Mount Vesuvius; she gives Arbaces a potion which causes Glaucus to become temporarily insane in Edward Bulwer-Lytton's *The Last Days of Pompeii.*

Sagacity Old man who tells the narrator the story of Christiana and her sons in Part 2 of John Bunyan's *The Pilgrim's Progress From this World to That Which Is to Come.*

Sagaris Deceitful Syrian slave of Marcian in George Gissing's *Veranilda.*

Mrs. Sagely Old woman in Sussex; she is called a witch by her neighbors; she nurses Roderick Random after his shipwreck and helps him with his courtship of Narcissa in Tobias Smollett's *The Adventures of Roderick Random.*

Mother St. Agatha Proud, inflexible, and cruel Prioress of St. Clare; she punishes Agnes de Medina for her pregnancy by feigning her death and imprisoning her in the vaults of the Convent of St. Clare without hope of release; eventually accused of murder, she is killed by the Madrid mob in Matthew Lewis's *The Monk.*

Madame St. Aubert French gentlewoman, whose death from a fever causes her husband's health to decline and her daughter Emily's strength of character to be tested in Ann Radcliffe's *The Mysteries of Udolpho.*

Monsieur St. Aubert Melancholy French gentleman, whose integrity and love of nature are instilled in his daughter Emily; his death orphans Emily and leads to her becoming a ward of her murderous step-uncle, Signor Montoni, in Ann Radcliffe's *The Mysteries of Udolpho.*

Emily St. Aubert Modest young Frenchwoman of sensibility, who falls in love with Chevalier Valancourt but is orphaned before she can marry him; she becomes the ward of her aunt, Madame Cheron, whose marriage to the evil Montoni makes Emily a pawn in Montoni's schemes to extort money; she is imprisoned in the Castle di Udolpho, where her aunt dies; she escapes from Udolpho and finds friends in the family of Count de Villefort; ultimately she finds herself heiress to the Villeroi and Udolpho fortunes and marries Valancourt in Ann Radcliffe's *The Mysteries of Udolpho.*

Chevalier St. Aumar A handsome gallant who is devoted to the Baroness de Tortillee in Eliza Haywood's *The Injur'd Husband; or, the Mistaken Resentment.*

St. Barbe (characterization of William Makepeace Thackeray) Part-time journalist and one of Endymion Ferrars's fellow clerks; he finds being a clerk very degrading in Benjamin Disraeli's *Endymion.*

Duchess of St. Bungay Regal wife of the powerful Duke, formidable in appearance and manner but always conscious of imagined slights to her rank and thus a constant source of anxiety to her husband in Anthony Trollope's *Can You Forgive Her?.* She is a patroness of the Negro Soldiers' Orphan Bazaar in *Miss Mackenzie.*

Duke of St. Bungay Aristocratic Knight of the Garter and Liberal pillar of the realm often consulted in the making of Prime Ministers; he offers the post of Chancellor of the Exchequer to Plantagenet Palliser in Anthony Trollope's *Can You Forgive Her?.* He is a powerbroker behind the scenes as head of the old Whigs of the country in *Phineas Finn* and in *Phineas Redux*. He does his best to sustain and encourage the Duke of Omnium (Palliser) throughout his miseries as leader of the nation in *The Prime Minister*. He appears briefly in *The Duke's Children*.

Marquis de St. Clair   Swiss nobleman, Louisa's father, who betroths her to Malcolm's brother in Ann Radcliffe's *The Castles of Athlin and Dunbayne*.

Jocelyn St. Cleeve   A physician whose ample legacy to his great-nephew, Swithin St. Cleeve, depends on the young man's not marrying before the age of twenty-five in Thomas Hardy's *Two on a Tower*.

Swithin St. Cleeve   Handsome aspiring astronomer, several years younger than Lady Constantine; having set up his telescope on a lonely, ruined tower on the Constantine property, he attracts her attention and gradually her love; that astronomy remains of primary importance to him is central to their tragedy, though he loves her and means to behave honorably in Thomas Hardy's *Two on a Tower*.

Piers St. Cloud   High-spending, unscrupulous son of a nobleman; a member of the fast set at St. Ambrose's College, Oxford, he attempts to ruin Mary Porter's reputation in Thomas Hughes's *Tom Brown at Oxford*.

Jules St. Croix   Young French prisoner of war set free by Charles O'Malley; he tries later to arrange O'Malley's escape after capture in his turn by the French in Charles Lever's *Charles O'Malley*.

St. Elmo   High-minded and idealistic Corsican robber baron, whom Julian Danvers and Francesco Perfetti join, and with whom they are caught and imprisoned in Palermo in William Godwin's *Cloudesley*.

Lord St. Erme   Theodora Martindale's unsuccessful suitor, who gives up his dilettantish ways to tackle social problems in Charlotte Yonge's *Heartsease*.

Marquis St. Evremond   Angelo D'Albini's aristocratic friend, who keeps him informed of the whereabouts of Milborough in Charlotte Dacre's *The Libertine*.

Marquis St. Evrémonde (1)   The deceased elder brother of the present marquis; he was the seducer of Madame Defarge's sister and father of Charles St. Evrémonde in Charles Dickens's *A Tale of Two Cities*.

Marquis St. Evrémonde (2)   The younger of twin brothers and uncle of Charles St. Evrémonde; he is a vicious aristocrat who, when his coach runs over a girl in St. Antoine, contemptuously throws money at the grieving father and verbally scorns the village people when the money is thrown back into his coach; he is murdered in his bed in Charles Dickens's *A Tale of Two Cities*.

Marquise St. Evrémonde   Charles's mother, who wanted her son to make amends for his father's crime; the name he assumes on renouncing his patrimony, Darnay, is derived from her family name, D'Aulnais, in Charles Dickens's *A Tale of Two Cities*.

Charles St. Evrémonde   French aristocrat who renounces his estate out of sympathy for the poor and horror of his father's and uncle's wickedness; he emigrates to England, where he uses the name Charles Darnay; he is acquitted of being a spy for the French by the Old Bailey court when Sydney Carton's testimony undermines John Barsad's identification; he falls in love with Lucie Manette and marries her; returning to France in answer to Théophile Gabelle's plea, he is himself condemned to the guillotine but rescued by Sydney Carton's self-sacrifice in Charles Dickens's *A Tale of Two Cities*.

Baron de St. Foix   Superstitious friend of Count de Villefort and father of Chevalier St. Foix in Ann Radcliffe's *The Mysteries of Udolpho*.

Chevalier St. Foix   French officer who falls in love with Blanche de Villefort, is wounded in rescuing her from mountain bandits, and recovers to marry her in Ann Radcliffe's *The Mysteries of Udolpho*.

Lord St. George   Sensible son of the Marquis of Trowbridge; he warns his father against building a Methodist chapel and tactfully negotiates for its removal in Anthony Trollope's *The Vicar of Bullhampton*.

Mr. St. George   False, shallow friend of Clarence Hervey; along with Mr. Rochfort he stands by and does nothing while Hervey nearly drowns in Maria Edgeworth's *Belinda*.

Albert St. George   Lady Madeline Trevor's brother, who is saved from ruin at the hands of unscrupulous gamblers by Vivian Grey in Benjamin Disraeli's *Vivian Grey*.

James Stewart (or Stuart), Chevalier de St. George (the "Old Pretender")   Son of the exiled King James II; Horatio becomes his attendant through the offices of the Baron de la Valiers in Eliza Haywood's *The Fortunate Foundlings*. Regarded by the Jacobites as king of England, he is brought to England from France by Colonel Henry Esmond in a plot to have him named successor to Queen Anne; his pursuit of Beatrix Esmond dooms the scheme in William Makepeace Thackeray's *The History of Henry Esmond*.

Lord Robert St. George   A man known for his many conquests of women; his attempt to seduce Lady Mary Jones causes her to reform her manners; his later proposal to Harriot Selvyn is eloquently refused in Sarah Scott's *A Description of Millenium Hall*.

Eloise de St. Irvyne   Wolfstein's virtuous sister, who is captured by Frederic de Nempere (Ginotti); freed, she ultimately falls in love with Fitzeustace in Percy Bysshe Shelley's *St. Irvyne*.

Sir Arthur St. Ives   Baronet and father to Anna St. Ives; his undiscerning benevolence prevents him from recognizing Abimelech Henley's deceit; he later encourages the relationship between Anna and Frank Henley in Thomas Holcroft's *Anna St. Ives*.

Anna Wenbourne St. Ives   Forthright, truth-loving heroine, who succeeds in convincing her suitor Coke Clifton to forsake vice and who, at the end of the novel, is soon to marry the noble, honest Frank Henley in Thomas Holcroft's *Anna St. Ives*.

Captain Edward St. Ives   Anna St. Ives's brother, who is threatened by Phelim Mac Fane over a gambling debt and who is relieved, thanks to the wit and generosity of Frank Henley, in Thomas Holcroft's *Anna St. Ives*.

George Augustus Frederick, Duke of St. James   Ruinously prodigal young duke; he nearly destroys his fortune and health with irresponsible feats of spending and excess; he has a youthful infatuation with his cousin Caroline St. Maurice, has a disastrous affair with Lady Aphrodite Grafton, and finally falls in love with May Dacre, the Catholic daughter of his estranged former guardian; May Dacre's influence encourages his essentially generous and virtuous nature, ultimately leading to his salvation in Benjamin Disraeli's *The Young Duke*.

Miss Sainthill   Upper-class intellectual and friend of Lady Forester; she argues for Methodism to spite the fashionably atheistic Colonel Rappee in Richard Graves's *The Spiritual Quixote*.

Lady St. Jerome   Roman Catholic noblewoman, who uses her influence in an attempt to inspire Lothair to join her church in Benjamin Disraeli's *Lothair*.

Miles St. John   Wealthy landowner, who disinherits his niece Lucretia Clavering after learning that she seeks his death; he leaves his estate to the next heir, Charles Vernon, in Edward Bulwer-Lytton's *Lucretia*.

Percival St. John   Son of Charles Vernon; he courts his cousin, Helen Mainwaring, while both are objects of a murderous plot devised by their aunt, Lucretia Clavering, in Edward Bulwer-Lytton's *Lucretia*.

Lady St. Julians   Rival of Lady Marney, with whom she competes to advance the political career of her own son in Benjamin Disraeli's *Sybil*.

Mr. St. Leger   Member of the Brotherhood of the Rose and son of Sir Warham in Charles Kingsley's *Westward Ho!*.

Sir Warham St. Leger   Marshal of Munster, Ireland, who takes part in the Irish campaign against the Spanish in Charles Kingsley's *Westward Ho!*.

Charles de St. Leon (Chevalier de Damville)   High-minded son of Reginald de St. Leon; he becomes disillusioned with his father's vices and takes his mother's maiden name; after befriending the handsome and charming D'Aubigny, whom he found in the smoldering ruins of Bethlem Gabor's castle, he discovers that D'Aubigny, the notorious outlaw Chattilon, and his father are the same man in William Godwin's *St. Leon*.

Reginald de St. Leon (the elder)   Brave, virtuous soldier, who falls in Italy under the banner of Louis XII; he is father of the addicted gambler and alchemist, Reginald de St. Leon (Chattilon, D'Aubigny), in William Godwin's *St. Leon*.

Reginald de St. Leon (Chattilon, D'Aubigny)   Scion of a noble family of France; addicted to gambling, he is frequently forced to uproot his family and flee creditors and bailiffs, thereby losing honor and alienating his son, Charles; in Switzerland, at the nadir of his fortunes, he encounters Francesco Zampieri, who promises to bestow opulence upon him if only he will keep secret "the art of multiplying gold, and the power of living forever"; on his subsequent travels he spends twelve years as a prisoner of the Inquisition, surfaces as a philanthropist in Budapest, and is rescued from the ruins of Bethlem Gabor's castle; he is befriended but not recognized by his own son; although he exploits the powers of the philosopher's stone, which preserve his youth and provide him with riches aplenty, he suffers from the curse of the *opus magnum*: "I was utterly alone in the world, separated by an insurmountable barrier from every being of my species" in William Godwin's *St. Leon*.

Aubrey St. Lys   Vicar of Mowbray, who views Christianity as "completed Judaisim" and devotes himself wholeheartedly to improving the living conditions of the poor in Benjamin Disraeli's *Sybil*.

Lady Caroline St. Maurice   Gentle daughter of the Earl of Fitz-pompey and cousin of the young Duke of St. James; she develops an adolescent love for the young duke and is widely expected to marry him, but he disappoints her, and she finally marries Arundel Dacre in Benjamin Disraeli's *The Young Duke*.

Miss St. Omar   Grace Nugent's scandalous mother, ostracized for having a supposedly illegitimate daughter in Maria Edgeworth's *The Absentee*.

Eustace St. Pierre   The commander of the defense of Calais against English siege in a parable told by Charles Meekly in Henry Brooke's *The Fool of Quality*.

Virginia (Rachel) St. Pierre   Lovely, simple, artless young protégée of Clarence Hervey; having been discovered by him living secluded and innocent in the woods, she is taken away by him to be molded into the "perfect" wife; luckily, Harvey does not marry her and she instead is united with the man she truly loves in Maria Edgeworth's *Belinda*.

Zelie de St. Pierre   A French teacher at Mme. Beck's school; she would like to seduce M. Paul Emanuel; her overtures of friendship are not returned by Lucy Snowe in Charlotte Brontë's *Villette*.

Mother St. Ursula   Compassionate nun who opposes Mother St. Agatha's vicious punishment of Agnes de Medina and accuses the prioress of murder in Matthew Lewis's *The Monk*.

Valerie de St. Ventadour   Parisian once beloved by Ernest Maltravers in Edward Bulwer-Lytton's *Ernest Maltravers*. She helps him save Evelyn Templeton in *Alice*.

Old Sal   Nanny's "wicked, old grannie" in George MacDonald's *At the Back of the North Wind*.

Conde (Senor Silva Diaz) De Saldar   Portuguese diplomat, who marries Louisa Harrington in George Meredith's *Evan Harrington*.

Louisa Harrington, Countess De Saldar   Evan Harrington's snobbish sister, who will stoop to deception to conceal her father's occupation as a tailor and to arrange a marriage between Evan and the wealthy Rose Jocelyn in George Meredith's *Evan Harrington*.

Saladin (Ilderim, Hakim Adonbec)   Sultan of Moslem forces; disguised as Ilderim, a Saracen warrior, he battles with Sir Kenneth; disguised as Hakim Adonbec, he arbitrates Richard's quarrel with Conrade, Marquis of Montserrat; he executes Giles Amaury, the grand master of the Templars, in Sir Walter Scott's *The Talisman*.

Jem Salisbury   Thief and former pal of Tom Robinson; he becomes his reformed friend and defender in Charles Reade's *It is Never Too Late to Mend*.

Mr. Salisbury   Distinguished gentleman intended as a husband for Grace Nugent in Maria Edgeworth's *The Absentee*.

Sallust   Glaucus's friend, who tardily saves him from the lions in Edward Bulwer-Lytton's *The Last Days of Pompeii*.

Sally   Dr. Walsingham's kind and faithful housekeeper; she tells stories of the haunting of Tiled House to his daughter Lilias and nurses her during her illness in J. Sheridan Le Fanu's *The House by the Churchyard*.

Sally   The Greys' maid, who stays with them after they find themselves in straitened circumstances in Anne Brontë's *Agnes Grey*.

Sally   Any of a series of Martha Honeyman's young servant girls from the workhouse; Martha gives them all the same name in William Makepeace Thackeray's *The Newcomes*.

Sally   The shrewd and faithful old servant of the Bensons, who provides practical sense as well as some humor in helping Ruth Hilton adjust to her new life in Elizabeth Gaskell's *Ruth*.

Sally   Miss Galindo's odd little maidservant in Elizabeth Gaskell's *My Lady Ludlow*.

Old Sally   Old woman in the workhouse who confesses on her deathbed that she stole gold from Oliver Twist's mother that was meant for him in Charles Dickens's *Oliver Twist*.

Captain Salmonet   Major O'Hara's friend, who accompanies him and his wife on a visit intended to force access to her daughter, Emily Jervois, in Samuel Richardson's *Sir Charles Grandison*.

Jim Salt   One of Jonathan Burge's employees in George Eliot's *Adam Bede*.

Bess Salt (Timothy's Bess)   A cousin of Bess Cranage and wife of Jim Salt in George Eliot's *Adam Bede*.

Rose Salterne   Beautiful daughter of the mayor of Bideford; known as the Rose of Torridge, she inspires passion in the young men who form the Brotherhood of the Rose; she falls in love with Don Guzman de Soto and flees to Caracas to join him, marries him, and is finally burned by the Inquisitors in Charles Kingsley's *Westward Ho!*.

William Salterne   Mayor of Bideford, merchant, and father of Rose; he cultivates Don Guzman de Soto, hoping to obtain useful commercial information, without appreciating the danger to Rose; after her flight, he asks Amyas to bring him Guzman's head and leaves money for vengeance in his will in Charles Kingsley's *Westward Ho!*.

Lord Saltstream   Mad peer, who sees the arrival in London of Lucilla Volktman as a portent of impending revolution in Edward Bulwer-Lytton's *Godolphin*.

Sam   Footman at Thornfield Hall, who announces the gypsy fortune-teller (Mr. Rochester in disguise) to his house guests in Charlotte Brontë's *Jane Eyre*.

Sam   A turf-cutter and a voice of rural commentary in Thomas Hardy's *The Return of the Native*.

Sambo   Mr. Sedley's black servant in William Makepeace Thackeray's *Vanity Fair*.

Sammy   Cab driver at St. Martin's-le-Grand coach station, who picks a fight with Samuel Pickwick in Charles Dickens's *The Posthumous Papers of the Pickwick Club*.

Anne Sample   Spinster landlady of Bob Bagshot; her writ for his failure to pay rent causes his detention by Mr. Snap in Henry Fielding's *The Life of Mr. Jonathan Wild the Great*.

Dr. Sampson   Scottish practitioner of the "chronothairmal system of diagnosis," infuriating and endearing, whose loyalty is invaluable to the Dodd family during the disappearance and insanity of David Dodd and the disappearance and incarceration of Alfred Hardie in Charles Reade's *Hard Cash*.

Mr. Sampson   Merry but profligate chaplain to (Eugene) Lord Castlewood; he is a faithful friend to Harry and George Warrington, especially when his discovery of a lost deed preserves their claim to their estate in America; he marries Hermann Foker's widow in William Makepeace Thackeray's *The Virginians*.

Mr. Sampson   The coachman who describes the country areas he travels and complains bitterly about the railroad in George Eliot's *Felix Holt, the Radical*.

Dominie Abel Sampson   Absent-minded, affectionate, and awkward scholar, who faithfully serves as Henry and Lucy Bertram's tutor before becoming Colonel Mannering's librarian; he has studied to become a clergyman, and his language is filled with scriptural phraseology in Sir Walter Scott's *Guy Mannering*.

George Sampson   Weak-minded suitor of Bella Wilfer; he transfers his affections to Lavinia Wilfer after Bella moves in with the Boffins in Charles Dickens's *Our Mutual Friend*.

Samson   Executioner who operates the guillotine in Paris in Charles Dickens's *A Tale of Two Cities*.

Samuel   Second son of Christian and Christiana; he marries Grace, daughter of Mnason, in John Bunyan's *The Pilgrim's Progress From this World to That Which Is to Come*.

Marco Sana   One of the Italian revolutionists who fight with Carlo Ammiani in George Meredith's *Vittoria*.

Madame de Sancerre   Witty woman of letters; she spends time at Montauban castle shortly after the wedding of Julia de Roubigné and Count Louis de Montauban in Henry Mackenzie's *Julia de Roubigné*.

Father Sancta Clara (Mr. Hall)   Jesuit priest and advisor to queen Henrietta Marie; he trains John Inglesant to be liaison between Church of England and papist factions during the reign of Charles I in J. Henry Shorthouse's *John Inglesant, A Romance*.

John Sandal   Grandson of Sir Roger Mortimer; he leaves Elinor Mortimer, his cousin, at the altar after he discovers a codicil in Sir Roger's will which limits Elinor's inheritance if she marries Sandal; he then marries Elinor's sister, Margaret, the heiress of the Mortimer estates in Charles Maturin's *Melmoth the Wanderer*.

Lucilla Sandbrook   Strong-willed daughter of the elder Owen Sandbrook; she resents her guardian, Honora Charlecote, scandalizes her lover, Robert Fulmort, loses her health, and marries her father's curate in Charlotte Yonge's *Hopes and Fears*.

Owen Sandbrook   Handsome, unstable clergyman, who goes to Canada as a missionary among the Indians but deserts them and his promise to Honora Charlecote in order to marry a wealthy woman in Charlotte Yonge's *Hopes and Fears*.

Owen Sandbrook (the younger)   Adopted son of Honora Charlecote; his uncertainty as to her intentions toward him and his weak character lead to an imprudent marriage in Charlotte Yonge's *Hopes and Fears*.

Susannah Sanders   Fat, heavy-faced friend of Martha Bardell in Charles Dickens's *The Posthumous Papers of the Pickwick Club*.

Dr. Sanderson   Friend to whom Henry Lambert turns for advice despite cruel rumors that he has adopted democratic principles in William Beckford's *Modern Novel Writing; or, the Elegant Enthusiast*.

Grant Sanderson   Owner of the yacht *Dream*, which is renamed *Currency Lass* by Captain Joe Wicks and crew in Robert Louis Stevenson's *The Wrecker*.

Sandford   Jesuit priest and mentor to Dorriforth, Lord Elmwood; a crusty curmudgeon, he shows a heart of gold as Dorriforth's cruelty grows excessive in Elizabeth Inchbald's *A Simple Story*.

Billy Sandwith   A leading Muskegon businessman who "bit the dust" in Robert Louis Stevenson's *The Wrecker*.

Captain Sang   Hearty captain of the ship that ferries David Balfour and Catriona Drummond to Leyden, Holland, in Robert Louis Stevenson's *Catriona*.

Mademoiselle Sansfay   A vain coquette, who is never happier than when giving pain in Eliza Haywood's *The Injur'd Husband; or, the Mistaken Resentment*.

Count de Santmorin   Swiss nobleman, a distant relative of Louisa; his ship is wrecked at Castle Athlin; he befriends Osbert and falls in love with Mary, only to be refused by her; he kidnaps Mary and is caught by Osbert and Alleyn (Philip) in Ann Radcliffe's *The Castles of Athlin and Dunbayne*.

Sappho   Poet whose soul the author encounters in Elysium in Henry Fielding's *A Journey From This World to the Next*.

Ethelinda Brobity Sapsea   Late wife of Thomas Sapsea; as Miss Brobity she kept a girls' school in competition with Miss Twinkleton's in Charles Dickens's *The Mystery of Edwin Drood*.

Thomas Sapsea   Cloisterham's auctioneer and mayor who takes a lively interest in the fight between Edwin Drood and Neville Landless and is a "type of self-sufficient stupidity and conceit" in Charles Dickens's *The Mystery of Edwin Drood*.

Lady Sara   Daughter of an English nobleman; she is an honest though proud young woman, who attends the concert with Ginevra Fanshawe in Charlotte Brontë's *Villette*.

Luigi Saracco   Spy for both Pericles and Barto Rizo on Vittoria Campa and others in George Meredith's *Vittoria*.

Sarah   Millward family's maid who relays gossip from the Lawrence residence to Eliza Millward in Anne Brontë's *The Tenant of Wildfell Hall*.

Sarah   Wife of Abraham; she is nearly seduced by Totis in the appended romance "The History of Charoba, Queen of Egypt" in Clara Reeve's *The Progress of Romance*.

Sarah   The pretty servant who works for Robert and Hortense Moore in Charlotte Brontë's *Shirley*.

Sarah   Maidservant at the girls' boarding school at Westgate House in Charles Dickens's *The Posthumous Papers of the Pickwick Club*.

Sarah   Housemaid at Gateshead Hall for Mrs. Reed in Charlotte Brontë's *Jane Eyre*.

Sarah   Young wet nurse who is engaged to care for Jack Easy in Captain Frederick Marryat's *Mr. Midshipman Easy*.

Sarah   Silas Marner's betrothed in his youth; she marries William Dane after Marner is publicly shamed in George Eliot's *Silas Marner*.

Sarah (Sally) (Wilkins)   Third and youngest daughter of Peter Wilkins and Youwarkee in Robert Paltock's *The Life and Adventures of Peter Wilkins*.

Samuel Sarcasm   Steward to Sir Benjamin Beauchamp in S. J. Pratt's *Shenstone-Green*.

Mr. Sarcastic   Politician who expresses normal human conduct as his own original theories and is accused of expressing pernicious doctrine in Thomas Love Peacock's *Melincourt*.

Mrs. Sarsenet   Milliner, friend of Squire Townsend's first wife, and chaperon to Julia Townsend; she worsens Julia's relationship with her stepmother by expressing her dislike for the latter; later she becomes a disciple of Geoffry Wildgoose in Richard Graves's *The Spiritual Quixote*.

Leonora Sarsfield   Young Protestant woman of Richmondshire; she marries a French Catholic named Burke and is beaten cruelly by him in his attempt to convert her to Catholicism; she escapes into a reclusive existence near John Buncle's Orton Lodge in Thomas Amory's *The Life of John Buncle, Esq.*

Satchell   The Donnithorne steward in George Eliot's *Adam Bede*.

Samuel Saul   Thin, hard-working curate of the Reverend Henry Clavering, who looks with distaste on Saul's earnest piety; he falls in love with Fanny Clavering and finally wins her as his wife despite family opposition; he becomes rector of Clavering parish after Henry Clavering becomes Sir Henry and resigns the living to him in Anthony Trollope's *The Claverings*.

Miss Saunders   Daughter of Mr. Saunders; Lucius's generosity makes it possible for Mr. Trueman's son to have a fortune sufficient to make a match with her in Mary Collyer's *Felicia to Charlotte*.

Mr. Saunders   Virtuous tenant of Lucius Manly; facing imprisonment for debt, he reacts violently to the suggestion of a stranger (really Lucius) that he could clear his debts by stealing trees from his landlord; Lucius rescues this honest farmer in Mary Collyer's *Felicia to Charlotte*.

Mrs. Saunders　　Mother of Esther Waters and widow of a shopkeeper; though she is sympathetic to Esther, because of ill health from frequent childbearing and duty to her abusive second husband and his children she is unable to help Esther in George Moore's *Esther Waters*.

Betty Saunders　　Good wife of farmer Saunders; her emotionally violent response to the disguised Lucius's suggestion that her husband clear his debts by stealing from his landlord makes her think they were visited by the devil in Mary Collyer's *Felicia to Charlotte*.

Jim Saunders　　Esther Waters's alcoholic stepfather, who maltreats Esther's mother and three stepsisters; on the death of Mrs. Saunders he decides to go to Australia, making the daughters demand money of Esther for passage in George Moore's *Esther Waters*.

Nick Saunders　　Catholic legate and plotter for the overthrow of the English presence in Ireland whom Sir Walter Raleigh and Amyas Leigh find dead in an Irish bog with incriminating documents in Charles Kingsley's *Westward Ho!*.

Sukey Saunders　　Young woman known for a scandalous intrigue in William Beckford's *Modern Novel Writing; or, the Elegant Enthusiast*.

Justine-Marie Sauveur　　Goddaughter of M. Paul Emanuel and niece of his former bride-to-be, Justine-Marie; she is engaged to Heinrich Muhler, but some would like to see her married to M. Paul in Charlotte Brontë's *Villette*.

Save-all　　One of three friends of By-ends; he uses religion for selfish and worldly ends in John Bunyan's *The Pilgrim's Progress From this World to That Which Is to Come*.

Madame Savelli　　Famous voice teacher, who is impressed by Evelyn Innes and trains her to become an opera star in George Moore's *Evelyn Innes*.

Agnes de Saverne　　Heroine of the novel, brought to England as a young child; after being orphaned she has an innocent romance with Denis Duval, whom after many trials she would marry in William Makepeace Thackeray's unfinished *Denis Duval*.

Clarisse, Comtesse de Saverne　　Unhappy mother of Agnes, after whose birth she loses her mind, becomes converted to Catholicism, and flees to England, where she dies in William Makepeace Thackeray's *Denis Duval*.

Francis Stanislas, Comte de Saverne　　Foul-tempered, gloomy husband of Clarisse, whom he pursues to England, imagining that she is the mistress of the Chevalier de la Motte; he challenges la Motte to a duel and is killed in William Makepeace Thackeray's *Denis Duval*.

Mesdemoiselles de Saverne　　Unmarried sisters of Francis Stanislas, Comte de Saverne; they contentedly act as their brother's domestic servants in William Makepeace Thackeray's *Denis Duval*.

Comte de Saverne (the elder)　　Cheerful French Protestant nobleman, whose disposition is in contrast to that of his son in William Makepeace Thackeray's *Denis Duval*.

Augustus Saville　　Aesthete and guide of Percy Godolphin; he arranges Godolphin's marriage to Constance Vernon (Countess of Erpingham) in Edward Bulwer-Lytton's *Godolphin*.

George Saville　　A friend and employer of Bryan Perdue's governor (tutor); he employs Bryan after his father's death; his note is appropriated by Bryan, resulting in Bryan's trial for forgery in Thomas Holcroft's *The Memoirs of Bryan Perdue*.

George Saville (the son)　　Bryan Perdue's friend and fellow gambler in Thomas Holcroft's *The Memoirs of Bryan Perdue*.

Henrietta Saville　　The beautiful and virtuous daughter of the elder George Saville; Bryan Perdue saves her from a fire; she becomes Lord Campion's wife in Thomas Holcroft's *The Memoirs of Bryan Perdue*.

Lady Jane Saville　　The second wife of the elder George Saville; a woman of high fashion, she competes with her daughter, Henrietta, to look young in Thomas Holcroft's *The Memoirs of Bryan Perdue*.

Savillon　　Tenderhearted childhood companion to Julia de Roubigné and beloved of her but forced to seek his fortune in Martinique; his clandestine visit with Julia after her marriage triggers Count Louis de Montauban's murderous rage when he discovers it in Henry Mackenzie's *Julia de Roubigné*.

Savillon's Uncle　　Wealthy Martinique businessman, who offers his nephew the chance to make his fortune in Henry Mackenzie's *Julia de Roubigné*.

Young Saving　　Young fop in love with Betsy Thoughtless in Eliza Haywood's *The History of Miss Betsy Thoughtless*.

Fra Girolamo Savonarola　　Prior of the Dominican

monastery of San Marco in Florence; he believes he has a divine mission to foretell doom like the Hebrew prophets; the first time Romola de' Bardi attempts to leave Florence, his compelling speech forces her to stay; he is eventually considered too politically powerful and is burned as a heretic in George Eliot's *Romola*.

Mr. Sawbridge   First lieutenant of H.M.S. *Harpy*, later captain of H.M.S. *Aurora* and of H.M.S. *Latona*; he comes to appreciate Jack Easy's qualities in Captain Frederick Marryat's *Mr. Midshipman Easy*.

Dr. Sawyer   Skillful young surgeon from Brotherton; he treats Adelaide Houghton's arm after her hunting spill at Pugsby Brook in Anthony Trollope's *Is He Popenjoy?*.

Bob Sawyer   Coarse, dissolute, and slovenly medical student, then medical partner of Ben Allen and a suitor of Arabella Allen in Charles Dickens's *The Posthumous Papers of the Pickwick Club*.

Lord Saxingham   Political leader and the affectionate, though worldly, father of Lady Florence Lascelles in Edward Bulwer-Lytton's *Ernest Maltravers*. His political misfortune is eluded by his ally, the scheming Lumley Ferrers, in *Alice*.

Master Sayers   Mrs. Sayers's son, whose affected manners and pedantic discussion of painting while visiting the Bidulphs contrast him to Orlando Faulkland in Frances Sheridan's *Memoirs of Miss Sidney Bidulph*.

Mrs. Sayers   Controlling mother of Master Sayers; she tries to show off her son to the Bidulphs in Frances Sheridan's *Memoirs of Miss Sidney Bidulph*.

Zephaniah Scadder   Sleazy, dishonest American agent for the Eden Land Corporation, who cheats Mark Tapley and the younger Martin Chuzzlewit by selling them uninhabitable swampland in Eden in Charles Dickens's *The Life and Adventures of Martin Chuzzlewit*.

Harry Scaddon   Philip Debarry's scheming servant, who changed identities with the dying Maurice Christian Bycliffe and is known as "Mr. Christian"; he loses papers belonging to Sir Maximus Debarry which are found by Felix Holt and help to prove Esther Lyon's true identity in George Eliot's *Felix Holt, the Radical*.

Alessandra Scala   Bartolomeo Scala's beautiful daughter in George Eliot's *Romola*.

Bartolomeo Scala   Florentine Republic secretary, who buys gems from Tito Melema in George Eliot's *Romola*.

Mr. Scales   The Debarrys' butler, whose action of discarding the purse of the sleeping "Mr. Christian" (Henry Scaddon) leads to Rufus Lyon's discovery of Esther Lyon's paternity in George Eliot's *Felix Holt, the Radical*.

Earl of Scamperdale ("Lord Hardup")   Sporting nobleman who invites Soapey Sponge to his house, mistakenly believing Sponge to be a sportswriter traveling incognito, to better evaluate the hounds and the field in Robert Surtees's *Mr. Sponge's Sporting Tour*.

Mr. Scarborough   Neighbor of Casimir and Mary Fleetwood in Merionetshire; he reveals the truth about Gifford Kenrick's misdeeds and exposes to ridicule Fleetwood's suspicions concerning Mary's supposed liaison with his nephew, Edward Kenrick, in William Godwin's *Fleetwood*.

Augustus Scarborough   Cynical, devious, and thoroughly selfish younger son of John Scarborough of Tretton Park; he becomes his father's chosen heir for a time, but his avarice causes his father to reinstate his other son, Mountjoy, as heir; he tries to steal Florence Mountjoy from Harry Annesley; he schemes to consolidate his position over his brother and is at last ruined in Anthony Trollope's *Mr. Scarborough's Family*.

John Scarborough   Manipulative, intelligent, and amoral dying landowner, who wishes to defy social conventions, particularly the laws of entail; he devotes his life to deceptions within the law to circumvent the entail leaving his estate to his elder son, Mountjoy, so that he may bestow the land as he pleases, perhaps on his younger son, Augustus; his scheme is based on his two marriages abroad to the same woman, before and after the birth of his elder son; he declares and seems to prove Mountjoy illegitimate because Mountjoy has gambled away his entire inheritance, the bills to be paid after Mr. Scarborough's death; he comes to hate his malicious and greedy younger son, and after the money-lenders have reluctantly accepted repayments of principal, he validates Mountjoy's legitimacy, reinstating him as heir before dying in Anthony Trollope's *Mr. Scarborough's Family*.

Louisa Scarborough   Bride-to-be of Lieutenant Edward Kenrick, for whom Mary Fleetwood acts as a go-between and in so doing inadvertently arouses the jealousy of her husband, Casimir Fleetwood, in William Godwin's *Fleetwood*.

Martha Scarborough   Unmarried sister of John Scarborough; she lives on the family estate at Tretton Park in Anthony Trollope's *Mr. Scarborough's Family*.

Captain Mountjoy Scarborough   Dashing, reckless, profligate gambler, an officer in the Coldstream Guards and elder son of John Scarborough of Tretton Park; when his debts threaten to put the entire estate into the hands of the moneylenders, his father disinherits him by apparently proving him illegitimate but later provides evidence of his legitimacy; reinstated to his inheritance, when his father dies he goes to Monte Carlo, resuming his wastrel existence, in Anthony Trollope's *Mr. Scarborough's Family.*

Lady Scatcherd   Loyal wife of Sir Roger overwhelmed by her elevated status as mistress of Boxall Hill; to her husband's annoyance she retains a devotion to Frank Gresham, whom she nursed in his infancy in Anthony Trollope's *Doctor Thorne.* She appears briefly in *Framley Parsonage.*

Miss Scatcherd   Bad-tempered teacher of history and grammar at Lowood School, who continually and unjustly singles out Helen Burns as her example of laziness and untidiness in Charlotte Brontë's *Jane Eyre.*

(Sir) Louis Philippe Scatcherd   Dissipated, dying son of Sir Roger Scatcherd, who encourages his unsuccessful suit for Mary Thorne; he does not long survive his father in Anthony Trollope's *Doctor Thorne.*

Sir Roger Scatcherd   Former stonemason, who has become a wealthy railway contractor and baronet and is narrowly elected a Member of Parliament; he is dying of alcoholism, as is his worthless son, Louis Philippe; his will makes his illegitimate niece, Mary Thorne, an heiress in Anthony Trollope's *Doctor Thorne.*

Lady Scattercash   Sir Harry's wife, a former actress who smokes cigars in Robert Surtees's *Mr. Sponge's Sporting Tour.*

Sir Harry Scattercash   A rake in Robert Surtees's *Mr. Sponge's Sporting Tour.*

Scawthorne   Scheming lawyer's clerk, who collaborates with his unscrupulous client Joseph Snowdon to gain a fortune in George Gissing's *The Nether World.*

Schemzeddin (Cozro, Schemerzad)   Wise, popular young sultan of Persia; he loves Nourjahad like a brother; disquieted by reports of Nourjahad's flaws, he devises an elaborate scheme in which he plays the roles of Cozro, Nourjahad's servant and guide, and Schemerzad, his own successor as sultan and ostensibly his own son, to exact Nourjahad's repentance in Frances Sheridan's *The History of Nourjahad.*

Alexis Scherbatoff   Friend of William Meadows and fellow clerk in the office of his mother's half-brother, John Ernest Biren, consort of the Czarina Anne and real holder of power in the Empire in William Godwin's *Cloudesley.*

Isabella Scherbatoff   Sister of Alexis Scherbatoff and niece of John Ernest Biren; she is the object of William Meadows's affection in William Godwin's *Cloudesley.*

Schirene   Daughter of the caliph who rules the occupied country reclaimed by David Alroy; she falls in love with Alroy and distracts him from the altruistic path that led to his success in Benjamin Disraeli's *The Wondrous Tale of Alroy.*

Ludmilla Schnetterling   Half sister of Gerald Underwood; she is protected by him from her corrupt mother and accompanies him to the United States in Charlotte Yonge's *The Long Vacation.*

Scholar   (persona of William Morris)   Nineteenth-century man who dreams that he is a medieval scholar in a Kentish village during Wat Tyler's Rebellion of 1381; he admires the way of life, sees a skirmish of the king's men, and discusses the waning of feudalism and the rise of commercialism with John Ball in William Morris's *A Dream of John Ball.*

Lawrence Scholey   Magnus Troil's quick-thinking servant in Sir Walter Scott's *The Pirate.*

Ital Schreckenwald   Steward and henchman of Count Albert of Geierstein; he undertakes responsibility for the count's daughter, Anne, when she returns to her father in Sir Walter Scott's *Anne of Geierstein.*

Jonas Schwanker   Court jester who entertains and warns Leopold, Archduke of Austria, in Sir Walter Scott's *The Talisman.*

Scipiana   Clelia's cousin disguised as a page, then as the exile Exilia; she has a man's education and is the heroine of Jane Barker's *Exilius; or, The Banish'd Roman.*

Scipio   See Asisticus.

Scorbutia   Genteel, ugly youngest daughter of Maladie Alamode; her name is translated as "scurvy"; she denies her relation to her mother in Henry Fielding's *A Journey From This World to the Next.*

Alberto Scoto   Exiled Italian general fighting on the French side in the French-Flemish war; he introduces Castruccio dei Antelminelli to unscrupulous methods of power politics in Mary Shelley's *Valperga.*

Captain Valentine Scott   Impecunious scoundrel and brother of Undecimus; he demands a share in money Alaric Tudor has misappropriated in Anthony Trollope's *The Three Clerks.*

Mrs. Valentine Scott   Widowed mother of Clementina Golightly and wife of Captain Valentine Scott; she patronizes the Tudors in Anthony Trollope's *The Three Clerks.*

Harry Scott   Joe Scott's son, who spends his time at Moore's mill in Charlotte Brontë's *Shirley*.

Joe Scott   Overseer at Robert Moore's mill, who is well informed about the issues facing mill owners and believes this is not information that is of any use to young ladies in Charlotte Brontë's *Shirley*.

Tom Scott   Boy who works for Daniel Quilp and likes to walk on his hands; he is the only mourner when Quilp dies in Charles Dickens's *The Old Curiosity Shop*.

Undecimus (Undy) Scott   Unscrupulous stockjobber, who involves Alaric Tudor in shady business ventures in Anthony Trollope's *The Three Clerks*.

Brother Scotton   Deacon in the Reverend Broad's chapel, who gives legalistic advice on a way to eject the Allens in Mark Rutherford's *The Revolution In Tanner's Lane*.

Andie Scougal   Captain of the *Thistle*; he agrees to give Alan Breck Stewart clandestine passage to France in Robert Louis Stevenson's *Catriona*.

James Scout   Mrs. Slipslop's lover and Lady Booby's lawyer; he prepares false charges to prevent the marriage of Fanny Goodwill and Joseph Andrews in Booby's parish in Henry Fielding's *The History of the Adventures of Mr. Joseph Andrews and of his Friend Mr. Abraham Adams*.

Scragga   Son of Twala; a brutal executioner, he is killed by Sir Henry Curtis when he attempts to murder a tribeswoman, Foulata, as a sacrifice to their stone gods in H. Rider Haggard's *King Solomon's Mines*.

Lord Scrape   The author's former acquaintance, whose punishment for past usury and avarice is to give away his hoard as fee money to visiting souls in the City of Disease in Henry Fielding's *A Journey From This World to the Next*.

Samuel Scrape   Scots-speaking servant of Robert Colwan as Laird of Dalcastle; he warns him through anecdotes of the devil's deceitfulness in James Hogg's *The Private Memoirs and Confessions of a Justified Sinner*.

Mr. Scrobby   Litigious retired grocer with a grudge against Lord Rufford; he acquires the strychnine with which to poison a fox, causing uproar among the hunting set in Anthony Trollope's *The American Senator*.

Scroggs   Lord chief justice, trial judge when the Peverils are accused of treason in the Popish Plot in Sir Walter Scott's *Peveril of the Peak*.

Ebenezer Scrooge   Flint-hearted miser, whose typical response to others' good humor is "Bah! Humbug!"; he receives Christmas Eve visits from the ghost of his former partner and three Christmas Spirits, learns about human suffering and happiness and the importance of the Christmas season, and becomes a more humane, generous, and joyful employer, uncle, and citizen in Charles Dickens's *A Christmas Carol*.

Josiah Scroome   American congressman from the state of Mickewa who receives letters describing English customs from his friend Elias Gotobed in Anthony Trollope's *The American Senator*.

Earl of Scroope   Tall, thin, Dorsetshire landowner, who makes his nephew, Fred Neville, heir to Scrope Manor; after Fred's death, the estate comes to Fred's brother, Jack, in Anthony Trollope's *An Eye for an Eye*.

Lady Scroope (1)   Wife of Lord Scroope (1) and kind stepmother of Gertrude Marlowe in Sophia Lee's *The Recess*.

Lady Scroope (2)   Sister of the Duke of Norfolk and wife of Lord Scroope (2); she becomes the confidante of Mary, Queen of Scots in Sophia Lee's *The Recess*.

Lord Scroope (1)   Father of the illegitimate Gertrude Marlowe and Anthony Colville, the former of whom he raises with his legitimate heir in Sophia Lee's *The Recess*.

Lord Scroope (2)   The victim of Lord Burleigh's plotting; he falls from Queen Elizabeth's favor, loses his estate, and dies in confinement in Sophia Lee's *The Recess*.

Mary, Lady Scroope   Young second wife of the Earl of Scroope; when she learns that Fred Neville, the future heir, has seduced Kate O'Hara, she insists that no marriage take place and has her husband extract Fred's promise on that score; pangs of conscience later cause her to become a recluse in Anthony Trollope's *An Eye for an Eye*.

Lord Scrope   Young nobleman who is Plantagenet Cadurcis's drinking companion and attends him in his duel with Lord Monteagle in Benjamin Disraeli's *Venetia*.

George Scruby   Knowledgeable huntsman, who leads the way in the hunt at Manor Cross in which Adelaide Houghton dislocates her shoulder in Anthony Trollope's *Is He Popenjoy?*.

Mr. Scruby   Devious attorney, who masterminds George Vavasor's electioneering and helps him win a seat in Parliament briefly for Chelsea Districts in Anthony Trollope's *Can You Forgive Her?*.

Mr. Scruple   Lawyer and friend of Barnaby Boniface; his obstructionist tactics keep a simple lawsuit in British courts for thirteen years in an anecdote told by Mr. Fielding in Henry Brooke's *The Fool of Quality.*

Lord Scudabout   Impish aristocrat and an unwanted admirer of Azemia; he frightens her in a mausoleum in William Beckford's *Azemia.*

Fred Scully   Brother of Violet and in love with May Gould but interested in horses and a good time; he is unaware that May has had his child in George Moore's *A Drama in Muslin.*

Violet Scully   One of five graduating debutantes; thin and elegant, but with narrow intelligence, she successfully schemes to defeat Olive Barton in becoming titled in George Moore's *A Drama in Muslin.*

Jem Scuttle   Stableboy at the Dragon of Wantly inn who, according to Dan Stringer's belated testimony, stole the cheque and then emigrated to New Zealand, causing the chain of disasters involving Mr. Crawley in Anthony Trollope's *The Last Chronicle of Barset.*

Sea Captain   Intermediary between Savillon in Martinique and the de Roubignés; he brings that family erroneous news of Savillon's engagement to a wealthy heiress in Henry Mackenzie's *Julia de Roubigné.*

John Seacombe   William Crimsworth's uncle on his mother's side who does little to help the Crimsworth family after Mr. Crimsworth's death in Charlotte Brontë's *The Professor.*

Sarah Seacombe   One of John Seacombe's six daughters; William Crimsworth's rejection of her as a possible wife leads to her father's indifference to his welfare in Charlotte Brontë's *The Professor.*

Sea Eagle (Long-hoary)   Ancient sea rover and grandfather of Puny Fox; he accompanies Hallblithe of the Raven to the Glittering Plain and thereby renews his youth in William Morris's *The Story of the Glittering Plain.*

Earl of Seaforth   A general in the Covenanters' service who forms a second army against Montrose in Sir Walter Scott's *A Legend of Montrose.*

Sea-goddess   Sea nymph who reveals to Gebirus how to keep Charoba's demons from destroying the city he wishes to build for her in the appended romance "The History of Charoba, Queen of Egypt" in Clara Reeve's *The Progress of Romance.*

Goody Seagrim   Black George's wife, who tries to advance her daughter, Molly, first as a maid to Sophia, then as mistress to Thomas Square in Henry Fielding's *The History of Tom Jones.*

Betty Seagrim   Molly's elder sister; she informs Tom Jones of Molly's infidelities to punish her for her affair with Betty's former beau, Will Barnes, in Henry Fielding's *The History of Tom Jones.*

George (Black George) Seagrim   Allworthy's gamekeeper, father of Molly; despite Tom's past generosity, he ungratefully steals Tom's five hundred pounds; later, he carries Tom's messages to Sophia in Henry Fielding's *The History of Tom Jones.*

Molly Seagrim   Black George's comely, coarse second daughter, who charms Tom Jones; the discovery that her favorite and first love is Will Barnes relieves Tom of responsibility for her pregnancy in Henry Fielding's *The History of Tom Jones.*

Granny Seamore   Village gossip who encourages Martha Garland's belief that Anne Garland favors the braggart Festus Derriman in Thomas Hardy's *The Trumpet-Major.*

Anne Seaway   Woman whom Aeneas Manston prevails on to act the part of his returned first wife; her suspicions of his motives aroused, she follows him and witnesses his removal and burying of Eunice Manston's body in Thomas Hardy's *Desperate Remedies.*

Sebastes of Mitylene   Robber and assassin of the Immortal Guard, slain by Robert of Paris in his escape from the Blacquernal dungeons in Sir Walter Scott's *Count Robert of Paris.*

Sebastian   Octavio's elderly, misogynist uncle, who becomes so enamored of Sylvia that he asks her to marry him in spite of her affair with Octavio; he discovers Octavio and Sylvia together in his house and is killed when a gun misfires in the ensuing scuffle in Aphra Behn's *Love Letters Between a Nobleman and His Sister.*

Sebastian   Italian colonel from Modena; he comes to plead with Lord Grey in Ireland for the Spaniards but behaves badly, attacking Amyas Leigh, in Charles Kingsley's *Westward Ho!.*

The Sebastocrator (Protosebastos)   Official next in rank to Emperor Alexius Comnenus in Sir Walter Scott's *Count Robert of Paris.*

Mr. Sebright   Oculist opposed to Herr Gross's operation on Lucilla Finch; he regards her blindness as incurable and is not surprised when it recurs in Wilkie Collins's *Poor Miss Finch.*

Lieutenant J. Lascelles Sebright   First officer of H.M.S. *Tempest* who recognizes Norris Carthew when he boards; he gives first Loudon Dodd, then Harry Bellairs,

Carthew's address in Robert Louis Stevenson's *The Wrecker*.

Secret Messenger from the king; he tells Christiana to go on her pilgrimage in John Bunyan's *The Pilgrim's Progress From this World to That Which Is to Come*.

Secretary of the Charity A former attorney's clerk, who uses the charity as a means of providing for himself in Charles Johnstone's *Chrysal: or, The Adventures of a Guinea*.

Mr. Secretary Secretary for a London radical political club, who is bribed to spy for the government, and who is assassinated in Mark Rutherford's *The Revolution In Tanner's Lane*.

Miss Sedate Temporary object of George Edwards's love in John Hill's *The Adventures of Mr. George Edwards, a Creole*.

Mr. Sedate Father of Miss Sedate and, as member of the Royal Society, butt of the satire on projectors (originators of philosophic projects) in John Hill's *The Adventures of Mr. George Edwards, a Creole*.

Sir Francis Seddley Skilled surgeon from London who operates on Stanley Lake and saves his life after his duel with Sir Harry Bracton in J. Sheridan Le Fanu's *Wylder's Hand*.

Caroline Sedgeley Niece of Lord and Lady Bendham; she accepts the younger William Norwynne as husband, though she cares as little for him as he does for her; her unspoken passion is for his cousin, Henry; she later is caught in adultery, is divorced, and marries her libertine lover in Elizabeth Inchbald's *Nature and Art*.

Susan (Suky) Sedgemoor Greaves Oakley's beloved, who nearly dies of grief at his disappearance and is restored to life by his return in Tobias Smollett's *The Adventures of Sir Launcelot Greaves*.

Nic Sedgett Robert Armstrong Eccles's churlish enemy; he marries Dahlia Fleming, Edward Blancove's cast-off mistress, for a large sum of money, but the discovery of his previous marriage invalidates their union in George Meredith's *Rhoda Fleming*.

Lady Alice Sedgewick Sister of the Marquis of Worthing and a member of the aristocratic society in George Moore's *A Modern Lover*.

Sedley Young traveler, who, like Harley, must learn to distinguish between true benevolence and the appearance of it in Henry Mackenzie's *The Man of Feeling*.

Mr. Sedley Rakish anti-hero stabbed to death by Mr. Mortimer, whose wife Sedley has raped in S. J. Pratt's *Pupil of Pleasure*.

Mrs. Sedley Good-natured wife of John Sedley in her prosperity but harsh toward Amelia Sedley when she becomes poor in William Makepeace Thackeray's *Vanity Fair*.

Amelia Sedley Amiable, gentle, and loving daughter of John Sedley, whose bankruptcy nearly breaks off her marriage to George Osborne but who marries him against his father's wishes and is widowed at Waterloo; financial need and her son's perceived best interests impel her to give him up to his paternal grandfather; her eyes opened by Becky Sharp to the true character of her late husband, she finally marries the faithful William Dobbin in William Makepeace Thackeray's *Vanity Fair*.

Joan Sedley (John Matcham) Tall, brave, beautiful orphan, whose marriage has been bought by Sir Daniel Brackley; disguised as John Matcham, she has many adventures traveling to Hollywood with Dick Shelton; she runs away from Brackley; after several mishaps she marries Shelton in Robert Louis Stevenson's *The Black Arrow: A Tale of Two Roses*.

John Sedley Stockbroker whose failure drags down his family in William Makepeace Thackeray's *Vanity Fair*.

Joseph (Jos) Sedley Fat and gluttonous Collector of Boggley Wallah; he is attracted to Becky Sharp when she comes from school to the Sedleys' house and is subsequently ensnared by her at Pumpernickel; he insures his life in her favor and dies in William Makepeace Thackeray's *Vanity Fair*.

Superintendent Seegrave Plodding officer of the Frizinghall police force; he carries out an initial inquiry into the theft of a priceless diamond from the Verinder household; he offends several people before Sergeant Cuff is called in on the case in Wilkie Collins's *The Moonstone. A Romance*.

Seekers of the Land Three drooping horsemen seeking the Acre of Undying; they pass Hallblithe of the Raven at his home garth; later they save his life in the mountains adjoining the Glittering Plain in William Morris's *The Story of the Glittering Plain*.

Captain Seelencooper Brutal superintendent of the East India Company's hospital, from which Adam Hartley rescues Richard Middlemas in Sir Walter Scott's *The Surgeon's Daughter*.

Mr. Seely Attorney for John Caldigate in the bigamy

trial; he is tempted to throw up the case, believing his client guilty in Anthony Trollope's *John Caldigate*.

Lady Helen Seely (Mrs. Seymour) Beautiful, strong-minded daughter of Lord and Lady Granderville; invited with her parents to Lucy Bentham's estate, she falls in love and elopes with Lewis Seymour, an artist Mrs. Bentham has sponsored and loved; after marriage she becomes disillusioned with Lewis's shallowness, his use of her social position for self-promotion and money, and his infidelity in George Moore's *A Modern Lover*. Disillusioned, she commits suicide; her body is discovered by Mike Fletcher, John Harding, John Norton, and Frank Escott, who make the action a subject of their aesthetic discussion; she leaves her estate to Mike in *Mike Fletcher*.

Segarva Epistolary intimate of Count Louis de Montauban in Henry Mackenzie's *Julia de Roubigné*.

Seithenyn ap Seithyn Saidi Lord High Commissioner of Royal Embankments who drinks up the profits and allows the walls to collapse; having apparently ended his life by throwing himself into the flood, he reappears years later, assists Taliesin in the restoration of Queen Gwenyvar to King Arthur, and becomes second butler to Arthur in Thomas Love Peacock's *The Misfortunes of Elphin*.

George Selby Husband of Harriet Byron's aunt, Marianne Selby, and father of Nancy and Lucy in Samuel Richardson's *Sir Charles Grandison*.

Lucy Selby Daughter of George and Marianne Selby and Harriet Byron's principal correspondent in Samuel Richardson's *Sir Charles Grandison*.

Marianne Selby Aunt and occasional advice-giving correspondent of Harriet Byron in Samuel Richardson's *Sir Charles Grandison*.

Nancy Selby Lucy Selby's sister in Samuel Richardson's *Sir Charles Grandison*.

Selden One of Sir Daniel Brackley's aides sent to capture Joan Sedley; he and his six men are ambushed, taunted, and killed by Ellis Duckworth and his men as Dick Shelton and Joan watch in Robert Louis Stevenson's *The Black Arrow: A Tale of Two Roses*.

Selden Convicted murderer sentenced to life imprisonment, who escapes from Dartmoor and is found dead in Arthur Conan Doyle's *The Hound of the Baskervilles*.

Self-will Character in a story told by Honest; he believed that he could practice the vices of biblical figures if he possessed their virtues in John Bunyan's *The Pilgrim's Progress From this World to That Which Is to Come*.

Mr. Selkirk Village schoolmaster, who teaches Latin by means of games and physical exercises in Richard Graves's *The Spiritual Quixote*.

Mr. Selvin Ignorant, pedantic windbag whom Arabella innocently exposes at Bath; he is part of a complicated farce in which he competes with Mr. Tinsel to alternately insult and court Arabella in Charlotte Lennox's *The Female Quixote*.

Harriot Selvyn Lady Emilia Reynolds's illegitimate child, who is raised by Mr. Selvyn, and who sets an example of female propriety for Lady Mary Jones in Sarah Scott's *A Description of Millenium Hall*.

Mr. Selvyn Gentleman who brings up the illegitimate daughter of Lady Emilia Reynolds to be a model of female propriety in Sarah Scott's *A Description of Millenium Hall*.

Mrs. Selwyn Neighbor of Arthur Villars; she escorts Evelina Anville Belmont to Bristol for her health and forces Sir John Belmont to meet Evelina in Frances Burney's *Evelina*.

Mrs. Selwyn Ill-natured aunt of Sir Thomas Sindall; she fancies herself a philosopher in Henry Mackenzie's *The Man of the World*.

Mr. Popular Sentiment (caricature of Charles Dickens) Famous novelist of the day, active in social causes; he dashes off a novel, *Almshouse*, causing Mr. Harding further grief in Anthony Trollope's *The Warden*.

Lord Senton Member of the landed gentry, a neighbor of Lucy Bentham; he desperately woos her and then Lady Helen Seely in George Moore's *A Modern Lover*.

Baron Sergius (characterization of Metternich) Ambassador and political mastermind of an unnamed Continental kingdom in Benjamin Disraeli's *Endymion*.

Serjeant Man who gives Chrysal to the Sutler for a meal in Charles Johnstone's *Chrysal: or, the Adventures of a Guinea*.

Serjeant Traveler on the wagon who speaks of his war exploits and proves his valour with an oath at every word in Charles Johnstone's *Chrysal: or, The Adventures of a Guinea*.

Serjeant Soldier who encourages Tom Jones to fight the Pretender in the Jacobite rebellion; he tries to cheat Tom when selling him a sword in Henry Fielding's *The History of Tom Jones*.

Serle Mr. Woodhouse's trusted and lauded cook,

whose productions are nevertheless sometimes rejected as unwholesome in Jane Austen's *Emma*.

Servant Lover Servant of the Keeper of Mock Monastery; he was deprived of an inheritance and is hanged for forgery in Charles Johnstone's *Chrysal: or, The Adventures of a Guinea*.

Servant-Maid Traveler on the wagon who is going to London to repair a cracked reputation and who listens to the Methodist Preacher with complacency and attention in Charles Johnstone's *Chrysal: or, The Adventures of a Guinea*.

Servant's Servant A man who sprang from the dregs of the people and yet acquires vast wealth by studying the tempers of those around him and using what he has learned to his own advantage in Charles Johnstone's *Chrysal: or, The Adventures of a Guinea*.

Major Settle Neighbor of the Moreland estate who talks importantly about unimportant subjects in Henry Brooke's *The Fool of Quality*.

Helen Sevely Titled, rich widow of thirty-three; she attracts Frank Escott; at the music hall and at Mount Rorke they meet Mike Fletcher and the novelist John Harding, whom she also attracts in George Moore's *Spring Days*.

Julia Severn Pupil at Lowood School who is forced by a raging Mr. Brocklehurst to have her natural red curls cut off to conform to the plain style he demands in Charlotte Brontë's *Jane Eyre*.

Dr. John (Jack) Seward Unsuccessful suitor of Lucy Westenra and director of a hospital for mental patients; when Lucy falls ill, he summons his old teacher, Dr. Van Helsing, who is essential in the defeat of Dracula in Bram Stoker's *Dracula*.

Lewis Seymour Handsome, struggling artist who succeeds through women, including Lucy Bentham and Lady Helen Seely, the wealthy, beautiful aristocrat whom he marries; he connives to gain commissions and Academy membership; his shallowness is recognized by those who love him in George Moore's *A Modern Lover*.

Catherine Seyton Lord Seyton's beautiful and charming daughter; she waits upon Queen Mary of Scotland during her captivity in Lochleven Castle, using her wit to entertain the queen; she encourages her lover, Roland Graeme, to assist in Mary's escape and returns to Scotland to marry him in Sir Walter Scott's *The Abbot*.

Lord George Seyton Catherine and Henry Seyton's father; a loyal supporter of Queen Mary of Scotland, he becomes impoverished following the battle at Langside;

by gaining the favor of James VI, however, he recovers his estates in Sir Walter Scott's *The Abbot*.

Henry Seyton Lord Seyton's daring and temperamental son, who bears a striking resemblance to his twin sister, Catherine, a fact which causes some consternation for Roland Graeme; a key figure in Queen Mary of Scotland's escape, he falls in the battle at Langsfield in Sir Walter Scott's *The Abbot*.

Signora Juliana Sforza Sister to the Marchese della Porretta; she is entrusted with the custody of Lady Clementina della Porretta, whom she abuses with the hope of driving her into a nunnery and thereby freeing her fortune in Samuel Richardson's *Sir Charles Grandison*.

Laurana Sforza Daughter of Signora Juliana Sforza; she conspires in the cruel treatment of her cousin, Lady Clementina della Porreta, hoping to marry Clementina's suitor the Count of Belvedere and to acquire Clementina's fortune; the destruction of her hopes drives her to suicide in Samuel Richardson's *Sir Charles Grandison*.

Shaban Dwarf and a loyal friend of Emir Fakreddin; he helps stage the feigned deaths of Nouronihar and Gulchenrouz in William Beckford's *Vathek*.

Bernard Shackle Owner of a private madhouse in London who is forced to free Sir Launcelot Greaves in Tobias Smollett's *The Adventures of Sir Launcelot Greaves*.

Shadow Anodos's acquisition in the Church of Darkness (the house of the ogre), which blights nature and disenchants reality and is lost by Anodos when he learns the nature of love in George MacDonald's *Phantastes*.

Edris al Shafei Religious emissary to Mecca who watches with horror as Vathek defiles a religious relic brought from the holy city in William Beckford's *Vathek*.

Ettie Shafter American woman who is the first wife of Birdy Edwards; she dies in California in Arthur Conan Doyle's *The Valley of Fear*.

Ned Shafton Condemned Jacobite imprisoned at Newgate in Sir Walter Scott's *Rob Roy*.

Sir Piercie Shafton (The Knight of Wilverton) Handsome and brave courtier; he is blamed for a Catholic plot, which he has undertaken with the Earl of Northumberland, and is imprisoned in the Tower of Glendearg; he duels with Halbert Glendinning over Mary Avenel and marries Mysie Happer in Sir Walter Scott's *The Monastery*.

Mr. Shagg The London dressmaker of the recently returned and newly wealthy Lady Juliana Douglas in Susan Ferrier's *Marriage*.

Shagpat   Clothier upon whom Noorna bin Noorka plants the Identical in order to outwit Karaz; he becomes the object of adoration in Oolb, renamed Shagpat, where no one shaves, following the fashion of Shagpat himself, who remains unaware of the source of people's adoration; after the Identical is shaved off he loses his followers in George Meredith's *The Shaving of Shagpat*.

Shagram   Martin Tacket's old pony in Sir Walter Scott's *The Monastery*.

William Shakespeare   Poet and player; Robert Dudley, Earl of Leicester, meeting him, accuses him of wizardry in an elaborate compliment in Sir Walter Scott's *Kenilworth*. The author encounters his soul in Elysium in Henry Fielding's *A Journey From This World to the Next*.

Shame   Faithful's adversary, who argues that religion is foolish and unworthy of man in John Bunyan's *The Pilgrim's Progress From this World to That Which Is to Come*.

Dr. Shand   Country physician and father of a large family, including a son, Dick, who emigrates to Australia in Anthony Trollope's *John Caldigate*.

Dick Shand   Jovial friend of John Caldigate; both try their fortunes gold prospecting in Australia, but Dick takes to drink and disappears; he returns to England and gives testimony which releases his former partner from jail after his trial for bigamy in Anthony Trollope's *John Caldigate*.

Maria Shand   Third daughter of an Essex physician; she falls hopelessly in love with John Caldigate in Anthony Trollope's *John Caldigate*.

Charles Shandon   Attractive but improvident journalist; his debts send him to Fleet Prison, where he continues to work in William Makepeace Thackeray's *The History of Pendennis*. He also appears in *The Newcomes* and in *The Adventures of Philip on His Way through the World*.

Mrs. Charles Shandon   Loyal, admiring, good-hearted wife of Captain Charles Shandon in William Makepeace Thackeray's *The History of Pendennis*. Widowed, she marries Shandon's friend Jack Finucane in *The Adventures of Philip on His Way through the World*.

Mrs. Shandy   Walter Shandy's wife and Tristram Shandy's mother; not stupid, but unlearned and intellectually eclipsed by her husband, she is well equipped to bear his eccentricities by virtue of her remarkable insouciance in Laurence Sterne's *The Life and Opinions of Tristram Shandy, Gentleman*.

Bobby Shandy   Tristram Shandy's older brother, ungifted and fat, who dies just in time to save his father the expense of launching him on his European tour in Laurence Sterne's *The Life and Opinions of Tristram Shandy, Gentleman*.

Toby (Captain, Uncle Toby) Shandy   Tristram Shandy's uncle, a retired soldier, modest and kindhearted almost to the point of simple-mindedness; he was wounded in the groin at the Siege of Namur and became obsessed with constructing scale-model fortifications and reenacting military sieges in Laurence Sterne's *The Life and Opinions of Tristram Shandy, Gentleman*.

Tristram Shandy   First-person narrator, who is not born until approximately one hundred pages into his memoirs and appears rarely afterwards in his own narrative in Laurence Sterne's *The Life and Opinions of Tristram Shandy, Gentleman*.

Walter Shandy   Tristram Shandy's father, master of Shandy Hall; a wealthy, retired tradesman and dilettante scholar, he is an obstinate, peevish, but essentially generous man, of eccentric views and paradoxical notions defended with a great show of learning in Laurence Sterne's *The Life and Opinions of Tristram Shandy, Gentleman*.

Reuben Shapcott   Unsuccessful minister and journalist friend of Mark Rutherford; he helps him find his way in London, and he edits all Mark's novels after his death as Mark Rutherford's *The Autobiography of Mark Rutherford, Mark Rutherford's Deliverance, The Revolution in Tanner's Lane, Miriam's Schooling, Catherine Furze,* and *Clara Hopgood*.

Squire Shapely   Generic example of the "London Esquire" who leads a pretentious suburban existence; his description appears along with a humorous definition of a "country squire" in Richard Graves's *The Spiritual Quixote*.

Rebecca (Becky) Sharp   An impecunious artist's daughter, who becomes a free pupil at Miss Pinkerton's school; she makes friends with the Sedley family and nearly entraps Joseph Sedley before becoming governess to the Crawleys and marrying Rawdon Crawley, whom she supports by her wits until, being caught in a compromising situation with Lord Steyne, she loses her reputation, affluence, husband, and son; she recoups financial security through her dominance of Jos Sedley and is suspected of his death; she disinterestedly opens Amelia (Sedley) Osborne's eyes to the true character of her late husband in William Makepeace Thackeray's *Vanity Fair*.

Sharpe   Wizened smuggler, who meets Loudon Dodd in Hawaii with Speedy, Billy Fowler's partner who supplies capital in Robert Louis Stevenson's *The Wrecker*.

Jawster Sharpe   Liberal party candidate who runs against Nicholas Rigby for Parliament in Benjamin Disraeli's *Coningsby; or, The New Generation.*

Gideon Sharpitlaw   Edinburgh procurator-fiscal; he is an intelligent and observant police officer in Sir Walter Scott's *The Heart of Midlothian.*

Mr. Shatterbrain   London innkeeper who has made elaborate provisions for his own funeral, thus drawing the contempt of Dr. Greville in Richard Graves's *The Spiritual Quixote.*

Mr. Shaw   A tinker and free thinker; he gives Ernest Pontifex rejoinders to his religious statements that unnerve him in Samuel Butler's *The Way of All Flesh.*

Mrs. Shaw   Margaret Hale's aunt, whose comfortably wealthy house is a second home to Margaret in Elizabeth Gaskell's *North and South.*

Edith Shaw   Margaret Hale's fashionable, wealthy cousin, who marries Captain Cosmo Lennox; her London life is a contrast to Margaret's in Elizabeth Gaskell's *North and South.*

She (Ayesha, Hija, She-Who-Must-Be-Obeyed)   Fatally attractive white queen of the Amahagger who has waited two thousand years for the arrival of Leo Vincey, the reincarnation of her lover Kallikrates whom she murdered in a jealous rage; she undergoes a horrible transformation into a mummy and dies upon reentering the pillar of fire which first gave her the gift of longevity in H. Rider Haggard's *She.*

Sheelah   Old woman who, with the help of her herbal preparations and folk wisdom, looks after Cornelius O'Shane in Maria Edgeworth's *Ormond.*

Solomon Sheeppen   Nephew of Miss Griselda Ursula Ironside; he is a resident of Cambridge and a prize-winning poet who cannot write a line of poetry; he falls in love with Azemia and searches for her in William Beckford's *Azemia.*

Lady Sheerness   Pleasure-loving aunt of Lady Mary Jones; she dies unprepared and indebted, leaving Lady Mary without support in Sarah Scott's *A Description of Millenium Hall.*

Anne Shelburne   Nurse to Clarissa Harlowe in her final days in Samuel Richardson's *Clarissa: or, The History of a Young Lady.*

Sir Henry (Harry) Shelton   Dick's noble father, murdered by Sir Daniel Brackley at Moat House when Dick was a young child; the murder is avenged by Ellis Duckworth in Robert Louis Stevenson's *The Black Arrow: A Tale of Two Roses.*

Richard (Dick) Shelton   Sir Daniel Brackley's athletic young ward, raised in ignorance of his father's death; he aids John Matcham (Joan Sedley) in ignorance of her sex; he escapes Brackley, joins Ellis Duckworth's band, and is knighted by the future Richard III after the Battle of Shoreby; he marries Joan Sedley in Robert Louis Stevenson's *The Black Arrow: A Tale of Two Roses.*

Mr. Shenstone   Vicar at the village of Ipscombe; he is hopelessly in love with Rachel Henderson in Mrs. Humphry Ward's *Harvest.*

Mr. Shenstone   Learned gentleman and an old acquaintance of Geoffry Wildgoose; Wildgoose admires his elaborate landscaping at Leasowes but leaves the house during the night because, as he says in a note, he fears his friend has begun to worship the "idols" in his garden in Richard Graves's *The Spiritual Quixote.*

Shepherd   Disguised genius responsible for watching over Vathek; encountered by Vathek near Eblis's palace, he offers a last chance for salvation but is ignored by the prince in William Beckford's *Vathek.*

Shepherd near Hawick   Poor man who exchanges clothes with Robert Colwan, providing him with a disguise in James Hogg's *The Private Memoirs and Confessions of a Justified Sinner.*

Miss Shepherd   Pretty girl David Copperfield loves when he is a boy in Canterbury in Charles Dickens's *The Personal History of David Copperfield.*

John Shepherd   Agent to Sir Walter Elliot and father of Mrs. Clay; adept at flattery like his daughter, he persuades Sir Walter to rent his estate to Admiral Croft in Jane Austen's *Persuasion.*

Joan Sheppard   Destitute, widowed mother of Jack Sheppard, befriended by Owen Wood; she becomes distraught at her son's criminal career, falls into the power of Jonathan Wild, and dies before she can enjoy her actual station in life; she is revealed to be the long lost Constance Trenchard, kidnapped by Gypsies as an infant; sister of Sir Rowland Trenchard, she is heir to the family fortune in William Harrison Ainsworth's *Jack Sheppard.*

John (Jack) Sheppard   Thief and jail-breaker, adopted and apprenticed by Owen Wood, despite whose care he takes to crime; he falls under the fatal influence of Jonathan Wild, makes various celebrated escapes from prison, and is finally hanged at Tyburn, though he turns out to be, through his mother, the heir to a fortune in William Harrison Ainsworth's *Jack Sheppard*.

Peggy Sheridan   A gardener's attractive daughter, who is almost seduced by Harry Ormond; realizing his error, Ormond is quick to help her marry her love and his friend, Moriarty Carroll, in Maria Edgeworth's *Ormond*.

Theodore Sherlock   Young clergyman who becomes involved in public theological debates against Rufus Lyon in George Eliot's *Felix Holt, the Radical*.

Mr. Sherrick   Vulgar, socially ambitious wine merchant and moneylender; he increases the popularity of Charles Honeyman's chapel after taking it on as a business investment in William Makepeace Thackeray's *The Newcomes*.

Mrs. Sherrick   Mr. Sherrick's wife, a former opera singer in William Makepeace Thackeray's *The Newcomes*.

Julia Sherrick   Mr. Sherrick's handsome daughter, who marries Charles Honeyman in William Makepeace Thackeray's *The Newcomes*.

Mr. Sherwin   Prosperous linen draper, vulgar, assertive, and greedy for wealth and social advancement; he expects to rise by Basil's passion for his beautiful daughter, Margaret; his vanity and misunderstanding of Margaret's nature have tragic consequences in Wilkie Collins's *Basil: A Story of Modern Life*.

Mrs. Sherwin   Margaret Sherwin's timid and suppressed but observant mother; her dying testimony to Basil infuriates her husband by confirming Margaret's guilt in Wilkie Collins's *Basil: A Story of Modern Life*.

Margaret Sherwin   Linen draper's beautiful but corrupt daughter, with whom Basil falls so helplessly in love that he agrees to a year-long unconsummated marriage; she is caught by her husband in a tryst with Robert Mannion; she contracts typhoid from another hospital patient when she visits the wounded Mannion; her guilt and vicious nature are confirmed by her delirious deathbed ravings in Wilkie Collins's *Basil: A Story of Modern Life*.

Godfrey Sherwood   Unreliable business partner of Will Warburton; he loses Will's money in a speculation but continues in vain to hope for better luck in George Gissing's *Will Warburton*.

Lady Sherwood   Noblewoman who, having become bored by pseudo-pastoralism, summons Geoffry Wildgoose for a discussion of religion in Richard Graves's *The Spiritual Quixote*.

William Shiel   One of the young men who first dig up the suicide's grave more than one hundred years after his death in James Hogg's *The Private Memoirs and Confessions of a Justified Sinner*.

Fred Shiner   Rich farmer and the one of Fancy Day's suitors preferred by her father; as churchwarden, he introduces an organ which supplants the parish choir in Thomas Hardy's *Under the Greenwood Tree*.

Shingfu   Chinese man, positive example of resilience after grief, in a story told by Lien Chi Altangi in Oliver Goldsmith's *The Citizen of the World*.

Henrietta Shirley   Exemplary grandmother of the orphaned Harriet Byron; she gives high-minded but practical advice as to suitors in Samuel Richardson's *Sir Charles Grandison*.

General Shoeneck   Austrian commander who allows Wilfrid Pole another chance in the army after his involvement in the escape of an Italian revolutionist in George Meredith's *Vittoria*.

Bartholomew Sholto   A son of the late Major John Sholto and twin brother of Thaddeus Sholto; he is found poisoned in Arthur Conan Doyle's *The Sign of Four*.

Thaddeus Sholto   A son of the late Major John Sholto and twin brother of Bartholomew Sholto in Arthur Conan Doyle's *The Sign of Four*.

Shoplifter   A sailor's poor widow, who tries to steal bread and cheese to feed her starving children in Charles Johnstone's *Chrysal: or, The Adventures of a Guinea*.

Lord Shoreby   Bald, gouty, infamous Lancastrian nobleman and Sir Daniel Brackley's ally, who meets secretly with Brackley to arrange his marriage to Joan Sedley in Robert Louis Stevenson's *The Black Arrow: A Tale of Two Roses*.

Harris (Trotters) Short   Partner with Tom Codlin in a traveling Punch and Judy show; he is friendly and affable but wonders if someone would pay to know where Nell Trent and her grandfather are in Charles Dickens's *The Old Curiosity Shop*.

Dr. Shrapnel   Nevil Beauchamp's radical mentor, horsewhipped by Beauchamp's uncle Everard Romfrey; Romfrey and Dr. Shrapnel are drawn together when Beauchamp is drowned after marrying Shrapnel's ward, Jenny Denham, in George Meredith's *Beauchamp's Career*.

Countess of Shrewsbury   Lady who claims to have shown King James proof of the marriage of Mary, Queen of Scots and the Duke of Norfolk in Sophia Lee's *The Recess*.

Earl of Shrewsbury   Guard of the imprisoned Mary, Queen of Scots and supporter of the Duke of Norfolk's plan to free her in Sophia Lee's *The Recess*. He is the fourth husband of Bess of Hardwicke (Elizabeth Cavendish) and the perplexed jailer of Queen Mary in Charlotte Yonge's *Unknown to History*.

Mr. Shuan   Sullen, dark, and cruel chief mate of the Scottish brig *Covenant*; he is peaceable when sober but abusive and dangerous when drunk; he beats Ransome the cabin-boy to death in Robert Louis Stevenson's *Kidnapped*.

Shufle   Curate who complains of his vicar's irresponsibility and whose background includes pimping in Tobias Smollett's *The Adventures of Roderick Random*.

Percy Sibwright   Young lawyer who is George Warrington and Arthur Pendennis's neighbor at Shepherd's Inn in William Makepeace Thackeray's *The History of Pendennis*.

Henry Sidney   Amiable friend of Harry Coningsby and third son of the Duke of Beaumanoir in Benjamin Disraeli's *Coningsby; or, The New Generation*.

Sir Philip Sidney (Sydney)   Gallant and refined nephew of Lord Leicester; after being disappointed in his passionate love for Matilda, he marries Miss Walsingham, who later becomes Lady Essex in Sophia Lee's *The Recess*.

Lady Theresa Sidney   One of Henry Sidney's beautiful sisters; Harry Coningsby is falsely rumored to be engaged to her in Benjamin Disraeli's *Coningsby; or, The New Generation*.

Sidonia   Incredibly wealthy and politically powerful Jewish intellectual and Harry Coningsby's mentor, who has exhausted all sources of human knowledge and devoted himself to the "eternal principles of human nature" in Benjamin Disraeli's *Coningsby; or, The New Generation*. He sympathizes with Tancred, Lord Montacute's wish to tour the Holy Land and provides letters of credit and introductions in *Tancred; or, The New Crusade*.

Nancy Sievewright   Pretty blacksmith's daughter, with whom Henry Esmond flirts in his youth; he catches smallpox from her brother, thus bringing the disease to the Castlewood family; Nancy dies of smallpox in William Makepeace Thackeray's *The History of Henry Esmond*.

Mr. Signsealer   Foolish magistrate and colleague of Squire Mountmeadow in Benjamin Disraeli's *Venetia*.

William (Bill) Sikes   Stout criminal, who works for Fagin as a burglar; he lives with Nancy and murders her when he finds out that she betrayed Fagin and Monks (Edward Leeford) in Charles Dickens's *Oliver Twist*.

Pere Silas   The French Jesuit priest who hears Lucy Snowe's confession; a former tutor of M. Paul, he counsels him against marrying Lucy in Charlotte Brontë's *Villette*.

Lucy Silborn (Brawn)   Prostitute who dupes the hero Benignus in S. J. Pratt's *Liberal Opinions upon Animals, Man, and Providence*.

Ben Silton   Crusty, right-minded baronet, who shares with Harley a coach ride from London and a discussion about poetry in Henry Mackenzie's *The Man of Feeling*.

Long John Silver (Barbecue)   One-legged, duplicitous pirate, Flint's quartermaster, who owns the Spy Glass pub and the parrot Captain Flint; hired as cook on the *Hispaniola*, he engineers the mutiny and later makes a deal for his life with Dr. Livesey; at a port on the return journey Ben Gunn allows him to escape with a small portion of the treasure in Robert Louis Stevenson's *Treasure Island*.

Plantagenet Palliser, Lord Silverbridge   Eldest child of Plantagenet and Lady Glencora Palliser; his birth delights his great-uncle, the old Duke of Omnium, in Anthony Trollope's *Can You Forgive Her?*. Lady Glencora, alive to his rights as heir, takes him with her to call on Madame Max Goesler in *Phineas Finn*. Having become Lord Silverbridge when his father succeeds to the title of Duke of Omnium, he is wild and undisciplined but not unprincipled; expelled from Oxford, he further disappoints his father by becoming a Conservative, running up huge racing debts, and wanting to marry an American, Isabel Boncassen; the duke pays his bills and becomes reconciled to the marriage and is gratified by Silverbridge's return to the Liberal politics of the family tradition in *The Duke's Children*.

Anne, "Mrs." Silvester (Mrs. John Vanborough)   Beautiful, talented singer, a Roman Catholic who is put aside at the age of forty-two by her husband on his discovering that the pre-nuptial date of his own conversion has invalidated the marriage; she resumes her maiden name with the prefix "Mrs." and becomes a music teacher but soon dies, leaving her now illegitimate daughter in the care of her lifelong friend Blanche, Lady Lundie in Wilkie Collins's *Man and Wife*.

Anne Silvester   Victim, first, of a technicality which invalidates the marriage of her parents, Anne ("Mrs." Silvester) and John Vanborough; a refined and high-minded governess to her beloved friend Blanche Lundie, she nevertheless falls victim to a seducer, Geoffrey Delamayn; expecting him to marry her, she waits at an inn and is surprised at the arrival, with Geoffrey's written promises and excuses, of his friend and Blanche's betrothed, Arnold Brinkworth; to prove Anne has no claim of any kind on him, Geoffrey later concocts the credible fraud of her "Scotch Marriage" to Arnold; in order to validate the marriage of Arnold and Blanche, Anne produces Geoffrey's letter which constitutes his own prior "Scotch Marriage" to her; thwarting Geoffrey, Anne knowingly endangers her life; after his death in the act of attempting her murder she marries Sir Patrick Lundie in Wilkie Collins's *Man and Wife*.

José da Silvestra Sixteenth-century Portuguese political refugee, who finds King Solomon's mines, makes a map, and freezes to death in a mountain cave before he can return; his body is found three hundred years later by Allan Quatermain in H. Rider Haggard's *King Solomon's Mines*.

José Silvestre Portuguese don who dies attempting to find King Solomon's mines but not before he gives his sixteenth-century ancestor's map to Allan Quatermain in H. Rider Haggard's *King Solomon's Mines*.

Donna Inez da Silviero The beautiful daughter of a wealthy Portuguese; she attracts a number of suitors but eventually marries Charles O'Malley's friend Fred Power in Charles Lever's *Charles O'Malley*.

Mr. Simkins A London borough man who is a guest at the party when Harrel kills himself in Frances Burney's *Cecilia*.

Mr. Simmery Stockbroker who shares an office and bets with Wilkins Flasher in Charles Dickens's *The Posthumous Papers of the Pickwick Club*.

Mr. Simmonds Bedfordshire surgeon in Samuel Richardson's *Pamela, or Virtue Rewarded*.

Miss Simmons Owner of the dressmaker's shop that employs Mary Barton in Elizabeth Gaskell's *Mary Barton*.

Henrietta Simmons Mrs. Jiniwin's friend, who has tea with her in Charles Dickens's *The Old Curiosity Shop*.

Simnel Sir Daniel Brackley's neighbor and one of his victims in Robert Louis Stevenson's *The Black Arrow: A Tale of Two Roses*.

Simon of Hackburn Spirited young borderer in favor of raiding an English farm to avenge the destruction of Hobbie (Halbert) Elliot's in Sir Walter Scott's *The Black Dwarf*.

Simon Peter Fisherman who, with his brothers, owns fishing boats in the employ of Dan of Arimathea; he and his brothers leave their business to follow Jesus in George Moore's *The Brook Kerith*.

Mr. Simper Surgeon who replaces Mackshane when Captain Whiffle takes command of the *Thunder* in Tobias Smollett's *The Adventures of Roderick Random*.

Simple One of three men Christian finds fettered and sleeping; he ignores Christian's warning and goes back to sleep in John Bunyan's *The Pilgrim's Progress From this World to That Which Is to Come*.

Camilla Simple Stepdaughter of Livia, who falsely charges her with the crime of incest with her brother Valentine; she marries David Simple in the happy ending of Sarah Fielding's *The Adventures of David Simple in Search of a Faithful Friend*. She writes to Cynthia about Leontine's envy of his wife Leontia's greater intelligence in *Familiar Letters between the Principal Characters of David Simple and Some Others*. She dies of sorrow after a series of overwhelming calamities in *David Simple. Volume the Last*.

Daniel Simple David Simple's cunning brother; he forges their father's will in order to disinherit the ingenuous David in Sarah Fielding's *The Adventures of David Simple in Search of a Faithful Friend*.

David Simple An ingenuous youth who is betrayed by his brother, Daniel; he searches the world for true friends and finds them in Valentine and Valentine's sister, Camilla, whom he marries in the happy ending of Sarah Fielding's *The Adventures of David Simple in Search of a Faithful Friend*. The persecution of the virtuous culminates in the deaths of David and Camilla in *David Simple. Volume the Last*.

Mr. Simpson Former horse changer imprisoned for debt in the Fleet prison; Samuel Pickwick is assigned to share his room in Charles Dickens's *The Posthumous Papers of the Pickwick Club*.

Mr. Simpson Cantankerous travelling companion to Henry Willoughton in Ann Radcliffe's *Gaston de Blondeville*.

Dick Simpson The shiftless help at the press-gang headquarters, whose evidence convicts Daniel Robson in Elizabeth Gaskell's *Sylvia's Lovers*.

Luckie Simson Zilia de Monçada's midwife during the birth of Richard Middlemas in Sir Walter Scott's *The Surgeon's Daughter*.

Sincere One of four Shepherds who show Christian

and Hopeful, and later Christiana and her party, the hills of Error, Caution, and Clear, and advise them on their journey in John Bunyan's *The Pilgrim's Progress From this World to That Which Is to Come.*

Mrs. Sinclair   See Sally Martin.

Lucy Sindall   Illegitimate daughter of Sir Thomas Sindall and Harriet Annesly; her evil father, ignorant of her identity, is determined to debauch her in Henry Mackenzie's *The Man of the World.*

Sir Thomas Sindall   Self-indulgent, manipulative, and dissipated villain, whose lust for Harriet Annesly leads him to deceive the father, corrupt the son, and rape Harriet; he eventually attempts to seduce his own daughter in Henry Mackenzie's *The Man of the World.*

Mr. Singleton   Sailor friend of the younger James Harlowe; he is said to be plotting to spirit Harlowe's sister Clarissa away from Robert Lovelace in Samuel Richardson's *Clarissa: or, The History of a Young Lady.*

Adrian Singleton   Young man whom Dorian Gray leads into a life of utter ruin and degradation in Oscar Wilde's *The Picture of Dorian Gray.*

Captain Bob Singleton (Seignior Capitano)   Pirate who was stolen at birth and sold to gypsies; left on an island with fellow crew members after a failed mutiny, he escapes from the island and travels through Africa; he becomes a pirate until he is later persuaded to give up that trade and become a penitent in Daniel Defoe's *The Life, Adventures, and Pyracies of the Famous Captain Singleton.*

Mr. Sink   Aged attorney; his refusal to pay his bills lands him and his creditors, now unable to pay their debts, in Fleet Prison for debt in Henry Brooke's *The Fool of Quality.*

Mrs. Sinnott   Housekeeper at Marlowe after Donica Gwynn moves to Wardlock Manor with Lady Alice Redcliffe in J. Sheridan Le Fanu's *Guy Deverell.*

Mr. Sircome   A miller in George Eliot's *Felix Holt, the Radical.*

Madame Siron   Owner of a hotel in Barbizon; she tells Norris Carthew of Loudon Dodd's arrival in Robert Louis Stevenson's *The Wrecker.*

Monsieur Siron   Six-foot owner of a hotel in Barbizon; he waits on Loudon Dodd and Norris Carthew in Robert Louis Stevenson's *The Wrecker.*

Carolina Wilhelmina Amelia Skeggs   Strumpet posing as a town lady; she is an acquaintance of Squire Thornhill in Oliver Goldsmith's *The Vicar of Wakefield.*

Mrs. Skelton   London procuress who poses as Julia Townsend's guide and protector and temporarily persuades her to trust the lascivious Mr. Blackman in Richard Graves's *The Spiritual Quixote.*

Lady Skettles   Wife of Sir Barnet Skettles in Charles Dickens's *Dombey and Son.*

Barnet Skettles   Son of Sir Barnet Skettles; he attends Dr. Blimber's school in Charles Dickens's *Dombey and Son.*

Sir Barnet Skettles   Man who meets Florence Dombey at the dance at Dr. Blimber's school, which his son will be attending; he later has Florence as a guest in his house in Charles Dickens's *Dombey and Son.*

Mrs. Skewton   Blooming, false old lady in a wheelchair and a devotee of nature; she is attended by her daughter, Edith Granger, whom she manipulated into a disastrous first marriage; she meets Paul Dombey in Leamington and lives with the Dombeys after their marriage; she dies from a stroke in Charles Dickens's *Dombey and Son.*

Miss Skiffins   John Wemmick's sweetheart in Charles Dickens's *Great Expectations.*

Charlotte, Lady Skifton   Selfish, neurotic mother of Gertrude Ross; she is dependent on her beautiful daughter, who therefore lacks a wise mother's counsel in Caroline Norton's *Old Sir Douglas.*

Skill   Physician who treats Matthew at House Beautiful in John Bunyan's *The Pilgrim's Progress From this World to That Which Is to Come.*

Mr. Skimpkin   Lawyer who is "junior" to Serjeant Buzfuz in Charles Dickens's *The Posthumous Papers of the Pickwick Club.*

Mrs. Skimpole   Delicate invalid wife of Harold Skimpole in Charles Dickens's *Bleak House.*

Arethusa Skimpole   The beautiful daughter of Harold Skimpole in Charles Dickens's *Bleak House.*

Harold Skimpole   John Jarndyce's friend who calls himself a "child"; he goes through life with a cheerful and whimsical irresponsibility, sponging off his friends; he receives a commission for bringing Mr. Vholes and Richard Carstone together, leading to Richard's ruin in Charles Dickens's *Bleak House.*

Kitty Skimpole   The funny daughter of Harold Skimpole in Charles Dickens's *Bleak House.*

Laura Skimpole　The sentimental daughter of Harold Skimpole in Charles Dickens's *Bleak House*.

Skinker　Boy who plays too roughly with young Harry Clinton and gets beaten in return in Henry Brooke's *The Fool of Quality*.

Dr. Skinner　Head of the school at Roughborough and a friend of Theobald Pontifex at Cambridge; universally acknowledged to be a genius, he is believed by the narrator to be a humbug; when he retires, he becomes dean of a cathedral in a Midland county in Samuel Butler's *The Way of All Flesh*.

Miss Skinner　Eldest daughter of Dr. Skinner; she is horrified that Ernest Pontifex does not like modern music (beginning with Bach); for her, one chord of Beethoven is happiness in Samuel Butler's *The Way of All Flesh*.

Deborah Skinner　Housemaid to the Clements; she robs the corpse of Lord Stivers and accuses Arabella Clement of the theft in Henry Brooke's *The Fool of Quality*.

Noah Skinner (Mr. Barkington)　Richard Hardie's clerk, who has observed his employer's financial manipulations; he was present when Captain Dodd deposited his £14,000 and snatched up the banker's receipt, using it to blackmail Hardie; he accidentally asphixiates himself, leaving his money to Julia Dodd and holding the missing receipt in his dead hand in Charles Reade's *Hard Cash*.

Mr. Skionar　(caricature of Samuel Taylor Coleridge) Poetical philosopher who settles all problems by means of sentiment and intuition in Thomas Love Peacock's *Crotchet Castle*.

Andrew Skurliewhitter　London scrivener, who serves Lord Dalgarno in the plot to take possession of Nigel Olifaunt's Scottish estate, plots for the murder of Lord Dalgarno by Captain Colepepper, and is a fugitive from the king's justice in Sir Walter Scott's *The Fortunes of Nigel*.

Mr. Slackbridge　Union organizer who reveals himself to be more concerned with political rhetoric than with the plight of the workers in Charles Dickens's *Hard Times*.

Dr. Slammer　Small, fat, bald surgeon of the Ninety-seventh Regiment, who attends the ball at the Bull Inn and challenges Nathaniel Winkle to a duel in Charles Dickens's *The Posthumous Papers of the Pickwick Club*.

Dr. Slash　Elderly surgeon, who reluctantly and incompetently examines Geoffry Wildgoose's head injury in Richard Graves's *The Spiritual Quixote*.

Dr. Slasher　Knife-happy surgeon and instructor at St. Bartholomew's Hospital, where Ben Allen and Bob Sawyer acquire their medical training in Charles Dickens's *The Posthumous Papers of the Pickwick Club*.

Hafen Slawkenbergius　Author of a treatise on noses which the narrator cites at length in Laurence Sterne's *The Life and Opinions of Tristram Shandy, Gentleman*.

Slay-good　Giant tormenting Feeble-mind; he is killed by Great-heart in John Bunyan's *The Pilgrim's Progress From this World to That Which Is to Come*.

Mr. Sleary　Kindhearted, lisping circus master, whose circus represents the human need for entertainment and amusement in opposition to the humorless values embodied in utilitarianism in Charles Dickens's *Hard Times*.

Josephine Sleary　Circus master Sleary's daughter, who marries horseback performer E. W. B. Childers and has a son who becomes a circus rider in Charles Dickens's *Hard Times*.

Sleddon　Groom to lawyer Josiah Larkin in J. Sheridan Le Fanu's *Wylder's Hand*.

Mr. Sleigh　Unpleasant attorney sent by Silas Ruthyn to the reading of his brother Austin Ruthyn's will in J. Sheridan Le Fanu's *Uncle Silas*.

Brother Slender　Staymaker who, as a follower of the Methodist leader Mr. Whitfield, has renounced his profession as sinful; he is introduced to Geoffry Wildgoose as a man who has not sinned for five years in Richard Graves's *The Spiritual Quixote*.

Mr. Slicer　Hypochondriac and enthusiastic user of patent medicines who introduces Geoffry Wildgoose to Mr. Selkirk and Gregory Griskin in Richard Graves's *The Spiritual Quixote*.

Quintus Slide　Muckraking editor of a gutter-press journal ostensibly dedicated to people's rights; he objects to Phineas Finn's condescension and attacks him in print; he later offers him a post as leader writer, and his enmity is cemented when Finn angrily refuses in Anthony Trollope's *Phineas Finn*. He steps up his attacks in *Phineas Redux*. Refused access to the (younger) Duke of Omnium's country estate, he launches thunderbolts against the Duke in *The Prime Minister*.

Peg Sliderskew　Housekeeper of Arthur Gride; conspiring with Wackford Squeers, she steals documents from Gride concerning Madeline Bray's inheritance; she is tried and transported for life for their theft in Charles Dickens's *The Life and Adventures of Nicholas Nickleby*.

Slimy　Demented drunkard, who robs Osmond Waymark and imprisons him when he comes to collect the rent in George Gissing's *The Unclassed.*

Slingo   Horse dealer for whom Edward (Tip) Dorrit works for a short time in Charles Dickens's *Little Dorrit.*

Mrs. Slipslop   Lady Booby's waiting-gentlewoman, who is given to malapropisms; she encourages and shares her lady's passion for Joseph Andrews; self-interest guides her actions throughout Henry Fielding's *The History of the Adventures of Mr. Joseph Andrews and of his Friend Mr. Abraham Adams.*

Dr. Slop   Short and squat Roman Catholic "man-midwife" who delivers Tristram Shandy, causing the malformation of his nose by misuse of the forceps in Laurence Sterne's *The Life and Opinions of Tristram Shandy, Gentleman.*

Obadiah Slope   Greasy chaplain of Bishop Proudie intent on holding supreme power in Barchester close and on marrying the propertied widow, Eleanor Bold; his rebellion against Mrs. Proudie and his unexpected passion for the Signora Neroni prove his undoing in Anthony Trollope's *Barchester Towers.*

Sloppy   Child who is looked after by Betty Higden; later, taken in by the Boffins, he learns woodworking in Charles Dickens's *Our Mutual Friend.*

Sloth   One of three men Christian finds fettered and sleeping; he ignores Christian's warning and goes back to sleep in John Bunyan's *The Pilgrim's Progress From this World to That Which Is to Come.*

Tilly Slowboy   Adolescent nursemaid to the Peerybingle baby; she is a foundling with a curious knack for endangering her infant charge in Charles Dickens's *The Cricket on the Hearth.*

Arthur Slowe   Resident of Chapelizod whom Magnolia Macnamara would like to marry for his money in J. Sheridan Le Fanu's *The House by the Churchyard.*

Richard Sludge (Dickie, Dickon, Flibbertigibbet)   Ugly, impish boy, who introduces Edmund Tressilian and Wayland Smith; at the Kenilworth revels he obtains entrance for Wayland and Amy Robsart Dudley but later steals the letter in which she explains her situation to her husband, Robert Dudley, Earl of Leicester; the loss of this letter makes plausible Richard Varney's accusation of adultery against Amy in Sir Walter Scott's *Kenilworth.*

Mr. Slum   Military gentleman who writes poetical advertisements for Mrs. Jarley's waxworks in Charles Dickens's *The Old Curiosity Shop.*

Samuel Slumkey   The Blue Party's candidate to Parliament from Eatanswill, who is running against Horatio Fizkin in Charles Dickens's *The Posthumous Papers of the Pickwick Club.*

Mr. Slurk   Editor of *The Eatanswill Independent* and rival of Mr. Pott in Charles Dickens's *The Posthumous Papers of the Pickwick Club.*

James Sly   Fellow thief who impeaches Thomas Fierce to save his own skin in Henry Fielding's *The Life of Mr. Jonathan Wild the Great.*

Lucy Sly   One of the nine pupils of Mrs. Teachum's school; her cunning is made the object of critical scrutiny in Sarah Fielding's *The Governess.*

Richard Sly   Thief and thief-taker in Charles Johnstone's *Chrysal: or, The Adventures of a Guinea.*

Sam Slybore   Young painter in William Beckford's *Modern Novel Writing; or, the Elegant Enthusiast.*

Chevy (Chiv) Slyme   Disreputable, unkempt nephew of Martin Chuzzlewit; he believes himself to be a man of unappreciated literary talents and begs through his agent Montague Tigg in Charles Dickens's *The Life and Adventures of Martin Chuzzlewit.*

Mr. Smales   A kindly chemist, father of Harriet and uncle of Julian Casti; he kills himself when he goes bankrupt, having made Julian promise to care for Harriet in George Gissing's *The Unclassed.*

Harriet Smales   Shop girl and cousin of Julian Casti; she tricks him into marriage, becomes a shrew, and jealously accuses Ida Starr of theft and has her sent to prison in George Gissing's *The Unclassed.*

Jonathan Small   Former soldier who served in India, where he was maimed by a crocodile; later convicted of murdering a wealthy merchant, he served a prison sentence in the Andaman Islands; he is guilty of the murder of Bartholomew Sholto in Arthur Conan Doyle's *The Sign of Four.*

Dr. Polycarp Small   Rigidly orthodox vicar of Rookwood in William Harrison Ainsworth's *Rookwood.*

Lydia (Liddy) Smallbury   Bathsheba Everdene's servant girl who consistently demonstrates a selfless concern for Bathsheba; remarkably straightforward and daring, she participates in her mistress's scheme to taunt farmer Boldwood with an anonymous "love note" in Thomas Hardy's *Far from the Madding Crowd.*

Mrs. Smallridge   Mrs. Suckling's friend in whose

household Jane Fairfax accepts employment as a governess, breaking her secret engagement to Frank Churchill; the renewal and the acknowledgement of the engagement make the employment unnecessary in Jane Austen's *Emma*.

Mrs. Smallweed   Senile wife of Joshua Smallweed; she speaks in terms of quantities of money and is continually irritating her husband in Charles Dickens's *Bleak House*.

Bartholomew (Bart, Chick) Smallweed   Fourteen-year-old clerk for Kenge and Carboy; small, sharp, and precociously aged, he exhibits the family characteristics of rapaciousness and miserliness; he is a crony of Mr. Guppy in Charles Dickens's *Bleak House*.

Joshua Smallweed   Bart Smallweed's aged and physically helpless grandfather; a miserly moneylender, he works with Mr. Tulkinghorn by threatening Trooper George (George Rouncewell) with foreclosure on his shooting gallery unless George can deliver a sample of Hawdon's handwriting to Tulkinghorn in Charles Dickens's *Bleak House*.

Judith (Judy) Smallweed   Hard, sharp twin sister of Bart Smallweed; her frequent task is to shake up and straighten in his chair her grandfather, Joshua Smallweed, in Charles Dickens's *Bleak House*.

Mr. Smangle   Flashy cellmate of Samuel Pickwick in the Fleet debtors' prison in Charles Dickens's *The Posthumous Papers of the Pickwick Club*.

Mr. Smart   Delicate, limp-looking first master at the Salem House school in Charles Dickens's *The Personal History of David Copperfield*.

Tom Smart   Salesman for Bilson and Slum in "The Bagman's Tale," told by a one-eyed bagman in Charles Dickens's *The Posthumous Papers of the Pickwick Club*.

John Smauker   Angelo Cyrus Bantam's footman, who invites Sam Weller to a "swarry" of select footmen in Bath in Charles Dickens's *The Posthumous Papers of the Pickwick Club*.

Nabal Smeddum   Tobacconist who stirs up opposition to James Pawkie, the town provost, over repairs to the kirk; Pawkie defeats him in a legal action financed from "the public purse" in John Galt's *The Provost*.

Andrew Smee   Drawing teacher who wants to marry Jane Osborne and is turned out of the house by her father in William Makepeace Thackeray's *Vanity Fair*.

Smelfungus   (parody of Tobias Smollett) Learned but

splenetic traveler Yorick encounters in Calais in Laurence Sterne's *A Sentimental Journey through France and Italy*.

Smid   Goth warrior, armorer to the party led by Amalric in Charles Kingsley's *Hypatia*.

Putnam Smif   Poetic, self-exalted clerk in an American dry-goods store, who petitions young Martin Chuzzlewit for introductions to Englishmen who would pay his expenses in visiting their country in Charles Dickens's *The Life and Adventures of Martin Chuzzlewit*.

Joseph Smiggers   Perpetual vice-president and member of the Pickwick Club in Charles Dickens's *The Posthumous Papers of the Pickwick Club*.

Smike   Son of Ralph Nickleby, but hidden away from the world, beaten, and starved by Wackford Squeers at Dotheboys Hall in Yorkshire; Nicholas Nickleby befriends him and takes him along when they leave the school; Smike later dies in Charles Dickens's *The Life and Adventures of Nicholas Nickleby*.

Mr. Smiler   Thief convicted with Mr. Benjamin of the theft of the Eustace necklace in Anthony Trollope's *The Eustace Diamonds*.

Maria Smiley   Robust widow friend of Mrs. Moulder, who pushes her reluctant brother, John Kenneby, into marriage with Maria in Anthony Trollope's *Orley Farm*.

Tom Smirk   Foppish clerk, to whom Laetitia Snap surrenders her charms; she has just repulsed Jonathan Wild, citing her chastity and virtue, in Henry Fielding's *The Life of Mr. Jonathan Wild the Great*.

Mr. Smirke   Curate at Clavering and Arthur Pendennis's tutor; he foolishly confesses his love for Helen Pendennis in William Makepeace Thackeray's *The History of Pendennis*.

Augustus Smirkie   Harassed rector of modest means and a widower with five children; he marries Julia Babington in Anthony Trollope's *John Caldigate*.

Smith   One of the partners in Burlington and Smith, a London law firm that conspires with the lawyer Josiah Larkin in his machinations against William Wylder in J. Sheridan Le Fanu's *Wylder's Hand*.

Smith   One of Sir Daniel Brackley's men killed in battle at Risingham in Robert Louis Stevenson's *The Black Arrow: A Tale of Two Roses*.

Miss Smith   Needlework teacher at Lowood School, who looks after the children's clothing in Charlotte Brontë's *Jane Eyre*.

Mr. Smith A grocer and the second man with whom Agnes Grey's father overextends his credit in Anne Brontë's *Agnes Grey*.

Mr. Smith Lodger in Mr. Branghton's London house; he tries to court Evelina Anville Belmont and is himself the object of Biddy Branghton's marital designs in Frances Burney's *Evelina*.

Mr. Smith Mary Smith's kindly father, who becomes adviser to Matilda Jenkyns in Elizabeth Gaskell's *Cranford*.

Mrs. Smith Widowed invalid and former school friend of Anne Elliot; her late husband lost his fortune when led into extravagance by William Elliot; she reveals William's wickedness to Anne in Jane Austen's *Persuasion*.

Mrs. Smith Owner of Allenham Court and the strict, invalid, elderly cousin of John Willoughby; her disinheriting Willoughby for his behavior to Eliza Williams drives him to leave Marianne Dashwood in order to secure an heiress in Jane Austen's *Sense and Sensibility*.

Mrs. Smith Poor old woman whom Colonel Jack robs; he later feels remorse and restores the money to her in Daniel Defoe's *The History and the Remarkable Life of the Truly Honourable Colonel Jacques, Commonly Call'd Col. Jack*.

Mrs. Smith Farmer's wife who cares for Virginia St. Pierre in Maria Edgeworth's *Belinda*.

Mrs. ("Goody") Smith Glove maker and seller, who runs the rooming house in Covent Garden where Clarissa Harlowe dies, and whose kindness eases Clarissa's final days in Samuel Richardson's *Clarissa: or, The History of a Young Lady*.

Annette (Netty) Smith Loyal daughter of Van Dieman Smith (Ribstone), beloved of Herbert Fellingham; she is courted by Martin Tinman, her senior by some twenty years, and is nearly forced to marry him until his duplicity finally destroys the bond between her father and Tinman in George Meredith's *The House on the Beach*.

(Diogenes) Smith Captain of the rowing eight at St. Ambrose's College, Oxford, in Thomas Hughes's *Tom Brown at Oxford*.

Euphemia Smith Licentious adventuress, who entices John Caldigate while traveling to Australia; he lives with her while digging for gold; after his return to England and marriage to Hester Bolton, she turns up accusing him of bigamy, for which he is briefly imprisoned before her scheming is exposed in Anthony Trollope's *John Caldigate*.

Harold Smith Pompous brother-in-law of the spendthrift squire Nathaniel Sowerby and a minor official in Treasury and Admiralty in Anthony Trollope's *Framley Parsonage*. He appears in *The Last Chronicle of Barset*.

Mrs. Harold Smith Nathaniel Sowerby's devoted sister, who tries to use her husband's position in government circles to help her feckless brother; she is ultimately unsuccessful also in uniting him with an heiress in Anthony Trollope's *Framley Parsonage*.

Harriet Smith Docile, seventeen-year-old, illegitimate beauty, open-hearted and simple, who boards at school near Hartfield; Emma Woodhouse takes her up as friend and project, persuading her to reject a suitable proposal from farmer Robert Martin and talking her into an unrequited fancy for clergyman Mr. Elton; she finally marries Martin in Jane Austen's *Emma*.

Henry Gow Smith Powerful Scottish blacksmith and armor maker, who courts Catherine Glover though she dislikes his life of violence; he cuts off the hand of John Ramorny when the Duke of Rothsay's gang tries to kidnap Catherine; he challenges MacIan (Conachar) to a combat from which MacIan flees; he finally is accepted in marriage by Catherine in Sir Walter Scott's *The Fair Maid of Perth*.

Jack Smith Rakish friend and traveling companion of Felicia's cousin; unlike Felicia's cousin, he reforms after hearing an ironic lecture in praise of swearing delivered by Lucius Manly in Mary Collyer's *Felicia to Charlotte*.

Jane Smith John's wife and Stephen's mother in Thomas Hardy's *A Pair of Blue Eyes*.

John Smith A master mason whose social status advances with the professional success of his architect son, Stephen, in Thomas Hardy's *A Pair of Blue Eyes*.

John Smith Glove maker and seller, at whose lodgings Clarissa Harlowe dies in Samuel Richardson's *Clarissa: or, The History of a Young Lady*.

John Smith San Francisco chandler who supplies the *Norah Creina* in Robert Louis Stevenson's *The Wrecker*.

Mary Smith Young friend of the Jenkynses and a frequent visitor from the commercial center of Drumble; she is the sympathetic observer who is the concerned yet mildly ironic narrator in Elizabeth Gaskell's *Cranford*.

Stephen Smith A stonemason's talented son, who becomes an architect and returns to the parental village as a restoration consultant; he and Elfride Swancourt become engaged; her father's opposition causes them to plan an elopement, of which they repent before it is completed; the older, more worldly, and intellectual Henry Knight comes her way and she writes breaking with Stephen; he loves her unselfishly and returns at last to find she is dead in Thomas Hardy's *A Pair of Blue Eyes*.

Sullivan Smith   Hot-tempered Irish rejected suitor of Diana Merion (Warwick); he remains a defender of her honor in George Meredith's *Diana of the Crossways*.

Tom Smith   One of three mutineers; he turns against the English Captain but is eventually captured by the captain, Friday, and Robinson Crusoe in Daniel Defoe's *The Life and Strange Surprizing Adventures of Robinson Crusoe of York, Mariner*.

Van Dieman Smith   Convict and benefactor of Philip Ribstone, who takes his name in compliance with Smith's last request in George Meredith's *The House on the Beach*.

Van Dieman Smith (Ribstone)   See Philip Ribstone.

Wayland Smith   A blacksmith, juggler, magician, and alchemist, who joins Edmund Tressilian in trying to aid Amy Robsart Dudley; he cures Sir Hugh Robsart of illness brought on by grief, provides an antidote for the poison that would have killed Thomas Ratcliffe, Earl of Sussex, and conducts a disguised Amy from Cumnor-Place to Kenilworth; Queen Elizabeth takes him into her service, and he marries Janet Foster in Sir Walter Scott's *Kenilworth*.

Miss Smithers   Inquisitive boarder at the girls' school at Westgate House in Charles Dickens's *The Posthumous Papers of the Pickwick Club*.

The Misses Smithie   Two daughters of Mr. and Mrs. Smithie in Charles Dickens's *The Posthumous Papers of the Pickwick Club*.

Mr. Smithie   Employee at the Chatham dockyard who attends the ball at the Bull Inn in Rochester in Charles Dickens's *The Posthumous Papers of the Pickwick Club*.

Mrs. Smithie   Wife of Mr. Smithie in Charles Dickens's *The Posthumous Papers of the Pickwick Club*.

Madame de Smolensk   Hardworking, respectable proprietor of the select Paris boarding house in which the Bayneses lodge; she befriends Philip Firmin and Charlotte Baynes in William Makepeace Thackeray's *The Adventures of Philip on His Way through the World*.

Captain Alexander Smollett   Sensible captain of the *Hispaniola*; his distrust of the crew irritates Squire Trelawney until its wisdom is demonstrated; he runs a tight ship, keeps order in the stockade, and is wounded

by Job Anderson in a pirate attack in Robert Louis Stevenson's *Treasure Island*.

Count Smorltork   Admired foreign guest at Mrs. Leo Hunter's fancy-dress breakfast; he collects and misinterprets information on numerous tablets in Charles Dickens's *The Posthumous Papers of the Pickwick Club*.

Stephen Smotherwell   Public executioner who conspires with Henbane Dwining to pretend to hang Bonthron in Sir Walter Scott's *The Fair Maid of Perth*.

Mr. Smouch   Shabby accomplice of the sheriff's deputy Mr. Namby in Charles Dickens's *The Posthumous Papers of the Pickwick Club*.

Smuggler   Traveler on the wagon who seizes the Exciseman by the throat in Charles Johnstone's *Chrysal: or, The Adventures of a Guinea*.

Major Smyth   Army officer visiting the Bonds; he attracts not only Miss Bond, to whom he becomes engaged, but also Mrs. Faulkland (formerly Miss Burchell), with whom he is found in bed by Orlando Faulkland; after firing a pistol at the angry husband, he is fatally shot by Faulkland in Frances Sheridan's *Memoirs of Miss Sidney Bidulph*.

Mr. Snack   Unscrupulous attorney who helps Sir Freestone Hardgrave steal the farm of Giffard Homely in Henry Brooke's *The Fool of Quality*.

Mrs. Snagsby   Mr. Snagsby's shrewish, jealous wife, who suspects that Jo is his illegitimate boy and continually spies on him in Charles Dickens's *Bleak House*.

Paul Snagsby   Mild and timid law-stationer in Cook's Court, who employed Nemo (Captain Hawdon) to copy documents and befriends Jo in Charles Dickens's *Bleak House*.

Bryce Snailsfoot   Coarse and offensive little peddler, called a *jagger* by the Zetlanders in Sir Walter Scott's *The Pirate*.

Mr. Snale   Draper who is deacon at Mark Rutherford's first chapel; opposed to Mark, he anonymously attacks him in letters to the newspaper and drives him from town with gossip about his broken engagement in Mark Rutherford's *The Autobiography of Mark Rutherford*.

Mrs. Snale   Wife of the deacon/draper; she is occasional hostess to chapel society gatherings but never shows generosity to her guests in Mark Rutherford's *The Autobiography of Mark Rutherford*.

Snap   Family dog mentioned by Jeremiah Tugwell during his fits of homesickness in Richard Graves's *The Spiritual Quixote*.

Mr. Snap   Bailiff who acts as tutor to Jonathan Wild; he is father of Laetitia and Theodosia Snap in Henry Fielding's *The Life of Mr. Jonathan Wild the Great*.

Laetitia (Miss Tishy) Snap   Younger Snap daughter, whose feigned virtue kindles Jonathan Wild's lust; they marry and hate each other in Henry Fielding's *The Life of Mr. Jonathan Wild the Great*.

Theodosia (Miss Doshy) Snap   Eldest Snap daughter, who bears a child by Count La Ruse; she is transported to America, where she reforms and lives happily in Henry Fielding's *The Life of Mr. Jonathan Wild the Great*.

Thomas Snape   Senior clerk in the Internal Navigation Office whose fawning towards authority makes him unpopular among the junior clerks in Anthony Trollope's *The Three Clerks*.

Miss Snapper   Heiress whom Banter recommends to Roderick Random and who meets Roderick in a coach to Bath in Tobias Smollett's *The Adventures of Roderick Random*.

Mr. Snapper   Bishop Proudie's domestic chaplain, successor to Mr. Slope; he takes over the pastoral duties of Hogglestock when Mr. Crawley resigns in Anthony Trollope's *The Last Chronicle of Barset*.

Mr. Snarle   Peevish old man; a victim of the exuberance of Ned (Fielding), he retaliates too fiercely and is in turn the comical object of Ned's vengeance in Henry Brooke's *The Fool of Quality*.

Mr. Snarler   Examiner who insults Roderick Random during his examination for qualification as a surgeon's mate in Tobias Smollett's *The Adventures of Roderick Random*.

Mr. Snawley   Stepfather who places his wife's sons at Squeers's Dotheboys Hall in order to be able spend their mother's money, for which he married her in Charles Dickens's *The Life and Adventures of Nicholas Nickleby*.

Mrs. Snawley   Mr. Snawley's wife, whose boys are among those mistreated at Dotheboys Hall by Wackford Squeers in Charles Dickens's *The Life and Adventures of Nicholas Nickleby*.

Joshua Sneakington   Country mischief-maker, village lawyer, and secretary to John Jorrocks; he is eventually prosecuted by Jorrocks for stealing his partridges in Robert Surtees's *Hillingdon Hall*.

John Snell   The landlord of the Rainbow Tavern of Ravenloe in George Eliot's *Silas Marner*.

Samuel Snell   Calcutta indigo smuggler, whose large fortune is a factor in both unhappy marriages of his daughter, Lady Clavering, in William Makepeace Thackeray's *The History of Pendennis*.

Miss Snevellicci   Leading lady in the Vincent Crummles Theatrical Company, who flirts unsuccessfully with Nicholas Nickleby and later marries a tallow chandler in Charles Dickens's *The Life and Adventures of Nicholas Nickleby*.

Mr. Snicks   The Life Office secretary and a guest at Mr. Perker's in Charles Dickens's *The Posthumous Papers of the Pickwick Club*.

Lord Snigsworth   Melvin Twemlow's noble first cousin, who reigns at Snigsworthy Park in Charles Dickens's *Our Mutual Friend*.

Wilmot Snipe   Ensign from a good family who is in the Ninety-seventh Regiment and is present at a ball at the Bull Inn in Rochester in Charles Dickens's *The Posthumous Papers of the Pickwick Club*.

Mrs. Snitchey   Jonathan Snitchey's wife, who is suspicious of Thomas Craggs on principle in Charles Dickens's *The Battle of Life*.

Jonathan Snitchey   Conservative lawyer and family friend of the Jeddlers and best friend of his partner, Thomas Craggs, whose death leaves him bereft in Charles Dickens's *The Battle of Life*.

Augustus Snodgrass   Samuel Pickwick's young companion, who has a poetic nature (although he never writes any poetry) and falls in love with Emily Wardle in Charles Dickens's *The Posthumous Papers of the Pickwick Club*.

Mary Snow   Winsome daughter of a drunken engraver; she is groomed by Felix Graham to make her his ideal wife; when she falls in love with the apothecary's assistant, Albert Fitzallen, Graham assists their match in Anthony Trollope's *Orley Farm*.

Jane Snowdon   An oppressed servant girl; she is rescued by her grandfather, who returns from the colonies a rich man; she tries unsuccessfully to fulfill his wish that she become a charity worker; she is rejected by her lover in George Gissing's *The Nether World*.

Joseph Snowdon   Irresponsible father who abandons his daughter, Jane Snowdon; he finds that his father, Michael Snowdon, intends to leave his money to Jane, but

Joseph inherits when the old man dies without leaving a will in George Gissing's *The Nether World*.

Michael Snowdon Character who returns from Australia a wealthy man to find his granddaughter, Jane Snowdon, and enable her to become a charity worker; she disappoints him, and he destroys the will making her his heiress in George Gissing's *The Nether World*.

Lord Snowdown Fashionable young aristocrat, who likes the company of young artists and writers in George Moore's *Mike Fletcher*.

Snowdrop Offspring of Dinah, the cat; constantly being washed, it is a counterpart of the always-untidy White Queen in Lewis Carroll's *Through the Looking-Glass*.

Lucy Snowe Imaginative and passionate young Englishwoman, born to suffering, who works first as a lady's companion and then goes to Labassecour; she is hired by Mme. Beck as a nursemaid and then is promoted to English teacher; her unspoken interest in Dr. John Bretton is followed by a more reciprocal attraction to M. Paul Emanuel, but he likely does not survive a storm at sea on his return from three years' absence in Charlotte Brontë's *Villette*.

Serjeant Snubbin Slovenly defense attorney, who sacrifices tidiness for professional purposes and is retained by Mr. Perker to represent Samuel Pickwick in the breach-of-promise suit in Charles Dickens's *The Posthumous Papers of the Pickwick Club*.

Lady Snuphanuph Distinguished dowager in Bath, with whom Samuel Pickwick plays whist in Charles Dickens's *The Posthumous Papers of the Pickwick Club*.

Mr. Soames Business manager for Lord Lufton; by losing a cheque for £20 and believing he left it at Mr. Crawley's house, he precipitates the celebrated Crawley case in Anthony Trollope's *The Last Chronicle of Barset*.

John Soberton Gentleman to whose house Anna Howe tells her friend Clarissa Harlowe to direct her letters after Mrs. Howe forbids the correspondence between Anna and Clarissa in Samuel Richardson's *Clarissa: or, The History of a Young Lady*.

Madame Socani Temperamental opera singer and former mistress of Mahomet M. Moss; she is the jealous rival of Rachel O'Mahony in Anthony Trollope's *The Landleaguers*.

Count von Sohnspeer Field Marshal of the Austrian army, who is Vivian Grey's rival suitor for the Baroness Sybilla in Benjamin Disraeli's *Vivian Grey*.

Mr. Soho Flamboyant interior designer whom fashionable English society employs to decorate its homes in Maria Edgeworth's *The Absentee*.

Soles Shoemaker whose measurement of the footprints left in the sand by Francis Kennedy's murderers results in the arrest of Dirk Hatteraick in Sir Walter Scott's *Guy Mannering*.

Solmes Manservant to the usurping Earl of Etherington (Valentine Bulmer); he reveals all his master's secrets to Touchwood in Sir Walter Scott's *St. Ronan's Well*.

Roger Solmes A narrow, mean-spirited, avaricious gentleman, whose marriage settlement with Clarissa Harlowe is concluded by Clarissa's father without her knowledge and consent; her continued refusal of him on moral and personal grounds and the family's insistence that they marry finally drive Clarissa into flight with Robert Lovelace in Samuel Richardson's *Clarissa: or, The History of a Young Lady*.

Nehemiah Solsgrace Presbyterian parson who is turned out by Sir Geoffrey Peveril at the time of the Restoration and emigrates to New England in Sir Walter Scott's *Peveril of the Peak*.

Isabella Somerive Orlando Somerive's older sister, whom General Tracey first wants as mistress, later as wife; she soon regrets the engagement she has agreed to and elopes to America with his nephew, Captain Warwick, before they return to London in Charlotte Smith's *The Old Manor House*.

Orlando Somerive Miss Rayland's favorite relative; he has the use of her library, where he reads poetry and fiction, and comes to love Monimia Morysine; he leaves home to fight in the American War, but fails to achieve financial independence so that, after returning and finding and marrying Monimia, he must prove himself to be Miss Rayland's heir in order to rescue his family from poverty in Charlotte Smith's *The Old Manor House*.

Philip Somerive Clergyman and closest relative of Miss Rayland, whose estate he hopes one of his sons, Philip and Orlando, will inherit; he opposes Orlando Somerive's marriage to Monimia Morysine but dies before the event, leaving his family in penury in Charlotte Smith's *The Old Manor House*.

Philip Somerive (the younger) Orlando's older brother, whose expensive education and gambling debts are ruinous to the small family fortune, and whose dissipation ends in early death in Charlotte Smith's *The Old Manor House*.

Selina Somerive   Orlando Somerive's younger sister, who alone befriends Monimia Morysine and who sustains secret communication between them when Orlando is absent; she marries Lieutenant Fleming in Charlotte Smith's *The Old Manor House*.

Mr. Somers   Highly respected agent of the Castle Richmond property; he chairs a relief committee for victims of the potato famine in Anthony Trollope's *Castle Richmond*.

Alfred Somers   Popular landscape painter and Jocelyn Pierston's old friend, who counsels Pierston through his several love affairs; Somers himself marries the well-connected Nichola Pine-Avon in Thomas Hardy's *The Well-Beloved*.

Denzil Somers   Poet and closest friend of Sir Austin Feverel; he runs off with Lady Feverel, turning Sir Austin against women and leading him to raise his son according to a disastrous system; Somers uses the pseudonym Diaper Sandoe in George Meredith's *The Ordeal of Richard Feverel*.

Earl of Somerset   Formerly the Viscount Rochester; a favorite of King James, he conducts an illicit correspondence with the imprisoned (younger) Mary in Sophia Lee's *The Recess*.

George Somerset   Young, talented architect in love with Paula Power; he agrees to restore her castle; plotted against by William Dare through a method of photographic distortion, he nevertheless succeeds in marrying Paula in Thomas Hardy's *A Laodicean*.

Countess of Somerset (1)   Attendant to Queen Elizabeth; she conveys a portrait of Mary, Queen of Scots from the enraged Elizabeth to Lord Leicester in Sophia Lee's *The Recess*.

Countess of Somerset (2)   Cruel and ambitious divorced woman, who marries the Earl of Somerset after failing to attach herself to Prince Henry; she has (the younger) Mary poisoned in Sophia Lee's *The Recess*.

Soorcrout   Colleague of Sucrewasser and a proponent of egg white as canvas varnish; he loses a dispute with Og of Basan, who extolls nut oil as the best varnish in William Beckford's *Biographical Memoirs of Extraordinary Painters*.

Sophia   Daughter of the brass-and-copper-founder's family and Ruth Pinch's pupil, whose rudeness to Ruth is encouraged by her parents in Charles Dickens's *The Life and Adventures of Martin Chuzzlewit*.

Sophia   Jenny Jessamy's school friend who falls in love with a scoundrel in Eliza Haywood's *The History of Jemmy and Jenny Jessamy*.

Sophie   The French nursemaid who accompanies Adèle Varens to Thornfield Hall and speaks French to Jane Eyre in Charlotte Brontë's *Jane Eyre*.

Lady Sophister   A divorced lady of quality, who is a friend of Lady Tempest; she is a famous wit, whose opinions are often very absurd and owe more to whim and caprice than to understanding in Francis Coventry's *The History of Pompey the Little*.

Sophronia   Lady who recounts her attachment to philosophy to her correspondent Celia, who pursues only personal pleasure in Sarah Fielding's *Familiar Letters between the Principal Characters of David Simple and Some Others*.

Sophronia   Minor interlocutor, who asks leading questions and offers occasional illustrative anecdotes supporting the value and attraction of Romances in Clara Reeve's *The Progress of Romance*.

Sophy   Mysterious orphan and actress known as The Phenomenon; she is protected by William Waife, preyed on by Jasper Losely, and beloved by Lionel Haughton in Edward Bulwer-Lytton's *What Will He Do With It? by Pisistratus Caxton*.

Miss Sophy   Emilia Gauntlet's cousin, who marries Godfrey Gauntlet and assists Perry Pickle in his courtship of Emilia in Tobias Smollett's *The Adventures of Peregrine Pickle*.

Sorais (Lady of the Night)   Dark-haired and beautiful but cruel and treacherous queen of the Zu-Vendis and twin sister of Nyleptha; when Sir Henry Curtis rejects her love and chooses her sister, she joins General Nasta in a rebellion and commits suicide after their defeat in H. Rider Haggard's *Allan Quatermain*.

Madame di Soranzo   An Italian woman brought to England and wooed unsuccessfully by Captain Maurice; she suffers from a nervous breakdown but eventually recovers fully and becomes the close friend and housemate of Mrs. Darnford in Clara Reeve's *Plans of Education*.

Edward Sorell   Young Oxford professor, whose friendship with the Hooper family and Lady Connie Bledlow turns into love for the young Nora Hooper in Mrs. Humphry Ward's *Lady Connie*.

Mrs. Sorling   Widowed sister of the housekeeper on Lord M—'s estate; Robert Lovelace brings Clarissa Harlowe to her lodgings after Clarissa flees with him in Samuel Richardson's *Clarissa: or, The History of a Young Lady*.

Hetty Sorrel   Niece of the younger Martin Poyser; she is a vain, beautiful woman full of false innocence and artful displays of her charms; although she has encouraged some advances from Adam Bede, she dallies with Arthur Donnithorne, becomes pregnant, and abandons her baby; Adam finds difficulty in separating her physical perfection from his ideas of moral virtue, so her decline as a "pleasure craving nature" is the beginning of Bede's better understanding of humanity; she is sentenced to death for the death of her baby, but the sentence is commuted to transportation in George Eliot's *Adam Bede*.

Sorrow   Tess Durbeyfield's illegitimate son by Alec Stoke-D'Urberville; when Tess learns that her baptism of the infant just before his death will not qualify him for burial in holy ground, the injustice hardens her against institutional religion in Thomas Hardy's *Tess of the D'Urbervilles*.

Don Guzman de Soto   Treacherous Spanish nobleman, captured in Ireland by Amyas Leigh; later Sir Richard Grenville's guest, he woos and marries Rose Salterne and becomes Governor of Caracas after his ransom; he dies when his ship sinks during the Battle of the Spanish Armada in Charles Kingsley's *Westward Ho!*.

Mr. South   Idealized clergyman who twice helps Ophelia to escape from her persecutors despite her refusal to marry him in Sarah Fielding's *The History of Ophelia*.

John South   Marty South's father, whose leases of land are written to expire at his death; his death therefore has a calamitous effect on the fortunes of Giles Winterborne in Thomas Hardy's *The Woodlanders*.

Marty South   The plain, orphaned, poor young woman who hopelessly loves Giles Winterborne; her letter to Edred Fitzpiers results in a dispute which, by taking him away from Felice Charmond, saves him from scandal when Charmond is killed; after Giles dies, Marty visits his grave faithfully in Thomas Hardy's *The Woodlanders*.

Lady Southampton   Elizabeth Vernon, wife of Lord Southampton and friend of Matilda and Ellinor; she meets Ellinor in Ireland and is detained with her in Scotland in Sophia Lee's *The Recess*.

Lord Southampton   Supporter of both the Duke of Norfolk and the Earl of Essex (2); his political intriguing is pardoned at the request of the condemned Essex in Sophia Lee's *The Recess*.

Dowager Countess of Southdown   Sternly evangelical mother of Lady Jane Sheepshanks (Crawley); she terrifies the Crawley family with her tracts in William Makepeace Thackeray's *Vanity Fair*. She is mentioned in *The History of Pendennis*.

Earl of Southdown   Easy-going brother-in-law of the younger Pitt Crawley; Rawdon and Becky (Sharp) Crawley live at his expense in London in William Makepeace Thackeray's *Vanity Fair*.

Mr. Sowerberry   Tall, gaunt, parochial undertaker, who apprentices Oliver Twist to work for him as a houselad and mute at children's funerals in Charles Dickens's *Oliver Twist*.

Mrs. Sowerberry   Thin, vixenish wife of Mr. Sowerberry in Charles Dickens's *Oliver Twist*.

Dudley Sowerby   Heir to an earldom, chosen by Victor Radnor to marry his daughter, Nesta; Sowerby gives up his suit when he finds that Nesta is illegitimate, takes it up again when his family decides in favor of the Radnor fortune, but is ultimately rejected by Nesta, who cannot accept his conventional moralism in George Meredith's *One of Our Conquerers*.

Nathaniel Sowerby   Spendthrift, debt-burdened Member of Parliament for West Barsetshire; he persuades Mark Robarts to sign bills for debts comparatively inconsequential to himself but almost ruinous to Mark; he finally loses his beloved estate, Chaldicotes, to the creditor of his choice, Martha Dunstable, instead of to the (old) Duke of Omnium, but has no other triumph in Anthony Trollope's *Framley Parsonage*.

Mr. Sownds   The beadle of the Dombeys' district; he is present at the ceremony of Paul Dombey's second marriage in Charles Dickens's *Dombey and Son*.

Spalatro   Haunted assassin hired by Father Schedoni (Ferando di Bruno) to kill Count di Bruno and to confine Ellena Rosalba in a remote house to await her murder in Ann Radcliffe's *The Italian*.

Caroline Spalding   Spirited niece of the American minister to Italy; she falls in love with the Honourable Charles Glascock and marries him in Anthony Trollope's *He Knew He Was Right*.

Jonas Spalding   American minister to Italy based in Florence; he proclaims loudly the virtues of American ways and institutions in Anthony Trollope's *He Knew He Was Right*.

Olivia (Livy) Spalding   Younger sister and traveling companion of Caroline; her intelligence, humor, and wit encourage the developing romance between Caroline and the Honourable Charles Glascock in Anthony Trollope's *He Knew He Was Right*.

Spaniard   Military leader who is brought to Robinson Crusoe's island by hostile natives to be killed and eaten;

he is rescued by Crusoe and Friday in Daniel Defoe's *The Life and Strange Surprizing Adventures of Robinson Crusoe of York, Mariner*.

Spanish Commander in Jamaica   Amelia's husband, who commutes Traffick's sentence for piracy from death to labor for life in the gold mines of Peru in Charles Johnstone's *Chrysal: or, The Adventures of a Guinea*.

Mrs. Conway Sparkes   Outspoken literary lady, whose presence at Lady Glencora Palliser's house party enrages the Duchess of St. Bungay in Anthony Trollope's *Can You Forgive Her?*. She is a patroness of the Negro Soldiers' Orphan Bazaar in *Miss Mackenzie*. She attends Lady Monk's reception in *Phineas Finn*.

Ebenezer Sparkes   Veteran waiter concerned about his errant daughter in George Gissing's *The Town Traveller*.

Polly Sparkes   An independent and hot-tempered young girl, who sets off the search for Lord Polperro, her mysteriously missing uncle, after she sees him at the theatre where she sells programs in George Gissing's *The Town Traveller*.

Master Sparkish   Susceptible youth in love with Miss Forward in Eliza Haywood's *The History of Miss Betsy Thoughtless*.

Elizabeth Sparkle   Prostitute introduced to George Edwards by her pimp, M. Le Guardien; she relieves George of large sums in John Hill's *The Adventures of Mr. George Edwards, a Creole*.

Edmund Sparkler   Empty-headed son of Mrs. Merdle by her first husband; devoted to Fanny Dorrit since her days as a dancer, he becomes her husband, lands a position in the Circumlocution Office, and eventually supports his wife and mother on his salary in Charles Dickens's *Little Dorrit*.

Sparks   Tender and romantically inclined young military officer of great simplicity; he marries Mary (Baby) Blake in Charles Lever's *Charles O'Malley*.

Mrs. Sparsit   Genteel but nosy housekeeper of Josiah Bounderby; she finally gets revenge for his insufferable bragging in Charles Dickens's *Hard Times*.

Mr. Spatter   One of David Simple's potential soulmates who proves to be false after introducing David to high life in London in Sarah Fielding's *The Adventures of David Simple in Search of a Faithful Friend*. He is a vituperative commentator on others' flaws in *Familiar Letters between the Principal Characters in David Simple and Some Others*.

Lieutenant Jack Spatterdash   A friend of Captain

Rawdon Crawley and an admirer of Becky (Sharp) Crawley in William Makepeace Thackeray's *Vanity Fair*.

Rosanna Spearman   Reserved and lonely deformed servant in the Verinder household; having once been placed in a reformatory, she becomes a prime suspect in the theft of a huge diamond; madly in love with Franklin Blake, whom she believes to be the thief, she tries to protect him; she commits suicide in Wilkie Collins's *The Moonstone. A Romance*.

Lady Speck   Survivor of an unhappy marriage who falls in love with Celadine and is very jealous of Jenny Jessamy in Eliza Haywood's *The History of Jemmy and Jenny Jessamy*.

Mr. Speckle   Successor to Mr. Cayenne as director of the weaving mill; his bankruptcy gives Dalmailing its first experience of mass unemployment in John Galt's *Annals of the Parish*.

Mr. Speedwell   Physician who attends Geoffrey Delamayn and vainly warns him to abstain from brandy and excitement in Wilkie Collins's *Man and Wife*.

Mr. Speedy   Irishman who gives Loudon Dodd wildcat stock for picnic hampers; he is sent by Jim Pinkerton to Hawaii to deal with opium smugglers in Robert Louis Stevenson's *The Wrecker*.

Mrs. Speedy   Motherly Irishwoman, who gambles in mining stocks for fifteen years and becomes Loudon Dodd's and her husband's partner in the Catamount Silver Mine in Robert Louis Stevenson's *The Wrecker*.

Mr. Spelling   Most eligible gentleman suitor rejected by Matilda Golding because of her secret love of Henry Clinton in Henry Brooke's *The Fool of Quality*.

Mr. Spence   See Mr. Wentworth.

Edward Spence   Businessman of studious tastes who has retired and lives in Italy in George Gissing's *The Emancipated*.

Eleanor Spence   Cousin of Miriam Baske in George Gissing's *The Emancipated*.

Maria Spence   John Buncle's fourth wife, whom he meets first at Harrogate and later at her home in Cleator, Westmoreland, and who is a Christian deist and adept at calculus; she dies six months after her wedding of a fever and complications resulting from her treatment by four doctors in Thomas Amory's *The Life of John Buncle, Esq*.

Clarissa Spenlow   Unmarried sister of Francis Spenlow; her niece, Dora, lives with her and her sister,

Lavinia, after Francis dies in Charles Dickens's *The Personal History of David Copperfield*.

Dora (Little Blossom) Spenlow Francis Spenlow's pretty daughter, whom David Copperfield falls in love with and marries; though loving, she is childish and incapable of responsibility in household matters; she dies after the death of their baby in Charles Dickens's *The Personal History of David Copperfield*.

Francis Spenlow Partner in the law firm of Spenlow and Jorkins, to which David Copperfield is apprenticed; he is father of the pretty Dora Spenlow, with whom David falls in love, but he forbids their engagement; he dies of apoplexy in Charles Dickens's *The Personal History of David Copperfield*.

Lavinia Spenlow Unmarried sister of Francis Spenlow; her niece, Dora, lives with her and her sister, Clarissa, after he dies; she is supposed to be an expert on affairs of the heart in Charles Dickens's *The Personal History of David Copperfield*.

Edmund Spenser Poet and soldier, who discusses hexameters with Sir Walter Raleigh during the voyage to Ireland in Charles Kingsley's *Westward Ho!*.

Mr. Spicer Mustard-maker at Percycross; his support is wooed by Griffenbottom's conservatives since he directs votes of his employees in Anthony Trollope's *Ralph the Heir*.

Henry Spiker Cold solicitor present at the Waterbrooks' dinner party in Charles Dickens's *The Personal History of David Copperfield*.

Mrs. Henry Spiker Awful wife of Henry Spiker; she reminds David Copperfield of Hamlet's aunt in Charles Dickens's *The Personal History of David Copperfield*.

Adam Spindlemans Wealthy merchant who presents Aldrovandus Magnus's paintings to nobles, thereby introducing the painter at court in William Beckford's *Biographical Memoirs of Extraordinary Painters*.

Ann Spindlemans Charming daughter of Adam Spindlemans and the dangerous object of young Aldrovandus Magnus's admiration in William Beckford's *Biographical Memoirs of Extraordinary Painters*.

Dolfo Spini The cocky captain of the Compagnacci, a gang of Florence, who always wears a red feather in his hat in George Eliot's *Romola*.

Mrs. Spires A baby-farmer (woman who takes care of or disposes of unwanted babies); her offer to Esther Wa-

ters to rid her of her son drives Esther with her child to the workhouse in George Moore's *Esther Waters*.

Mr. Spiveycomb Paper-maker in Percycross; he supports the Conservatives in the election because of contracts that come his way from the local Tory paper in Anthony Trollope's *Ralph the Heir*.

Mr. Spondy Poet who is a member of the London College of Authors, which Perry Pickle joins, in Tobias Smollett's *The Adventures of Peregrine Pickle*.

Soapey Sponge Rider to hounds and con artist superb, who hates work but despises poverty; he marries Lucy Glitters and settles down in London with a successful tobacco shop and betting room in Robert Surtees's *Mr. Sponge's Sporting Tour*.

Spontoon Colonel Talbot's trustworthy servant, who assists Talbot in keeping Edward Waverly's presence in London a secret in Sir Walter Scott's *Waverly*.

Miss Spooner Bosom friend of Clarissa and Patience Underwood and their neighbor in Fulham in Anthony Trollope's *Ralph the Heir*.

Mrs. Spooner The former Miss Leatherside and an ardent rider to hounds, always to the fore and an authority in any dispute; Lady Chiltern (Violet Effingham) recommends her as a Master of Hounds in Anthony Trollope's *The Duke's Children*.

Ned Spooner Cousin and manager of Tom Spooner's estate; he helps Tom concoct a love letter to Adelaide Palliser in Anthony Trollope's *Phineas Redux*.

Thomas Platter Spooner Ardent huntsman and neighbor of the Chilterns; he falls in love with Adelaide Palliser; his disappointment at her rejection is the more acute because he finds it incredible in Anthony Trollope's *Phineas Redux*. He and his stables are taken over by his bride, the former Miss Leatherside, in *The Duke's Children*.

Mr. Spottletoe Quarrelsome husband of Mrs. Spottletoe; he accuses Seth Pecksniff of conspiring with old Martin Chuzzlewit against the interests of Chuzzlewit's other relatives in Charles Dickens's *The Life and Adventures of Martin Chuzzlewit*.

Mrs. Spottletoe Mr. Spottletoe's thin wife and a Chuzzlewit kinswoman in Charles Dickens's *The Life and Adventures of Martin Chuzzlewit*.

Spraggon Lord Scamperdale's servant in Robert Surtees's *Mr. Sponge's Sporting Tour*.

Dr. Sprague   A Middlemarch physician in George Eliot's *Middlemarch*.

Mr. Spratt   A Tory who is rescued from the rioters by Felix Holt in George Eliot's *Felix Holt, the Radical*.

Edward Springrove (the elder)   Tenant of Cytherea Aldclyffe, landlord of the Three Tranters inn, and affectionate father of Edward Springrove, the architect, in Thomas Hardy's *Desperate Remedies*.

Edward Springrove   Somber young architect, who falls in love with Cytherea Graye, though long betrothed to his cousin; he helplessly watches Cytherea marry another man who, after the marriage, is suspected of foul doings with his first wife; the devoted Edward, freed from his engagement, investigates and solves the mystery and is finally rewarded when he and Cytherea are married in Thomas Hardy's *Desperate Remedies*.

Sally Sprodgkin   Frank Milvey's troublesome parishioner, who always shows up at the parsonage at the most inconvenient times in Charles Dickens's *Our Mutual Friend*.

Mr. Sandie Sprott   Ruddy, hard, and uncivil Scottish merchant who, soured by unprofitable dealings with James More MacGregor, refuses aid to his daughter, Catriona, in Holland in Robert Louis Stevenson's *Catriona*.

Mr. Sprout   Local shoemaker who specializes in cork soles, active in the attempt of Ferdinand Lopez to become Member of Parliament for Silverbridge in Anthony Trollope's *The Prime Minister*. He supports Lord Silverbridge's election in *The Duke's Children*.

Sarah Sprowl   Dealer in cheap liquor who exercises an evil influence on Harriet Smales and helps to implicate Ida Starr in George Gissing's *The Unclassed*.

Nancy Spruce   One of the nine pupils of Mrs. Teachum's school; she learns the folly of personal vanity in Sarah Fielding's *The Governess*.

Sally Spruce   Mrs. Roper's elderly spinster cousin, who lives at the Roper establishment in Anthony Trollope's *The Small House at Allington*.

Mr. Sprugeon   Silverbridge ironmonger active in the Parliamentary candidacy of Ferdinand Lopez so long as he believes Lopez to be the (younger) Duke of Omnium's choice; finding this not to be the case, he withdraws his support in Anthony Trollope's *The Prime Minister*.

Dick Spur'em   Jailor MacGuffog's shady assistant, who is most useful in capturing criminals in Sir Walter Scott's *Guy Mannering*.

Mrs. Spurling   Much-widowed barkeeper, who helps Jack Sheppard escape from Newgate and marries Marvel, the hangman, in William Harrison Ainsworth's *Jack Sheppard*.

Mr. Spurrell   A poor watchmaker, who lost his son six months before he meets Caleb Williams; Caleb becomes his apprentice and his ersatz son; Mr. Spurrel turns in Caleb for the reward in William Godwin's *Caleb Williams*.

Jem Spyers   Bow Street officer who arrests Conkey Chickweed, as related by Mr. Blathers, a Bow Street runner, in Charles Dickens's *Oliver Twist*.

Dr. Squably   Clergyman who advises the Reverend Sheeppen he can marry a Turkish infidel if he converts her, inspiring Sheeppen's pursuit of Azemia in William Beckford's *Azemia*.

Thomas Square   Philosopher who instructs Allworthy's nephews; he persecutes Tom until Tom finds him in bed with Molly Seagrim; eventually he regrets ill-using Tom in Henry Fielding's *The History of Tom Jones*.

Mr. Squares   Acrimonious clergyman who loves royalty and detests liberty; he saves Lucinda Howard from drowning but coldly ignores her professions of love; his asperity partly causes her death in William Beckford's *Modern Novel Writing; or, the Elegant Enthusiast*.

Mrs. Squeers   Wife of Wackford Squeers; she doses the Dotheboys Hall inmates with brimstone and treacle to take away their appetites; she is cruel, vicious, and loudmouthed in Charles Dickens's *The Life and Adventures of Nicholas Nickleby*.

Fanny Squeers   Daughter of Wackford Squeers; she attempts to capture Nicholas Nickleby romantically, but hates him when he repulses her in Charles Dickens's *The Life and Adventures of Nicholas Nickleby*.

Wackford Squeers   Head of Dotheboys Hall in Yorkshire, a year-round, no-vacation boarding school where no learning takes place; it specializes in unwanted boys, who are starved and beaten; Squeers conspires with Ralph Nickleby to take vengeance on Nicholas Nickleby, who has beaten him with a whip; he ends up in prison in Charles Dickens's *The Life and Adventures of Nicholas Nickleby*.

Master Wackford Squeers   Fat, spoiled son of Wackford Squeers; he enjoys taunting the students at his father's school in Charles Dickens's *The Life and Adventures of Nicholas Nickleby*.

Mr. Squercum Scruffy, sharp lawyer retained by Dolly Longestaffe to look after his interests, especially in opposition to those of his father in Anthony Trollope's *The Way We Live Now.*

Squire Narcissa's hard-drinking, fox-hunting brother; their aunt calls him "the Savage"; he opposes Narcissa's marrying Roderick Random and tries to forward other suitors; he marries Melinda Goosetrap in Tobias Smollett's *The Adventures of Roderick Random.*

Squire Unnamed landowner who invites Parson Adams, Joseph Andrews, and Fanny Goodwill to his manor for dinner to play practical jokes on them and to debauch Fanny in Henry Fielding's *The History of the Adventures of Mr. Joseph Andrews and of his Friend Mr. Abraham Adams.*

Sir Giles Squirrel English sharper, who meets Ferdinand in Paris and joins with Sir Stentor Stile to win all of Ferdinand's money at dice in Tobias Smollett's *The Adventures of Ferdinand Count Fathom.*

Phil Squod Dwarf who works for Trooper George (George Rouncewell) in the shooting gallery in Charles Dickens's *Bleak House.*

M. Le Chevalier Staas A man of consequence in Villette who attends the oration in honour of the prince's birthday in Charlotte Brontë's *Villette.*

Bob Stables Horsey young man, who approves of Lady Dedlock in equestrian terms in Charles Dickens's *Bleak House.*

Charles Stacey Sailor whose home is in the despised Southdown street; he frequents the Brookes house to visit James Brookes's daughters; he is forbidden the house by Willy Brookes in George Moore's *Spring Days.*

Mr. Stackpoole Racing crony of George Hotspur; he tells Emily Hotspur that George lied when he told her that he had not attended a race meeting in Anthony Trollope's *Sir Harry Hotspur of Humblethwaite.*

Colonel Stafford Wealthy, hospitable member of the Royal Irish Artillery, second-in-command to General Chattesworth; he is host of the party at which the two couples, Mr. Mervyn and Gertrude Chattesworth and Lilias Walsingham and Richard Devereux, come to secret understandings in J. Sheridan Le Fanu's *The House by the Churchyard.*

Mrs. Stafford Colonel Stafford's wife, who often entertains members of the Royal Irish Artillery in her home in J. Sheridan Le Fanu's *The House by the Churchyard.*

C. Stafford Wife of a spendthrift threatened by imprisonment for debts; she befriends, shelters, tutors, and advises Emmeline Mobray in Charlotte Smith's *Emmeline: The Orphan of the Castle.*

Stagg Blind operator of a squalid drinking establishment where the "Prentice Knights" meet; he encourages Barnaby Rudge to come to London to participate in the riots and acts as a messenger to Mary Rudge from her husband, terrorizing her in Charles Dickens's *Barnaby Rudge.*

Baron Stahlhoffen Member of a hunting party, who witnesses the duel fought on the outskirts of Salzburg between Arthur Danvers, Lord Alton and Signor Fabroni, and to whose estate the fatally wounded Arthur is conveyed by his brother Richard (later Lord Alton) in William Godwin's *Cloudesley.*

Stamford John H. Watson's old friend and colleague, a dresser at St. Bartholomew's Hospital; he introduces Sherlock Holmes and Watson in Arthur Conan Doyle's *A Study in Scarlet.*

Sir Robert Stamford Erasmus Bethel's attorney, who rises through a seat in Parliament to a position of considerable wealth, buys one of the Verney residences, and disfigures an elegant estate in order to supply delicacies for his table in Charlotte Smith's *Desmond.*

Mrs. Stanbury A clergyman's almost indigent widow and mother of Priscilla, Dorothy, and Hugh; she occupies a modest cottage at Nuncombe Putney and is kept from absolute want by the severe economies of Priscilla in Anthony Trollope's *He Knew He Was Right.*

Dorothy Stanbury Retiring, loving, unaffected niece of Jemima Stanbury; she rejects her aunt's choice of husband and falls in love with and becomes engaged to Brooke Burgess; she finally overcomes her aunt's displeasure at the match in Anthony Trollope's *He Knew He Was Right.*

Hugh Stanbury Brilliant, attractive, moderately Bohemian friend of Louis Trevelyan; unable to begin to make a living as a barrister, he has become a journalist for the *Daily Record*, causing a complete break between him and his aunt, Jemima Stanbury; he falls in love with and eventually marries Nora Rowley in Anthony Trollope's *He Knew He Was Right.*

Jemima Stanbury Wealthy spinster, whose property was the legacy of a former betrothed; she has resolved that it shall go back to a member of his family, the Burgesses, and not enrich her own; she lives in the cathedral close at Exeter and rules the roost in the county set; she breaks with her nephew, Hugh Stanbury, when he becomes a journalist; for a while she tries to prevent the marriage of her niece, Dorothy, to Brooke Burgess, whom she has selected as her heir, but her affection triumphs over self-imposed principle in Anthony Trollope's *He Knew He Was Right*.

Priscilla Stanbury High-principled elder daughter of Mrs. Stanbury; she writes letters, manages her mother's affairs, and gives wise counsel to her sister, Dorothy, about marrying for love in Anthony Trollope's *He Knew He Was Right*.

Captain Stanchells Principal jailer of the Glasgow prison in Sir Walter Scott's *Rob Roy*.

Captain Standard An officer's talented and distinguished son, who expects gratitude from a general whom his father had assisted in Charles Johnstone's *Chrysal: or, The Adventures of a Guinea*.

Colonel Standard Courageous duelling opponent of Charles Meekly, whom he teaches that duelling is the refuge of cowards, causing Meekly to become a Christian in Henry Brooke's *The Fool of Quality*.

Stand-fast Pilgrim who joins Christiana and her party after the Enchanted Ground; he resists the temptation of Madam Bubble; his death is the last described and is given the most detail in John Bunyan's *The Pilgrim's Progress From this World to That Which Is to Come*.

Mr. Standish Peter Featherstone's lawyer in George Eliot's *Middlemarch*.

Squire Standish Avid persecutor of the Jacobites in Sir Walter Scott's *Rob Roy*.

Joseph Stangerson Mormon and private secretary to Enoch Drebber, Principal Elder of the Church of Latter Day Saints; he is a murder victim in Arthur Conan Doyle's *A Study in Scarlet*.

Mrs. Stanhope Handsome, middle-aged wife of Dr. Vesey Stanhope; her one purpose in life, at which she is a complete success, is to dress well in Anthony Trollope's *Barchester Towers*.

Charlotte Stanhope Elder daughter of Dr. Vesey Stanhope; ever vigilant for family dignity, she abets her brother Bertie in his wooing of Eleanor Bold in Anthony Trollope's *Barchester Towers*.

Ethelbert (Bertie) Stanhope Handsome, artistic, utterly indolent son of Dr. Vesey Stanhope, on whom he is content to sponge; he is encouraged by his sister Charlotte to woo widow Eleanor Bold for her fortune in Anthony Trollope's *Barchester Towers*.

Selena Stanhope Worldly aunt of Belinda Portman, who, having established her six other nieces in wealthy marriages, tries to do the same with Belinda in Maria Edgeworth's *Belinda*.

Dr. Vesey Stanhope Leonine-featured absentee Vicar of Crabtree Canonicorum in Barchester; summoned back to his duties from his Lake Como retreat by the Proudie faction in the cathedral power struggle, he is accompanied by his adult children, who make considerable mischief before he is allowed to return to Italy in Anthony Trollope's *Barchester Towers*. His death abroad is mentioned in *Framley Parsonage* and in *Doctor Thorne*.

Sir Charles Stanley Wealthy, handsome would-be seducer of Harriot Darnley; he falls in love honorably with Sophia Darnley and becomes her family's benefactor but then doubts the sincerity of her love and removes his favor; he is reconciled to Sophia through the offices of Mr. Herbert in Charlotte Lennox's *Sophia*.

Frank Stanley Colonel Talbot's adventurous nephew, whose passport Edward Waverly uses to travel through England and Scotland in Sir Walter Scott's *Waverly*.

Juliana Stantiloup Disgruntled parent of a pupil at Dr. Wortle's school; bearing a grudge over fees, she leads a campaign of gossip concerning two members of his staff and their marital circumstances in Anthony Trollope's *Dr. Wortle's School*.

Stanton Englishman who wrote the manuscript which introduces John Melmoth to the terrifying truth about Melmoth's relative, the Wanderer; Stanton encountered the Wanderer in Spain, offended him, and was cursed; he was placed in Bedlam as a madman and visited by the Wanderer, who offered to free Stanton if he would give his soul to Satan; Stanton refuses to do so in Charles Maturin's *Melmoth the Wanderer*.

Dr. Stanvil Physician who exhumes the apparently dead Agnes Dunk and marries her after she revives on his dissection table; he dies suddenly, leaving her free to marry John Buncle in Thomas Amory's *The Life of John Buncle, Esq.*

Mr. Staple Betsy Thoughtless's suitor recommended by her guardian; he fights a duel with Charles Trueworth in Eliza Haywood's *The History of Miss Betsy Thoughtless*.

Mr. Staple Speaker at the cricket banquet at the Blue Lion Inn, Muggleton, in Charles Dickens's *The Posthumous Papers of the Pickwick Club*.

Marquis of Stapledean Miserly landowner, who gives the living of Hurst Staple to Arthur Wilkinson on condition that he pay part of his stipend to his mother in Anthony Trollope's *The Bertrams*.

Beryl Stapleton   Beautiful neighbor of the Baskerville family; she warns Sir Henry Baskerville to return to London in Arthur Conan Doyle's *The Hound of the Baskervilles*.

John Stapleton   Naturalist, discoverer of a species of moth, and neighbor of the Baskerville family; he lives with his supposed sister, Beryl, in Arthur Conan Doyle's *The Hound of the Baskervilles*.

Justice Stareleigh   Short, fat judge, who presides over Martha Bardell's breach-of-promise suit against Samuel Pickwick in Charles Dickens's *The Posthumous Papers of the Pickwick Club*.

Mr. Starkweather   Clergyman, uncle, and guardian of the orphaned Valeria Brinton; he officiates at her marriage to Eustace Woodville (really Macallan) in Wilkie Collins's *The Law and the Lady*.

Ida Starr   Orphaned working girl, the granddaughter of Abraham Woodstock; she is unjustly sentenced to prison but inherits her grandfather's money and eventually agrees to marry Osmond Waymark in George Gissing's *The Unclassed*.

Lotty Starr   Ida Starr's mother, a prostitute who dies early and leaves her little daughter an orphan in George Gissing's *The Unclassed*.

Startop   Gentleman friend of Pip Pirrip; he aids Pip and Herbert Pocket in their attempt to get Abel Magwitch out of England in Charles Dickens's *Great Expectations*.

Sir Standish Stately   Stereotypical member of the gentry who is highest in his own esteem in Henry Brooke's *The Fool of Quality*.

Mr. Staunton   Kindly rector of Willingsham and George Staunton's father; he assists Jeanie Deans in Sir Walter Scott's *The Heart of Midlothian*.

Eleanor Staunton   See Lady Ellerton.

George Staunton (Geordie Robertson, Gentle George)   Heir of Willingsham, disowned for his dissolute lifestyle; as Geordie (Gentle George) Robertson, he is Andrew Wilson's smuggling associate; he seduces Effie Deans and then must desert her; they later marry, and he becomes an arrogant and upstanding citizen, proud of his family honor; he is killed in a robbery attempt by his and Effie's outlaw son, the Whistler, while he is seeking him in Sir Walter Scott's *The Heart of Midlothian*.

Judge Staveley   Gentle and much-loved father of Au-

gustus, Madeline, and Isabella (Arbuthnot); his tolerant attitudes assist the love of Madeline and Felix Graham in Anthony Trollope's *Orley Farm*.

Augustus Staveley   Young lawyer brother of Madeline and confidant of Felix Graham; he engages in a tepid wooing of Sophia Furnival in Anthony Trollope's *Orley Farm*.

Lady Isabella Staveley   Devoted wife of Judge Staveley; she prides herself on keeping the family home at Noningsby well supplied with creature comforts in Anthony Trollope's *Orley Farm*.

Madeline Staveley   Judge Staveley's vivacious daughter, with whom young Peregrine Orme falls hopelessly in love; she becomes engaged to her sweetheart, Felix Graham, in Anthony Trollope's *Orley Farm*.

Mr. Staytape   Tailor to whom Cringer recommends Roderick Random for help without saying what his business is in Tobias Smollett's *The Adventures of Roderick Random*.

Anne Steele   Plain and vulgar elder sister of Lucy; she can talk of nothing but beaux until she lets slip the news of Lucy's secret engagement in Jane Austen's *Sense and Sensibility*.

Lucy Steele   A successful schemer, a clever and pretty flatterer, but inelegant; she holds Edward Ferrars to their youthful secret engagement, torments her suspected rival, Elinor Dashwood, and finally elopes with Robert Ferrars, who has gained the inheritance Edward has lost in Jane Austen's *Sense and Sensibility*.

Richard Steele   Playright and politician, a generous, dissipated, charming man and Henry Esmond's friend in William Makepeace Thackeray's *The History of Henry Esmond*.

Steelhead   Osberne Wolfsson's nonmortal guardian, who appears at need, advises him, and bestows the unconquerable sword Boardcleaver in William Morris's *The Sundering Flood*.

Steenie Steenson   Ancestor of Wandering Willie Steenson; he was a famous piper and visited the ghost of his landlord, Sir Robert Redgauntlet, in hell in Sir Walter Scott's *Redgauntlet*.

Wandering Willie Steenson   Blind fiddler, who befriends Darsie Latimer (Arthur Redgauntlet) and sings ballads to communicate with the kidnapped Darsie in Sir Walter Scott's *Redgauntlet*.

Mrs. Steerforth   Indulgent, elderly mother of James

Steerforth in Charles Dickens's *The Personal History of David Copperfield*.

James Steerforth   Proud, handsome student at Salem House school; he is David Copperfield's friend and protector; later he accompanies David on a visit to the Peggotty household at Yarmouth; he seduces Emily Peggotty and abandons her after she runs away with him; he is drowned in a shipwreck in Charles Dickens's *The Personal History of David Copperfield*.

Sir Steady Steerwell   Government minister who betrays the confidence of Perry Pickle in London; he instigates the move which forces Perry to seek refuge in the Fleet in Tobias Smollett's *The Adventures of Peregrine Pickle*.

Timothy Steighton   Clerk with Edward Crimsworth's manufacturing firm, who spies on William Crimsworth for his master in Charlotte Brontë's *The Professor*.

Stephen Steinernherz   Executioner who wishes to become a noble; he turns against and executes his master, Archibald von Hagenbach, and tries to steal diamonds taken by von Hagenbach from John Philipson (John de Vere) in Sir Walter Scott's *Anne of Geierstein*.

Baron Steinhaussen   Adoptive parent of Agnes D'Albini; his ill health causes Agnes to give up his son, whom he has promised to another as part of a gambling debt, in Charlotte Dacre's *The Libertine*.

Baroness Steinhaussen   Agnes D'Albini's adoptive parent, who helps her escape from Switzerland to Germany in Charlotte Dacre's *The Libertine*.

Darlowitz Steinhaussen   German aristocrat and lover of Agnes D'Albini; he comes to marry her the night she has taken her nun's vows; he is killed by her father in Charlotte Dacre's *The Libertine*.

Stella   The mysterious person in a painting which is the subject of one of Mark Rutherford's essays appended by Reuben Shapcott to Mark Rutherford's *Mark Rutherford's Deliverance*.

Walter Stelling   The ambitious clergyman who takes Tom Tulliver as a pupil in his school, King's Lorton, and attempts to give him a "gentleman's education," which consists mainly of monotonous Latin drills of no use to the uninterested boy; he also tutors Philip Wakem and allows Maggie Tulliver to study with the boys a bit, although he is convinced that women have shallower minds in George Eliot's *The Mill on the Floss*.

Joseph Stemm   General factotum and law clerk of Sir Thomas Underwood; he is constantly reproving his master; when Sir Thomas finally decides to settle down with

his daughter, Patience, at Fulham, the elderly retainer is given a place there in Anthony Trollope's *Ralph the Heir*.

Stennis(es)   Brothers, a "pair of hare-brained Scots," Loudon Dodd's friends, present at Genius of Muskegon's judging in Robert Louis Stevenson's *The Wrecker*.

Stephano   Servant of Alphonso d'Alvarada (Raymond, Marquis de la Cisternas); he unintentionally gives bandits knowledge of his master's effects and is later murdered by them in Matthew Lewis's *The Monk*.

Stephanoff   William Meadows's friend, who is a clerk in John Ernest Biren's Bureau de Ministre; upon discovering that Biren has ordered that Meadows be arrested, he helps his English friend escape to Amsterdam in William Godwin's *Cloudesley*.

Stephen   A favorite eunuch of Justinian II; Julian the Apostate, incarnated as a monk, flatters him to gain introduction to the emperor in Henry Fielding's *A Journey From This World to the Next*.

Stephen the Eater   Hired man employed by Master Nicholas of Wethermel; he is a smith, skilled craftsman, and ingenious spy in William Morris's *The Sundering Flood*.

Stephen-a-Hurst   Swevenham man eager to leave Cheaping Knowe; he joins Ralph and leads the Champions of the Dry Tree in the Battle of Upmeads in William Morris's *The Well at the World's End*.

Ann (Nanny) Roche Stern   Wife of Tom and mother of Diana Stern; she dies from grief and fright caused by her daughter's plight in Henry Brooke's *The Fool of Quality*.

Diana Stern   Beautiful daughter of Tom Stern; a scheme by the lecherous Delville to seduce her lands her in debtor's prison; she is rescued by the charity of Henry Clinton, exercised through young Harry Clinton in Henry Brooke's *The Fool of Quality*.

Tom Stern   A respectable squire's second son, who becomes a house painter; he marries Ann Roche and has a daughter, Diana; his father-in-law tries to separate Diana from him by bribing her in Henry Brooke's *The Fool of Quality*.

Duchess de Sternach   Amelia Darlowitz's aristocratic mother, who taught her daughter "ideal" virtues and died at her bedside in Charlotte Dacre's *The Passions*.

Duchess of Stevenage   Leader of fashion whose social acceptance of the Melmottes is traded for Augustus Melmotte's rescue of her brother, Lord Alfred Grendall, from bankruptcy in Anthony Trollope's *The Way We Live Now*.

Mr. Stevens Affable country squire and brother of Prudilla; he is angry at Prudilla's bequest of her fortune to a daughter born of an illicit relationship with Lucius Manly, but he is brought to see the justice of his sister's action in Mary Collyer's *Felicia to Charlotte*.

Prudilla Stevens Scheming Calvinist spinster, who delights in attacking the moral faults of others; her conviction that she belongs to the elect gives free reign to her lust for Lucius Manly; she plots the destruction of the budding relationship between Felicia and Lucius; on her deathbed, she confesses to having seduced Lucius in his sleep in Mary Collyer's *Felicia to Charlotte*.

"Mr. Steward" Peter Wilkins's predecessor as captain's steward in Robert Paltock's *The Life and Adventures of Peter Wilkins*.

Steward of Charity A man who looks after his own interests before those of the charity in Charles Johnstone's *Chrysal: or, The Adventures of a Guinea*.

Mr. Stewart One of the four Scottish counsels to alleged murderer James Stewart in the Appin murder trial in Robert Louis Stevenson's *Catriona*.

Mrs. Stewart James Stewart's wife, who copiously thanks and blesses David Balfour for his loyalty to her husband in Robert Louis Stevenson's *Kidnapped*.

Alan Black Stewart See Alan Breck Stewart.

Alan Breck Stewart Brash but loyal Highland Jacobite who is outlawed as a traitor in Scotland and later becomes an alleged conspirator in the murder of Colin Ray Campbell; he is befriended by David Balfour in a fight aboard the *Covenant*, and the two travel as fugitives across Scotland in Robert Louis Stevenson's *Kidnapped*. He may be the Alan Black Stewart, suspected by Ephran Mackellar of being the Appin murderer, who challenges the Master (James Durie) in *The Master of Ballantrae: A Winter's Tale*. He is helped to escape to France in *Catriona*.

Arabella Stewart Hapless granddaughter of Bess of Hardwicke (Elizabeth Cavendish) and a pawn in her relatives' scramble for power in Charlotte Yonge's *Unknown to History*.

Charles Stewart Small and brisk lawyer, agent, and kinsman to the Appin Stewarts; he helps David Balfour procure secret passage to France for Alan Breck Stewart in Robert Louis Stevenson's *Catriona*.

Charles Edward Stewart (or Stuart) ("Bonny Prince Charlie," the "Young Pretender") Son of the Chevalier de St. George and grandson of King James II; he leads an insurrection, at first successful but ultimately doomed, to place his exiled father on the throne of England in Sir Walter Scott's *Waverly*. Using the pseudonym Father Bonaventure he travels to England to head a new rebellion led by Hugh Redgauntlet, is captured with Jacobites, and is magnanimously released by orders of the king in *Redgauntlet*.

Francis Stewart, Sergeant Bothwell Soldier in the army of King James II, who fights against Burley (John Balfour) and arrests Henry Morton; he is killed by Balfour after being disarmed in Sir Walter Scott's *Old Mortality*.

James Stewart (or Stuart) See Chevalier de St. George.

James (of the Glens) Stewart Highland Jacobite clansman of the Appin Stewarts suspected of the murder of Colin Ray Campbell; David Balfour and Alan Breck Stewart believe him innocent and meet him at his home in Robert Louis Stevenson's *Kidnapped*. He is tried and executed in *Catriona*.

Robin (Rob, Robbie) Stewart Law clerk to Charles Stewart in Robert Louis Stevenson's *Catriona*.

George Gustavus, Marquis of Steyne Aristocratic and lecherous patron of Becky (Sharp) Crawley, with whom he is caught by her husband in a compromising situation; the humiliation resulting from the scandal creates his implacable hatred for Becky in William Makepeace Thackeray's *Vanity Fair*. He appears in *The History of Pendennis* and is mentioned in *The Newcomes*.

George Stickatit Junior member of the law firm of Dry and Stickatit, executors of the elder George Bertram's estate in Anthony Trollope's *The Bertrams*.

Jeremy Stickles John Ridd's friend from London who works for the king; loyal friends, John and Jeremy fight together in a successful attack against the Doones in R. D. Blackmore's *Lorna Doone*.

Stiggins An influential and cynical critic, who runs down Hubert Price's play in George Moore's *Vain Fortune*.

Mr. Stiggins Dissenting, red-nosed, rum-guzzling clergyman, who is befriended by Susan Weller and takes advantage of her in Charles Dickens's *The Posthumous Papers of the Pickwick Club*.

Mrs. Stiggs Tenant of Trotter's Buildings; she provides board and lodging for Carry Brattle, paid by Frank Fenwick in Anthony Trollope's *The Vicar of Bullhampton*.

Sir Stentor Stile English sharper, who meets Ferdinand in Paris and joins with Sir Giles Squirrel to win all of Ferdinand's money at dice in Tobias Smollett's *The Adventures of Ferdinand Count Fathom*.

Edward Stiles Mutinous member from Wapping of John Oxenham's expedition; he is killed by Oxenham's fist in Charles Kingsley's *Westward Ho!*.

Lord Lancaster Stiltstalking Retired member of the British embassy; he is maintained in Parliament by the Circumlocution Office and referred to as the "noble Refrigerator" in Charles Dickens's *Little Dorrit*.

Stirling Brother-in-law of William Meadows and a tenant on property belonging to Richard Danvers, Lord Alton; he invites Meadows to stay with him and his wife, and during this visit Meadows is unexpectedly summoned to call on the lord himself in William Godwin's *Cloudesley*.

Mr. Stistick Member of Parliament for Peterloo; he and his wife are guests at Sir Henry Harcourt's dinner in Anthony Trollope's *The Bertrams*.

Mrs. Stistick Indolent, complacent, silent wife of Mr. Stistick in Anthony Trollope's *The Bertrams*.

Lord Stivers Ministerial agent who hires Hammel Clement to write pro-administration pamphlets; he is eventually killed by Arabella Clement during an attempted rape; robbery of his corpse leads to murder and robbery charges against her in Henry Brooke's *The Fool of Quality*.

Ruth Stockwool Neighbor who gives protection to Ann Avice Caro after her mother's death in Thomas Hardy's *The Well-Beloved*.

Mrs. Stoke-D'Urberville Alec Stoke-D'Urberville's blind mother, whose late husband appropriated the ancient D'Urberville name for its aristocratic implications; her great pride is her poultry farm; Alec's letter offering employment to Tess Durbeyfield is written as though from his mother in Thomas Hardy's *Tess of the D'Urbervilles*.

Alec Stoke-D'Urberville Wealthy, arrogant, calculating seducer of Tess Durbeyfield; he experiences a religious conversion and takes up itinerant preaching, but reencountering Tess, he relapses completely; his proposal of marriage cannot be accepted by her, but in desperate need she becomes his mistress; upon the return of her husband, her detestation of Stoke-D'Urberville is so great

that she kills him in Thomas Hardy's *Tess of the D'Urbervilles*.

Mr. Stokes Old-fashioned country solicitor of the Germain family; he dislikes making decisions or causing trouble in Anthony Trollope's *Is He Popenjoy?*.

Mrs. Stokes Highbury innkeeper; the Westons give a ball at the Crown inn in Jane Austen's *Emma*.

Mrs. Stone Officer's widow who assumes the duties of hostess at Grondale Castle after Lady Grondale dies and who hopes to become the next Lady Grondale in Robert Bage's *Hermsprong*.

Sarah Stone A widow who cares for Hetty Sorrel when her baby is born and later recognizes the clothes she has dressed the newborn with as the same as those on the dead child found by John Olding; her testimony at the trial removes any chance that Hetty will be found innocent in George Eliot's *Adam Bede*.

Stone-face Older warrior of Burgdale; he is foster father of Iron-face in William Morris's *The Roots of the Mountains*.

Mr. Story Butler at Marlowe in J. Sheridan Le Fanu's *Guy Deverell*.

Elias Strachen Covenanter who bought Drumthwacket, causing Dalgetty to side with Montrose in Sir Walter Scott's *A Legend of Montrose*.

Hannah Strachen Elderly widow of Elias Stachen; through marriage with her, Dalgetty regains his paternal estate of Drumthwacket in Sir Walter Scott's *A Legend of Montrose*.

Lord Straddle Son of an influential aristocrat in London; he introduces Roderick Random to Lord Strutwell and receives a diamond ring from Roderick in Tobias Smollett's *The Adventures of Roderick Random*.

Molly Straddle Prostitute friend of Jonathan Wild; she steals nine hundred pounds from him during an amorous dalliance in Henry Fielding's *The Life of Mr. Jonathan Wild the Great*.

Mr. Stradling Law printer and friend of Mr. Rudge and Mr. Trottman; he engages in disputes over legal technicalities in Thomas Holcroft's *The Adventures of Hugh Trevor*.

Thomas, Lord Strafford Charles I's appointee as Lord Lieutenant of Ireland, in whose absence the rebellion led by Sir Phelim O'Neile and his fellow conspirators takes place in William Godwin's *Mandeville*.

Straightener Any therapist hired to correct the vice practiced by family members; straighteners use torture and lectures on practitioners of vice and make their own forays into vice so as to know how best to deal with the problems of their clients in Samuel Butler's *Erewhon* and in *Erewhon Revisited Twenty Years Later.*

Mrs. Herbert Strangeways Woman of intrigue who introduces women to the disreputable Cyrus Redgrave and practices blackmail in George Gissing's *The Whirlpool.*

Guy Strangways (the younger Guy Deverell) Handsome, noble young nephew of Varbarriere; he is revealed to be the son of the Guy Deverell killed by Sir Jeckyl Marlowe; he falls in love with Beatrix Marlowe; unaware of his uncle's plans for revenge, he quarrels with his uncle over the proposed lawsuit against Marlowe but is eventually reunited with him and, through the machinations of Lady Alice Redcliffe, with Beatrix, whom he marries in J. Sheridan Le Fanu's *Guy Deverell.*

Herbert Strangways See Varbarriere

Hugh Strap Schoolmate of Roderick Random; he once saved Roderick's life, assists in punishment of the schoolmaster, becomes a barber, is wounded by Rifle, becomes Roderick's companion on the road to London, is employed by a periwig maker in London, separates from Roderick until they meet again near Rheims, France, returns with Roderick to London, and marries Nancy Williams when he returns with Roderick to Scotland in Tobias Smollett's *The Adventures of Roderick Random.*

Monsieur de Strasbourg Public executioner who privately beheads Princess Olivia on her husband's order in William Makepeace Thackeray's *The Luck of Barry Lyndon.*

Mrs. Stratton A strong-minded colonel's wife, friend of Isabel Clarendon, and mother of four athletic and combative sons in George Gissing's *Isabel Clarendon.*

Strauchan Old soldier who is Sir Kenneth's only surviving follower and who knows his real identity in Sir Walter Scott's *The Talisman.*

Jack Straw Leader of the Men of Kent in a skirmish with the king's men during Wat Tyler's Rebellion of 1381 in William Morris's *A Dream of John Ball.*

Mrs. Strictland Occasional recipient of Mrs. Darnford's letters discussing her life and activities in Clara Reeve's *Plans of Education.*

Major Strike Caroline's cruel and arrogant husband, a marine who fortunately dies in George Meredith's *Evan Harrington.*

Caroline Strike Evan Harrington's unhappily married sister; the only one of the three who maintains a sense of honor, she tries to arrange a liaison between her brother and Julianna Bonner, whom she nurses in George Meredith's *Evan Harrington.*

Daniel Stringer Dishonest assistant of his cousin, the landlord of the Dragon of Wantly inn; his belated testimony names Jem Scuttle as the thief of the check that Josiah Crawley has already been cleared of stealing; Stringer is punished and driven out of Barset by popular though not legal means in Anthony Trollope's *The Last Chronicle of Barset.*

John Stringer Landlord of the Dragon of Wantly inn; its owner, Mrs. Arabin, accepts as rent a cheque lost there by Mr. Soames; by quietly adding it to her husband's gift of money to Mr. Crawley, she unknowingly brings about his troubles in Anthony Trollope's *The Last Chronicle of Barset.*

Dr. Strong Tall, elderly, kind schoolmaster in Canterbury whose school David Copperfield attends; he later employs David as his secretary in Charles Dickens's *The Personal History of David Copperfield.*

Mayor Strong Husband of Yram and a man of few words, who leaves the running of things to Yram; he knows Jack Higgs is the father of George but loves Yram enough not to care; he aids in Higgs's escape in Samuel Butler's *Erewhon Revisited Twenty Years Later.*

Annie Strong Young, pretty wife of Dr. Strong; she used to love her cousin Jack Maldon but now loves her husband; suspected of still loving Maldon, she vindicates herself in Charles Dickens's *The Personal History of David Copperfield.*

Captain Edward Strong Factotum and friend of Sir Francis Clavering, whose interests he loyally serves in spite of his own and his patron's poverty in William Makepeace Thackeray's *The History of Pendennis.*

George Strong Head Ranger and son of Yram and Jack Higgs; after Higgs reveals his bravery and love of truth, George loves him as his father; he aids Yram in helping Higgs escape in Samuel Butler's *Erewhon Revisited Twenty Years Later.*

Megalena Strozzi Manipulative mistress of Il Conte Berenza; she uses her new lover to attempt his murder and then flees with him to the forest in Charlotte Dacre's *Zofloya; or, The Moor.*

Mr. Struggles Top bowler of the Dingley Dell cricket club in Charles Dickens's *The Posthumous Papers of the Pickwick Club.*

Nick Strumpfer (Pacolet) A hideously deformed, mute dwarf who serves Norna Troil in Sir Walter Scott's *The Pirate*.

Earl Strutwell Influential homosexual English lord, who unsuccessfully tries to seduce Roderick Random in Tobias Smollett's *The Adventures of Roderick Random*.

Mr. Stryver Barrister who aids Sydney Carton at Charles Darnay's trial for spying in England; he later expresses the view that Charles St. Evrémonde (Darnay) is not a gentleman for renouncing his rights as a French aristocrat in Charles Dickens's *A Tale of Two Cities*.

David Stuart (Stuart of Dunleath) Hero of the novel; he is loved by Eleanor Raymond, for whom he is appointed guardian by her father on the latter's deathbed; poor because of his own father's extravagance, and unfairly accused of a crime in regard to Eleanor's money, he pretends suicide but goes to America to earn back the money he has lost; his misunderstanding of Eleanor's love and his pretense of being dead cause the tragedy of the novel; he reveals his love of Eleanor but marries Lady Margaret after Eleanor's death in Caroline Norton's *Stuart of Dunleath*.

Sir George Stuart Nobleman to whom Mr. B— holds forth on the virtues of Scots as tutors in Samuel Richardson's *Pamela, or Virtue Rewarded*.

Jack Stuart Owner of the yacht which takes Sir Hugh and Archibald Clavering on their fatal fishing trip to Norway in Anthony Trollope's *The Claverings*.

Captain Stubber Small-time moneylender working for a shady firm of attorneys; he pesters George Hotspur for outstanding debts in Anthony Trollope's *Sir Harry Hotspur of Humblethwaite*.

Ensign Stubble Young officer in Captain Osborne's regiment who admires Osborne and Amelia (Sedley) Osborne; she nurses him after he is wounded at Waterloo in William Makepeace Thackeray's *Vanity Fair*.

Dr. Stubbs Traveling quack, whose audience Geoffry Wildgoose tries to appropriate; in retaliation, Stubbs tells the local constable that Wildgoose is a Jesuit in Richard Graves's *The Spiritual Quixote*.

Charlie Stubbs (Stobbs) The "Yorkshireman" who travels throughout England and France with John Jorrocks at Jorrocks's expense; he is a connoisseur of art and cuisine and the favorite suitor of Belinda Jorrocks in Robert Surtees's *Jorrocks's Jaunts and Jollities* and in *Handley Cross*.

Colonel Jonathan Stubbs Bearish, red-faced professional soldier, who scoffs at marriage but falls in love with Ayala Dormer; although he in no way accords with her beau ideal, she comes to see his worth and marries him in Anthony Trollope's *Ayala's Angel*.

Mr. Stultz Bond Street master tailor admired by Alton Locke for his wisdom, kindness, and humanity in Charles Kingsley's *Alton Locke*.

Mr. Stumfold Narrow-minded evangelical clergyman dead set against card-playing, dancing, and hunting; he is popular with the ladies of Littlebath, among whom he presides with his censorious wife in Anthony Trollope's *Miss Mackenzie*.

Mrs. Stumfold Nagging wife of a Littlebath clergyman; her favorite pastime is chiding ladies in the parish for their behavior; she warns Margaret Mackenzie not to encourage the curate Maguire and departs in high dudgeon to poison the local atmosphere still further in Anthony Trollope's *Miss Mackenzie*.

Bill Stumps Laborer and perhaps inscriber of a message on a small stone in Charles Dickens's *The Posthumous Papers of the Pickwick Club*.

Mrs. Sturgis Wife of the old boatman who shelters Mary Barton in Elizabeth Gaskell's *Mary Barton*.

Ben Sturgis Old boatman who shelters Mary Barton when she collapses with fever after the chase for Will Wilson in Elizabeth Gaskell's *Mary Barton*.

Dr. Barney Sturk Surgeon to the Royal Irish Artillery; he believes himself a shrewd businessman and wants to replace Charles Nutter as manager of Lord Castlemallard's estate but ends up in debt; he tries to blackmail Paul Dangerfield when he realizes the latter's true identity as Charles Archer; Dangerfield beats him and leaves him for dead; he is found in a coma from which, after a few months, he awakes long enough to identify Dangerfield as his attacker and the murderer of Beauclerc, but dies shortly thereafter in J. Sheridan Le Fanu's *The House by the Churchyard*.

Letitia Sturk Kindly but cowed wife of Dr. Barney Sturk; garrulous when her husband isn't present, she tells Paul Dangerfield gossip of the town and its inhabitants; she believes him a friend when he gives the family money in J. Sheridan Le Fanu's *The House by the Churchyard*.

Mrs. Sturt Friendly rustic neighbor of Mrs. Ray; she counsels her friend's daughter, Rachel, not to let anybody stand in the way of the man she loves; she provides the opportunity for the lovers to pledge themselves finally in Anthony Trollope's *Rachel Ray*.

Father Henry Sturt   A force for morality and goodness in the Jago; he tries unsuccessfully to help Dicky Perrott go straight and plans to build a new church in Arthur Morrison's *A Child of the Jago*.

Stuzza   Assassin brought to justice by Abellino/Flodoardo (Count Rosalvo) in Matthew Lewis's *The Bravo of Venice*.

Stygee   Daughter of Oniwheske; she marries Georigetti and with him rules three kingdoms in Robert Paltock's *The Life and Adventures of Peter Wilkins*.

Subaltern   Military enthusiast, who thinks that rank in the army is determined by merit, and who proves himself worthy in Charles Johnstone's *Chrysal: or, The Adventures of a Guinea*.

Cecilia (Cissy) Subbs   Buxom daughter of a local squire; she fancies herself as Edward Waverly's wife in Sir Walter Scott's *Waverly*.

Sub-Warden (Vice-Warden, Sibby)   Brother of the Warden; he doctors legal papers in the Warden's absence and falsely reports the death of his brother in order to usurp control of Outland; he places his son, Uggug, in line of succession instead of Bruno in Lewis Carroll's *Sylvie and Bruno*. He is the Emperor who eventually repents his misdeeds and learns to rule with wisdom in *Sylvie and Bruno Concluded*.

Tom Suckbribe   Incompetent constable, who allows the highwayman who robbed and beat Joseph Andrews to escape from the Dragon Inn in Henry Fielding's *The History of the Adventures of Mr. Joseph Andrews and of his Friend Mr. Abraham Adams*.

Lord Suckling   Nobleman who nearly duels with Algernon Blancove over Mrs. Lovell in George Meredith's *Rhoda Fleming*.

Polly Suckling   One of the nine pupils of Mrs. Teachum's school; she learns respect for the aged in Sarah Fielding's *The Governess*.

Selina Suckling   Sister of Mrs. Elton; her husband's wealth, house, and style of living are the chief subjects of Mrs. Elton's boasts in Jane Austen's *Emma*.

Sucrewasser of Vienna   Mid sixteenth-century painter, trained as a herald painter and admired for his colorful and correct renderings of his only subjects, the Three Graces and Four Seasons; his fortunes decline when Og of Basan demonstrates that nut oil is a better canvas varnish than egg white in William Beckford's *Biographical Memoirs of Extraordinary Painters*.

Benjamin Suddlechop   London barber who keeps a tavern as a cover for his wife's dark dealings in Sir Walter Scott's *The Fortunes of Nigel*.

Ursula Suddlechop   A bawd and the wife of barber Benjamin Suddlechop; she serves Margaret Ramsay in the plan to rescue Nigel Olifaunt from the Tower in Sir Walter Scott's *The Fortunes of Nigel*.

Lady Matilda Sufton   The newly widowed neighbor of Frederick, Lord Lindore and Lady Juliana Douglas; she is known for her theatrics and hypocrisy in Susan Ferrier's *Marriage*.

Sugden   The constable who is called by Robert Moore to arrest the machine breakers in Charlotte Brontë's *Shirley*.

Sukoh   Royal Professor of Worldly Wisdom at Bridgeford and one of the first people Jack Higgs meets on his return to Erewhon; Sukoh reveals enormous changes in Erewhon; he gives the sermon at the christening of Sunchild Temple; he threatens to have Higgs killed as an imposter, all the while knowing Higgs's true identity in Samuel Butler's *Erewhon Revisited Twenty Years Later*.

Sukop   Royal Professor of Unworldly Wisdom at Bridgeford; he wears his English-style clothes reversed; the second of the two whom Jack Higgs meets upon re-entering Erewhon, he reveals enormous changes in Erewhon in Samuel Butler's *Erewhon Revisited Twenty Years Later*.

Squire Sulky   Brutal neighbor of the Moreland estate; he tyrannizes over women in Henry Brooke's *The Fool of Quality*.

Sullenness   A native slave so named by William John Attwater; repeatedly punished for minor crimes committed by another native slave, Obsequiousness, he finally hangs himself out of pride and desperation in Robert Louis Stevenson's *The Ebb-Tide: A Trio and a Quartette*.

Moggy Sullivan   Spunky and faithful servingwoman to the Nutters; she tries to save her mistress by going for help when Mary Matchwell attempts to take over the household in J. Sheridan Le Fanu's *The House by the Churchyard*.

Sir Thomas Sullivan   One of the Irish whom the Master (James Durie) "truckles to" during his campaign with Prince Charlie in Robert Louis Stevenson's *The Master of Ballantrae: A Winter's Tale*.

Mr. Sumelin   Respectable banker, who handles Charles Hermsprong's English financial business in Robert Bage's *Hermsprong*.

Harriet Sumelin Daughter of Mr. Sumelin; she runs away to marry Mr. Fillygrove, realizes her folly, and is rescued by Charles Hermsprong in Robert Bage's *Hermsprong*.

Summer Handsome scholar befriended by Squire Allworthy; he contracted and died of smallpox after living a year at Allworthy's but before the clandestine birth of his son, Tom Jones, to the squire's sister in Henry Fielding's *The History of Tom Jones*.

Professor Summerlee Professor Challenger's chief scientific antagonist, who accompanies his great expedition and ultimately comes to agree with him in Arthur Conan Doyle's *The Lost World*.

William Summers Robert Lovelace's servant and conspirator in persecuting Clarissa Harlowe in Samuel Richardson's *Clarissa: or, The History of a Young Lady*.

Esther Summerson Illegitimate, humble heroine, who is Ada Clare's companion and John Jarndyce's housekeeper; resolved in her lonely, loveless childhood to be industrious, contented, true-hearted, and to do good to someone, she succeeds in being loved by all around her, eventually marrying Allan Woodcourt in Charles Dickens's *Bleak House*.

Mr. Sumner Grammar school headmaster in Charlotte Brontë's *Shirley*.

Freshfield Sumner A suitor of the frigid Pole sisters; his attention, like that of his rivals, is sought by more than one of the sisters in George Meredith's *Emilia in England*.

Knight of the Sun Jealous slayer of the Lady of Abundance, whom he had forced to marry him; he is killed by Ralph in William Morris's *The Well at the World's End*.

Sun-beam Sister of Folk-might; she participates in the battle of Silver-dale and subsequently marries Face-of-god in William Morris's *The Roots of the Mountains*.

Captain Sunderland The hero of Virginia St. Pierre's dreams; she adores his picture first and later learns to love the real man in Maria Edgeworth's *Belinda*.

Superior The head of the convent, who allows Alonzo de Monçada to attempt to escape the convent so that Monçada may be imprisoned during the Inquisition in Charles Maturin's *Melmoth the Wanderer*.

Superstition One of three men who give evidence against Faithful and Christian at their trial at Vanity Fair in John Bunyan's *The Pilgrim's Progress From this World to That Which Is to Come*.

Supervisor of Mock Monastery Well-born, well-connected man, who is educated abroad and corrupted by the religious and political principles of the foreign country; he establishes the Mock Monastery to invalidate his youthful conversion in Charles Johnstone's *Chrysal: or, The Adventures of a Guinea*.

Mr. Supple Somersetshire curate who tries weakly to curtail Squire Western's violent anger when Sophia Western continues to refuse the match with Master Blifil in Henry Fielding's *The History of Tom Jones*.

Mrs. Supple Servant to Lord B—'s mother, the countess; she is a prying busybody sent by Henrietta Courteney to get her a coach when Lord B—'s attentions become oppressive in Charlotte Lennox's *Henrietta*.

Supplehough A dissenting preacher who, because he works harder than the curates, wins many converts in Charlotte Brontë's *Shirley*.

Mr. Supplehouse Nathaniel Sowerby's journalist friend on the great newspaper, the *Jupiter*; his published attacks add to Mark Robarts's distress in Anthony Trollope's *Framley Parsonage*.

Surgeon Unnamed medical man who exaggerates the seriousness of Tom Jones's wounded temple, then abandons his patient when he realizes Tom isn't rich in Henry Fielding's *The History of Tom Jones*.

Surgeon Member of the group which is led by Captain Singleton through Africa; he helps heal the young Black Prince's wounds in Daniel Defoe's *The Life, Adventures, and Pyracies of the Famous Captain Singleton*.

Susan Upton Inn chambermaid who delivers Sophia Western's muff to Tom Jones to punish him for his indiscretion with Mrs. Waters in Henry Fielding's *The History of Tom Jones*.

Susan Peter's sister, a Savoy peasant who temporarily shelters Adeline during her flight from Phillippe, Marquis de Montalt in Ann Radcliffe's *The Romance of the Forest*.

Susan Maid in the workhouse where Oliver Twist lives in Charles Dickens's *Oliver Twist*.

Susan (Susanna) Roxana's eldest daughter by the brewer, though she initially believes her mother to be Roxana's servant Amy; later Amy has her falsely imprisoned for debt in Daniel Defoe's *The Fortunate Mistress*.

Mrs. Susan Housemaid who interrupts Amelia Booth's hysterics over the challenge from Colonel James to deliver Booth's remorseful letter from prison in Henry Fielding's *Amelia*.

Mrs. Susan   Favorite domestic of Matilda Golding; after her mistress's death, she is promised financial support for life by Henry Clinton in Henry Brooke's *The Fool of Quality*.

Susannah   Shandy family maid; she forgets the baby's intended Christian name, Trismegistus, on the way to tell it to the curate, who consequently names him Tristram; she nearly emasculates Tristram when he is five years old by accidentally dropping the window sash on him in Laurence Sterne's *The Life and Opinions of Tristram Shandy, Gentleman*.

Thomas Ratcliffe, Earl of Sussex   A military leader who has been of great service to Queen Elizabeth in quelling rebellions; as the leader of a court faction, he is the archrival of Robert Dudley, Earl of Leicester; because Edmund Tressilian is Sussex's supporter as well as his kinsman, Leicester is the more willing to believe Richard Varney's accusations that Tressilian is guilty of adultery with Amy Robsart Dudley in Sir Walter Scott's *Kenilworth*. He is a supporter of the Duke of Norfolk's plan to free the pregnant Mary, Queen of Scots in Sophia Lee's *The Recess*.

Sutlememe   Dwarf and a loyal friend of Emir Fakreddin; he helps stage the feigned deaths of Nouronihar and Gulchenrouz in William Beckford's *Vathek*.

Sutler   Venial, vicious man, who, in business with the Admiral's Clerk, cheats soldiers and sailors, their masters, and the English public in Charles Johnstone's *Chrysal: or, The Adventures of a Guinea*.

Suzette   A teacher at Mlle. Reuter's school who is common and ordinary in all respects in Charlotte Brontë's *The Professor*.

Svengali   A sinister German musician, who is first a friend of Taffy Wynne, the Laird (Sandy McAllister), and Little Billie (Billy Bagot) but becomes a vile enemy; a vain, brilliant man possessing a talent to make beautiful, feeling music, he is also mysterious and violent; Svengali marries Trilby O'Ferrall and makes her his instrument and servant in George Du Maurier's *Trilby*.

Jack Swagger   Irish bawdy-house bully and friend of Molly Straddle, who gives him two hundred pounds of the money she stole from Jonathan Wild in Henry Fielding's *The Life of Mr. Jonathan Wild the Great*.

Charlotte Troyton Swancourt   A plain, middle-aged widow of means, who marries Christopher Swancourt; she is good humored and amusing; Henry Knight is her cousin in Thomas Hardy's *A Pair of Blue Eyes*.

Christopher Swancourt   Elfride's father, a clergyman; he will not countenance her engagement to Stephen Smith, the son of village peasants, in Thomas Hardy's *A Pair of Blue Eyes*.

Elfride Swancourt   Intelligent, charming, emotionally developing heroine, who falls in love with the young architect Stephen Smith but in his absence rejects him for the more sophisticated Henry Knight; forsaken by Knight, she marries Lord Luxellian, a wealthy widower with two children, and dies in miscarriage in Thomas Hardy's *A Pair of Blue Eyes*.

Rhoda Swartz   Mulatto heiress whom Mr. Osborne unsuccessfully orders his son George to marry; she refuses Mr. Osborne's own proposal and marries the Hon. James McMull in William Makepeace Thackeray's *Vanity Fair*.

Paul (Poll) Sweedlepipe   Barber and bird fancier; he is a tenderhearted friend to Bailey and landlord to Sarah Gamp in Charles Dickens's *The Life and Adventures of Martin Chuzzlewit*.

Mme. Sweeny   Former nursemaid at Mme. Beck's school who lasts only a month because of her coarse, drunken manner in Charlotte Brontë's *Villette*.

David Sweeting   The small, good-natured Nunnely curate, who marries the hefty Miss Dora Sykes in Charlotte Brontë's *Shirley*.

Mabel Sweetwinter   Daughter of a miller; a childhood friend of Harry Richmond, she is courted by him, then seduced by Edbury; she and the pursuing Edbury are lost at sea on Captain Welsh's ship in George Meredith's *The Adventures of Harry Richmond*.

Mrs. Swertha   Basil (Vaughan) Mertoun's greedy and unprincipled housekeeper; though affectionate towards Basil's son Mordaunt, she fears Basil and slyly fleeces them both in Sir Walter Scott's *The Pirate*.

Sage of Swevenham   Sturdy older man, who advises Ralph and Ursula on reaching the Well; he later accompanies them to Upmeads in William Morris's *The Well at the World's End*.

George Swidger   William's sick brother, who is depressed, scared, and cannot die the way he wants to after Redlaw's visit in Charles Dickens's *The Haunted Man and the Ghost's Bargain*.

Milly Swidger   William's wife, a kind, motherly hard worker, who loves people and tries to better the lives of those around her; her goodness shines light into Mr. Redlaw's lonely life, and her neat simplicity reflects happiness in Charles Dickens's *The Haunted Man and the Ghost's Bargain*.

Philip Swidger   William's father and custodian of the school building Mr. Redlaw lives in; at eighty-seven, he has a good memory, has lived a happy life, and enjoys his son and his son's wife, Milly, always speaking to them kindly in Charles Dickens's *The Haunted Man and the Ghost's Bargain*.

William Swidger   Friendly, caring, talkative caretaker of Mr. Redlaw; his wife, Milly, and father, Philip, make his life much less lonely than Redlaw's in Charles Dickens's *The Haunted Man and the Ghost's Bargain*.

Little Swills   The comic soloist at the Sol's Arms in Cook's Court in Charles Dickens's *Bleak House*.

Captain Swinger   Agent of Sir John Harthover in Charles Kingsley's *The Water-Babies*.

Laird of Swinton   A Gudetown rake who injures the nephew of James Pawkie, the provost, over an actress; Pawkie generously saves him from the legal consequences of his actions in John Galt's *The Provost*.

Richard (Dick) Swiveller   Comic, imaginative, and careless young man, who likes to drink; he is originally in Daniel Quilp's plot to get Nell Trent's supposed fortune and breaks his engagement to Sophy Wackles to be free to marry Nell; he works as a clerk for Sampson Brass, where he meets the Marchioness, whom he eventually marries; he is instrumental in clearing Kit Nubbles in Charles Dickens's *The Old Curiosity Shop*.

Roger Swizzle   Red-faced quack doctor; an apothecary from London who purchases a lease to the mineral springs in Handley Cross, he touts the springs as a cureall to the upper class, whose complaints arise generally from overeating and indolence; through his scheme Handley Cross gains notoriety in Robert Surtees's *Handley Cross*.

W. Sword   One of the young men who first dig up the suicide's grave more than one hundred years after his death in James Hogg's *The Private Memoirs and Confessions of a Justified Sinner*.

Captain Swosser   The first of Mrs. Bayham Badger's often-mentioned late husbands in Charles Dickens's *Bleak House*.

Sir Jacob Swynford   Insolent, stupid, and proud uncle by half blood to Mr. B——, whose marriage disappoints his expectation that his children will inherit Mr. B——'s estate; his foolish refusal to acknowledge Mr. B——'s wife Pamela (Andrews) is confounded through a masquerade

perpetrated by Lady Davers and Pamela in Samuel Richardson's *Pamela, or Virtue Rewarded*.

Baroness Sybilla   Naive and beautiful woman, actually an Imperial Archduchess of Austria who, posing as Beckendorff's daughter, goes incognito to the court of her betrothed, the Crown Prince of Reisenburg, where she and Vivian Grey fall in love but cannot marry in Benjamin Disraeli's *Vivian Grey*.

Sybrandt   Gerard's worthless brother, who replaces the letter of pardon with the forged announcement of Margaret Brandt's death; after Gerard's curse, he falls and breaks his back; Margaret and Gerard care for him until he dies in the arms of the two lovers he parted in Charles Reade's *The Cloister and the Hearth*.

Sir Lyell Sycamore   Young English baronet, who tries to seduce Juliet Granville at Brightelmstone in Frances Burney's *The Wanderer*.

Squire Philip Sycamore   Young man of ill repute; intended by Anthony Darnel to be the husband of Aurelia Darnel, he fights a duel with Sir Launcelot Greaves, conspires to imprison Sir Launcelot in a London madhouse, and flees to the Continent when found out in Tobias Smollett's *The Adventures of Sir Launcelot Greaves*.

Anthony Syddall   Faithful and enigmatic old butler and major-domo at Osbaldistone Hall in Sir Walter Scott's *Rob Roy*.

Mr. Sydenham   Louisa Delmont's eventual husband; when George Delmont and Medora Glenmorris emigrate to America, the Sydenhams become tenants of George's English farm in Charlotte Smith's *The Young Philosopher*.

Sykes   Worker at Robert Moore's mill in Charlotte Brontë's *Shirley*.

Mrs. Sykes   A kind woman, who spends her time matchmaking in Charlotte Brontë's *Shirley*.

Christopher Sykes   A mill owner, who becomes brave only after drinking his gin in Charlotte Brontë's *Shirley*.

Dora Sykes   One of several self-possessed daughters of Christopher Sykes; she marries David Sweeting in Charlotte Brontë's *Shirley*.

John Sykes   Son of Christopher Sykes in Charlotte Brontë's *Shirley*.

Syllalippe   Princess of Affadid, attended from her infancy by Atamadoul; she is wooed by, and loves, Ochihatou, but she does not flout her parents' rejection of the match in Eliza Haywood's *Adventures of Eovaai, Princess of Ijaveo*.

Don Pedro de Sylva   Cruel and corrupt governor of Jamaica and brother-in-law of Mr. Mortimer in Sophia Lee's *The Recess*.

Sylvanus   Powerful orangutan from the imperial menagerie, trained to guard the Blaquernal dungeons; he is overcome by Robert of Paris and strangles Michael Agelastes in Sir Walter Scott's *Count Robert of Paris*.

Mr. Sylvester   Danby family lawyer in Samuel Richardson's *Sir Charles Grandison*.

Sylvia   Orphan who is saved from creditors and bailiffs when Bernardo steps in and manages to restore her mother's lost fortune to her; she refuses Monsieur De Vaux's offer of marriage in order to raise and educate her siblings in Sarah Scott's *The History of Cornelia*.

Sylvia   Beautiful young sister of Myrtilla; she runs off with her brother-in-law, Philander, marries his friend Brilliard to escape her father, and on occasion dresses as a man for greater freedom of movement; she becomes increasingly vain, promiscuous, and greedy, exploiting Brilliard in order to deceive Philander, Octavio, and Alonzo in Aphra Behn's *Love Letters Between a Nobleman and His Sister*.

Sylvie   Ten-year-old, angelic daughter of the Warden of Outland and older sister, teacher, and mother-figure of Bruno; she is sometimes seen as an Outlander, sometimes as a fairy, sometimes as a human child; she wears the magic locket of love bestowed by her father; she is the counterpart of Lady Muriel Orme in Lewis Carroll's *Sylvie and Bruno*. She returns to Outland for Uggug's banquet and is reunited with her father but remains a fairy in *Sylvie and Bruno Concluded*.

Mr. Symmes   Gentleman who makes an unsuccessful proposal of marriage to Clarissa Harlowe on the encouragement of her brother James in Samuel Richardson's *Clarissa: or, The History of a Young Lady*.

Mr. Symmonds   Innkeeper who tells Dr. Charles Primrose of Squire Thornhill's wicked reputation; Olivia Primrose is staying at his inn after being deserted by the squire in Oliver Goldsmith's *The Vicar of Wakefield*.

Dr. Symonds   William John Attwater's absent English partner in the South Sea fishing and export of pearls in Robert Louis Stevenson's *The Ebb-Tide: A Trio and a Quartette*.

Mr. Sympson   Shirley Keeldar's respectable but worldly uncle, who attempts to guide Shirley in her marital plans in Charlotte Brontë's *Shirley*.

Mrs. Sympson   A good but narrow-minded woman, who rules her own household in Charlotte Brontë's *Shirley*.

Gertrude Sympson   Shirley Keeldar's cousin, who condemns her unconventional conduct in Charlotte Brontë's *Shirley*.

Henry (Harry) Sympson   Shirley Keeldar's favorite cousin, a lame, pale boy, who is "desperately fond" of her in Charlotte Brontë's *Shirley*.

Isabella Sympson   Shirley Keeldar's cousin, who condemns her unconventional conduct in Charlotte Brontë's *Shirley*.

Richard Sympson   Lemuel Gulliver's cousin and correspondent in Jonathan Swift's *Travels into Several Remote Nations of the World. In Four Parts. By Lemuel Gulliver*.

Synesius   Genial, hospitable, hunting squire-bishop of Cyrene, admirer of Hypatia and confidant of the lovesick Raphael Aben-Ezra; in his house Augustine of Hippo converts Raphael, and Raphael meets again his future wife, Victoria, in Charles Kingsley's *Hypatia*.

Mr. Syntax   Assistant schoolmaster, who is thrashed by Roderick Random, Tom Bowling, and others; he reads a Latin speech in honor of the return of Roderick to Scotland in Tobias Smollett's *The Adventures of Roderick Random*.

Syphax   Groom to Synesius, bishop of Cyrene, in Charles Kingsley's *Hypatia*.

T

Andrew Tacchi   Giacomo Tacchi's son, who is sent to clerk in his uncle's London shop, and who becomes so alcoholic he must return to his father's for recovery in Mark Rutherford's *Miriam's Schooling*.

Giacomo Tacchi   Watchmaker son of Italian immigrants in the English village of Cowfold; he marries the daughter of a local farmer, has two children, is widowed, and marries Mrs. Brooks in Mark Rutherford's *Miriam's Schooling*.

Miriam Tacchi   Giacomo Tacchi's daughter, who goes to London with her brother, Andrew; she loves and denounces George Montgomery; she tries to support herself and Andrew, considers suicide, and fails as a nursing apprentice; she finally learns astronomy and love when she marries Didymus Farrow in Mark Rutherford's *Miriam's Schooling*.

Martin Tacket   Lady Alice Avenel's reverent and steadfast elderly shepherd, who tries to restrain Halbert Glendinning's temper in Sir Walter Scott's *The Monastery*.

Tibbie Tacket   Martin Tacket's wife and Lady Alice Avenel's loyal bower-woman; she remains faithful to her mistress in her misfortune in Sir Walter Scott's *The Monastery*.

Mr. Tackleton   Toy merchant and "domestic ogre," who delights in designing frightening toys, and who wishes to wed the much younger May Fielding despite her lack of affection for him; he becomes more sociable and kindly after May elopes with her true love in Charles Dickens's *The Cricket on the Hearth*.

Brother Tadger   Member of the Brick Lane Branch of the United Grand Junction Ebeneezer Temperance Association in Charles Dickens's *The Posthumous Papers of the Pickwick Club*.

Mr. Tadpole   Comic and unprincipled politico and companion of Nicholas Rigby in Benjamin Disraeli's *Coningsby; or, The New Generation*. He is a political opportunist and Member of Parliament, whose constant political scheming is satirized in *Sybil*.

Tae   Eldest son of the Tur (chief magistrate) of the community of Vril-ya described by the Tish in Edward Bulwer-Lytton's *The Coming Race*.

Lieutenant Daniel Taffril   Young naval officer who serves as William Lovel's second at the duel with Hector M'Intyre and helps Lovel escape on his ship in Sir Walter Scott's *The Antiquary*.

Mum Taft   A silent carpenter employed by Jonathan Burge in George Eliot's *Adam Bede*.

Count Tag   Aurora's admirer, who merits his title by his exploits and who proportions his respect and time according to the rank and fortune of his company in Francis Coventry's *The History of Pompey the Little*.

Lady Emily Tagmaggert   Red-nosed youngest, though not young, daughter of an earl; she becomes the wife of the snobbish Captain Aylmer in Anthony Trollope's *The Belton Estate*.

Cecily Talbot   Daughter of Mary Stewart, Queen of Scots; she is raised by Richard Talbot as his daughter and chooses exile rather than involve herself in intrigues over who shall succeed Queen Elizabeth in Charlotte Yonge's *Unknown to History*.

Humfrey Talbot   Son of Richard Talbot; he grows up believing Cecily Talbot is his sister but ultimately chooses exile in order to marry her in Charlotte Yonge's *Unknown to History*.

Colonel Philip Talbot   Royal Dragoon officer whose obligations to Sir Everard Waverly send him to Scotland searching for Edward Waverly, who takes him prisoner and later arranges his release; Talbot returns the favor, providing Waverly with money and an alias in Sir Walter Scott's *Waverly*.

Richard Talbot   Relative of the Earl of Shrewsbury; he rescues from a shipwreck an infant who proves to be the daughter of Queen Mary of Scotland in Charlotte Yonge's *Unknown to History*.

Susan Talbot   Wife of Richard Talbot; she raises the daughter of Queen Mary of Scotland as her own child in Charlotte Yonge's *Unknown to History*.

Clara Talboys   George Talboys's sister; she is loved by Robert Audley, whom she helps to uncover the plot of her brother's disappearance and marries in Mary Elizabeth Braddon's *Lady Audley's Secret*.

George Talboys   Friend of Robert Audley; the first husband of Lucy (later Lady Audley) and the father of her son, he has left her to go to the colonies to make money; he returns to find her remarried in Mary Elizabeth Braddon's *Lady Audley's Secret*.

George Talboys (the younger)   Lady Audley's son from her first marriage, to George Talboys; he lives first with Lady Audley's father, Mr. Maldon, and then with Clara Talboys and Robert Audley after their marriage in Mary Elizabeth Braddon's *Lady Audley's Secret.*

Harcourt Talboys   Father of Clara Talboys and of George, whom he rejects when the young man marries Lucy Maldon (later Lady Audley); finally he is reunited with George and Lucy's son in Mary Elizabeth Braddon's *Lady Audley's Secret.*

Taliesin   Foundling reared by Elphin; he becomes a bard and by clever diplomacy restores Queen Gwenyvar to King Arthur; he traps Rhûn and so effects the rescue of Elphin; he is rewarded with marriage to Melanghel in Thomas Love Peacock's *The Misfortunes of Elphin.*

Talkative   Hypocrite who meets with Christian and Faithful; he seems a true Christian, but Christian exposes his hypocrisy in John Bunyan's *The Pilgrim's Progress From this World to That Which Is to Come.*

Miss Tallowax   Great-aunt of Lady George Germain; she bestows £20,000 on the newborn son of Lady George (now Marchioness of Brotherton) on condition that she can be godmother and that Tallowax be included in the boy's name in Anthony Trollope's *Is He Popenjoy?.*

Mr. Tallowax   Wealthy grandfather of Mary Lovelace; he leaves his fortune to her, thus promoting her marriage to Lord George Germain in Anthony Trollope's *Is He Popenjoy?.*

Tamar   Somber childhood nurse of Rachel and Stanley Lake; she is devoted to Rachel, whom she lives with at Redman's Farm, but recognizes Stanley's vices; she urges Stanley to confess his crimes but to no avail in J. Sheridan Le Fanu's *Wylder's Hand.*

Tamaroo   Ancient and uncomprehending female successor to Benjamin Baily in Mrs. Todgers's boarding house in Charles Dickens's *The Life and Adventures of Martin Chuzzlewit.*

Tancred, Prince of Otranto   Exceedingly beautiful young nobleman, who becomes a crusader in Sir Walter Scott's *Count Robert of Paris.*

Tim Tang   Suke Damson's husband; jealous of her affection for her former lover, Dr. Edred Fitzpiers, he sets a man-trap which narrowly misses seriously injuring Grace (Melbury) Fitzpiers instead of her husband; Tang and Suke emigrate to New Zealand in Thomas Hardy's *The Woodlanders.*

Anthony Tangle   Attorney and leading expert in the Jarndyce and Jarndyce case, who brings up the issue of

the guardianship of Ada Clare and Richard Carstone in Charles Dickens's *Bleak House.*

Taniera   Pretty native girl on William John Attwater's secluded island; to avoid the temptation of sin, the religious Attwater has her married to another native against her will in Robert Louis Stevenson's *The Ebb-Tide: A Trio and a Quartette.*

M. Tanneguy   Frenchman who marries Alice Knevett; he forces a duel upon Edgar Underwood and dies of his wound in Charlotte Yonge's *The Pillars of the House.*

Dick Tanner   Former Canadian neighbor of Rachel Henderson; they had a brief affair that left her feeling morally guilty in Mrs. Humphry Ward's *Harvest.*

Tantripp   Faithful maid of Dorothea Brooke in George Eliot's *Middlemarch.*

Mrs. Tantrum   Proprietress of an inn who, having misconstrued Geoffry Wildgoose's intentions toward her daughter-in-law, throws a hot breakfast at Wildgoose and Jeremiah Tugwell in Richard Graves's *The Spiritual Quixote.*

Counsellor Tanturion   An avaricious, unsuccessful lawyer, who, through usury, accumulates £1000, which he hoards and does not enjoy in Francis Coventry's *The History of Pompey the Little.*

Mr. Taper   Mr. Tadpole's cohort, who assists him in his political machinations in Benjamin Disraeli's *Sybil.* He is Nicholas Rigby's gossiping associate, whose self-serving political aspirations are satirized in *Coningsby; or, The New Generation.*

Mrs. Tapkins   Lady who leaves her calling card with the Boffins in Charles Dickens's *Our Mutual Friend.*

Mr. Tapley   Brewer who is in London debtor's prison, where he fights with Dr. Crabclaw in Tobias Smollett's *The Adventures of Sir Launcelot Greaves.*

Mark Tapley   Hostler at the Blue Dragon Inn, afterwards servant/companion to the younger Martin Chuzzlewit; he desires adverse circumstances in order to test the worth of his good humor; in America he aids in Martin's moral transformation and professes disappointment that Martin's reformation reduces the merit of his jollity; reconciled to comfort, he marries Mrs. Lupin in Charles Dickens's *The Life and Adventures of Martin Chuzzlewit.*

Simon (Sim) Tappertit   Gabriel Varden's apprentice, who is ugly in appearance; he pursues Dolly Varden but is loved by Miss Miggs; he is revered as leader of the "Prentice Knights"; he participates in the Gordon riots and is injured in Charles Dickens's *Barnaby Rudge*.

Augusta Tappitt The second of Thomas Tappitt's three good-humored, ordinary daughters in Anthony Trollope's *Rachel Ray*.

Cherry Tappitt The youngest of Thomas Tappitt's three similar daughters; their mother believes it Luke Rowan's duty to marry one of them in Anthony Trollope's *Rachel Ray*.

Margaret Tappitt Snobbish wife of a Devon brewery owner; she takes against his clerk and would-be partner, Luke Rowan, when the young man courts Rachel Ray instead of one of her own daughters; she tries to enter society by giving a grand party, but she stays loyal and loving to her husband when he relinquishes management of the brewery in Anthony Trollope's *Rachel Ray*.

Martha Tappitt The eldest of Thomas Tappitt's three good-humored daughters, any one of whom, in her mother's eyes, would be superior to Rachel Ray as a wife for their distant cousin, Luke Rowan, in Anthony Trollope's *Rachel Ray*.

Thomas Tappitt Part owner of a Baslehurst district brewery in Devon always at odds with his clerk, Luke Rowan, about the quality of the beer; he finally loses management of the business to Luke in Anthony Trollope's *Rachel Ray*.

Lieutenant Tappleton Second to Dr. Slammer in the duel with Nathaniel Winkle in Rochester in Charles Dickens's *The Posthumous Papers of the Pickwick Club*.

Jack Tar Honest and generous sailor, who pays the debts of the Shoplifter, a destitute widow, in Charles Johnstone's *Chrysal: or, The Adventures of a Guinea*.

Mrs. Tarbat Landlady who gives assistance to Medora Glenmorris in her flight in Charlotte Smith's *The Young Philosopher*.

Prince Tarquin A nobleman who claims to be descended from the kings of Rome; he is charmed by Miranda and marries her against all advice; persuaded by Miranda to murder Alcidiana, he fails at the attempt and is sentenced to a beheading which he miraculously survives; he lives to settle in Holland with the reformed Miranda in Aphra Behn's *The Fair Jilt*.

Lionel Tarrant Handsome, idle young man, who seduces and feels compelled to marry Nancy Lord; the terms of her father's will make it advisable to conceal the marriage; believing that husband and wife should not live

together, he arranges to live apart from his wife even after they are reconciled in George Gissing's *In the Year of Jubilee*.

Captain Tartar Stern commander of H.M.S. *Aurora*; he places Jack Easy and Ned Gascoigne in irons after one of their adventures in Captain Frederick Marryat's *Mr. Midshipman Easy*.

Lieutenant Tarter Retired Royal Navy man who appears in Cloisterham about the time of Edwin Drood's disappearance; he may be a detective or private investigator connected with Dick Datchery in Charles Dickens's *The Mystery of Edwin Drood*.

Mr. Tatham Lawyer consulted by Major Pendennis in William Makepeace Thackeray's *The History of Pendennis*.

Achilles Tatius Commander of the Varangians; his principal duty is constant attendance upon the emperor; vain and cowardly, he considers himself politically adept and conspires for the crown in Sir Walter Scott's *Count Robert of Paris*.

Lady Tattle Town lady traveling with Lady Tittle; she comments on Lady Booby and Joseph Andrews walking together in Hyde Park in Henry Fielding's *The History of the Adventures of Mr. Joseph Andrews and of his Friend Mr. Abraham Adams*.

Tattycoram See Harriet Beadle.

Tavern-Keeper A notorious brothel-keeper, who professes himself a reformer of religion in Charles Johnstone's *Chrysal: or, The Adventures of Guinea*.

Taylor Warwick peasant who claims to have seen Queen Elizabeth's ghost in Ann Radcliffe's *Gaston de Blondeville*.

Taylor London coal porter who is rescued from despair by M'Kay and Mark Rutherford in the London mission in Mark Rutherford's *Mark Rutherford's Deliverance*.

Mrs. Taylor Taylor's wife, who helps nurse Ellen (Butts) during her illness after the family holiday in Mark Rutherford's *Mark Rutherford's Deliverance*.

Teach Blustering, cowardly pirate captain of the *Sarah*, on which the Master (James Durie) and Colonel Francis Burke are taken for recruits; Mackellar denies that he is the historical Blackbeard in Robert Louis Stevenson's *The Master of Ballantrae: A Winter's Tale*.

Teacher of Lore Wise older woman who, in the Dale of Lore, instructs the girl who becomes the Lady of Abundance; both are later rejuvenated at the Well in William Morris's *The Well at the World's End*.

Mrs. Teachum Exemplary governess of the nine pupils to whom she imparts the norms of female behavior in Sarah Fielding's *The Governess*.

Mr. Tedman Wealthy grocer, who provides Juliet Granville with friendship and financial aid at Brightelmstone in Frances Burney's *The Wanderer*.

Teithrin ap Tathral A conscientious Commissioner of Royal Embankments for Gwythno Garanhir in Thomas Love Peacock's *The Misfortunes of Elphin*.

Telamine Mythical wife of Arco, with whom she founds a cruel race in Robert Paltock's *The Life and Adventures of Peter Wilkins*.

Toby Telford Robust fool who dances attendance on Dr. Lundin in Sir Walter Scott's *The Abbot*.

Dr. Mortimer Tempest Rector of Silverbridge, who becomes chairman of the commission set up to examine Josiah Crawley about the stolen-cheque scandal; Dr. Tempest's refusal to discuss the matter in Mrs. Proudie's presence immediately precedes her death in Anthony Trollope's *The Last Chronicle of Barset*. He seconds the nomination of Lord Silverbridge as Parliamentary candidate in *The Duke's Children*.

Lady Tempest A lady of quality, a widow, and frequent visitor of Hillario; she acquires Pompey in exchange for a promise to admit Hillario at any time and loses Pompey in St. James's Park; she is reunited with Pompey at the end of Francis Coventry's *The History of Pompey the Little*.

Augustus Temple Friend of Harry Richmond from the time they are at Rippenger's school; he accompanies Harry on many of his adventures in George Meredith's *The Adventures of Harry Richmond*.

Fanny, Lady Temple Widow with several young children; she rescues the girls being mistreated by the imposter Mauleverer in Charlotte Yonge's *The Clever Woman of the Family*.

Henrietta Temple Beautiful but penurious young woman, who falls in love with Ferdinand Armine after he is committed to marry Katherine Grandison; she turns out to be a greater heiress than her rival and, after Katherine releases Ferdinand from his promise, is able to marry him in Benjamin Disraeli's *Henrietta Temple: A Love Story*.

John Temple Friend and correspondent of Ed. Rivers;

his libertine inclinations are ostensibly reformed upon his marriage to Rivers's younger sister, Lucy, in Frances Brooke's *The History of Emily Montague*.

Maria Temple Tranquil headmistress of Lowood School, who becomes a gentle guiding companion to Jane Eyre; when she leaves to marry a clergyman, Jane's restive nature returns immediately in Charlotte Brontë's *Jane Eyre*.

Evelyn Templeton Supposed daughter of Alice (Darvil) Templeton; she inherits Richard Templeton's fortune in Edward Bulwer-Lytton's *Ernest Maltravers*. She is discovered to be Templeton's beloved unacknowledged though legitimate daughter; rescued from a fraudulent marriage with Lumley Ferrers, she is united with George Legard in *Alice*.

Richard Templeton Lumley Ferrers's uncle, a provincial banker; he becomes Lord Vargrave and dies, having left his fortune to Evelyn Cameron (Templeton), the supposed daughter of his wife, Alice Darvil, in Edward Bulwer-Lytton's *Ernest Maltravers*. It is discovered that Evelyn is Templeton's daughter by an earlier, secret marriage; his dying wish that Evelyn acquire the Vargrave title through marriage to Ferrers is fortunately unfulfilled in *Alice*.

Mr. Tench Wealthy Irish clergyman from the County Galway; he converts Carola Bennet to Christianity and marries her after her exploitation as a prostitute in Thomas Amory's *The Life of John Buncle, Esq.*

Bob Tench Upper-class sportsman and guest of Sir William Forester; he summons a surgeon after Geoffry Wildgoose has been hit in the head in Richard Graves's *The Spiritual Quixote*.

Teresa Carmina Graywell's old servant, who accompanies her to England but must return to Italy to nurse a dying husband; passionately devoted to Carmina, she returns to England to assist the frustration of Mrs. Gallilee's cruel schemes in Wilkie Collins's *Heart and Science*.

Teresa Maid for Mademoiselle de Melvil; she loves Ferdinand, conspires with him to cheat Mademoiselle de Melvil, and believes herself married to Ferdinand in Tobias Smollett's *The Adventures of Ferdinand Count Fathom*.

Teresa Roman matron who is saved from drowning by Gerard, who lashes mother and child to a large wooden Madonna; she is wife of the criminal Lodovico in Charles Reade's *The Cloister and the Hearth*.

Mrs. Terwitt Harry Bolton's loquacious London landlady in Henry Mackenzie's *The Man of the World*.

Teshoo Lama Simple, wise, and good Abbot of Suchzen in Tibet; he travels to India on pilgrimage to retrace the Buddha's footsteps and find the Holy River when he meets and befriends young Kim in Rudyard Kipling's *Kim*.

Benjamin Testy Hotheaded friend of Peter Patience in Henry Brooke's *The Fool of Quality*.

Adolphus Tetterby Poor but content father of seven, who owns a small paper shop in a poor building; he loves his children and his wife, Sophia, in Charles Dickens's *The Haunted Man and the Ghost's Bargain*.

'Dolphus Tetterby Adolphus and Sophia Tetterby's elder son, who sells newspapers in a railway station in Charles Dickens's *The Haunted Man and the Ghost's Bargain*.

Johnny Tetterby Little boy who is the sole caretaker of his infant sister and so cannot play with the other boys; he devotes his life to his sister without resentment or bitterness in Charles Dickens's *The Haunted Man and the Ghost's Bargain*.

Sophia Tetterby Frazzled mother who is working to keep her family from starving; though poor, she loves her children and husband, values her time with them, and is grateful for what she has in Charles Dickens's *The Haunted Man and the Ghost's Bargain*.

Sir Griffin Tewett Seemingly frail but sadistic baronet, friendly with Lord George de Bruce Carruthers; his determination to marry Lucinda Roanoke is intensified by her open hatred of him; on the wedding day she passionately refuses to go through with her self-sacrifice in Anthony Trollope's *The Eustace Diamonds*.

Theanor The Duke of Malfy's brother, who hates Gigantilla because he sees her as she really is in Eliza Haywood's *The Perplex'd Dutchess; or, Treachery Rewarded*.

Theatre Manager Judge of poets and their plays; he decides which new plays will be performed in Charles Johnstone's *Chrysal: or, the Adventures of a Guinea*.

Theodora Wife of the Bohemian Petitioner; although she has changed hands frequently, she comes back to her husband unchanged in Charles Johnstone's *Chrysal: or, The Adventures of a Guinea*.

Theodore Marguerite's stalwart son, who defends Alphonso d'Alvarada (Raymond, Marquis de la Cisternas) against murderous bandits and, as his page, helps rescue Agnes de Medina in Matthew Lewis's *The Monk*.

Theodore The rightful heir to Otranto; he appears disguised as a peasant and falls in love with Manfred's daughter, Matilda, but marries Isabella after Matilda's murder in Horace Walpole's *The Castle of Otranto*.

Theodosia Aurora's elder sister, a woman of forty, who is of good temper and education in Francis Coventry's *The History of Pompey the Little*.

Theodosius Correspondent with Ferdinand on the subject of wit and judgment in Sarah Fielding's *Familiar Letters between the Principal Characters of David Simple and Some Others*.

Theon Elderly, debt-ridden father of the philosopher Hypatia; he is himself a philosopher and teacher of mathematics in Charles Kingsley's *Hypatia*.

Theophilus Christian patriarch of Alexandria prior to Cyril; under him much pagan violence has occurred in Charles Kingsley's *Hypatia*.

Theresa Elderly housekeeper at La Vallee, family home of the St. Auberts; she is evicted by Monsieur Quesnel and rescued by Valancourt; later she urges Valancourt's suit to marry Emily St. Aubert in Ann Radcliffe's *The Mysteries of Udolpho*.

Sir Timothy Thicket Brutal country squire, who courts Narcissa, tries to rape her, and is driven away by Roderick Random; he vows to avenge himself and dies of apoplexy after confessing his designs on Narcissa in Tobias Smollett's *The Adventures of Roderick Random*.

Thiebault Native of Provence who guides Arthur de Vere from the Duke of Burgundy's court to King René in Sir Walter Scott's *Anne of Geierstein*.

Schwartz Thier Rough and ready member of Werner's band; he accosts Margarita Groschen, earning himself a beating from Guy the Goshawk; he is again bested by Guy; the two become friends, and Thier assists Guy and Farina when they liberate Margarita from captivity in Werner's Eck in George Meredith's *Farina*.

Thomas Thimble Tailor whose bond against Count La Ruse caused the latter's incarceration at Mr. Snap's and his introduction to Jonathan Wild in Henry Fielding's *The Life of Mr. Jonathan Wild the Great*.

Mr. Thims Cashier at the musical bank, who becomes Jack Higgs's friend when others desert him; he invites Higgs to the country and explains the College of Unreason to him in Samuel Butler's *Erewhon*.

Thiodolf Chief of the Wolfing clan of the Gothic Markmen; he leads his folk against invading Romans and dies in victory when he scorns the personal safety of a magic hauberk that would bring defeat in William Morris's *A Tale of the House of the Wolfings.*

Mr. Thistlewood   Schoolmaster who has had love adventures in Paris as a student and marries a respectable widow in George Gissing's *The Whirlpool.*

Thomas   Roxana's eldest son, whom her Dutch husband hires as a servant; the Dutch husband buys him a large plantation in Virginia after discovering that he is Roxana's son in Daniel Defoe's *The Fortunate Mistress.*

Thomas   Servant of Helen Huntingdon's aunt and uncle, the Maxwells, in Anne Brontë's *The Tenant of Wildfell Hall.*

Thomas   One of Miss Marchmont's servants when she was young in Charlotte Brontë's *Villette.*

Thomas   A farmer and close friend of Caleb Williams's father; he is horrified by Caleb's crime, yet is moved to help him escape from jail; on another occasion, he serves as a messenger, delivering money to Caleb from Ferdinando Falkland in William Godwin's *Caleb Williams.*

Thomas (Tom)   Mr. Helstone's assistant in Charlotte Brontë's *Shirley.*

Thomas (Tom, Brother Tom)   Sail-maker and brother of John; he sets out with his brother and Richard the joiner in leaving Wapping in Daniel Defoe's *A Journal of the Plague Year.*

Sir Thomas   Governor of Malta, who is always amused by Jack Easy's tales of adventures in Captain Frederick Marryat's *Mr. Midshipman Easy.*

Mrs. Thomas   Unsuccessful teacher, to whom Felix Graham entrusts the grooming of Mary Snow as his future ideal wife in Anthony Trollope's *Orley Farm.*

Mrs. Thomas   Bedfordshire midwife who attends Pamela B——- during her first childbirth in Samuel Richardson's *Pamela, or Virtue Rewarded.*

John Thomas   Footman who quits the service of Matthew Bramble when he has an encounter with Tabitha Bramble's dog, Chowder, in Tobias Smollett's *The Expedition of Humphry Clinker.*

John Thomas   Man who runs the delft, ironmongery, sponge, and umbrella shop in the town of Gylingden; with the baker, Mr. Crump, he brings news of Sir Harry Bracton's entry into the town to try to win the election from Lake, precipitating Lake's fateful ride past Wylder's hand in J. Sheridan Le Fanu's *Wylder's Hand.*

Thomasine (Belton)   Adulterous common-law wife of Thomas Belton, Robert Lovelace's libertine friend, in Samuel Richardson's *Clarissa: or, The History of a Young Lady.*

Thomaso   Assassin brought to justice by Abellino/Flodoardo (Count Rosalvo) in Matthew Lewis's *The Bravo of Venice.*

Mr. Thompson   Police Superintendent for Silverbridge who brings Josiah Crawley before the magistrate in Anthony Trollope's *The Last Chronicle of Barset.*

Mrs. Thompson   Wife of a farmer in Theobald Pontifex's parish and constantly near death; she is the object of Theobald's reassurances and presents of meat and beverages in Samuel Butler's *The Way of All Flesh.*

Mrs. Thompson   Farmer's wife who, having reason to believe that Captain Mahoney has designs on Julia Townsend, hides the girl in her home in Richard Graves's *The Spiritual Quixote.*

Frank Thompson   Artist, head of the new Modern school of art; he is one of the young intelligentsia and a man about town in George Moore's *Mike Fletcher.* He becomes a member of the Academy and discusses the relation of art and logic with critics and Lewis Seymour's friends attending a showing in *A Modern Lover.*

Goody Thompson   Loyalist soldier who disguises himself as an old woman in order to flee after the defeat at Marston Moor; he goes with the Cavalier and another soldier, who are also disguised in Daniel Defoe's *Memoirs of a Cavalier.*

Ripton Thompson   Awkward, unassuming son of Sir Austin Feverel's lawyer and friend of Richard Feverel; he is involved in the burning of the hayrick and assists Richard and Lucy Desborough at various times, often providing a comic foil to the intense Richard in George Meredith's *The Ordeal of Richard Feverel.*

Thomson   Exciseman who suggests capturing the madman, Tom Jones, and returning him to Squire Allworthy's house after Partridge exaggerates Tom's history in Henry Fielding's *The History of Tom Jones.*

Lieutenant Jack Thomson   A crippled resident of the Mandeville estate, whom Commodore Mandeville persuades to marry Amelia Montfort, thus thwarting Audley Mandeville's hopes of marrying her in William Godwin's *Mandeville.*

William Thomson   Surgeon who has qualified for navy third mate and who tells Roderick Random about John Jackson's background; he waits for an assignment at the Navy Office in London, where Roderick meets him; the surgeon's second mate aboard the *Thunder*, he jumps ship and is presumed dead; he is discovered alive in Jamaica, where he is a surgeon and overseer for a wealthy landowner in Tobias Smollett's *The Adventures of Roderick Random*.

Thorkettle   See Wood-Sun.

Thomas Thorl   Handloom weaver and "pious zealot" who opposes Micah Balwhidder's appointment as minister but becomes a supporter upon closer acquaintance in John Galt's *Annals of the Parish*.

Job Thornberry   Son of the farmer who was neighbor of the Ferrarses during their country exile; he becomes a political activist in favor of the Charter and free trade in Benjamin Disraeli's *Endymion*.

Emma Thornburgh   Vicar's wife at Long Whinsdale and cousin of Robert Elsmere; she employs her matchmaking skills to unite Catherine Leyburn and Robert Elsmere in marriage in Mrs. Humphry Ward's *Robert Elsmere*.

Mr. Thornby   Mr. Wakefield's uncle and greedy executor of the rector's estate; he repents of and attempts to rectify his injustices before his death in Thomas Holcroft's *The Adventures of Hugh Trevor*.

Mrs. Thornby   Louisa Mancel's mother, who, long separated from her child, hires Louisa under an assumed name, discovers her identity, and leaves her the fortune with which she co-founds Millenium Hall in Sarah Scott's *A Description of Millenium Hall*.

Thorne   Puritan landowner and suitor of Mary Collet Farrar; he is the jealous rival of John Inglesant in J. Henry Shorthouse's *John Inglesant, A Romance*.

Henry Thorne   Dr. Thorne's brother, the black sheep of the family, who seduced Mary Scatcherd (now Tomlinson) and fathered an illegitimate child adopted by his brother in Anthony Trollope's *Doctor Thorne*.

Mary Thorne   Illegitimate niece and adopted daughter of Dr. Thorne; Frank Gresham defies his family to form and stand by an engagement to her; until the engagement is formalized only Dr. Thorne knows that she has prospects of great wealth; she becomes heiress to the Scatcherd fortune and marries Frank Gresham in Anthony Trollope's *Doctor Thorne*. She assists the union of her uncle and Martha Dunstable in *Framley Parsonage*.

Maude Hippesley, Mrs. Thorne   Close friend and confidante of Cecilia Holt and niece of Sir Francis Geral-

dine; her father is the Dean of Exeter Cathedral in Anthony Trollope's *Kept in the Dark*.

Monica Thorne   Sister of Wilfred Thorne; her similar passion for genealogy and medievalism is indulged at Ullathorne Court by means of a garden party with Elizabethan sports in Anthony Trollope's *Barchester Towers*. She appears briefly in *Doctor Thorne* and in *The Last Chronicle of Barset*.

Dr. Thomas Thorne   Hard-working, forthright general practitioner in Greshamsbury village; he brings up his brother's illegitimate daughter, Mary, in Anthony Trollope's *Doctor Thorne*. He makes a happy marriage of mutual affection to the heiress Martha Dunstable in *Framley Parsonage*. He serves on the commission in the Crawley case in *The Last Chronicle of Barset*.

Wilfred Thorne   Genial squire of Ullathorne, whose love of the past is celebrated by the Ullathorne sports and garden party in Anthony Trollope's *Barchester Towers*. He also appears in *Doctor Thorne*, in *Framley Parsonage*, and in *The Last Chronicle of Barset*.

Squire Thornhill   Villainous seducer responsible for most of the Primrose family's misfortunes; he is defeated at the end and shows signs of potential reformation in Oliver Goldsmith's *The Vicar of Wakefield*.

Master Billy, Sir William Thornhill   Sir Spranger Thornhill's son; a benevolent landlord, he restores property unjustly confiscated by the greedy Sir Freestone Hardgrave from Giffard Homely, his tenant farmer, in Henry Brooke's *The Fool of Quality*.

Sir Spranger Thornhill   Decent landowner, whose death occasions the loss of Giffard Homely's property in Henry Brooke's *The Fool of Quality*.

Sir William Thornhill   High-principled uncle of the infamous Squire Thornhill; under the alias Mr. Burchell he befriends the Primrose family, thereby assured that they love him for himself, not for his money and social stature; he rescues them by disinheriting his nephew and marries Sophia Primrose in Oliver Goldsmith's *The Vicar of Wakefield*.

Thornton   Son of one of Deloraine's oldest friends; he treats Deloraine and his daughter, Catherine, with kindness, sympathy, and offers of protection from their pursuers; so attached is he to Deloraine that he follows him into lifelong exile and eventually marries Catherine in William Godwin's *Deloraine*.

Captain Thornton   Courageous English officer; having received orders to arrest Rob Roy McGregor, he is betrayed by Dougal into an ambush by the MacGregors, where his men are slaughtered and he is taken prisoner in Sir Walter Scott's *Rob Roy*.

Mr. Thornton   Libertine who reforms in S. J. Pratt's *Pupil of Pleasure*.

Mrs. Thornton   Mother of John and Fanny; her strong-minded suspicion of Margaret Hale and "southern" ways creates tensions with her son in Elizabeth Gaskell's *North and South*.

Fanny Thornton   Docile younger sister of John Thornton in Elizabeth Gaskell's *North and South*.

John Thornton   Independent-minded mill owner, who represents the attitudes and positive values of the "north"; he comes to terms with the unionist Higgins and Margaret Hale; when conditions and his principles of action threaten bankruptcy, Margaret rescues and then marries him in Elizabeth Gaskell's *North and South*.

Thomas Thornton   Coarse gamester, who murders Sir John Tyrrell during a robbery and then blackmails Sir Reginald Glanville for the crime in Edward Bulwer-Lytton's *Pelham*.

Joe Thoroughbung   Prosperous young brewer of Buntingford who wins the heart of Mary Annesley and marries her, to her parents' satisfaction in Anthony Trollope's *Mr. Scarborough's Family*.

Matilda Thoroughbung   Wide-awake, middle-aged, well-off spinster, somewhat vulgar but full of good-humored fun, who drives such a hard bargain with Peter Prosper that he takes fright and breaks off the marriage negotiations in Anthony Trollope's *Mr. Scarborough's Family*.

Mrs. Thorpe   Older cousin and chaperon of Lucy Bentham; she succumbs to Lewis Seymour's charm in George Moore's *A Modern Lover*.

Mrs. Thorpe   Zack's warm-hearted mother, overruled by her severe husband in the boy's upbringing in Wilkie Collins's *Hide and Seek*.

Mrs. Thorpe   A widow and an old school acquaintance of Mrs. Allen; their reunion in Bath is opportune, for Mrs. Allen has been lamenting knowing nobody there; Mrs. Thorpe is mother of John and Isabella and two younger daughters in Jane Austen's *Northanger Abbey*.

Anne Thorpe   Isabella's younger sister who is contemptuously excluded from an excursion by her brother, John, because of the thickness of her ankles in Jane Austen's *Northanger Abbey*.

Isabella Thorpe   Shallow and flirtatious beauty, already acquainted with James Morland; she claims Catherine Morland as an immediate intimate friend; she becomes engaged to James but drops him when she discovers him to be less wealthy than expected in Jane Austen's *Northanger Abbey*.

John Thorpe   Impudent, boorish, and conceited brother of Isabella; he courts Catherine Morland, believing that she is rich, misleads General Tilney to believe so also, and then disparages her to the general in Jane Austen's *Northanger Abbey*.

Maria Thorpe   John and Isabella's younger sister who substitutes for Catherine Morland on an outing of which the failed objective is Blaize Castle in Jane Austen's *Northanger Abbey*.

Zack Thorpe   Rebellious, brave, good-hearted youth, estranged from his father and looked after by the kind-hearted painter Valentine Blyth; his chance service to Mat Grice results in their friendship and his discovery that a young woman who admires him is his half sister in Wilkie Collins's *Hide and Seek*.

Zachary Thorpe (Arthur Carr)   Severe, pious father of Zack, from whom he becomes estranged; as a young man he retreated under an assumed name, Arthur Carr, for the purpose of studying botany undisturbed; he fell in love with a village girl; his apparent neglect of her, leading to her death, was largely the doing of her aunt, Joanna Grice; Mat Grice confronts him but does not pursue his revenge; Thorpe is reconciled to his son before dying in Wilkie Collins's *Hide and Seek*.

Betsy Thoughtless   Heroine, who, at first, is excessively flirtatious and vain; she has a good heart and is eager to help anyone in need in Eliza Haywood's *The History of Miss Betsy Thoughtless*.

Francis Thoughtless   Betsy's brother who has a fiery disposition in Eliza Haywood's *The History of Miss Betsy Thoughtless*.

Thomas Thoughtless   Betsy's even-tempered brother in Eliza Haywood's *The History of Miss Betsy Thoughtless*.

Jonathan Thrasher   Westminster justice of the peace who, ignorant of the law, decides legal cases according to his own self-interest in Henry Fielding's *Amelia*.

Mr. Threeper   The advocate who successfully argues George Walkinshaw's case against his brother Walter on grounds of fatuity and thus enables George to control the Kittlestonheugh estate in John Galt's *The Entail*.

Throgmorton   Dependable servant of Sir Daniel

Brackley, picked by him to deliver a letter to Wensleydale; he is hanged by Black Arrow's band; Dick Shelton finds the letter on his corpse in Robert Louis Stevenson's *The Black Arrow: A Tale of Two Roses.*

Thomas Thumb Spirit in Elysium in the company of Ulysses, Achilles, and Julius Caesar; he clarifies aspects of legends that evolved about him in Henry Fielding's *A Journey From this World to the Next.*

Caleb Thumble Obsequious cleric, who is Mrs. Proudie's choice to replace Josiah Crawley at Hogglestock in Anthony Trollope's *The Last Chronicle of Barset.*

Mr. Thurle A stranger who wants to buy part of Chase Farm from Squire Donnithorne and thus provokes Mrs. Poyser's witty tirade against the squire's tight-fisted ways in George Eliot's *Adam Bede.*

Mrs. Thurloe Old lady who owns a home in Westmoreland where John Buncle meets two young ladies in Thomas Amory's *The Life of John Buncle, Esq.*

Roger Thwackum Hypocritical clergyman, who instructs Squire Allworthy's nephews; he persecutes Tom Jones and teaches hypocrisy to Master Blifil in Henry Fielding's *The History of Tom Jones.*

Daniel Thwaite Educated worker, philosopher, socialist, and son of the tailor Thomas Thwaite; he loves and wishes to marry Anna Murray (Lady Anna Lovel) but is impoverished by his father's quixotic attempts to help her and her mother, Josephine (Countess Lovel); when Lady Anna's inheritance and rank are restored, she insists on their marriage and they emigrate to Australia in Anthony Trollope's *Lady Anna.*

Thomas Thwaite Romantic democrat tailor imbued with ideas of helping his fellow man; when Countess Lovel is abandoned by her wicked husband, he spends his fortune trying to restore the lady's name and the legitimacy of her daughter, Anna; bitterly disappointed when the countess forbids a match between Anna and his son, Daniel, he dies leaving accounts showing how much the countess owed him in Anthony Trollope's *Lady Anna.*

Lady Isabella Thynne Beautiful and popular member of the court of Charles I; she is noted for her love of intrigue in J. Henry Shorthouse's *John Inglesant, A Romance.*

John (Uncle Jack) Tibbetts Maternal uncle of Pisistratus Caxton; his harebrained schemes for enriching the family create financial disaster in Edward Bulwer-Lytton's *The Caxtons.*

Mrs. Tibbs Wife and social-climbing feminine counter-

part of Ned Tibbs in Oliver Goldsmith's *The Citizen of the World.*

Ned (the Little Beau) Tibbs Name-dropping hanger-on of high society who befriends Lien Chi Altangi in Oliver Goldsmith's *The Citizen of the World.*

Tibby The middle-aged womanservant of Glenfern Castle in Susan Ferrier's *Marriage.*

Mrs. Tickit Cook and housekeeper for the Meagleses in Charles Dickens's *Little Dorrit.*

Jemima Tickle Long-time companion of Matilda Thoroughbung; having come to dread the prospect of marriage to Miss Thoroughbung, Peter Prosper clings to a refusal to maintain Miss Tickle and a pair of ponies in order to effect an escape in Anthony Trollope's *Mr. Scarborough's Family.*

Tobias Tickler Forty-three-year-old widowed clergyman with three children; he marries Olivia Proudie in Anthony Trollope's *Framley Parsonage.*

Thomas Tickletext Ingenuous parson whose commendation of the novel *Pamela* (by Samuel Richardson) to Parson J. Oliver contains numerous unintentional double entendres in Henry Fielding's *An Apology for the Life of Mrs. Shamela Andrews.*

Mr. Tiffey Old clerk at Spenlow and Jorkins in Charles Dickens's *The Personal History of David Copperfield.*

Major Tifto Dapper, shifty-eyed man of the turf and partner with Lord Silverbridge in owning a racehorse; when Silverbridge snubs him, he nobbles the horse on the eve of the St. Leger and plunges his former partner into debt; repentant and stripped of his reputation, he becomes an object of Silverbridge's charity in Anthony Trollope's *The Duke's Children.*

Montague Tigg Beggarly agent to Chevy Slyme; as Tigg Montague he becomes Chairman of the Board of the (fraudulent) Anglo-Bengalee Disinterested Loan and Life Assurance Company and a wealthy man before his sideline of blackmail results in his murder in Charles Dickens's *The Life and Adventures of Martin Chuzzlewit.*

Lord Tillibody Lady Ann Carthew's brother, who dies two months after her husband in Robert Louis Stevenson's *The Wrecker.*

Count Tilly Invading general, who is killed in a battle with King Gustavus Adolphus's forces along the river Lech in Daniel Defoe's *Memoirs of a Cavalier.*

General Tilney Bad-tempered and greedy owner of

the estate called Northanger Abbey; perceiving affection between his younger son and Catherine Morland and misled into believing Catherine wealthy, he invites her to accompany his daughter on a visit to his home; he sends her packing when he discovers her lack of fortune in Jane Austen's *Northanger Abbey*.

Mrs. Tilney   Deceased wife of General Tilney; her death is foolishly suspected by romantic Catherine Morland to be shrouded in mystery and crime in Jane Austen's *Northanger Abbey*.

Eleanor Tilney   Sweet and refined daughter of General Tilney and an affectionate friend to Catherine Morland; she suffers under her father's bad temper and desire for moneyed connections but eventually marries happily in Jane Austen's *Northanger Abbey*.

Captain Frederick Tilney   General Tilney's heir; a fashionable, expensive young man, he flirts with Isabella Thorpe, awakening hopes of a superior marriage and causing her to break her engagement with James Morland in Jane Austen's *Northanger Abbey*.

Henry Tilney   Clergyman and younger son of General Tilney; clever and handsome, he is attracted by Catherine Morland's admiration of him and defies his father to propose to her in Jane Austin's *Northanger Abbey*.

Martha Tilston   Ward of the cruel lawyer Old Cock; she escapes his clutches with the aid of John Buncle and his servant, Soto O'Fin, and takes refuge at Buncle's retreat, Orton Lodge, until her guardian's death in Thomas Amory's *The Life of John Buncle, Esq.*

Tim   One of the two servants acquired from the Harcourts; he assists John Buncle on the way to Ulubrae in Thomas Amory's *The Life of John Buncle, Esq.*

Timasius   Officer in the Roman army who employs Julian the Apostate, now freed in his incarnation as a slave, conferring upon him many honors to which Julian responds by betraying his benefactor in Henry Fielding's *A Journey From This World to the Next*.

Timorous   Mistrust's companion in fleeing the lions away from the Celestial City in John Bunyan's *The Pilgrim's Progress From this World to That Which Is to Come*.

Mrs. Timorous   Wife of Timorous and neighbor of Christiana; she tries to dissuade Christiana from her pilgrimage in John Bunyan's *The Pilgrim's Progress From this World to That Which Is to Come*.

Mrs. Tinker   Sir Pitt Crawley's servant in William Makepeace Thackeray's *Vanity Fair*.

Mr. Tinkler   Valet to William Dorrit in Charles Dickens's *Little Dorrit*.

Albert Tinley   A member of the wealthy Tinley family, the Poles' neighbors, and a suitor of Arabella Pole in George Meredith's *Emilia in England*.

Laura Tinley   One of the principal combatants in a struggle for superior social status carried on between the Tinley and Pole families; the wealthier Laura manages to win Mr. Pericles from the Poles in George Meredith's *Emilia in England*.

Martin Tinman   Vain, parsimonious retired merchant with social aspirations; his parsimony begets a feud with his friend Van Dieman Smith (Ribstone), whose daughter he courts but fails to win, both despite and because of his attempts to blackmail his old friend in George Meredith's *The House on the Beach*.

Mr. Tinsel   Fop, friend, and rival of Mr. Selvin; a scandal-monger, he is satirized and humiliated by Arabella; he is a typical Bath acquaintance of Charlotte Glanville in Charlotte Lennox's *The Female Quixote*.

Lady Tippins   Charming old lady, who is conspicuously painted, wigged, and gowned, and who dines regularly with the Veneerings and keeps her Cupidon, a ledger of her lovers, in Charles Dickens's *Our Mutual Friend*.

Miss Tippit   London landlady, religious, demure, and fifty, who befriends the hostile Miriam Tacchi, and who nurses Miriam during her illness in Mark Rutherford's *Miriam's Schooling*.

Andrew Tipple   Friend and former apprentice of Jeremiah Tugwell; he informs Tugwell that his wife is angry at him for leaving home in Richard Graves's *The Spiritual Quixote*.

Prince Tippoo Saib   Son of Prince Hyder Ali Kahn Bahauder and Vice-Regent of Bangalore; it is to his seraglio that Richard Middlemas intends to send Menie Gray in Sir Walter Scott's *The Surgeon's Daughter*.

Earl of Tiptoff   Good-hearted young nobleman, who assists Samuel Titmarsh by making him his steward; his kindness leads to Titmarsh's restoration to the favor of his aunt, Susan Hoggarty, in William Makepeace Thackeray's *The History of Samuel Titmarsh and the Great Hoggarty Diamond*.

Marchioness of Tiptoff   The marquess's wife, who is unsuccessful in opposing the marriage of Lady Lyndon to Redmond Barry in William Makepeace Thackeray's *The Luck of Barry Lyndon*.

Marquess of Tiptoff Lady Lyndon's kinsman and the Viscount Bullingdon's guardian in William Makepeace Thackeray's *The Luck of Barry Lyndon.*

Lady Fanny Rakes, Lady Tiptoff Lady Drum's granddaughter and the Earl of Tiptoff's wife; she hires Mary Titmarsh as her baby's nurse and assists the Titmarshes in other ways in William Makepeace Thackeray's *The History of Samuel Titmarsh and the Great Hoggarty Diamond.*

Earl of Tiroen Formerly General O'Neil; he is an Irish rebel, who captures and attempts to rape Ellinor; he notifies Queen Elizabeth of the alleged misconduct of the Earl of Essex (2) in Sophia Lee's *The Recess.*

Barnabas (Barnaby, John) Tirrel As John, the favorite domestic of Mr. Golding and later the personal friend of Henry Clinton; on his deathbed he gives his savings to the first beggar Clinton finds in the street; the recipient turns out to be Eleanor Tirrel, the wife he abandoned after stabbing her brother, whom he mistook for a paramour in Henry Brooke's *The Fool of Quality.*

Eleanor (Nelly) Damer Tirrel Beggar woman reduced to poverty because she could not run her husband's chandler shop after his disappearance; she is reunited with her husband, Barnabas, just before he dies in Henry Brooke's *The Fool of Quality.*

The Tish Unnamed narrator, who by chance finds a civilization deep within the earth, the land of the Vril-ya, and is loved by Zee, who finally helps him to return to earth before he is to be executed in Edward Bulwer-Lytton's *The Coming Race.*

Mrs. Tisher "Deferential widow" and companion of Miss Twinkleton at the boarding school; she especially looks after Rosa Bud in Rosa's interviews with Edwin Drood in Charles Dickens's *The Mystery of Edwin Drood.*

Mrs. Titmarsh Widowed mother of Samuel and nine daughters in William Makepeace Thackeray's *The History of Samuel Titmarsh and the Great Hoggarty Diamond.*

Michael Angelo Titmarsh (the author's self-caricature) A character who makes an appearance in William Makepeace Thackeray's *The History of Samuel Titmarsh and the Great Hoggarty Diamond.*

Mary Smith Titmarsh Devoted wife of Samuel Titmarsh, whom she eventually saves from ruin when, after the death of her infant child, she becomes wet nurse to Lady Tiptoff's child in William Makepeace Thackeray's *The History of Samuel Titmarsh and the Great Hoggarty Diamond.*

Samuel Titmarsh The narrator, an honest, unassuming clerk in the Independent West Diddlesex Fire and Life Insurance Co.; his ownership of his aunt's diamond pin brings him unexpected wealth and friendships, which lead to disaster until tragedy forces him to sell the diamond in William Makepeace Thackeray's *The History of Samuel Titmarsh and the Great Hoggarty Diamond.*

Winny Titmarsh One of the nine sisters of Samuel Titmarsh; she marries Gus Hoskins in William Makepeace Thackeray's *The History of Samuel Titmarsh and the Great Hoggarty Diamond.*

Lady Tittle Town lady who spreads gossip about Lady Booby and Joseph Andrews in Henry Fielding's *The History of the Adventures of Mr. Joseph Andrews and of his Friend Mr. Abraham Adams.*

Maid of Tivoli Young woman whose suicide after a brief encounter with Og of Basan results in guilt which, with her brother's threat, torments him for the rest of his life in William Beckford's *Biographical Memoirs of Extraordinary Painters.*

Stapylton Toad Manipulative and unscrupulous attorney, whose social advancement and great professional success result from his restoration of a lord to fiscal solvency in Benjamin Disraeli's *Vivian Grey.*

Sally Todd Jovial traveling companion and friend of Mary Baker; she delights in giving card parties and is a target for Sir Lionel Bertram's mercenary marital schemes in Anthony Trollope's *The Bertrams.* She is a neighbor of Miss Mackenzie in the Paragon Bath in *Miss Mackenzie.*

Mrs. Todgers Proprietress of Todgers's Commercial Boarding House, London, where the Pecksniffs stay, and special friend of Mercy and Charity Pecksniff in Charles Dickens's *The Life and Adventures of Martin Chuzzlewit.*

Todhunter Lord Farintosh's toady in William Makepeace Thackeray's *The Newcomes.*

John James, Lord Todmorden Samuel Ridley's master in William Makepeace Thackeray's *The Newcomes.* He is mentioned in *The Adventures of Philip on His Way through the World.*

Mrs. Toff Housekeeper at the Marquis of Brotherton's property, Manor Cross, and well aware of her power in the establishment in Anthony Trollope's *Is He Popenjoy?.*

Mr. Toffy Wiltshire police head constable, contemptuous of efforts by other county constabularies to apprehend the killers of Farmer Trumbull; his investigations clear Sam Brattle of the crime in Anthony Trollope's *The Vicar of Bullhampton*.

Toison d'Or   Quick-witted Burgundian herald, who examines Rouge Sanglier (Hayraddin Maugrabin) and discovers he is an impostor in Sir Walter Scott's *Quentin Durward*.

Samuel Tollady   Kindly printer who employs and befriends Arthur Golding in George Gissing's *Workers in the Dawn*.

Harry Toller   A brewer in George Eliot's *Middlemarch*.

Sophy Toller   Harry Toller's daughter, who marries Ned Plymdale in George Eliot's *Middlemarch*.

Mr. Tolson   Derbyshire bachelor determined never to marry a widow, especially one with a child and without a fortune, and who detests red hair, but marries Mrs. Turner in an anecdote related by Harriet Byron in Samuel Richardson's *Sir Charles Grandison*.

Tom   The sentimental, well-traveled assembler of the letters and papers that tell the story in Henry Mackenzie's *The Man of the World*. He saves the manuscript of Harley's biography in *The Man of Feeling*. He fulfills the request of a sentimental French visitor that he publish the letters that comprise the story of *Julia de Roubigné*.

Tom   Honest hand on the *Hispaniola*, killed by Long John Silver because he won't join the mutiny in Robert Louis Stevenson's *Treasure Island*.

Tom   Grimy little chimney-sweep employed by Mr. Grimes; he descends mistakenly into Ellie Harthover's bedroom; chased away, he tumbles into a river, is transformed by the fairies into a water-baby, and journeys to the sea; finally, after a moral cleansing, he becomes a scientist and spends time with Ellie in Charles Kingsley's *The Water-Babies*.

Tom   Groom at the Manor Farm, Dingley Dell, in Charles Dickens's *The Posthumous Papers of the Pickwick Club*.

Tom   Pimp and footman whom the naive Harley mistakes for a gentleman in Henry Mackenzie's *The Man of Feeling*.

Tom   Arblaster's suspicious crewman, who distrusts Lawless and Dick Shelton; he is killed by a knave in russet during the battle of Shoreby in Robert Louis Stevenson's *The Black Arrow: A Tale of Two Roses*.

Tom   John's son, whose education gives his father

something to live for in Mark Rutherford's *Mark Rutherford's Deliverance*.

Tom   Clergyman son of Dr. Harrison's impoverished friend; vanity leads him to dispute his learning with Dr. Harrison, his benefactor, in Henry Fielding's *Amelia*.

Tom   Driver of the coach with the Dover mail in Charles Dickens's *A Tale of Two Cities*.

Black Tom   Black San Francisco saloon owner and ward politician; Johnson hangs out at his bar in Robert Louis Stevenson's *The Wrecker*.

Captain Tom   Scottish sea captain who scornfully orders the three begging beachcombers, Mr. Huish, Robert Herrick, and Captain John Davies, off his ship and warns them of their upcoming arrest in Robert Louis Stevenson's *The Ebb-Tide: A Trio and a Quartette*.

Tom the Stable-boy   Stand-in for the amorous Mrs. Molly in a mock seduction scene arranged by servants to fool Geoffry Wildgoose in Richard Graves's *The Spiritual Quixote*.

Marco Toma   Old fisherman who seeks refuge from a storm at Spalatro's house, only to discover a corpse in Ann Radcliffe's *The Italian*.

May Tomalin   Young woman who belongs to Lady Ogram's lost family and is courted by Dyce Lashmar when he thinks she will be an heiress in George Gissing's *Our Friend the Charlatan*.

Chevalier Tomaso   A follower of Cesario; he relates the story of Cesario's affair with Hermione as well as his own intrigues with women and politics in Aphra Behn's *Love Letters Between a Nobleman and His Sister*.

Mr. Tombe   Deferential, astute lawyer of John Grey; he arranges the payment of George Vavasor's election costs from Grey's funds rather than Alice Vavasor's in Anthony Trollope's *Can You Forgive Her?*.

Tomkins   The manservant at the Beech Park residence of Frederick, Lord Lindore, Lady Juliana Douglas, and their respective children in Susan Ferrier's *Marriage*.

Miss Tomkins   Headmistress of the girls' boarding school at Westgate House, who interviews Samuel Pickwick after he is trapped in the kitchen closet in Charles Dickens's *The Posthumous Papers of the Pickwick Club*.

Joseph Tomkins (Philip Hazeldine)   Colonel Desborough's secretary, who spies for both Oliver Cromwell's men and for King Charles II's followers; he is killed by Joceline Joliffe when he tries to rape Phoebe Mayflower in Sir Walter Scott's *Woodstock*.

Miss Tomlins   A young woman proposed in the past as a match for Mr. B—— but refused by him because of her masculine air in Samuel Richardson's *Pamela, or Virtue Rewarded*.

Mr. Tomlins   Surgeon on the *Lizzard*, who befriends Roderick Random; later he tries to prevent Narcissa's marrying Roderick in Tobias Smollett's *The Adventures of Roderick Random*.

Tomlinson   Sir Jeckyl Marlowe's manservant who keeps his master's secrets in J. Sheridan Le Fanu's *Guy Deverell*.

Mrs. Tomlinson   Post-office keeper of Rochester, who attends the ball at the Bull Inn in Charles Dickens's *The Posthumous Papers of the Pickwick Club*.

Augustus Tomlinson   Foppish highwayman, who leads Paul Clifford astray in Edward Bulwer-Lytton's *Paul Clifford*.

Mary Scatcherd Tomlinson   Roger Scatcherd's sister, seduced in her youth by Henry Thorne, and mother of the illegitimate Mary Thorne; she married a village workman and emigrated with him in Anthony Trollope's *Doctor Thorne*.

Peggy Tomlinson   Absent-minded housemaid in the household of Sir George Darlington in William Beckford's *Modern Novel Writing; or, the Elegant Enthusiast*.

Tommy   Waterman at the coach stand in St. Martin's-le-Grand in Charles Dickens's *The Posthumous Papers of the Pickwick Club*.

Tommy (Wilkins)   Second son of Peter Wilkins and Youwarkee; he is adopted by Yaccombourse and later given preferment by Georigetti in Robert Paltock's *The Life and Adventures of Peter Wilkins*.

Peg Tomson   One of the old women present at Richard Middlemas's birth; she is Bet Jamieson's mother in Sir Walter Scott's *The Surgeon's Daughter*.

Mercus Tonans   A newspaper editor who publishes secret political information sold to him by Diana Warwick, who was told it in confidence by Percy Dacier, in George Meredith's *Diana of the Crossways*.

Toncarr   A pimp for DouLache and an experienced villain in Eliza Haywood's *The Injur'd Husband; or, the Mistaken Resentment*.

Tonga   Native of the Andaman Islands, who helped Jonathan Small escape and accompanied him to London, where he dies, in Arthur Conan Doyle's *The Sign of Four*.

Mr. Toobad   Manichean Millenarian; he believes the evil principle rules the world and constantly warns, "The Devil has come among you, having great wrath," in Thomas Love Peacock's *Nightmare Abbey*.

Celinda Toobad   Solemn young woman who, disguised as "Stella," uses a melancholy personal tale to arouse the love of Scythrop Glowry; she accepts Mr. Flosky's proposal in Thomas Love Peacock's *Nightmare Abbey*.

Mr. Toodle   Apple-cheeked husband of Polly Toodle; he works as a stoker for a steam engine and later works on the railroad, representing a new type of worker on a new and powerful type of transportation in Charles Dickens's *Dombey and Son*.

Polly ("Richards") Toodle   Wet nurse hired for the motherless infant Paul Dombey; kind and motherly to Florence, she is fired when she takes Paul and Florence to her home in Staggs' Gardens and Florence becomes lost in Charles Dickens's *Dombey and Son*.

Robin (Rob, Biler) Toodle   Oldest Toodle child, who is put into the Charitable Grinder school through the patronage of Paul Dombey; sneaky and untrustworthy, he works for Sol Gills in the shop and spies for James Carker in Charles Dickens's *Dombey and Son*.

Mrs. Toogood   Thomas Toogood's wife and mother of a large family; she worries that his costly and unremunerated efforts on behalf of Josiah Crawley will reduce the family income in Anthony Trollope's *The Last Chronicle of Barset*.

Thomas Toogood   Lawyer of Gray's Inn and cousin of Mrs. Crawley; his efforts on behalf of Josiah Crawley in the stolen-cheque affair clear Mr. Crawley's name in Anthony Trollope's *The Last Chronicle of Barset*.

Fitzwalker Tookey   Former partner of John Gordon in the Stick-in-the-Mud claim of the Great Kimberley diamond mine; he returns to England to persuade Gordon to sell his share to him in Anthony Trollope's *An Old Man's Love*.

Matilda Tookey   Long-suffering wife of Fitzwalker Tookey; although he abused her during their spell in South Africa, she returns with him to England in Anthony Trollope's *An Old Man's Love*.

Dr. Tom Toole   Jovial, gossipy, kind-hearted local practitioner who likes to know everything about everybody and is involved in most situations in J. Sheridan Le Fanu's *The House by the Churchyard*.

Dr. Tootle   Headmaster of the disorderly school where Osmond Waymark teaches in George Gissing's *The Unclassed*.

Mrs. Tootle   Shrewish and ignorant wife of the headmaster; she oppresses the teachers of the school where Osmond Waymark is a schoolmaster in George Gissing's *The Unclassed*.

Felix Tootle   Impudent son of the headmaster; he is beaten for misbehavior by Osmond Waymark in an incident that leads to Waymark's leaving Dr. Tootle's school in George Gissing's *The Unclassed*.

Tom Tootle   Customer at the Six Jolly Fellowship Porters who helps to rescue Roger Riderhood from the river in Charles Dickens's *Our Mutual Friend*.

Captain Tootles   Captain of H.M.S. *Tempest*, scared of currents around Midway, according to a hand Loudon Dodd meets in Hawaii in Robert Louis Stevenson's *The Wrecker*.

P. Toots   Head boy at Dr. Blimber's school, where his mind went weak after the stress of too much learning; he becomes little Paul and Florence Dombey's friend, falls in love with Florence, and remains her friend but eventually marries Susan Nipper in Charles Dickens's *Dombey and Son*.

Mr. Tope   Chief verger of Cloisterham Cathedral and husband of Mrs. Tope; he is fond of Edwin Drood and of John Jasper but knows nothing of Jasper's opium habits or secret love for Rosa Bud in Charles Dickens's *The Mystery of Edwin Drood*.

Mrs. Tope   Wife of the chief verger in Charles Dickens's *The Mystery of Edwin Drood*.

Mr. Topelius   Cohen & Co.'s agent in Butaritari who makes a deal with Captain Joe Wicks because of the wreck of the *Leslie* in Robert Louis Stevenson's *The Wrecker*.

Charles Topham   Soldier who carries the king's warrant to arrest suspects during the time of the Popish Plot; he arrests Sir Geoffrey Peveril and returns him a prisoner to London in Sir Walter Scott's *Peveril of the Peak*.

Mrs. Toplady   Influential, wealthy widow who sees through the many intrigues of Lady Ogram in George Gissing's *Our Friend the Charlatan*.

Mr. Topper   Merry, flirtatious bachelor, friend of

Ebenezer Scrooge's nephew, Fred, in Charles Dickens's *A Christmas Carol*.

George Torfe   Elderly but capable and resolute provost in Sir Walter Scott's *The Pirate*.

Mr. Torkingham   Well-intended clergyman whose conventional counsel never addresses Lady Constantine's problems in Thomas Hardy's *Two on a Tower*.

Lorenzo Tornabuoni   Wealthy friend of Tito Melema; he supports the Medici and is imprisoned in George Eliot's *Romola*.

Torpenhow   Gruff, staunch war correspondent for a British newspaper syndicate; he befriends Dick Heldar in Rudyard Kipling's *The Light That Failed*.

Torquil   A seer and warrior of a Highland clan; he dies protecting his chief and foster son, Eachin MacIan (Conachar), from Henry Smith during battle with a rival clan in Sir Walter Scott's *The Fair Maid of Perth*.

Mr. Torrance   Aged minister of the local Hermiston estate church in Robert Louis Stevenson's *Weir of Hermiston: An Unfinished Romance*.

Baron de Tortillee   A very gullible husband, who easily believes the Baroness de Tortillee and all her lies in Eliza Haywood's *The Injur'd Husband; or, the Mistaken Resentment*.

Mademoiselle La Motte, Baroness de Tortillee   Woman devoid of honor and gratitude who wants only to gratify herself; she totally mesmerizes the baron and marries him; she continues to sell herself after marriage in Eliza Haywood's *The Injur'd Husband; or, the Mistaken Resentment*.

Totila   King of the Goths who is campaigning in southern Italy; he invites Basil to join him during an interview at the Abbey of Cassino and later promises that he will allow him to marry Veranilda in George Gissing's *Veranilda*.

Totis   King of Egypt, who almost seduces Sarah, not knowing she is the wife of Abraham; he is poisoned by an unknown hand in the appended romance "The History of Charoba, Queen of Egypt" in Clara Reeve's *The Progress of Romance*.

Susanna Touchandgo   A teacher of the children of a farmer; she must support herself because she was left penniless by her absconding father; she was also abandoned by her suitor, young Crotchet; she seeks the healing power of nature in rural Wales and marries Mr. Chainmail in Thomas Love Peacock's *Crotchet Castle*.

Peregrine Scrogie Touchwood Wealthy world traveler who intrudes into the affairs of the Mowbrays with Francis Tyrrell and the Earl of Etherington (Valentine Bulmer), reveals himself to John Mowbray as a distant relative anxious to lend financial assistance, and assists Mowbray in his flight from Britain after the killing of Etherington in Sir Walter Scott's *St. Ronan's Well*.

Pasteur Tourneur French Protestant clergyman of powerful presence; he marries Caroline Gilmour in Anne Thackeray Ritchie's *The Story of Elizabeth*.

Anthony Tourneur Adolescent son of Pasteur Tourneur; he pursues Elizabeth Gilmour, much to her distress in Anne Thackeray Ritchie's *The Story of Elizabeth*.

James Tourville Foppish libertine friend of Robert Lovelace in Samuel Richardson's *Clarissa: or, The History of a Young Lady*.

Mr. Touthope Clever, devious justice's clerk in Sir Walter Scott's *Rob Roy*.

Lady Towers Unmarried, witty, satirical Bedfordshire neighbor of Mr. B——; her humor stings Pamela Andrews the maid but not Pamela the married Mrs. B—— in Samuel Richardson's *Pamela, or Virtue Rewarded*.

Sir Harry Towers Neighbor, suitor, and finally husband of Alicia Audley in Mary Elizabeth Braddon's *Lady Audley's Secret*.

Tom Towers Powerful journalist on the *Jupiter* who takes up John Bold's crusade against abuse of charity funds in Anthony Trollope's *The Warden*. He supports Mr. Slope's bid to become Dean of Barchester in *Barchester Towers*. He also appears in *Framley Parsonage*.

Sir Thomas Towler President of the Royal Academy in George Moore's *A Modern Lover*.

Towlinson Servant of Mr. Dombey in Charles Dickens's *Dombey and Son*.

Towneley Good looking and popular classmate of Ernest Pontifex from Cambridge; Ernest cuts him out of his life in order to be free to write what he wants in Samuel Butler's *The Way of All Flesh*.

"Colonel" Townley An elderly stranger, who draws the reader into the story as he rides his horse into Hayslope; he admires both Adam Bede and Dinah Morris; at the conclusion of the novel, he is a magistrate of Stoniton and allows Dinah to stay in prison to soften Hetty Sorrel's heart in George Eliot's *Adam Bede*.

Captain Townsend Deceased naval officer, distantly related to the family of Squire Townsend; he was the Widow Townsend's first husband and is eventually revealed by Joseph Tugwell to have been a rival to Captain Mahoney in Richard Graves's *The Spiritual Quixote*.

Mrs. Townsend Letty Fitzgerald's intimate friend, even more intolerant in her anti-Catholicism than her clergyman husband, Aeneas Townsend, in Anthony Trollope's *Castle Richmond*.

Squire Townsend Julia Townsend's father, a dreamy, pseudoscholarly gentleman, with whom Geoffry Wildgoose has a good-natured dispute over aesthetics and religion in Richard Graves's *The Spiritual Quixote*.

Widow Townsend Second wife of Squire Townsend and earlier the wife of his distant relative Captain Townsend; she unsuccessfully schemes to marry her stepdaughter Lucia to her own purported brother (actually, her lover), the already married Captain Mahoney, in order to get a share of the Townsend fortune in Richard Graves's *The Spiritual Quixote*.

Aeneas Townsend Rabidly anti-Catholic rector of Drumbarrow and an uncompromising foe of the parish priest, Father Bernard McCarthy, in Anthony Trollope's *Castle Richmond*.

Julia Townsend Geoffry Wildgoose's beloved, who runs away to London to escape her stepmother, narrowly escapes the familiarities of Mr. Blackman, finds refuge with her deceased mother's friend, Mrs. Sarsenet, and is briefly the object of Captain Mahoney's desire; she is unimpressed by Wildgoose's religious enthusiasm but marries him after he gives up his roving Methodist ministry in Richard Graves's *The Spiritual Quixote*.

Lucia Townsend Julia Townsend's sister and heir to an aunt's fortune; she is the main object of Captain Mahoney's desire and ambition in Richard Graves's *The Spiritual Quixote*.

Mr. Tow-wouse Innkeeper of the Dragon, where the stagecoach delivers the injured Joseph Andrews; he is inclined to aid Joseph but bows to wife's command to neglect an obviously penniless customer in Henry Fielding's *The History of the Adventures of Mr. Joseph Andrews and of his Friend Mr. Abraham Adams*.

Mrs. Tow-wouse Ugly wife of innkeeper Tow-wouse; hypocrisy and self-interest make her neglect poor customers and patronize wealthy ones in Henry Fielding's *The History of the Adventures of Mr. Joseph Andrews and of his Friend Mr. Abraham Adams*.

Lucretia Tox Kind-hearted, middle-aged spinster of limited income; she is encouraged by Mrs. Chick to consider Paul Dombey as a prospective spouse and takes an active interest in his welfare and household; she is disappointed and rejected by Mrs. Chick when Dombey marries Edith Granger in Charles Dickens's *Dombey and Son*.

Toxartis   Scythian soldier who insults the Countess Brenhilda and is killed by her in Sir Walter Scott's *Count Robert of Paris*.

Tozer   Stony young roommate of little Paul Dombey at Dr. Blimber's boarding school in Charles Dickens's *Dombey and Son*.

Mr. Tozer   Senior deacon in Salem Chapel and Arthur Vincent's warmest supporter in his tribulations; in spite of his humble work as a butterman, his self-satisfaction, and his lack of spiritual depth he achieves a certain heroic dignity in Margaret Oliphant's *Salem Chapel*.

Phoebe Tozer   Young lady, pink, plump, and full of dimples, who makes obvious if kindly advances to Arthur Vincent but eventually marries his successor Mr. Beecher in Margaret Oliphant's *Salem Chapel*.

Tom Tozer   Moneylender who with his brother holds promissory notes Mark Robarts has signed for Nathaniel Sowerby in Anthony Trollope's *Framley Parsonage*.

Mr. Trabb   A tailor who outfits Pip Pirrip for London and whose attitude toward money sharply reveals England's attitude about social class in Charles Dickens's *Great Expectations*.

Trabb's boy   Mr. Trabb's errand boy, from whom, Pip Pirrip says, he learns the moral value and power of money; he later helps to rescue Pip from Dolge Orlick in Charles Dickens's *Great Expectations*.

General Tracey   Aristocratic client of Orlando Somerive's maternal uncle; he secures a commission for Orlando in hopes that his aid will facilitate his plans to either lure or coerce Isabella Somerive into becoming his mistress in Charlotte Smith's *The Old Manor House*.

Henry Tracey   Faithful aide-de-camp to the Earl of Essex (2); he delivers Ellinor and Lady Southampton from Scotland and dies fighting for his master in Sophia Lee's *The Recess*.

John Tracy   Hugh Walsingham's faithful butler; he always accompanies Walsingham when the rector is called out at night in J. Sheridan Le Fanu's *The House by the Churchyard*.

Thomas (Tommy) Traddles   Student at Salem House school; he is David Copperfield's first friend; he draws skeletons on his school assignments; he goes into the law

and marries Sophy Crewler in Charles Dickens's *The Personal History of David Copperfield*.

Traffick   Prisoner in the mines of Peru; he first digs out the gold which contains Chrysal in Charles Johnstone's *Chrysal: or, The Adventures of a Guinea*.

Augusta Tringle Traffick   Snobbish, mean-spirited elder daughter of Sir Thomas Tringle; her huge dowry guarantees her a husband in Septimus Traffick, who happily sponges on her father; Augusta cordially loathes Ayala Dormer for having the charm and beauty she lacks in Anthony Trollope's *Ayala's Angel*.

E. Traffick   Amoranda's uncle in Mary Davys's *The Reform'd Coquet*.

Septimus Traffick   Balding Member of Parliament for Port Glasgow; he marries Augusta Tringle and her huge dowry and still contrives to sponge on her father, Sir Thomas Tringle, in Anthony Trollope's *Ayala's Angel*.

Mr. Trafford   Honest and diligent factory worker, who has become the wealthy owner of a large factory, which he operates humanely for the benefit of his workers in Benjamin Disraeli's *Sybil*.

Lord Augustus Trafford   One of three sons of the Marquis of Kingsbury by his second marriage in Anthony Trollope's *Marion Fay*.

Sir Cecil Trafford   Roman Catholic and Jacobite sympathiser, who marries Aliva Trenchard, sister of his friend Sir Rowland Trenchard, in William Harrison Ainsworth's *Jack Sheppard*.

Lady Frances Trafford   Only daughter of the Marquis of Kingsbury; she is disliked by her stepmother, the Marchioness; she is in love with George Roden, a post office clerk, and her family oppose the match; she finally marries when George turns out to be the Duca di Crinola in Anthony Trollope's *Marion Fay*.

Lord Frederic Trafford   One of three sons of the Marquis of Kingsbury by his second marriage in Anthony Trollope's *Marion Fay*.

Lord Gregory Trafford   One of three sons of the Marquis of Kingsbury by his second marriage; ambition for her sons partly motivates the Marchioness's scheming against her husband's eldest son, Lord Hampstead, in Anthony Trollope's *Marion Fay*.

Ursula Trafford   Mother Superior of the convent in which Sybil Gerard was raised; she counsels Sybil to acknowledge her love for Charles Egremont instead of becoming a nun in Benjamin Disraeli's *Sybil*.

Gaffer Tramp Cumbrian peasant who approves of Meg Murdockson's hanging because he believes she is a witch in Sir Walter Scott's *The Heart of Midlothian*.

Lady Harriet Tranmere Youngest daughter of Lord and Lady Cumnor; she champions Molly Gibson and uses her social power to rescue Molly's reputation in Elizabeth Gaskell's *Wives and Daughters*.

Lord Tranmore William Ashe's father in Mrs. Humphry Ward's *The Marriage of William Ashe*.

Elizabeth, Lady Tranmore Mother of William Ashe; she upholds the standards of her society; although she attempts to see her son and his wife, Lady Kitty, reconciled, Lady Tranmore cannot forgive in Mrs. Humphry Ward's *The Marriage of William Ashe*.

Arabella Transome The proud, slim wife of the incapicated elder Harold Transome; she holds Transome Court together by herself until her younger son, the apparent heir, returns after his brother's death; she must live with the guilt of an old love affair with Matthew Jermyn which produced her son Harold, whom she adores in George Eliot's *Felix Holt, the Radical*.

Durfey Transome The weak, foolish, older Transome son, who is hated by his mother; his death causes his brother, Harold, to return from Smyrna in order to manage the family estate in George Eliot's *Felix Holt, the Radical*.

Harold Transome (the elder) A dim-witted old man, who is mastered by his wife, suffers a stroke, and spends his time in the library of his home rearranging his bug specimens in George Eliot's *Felix Holt, the Radical*.

Harold Transome The apparent second son of a wealthy family; he returns after fifteen years as a merchant and banker in Smyrna when his older brother dies; he runs for Parliament as a Radical candidate with the help of Matthew Jermyn, a corrupt lawyer and Harold's real father; he is rejected as a husband by Esther Lyon, but she does return the Transome Court estate to him although it is legally hers in George Eliot's *Felix Holt, the Radical*.

Harry Transome Child who accompanies his father, the younger Harold Transome, to England; his mother, a native of Smyrna, is dead in George Eliot's *Felix Holt, the Radical*.

Thomas Transome (Tommy Trounsem) Old alcoholic trampled in the Election Day riot in George Eliot's *Felix Holt, the Radical*.

Trapbois Miserly old man who owns the house in Alsatia where Nigel Olifaunt hides; he steals Nigel's legal documents and is murdered by Captain Colepepper and Andrew Skurliewhitter in Sir Walter Scott's *The Fortunes of Nigel*.

Martha Trapbois Trapbois's daughter, who keeps the house in Alsatia where Nigel Olifaunt hides, is rescued by Nigel from the murderers of her father, and marries Richie Moniplies after he kills Captain Colepepper, one of her father's murderers, in Sir Walter Scott's *The Fortunes of Nigel*.

Mrs. Trapwell Englishwoman who conspires with her husband to seduce and then rob Ferdinand, whom they believe to be a physician, in Tobias Smollett's *The Adventures of Ferdinand Count Fathom*.

Travers A Jamaican of Creole stock; he is William's boon companion on his adventures in the West Indies; he feels indebted to William, who saved him in a shark attack, and vows to track down Deloraine and bring him to justice; in the face of Catherine's anguished plea for mercy, he experiences a change of heart and insists only that Deloraine remain in exile on the Continent in William Godwin's *Deloraine*.

Captain Traverse Impoverished discharged soldier for whom Lord Dorchester secures a commission in Sarah Fielding's *The History of Ophelia*.

Thomas Traverse Servant who apes the viciousness of his master Sedley in S. J. Pratt's *Pupil of Pleasure*.

Mrs. Travis A friend of Cecily Doran; she leaves her unfaithful husband but ultimately returns to him in George Gissing's *The Emancipated*.

Fernando (The Cacique) Travis Mexican-American who is won over to Tractarian devotional practices by the Underwoods, travels around the world in search of Edgar Underwood, recovers his family fortune, and marries Marilda Underwood in Charlotte Yonge's *The Pillars of the House*. He appears in *The Long Vacation*.

Treasurer of the Charity A man who looks after his own interests before the interests of the charity in Charles Johnstone's *Chrysal: or, The Adventures of a Guinea*.

Count Trebasi Hungarian who marries the widowed mother of Renaldo de Melvil, fights with Renaldo, and repents of his mistreatment of Renaldo's mother and sister in Tobias Smollett's *The Adventures of Ferdinand Count Fathom*.

Young Tredwell Emanthe's beloved, shipped off by his father to avoid her; true love triumphs, and he is reunited with her in Eliza Haywood's *Philidore and Placentia; or, L'Amour trop delicat*.

Diego de Trees   Courteous Spanish commander, who captures the band led by John Oxenham, but who has a litter made for Oxenham's mistress in Charles Kingsley's *Westward Ho!*.

Miss Trefoil   Dean Trefoil's spinster daughter, who keeps house for him while indulging her passion for botany in Anthony Trollope's *Barchester Towers*.

Mr. Trefoil   Dean of Barchester Cathedral whose death precipitates the battle for his succession won by Mr. Arabin in Anthony Trollope's *Barchester Towers*.

Arabella Trefoil   Mercenary, self-centered beauty dedicated to becoming a great lady; she shamelessly pursues Lord Rufford and claims he has proposed; she confesses this falsehood to her betrothed, John Morton; he dies, leaving her a legacy; she marries Mounser Green in Anthony Trollope's *The American Senator*.

Lady Augustus Trefoil   Discontented, scheming mother of Arabella; obsessed with marrying her daughter off to the best bidder, she supports Arabella's claims on Lord Rufford for breach of promise in Anthony Trollope's *The American Senator*.

Lord Augustus Trefoil   The Duke of Mayfair's younger brother and the indolent father of Arabella; he is intent only on his whist, creature comforts, and not getting involved with family squabbles involving his daughter's matrimonial prospects in Anthony Trollope's *The American Senator*.

Trefry   An Englishman who buys Oroonoko in Surinam; impressed by his nobility, Trefry promises to help Oroonoko, and allows him to marry Imoinda in Aphra Behn's *Oroonoko*.

Sir John Tregarvan   Cornish Member of Parliament and founder of the *European Review*, for which Philip Firmin writes in William Makepeace Thackeray's *The Adventures of Philip on His Way through the World*.

Francis (Frank) Tregear   Former Oxford classmate of Lord Silverbridge, to whose sister, Lary Mary Palliser, he is secretly engaged; her father, the (younger) Duke of Omnium, forbids the match; Frank's integrity and consistency finally convince the duke of his manliness, and the couple are allowed to marry in Anthony Trollope's *The Duke's Children*.

Frank Treherne   Child of Beatrice Brooks; he dies at age two in Caroline Norton's *Lost and Saved*.

Montague Treherne   Cousin of Lady Eudocia Wallingham and considered a good match because of the fortune he will have when he comes of age; he loves Beatrice Brooks and pretends to marry her in a mock ceremony, then later leaves her; having come to regret his behavior, he dies as a young man in Caroline Norton's *Lost and Saved*.

John Trelawney   Rather dense and foolish yet brave squire, who finances and accompanies the treasure hunt; his marksmanship allows his party to escape to the stockade in Robert Louis Stevenson's *Treasure Island*.

Lady Adelina Trelawny   Sister of Lord Westerhaven and of George Godolphin and victim of an early and loveless marriage to a profligate who dies bankrupt; she falls in love with George Fitz-Edward, bears his child, and, when widowed, is encouraged to marry him in Charlotte Smith's *Emmeline: The Orphan of the Castle*.

Miss Tremenhere   George Western's betrothed, who jilts him in order to marry Captain Walter Geraldine in Anthony Trollope's *Kept in the Dark*.

Aliva Trenchard   Younger sister of Sir Rowland Trenchard, mother of Thames Darrell by her first husband, a French aristocrat, and later the wife of Sir Cecil Trafford in William Harrison Ainsworth's *Jack Sheppard*.

Constance Trenchard   See Joan Sheppard.

Oliver Trenchard   Frank Henley's virtuous intimate and correspondent in Thomas Holcroft's *Anna St. Ives*.

Sir Rowland Trenchard   Roman Catholic, Jacobite, and knight of Ashton Hall, near Manchester; he kills the lover of his sister, Aliva, and attempts to kill her son, Thames Darrell, to ensure his own hold on the family fortune, but is himself murdered by Jonathan Wild in William Harrison Ainsworth's *Jack Sheppard*.

Grandfather Trent   Grandfather and guardian of Nell Trent; he owns the curiosity shop and is addicted to gambling; his debts force him to flee London with Nell, but he continues to gamble with the goal of making Nell a rich lady; he grows feebler and dies shortly after Nell's death in Charles Dickens's *The Old Curiosity Shop*.

Mrs. Trent   Attractive stepsister, then wife, to George Trent; she cultivates the Noble Lord's attentions when she finds Trent's affections cooling in Henry Fielding's *Amelia*.

Single Gentleman [Trent]   Energetic, restless, strong-minded man, who lodges at the Brasses' home and searches for Nell Trent and her grandfather, who is his older brother, in Charles Dickens's *The Old Curiosity Shop*.

Fred Trent   Nell Trent's handsome and dissolute older brother; he and Daniel Quilp plot to have Dick Swiveller marry Nell so that he can gain access to his grandfather's supposed fortune in Charles Dickens's *The Old Curiosity Shop*.

George Trent   Fellow captain, former friend of William Booth; now gamester and pimp, he makes his fortune off the Noble Lord in Henry Fielding's *Amelia*.

Captain Jacob Trent   English captain of the *Flying Scud*, knifed by Mack when he demands an exorbitant price for the *Currency Lass* crew's passage home; his identity is assumed by Captain Joe Wicks in Robert Louis Stevenson's *The Wrecker*.

Lydia Trent   Older sister and faithful guardian and attendant of Thyrza Trent in George Gissing's *Thyrza*.

Nell (Little Nell) Trent   Child and heroine, who lives with her grandfather in an old curiosity (antiques) shop; she accompanies and cares for her grandfather during their wanderings in the country while fleeing Daniel Quilp and dies pathetically at the end of Charles Dickens's *The Old Curiosity Shop*.

Thyrza Trent   Working girl with beauty and refinement above her station; she is engaged to a workingman but falls in love with the wealthy idealist Walter Egremont; she is taken in and educated by a benevolent matron but does not marry and dies suddenly in George Gissing's *Thyrza*.

Marchioness of Trente   Kidnapper of Ophelia, whom she sees as an impediment to her own salacious love for Lord Dorchester in Sarah Fielding's *The History of Ophelia*.

Harriot Trentham   Granddaughter of Mrs. Alworth who, when her married cousin, Mr. Alworth, realizes he loves her, leaves home and contracts smallpox, which lessens her beauty but helps reconcile her to the idea of single life in Sarah Scott's *A Description of Millenium Hall*.

Mr. Tresham   Will Tresham's father and the silent partner in the firm of Osbaldistone and Tresham in Sir Walter Scott's *Rob Roy*.

Richard Tresham (Middlemas, General Witherington)   Zilia de Monçada's belated husband and Richard Middlemas's father; he assumes the name Middlemas while in Scotland for Richard's birth; a high-born Jacobite, he becomes a political exile and flees England; assuming his mother's maiden name, Witherington, he gains fortune and rank in the service of the East India Company in Sir Walter Scott's *The Surgeon's Daughter*.

Will Tresham   The friend for whom Francis Os-baldistone writes his autobiography in Sir Walter Scott's *Rob Roy*.

Mrs. Tresilian   Charitable woman who is loved by Louis Reed and is disapproved of by his guardian, Lady Revill, in George Gissing's *Sleeping Fires*.

Amelia, Lady Tressady   Spendthrift mother of Sir George Tressady; she brings financial ruin on her son through her gambling in Mrs. Humphry Ward's *Sir George Tressady*.

Sir George Tressady   Aristocratic, Conservative Member of Parliament, who, because of his admiration for Lady Maxwell, breaks with his party and votes for the coalition sponsoring the Maxwell Factory bill; he dies in his own coal mines when he goes to the aid of his trapped miners in Mrs. Humphry Ward's *Sir George Tressady*.

Letty Sewell, Lady Tressady   Giddy young wife of Sir George Tressady; she bewitches him but is not his intellectual equal; after two years the marriage has foundered in Mrs. Humphry Ward's *Sir George Tressady*.

Mr. Tressels   Jolly undertaker, who assists with the secret burial of the coffin Mervyn brings to Chapelizod in J. Sheridan Le Fanu's *The House by the Churchyard*.

Edmund Tressilian   Former suitor of Amy Robsart (Dudley), her father's friend, and a follower of the Earl of Sussex; believing Amy to have been seduced by Richard Varney, he petitions Queen Elizabeth through Sussex to discipline her seducer and restore Amy to her father; at Kenilworth revels, he discovers Amy in his room and promises to keep silent about her plight, a promise that proves fatal to her in Sir Walter Scott's *Kenilworth*.

Colonel von Tresten   Friend of Sigismund Alvan and liaison between Alvan and the von Rüdigers; he is unimpressed with Clotilde and conducts himself with a strict formality that keeps Clotilde from sending her true thoughts to Alvan through him in George Meredith's *The Tragic Comedians*.

Captain Trevanion   Capable army friend of Harry Lorrequer; he assists Harry in extricating himself from his problems and involvements in Paris in Charles Lever's *The Confessions of Harry Lorrequer*.

Fanny Trevanion   The beloved of both Pisistratus Caxton and his wild cousin, Herbert Caxton; she is unwillingly married to the Marquess of Castleton in Edward Bulwer-Lytton's *The Caxtons*.

Emily Rowley Trevelyan   Married daughter of Sir Marmaduke Rowley; her defiance of her husband, Louis Trevelyan, over her friendship with Colonel Osborne inflames his jealousy; she pursues him to Italy after he abducts their son and persuades him to return to England for treatment in Anthony Trollope's *He Knew He Was Right*.

Louey Trevelyan   Baby son of the Trevelyans used as a pawn in their terrible marital feud; he is kidnapped and taken to Italy by his half-mad father, Louis Trevelyan, in Anthony Trollope's *He Knew He Was Right*.

Louis Trevelyan   Self-willed husband of Emily (Rowley); he becomes jealous when she appears to relish the attentions of the mischief-making Colonel Osborne; in vengefulness and desperation, after they have been living for some months apart, he abducts their child and flees to Italy, where he descends into madness; she persuades him to return with her to England, but his health is gone, and he dies at a moment of reconciliation and what Emily convinces herself is at last an expression of his belief in her honor in Anthony Trollope's *He Knew He Was Right*.

Hugh Trevor (the elder)   Hugh Trevor's father, a handsome and fun-loving farmer's son who becomes bankrupt, flees his family, and dies on a ship in Thomas Holcroft's *The Adventures of Hugh Trevor*.

Hugh Trevor   Narrator and hero whose naiveté and youth cause him to suffer at the hands of both the foolish and the deceitful, and whose basic honesty eventually brings him wealth, position, and happiness in Thomas Holcroft's *The Adventures of Hugh Trevor*.

Lady Madeline Trevor   Violet Fane's charming guardian, to whom Vivian Grey is devoted and whom he assists by saving her brother from unscrupulous gamblers in Benjamin Disraeli's *Vivian Grey*.

Captain Trevyllian   Friend of Captain Hammersley; he fights a duel with Charles O'Malley in Charles Lever's *Charles O'Malley*.

Daniel Tribbledale   Plodding clerk for a firm of commission merchants where Zachary Fay is his chief; he marries Clara Demijohn in Anthony Trollope's *Marion Fay*.

Mrs. Trickmaid   Procuress for Lucy Silborn (Brawn) in S. J. Pratt's *Liberal Opinions upon Animals, Man, and Providence*.

Ann Tricksy   Syrena's mother, who teaches her to be deceitful and vain, in Eliza Haywood's *Anti-Pamela: or, Feign'd Innocence Detected*.

Syrena Tricksy   A great beauty and a dissembler; she is an actress and a hypocrite who wants to get money out

of every man in Eliza Haywood's *Anti-Pamela: or, Feign'd Innocence Detected*.

Mr. Trigger   Cynical agent for Mr. Griffenbottom and his running-mate, Sir Thomas Underwood, in the Percycross election; his vote buying and dishonesty lead to the borough's disenfranchisement in Anthony Trollope's *Ralph the Heir*.

Tom Trim   Brother of Corporal Trim (James Butler) and very like him in appearance and manner; he married "a Jew's widow" who kept a sausage shop in Lisbon and was thrown into a dungeon by agents of the Inquisition; he is forever mourned by Corporal Trim in Laurence Sterne's *The Life and Opinions of Tristram Shandy, Gentleman*.

Trinette   The Beck children's maid in Charlotte Brontë's *Villette*.

Parson Tringham   Clergyman whose antiquarian research leads to John Durbeyfield's consciousness of his ancient lineage in Thomas Hardy's *Tess of the D'Urbervilles*.

Emmeline, Lady Tringle   Anxious wife of Sir Thomas and sister of Reginald Dosett; surrounded by luxury and told by her husband that cash flow is unlimited, she worries constantly over the marriage prospects and love entanglements of her children, Tom, Augusta, and Gertrude, in Anthony Trollope's *Ayala's Angel*.

Gertrude Tringle   Sir Thomas's younger daughter, anxious to secure the same huge dowry when she marries that her sister Augusta engineered; her choice of Frank Houston as husband meets parental veto; she elopes with Captain Batsby, who gambles on her father's relenting and making a generous endowment on his daughter in Anthony Trollope's *Ayala's Angel*.

Sir Thomas Tringle   Wealthy senior partner in a London banking firm sorely beset by the loves and matrimonial scrapes of his daughters, Augusta and Gertrude, and his son, Tom, in Anthony Trollope's *Ayala's Angel*.

Tom Tringle   Hobbledehoy puppyish son of Sir Thomas; his mad infatuation for Ayala Dormer involves him in assaulting a policeman after overindulgence in champagne and issuing a challenge to his rival, Jonathan Stubbs; his father packs him off to New York in Anthony Trollope's *Ayala's Angel*.

Battista Tripalda   Infidel priest of Castruccio dei Antelminelli's court; he is Euthanasia dei Adimari's ally in a conspiracy against Castruccio and then doublecrosses her by confiding in Castruccio's governor in Mary Shelley's *Valperga*.

Tripp Carman at Murdstone and Grinby in Charles Dickens's *The Personal History of David Copperfield*.

Joanna Trista A Belgian-Spanish pupil of Mlle. Reuter's school, whose frequent disturbances in class are snuffed out when she is locked in a cupboard one day in Charlotte Brontë's *The Professor*.

Brenda Troil Magnus Troil's beautiful and high-spirited younger daughter; after a lengthy acquaintance, she and Mordaunt Mertoun fall in love and marry in Sir Walter Scott's *The Pirate*.

Magnus Troil Kindly and generous Udall of Jarlshof and master of Burgh Westra; he is somewhat intemperate in his habits but a proud and doting father; steeped in Norwegian traditions, he passionately resents Scottish encroachments on Zetland in Sir Walter Scott's *The Pirate*.

Minna Troil Magnus Troil's serious and beautiful elder daughter; having fallen in love with the dashing Captain Clement Cleveland, she has her romantic illusions of pirates swept away when she is kidnapped by Cleveland's crew, after which she sadly parts from her lover in Sir Walter Scott's *The Pirate*.

Norna Troil (Norna of the Fitful-head, Ulla Troil) Kinswoman of Magnus Troil and a sibyl who inhabits a remote cavern with the dwarf Nick Strumpfer; she has an extraordinary knowledge of the weather, prophetic pretensions, and magical powers of healing, which she successfully practices on Minna Troil; mistaking Mordaunt Mertoun for her long-lost son, she jealously endangers Clement Cleveland's life before discovering he is actually her son in Sir Walter Scott's *The Pirate*.

Trois-Eschelles A tall, gaunt, and somber hangman, Provost L'Hermite's assistant and Petit-André's colleague in Sir Walter Scott's *Quentin Durward*.

Betty Trollop A bed-maker at Cambridge who gives birth to an illegitimate child and, at Young Qualmsick's instigation, sends Pompey, instead of the child, to Williams in Francis Coventry's *The History of Pompey the Little*.

Colonel Trompington Uneducated, shallow mercenary whom Dr. Harrison is asked to support for mayor in exchange for preferment for William Booth in Henry Fielding's *Amelia*.

Dan Troop Fifteen-year-old son of Disko, the skipper of a cod-fishing boat off the Great Banks; he befriends spoiled young Harvey Cheyne in Rudyard Kipling's *"Captains Courageous": A Story of the Grand Banks*.

Disko Troop Crusty, crafty skipper of the *We're Here*, a cod-fishing boat; he makes a man out of spoiled young Harvey Cheyne in Rudyard Kipling's *"Captains Courageous": A Story of the Grand Banks*.

Salters Troop The farmer-turned-fisherman brother of Disko and uncle of young Dan; he befriends mad Pennsylvania Pratt and spoiled young Harvey Cheyne in Rudyard Kipling's *"Captains Courageous": A Story of the Grand Banks*.

Mrs. Trotter Neighborhood gossip and mother of Eliza Trotter in Robert Surtees's *Hillingdon Hall*.

Eliza Trotter Daughter of John Jorrocks's neighbor and a rival to Emma Flather for the affections of James, Marquis of Bray in Robert Surtees's *Hillingdon Hall*.

Jemmy (Dismal Jemmy, Jem Hutley) Trotter Careworn transient, who relates "The Stroller's Tale" to Samuel Pickwick, Tracy Tupman, Augustus Snodgrass, and Nathaniel Winkle and is Job Trotter's brother in Charles Dickens's *The Posthumous Papers of the Pickwick Club*.

Job Trotter Alfred Jingle's pious and loyal servant, who assists in his master's deceptions and is prone to tears in Charles Dickens's *The Posthumous Papers of the Pickwick Club*.

Nelly Trotter Fishwife who carries gossip from St. Ronan's Well to Meg Dods's inn in Sir Walter Scott's *St. Ronan's Well*.

Thomas Trotter Yeoman who witnesses Joseph Andrews cutting a twig on Lawyer Scout's land; his deposition brings larceny charges against Joseph and Fanny Goodwill in Henry Fielding's *The History of the Adventures of Mr. Joseph Andrews and of his Friend Mr. Abraham Adams*.

Mr. Trottman Student of the law and an intimate of Mr. Hilary; along with Mr. Rudge, he introduces Hugh Trevor to legal absurdities in Thomas Holcroft's *The Adventures of Hugh Trevor*.

Betsey Trotwood David Copperfield's great-aunt, who appears at his birth but walks out in disappointment that he is not a girl; she later adopts him when he runs away to her house in Dover; kindhearted under a sharp exterior, she secretly supports her vagabond husband in Charles Dickens's *The Personal History of David Copperfield*.

Farmer Troutham Neighbor of Jude Fawley and his aunt; as a child, Jude is employed by Troutham to keep birds out of his fields; being too sensitive to harm these animals, Jude fails in his duty and is discharged from his job in Thomas Hardy's *Jude the Obscure*.

John Augustus Stowte, Marquis of Trowbridge Silly, self-important, easily offended landowner in dispute with Harry Gilmore when the latter refuses to evict Jacob Brattle, whose son Sam is accused of murder; having fallen out also with the vicar, Frank Fenwick, the Marquis donates land to allow Methodists to build a chapel opposite the vicarage gates; when records disclose that the site is part of church domain he is forced to remove the chapel in Anthony Trollope's *The Vicar of Bullhampton*.

Sergeant Francis (Frank) Troy Deceptive, shallow, and greedy husband of Bathsheba Everdene; he marries her for her looks and money, although he has previously seduced and impregnated one of her servants, Fanny Robin; upon Fanny's death, the repentant Troy leaves Bathsheba only to return years later to be killed by John Boldwood, who has obsessively and, of late, hopefully pursued Bathsheba in Thomas Hardy's *Far from the Madding Crowd*.

Tommy Truck Bully beaten up by young Harry Clinton because the ruffian hit Harry's brother; as young adults they become friends despite a difference in social position in Henry Brooke's *The Fool of Quality*.

Mr. Trueman Retired businessman and neighbor of Lucius Manly; his son is his only support; he found trade unpleasant because he constantly worried that honest merchants would suffer from his misfortunes; Lucius hires his son as steward in Mary Collyer's *Felicia to Charlotte*.

Mr. Trueman Honest and honorable gentleman companion, who is entrusted to keep the Nobleman of the First Rank out of trouble, and who proves to be beyond all temptation in Charles Johnstone's *Chrysal: or, The Adventures of a Guinea*.

Timothy Trueman Servant who apes the virtue of his master Michael Bankwell in S. J. Pratt's *Pupil of Pleasure*.

Charles Trueworth Betsy Thoughtless's true suitor and love; he has a stable disposition in Eliza Haywood's *The History of Miss Betsy Thoughtless*.

Miss Trufle Well-off, homely woman at Bath who, having alienated all possible suitors, collects small companion animals in Richard Graves's *The Spiritual Quixote*.

Mrs. Trulliber Parson Trulliber's thoroughly cowed wife, who fears and worships her husband and takes his part against her own conscience to avoid repercussions in Henry Fielding's *The History of the Adventures of Mr. Joseph Andrews and of his Friend Mr. Abraham Adams*.

Parson Trulliber Farmer-clergyman, who rudely mis-takes Parson Adams for a hog dealer, then refuses to lend him seven shillings in Henry Fielding's *The History of the Adventures of Mr. Joseph Andrews and of his Friend Mr. Abraham Adams*.

Bailie Trumbull Touthope's accomplice in Sir Walter Scott's *Rob Roy*.

Farmer Trumbull Tenant farmer of the Marquis of Trowbridge; he is robbed and beaten to death, and Sam Brattle is accused of the crime in Anthony Trollope's *The Vicar of Bullhampton*.

Borthrup Trumbull Peter Featherstone's cousin, who briefly courts Mary Garth because he believes that Peter may have left her a large sum of money in his will in George Eliot's *Middlemarch*.

Mr. Trundle Betrothed and later husband of Isabella Wardle in Charles Dickens's *The Posthumous Papers of the Pickwick Club*.

Commodore Hawser Trunnion Retired naval man who has only one eye; he resists the seduction of Mrs. Grizzle but finally gives in and marries her and adopts Peregrine Pickle when the boy's mother turns against him; he dies leaving his estate to Peregrine in Tobias Smollett's *The Adventures of Peregrine Pickle*.

Lady Trusty Sir Ralph's wife whom Betsy Thoughtless considers her second mother in Eliza Haywood's *The History of Miss Betsy Thoughtless*.

Sir Ralph Trusty Betsy Thoughtless's guardian in Eliza Haywood's *The History of Miss Betsy Thoughtless*.

Mrs. Tubbs Fenmarket brewer's wife, who attributes the strange ways of the Hopgood sisters to their German education in Mark Rutherford's *Clara Hopgood*.

Friar Tuck Jolly friar of Robin Hood's band, who revels with the Black Knight; he is ashamed of their exchange of hard blows when he discovers the Black Knight to be his revered king, Richard, in Sir Walter Scott's *Ivanhoe*.

Tucker The constable killed accidentally by Felix Holt's efforts to disperse the Election Day rioters in George Eliot's *Felix Holt, the Radical*.

Sarah (Sally) Tucker Esther Waters's fellow servant at the Barfields'; she is jealous of Esther; she loses her position when the estate goes to ruin; she renews her acquaintance with Esther and William Latch at William's pub; charged with robbery, she unwittingly reveals the illegal gambling at the pub, causing William to lose his license in George Moore's *Esther Waters*.

Blackburn Tuckham　Nevil Beauchamp's stodgy and conservative cousin; he wins Beauchamp's beloved, Cecilia Halkett, from him but honorably insures he doesn't receive Beauchamp's inheritance as well in George Meredith's *Beauchamp's Career*.

Mr. Tuckle　One of the select footmen at John Smauker's "swarry" in Bath in Charles Dickens's *The Posthumous Papers of the Pickwick Club*.

Job Tudge　Independent, friendly child, who attracts the interest of Esther (Lyon) and Felix Holt in George Eliot's *Felix Holt, the Radical*.

Alaric Tudor　Ambitious civil servant, whose dubious financial ventures lead to a prison term for embezzlement; he ultimately marries Gertrude Woodward and emigrates in Anthony Trollope's *The Three Clerks*.

Charley Tudor　Alaric Tudor's cousin, a junior clerk in government office often in trouble until reformed by his sweetheart, Katie Woodward, in Anthony Trollope's *The Three Clerks*.

Lady Tufto　The general's long-suffering wife in William Makepeace Thackeray's *Vanity Fair*.

Sir George Tufto　Elderly general who has amorous intentions towards Becky (Sharp) Crawley in William Makepeace Thackeray's *Vanity Fair* He is mentioned in *The Newcomes*.

Mr. Tufton　Arthur Vincent's predecessor as minister; his stupidity makes him an ineffective supporter of his more sensitive successor in Margaret Oliphant's *Salem Chapel*.

Mrs. Tufton　Well-meaning and tenderhearted friend of Arthur Vincent during his time of trouble in Margaret Oliphant's *Salem Chapel*.

Adelaide Tufton　Sharp-eyed and sharp-tongued invalid, who is quick to see the difficulties of the Vincent family in Margaret Oliphant's *Salem Chapel*.

Tugby　Porter to Sir Joseph Bowley in Charles Dickens's *The Chimes*.

Dorothy Tugwell　Wife of Jeremiah Tugwell; her anger at his leaving home is appeased when he returns with money and their long-lost son in Richard Graves's *The Spiritual Quixote*.

Jeremiah Tugwell　Cobbler who accompanies Geoffry Wildgoose during his career as an itinerant Methodist preacher; he gets into fistfights, reveals his susceptibility to superstitious fears, and frequently complains of hunger, thirst, and homesickness in Richard Graves's *The Spiritual Quixote*.

Joseph Tugwell　A soldier and the long-lost son of Jeremiah Tugwell, who supposes him to have been killed overseas; he finds his father at a Methodist assembly and reveals the true relationship between the Widow Townsend and Captain Mahoney in Richard Graves's *The Spiritual Quixote*.

Mr. Tulkinghorn　Secretive lawyer of Sir Leicester Dedlock; he collects information about Lady Dedlock and discovers her secret, but is then shot to death by Hortense, Lady Dedlock's maid, in Charles Dickens's *Bleak House*.

Corporal Tullidge　Middle-aged beacon watchman with Simon Burden; he is a war veteran who has worn a hat in public to protect the squeamish ever since his head injury in Valenciennes in 1793 in Thomas Hardy's *The Trumpet-Major*.

Edward Tulliver　The owner of Dorlcote Mill on the river Floss; he recognizes that his daughter, Maggie, is more clever than naughty and is kind to her; John Waken's getting the mortgage on the mill causes Tulliver to decline in health and quickly die in George Eliot's *The Mill on the Floss*.

Elizabeth (Bessy) Dodson Tulliver　Dull-witted, ineffectual woman, who is dependent on her more prosperous sisters; she never says the right thing; she cares more for her son, Tom, than for her daughter, Maggie, and cares much more for her china and linens than for either of her children; she softens towards Maggie near the end and goes to live with her at Bob Jakin's house in George Eliot's *The Mill on the Floss*.

Maggie Tulliver　Imaginative, acute, and difficult child, who never escapes the unhappiness her intelligence causes her, even as an adult; her cousin Lucy's suitor, Stephen Guest, nearly succeeds in persuading her to elope with him, but she cannot hurt her family and friends; she returns the next day only to find that the world believes she has sinned; Tom, her brother, whom she loves dearly, disowns her, but they are reconciled in death as they drown clasped in each others' arms in George Eliot's *The Mill on the Floss*.

Tom Tulliver　Placidly arrogant boy, who reaches manhood still full of the same assurance that his moral outlook is impeccable; he disowns his sister, Maggie, when he believes her to have fallen prey to Stephen Guest, but is reconciled with her just before they drown together in the flood in George Eliot's *The Mill on the Floss*.

Mr. Tungay　Man with a wooden leg who works for

Mr. Creakle at the Salem House school and considers everyone there his enemy except Mr. Creakle in Charles Dickens's *The Personal History of David Copperfield*.

Tunley   Landlord of the alehouse near Perry Pickle's home; he is the victim of a practical joke by Perry and Jack Hatchway in Tobias Smollett's *The Adventures of Peregrine Pickle*.

Thomas Tunny   Charles Hermsprong's landlord at The Golden Ball; he introduces Charles to the Reverend Woodcock in Robert Bage's *Hermsprong*.

Francis Tunstall   Junior apprentice to David Ramsay; he helps Jin Vin (Jenkin Vincent) in a London brawl in Sir Walter Scott's *The Fortunes of Nigel*.

Tracy Tupman   Samuel Pickwick's middle-aged, portly, sentimental companion, who enjoys flirting with women and has a short-lived romance with Rachael Wardle in Charles Dickens's *The Posthumous Papers of the Pickwick Club*.

Tur   Chief magistrate of a community of the Vril-ya; he plans to destroy the Tish rather than allow his daughter to marry this carnivorous, inferior earthling in Edward Bulwer-Lytton's *The Coming Race*.

Timothy Turbot   An Irish journalist orator who aids in Nevil Beauchamp's campaign for Parliament in George Meredith's *Beauchamp's Career*.

Mr. Turl   Hugh Trevor's extraordinary schoolmate, who uses his intellect to promote justice and encourages Hugh to distinguish vice from virtue in Thomas Holcroft's *The Adventures of Hugh Trevor*.

Turnbull   Family lawyer of the Warburtons in George Gissing's *Will Warburton*.

Dr. Turnbull   Atheist, a kindly man and the best doctor in Eastthorp, who tends to Catharine Furze during her illnesses in Mark Rutherford's *Catharine Furze*.

Mr. Turnbull   Popular radical politician and something of a maverick among the Liberals; his great powers of oratory enable him to carry the popular vote, but his principles on electoral reform are questionable in Anthony Trollope's *Phineas Finn*. He appears in *Phineas Redux*.

Michael Turnbull   Sir James Douglas's huntsman, a daring outlaw who attempts to assassinate Sir John de Walton and recover Douglas Castle in Sir Walter Scott's *Castle Dangerous*.

Miss Turner   A weak-willed English teacher, who is let go by Mme. Beck because she cannot govern her pupils in Charlotte Brontë's *Villette*.

Miss Turner   John Buncle's fifth wife; the sister of his close friend, Charles Turner of Skelsmore-Vale, she is well educated in antiquity, history, geography, and music; she dies in a carriage accident six weeks after her marriage in Thomas Amory's *The Life of John Buncle, Esq.*

Mrs. Turner   Portionless, red-haired widow and mother who marries Mr. Tolson in an anecdote related by Harriet Byron in Samuel Richardson's *Sir Charles Grandison*.

Mr. Turner (Thomasine Fuller)   Lawyer whose pseudonymous letter warns Pamela (Andrews) B—— of Mr. B——'s attempted bigamy in Samuel Richardson's *Pamela, or Virtue Rewarded*.

Charles Turner   Close university friend whom John Buncle hopes to find; Buncle finds only his home, Skelsmore-Vale, in Westmoreland but marries his sister, Buncle's fifth wife; later Turner dies in Italy in Thomas Amory's *The Life of John Buncle, Esq.*

Turnham-Green Gentleman   Intended victim, who captures a Highway Man in the act of robbing him in Charles Johnstone's *Chrysal: or, The Adventures of a Guinea*.

Lord Turntippet   Politically savvy member of the Scottish Privy Council in Sir Walter Scott's *The Bride of Lammermoor*.

Richard (Dick) Turpin   Noted highwayman, also known as Jack Palmer; he is a friend of Luke Bradley and the Gypsies; he accomplishes his celebrated nonstop ride from London to York on his famous horse, Black Bess, in William Harrison Ainsworth's *Rookwood*.

Turpius   Father of the bastard Valerius and of Clarenthia, whom he seduces; he gets very sick as a punishment for his sins in Jane Barker's *Exilius; or, The Banish'd Roman*.

Mr. Turvey   Principal of the Provincial Deformatory for Boys; in a corruption of Higgs's philosophy, boys are taught vice so as not to be too good in Samuel Butler's *Erewhon Revisited Twenty Years Later*.

Mr. Turveydrop   Prince Turveydrop's fat old father, who is an admirer of the late George IV and famed for his deportment; he lives off his son's labor while contributing nothing to his upkeep in Charles Dickens's *Bleak House*.

Prince Turveydrop   Fair young dancing-master, who supports and looks up to his indolent father and eventually marries Caddy Jellyby in Charles Dickens's *Bleak House*.

Tuscan   A slave who initially resists Oroonoko's call to war because of wife and family, but is inspired to action by Oroonoko's speech about loyalty and glory; later, he is the only slave to stand by Oroonoko when he has been defeated by white colonists in Aphra Behn's *Oroonoko*.

Mrs. Tusher   The vicar's wife, formerly waiting-woman of the Dowager Viscountess Castlewood (Isabel), in William Makepeace Thackeray's *The History of Henry Esmond*.

Dr. Robert Tusher   Pompous, obsequious vicar at Castlewood in William Makepeace Thackeray's *The History of Henry Esmond*.

Thomas Tusher   Henry Esmond's contemporary, a sycophant by nature rather than by craft; he becomes vicar at Castlewood and eventually marries Beatrix Esmond and becomes dean and bishop in William Makepeace Thackeray's *The History of Henry Esmond*.

Tutor   Servant on Colonel Jack's plantation who teaches him Latin and who becomes a devout Christian; he falls in love with Colonel Jack's housekeeper but discovers she is married in Daniel Defoe's *The History and the Remarkable Life of the Truly Honourable Colonel Jacques, Commonly Call'd Col. Jack*.

Tutor   Teacher of the Erewhonian language to Jack Higgs; he is impressed with Higgs's progress and tells him about straighteners in Samuel Butler's *Erewhon*. He identifies Higgs as the Sunchild but later is forced to rescind his testimony in *Erewhon Revisited Twenty Years Later*.

Twala (The One Eyed, The Mighty, Husband of One Thousand Wives)   Murderer of his brother, Imotu, the rightful king; he usurped the throne of Kukuanaland; he is overthrown by Ignosi (Umbopa), son of Imotu, in a civil war and beheaded by Sir Henry Curtis in H. Rider Haggard's *King Solomon's Mines*.

Mr. Twangdillo   Methodist preacher who is enthusiastically recommended by the scullery maid Deborah in Richard Graves's *The Spiritual Quixote*.

Tweedledee   Tweedledum's identical twin, who resembles an oversized school boy; he recites "The Walrus and the Carpenter" and explains to Alice that she exists only in the Red King's dream; his destruction of his brother's rattle leads to preparations for a battle between them in Lewis Carroll's *Through the Looking-Glass*.

Tweedledum   Tweedledee's identical twin, who resembles an oversized school boy; he dances and sings

with his brother and Alice and supports his brother's opinion that Alice is only part of the Red King's dream; his rage over a broken rattle leads to preparations for battle with his brother in Lewis Carroll's *Through the Looking-Glass*.

Melvin Twemlow   Wizened friend of the Veneerings; his social value lies in his being first cousin to Lord Snigsworth in Charles Dickens's *Our Mutual Friend*.

Lawrence Twentyman   Amiable gentleman-farmer, who rides with the Dillsborough Hunt; he asks Mary Masters to marry him; when she refuses, he falls in love with her sister Kate in Anthony Trollope's *The American Senator*. He appears as a guest of Sir Harry Albury in *Ayala's Angel*.

Mr. Twineall   Young coxcomb employed by the mercantile firm Osbaldistone and Tresham in Sir Walter Scott's *Rob Roy*.

Miss Twinkleton   Mistress of the boarding school where Rosa Bud is a resident pupil; she is a proper Victorian lady in Charles Dickens's *The Mystery of Edwin Drood*.

Oliver Twist   Boy who is orphaned at birth and named by the beadle; he lives in a workhouse, then is apprenticed to an undertaker; having run away to London, he falls in with Fagin and his boys; he is rescued by Mr. Brownlow and later the Maylies, is pursued by Fagin and Bill Sikes, and is finally adopted by Mr. Brownlow after the death of Nancy in Charles Dickens's *Oliver Twist*.

Two, Five, and Seven   Playing-card gardeners in the service of the Queen of Hearts; their attempt to correct a gardening mistake by painting white roses red is discovered, fueling the wrath of the queen in Lewis Carroll's *Alice's Adventures in Wonderland*.

Andrew Twyford   Edmund Lovel's adoptive peasant father, who maltreats the young Edmund until he is taken into the Fitz-Owen household in Clara Reeve's *The Old English Baron*.

Margery Twyford   Edmund Lovel's adoptive peasant mother, who provides him with information and evidence proving his true lineage in Clara Reeve's *The Old English Baron*.

Agnes Twysden   First cousin and first love of Philip Firmin; she jilts him in favor of Captain Woolcomb, to whom she is subsequently unfaithful in William Makepeace Thackeray's *The Adventures of Philip on His Way through the World*.

Blanche Twysden   Scientific, lecture-attending elder

daughter of Talbot and Maria Twysden in William Makepeace Thackeray's *The Adventures of Philip on His Way through the World*.

Maria Ringwood Twysden　Snobbish and mean maternal aunt of Philip Firmin and niece to Lord Ringwood, to whom she toadies and who treats her with contempt in William Makepeace Thackeray's *The Adventures of Philip on His Way through the World*.

Ringwood Twysden　Odious cousin of Philip Firmin, who kicks him into a fountain in William Makepeace Thackeray's *The Adventures of Philip on His Way through the World*.

Talbot Twysden　Snobbish, toadying husband of Maria Ringwood Twysden and father of Agnes and Ringwood; greedy for money, he unsuccessfully tries to persuade Caroline Brandon to press claims against Dr. Firmin which would make Philip Firmin illegitimate in William Makepeace Thackeray's *The Adventures of Philip on His Way through the World*.

Tygrinonniple　Evil queen of Icinda; she helps Broscomin in Eliza Haywood's *Adventures of Eovaai, Princess of Ijaveo*.

Walter Tyke　Curate of St. Peter's, who becomes the hospital chaplain instead of the Reverend Farebrother when Dr. Tertius Lydgate delivers his tie-breaking vote in George Eliot's *Middlemarch*.

Lord Tynedale　William Crimsworth's uncle on his mother's side, who pays for William's education only after pressure is exerted on him, and who expects William to enter the Church in Charlotte Brontë's *The Professor*.

Dr. Titus Tyrconnel　Irish doctor attendant upon Sir Piers Rookwood; he is the intrusively convivial inmate of Rookwood Place in William Harrison Ainsworth's *Rookwood*.

Mrs. Tyrrel　Barnabas Tyrrel's mother, who raised her son to be uncultured and wild; she treats her niece, Emily Melville, as part relative, part servant, setting the foundation for Tyrrel's later charge against Emily of a bill for her living expenses in William Godwin's *Caleb Williams*.

Barnabas Tyrrel　Ferdinando Falkland's aristocratic neighbor, who is eventually murdered by Falkland; Tyrrel is a bully whose desire for center stage in the town is upset by Falkland's popularity; he forms a great hatred towards Falkland and anything else that he is unable to control; he destroys his tenants Benjamin and Leonard Hawkins, his cousin Emily Melville, and ultimately, Falkland in William Godwin's *Caleb Williams*.

Francis Tyrrel　Young painter, who is the legitimate son of the late Earl of Etherington and contests the claim of his half brother, Valentine Bulmer, to the title; loving Clara Mowbray despite her mock marriage to Bulmer, he disappears without claiming his title after Clara dies in Sir Walter Scott's *St. Ronan's Well*.

Paula Tyrrel　Beautiful and wealthy young girl, who marries a politician and is persecuted by her husband in George Gissing's *Thyrza*.

Sir John Tyrrell　Former associate of Sir Reginald Glanville; his rape of Gertrude Douglas deranges her mind and leaves Glanville obsessed with vengeance; Tyrell refuses Glanville's challenge and evades his pursuit, only to be robbed and murdered by Thomas Thornton in Edward Bulwer-Lytton's *Pelham*.

Mr. Tyrrwhit　Avaricious moneylender, who lends Mountjoy Scarborough large sums in anticipation of becoming owner of Tretton Hall upon the imminent death of John Scarborough in Anthony Trollope's *Mr. Scarborough's Family*.

U

Laurentini di Udolpho Former heir to Udolpho; her love for the Marquis de Villeroi causes her to reject Montoni's proposal of marriage; she disappears; years later she is revealed to be the deranged nun Sister Agnes and the murderer, with Villeroi as accomplice, of the Marchioness de Villeroi in Ann Radcliffe's *The Mysteries of Udolpho*.

Uggug (His Exalted Fatness) Son of the Sub-Warden and My Lady, spoiled by his mother, and completely selfish and inept at his studies; he is the false heir of Outland in Lewis Carroll's *Sylvie and Bruno*. He is the birthday banquet honoree, who fails to attend after he has turned into a porcupine because of a loveless life in *Sylvie and Bruno Concluded*.

The Uglies Forty-nine grotesquely ugly, abnormal animals, who are subdued by Lina on the way to Gwyntystorm; they help Curdie Peterson defeat the conspirators and become the main body of the king's army in his battle against the King of Borsagrass in George MacDonald's *The Princess and Curdie*.

Ugo One of two thugs hired by Montoni to transport Emily St. Aubert from Udolpho to Tuscany in Ann Radcliffe's *The Mysteries of Udolpho*.

Ulric (Martha) A Saxon and Bertha's mother, captured with her by the Norman Knight of Aspramonte and renamed Martha in Sir Walter Scott's *Count Robert of Paris*.

Ulrica (Urfried) Bitter old Saxon hag and Sir Reginald Front-de-Boeuf's former mistress, whom he now despises; she assumes the name Urfried to hide her shame at having been a Norman's mistress; she helps the besiegers and sets fire to Torquilstone Castle in Sir Walter Scott's *Ivanhoe*.

Ulysses Hero whose spirit the author encounters in Elysium in Henry Fielding's *A Journey From This World to the Next*.

Umbopa Magnificent Zulu tribesman, servant to Henry Curtis; after revealing his true identity as Ignosi, the rightful king of Kukuanaland, he wrests the throne from the usurper, his uncle, Twala, with the help of Allan Quatermain and his party of Englishmen in H. Rider Haggard's *King Solomon's Mines*.

Duke of Umbria Elderly nobleman and patron of John Inglesant, upon whom he bestows a small estate in the Apennines in J. Henry Shorthouse's *John Inglesant, A Romance*.

Barbara Umfraville Forbidding great aunt of Katharine Umfraville; upon reluctantly becoming her guardian, she tries to alienate her from Mr. Wardour, who has raised her, in Charlotte Yonge's *Countess Kate*.

Giles Umfraville Katharine Umfraville's great-uncle, who has lost all his children in India; on returning to England, he provides a sympathetic home for his niece, now Countess of Caergwent, in Charlotte Yonge's *Countess Kate*.

Jane Umfraville Invalid sister of Barbara Umfraville and great aunt of Countess Kate; she shows her some affection but lacks the force to challenge her sister's sternness in Charlotte Yonge's *Countess Kate*.

Katharine Umfraville Unruly, imaginative ten-year-old who has been ignored by her noble relatives until a series of deaths makes her Countess of Caergwent; she must leave her Wardour relatives and live with an unsympathetic aunt in Charlotte Yonge's *Countess Kate*. She appears in *The Pillars of the House*.

Umslopogaas (Woodpecker, Slaughterer) Fierce, handsome Zulu chief known for his skill with a battle axe, Inkosi-Kaas; he accompanies Allan Quatermain to the Zu-Vendis, where he dies during a civil war defending Queen Nyleptha in H. Rider Haggard's *Allan Quatermain*.

Una Throned figure representing Truth; she offers impartial judgments that are scorned by the false Duessa in Sarah Fielding's *The Cry*.

Edward Undercliff Handwriting expert who, with his mother's help, proves that Arthur Wardlaw forged the note which sent Robert Penfold to prison in Charles Reade's *Foul Play*.

Squire Underwood Benjamin Hawkins's former landlord, whose estate Hawkins left because he wanted Hawkins to vote for a political candidate to whom Hawkins objected in William Godwin's *Caleb Williams*.

Alda Underwood Worldly, devious twin sister of Wilmet Underwood; she is adopted by her wealthy uncle, Thomas Underwood; she jilts Fernando Travis, and bears eight daughters to her brutal husband, Sir Adrian Vanderkist, in Charlotte Yonge's *The Pillars of the House*. She appears in *The Long Vacation*.

Angela Underwood Young sister of Felix and Wilmet Underwood; her unstable behavior contributes to Felix's decline and the death of her brother Theodore before she finds peace in a sisterhood in Charlotte Yonge's *The Pillars of the House*. She appears in *The Long Vacation*.

Bernard (Bear) Underwood Athletic youngest

brother of the Underwood family; he is matured by the death of his brother Felix in Charlotte Yonge's *The Pillars of the House*. He marries Phyllis Merrifield in Ceylon in *Beechcroft at Rockstone*.

Clarissa Underwood   Younger daughter of Sir Thomas; she is attracted to Ralph Newton, heir to Newton Priory, and gradually discovers his inconstancy; eventually she grows to love his clergyman brother, Gregory, who has long been devoted to her, and they become engaged in Anthony Trollope's *Ralph the Heir*.

Clement Underwood   Clerical brother of Wilmet and Felix Underwood; he belongs to the High Church, ritualistic wing of the Church of England and becomes Vicar of Vale Leston and then director of the London mission founded by Robert Fulmort in Charlotte Yonge's *The Pillars of the House*. He appears in *The Long Vacation*.

Edgar Underwood   Son of Edward Underwood; his moral and artistic decline is attributed to his agnosticism; he is jilted by Alice Knevett and later is forced into a duel by her husband, M. Tanneguy; he dies in an Indian attack in California in Charlotte Yonge's *The Pillars of the House*.

Edward Underwood   Impoverished, charismatic curate, who dies of tuberculosis, leaving the burden for the support of his thirteen children on his eldest son, Felix, and daughter, Wilmet, in Charlotte Yonge's *The Pillars of the House*.

Felix (Blunderbore) Underwood   Heroically responsible eldest son of Mary and Edward Underwood; he forgoes his University career to support his orphaned siblings by working for the provincial bookseller, Mr. Froggatt, in Charlotte Yonge's *The Pillars of the House*.

Fulbert Underwood   Relentless son of Edward Underwood; he emigrates to Austrialia with Charles Audley in Charlotte Yonge's *The Pillars of the House*.

Fulbert (Old Fulbert) Underwood   Disreputable cousin of Mary Underwood; he successfully challenges her claim to the Vale Leston property but, dying childless, restores it to her children in Charlotte Yonge's *The Pillars of the House*.

Gerald Underwood   Son of Edgar Underwood and Zoraya Prebel; he is raised as the heir to Vale Leston in Charlotte Yonge's *The Pillars of the House*. He protects his half sister, Ludmilla Schnetterling, and cares for his dying mother; he dies at twenty-one in *The Long Vacation*.

Geraldine Underwood   Favorite sister of Edgar Underwood; her artistic success, the result of self-discipline,

is in contrast to his dilettantism and self-indulgence in Charlotte Yonge's *The Pillars of the House*.

Lancelot Underwood   Musically gifted brother of Felix and Wilmet Underwood; disabled by illness from a university career, he joins his brother in the bookselling business at Bexley, marries Gertrude May, and ultimately inherits Vale Leston in Charlotte Yonge's *The Pillars of the House*. He appears in *The Long Vacation*.

Mary Underwood   Wife of Edward Underwood; she loses her title to the Vale Leston estate and is worn down by poverty and the cares of her large family in Charlotte Yonge's *The Pillars of the House*.

Mary (Marilda) Underwood   Kindly but often tactless daughter of Thomas Underwood; she directs the family importing firm on his death, tries to save Edgar Underwood from his follies, and marries Fernando Travis in Charlotte Yonge's *The Pillars of the House*. She appears in *The Long Vacation*.

Patience Underwood   Elder daughter of Sir Thomas; intelligent, well-read, and capable, she frets over the attachment of her sister, Clarissa, to the feckless Ralph Newton, heir of Newton Priory; she keeps track of household affairs at Popham Villa, Fulham, and persuades her father to settle down there at last in Anthony Trollope's *Ralph the Heir*.

Robina Underwood   Sister of Wilmet and Felix Underwood; she becomes a beloved governess in the family of Lord Ernest De la Poer and then marries William Harewood in Charlotte Yonge's *The Pillars of the House*.

Stella Underwood   Lovely youngest daughter of Edward Underwood and twin sister of the retarded Theodore; after his death she marries into the aristocratic Audley family in Charlotte Yonge's *The Pillars of the House*. She appears in *The Long Vacation*.

Theodore Underwood   Retarded son of Edward Underwood and twin of Stella; he dies in Charlotte Yonge's *The Pillars of the House*.

Thomas Underwood   Wealthy cousin of Edward Underwood, after whose death he adopts Alda and Edgar Underwood with disastrous consequences in Charlotte Yonge's *The Pillars of the House*.

Sir Thomas Underwood   Shy, solitary former Solicitor General, who is tempted to reenter politics by contesting the corrupt borough of Percycross; in a dirty campaign, his arm is broken and, although he enjoys brief election triumph, the borough is disenfranchised; guilt and failure dog Sir Thomas as he ponders fruitlessly on a life of

Bacon, suffering a perpetual writer's block in Anthony Trollope's *Ralph the Heir*.

Wilmet Underwood   Eldest daughter of Edward and Mary Underwood; after her father's death she manages their impoverished household with her brother Felix; she marries Major John Harewood in Charlotte Yonge's *The Pillars of the House*.

Unicorn   Creature developed from the traditional nursery rhyme; he fights with the Lion for the White King's crown; he calls Alice a "fabulous monster" in Lewis Carroll's *Through the Looking-Glass*.

Unity   The Swancourts' maidservant in Thomas Hardy's *A Pair of Blue Eyes*.

Marchioness of Updown   Prototype of the stupid aristocrat; fat, large, and selfish, she is cruel to Beatrice Brooks in Caroline Norton's *Lost and Saved*.

George Uploft   Relater of some stories about the Great Mel Harrington which embarrass his daughters and others; he once tried to run off with Louisa Harrington in George Meredith's *Evan Harrington*.

Miss Uppish   Fashionable young heiress, disdainful in spite of her physical deformities in Henry Brooke's *The Fool of Quality*.

Richard Upwitch   A greengrocer and juryman for the Bardell v. Pickwick breach-of-promise suit in Charles Dickens's *The Posthumous Papers of the Pickwick Club*.

Dr. Urquart   Gallant physician of H.M.S. *Tempest*; he conceals Norris Carthew's identity, smuggles him ashore, and obtains Douglas Longhurst's help in Robert Louis Stevenson's *The Wrecker*.

Sir John Urrie   Presently an officer in the Covenanters' army; he is unable to choose sides decisively and occasionally switches loyalties in Sir Walter Scott's *A Legend of Montrose*.

Zedekias Ursel   Capable and popular rival whom Emperor Alexius Comninus imprisons for three years; his liberty is restored after he agrees to assist the emperor through a political crisis in Sir Walter Scott's *Count Robert of Paris*.

(Dorothea) Ursula   Lovely and valiant young woman, who hears of the Well from the Lady of Abundance and thereafter endures vicissitudes until, escaping from the lustful Gandolf, King of Utterbol, she meets Ralph, with whom she reaches the Well; she returns with him to become Queen of Upmeads in William Morris's *The Well at the World's End*.

Margaret, Lady Ushant   Lonely, widowed occupant of Bragton House, where she had made a home for Mary Masters; priding herself on not interfering, she rejoices at last in Mary's promised marriage to her nephew Reginald Morton in Anthony Trollope's *The American Senator*.

Captain Myles Ussher   Protestant revenue officer who seduces Feemy Macdermot and is murdered by her brother, Thady, in Anthony Trollope's *The Macdermots of Ballycloran*.

Ustane   Handsome woman of the Amahagger people; she chooses Leo Vincey as her husband, nurses him to health, and defies She's command to relinquish Leo as her lover; as punishment she is first marked, then murdered by She's supernatural powers in H. Rider Haggard's *She*.

Utaldo   Italian army captain with whom Montoni is friendly in Ann Radcliffe's *The Mysteries of Udolpho*.

Queen of Utterbol   Disillusioned wife of Gandolf; she marries Bull Shockhead after he slays the king in William Morris's *The Well at the World's End*.

Gabriel John Utterson   Arid, lean, and dreary lawyer and friend to Dr. Henry Jekyll; he receives the many strange documents (Jekyll's will and Dr. Hastie Lanyon's letter) which help to unravel the mysterious behavior of Dr. Jekyll and his relationship to Edward Hyde in Robert Louis Stevenson's *The Strange Case of Dr. Jekyll and Mr. Hyde*.

V

Madame de V*** Superficial woman, who finds Yorick has said more of revealed religion than the entire Encyclopedia in Laurence Sterne's *A Sentimental Journey through France and Italy*.

Lady V—— Admirable and amiable visitor to Sidney Bidulph Arnold at South Park; she acts with maternal kindness toward Sidney, and with her husband endeavors to reunite the Arnolds; later she confirms Orlando Faulkland's devotion while respecting Sidney's delicate sentiments in Frances Sheridan's *Memoirs of Miss Sidney Bidulph*.

Lord V—— Frank and affable visitor to Sidney Bidulph Arnold at South Park; he acts with fatherly concern toward Sidney, and with his wife endeavors to reunite the Arnolds; his death from an apoplexy numbers among Sidney's losses in Frances Sheridan's *Memoirs of Miss Sidney Bidulph*.

Lord V—— (the younger) Profligate eldest son of Lord and Lady V—; upon inheriting his father's estate, he disrupts Sidney Bidulph Arnold's domestic felicity by mercilessly calling in the loans made to the Arnolds by his contrastingly benevolent father in Frances Sheridan's *Memoirs of Miss Sidney Bidulph*.

Vaekehu Native queen of Marquesas Islands, who watches the arrival of Loudon Dodd's ship with other natives in Robert Louis Stevenson's *The Wrecker*.

Maestro Vaiano Astrologer from whom Tito Melema rescues Tessa (Melema) at the carnival in George Eliot's *Romola*.

Chevalier Valancourt Kind-hearted younger son of French nobility who falls in love with Emily St. Aubert, is rejected by her evil guardian Montoni, succumbs to Parisian vices, and is imprisoned for debt; he sacrifices his fortune and his chance to marry Emily in order to purchase the release of Monsieur Bonnac; he ultimately marries Emily in Ann Radcliffe's *The Mysteries of Udolpho*.

Sir Aymer de Valence Nephew to the Earl of Pembroke and deputy governor of Douglas Castle; he is brave and courteous but guards his dignity with youthful jealousy and has a lengthy misunderstanding with his governor in Sir Walter Scott's *Castle Dangerous*.

Valentine Stepson of Livia, who falsely charges him with the crime of incest with his sister, Camilla (Simple); he marries Cynthia and lives a virtuous life in the happy ending of Sarah Fielding's *The Adventures of David Simple in Search of a Faithful Friend*. Financial problems force his retreat to Jamaica, where he dies, leaving his wife in great distress in *David Simple. Volume the Last*.

Valerius Bastard son of Turpius and Asbella; he is supposed to marry Clarenthia but kidnaps her instead in Jane Barker's *Exilius; or, The Banish'd Roman*.

Valiant-for-Truth Champion who defeats the three robbers who attack Little-faith, relying on God and his "Jerusalem blade"; inspired by the story of Christian to become a pilgrim, he joins Christiana and her party in John Bunyan's *The Pilgrim's Progress From this World to That Which Is to Come*.

Count Henrik de Vallary Isabella's father, who takes holy orders after his wife's death and has his daughter raised in a convent, promising her fortune to the church should she decide to take the vows in Aphra Behn's *The History of the Nun*.

Van Brune Miranda's page, who loves her obsessively and, at her demand, attempts to poison Alcidiana; he is hanged for his crime, and Miranda is sentenced to stand below his gibbet for the day with a rope about her neck in Aphra Behn's *The Fair Jilt*.

Mr. Van der Bosch Shrewd, rich Dutchman from Albany, New York, who acts as steward to his son-in-law, Eugene, Earl of Castlewood, putting his estate in order in William Makepeace Thackeray's *The Virginians*.

Lydia Van der Bosch Self-important, pretty young woman from Albany, New York, whose fortune is her greatest charm; unable to attract George Warrington, she makes an unhappy marriage with the selfish Eugene, Earl of Castlewood, over whom she rules with the help of her father in William Makepeace Thackeray's *The Virginians*.

Margaret Van Eyck Sister and survivor of the famous Van Eyck artist brothers; she teaches Gerard the Van Eyck color secrets for the illumination of manuscripts; she urges Gerard to forsake his vocation and marry Margaret Brandt and to seek their fortune in Italy; when she dies all her property goes to Margaret Brandt, save for a bequest to her faithful housekeeper, Reicht Heynes, in Charles Reade's *The Cloister and the Hearth*.

Burgomaster Van Gulph Subject of a portrait by Jeremy Watersouchy, whose precise rendering of the subject's jewelry, carbuncle, and eyelashes leads to a commission from Van Gulph's wife in William Beckford's *Biographical Memoirs of Extraordinary Painters*.

Madam Van Gulph Patron who commissions Watersouchy for a portrait; his desire for precision surpassing that of his master causes him to spend a month on her fingers alone; the effort exhausts and weakens him in William Beckford's *Biographical Memoirs of Extraordinary Painters*.

Van Hagan   Dutch merchant who believes that money can buy anything including governments in Charles Johnstone's *Chrysal: or, The Adventures of a Guinea*.

Mrs. Van Siever   Widowed mother of Clara; she involves herself in the monetary swindles practiced by Augustus Musselboro and Dobbs Broughton; her belief that Musselboro is cheating her at last reconciles her to Conway Dalrymple as son-in-law in Anthony Trollope's *The Last Chronicle of Barset*.

Clara Van Siever   Statuesque beauty who poses for the artist Conway Dalrymple, whom she eventually marries in Anthony Trollope's *The Last Chronicle of Barset*.

Ghysbrecht Van Swieten   Miserly burgomaster of Tergou, who has been withholding Margaret Brandt's patrimony and fears Gerard has discovered his secret; earlier struck down by the staff of the fleeing Gerard, he finally receives the last rites from Gerard, restoring land and 340 gold angels to Margaret Brandt in Charles Reade's *The Cloister and the Hearth*.

Dorothea Vanborough   Protagonist, whose yearning for understanding and love is not fully satisfied by her mother, Philippa Palmer, or her aunt, Lady Sarah Francis; overwhelmed into an engagement with Robert Henley, she finally marries Frank Raban, the man who values her direct, generous nature in Anne Thackeray Ritchie's *Old Kensington*.

George Vanborough   Melancholy brother of Dorothea Vanborough; he falls victim to the deceits of Rhoda Parnell and dies in the Crimea in Anne Thackeray Ritchie's *Old Kensington*.

John Vanborough   Well-to-do, ambitious gentleman, who regrets his marriage to a beautiful, charming, well-educated singer as socially limiting and puts her and their daughter aside on finding a legal technicality invalidating their marriage; he marries for ambition and becomes a Member of Parliament but, disappointed in his failure to rise, takes his own life in Wilkie Collins's *Man and Wife*.

Frank Vance   Artist and friend of Lionel Haughton; he is revealed as the uncle of Sophy in Edward Bulwer-Lytton's *What Will He Do With It? by Pisistratus Caxton*.

Vandam   One of two earnest but soulless Flemish ushers who supervise the pupils and for whom the headmaster, M. Pelet, has only contempt in Charlotte Brontë's *The Professor*.

Jean Baptiste Vandenhuten   An awkward young pupil of M. Pelet's school, who is rescued by William Crimsworth during a boating accident in Charlotte Brontë's *The Professor*.

Victor Vandenhuten   Father of Jean Baptiste and a rich businessman, who, in gratitude for the rescue of his son, uses his influence to find William Crimsworth a job as professor of English at one of the colleges in Brussels in Charlotte Brontë's *The Professor*.

Jules Vanderkelkov   One of the pupils at M. Pelet's school, whose poor English accent belies his self-complacent attitude in Charlotte Brontë's *The Professor*.

Sir Adrian Vanderkist   Vicious baronet, whose addiction to gambling and alcohol impoverishes his children and brings misery to his wife, Alda Underwood, in Charlotte Yonge's *The Pillars of the House*. He dies in *The Long Vacation*.

Adrian (The Little Baronet) Vanderkist   Posthumous son of Sir Adrian Vanderkist; he is sent to school at Rockstone to emancipate him from the overprotectiveness of his mother, Alda (Underwood), and sisters in Charlotte Yonge's *The Long Vacation*.

Emilia Vanderkist   Daughter of Sir Adrian and Alda (Underwood) Vanderkist; she flirts with her cousin Gerald Underwood but marries into the firm of Travis and Underwood in Charlotte Yonge's *The Long Vacation*.

Franceska Vanderkist   Daughter of Sir Adrian and Alda (Underwood) Vanderkist; she realizes her mother's ambitions by marrying the heir to the Marquess of Rotherwood in Charlotte Yonge's *The Long Vacation*.

Mr. Vandernoodt   Gentleman of wealth staying at Leubronn in George Eliot's *Daniel Deronda*.

Isaac Vanderpelft   Jewish stock-jobber, who contests Sir Valentine Quickset for election to Parliament; he drops through a barrel after his oration in Tobias Smollett's *The Adventures of Sir Launcelot Greaves*.

Mr. Vane   Ineffective protagonist who attempts to help the Lovers (Little Ones) against the Bags and to find mothers; in his loneliness, he restores Lilith's vitality with his blood; he falls in love with Lona and must learn to sleep in the House of the Dead; he buries Lilith's severed hand to restore water and fertility to the land in George MacDonald's *Lilith*.

Mrs. Vane   Mother of Sibyl and James; she is a foolish stage mother, who manages Sibyl's acting career in Oscar Wilde's *The Picture of Dorian Gray*.

Agnes Vane Beautiful young cousin and companion of Antonia Cranmer in Thomas Amory's *The Life of John Buncle, Esq.*

James Vane Sibyl Vane's brother, who vows revenge upon Dorian Gray for destroying his sister's life; James finally catches up with Dorian eighteen years later, but Dorian convinces him that he looks too young to be the same man; Dorian finally kills James in a hunting accident in Oscar Wilde's *The Picture of Dorian Gray.*

Sibyl Vane A beautiful actress whose character portrayals Dorian Gray falls in love with; when her love for Dorian becomes more real for her than her acting, her acting deteriorates, causing Dorian to reject her; his rejection causes her finally to commit suicide in Oscar Wilde's *The Picture of Dorian Gray.*

Andrew Vanstone Cheerful, easygoing father of Norah and Magdalen; after his sudden death, questions concerning his marriage and will render his children illegitimate and almost penniless in Wilkie Collins's *No Name.*

Magdalen Vanstone Hot-tempered, ruthless younger daughter of Andrew Vanstone; embittered by the loss of name and family fortune, she turns her talents as an actress to ensnaring her cousin, Noel, into marriage; still in pursuit of her lost inheritance, she disguises herself as a maid in the service of Admiral Bartram; she finally marries Captain Kirke in Wilkie Collins's *No Name.*

Michael Vanstone Estranged brother of Andrew; he inherits the Somerset estate and fortune when Andrew dies in a railway accident; he rejects any claims of his brother's daughters, Norah and Magdalen, and the estate passes to his weakling son, Noel, in Wilkie Collins's *No Name.*

Noel Vanstone Petulant and weak but stubborn hypochondriac son of Michael Vanstone; having inherited the family fortune, he is pursued by one of the displaced heirs, his cousin Magdalen, who entraps him into marriage despite the vigilance of his cunning housekeeper, Mrs. Lecount; under the housekeeper's direction, he makes a will consigning the fortune to the hands of Admiral Bartram before he dies in Wilkie Collins's *No Name.*

Norah Vanstone Gentle elder sister of Magdalen; she reacts stoically to loss of the family name and fortune and becomes a governess; she later marries her cousin George Bartram in Wilkie Collins's *No Name.*

Pietro Vanucci Unappreciated artist rescued from despair by Gerard, who later becomes his companion in debauchery in Charles Reade's *The Cloister and the Hearth.*

Varbarriere (Herbert Strangways) Wealthy, mysterious houseguest with his nephew, Guy Strangways, at Marlowe; when young, he saw Sir Jeckyl Marlowe kill Guy Deverell in an unfair duel; he plots his revenge by telling General Lennox of Sir Jeckyl's affair with Lady Jane Lennox and by planning a lawsuit to reveal that Sir Jeckyl has hidden a paper proving Marlowe belongs to the Deverells; after Sir Jeckyl dies of a wound inflicted by Lennox, he does not pursue the lawsuit and is eventually reconciled to his nephew's marrying Beatrix Marlowe in J. Sheridan Le Fanu's *Guy Deverell.*

Dolly Varden Beautiful daughter of Gabriel and Martha Varden; she fascinates Simon Tappertit, apprentice to Gabriel; she acts as a go-between for Emma Haredale and Edward Chester; she marries Joe Willet after he rescues her from the Gordon rioters in Charles Dickens's *Barnaby Rudge.*

Gabriel Varden Locksmith and supporter of the law during the Gordon riots; he helps to secure Barnaby Rudge's release from prison after he is charged; he endures his wife's verbal assaults upon him in Charles Dickens's *Barnaby Rudge.*

Martha Varden Gabriel Varden's fanatical Protestant wife, who browbeats her husband; after Gabriel's display of courage in the Gordon riots, Martha recognizes her husband's virtues in Charles Dickens's *Barnaby Rudge.*

Vardine Syrena Tricksy's first love in Eliza Haywood's *Anti-Pamela: or, Feign'd Innocence Detected.*

Adèle Varens Mr. Rochester's ward, brought up by him after she is abandoned by his former mistress, Céline Varens; she becomes Jane Eyre's pupil at Thornfield Hall in Charlotte Brontë's *Jane Eyre.*

Céline Varens Mr. Rochester's first mistress, a French opera dancer, who is unfaithful to him and abandons a child she claims is his, although there is no resemblance in Charlotte Brontë's *Jane Eyre.*

Lady Vargrave See Alice Darvil.

Lord Vargrave See both Richard Templeton and Lumley Ferrers.

Helen, Lady Varley Pretty sister of Hugh Flaxman and a relation of the Wendovers; she aids the marriage of her brother to Rose Leyburn in Mrs. Humphry Ward's *Robert Elsmere.*

Gabriel Varney Artist son of Olivier Dalibard; he embarks with his stepmother, Lucretia Clavering, on a career of poisoning and robbery; he is transported to Australia for life in Edward Bulwer-Lytton's *Lucretia.*

Richard Varney   Villainous and ambitious Master of the Horse to Robert Dudley, Earl of Leicester; his ambitions spur the earl's, and he is utterly without scruple; he commits suicide following his arrest for the murder of the Countess of Leicester, Amy Robsart Dudley, in Sir Walter Scott's *Kenilworth.*

Mr. Varnish   Potential friend whose lack of sensibility finally disgusts David Simple in Sarah Fielding's *The Adventures of David Simple in Search of a Faithful Friend.* He is an example of insensibility to others' suffering in *Familiar Letters between the Principal Characters in David Simple and Some Others.*

Vashti   Epitome of the celebrated, passionate actress; her performance magnetizes Lucy Snowe in Charlotte Brontë's *Villette.*

Vasili   Albanian Greek soldier, who befriends and protects John Falkner during his suicidal impulses during the Greek-Turkish War in Mary Shelley's *Falkner.*

Caliph Vathek   Viceregent of Mohamet on earth, ruled by his appetites, physical and intellectual; he is lured on a pilgrimage to eternal damnation by the unlimited wealth, knowledge, and power promised him by the powers of darkness if he will deny his god and travel to the palace of Eblis; his first and last exercise of his unlimited power is to have his mother brought to the subterranean palace, where he, Princess Carathis, and Nouronihar suffer eternal perdition in William Beckford's *Vathek.*

Monsieur Vaublanc   Cruel owner of a silk factory in Lyons, to whom the young William Ruffigny is apprenticed by his dishonest uncle in William Godwin's *Fleetwood.*

Ferrand de Vaudemont   Grandson of King René; he opposes plans to cede Provence to Charles, Duke of Burgundy, and joins the Swiss to defeat Burgundy in Sir Walter Scott's *Anne of Geierstein.*

Mrs. Vaughan   A virtuous and well-bred woman, who educates Henrietta Saville and other young women in Thomas Holcroft's *The Memoirs of Bryan Perdue.*

Frederic Vaughan   Son of Mrs. Vaughan; he is nearly ruined in a gambling match with Bryan Perdue in Thomas Holcroft's *The Memoirs of Bryan Perdue.*

Basil Vaughan (Mertoun)   Cynical recluse, whose youthful misfortunes with women cause him to become a pirate; maturity brings remorse and, changing his name from Vaughan to Mertoun, he retreats to the Zetland Islands; years of searching disclose that his beloved son

is the condemned pirate Clement Cleveland in Sir Walter Scott's *The Pirate.*

Monsieur De Vaux   Mr. De Rone's friend, who testifies to Bernardo's faithfulness during the period of his separation from Cornelia in Sarah Scott's *The History of Cornelia.*

Squire Vavasor   Country gentleman of breeding and principle who owns Vavasor Hall in Westmoreland and provides a home for his granddaughter, Kate; he disinherits his grandson, George, and dies with Kate at his bedside in Anthony Trollope's *Can You Forgive Her?.*

Alice Vavasor   Headstrong beauty under the spell of her dangerous cousin, George Vavasor, who wheedles money from her so that he can run for Parliament; she is loved by the kind, gentle, reliable John Grey, and she finally marries him; her streak of wildness attracts Lady Glencora Palliser in Anthony Trollope's *Can You Forgive Her?.* As Mrs. Grey she is Lady Glencora's guest in *The Eustace Diamonds.*

George Vavasor   Scarred Byronic cousin of Alice Vavasor; he exercises a strong influence over her, causing her to part with money so that he can run for Parliament; losing his seat, he quarrels with her and fires his pistol at her husband-to-be, John Grey; he finally emigrates to America in Anthony Trollope's *Can You Forgive Her?.*

John Vavasor   Self-centered father of Alice; he lives on a modest sinecure, and the main business of his life is not to be bothered by his daughter's problems in Anthony Trollope's *Can You Forgive Her?.*

Kate Vavasor   Adoring sister of George; she tries to encourage Alice Vavasor to abandon John Grey and return to George; she persuades Alice to put up enough money to enable George to contest a seat in Parliament in Anthony Trollope's *Can You Forgive Her?.*

Mr. Vavasour   Tory candidate in the Fanchester election who resigns because he realizes he cannot possibly defeat the popular Aubrey Bohun in Benjamin Disraeli's *A Year at Hartlebury; or, The Election.*

Meg Veck   Affectionate daughter of Toby Veck in Charles Dickens's *The Chimes.*

Toby (Trotty) Veck   Old but energetic ticket porter (messenger), whose trotting gait has earned him his nickname; his fanciful relationship with the church chimes leads him on a morally educative journey with the Spirit of the Chimes, after which he awakens with a greater understanding of human suffering and belief in human goodness in Charles Dickens's *The Chimes.*

Mr. Veer　Principal court writer, convinced to reexamine his antidemocratic views by young Harry Clinton in Henry Brooke's *The Fool of Quality*.

Annette Veilchen　Attendant to Anne of Geierstein; she leads Arthur Philipson (Arthur de Vere) to meet Anne at her father's castle in Sir Walter Scott's *Anne of Geierstein*.

Count Velasquez　An admirer of Amelia de Gonzales; he is loved by Adeline de Guides in William Beckford's *Modern Novel Writing; or, the Elegant Enthusiast*.

Maria de Vellorno　Beautiful, deceitful second wife of the Marquis de Mazzini; she plots against her stepchildren, only to be discovered in an illicit affair with Cavalier de Vincini; she ultimately poisons the Marquis and commits suicide in Ann Radcliffe's *A Sicilian Romance*.

Mr. Vellum　Old schoolmaster whom Lady Manning wishes to force Henrietta Courteney to marry in Charlotte Lennox's *Henrietta*.

Mr. Vellum　Bookseller who publishes and sells scandal sheets, romances, and secret histories, and cheats his authors in Charles Johnstone's *Chrysal: or, The Adventures of a Guinea*.

Charlotte Venables　Eldest daughter of a newcomer merchant family and the person whom Maria selects for a friend prior to her infatuation with the family's second son, her future husband, George Venables, in Mary Wollstonecraft's *Maria; or The Wrongs of Woman*.

George Venables　Weak, selfish, and ultimately dissolute young man of business whom Maria marries after her mother's death, only to discover, too late, that he is a "heartless, unprincipled wretch," who abuses her emotionally and legally in Mary Wollstonecraft's *Maria; or The Wrongs of Woman*.

Maria Venables　Tortured, virtuous heroine, who leaves her morally dissipated husband and in return is harassed, forcibly separated from her newborn child, and imprisoned in a private madhouse, where she writes a memoir indicting the legal double standards oppressing women in Mary Wollstonecraft's *Maria; or The Wrongs of Woman*.

Venantius　Roman nobleman and military commander who resists the Greek domination and befriends Basil in George Gissing's *Veranilda*.

Anastatia Veneering　Hamilton Veneering's brand-new wife, who produces a brand-new baby in Charles Dickens's *Our Mutual Friend*.

Hamilton Veneering　One of the middle-class new rich whose fortunes rise and fall through speculation; the dinners at his home serve as a rallying place for "the chorus of society" to comment on the events in Charles Dickens's *Our Mutual Friend*.

The Vengeance　A confederate of Madame Defarge and a leading militant among the revolutionary women; she particularly enjoys seeing the French aristocrats lose their heads on the guillotine in Charles Dickens's *A Tale of Two Cities*.

Diggory Venn　Reddleman (carter who supplies farmers with redding for their sheep) who eventually becomes a successful dairyman; constant in his devotion to Thomasin Yeobright, he tries to promote her happiness by circumventing her husband's elopement with Eustacia Vye; he is eventually rewarded by marriage to the widowed Thomasin in Thomas Hardy's *The Return of the Native*.

Mr. Venning　Flute maker and father of Lucy Venning; Arthur Golding lodges with him in George Gissing's *Workers in the Dawn*.

Lucy Venning　Associate in Helen Norman's charitable work; she falls in love with the clergyman who supervises it in George Gissing's *Workers in the Dawn*.

Lucille Ventadour　French Canadian bride of Edward Holdsworth; news of the marriage shatters Phillis Holman's hopes in Elizabeth Gaskell's *Cousin Phillis*.

Counsellor Ventilate　Conceited, ridiculous lawyer holding a seat in the House of Commons; Hugh Trevor was to be apprenticed to him in Thomas Holcroft's *The Adventures of Hugh Trevor*.

Mr. Venus　Weak-eyed articulator and taxidermist, who conspires with Silas Wegg against Noddy Boffin; his unrequited love for Pleasant Riderhood renders him melancholy, but he later tells Boffin of the conspiracy and wins Pleasant in the end in Charles Dickens's *Our Mutual Friend*.

Veranilda　Gothic princess loved by Basil; she is abducted and alienated from her lover by deceptions but is ultimately reunited with him in George Gissing's *Veranilda*.

Mrs. Vere　Youngest daughter of Lady Grimston; she tells Sidney Bidulph Arnold the melancholy story of her disinheritance through her own mother's actions and otherwise acts as companion to Sidney while she is at Grimston Hall in Frances Sheridan's *Memoirs of Miss Sidney Bidulph*.

Bertha Vere Young widow and an ally and fellow conspirator of Sir Lucius Grafton in Benjamin Disraeli's *The Young Duke*.

Isabella Vere Richard Vere's beautiful and high-spirited daughter, who gains the respect of Elshender (Sir Edward Mauley) when she behaves compassionately toward him; abducted through her father's scheme, she is rescued by Hobbie (Halbert) Elliot and by Patrick Earnscliff, whom she later marries in Sir Walter Scott's *The Black Dwarf*.

Lord Edwin Vere A member of the aristocracy, whose planned elopement to Georgiana Reed is thwarted by her sister Eliza in Charlotte Brontë's *Jane Eyre*.

Ovid Vere Renowned scientific prodigy who is also a physician of great industry and compassion; he falls in love with his cousin, Carmina Graywell, but must travel to America to recover his health; in Canada he considerately attends a dying, broken-down man of science, who bequeaths him the manuscript which enables him to cure Carmina and scoop the medical discoveries of the heartless vivisectionist Dr. Benjulia in Wilkie Collins's *Heart and Science*.

Richard Vere Laird of Ellieslaw and Isabella's father; an arrogant and selfish schemer, he was an accessory to the murder of Patrick Earnscliff's father and instigates Jacobite intrigues to further his own ends in Sir Walter Scott's *The Black Dwarf*.

Arthur de Vere (Philipson) Son of the Earl of Oxford; he travels in disguise with his father on a secret mission to the Duke of Burgundy, falls in love with Anne of Geierstein, fights for Burgundy against the Swiss, and marries Anne in Sir Walter Scott's *Anne of Geierstein*.

John de Vere (Philipson) English Earl of Oxford, exiled after the victory of the House of York over the House of Lancaster in the War of the Roses; he travels with his son in disguise as a merchant through Switzerland on a secret mission to Charles, Duke of Burgundy, in Sir Walter Scott's *Anne of Geierstein*.

Cornelia de Vereza Melancholy sister of Hippolitus de Vereza; she becomes a nun in the mistaken belief that her lover is dead; she befriends Julia de Mazzini in the Saint Augustin monastery; she dies of a broken heart when she discovers her lover has become a priest in Ann Radcliffe's *A Sicilian Romance*.

Hippolitus de Vereza Young Neapolitan nobleman, who falls in love with Julia de Mazzini; he is stabbed by the Marquis de Mazzini in an attempt to rescue Julia from a forced engagement to the Duke de Luovo; he recovers in time to rescue Julia from bandits and from a cave beneath her father's castle; ultimately he marries Julia in Ann Radcliffe's *A Sicilian Romance*.

Verezzi The Countess Julia's virtuous lover, who is tricked by Zastrozzi and seduced by Matilda di Laurentini and who finally kills himself in Percy Bysshe Shelley's *Zastrozzi*.

Signor Verezzi Volatile Venetian gambler, who is a partner in Montoni's plan to use Udolpho as a fortress for mercenaries in Ann Radcliffe's *The Mysteries of Udolpho*.

Sir John Verinder Kindly, indolent owner of an estate at Frizinghall, Yorkshire, and father of Rachel; his will protects Rachel from fortune hunters by instructing that she have only a life-interest in the property in Wilkie Collins's *The Moonstone. A Romance*.

Julia, Lady Verinder Widowed mother of Rachel; she calls in Sergeant Cuff to investigate the theft of the Verinder diamond, then discharges him when his suspicions fall on Rachel; stress and misery over the mystery cause her early death in Wilkie Collins's *The Moonstone. A Romance*.

Rachel Verinder Fiery, lively daughter of Lady Verinder; forced by the evidence of her own eyes to believe falsely that her beloved Franklin Blake has stolen a diamond given to her on her birthday, she is heartbroken; when Blake is proved innocent, the lovers are reunited in Wilkie Collins's *The Moonstone. A Romance*.

Lord Frederick Verisopht Aristocratic fop flattered and fleeced by Sir Mulberry Hawk, who secretly despises him; they later quarrel over debts to Ralph Nickleby and fight a duel over Kate Nickleby's honor; Hawk kills Verisopht but is financially ruined by doing so in Charles Dickens's *The Life and Adventures of Nicholas Nickleby*.

Hugh the Great, Count of Vermandois Crusader and brother to the King of France in Sir Walter Scott's *Count Robert of Paris*.

Monsieur Verneuil Gentleman of sensibility, who befriends Arnand La Luc and falls in love with Clara La Luc; he is discovered to be a distant relative of Adeline's and acts in her interest; finally he marries Clara in Ann Radcliffe's *The Romance of the Forest*.

Geraldine Waverly Verney Young mother of three young children; she bears the shame of her husband's notorious infidelities, of his abuse, and of harassment by creditors, yet remains persuaded that her own honor lies in dutiful obedience, no matter how exploitative her husband is of her property and her person in Charlotte Smith's *Desmond*.

Lionel Verney A commoner; the last man on earth, he narrates his history of the last decade of the twenty-first century; he details mankind's prosperity destroyed by a virulent plague; he is the husband of Idris and the friend of Adrian, with whom he leads the remnant of the human race to the Alps in Mary Shelley's *The Last Man*.

Charles Vernon Man about town who inherits a rich estate from Miles St. John and then rejects the advances of the disinherited Lucretia Clavering in Edward Bulwer-Lytton's *Lucretia*.

Diana (Die) Vernon Sir Frederick Vernon's daughter and Sir Hildebrand Osbaldistone's niece and dependent; a Catholic Jacobite, she is beautiful, well-educated, and self-possessed; though destined for the convent or one of her brutish cousins, she loves Francis Osbaldistone; befriended by Rob Roy MacGregor, she works tirelessly for the Jacobite interests in Sir Walter Scott's *Rob Roy*.

Sir Frederick Vernon (Viscount Beauchamp, Father Vaughn) Diana Vernon's father; brave and honorable, he is a trusted agent of the Stuart faction; with the failure of the rebellion of 1715, he flees to France; he assumes the guise of Father Vaughn when residing at Osbaldistone Hall in Sir Walter Scott's *Rob Roy*.

Sister Veronica Young novice at The Passionist Sisters; she is attracted to Evelyn Innes in George Moore's *Evelyn Innes* and in *Sister Teresa*.

Il Conte Verospi Italian aristocrat, who helps Angelo D'Albini escape following Darlowitz Steinhaussen's murder, and who watches over Agnes D'Albini in the convent in Charlotte Dacre's *The Libertine*.

Mrs. Vesey Mild, vacuous former governess of Laura Fairlie, always in the background and always anxious to please in Wilkie Collins's *The Woman in White*.

Vespasian Negro comic character who saves Joshua Fullalove and a sailor from drowning and Captain Dodd from French thugs in Charles Reade's *Hard Cash*.

Mildred Vesper Studious girl who rooms for a time with Monica Madden in George Gissing's *The Odd Women*.

Veteran Soldier who loses a leg, arm, and scalp to the French in America and who falls down dead drunk in Charles Johnstone's *Chrysal: or, The Adventures of a Guinea*.

Vexhelia Brenhilda's attendant and Osmund's wife in Sir Walter Scott's *Count Robert of Paris*.

Miss Veyssiere A beauty remarkable for her dancing ability; she is sacrificed to an old man for a great jointure;

she meets John Buncle at a dance at Oliver Wincup's in Thomas Amory's *The Life of John Buncle, Esq.*

Mr. Vholes Sallow, lifeless-looking lawyer in black, who represents Richard Carstone's interest in Jarndyce and Jarndyce and slowly bleeds his client of all his money under the guise of providing for the three Misses Vholes and their grandfather in Charles Dickens's *Bleak House*.

Carolina Vholes One of three daughters of Mr. Vholes in Charles Dickens's *Bleak House*.

Emma Vholes One of three daughters of Mr. Vholes in Charles Dickens's *Bleak House*.

Jane Vholes One of three daughters of Mr. Vholes in Charles Dickens's *Bleak House*.

Scatchard Vialls Clergyman favored as a suitor for Serena Mumbray by her mother, and a political opponent of Denzil Quarrier in George Gissing's *Denzil Quarrier*.

Frederic, Marquis of Vicenza Father of Isabella; he appears disguised as the "Knight of the Gigantic Sabre" to rescue her in Horace Walpole's *The Castle of Otranto*.

Mr. Vicome Invalid father of Lucy Bentham; wealthy, he encourages Lewis Seymour's art project in George Moore's *A Modern Lover*.

Victor Dorian Gray's valet, from whom Dorian strives to conceal his changing portrait in Oscar Wilde's *The Picture of Dorian Gray*.

Victoria Beautiful, saintly Christian daughter of the prefect Majoricus; she is to enter a convent but falls in love with Raphael Aben-Ezra and marries him after his conversion to Christianity in Charles Kingsley's *Hypatia*.

Donna Victoria Sister to Don Pedro de Sylva and first wife of Mr. Mortimer in Sophia Lee's *The Recess*.

Victorine Poor, unwed French mother of Pauline Caillaud; she helps rescue her lover Dupin from prison during the French Revolution in 1793 in Mark Rutherford's *The Revolution In Tanner's Lane*.

Victorinus Child of Emanuella and Emilius in Eliza Haywood's *The Rash Resolve; or, the Untimely Discovery*.

Victorius Soldier and Christian, son of the prefect Majoricus and brother of Victoria in Charles Kingsley's *Hypatia*.

Whip Vigil Zealous government whip, who opposes a project in which Alaric Tudor and Undecimus Scott have invested in Anthony Trollope's *The Three Clerks*.

Captain Vignolles Professional card player, who sits down with Mountjoy Scarborough in a private room and cheerfully fleeces him in Anthony Trollope's *Mr. Scarborough's Family*.

Vigors Seventeen-year-old midshipman serving on H.M.S. *Harpy*; he is thrashed by Jack Easy for bullying in Captain Frederick Marryat's *Mr. Midshipman Easy*.

Mr. Vigors Magistrate who blames Allen Fenwick for the death of his cousin, Dr. Lloyd, in Edward Bulwer-Lytton's *A Strange Story*.

Vilbert Peddler, quack doctor, and con artist, who takes Jude Fawley's money in exchange for promising to obtain certain scholarly books; he keeps the money and never delivers Jude's long-hoped-for books, initiating Jude's disillusionment in Thomas Hardy's *Jude the Obscure*.

Virginia de Villa Franca Beautiful, accomplished, virtuous convent pensioner, who nurses Agnes de Medina and marries Lorenzo de Medina in Matthew Lewis's *The Monk*.

Matilda de Villanegas Lustful beauty disguised as Rosario, a monastic novice, in order to seduce Abbot Ambrosio, later assisting his rape of Antonia de las Cisternas through demonic means; eventually she is revealed as a succubus, leading Ambrosio toward damnation in Matthew Lewis's *The Monk*.

Arthur Villars Clergyman and guardian of Evelina Anville Belmont since infancy; he distrusts Madame Duval's interest in Evelina and writes Evelina to warn her about London temptations; he celebrates Evelina's reconciliation with her father when she marries in Frances Burney's *Evelina*.

Villebecque Enterprising manager of Lord Monmouth's theater troupe and stepfather of Mademoiselle Flora in Benjamin Disraeli's *Coningsby; or, The New Generation*.

Countess de Villefort The Count de Villefort's flighty second wife, who longs for Parisian society in Ann Radcliffe's *The Mysteries of Udolpho*.

Blanche de Villefort Daughter of Count de Villefort; she spends her adolescence in a convent; upon reunion with her family, she befriends Emily St. Aubert, is captured by bandits, and falls in love with and finally marries Chevalier St. Foix in Ann Radcliffe's *The Mysteries of Udolpho*.

Francis Beaveau, Count de Villefort Honest French nobleman, who takes in Emily St. Aubert after a shipwreck; he acts in her interest in retrieving property stolen by Montoni and in advising her suitors, Du Pont and Valancourt, in Ann Radcliffe's *The Mysteries of Udolpho*.

Henri de Villefort The Count de Villefort's son, who, upon the disappearance of Ludovico, stands watch in the mysterious chamber where the Marchoness de Villeroi died in Ann Radcliffe's *The Mysteries of Udolpho*.

Count de Villenoys Young man who loves Isabella before she takes her vows; he is later Bernardo Henault's friend in battle and marries Isabella after Bernardo's supposed death; later, unaware that Isabella has murdered Bernardo, he is drowned through Isabella's cunning as he throws Bernardo's body into the river in Aphra Behn's *The History of the Nun*.

Marchioness de Villeroi The Marquis de Villeroi's faithful wife, who is murdered by her husband's mistress; later she is discovered to be Emily St. Aubert's aunt in Ann Radcliffe's *The Mysteries of Udolpho*.

Marquis de Villeroi Laurentini di Udolpho's lover, who conspires with her to kill his wife; remorseful, he ultimately dies in self-exile in Ann Radcliffe's *The Mysteries of Udolpho*.

Marquis de Villeroy Maternal uncle of Reginald de St. Leon and his guardian on the occasion of the meeting between brother monarchs, Henry VIII and King Francis; he is slain as the seige of Pavia is broken in William Godwin's *St. Leon*.

Vincent Dependent of the Marquis de Mazzini; he is forced to jail Louisa Bernini in a cave beneath the castle; he repents on his deathbed in Ann Radcliffe's *A Sicilian Romance*.

Lord Vincent Pedantic friend of Henry Pelham, whom he attempts to entangle in Tory party intrigues which would advance both their interests in Edward Bulwer-Lytton's *Pelham*.

Mr. Vincent Junior Tutor at St. Saviour's College, Oxford; reputed a clever scholar but actually a muddler, he cautions Charles Reding against religious partisanship, describing abuses in Continental Catholicism, in John Henry Newman's *Loss and Gain*.

Mr. Vincent Frank, good-natured Creole from the West Indies; he is the ward of Mr. Percival; he courts Belinda but is refused by her after he is discovered to have gambled at Mrs. Luttridge's in Maria Edgeworth's *Belinda*.

Mrs. Vincent Frail but indomitable old lady, who fights to save her daughter's health and reputation while simultaneously defending her son's career against petty gossip in Margaret Oliphant's *Salem Chapel*.

Mrs. Vincent   Friend and confidante of Mrs. Roden; she takes tea with her regularly and gossips about Mrs. Roden's son, George, and his attachment to Lady Frances Trafford in Anthony Trollope's *Marion Fay*.

Arthur Vincent   Young and idealistic nonconformist minister; he finds himself entrapped in a small-minded provincial society he despises, while pining for an aristocratic beauty whom he cannot win and simultaneously trying to save his sister, who is caught up in a melodramatic adventure involving attempted seduction and murder in Margaret Oliphant's *Salem Chapel*.

Jenkin (Jin Vin) Vincent   David Ramsay's apprentice, who is in love with Margaret Ramsay, conspires with Dame Ursula Suddlechop to send Nigel Olifaunt out of London, and assists in a fight with the murderers of Lord Dalgarno in Sir Walter Scott's *The Fortunes of Nigel*.

Susan Vincent   Victim of Colonel Mildmay's attempted seduction; she is accused of his murder and falls into a stupor from which she is roused by the arrival of his daughter Alice in Margaret Oliphant's *Salem Chapel*.

Leo Vincey   Extraordinarily handsome adopted son of Ludwig Horace Holly and reincarnation of his Egyptian ancestor Kallikrates; he travels to the African interior, following instructions on an ancient potsherd, meets and falls under the spell of Ayesha (She), who has waited two thousand years for this "return" of her dead lover in H. Rider Haggard's *She*.

M. L. Vincey   Father of Leo Vincey; he ends a fatal illness with suicide and leaves his five-year-old son Leo in the care of his friend and colleague Ludwig Horace Holly in H. Rider Haggard's *She*.

Fiorenza de Vinci   Pretended brother of Oriana but actually her lover, who is killed mistakenly in a plot to murder Angelo D'Albini in Charlotte Dacre's *The Libertine*.

Cavalier de Vincini   Flattering lover of the Marquis de Mazzini's second wife, Maria de Vellorno, in Ann Radcliffe's *A Sicilian Romance*.

Walter Vincy   Mayor of Middlemarch; he is occasionally threatening to his children, Fred and Rosamond, but usually backs down in George Eliot's *Middlemarch*.

Fred Vincy   Irresponsible boy, who spends all of his borrowed money on a worthless horse and is unable to repay the debt, for which Caleb Garth becomes responsible as co-signer; he would have been rich if Peter Featherstone had not changed his will shortly before he died; eventually he becomes a practical farmer and marries Mary Garth in George Eliot's *Middlemarch*.

Lucy Vincy   Mayor Walter Vincy's wife, who dotes on her children and begs help from Dr. Tertius Lydgate when her son, Fred, is sick in George Eliot's *Middlemarch*.

Rosamond Vincy   Beautiful, vain daughter of Middlemarch's mayor; she marries Tertius Lydgate because she imagines him to be a rich, exciting stranger; her refusal to realize the reality of their situation causes financial ruin and forces her and Lydgate to move away in George Eliot's *Middlemarch*.

Mr. Vindex   Misguided tutor to Harry Clinton and Ned (Fielding); he is dismissed for injudicious use of the rod; the victim of a practical joke by Ned that leads to his ruin, he is eventually rescued from Fleet Prison by young Harry's payment of his debts in Henry Brooke's *The Fool of Quality*.

Susanna Vindex   Pretty daughter of Mr. Vindex; she is instinctively attracted by the purity of young Harry Clinton in Henry Brooke's *The Fool of Quality*.

Emma Vine   Working-class sweetheart of Richard Mutimer; she is abandoned when he marries a middle-class girl in George Gissing's *Demos*.

Jane Vine   Sister of Emma; her illness delays and ultimately prevents Emma's marriage in George Gissing's *Demos*.

Count de Vinevil   Rash but goodhearted widower, father of Ardelisa; he sells his estate in France and takes his daughter and his ward, Count de Longueville, to Constantinople, where he is killed by a lustful Turk who pursues Ardelisa in Penelope Aubin's *The Strange Adventures of the Count de Vinevil and His Family*.

Ardelisa de Vinevil   Beautiful, virtuous daughter of Count de Vinevil and later the wife of Count de Longueville; in Constantinople she is pursued by several lustful Turks; she escapes but is shipwrecked on the island of Delos; rescued and taken to Venice, she stays with friends until a ship leaves for France; she sends Father Francis to test Longueville's love for her, then is happily reunited with him in Penelope Aubin's *The Strange Adventures of the Count de Vinevil and His Family*.

Henry Viney   Lewis Marr's ex-partner in shipping; he is responsible for giving the orders for the *Juno* to founder, resulting in the death of Stephen Kemp's father; he conspires with Dan Ogle to get Marr's money from Captain Nat Kemp and apparently drowns at the end in Arthur Morrison's *The Hole in the Wall*.

Mr. Vining A tutor employed to teach Lord Ingram but dismissed for his suspected involvement with the governess in Charlotte Brontë's *Jane Eyre*.

Violante (The Muse) Talented vocal and instrumental musician; she is Anna Comnena's slave and a companion to Astarte in Sir Walter Scott's *Count Robert of Paris*.

Violetta Venetian lady who is imprisoned by the Turk Osmin; she flees with Ardelisa de Vinevil but is shipwrecked on Delos until rescued by a ship captained by her father, Don Manuel; she marries Monsieur de Feuillade after she knows Osmin is dead and her honor restored; they accompany Ardelisa back to France, where they live near one another in great joy and prosperity in Penelope Aubin's *The Strange Adventures of the Count de Vinevil and His Family*.

Carr Vipont Kinsman of the Marquess of Montfort; he looks after the business interests of the house of Vipont in Edward Bulwer-Lytton's *What Will He Do With It? by Pisistratus Caxton*.

Selina Vipont Carr Vipont's wife, who hopes to marry her daughter to Guy Darrell in Edward Bulwer-Lytton's *What Will He Do With It? by Pisistratus Caxton*.

Virgil Epic poet whose soul the author encounters in Elysium in Henry Fielding's *A Journey From This World to the Next*.

Virginie Pupil at Mme. Beck's school in Charlotte Brontë's *Villette*.

Viridis Beloved of Sir Hugh; she is one of the damsels imprisoned by the Witch-Wife's Sister in William Morris's *The Water of the Wondrous Isles*.

Galleazo Visconti Matteo Visconti's son and Castruccio dei Altiminelli's friend; he encourages Castruccio to conquer Florence and clandestinely destroys his engagement to Euthanasia dei Adimari in Mary Shelley's *Valperga*.

Matteo Visconti Galleazo Visconti's father, the chief of the Ghibelline party in Milan, and a courtier of Emperor Henry in Mary Shelley's *Valperga*.

Mr. Vissian Clergyman and book lover who befriends Bernard Kingcote and is part of the social scene in George Gissing's *Isabel Clarendon*.

Marquis of Viterbo Father of Juliana, who has been promised in marriage to Aurelian to end the Marquis's feud with Don Fabio in William Congreve's *Incognita*.

Vitricus Farm bailiff and superior of Agellius in John Henry Newman's *Callista*.

Marchesa di Vivaldi Ambitious and deceitful Neapolitan, who plots with Father Schedoni (Ferando di Bruno) to abduct, imprison, and finally assassinate Ellena Rosalba; ultimately she feels remorse and confesses all on her deathbed in Ann Radcliffe's *The Italian*.

Marchese di Vivaldi Influential Neapolitan nobleman, who, through familial pride, denies his son Vincentio's request to marry the orphaned Ellena Rosalba; he attempts to effect Vincentio's release from the Inquisition; finally he approves Vincentio's marriage to Ellena in Ann Radcliffe's *The Italian*.

Vincentio di Vivaldi Only son of a Neapolitan nobleman; he falls in love with the orphaned Ellena Rosalba against his parents' wishes; he rescues Ellena from a convent, only to be accused of heresy and imprisoned by the Inquisition; he witnesses the death of his enemy and accuser, the evil Father Schedoni (Ferando di Bruno), is released, and marries Ellena in Ann Radcliffe's *The Italian*.

Vivian Heliodora's dissolute follower, who threatens Basil and fights with him but is overcome in George Gissing's *Veranilda*.

Mr. Vivian Snobbish friend of Lord Hampstead and a junior private secretary to Lord Persiflage in Anthony Trollope's *Marion Fay*.

Camilla Vivian Former betrothed of Raymond Charnock Poynsett; she relieves her continuing passion for him by undermining his marriage in Charlotte Yonge's *The Three Brides*.

Eleonora Vivian Younger sister of Camilla Vivian; she resists her sister's schemes to marry her to wealthy men and weds Frank Charnock in Charlotte Yonge's *The Three Brides*.

Harry Vivian Julia Charnock Poynsett's dissolute neighbor, who lures young men into gaming; he is the father of Camilla and Eleonora in Charlotte Yonge's *The Three Brides*.

Signor Volanti Italian entertainer who helps young Harry Clinton play an April Fool's joke on the public in Henry Brooke's *The Fool of Quality*.

Volktman Reclusive Danish sculptor and astrologer, who instructs Percy Godolphin and casts a horoscope which predicts both Godolphin's death and that of Volktman's daughter, Lucilla Volktman, in Edward Bulwer-Lytton's *Godolphin*.

Lucilla Volktman Clairvoyant and betrayed mistress of Percy Godolphin; she pursues him to England and lures him to his death in Edward Bulwer-Lytton's *Godolphin*.

Herr Vossner Agreeably obliging manager of the Beargarden Club, always ready to advance money to members at alarming interest rates; he absconds with the club funds, leaving the members in grief for their vanished comfort and convenience in Anthony Trollope's *The Way We Live Now*.

Mr. Vuffin Traveling showman and proprietor of a giant and a little woman missing one leg; he meets Nell Trent, her grandfather, Tom Codlin, and Harris Short in an inn in Charles Dickens's *The Old Curiosity Shop*.

Miss Vulcany A gossip in George Eliot's *Daniel Deronda*.

Mr. Vulture Bailiff of the Marshalsea; he mistakenly arrests Nancy Williams in Tobias Smollett's *The Adventures of Roderick Random*.

Captain Vye Seaman and grandfather of Eustacia Vye, who lives with him in his retirement on Egdon Heath; he does not recognize the tragic possibilities of her restlessness in Thomas Hardy's *The Return of the Native*.

Eustacia Vye Beautiful, restless granddaughter of Captain Vye; determined to escape her dull life, she marries Clym Yeobright, who has returned to Egdon Heath from Paris; her disappointment at his decision to remain turns to despair when ill fortune strikes; she plans an elopement with Damon Wildeve, but drowns—probably by her own intention—in Thomas Hardy's *The Return of the Native*.

W

Lord W.   Maternal uncle of Sir Charles Grandison; unwilling to make the allowance necessary to rid himself of a difficult mistress, he requests the advice of Sir Charles, who solves the problem by taking on the financial obligation; chagrined, Lord W. pledges moral reformation and matrimony to a woman of Sir Charles's selection in Samuel Richardson's *Sir Charles Grandison.*

Mrs. Wackles   Mother of Sophy, Jane, and Melissa Wackles; she keeps a day school for girls in Charles Dickens's *The Old Curiosity Shop.*

Jane Wackles   Sister of Sophy and Melissa and a teacher in their mother's day school for girls in Charles Dickens's *The Old Curiosity Shop.*

Melissa Wackles   Sister of Sophy and Jane and a teacher in their mother's day school for girls in Charles Dickens's *The Old Curiosity Shop.*

Sophy Wackles   Pretty young woman who is beloved by Dick Swiveller but is dropped by him when he plots with Fred Trent for Fred's sister, Nell; she marries instead Mr. Cheggs, a market gardener, in Charles Dickens's *The Old Curiosity Shop.*

Mr. Waddle   Ledger clerk in Mr. Neefit's breeches-making business and colleague of Herr Bawwah in Anthony Trollope's *Ralph the Heir.*

Sawyny Waddle   Peddler who flees the inn when he overhears Rifle in the room next to his in Tobias Smollett's *The Adventures of Roderick Random.*

Sam Waddy   One of the guests at Edward Crimsworth's birthday dance, who is thwarted by Yorke Hunsden in his attempts to attract one of the pretty young girls in Charlotte Brontë's *The Professor.*

Miss Wade   Reserved and haughty genteel Englishwoman with a twisted, passionate nature; she influences Tattycoram (Harriet Beadle) to live with her, keeps the iron box for Rigaud/Blandois, and hinders Mr. Meagles's and Arthur Clennam's attempts to bring back Tattycoram and to find the box in Charles Dickens's *Little Dorrit.*

Mrs. Wade   Advocate of women's rights and an ideological opponent of Denzil Quarrier; she nevertheless helps Lilian Quarrier when her estranged husband appears in George Gissing's *Denzil Quarrier.*

Widow Wadman   Aging femme fatale who captures Uncle Toby's affection and elicits his proposal of marriage in the last book in Laurence Sterne's *The Life and Opinions of Tristram Shandy, Gentleman.*

Mr. Waffles   Master of the Laverick Wells hounds and a victim of Soapey Sponge, who bilks him twice for money over the sale of a horse in Robert Surtees's *Hillingdon Hall.*

Mr. Wagg   Witty author, proud of his fashionable position, in William Makepeace Thackeray's *The History of Pendennis.* He is Lord Steyne's toady in *Vanity Fair.*

Carrie Waghorn   Young woman who shares her room with Polly Sparkes in George Gissing's *The Town Traveller.*

John Waghorn   Railway director who marries Maud Gresham in George Gissing's *Workers in the Dawn.*

Walter Waglock   Comical turnpike keeper in William Beckford's *Azemia.*

Sir Joseph Wagstaff   One of the chief officers in the Royalist army; he escapes capture by the insurgent forces owing to the efforts of Charles Mandeville in William Godwin's *Mandeville.*

Dr. Wagtail   London physician who is introduced to Roderick Random by Mr. Medlar and introduces Roderick to tavern companions including Mr. Banter; he is "roasted" by a trick at the tavern; he has a scheme to invent a new medicine in Tobias Smollett's *The Adventures of Roderick Random.*

William Waife   Christ-like father of Jasper Losely, protector of Sophy, and tutor to George Morley in Edward Bulwer-Lytton's *What Will He Do With It? by Pisistratus Caxton.*

Brother Wainwright   Deacon in the Reverend Broad's chapel, who echoes Brother Bushel's enmity for the Allens in Mark Rutherford's *The Revolution In Tanner's Lane.*

Mr. Wakefield (Belmont)   Mr. Thornby's amoral nephew, who marries Hugh Trevor's mother, ruins her estate, taunts Hugh under the pseudonym of Belmont, and finally repents and marries Miss Wilmot in Thomas Holcroft's *The Adventures of Hugh Trevor.*

Jane Trevor Wakefield   Hugh Trevor's mother, whose infelicitous second marriage, to Mr. Wakefield, threatens to ruin Hugh's prospects in Thomas Holcroft's *The Adventures of Hugh Trevor.*

John Wakem   A lawyer whose acquisition of the mortgage to the mill prompts Edward Tulliver to assault him;

he is the devoted father of Philip Wakem in George Eliot's *The Mill on the Floss.*

Philip Wakem   John Wakem's son, a sensitive, hunchbacked artist, who falls in love with Maggie Tulliver when they meet as children at King's Lorton school in George Eliot's *The Mill on the Floss.*

Everhard Walberg   Husband of Ines Guzman Walberg; he moves his family from Germany to Spain when Don Guzman is near death; after a lengthy litigation period to contest Guzman's false will, Walberg goes temporarily mad and tries to kill his family in Charles Maturin's *Melmoth the Wanderer.*

Ines Walberg   Sister of Don Guzman and wife of Everhard Walberg; she reluctantly returns to Spain from Germany to inherit her brother's estate, a move which nearly causes her family's deaths in Charles Maturin's *Melmoth the Wanderer.*

Mr. Walcot   Surgeon brought to Deerbrook by the manipulative Priscilla Rowland to replace the hated Edward Hope as village surgeon; he reveals his immaturity by repeated appeals to the judgment of his parents and by his inability to treat the fever epidemic in Harriet Martineau's *Deerbrook.*

Martin Waldeck   Hero of a German folktale recited by Isabel Wardour in Sir Walter Scott's *The Antiquary.*

Mr. Walden   Harriet Byron's opinionated London acquaintance, who, being an Oxford scholar, despises everyone who does not have a university education; Harriet's triumph in their conversational debate earns the admiration of her hearers in Samuel Richardson's *Sir Charles Grandison.*

Mr. Waldershare   Brilliant and sentimental but erratic and profligate friend of Endymion Ferrars; he marries Adriana Neuchatel in Benjamin Disraeli's *Endymion.*

Mr. Waldlaw   Honest, practical land steward at Osbaldistone Hall in Sir Walter Scott's *Rob Roy.*

M. Waldman   Professor of chemistry at the University of Ingolstadt; his benevolence, dignity and wisdom encourage Victor Frankenstein to study chemistry in Mary Shelley's *Frankenstein; or, The Modern Prometheus.*

Lady Walham   Lord Kew's pious mother; his worldly behavior estranges them until he is wounded in a duel in William Makepeace Thackeray's *The Newcomes.*

Mr. Walker   Victim of George Hotspur's cheating at the card table; he is ready to give evidence before magis-

trates in Anthony Trollope's *Sir Harry Hotspur of Humblethwaite.*

George Walker   Silverbridge attorney for the law firm handling local business on behalf of the Dukes of Omnium; he works in the case against Josiah Crawley for alleged theft in Anthony Trollope's *The Last Chronicle of Barset.* He proposes the election of Lord Silverbridge to Parliament in *The Duke's Children.*

Green Walker   Member of Parliament for Crewe Junction with aristocratic connections in Anthony Trollope's *Framley Parsonage.*

H. Walker   Tailor and convert to temperance, mentioned in the "Report of the Committee of the United Grand Junction Ebeneezer Temperance Association" in Charles Dickens's *The Posthumous Papers of the Pickwick Club.*

Mick Walker   Oldest boy at the firm of Murdstone and Grinby; he shows the apprentice David Copperfield what needs to be done in Charles Dickens's *The Personal History of David Copperfield.*

Sir Sidney Walker   Unwanted admirer of Lucinda Howard; he has a fine estate but lacks a seat in Parliament; he pays occasional lengthy visits to Lady Fairville in William Beckford's *Modern Novel Writing; or, the Elegant Enthusiast.*

Charles Walkinshaw   Claud's eldest son and heir; Charles dies from the shock of betrayal, exacerbated by a fever, when he learns of his disinheritance in John Galt's *The Entail.*

Claud Walkinshaw   Man whose ancestors were the lairds of Grippy; raised in poverty because of his grandfather's loss of the family estate through bankruptcy, he is tragically obsessed with regaining and retaining it whole by means of the legal instrument of entail; his manipulations to this end, against his better judgment, almost destroy his family, and he dies in despair in John Galt's *The Entail.*

George Walkinshaw   Claud Walkinshaw's third son, who is a wealthy merchant more avaricious than his father; he wrests Kittlestonheugh from his brother Walter, leaving him to lead a miserable life in Glasgow; George lacks male heirs and dies an early death in John Galt's *The Entail.*

James Walkinshaw   Charles Walkinshaw's eldest son and rightful heir to Kittlestonheugh; he marries Ellen Frazer and inherits the estate to which his father once was heir in John Galt's *The Entail.*

Margaret (Meg) Walkinshaw   Claud Walkinshaw's only daughter; she marries Milrookit, laird of Dirdumwhamle; their son is Walkinshaw Milrookit in John Galt's *The Entail*.

Robina Walkinshaw   George's surviving twin daughter who secretly marries her cousin, Walkinshaw Milrookit, and thus destroys George's plan for her to marry James, the male heir to Kittlestonheugh, in John Galt's *The Entail*.

Walter (Watty) Walkinshaw   Claud's second son, of feeble mind, to whom Claud entails Kittlestonheugh in order to add it to the estate of Plealands, entailed on Walter by his grandfather, in John Galt's *The Entail*.

Sir Thomas Wallace   Lord Craigie and Lord Justice Clerk, uncle to Thomas Drummond; he produces evidence of his nephew's innocence and aids the women seeking Robert Colwan's conviction for young George Colwan's murder in James Hogg's *The Private Memoirs and Confessions of a Justified Sinner*.

John Wallen   Finnish hand on the *Flying Scud*, reported drowned; he was shot to death after his jaw was broken in Robert Louis Stevenson's *The Wrecker*.

James Walling   Laborer whose courage inspires the cowardly Mr. Jackson to be concerned about the nearly dead woman (Eleanor Grimshaw) who appears in the night at his door in a ghost story interpolated into the narrative of William Beckford's *Azemia*.

Lady Wallinger   Wife of Sir Joseph Wallinger and aunt of Edith Millbank; she reveals to Harry Coningsby that Edith's intimacy with Sidonia is respect for a family counselor rather than romantic love, thereby encouraging Coningsby to woo Edith in Benjamin Disraeli's *Coningsby; or, The New Generation*.

Sir Joseph Wallinger   Whig baronet and brother of Mr. Millbank; he favors Harry Coningsby in spite of Mr. Millbank's hatred of Harry's grandfather in Benjamin Disraeli's *Coningsby; or, The New Generation*.

Mrs. Wallingford   Silly flirt who passionately admires Henry Lambert in William Beckford's *Modern Novel Writing; or, the Elegant Enthusiast*.

Lady Eudocia Wallingham   Cousin and neighbor of the Brooks family; a selfish and cold social snob, she is mother of five daughters in Caroline Norton's *Lost and Saved*.

Helen Wallingham   Daughter of Lady Eudocia; she is a friend of Beatrice Brooks, whom she sees when Beatrice

is poor, and whom she tries to help in Caroline Norton's *Lost and Saved*.

Colonel Wallis   William Elliot's friend who is privy to his schemes and aspirations in Jane Austen's *Persuasion*.

Mrs. Wallis   Colonel Wallis's pretty young wife and confidante; a new mother, she gossips to Nurse Rooke, indirectly giving Anne Elliot important information about William Elliot's motives in Jane Austen's *Persuasion*.

Barbara (Bab) Wallis   Woman of ill repute, who impersonates Robert Lovelace's aunt, Lady Betty Lawrence, in Lovelace's kidnapping of Clarissa Harlowe in Samuel Richardson's *Clarissa: or, The History of a Young Lady*.

Magloire Walravens   Malign, dwarfish widow of ninety who exploits M. Paul Emanuel; he supports her despite her earlier disapproval of his planned marriage to her granddaughter, Justine-Marie, in Charlotte Brontë's *Villette*.

Walrus   A character in Tweedledee's poem; on the beach with the Carpenter, he coaxes the oysters to come for a walk; he makes a show of mourning their fate while he devours them in Lewis Carroll's *Through the Looking-Glass*.

Nora Walsh   Tough, fighting woman in the Rann gang who brawls with Sally Green and is partially scalped in Arthur Morrison's *A Child of the Jago*.

Lady Walsingham   Stern mother whose death liberates her daughter (Lady Essex) in Sophia Lee's *The Recess*.

Sir Frederick Walsingham   Father of the future Lady Essex in Sophia Lee's *The Recess*.

Dr. Hugh Walsingham   Kind, wise, and firm rector of Chapelizod and Lilias's father; he presides at the burial of the coffin Mervyn brings to town; he knows Mervyn's true identity and warns Lilias and the Chattesworths of his family's disgrace; though heartbroken over his daughter's death, he expresses great happiness over the union of Gertrude Chattesworth and Mervyn and the clearing of Mervyn's father and the family name in J. Sheridan Le Fanu's *The House by the Churchyard*.

Lilias (Lily) Walsingham   Pretty, bright, tender daughter of the rector; she loves Richard Devereux but refuses him because of his wild reputation; she dies at a very young age in J. Sheridan Le Fanu's *The House by the Churchyard*.

Walter   Ellenshaws farm worker sharing a loft with Robert Colwan while Gil-martin and fiends contend out-of-doors for possession of Colwan in James Hogg's *The Private Memoirs an Confessions of a Justified Sinner.*

William Walters (Captain William, Senior Constantine Alexion of Ispahan)   Comic and merry Quaker surgeon, who is cheerfully "forced" to join Wilmot's group; he goes with Captain Singleton and becomes his good friend, later persuading Singleton to give up piracy in Daniel Defoe's *The Life, Adventures, and Pyracies of the Famous Captain Singleton.*

Mrs. Waltham   Matron who persuades her daughter Adela to give up her disinherited lover and marry the newly enriched proletarian Richard Mutimer in George Gissing's *Demos.*

Adela Waltham   Middle-class girl of pious and conservative tendencies; she enters into an unhappy marriage with the wealthy Socialist Richard Mutimer because of her mother's prompting in George Gissing's *Demos.*

Alfred Waltham   Younger brother of Adela Waltham; he becomes a Socialist enthusiast in George Gissing's *Demos.*

Miss Walton   Harley's young, tenderhearted female neighbor, whom he secretly loves in Henry Mackenzie's *The Man of Feeling* She is a benevolent neighbor of one of Sir Thomas Sindall's estates in *The Man of the World.*

Mr. Walton   Father of Miss Walton and advisor to Harley in trying to secure a lease to crown lands that would enrich the impoverished Harley estate in Henry Mackenzie's *The Man of Feeling.*

John Walton   John Smith's neighbor, who writes to the parson Elias Brand in order to correct the false report of Clarissa Harlowe's behavior in Samuel Richardson's *Clarissa: or, The History of a Young Lady.*

Captain Robert Walton   English explorer who encounters Victor Frankenstein and his demon when his ship is frozen in polar ice; like Victor, he pursues dangerous knowledge, the secret of magnetism, in Mary Shelley's *Frankenstein; or, The Modern Prometheus.*

Sir John de Walton   Governor of Douglas Castle and Lady Augusta de Berkely's lover; handsome and noble, he is a poor but famous knight known for his loyalty and generosity; when Sir James Douglas demands the castle as ransom for Lady Augusta's freedom, Sir John refuses to surrender, instead engaging in personal combat with Douglas in Sir Walter Scott's *Castle Dangerous.*

Wamba   Cedric's faithful fool, who secretly exchanges places with his master to allow Cedric to escape Torquilstone Castle in Sir Walter Scott's *Ivanhoe.*

The Wandering Jew   Spirit who helps Alphonso d'Alvarada (Raymond, Marquis de la Cisternas) free himself from the Bleeding Nun ghost of Beatrice de las Cisternas in Matthew Lewis's *The Monk.*

Captain Josiah Wappingshot   Master of the British warship *Amputator*; he captures Azemia when he takes a French merchant ship and imprisons her in the home of Mrs. Periwinkle until he can give her to the duke, whose favor he is courting in William Beckford's *Azemia.*

F. Wapshot   Clergyman, a master of Clavering Grammar School in William Makepeace Thackeray's *The History of Pendennis.*

Mr. Warburton   Efficient private secretary to the (younger) Duke of Omnium; he uses his diplomacy to avoid clashes between his master and the duchess in Anthony Trollope's *The Prime Minister.*

Mrs. Warburton   Invalid mother of Will; she gives up her home to spare him expense in George Gissing's *Will Warburton.*

Jane Warburton   Sister of Will Warburton; she takes a job to relieve him of the need to support her and their mother in George Gissing's *Will Warburton.*

Will Warburton   Businessman who opens a grocer's shop after his partner loses his capital in a speculation, keeping his humble occupation a secret from his friends and family; when his secret is discovered, he is rejected by Rosamund Elvan and marries Bertha Cross in George Gissing's *Will Warburton.*

Mr. Ward   Ignorant, pompous tutor to George and Harry Warrington in William Makepeace Thackeray's *The Virginians.*

Averil Ward   Proud, musically gifted sister of Leonard Ward; taken to the United States after he is convicted of murder, she undergoes many privations before being rescued by Tom May in Charlotte Yonge's *The Trial.* She appears in *The Pillars of the House.*

Henry Ward   Physician and eldest of the Ward children; he takes his sisters to the United States after their brother's conviction for murder and finally joins the Union Army at Vicksburg in Charlotte Yonge's *The Trial.*

Leonard Ward   Teenager falsely accused of murdering his wealthy uncle; retaining a feeling of guilt even after his release, he goes as a missionary to Melanesia in Charlotte Yonge's *The Trial.* He also appears in *The Long Vacation.*

Warden (Elfin-king, the beggar)   Wise and kind ruler

of Outland and father of Sylvie and Bruno; he leaves Bruno in charge but returns disguised as a beggar; having revealed to Sylvie and Bruno that he has become the Elfin-king of Fairyland, he gives Sylvie a magic locket of love, which has the power to make objects and people invisible; he is later presumed dead in Lewis Carroll's *Sylvie and Bruno*. The Elfin-king is disguised as the old beggar, who reveals himself to the children and offers his brother his forgiveness in *Sylvie and Bruno Concluded*.

Warden of the Uttermost House   Disagreeable keeper of a house near the edge of the Glittering Plain in William Morris's *The Story of the Glittering Plain*.

Henry Warden   Zealous and principled Protestant preacher; sheltered by the border baron Julian Avenel when he must flee Edinburgh, he soon angers the baron, who imprisons him at the Monastery of St. Mary's; reunited with his old friend the sub-prior, who protects him, Warden is able to prevent the destruction of the monastery in Sir Walter Scott's *The Monastery*. A political exile residing in Avenel Castle, he wrathfully castigates Roland Graeme for lack of respect towards himself and his holy office in *The Abbot*.

Michael Warden   A mysterious, determined client of Snitchey and Craggs; he loves Marion Jeddler but leaves because of financial problems; on his return he misleads Clemency Newcome, Benjamin Britain, and Jonathan Snitchey about Marion; he finally weds her in Charles Dickens's *The Battle of Life*.

Arthur Wardlaw   Handsome but weak young man with the fatal gift of mimicry; he lets his tutor and friend, Robert Penfold, go to prison for his forgery; he arranges to have his own ship scuttled for the insurance and, when exposed, goes insane in Charles Reade's *Foul Play*.

John Wardlaw   Very respectable merchant who assists Lieutenant-General Rolleston to achieve full generalship, pays back the defrauded underwriters of the *Proserpine*, and makes over the family firm to Penfold and son in Charles Reade's *Foul Play*.

Mrs. Wardle   Deaf and outspoken mother of Jem Wardle in Charles Dickens's *The Posthumous Papers of the Pickwick Club*.

Emily Wardle   Daughter of Jem Wardle in Charles Dickens's *The Posthumous Papers of the Pickwick Club*.

Isabella Wardle   Daughter of Jem Wardle in Charles Dickens's *The Posthumous Papers of the Pickwick Club*.

Jem Wardle   Good-humored, hospitable owner of the Manor Farm, Dingley Dell, who invites Samuel Pickwick, Tracy Tupman, Augustus Snodgrass, and Nathaniel

Winkle to his home for Christmas; he is brother of Rachael Wardle and father of Emily and Isabella Wardle in Charles Dickens's *The Posthumous Papers of the Pickwick Club*.

Rachael Wardle   Jem Wardel's middle-aged, vain sister, who flirts with Tracy Tupman and elopes with Alfred Jingle in Charles Dickens's *The Posthumous Papers of the Pickwick Club*.

Mr. Wardour   Clergyman uncle of Katharine Umfraville; he raises her as one of his own children but must relinquish her when she becomes Countess of Caergwent in Charlotte Yonge's *Countess Kate*.

Sir Arthur Wardour   Baronet of Knockwinnock, who shares antiquarian interests with Oldbuck (Jonathan Oldenbuck), has Jacobite sympathies, and is in danger of bankruptcy; he is helped by his friend Oldbuck to escape losing money to Herman Dousterswivel and is saved by the financial aid of his son and by William Lovel's trick of buried silver in Sir Walter Scott's *The Antiquary*.

Isabel Wardour   Daughter of Sir Arthur; with her father, she is saved from drowning by William Lovel; she marries Lovel after his true identity is discovered in Sir Walter Scott's *The Antiquary*.

Reginald Gamelyn Wardour   Son of Sir Arthur; his letter brings timely financial relief to Sir Arthur in Sir Walter Scott's *The Antiquary*.

Sylvia Wardour   Katharine Umfraville's cousin, who has been raised with her since infancy and eventually is able to live with her at Caergwent Castle in Charlotte Yonge's *Countess Kate*.

Miss Ware   Young Mr. Ware's sister, whose absence from the household leaves Miss Price more vulnerable to Ware's advances in Frances Sheridan's *Memoirs of Miss Sidney Bidulph*.

Mr. Ware   Gentleman of a large estate; he hires Mr. Price as tutor for his son and acts as friend and guardian to both Price and his daughter in Frances Sheridan's *Memoirs of Miss Sidney Bidulph*.

Mr. Ware (the younger)   Mr. Ware's son, who initially acknowledges his obligation to the Prices but after his father's death treats them shamefully when Miss Price rebuffs his advances in Frances Sheridan's *Memoirs of Miss Sidney Bidulph*.

Major Percy Waring   Man who aids Robert Armstrong Eccles in finding Dahlia Fleming by getting her address from Mrs. Lovell; his reproach of Mrs. Lovell for her continuing poor conduct calls forth her more honorable conduct in George Meredith's *Rhoda Fleming.*

Colonel Markham Warington   Mysterious friend of Madame d'Estrees; he rescues her from bitter poverty by marrying her in Mrs. Humphry Ward's *The Marriage of William Ashe.*

Captain Harry Warkworth   Fortune-hunting professional soldier, who seeks an appointment to Mokembe, Africa, and falls in love with Julie Le Breton in Mrs. Humphry Ward's *Lady Rose's Daughter.*

Miss Warley   Woman who swallows a pin during a dinner party at Sir George Darlington's in William Beckford's *Modern Novel Writing; or, the Elegant Enthusiast.*

Walter Warmhouse   Substantial farmer who rejects a neighborly arbitration of a property claim and sues; his suit fails to advance despite thirteen years in the British courts in an anecdote recited by Mr. Fielding in Henry Brooke's *The Fool of Quality.*

Edward Warner   Nephew of Lady Bidulph's late husband and "Cousin Ned" to Sidney Bidulph Arnold; after a twenty-five-year absence in the West Indies, he returns to England in rags, though wealthy, and is rebuffed by Sir George Bidulph but embraced by Sidney, to whom he bequeaths his fortune in Frances Sheridan's *Memoirs of Miss Sidney Bidulph.*

Phillip Warner   Father of a large, destitute family, whose poverty reveals to Charles Egremont the hardship and squalor of lower working-class life, and who helps Aubrey St. Lys quell the rioting workers who have besieged Mowbray Castle in Benjamin Disraeli's *Sybil.*

Warren   Mrs. Bretton's servant in Charlotte Brontë's *Villette.*

Ada Warren   The illegitimate daughter of Mr. Clarendon; she comes to live with his widow, Isabel, when she is a child and later rebels against her; she is courted and then rejected by the fortune-hunting Vincent Lacour; although Clarendon's will stipulates that she is to inherit his property when she comes of age, she prefers to win independence as a writer and nobly lets Isabel keep the inheritance in George Gissing's *Isabel Clarendon.*

Buckland Warricombe   Friend and schoolfellow of Godwin Peak and brother of the upper-class girl Godwin courts; he discovers and exposes Godwin's deception in George Gissing's *Born in Exile.*

Martin Warricombe   Well-to-do father of Buckland and Sidwell, the girl Godwin Peak hopes to marry; a religious man with an interest in geology, he is the victim of Peak's pretense at piety in George Gissing's *Born in Exile.*

Sidwell Warricombe   Conventionally religious girl of a refined and wealthy family; she accepts Godwin Peak's advances and falls in love with him but cannot accept him after his deception is exposed and her family disapproves of him in George Gissing's *Born in Exile.*

Lady Warrington   Religious, uncharitable wife of Sir Miles Warrington in William Makepeace Thackeray's *The Virginians.*

Dora Warrington   Sir Miles's daughter, whose interest in Harry Warrington evaporates when he loses his money; she marries the Reverend Mr. Juffles in William Makepeace Thackeray's *The Virginians.*

Flora Warrington   Sir Miles's handsome eldest daughter, who marries Tom Claypool in William Makepeace Thackeray's *The Virginians.*

George Warrington (the elder)   Younger brother of Sir Miles; he is husband of Rachel Esmond (Madam Esmond) and father of the twins George and Harry Esmond Warrington, but dies not long after his marriage in William Makepeace Thackeray's *The Virginians.*

George Esmond Warrington   Introspective, virtuous elder twin son of Madam Esmond; thought to have died in a campaign against the French in America, he escapes from captivity and visits England, where after mixed success as a playright he marries Theo Lambert and settles down as a country squire; he remains attached to his brother, Harry, and withdraws from the British army rather than risk meeting him in combat; he yields to Harry his claim on the Virginia estates in William Makepeace Thackeray's *The Virginians.* He is grandfather of George Warrington of *The History of Pendennis.*

George Warrington   Arthur Pendennis's stouthearted friend, whose life has been darkened by a disastrous early marriage, dooming his love for Laura Bell; he remains devoted to her and Arthur Pendennis after their marriage in William Makepeace Thackeray's *The History of Pendennis.* He appears in *The Newcomes.* He is the grandson of George Esmond Warrington and Theo (Lambert) Warrington of *The Virginians.*

Harry Esmond Warrington   Dashing younger twin son of Madam Esmond; he is briefly arrested for debt but becomes a soldier and earns high praise fighting for England on the Continent and for America in the War of Independence; his marriage to Fanny Mountain is somewhat unfortunate; years later, widowed, he visits his brother, George, in England and proposes to Hetty Lambert; though she has long loved him, the proposal comes too late, and she refuses in William Makepeace Thackeray's *The Virginians*.

Henry (Hal) Warrington   Theo (Lambert) and George Warrington's younger son in William Makepeace Thackeray's *The Virginians*.

Hester Mary Warrington   Theo (Lambert) and George Warrington's daughter in William Makepeace Thackeray's *The Virginians*.

Sir Miles Warrington   Genial if thrifty Norfolk baronet, paternal uncle to George and Harry Warrington; he makes much of them in their prosperity but does not help them in adversity in William Makepeace Thackeray's *The Virginians*.

Miles Warrington   Sir Miles's son and heir, fond of his cousins George and Harry Warrington; his death in a shooting accident makes George heir to the baronetcy in William Makepeace Thackeray's *The Virginians*.

Captain Miles Warrington   Eldest son of Theo (Lambert) and George Warrington in William Makepeace Thackeray's *The Virginians*.

Captain Warwick   Orlando Somerive's mentor when he enters the army and General Tracey's nephew; he is the general's heir until he elopes with Isabella Somerive to America; returning to London, he briefly supports his family by writing until he is reconciled with his uncle in Charlotte Smith's *The Old Manor House*.

Earl of Warwick   Hospitable nobleman, who invites Henry III to his castle in Ann Radcliffe's *Gaston de Blondeville*.

Augustus Warwick   Ambitious politician who marries the lovely, intelligent Diana Merion; he sues for divorce based on her innocent relationship with Lord Dannisburgh but cannot prove his case; the two separate, and Diana is freed only by his accidental death in George Meredith's *Diana of the Crossways*.

Diana Antonia (Tony) Merion Warwick   Witty Irish beauty more suited to intellectual than romantic pursuits; she marries Augustus Warwick, whose legal actions against her for a suspected affair estrange the two; she is again gossiped about for her relationship with the politician Percy Dacier; when he repudiates her, she marries her faithful friend Thomas Redworth in George Meredith's *Diana of the Crossways*.

George Washington   Neighbor of the Warringtons in Virginia; thinking he means to marry Madam Esmond, George Warrington wants to duel with him; fighting with him under General Braddock, George Warrington is be-

lieved dead; Harry Warrington fights under his command in the War of Independence in William Makepeace Thackeray's *The Virginians*.

Wasp   Henry Bertram's faithful little dog in Sir Walter Scott's *Guy Mannering*.

Watchful   Porter of the Palace Beautiful on the Hill of Difficulty in John Bunyan's *The Pilgrim's Progress From this World to That Which Is to Come*.

Watchful   One of four Shepherds who show Christian and Hopeful, and later Christiana and her party, the hills of Error, Caution, and Clear, and advise them on their journey in John Bunyan's *The Pilgrim's Progress From this World to That Which Is to Come*.

Watchman   Finder of Pompey, who is lost; he carries him to the Watch-house, where he gives the dog to a Blind Beggar of his acquaintance in Francis Coventry's *The History of Pompey the Little*.

Mr. Waterbrook   Mr. Wickfield's agent in London in Charles Dickens's *The Personal History of David Copperfield*.

Mrs. Waterbrook   Large wife of Mr. Waterbrook in Charles Dickens's *The Personal History of David Copperfield*.

The Water-Lady   A spirit that assists Farina and Guy the Goshawk in their rescue of Margarita from Werner in George Meredith's *Farina*.

Mrs. Waters   See Jenny Jones.

Esther Waters   Cook's slavey in the racing, betting Barfield household; a pious Dissenter, she is a butt of the servants but favored by Mrs. Barfield, a fellow-worshipper; seduced by William Latch, the cook's son, she is reluctantly packed off to London, where poverty, the workhouse, rare kindnesses, and devotion to her son make up her drab existence until William's reappearance; after their marriage and the establishment of a pub, she struggles between religion and enjoyment of Williams's business, which is dependent on illegal betting; when William's health and business are ruined by gambling, Esther returns to servant life on the ruined Barfield estate with Mrs. Barfield in George Moore's *Esther Waters*.

Jeremy Watersouchy   Mid seventeenth-century Dutch painter admired for his obsession with peripheral details in his paintings, especially clothing and jewelry; he expires from exhaustion after his last expression of genius, a painting depicting a flea, in William Beckford's *Biographical Memoirs of Extraordinary Painters*.

Mrs. Crambourne Wathin   The socially ambitious, and thus ultra-conventional, wife of a tradesman; she is one of the many who impugn the character of Diana Warwick, who she feels has insulted her in George Meredith's *Diana of the Crossways*.

Mr. Watson School friend who introduces Jack, Man of the Hill, to gambling; he later betrays Jack as a traitor in Henry Fielding's *The History of Tom Jones*.

Dorick Watson Reclusive English gentleman of Bishoprick; he marries a sister of the French theologian Abbé le Blanc; he converts himself and his wife to Protestantism, though she dies shortly thereafter; he encourages John Buncle to pursue Antonia Cranmer in Thomas Amory's *The Life of John Buncle, Esq.*

Emily Watson Seventeen-year-old disinherited cousin of Hubert Price; he invites her to continue living at Ashwood with her companion, Julia Bentham; in love with Hubert, she becomes morbidly jealous of Mrs. Bentham and commits suicide in George Moore's *Vain Fortune*.

James Watson Queen's printer in Scotland; he orders the new-printed copies of Robert Colwan's memoirs burned as blasphemous in James Hogg's *The Private Memoirs and Confessions of a Justified Sinner*.

John H. Watson British former army surgeon, whose health is impaired by a wound and convalescence in India; home in London, he needs to conserve income by sharing rooms and is introduced to Sherlock Holmes; he shares in Holmes's investigations and begins his long service as chronicler of them in Arthur Conan Doyle's *A Study in Scarlet*. He marries Mary Morstan at the conclusion of *The Sign of Four*. A widower, and having sold his medical practice, he is again residing with Holmes when he agrees to go to Devonshire to make preliminary investigations in *The Hound of the Baskervilles*. He accompanies Holmes to Birlstone in *The Valley of Fear*.

Richard Watson Laborer murdered in 1859 whose ghost is said to walk Great End Farm in 1918 in Mrs. Humphry Ward's *Harvest*.

S. Watson Former Berkshire curate, now a thirty-year-old parson ministering in an impoverished London parish; Richard mistakenly supposes him to be a rival for Lucy Hurst's hand in Thomas Hughes's *The Scouring of the White Horse*.

Mr. Watty Bankrupt client of Mr. Perker in Charles Dickens's *The Posthumous Papers of the Pickwick Club*.

Jane Waule Peter Featherstone's rich sister, who tries to convince her brother not to leave an inheritance to Fred Vincy in George Eliot's *Middlemarch*.

Miss Wavel Woman who attends Harriet Sumelin

when she elopes with Mr. Fillygrove, though she is in love with Mr. Fillygrove too in Robert Bage's *Hermsprong*.

Waverly Geraldine Waverly Verney's irresolute and impulsive brother, whom Lionel Desmond extricates from an unsuitable engagement in France by way of a duel during which he is shot in the arm in Charlotte Smith's *Desmond*.

Mrs. Waverly Mother of Waverly, Geraldine Verney, and Frances Waverly; her selfishness and fatuity constrain Frances's role as mediator in family affairs; she promotes her son's interests and neglects those of his sisters in Charlotte Smith's *Desmond*.

Edward Waverly Unworldly and romantic young English noble, who is raised by his uncle; he becomes an honorary Highlander and fast friend of Fergus MacIvor; swept into the ranks of Prince Charles Stuart's army, he is charged with, then pardoned for, high treason before settling down and marrying Rose Bradwardine in Sir Walter Scott's *Waverly*.

Sir Everard Waverly Old-school Tory, who raises his nephew, Edward Waverly, as his heir after the boy is abandoned by his father; it is through his upbringing that Edward has Scottish sympathies in Sir Walter Scott's *Waverly*.

Frances (Fanny) Waverly Geraldine Waverly Verney's pert and candid younger sister; too much a social critic and satirist by English standards, she finds in the Marquis de Montfleuri a husband tolerant of her sardonic wit in Charlotte Smith's *Desmond*.

Rachel Waverly Sir Everard's sister and Edward's aunt; a kind-hearted spinster, she provides the feminine influence in Edward's upbringing in Sir Walter Scott's *Waverly*.

Richard Waverly Second son of a noble; he becomes a Whig and a supporter of King George II; he abandons his son, Edward, at an early age to his older brother in order to enjoy life unencumbered in Sir Walter Scott's *Waverly*.

Osmond Waymark Impoverished schoolmaster and aspiring social novelist; he leaves teaching to work as a rent collector in the slums owned by Abraham Woodstock and loves both the conventional Maud Enderby and the Bohemian Ida Starr in George Gissing's *The Unclassed*.

Tom Wealdon Frank, good-humored town clerk of Gylingden; expert at electioneering, he is called in by Stanley Lake to aid him in his efforts to win office in J. Sheridan Le Fanu's *Wylder's Hand*.

Captain Weatherport   Honorable and compassionate commander of the British man-of-war *Halcyon*; he captures the pirates and their ship in Sir Walter Scott's *The Pirate*.

Captain Weazle   Cowardly officer, who is jealous of his wife, objects to letting Roderick Random and Hugh Strap board the wagon to London, and is cuckolded by Strap at an inn; he hides beneath his wife's petticoats from a highwayman in Tobias Smollett's *The Adventures of Roderick Random*.

Mr. Webb   Nephew to Mrs. Clarke; working as a highwayman, he threatens Anna St. Ives's carriage and is consequently shot by Frank Henley; later he assists Anna's family in their effort to discover her whereabouts in Thomas Holcroft's *Anna St. Ives*.

General John Webb   Henry Esmond's commanding officer, an able soldier and a handsome, accomplished politician; his rivalry with the Duke of Marlborough both stimulates and injures his pride and his career in William Makepeace Thackeray's *The History of Henry Esmond*.

Francis Webber   Riotous scapegrace student, eventually expelled from Trinity College, Dublin, whose chambers are shared briefly by Charles O'Malley in Charles Lever's *Charles O'Malley*.

Dorothy Webster   Servant of the Marchioness of Oakley; she guards the imprisoned Amelia de Gonzales in William Beckford's *Modern Novel Writing; or, the Elegant Enthusiast*.

Aaron Weech   A fence for stolen goods; he is crafty and tricks Dicky Perrott into working for him and rats on Josh Perrott to help send him to prison; Josh finally murders him in revenge in Arthur Morrison's *A Child of the Jago*.

Mr. Weeley   Deacon at Mark Rutherford's first chapel; he is a builder and an undertaker, who uses his religious connection to help his businesses in Mark Rutherford's *The Autobiography of Mark Rutherford*.

Silas Wegg   Knotty, hard, wooden-legged man hired by the illiterate Noddy Boffin to read to him; he conspires with Mr. Venus to find the latest will of old Mr. Harmon in the mounds; his plot to blackmail Boffin is frustrated in Charles Dickens's *Our Mutual Friend*.

Cosmo von Wehrstahl   Student at the University of Prague in the independent story contained within the novel; he buys an enchanted mirror in which he sees a woman clothed in white (Princess von Hohenweiss); he falls in love with the woman, smashes the mirror to free her from enchantment, and dies in George MacDonald's *Phantastes*.

Archibald (Archie) Weir   Fair-skinned, intelligent, and introverted son of Adam Weir (Lord Hermiston), Lord Advocate of Scotland; his indiscreet denunciation of a death sentence passed by his father results in his father's edict that he live an isolated life as estate lord of Hermiston, for which he in one sense compensates by falling in love with the unequally suited farmer's daughter, Christina Elliot, in Robert Louis Stevenson's *Weir of Hermiston: An Unfinished Romance*.

Jean Weir   Pale, pious, and tender but ineffectual mother of Archibald Weir and wife of Adam Weir, Lord Hermiston; she is the last descendant of the Rutherfords, known for their bloodthirsty men and white, trembling women in Robert Louis Stevenson's *Weir of Hermiston: An Unfinished Romance*.

Weird Old Wife   Strange old woman whom David Balfour meets talking to herself beside two executed criminals hanging from a gibbet; she foretells David's threatened future in Robert Louis Stevenson's *Catriona*.

Johann Nepomuk, Freiherr Von Sheppenhausen, Captain/Major Weisspreiss   Austrian army officer engaged to Countess Anna von Lenkenstein; he aids in the kidnapping of Vittoria Campa; a frequent duelist, he finally meets his death at the hand of Carlo Ammiani in George Meredith's *Vittoria*.

Sir Thomas Welby   Friend of Mr. Huntley and Sir Robert Manley in Eliza Haywood's *The History of Jemmy and Jenny Jessamy*.

Mr. Weldon   Surgeon who extracts a pistol ball from the shoulder of Hammel Clement, leaving him obligated for the subsequent care Mrs. Graves gives him in Henry Brooke's *The Fool of Quality*.

Mr. Wellcot   London bookseller and printer who complains he can hire educated gentlemen for less money than he can hire a porter; he inspires Hammel Clement's pamphlet writing, then betrays him to the government in Henry Brooke's *The Fool of Quality*.

Sam Weller   Samuel Pickwick's faithful cockney manservant, who is street-smart and wordly-wise; he accompanies his master on his travels, assists him in his schemes, faithfully attends him in the Fleet prison, and is known for his witty sayings in Charles Dickens's *The Posthumous Papers of the Pickwick Club*.

Susan Clarke Weller   Shrewish second wife of Tony Weller and owner of the Marquis of Granby Inn in Dorking; she is a disciple of the Reverend Stiggins and later dies in Charles Dickens's *The Posthumous Papers of the Pickwick Club*.

Tony Weller   Corpulent, good-hearted, but childlike father of Sam; he is a coachman and marries the widow Susan Clarke in Charles Dickens's *The Posthumous Papers of the Pickwick Club*.

Wells   Robinson Crusoe's neighbor in Brazil; they help each other start plantations in that country in Daniel Defoe's *The Life and Strange Surprizing Adventures of Robinson Crusoe of York, Mariner*.

Captain Jasper Welsh   Sea captain who kidnaps Harry Richmond and his friend Augustus Temple because he fears that they lead a life of sin; it is aboard his boat that Lord Edbury, Janet Ilchester's betrothed, drowns when the ship goes down in George Meredith's *The Adventures of Harry Richmond*.

Mr. Wemmick ("The Aged P")   Deaf old man who lives with his son, John, and enjoys being nodded at while reading the newspaper and shooting off the toy cannon outside of his house in Charles Dickens's *Great Expectations*.

John Wemmick   Mr. Jaggers's clerk, who represents the ability to distinguish between the "public" life, often morally repugnant, and the "private" life, in which he shows great tenderness to his father in a home they call a castle because a drawbridge provides the entrance in Charles Dickens's *Great Expectations*.

Aunt Wenbourne   Anna St. Ives's aunt, who favors her match with Frank Henley in Thomas Holcroft's *Anna St. Ives*.

Roger Wendover   Squire of Wendover, an anti-Christian scholar and author, who befriends Robert Elsmere in Mrs. Humphry Ward's *Robert Elsmere*.

Mr. Wenham   Friend of Lord Steyne, for whom he provides something of an alibi in William Makepeace Thackeray's *Vanity Fair*. He also appears in *The History of Pendennis*.

Richard Wenlock   Aristocratic cousin of Robert and William Fitz-Owen; he turns against Edmund Lovel out of jealousy in Clara Reeve's *The Old English Baron*.

Lady Alice (Bristol) Wensleydale   Lady Kitty Ashe's prematurely aged, widowed half sister, who lives in seclusion; her fortune was squandered in a conspiracy between her father, her stepmother, and her husband; she rebuffs Lady Kitty's girlish sisterly overtures; though she provides Lady Kitty protection after she leaves her husband, there is no intimacy between them in Mrs. Humphry Ward's *The Marriage of William Ashe*.

Mr. Wentworth   Uncle of July Wentworth; using the name Spence, he travels incognito with George Edwards from his brother's plantations in the West Indies to London to serve as George's secret protector in John Hill's *The Adventures of Mr. George Edwards, a Creole*.

Captain Frederick Wentworth   Naval captain who loved Anne Elliot eight years earlier and who left in anger after Anne was persuaded to end the engagement; he returns to visit his sister, Mrs. Croft, and becomes romantically entangled with the Musgrove girls, but eventually comes to love Anne again in Jane Austen's *Persuasion*.

July (Juliet) Wentworth   Young woman whose reciprocated love for the hero, George Edwards, is the cause of his being sent away to England; the account of her death at the novel's beginning is revealed to be false at the novel's conclusion, when the lovers are reunited, marry, and return to the West Indies in John Hill's *The Adventures of Mr. George Edwards, a Creole*.

Werner   A daring and criminal baron; he abducts Margarita Groschen and carries her off to his stronghold, where Guy the Goshawk fights and defeats him in George Meredith's *Farina*.

Count de Wertheim   Father-in-law of Frank, fifth Viscount Castlewood in William Makepeace Thackeray's *The History of Henry Esmond*.

Roger de Wesham   Bishop whose illness calls the Archbishop of York away from Hugh Woodreeve's trial in Ann Radcliffe's *Gaston de Blondeville*.

John Wesley   The Methodist divine; on meeting his admirer Geoffry Wildgoose, he urges him to avoid the threatening, anti-Methodist crowd of miners in the next town in Richard Graves's *The Spiritual Quixote*.

George Westall   Unpleasant gamekeeper of old Lord Maxwell; he is shot by his old enemy, the poacher Jim Hurd, while protecting his master's shooting preserve in Mrs. Humphry Ward's *Marcella*.

Isabella Westall   Working-class wife of George Westall, gamekeeper of Lord Maxwell; when Westall is shot by poachers, Isabella loses her sanity in Mrs. Humphry Ward's *Marcella*.

Westbrook   Wealthy, land-buying neighbor of whom Lord Belmont and Lady Anne Wilmot disapprove for his ostentation and injudicious behavior toward his tenants and financial inferiors in Frances Brooke's *The History of Lady Julia Mandeville*.

Miss Westbrook Husband-hunting daughter of a newly rich father; she marries Lord Fondville in Frances Brooke's *The History of Lady Julia Mandeville*.

Eleanor Westbrook Edward Aubrey's long-dead sweetheart, who married for money but became an impecunious widow with a daughter, Mary, in Edward Bulwer-Lytton's *Alice*.

Mary Westbrook Pretty young woman, orphaned early, who attracts the guilty love of the publicly pious Mr. Templeton; his wife's death allows him to marry her before the birth of her child, but he conceals the marriage to preserve his reputation; she dies after giving birth to Evelyn "Cameron" in Edward Bulwer-Lytton's *Alice*.

Mr. Westbury Owner of Hillingdon Hall, which John Jorrocks purchases in Robert Surtees's *Hillingdon Hall*.

Sir Warwick Westend Senior civil servant and strong advocate of competitive examinations in Anthony Trollope's *The Three Clerks*.

Lucy Westenra Mina Harker's best friend, who is engaged to Arthur Holmwood and beloved by Quincey Morris and John Seward; she is attacked by Dracula and turned into a vampire, but her friends save her soul by driving a stake through her heart in Bram Stoker's *Dracula*.

Lord Westerhaven George Godolphin's elder brother, who marries Lady Augusta Delamere and helps Emmeline Mobray evade his cousin Bellozane's insulting advances; he mediates between her and a frenzied Frederick Delamere and negotiates the restitution of her estate in Charlotte Smith's *Emmeline: The Orphan of the Castle*.

Captain Westerho Craigengelt's colleague, a corrupt adventurer employed by Lady Ashton in Sir Walter Scott's *The Bride of Lammermoor*.

Lady Western Young and beautiful queen of Carlingford society; she arouses the love of Arthur Vincent to the horror of his congregation but eventually marries Mr. Fordham in Margaret Oliphant's *Salem Chapel*.

Squire Western Neighbor of Thomas Allworthy and vulgar father of Sophia; loving his daughter, he insists upon her marriage against her will to Master Blifil in order to enrich her; when Tom Jones's and Blifil's fortunes are reversed in the end, he is equally but less objectionably determined that she marry Tom in Henry Fielding's *The History of Tom Jones*.

George Western Silent, shy, but pig-headed husband of Cecilia (Holt); learning that she had concealed an earlier, broken engagement with Sir Francis Geraldine, he becomes jealous, imagining further intrigue than had been acknowledged; when the gulf between husband and wife seems unbridgeable, his sister, Lady Grant, acts as mediator and they agree to bury the past in Anthony Trollope's *Kept in the Dark*.

Bell (Di) Western Vain sister of Squire Western, aunt to Sophia Western and Harriet Fitzpatrick, and cousin to Lady Bellaston; she causes Sophia's trials when she mistakes her love for Tom Jones as love for Master Blifil and fiercely promotes the wrong match; later she is led by social pretension to try to marry Sophia to Lord Fellamar in Henry Fielding's *The History of Tom Jones*.

Sophia Western Beautiful, compassionate, and good-hearted daughter of Squire Western; she refuses a match with Master Blifil and escapes parental tyranny by running away to London, where her trust is betrayed and her virtue endangered; she eventually forgives Tom's philandering and marries him with her father's consent in Henry Fielding's *The History of Tom Jones*.

Mr. Westlake Socialist intellectual and writer in George Gissing's *Demos*.

Stella Westlake An idealistic Socialist to whom Adela Waltham becomes passionately attached in George Gissing's *Demos*.

John Westlock Frank and generous former pupil of Seth Pecksniff and dear friend of Tom Pinch; he recognizes Pecksniff's exploitation of Tom and later marries Tom's sister, Ruth, in Charles Dickens's *The Life and Adventures of Martin Chuzzlewit*.

Mr. Westmacott Radical candidate in the Percycross election; he partners Ontario Moggs in opposing the Conservative standing member, Mr. Griffenbottom, and his running-mate, Sir Thomas Underwood, in Anthony Trollope's *Ralph the Heir*.

Earl of Westmoreland Supporter of the Duke of Norfolk's plan to free the pregnant Mary, Queen of Scots in Sophia Lee's *The Recess*.

Mr. Weston Good-hearted man of excellent character and possessed of a comfortable earned income; the widower father of Frank Churchill, he has recently married Emma Woodhouse's former governess in Jane Austen's *Emma*.

Mrs. Weston George Weston's wife, in whose kindly care Agnes de Saverne is placed after her mother's death in William Makepeace Thackeray's *Denis Duval*.

Anna Taylor Weston Former governess and companion to Emma Woodhouse; intelligent and gentle, she believes Emma is faultless and defends her against Mr. Knightly's criticism; she and her husband hope that Emma and Frank Churchill will marry in Jane Austen's *Emma*.

Edward Weston   Mr. Hatfield's thoughtful curate at Horton, whose quiet good works do more for the villagers than all of Mr. Hatfield's blustery sermons, but who leaves to become Vicar of F–– and marries Agnes Grey in Anne Brontë's *Agnes Grey*.

George Weston   Catholic squire much engaged with the "Mackerels Party," an organization of Winchelsea smugglers; an apparent victim, he is in fact an accomplice of his brother's attempted highway robbery in William Makepeace Thackeray's *Denis Duval*.

Joseph Weston   George Weston's brother and partner in criminality; acting as a highwayman, he is wounded by Denis Duval, who is finally sent to sea to escape Weston's implacable vengeance in William Makepeace Thackeray's *Denis Duval*.

Tiel Wetzweiler, Le Glorieux   The Duke of Burgundy's jester, who rescues his master at the battle of Montl'hery; not wishing to make enemies of the duke's bodyguard, he exaggerates his exploits for laughs and receives the name Le Glorieux, or the boastful, in Sir Walter Scott's *Quentin Durward*.

Matthew (Matey) Weyburn   Intelligent, sympathetic secretary to Lord Ormont; as an ambitious young man he was the sweetheart of Aminta Farrell, now Lady Ormont, and their acquaintance is renewed when Matey, lacking the money necessary for a military career, becomes secretary to Ormont; he declares his love for Aminta after she has broken with Lord Ormont in George Meredith's *Lord Ormont and his Aminta*.

Whackbairn   Tyrant schoolmaster, under whom Reuben Butler works in a parochial school near Edinburgh in Sir Walter Scott's *The Heart of Midlothian*.

Dr. Whackdeil   Successor to Mr. Pittle as minister of Gudetown; he is a serious and effective divine who does not embarrass the provost, James Pawkie, as did the unworthy Pittle in John Galt's *The Provost*.

Dr. Whaley   Dean of Derry, whom John Buncle meets while sailing to England from Dublin and whose unusual fears cause him to scream aloud during a storm; he discusses the decay of Christianity with Buncle in Thomas Amory's *The Life of John Buncle, Esq.*

Whang   Avaricious miller, who digs beneath his mill seeking a cache of diamonds but only undermines his mill in a parable told by Lien Chi Altangi in Oliver Goldsmith's *The Citizen of the World*.

Miss Wharton   Mrs. Wharton's daughter, who is about to be married and has her antique lace veil mended by Frances Henri in Charlotte Brontë's *The Professor*.

Mr. Wharton   A clergyman with principles and integrity worthy of his position, who marries Mary Rivers in Charlotte Brontë's *Jane Eyre*.

Mrs. Wharton   A benevolent Englishwoman, who befriends Frances Henri, employs her as a lace-mender, and then finds her a job teaching French in an English school in Charlotte Brontë's *The Professor*.

Abel Wharton   Prosperous, imposing, upright barrister much beset by troubles caused by his feckless son, Everett, and by his headstrong daughter, Emily, who marries against his will the adventurer Ferdinand Lopez; the death of Lopez removes the incubus and, when Everett reforms and marries, the old man is content at last in Anthony Trollope's *The Prime Minister*.

Sir Alured Wharton   Cousin of Abel; a baronet and the head of the Wharton family, he is proud of his lineage and estate in Herefordshire; he is made happy by the marriage of his beloved daughter, Mary, to Everett Wharton, in Anthony Trollope's *The Prime Minister*.

Everett Wharton   Amiable son of Abel; his indolence is a constant source of anxiety to his father until, having become heir to Sir Alured, he reforms and marries his cousin Mary in Anthony Trollope's *The Prime Minister*.

Harry Wharton   Upper-class Labour-party Member of Parliament, who loves Marcella Boyce but marries an heiress, Lady Selina Farrell, after his public disgrace as a bribe-taker in Mrs. Humphry Ward's *Marcella*.

Mary Wharton   Beloved daughter of Sir Alured; she is impatient with her cousin Emily (Lopez) for not encouraging Arthur Fletcher; she marries her cousin Everett, much to her father's delight, in Anthony Trollope's *The Prime Minister*.

Polly Wheedle   Rose Jocelyn's maid; she marries Jack Raikes in George Meredith's *Evan Harrington*.

Susan Wheedle   The near-suicidal mother of Harry Jocelyn's illegitimate child; she is rescued by Evan Harrington in George Meredith's *Evan Harrington*.

Whelpdale   Cheap journalist, who escapes starvation in America by writing stories for newspapers, specializes in writing for uneducated readers, gains a fine editorial position, and marries Dora Milvain in George Gissing's *New Grub Street*.

Mr. Whiffer The town crier of Eatanswill in Charles Dickens's *The Posthumous Papers of the Pickwick Club*.

Mr. Whiffers One of the select footmen present at John Smauker's "swarry"; he resigns from his position in Charles Dickens's *The Posthumous Papers of the Pickwick Club*.

Captain Whiffle Young, delicate dandy, who replaces Captain Oakhum on the *Thunder* in Jamaica in Tobias Smollett's *The Adventures of Roderick Random*.

Augustus Whiffle Orlando Whiffle's son, the unscrupulous seducer of Carrie Mitchell and lover of Maud Gresham in George Gissing's *Workers in the Dawn*.

Orlando Whiffle Hypocritical clergyman, father of Augustus Whiffle, and tutor of Arthur Golding in George Gissing's *Workers in the Dawn*.

Mrs. Whimple Lady who runs the house where Pip Pirrip hides Abel Magwitch from the police under the name of Provis in London in Charles Dickens's *Great Expectations*.

Mrs. Whipp An exasperated landlady, whose tenant is David Sweeting in Charlotte Brontë's *Shirley*.

Tom Whipwell Coachman who, fearing legal reprisals for neglecting the beaten and robbed Joseph Andrews should he die, conveys him to the Dragon Inn in Henry Fielding's *The History of the Adventures of Mr. Joseph Andrews and of his Friend Mr. Abraham Adams*.

The Whistler Illegitimate son of Effie Deans and George Staunton; sold as an infant to a Highland outlaw, he becomes an outlaw and kills his father in an attempted robbery in Sir Walter Scott's *The Heart of Midlothian*.

White Fellow-student of Charles Reding, an Anglo Catholic who to Reding's contempt returns from the Roman to the Anglican church, is ordained, and marries in John Henry Newman's *Loss and Gain*.

Mrs. White Lady Meadows's servant; pitying Henrietta Courteney, she warns her of her danger and is dismissed, to be reinstated later when Mr. Danvers is exposed in Charlotte Lennox's *Henrietta*.

Alexis White Son of a dead colleague of Sir Jasper Merrifield; his misinterpretation of Gillian Merrifield's interest in his academic progress leads to serious consequences in Charlotte Yonge's *Beechcroft at Rockstone*.

James White Wealthy quarry owner with claims to a title in Italy; he marries Adeline Mohun to provide a socially impeccable chaperon for his niece, Maura White, in Charlotte Yonge's *Beechcroft at Rockstone*. He appears in *The Long Vacation*.

Kalliope White Beautiful artist who supports her family as chief designer at James White's quarry and is patronized by Gillian Merrifield in Charlotte Yonge's *Beechcroft at Rockstone*. On her marriage to a wealthy man she continues at her work in *The Long Vacation*.

Maple White American who first discovered the mysterious plateau to which Professor Challenger leads his expedition in Arthur Conan Doyle's *The Lost World*.

Maura White Self-centered beauty, who embarrasses her sister, Kalliope, in Charlotte Yonge's *Beechcroft at Rockstone*. She is the rival of Franceska Vanderkist in *The Long Vacation*.

Wully White A highly religious man who, after rebuking the Master (James Durie), is harassed to death with fireworks in Robert Louis Stevenson's *The Master of Ballantrae: A Winter's Tale*.

Mr. Whitfield Methodist leader, who becomes a spiritual and practical mentor to Geoffry Wildgoose in Richard Graves's *The Spiritual Quixote*.

Mrs. Whitfield Innkeeper, sister-in-law to the Methodist leader Mr. Whitfield; she scoffs at Geoffry Wildgoose and Jeremiah Tugwell until she learns of their allegiance to Whitfield in Richard Graves's *The Spiritual Quixote*.

White King Chess piece who sends all his soldiers and horses (except two left for the chess game), presumably to the rescue of Humpty Dumpty; he speaks with his messengers on the battle between the Lion and the Unicorn and takes Alice to the battle in Lewis Carroll's *Through the Looking-Glass*.

White Knight Chess piece who rescues Alice from the Red Knight and escorts her to the eighth square; gentle in manner and appearance, he is mildly vexed at the inefficacy of his various inventions; he continually falls off his horse in Lewis Carroll's *Through the Looking-Glass*.

White Lady Beautiful guardian spirit of the House of Avenel; she oversees Lady Alice Avenel's Protestant Bible, regaining it from Father Philip; she is responsible for the Protestant conversions of both Mary Avenel and Halbert Glendinning but opposes their marriage before ultimately rejoicing in it in Sir Walter Scott's *The Monastery*.

Lady Whitelaw Sponsor of Godwin Peak's college

scholarship; she agrees to support him for a year of study in London when he leaves college in George Gissing's *Born in Exile*.

White Man   South-Sea native crew member aboard the schooner *Farallone* in Robert Louis Stevenson's *The Ebb-Tide: A Trio and a Quartette*.

White Queen   Chess piece foolishly helpless in personality and untidy in appearance; because she lives "backwards," she can "remember" future events; she turns into a sheep who knits in a shop which turns into a boat on a river and back into a shop, where she sells Alice an egg that becomes Humpty Dumpty; as the White Queen she assists the Red Queen in instructing Queen Alice and recites a riddle poem at Alice's feast in Lewis Carroll's *Through the Looking-Glass*.

White Rabbit   The catalyst for Alice's fantastic journey; he is late for the Queen of Hearts's party and continually loses items of apparel, which Alice tries to retrieve; he becomes the herald at the trial of the Knave of Hearts in Lewis Carroll's *Alice's Adventures in Wonderland*.

Mr. Whitefield   Bell Inn landlord of Gloucester whose wife mistreats Tom Jones because she hears bad things about him in Henry Fielding's *The History of Tom Jones*.

Mrs. Whitefield   Bell Inn landlady of Gloucester who believes Petty-fogger's lies about Tom and treats Tom poorly during his stay in Henry Fielding's *The History of Tom Jones*.

Vernon Whitford   Penniless intellectual who wins the love of his cousin Sir Willoughby Patterne's disenchanted betrothed, Clara Middleton, in the process of helping her to avoid a loveless marriage in George Meredith's *The Egoist*.

George Whitstable   Rural landowner of limited intelligence but sufficient means to enable Sophia Longestaffe to be complacent in her successful nuptials, despite her sister's voluble contempt in Anthony Trollope's *The Way We Live Now*.

Thomas Whitteret   Former law clerk of Mr. Keelevin; he uncovers the terms of entail and is instrumental in restoring Kittlestonheugh to Charles Walkinshaw's family in John Galt's *The Entail*.

Abel Whittle   Young, simple-minded employee of Michael Henchard; the question of appropriate punishment for his fecklessness occasions the first major conflict between Henchard and Donald Farfrae; it is Abel who takes care of Henchard in his final illness in Thomas Hardy's *The Mayor of Casterbridge*.

William Whittlestaff   Middle-aged guardian of Mary Lawrie; he falls in love with her, and she agrees to marry him out of gratitude, although she loves John Gordon; after Gordon returns with a moderate fortune from the South Africa diamond mines, Whittlestaff realizes he must release her from her engagement in Anthony Trollope's *An Old Man's Love*.

Whitwell   Polite, educated mate of the passenger boat on which John Buncle meets Charlotte Melmoth and later East India Company captain; his loss of two wives leaves him only the consolation of his religion in Thomas Amory's *The Life of John Buncle, Esq*.

Mrs. Wickam   Little Paul Dombey's melancholy and pessimistic nurse who replaces Richards (Polly Toodle) in Charles Dickens's *Dombey and Son*.

Mr. Wickerby   Zealous attorney, who defends Phineas Finn on trial for Mr. Bonteen's murder in Anthony Trollope's *Phineas Redux*.

Mr. Wickfield   Handsome, middle-aged lawyer of Betsey Trotwood in Canterbury; David Copperfield boards with him while attending school; he and his pretty, gentle daughter, Agnes, fall under the power of his scheming, blackmailing clerk, Uriah Heep, but are rescued by Wilkins Micawber and David in Charles Dickens's *The Personal History of David Copperfield*.

Agnes Wickfield   Mr. Wickfield's pretty, tranquil daughter, who is his housekeeper; she is David Copperfield's good friend from his childhood through adulthood and his first marriage, loving him the whole time; she is almost forced to marry Uriah Heep but finally marries David in Charles Dickens's *The Personal History of David Copperfield*.

George Wickham   Handsome and ingratiating but extravagant and unprincipled officer, who joins the regiment stationed near the Bennet estate; he attracts Elizabeth Bennet and easily convinces her of the arrogance and wickedness of Mr. Darcy; Darcy's revelation to Elizabeth that he had prevented Wickham's elopement with his sister initiates the change in Elizabeth's feelings for both men; Wickham elopes with Lydia Bennet in Jane Austen's *Pride and Prejudice*.

Captain Joe Wicks   Shrewd captain of the *Currency Lass*, accused of murdering a hand on the *Grace Darling*; disguised as a cabman, he buys Captain William Kirkup's papers and assumes Captain Jacob Trent's identity in Robert Louis Stevenson's *The Wrecker*.

Mr. Wicks   Law clerk for Dodson and Fogg in Charles Dickens's *The Posthumous Papers of the Pickwick Club*.

Edmund Widdowson Prosperous businessman, who marries Monica Madden, jealously forbids her any freedom, and quarrels with her when he discovers that she has had a lover in George Gissing's *The Odd Women*.

Mrs. Luke Widdowson Fashionable matron who is critical when her brother-in-law, Edmund, marries a shop girl, but accepts her with good humor in George Gissing's *The Odd Women*.

Widow Elderly woman who welcomes Halbert Glendinning because he resembles her dead son in Sir Walter Scott's *The Monastery*.

Widow of Great Distinction Young woman who plunges into all the fashionable follies following her husband's death, and who, since vanity is her ruling passion, schemes to take precedence over everyone in Charles Johnstone's *Chrysal: or, The Adventures of a Guinea*.

Count Wiemar Venetian aristocrat who marries an innocent orphan, subjects her to the plottings of the woman he scorned and the lusts of his best friend, and then refuses to forgive her for her mere thoughts of infidelity because of his pride in Charlotte Dacre's *The Passions*.

Julia Wiemar Venetian countess whose innocence makes her the victim of others' passions and leads her into subsequent isolation and madness in Charlotte Dacre's *The Passions*.

Wife of Charity Supporter Number Seven Heiress who is vain, imperious, extravagant, and has a temper but who has pretensions to taste and judgment in Charles Johnstone's *Chrysal: or, The Adventures of a Guinea*.

Wife of Charity Supporter Number Six A woman of fashion, who sets her card parties on Sundays, causing her husband numerous embarrassments and discomforts, and who also lavishes excessive care on her pets in Charles Johnstone's *Chrysal: or, The Adventures of a Guinea*.

Wife of Messenger Woman who spends money on card parties rather than household accounts in Charles Johnstone's *Chrysal: or, The Adventures of a Guinea*.

Wife of the Chaplain Successful schemer, who works on the Bishop and his Lady's belief in dreams to get her husband the place of Rector in Charles Johnstone's *Chrysal: or, The Adventures of a Guinea*.

Wiggins Leader of the Baker Street Irregulars, the band of "street Arabs" who first assist Sherlock Holmes in Arthur Conan Doyle's *A Study in Scarlet*.

Mr. Wiglinton Grim, bilious, elderly clergyman with antinomian tendencies, disliked by young Alton Locke; he drinks tea with Mrs. Locke and Mr. Bowyer and marries Alton's sister, Susan, in Charles Kingsley's *Alton Locke*.

Nehemiah Wikins Lower-class labor leader who ruins the career of Harry Wharton in Mrs. Humphry Ward's *Marcella*.

Thomas Wilcocks Captain of the ship which rescues Lemuel Gulliver after he has left Brobdingnag in Jonathan Swift's *Travels into Several Remote Nations of the World. In Four Parts. By Lemuel Gulliver*.

Mr. Wild Jonathan Wild's father, who attempts to reconcile Bob Bagshot and Mr. Grave after Grave accuses Bagshot of picking his pocket in Henry Fielding's *The Life of Mr. Jonathan Wild the Great*.

Jonathan Wild Protagonist who cheats and swindles friend and foe alike; his plot to ruin Thomas Heartfree fails only because the gang member Fireblood betrays Wild to reduce his own sentence in Henry Fielding's *The Life of Mr. Jonathan Wild the Great*. He is a repulsive and murderous thief-taker, who with blackmail, treachery, and terror pursues Jack Sheppard throughout his life until he sees him hanged at Tyburn in William Harrison Ainsworth's *Jack Sheppard*.

Wolfstan Wild First in a list of immoral ancestors of Jonathan Wild in Henry Fielding's *The Life of Mr. Jonathan Wild the Great*.

Mr. Wildcodger Sycophant who conducts experiments in practical agricultural science and assumes custody of the captive Azemia from Lady Belinda in William Beckford's *Azemia*.

Mrs. Wildcodger Fertile, ignorant wife of Mr. Wildcodger; she is threatened by the presence of the beautiful captive in William Beckford's *Azemia*.

Damon Wildeve Handsome, selfish lover of Eustacia Vye; losing her to Clym Yeobright, he spitefully marries Thomasin Yeobright, whom he mistreats; Eustacia's domestic troubles give him opportunity to elope with her; he dies trying to save her from drowning in Thomas Hardy's *The Return of the Native*.

Madge Wildfire Meg Murdockson's insane daughter, who mourns the loss of her illegitimate baby by George Staunton; verbose and lively, she is Jeanie Deans's keeper before being killed by a witch-hunting crowd in Sir Walter Scott's *The Heart of Midlothian*.

Mr. Wildgoose Father of Geoffry Wildgoose; though unschooled himself, he sends his son to Oxford; his death brings Geoffry back home just before completing his degree in Richard Graves's *The Spiritual Quixote*.

Mrs. Wildgoose   Mother of Geoffry Wildgoose; she unsuccessfully opposes his calling to be a traveling Methodist preacher and literally worries herself sick during his absence in Richard Graves's *The Spiritual Quixote*.

Geoffry Wildgoose   Young gentleman farmer who becomes an itinerant Methodist preacher; he roams the countryside with his companion, Jeremiah Tugwell, preaching mainly to working-class sympathizers and discussing religion privately with upper-class skeptics; his ingenuousness makes him the butt of several practical jokes, and after getting hit in the head with a bottle he is finally persuaded to give up preaching, whereupon he marries Julia Townsend in Richard Graves's *The Spiritual Quixote*.

Mr. Wildly   Father of Flora Mellasin's baby in Eliza Haywood's *The History of Miss Betsy Thoughtless*.

Roger Wildrake   Drunken clerk for Markham Everard; he negotiates with Oliver Cromwell for Everard to rescind the order to possess Woodstock, and he attempts to stab Cromwell before the assault on Woodstock Lodge in Sir Walter Scott's *Woodstock*.

Mrs. Wilfer   Reginald Wilfer's majestic and dour wife, who likes to see herself as a martyr in Charles Dickens's *Our Mutual Friend*.

Bella Wilfer   Beautiful but mercenary and spoiled young woman, who was "willed" to John Harmon; she lives with the wealthy Boffins, rejects Harmon's marriage proposal, but changes for the better as she witnesses Mr. Boffin's miserly behavior and finally marries Harmon in Charles Dickens's *Our Mutual Friend*.

Lavinia (Lavvy) Wilfer   Bella Wilfer's sassy and contradictory younger sister, who inherits Bella's former suitor, George Sampson, in Charles Dickens's *Our Mutual Friend*.

Reginald (R., Rumty) Wilfer   Chubby, cherubic, mild-mannered head of the Wilfer household; he is henpecked by his wife and adored by his daughter Bella in Charles Dickens's *Our Mutual Friend*.

Wilhelmina   Daughter of a rich Vienna jeweller; she is seduced by Ferdinand, becomes the victim of his fraud, is abandoned by him, and enters a nunnery; she accompanies Mademoiselle de Melvil to meet Renaldo de Melvil in Tobias Smollett's *The Adventures of Ferdinand Count Fathom*.

Wilhemina of Bohemia   An executed heretic in Mary Shelley's *Valperga*.

Wilkins   Subgardener of Captain Bolwig in Charles Dickens's *The Posthumous Papers of the Pickwick Club*.

Mrs. Wilkins   An innkeeper who finds the Blind Beggar dead and orders Pompey executed, but changes her mind when she sees how beautiful he is in Francis Coventry's *The History of Pompey the Little*.

Alice Wilkins   Mother of Peter Wilkins; she marries the opportunistic J. G. in Robert Paltock's *The Life and Adventures of Peter Wilkins*.

Deborah Wilkins   Squire Allworthy's unmarried, elderly, self-interested servant, who ingratiates herself with Captain Blifil by revealing the apparent identity of Tom Jones's father in Henry Fielding's *The History of Tom Jones*.

Dick Wilkins   Fellow apprentice of Ebenezer Scrooge at Fezziwig's; he was fond of Ebenezer in Charles Dickens's *A Christmas Carol*.

Patty Wilkins   A maidservant with whom young Peter Wilkins has an amorous intrigue; she becomes his first wife and bears two children in Robert Paltock's *The Life and Adventures of Peter Wilkins*.

Peter Wilkins (the father)   A Protestant zealot who is executed for his role in Monmouth's Rebellion before the birth of his son, Peter, in Robert Paltock's *The Life and Adventures of Peter Wilkins*.

Peter Wilkins   Cornish sailor who is shipwrecked near the land of Normnbdsgrsutt, where, in fulfillment of an ancient prophecy, he routs King Georigetti's enemies; he then institutes an ambitious program of colonial expansion, commercial development, and social and religious reform in Robert Paltock's *The Life and Adventures of Peter Wilkins*.

Arthur Wilkinson (the elder)   Vicar of Hurst Staple and the ineffectual father of Arthur Wilkinson; his death leaves his four daughters and his wife dependent on his son in Anthony Trollope's *The Bertrams*.

Arthur Wilkinson   Harrassed Vicar of Hurst Staple forced to support his widowed mother and for a long time unable to marry Adela Gauntlet in Anthony Trollope's *The Bertrams*. He appears at one of Miss Todd's parties in *Miss Mackenzie*.

James Wilkinson   Chief servant in the household of Fairford in Sir Walter Scott's *Redgauntlet*.

Mrs. Arthur Wilkinson   Vicar's widow, who benefits

from Lord Stapledean's insistence when bestowing the living of Hurst Staple on her son that he pay her the major portion of his stipend; she comes to regard the money as hers by right in Anthony Trollope's *The Bertrams*.

Will   Servant boy Fanny Hill seduces and uses to avenge Mr. H——'s infidelities in John Cleland's *Memoirs of a Woman of Pleasure*.

Will   Older and more daring pickpocket, who works with Colonel Jack and begins working with a gang involved in burglary and robbery; he is arrested and put in Newgate in Daniel Defoe's *The History and the Remarkable Life of the Truly Honourable Colonel Jacques, Commonly Call'd Col. Jack*.

Will   Guilbert Girder's foreman in Sir Walter Scott's *The Bride of Lammermoor*.

Black Will   Thug and former pal of Tom Robinson; he dies of hunger and exposure when he sets out to kill Tom and George Fielding in Charles Reade's *It Is Never Too Late to Mend*.

John Willett   Landlord of the Maypole Inn, who is considered a wise man by the patrons of his establishment; he is devastated by the burning of the Maypole Inn during the Gordon riots in Charles Dickens's *Barnaby Rudge*.

Joe Willett (Tom Green)   John Willett's son, who is considered a mere child and is humiliated by his father; as Tom Green he enlists in the army and loses an arm fighting in America; he returns to rescue Dolly Varden during the Gordon riots; after they marry they reopen the Maypole Inn in Charles Dickens's *Barnaby Rudge*.

William   General's servant; a son of the regiment who was educated by Captain Standard's father, he goes into profitable service in Charles Johnstone's *Chrysal: or, The Adventures of a Guinea*.

William   Coachman on the London coach from Canterbury in Charles Dickens's *The Personal History of David Copperfield*.

William   Farmer, the brother of Lucy, Arabella's maid; at his home Lucy meets Mr. Hervey to be bribed to receive love letters for Arabella in Charlotte Lennox's *The Female Quixote*.

William   Bryan Perdue's footman and friend, who informs Bryan of his father's death in Thomas Holcroft's *The Memoirs of Bryan Perdue*.

William   Margaret Borredale's impetuous and vital suitor of inferior social station; rejected by her father,

Lord Borradale, he emigrates to Canada; learning that Margaret is free to marry him, he hurries home but is apparently lost at sea; rescued, he returns to England after three years, ignorant of Margaret's marriage; his reunion with her is interrupted by pistol shots fired by Deloraine in William Godwin's *Deloraine*.

Duke (William Longsword) William of Normandy   High-minded father of Duke Richard; he is betrayed and murdered by Arnulf of Flanders in Charlotte Yonge's *The Little Duke*.

Sweet William   A silent man who earns money by card tricks and stops at the same inn as Nell Trent, her grandfather, Tom Codlin, and Harris Short in Charles Dickens's *The Old Curiosity Shop*.

Williams   Pompous prison justice (inspector) who considers the prisoners subhuman and approves of everything Hawes does in Charles Reade's *It Is Never Too Late to Mend*.

Williams   A most egregious trifler and young Master of Arts at Cambridge, on whom Young Qualmsick plays a trick in Francis Coventry's *The History of Pompey the Little*.

Williams   Attendant to Lord Leicester; he is frustrated in his design to wed Ellinor and blackmail Matilda; he murders Anthony Colville and imprisons Matilda and Leicester before Leicester kills him in Sophia Lee's *The Recess*.

Miss Williams   Lady Betty Williams's daughter, brought up at a distance from maternal supervision; her mother boasts of their consequentially good relationship, but Miss Williams elopes in Samuel Richardson's *Sir Charles Grandison*.

Miss Williams   Dressmaker of Gylingden for the Hunt Ball in J. Sheridan Le Fanu's *Wylder's Hand*.

Mr. Williams   Neighboring farmer and would-be bridegroom of Olivia Primrose; he is dismayed when she elopes in Oliver Goldsmith's *The Vicar of Wakefield*.

Alison Williams   Sister of Ermine Williams; employed as governess, she becomes the very intimate friend of Lady Temple in Charlotte Yonge's *The Clever Woman of the Family*.

Arthur Williams   Young Lincolnshire curate who is dependent upon Mr. B——'s patronage; Pamela appeals to him for help after she is kidnapped and taken to Mr. B——'s Lincolnshire estate; his timidity and naïveté impede his helpfulness; he eventually marries an heiress in Samuel Richardson's *Pamela, or Virtue Rewarded*.

Arthur Williams Hypocritical parson, who seduces Shamela Andrews and fathers her child; they continue their affair throughout Shamela's courtship by Squire Booby and after the marriage; he uses Scripture and sermons to justify his exploitation of Shamela in Henry Fielding's *An Apology for the Life of Mrs. Shamela Andrews*.

Lady Betty Williams A lively, flattering widow, who cannot understand Harriet Byron's dislike of Sir Hargrave Pollexfen; she is wrongly suspected of complicity in Harriet's disappearance in Samuel Richardson's *Sir Charles Grandison*.

Bill Williams Advance-booking agent for the acting company; he books Dick Lennox a room in the Ede household in George Moore's *A Mummer's Wife*.

Caleb Williams A former tenant of Ferdinando Falkland; because of his inquisitive mind, he is hired as Falkland's secretary; Caleb's insatiable curiosity leads him to discover Falkland's triple crime: the murder of Barnabas Tyrrel and the unnecessary deaths of the Hawkinses; as a result of his knowledge, he is falsely accused of a crime, and for the next several years is hounded and his life made unbearable; finally, he forces a confession from Falkland and plunges into a deep depression in William Godwin's *Caleb Williams*.

Edward Williams Laboring-class artist, who converts to Catholicism and then recants in order to resume his painting in Mrs. Humphry Ward's *Helbeck of Bannisdale*.

Eliza Williams Colonel Brandon's unfortunate ward, the orphaned, illegitimate daughter of the woman whom he formerly loved (also named Eliza Williams); she is seduced and abandoned by John Willoughby in Jane Austen's *Sense and Sensibility*.

Ermine Williams Crippled magazine editor, who befriends Rachel Curtis, marries her long-lost lover Colonel Colin Keith, and adopts the orphaned son of Lord and Lady Keith in Charlotte Yonge's *The Clever Woman of the Family*.

Fanny Williams Young, modest, and well-bred neighbor of Arabella (Fermor) and Captain Fitzgerald in rural England; she is guardian of the offspring of a deceased friend in Frances Brooke's *The History of Emily Montague*.

Nancy Williams A prostitute to whom Roderick Random gives medical assistance; she becomes Narcissa's attendant and eventually marries Hugh Strap in Tobias Smollett's *The Adventures of Roderick Random*.

William Williams Customer at the Six Jolly Fellowship Porters who helps to revive Roger Riderhood in Charles Dickens's *Our Mutual Friend*.

Williamsburg Landlord Traveler who invites Billy Annesly into his home and then tries to indenture him in Henry Mackenzie's *The Man of the World*.

Williamson Servant of the Murrays at Horton Lodge in Anne Brontë's *Agnes Grey*.

Clara Williamson Abandoned wife of the unscrupulous Willis Rodman in George Gissing's *Demos*.

Jane Williamson Narrator of Anne Thackeray Ritchie's *The Village on the Cliff*.

Willie A workingman and a problem drinker; stopped by Sylvie and Bruno from entering a tavern, he goes home to his wife and child; he vows to give up liquor in Lewis Carroll's *Sylvie and Bruno Concluded*.

William Willieson Scottish Jacobite skipper in league with Richard Vere; he is convinced that the piracies on the East India trade route permit rebellion against the government in Sir Walter Scott's *The Black Dwarf*.

Willis Fellow student of Charles Reding and largely instrumental in his conversion; he becomes a Passionist Father in John Henry Newman's *Loss and Gain*.

Mr. Willis James's Street master tailor, admired by Alton Locke for his wisdom, kindness, and humanity in Charles Kingsley's *Alton Locke*.

Mrs. Willis Childhood friend of Charles Mandeville's mother; following a visit to the Mandeville family in Ireland, she takes the infant Henrietta back with her to England, thus saving Charles's sister from the mob that kills her parents in William Godwin's *Mandeville*.

Mrs. Willis Old friend of the elder Mr. Bale; she takes Henrietta Courteney in and advises her to reconcile with her aunt, Lady Meadows, and to obey her elders whenever possible; she protects her against the younger Mr. Bale's plot in Charlotte Lennox's *Henrietta*.

Letty Willis Gloucester boarding-school friend and confidential correspondent of Lydia Melford; she travels to attend Lydia's wedding at the end of Tobias Smollett's *The Expedition of Humphry Clinker*.

Colonel Willmott Middle-aged gentleman who returns to England after making his fortune in the East Indies; his identity as the father of Emily Montague is revealed after the happy, coincidental conformity of her marriage to Ed. Rivers with his prior arrangement for her in Frances Brooke's *The History of Emily Montague*.

Sir Clement Willoughby Foppish young London baronet who pursues Evelina Anville Belmont in competition with Lord Orville, and who goes to the Continent when he hears Evelina will marry Orville in Frances Burney's *Evelina*.

John Willoughby   Handsome, clever, dashing realization of Marianne Dashwood's romantic ideal; in love with and loved by Marianne, he leaves abruptly to court an heiress after he is disinherited by his elderly cousin, Mrs. Smith, in punishment for his earlier seduction of Colonel Brandon's ward in Jane Austen's *Sense and Sensibility*.

Harry Willoughton   Amateur antiquary, whose curiosity leads him to buy the manuscript relating Gaston de Blondeville's story in Ann Radcliffe's *Gaston de Blondeville*.

Miss Willow   Neighbor of the Moreland estate who has discovered the problems created by possessing wit, beauty, and affluence in Henry Brooke's *The Fool of Quality*.

Wilmot   Lucy Snowe's uncle whom she does not resemble in Charlotte Brontë's *Villette*.

Captain Wilmot   Sailor aboard an English ship who plots a mutiny and succeeds, becoming a pirate in league with Captain Singleton; eventually his group splits from Singleton and joins Captain Avery in Daniel Defoe's *The Life, Adventures, and Pyracies of the Famous Captain Singleton*.

Miss Wilmot   Mr. Wilmot's sister, who suffers at the hands of her lover, Mr. Wakefield; she later assists in the reconciliation of Hugh Trevor and Olivia Mowbray; she finally marries the repentant Wakefield in Thomas Holcroft's *The Adventures of Hugh Trevor*.

Mr. Wilmot   An obnoxious, elderly, wealthy friend of Mr. Maxwell; he does not relent in his pursuit of Helen until she marries Arthur Huntingdon in Anne Brontë's *The Tenant of Wildfell Hall*.

Mr. Wilmot   Thrice-married father of Arabella Wilmot in Oliver Goldsmith's *The Vicar of Wakefield*.

Mr. Wilmot   Amiable, educated poet, who serves as usher at Hugh Trevor's school, is saved from an attempted suicide by Hugh's schoolmate Mr. Turl, and becomes an advocate for justice and an intimate friend of Hugh Trevor in Thomas Holcroft's *The Adventures of Hugh Trevor*.

Annabella Wilmot   Mr. Wilmot's niece and Milicent Hargrave's cousin, who marries Lord Lowborough but flirts with Arthur Huntingdon and later becomes his mistress; she has two children, is divorced by Lord Lowborough, and dies in misery in Anne Brontë's *The Tenant of Wildfell Hall*.

Lady Anne Wilmot   Self-proclaimed coquette, a friend of both Lady Julia Belmont and Henry Mandeville, and the chief letter-writer of the novel; she is constrained by jointure arrangements made by her deceased husband from marrying her beloved correspondent, the absent Colonel Belville, in Frances Brooke's *The History of Lady Julia Mandeville*.

Arabella Wilmot   Sweetheart of George Primrose; their engagement is broken off when the Primroses are ruined; she becomes engaged to the villainous Squire Thornhill but marries George after all when the squire's villainy is exposed in Oliver Goldsmith's *The Vicar of Wakefield*.

Captain Wilson   Captain of H.M.S. *Harpy*; he accepts Jack Easy as a midshipman to oblige Nicodemus Easy, from whom, being a married man with many children, he has to borrow money in Captain Frederick Marryat's *Mr. Midshipman Easy*.

Dr. Wilson   Ferdinando Falkland's doctor, called in to help Emily Melville while she is dying in jail in William Godwin's *Caleb Williams*.

Miss Wilson   Blanche and Mary Ingram's former governess who was dismissed for her suspected involvement with the tutor in Charlotte Brontë's *Jane Eyre*.

Mr. Wilson   The English teacher at Mme. Beck's school who is replaced by Lucy Snowe because of his lack of punctuality in Charlotte Brontë's *Villette*.

Mr. Wilson   Gentleman leading a retired country life after a debauched young adulthood; he is Joseph Andrews's real father; he shelters Fanny Goodwill, Parson Adams, and Joseph after their flight from some sheep stealers in Henry Fielding's *The History of the Adventures of Mr. Joseph Andrews and of his Friend Mr. Abraham Adams*.

Mr. Wilson   Schoolmaster who is deceived by Robert Colwan into punishing the innocent McGill in James Hogg's *The Private Memoirs and Confessions of a Justified Sinner*.

Mrs. Wilson   Widowed mother of Robert, Richard, and Jane in Anne Brontë's *The Tenant of Wildfell Hall*.

Alice Wilson   The sister of George Wilson; she still retains her old country ways and simplicity though working in Manchester; her illness and death affect all who have known her in Elizabeth Gaskell's *Mary Barton*.

Alison Wilson   Old housekeeper at Milnwood, who recognizes Henry Morton when he returns from exile in Sir Walter Scott's *Old Mortality*.

Andrew (Handy Dandi) Wilson   Smuggler associate of Geordie Robertson (George Staunton); he is caught robbing a revenue collector and hanged in Sir Walter Scott's *The Heart of Midlothian.*

Bob Wilson   Henry Ashton's groom and companion in Sir Walter Scott's *The Bride of Lammermoor.*

Sir Broadley Wilson   The one of Rosalie Murray's admirers at her coming-out ball to whom she is least attracted in Anne Brontë's *Agnes Grey.*

George Wilson   Friend of John Barton and father of Jem Wilson; his family is a support to the Bartons during their troubles, even when Jem is on trial for the murder of Harry Carson in Elizabeth Gaskell's *Mary Barton.*

Jane Wilson   George Wilson's wife; she blames Mary Barton when her son, Jem Wilson, is arrested but later gladly accepts her as Jem's wife and goes with them to Canada in Elizabeth Gaskell's *Mary Barton.*

Jane Wilson   An ambitious young woman, who aspires to marry a country gentleman like Frederick Lawrence but whose plans are thwarted by Gilbert Markham, who dislikes her pretentious manner; she remains a spinster in Anne Brontë's *The Tenant of Wildfell Hall.*

Jem Wilson   A mechanic with a good reputation; he is in love with Mary Barton, who refuses to admit she loves him; he is accused of murdering Harry Carson after a fight about Mary but is finally acquitted through Mary's efforts to prove an alibi; they marry and emigrate in Elizabeth Gaskell's *Mary Barton.*

John Wilson   Godfrey Bertram's groom, who witnesses Meg Merriles's curse on Godfrey Bertram in Sir Walter Scott's *Guy Mannering.*

Legge Wilson   Secretary for War in Mr. Mildmay's cabinet and friend to Phineas Finn in Anthony Trollope's *Phineas Finn* and in *Phineas Redux.* He is Secretary for India in *The Eustace Diamonds.* He is mentioned in *The Way We Live Now.*

Mary Ann Wilson   An older pupil who becomes Jane Eyre's friend at Lowood School because she is witty and original in Charlotte Brontë's *Jane Eyre.*

Richard Wilson   Quiet, studious younger son, who is engaged to Mary Millward and eventually becomes Vicar of Lindenhope in Anne Brontë's *The Tenant of Wildfell Hall.*

Robert Wilson   Elder son and rough farmer in Anne Brontë's *The Tenant of Wildfell Hall.*

Sarah Wilson   Helen Rolleston's maid who falls in love with James Seaton (Robert Penfold) and reveals the gardener's passion for Helen to her father in Charles Reade's *Foul Play.*

Will Wilson   The sailor cousin of Jem Wilson; he provides the alibi that proves Jem's innocence in Elizabeth Gaskell's *Mary Barton.*

William Wilson   Servant hired by Harriet Byron on the recommendation of James Bagenhall; he is in fact in the employ of Sir Hargrave Pollexfen and is an essential part of Sir Hargrave's plot to kidnap Harriet; Sir Charles Grandison's magnanimity makes possible his reformation and marriage to Deb Awberry in Samuel Richardson's *Sir Charles Grandison.*

Sidney Wilton   Cabinet minister to whom Endymion is promoted as private secretary; he becomes Prime Minister and grooms Endymion to be his successor in Benjamin Disraeli's *Endymion.*

Mr. Winbrooke   Cold-blooded seducer of Emily Atkins in Henry Mackenzie's *The Man of Feeling.*

Harry Winburn   Boyhood chum of Tom Brown; he becomes a poacher and social outcast, reverts to good character on joining the army, and goes to New Zealand with Henry East after marrying Patty Gibbons in Thomas Hughes's *Tom Brown at Oxford.*

Madge Winch   Maid and companion of Lady Fleetwood (Carinthia Kirby); she takes Carinthia home with her to Whitechapel after Lord Fleetwood deserts her; her character wins her the love of Gower Woodseer in George Meredith's *The Amazing Marriage.*

Sarah (Sally) Winch   The sister of Madge Winch; Lord Fleetwood's generosity in fitting a new shop out for Sally contrasts sharply with his mean treatment of his wife, Carinthia (Kirby), in George Meredith's *The Amazing Marriage.*

Frank Winchester   Earl's son who persuades George Fielding to go with him to Australia and who gives George his initial start there in Charles Reade's *It Is Never Too Late to Mend.*

Mr. Winckworth   Wealthy squire who courts Amelia Harris, prompting Mrs. Harris to withdraw her consent to Amelia's match with William Booth in Henry Fielding's *Amelia.*

Oliver Wincup   Recently married gentleman of Woodcester; he provides John Buncle with the diversion of country dances, at which he becomes briefly acquainted with new friends in Thomas Amory's *The Life of John Buncle, Esq.*

Mr. Windrush Eloquent Emersonian American preacher, much admired by John Crosthwaite and other Chartists in Charles Kingsley's *Alton Locke.*

Countess of Windsor Haughty ex-queen of England and princess of the house of Austria; she becomes embittered by her husband's abdication of the throne and her daughter's marriage to a commoner in Mary Shelley's *The Last Man.*

Jasper Wingate Cunning and conceited steward of Avenel Castle in Sir Walter Scott's *The Abbot.*

Ambrose Wingfield Lancie Wingfield's honest brother in Sir Walter Scott's *Rob Roy.*

Lancie Wingfield Ambrose Wingfield's immoral brother, who spies upon the Jacobites for clerk Joseph Jobson in Sir Walter Scott's *Rob Roy.*

Miss Wingman Volatile and light-hearted young woman, who marries Mr. Huntley in Eliza Haywood's *The History of Jemmy and Jenny Jessamy.*

Michael Wing-the-Wind The favorite attendant of James Stuart, Earl of Murray and Regent of Scotland; though elderly, he devotedly serves the earl in Sir Walter Scott's *The Abbot.*

Mr. Winkle A wharfinger and the strict father of Nathaniel Winkle; he is angry about the elopement of Nathaniel and Arabella Allen but is later reconciled to it by Arabella in Charles Dickens's *The Posthumous Papers of the Pickwick Club.*

Nathaniel Winkle Samuel Pickwick's young companion, who has a reputation for being a sportsman though he is actually inept, and who elopes with Arabella Allen in Charles Dickens's *The Posthumous Papers of the Pickwick Club.*

Winks Deputy who aids Durdles in caring for the Cloisterham Cathedral graveyard and is suspicious of John Jasper's interests in the crypts in Charles Dickens's *The Mystery of Edwin Drood.*

Annie Winnie Lame madwoman and Ailsie Gourley's crony in Sir Walter Scott's *The Bride of Lammermoor.*

Dean Winnstay Benevolent cleric and naturalist, father of Lillian and benefactor of Alton Locke; he invites Alton to his house, tutors him in natural science, and arranges for the publication of his poems after their rad-

ical content has been toned down in Charles Kingsley's *Alton Locke.*

Lillian Winnstay Beautiful, shallow daughter of Dean Winnstay; idolized by Alton Locke, she marries Alton's cousin, George Locke, and is finally worn down by sorrow, sickness, and widowhood in Charles Kingsley's *Alton Locke.*

Dr. Winslow A well-to-do, middle-aged clergyman, complacent and comfortably worldly; he is disappointed in his confident expectation that his son will marry his wealthy ward, Martha Goldthorp, in Charlotte Smith's *The Young Philosopher.*

Mrs. Winslow Dr. Winslow's fretful wife in Charlotte Smith's *The Young Philosopher.*

Middleton Winslow Dr. Winslow's foolish son, willing to marry the heiress Martha Goldthorp but insufficiently devoted, even to her money, to bother with courtship in Charlotte Smith's *The Young Philosopher.*

Mrs. Winstanly Servant-companion of Sir Thomas Sindall's mother; she is teacher of and mother figure to the Annesly children in Henry Mackenzie's *The Man of the World.*

Dean Winston Upper-class religious leader and a Latitudinarian in Mrs. Humphry Ward's *Marcella.* He helps to reunite William Ashe and his wife, Lady Kitty, as she lies dying in Switzerland in *The Marriage of William Ashe.*

Winter Artist, friend, and sage/counselor of Contarini Fleming in Benjamin Disraeli's *Contarini Fleming.*

Winter Old and faithful servant of General Witherington (Richard Tresham); he prevents the general from harming Richard Middlemas at his wife's death in Sir Walter Scott's *The Surgeon's Daughter.*

Admiral Winter Commander of Amyas Leigh and Will Carey in Ireland; he is disliked by Amyas because of his earlier cowardly behavior at the Straits of Magellan in Charles Kingsley's *Westward Ho!.*

Katie Winter Daughter of a valetudinarian father and cousin of Tom Brown, whom she visits in Oxford with Mary Porter; she marries John Hardy in Thomas Hughes's *Tom Brown at Oxford.*

Mr. Winterblossom Retired gentleman who moves in the social circle of gossips at St. Ronan's Well in Sir Walter Scott's *St. Ronan's Well.*

Lady Winterbourne Old lady who is kind to Marcella

Boyce because she has sympathy for her causes in Mrs. Humphry Ward's *Marcella*.

Giles Winterborne Grace Melbury's steadfast, honest admirer, a young timberman who becomes an itinerant worker after losing his lands through happenstance; jilted by Grace, he—although very ill—gallantly helps her escape from her faithless husband; his self-sacrificial death and noble nature assist Grace's emotional growth in Thomas Hardy's *The Woodlanders*.

Mrs. Winterfield Pious, wealthy widow expected to leave her fortune to her niece, Clara Amedroz; Captain Aylmer instead becomes her heir; Mrs. Winterfield's understanding is that he will marry Clara, but the change of beneficiary removes Lady Aylmer's satisfaction in the match in Anthony Trollope's *The Belton Estate*.

Jack Winterfield Gentleman highwayman to whom Squire Inglewood likens Francis Osbaldistone in Sir Walter Scott's *Rob Roy*.

Lord Winterset Nobleman in love with Isabel Clarendon, who refuses him in favor of the penniless Bernard Kingcote in George Gissing's *Isabel Clarendon*.

Aaron Winthrop The son of the wheelwright; when he is a boy, his mother, Dolly, takes him to sing hymns to Silas Marner; he grows up to marry Eppie in George Eliot's *Silas Marner*.

Ben Winthrop The wheelwright of Ravenloe; he is father of Aaron and husband of Dolly in George Eliot's *Silas Marner*.

Dolly Winthrop The good woman who helps Silas Marner in his efforts to raise the orphan child Eppie; her kindness forces Marner to confess the horrors of his early life, and her religious views help him to stop hoping for his idea of justice in the world in George Eliot's *Silas Marner*.

Zachary Winthrop Partner in a law firm with George Walker and clerk to the Silverbridge magistrates in Anthony Trollope's *The Last Chronicle of Barset*.

Miss Wintletop Kindly, rustic old maid, a houseguest of Lady Knollys and a treasure trove of stories about the county and its families in J. Sheridan Le Fanu's *Uncle Silas*.

Marianne Tilney, Lady Winton Sister of the drunkard Roger Delane; she is forced to accede to his demands for money in Mrs. Humphry Ward's *Harvest*.

Dutch Merchant (Count de Wintselshiem) Roxana's friend who counsels her on how to dispose of the jewels given to her by the Prince of ——; he helps her to flee to England, and after four years of searching for her, he becomes ennobled by buying a title and marries her; outraged at the discovery of Roxana's past, he comes to hate her so much that he leaves virtually nothing to her in his will in Daniel Defoe's *The Fortunate Mistress*.

Mr. Winyard Charles Arnold's benevolent uncle, who shelters the rescued Azemia and gives the favorite nephew £1500 so he can marry Azemia in William Beckford's *Azemia*.

Miss Wirt German governess to the Osborne family in William Makepeace Thackeray's *Vanity Fair*.

Wischard Monk of Saint Mary's Priory who is enlisted by the prior in a scheme to poison Hugh Woodreeve in Ann Radcliffe's *Gaston de Blondeville*.

Dr. Wiseheart Montrose's military chaplain in Sir Walter Scott's *A Legend of Montrose*.

Captain Wiseman Former irresponsible captain of the schooner *Farallone*, who died drunken and disfigured by smallpox, allowing Captain John Davies to command the schooner in Robert Louis Stevenson's *The Ebb-Tide: A Trio and a Quartette*.

Wise Woman of Sarras Seer who advises Dame Katherine how to reach the Well and gives her the beads which make the journey possible in William Morris's *The Well at the World's End*.

Wishart Captain Wiseman's first mate, who also died of smallpox aboard the schooner *Farallone* before it passed on to Captain John Davies's command in Robert Louis Stevenson's *The Ebb-Tide: A Trio and a Quartette*.

Miss Wisk Mission-minded bride-to-be of Mr. Quale in Charles Dickens's *Bleak House*.

James Wissant Calais citizen who urges Eustace St. Pierre to sacrifice his kinsmen to the English conquerors in a parable told by Charles Meekly in Henry Brooke's *The Fool of Quality*.

Peter Wissant Calais citizen who urges Eustace St. Pierre to sacrifice his kinsmen to the English victors in a parable told by Charles Meekly in Henry Brooke's *The Fool of Quality*.

Witch-Wife Kidnapper of the infant Birdalone and her captor for seventeen years in William Morris's *The Water of the Wondrous Isles*.

Witch-Wife's Sister Cruel and stupid queen of the Isle of Increase Unsought and the recipient of the Witch-

Wife's gift of the three damsels in William Morris's *The Water of the Wondrous Isles*.

Mr. Witherden   Pompous and brisk notary, who is a friend of the Garlands; he is the employer of their son, Abel, and assists the single gentleman (Trent) and the Garlands in finding Little Nell Trent and clearing Kit Nubbles in Charles Dickens's *The Old Curiosity Shop*.

Miss Witherfield   Middle-aged woman in curlpapers in Ipswich, who is courted by Peter Magnus and who is surprised when Samuel Pickwick accidentally visits her room one night at the inn where both are staying in Charles Dickens's *The Posthumous Papers of the Pickwick Club*.

Withers   Page of Mrs. Skewton in Charles Dickens's *Dombey and Son*.

Withers   Naive author of the verse epic, *The Fifth Labour of Hercules*, who is humiliated by a cruel hoax staged by fellow-Oxonians Morrison and Frewen; as a result of the humiliation he suffers, he loses his mind and drowns himself in the Isis in William Godwin's *Fleetwood*.

Miss Withers   Very old woman, who pretends to be the beautiful heiress Miss Sparkle and unsuccessfully tries to seduce Roderick Random in Tobias Smollett's *The Adventures of Roderick Random*.

Martin Wittenhaagen   Old soldier, archer to Duke Philip; he helps Gerard escape from the burgomaster, gets a pardon for Gerard and himself from the duke, cares for Margaret and her child, and dies peacefully in Rotterdam in Charles Reade's *The Cloister and the Hearth*.

Henry Wittitterly   Extravagently solicitous husband of Julia; they live an affected life in fashionable Belgravia in Charles Dickens's *The Life and Adventures of Nicholas Nickleby*.

Julia Wittitterly   Languid woman who affects delicate health; she hires Kate Nickleby as a companion; flattered by Sir Mulberry Hawk's visits, though they are painful to Kate, she becomes aware that Kate is the object of the attention and dismisses her in Charles Dickens's *The Life and Adventures of Nicholas Nickleby*.

Anne Wixted   Good-natured chambermaid at Knowl; she is tricked by Mme. de la Rougierre into obtaining brandy for her in J. Sheridan Le Fanu's *Uncle Silas*.

Mr. Wobbler   Employee in the Circumlocution Office who refuses to assist Arthur Clennam in his inquiries in Charles Dickens's *Little Dorrit*.

Captain Wogan   Legendary Highland soldier who

died valiantly; Flora MacIvor is in love with his memory and uses him as a standard for men in Sir Walter Scott's *Waverly*.

Wolf   Favored stag-greyhound at Avenel Castle; though he rescues Roland Graeme from drowning, he becomes exceedingly jealous of the pampered page in Sir Walter Scott's *The Abbot*.

Dr. Wolf   Owner and operator of Drayton House, run on the penal system; he is Edith Archbold's lover in Charles Reade's *Hard Cash*.

Miss Wolf   Hostess at Clankford, Yorkshire, where John Buncle meets an old love from his childhood, Imoinda Fox, in Thomas Amory's *The Life of John Buncle, Esq.*

Mr. Wolf   Literary man, who refers frequently to aristocratic and powerful friends eager to honor him, at the dinner Tigg Montague gives for Jonas Chuzzlewit in Charles Dickens's *The Life and Adventures of Martin Chuzzlewit*.

Wolf-hunter   American Indian mercenary of the "noble savage" type, although less noble than savage, who befriends Orlando Somerive in Charlotte Smith's *The Old Manor House*.

Wolfkettle   Mighty warrior of the Wolfings; in the last encounter he slays the Chief Captain of the Romans as the latter stabs Thiodolf in William Morris's *A Tale of the House of the Wolfings*.

Wolfram   Dishonest Abbot of St. Edmund's; his quarrel with Athelstane leads to the Saxon's near burial in Sir Walter Scott's *Ivanhoe*.

Wolfstein   Brooding German nobleman, who joins a group of bandits, becomes hardened, pursues a mutually destructive romance with Megalena de Metastasio, and is relentlessly hunted by Ginotti in Percy Bysshe Shelley's *St. Irvyne*.

Wollaston   Freethinking London publisher, who hires Mark Rutherford after Mark leaves preaching forever in Mark Rutherford's *The Autobiography of Mark Rutherford*.

Theresa Wollaston   Wollaston's musically talented and intellectual niece, who shares his free thinking and who wins Mark Rutherford's heart when she saves his job but whom he does not offer to marry because his attention is diverted by the return of Mary and Edward Mardon into his life in Mark Rutherford's *The Autobiography of Mark Rutherford*.

Cardinal Wolsey   Henry VIII's henchman, who informs Lord Percy that he may not marry Anna Boleyn in Henry Fielding's *A Journey From This World to the Next*.

Mr. Wood   Clergyman at Hay Church near Thornfield Hall, who begins the interrupted marriage ceremony between Jane Eyre and Mr. Rochester in Charlotte Brontë's *Jane Eyre*.

Mrs. Wood   Nagging wife of Owen Wood; she is murdered in the course of a robbery at their home in William Harrison Ainsworth's *Jack Sheppard*.

Alice Wood   An orphan girl who serves as Jane Eyre's handmaid while she is living in her cottage at Morton in Charlotte Brontë's *Jane Eyre*.

Mark Wood   A farmhand who is dying of consumption and who tells Agnes Grey of Mr. Weston's compassion and consideration in Anne Brontë's *Agnes Grey*.

Owen Wood   Kindly London carpenter, who adopts Jack Sheppard and Thames Darrell as infants, apprentices them to his trade, sees the one become a thief and finally hang at Tyburn, and the other, after many misfortunes, inherit title and fortune, in William Harrison Ainsworth's *Jack Sheppard*.

Winifred Wood   Owen Wood's daughter, who loves and eventually marries Thames Darrell in William Harrison Ainsworth's *Jack Sheppard*.

Mr. Woodbind   The Marquis of —'s head gardener, who catches Edward stealing carp from the fish pond in Charlotte Lennox's *The Female Quixote*.

Miss ("Celinda") Woodby   Henrietta Courteney's ugly, romantic confidante; she betrays her friend's real name and whereabouts to Lord B—, an intended ravisher, and then reports scandal about her to Lady Meadows in Charlotte Lennox's *Henrietta*.

Woodcock   Prison justice (inspector) who follows Williams's lead in approving of Hawes's cruel prison procedures in Charles Reade's *It Is Never Too Late to Mend*.

Mr. Woodcock   Dr. Blick's poor, honest curate, who is forced to support himself by selling sermons; he becomes Charles Hermsprong's friend and eventually takes over Dr. Blick's position in Robert Bage's *Hermsprong*.

Adam Woodcock   Forthright and pretentious English falconer at Avenel Castle; he believes himself a poet and a jester and plays the character of the Abbot of Unreason with bawdy relish during the masque which mocks the Monastery of St. Mary's in Sir Walter Scott's *The Abbot*.

Mrs. Woodcourt   Allan Woodcourt's mother from Wales, who has great pride in her Welsh ancestors; she discourages Esther Summerson from regarding Allan as a possible husband in Charles Dickens's *Bleak House*.

Allan Woodcourt   Dark young surgeon, who is present when the bodies of Nemo (Captain Hawdon) and Lady Dedlock are found; he befriends Richard Carstone in London, generously works among the poor, and eventually marries Esther Summerson in Charles Dickens's *Bleak House*.

Wood-father   Uncle of Bow-may and father of three "doughty" young men of the Kindred of the Wolf in William Morris's *The Roots of the Mountains*.

Emma Woodhouse   Handsome, clever, rich, and spoiled heroine, deluded in her matchmaking efforts; she nearly destroys Harriet Smith's romance with a young farmer and believes Frank Churchill to be in love with herself when he is really secretly engaged to Jane Fairfax; she comes to comprehend the dangers of her interference and is rewarded by marriage to Mr. Knightly in Jane Austen's *Emma*.

Henry Woodhouse   Amiable valetudinarian father of Emma and the well-to-do owner of Hartfield; he fancies himself and everyone around him ill and hates marriage as an agent of change in Jane Austen's *Emma*.

Miss Woodley   Kindly spinster who befriends Lady Elmwood (formerly Miss Milner) when Dorriforth abandons her in Elizabeth Inchbald's *A Simple Story*.

Mrs. Woodreeve   Wife of Hugh Woodreeve; she attempts to rescue her husband from imprisonment in Ann Radcliffe's *Gaston de Blondeville*.

Hugh Woodreeve   Bristol merchant incarcerated for accusing Gaston de Blondeville of murdering Reginald de Folville; he escapes with the help of the evil Prior of Saint Mary's only to be recaptured, tried for sorcery, and sentenced to death; vindicated by the ghost of Folville, he is released in Ann Radcliffe's *Gaston de Blondeville*.

Mary Woodruff   Faithful old servant who acts as guardian and companion to Nancy Lord in George Gissing's *In the Year of Jubilee*.

Mr. Woodseer   Gower's father, a cobbler who ministers to the poor of Whitechapel in George Meredith's *The Amazing Marriage*.

Gower Woodseer   Natural philosopher, Lord Fleetwood's secretary, and an advocate for Carinthia (Kirby), whom he accurately describes as "a beautiful Gorgon—a haggard Venus"; he marries Carinthia's maid,

Madge Winch, in George Meredith's *The Amazing Marriage*.

Abraham Woodstock Cold-hearted businessman and owner of tenements; he is grandfather of Ida Starr; he hires Osmond Waymark to collect rents and takes Ida in when she is released from prison in George Gissing's *The Unclassed*.

Wood-Sun Nonhuman "daughter of the gods," mother of Hall-Sun, and lover of Thiodolf; she disguises herself as Thorkettle in order to procure a magic, dwarf-wrought hauberk in a vain attempt to protect Thiodolf from death in battle in William Morris's *A Tale of the House of the Wolfings*.

Mr. Woodville Good-natured farmer who, in spite of his wife's objections, does not block the marriage of his daughter Charlotte to Mr. Rivers in Richard Graves's *The Spiritual Quixote*.

Mrs. Woodville Farmer's wife who unsuccessfully discourages the impecunious Mr. Rivers's courtship of her stepdaughter Charlotte in Richard Graves's *The Spiritual Quixote*.

Betsy Woodville Ill-tempered older sister of Charlotte Woodville; she is bribed by their stepmother to spy and report on Charlotte's innocent tryst with Mr. Rivers in Richard Graves's *The Spiritual Quixote*.

Charlotte Woodville Virtuous and beautiful farmer's daughter, who is wooed and won by Mr. Rivers despite the objections of her stepmother; while she and Rivers are living separately due to the terms of his university fellowship, she staves off the advances of several men; as Mrs. Rivers she greatly impresses Geoffry Wildgoose in Richard Graves's *The Spiritual Quixote*.

Bessie Woodward Clergyman's widow, whose three daughters eventually marry three civil servants in Anthony Trollope's *The Three Clerks*.

Gertrude Woodward Beloved of Henry Norman; she marries Alaric Tudor and emigrates with him to Australia after he has served a prison sentence in Anthony Trollope's *The Three Clerks*.

Katie Woodward Sweetheart of scapegrace Charley Tudor; she falls ill when her mother attempts to separate the lovers in Anthony Trollope's *The Three Clerks*.

Linda Woodward Second daughter of Bessie Woodward; she falls in love with Alaric Tudor but eventually marries Harry Norman in Anthony Trollope's *The Three Clerks*.

Mr. Woodwell The Baptist minister in Thomas Hardy's *A Laodicean*.

Wood-wicked Wood-father's son, who is killed in the battle of Silver-stead in William Morris's *The Roots of the Mountains*.

Wood-wise Son of Wood-father; archer and swordsman in the battle of Silver-stead, he is wounded in the leg in William Morris's *The Roots of the Mountains*.

Wood-wont Musical son of Wood-father; he participates in the battle of Silver-stead in William Morris's *The Roots of the Mountains*.

Captain Grenville Woolcomb Immensely wealthy young mulatto, for whom Agnes Twysden jilts Philip Firmin; he is ignorant and stingy and mistreats Agnes, who is unfaithful to him in William Makepeace Thackeray's *The Adventures of Philip on His Way through the World*.

Iris Woolstan Young widow who employs Dyce Lashmar as a tutor for her son, lends him money, and ultimately marries him but loses her money to a swindler in George Gissing's *Our Friend the Charlatan*.

Mr. Wopsle (Waldengarver) A church clerk and a friend of Mrs. Joe Gargery; he enjoys lecturing Pip Pirrip about how he should be grateful to the people who raised him; Pip and Herbert Pocket later join in the derision that Mr. Wopsle receives from the audience when, under the pseudonym Waldengarver, he plays Hamlet at a London theater in Charles Dickens's *Great Expectations*.

Mr. Wopsle's Great Aunt Mistress of an evening school in the village where Pip Pirrip takes classes; she falls asleep every evening during lessons, and the pupils have nothing to do but watch her in Charles Dickens's *Great Expectations*.

Worboys Archaelogist of ancient Greece and tutor and traveling companion to Louis Reed in George Gissing's *Sleeping Fires*.

Worldly Wiseman Counselor who tries to persuade Christian to turn back from his journey and tempts him with the things of this world in John Bunyan's *The Pilgrim's Progress From this World to That Which Is to Come*.

William Worm Rustic servant in the Swancourt household in Thomas Hardy's *A Pair of Blue Eyes*.

Marquis of Worthing Social head of the county and sympathetic to his niece, Lady Helen Seely; he helps promote Lewis Seymour's candidacy to the Academy; he is an admirer of Mrs. Campbell-Ward in George Moore's *A Modern Lover*.

Dr. Jeffrey Wortle   Kindly head of the Bowick boys' school; his determination to defend the Peacockes from calumny over their marital status brings him almost to ruin; he is harried by the gutter press and quizzed by his bishop but remains loyal throughout until the Peacockes are reinstated in his school in Anthony Trollope's *Dr. Wortle's School*.

Mrs. Jeffrey Wortle   Sunny-tempered, self-effacing wife of the head of a school; she supports her husband when he is attacked in the community for harboring the Peacockes, about whom gossip circulates concerning their marital status; she befriends Mrs. Peacocke at her most desolate phase in Anthony Trollope's *Dr. Wortle's School*.

Mary Wortle   Only daughter of Dr. Wortle; she falls in love with Lord Carstairs, a student at her father's school; she rejects his marriage proposal on grounds of his youth and rank but she accepts him at last in Anthony Trollope's *Dr. Wortle's School*.

Mr. Worts   Brewery foreman for Thomas Tappitt won over by the notion of improving the beer against his employer's wishes; he supports Butler Cornbury's bid for a seat in Parliament in Anthony Trollope's *Rachel Ray*.

Lord Henry (Harry) Wotton   Amoral, cynical, witty philosopher of decadence and decay; he helps to corrupt Dorian Gray into a depraved life of hedonism and decadence in Oscar Wilde's *The Picture of Dorian Gray*.

Captain Horatio Wragge   Wily adventurer with one green eye and one brown; he develops Magdalen Vanstone's acting talents, intending to profit from her attempts to recover her fortune by marrying her cousin, Noel Vanstone; he matches wits with Noel's cunning housekeeper, Virginie Lecount, and finally enriches himself by investing in patent medicine in Wilkie Collins's *No Name*.

Matilda Wragge   Captain Wragge's huge, slatternly wife, constantly bemused by her husband's ridicule; Magdalen Vanstone pities her and becomes her friend in Wilkie Collins's *No Name*.

Magog Wrath   Leader of the Liberal mob; he supports Mr. Millbank during the Darlford Parliamentary elections in Benjamin Disraeli's *Coningsby; or, The New Generation*.

Mrs. Wrattles   Sextonness at the church attended by Lady Alice Redcliffe in J. Sheridan Le Fanu's *Guy Deverell*.

Eugene Wrayburn   Indolent upper-class barrister, who has no clients; he falls in love with Lizzie Hexam and pursues her, stirring the jealousy of Bradley Headstone, who murderously attacks him and throws him in the river; he is rescued by Lizzie, whom he marries in Charles Dickens's *Our Mutual Friend*.

Mr. Wrench   Medical man who incorrectly diagnoses Fred Vincy's illness as unthreatening when it is actually typhoid fever in George Eliot's *Middlemarch*.

Allan Wrentmore   Dying son of Matthew Wrentmore; by changing his name to Allan Armadale, he had been made heir to a fortune out of which Fergus Ingleby had cheated him as prelude to events in Wilkie Collins's *Armadale*.

Matthew Wrentmore   Dead father of Allan; his will made the son heir to land and fortune in the West Indies on condition that he change his name to Allan Armadale, a prelude to events in Wilkie Collins's *Armadale*.

Mr. Wright   Malicious rector of Belton parish; he spreads rumors about the marital status of the Askertons in Anthony Trollope's *The Belton Estate*.

Downe Wright   The son of Mrs. Downe Wright and Lady Juliana Douglas's choice of a husband for her daughter, Mary Douglas; he eventually becomes Lord Glenallan in Susan Ferrier's *Marriage*.

Mrs. Downe Wright   The socialite matron and neighbor of Frederick, Lord Lindore and Lady Juliana Douglas, she is mother of Downe Wright, whom Lady Juliana is determined to get as a husband for Mary Douglas in Susan Ferrier's *Marriage*.

Robert Wringhim   Reformist preacher who is the close companion of Lady Dalcastle (Rabina Colwan) and suspected to be the father of Robert Colwan; he guides the younger Robert to a belief in his irreversible election and in his duty to punish the wicked in James Hogg's *The Private Memoirs and Confessions of a Justified Sinner*.

Wrybolt   Financier and trustee of Iris Woolstan's money who proposes to her and fails in business, losing her money in George Gissing's *Our Friend the Charlatan*.

Mrs. Colonel Wugsby   Lady Snuphanuph's card-playing companion in Bath with whom Samuel Pickwick plays whist in a cutthroat match in Charles Dickens's *The Posthumous Papers of the Pickwick Club*.

Jane Wugsby   Pretty younger daughter of Mrs. Colonel Wugsby in Bath; she is in love with Mr. Crawley in Charles Dickens's *The Posthumous Papers of the Pickwick Club*.

Wulf Sympathetic Goth warrior prince and sagaman, fond of Philammon; he wants his leader Amalric to abandon Pelagia and marry Hypatia; he is elected chieftain after Amalric's death in Charles Kingsley's *Hypatia*.

Osberne Wulfsson (Red Lad) Lover of Elfhild, though separated from her by the Sundering Flood; he wins fame as a warrior and eventually is united with Elfhild in William Morris's *The Sundering Flood*.

Mr. Wurley Foul-mouthed, heavy-drinking, rich squire, who refuses to heed Tom Brown's pleas for humane treatment of Harry Winburn in Thomas Hughes's *Tom Brown at Oxford*.

Lucy (L'Amour) Wyat Ill-tempered old personal servant to Silas Ruthyn; while spiteful to Silas's niece and ward, Maud Ruthyn, she knows nothing of Silas's plots against Maud in J. Sheridan Le Fanu's *Uncle Silas*.

John Wyatt Peasant boy who becomes the loyal servant of Sir Philip Harclay and, later, Edmund Lovel in Clara Reeve's *The Old English Baron*.

Dr. Wycherley Amiable but slightly mad doctor, who becomes a connoisseur of madness and makes Alfred Hardie his "pet maniac" because of his intellectual superiority in Charles Reade's *Hard Cash*.

Alexander Wyerley A gentleman whose proposal to Clarissa Harlowe is rejected because of his "free opinions"; he repeats his offer with sincere affection once Robert Lovelace's treatment of Clarissa becomes public knowledge in Samuel Richardson's *Clarissa: or, The History of a Young Lady*.

Dolly Wylder Plain but good-humored wife of William Wylder; at Rachel Lake's urging she tries to convince her husband not to trust lawyer Larkin in J. Sheridan Le Fanu's *Wylder's Hand*.

Fairy Wylder Sprightly young son of William Wylder, whom he adores and is adored by; he grows sick but recovers just as his life is despaired of in J. Sheridan Le Fanu's *Wylder's Hand*.

Mark Wylder Aggressive and conceited former sailor, heir to a Wylder fortune which may be disputed by the Brandons; he agrees to a marriage with Dorcas Brandon but disappears before it takes place; at the end it is revealed he was killed and buried by Stanley Lake, but his family motto, *resurgam* ("I will rise again"), is fulfilled when rain shifts the bank where he is buried, uncovering his hand; the smell of the corpse spooks a horse ridden by Lake, who is thrown and fatally injured in J. Sheridan Le Fanu's *Wylder's Hand*.

William Wylder Quiet, moral Gylingden vicar, brother of Mark Wylder; when having trouble with debts, he is almost manipulated out of his inheritance by lawyer Josiah Larkin but is saved by Lord Chelford and Rachel Lake in J. Sheridan Le Fanu's *Wylder's Hand*.

Joseph Wylie Mate of the *Proserpine* and sweetheart to Nancy Rouse; he scuttles the ship for £2,000 to make it possible for him to marry Nancy in Charles Reade's *Foul Play*.

Mr. Wylmot Gentleman farmer and friend of Mr. Rivers; he enables Rivers to marry Charlotte Woodville by giving the couple a house in Richard Graves's *The Spiritual Quixote*.

Fanny Wyndham Striking, spirited ward of Lord Cashel; her guardian insists that she break her engagement to Francis O'Kelly, Lord Ballindine; she refuses to marry Lord Cashel's dissipated son, Lord Kilcullen, and eventually marries Ballindine in Anthony Trollope's *The Kellys and the O'Kellys*.

Mr. Wynne The magistrate who owns De Walden Hall; his two daughters' names are linked with Robert Moore's in Charlotte Brontë's *Shirley*.

Samuel Fawthrop Wynne Profligate, vulgar, stupid son of Mr. Wynne; he unsuccessfully proposes to Shirley Keeldar in Charlotte Brontë's *Shirley*.

Talbot (Taffy) Wynne A gentleman, sportsman, and realist painter; large and strong, he enjoys physical activity with his friends and is outgoing and fashionably attired; after Billy Bagot's death, he marries Billy's sister Blanche Bagot in George Du Maurier's *Trilby*.

Charlotte, Lady Wynnstay Formidable, snobbish aunt of Hugh Flaxman; she thinks his marriage with Rose Leyburn beneath him in Mrs. Humphry Ward's *Robert Elsmere*.

Owain Wythan A neighbor of Lord Fleetwood's Welsh estate, where Carinthia (Kirby), Lady Fleetwood goes to give birth to her son; he proves a loyal friend, and after the deaths of his and Carinthia's spouses, the two marry in George Meredith's *The Amazing Marriage*.

Rebecca Wythan Owain Wythan's invalid wife; she befriends Carinthia (Kirby), Lady Fleetwood and promotes the friendship of Carinthia and Wythan on her deathbed in George Meredith's *The Amazing Marriage*.

Mr. Wyvern Clergyman of conservative views who refuses to ally himself with the Socialists in George Gissing's *Demos*.

XYZ

Dr. X Clarence Hervey's old friend, who offers wise counsel to all, and who assures Lady Delacour that her wound is easily cured in Maria Edgeworth's *Belinda*.

Prince Victor of X—— Stern eldest son of the Duke of X——; he becomes estranged from his wife, the profligate Princess Olivia, and avenges her faithlessness by having her privately executed in William Makepeace Thackeray's *The Luck of Barry Lyndon*.

Duke of X—— Pleasure-loving old prince and the Baron de Magny's friend; he has in effect abdicated duties of state to his son, Prince Victor, in William Makepeace Thackeray's *The Luck of Barry Lyndon*.

Don Francisco de Xarate Unpleasant husband of John Oxenham's mistress; he bought her from her parents in Charles Kingsley's *Westward Ho!*.

Dona de Xarate Wife of Don Francisco and mistress of John Oxenham; she is known as "the lady"; she bears Oxenham's daughter and kills herself rather than return to her husband in Charles Kingsley's *Westward Ho!*.

Xury Young Moor who is in the boat when Robinson Crusoe escapes from slavery; they become friends, and when they are rescued by a Portuguese vessel, he stays with the captain of that vessel in Daniel Defoe's *The Life and Strange Surprizing Adventures of Robinson Crusoe of York, Mariner*.

Dr. Y Officiating physician who proclaims Captain Blifil dead from apoplexy; he treats the extravagantly grieving widow for a month's imaginary illness in Henry Fielding's *The History of Tom Jones*.

Yaccombourse Ambitious mistress of Georigetti; with her lover Barbarsi, she is executed for sedition in Robert Paltock's *The Life and Adventures of Peter Wilkins*.

Yamatalallabec Prince in love with and loved by Yximilla; abandoned by those who he hoped would help him rescue her, he advises her to yield to fate in Eliza Haywood's *Adventures of Eovaai, Princess of Ijaveo*.

Yambu Black slave prince, whom Savillon befriends and with whom he institutes a more humane and equitable way of managing the slaves on his uncle's plantations in Henry Mackenzie's *Julia de Roubigné*.

Yaoua Chinese lady, author of a letter cited by Lien Chi Altangi as an example of Chinese good breeding in Oliver Goldsmith's *The Citizen of the World*.

Countess Yarmouth-Walmoden Card-playing friend of the Baroness Bernstein (Beatrix Esmond) in William Makepeace Thackeray's *The Virginians*.

Mr. Yates Foolish younger son of a nobleman and friend of Tom Bertram, whom he accompanies to Mansfield Park; he proposes the ill-fated play-acting plan and eventually elopes with Julia Bertram in Jane Austen's *Mansfield Park*.

Ydgrun Sometimes absurd and cruel omnipresent and omnipotent mythical god of the Erewhonians in Samuel Butler's *Erewhon* and in *Erewhon Revisited Twenty Years Later*.

Bishop Yeld Lazy but good-natured Bishop of Elmham who graces local tables, especially that of his neighbor Roger Carbury in Anthony Trollope's *The Way We Live Now*.

Admiral Yellowchops The long-time friend and dining companion of Dr. Redgill in Susan Ferrier's *Marriage*.

Barbara Yellowley Triptolemus Yellowley's economical sister; gaunt and unattractive, she works her servants long and feeds them little in Sir Walter Scott's *The Pirate*.

Triptolemus Yellowley Opinionated and innovative agriculturist, brought as a farming agent to the Orkney and Zetland Islands by a nobleman; he angers the locals by insisting on his own judgments and lives in constant misery because of his sister Barbara's miserliness in Sir Walter Scott's *The Pirate*.

Salvation Yeo Gunner to John Oxenham; he gives young Amyas Leigh a horn; after Oxenham's death he is tortured by the Inquisition; he escapes, tells his story to Amyas and Sir Richard Grenvile, and is killed by lightning in the Battle of the Armada in Charles Kingsley's *Westward Ho!*.

Clement (Clym) Yeobright Protagonist who returns from his travels to his native area of Egdon Heath, marries Eustacia Vye, and decides to open a school; fortune turns against him: he temporarily loses his sight from overreading and must earn a living as a furze-cutter, and then he realizes that Eustacia married him because of her error in perceiving him as a means of escape from the boredom of Egdon Heath; after the deaths of his mother and Eustacia, he becomes a lay preacher in Thomas Hardy's *The Return of the Native*.

Mrs. Yeobright   Mother of Clym Yeobright and aunt of Thomasin Yeobright; she sensibly opposes their marriages; estranged from her son, she finally tries to make amends by visiting his house; when Eustacia (Vye) does not admit her, she mistakenly believes that she is unwelcome to her son, and on her return home she dies of snakebite, exhaustion, and a broken heart in Thomas Hardy's *The Return of the Native*.

Thomasin (Tamsin) Yeobright   Pretty, gentle, true-hearted cousin of Clym Yeobright; she unwisely marries the greedy, deceitful Damon Wildeve, by whom she has a daughter; her loyalty to her husband survives ill-treatment, but after Wildeve dies, she eventually marries the devoted Diggory Venn in Thomas Hardy's *The Return of the Native*.

Lucy Yolland   Ugly, clubfooted neighbor of the Verinders; she is trusted by Rosanna Spearman and keeps secret for a year her suicide letter in Wilkie Collins's *The Moonstone. A Romance*.

Aaron Yollop   Grim clergyman spiritually called in aid in the punishment of young Zack Thorpe in Wilkie Collins's *Hide and Seek*.

Yorick   The self-conscious narrator of the journey from Calais to Paris; he writes not conventionally of sights and scenes, but of his various emotional encounters, particularly with women, in Laurence Sterne's *A The Life and Opinions of Tristram Shandy, Gentleman*.

Archbishop of York   Wise clergyman and counselor to Henry III; he suspects Gaston de Blondeville of murdering Reginald de Folville in Ann Radcliffe's *Gaston de Blondeville*.

Hesther Yorke   Hiram Yorke's strong-minded wife, who has six children to keep her very busy, and who disapproves of signs of weakness and frivolity of any kind in Charlotte Brontë's *Shirley*.

Hiram Yorke   Proud, shrewd, and blunt landowner from an old family, who attacks Matthewson Helstone because he disagrees with him politically and because he once loved Helstone's wife, Mary Cave, in Charlotte Brontë's *Shirley*.

Jessie Yorke   Pert younger daughter of Hiram Yorke and her father's pet in Charlotte Brontë's *Shirley*.

Mark Yorke   Hiram Yorke's middle son, who acts twice his years in Charlotte Brontë's *Shirley*.

Martin Yorke   Hiram Yorke's precocious younger son, who possesses a healthy imagination and develops an affection for Caroline Helstone, whom he helps to visit the wounded Robert Moore in Charlotte Brontë's *Shirley*.

Matthew Yorke   Good-looking, bad-tempered eldest son of Hiram Yorke in Charlotte Brontë's *Shirley*.

Rose Yorke   Quiet, obedient elder daughter of Hiram Yorke; she travels abroad after her sister's death in Charlotte Brontë's *Shirley*.

Anna Young   Hard, mercenary friend of Euphemia Smith; she voyages from Australia to England to give evidence of John Caldigate's marriage to Euphemia; she confesses to perjury and thereby helps clear Caldigate from a bigamy charge in Anthony Trollope's *John Caldigate*.

Lily Young   Young girl who has left a nunnery, an action that attracts Mike Fletcher before her person does; she refuses his advances as immoral; after her health fails, Mike follows her to Italy; they plan marriage but her illness is fatal in George Moore's *Mike Fletcher*.

Maria Young   Wise and resigned governess of the Grey and Rowland children; her position in life was radically altered by her father's financial reverse and an accident that left her lame; she develops an enduring friendship with Margaret Ibbotson and offers her reflections about governessing, marriage, and the role of women in Harriet Martineau's *Deerbrook*.

Young Beauty   A clever young woman of honor and principle who foils the Rake with his own weapons and suffers for it in Charles Johnstone's *Chrysal: or, The Adventures of a Guinea*.

Young Gentleman   Roxana and the brewer's youngest son, whom Amy "adopts" and who goes to work for an Italian merchant in Daniel Defoe's *The Fortunate Mistress*.

Young Hollander   Dull, spiritless son of the Old Dutchman; he leads David Balfour and Catriona Drummond to their lodgings in Leyden, Holland, in Robert Louis Stevenson's *Catriona*.

Two Young Lords   Men about town who are arrested by the Watch for drunkenness and who insist on their prerogative to do as they please in Francis Coventry's *The History of Pompey the Little*.

Young Miss   A rich young woman whose father's death prevented her marriage to the Younger Son; she elopes with him in Charles Johnstone's *Chrysal: or, The Adventures of a Guinea*.

Young Nobleman   Aurora's fortunate lover, who has an excellent character, an uncommon uprightness of heart, and a benevolent temper in Francis Coventry's *The History of Pompey the Little*.

Young preacher of Glasgow   Man falsely condemned in the murder of Mr. Blanchard through Gil-martin's assumption of his physical appearance in James Hogg's *The Private Memoirs and Confessions of a Justified Sinner*.

Young Prince (Black Prince)   Tall, handsome African captured by Captain Singleton and his men during a skirmish with natives while traveling through Africa; he is healed of his wounds to the amazement of other natives and becomes a servant and guide to Singleton in Daniel Defoe's *The Life, Adventures, and Pyracies of the Famous Captain Singleton*.

Mrs. Younge   Matron in whose care Georgiana Darcy was formerly placed and who was dismissed after her unprincipled connivance in George Wickham's attempted elopement with Miss Darcy; through Mrs. Younge Mr. Darcy traces Wickham and Lydia Bennet after their elopement to London in Jane Austen's *Pride and Prejudice*.

Younger Son   Virtuous younger son of a noble family; he loves and elopes with a Young Miss in Charles Johnstone's *Chrysal: or, The Adventures of a Guinea*.

Youwarkee (Youwee)   Pendlehamby's daughter, an ingenious and beautiful *gawry* (flying woman), who crashes into Peter Wilkins's hut, and who becomes his devoted second wife and the mother of eight of his children in Robert Paltock's *The Life and Adventures of Peter Wilkins*.

Ypres   Bad genii who assist Ochihatou in black magic; they teach the seven deadly sins in Eliza Haywood's *Adventures of Eovaai, Princess of Ijaveo*.

Yram   Jailer's daughter, who is the first to befriend Jack Higgs; she helps him learn the Erewhonian language and explains the Erewhonian belief that illness is a crime; she jealously shields him from townspeople and is sad upon his leaving jail to meet the king in Samuel Butler's *Erewhon*. An influential mayoress, now the mother of Jack Higgs's son, George Strong, she is skeptical about Sunchildism and is considered dangerous by Sukop and Sukoh; she helps Higgs escape from Erewhon in *Erewhon Revisited Twenty Years Later*.

Alfred Yule   Hard-working veteran writer and scholar, who fails to gain the editorship he wants, goes blind, and must be cared for by his daughter, Marian, in George Gissing's *New Grub Street*.

Edmund Yule   The youngest of the Yule brothers and father of Amy Reardon; he leaves his wife and two children a modest income when he dies in George Gissing's *New Grub Street*.

Mrs. Edmund Yule   Amy Reardon's conventional-minded mother, to whose house Amy goes after she leaves her husband in George Gissing's *New Grub Street*.

John Yule   The eldest and most prosperous of the Yule brothers; he leaves a sizable estate when he dies in George Gissing's *New Grub Street*.

Marian Yule   Faithful assistant in her father's work as a writer; she hopes to free herself from editorial drudgery when she is told she has inherited money; she becomes engaged to Jasper Milvain, but he leaves her when her inheritance falls through; she becomes a librarian in the provinces, forced to support her mother and her blind father in George Gissing's *New Grub Street*.

Yximilla   Princess who ascended the throne of Ginsky after the death of her father; in love with Yamatalallabec, she is tortured by Tygrinonniple and forced to marry Broscomin in Eliza Haywood's *Adventures of Eovaai, Princess of Ijaveo*.

Dr. Z   Officiating physician who proclaims Captain Blifil dead of epilepsy; he treats the extravagantly distressed widow for a month's imaginary illness in Henry Fielding's *The History of Tom Jones*.

M. Z——   A polite Frenchman, who dines with M. Home de Bassompierre and speaks to his daughter, Paulina, in Charlotte Brontë's *Villette*.

Zadisky   Sir Philip Harclay's loyal Greek servant, who escorts Sir Walter Lovel into banishment in Clara Reeve's *The Old English Baron*.

Evadne Zaimi   Proud daughter of the Greek ambassador to England; destitute, she must support herself as a designer and a painter; she becomes the lover of Lord Raymond in Mary Shelley's *The Last Man*.

Zambo   Black man who remains loyal to the Challenger expedition and helps to keep its participants supplied for part of their time on the plateau in Arthur Conan Doyle's *The Lost World*.

Zamgrad   Officer and messenger in Schemzeddin's

court; Nourjahad gives him a diamond in exchange for fidelity and friendship; he is reported by Cadiga to have died during Nourjahad's second sleep in Frances Sheridan's *The History of Nourjahad*.

Nicola di Zampari   Companion to the evil Father Schedoni (Ferando di Bruno) and later discovered to be the mysterious monk who warns Vincentio di Vivaldi away from Villa Altieri; ultimately he is poisoned by Schedoni and dies in Ann Radcliffe's *The Italian*.

Franceso Zampieri   Mysterious stranger who imparts to Reginald de St. Leon the secrets of eternal life and multiplying gold in William Godwin's *St. Leon*.

Zanoni   Possessor of the wisdom of the Chaldean Brotherhood; he influences the destiny of Clarence Glyndon and many others; he surrenders his own immortality for the love of Viola Pisani in Edward Bulwer-Lytton's *Zanoni*.

Signor Zappi   Nobleman who aids the wandering Leonardo di Loredani in Charlotte Dacre's *Zofloya; or, The Moor*.

Signora Zappi   Noblewoman who attempts to seduce Leonardo di Loredani but is rejected in Charlotte Dacre's *Zofloya; or, The Moor*.

Zara   Daughter of the Muscovite general who captures Count de Beaumont; she falls in love with the count but dies of grief when he refuses to forget his wife, Belinda (Madam de Beaumont), in Penelope Aubin's *The Life of Madam de Beaumont*.

Zarah (Fenella)   Dark-skinned, diminutive train bearer to Charlotte de la Tremouille, the Countess of Derby; a spy for Edward Christian against the Countess, she tries to detach Julian Peveril from Alice; she discovers that Edward Christian is her real father in Sir Walter Scott's *Peveril of the Peak*.

Zastrozzi   Gothic villain and atheist, who plots against Verezzi to avenge his mother's betrayal at the hands of Verezzi's father in Percy Bysshe Shelley's *Zastrozzi*.

Zee   A Gy (woman) of a community of Vril-ya and a professor in the College of Sages; she loves the Tish and helps him escape destruction at the hands of the Tur in Edward Bulwer-Lytton's *The Coming Race*.

Ferdinand Zeilnitz   Matilda di Laurentini's German servant, who lies to protect her in Percy Bysshe Shelley's *Zastrozzi*.

Don Diego de Zelos   Castilian nobleman who disguises himself as a Persian named Ali Beker in Paris, where he tells Ferdinand his life story; he suffers guilt for killing his daughter's lover and then poisoning his wife and daughter, Serafina; robbed by Ferdinand and abandoned without resources, he is saved from brigands by Renaldo de Melvil, whom he discovers to be the man he thought he murdered in Spain; he finds his daughter alive and well in London, and he marries Madam Clement in Tobias Smollett's *The Adventures of Ferdinand Count Fathom*.

Serafina (Monimia) de Zelos   Daughter of Don Diego; separated from her lover, Renaldo de Melvil, by Ferdinand in London, she is believed to have died from Ferdinand's mistreatment; she reveals herself to Renaldo as a ghost in her tomb and explains her real identity to her father, relieving him of his guilt; she marries Renaldo after forgiving Ferdinand in Tobias Smollett's *The Adventures of Ferdinand Count Fathom*. She appears as the Countess de Melville in *The Expedition of Humphry Clinker*.

Zeno   Emperor of Thrace, with whom Julian the Apostate ingratiates himself to the exalted position of general in Henry Fielding's *A Journey From This World to the Next*.

Lady Zenobia   Garrulous queen of London society hostesses in Benjamin Disraeli's *Endymion*.

Mlle. Zephyrine   One of the teachers at Mlle. Reuter's school, who stands out because she is more of a Parisian coquette than the others in Charlotte Brontë's *The Professor*.

Zerubbabel   A Jew who attempts to convert Charles Reding as he is about to become a Roman Catholic in John Henry Newman's *Loss and Gain*.

Count Zigzaggi   Italian nobleman who becomes patron of Og of Basan in Naples; he receives two striking paintings on antediluvian subjects produced by Og and Andrew Gulph as repayment for his generosity in William Beckford's *Biographical Memoirs of Extraordinary Painters*.

Zillah   Maidservant at Wuthering Heights who relates the death of Linton Heathcliff in Emily Brontë's *Wuthering Heights*.

Zillah   Lucilla Finch's old nurse in Wilkie Collins's *Poor Miss Finch*.

Zofloya   The noble Moor in turban and jewels, who serves Henriquez and later Victoria di Loredani; he finally reveals himself as Satan in Charlotte Dacre's *Zofloya; or, The Moor*.

Zoroaster   Former boxer and member of the Gypsy gang in William Harrison Ainsworth's *Rookwood*.

Zosimus   Elderly, bigoted patriarch of the Greek

Church; in exchange for his support of the flagging throne, he extracts extensive favors from the Emperor Alexius Comnenus in Sir Walter Scott's *Count Robert of Paris.*

Antonio Zucchi   Venetian painter, who aids the career of Angelica Kauffmann and finally marries her years after her disastrous entanglement with Frederick DeHorn in Anne Thackeray Ritchie's *Miss Angel.*

Zulika   Glanlepze's devoted wife in Robert Paltock's *The Life and Adventures of Peter Wilkins.*

Apollonia Zulmer   Venetian countess, a woman scorned, who lets her passions overcome her reason and manipulates her lover's wife into sin by pretended friendship and the aid of nontraditional books in Charlotte Dacre's *The Passions.*

Index

A name in brackets indicates an additional name by which the character can be located in the Dictionary.

William Harrison Ainsworth (1805-1882)

Jack Sheppard (1839)—JHi
Quilt Arnold
Edgeworth Bess
Blueskin
Thames Darrell
Mynheer Van Galgebrook
Baptist Kettleby
William Kneebone
Polly Maggot
Abraham (Nab) Mendez
Terence (Terry) O'Flaherty
Joan Sheppard [Constance Trenchard]
John (Jack) Sheppard
Mrs. Spurling
Sir Cecil Trafford
Aliva Trenchard
Sir Rowland Trenchard
Jonathan Wild
Mrs. Wood
Owen Wood
Winifred Wood

Rookwood (1834)—JHi
Agnes
Hugh Badger
Balthazar
Black Bess
Father Checkley [Father Ambrose]
Codicil Coates
Handassah
Conkey Jem
Jerry Juniper
Knight of Malta
Barbara Lovel
Sybil Lovel
Major Mowbray
Eleanor Mowbray
Eleanor Rookwood Mowbray
Alan Rookwood [Peter Bradley]
Eleanor, Lady Rookwood
Luke Rookwood [Luke Bradley]
Maud D'Aubeny, Lady Rookwood
Sir Piers Rookwood
Ranulph Rookwood
Sir Reginald Rookwood
Susan Rookwood [Susan Bradley]
Dr. Polycarp Small
Richard (Dick) Turpin
Dr. Titus Tyrconnel

Zoroaster

Thomas Amory (1691?-1788)

The Life of John Buncle, Esq (1756, 1766)—GS
Mrs. Asgill
Mrs. Benlow
Carola Bennet
Bob Berrisfort
Juliet Berrisfort
John Bruce
John Buncle (the elder)
John Buncle
Mr. Burcot
Azora Burcot
Mr. Burke
Cantalupe
Agnes de Castra
Christopher
Tom Clancy
Old Cock
Belinda Coote
Maria Coote
Alcmena Cox
Mrs. Crafton
Antonia Cranmer
Edmund Curll
Frederic Dancer
Old Dunk
Agnes Dunk
Mr. Dunkley
Orlando Eustace
Downe Falvey
Dr. Fitzgibbons
Julia Fitzgibbons
Sir Loghlin Fitzgibbons
Friar Fleming
Jemmy Fleming
Tom Fleming
Antonia Fletcher
Miss Fox
Imoinda Fox
Tom Gallagher
Jack Gallaspy
Pierce Gavan
Mr. Harcourt
Eusebia Harcourt
Mr. Henley
Charles Henley (1)
Charles Henley (2)
Statia Henley
Miss Hinxworth

Claudius Hobart
Mrs. Hunfleet
Charles Hunt
Elizabeth Hunt
Martha Jacquelot
Jemmy King
Alithea Llansoy
Mr. (Ugly) Makins
John Mansel
Charlotte Melmoth
Mr. Monaghan
Avery Moncton
Martin Murdoch
Paddy (Little Beau) Murphy
John Nixon
Harriet Noel
Terelah O Crohane
Soto O'Fin
Mrs. O'Hara
Mr. O'Keefe
Old Doctor
Mr. O'Regan
John Orton
Antiope Pearson
John Price
Jack Railton
Ralph
Mr. Ribble
Mr. Richmond
Leonora Sarsfield
Maria Spence
Dr. Stanvil
Mr. Tench
Mrs. Thurloe
Martha Tilston
Tim
Miss Turner
Charles Turner
Agnes Vane
Miss Veyssiere
Dorick Watson
Dr. Whaley
Whitwell
Oliver Wincup
Miss Wolf

Penelope Aubin (1685-1731)

The Life and Adventures of the Lady Lucy (1726)—KW
Lady Abbess
Henrietta Albertus
Lewis Augustus Albertus

Sir Marmaduke Manchet
Lady Harriet Marlow
Citizen Moutard
Oglow Muley
Muzzled-Abi
Hannah Pegham
Mrs. Periwinkle
Sally Periwinkle
Courtney Perkly
Dr. Prose
Paridel Puffwell
Mrs. Quackly
Rebecca
Lord Scudabout
Solomon Sheeppen
Dr. Squably
Walter Waglock
James Walling
Captain Josiah Wappingshot
Mr. Wildcodger
Mrs. Wildcodger
Mr. Winyard

Biographical Memoirs of Extraordinary Painters (1780)–DJN
Monsieur Baise-la-main
Benboaro Benbacaio
Blunderbussiana
Rouzinski Blunderbussiana
Andrea Boccadolce
Mynheer Bootersac
Princess Dolgoruki
Gerard Dow
Princess Ferdinanda Joanna Maria
Cardinal Grossocavallo
Andrew Guelph
Jean Hemmelinck
Insignificanti
Joan Jablinouski
The Jew
Clod Lumpewitz
Anthony Aldrovandus Magnus
Madam Merian
Francis Van Cuyck de Mierhop
Mieris
Og of Basan
John Ogilby
George Podebrac
Joseph Porta
Soorcrout
Adam Spindlemans
Ann Spindlemans
Sucrewasser of Vienna
Maid of Tivoli

Burgomaster Van Gulph
Madam Van Gulph
Jeremy Watersouchy
Count Zigzaggi

Modern Novel Writing; or, the Elegant Enthusiast (1796)–DJN
Don Gomez d'Aldova
Mr. Bangrove
Mr. Barlow
General Barton
Lady Barton
Lord Belgrave
Mr. Beloe
Chevalier de Berlingier
Captain Beville
Mr. Bilbo
Colonel Frank Birch
Lawyer Blackingson
Arabella Bloomville
Bridget Cawthorne
Mr. Chapman
Lord Damplin
Sir Paul Danbury
Lucy Danton
Sir George Darlington
Jack Deepley
Mrs. De Malthe
Philip Duvergois
Earl of Fairville
Wilhelmina, Countess of Fairville
Ferguson
Miss Ford
Earl of Frolicsfun
Gabble
Mr. Gifford
Amelia de Gonzales
Don Pedro de Gonzales
Margaret Grimes
Adeline de Guides
Lucinda Howard
Mr. Ireland
Jennings
Lady Maria Jones
Colonel Lambert
Henry Lambert
Lady Maria Lambert
Tommy Lambert
Lady Langly
Father Laurence
Miss Macnamara
Lord Mahogany
Mrs. Maleverer
Mrs. Maltrever

Mr. Mandrake
Mrs. Mandrake
Maria Helen
Lady Harriet Marlow
Marquis of Mushroom
La Contessa Negri
Marchioness of Oakley
Lord Charles Oakley
Mr. Oldfield
Old Man
Mrs. Ormsby
Peter Perkins
Dr. Sanderson
Sukey Saunders
Sam Slybore
Mr. Squares
Peggy Tomlinson
Count Velasquez
Sir Sidney Walker
Mrs. Wallingford
Miss Warley
Dorothy Webster

Vathek (1815)–DJN
Bababalouk
Cafour
Princess Carathis
Soliman Ben Daoud
Dilara
Eblis
Emir Fakreddin
The Giaour
Good old Genius
Gulchenrouz
Ali Hassan
Morakanabad
Motavakel
Al Mouhateddin
Nerkes
Nouronihar
Shaban
Edris al Shafei
Shepherd
Sutlememe
Caliph Vathek

Aphra Behn (1640?-1689)
The Fair Jilt (1688)–RSm
Alcidiana
Cornelia
Prince Henrik
Miranda
Prince Tarquin
Van Brune

Wilmot
Mr. Wilson
M. Z––

Emily Brontë (1818-1848)

Wuthering Heights (1847)–TW
Ellen (Nelly) Dean
Mr. Earnshaw
Catherine Earnshaw
Frances Earnshaw
Hareton Earnshaw
Hindley Earnshaw
Heathcliff
Linton Heathcliff
Joseph
Catherine Linton
Edgar Linton
Isabella Linton
Mr. Lockwood
Zillah

Frances Brooke (1724-1789)

The History of Emily Montague (1769)–JS
Mrs. Clayton
Sir George Clayton
Arabella Fermor
Captain William Fermor
Captain Fitzgerald
Mrs. Melmoth
Emily Montague
Colonel Ed. Rivers
Lucy Rivers
Mme. des Roches
John Temple
Fanny Williams
Colonel Willmott

The History of Lady Julia Mandeville
(1763)–JS
Lady Belmont
Lord Belmont
Lady Julia Belmont [Lady Julia
    Mandeville]
Lady Mary Belmont
Colonel Belville
Lord Fondville
Bell Hastings
Emily Howard
Colonel John Mandeville
Henry Mandeville
Countess Melespini
Lord Melvin
George Mordaunt
Lord Rochdale

Westbrook
Miss Westbrook
Lady Anne Wilmot

Henry Brooke (1703?-1783)

The Fool of Quality (1765-1770)–DJN
Princess Abenaide of Morocco
Emperor Abenamin of Morocco
Abencerrage
John de Aire
Earl of Albemarle
Mr. Andrew
Araspes
Mr. Archibald
Eloisa, Marchioness D'Aubigny
Lewis, Marquis D'Aubigny
Barnaby Boniface
(Jemmy) Lord Bottom
Robert Callan
Marmaduke Catharines
Lady Childish
Mrs. Clement
Arabella Graves Clement
Bartholomew Clement
(Sergeant) Hammel (Hammy) Clem-
    ent (Stapleton)
Richard (Dicky) Clement
Eloisa Clinton
Harriet Clinton
Harry (Henry) Clinton
Henry (Harry, Dada) Clinton [Mr.
    Fenton]
Jacky Clinton
Louisa D'Aubigny Clinton
Lady Cloudy
Sir Christopher Cloudy
Sergeant Craw
Humphrey Cypher
Cyrus
Tommy Damer
Mr. De Wit
Jonathan Delvile
Goodman Gaffer Dobson
Nurse Kate Dobson
Mr. Fielding
Mrs. Fielding
Edward (Neddy or Ned) Fielding
Lord Flippant
Mr. Frank
Lady Gentle
Mr. Gentle
Mr. Giles
Mr. Golding

Matilda (Matty) Golding
Fanny Goodall (Countess of Mait-
    land, Marchioness D'Aubigny)
Mr. Goodville
Anthony Granger
Mrs. Graves
Mrs. Hannah
Sir Freestone Hardgrave
Harriet
Mr. Heartless
Hercules
Miss Hodgins
Mr. Hollow
Giffard Homely
Peggy Granger Homely
Mr. James
Rose Jenkins
Mrs. Jennett
John
Colonel Jolly
Maria (Pierre) de Lausanne
Lord Lechmore
Edward Longfield
Miss Lovely
Madame Maintenon
Earl of Maitland
Lady Mansfield
Lord Mansfield
Louisa Mansfield
Mr. Marfelt
Sir Walter Mauny
Charles Meekly
Mrs. Mirror
Mr. Mole
Richard Clinton, first Earl of More-
    land
Richard Clinton, second Earl of
    Moreland
Richard (Dicky) Clinton, third Earl
    of Moreland
Mrs. Neighborly
Mr. Niggards
Panthea
Gatty Patience
Peter Patience
Hector Pluck
Lord Portland
Lord Prim
Lady Jane Quirp
Mr. Roche
Mr. Ruth
Belinda Ruth
Harry Ruth

Eustace St. Pierre
Mr. Scruple
Major Settle
Mr. Sink
Skinker
Deborah Skinner
Mr. Snack
Mr. Snarle
Mr. Spelling
Colonel Standard
Sir Standish Stately
Ann (Nanny) Roche Stern
Diana Stern
Tom Stern
Lord Stivers
Squire Sulky
Mrs. Susan
Benjamin Testy
Master Billy, Sir William Thornhill
Sir Spranger Thornhill
Barnabas (Barnaby, John) Tirrel
Eleanor (Nelly) Damer Tirrel
Tommy Truck
Miss Uppish
Mr. Veer
Mr. Vindex
Susanna Vindex
Signor Volanti
Walter Warmhouse
Mr. Weldon
Mr. Wellcot
Miss Willow
James Wissant
Peter Wissant

Edward Bulwer-Lytton (1803-1873)

Alice (1838)—BJD
Edward Aubrey
Mr. Cleveland
Castruccio Caesarini
Alice Darvil
Monsieur DeMontaigne
Teresa DeMontaigne
Lord Doltimore
Gustavus Douce
Lumley Ferrers
Sarah Elton
Mr. Howard
George Legard
Mrs. Leslie
Ernest Maltravers
Mrs. Merton
Caroline Merton

Charles Merton
Valerie de St. Ventadour
Lord Saxingham
Evelyn Templeton
Richard Templeton
Eleanor Westbrook
Mary Westbrook

The Caxtons (1849)—BJD
Marquess of Castleton
Austin Caxton
Blanche Caxton
Herbert Caxton
Katharine (Kitty) Caxton
Pisistratus Caxton
Roland Caxton
John (Uncle Jack) Tibbetts
Fanny Trevanion

The Coming Race (1871)—BJD
Aph-Lin
Bra
Lo
Tae
The Tish
Tur
Zee

Devereux (1829)—BJD
Isora D'Alverez
Signor Bezoni
Jean Desmarais
Countess Devereux
Aubrey Devereux
Gerald Devereux
Morton Devereux
William Devereux
Julian Montreuil
Marie Osward

Ernest Maltravers (1837)—BJD
Castruccio Caesarini
Mr. Cleveland
Monsieur DeMontaigne
Teresa DeMontaigne
Alice Darvil [Lady Vargrave]
Luke Darvil
Lumley Ferrers [Lord Vargrave]
Lady Florence Lascelles
Ernest Maltravers
Lord Saxingham
Valerie de St. Ventadour
Evelyn Templeton [Evelyn Cameron]

Richard Templeton [Lord Vargrave]

Eugene Aram (1832)—BJD
Eugene Aram
Jacob Bunting
Peter Dealtry
Richard Houseman
Ellinor Lester
Geoffrey Lester [Daniel Clarke]
Madeline Lester
Rowland Lester
Walter Lester

Godolphin (1833)—BJD
Constance Vernon, Countess of Erpingham
Percy Godolphin
Fanny Millinger
Stainsforth Radclyffe
Lord Saltstream
Augustus Saville
Volktman
Lucilla Volktman

The Last Days of Pompeii (1834)—BJD
Apaecides
Arbaces
Calenus
Marcus Clodius
Glaucus
Ione
Julia
Nydia
Olinthus
Saga
Sallust

Lucretia (1846)—BJD
John Ardworth
Beck [Vincent Braddell]
Lucretia Clavering
Olivier Dalibard
Helen Mainwaring
William Mainwaring
Susan Mivers
Miles St. John
Percival St. John
Gabriel Varney
Charles Vernon

"My Novel," by Pisistratus Caxton (1852)—BJD
Leonora Avenel

John Cleland (1710-1789)

Memoirs of a Woman of Pleasure (1748-1749)—JB
Phoebe Ayres
Mr. Barvile
Mrs. Brown
Mrs. Cole
Mr. Crofts
Esther Davis
Good-natured Dick
Emily
Mr. H——
Harriet
Frances (Fanny) Hill
Mrs. Jones
Louisa
Mr. Norbert
Charles O——
Will

Wilkie Collins (1824-1889)

Armadale (1866)—RCT
Allan Armadale
Felix Bashwood
James (Jemmy) Bashwood
Mrs. Blanchard
Jane Blanchard
Decimus Brock
Dr. Downward
Lydia Gwilt
Mr. Hawbury
Fergus Ingleby
Captain Manuel
Ozias Midwinter
Major Milroy
Mrs. Milroy
Eleanor (Neelie) Milroy
Mr. Neal
Maria Oldershaw
Mr. Pedgift
Mr. Pedgift (the younger)
Mrs. Pentecost
Samuel Pentecost
Allan Wrentmore
Matthew Wrentmore

Basil: A Story of Modern Life (1852)—AB
Basil
Basil's Father
John Bernard
Clara
Robert Mannion
Susan Penhale
William Penhale

Ralph
Mr. Sherwin
Mrs. Sherwin
Margaret Sherwin

Heart and Science (1883)—AB
Mr. Baccani
Lemuel Benjulia
Dr. Nathan Benjulia
Cook
Mr. Gallilee
Maria Gallilee
Maria Graywell Gallilee
Zoe (Zo) Gallilee
Carmina Graywell
Robert Graywell
Mr. Le Frank
Marcelline
Frances Minerva
Mr. Mool
Mr. Morphew
Lord Northlake
Susan Graywell, Lady Northlake
Mr. Null
Teresa
Ovid Vere

Hide and Seek (1854)—AB
Mr. Blyth
Lavinia-Ada (Lavvie) Blyth
Valentine Blyth
Dowager Countess of Brambledown
Mr. Bullivant
Mr. Gimble
Mr. Goodworth
Ellen Gough
Joanna Grice
Joshua Grice
Mary (Madonna) Grice
Mat (Marksman) Grice
Jane Holdsworth
Mr. Joyce
Mr. Jubber
Martha Peckover
Mrs. Thorpe
Zack Thorpe
Zachary Thorpe [Arthur Carr]
Aaron Yollop

The Law and the Lady (1875)—AB
Ariel
Helena Beauly
Mr. Benjamin

Lady Brydehaven
Lady Clarinda
Miserrimus Dexter
Major Fitz-David
Miss Hoighty
Andrew Kirlay
Mrs. Macallan
Eustace Macallan
Sara Macallan
Valeria Brinton, Mrs. Eustace Macallan (also Woodville)
Christina Ormsay
Phoebe
Mr. Playmore
Mr. Starkweather

Man and Wife (1870)—AB
Mr. Babchild
Mr. Bishopriggs
Arnold Brinkworth
Geoffrey Delamayn
Hester Limbrick Dethridge
Joel Dethridge
Mrs. Glenarm
Mr. Delamayn, Lord Holchester
Julian Delamayn, Lord Holchester
Mr. Kendrew
Reuben Limbrick
Blanche Lundie
Blanche, Lady Lundie
Julia, Lady Lundie
Sir Patrick Lundie
Sir Thomas Lundie
Mr. Moy
Captain Newenden
Lady Jane Parnell
Perry
Anne, "Mrs." Silvester (Mrs. John Vanborough)
Anne Silvester
Mr. Speedwell
John Vanborough

The Moonstone. A Romance (1868)—RCT
The Misses Ablewhite
Mr. Ablewhite
Mrs. Ablewhite
Godfrey Ablewhite
Gabriel Betteredge
Penelope Betteredge
Franklin Blake
Matthew Bruff
Thomas Candy
Drusilla Clack

Count Tag
Counsellor Tanturion
Lady Tempest
Theodosia
Betty Trollop
Two Young Lords
Watchman
Mrs. Wilkins
Williams
Young Nobleman

Charlotte Dacre (1782-1841?)

The Libertine (1807)—VB
Agnes D'Albini (Ida)
Angelo D'Albini
Felix D'Albini
Cecile Bertrand
Pierre Bouffuet
Claudio
Ellesmere
Fitzgarden
Madame la Marquise
Paulina Mezzotetto
Milborough
Montmorency
Gabrielle di Montmorency
    (D'Albini)
Oriana
Promlino
Marquis St. Evremond
Baron Steinhaussen
Baroness Steinhaussen
Darlowitz Steinhaussen
Il Conte Verospi
Fiorenza de Vinci

The Passions (1811)—VB
Count Darlowitz
Amelia Darlowitz
Catherine Glatz
Madame de Hautville
Jeanette
Pietro Mondovi
Pierre
Baron Rosendorf
Duchess de Sternach
Count Wiemar
Julia Wiemar
Apollonia Zulmer

Zofloya; or, The Moor (1806)—VB
Count Ardolph
Il Conte Berenza
Catau

Ginotti
Henriquez
Latoni
Lilla
Marchese di Loredani
Laurina di Loredani
Leonardo di Loredani
Victoria di Loredani
Signora di Modena
Nina
Megalena Strozzi
Signor Zappi
Signora Zappi
Zofloya

Mary Davys (1674-1732)

The Reform'd Coquet (1724)—MAS
Alanthus (Formator)
Altemira
Amoranda
Arentia
Biranthus (Berentha)
Callid
Froth
Jenny
Lord Lofty
E. Traffick

Daniel Defoe (1660-1731)

The Fortunate Mistress (1724)—AGL
Amy (Cherry, Mrs. Amy, Madam
    Collins)
Amy's Gentleman
Brewer
Brewer's Brother-In-Law
Brewer's Sister
Sir Robert Clayton
Prince of —— (Count de Clerac)
Good Poor Woman
Jewish Jeweller
Isabel Johnson
Landlord
Little Son of Honour
Lord——
Princess of ——
Quaker Gentlewoman
Roxana (Susan, Mlle. Beleau,
    Countess de Wintselsheim)
Susan (Susanna)
Thomas
Dutch Merchant (Count de
    Wintselshiem)
Young Gentleman

The Fortunes and Misfortunes of the Famous Moll Flanders (1722)—AGL
Bank Clerk
Baronet ("handsome Sir ——")
Captain
Captain's Widow
Jemy (James) E
Elder Brother
Moll (Mary) Flanders (Mrs. Betty,
    Lady Cleave, Gabriel Spencer)
Gentleman Draper
Gentleman of Bath
Gentlewoman
North Country Gentlewoman
Humphrey (the elder)
Humphrey
Anthony Johnson
Minister
Mistress Nurse
Mother Midnight (Mrs. B——, "the
    governess")
Robin (Robert, Brother Robin)

The History and the Remarkable Life of the Truly Honourable Colonel Jacques, Commonly Call'd Col. Jack (1722)—AGL
Bill Collector
Clerk of the Custom-House
Constable
French Captain
Gilliman
Mrs. Housekeeper
Major Anthony Jack
Captain Jack ("horrid Jack")
Colonel Jack (John, Colonel
    Jacque, Monsieur Charnot, Monsieur Charnock)
Colonel Jack's Second Wife
Colonel Jack's Third Wife
Mrs. Margaret (Moggy)
Marquis
Master
Mouchat
Nurse
Robin
Mrs. Smith
Tutor
Will

A Journal of the Plague Year (1722)—AGL
John Cock
Constable
Solomon Eagle

Tom Pinch
Mr. Pip
Elijah Pogram
Betsey Prig
Zephaniah Scadder
Chevy (Chiv) Slyme
Putnam Smif
Sophia
Mr. Spottletoe
Mrs. Spottletoe
Paul (Poll) Sweedlepipe
Tamaroo
Mark Tapley
Montague Tigg [Tigg Montague]
Mrs. Todgers
John Westlock
Mr. Wolf

The Life and Adventures of Nicholas Nickleby (1837-1839)—RC
Miss Belvawney
Miss Bravassa
Madeline Bray
Walter Bray
Brooker
John Browdie
Charles Cheeryble
Edwin Cheeryble
Frank Cheeryble
Mr. Crowl
Mrs. Crummles
Charles Crummles
Ninetta Crummles (The Infant Phenomenon)
Percy Crummles
Vincent Crummles
Mr. Folair
Mr. Gregsbury
Arthur Gride
Mrs. Grudden
Sir Mulbery Hawk
Mr. Kenwigs
Morleena Kenwigs
Susan Kenwigs
Miss Knag
Miss LaCreevy
Miss "Led" Ledbrook
Mrs. Lenville
Thomas Lenville
Mr. Lillyvick
Miss Linkinwater
Tim Linkinwater
Madame Mantalini
Alfred Mantalini

Mrs. Nickleby
Kate Nickleby
Nicholas Nickleby
Ralph Nickleby
Newman Noggs
Henrietta Petowker
Mr. Pluck
Matilda ('Tilda) Price
Mr. Pyke
Peg Sliderskew
Smike
Mr. Snawley
Mrs. Snawley
Miss Snevellicci
Mrs. Squeers
Fanny Squeers
Wackford Squeers
Master Wackford Squeers
Lord Frederick Verisopht
Henry Wittitterly
Julia Wittitterly

Little Dorrit (1855-1857)—AW
Mrs. Bangham
Clarence Barnacle
Lord Decimus Tite Barnacle
Ferdinand Barnacle
Tite Barnacle
Mrs. Tite Barnacle (née Stilt-stalking)
William Barnacle
Madame Barronneau
Henri Barronneau
Harriet Beadle [Tattycoram]
Bob
Christopher Casby
Jean Baptist Cavalleto
Mr. Chivery
Mrs. Chivery
John Chivery
Mrs. Clennam
Arthur Clennam
Mrs. Dorrit
Amy (Little Dorrit) Dorrit
Edward (Tip) Dorrit
Fanny Dorrit
Frederick Dorrit
William Dorrit
Daniel Doyce
Flora Finching
Mr. F's (Finching's) Aunt
Affery Flintwich
Ephraim Flintwich
Jeremiah Flintwich

Mrs. General
Mrs. Gowan
Henry Gowan
Dr. Haggage
Jenkinson
Maggy
Captain Maroon
Mr. Meagles
Mrs. Meagles
Minnie (Pet) Meagles
Mr. Merdle
Mrs. Merdle
Mr. Nandy
Mr. Pancks
Mr. Plornish
Sally Plornish
M. Rigaud (Blandois/Lagnier)
Miss Rugg
Mr. Rugg
Slingo
Edmund Sparkler
Lord Lancaster Stiltstalking
Mrs. Tickit
Mr. Tinkler
Miss Wade
Mr. Wobbler

The Mystery of Edwin Drood (1870)—RC
Mr. Bazzard
Mrs. Billickin
Rosa Bud
Jack Chinaman
Mrs. Crisparkle
Septimus Crisparkle
Dick Datchery
Edwin Drood
Durdles
Hiram Grewgious
Luke Honeythunder
John Jasper
Helena Landless
Neville Landless
Princess Puffer
Ethelinda Brobity Sapsea
Thomas Sapsea
Lieutenant Tarter
Mrs. Tisher
Mr. Tope
Mrs. Tope
Miss Twinkleton
Winks

The Old Curiosity Shop (1841)—AW
The Bachelor

Mr. Barkis
Charley
Mr. Chestle
Mr. Chillip
Clickett (The Orfling)
David (Daisy, Trotwood, Doady)
  Copperfield
Miss Creakle
Mr. Creakle
Mrs. Creakle
Caroline Crewler
Horace Crewler
Mrs. Horace Crewler
Louisa Crewler
Lucy Crewler
Margaret Crewler
Sarah Crewler
Sophy Crewler
Mrs. Crupp
Rosa Dantle Dartle
George Demple
Mr. Dolloby
Martha Endell
Mrs. Fibbitson
Mr. Grainger
Mr. and Mrs. Grayper
Gregory
Mr. and Mrs. Gulpidge
Mrs. Gummidge
Mrs. Heep
Uriah Heep
Captain Hopkins
The Misses Hopkins
Mrs. Hopkins
Janet
Master Jones
Mr. Joram
Joe Joram
Minnie Joram
Minnie Omer Joram
Mr. Jorkins
Mrs. Kidgebury
Miss Kitt
Miss Larkins
Mr. Larkins
Littimer
Jack Maldon
Mr. Markham
Mrs. Markleham (Old Soldier)
Mary Anne
"Mealy Potatoes"
Mrs. Mell
Charles (Charley) Mell

Emma Micawber
Emma Micawber (the younger)
Wilkins Micawber
(Master) Wilkins Micawber
Julia Mills
Mr. Mills
Miss Mowcher
Clara Murdstone [Clara
  Copperfield]
Edward Murdstone
Jane Murdstone
The Misses Nettingall
Mr. Omer
Mr. Passnidge
Clara Peggotty
Daniel (Dan'l) Peggotty
Emily Peggotty [Little Em'ly]
Ham Peggotty
Mr. Quinion
Miss Shepherd
Mr. Smart
Clarissa Spenlow
Dora (Little Blossom) Spenlow
  [Dora Copperfield]
Francis Spenlow
Lavinia Spenlow
Henry Spiker
Mrs. Henry Spiker
Mrs. Steerforth
James Steerforth
Dr. Strong
Annie Strong
Mr. Tiffey
Thomas (Tommy) Traddles
Tripp
Betsey Trotwood
Mr. Tungay
Mick Walker
Mr. Waterbrook
Mrs. Waterbrook
Agnes Wickfield
Mr. Wickfield
William

*The Posthumous Papers of the Pickwick
  Club* (1836-1837)—AW
Arabella Allen
Benjamin Allen
Mr. Ayresleigh
Jack Bamber
Angelo Cyrus Bantam
Martha Bardell
Tommy Bardell
Harry Beller

Betsy
Prince Bladud
Colonel Sir Thomas Blazo
Mr. Blotton
Captain Boldwig
Miss Bolo
Mr. Brooks
Mrs. Budger
Colonel Bulder
Miss Bulder
Mrs. Bulder
Mrs. Bunkin
Thomas Burton
Serjeant Buzfuz
Charley
Lady Clubber
The Misses Clubber
Sir Thomas Clubber
Elizabeth Cluppins
Mrs. Craddock
Mr. Crawley
Mr. Crushton
Tom Cummins
Mr. Dibdin
Mr. Dodson
Mr. Dowler
Mrs. Dowler
Dubbley
Mr. Dumkin
Edmunds
John Edmunds
Emma
Horatio Fizkin
Don Bolaro Fizzgig
Donna Christina Fizzgig
Wilkins Flasher
Mr. Fogg
George
Thomas Groffin
Gabriel Grub
Daniel Grummer
Mr. Grundy
Mr. Gunter
Miss Gwynn
Mr. Harris
Henry
George Heyling
Mary Heyling
Jack Hopkins
Lud Hudibras
Anthony Humm
Hunt
The Misses Hunter

Lord Oranmore
Mrs. Raffarty
Mr. Reynolds (the elder)
Mr. Reynolds
Mr. Salisbury
Miss St. Omar
Mr. Soho

Belinda (1801)–RS
Sir Philip Baddely
Lady Boucher
Champfort
Lady Delacour
Lord Delacour
Helena Delacour
Margaret Delacour
Harriot Freke
Mr. Hartley
Clarence Hervey
Juba
Colonel Lawless
Mr. Luttridge
Mrs. Luttridge
Anabella Luttridge
Marriott
Miss Moreton
Mr. Moreton
Mrs. Ormond
Henry Percival
Lady Anne Percival
Belinda Portman
Mr. Rochfort
Mr. St. George
Virginia (Rachel) St. Pierre
Mrs. Smith
Selena Stanhope
Captain Sunderland
Mr. Vincent
Dr. X

Castle Rackrent (1800)–VB
Jason Quirk
Judy Quirk
Thady Quirk
Sir Conolly (Sir Condy) Rackrent
Isabella Moneygawl Rackrent
Jessica Rackrent
Sir Kit Rackrent
Sir Murtagh Rackrent
Sir Patrick (O'Shaughlin) Rackrent

Ormond (1817)–RSy
Lady Annaly
Florence Annaly
Sir Herbert Annaly

Miss Black [Mrs. M'Crule]
Dr. Cambray
Moriarty Carroll
Black (Captain Connal, Monsieur
    de Connal) Connal
White Connal
Miss Darrell
Michael Dunne
Betty Dunshaughlin
Tommy Dunshaughlin
Father Jos
Miss Lardner
Lady Millicent
Abbe Morellet
Lady Norton
Mademoiselle O'Faley
Harry Ormond
Lady O'Shane
Cornelius (King Corny) O'Shane
Dora O'Shane
Emmy Annaly O'Shane
Marcus O'Shane
Lady Theodosia O'Shane
Sir Ulick O'Shane
Patrickson
Sheelah
Peggy Sheridan

George Eliot (Mary Ann Evans, 1819-1880)

Adam Bede (1859)–LCL
Alick
Adam Bede
Adam Bede (the younger)
Lisbeth Bede
Lisbeth Bede (the younger)
Matthias Bede
Seth Bede
Mrs. Best
Jonathan Burge
Mary Burge
Mr. Casson
Mr. Craig
Ben Cranage (Wiry Ben)
Bessy Cranage (Chad's Bess)
Chad Cranage
Dolly
Arthur Donnithorne
Lydia Donnithorne
Squire Donnithorne
Mrs. Irwine
Adolphus Irwine
Anne Irwine

Kate Irwine
Will Maskery
Bartle Massey
Molly
Dinah Morris
John Olding
Mrs. Pomfret
Charlotte ("Totty") Poyser
Martin Poyser (the elder)
Martin Poyser
Marty Poyser
Rachel Poyser
Tommy Poyser
Pym
Joshua Rann
Jim Salt
Bess Salt (Timothy's Bess)
Satchell
Hetty Sorrel
Sarah Stone
Mum Taft
Mr. Thurle
"Colonel" Townley

Daniel Deronda (1876)–LCL
Mr. Arrowpoint
Mrs. Arrowpoint
Catherine Arrowpoint
Lady Brackenshaw
Lord Brackenshaw
Mrs. Cohen
Addy Cohen
Adelaide Rebekah Cohen
Ezra Cohen
Jacob Alexander Cohen
Alice Davilow
Bertha Davilow
Fanny Davilow
Fanny Davilow (the younger)
Isabel Davilow
Daniel Deronda
Anna Gascoigne
Henry Gascoigne
Nancy Gascoigne
Rex Gascoigne
Lydia Glasher
Henleigh Mallinger Grandcourt
Princess Leonora Halm-Eberstein
Gwendolen Harleth
Joseph Kalonymos
Julius Klesmer
Baron von Langen
Baroness von Langen
Mr. Lapidoth

Edward the Confessor
Eutropius
Fausta
William Fitz-Osborne
Goddess of Fortune
Earl Goodwin
Editha Goodwin
Swane Goodwin
Homer
Hypatia
Julian the Apostate
Julius Caesar
Justinian II
King-Spirit
Leonidas of Sparta
Lepra
Lucilius
Maladie Alamode
Lady Mary
Mauregas
Mercury
John Milton
Judge Minos
Orpheus
Lord Percy
Robert Powney
Rodoric
Sabina
Sappho
Scorbutia
Lord Scrape
William Shakespeare
Stephen
Thomas Thumb
Timasius
Ulysses
Virgil
Cardinal Wolsey
Zeno

The Life of Mr. Jonathan Wild the Great
(1743)—HG
Bob Bagshot
Blueskin
Thomas Fierce
Fireblood
Jack Friendly
Grave
Mrs. Heartfree
Nancy Heartfree
Thomas Heartfree
Roger Johnson
Mr. Ketch
Count La Ruse

Mr. Marybone
Titus Oates
Anne Sample
James Sly
Tom Smirk
Mr. Snap
Laetitia (Miss Tishy) Snap
Theodosia (Miss Doshy) Snap
Molly Straddle
Jack Swagger
Thomas Thimble
Mr. Wild
Jonathan Wild
Wolfstan Wild

Sarah Fielding (1710-1768)

*The Adventures of David Simple in Search
of a Faithful Friend* (1744)—AL
Cynthia
Isabelle
Nanny Johnson
Livia
Peter Ratcliff
Camilla Simple
Daniel Simple
David Simple
Mr. Spatter
Valentine
Mr. Varnish

The Cry (1754)—AL
Cordelia
Cylinda
Duessa
Ferdinand
Melantha
Nicanor
Oliver
Portia
Una

David Simple. Volume the Last (1753)—AL
Cynthia
Mrs. Dunster
Mr. and Mrs. Orgueil
Camilla Simple
David Smiple
Valentine

*Familiar Letters between the Principal Char-
acters of David Simple and Some Others*
(1747)—AL
Belinda
Celia

Cleomenes
Cleora
Cratander
Cynthia
Delia
Ferdinand
Prudentia Flutter
Isabinda
Lavinia
Leontia
Lindamira
Lydia
Lysimachus
Pharamond
Lucy Rural
Camilla Simple
Sophronia
Mr. Spatter
Theodosius
Mr. Varnish

The Governess (1749)—AL
Betty Ford
Henny Frett
Dolly Friendly
Sukey Jennett
Patty Lockit
Jenny Peace
Lucy Sly
Nancy Spruce
Polly Suckling
Mrs. Teachum

The History of Ophelia (1760)—AL
Lord Dorchester
Rumford Dorking
Mrs. Herner
Lord Larborough
Sir Charles Lisdale
Ophelia
Mr. South
Captain Traverse
Marchioness of Trente

The History of the Countess of Dellwyn
(1759)—AL
Mr. Bilson
Mrs. Bilson
Lady Chlegen
Lord Clermont
Sir Harry Cleveland
Miss Cummyns
Lord Dellwyn
Lady Dellwyn (Charlotte Lucum)

Richard Danvers, Lord Alton
Borromeo
Bozzari
Frederigo, Count of Camaldoli
Camilla
Cloudesley
Colocotroni
Irene Colocotroni
Corrado
John Ernest Biren, Duke of Courland
Julian Danvers
Sergius Dolgorouki
Elliot
Eudocia
Signor Fabroni
Selina Fortescue
Giuseppe
Helena Ludolfski
William Meadows
Bernardino Perfetti
Francesco Perfetti
Alexis Scherbatoff
Isabella Scherbatoff
St. Elmo
Baron Stahlhoffen
Stephanoff
Stirling

Deloraine (1833)—GM
Ambrose
Lord Borradale
Margaret Borradale
Maurice Borradale
Colonel Bouverie
Catherine Deloraine
Emilia Fitzcharles Deloraine
P. Deloraine
Catherine Fanshaw
Monsieur Jerome
Monsieur Morlaix
John Rowland
Thornton
Travers
William

Fleetwood (1805)—GM
Sir George Bradshaw
Mrs. Comorin
Ambrose Fleetwood
Casimir Fleetwood (the elder)
Casimir Fleetwood
Mary Macneil Fleetwood
Frewen

Mrs. Gifford
Sir Charles Gleed
Mr. Kenrick
Edward Kenrick
Gifford Kenrick
Mr. Macneil
Mr. Matthews
Morrison
Mr. Parkhurst
Laetitia Philips
Mathilda Rancliffe
William Ruffigny
Mr. Scarborough
Louisa Scarborough
Monsieur Vaublanc
Withers

Mandeville (1817)—GM
Hilkiah Bradford
William, Lord Caulfield
Sir Arthur Chicester
Lionel Clifford
Sir Anthony Ashley Cooper
Captain Unton Croke
Marquis de Grevres
Colonel Hugh Grove
Josiah Hampole
Holloway
Judith
Mrs. Landseer
Mallison
Commodore Mandeville
Audley Mandeville
Charles Mandeville
Dorothy Mandeville
Henrietta Mandeville
Edward Montagu
Ralph Montagu
Amelia Montfort
Sir Phelim O'Neile
Colonel John Penruddock
Dr. Pottinger
Thomas, Lord Strafford
Lieutenant Jack Thomson
Sir Joseph Wagstaff
Mrs. Willis

St. Leon (1799)—GM
Duke of Alencon
Bernardin
Muzaffer Bey
Gian-Battasta Castaldo (Count of Piadena)
Marian Chabot

Gaspar de Coligny
Marquis de Damville
Marguerite de Damville
Chevalier Dupont
Andrea Filosanto
Marchese Filosanto
King Francis
Bethlem Gabor
Monsieur Grimseld
Hector
King Henry VIII
Antonio de Leyva
Monsieur Monluc
Mordecai
Pandora Nadasti
King Philip II
Charles de St. Leon (Chevalier de Damville)
Reginald de St. Leon (the elder)
Reginald de St. Leon (Chattilon, D'Aubigny)
Marquis de Villeroy
Franceso Zampieri

Oliver Goldsmith (1730-1774)

The Citizen of the World (1762)—NT
Catharina Alexowna
Barbacela (Queen of Emmets)
Bonbennin bonbobbin-bonbobbinet
Choang
Will Drybone
Mr. Fudge
Fum Hoam
Hansi
Jack
Lien Chi Altangi
Nanhoa (Queen of the Scarlet Dragons)
Shingfu
Mrs. Tibbs
Ned (the Little Beau) Tibbs
Whang
Yaoua

The Vicar of Wakefield (1766)—NT
Timothy Baxter
Lady Blarney
Solomon Flamborough
Ephram Jenkinson
Bill Primrose
Dr. Charles Primrose
Deborah Primrose
Dick Primrose
George Primrose

Moses Primrose
Olivia (Livy) Primrose
Sophia (Sophy) Primrose
Carolina Wilhelmina Amelia Skeggs
Mr. Symmonds
Sir William Thornhill [Mr. Burchell]
Squire Thornhill
Mr. Williams
Mr. Wilmot
Arabella Wilmot

Richard Graves (1715-1804)

The Spiritual Quixote (1773)—ACS

Mr. Alcock
Mr. Aldworth
Lord B——
Mrs. Bardolph
Mr. Blackman
Mrs. Booby
Dr. Brewer
Mrs. Brewer
Mr. Calomel
Captain
Mr. Clayton
Christopher Collop
Alderman Cullpepper
Mrs. Cullpepper
Deborah
Mrs. Enville
Isabella Fairfax
Mrs. Filch
Fillpot
Lady Fanny Flurry
Lady Forester
Kitty Forester
Sir William Forester
Mr. George
Captain Gordon
Mr. Graham
Mr. Grandison
Dr. Greville
Mrs. Greville
Gregory Griskin
Mr. Hammond
Howel Harris
Johnny
Captain Johnson
Jonathan
Tom Keen
Lavinia
Captain Mahoney
Mrs. Mahoney

Maritornes
Mrs. Molly
Nan
Mr. Nash
Mr. Newland
Mr. Pennywise
Mrs. Placket
Mr. Pottle
Mr. Powell
Mrs. Quick
Colonel Rappee
Lady Riot
Mr. Rivers
Mr. Rouvell ("Beau Rueful")
Lady Ruelle
Miss Sainthill
Mrs. Sarsenet
Mr. Selkirk
Squire Shapely
Mr. Shatterbrain
Mr. Shenstone
Lady Sherwood
Mrs. Skelton
Dr. Slash
Brother Slender
Mr. Slicer
Snap
Dr. Stubbs
Mrs. Tantrum
Bob Tench
Mrs. Thompson
Andrew Tipple
Tom the Stable-boy
Captain Townsend
Squire Townsend
Widow Townsend
Julia Townsend
Lucia Townsend
Miss Trufle
Dorothy Tugwell
Jeremiah Tugwell
Joseph Tugwell
Mr. Twangdillo
John Wesley
Mr. Whitfield
Mrs. Whitfield
Mr. Wildgoose
Mrs. Wildgoose
Geoffry Wildgoose
Mr. Woodville
Mrs. Woodville
Betsy Woodville
Charlotte Woodville

Mr. Wylmot

H. Rider Haggard (1856-1925)

Allan Quatermain (1887)—MT

Agon
Alphones
Annette
Sir Henry (Incubu) Curtis
Captain John (Bougwan) Good
Mr. Mackenzie
Mrs. Mackenzie
Flossie (Waterlily) Mackenzie
General Nasta
Nyleptha
Allan (Hunter, Macumazahn) Quatermain
Harry Quatermain
Sorais (Lady of the Night)
Umslopogaas (Woodpecker, Slaughterer)

King Solomon's Mines (1885)—MT

George Curtis [Neville]
Sir Henry (Icubu) Curtis
Evans
Foulata
Gagool
Captain John (Bougwan) Good
Imotu
Infadoos
Jim
Allan Quatermain
Scragga
José da Silvestra
José Silvestre
Twala (The One Eyed, The Mighty, Husband of One Thousand Wives)
Umbopa [Ignosi]

She (1886)—MT

Amenartas
Billali
Ludwig Horace Holly
Job
Kallikrates
Mohammed
Noot
She (Ayesha, Hija, She-Who-Must-Be-Obeyed)
Ustane
Leo Vincey
M. L. Vincey

Ann Radcliffe (1764-1823)

The Castles of Athlin and Dunbayne
(1789)–JM
Earl of Athlin
Edmund
Edric
James
Laura
Louisa
Malcolm
Mary
Matilda
Osbert
Patrick
(Alleyn) Philip
Robert
Count de Santmorin
Marquis de St. Clair

Gaston de Blondeville (1826)–JM
Aaron
Lady Barbara
Gaston de Blondeville
Aveline de Bohun
Carle
Cincia
Timothy Crabbe
Eadwyn
Prince Edmund
Prince Edward
Eleanor
Queen Eleanor
Ewdwyn
Reginald de Folville
William de Fortibus
Robert de Grendon
Guy
Maister Henry
King Henry III
Earl of Huntingdon
Lady Huntingdon
Lady Isabel
Lord de Lomene
Maria
Simon de Montfort
William de Mowbray
Earl of Norfolk
Norroy
Old Man
Pierre
Prior of Saint Mary's
Richard
Mr. Simpson
Taylor

Earl of Warwick
Roger de Wesham
Harry Willoughton
Wischard
Hugh Woodreeve
Mrs. Woodreeve
Archbishop of York

The Italian (1797)–JM
Abate
Abbess
(Sacchi) Father Ansaldo
Beatrice
Signora Bianchi
Bonamo
Count di Bruno
Ferando di Bruno (Father Schedoni)
Olivia di Bruno (Sister Olivia)
Signor Giotto
Giovanni
Inquisitor
Friar Jeronimo
Sister Margaritone
Count di Maro
Paulo
Ellena Rosalba
Spalatro
Marco Toma
Marchesa di Vivaldi
Marchese di Vivaldi
Vincentio di Vivaldi
Nicola di Zampari

The Mysteries of Udolpho (1794)–JM
Annette
Barnardini
Monsieur Barreaux
Count Bauvillers
Madame Bearn
Signor Bertolini
Bertrand
Sir Bevys
Monsieur Bonnac
Signor Brochio
Baron de Brunne
Carlo
Caterina
Signor Cavigni
Cesario
Marchioness Champfort
Madame Cheron, later Madame Montoni
Madame Clairval
Dorina

Dorothee
Mademoiselle Feydeau
Sister Frances
Signora Herminia
Countess Lacleur
La Voisin
Signora Livona
Ludovico
Maddelina
Marco
Michael
Signor Montoni
Count Morano
Monsieur Motteville
Signor Orsino
Chevalier Du Pont
Madame Quesnel
Monsieur Quesnel
Madame St. Aubert
Monsieur St. Aubert
Emily St. Aubert
Baron de St. Foix
Chevalier St. Foix
Theresa
Laurentini di Udolpho [Sister Agnes]
Ugo
Utaldo
Chevalier Valancourt
Signor Verezzi
Countess de Villefort
Blanche de Villefort
Francis Beaveau, Count de Villefort
Henri de Villefort
Marchioness de Villeroi
Marquis de Villeroi

The Romance of the Forest (1791)–JM
Adeline
Monsieur Amand
Monsieur Audley
Jean d'Aunoy (Louis de St. Pierre)
Francis Balliere
de Bosse
Jacques
Lafance
Madame La Luc
Arnand La Luc
Clara La Luc
Constance de La Mott
Louis de La Mott
Pierre de La Mott
Jacques Martigny
Monsieur Mauron

William Fitz-Owen
Lord Graham
Sir Philip Harclay
Thomas Hewson
Joseph Howell
Edmund Lovel
Sir Walter Lovel
John Markham
Father Oswald
Andrew Twyford
Margery Twyford
Richard Wenlock
John Wyatt
Zadisky

Plans of Education (1792)–JV
Lord A––
Louisa, Lady A––
Charlotte Brady
Frances Darnford
Mrs. Langston
Captain Maurice
Madame di Soranzo
Mrs. Strictland

The Progress of Romance (1785)–JV
Abraham
Charoba
Dalica
Euphrasia
Gebirus
Hagar
Hortensius
Nurse
Sarah
Sea-goddess
Sophronia
Totis

Samuel Richardson (1869-1761)

Clarissa: or, The History of a Young Lady
(1747-1748)–MMa
Betty Barnes
Johnny Barton
John ("Jack") Belford
Thomas Belton
Betsy ("Rosebud")
Miss Betterton
Mrs. Bevis
Elias Brand
Hannah Burton
Deb Butler (Dorcas Wykes, Dorcas
    Martindale)
Sir George Colmar

F. J. de la Tour
Mr. Diggs
Thomas Doleman
Sir Harry Downeton
Mrs. Fortescue
Mr. Goddard
Johanetta Golding
Mrs. Greme
Dr. H–
Anthony Harlowe
Arabella Harlowe
Charlotte Harlowe
Clarissa (Clary) Harlowe
James Harlowe
James Harlowe (the younger)
John Harlowe
Aunt Harman
Dolly Hervey
Dorothy Hervey
Charles Hickman
Polly Horton
Anna ("Nancy") Howe
Annabella Howe
Joseph
Mrs. Knolly
Miss Lardner
Lady Betty Lawrence
Joseph Leman
Dr. Lewen
Miss Lockyer
Robert (Bob, Bobby) Lovelace
Mrs. Lovick
Lord M–
Mabel
Sally Martin (Mrs. Sinclair)
Patrick McDonald (M'Donald)
Mr. Melvill
Captain Mennell
Richard Mobray
Charlotte Montague
Martha (Patty, Patsey) Montague
Mrs. Moore
Colonel William Morden
Susan Morrison
Mr. Mullins
Judith ("Goody") Norton
Mr. Osgood
Miss Rawlins
Mr. Rowland
Mrs. Rowland
Anne Shelburne
Mr. Singleton
John Smith

Mrs. ("Goody") Smith
John Soberton
Roger Solmes
Mrs. Sorling
William Summers
Mr. Symmes
Thomasine (Belton)
James Tourville
Barbara (Bab) Wallis
John Walton
Alexander Wyerley

Pamela, or Virtue Rewarded (1740)–MMa
Elizabeth Andrews
John (Goodman, Goody) Andrews
Pamela Andrews (later Pamela
    B––)
Thomas Andrews
John Arnold
Mrs. Arthur
William B––
William (Billy) B––
Polly (Mary) Barlow
Mr. Barrow
Lady Betty
Cousin Borroughs
Mrs. Brooks
Countess of C––
Mr. Carlton
Mr. Chapman
Mrs. Chapman
Monsieur Colbrand
Countess, Dowager of ––
Earl and Countess of D––
Mary (Polly) Darnford
Nancy Darnford
Sir Simon Darnford
Barbara, Lady Davers
Mrs. Dobson
Sir William G––
Gipsy
Sally Godfrey (Wrightson)
Sally Goodwin
Jackey (John), Lord H––
Sir Charles Hargrave
Mrs. Harris
Mrs. Jervis
Mrs. Jewkes
Lady Jones
Mr. Longman
Dr. M
Squire Martin
Mr. Murray
Nan

Contributors

LA Lionel Adey
RA Rebecca Arnould

AB Arlyn Bruccoli
CB Charles Burkitt
DBo Diana Bowstead
DBr David Brailow
JB James Basker
MB Myra Best
VB Virginia Busskohl

CC Cynthia Caywood
KCl Katherine Clark
KCo Keith Costain
NBC Natalie Bell Cole
RC Richard Currie

BJD Barbara J. Dunlap
JD Joseph Dunlap
TD Tim Dayton

EE Elisabeth Ebert
DE-M Dawn Elmore-McCrary

LJF Lois Josephs Fowler
PF Pamela Fetters
RF Ruth Faurot

A-LG Anne-Louise Gibbons
CG-C C. Gordon-Craig
GG George Grella
HG Heather Graves
JG John Greenfield

AH Angela Hubler
CH Cherie Hutchison
JHa Jill Hall
JHi Jonathan Hill

AI Andrea Invanov

JJ John Jones

CK Cindy Kelly
JK Jacob Korg
MK Melissa Kaegel
PK Patricia Koster

AGL Alfred G. Litton
AL April London
LCL Laura Cooner Lambdin
RL Robert Lambdin
RJL Rachael Jane Lynch

CM Cecilia Macheski
GM Gregory Maertz
JM Julie Miller
MMa Maureen Mann
MMc Michael McCully
RM Richard McGhee
WM William McInvaille

DJN Donald J. Newman

TO Toni Oplt

AP Alexander Pettit
KP Kevin Paul

DR Deborah Ross
FR Frank Riga
JR John Rogers
SR Susan Rodstein

ACS Ann Chandler Scott
BS Betty Schellenberg
CNS C. N. Smith
ES Elton Smith
GS Garry Sherbert
JS Jane Sellwood
MAS Mary Anne Schofield
MSS Mary S. Smith
KS Kate Spencer
PS Peter Slade
RSm Ruth Smalley
RSy Rene Sykes

AT Alison Thompson
DMT Dorothea M. Thompson
MT Maureen Thum
NT Nancy Tyson
RCT R. C. Terry

TU Troy Underwood

JV Jack Voller

AW Ann Werner
ALW Andrea L. Westcott
EW Edgar Wright
KW Kathryn West
NW Nancy West
TW Tom Winnifrith